The Victoria History of the Counties of England

EDITED BY WILLIAM PAGE, F.S.A.

A HISTORY OF
SUSSEX
VOLUME I

THE
VICTORIA HISTORY
OF THE COUNTIES
OF ENGLAND

SUSSEX

PUBLISHED FOR

THE UNIVERSITY OF LONDON

INSTITUTE OF HISTORICAL RESEARCH

REPRINTED FROM THE ORIGINAL EDITION OF 1905

BY

DAWSONS OF PALL MALL

FOLKESTONE & LONDON

1973

Issued by
Archibald Constable and Company Limited
in 1905

Reprinted for the University of London
Institute of Historical Research
by
Dawsons of Pall Mall
Cannon House
Folkestone, Kent, England
1973

ISBN: 0 7129 0585 5

Originally printed in Great Britain by
Butler & Tanner of Frome and London
Reprinted in Belgium by Jos Adam, Brussels

INSCRIBED
TO THE MEMORY OF
HER LATE MAJESTY
QUEEN VICTORIA
WHO GRACIOUSLY GAVE
THE TITLE TO AND
ACCEPTED THE
DEDICATION OF
THIS HISTORY

THE ADVISORY COUNCIL
OF THE VICTORIA HISTORY

GENERAL ADVERTISEMENT

The Victoria History of the Counties of England is a National Historic Survey which, under the direction of a large staff comprising the foremost students in science, history, and archæology, is designed to record the history of every county of England in detail. This work was, by gracious permission, dedicated to Her late Majesty Queen Victoria, who gave it her own name. It is the endeavour of all who are associated with the undertaking to make it a worthy and permanent monument to her memory.

Rich as every county of England is in materials for local history, there has hitherto been no attempt made to bring all these materials together into a coherent form.

Although from the seventeenth century down to quite recent times numerous county histories have been issued, they are very unequal in merit ; the best of them are very rare and costly; most of them are imperfect, and many are now out of date. Moreover they were the work of one or two isolated scholars, who, however scholarly, could not possibly deal adequately with all the varied subjects which go to the making of a county history.

In the VICTORIA HISTORY each county is not the labour of one or two men, but of many, for the work is treated scientifically, and in order to embody in it all that modern scholarship can contribute, a system of co-operation between experts and local students is applied, whereby the history acquires a completeness and definite authority hitherto lacking in similar undertakings.

The names of the distinguished men who have joined the Advisory Council are a guarantee that the work represents the results of the latest discoveries in every department of research, for the trend of modern thought insists upon the intelligent study of the past and of the social, institutional and political developments of national life. As these histories are the first in which this object has been kept in view, and modern principles applied, it is hoped that they will form a work of reference no less indispensable to the student than welcome to the man of culture.

THE SCOPE OF THE WORK

The history of each county is complete in itself, and in each case its story is told from the earliest times, commencing with the natural features and the flora and fauna. Thereafter follow the antiquities, pre-Roman, Roman and post-Roman; ancient earthworks; a new translation and critical study of the Domesday Survey; articles on political, ecclesiastical, social and economic history; architecture, arts, industries, sport, etc.; and topography. The greater part of each history is devoted to a detailed description and history of each parish, containing an account of the land and its owners from the Conquest to the present day. These manorial histories are compiled from original documents in the national collections and from private papers. A special feature is the wealth of illustrations afforded, for not only are buildings of interest pictured, but the coats of arms of past and present landowners are given.

HISTORICAL RESEARCH

It has always been, and still is, a reproach that England, with a collection of public records greatly exceeding in extent and interest those of any other country in Europe, is yet far behind her neighbours in the study of the genesis and growth of her national and local institutions. Few Englishmen are probably aware that the national and local archives contain for a period of 800 years in an almost unbroken chain of evidence, not only the political, ecclesiastical, and constitutional history of the kingdom, but every detail of its financial and social progress and the history of the land and its successive owners from generation to generation. The neglect of our public and local records is no doubt largely due to the fact that their interest and value is known to but a small number of people, and this again is directly attributable to the absence in this country of any endowment for historical research. The government of this country has too often left to private enterprise work which our continental neighbours entrust to a government department. It is not surprising, therefore, to find that although an immense amount of work has been done by individual effort, the entire absence of organization among the workers and the lack of intelligent direction has hitherto robbed the results of much of their value.

In the VICTORIA HISTORY, for the first time, a serious attempt is made to utilize our national and local muniments to the best advantage by carefully organizing and supervising the researches required. Under the direction of the Records Committee a large staff of experts has been engaged at the Public Record Office in calendaring those classes of records which are fruitful in material for local history, and by a system of interchange of communication among workers under the direct supervision of the general editor and sub-editors a mass of information is sorted and assigned to its correct place, which would otherwise be impossible.

THE RECORDS COMMITTEE

Sir Edward Maunde Thompson, K.C.B.
Sir Henry Maxwell-Lyte, K.C.B.
W. J. Hardy, F.S.A.
F. Madan, M.A.
F. Maitland, M.A., F.S.A.

C. T. Martin, B.A., F.S.A.
J. Horace Round, M.A., LL.D.
S. R. Scargill-Bird, F.S.A.
W. H. Stevenson, M.A.
G. F. Warner, M.A., F.S.A.

FAMILY HISTORY

Family History is, both in the Histories and in the supplementary genealogical volumes of chart Pedigrees, dealt with by genealogical experts and in the modern spirit. Every effort is made to secure accuracy of statement, and to avoid the insertion of those legendary pedigrees which have in the past brought discredit on the subject. It has been pointed out by the late Bishop of Oxford, a great master of historical research, that 'the expansion and extension of genealogical study is a very remarkable feature of our own times,' that 'it is an increasing pursuit both in America and in England,' and that it can render the historian most useful service.

CARTOGRAPHY

In addition to a general map in several sections, each History contains Geological, Orographical, Botanical, Archæological, and Domesday maps; also maps illustrating the articles on Ecclesiastical and Political Histories and the sections dealing with Topography. The Series contains many hundreds of maps in all.

ARCHITECTURE

A special feature in connexion with the Architecture is a series of ground plans, many of them coloured, showing the architectural history of castles, cathedrals, abbeys, and other monastic foundations.

In order to secure the greatest possible accuracy, the descriptions of the Architecture, ecclesiastical, military, and domestic are under the supervision of Mr. C. R. PEERS, M.A., F.S.A., and a committee has been formed of the following students of architectural history who are referred to as may be required concerning this department of the work :—

ARCHITECTURAL COMMITTEE

J. BILSON, F.S.A., F.R.I.B.A.

R. BLOMFIELD, M.A., F.S.A., A.R.A.

HAROLD BRAKSPEAR, F.S.A., A.R.I.B.A.

PROF. BALDWIN BROWN, M.A.

ARTHUR S. FLOWER, F.S.A., A.R.I.B.A.

GEORGE E. FOX, M.A., F.S.A.

J. A. GOTCH, F.S.A., F.R.I.B.A.

W. H. ST. JOHN HOPE, M.A.

W. H. KNOWLES, F.S.A., F.R.I.B.A.

J. T. MICKLETHWAITE, F.S.A.

ROLAND PAUL, F.S.A.

J. HORACE ROUND, M.A., LL.D.

PERCY G. STONE, F.S.A., F.R.I.B.A.

THACKERAY TURNER

GENEALOGICAL VOLUMES

The genealogical volumes contain the family history and detailed genealogies of such houses as had at the end of the nineteenth century seats and landed estates, having enjoyed the like in the male line since 1760, the first year of George III., together with an introductory section dealing with other principal families in each county.

The general plan of Contents and the names among others of those who are contributing articles and giving assistance are as follows :—

Natural History.

    Geology. CLEMENT REID, F.R.S., HORACE B. WOODWARD, F.R.S., and others

    Palæontology. R. L. LYDEKKER, F.R.S., etc.

    Flora } Contributions by G. A. BOULENGER, F.R.S., H. N. DIXON, F.L.S., G. C. DRUCE, M.A., F.L.S., WALTER GARSTANG, M.A., F.L.S., HERBERT GOSS, F.L.S., F.E.S., R. I. POCOCK, REV. T. R. R. STEBBING, M.A., F.R.S.,etc., B. B. WOODWARD, F.G.S.,F.R.M.S., etc., and other Specialists
    Fauna }

Prehistoric Remains. SIR JOHN EVANS K.C.B., D.C.L., LL.D., W. BOYD DAWKINS, D.Sc., LL.D., F.R.S., F.S.A., GEO. CLINCH, F.G.S., JOHN GARSTANG, M.A., B.LITT., and others

Roman Remains. F. HAVERFIELD, M.A., LL.D., F.S.A.

Anglo-Saxon Remains. C. HERCULES READ, F.S.A., REGINALD A. SMITH, B.A., F.S.A., and others

Domesday Book and other kindred Records. J. HORACE ROUND, M.A., LL.D., and other Specialists

Architecture. C. R. PEERS, M.A., F.S.A., W. H. ST. JOHN HOPE, M.A., and HAROLD BRAKSPEAR, F.S.A., A.R.I.B.A.

Ecclesiastical History. R. L. POOLE, M.A., and others

Political History. PROF. C. H. FIRTH, M.A., LL.D., W. H. STEVENSON, M.A., J. HORACE ROUND, M.A., LL.D., PROF. T. F. TOUT, M.A., PROF. JAMES TAIT, M.A., and A. F. POLLARD

History of Schools. A. F. LEACH, M.A., F.S.A.

Maritime History of Coast Counties. PROF. J. K. LAUGHTON, M.A., M. OPPENHEIM, and others

Topographical Accounts of Parishes and Manors. By Various Authorities

History of the Feudal Baronage. J. HORACE ROUND, M.A., LL.D., and OSWALD BARRON, F.S.A.

Agriculture. SIR ERNEST CLARKE, M.A., Sec. to the Royal Agricultural Society, and others

Forestry. JOHN NISBET, D.Oec., and others

Industries, Arts and Manufactures
} By Various Authorities
Social and Economic History

Ancient and Modern Sport. E. D. CUMING and others.

    Hunting
    Shooting } By Various Authorities
    Fishing, etc.
    Cricket. HOME GORDON
    Football. C. W. ALCOCK

The Weald of Sussex from the South Downs

THE
VICTORIA HISTORY
OF THE COUNTY OF
SUSSEX

EDITED BY WILLIAM PAGE, F.S.A.

VOLUME ONE

PUBLISHED FOR
THE UNIVERSITY OF LONDON
INSTITUTE OF HISTORICAL RESEARCH
REPRINTED BY
DAWSONS OF PALL MALL
FOLKESTONE & LONDON

County Committee for Sussex

THE MOST HON. THE MARQUESS OF ABERGAVENNY, K.G.

Lord Lieutenant, Chairman

His Grace The Duke of Norfolk, K.G., G.C.V.O.

The Rt. Hon. The Earl of March

The Rt. Hon. The Earl De La Warr

The Rt. Hon. The Viscount Gage

The Rt. Hon. The Lord Leconfield

The Rt. Hon. The Lord Monk Bretton, C.B.

The Rt. Hon. The Lord Brassey, K.C.B.

The Hon. T. A. Brassey

The Rt. Hon. Sir Henry Aubrey-Fletcher, Bart., C.B.

The Hon. A. G. Brand, M.P.

Sir Weetman W. Pearson, Bart:

Sir Richard Farrant

W. C. Alexander, Esq., J.P.

Col. A. M. Brookfield

William H. Campion, Esq., C.B.

W. L. Christie, Esq., D.L., J.P.

William V. Crake, Esq.

Robert Payne Crawfurd, Esq.

W. Galsworthy Davie, Esq.

Charles Aug. Egerton, Esq., D.L., J.P.

Charles J. Fletcher, Esq., D.L., J.P.

Col. Edward Frewen, D.L., J.P.

J. Anderton Greenwood, Esq.

Lindsay Hogg, Esq., M.P.

James Fitzalan Hope, Esq., M.P.

Edward Huth, Esq., M.D., D.L., J.P.

William D. James, Esq., D.L., J.P.

Gerald E. Loder, Esq., D.L., J.P.

C. J. Lucas, Esq.

Major T. Astley Maberly

Hugh Penfold, Esq., M.A.

Walter C. Renshaw, Esq., LL.M., K.C

J. Hall Renton, Esq.

J. Compton Rickett, Esq., M.P.

Herbert A. Rigg, Esq., M.A., F.S.A.

J. Horace Round, Esq., M.A. LL.D., Hon. Member of the Sussex Archæological Society

Lieut.-Col. Dudley Sampson, D.L., J.P.

F. H. Scott, Esq., D.L., J.P.

Frederick S. Shenstone, Esq., D.L., J.P.

R. Denny Urlin, Esq., F.L.S.

R. G. Wilberforce, Esq., D.L., J.P.

The Worshipful The Mayor of Arundel

The Worshipful The Mayor of Brighton

The Worshipful the Mayor of Chichester

The Worshipful The Mayor of Eastbourne

The Worshipful The Mayor of Hastings

The Worshipful The Mayor of Hove

CONTENTS OF VOLUME ONE

CONTENTS OF VOLUME ONE

LIST OF ILLUSTRATIONS

LIST OF ILLUSTRATIONS

LIST OF MAPS

★ *Not reproduced in this edition owing to technical difficulties.*

† *Reproduced in black and white in this edition.*

PREFACE

ONE of the first to make collections for the history of Sussex was Sir William Burrell, LL.D., F.R.S., F.S.A., an eminent lawyer who visited many of the parishes, collected drawings of the objects of interest, and spent a considerable amount of time on the genealogy of the county families. He however never printed the result of his labours, and at his death in 1796 he bequeathed the whole of his valuable collections to the British Museum, where they now lie among the Additional MSS. These collections have been very considerably used by subsequent historians of the county, and particularly, perhaps, by Rev. James Dallaway, M.A., who compiled from this source, at the expense of the Duke of Norfolk, *The History of the Three Western Rapes of Sussex*. The first volume of this history, comprising the account of the rape and city of Chichester, was published in 1815, and the first part of the second volume, containing the rape of Arundel, in 1819. The rape of Bramber, forming the second part of the second volume, was undertaken at Dallaway's request by Rev. Edmund Cartwright, but was not published till 1830. Dallaway's history is a useful book, but it cannot be considered reliable according to the modern standard of historical research.

The next historian of the county was Rev. Thomas Walker Horsfield, F.S.A., a Presbyterian minister who, in 1835, published in two volumes *The History and Antiquities and Topography of the County of Sussex*. The first volume, dealing with East Sussex, in which he was assisted by William Durrant Cooper, is of greater value than the second, which relies almost entirely upon Dallaway.

Mark Anthony Lower, a schoolmaster at Lewes, issued in 1870 *A Compendious History of Sussex: Topographical, Archæological and Anecdotal*, which contains an index to the first twenty volumes of the *Sussex Archæological Collections*, and is a valuable book of reference to all those concerned with the history of this county.

The Editor wishes to express his indebtedness to Dr. J. Horace Round for much help and many kind suggestions while passing this volume through the press. He also has to thank the Society of Antiquaries, the Geological Society, the Archæological Institute and the Sussex Archæological Society for the use of blocks for illustrations, and the authorities of the Brighton Museum for their courtesy in permitting various objects in their custody to be photographed.

TABLE OF ABBREVIATIONS

Abbrev. Plac. (Rec. Com.)	Abbreviatio Placitorum (Record Commission)
Acts of P.C. . .	Acts of Privy Council
Add.	Additional
Add. Chart. . .	Additional Charters
Admir.	Admiralty
Agarde	Agarde's Indices
Anct. Corresp. . .	Ancient Correspondence
Anct. D. (P.R.O.) A 2420	Ancient Deeds (Public Record Office) A 2420
Ann. Mon. . . .	Annales Monastici
Antiq.	Antiquarian or Antiquaries
App.	Appendix
Arch.	Archæologia or Archæological
Arch. Cant. . .	Archæologia Cantiana
Archd. Rec. . .	Archdeacons' Records
Archit.	Architectural
Assize R. . . .	Assize Rolls
Aud. Off. . . .	Audit Office
Aug. Off. . . .	Augmentation Office
Ayloffe	Ayloffe's Calendars
Bed.	Bedford
Beds	Bedfordshire
Berks	Berkshire
Bdle.	Bundle
B.M.	British Museum
Bodl. Lib. . . .	Bodley's Library
Boro.	Borough
Brev. Reg. . . .	Brevia Regia
Brit.	Britain, British, Britannia, etc.
Buck.	Buckingham
Bucks	Buckinghamshire
Cal.	Calendar
Camb.	Cambridgeshire or Cambridge
Cambr.	Cambria, Cambrian, Cambrensis, etc.
Campb. Ch. . .	Campbell Charities
Cant.	Canterbury
Cap.	Chapter
Carl.	Carlisle
Cart. Antiq. R. .	Cartæ Antiquæ Rolls
C.C.C. Camb. . .	Corpus Christi College, Cambridge
Certiorari Bdles. (Rolls Chap.)	Certiorari Bundles (Rolls Chapel)
Chan. Enr. Decree R.	Chancery Enrolled Decree Rolls
Chan. Proc. . .	Chancery Proceedings
Chant. Cert. . .	Chantry Certificates (or Certificates of Colleges and Chantries)
Chap. Ho. . . .	Chapter House
Charity Inq. . .	Charity Inquisitions
Chart. R. 20 Hen. III. pt. i. No. 10	Charter Roll, 20 Henry III. part i. Number 10

Chartul. . . .	Chartulary
Chas.	Charles
Ches.	Cheshire
Chest.	Chester
Ch. Gds. (Exch. K.R.)	Church Goods (Exchequer King's Remembrancer)
Chich.	Chichester
Chron.	Chronicle, Chronica, etc.
Close	Close Roll
Co.	County
Colch.	Colchester
Coll.	Collections
Com.	Commission
Com. Pleas . . .	Common Pleas
Conf. R. . . .	Confirmation Rolls
Co. Plac. . . .	County Placita
Cornw.	Cornwall
Corp.	Corporation
Cott.	Cotton or Cottonian
Ct. R.	Court Rolls
Ct. of Wards . .	Court of Wards
Cumb.	Cumberland
Cur. Reg. . . .	Curia Regis
D.	Deed or Deeds
D. and C. . . .	Dean and Chapter
De Banc. R. . .	De Banco Rolls
Dec. and Ord. . .	Decrees and Orders
Dep. Keeper's Rep.	Deputy Keeper's Reports
Derb.	Derbyshire or Derby
Devon	Devonshire
Dioc.	Diocese
Doc.	Documents
Dods. MSS. . .	Dodsworth MSS.
Dom. Bk. . . .	Domesday Book
Dors.	Dorsetshire
Duchy of Lanc. .	Duchy of Lancaster
Dur.	Durham
East.	Easter Term
Eccl.	Ecclesiastical
Eccl. Com. . . .	Ecclesiastical Commission
Edw.	Edward
Eliz.	Elizabeth
Engl.	England or English
Engl. Hist. Rev. .	English Historical Review
Enr.	Enrolled or Enrolment
Epis. Reg. . . .	Episcopal Registers
Esch. Enr. Accts. .	Escheators Enrolled Accounts
Excerpta e Rot. Fin. (Rec. Com.)	Excerpta e Rotulis Finium (Record Commission)
Exch. Dep. . .	Exchequer Depositions
Exch. K.B. . .	Exchequer King's Bench
Exch. K.R. . .	Exchequer King's Remembrancer
Exch. L.T.R. . .	Exchequer Lord Treasurer's Remembrancer

TABLE OF ABBREVIATIONS

Exch. of Pleas, Plea R.	Exchequer of Pleas, Plea Roll
Exch. of Receipt .	Exchequer of Receipt
Exch. Spec. Com. .	Exchequer Special Commissions
Feet of F. . . .	Feet of Fines
Feod. Accts. (Ct. of Wards)	Feodaries Accounts (Court of Wards)
Feod. Surv. (Ct. of Wards)	Feodaries Surveys (Court of Wards)
Feud. Aids . .	Feudal Aids
fol.	Folio
Foreign R. . .	Foreign Rolls
Forest Proc. . .	Forest Proceedings
Gaz.	Gazette or Gazetteer
Gen.	Genealogical, Genealogica, etc.
Geo. . . .	George
Glouc. . . .	Gloucestershire or Gloucester
Guild Certif.(Chan.) Ric. II.	Guild Certificates (Chancery) Richard II.
Hants	Hampshire
Harl.	Harley or Harleian
Hen.	Henry
Heref. . . .	Herefordshire or Hereford
Hertf. . . .	Hertford
Herts	Hertfordshire
Hil.	Hilary Term
Hist.	History, Historical, Historian, Historia, etc.
Hist. MSS. Com. .	Historical MSS. Commission
Hosp.	Hospital
Hund. R. . . .	Hundred Rolls
Hunt.	Huntingdon
Hunts	Huntingdonshire
Inq. a.q.d. . . .	Inquisitions ad quod damnum
Inq. p.m. . . .	Inquisitions post mortem
Inst.	Institute or Institution
Invent.	Inventory or Inventories
Ips.	Ipswich
Itin.	Itinerary
Jas.	James
Journ.	Journal
Lamb. Lib. . .	Lambeth Library
Lanc. . . .	Lancashire or Lancaster
L. and P. Hen. VIII.	Letters and Papers, Hen. VIII.
Lansd.	Lansdowne
Ld. Rev. Rec. . .	Land Revenue Records
Leic.	Leicestershire or Leicester
Le Neve's Ind. .	Le Neve's Indices
Lib.	Library
Lich.	Lichfield
Linc.	Lincolnshire or Lincoln
Lond.	London
m.	Membrane
Mem.	Memorials

Memo. R. . . .	Memoranda Rolls
Mich.	Michaelmas Term
Midd.	Middlesex
Mins. Accts. . .	Ministers' Accounts
Misc. Bks. (Exch. K.R., Exch. T.R. or Aug. Off.)	Miscellaneous Books (Exchequer King's Remembrancer, Exchequer Treasury of Receipt or Augmentation Office)
Mon.	Monastery, Monasticon
Monm.	Monmouth
Mun.	Muniments or Munimenta
Mus.	Museum
N. and Q. . . .	Notes and Queries
Norf.	Norfolk
Northampt. . .	Northampton
Northants . . .	Northamptonshire
Northumb. . .	Northumberland
Norw.	Norwich
Nott.	Nottinghamshire or Nottingham
N.S.	New Style
Off.	Office
Orig. R. . . .	Originalia Rolls
O.S.	Ordnance Survey
Oxf.	Oxfordshire or Oxford
p.	Page
Palmer's Ind. . .	Palmer's Indices
Pal. of Chest. . .	Palatinate of Chester
Pal. of Dur. . .	Palatinate of Durham
Pal. of Lanc. . .	Palatinate of Lancaster
Par.	Parish, parochial, etc.
Parl.	Parliament or Parliamentary
Parl. R. . . .	Parliament Rolls
Parl. Surv. . . .	Parliamentary Surveys
Partic. for Gts. .	Particulars for Grants
Pat.	Patent Roll or Letters Patent
P.C.C.	Prerogative Court of Canterbury
Pet.	Petition
Peterb.	Peterborough
Phil.	Philip
Pipe R. . . .	Pipe Roll
Plea R.	Plea Rolls
Pop. Ret. . . .	Population Returns
Pope Nich. Tax. (Rec. Com.)	Pope Nicholas' Taxation (Record Commission)
P.R.O.	Public Record Office
Proc.	Proceedings
Proc. Soc. Antiq. .	Proceedings of the Society of Antiquaries
pt.	Part
Pub.	Publications
R.	Roll
Rec.	Records
Recov. R. . . .	Recovery Rolls
Rentals and Surv. .	Rentals and Surveys
Rep.	Report
Rev.	Review
Ric.	Richard

TABLE OF ABBREVIATIONS

Roff.	Rochester diocese
Rot. Cur. Reg. .	Rotuli Curiæ Regis
Rut.	Rutland
Sarum	Salisbury diocese
Ser.	Series
Sess. R. . . .	Sessions Rolls
Shrews. . . .	Shrewsbury
Shrops	Shropshire
Soc.	Society
Soc. Antiq. . .	Society of Antiquaries
Somers. . . .	Somerset
Somers. Ho. . .	Somerset House
S.P. Dom. . . .	State Papers Domestic
Staff.	Staffordshire
Star Chamb. Proc.	Star Chamber Proceedings
Stat.	Statute
Steph.	Stephen
Subs. R. . . .	Subsidy Rolls
Suff.	Suffolk
Surr.	Surrey
Suss.	Sussex
Surv. of Ch. Livings (Lamb.) or (Chan.)	Surveys of Church Livings (Lambeth) or (Chancery)

Topog.	Topography or Topographical
Trans.	Transactions
Transl.	Translation
Treas.	Treasury or Treasurer
Trin.	Trinity Term
Univ.	University
Valor Eccl. (Rec. Com.)	Valor Ecclesiasticus (Record Commission)
Vet. Mon. . . .	Vetusta Monumenta
V.C.H.	Victoria County History
Vic.	Victoria
vol.	Volume
Warw.	Warwickshire or Warwick
Westm.	Westminster
Westmld. . . .	Westmorland
Will.	William
Wilts	Wiltshire
Winton. . . .	Winchester diocese
Worc. . . .	Worcestershire or Worcester
Yorks	Yorkshire

A HISTORY OF
SUSSEX

GEOLOGY

I T is not easy to fix on any point in time at which we can say that the history of Sussex began. We commonly speak of history as commencing with the first obscure and mutilated chronicles. Or perhaps we go back to somewhat earlier periods, for which we have only rude tradition, folklore or antiquities of uncertain age to act as guides. But history as we here understand it commences at an earlier date. It begins with the gradual building up of the solid earth on which we stand ; it deals with the rise of this land above the sea, its sculpture into hill and valley, and as a result its preparation and adaptation for man's occupation. We do not intend to go back, like the old chronicles, to the creation, or to start with a cosmogony. It will be sufficient for our purpose to indicate how the foundations of Sussex were laid, and to suggest what the world was like in those early days, what were its inhabitants, and what each successive period added to its mineral wealth, to its beauty, to its suitability for man. In thus treating the science of geology it is evident that attention must principally be devoted to the later geological periods, those which either lead up to or are directly concerned with the occupation of the county by man. Space will not allow us to deal fully with the earlier periods, or with the successive changes of their faunas and floras ; full information, however, will be found in the books and papers mentioned in the footnotes, which give references to the leading sources of information.

Sussex in its geological structure is one of the counties most easy to understand. It is also a district each of whose surface features is intimately connected with the subterranean arrangement of the strata, or is due to erosive forces such as we can readily comprehend. In a general way we now find in the county four distinct types of scenery, corresponding with different productions, different agriculture and different settlements and history. First, on the south there is the coastal plain, a low-lying sharply-defined tract of flat land, beginning narrow at Brighton and widening westward to about 8 miles at Selsey. This coastal plain, it should be remembered, was much wider formerly, and is still rapidly wasting away under the attacks of the sea. It was probably fully a mile wider in the Roman period. Next comes a wide belt of high, undulating, bare and almost waterless chalk downs, stretching from Beachy Head throughout the county to its western border, and ending abruptly in a steep scarp overlooking the Weald. Then to the north

A HISTORY OF SUSSEX

comes the lower region of the Weald, divisible into two belts : the one generally fertile and formed by the alternating marl flats and ridges of ferruginous sand, which lie between the foot of the chalk downs and the wide plain of the Weald Clay ; the other consisting of less fertile alternate wastes of sand and wide flats of clay. Both of these latter belts till well into historic times were covered with dense forest. We have thus in the first two regions an area, open, settled and well peopled even in times long before written history, and this part of the county has definite and well marked physical boundaries—on the south the sea, on the east the marshes about Dunge Ness, on the west a tidal harbour. Behind this settled region extended the wide 'hinterland' of the Weald, which was gradually annexed by the settlers on the north and south till they met at what is now the northern boundary of the county ; this line however is very irregular and has no regard to physical features. On the north-west the county has a similarly artificial boundary ; but here also were extensive woodlands, for the Tertiary strata are here bare of gravel and still support considerable oak woods, while even the chalk of this particular area is covered by so deep a clay soil that it still supports much beech. For a long period therefore the earlier settlements of Sussex were almost isolated from the rest of the country by water or by wide tracts of dense forest. Thus the county of Sussex has probably existed as a natural division of Britain from very early prehistoric times, though the fixing of its exact limits is of comparatively late date. It is not unlikely that with better information we may be able to trace local peculiarities in the manufactures as far back as the Palæolithic period, for even then it was essentially an open country cut off and surrounded by water and forest. Subsequent articles relating to the history and archæology of the county will describe how this isolation was afterwards broken down ; in this sketch we deal with its origin, and with the leading changes which made Sussex as we now see it.

We naturally inquire, What is the meaning of the striking differences already alluded to, and why should the geological structure of a county like this, which contains no mountains and no hill reaching to 1,000 feet in altitude, have dominated so completely the position of its settlements and also the occupation of its inhabitants ? We need not go back to very early geological times ; the history of Sussex for our purpose begins with the oldest strata seen at the surface in the Weald, though other deposits somewhat older have been penetrated by a deep boring near Battle. The geological formations known to exist in Sussex may be grouped as in the following table ; but their thicknesses, it may be observed, vary greatly even within this limited area. Though it is not to be expected that a boring or shaft sunk at any one point would penetrate the whole of these strata, yet there is little doubt that at Selsey we should have to descend fully 6,000 feet to reach the lowest deposit shown in this table. Near Eastbourne and Newhaven on the other hand far older strata may possibly be reached in less than 2,000 feet below the surface ; though this remains to be proved.

GEOLOGY

TABLE OF STRATA FOUND IN SUSSEX

Period	Formation	Character of the Strata	Approximate thickness in feet
Recent	Peat	Very local	1 to 5
	Alluvium	Usually muddy.	up to 60
	Blown Sand	Clean sand	up to 20
	Shingle Beaches . . .	Flint pebbles	up to 20
Pleistocene and Palæolithic	Brickearth	Sandy loam	10
	Coombe Rock and Valley Gravel	Angular detritus, mainly flint and chalk	20
	Raised Beach	Shingle, sand and clay	10
	Glacial Deposit. . . .	Large erratics	thin
	Plateau Gravel	Angular gravel	thin
	Clay with Flints . . .	Angular flints and clay, on chalk .	10
Eocene	Bracklesham Beds . . .	Shelly sand, clay and thin rock . .	500 or 600
	Bagshot Sands	Greenish sands	thin
	London Clay	Clay, thin sands and Bognor Rock	300
	Woolwich and Reading Beds	Red-mottled clay, coarse sands, pebble beds, lignite and blue clay	80 to 130
Upper Cretaceous	Upper Chalk and Chalk Rock	Soft chalk, with flints	500 to 700
	Middle Chalk and Melbourn Rock	Harder chalk, with few or no flints	200
	Lower Chalk	Grey chalk, marly below. . . .	160 to 200
	Upper Greensand . . .	Greenish sand, sandstone and malm rock	40 to 80
	Gault	Blue marl, coarse sand at the base .	300
Lower Cretaceous	Folkestone Beds . . .	Coarse sand	0 to 140
	Sandgate Beds	Fine sand and clay	30 to 100
	Hythe Beds	Sand, sandstone and chert, calcareous above	25 to 200
	Atherfield Clay . . .	Shelly clay	thin
	Weald Clay	Blue and red-mottled clays, with thin sands, Sussex marble and Horsham stone	600
	Upper Tunbridge Wells Sand	⎰Sand and sandstone, with layers of Tilgate stone at the top . . .	115
		Cuckfield Clay	15
		⎱Sand and sandstone	70
	Grinstead Clay	Clay and sandstone	100
	Lower Tunbridge Wells Sand	Sand and sandstone	100
	Wadhurst Clay . . .	Shaly clay	130
	Ashdown Sand . . .	Fine sand	150
	Fairlight Clay	Clay and thin sands	360
Jurassic	Purbeck Beds	Shales and limestones with gypsum .	400
	Portland Beds	Soft sandstones and shales . . .	105
	Kimeridge Clay . . .	Black shale with ammonites, etc .	1,290
	Corallian Oolite . . .	Sands and thin oolitic limestones .	222
	Oxford Clay	Dark shale and thin limestone . .	over 120

On referring to the geological map of Sussex the reader will notice that it is coloured various tints, which form belts extending east and west throughout the county. These belts represent the strata coming to the surface, or 'cropping out,' as it is termed, in succession, the oldest appearing towards the north-east and the newest towards the south and south-west. The cross-sections appended to the map will better explain this peculiarity. The geological structure of the county consists essentially of one big wave, with its crest near Battle, Horsham and Haslemere, and its parallel trough extending east and west under the English Channel a few miles south of the coast. Minor ripples or undulations somewhat modify the perfect regularity of the big wave on which they ride ; but they are comparatively unimportant, for while the height of the dominant wave, measured from crest to trough, is fully 4,000 feet, the minor ripples do not exceed 600 feet.

The oldest rocks known within the county are the Jurassic deposits met with in the 'Sub-Wealden Boring,' a trial boring made in the year 1874 to explore the unknown deep-seated strata and to ascertain whether coal could be found within a workable depth. The most ancient strata exposed at the surface are those met with near Battle, where the crest of the high wave has been planed down so as to lay bare layers which elsewhere are only to be found far below the sea-level. To the neighbourhood of Battle therefore geologists turned their attention when it was proposed to attempt to reach Coal Measures by boring through the Secondary formations. It was naturally thought that the lower in the series it was possible to commence, the less the thickness to be penetrated before Coal Measures or other Palæozoic rocks were reached. The experimental boring at Limekiln Wood in the parish of Mountfield however proved to be a failure, its main result being to show an enormous and quite unexpected thickening of some of the Jurassic clays, so that at 1,905 feet from the surface the boring was still in Oxford Clay, with no sign of a change and perhaps several thousand feet of Secondary strata still to penetrate. The small size of the cores obtained makes it difficult to say much about the lower strata, though sufficient fossils were discovered to prove the age of certain beds. Divisions however shade into each other in such a way, and the characters of the rocks are so different from the nearest outcrops, a hundred miles distant, that there is still some difference of opinion as to the exact limits of each formation. In the following notes the grouping used by Mr. H. B. Woodward has been adhered to.[1]

The lowest strata reached consist of 100 feet or so of dark shale, with a 15 foot bed of limestone. In these shales were found specimens of *Ammonites chamusseti*, proving them to belong to the Oxford Clay. Next follow about 240 feet of more or less calcareous and sandy strata, with *Rhynchonella pinguis*, a fossil characteristic of the Corallian rocks of

---

[1] 'Jurassic Rocks of Britain,' v. 345-7, *Mem. Geol. Survey* (1895) ; see also H. Willett, *Record of the Sub-Wealden Exploration* (8vo, Brighton, 1878) ; and W. Topley, 'Geology of the Weald,' *Mem. Geol. Survey* (1875).

GEOLOGY

Dorset ; but the deposits are very unlike the Dorset type, half the thickness being shale. Above these come nearly 1,300 feet of shaly strata, with numerous ammonites and other characteristic fossils of the Kimeridge Clay. Of this enormous mass the upper 700 feet is entirely shale, the lower 600 consisting of alternations of shale, shaly sandstone and shaly limestone. The next 115 feet of strata are sandy shales and soft sandstones, yielding *Ammonites biplex* near the base and referable to the Portland series, though little resembling the hard rocks of the isle of Portland.

Next above the Portland occur Purbeck rocks to a thickness estimated by Topley at 400 feet. Of this the lower 70 feet is only known from the Sub-Wealden boring and from a mine which has since been sunk to work the beds of gypsum proved by that boring to occur at the base of the series. The upper half of the Purbeck series can be examined at the surface to the north and north-west of Battle, where it has also been exposed in bell-shaped pits, opened to obtain a calcareous sandstone and certain grey and blue limestones formerly much used for lime. The associated strata are mainly shales like those of the Isle of Purbeck, and contain a similar mixture of freshwater and marine fossils, the marine species being mostly stunted and small. The character of the rocks and of their included fossils suggests an estuarine or lagoon origin for these strata, for gypsum is a product of salt lakes and lagoons, and the abundant remains of brackish-water shells and entomostraca, belonging to few species and fewer genera, point to similar conditions. Two ferns and some insect remains have also been found ; but the curious small marsupials and the numerous cycads which occur in Dorset have not yet been discovered in the Purbeck rocks of Sussex.

Cretaceous follow the Jurassic strata without a break, estuarine deposits more than 1,000 feet thick, known as Wealden, indicating a continuance of conditions very similar to those which held during the Purbeck period. In their lower part the deposits of the Wealden period consist mainly of sands, the Hastings and Tunbridge Wells sands, with subordinate masses of sandstone, shale or clay ; but above these comes a mass of clay, with little sand, several hundred feet in thickness. So much interest has been excited by the occurrence of remains of the gigantic land reptile Iguanodon in Tilgate Forest[1] that it is scarcely realized that the Wealden strata are very sparingly fossiliferous. Beds of freshwater shells such as form the well known 'Sussex marble,' or shales rendered fissile by multitudes of the minute valves of a bivalve entomostracan, occasionally occur ; but it is quite possible to search closely a hundred feet of strata and not find a fossil. Those fossils that occur tend rather to link the Wealden with the Purbeck below than with the Cretaceous above ; but the Wealden fossils have been derived mainly from the lower part of the series, and we have still a most imperfect knowledge of those belonging to the Weald Clay. Besides land reptiles we find one or two small mammals closely allied to those of the Purbeck period,

[1] Mantell. *Fossils of the South Downs ; or, Illustrations of the Geology of Sussex* (4to, London, 1822).

numerous fish, and a fine series of plants, which last have been carefully studied by Mr. Seward.[1] These plants consist of ferns, cycads and conifers of Jurassic types, but include none of the higher flowering plants which mark the incoming of the Lower Cretaceous period abroad. Whilst recognizing the strikingly Jurassic appearance of the Wealden animals and plants, it should not be forgotten however that truly marine fossils, on which our geological classification is mainly based, are practically unknown in the Wealden strata. Until its marine fauna is better known the exact relation of the Wealden to the Upper Jurassic and Lower Cretaceous of other regions must remain somewhat doubtful.

The absence of lime and of certain compounds necessary for plant life, as well as the common occurrence of poisonous iron salts, make most of the country occupied by Wealden strata very infertile and more fitted for oak forest or permanent pasture than for tillage. Where orchards or fruit or hop-gardens thrive it will generally be found that the underlying strata are buried under several feet of superficial 'Drift,' which quite alters the character of the soil. The Hastings Sands form undulating country with steeper slopes than those of the Weald Clay, the beds of sand forming ridges roughly parallel to the folds with east and west axis, which are so marked a feature in Sussex geology. They rise in places to considerable heights, as will be seen on comparing the geological with the orographic map.

There is one important product of the Wealden strata that should be mentioned, though it will again be referred to in a later volume in the section on ironworks of the Weald. For many centuries the Weald was one of the most important iron-producing districts of Britain, the ore commonly used being the clay-ironstone nodules at the base of the Wadhurst Clay. These were dug in bell-pits of no great depth, and worked with oak charcoal, which yielded steely wrought-iron of excellent quality. Later on a considerable quantity of cast-iron was made; but the industry was finally abandoned in the early part of the nineteenth century, owing to the growing scarcity of charcoal and the gradual introduction of coal and of the associated Coal Measure ironstone.[2]

There is another product of the Wealden strata that deserves mention. Two borings for water at Waldron, the one at Heathfield railway station, the other at New Heathfield Hotel, struck inflammable gas in the Fairlight Clay.[3] This gas seems, according to the analysis by Mr. S. A. Woodhead, to be a genuine petroleum derivative, containing 72 per cent of marsh gas, mixed with enough oxygen (18 per cent) to make it slightly explosive. The gas has been used for lighting the railway station and offices.

As the main dome of the Wealden anticline causes the strata in Sussex to have a general dip to the south, if we leave out the minor

[1] *Catalogue of the Mesozoic Plants in the Department of Geology, British Museum*; *The Wealden Flora* (8vo).
[2] W. Topley, 'Geology of the Weald,' chap. xix. (1875).
[3] C. Dawson, 'On the Discovery of Natural Gas in East Sussex,' *Quart. Journ. Geol. Soc.* liv. 564–71 (1898).

folds we find higher Cretaceous deposits coming on in succession above the Weald Clay in the southern part of the county between Eastbourne and Midhurst. The earliest of these strata belongs undoubtedly to the Lower Cretaceous period; for this Atherfield Clay, so called from the place where it is best seen, Atherfield in the Isle of Wight, contains Lower Greensand marine fossils. The Atherfield Clay has only been traced as far east as Warminghurst, where Mr. Lamplugh recently noticed about 20 feet of clay with marine fossils, below the sandy Hythe Beds, and resting with a sharp division on the blue shaly Weald Clay. It is by no means clear yet whether there is not everywhere a break between the Atherfield Clay and the Weald Clay below; for there is a sudden change from estuarine to purely marine conditions, and near Eastbourne most of the Lower Greensand and probably much of the Weald Clay have been cut out or overlapped by deposits of somewhat newer date. Unfortunately however the junction of the two clay deposits is difficult to examine; for it usually occurs in flat land where natural sections are wanting and artificial sections are scarce. Wells are not sunk near the junction, for there is seldom any water to be had, and that found is not palatable.

The Lower Greensand above the Atherfield Clay consists mainly of sandy deposits with subordinate beds of harder rock. When met with in wells or excavations some depth below the level of the surface, the sands are commonly tinged more or less with green (hence the name 'Greensand') from the presence of small grains of a dark green mineral known as glauconite. This mineral, which is an iron compound, readily oxidizes on exposure, and then the sands take the familiar buff or rusty hue which makes people wonder why geologists ever called them Greensand. There is a remarkable change in the Lower Greensand when traced from west to east and south through Sussex. At Petersfield it has a thickness, according to Topley, of 425 feet; seventeen miles to the east, at Pulborough, it has decreased to 380 feet, through the thinning of the two lower divisions, the Atherfield Clay and the Hythe Beds. Another seventeen miles to the east, at Hassocks Gate, the total is only 130 feet, the Atherfield Clay having disappeared and the other three divisions having thinned considerably. Five miles or so further towards the south-east the bold pine-clad sandy ridges which characterize this formation sink and seem to melt away into an almost featureless undulating plain, which stretches to the sea near Eastbourne, where the Lower Greensand is represented by a few feet of coarse sand between the Gault and the Weald Clay, all the rest of the formation having disappeared. The question of the relation of the Lower Greensand to the Wealden strata in Sussex happens to be of more than purely scientific interest; for if Lower Cretaceous deposits can disappear so rapidly towards the south-east, it is evidently possible that the geological structure may correspond with that on the northern side of the Wealden anticline, and the Lower Cretaceous and perhaps the Jurassic strata may be entirely wanting around Newhaven. Palæozoic rocks may there occur much nearer to the surface than would otherwise be expected, and we may there find a counterpart of the Palæozoic ridge under Dover and London. Experiments at Dover however have not yet been so successful as to encourage deep borings in Sussex, and near London rocks older than the Coal Measures have been met with beneath the Cretaceous. The only deep boring on the south side of the Wealden anticline is that sunk at the Brighton Industrial School at Telscombe, where Lower Greensand was touched at 1,280 feet from the surface, but was only penetrated to a depth of about 5 feet. It is unfortunate that this boring was not carried a few feet lower, for within 20 feet the Lower Greensand would probably be pierced. What comes below is quite uncertain, and the determination of this point would throw much light on Sussex geology.

Owing to the absence of Lower Greensand cliff sections in Sussex few fossils have been found in this division compared with the prolific fauna of Kent and Hampshire. Selmeston yields drifted pine-wood perforated by boring molluscs. At Pulborough and Parham marine mollusca have been obtained from the Sandgate Beds, and at Pulborough the Hythe Beds also have yielded a good many species and the Folkestone Sands contain a few. These fossils are mainly bivalve shells, few of the characteristic ammonites or other cephalopods and few gasteropods having yet been found in Sussex.

The porous strata of the Lower Greensand are succeeded by a mass of stiff dark-blue clay known as Gault. This comes to the surface in the belt of flat heavy land which separates the sandy ridges of the Lower from the similar ridge formed by the Upper Greensand on the south. In Sussex the Gault reaches the exceptional thickness of 300 feet, and is nearly everywhere fossiliferous, though owing to the absence of cliff sections and the rarity of clear inland exposures fossils are not so readily obtained as at Folkestone. At the base is found a band of scattered phosphatic nodules, and this band seems to separate the true Gault from the Lower Greensand below—though the upper part of this latter (the only part preserved at Eastbourne) may be nothing but a gravelly base to the Gault, equivalent to beds with *Ammonites mammillatus* found elsewhere. Low down in the true Gault at Eastbourne *Ammonites lautus*, a characteristic fossil of the Lower Gault, has been found ; but the principal locality for Lower Gault fossils in Sussex is Ringmer, from which place Mr. Jukes-Browne gives a long list of fossils, cephalopods being particularly abundant.[1] At St. Anthony's Hill near Eastbourne Mr. F. G. H. Price discovered another set of fossils, which prove the Gault there seen to belong to the lower part of the Upper Gault. The highest beds of all are sometimes well exposed on the foreshore opposite Eastbourne, and they have been carefully examined below the Wish Tower by Mr. Price and Rev. H. E. Maddock, who there collected many fossils, including such characteristic Upper Gault forms as *Ammonites rostratus*, *A. varicosus*, *A. auritus* and *Anisoceras (Hamites) armatum*.

---

[1] 'The Cretaceous Rocks of Britain,' i. 121, *Memoirs Geol. Survey* (1900).

GEOLOGY

According to Mr. Price, the most fossiliferous part is a sandy bed about 3 feet below the Upper Greensand.

The sandy Upper Gault of Eastbourne is succeeded by loamy micaceous sands, which seem to pass laterally into the 'malmstone' of west Sussex. This malmstone is a rock of quite exceptional character; it is defined by Mr. Jukes-Browne as a 'fine-grained siliceous rock, the silica of which is either principally of the colloid variety, either in the form of a semigranular ground mass or of scattered microscopic spheroids, or in both forms. Sponge spicules, or the spaces once occupied by them, are always abundant, and seem to have supplied the silica which is now in the globular semigranular condition. Quartz, mica and glauconite are present, but generally in small quantities. There is always some calcareous matter, but in the purer varieties this does not amount to more than 2 or 3 per cent. Other varieties, however, contain as much as 20 or 25 per cent, and these are called *calcareous malmstones* or *fire-stones.*' Above the malmstone and loamy beds comes a mass of glauconitic sand or sandstone, calcareous in the upper part, and probably from 40 to 50 feet in thickness near Eastbourne. The total thickness of the Upper Greensand in western Sussex is estimated by P. J. Martin at about 90 to 100 feet,[1] and this is probably the maximum in the county. The formation has not yet yielded many fossils, and it is still doubtful whether any part of it in Sussex represents the zone of *Pecten asper*; the species found are not characteristic of particular zones. Upwards the Greensand passes gradually into the Chalk, the sand becoming more calcareous and marly, till it gives place to the somewhat sandy marl which here forms the base of the true Chalk. Though, as already mentioned, the Upper Greensand tends to form a ridge of sandy land, yet it is usually so dominated by the higher escarpment of the Chalk, that both the feature it makes and the character of the soil are masked and altered by material washed from the Chalk above. The Upper Greensand was probably woodland in prehistoric times.

Chalk, as will be seen by the geological map, occupies the surface of nearly a third of Sussex, forming a sharply defined region of character unlike any other in the county, and known as the South Downs. It is the only limestone, with the exception of the few thin bands already mentioned; and having a thickness of about 1,000 feet, hill and valley can be carved out of it without cutting into older rocks. Moreover, being without impervious beds except in the lowest 200 feet it forms a dry region, with no springs or flowing water except in the lowest valleys. The greater part of the Downs forms open rolling country, bare and treeless, but covered with excellent pasture, or with light, calcareous soil readily worked by the plough. These characteristics have always influenced the position of the settlements and the early history of the region; for when ploughs and cutting tools were ruder and more clumsy, open pasture land with light and fairly good soil, not encumbered by trees, was far more valuable than the woodland which

---

[1] *Geological Memoir on a part of Western Sussex* (4to, London, 1828).

overspread the clays, or the bare heaths which characterized the sands. The areas occupied by Chalk were probably in prehistoric times, and even much later, the most settled and highly civilized parts of Britain ; they are certainly the areas over which are found our finest and most extensive prehistoric antiquities. We in Sussex scarcely realize how peculiar and abnormal a deposit is this soft pure white limestone known as Chalk. It occupies a small part of western Europe, but in other regions of the world there is nothing very closely resembling it, except in comparatively thin beds. This thousand feet of strata is composed almost entirely of marine organisms—either recognizable or decayed— except in the lower part, in which there is a considerable admixture of clay and other detritus washed from the land. The rest of the formation is so uniform that the differences are not such as to strike the casual observer, who would describe the whole mass simply as chalk. On examining more closely we find at different levels slight differences in the character of the deposits and in their included fossils. These variations extend throughout the county, so that it is usually possible from an isolated chalk pit to tell approximately how high we are above the base of the deposit.[1]

The lower part of the Chalk consists essentially of greyish marl in alternate hard and soft beds, which make conspicuous ledges on the fore-shore and at the base of the cliff between Eastbourne and Beachy Head. These deposits form the Lower Chalk, which has a thickness of from 150 to 200 feet, and occupies the gently rising ground at the foot of the Chalk escarpment. Its soil is more retentive than that of the rest of the Chalk, and much of it was formerly woodland, though now it is mainly under the plough or changing to permanent pasture. The fossils are peculiar. Towards the base we find a narrow zone of hard sandy chalk with quartz grains and occasional phosphatic nodules. This zone is characterized by the small sponge *Stauronema carteri*. Then follow marls, breaking up into pieces with curved faces and containing *Ammonites varians*, *A. rotomagensis*, *Scaphites æqualis*, and *Holaster subglobosus*, as well as numerous bivalves and fish. Most of the beautifully-preserved fish remains found at Lewes and to be seen in every museum come from this division. At the top of the Lower Chalk is a band 10 or 20 feet thick of softer, darker, and more impervious marl, known as the 'Belemnite Marl,' from its characteristic fossil *Actinocamax* (*Belemnitella*) *plenus*. This marl holds up and throws out the water which falls on the higher beds of chalk ; many of the springs are therefore given out at the junction of the Lower with the Middle Chalk. Very little water is obtained from the Lower Chalk itself, except where it is much shattered, as near Eastbourne. This division of the Chalk, besides forming land of different agricultural character, produces hydraulic lime, which cannot be made from the beds above.

There is a sudden change from the soft Belemnite Marl to the hard

[1] The best account of the zones will be found in Dr. A. W. Rowe, 'The Zones of the White Chalk of the English Coast : I.—Kent and Sussex,' *Proc. Geol. Assoc.* vol. xvi. pt. 6 (1900).

and somewhat flaggy ' Melbourn Rock ' above, which forms the base of the Middle Chalk. This rock may be described as a hard, somewhat splintery, white chalk, with a curiously irregular wavy bedding and partings of grey marl, markedly in contrast with the evenly bedded grey marls below. The Melbourn Rock passes up into somewhat softer strata, but deposits of similar character form the whole 200 feet of the Middle Chalk. This chalk is full of fossils ; though the great majority of the fragments belong to a single species of bivalve shell, *Inoceramus mytiloides* (or *I. labiatus*), fragments of which form a considerable portion of the bulk of the rock and are easily recognizable from their peculiar fibrous structure. The upper part of the Middle Chalk is characterized by a small *Terebratulina* commonly referred to *T. gracilis*.

The Melbourn Rock projects as a distinct ledge in the face of the Chalk escarpment, or crowns projecting spurs, especially near Eastbourne ; this platform is often selected as a favourable site for building. The rest of the Middle Chalk forms the steep face of the escarpment, capped by the flinty chalk above ; it also stretches in long tongues up some of the valleys, as well as appearing in others as inliers. One series of these inliers, seen in the valley bottoms between Lewes and Patcham, is brought up by a prolongation of the anticline which passes through Beddingham and Kingstone. Another similar undulation brings Middle Chalk to the surface in the east and west valley between East Dean and Singleton ; and it is possible that Middle Chalk may also be exposed in the centre of the anticline near Littlehampton, though there the country is so covered with gravel, and the foreshore is so sandy, that it is difficult to examine the Chalk below.

The junction of the Middle and Upper Chalk in many parts of England is marked by a band of hard, splintery chalk known as the ' Chalk Rock.' This however is non-existent in Sussex, though the characteristic fossils, principally small gasteropods, can be found at Beachy Head. Beyond the gradual appearance of flints, there is no very obvious distinction between Middle and Upper Chalk, as seen in these vertical cliffs. The Upper Chalk is purer, whiter, softer, and contains fewer marl partings than the Middle Chalk. Flints are almost confined to it, though a few scattered nodules can be found 10 or 20 feet below the base. The lowest zone (including the Chalk Rock) is characterized by the echinoderm *Holaster planus* and a group of other fossils that are always found associated with it, but the lower limit of the zone seemingly does not quite coincide with the base of the Chalk Rock ; the thickness is about 50 feet. The next zones are specially characterized by different forms of *Micraster*, echinoderms which have lately yielded to Dr. A. W. Rowe[1] evidence of the gradual evolution of each succeeding form from an older one, so that by slight variations in the shape and pattern of the shell he can tell to within a few feet from what part of the Chalk a handful of these sea urchins was obtained. One result of this study is to show, as might have been expected, that when the missing

[1] *Quart. Journ. Geol. Soc.* lv. 494 (1899).

links are discovered species pass by imperceptible gradations into each other, so that the ordinary rules of zoological nomenclature break down, and it is exceedingly difficult to know what to call any but the extreme forms. Space will not permit any discussion of these variable fossils ; we can only observe that they are particularly abundant in the lower part of the Upper Chalk, *Micraster cor-bovis* being confined to the *Holaster planus* zone and the Chalk below ; while *Micraster cor-testudinarium* and *M. cor-anguinum* give their names to the next two zones, respectively 110 and 240 feet in thickness. Though still-varying micrasters extend throughout the Upper Chalk, other more abundant fossils have been selected to give their names to the higher zones. Next comes softer chalk with fewer flints, at any rate inland, belonging to the zone of *Marsupites*, curious purse-like echinoderms, two species of which are not uncommon, associated with *Uintacrinus* and the small sea urchin *Cardiaster pilula*. On the coast the thickness of this zone is nearly 80 feet.

The next zone, that of *Actinocamax quadratus*, is more flinty, and this superposition of flinty chalk on soft, easily eroded chalk with few flints has led to the formation of a series of isolated, flat-topped hills, with steep scarps towards the north and gentler slopes to the south, which form a chain extending east and west through the middle of the Downs. Each of these hills was fortified in prehistoric times, the best known of the fortresses being the conspicuous camp of Cissbury, where also the flints of this zone were mined for the manufacture of implements. According to Dr. Rowe, a thickness of 170 feet of Chalk belonging to this zone can be measured in the cliffs. It is doubtful whether there is more than this anywhere in the county, for the higher part of the zone and the whole of the zones above appear to be missing.

The best places to study the Chalk zones in Sussex are, for the Middle and Upper Chalk, the cliffs between Eastbourne and Brighton ; but for the Lower Chalk the large pits near Lewes are more satisfactory, for at Eastbourne the Lower Chalk is exceptionally hardened and disturbed. With regard to the zones into which the Chalk is divided, it may be remarked that these are belts corresponding roughly with the occurrence of certain faunas, and that the name of a particular fossil is only given to a zone as a matter of convenience. The name-fossil may be entirely absent from a particular district, or it may there range above or below the zone to which it gives its name ; and usually, as might be expected, most of the other species overlap towards the border and are found also in the zone above or below. Hard and fast boundaries are no more to be found between life-zones, except in rare cases, than they are to be found between species ; it is only our imperfect knowledge that in each case has allowed us to draw sharp lines.

Between the Chalk of Sussex and the oldest of the overlying Tertiary deposits there exists an enormous gap. Not only is great part of the Chalk missing, but several early Eocene deposits elsewhere well developed and containing peculiar faunas are absent ; even the Thanet

GEOLOGY

Sands of Kent cannot be traced into Sussex. The earliest Eocene strata preserved in the county are the highly variable estuarine deposits known as the Woolwich and Reading Series. These show a complete change of conditions, and contain animals and plants so different from those of the Chalk that comparison is almost impossible. The formation now stretches from the western border of the county in narrow belts through Chichester and Arundel to Bognor, Worthing and Lancing, and is continued eastward by a chain of outliers at Portslade, Brighton, Newhaven and Seaford. Originally however it must have overspread the whole county, for it corresponds closely with the deposits of the Thames basin and of the north of France. In the western half of the county the strata are of the ' Reading ' type, i.e. they consist mainly of red-mottled plastic or pottery clay, with occasional seams of lignite, flint pebbles and sand, and with a bed of unworn green-coated flints at the base. These deposits seem to be of lagoon or estuarine origin, though determinable fossils have not yet been found in them in Sussex. The eastern half of the county shows deposits more like the ' Woolwich ' type. At Lancing beneath or near the base of the red-mottled clay occurs a band of ironstone with marine fossils. At Portslade we find a mass of bluish-black shaly clays with a mixture of marine and freshwater fossils, principally oysters and *Cyrena*. At Brighton the thin outliers towards Preston yield moulds of marine fossils in ironstone, as well as traces of plants. Newhaven was formerly celebrated for its plant-beds, though these are now either washed away or hidden by the sloping of the cliffs under the fort ; the deposits there consisted mainly of laminated shelly or plant-bearing clays, with seams of sand and masses of lignite, to a thickness of 60 feet. Red-mottled plastic clays are absent. The shells recorded by Prestwich [1] are mainly estuarine and freshwater species such as *Dreissena*, *Unio*, *Cyrena*, *Cerithium*, *Melania inquinata* and *Ostrea bellovacina*. The flora is an interesting one, for it shows warm-temperate conditions, and the plants are closely allied to species still living in warmer regions. Unfortunately they are still only partially examined and described ; but according to Mr. J. S. Gardner the greater part of the leaves belong to a few species, amongst them being a palm and an aralia-like leaf. The Woolwich and Reading Series is from 90 to 130 feet thick ; but occupies so small an area in Sussex, and is so largely hidden by newer deposits, that it has had little influence on the position of settlements, except where the distruction of its outliers has overspread the Chalk with the sheet of clay known as ' Clay with Flints.' This last-mentioned deposit is often stated to be the insoluble residue of the Chalk dissolved by falling rain. Such however cannot be the case, for it has a curiously partial distribution, and only caps plateaus formerly overspread by Eocene strata. Its composition also shows it to be formed mainly of recognizable Eocene material, such as quartz sand, flint and quartz pebbles, green-

---

[1] 'On the Structure of the Strata between the London Clay and the Chalk in the London and Hampshire Tertiary Systems : Part II.—The Woolwich and Reading Series,' *Quart. Journ. Geol. Soc.* x. 83–4 (1854).

coated flints and pieces of ironstone. Some of the unworn flints in it undoubtedly are derived from the slow solution of the Chalk below, and a small part of the clayey matrix also may come from this source. The Upper Chalk of Sussex however is so pure that the removal of the soluble carbonate of lime would leave merely a stony desert of flints, without sufficient clay to fill the interstices. Such a stony waste is now gradually forming on parts of the Downs where no Tertiary material remains.

The London Clay in Sussex is more sandy than the corresponding deposit in the London basin, though not nearly so different as the local name, 'Bognor Beds,' formerly used would imply. It is a dark-blue clay, more or less sandy, containing beds of sand in the upper part, and in places it has a mass of flint shingle at the base. Two of the sand-beds near Bognor have been consolidated into hard sandstone; and as these sandstones form conspicuous rocky ledges, the Bognor Rocks and the Barn Rocks, projecting seaward from a coast otherwise flat and sandy, they have been given more importance than their small thickness would warrant. The Bognor Rock however is of considerable interest, for the fossils contained in it, now difficult to obtain, are well preserved and are not compressed like those ordinarily found in the London Clay. The most common are *Pectunculus brevirostris*, *P. decussatus*, *Cardita brongniarti*, *Panopæa intermedia*, *Pholadomya margaritacea*, *Pinna affinis*, all common fossils of the London Clay elsewhere. There is also a peculiar volute, *Voluta nodosa*, and the flat-coiled *Vermetus bognoriensis*. The total thickness of the London Clay is about 320 feet. Like the Reading Beds, much of it is hidden by newer deposits ; but where exposed it forms heavy clay land principally covered by oak plantations. Bricks are made from it ; but not to any great extent in Sussex, where better and more easily worked brick-earth is to be found in the same districts.

It is still somewhat uncertain whether Sussex contains any representative of the Lower Bagshot Beds. Sandy strata occur at the top of the London Clay on each side of the Selsey peninsula ; but they are difficult to examine, being hidden by gravel, and striking the coast just where everything is obscured by the mud of Pagham Harbour and of West Wittering. The sands cannot be thick, and no fossils have been obtained from them ; it is possible however that some of the deposits with driftwood occasionally to be seen on the foreshore near West Wittering may be referred to this formation.

The Bracklesham Beds form one of the most interesting deposits of the county from a scientific point of view ; but as they are entirely hidden by drift, except on the foreshore, and are confined to the Selsey peninsula, they have little influence on the character of the scenery, nature of the soil, or position of the settlements. The thickness of these strata reaches however as much as 500 feet. From top to bottom they consist of greenish, more or less carbonaceous clays and marls, alternating with glauconitic sands. Fossils are abundant, in fact

GEOLOGY

certain thin beds are so full of the coin-shaped nummulites or of the spindle-shaped *Alveolina* as to have become sandy limestones, while another bed is composed principally of the large handsome shells of *Cardita planicosta*. The fauna is extremely varied and has been carefully studied by the Rev. O. Fisher [1] and Dixon.[2] Mr. Fisher has made out a definite succession in the zones, certain fossils being characteristic of particular horizons throughout the Hampshire basin ; but it is not yet clearly understood to what extent these variations are the result of local conditions or of the lapse of time. Species confined to one thin bed in Selsey elsewhere have often much wider ranges. The constant changes in the character of the sediments, and probably in the saltness of the water, are enough to account for the appearance and disappearance of many of the more sensitive species.

Taking the strata in order, commencing with the lowest seen on the shore near Chichester Channel, we first meet with sandy loams with flint pebbles and much worm-eaten driftwood. This pebble bed is apparently the same as that forming the base of the Bracklesham Series in the Isle of Wight. Then follow bedded carbonaceous clays and sands, with much driftwood and an occasional oyster, till near West Wittering Beacon we find a sand full of the drifted fruits of the nipa-palm. This is a nut about the size of and somewhat like the cocoanut. A living species closely allied to the extinct form found at West Wittering is a low palm which always grows in tidal estuaries of the East Indies, dropping its nuts into the water in such profusion as to become an obstruction to the paddle-steamers which navigate these estuaries. The extinct species of *Nipa*, of which several have been found in Britain, seem all to have grown in similar positions, for they are found associated with oysters and *Teredo*-bored driftwood, not with plants and animals belonging entirely to the land or to fresh water.

More to the south, and consequently higher in the series (the dip is southward), follows bed after bed of carbonaceous clay and glauconitic sand, with driftwood and a few marine shells, till opposite Bracklesham farm commence the shelly beds from which most of the fossils are obtained. These continue to Selsey Bill, where the highest Eocene deposit in Sussex is met with in the Alveolina limestone of the Mixen Rocks, where it was formerly much quarried for building purposes.

The slightest acquaintance with the natural history of warmer regions brings out in a most striking manner the resemblance of the Bracklesham animals and plants to those of the tropics, and their comparatively small connection with the existing fauna and flora of Britain. Amongst the vertebrate animals the turtles, crocodiles, sea-snakes, and large sharks and rays find their nearest living allies in the tropics. The mollusca are distinctly sub-tropical, including numerous nautili, volutes, cones, mitres, olives, cowries, and other large and handsomely sculptured shells. True

[1] *Quart. Journ. Geol. Soc.* xviii. 65 (1862).
[2] *Geology of Sussex*, ed. 2, 4to, London (1878) ; see also Reid, 'Geology of Bognor,' pp. 4–8, *Mem. Geol. Survey* (1897).

15

reef-building corals are absent; but this may be due more to the muddiness of the water than to the absence of sufficient warmth. The large foraminifera also, though of extinct species, suggest tropical seas, and it is interesting to find in Egypt whole hills made up of nummulite limestone, belonging to a period not far removed from our Bracklesham. The palms also point to a high temperature, though the cones of pine occasionally found associated suggest a climate somewhat less warm. Few pines are now found in the tropics; but on the other hand in the Bracklesham Beds pine-cones are rare and may have drifted enormous distances, while nuts of nipa occur in profusion in certain beds, as do the tropical shells.

It has been asked, In what direction lay the continent or large island from which flowed the river that brought this mass of sediment and all this driftwood? The question is not easy to answer, for though slight indications point to land to the west or perhaps south-west, yet Bracklesham Beds of similar character, though much thinner, and containing the same nipa (*Nipa burtini*) are found in Belgium also. Perhaps the most probable analogy is with a tropical archipelago, such as the Malayan, with its dotted large and small islands. The few land animals found in the Bracklesham Beds are more suggestive of scattered islands than of a continent anywhere very near to Sussex.

From the Bracklesham period onward through several other periods the records have been destroyed in Sussex, and all that can be done is to outline roughly the probable course of events up to the Glacial epoch. This we are enabled to do through records preserved in adjoining counties, though for some stages the history is still so obscure that reconstruction is impossible. The marine Barton Beds, which complete the Eocene series, are well developed in Hampshire and the Isle of Wight, and they doubtless once extended over Sussex also. Whether this was the case with the fluvio-marine Oligocene strata which succeed is more doubtful; for the deposits, though 600 feet thick no further off than the Isle of Wight, consist so largely of lacustrine sediments that land cannot have been far distant. Slight indications however suggest that the land then lay to the south and west, and that the deposits became more marine towards Sussex, and are therefore more likely to have been continuous over that county.

The succeeding Miocene period has left no records either in Sussex or anywhere else in Britain; but it is almost certainly to this period that we may refer the great earth movements which caused the folding and bending of the strata to which reference has already been made. The mode by which we arrive at this date is as follows: The Eocene and Oligocene strata of the Isle of Wight form a continuous series without break up to the Middle Oligocene; but the whole of these rocks have been tilted and folded as one mass, so that in places the bedding is now vertical: therefore the great period of disturbance was later than Middle Oligocene. To ascertain the date when the great movements had ceased we reason thus: The earliest Pliocene Beds of Kent rest on an eroded

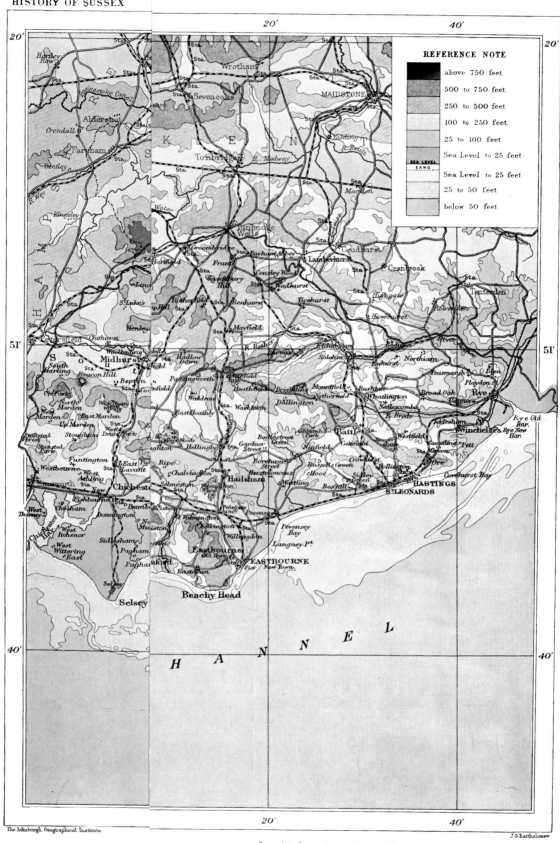

REFERENCE NOTE

above 750 feet
500 to 750 feet
250 to 500 feet
100 to 250 feet
25 to 100 feet
Sea Level to 25 feet
SEA LEVEL
SAND
Sea Level to 25 feet
25 to 50 feet
below 50 feet

The Edinburgh Geographical Institute

J.G.Bartholomew

ENGLAND

County Boundary shown thus _____

surface of Chalk, all the intermediate strata having been tilted up and denuded before the Pliocene were deposited : therefore the disturbance had taken place before the Pliocene period. This narrows the limit of time during which the great folding occurred to some part of the Miocene, or perhaps of the preceding Upper Oligocene. More direct evidence obtainable on the continent shows that the Miocene was one of the great periods of earth movement and mountain building, and to this period we may therefore safely refer most of the folding in Sussex. The movement in Sussex seems to have consisted of a horizontal compression of the strata from north to south, by which they were bent into a series of folds having an east and west axis. Thus was formed the large anticlinal arch of the Weald and the syncline of the Hampshire basin, as well as the numerous smaller ripples which will be found indicated on the geological map. To the same period belong the very curious overthrust faults so well seen on the foreshore between Eastbourne and Beachy Head, though these happen to run north and south for a short distance, for they apparently occur just where one fold is dying out and a fresh one commencing. All the folds are elongated domes, arranged *en échelon*, not in continuous ridges ; where one fold dies out a new one commences, but not exactly in the same line and not continuous with it.

The lateral compression of the rocks just referred to necessarily caused them to expand upwards, in the only direction in which they were free, to form east and west ridges. The largest of these undulations would now form a mountain chain over 6,000 feet in height in the centre of the Weald, were it not that rivers and sea combined to plane it down almost as fast as it rose. Its uprise however was sufficiently rapid to determine the course of the Wealden rivers, which flowed down the northward and southward slopes, diverging from the Wealden axis. During subsequent periods the country around this axis, being formed of rocks more easily denuded than the Chalk, has become lowered much below the level of the Downs through which the rivers now flow in narrow and deep valleys. A river once started tends to deepen its channel, but remains nearly in the same place long after the original slopes which first directed its course have been obliterated by the erosive action of its tributaries. The high cliff-like escarpment of the South Downs, which overlooks the Weald, is due to the erosive power of rain and rivers acting on strata some of which are hard and some soft ; it is not due to the waves of the sea as formerly thought. Standing on the Downs and overlooking the low-lying plain it is difficult to believe that we are not looking across the bed of an ancient sea, which once filled the Weald. But not only are newer Tertiary marine deposits absent from the Weald, but as Mr. Whitaker has pointed out, escarpments can readily be distinguished from sea-cliffs by certain characteristics. The foot of a sea-cliff keeps to one level, but cuts through various strata ; the foot of an escarpment formed by rain and rivers rises and falls considerably, but keeps to the same geological horizon. The northward-facing slope of the South Downs is an escarpment always having at its base the

soft Lower Chalk ; the southward-facing bluff (still to be described) is a
true sea-cliff, which sometimes leaves the Chalk altogether and cuts
through Tertiary strata.

The Sussex rivers and their peculiar courses will best be understood
from an examination of the accompanying orographic map. It will be
noticed that the principal streams, Arun, Adur, Ouse and Cuckmere,
rise on comparatively low ground towards the centre of the Weald and
make a short cut to the sea through gaps in the South Downs. The
Ashburn and the Rother, on the other hand, now flow over low country
to fall direct into the English Channel ; but it is possible that they also
at one time behaved like the other Wealden rivers and breached the
Chalk hills at a time when the Downs extended more to the east.
Topley, who did so much to elucidate the whole question of the origin
of the Wealden rivers, thought that formerly the Ashburn, which rises
on the south side of the axis, broke the South Downs a few miles east
of Beachy Head, and that the Rother, which rises north of the axis,
turned northward and breached the North Downs somewhere near the
middle of the present Straits of Dover.[1] It seems doubtful however
whether within the lifetime of the existing rivers the South Downs were
ever continuous with the Chalk hills of France,[2] though the North Downs
appear to have been so, for chalk has been traced across the bed of the
strait from shore to shore.

When we try to fix a date for the beginning of this peculiar valley
system it is obviously needless to look back to times anterior to the last
period when the county was submerged beneath the sea ; for the sea
tends to plane down the hills and to level up depressions, so that any
previously existing valleys are not likely to reappear when dry land again
emerges. The latest submergence to any considerable depth seems to
have been of older Pliocene date, marine deposits of this period capping
the North Downs at a height of over 600 feet near Lenham, though
they have not yet been discovered in Sussex. It does not seem probable
that any of the existing valleys date from an earlier period, though there
may have been an older system having a similar relation to the Wealden
uprise. It is not easy to follow the exact course of events in later Pliocene times, when the land rose and the streams began their work ; for
the rivers have long since entirely destroyed their earlier deposits, so that
no fossil relic now remains in Sussex of the interesting fauna and flora
which overspread Britain in preglacial times. From records preserved in
other counties we learn that these were times when large animals abounded
—elephants, rhinoceroses, hippopotami, numerous deer, mostly of species
unknown in later deposits, besides animals of more unfamiliar type, such
as the sabre-toothed tiger and mastodon. Towards the close of the Pliocene period Britain was still joined to the continent, the Thames and the
rivers north of the Wealden axis being tributaries of a larger Rhine, which
then seems to have reached the sea somewhere off the present Norfolk

[1] 'Geology of the Weald,' chap. xvi. and plate ii.
[2] Reid, 'Geology of Eastbourne,' *Mem. Geol. Survey* (1898), p. 13.

GEOLOGY

coast. The Sussex rivers however, except the Rother, belonged to a different system, the relations of which to the English Channel is by no means clear. The main river seems to have flowed eastward through the Hampshire Tertiary basin in a course similar to and parallel with that of the Thames. The southern side of the valley of this ancient Solent river has now been breached and destroyed by the sea everywhere except in the Isle of Purbeck and in the Isle of Wight. At one time however its basin was probably nearly as large as that of the Thames, for it drained most of Dorset, Wiltshire, Hampshire and Sussex, as well as the destroyed south side of the basin, the area of which we cannot now estimate. Between Brighton and Beachy Head the valley of this old river seems to have turned southward, probably opening into the English Channel in that direction within a few miles of the present coast.

Leaving speculation as to the probable course of the Pliocene rivers, we reach firmer ground when we examine the Pleistocene deposits of the Sussex levels ; for these yield valuable evidence as to what happened in the county during the Glacial epoch, and during that obscure period when man seems first to have occupied the county. Sussex, it so happens, has yielded for this period a clearer record than that preserved anywhere else on our south coast ; but unfortunately its superficial deposits have only yet been thoroughly examined over the southern part of the county. We must therefore devote most of our space to the region lying between the escarpment of the South Downs and the English Channel.[1]

It has already been mentioned that between the Downs and the sea there spreads a low-lying plain, which beginning at Brighton gradually widens to 8 miles between Chichester and Selsey. This plain is not, as might be thought, an area of soft, easily eroded rocks. It is composed of strata of varying hardness, folded and tilted at varying angles, but all planed down to one nearly uniform level. The levelling was obviously done by the sea ; for not only is the flat land bounded on the north by a partly-obliterated bluff or buried sea-cliff, sometimes of chalk, sometimes of clay, but against this cliff here and there are still to be found banked remains of the beaches cast up by the sea, and in these beaches occur well preserved sea shells. The deposits banked against the old cliff and scattered over the ancient sea bed belong however to more than one period and suggest, as does the wide extent of the levelled surface, that their formation occupied a considerable time. We will now describe these deposits as seen in the Selsey peninsula, for there the order of succession is clearest and the series most complete. Selsey gives the key to the succession in other parts of the county.

The Pagham erratics, the Coombe Rock, and the Pleistocene marine deposit of Selsey have been referred to by all writers on Sussex geology,[2]

---

[1] The following account is taken mainly from observations made in the course of the Geological Survey. See Reid, 'Pleistocene Deposits of the Sussex Coast,' *Quart. Journ. Geol. Soc.* xlviii. 344 (1892) ; 'Geology of the Country around Bognor,' *Mem. Geol. Survey* (1897).
[2] See Mantell, *Fossils of the South Downs* (1822) ; Dixon, *Geology of Sussex* (1850) and ed. 2 (1878) ; Godwin-Austen, 'Newer Tertiary Deposits of the Sussex Coast,' *Quart. Journ. Geol. Soc.* xiii. 40 (1857) ; Prestwich, 'Westward Extension of the Old Raised Beach of Brighton,' ibid. xv. 215 (1859).

but it was only during the later researches of the Geological Survey, when the superficial deposits were mapped, that the relation of these to each other was clearly made out. A series of storms in the autumn and winter of 1892 combined to cut back the cliff, scour away the beach and lay bare sections unlike any that had previously been noted. Nearly opposite Medmerry farm in Bracklesham Bay the foreshore thus bared exhibited the junction of the Glacial deposits with the Bracklesham Beds over a considerable area. The surface of the Bracklesham strata was neither smooth nor channelled, as in an ordinary shore ; but showed clear evidence of the action of floating ice, probably of 'ice-foot' such as forms every winter in the arctic regions on the shore beneath the cliffs. The ancient foreshore, which lay only a few feet above the level of the present tidal flats, was full of basins or pits from 2 to 6 feet across. Most of these pits contained nothing but loose gravel, with a few valves of *Balanus* and rare fragments of marine mollusca ; the others each contained a far-transported, erratic block, which had not merely been dropped, but showed signs of having been forcibly squeezed or screwed into the clay, until its upper surface was flush with the general level. The pits filled with finer material probably mark the spots where large

FIG. I.—DIAGRAM-SECTION TO SHOW THE RELATION OF THE ERRATIC BLOCKS TO THE FLOOR OF BRACKLESHAM BEDS.[1]

erratics were formerly deposited, though, becoming again frozen into the ice, they were lifted out and transported to fresh sites. Among the erratics found on this coast were blocks of Bembridge Limestone, large Chalk flints and Upper Greensand from the Isle of Wight ; many large masses of Bognor Rock from the ledge a few miles to the east ; and numerous more rounded blocks of harder rocks, such as peculiar granite, diorite, felsite, porphyry and hard sandstone. Most of these igneous and Palæozoic rocks seem to have come from the Channel Islands and the Brittany coast ; one granite with large crystals of white orthoclase felspar is more probably of Cornish origin. A large block of fossiliferous Bognor Rock, measuring 5 feet by 4, was beautifully striated. This is 50 miles south of the nearest glacial deposits of the Thames valley, and is the only glacially striated rock yet observed south of the Thames. Large granitic boulders of character similar to those of Selsey are scattered over the plain as far as Worthing, where two or three are preserved in the park ; other smaller pieces occur in the raised beach of Brighton, in which deposit however they were not originally dropped.

For the continuation of the Selsey record we must examine the coast nearly a mile to the south-east and nearer to the Bill, for there the series is more complete, though the glacial deposit just described has been

[1] Figs. I–4 have been reproduced, by kind permission of the Council, from the *Quarterly Journal of the Geological Society.*

FIG. 2.—GLACIALLY STRIATED ERRATIC FROM MEDMERRY NEAR SELSEY
(PORTION OF A BLOCK WEIGHING UPWARDS OF 2 TONS).

[From a photograph, half natural size, by Mr. J. J. H. Teall, F.R.S.]

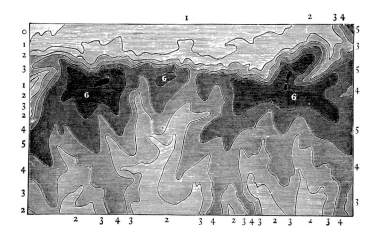

FIG. 3.—CONTOUR MAP OF A PORTION OF THE SOUTH DOWNS BETWEEN THE
VALLEY OF THE ADUR AND THE DEVIL'S DYKE.

(Scale, 1 inch to 1 mile)

EXPLANATION OF TINTS.

0 = 0–100 feet   1 = 100–200 feet   2 = 200–300 feet
3 = 300–400 feet   4 = 400–500 feet   5 = 500–600 feet
6 = 600–700 feet   7 (black) = 700–800 feet

To face page 20.

GEOLOGY

broken up and its materials have been redeposited, as at Brighton, in a newer stratum. Such also is the case at West Wittering, where numerous erratic blocks, derived from an underlying destroyed arctic deposit, are found mixed with the temperate or southern plants and mollusca of the stratum above. The section at Selsey Bill will be most readily understood from the subjoined sketch (fig. 4), made during the storms of 1892.

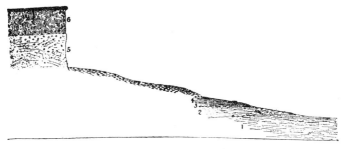

FIG. 4.—SECTION OF THE CLIFF AND FORESHORE AT SELSEY BILL.
(Scale : vertical, 20 feet = 1 inch ; horizontal, 100 feet = 1 inch)

feet
6. Stony loam, gravelly at base, chalky where unweathered (= Coombe Rock) . . . 6
5. Shingle, with occasional fragments of Greensand chert and other erratics (= raised beach of Brighton ?) 4
   Sand and shingle 3
   Hidden under recent beach (probably all sand and shingle, as above) 6
4. Black, stony, estuarine mud, with driftwood, acorns, Montpellier maple, *Scrobicularia* in the position of life, *Hydrobia ulvæ*, *Littorina obtusata*, *Rissoa parva*, *Utriculus*, *Tellina balthica*, *Cardium edule* 2
3. Stony clay with numerous re-deposited erratics (base of No. 4) . . . . $0\frac{1}{2}$
2. Hard, greenish clay, full of derivative Bracklesham fossils, and with Pleistocene marine mollusca. *Chiton siculus*, *Rissoa cimex*, etc. Occasional large chalk flints and erratic blocks (= raised beach of Goodwood ?). (This deposit is likely to be confounded with the underlying Eocene strata, for it is mainly formed of redeposited Bracklesham material, and contains more Eocene than Pleistocene fossils) 2
1. Bracklesham Beds.

The first thing to strike one in this section is that three different types of sediment are represented among the brackish-water and marine strata. The lowest bed (2) is a purely marine deposit, with a molluscan fauna of southern type, showing a depth probably of 10 or 25 fathoms. The next (3 and 4) is *Scrobicularia* mud, with estuarine shells and land plants, and was clearly formed between tide marks. The third (5) is a mass of littoral sand and shingle, resting irregularly on the fossiliferous strata, and within a short distance overlapping them and resting directly on Bracklesham Beds. All three deposits, notwithstanding their different lithological character and fossils, belong apparently to one series, and point to a gradual shoaling of the water and change from an open sea to a sheltered estuary.

The fossils of bed 2 clearly show the influence of warmer seas than those which now wash our shores ; for among the large number of mollusca already recorded several have a range exclusively southern and none are boreal. A raised beach and sand dune, banked against the old cliff in Goodwood Park, represent apparently the littoral deposits of the same period. Their level is about 130 feet above that of the Selsey clay. From beds 3 and 4 we have a much smaller list, and the species are

21

not characteristically southern, though certainly not arctic. The associated plants include the oak, blackberry, dog-rose, bird-cherry, wild cherry, and the maple of Montpellier, the last being a small tree of the Mediterranean region, found also in central Europe, but extinct in Britain. The plants point to a climate sufficiently mild for forest trees such as these, and therefore too mild to allow of the formation of ice-foot. Bed 5 does not appear yet to have yielded fossils at Selsey, but deposits probably of the same age at Worthing, Shoreham and Brighton contain only common littoral shells such as inhabit the English Channel at the present day.

West Wittering, near the western limit of the county, shows a still better exposure of peaty, estuarine loams with derived erratics, equivalent to beds 3 and 4 of the Selsey section. They yield quite an extensive series of land, freshwater and estuarine mollusca, flowering plants and mosses, as well as bones of elephant and rhinoceros. The lists are too long to reproduce; but among the mollusca are *Corbicula fluminalis*, *Helix ruderata*, and *Hydrobia marginata*, now extinct in Britain, as well as *Helix lamellata*, *Succinea oblonga* and *Hydrobia similis*, now having a restricted range and unknown living in Sussex. The forest trees include the holly, alder-buckthorn, sloe, wild cherry, cornel, elder, guelder-rose, wayfaring-tree, hazel, oak and sallow. The Montpellier maple has not yet been found ; but among the aquatic plants are two southern forms, *Najas minor* and *N. graminea*. A number of the plants are unrecorded elsewhere in the fossil state, and West Wittering has now yielded the largest flora of any Pleistocene deposit in Britain, or indeed in Europe.[1]

It has been thought advisable to deal with these comparatively recent strata at somewhat greater length than with the older rocks, for the reason that a thorough understanding of the climatic and orographic changes involved is needed before we can explain the origin of the existing fauna and flora of the county. Moreover, though the whole of the strata described up to this point have so far yielded no trace of the existence of man, yet it must be recognized that elsewhere strata apparently of the same date do yield such evidence. Thus at any moment the glacial and interglacial deposits of Sussex may turn out to be of absorbing interest in relation to the vexed question of the antiquity of man. To summarize : We learn from records preserved in Selsey that on the Sussex coast a deposit of glacial origin is overlain by one yielding a temperate fauna and flora, this latter being without admixture of arctic species, but including a few southern forms. Above these fossiliferous strata lie stony and chalky loam and Coombe Rock, which, if the interpretation of the evidence is correct, indicate a recurrence of arctic conditions. The strata yielding evidence of a temperate climate seem therefore to belong to an 'interglacial' mild episode.

The next deposit to be described, known as the Coombe Rock or Brighton Elephant-bed, is a mass of almost unstratified angular flint and chalk detritus spread over many square miles of country and becoming

---

[1] The fullest list will be found in Reid 'Origin of the British Flora' (1899), pp. 94–6.

more loamy and less chalky as we leave the rising Downs and cross the coastal plain. It is particularly well seen in the cliff at Black Rock, east of Brighton, where it overlies the raised beach, in the Portslade gravel pits, and in the enormous ballast pit by the side of the Brighton railway near Chichester. Selsey and Bognor cliffs show the loamy modification of this singular deposit, locally called ' shrave ' ; while when traced into the river gorges it tends to pass into a more stratified and cleaner river gravel, forming a terrace well above the present river level. The horse and the mammoth are everywhere the most common fossils in it ; but the teeth are always much battered and decayed, as though they had lain on the surface for some time before they reached their present resting-place. Implements used by man occur in it ; but these also may be of older date, for they are not nearly so plentiful as in the Bournemouth or Southampton gravels, which belong to a somewhat earlier period. Nothing like the Coombe Rock is now being formed in Britain, and we must go to regions having a more rigorous climate to find anything closely analogous. It is not however directly of glacial origin, for none of the stones are striated, and the few from distant sources are such as we know occur in the underlying marine Pleistocene deposit. The enormous sheet of Coombe Rock has evidently been derived from the Downs, and a study of the contours of the Downs (see orographic map) gives us the key to its mode of formation.[1]

The peculiar rolling outline of our Chalk Downs, the steep-sided valleys winding for miles among the hills, yet never, even in the wettest season, containing running water, are familiar types of English scenery. But, perhaps because so familiar, it does not at first strike one that these outlines point to conditions which have now entirely passed away. No streams now fill these upland valleys, and where streams do occupy the bottoms of coombes, their beds fall very gently, so that they do not assume the character of mountain torrents, as any stream in the steeper coombes must necessarily do. It is impossible, under present conditions, for any stream to exist in these dry valleys ; for the Chalk is so porous that the heaviest rain sinks in directly, and the most continued rainfall merely causes new springs to burst out at some point rather higher up the valley than usual. The upper and steeper portion of the valley still remains perfectly dry, and no running water can be found where the incline of the bottom of the valley exceeds the slope of the plane of saturation in the Chalk. The characteristic contour of these valleys is well shown in the Downs near Brighton (see fig. 3).

Though in Sussex the contemporaneous fossils of the Coombe Rock are insufficient to indicate the climatic conditions that held while it was being deposited and while the coombes were being excavated, yet in other districts this evidence can be obtained. At Fisherton near Salisbury corresponding beds yield many species of high northern mammals, such as the reindeer, musk ox and lemming, while at Bovey Tracey in

[1] Reid, ' On the Origin of Dry Chalk Valleys and of Coombe Rock,' *Quart. Journ. Geol. Soc.* xliii. 364 (1887).

Devon they yield arctic plants. Judging from the northern character of the fauna and flora, the mean temperature of north-western Europe at this period cannot have been less than 20° lower than it is now—probably it was 30° lower. This would give a mean temperature in the south of England very considerably below the freezing point; consequently all rocks not protected by snow would be permanently frozen to a considerable depth. This would modify the entire system of drainage of the country. All rocks would be equally and entirely impervious to water, and all springs would fail. While these conditions lasted, any rain falling in the summer would be unable to penetrate more than a few inches. Instead of sinking into the Chalk, or other pervious rock, and being slowly given out in springs, the whole rainfall would immediately run off any steep slopes like those of the Downs, and form violent and transitory mountain torrents. These would tear up a layer of rubble previously loosened by the frost and unprotected by vegetation, and would deposit this rubble on the low lands, where the slope becomes less and the streams had room to spread over fan-shaped deltas of the material thus brought down.

One result of this exceptional type of valley erosion is seen in the peculiar way in which the heads of the coombes almost touch but do not breach the escarpment. Coombe after coombe can be followed upwards till its slope suddenly steepens and it ends abruptly in a sort of 'cirque.' If the terminal wall of this cirque is climbed the sudden drop of the escarpment is seen just beyond; so that one can walk for miles along the edge of the Downs on a gently undulating ridge, which is often so narrow that from the same point a stone can be thrown down the escarpment on the one hand and into the coombe on the other. This shows that the escarpment has not been cut back since the coombes were formed, and it also shows that the coombes were formed when the escarpment had already receded to its present position. The abrupt ending of each coombe is obviously connected with its having cut back to a point beyond which, owing to the proximity of the escarpment, there could be no erosion, owing to the absence of any gathering ground for the rain.

The Downs are dead. Their flowing outlines and winding valleys point to bygone conditions, which can never recur till our climate again becomes arctic. The only noticeable change now going on is the gradual accumulation in the valleys of flints dislodged by sheep from the steep slopes above. Another less obvious change is caused by the gradual dissolving away of the Chalk by rain that falls on its surface. This is a slow process; but its tendency is to transform fertile Down into stony waste, through the accumulation beneath the turf of a thicker and thicker mass of the indestructible flints.

Before quitting the open Downs, with their short sweet pasture and easily worked soil, so valuable when most of the country was forest, reference should be made to a curious relic of the ancient settlers. At the foot of the Chalk hills is often found a thick bushy hedge, which can

24

be followed for long distances, and also occurs under similar circumstances in other counties. This hedge will at once strike the attention as something exceptional, for unless replanted in modern times it contains little hawthorn and is very wide. It consists of a belt of small trees, among which maple, cornel, sloe, hazel, buckthorn, wayfaring-tree, elder, holly and spindle-tree predominate, and are mixed with beech, ash, stunted oak, yew, crab-apple and service-tree. In short, it appears to be a relic of the vegetation of the original margin of the native forest, rendered denser and trimmed to a certain extent, but in other respects not greatly altered. At the present day this hedge separates the open Chalk pastures from the arable land, and as that has always been a convenient boundary, it has commonly been left undisturbed. In old days the presence of a barrier at this point was of even more importance. It now prevents the sheep from straying into the cultivated fields ; it then prevented the flocks and herds from straying into forests infested by wolves, or occupied by thieves and outlaws, or still worse haunted by the thing unseen.

We are still very ignorant as to what happened during the dark transition period which connects Palæolithic with Neolithic. While the Coombe Rock was being formed the climate was arctic, and the relative level of land and sea seems to have been much as at present, though perhaps the sea was a few feet lower than now. Next the land rose about 60 feet, so that the channels of all the main streams were cut far beneath the level of their present beds. No deposits belonging to this period of slow elevation are found, and we do not know what climatic change accompanied it. While at their maximum elevation the valleys were clothed with woods of oak and pine and thickets of hazel, which flourished well below the existing sea-level. Then, during the Neolithic period, the land seems to have sunk again step by step, so that the deeply excavated valleys above alluded to were flooded by the sea, which then penetrated as long fiords through the Downs into the Weald beyond. The submerged forests, seen between tide marks opposite each small valley, belong to this period of gradual subsidence, which ceased so recently that its close in all probability only dates about 3,000 years since. Subsequent changes have consisted mainly in the gradual silting up of the fiords, till they have mostly become alluvial flats ; but the last subsidence is of so recent a date that the fiords and harbours thus formed have not yet been completely obliterated. The Ouse, Adur and Arun, flowing through a clay country and bringing down much mud, have already filled their estuaries ; whilst Pagham and Emsworth Harbours receive little land-water, and consequently are silting up more slowly.

Since the period when the latest of the submerged forests sank beneath the tide there has been no further alteration in the relative level of land and sea. But for the last three thousand years the sea has continuously cut into the land, destroying large areas of the coastal plain and gradually forming longer and higher chalk cliffs. In Roman times the coastal plain probably masked the cliff for several miles east of Brighton, and the chalk cliffs were much lower and less conspicuous. The sea has also swept the shingle beach eastward before the prevalent wind, to accumulate in successive ridges or 'fulls' across Pevensey, Winchelsea and Rye Harbours. The mere fact that so enormous a proportion of this shingle beach is known to have accumulated well within the period of written history is sufficient evidence that the submergence which started the process cannot have taken place at a time historically very remote, otherwise the harbours of these cinque ports would have been obliterated long before. At this point we must leave the chronicle to be carried on by the archæologist and historian.

PALÆONTOLOGY

FEW English counties are of greater interest to the student of the past history of vertebrate animals than Sussex, since a very large number of species of extinct reptiles and fishes were named and described on the evidence of remains obtained from geological horizons within its borders. The most interesting of these are undoubtedly the reptiles of the Wealden and the fishes of the Chalk, whose remains were collected so assiduously in the early part of the last century by Mantell, and subsequently by Dixon. A large number of these fish remains were submitted to the French naturalist Agassiz, by whom they were described in his great work on *Poissons Fossiles* ; while others were named by Mantell himself. Unfortunately the affinities of many of these fossil fishes were but very imperfectly understood at that time, and it has consequently been found necessary in a large number of instances to change their generic titles. This must be borne in mind when readers of the present article refer back to the original works of Mantell and Dixon.

In addition to those from the Chalk and Wealden, remains of extinct vertebrates are also met with in the Middle Eocene deposits of Bracklesham Bay, and although the known species are comparatively few in number, their scientific interest is very considerable. The mammalian remains from the gravels, loams and raised beaches of Pleistocene or later age are, on the other hand, of less general interest, since they belong to species which occur abundantly in many other counties, as well as on the continent.

Commencing with the remains of these Pleistocene and later mammals (of which there is a fine series in the Brighton Museum), two localities in the county where they occur are Bracklesham Bay and Selsey. They were at times not unfrequently dredged up at Selsey by the fishermen ; but they also occur in the muddy deposit on the shore at both places. The species recorded from Bracklesham include the mammoth (*Elephas primigenius*), the straight-tusked elephant (*E. antiquus*), the horse (*Equus caballus*), the red deer (*Cervus elaphus*), and the wolf (*Canis lupus*). Remains of the goat and the Celtic shorthorn also occur, but these must be of later age than the mammoth. Teeth and bones of a rhinoceros, said to be *Rhinoceros leptorhinus*, were also discovered in 1877 by Mr. H. Willett in a deposit at East Wittering above the glacial beds of Selsea.[1] Mantell also records remains of the horse, red deer,

---

[1] Dixon, *Geology of Sussex*, ed. 2, pp. 19, 114.

27

and wild ox (*Bos taurus primigenius*) from other localities in the county, such as Hove, Burton Park and Peppering near Arundel. At the latter place it is believed that a whole skeleton of a mammoth occurred in gravelly loam some 80 feet above the level of the Arun. Red deer remains have also occurred near the barracks at Brighton, as well as in the Western Road ; and those of the mammoth at Patcham, Portslade, Bognor and near Hastings. Occasionally too mammoth teeth are dredged off Brighton. The neighbourhood of Lewes has likewise yielded remains of the red deer and the Celtic shorthorn ; while others from the same locality have been provisionally assigned to the southern right whale (*Balana biscayensis*) and the narwhal (*Monodon monoceros*).

From a deposit at West Wittering Mr. C. Reid[1] has recorded remains of *Elephas* and *Rhinoceros* in the lower strata, and those of *Bos* in a higher bed ; and to these species Mr. J. P. Johnson[2] has added the water-vole (*Microtus amphibius*) and the common frog (*Rana temporaria*).

But the most celebrated of these Sussex mammaliferous deposits is undoubtedly the Brighton 'elephant-bed,' first described by Mantell, and so named on account of the abundance of molars of the mammoth. This deposit also yields remains of the horse, the wild boar (*Sus scrofa ferus*), the woolly rhinoceros (*Rhinoceros antiquitatis*), and, it is said, the Pleistocene hippopotamus (*Hippopotamus amphibius major*). From the same deposit have been obtained a vertebra and part of the lower jaw, now in the British Museum, of Rudolphi's finner-whale (*Balænoptera borealis*).

Passing on to the Middle Eocene deposits of Bracklesham Bay— the 'Bracklesham beds' of geologists—we find that these have yielded teeth of a small mammal, *Lophiodon minimus*, distantly allied to the modern tapirs. The species in question was originally described from the Eocene deposits of France. Some of the teeth from Bracklesham are figured on page 311 of Owen's *British Fossil Mammals and Birds* ; they were collected by Bowerbank, and are now in the British Museum.

Remains of five different species of extinct reptiles have also been described from the Bracklesham beds. Of especial interest are those of a long-snouted crocodile, described by Owen under the name of *Garialis* (or *Gavialis*) *dixoni* ; but their inclusion in the same genus as the living gharial of the Ganges must be regarded as a provisional measure. They are the only known remains of the species, and are preserved in the British Museum. Most of the other reptilian remains from these deposits belong to the chelonian order. One of these is a species of soft tortoise, which has been named by the present writer[3] *Trionyx bowerbanki*. The remaining forms are marine turtles, of which the most abundant is *Lytoloma trigoniceps*, originally described by Owen (as *Chelone*) on the evidence of a skull from Bracklesham. The genus *Lytoloma* is confined to the Eocene period, the present species (like most of the reptiles from the same deposits) being peculiar to the Bracklesham beds. A single bone (humerus) indicates the occurrence of a species of logger-

[1] *Quart. Journ. Geol. Soc.* xlviii. 356 (1892).   [2] *Proc. Geol. Assoc.* xvii. 263 (1901).
[3] *Cat. Foss. Rept. Brit. Mus.* iii. 19.

head turtle which has been named by the writer *Thallasochelys eocænica* ; while a fragment of the shell is sufficient to prove the existence at the same epoch of a species belonging to an extinct genus (*Psephophorus*) of leathery turtle.[1]

Vertebræ of two species of large serpents belonging to an extinct family also occur in the Bracklesham beds. One of these, *Palæophis toliapicus*, is typified by specimens from the London Clay of Sheppey ; but the second, *P. typhæus*, was described on the evidence of Bracklesham fossils. These snakes, judging from the form of the vertebræ, appear to have been marine.

The list of Bracklesham fishes is considerably larger than that of the reptiles, and includes at least nine species first described from that formation, some of which are peculiar to the same. First on the list come two species of saw-fish, *Pristis contortus* and *P. bisulcatus*, the former of which is confined to the Bracklesham beds, while the latter also occurs at Barton, Hants. The flattened roller-like dental plates of eagle-rays are especially common in these deposits, and have been assigned to five species, namely *Myliobatis dixoni*, *M. striatus*, *M. goniopleurus*, *M. toliapicus*, and *M. latidens*, the last alone being typified by Bracklesham specimens. There are likewise two species of ray belonging to the allied genus *Aëtobatis*, of which *A. marginalis* is exclusively from Bracklesham, while *A. irregularis* also occurs in other Eocene deposits, and is typically from the London Clay.

Among sharks there are three representatives, *Odontaspis elegans*, *O. macrota*,[2] and *O. cuspidata*, of an extinct genus nearly related to the living porbeagle ; the three species are widely spread, and the first occurs at Newhaven as well as at Bracklesham Bay. There is also an extinct species of porbeagle, namely *Lamna vincenti*, not peculiar to the Bracklesham beds, as well as the so-called *Otodus obliquus*, occurring elsewhere in the county in the Middle Eocene beds of Bognor. Large teeth from Bracklesham have been assigned to *Carcharodon auriculatus*, a widely-spread extinct relative of the largest of living sharks (*C. rondeletii*). Another Bracklesham shark is *Galeocerdo latidens*, a species likewise with a wide geographical distribution.

Of fish allied to the living chimæra, or 'king of the herrings,' there are two representatives, *Edaphodon bucklandi* and *E. leptognathus*, both common to other Tertiary horizons. Fish-spines described as *Cælorhynchus rectus* are also found in the Bracklesham deposits, from which came the type specimens. Among the pycnodont ganoid fishes, in which the palate and lower jaw are armed with a pavement of spherical or oval crushing teeth, the species *Pycnodus kœnigi* was first described from Bracklesham, but has been subsequently identified from the corresponding formation of Belgium.

As 'cat-fishes' (*Siluridæ*) are comparatively rare as fossils, it is

---

[1] *Cat. Foss. Rept. Brit. Mus.* iii. 224.

[2] For the generic of this and two of the undermentioned species, see A. S. Woodward, *Proc. Geol. Assoc.* xvi. 10 ; in *Cat. Foss. Fish. Brit. Mus.* they are assigned to *Lamna*.

interesting to note the occurrence at Bracklesham of a species, *Arius egertoni*, belonging to an existing tropical genus, this species also occurring in the Belgian Eocene. Among the mackerel family (*Scombridæ*) remains of an undetermined species of the extinct genus *Scombrhamphodon* occur at Bracklesham, and these deposits have likewise yielded specifically indeterminable vertebræ referable to the genus *Xiphiorhynchus*, an extinct type of sword-fish. Another Bracklesham sword-fish, *Histiophorus eocænicus*, belonging to a genus still living, has been recently named by Dr. Smith Woodward on the evidence of a 'sword' in the British Museum. Lastly, we have *Platylæmus colei*, an extinct generic type of bass (*Labridæ*) described by Dixon on the evidence of specimens of the dental plates from Bracklesham, and at present unknown elsewhere. Dr. Woodward describes it as ' an extinct genus known only by the pharyngeals, each nearly or completely covered by a crushing plate, which consists of coarse vascular dentine invested with a very thin layer of gano-dentine.'

The Lower Eocene Bognor beds—the equivalent of the London Clay—seem to be exceptionally poor in vertebrate remains. They have however yielded an imperfect turtle-shell, which was made the type of a species by Owen, under the name of *Chelone declivis*, although it has since been provisionally identified[1] with one from the London Clay of Sheppey, now known as *Argillochelys convexa*. Vertebræ apparently referable to the long-nosed Lower Eocene crocodile known as *Crocodilus spenceri* also occur at Bognor.

The reptiles of the Sussex Chalk are not numerous, although some are of considerable interest. The great marine lizards known as Mosasauria are represented by *Liodon anceps*, a species which also occurs in the Chalk of Norfolk and Essex. A second species of the group has been described on the evidence of remains (now in the Brighton Museum) by Owen under the name of *Mosasaurus gracilis*. These remains were at one time considered by Dr. Smith Woodward to indicate a fish of the genus *Pachyrhizodus* rather than a reptile, but subsequent investigation has convinced the same palæontologist[2] that the original determination was correct, although it does not follow that the species belongs to the genus *Mosasaurus*. The crown of another mosasauroid tooth from the Chalk of the county has been provisionally assigned by the present writer[3] to the American Cretaceous genus *Platecarpus*. The most interesting of the Sussex Chalk lizards is however *Dolichosaurus longicollis*, a long-necked, snake-like, marine type also occurring in the Chalk of Kent ; in Sussex its remains have been found in Southeram pit, near Lewes. Remains from the Chalk of Washington near Worthing have been regarded as those of a small lizard, under the name of *Coniasaurus crassidens*. Another presumed lizard, *Rhaphiosaurus subulidens*, is now definitely known to have been named on teeth of a fish.

[1] *Cat. Foss. Rept. Brit. Mus.* iii. 48.   [2] *Cat. Foss. Fish. Brit. Mus.* iv. 45.
[3] *Cat. Foss. Rept. Brit. Mus.* i. 271.

PALÆONTOLOGY

Large conical fluted teeth from the Chalk of Falmer, Glynde, Lewes and Steyning belong to the huge reptile named *Polyptychodon interruptus*, which is a near ally of the better known Jurassic genus *Pliosaurus*, itself a large-headed and short-necked member of the group of marine saurians termed Plesiosauria. A tooth from Houghton in the Brighton Museum has been assigned to a second species of the former genus, *Polyptychodon continuus*. The Brighton Museum also contains remains of long-necked plesiosaurians from the Chalk of Clayton, Lewes, Houghton, Scellescomb and Southeram, which may be provisionally assigned to the Cretaceous genus *Cimoliosaurus*. To this type belong the plesiosaurians from the Sussex Chalk described by Owen under the names of *Plesiosaurus bernardi* and *P. constrictus*.

Two imperfectly known turtles complete the list of reptiles described from the Sussex Chalk. One is indicated by portions of the shell and vertebræ from Lewes and Clayton in the British and Brighton Museums, which are tentatively assigned to the typical genus *Chelone*. The other is represented by an imperfect bone (the humerus) in the British Museum from Lewes, referred to a species of leathery turtle, *Protostega anglica*, typified by a bone from the Cambridge Greensand.

The fishes from the Sussex Chalk number more than seventy, out of which over forty species were named on the evidence of specimens found in the county. Commencing with the rays, the first to be mentioned is a species of angel-fish, *Squatina cranei*, named by Dr. Smith Woodward in 1888 on the evidence of a unique specimen from Clayton in the Brighton Museum. The pavement-like teeth of the rays of the extinct genus *Ptychodus* are comparatively common in the Chalk of the county, and have been assigned to six species, of which all but the first and last were named from Sussex examples. Of these species *P. mammillaris* is recorded from Glynde and Lewes, *P. rugosus* from Arundel and elsewhere, *P. oweni* from Lewes, *P. decurrens* from Brighton and Lewes, *P. polygyrus* from Lewes and Seaford, and *P. latissimus* from Lewes. Nearly perfect sets of the dentition of the last-mentioned species and *P. decurrens* are preserved in the Brighton Museum. Of the existing comb-toothed sharks the common Cretaceous *Notidanus microdon* has been obtained at Brighton, Lewes and Newtimber. Among sharks with crushing teeth allied to the living Port Jackson *Cestracion philippi*, and included in the same family, *Synechodus illingworthi* was described by Dixon[1] from teeth obtained in Southeram pit near Lewes ; while a tooth from Glynde is provisionally assigned to *S. dubrisiensis*, of which Dover is the type locality. Neither are species referred to the same genus as the Port Jackson shark absent from the Chalk of the county, remains of *Cestracion canaliculatus* having been obtained from Southeram, and of *C. rugosus* from Lewes. Special interest attaches to the occurrence in the Chalk of the county of remains of a species of beaked shark, *Scapanorhynchus rhaphiodon*, since this genus was long supposed to be extinct, but has been recently discovered living in Japanese waters. Of

[1] As *Acrodus*.

31

the sharp-toothed sharks of the extinct genus *Oxyrhina*, one species, *O. mantelli*, was described by Agassiz from Lewes specimens; two other species, *O. angustidens* and *O. crassidens*, also occur in the Chalk of the county, remains of the latter (including a fine associated series of teeth and vertebræ in the Brighton Museum) having been obtained from Lewes, Houghton and Arundel. The porbeagle-sharks are represented by *Lamna appendiculata* from Lewes and Arundel, and *L. sulcata* from Lewes. Another shark, *Corax falcatus*, belonging to an extinct genus nearly allied to *Carcharodon*, but with smaller teeth, was named by Agassiz on the evidence of specimens collected by Mantell in Sussex.

Passing on to the chimæroid fishes, whose dentition takes the form of large triturating plates on the jaws, we find certain Sussex specimens identified with a species provisionally assigned to the Jurassic genus *Ischyodus* under the name of *I. incisus*. Of the allied Cretaceous genus *Edaphodon* four or five species are known to occur in the Chalk of the county, namely *E. sedgwicki*, *E. mantelli* (from Arundel, Brighton, Clayton, Glynde, Houghton and Lewes), *E. agassizi* (from Hamsey and Lewes), and *E. crassus*. A tooth from Glynde may possibly belong to *E. reedi*. The second and third of these were named from Sussex specimens. A fifth species, based on specimens in the Brighton Museum, was described in 1878 by Mr. E. T. Newton, but was subsequently made the type of a distinct genus, under the name of *Elasmodectes willetti*. The Brighton specimen, we believe, still remains the unique example of this fish. A fish-spine from the Sussex Chalk described under the name of *Cælorhynchus cretaceus* may, as in the case of the Bracklesham specimen with the same generic title, prove to belong to one of the sharks or chimæroids described upon the evidence of the teeth.

A fish from the Lewes Chalk described by Agassiz as *Macropoma mantelli* is of considerable interest as one of the comparatively few representatives in the later strata of the group of fringe-finned ganoids, which were so abundant in the Palæozoic, and of which the African bishir is the sole surviving member. The Sussex species is the only representative of its genus; its remains occur at North Stoke near Arundel, Lewes and elsewhere. Of the pycnodont ganoids, already briefly mentioned under the heading of the Bracklesham beds, the species *Gyrodus cretaceus* was described by Agassiz from Lewes specimens. Some imperfect remains of the group have been described as *Microdus occidentalis*, but their affinity is doubtful. The species *Cælodus parallelus* (*Pycnodus* of Dixon) is however a good one, of which the only known example is in the Brighton Museum. Another genus of pycnodonts is represented in the Sussex Chalk by *Anomæodus angustus* from Houghton, Lewes and Newtimber, and *A. willetti* from Glynde. The former was described by Agassiz (as *Gyrodus*) from a Lewes specimen, and the latter by Dr. Smith Woodward from the unique example in the Brighton Museum. Certain other pycnodont remains from the Chalk of the county are of uncertain affinity; one type has been identified with the so-called *Pycnodus scrobiculatus*, first described from the continent; the second was named by Dixon *Phacodus punctatus*, the type specimen, now in the British Museum, being from Lewes. A group of five teeth from Lewes in the British Museum has been made the type of a genus and species, with the name *Acrotemnus faba*.

Another group of extinct ganoids—the *Eugnathidæ*—are represented in the Chalk of Alfriston and Lewes by *Lophiostomus dixoni*, the only other species of the genus occurring in the Cambridge Greensand. In a third family, the *Pachycormidæ*, we find the spear-like teeth of the widely spread but still imperfectly known *Protosphyræna ferox* (often incorrectly called *Saurocephalus lanciformis*) in the Chalk of Amberley, Glynde, Lewes and Newtimber ; a second species of the same genus, *P. minor*, was named from a Lewes specimen. In yet another extinct ganoid family, the *Aspidorhynchidæ*, the species *Belonostomus cinctus* was described by Agassiz on the evidence of a specimen from Lewes ; another specimen from Southeram, now in the Brighton Museum, was named *B. attenuatus*, but its right to distinction is doubtful.

With the species known as *Elopopsis crassus*, named by Dixon (as *Osmeroides*) from a specimen in the Brighton Museum from Malling, Kent, but also known from Southeram, we come to a more modern type of fish, allied to the herrings. Another member of the same family (*Elopidæ*) is *Osmeroides lewesiensis*, which, as indicated by its name, was described on the evidence of a Lewes fossil ; a second species, *O. levis*, has been recently described by Dr. Smith Woodward,[1] the type being from Kent, but another specimen from the Lower Chalk of Lewes. The same writer[2] has also described a Lewes 'ichthyolite' as *Thrissopater* (?) *megalops*, an undoubted member of the same genus, *T. magnus*, also occurring in the Chalk of the county. The fishes of this genus belong to the *Elopidæ*, and are probably ancestral types of the modern herrings. To the same family probably belongs the genus *Pachyrhizodus*, of which the species *P. basalis*, *P. gardneri*, and *P. subulidens* occur in the Chalk of the county, although neither is based on Sussex specimens ; the third species was originally described as *Rhaphiosaurus* on the evidence of its teeth, which were believed to be those of a lizard. A fourth fish, from Glynde and Southeram, has been described as *Protelops anglicus*, the other species of the genus, which also belongs to the *Elopidæ*, being from the Bohemian Chalk.

To the family *Osteoglossidæ*, the existing members of which are restricted to the rivers of the southern hemisphere, or to the allied *Albulidæ*, may be provisionally assigned the fish described by Dixon as *Plethodus expansus* on the evidence of a dental plate from Kent now in the Brighton Museum, this species being probably also represented in Sussex ; a second species, *P. oblongus*, is typified by another dental plate from Clayton in the same collection ; while a third, *P. pentagon*, first described from Kent, also occurs in the Sussex Chalk. Large teeth from Lewes have been provisionally assigned to the genus *Portheus*, which occurs typically in the Cretaceous strata of North America, and

---

[1] *Cat. Foss. Fish. Brit. Mus.* iii. 16 (1901).   [2] *Ibid.* p. 35.

belongs to the family *Chirocentridæ*, now represented only by the Indian dorab ; a second species of the same genus, *P. mantelli*, has been named on the evidence of a Lewes specimen in the British Museum.   A lower jaw in the British Museum from the Lower Chalk of Halling has been provisionally assigned to *P. gaultinus*, typically from the Gault of Kent. To the same family belongs *Ichthyodectes minor*, a fish described on the evidence of a lower jaw from the Sussex Chalk in the British Museum ; other species of the same genus occur in the Chalk of the neighbouring counties.   Scales from Lewes have been made the type of *Cladocyclus lewesiensis*, a species of another Cretaceous genus of the same family. Possibly to this family should be assigned *Tomognathus mordax* of Dixon, a genus and species described on specimens from the Chalk of the south-east of England, which may have come from Sussex ; other specimens have been found at Amberley, Clayton and Southeram.

Ctenothrissa radians, one of three species of a Cretaceous genus typifying an extinct family closely allied to the herrings, was named by Agassiz (as *Beryx*) from Lewes specimens, the species also occurring in the Lower Chalk of Clayton and Southeram.   *Aulolepis typus*, the sole member of its genus, is another member of the same family named from Lewes fossils, and distinguished from the type genus by its smooth-edged scales.

Coming to the extinct family *Dercetidæ*, which is allied both to the herrings and salmonoids, we have *Leptotrachelus elongatus* typified from the Lewes Chalk, the specimens from which were originally described by Agassiz as *Dercetis*.   To an allied family belongs *Enchodus lewesiensis*, first described by Mantell as a fossil pike (*Esox*) ; a second species of the same genus, typically from Kent, has been recently described by Dr. Smith Woodward[1] as *E. pulchellus*, specimens from Lewes and Southeram being in the British Museum collection.   *Halec eupterygius*, typified by a specimen in the Brighton Museum from Southeram described by Dixon as *Pomognathus*, is another member of the same family.   The same is the case with *Cimolichthys lewesiensis*, of which the large spear-like teeth were long incorrectly known by the name of *Saurodon*.

With *Acrognathus boöps*, typically from Lewes, we come to the scopeloid fishes (*Scopelidæ*) ; the only other known species of the genus is from the Chalk of the Lebanon.   Another scopeloid is *Apateodus striatus*, perhaps identical with the *Saurocephalus striatus* of Agassiz, and typified by a skull from Lewes ; the two other species of the genus are from the Cretaceous of Kent.

Of especial interest is the occurrence of a fossil eel (*Urenchelys anglica*), known by a head from Lewes in the Brighton Museum, in the Sussex Chalk, since fish of this group are very scarce in the Secondary strata.   The other two representatives of the same genus are from the Chalk of the Lebanon.

Among the spiny-finned bony fishes the family *Berychidæ* is

[1] Op. cit. p. 194.

represented in the Chalk of the county by two species of the extinct genus *Hoplopteryx*. The first of these, *H. lewesiensis* (the *Zeus lewesiensis* of Mantell, and the *Beryx ornatus* of Agassiz and Dixon), was named on the evidence of a specimen from Lewes now in the British Museum ; the second, *H. superbus* (the *Beryx superbus* of Dixon), was described from a Southeram fossil, and has also been collected at Brighton. Another member of the same family, *Homonotus dorsalis*, described from a Kentish specimen in the Brighton Museum, and the only known representative of its genus, also occurs in the Sussex Chalk. A family (*Stromateidæ*) more nearly allied to the mackerels is represented in the Chalk of the county by *Berycopsis elegans*, a genus and species founded on a Lewes specimen in the Brighton Museum, and also recorded from Clayton. Another specimen in the same collection, from Steyning, described by Dixon as *Stenostoma pulchellum*, may indicate a second species of the same genus.

Finally, in the family of horse-mackerels or *Carangidæ* we have a species from Washington near Worthing, originally described as *Microdon nuchalis*, but now known as *Æpichthys nuchalis* ; the other member of the genus occurring in the Cretaceous of Istria and the Lebanon.

The Wealden formation being of freshwater origin, it is only natural to expect that it should yield remains of mammals, since those animals were in existence long before the epoch in question. Hitherto however only two specimens which can be regarded as undoubtedly mammalian have been obtained from Wealden strata, both of these coming from Hastings. The first is a molar tooth of a very small mammal identified by its describer, Dr. Smith Woodward,[1] with a Purbeck genus, and named *Plagiaulax dawsoni* ; its geological horizon is the Wadhurst Clay. The second specimen, an incisor tooth, is from the Tilgate Grit, and was described by the present writer,[2] although not named.

The lower end of a leg-bone (femur) from Ansty Lane near Cuckfield has been described by Professor H. G. Seeley[3] as probably belonging to a Wealden bird, but the opinion has been expressed that it is crocodilian rather than avian.

Among the reptiles of the Wealden, remains of several species of pterodactyles, or flying saurians, have been described, several of these specimens having been originally regarded as referable to birds. Provisionally, at any rate, all these pterodactyles may be included in the Cretaceous genus *Ornithochirus*. The species *O. clavirostris* was founded on part of an upper jaw from the Hastings Sands of St. Leonards ; *O. clifti*, which is known from Battle, Cuckfield, Hastings and Tilgate Forest, is typified by imperfect wing-bones (humerus) ; *O. curtus*, of which the exact locality is unknown, is represented by part of a leg-bone (tibia) in the collection of the British Museum ; and *O. cuvieri*, typically from Kent, appears to be represented by a specimen from Newtimber in the Brighton Museum. The so-called *Pterodactylus*

---

[1] *Proc. Zool. Soc. London*, 1891, 585.   [2] *Quart. Journ. Geol. Soc.* xlix. 281.   [3] Ibid. lv. 416.

sagittirostris, which certainly does not belong to the genus whose name it bears, is typified by a specimen from the Hastings Sands of St. Leonards, now preserved in the British Museum among the Beckles collection.

From an historical point of view the most interesting of the extinct reptiles from the Wealden of Sussex is however the huge dinosaur to which Mantell gave the name of *Iguanodon*, on account of a supposed resemblance between its teeth and those of the tropical American lizards known as iguanas. The history of the discovery, as told by Mantell,[1] is as follows : 'Soon after my first discovery of remains of large vertebrated animals in the strata of Tilgate Forest some teeth of a very remarkable character in a block of stone on the roadside particularly engaged my attention from their dissimilarity to any that had previously come under my notice. Additional examples were soon discovered, and at length I obtained a series of teeth in various conditions, from the pointed incised tooth of the young reptile to the obtuse, worn, flat crown of the adult.' To the reptile indicated by these teeth the name *Iguanodon* was applied by Mantell in 1825, but it was not till 1832 that H. von Meyer described the species as *I. mantelli*. Remains of this reptile were subsequently obtained from Battle, Cuckfield, Hawkbourne, Hastings, Horsham and Knellstone ; but it was not till comparatively recently, when entire skeletons were discovered in Belgium, that the true structure of the skeleton of the iguanodon was realized. These Belgian specimens showed individuals of two sizes, the smaller being identified with *I. mantelli*, and the larger described as a second species with the name of *I. bernissartensis*. Both types occur in the Sussex Wealden. Iguanodon was an herbivorous reptile, walking on its three-toed hind limbs, with the aid of some support from its long and powerful tail. The largest individuals stood but little short of 20 feet in height. Their three-toed footprints have been preserved in the Wealden sandstones of Hastings and Bexhill.

Two other species of iguanodon, *I. dawsoni* and *I. fittoni*, have been described from the Wadhurst Clay of Hastings, and a third (*I. hollingtoniensis*) from the same stratum at Hollington. The much smaller but allied dinosaur known as *Hypsilophodon foxi*, typically from the Wealden of the Isle of Wight, is also recorded from Cuckfield.

A totally different type of dinosaur is indicated by a huge bone of the fore-limb (humerus) from Tilgate Forest, described by Mantell under the name of *Pelorosaurus conybeari*, and now in the British Museum. American specimens show that the huge reptiles of this type were herbivorous and quadrupedal, with a length of 60 feet or more. The bodies of their vertebræ were excavated into large chambers. Such a vertebra has been obtained from the Wealden of Hastings, and may belong either to *Pelorosaurus* or to an allied form (typified by a tooth from the Isle of Wight) known as *Hoplosaurus armatus*. Smaller vertebræ of a similar type from Cuckfield and Hastings belong to a

[1] *Wonders of Geology*, i. 436.

species now known as *Morosaurus brevis*. Still smaller vertebræ of the same, together with teeth erroneously assigned by Mantell to the under-mentioned *Hylæosaurus*, from Cuckfield and Tilgate Forest, have been made the types of another species of dinosaur by the present writer under the name of *Pleurocœlus valdensis*, the generic name being first given to a North American dinosaur.

Quite another type of dinosaur is indicated by *Hylæosaurus armatus*, a genus and species known only from the Wealden of Battle, Bolney and Tilgate. It was armed with a number of large bony spines, probably carried in one or more rows along the back. A lower jaw from the Wealden of Cuckfield described by Mantell under the name of *Regnosaurus northamptoni* probably indicates a reptile nearly allied to, if not identical with, the last ; the specific name was applied in honour of a former Marquis of Northampton, and does not refer to the locality of the specimen. The carnivorous dinosaurs are represented by a species of the Jurassic genus *Megalosaurus*, which has been named by the present writer *M. oweni* ; its remains have been recorded from Battle, Cuckfield and Hastings. Some remains of the same genus from the Wealden of the county have been assigned to a continental species, *M. dunkeri*. Of the crocodiles of the Wealden of the county, one of the most abundant is *Goniopholis crassidens*, a genus and species first described by Mantell from the Purbeck of Swanage ; its remains occur at Cuckfield and Horsham, and a nearly perfect skull is preserved in the Brighton Museum. The bony plates protecting the body of this crocodile are articulated together by means of a peg-and-socket arrange-ment. Vertebræ from Cuckfield have been regarded as indicating a second species of the genus, named *G. carinata*. Crocodilian teeth from Cuckfield and Tilgate Forest of a different shape to those of *Goniopholis* —having a pair of sharp vertical ridges on opposite sides of the crown— have been made the type of a distinct genus under the name of *Sucho-saurus cultridens*. Finally, a more modern type of crocodile from the Wealden of Cuckfield and Hastings has been described as *Heterosuchus valdensis* ; but it does not seem certain that it is really distinct from a crocodile from the Belgian Wealden named *Hylæochampsa*.

Several kinds of freshwater tortoises are known from the Wealden strata of the county, most of these belonging to a group now restricted to the southern hemisphere. An exception in this respect is however a very remarkable Chelonian from Cuckfield and Tilgate Forest described by Mantell as *Trionyx bakewelli*, but now known as *Tretosternum bakewelli*. Although the shell is sculptured, the nearest living ally of the genus (unfortunately very imperfectly known) is the American snapper (*Chelhydra*). A second, unnamed, species of the genus occurs in the Wadhurst Clay of Hastings. The *Chelone belli* of Mantell, from Tilgate Forest, is now referred to the genus *Hylæochelys*, typically from the Purbeck of Swanage, where it is represented by *H. latiscutata*. To the latter species is assigned an imperfect shell in the British Museum from the Wealden of Burwash in the county under consideration. The tortoises of this genus are distinguished by the abnormal width of the row of horny shields covering the middle of the back. To a species of an allied genus, *Plesiochelys brodiei*, typically from the Wealden of the Isle of Wight, is assigned a young shell in the British Museum from the same formation at Hastings ; while fragments of a shell from Cuckfield in the same collection apparently indicate another species of the genus. It should be added that the species to which the names *Platemys mantelli* and *P. dixoni* have been applied belong to *Hylæochelys belli*. Very interesting are certain fragments of a chelonian shell from Cuckfield which have been made the type of a genus and species by the present writer under the name of *Archæochelys valdensis* ; but they are unfortunately too imperfect for the affinities of the genus to be properly determined.

Of long-necked plesiosaurians two small-sized species are known from the Wealden of the county. One of them, *Cimoliosaurus limnophilus*, from Cuckfield, was first described from the Wealden strata of the continent. The second, *C. valdensis*, which occurs at Cuckfield and in the Wadhurst Clay of Hastings, is peculiar to the county. The comparatively small dimensions of both these saurians are probably due to their being dwellers in brackish instead of salt water.

The fossil fishes of the Sussex Wealden are not numerous, although of considerable interest. Among the pavement-toothed sharks allied to the existing Port Jackson species the widely spread genus *Hybodus* is represented by *H. basanus*, a species first described from the Wealden of the Isle of Wight, but which also occurs at Hastings, Hollington, Pevensey Bay and in Tilgate Forest. Teeth from Hastings and Tilgate Forest indicate the occurrence of two other species of the same genus in the Wealden of the county. In the allied genus *Acrodus* the species *A. hirudo* was named by Agassiz on the evidence of a tooth, now in the British Museum, from Tilgate Forest ; and the same collection also contains a smaller tooth of this species from the Wealden of Telham near Battle. Fin-spines from Tilgate Forest have been made the types of *Asteracanthus granulosus*, a species of another widely spread genus of the same group of sharks.

Among the ganoid fishes, or those whose scales are bony, quadrangular and highly polished, the button-like teeth of *Lepidotus mantelli* occur in the Wealden strata of Billingshurst, Brightling, Heathfield, Hastings, Horsham, Tilgate Forest and other localities in the county, often accompanied by scales. In the neighbourhood of Hastings and in Tilgate Forest these teeth are extraordinarily abundant ; they are known to the quarrymen as 'fishes' eyes.' The Wealden species, which also occurs in Germany, was named by Agassiz on the evidence of Mantell's specimens ; many other species of the genus are known from Jurassic and Cretaceous strata. Of the pycnodont ganoids the species *Cælodus mantelli*, a member of another widely spread genus, was named by Agassiz from specimens of the dentition collected by Mantell in Tilgate Forest. A second and larger species, *C. parallelus*, was named by Dixon (as *Pycnodus*) on the evidence of a specimen of the dentition in the Brighton Museum from Cuckfield ; this specimen, we believe, still remains unique.

To a different group of ganoid fishes belongs *Neorhombolepis valdensis*, a species typified by a fossil fish coiled up in a waterworn sandstone boulder from the Wealden of Hastings now preserved in the British Museum. The genus to which this unique specimen belongs is typified by a species from the Kentish Chalk, and also includes a third representative from the Chalk of Kent and Surrey.

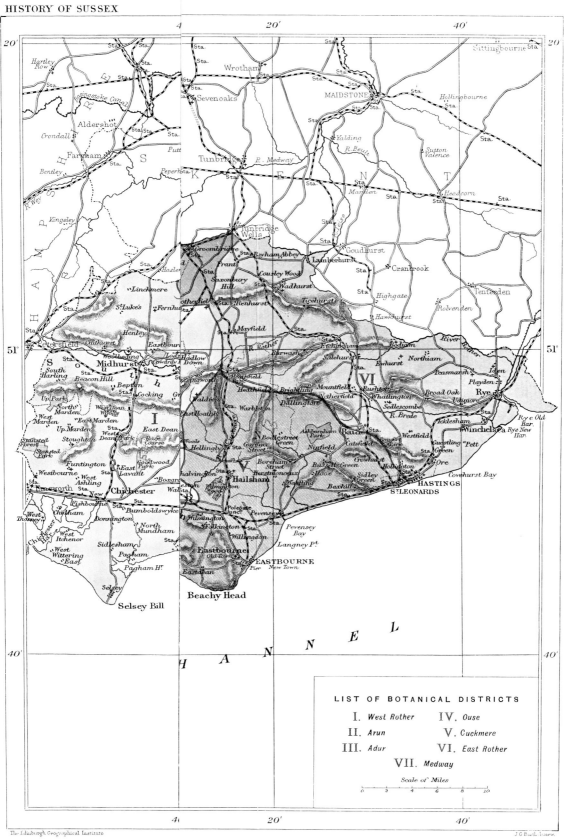

LIST OF BOTANICAL DISTRICTS

I. *West Rother*   IV. *Ouse*

II. *Arun*   V. *Cuckmere*

III. *Adur*   VI. *East Rother*

VII. *Medway*

Scale of Miles

The Edinburgh Geographical Institute

J. G. Bartholomew.

LAND

BOTANY

SUSSEX owing to its varied geological formations, its downs differing in elevation, its extensive weald, its forests, its cliffs, and its long seaboard, indented to the westward by estuaries, is one of the most interesting of our southern counties with respect to its flora.

It has been fortunate too in having attracted the attention of some of the more eminent of English naturalists in early times. As preliminary, therefore, a short history of the botany of the county is here sketched.[1]

In Gerarde's *Herball or General Historie of Plants*, 1633, we have the earliest account with which I am acquainted of plants with their localities in the county. Of the beech, the chief ornament of the Sussex hangers, he says : 'It groweth very plentifully in many forests and desart places of Sussex. The Sea Holly I found growing at Rye and Winchelsea, and the Rock Sampier.' He also gives a figure, without locality, of the spiked rampion now met with in Sussex only, well describing it as 'bearing at the top of the stalke a great thicke bushy eare, full of little long floures closely thrust together like a Fox-taile.' This plant, which occurs at Mayfield and its vicinity, is not known in any other district in Great Britain. Another woodcut of Gerarde may be mentioned here. It is an excellent one of the pease earth-nut, with its peculiar tubers, which ' by the Dutch are called tailled mise, of the similitude or likenesse of domesticall mise, which the blacke round and long nuts with a piece of string hanging out behind do represent '—and to a dead, shrivelled mouse they have certainly a quaint resemblance. Recorded only in Essex, Devon and Sussex, it was found at Eastbourne in 1888 by Mr. R. D. Postans.

In 1640 Parkinson mentions the bulbiferous coralwort not previously met with in England. It is still a very rare species in Sussex.

In 1690 John Ray, the 'father of English Botany' published his *Synopsis Methodica Stirpium Britannicarum*. He visited this county several times, and in a letter to Mr. Courthorpe, of Danny, April 28, 1692,

---

[1] I wish to express my thanks to the following friends and correspondents who have informed me of the discovery of additional species and stations : Miss R. L. Arnold, Miss Gould, Mrs. S. Butcher, Mrs. A. E. Lomax, Mr. B. Oakeshott, Messrs. J. Anderson, A. Bennett, F.L.S., P. Coombes, W. H. B. Fletcher, J. & H. Groves, F.L.S., J. H. A. Jenner, H. C. Miller, Dr. F. V. Paxton, F. Townsend, F.L.S., W. C. Unwin, the Revs. E. N. Bloomfield, E. R. Ellman, A. A. Evans, A. Fuller and W. Moyle Rogers, F.L.S., who have aided me both as to the phanerogams and cryptogams.

thus gives his observations : ' After you parted from us at Cuckfield I discovered growing about there *Anagallis aquatica surrectior, J. B. Cardamine impatiens, Pilosilla siliquosa Thalii. Astragalus sylvaticus Thalii, Bulbocastanum, Gramen nemorosum hirsutum* and another pretty sort of grasse.' These it would now be difficult to determine. To Gibbon's edition of Camden's *Britannia*, 1695, Ray contributed the plant list. It includes *Peucedanum officinale*, hog's fennel, growing in the marsh ditches about Shoreham, but of this there is no recent record. *Fœniculum vulgare* occurred in Pevensey Marsh, *Œnanthe crocata, Lathyrus sylvestris* near Poynings, *Chamædrys spuria* at Cuckfield. In Dillenius's third edition of Ray's Synopsis, 1724, a considerable number of Sussex plants is given. Of Sussex botanists of more recent date the most eminent was William Borrer, born at Henfield in 1781, whose knowledge of the flora of his native county was probably unequalled. His ardour in this pursuit began in early life. His brother tells us ' that he did not remember the time when he was not enthusiastic in his love for flowers and in his admiration of the vegetable world in general, so that there was no muddy ditch, no old wall, no stock of a tree, no rock or dell, no pool of water, or bay of the sea that did not add to his delight and open to him a wide field for investigation and enjoyment.' He first noticed *Isnardia palustris*, and *Leersia oryzoides* was first discovered by him in Henfield Levels. As an authority on the Rubi, Rosæ and Salices, the most difficult genera in our flora, he ranks among the highest. He resided at Henfield and continued his favourite recreation for more than half a century, dying in 1862. Mr. H. Collins of Aldsworth, himself an ardent botanist, accompanied him in some of his Sussex rambles, and his herbarium which contains many species collected by his friend Borrer is now in my possession.

In the old *Botanist's Guide*, by Turner and Dilwyn, 1805, we have an enumeration of the rarer Sussex plants, with localities, chiefly by Borrer. Watson's *New Botanical Guide*, 1835–7, has many additions to this. To Horsfield's *History of Sussex* Mr. T. H. Cooper in a supplement appended good lists of the less common species, especially as regards their climatic and geological distribution. In 1875 Mr. W. B. Hemsley published in the *Journal of Botany*, as an appendix, ' An Outline of the Flora of Sussex,' as showing the occurrence of our plants in the various districts, and in 1883 appeared Watson's *Topographical Botany*, which enumerates the plants of east and west Sussex. These are the chief works relating to the botany of Sussex in general, which so far as the standard species of British plants is concerned is probably now as well known as that of any county in England, while what are termed the critical species have received much attention.

As to its districts, hereafter to be described, our information may be thus summarized. The West Rother has been well explored by the Chichester and West Sussex Natural History Society, and having lived therein for many years I have myself paid special attention to its flora, and that of the Arun, the adjacent district. That of the Adur was the scene of Borrer's labours and those of Mr. W. Mitten of Hurstpierpoint, who contributed the list of flowering plants to Mr. Merrifield's *Sketch of the Natural History of Brighton*. The Ouse district has been well investigated by Mr. J. H. A. Jenner, Mr. W. C. Unwin and the members of the Lewes and East Sussex Natural History Society. In his *Flora of Eastbourne* Mr. F. C. S. Roper published an excellent account of that of the Cuckmere. The Rev. E. N. Bloomfield of Guestling, in his *Natural History of Hastings and St. Leonards*, with supplements in 1883 and 1888, has supplied a good catalogue of the plants of the East Rother, and for the Medway district we have Mr. E. Jenner's *Flora of Tunbridge Wells and its Neighbourhood*, with lists by the Rev. W. H. Coleman, Dr. Deakin, Dr. de Crespigny and other botanists.

Before considering our flora however, as it now presents itself to us, it will be well briefly to examine its origin—a very interesting subject—and this can only be done in connection with a wider one, that of the origin of the plants of Great Britain and the geographical distribution of our British plants which can merely be glanced at here.

That this island once formed part of an adjacent continent is now generally admitted. Its separation must have been gradual, and along the south coast we still find this constantly enlarged by the action of the sea. A thorough examination of the fossil plants of Sussex is still a desideratum. Those of the earlier geological periods have mostly perished from the intense cold which accompanied glaciation. Mr. Clement Reid, who has studied the plants of the latest Pliocene deposit, and the flora of various deposits from that ancient period to the time of the Roman occupation, has, by collecting the seeds and seed vessels of numerous species, shown that a considerable number of the plants we still meet with existed in prehistoric times. With respect to submerged forests he tells us that the newest he examined dates fully 3,000 years since. In Sussex one of these existed at Selsey, whence huge portions of trees are occasionally obtained, and at Hastings there was a submarine forest which contained the yew, oak and pine.

The geology of the county being treated of elsewhere, it is only pertinent to remember that its strata belong mainly to the Secondary formations. The Tertiary beds appear chiefly on the coast in its southwest extremity, and strips of these, chalk, greensand, and the sandstone of the Wealden formations, are its principal features. The range of chalk downs in Sussex is more than fifty miles long, with an average breadth of four miles and a half and an average altitude of about 500 feet, rising to between 800 and 900 feet eastwards. The ridge of the Weald attains its greatest height at Crowborough Beacon, where it is more than 800 feet above the level of the sea. The coast line has an extent of about ninety miles. With respect to the districts hereafter to be considered, five of them are physically very similar, each having a portion of coast and down and weald, whilst that towards the eastern extremity is altogether on the Wealden formation, extending also to the coast, and the seventh occupying the northern slope of the Wealden ridge has no seaboard.

A HISTORY OF SUSSEX

My friend, the late Mr. H. C. Watson, in his *Cybele Britannica*, mapped out our island into plant provinces and enumerated the species which occur in each. What have been called types have been thus established. Certain species have been found to extend over all Britain. These are denominated as of the British type. Other species occur chiefly or exclusively in England. Some are limited to Scotland or the north of England and Wales. These are of the Scottish type with which we are not concerned. Plants which are found chiefly in the south-east of England and the counties adjacent to the German Ocean are classified as of the Germanic type. These include the chalk plants of which we have so many examples in Sussex including the insectiform Orchids. Another group of species is met with in the south-west of England and Wales, and occasionally extending far along the western and southern district. This forms what is called the Atlantic type, and is of peculiar interest to us in considering the distribution of the flora of this county. A few of them call for our special notice. One of these is the Cornish money wort (*Sibthorpia Europæa*), an exquisite little pink trailing flower, which, extending from the Scilly Islands into Cornwall and Devon, passes over west Sussex and occurs in east Sussex near Waldron, and no further in England eastward. This is a fact seemingly inexplicable. Scarcely less so is the case of the yellow bartsia (*Bartsia viscosa*), which beginning in Cornwall extends through Devon, Dorset and Hants, misses west Sussex, and reappears near Bexhill Common, where it has been established for more than fifty years. It is not found further eastward.

The question as to whether certain plants are or are not truly native is often asked, but is one on which botanists differ very widely. Mr. Watson divides our introduced plants into Denizens, Colonists, Aliens and Casuals. Denizens may be described as maintaining their habitats, as if native, but liable to the suspicion of having been originally introduced by human agency. Colonists as weeds of cultivated land, seldom found except in places where the ground has been adapted for their production and continuance by the operations of man. Aliens as certainly or very probably of foreign origin. Casuals as stragglers from cultivation. We have examples of all, which will be differentiated in our account of the Sussex botanical districts, and we need only observe that certain foreign species may be noted which are gradually taking up their abode with us, and have evidently come to stay, as for instance those farm pests, the clover dodder (*Cuscuta trifolii*), not long known here and very destructive ; Bauxbaum's speedwell (*Veronica Bauxbaumii*), spreading rapidly in cornfields, and the lesser wart cress (*Senebiera didyma*), becoming common all along the Sussex coast, which manifests itself when trodden under foot by its pungent smell. To mention one other only, the sand mustard (*Diplotaxis muralis*), which is now becoming frequent, especially by the line of the London and South Coast Railway. This I first noticed but a few years ago, and observing it also near Torquay was able to add it to the flora of Devon.

BOTANY

We will now direct our attention to the habitats of the more interesting species which are to be met with in Sussex.

If we consider our county latitudinally, we have three divisions which differ greatly as to the character of their flora—the Coast, the Downs, and the Weald. Let us take a brief survey of each.

1. PLANTS OF THE COAST.—As preliminary it should be noted that starting from the western extremity of the county we have the London Clay extending from Hampshire along the coast south of Chichester to Worthing, and that this includes the Manhood, one of the most fertile districts in England. Beyond Worthing we come to the remarkable shingle beach at Shoreham, on which some interesting species occur. Thence we have the chalk, which in some places abuts close upon the shore, as far as Eastbourne. Beyond this, to Pevensey, the beach is composed almost entirely of rolled flints derived from the erosion of the chalk cliffs to the westward, and is known to be in some parts from 25 to 30 feet in thickness. The flora here is of considerable interest, as is that of Pevensey Marsh. Proceeding further eastwards we have the sand.

The estuaries which include the Sussex half of Emsworth Harbour, Bosham Creek and Chichester Harbour will repay examination. Some of the species, although not showy, from the peculiarities of their structure deserve notice, such as the greater ruppia (*R. spiralis*), uncoiling its stalk above the water, the horned pondweed (*Zannichellia pedicellata*), the fennel-leaved pondweed (*Potamogeton pectinatus*), and the curious little spathes of the grass wrack (*Zostera nana*), while the sides of these inlets of the Channel are everywhere clothed with the glasswort (*Salicornia herbacea*), at first of a bright green, then changing to yellow, fawn and reddish brown, and finally to deep mauve. At Thorney Island we have the horned poppy (*Glaucium luteum*) and the wild English clary (*Salvia verbenaca*), the fœtid iris or roast-beef plant (*I. fœtidissima*), and among the littoral *gramineæ* the scarce nit grass (*Gastridium lendigerum*), the very rare annual beard grass (*Polypogon monspeliensis*), the sea barley (*Hordeum maritimum*), and the sea hard grass (*Lepturus filiformis*). We next meet with the pretty pink sea heath (*Frankenia lævis*), which occurs along our shore in marshy flats. At Hermitage too we have the golden samphire (*Inula crithmoides*) in its vicinity. A little further on may be found the Danish scurvy grass (*Cochlearia Danica*) and the English scurvy grass (*C. Anglica*). The sea kale (*Crambe maritima*) still occurs occasionally, and among the crucifers to be sought for is the purple sea rocket (*Cakile maritima*), to be found at Brighton, Newhaven, Beachy Head and Eastbourne. One of our rarest flowers is the proliferous pink (*Dianthus prolifer*), as yet met with in Sussex only near Selsey, but which I have seen abundantly at Hayling Island, where it is extremely stunted. Amongst pebbles we have sometimes patches of the curious sea purslane (*Honkeneya peploides*). Our coast, too, well repays search for the various trefoils, as the soft-knotted trefoil (*Trifolium striatum*), the rough rigid trefoil (*T. scabrum*), the

45

dense-flowered trefoil (*T. suffocatum*), the teasel-headed trefoil (*T. maritimum*), the subterranean trefoil (*T. subterraneum*) and the strawberry-headed trefoil (*T. fragiferum*) are all to be found. A passing allusion can only be made to the starry-headed trefoil (*T. stellatum*), since rapacious collectors are to be dreaded. Allied to these is the elegant birdsfoot fenugreek (*Trigonella ornithopodiodes*), minute and rather rare. On sandy banks are to be seen the biting stonecrops (*Sedum acre*) and the English stonecrop (*S. Anglicum*). The samphire (*Crithmum maritimum*), once abundant with us, as on Beachy Head, is still to be met with in almost all our districts, but sparingly. It once gave employment to our cliffsmen, and is in perfection towards the end of May. Having tasted pickled samphire by way of experiment I am bound to commend it. This is however to be looked on as a lost Sussex industry, and it may be doubted whether it will ever give occupation to our seafaring men again.

From the coast we have derived divers of our vegetables. Here we find the wild carrot (*Daucus carota*), the wild celery (*Apium graveolens*), the alexanders (*Smyrnium olusatrum*), formerly cultivated and still to be seen around old gardens, the sea cabbage (*Brassica oleracea*), and the wild spinach or sea beet (*Beta maritima*). This I am of opinion surpasses the cultivated spinach as having a slightly saline flavour, and is less collected in the spring than it should be. The yellow horned poppy (*Glaucium luteum*) is not uncommon eastward. It usually grows along the beach just beyond the reach of the tide, but I have met with it on chalk as far inland as Bramber. On the cliffs below Shoreham we have the narrow-leaved flax (*Linum angustifolium*) and the star thistle (*Centaurea calcitrapa*), and as we approach Brighton two plants that are rare westward occur, namely, the seaside bindweed (*Convolvulus Soldanella*), and the sea holly (*Eryngium maritimum*), whose blanched shoots are sometimes substituted for asparagus, also a prostrate form of the woody nightshade (*Solanum Dulcamara*, known as *S. marinum*), which trails along the shore.

Onwards towards Eastbourne we come to the shingle beach extending to Pevensey, formed by rolled flints derived from the erosion of the chalk cliffs. Here some interesting species occur, including the least lettuce (*Lactuca saligna*), the stinking hawksbeard (*Crepis fœtida*), and the soapwort (*Saponaria officinalis*), while the lovely viper's bugloss (*Echium vulgare*) is very conspicuous. With the flora of Winchelsea and Rye we terminate our coast plants, coming upon the little bur medic (*Medicago minima*), and the sea buckthorn (*Hippophae rhamnoides*) on the Camber Sands, a very rare species, discovered there a few years ago.

2. PLANTS OF THE DOWNS.—After a journey into Sussex, Gilbert White enthusiastically described our South Downs as majestic mountains. They may better be termed a chain of bold chalk hills, which stretch away in a south-easterly direction from the Hampshire border to Beachy Head. On the north they are steep and abrupt in the direction of the Weald, while they descend on the south with a gentle declivity. The

summits of our downs are covered with a shallow layer of turf, which has been said to be the finest natural carpet in the world, and there is every reason to suppose that they were always open, dry, and as we now see them so they existed in primeval days. With the exception of the Hangers on the northern slope, which are also probably of very ancient date, the woods which now cover some of their summits, such as those near Goodwood and Arundel, have been all made within the memory of man or within the reach of record. From Shoreham to Eastbourne the average depth of the soil is not more than four or five inches, and on this some of our plants become so dwarfed and altered in appearance and habit as scarcely to be recognized as being of the same species with their representatives on lowland soil. The permeable nature of the chalk has a remarkable effect on the superincumbent vegetation and renders it well suited to our orchids, presently to be specially referred to.

Taking our down plants *seriatim* we notice first the pheasant's eye (*Adonis autumnalis*), with its bright scarlet petals not common in the county, but to be met with occasionally at Portslade and Rottingdean in cultivated fields, as is too that curious little species the mousetail (*Myosurus minimus*). The hairy violet (*V. hirta*) is not infrequent westward. Many leguminous plants love the downs. By Duncton Hill, near the chalk pits, grows the rare sweet milk vetch (*Astragalus glycyphyllos*), with leaves which taste like liquorice. At Bury, Parham and Amberley we find the pretty narrow-leaved everlasting pea (*Lathyrus sylvestris*), and in the same neighbourhood the yellow vetchling (*L. aphaca*). The horse-shoe vetch (*Hippocrepis comosa*) is rare westward but common on the eastern part of the range. Of the *Rosaceæ* we here note only the dropwort (*Spiræa Filipendula*), which abounding in some of the districts is absent from others. Among the *Compositæ* we have the flea wort (*Cineraria campestris*) on the downs between Shoreham and Brighton, but it is local and uncommon, while the beautiful musk thistle (*Carduus nutans*) and the curious carline thistle (*Carlina vulgaris*) are abundant. The bell-flowers are among the most lovely of our down plants. Every one knows the pale blue harebell (*Campanula rotundifolia*). The nettle-leaved bell-flower (*C. trachelium*) is to be found in chalky lanes, and certainly one of the handsomest ornaments of our hills is the clustered bell-flower (*C. glomerata*) with its blossoms of a deep rich purple. Occasionally it may be seen transferred to cottage gardens, and it certainly well deserves culture.

Allied to these is the round-headed rampion (*Phyteuma orbiculare*), locally known as the pride of Sussex, and by many considered the loveliest ornament of the British flora. It is confined to the south of England, occurring only in Sussex, Hants, Dorset, Wilts and Kent very sparingly. Old Gerarde quaintly describes it two hundred years ago as having 'flowers of a purple colour, which part themselves into fine slender strings with threads in the middle, which decaying are succeeded by little cups, ending in fine little pointels and containing a small yellow seed.' Ray in 1670 speaks of it as growing on the downs of Sussex in many places. It abounds on Beachy Head, and is to be frequently met with in the direction of Hampshire.

A pretty dark blue flower is the autumnal gentian (*G. amarella*), which decks the higher grounds in patches, and to the same family belongs that striking plant the yellow wort (*Chlora perfoliata*) of vivid hue and glaucous foliage. The tall mulleins are conspicuous in shady lanes. The great mullein (*Verbascum Thapsus*), known in Sussex as the blanket plant, which occasionally reaches six feet in height, is common. The dark mullein (*V. nigrum*) is local, occurring chiefly towards the west, as at Sutton, Harting and Racton. The white mullein (*V. lychnitis*) found at Halnaker and Dale Park is rare. The bastard toadflax (*Thesium humifusum*) is met with only on the chalk. It was discovered to be a parasite, attached by its roots to various plants, by the Sussex botanist Mitten. This curious little species has very small greenish white flowers and stems which creep along the ground, as its name implies. In Arundel Park I have noticed it in plenty.

Certain of the grasses which are found on the downs are beautiful and others useful. A handsome grass is the glabrous oat grass (*Avena pratensis*), shining with its bronzed plumes. Another is the rarer barren false brome (*Brachypodium pinnatum*) to be seen on Roche's Hill, Goodwood, and a pretty species is the crested hair grass (*Kœleria cristata*), but none is more useful than the sheep's fescue (*Festuca ovina*), to which is attributed the superiority of our South Down mutton, although some assert that this is owing to the zoned snail (*Helix virgata*), which we frequently find climbing up the stems of this grass, and of which no doubt the sheep eat quantities. To turn now to our orchids, in which Sussex is richer than any county in England, with the exception of Kent. A large proportion love the chalk, many delight in our beechen hangers, and others have their homes in the boggy lands at the foot of the downs. As to the insectiform species, we have the bee (*Ophrys apifera*), capricious in appearance, usually met with on the downs, but occasionally in low situations, as by Chichester Canal ; the pretty fly (*O. muscifera*), almost always at a considerable elevation ; the early spider (*O. aranifera*), in east Sussex, near Piecombe, and its variety the drone (*O. fucifera*), specimens of which I had sent me from Lewes. Some of our orchids flower at different seasons in different localities, so that one would suppose that they were of distinct species. As instances, the frog orchis (*Orchis viridis*), which flowers at Fishbourne in the low ground quite a month earlier than it does at Harting and Goodwood, and similarly with the fragrant orchis (*Gynadenia Conopsea*), which is comparatively small on the downs compared with its very luxuriant growth in the valley of the Ems. The pyramidal orchis (*Orchis pyramidalis*), with its dense spike of lovely rose, is common along the whole range. We have both the greater butterfly (*Habenaria chlorantha*) and the lesser butterfly (*H. bifolia*). The curious green man orchis (*Aceras anthropophora*) occurs at Horeham, and Hurstpierpoint. The dwarf dark-winged orchis (*O. ustulata*) is only found eastward, but

48

parForce

BOTANY

abounds near Beachy Head. In our hangers we have the brown bird's nest (*Neottia nidus-avis*) and the tway blade (*Listera ovata*), and there too we meet with the helleborines. The large white helleborine (*Cephalanthera grandiflora*), known in Sussex as the egg orchis, a handsome species, is common ; the lesser white (*C. ensifolia*) occurs near Goodwood, but is rare ; the broad-leaved helleborine (*Epipactis latifolia*), of purplish hue, is not uncommon westward. At Harting we have the narrow-leaved helleborine (*E. media*), and the rare and beautiful violet helleborine (*E. violacea*) at Stansted. We must not omit the pretty green musk orchis (*Herminium monorchis*), which occasionally peeps up amongst tall moss, as at Barlavington and Duncton. The latest flowering species is the fragrant ladies' tresses (*Spiranthes autumnalis*).

3. PLANTS OF THE WEALD.—The Weald Clay, says Professor Hull, forms a depressed tract of country between the elevated ground of the centre and the ridges of the Lower Greensand and Chalk, which enclose the Wealden area all round its circumference except along the eastern coast-line from Beachy Head to Shakespeare's Cliff near Dover. The Wealden area sinks down almost to the level of the high-water at Pevensey. The breadth of the Weald is from five to ten miles, and its length from thirty to forty miles. The Forest Ridge, which contains St. Leonards Forest and Ashdown Forest, is that portion of the county which, uniting with the Weald, forms the north-easterly division, stretching from Fairlight Down by Crowborough to St. Leonards Forest, and terminating gradually in the western part of the county in the angle formed by the sandhills of Petworth on the one side and by Black Down and Leith Hill on the other. It is composed of the more elevated portions of the sands and sandstones. The soil consists of a sandy loam, or iron sandstone, or of a poor black vegetable sand upon a soft clay marl. It is for the most part exceedingly barren. In Sussex the existing forests of St. Leonards, Ashdown, Tilgate and Waterdown are portions of the primeval forest of Anderida, which through the Roman and Saxon eras remained entire, and is spoken of by Bede in A.D. 731 as thick and inaccessible. At the time of the Conquest its dense woods were beyond the pale of the Norman survey, as a glance at the excellent map prefixed to the Sussex Domesday, published by the Sussex Archæological Society, plainly proves. A view of the Weald from the Devil's Dyke shows us how much of woodland still remains. This, together with its heaths, commons and bogs present many interesting localities to the botanist. As affecting its vegetation, it may be noted that in the Wealden district the temperature is more variable, and the rainfall heavier, than that along the coast, which is due mainly to the large extent of forest land and the fact that the South Downs rise in the track of the rain clouds. And here, by the way, it may be noted that while more bright sunshine is registered in the south of England than in any other part of the kingdom, according to the latest records, Sussex seems the sunniest county in the country, a circumstance which doubtless has a favourable influence on its flora.

I 49 7

As regards the plants to be met with, it may be noted that, beginning from the Hampshire border, we have Stansted Forest and Charlton Forest, both to a great extent planted. In these we have striking patches of the rosebay (*Epilobium angustifolium*), and beds of the meadow thistle (*Carduus pratensis*). Stansted contains some of the rarest of our helleborines, and near Colworth, in 1885, I found the very rare lesser winter green (*Pyrola minor*) growing in isolated patches. In St. Leonards Forest are the lovely ivy-leaved bell-flower (*Campanula hederacea*) and the bog pimpernel (*Anagallis tenella*). The columbine (*Aquilegia vulgaris*), both white and purple, occurs here, and the scarce intermediate winter green (*Pyrola media*) in considerable plenty. Large beds of the lily of the valley (*Convallaria majalis*) are one of its features, and in sandy bogs are the small chaffweed (*Centunculus minimus*) and the least gentianella (*Cicendia filiformis*), with the least spike rush (*Eleocharis acicularis*). In the forest meadows occurs the pale narcissus (*N. biflorus*), and in various places near Horeham grows the wild service-tree (*Pyrus torminalis*), rare westward. Ashdown Forest, which contains about 10,000 acres, was at one time an immense uncultivated tract, but it is now partly brought into tillage and partly broken up into separate forest districts. From its name it might be naturally supposed to be favourable to the growth of ash timber, but amongst the trees growing in some parts of the forest an ash is scarcely to be found,[1] while pine, beech and oak, some of the latter of extreme antiquity, abound. Here there were formerly many ironworks, and in the old Hammer ponds occur several very rare plants. In one of these at Buxted, in 1827, Borrer discovered the marsh isnardia (*Isnardia palustris*), previously unknown in Great Britain, and of this I have specimens taken from that place in my herbarium. He afterwards found it on Petersfield Heath in Hants, where it is now apparently lost by drainage. It has however been rediscovered in Hants, and although now considered lost in Sussex, it is to be hoped that therein also it may be met with afresh. Sussex and Hants are the only counties in which it has as yet been found. In the Forest the raspberry (*Rubus Idæus*) occurs in quantity, undoubtedly wild. Worth, Tilgate, and Dallington Forests were all to a great extent denuded of their timber by the Sussex ironworks. On the shore of the great pond at Tilgate Borrer found the hexandrous waterwort (*Elatine hexandra*), one of the scarcest species in our flora ; the plantain shoreweed (*Litorella lacustris*) occurs at Piltdown ; and in Tilgate Forest we have the beech fern (*Polypodium Phegopteris*), and three of the club mosses (*Lycopodium clavatum*, *L. inundatum* and *L. Selago*). Waterdown Forest approaches the border of Surrey, and here may be sought the bristle-leaved bent grass (*Agrostis setacea*), the wood small reed (*Calamagrostis setacea*), and the white beak rush (*Rhyncospora alba*).

In my *Flora of Sussex* I instituted a comparison with it and that of the adjacent counties of Hants, Kent and Surrey, which need not here

---

[1] Rev. E. Turner, *S.A.C.* xiv. 39.

BOTANY

be given. The plants of Great Britain include about 1,960 species, and from the following summary it will be seen that we have 1,159 in this county.

SUMMARY OF ORDERS, NUMBER OF GENERA AND OF SPECIES IN EACH ORDER

Sussex Flora

	Total Genera in each Order	Total Species in each Order		Total Genera in each Order	Total Species in each Order
			35. Araliaceæ	1	1
CLASS I			36. Cornaceæ	1	1
Exogeneæ			**Div. III.** *Corollifloræ*		
Div. I. *Thalamifloræ*			37. Loranthaceæ . . .	1	1
1. Ranunculaceæ . . .	10	33	38. Caprifoliaceæ . . .	4	8
2. Berberidaceæ . . .	1	1	39. Valerianaceæ . . .	3	6
3. Nymphæaceæ . . .	2	2	40. Rubiaceæ	4	14
4. Papaveraceæ	3	7	41. Dipsaceæ	2	5
5. Fumariaceæ	2	7	42. Compositæ	39	101
6. Cruciferæ	24	48	43. Campanulaceæ . . .	5	11
7. Resedaceæ	1	2	44. Ericaceæ	5	8
8. Cistaceæ	1	1	45. Jasminaceæ	2	2
9. Violaceæ	1	9	46. Apocynaceæ	1	1
10. Droseraceæ	1	2	47. Gentianaceæ . . .	6	10
11. Polygalaceæ	1	3	48. Convolvulaceæ . . .	2	7
12. Frankeniaceæ . . .	1	1	49. Solanaceæ	3	4
13. Caryophylleæ . . .	13	42	50. Scrophulariaceæ . .	13	39
13a. Illecebraceæ	1	1	51. Orobanchaceæ . . .	2	5
14. Portulaceæ	1	1	52. Verbenaceæ	1	1
15. Elatineæ	1	1	53. Labiatæ	18	43
16. Hypericaceæ . . .	1	9	54. Boraginaceæ	8	15
17. Malvaceæ	3	6	55. Pinguiculaceæ . . .	1	4
18. Tiliaceæ	1	3	56. Primulaceæ	8	12
19. Linaceæ	2	3	57. Plumbaginaceæ . . .	2	5
20. Geraniaceæ	3	13	58. Plantaginaceæ . . .	2	6
21. Ilicaceæ	1	1			
Div. II. *Calycifloræ*			**Div. IV.** *Monochlamydeæ*		
22. Celastraceæ	1	1	59. Amaranthaceæ . . .	1	1
23. Rhamnaceæ	1	2	60. Chenopodiaceæ . . .	7	23
24. Aceraceæ	1	2	61. Polygonaceæ . . .	2	24
25. Leguminosæ . . .	17	61	62. Elæagnaceæ	1	1
26. Rosaceæ	14	92	63. Thymeleaceæ . . .	1	2
27. Lythraceæ	2	3	64. Santalaceæ	1	1
28. Onagraceæ	3	11	65. Euphorbiaceæ . . .	2	11
29. Haloragiaceæ . . .	3	9	66. Ceratophyllaceæ . .	1	2
30. Cucurbitaceæ . . .	1	1	67. Urticaceæ	4	6
31. Grossulariaceæ . . .	1	3	68. Amentiferæ	10	30
32. Crassulaceæ	2	8			
33. Saxifragaceæ	2	3	**Div. V.** *Gymnospermæ*		
34. Umbelliferæ	29	42	69. Coniferæ	3	3

	Total Genera in each Order	Total Species in each Order		Total Genera in each Order	Total Species in each Order
CLASS II			**Div. II.** *Glumiferæ*		
ENDOGENÆ			83. Cyperaceæ	6	65
Div. I. *Petaloideæ*			84. Gramineæ	37	98
70. Typhaceæ	2	5	**CLASS III**		
71. Araceæ	2	3	CRYPTOGAMEÆ		
72. Lemnaceæ . . .	1	4	Div. I. *Vasculares*		
73. Naiadaceæ . . .	4	19			
74. Alismaceæ . . .	5	7	85. Filices	14	25
75. Hydrocharidaceæ . .	2	2	86. Lycopodiaceæ . . .	1	3
76. Orchidaceæ . . .	12	29	87. Marsiliaceæ	1	1
77. Iridaceæ	1	2	88. Equisetaceæ	1	5
78. Amaryllidaceæ . . .	3	4	Div. II. *Cellulares*		
79. Dioscoreaceæ . . .	1	1	89. Characeæ	4	11
80. Trilliaceæ . . .	1	1			
81. Liliaceæ	12	17			
82. Juncaceæ	2	19		431	1159

NOTES ON THE BOTANICAL DISTRICTS, WITH LISTS OF THE RARER PLANTS IN EACH DISTRICT

I. THE WEST ROTHER

This district, comprising the westernmost part of the county, is bounded on the east by a stream from the Surrey border, which flows by Shillinglee, Kirdford and Wisborough Green into the Arun, from which point the boundary runs along the west bank of the Arun to the sea. It is drained north of the Downs by the West Rother, a tributary of the Arun which it joins near Pulborough, and south into the Channel by two independent streams, the Lavant and the Ems. These are intermittent. The Lavant is usually dry during the summer. The Ems, which generally begins to flow in February, continues to carry down a considerable body of water until late in autumn.

In the northern part of this district we have the clay of the Weald, and in the neighbourhood of Midhurst and Petworth much of the greensand, with large tracts of boggy heath, common, and considerable woodland. Here we meet with many of our ferns, including *Lomaria spicant*, *Asplenium Trichomanes*, the lovely lady fern, *Athyrium Filix fœmina*, with its var. *Rhæticum*, *Cæterach officinarum*, sometimes in abundance, *Lastrea Thelypteris* rare, and *L. Oreopteris* local, *L. Spinulosa* and *Osmunda regalis*, which in a bend of the Rother I once found six feet in height. In this part of Sussex this latter plant is now becoming very rare, and one cannot give localities for it. Unfortunately our scarcer ferns are now of marketable value and the rapacity of collectors and dealers appears to be increasing. Midhurst, Graffham, and Duncton Common with their silver sand and boggy spots afford some interesting species, as *Gentiana Pneumonanthe*, *Filago minima*, *Eriophorum vaginatum* and *Malaxis paludosa*, and by the Rother we find the lovely flowering rush, *Butomus umbellatus*. We next come to the chalk with its plants already adverted to, and finally to the coast, which in this district presents features different from any other in the county. The estuaries of the extreme western portion are bounded by large tracts of moorland, some of which are now reclaimed. The Manhood and Thorney Island are on the London Clay, and beyond the latter is the vanishing islet of Pilsey, soon to be submerged in the Channel.

The rarer plants are :[1]—

[1] With respect to the districts I have used the term 'rarer' rather than 'peculiar' to them, because species formerly so considered have recently been found elsewhere in the county, and doubtless as research goes on this will continue to be the case. Plants printed in italics are naturalized or not quite wild. An asterisk before the specific name signifies that the plant may probably be extinct. Habitats

BOTANY

RANUNCULACEÆ
Ranunculus fluitans *Lam.*
Helleborus viridis *L.*

CRUCIFERÆ
Cochlearia anglica *L.*
C. Danica *L.*
Camelina sativa Crantz.
Lepidium Draba *L.*
L. latifolium *Br.*
Nasturtium amphibium *Br.*
Isatis tinctoria L.

CARYOPHYLLACEÆ
Dianthus prolifer *L.*
Silene conica *L.*
Arenaria tenuifolia *L.*
Stellaria aquatica *Scop.*

HYPERICACEÆ
Hypericum montanum *L.*

LEGUMINOSÆ
Melilotus parviflora *Lam.*
M. alba *Lam.*
Astragalus glycyphyllus *L.*
Lathyrus sylvestris *L.*

ROSACEÆ
Geum rivale *L.*
G. intermedium *Ehr.*

UMBELLIFERÆ
Bupleurum tenuissimum *L.*
Œnanthe pimpinelloides *L.*
Daucus carota v. maritimus *L. Gall.*

RUBIACEÆ
Rubia peregrina *L.*

DIPSACEÆ
Dipsacus pilosus *L.*

COMPOSITÆ
Petasites vulgaris *Desf.*
Inula Helenium *L.*
I. crithmoides *L.*
Lactuca virosa *L.*
Hieracium maculatum Sm.

CAMPANULACEÆ
Campanula patula *L.*
C. rapunculoides L.
C. rapunculus *L.*

ERICACEÆ
Pyrola minor *L.*

SCROPHULARIACEÆ
Verbasum Lychnitis *L.*

OROBANCHACEÆ
Lathræa squamosa *L.*

TRILLIACEÆ
Paris quadrifolia *L.*

LILIACEÆ
Ornithogalum pyrennicum *L.*

JUNCACEÆ
Juncus *acutus *L.*
Luzula albida

NAIADACEÆ
Zannichellia brachystemon *J. Gay*

ALISMACEÆ
Actinocarpus Damasonium *H. Br.*

ORCHIDACEÆ
Orchis incarnata × maculata
Epipactis media *Fries*
E. violacea *D. Dug.*
E. viridans *Cranz.*
Cephalanthera ensifolia *Rich.*

GRAMINEÆ
Spartina stricta *Roth.*
S. Townsendi *H & J. Groves.*
S. Alterni flora *Loisel.*
Polypogon monspeliensis *Desf.*

FILICES
Cystopteris fragilis *Bernh.*
Polypodium Robertianum *Hoffm.*

EQUISETACEÆ
Equisetum sylvaticum *L.*

II. THE ARUN

In tracing the boundaries of this district a start may be made at the Surrey border, and a line followed through Roughey Street across St. Leonards Forest, by Stone Lodge and Colegate to Pease Pottage Gate, thence south to Hand Cross, westward over Plummer's Plain to Monk's Gate, across country to the junction of the railways near Plumtree Cross, on to Bashurst and Ludwick, taking the main road to Billingshurst, then leaving it again and crossing the railway to the east of the station, on to Coneyhurst, Broadford Green, Chiltington, Thakeham, skirting Heath Common, through Washington, Highden, Findon, West Tarring and Heene to the sea, a little west of Worthing. This district includes the greater part of St. Leonards Forest, and stretches across the county in its widest part. It is drained by the Arun and a few tributary rivulets.

and localities for all the species are given at length in my *Flora of Sussex,* and the same nomenclature of genera and species is here adopted. Since its publication a considerable number of additions have been made.

53

A HISTORY OF SUSSEX

There is perhaps a greater diversity of soil in this district than in any other. In the north we have sands and sandstones alternating with beds of clay, and on these St. Leonards Forest of about 10,000 acres, in which many interesting plants previously referred to occur. The marsh and bog lands at the foot of the Downs, as at Chiltington Common, contain numerous species which delight the botanist, such as *Utricularia minor*, formerly questionable in Sussex, *Potentilla Comarum*, *Menyanthes trifoliata*, *Hydrocharis Morsus-ranæ*, and *Pilularia globulifera*, rare in the county. Further south are the Amberley Wild Brooks, in the valley of the Arun, an immense marshy tract for Sussex, which when flooded in winter resembles a lake in dimensions. Here grew formerly the black crowberry, *Empetrum nigrum*, perhaps not extinct, and the cranberry, *Vaccinium oxycoccos*, now rare, but which formerly so abounded that its fruit sold at a shilling a quart, and here are to be found *Stellaria glauca*, *Hypericum elodes*, *Myrica Gale*, *Viola palustris*, *Eriophorum vaginatum*, and *Carex teretiuscula*. Vegetable mould here first appears, and then from four to five feet of peat on a dark blue silt or clay.

The banks of the Arun well repay investigation, and near Arundel, on both sides of the river affected by the tide, we have *Scirpus carinatus* and *S. triqueter*, both very rare, the latter being found only by the Arun and the Thames. Clymping Sands near its mouth afford good botanising.

Among the rarer plants of this district are :—

RANUNCULACEÆ
Helleborus fœtidus *L.*

CRUCIFERÆ
Draba muralis *L.*
Erysimum cheiranthoides *L.*
Lepidium ruderale *L.*

LEGUMINIFERÆ
Trifolium ochroleucum *L.*
T. suffocatum *L.*

ROSACEÆ
Rubus fissus *Lindl.*
R. carpinifolius *W. & N.*
R. plicatus *W. & N.*

HALORAGIACEÆ
Callitriche truncata *Guss.*

CRASSULACEÆ
Sedum album v. micranthum Bast.

CAPRIFOLIACEÆ
Lonicera Xylosteum L.

RUBIACEÆ
Rubia peregrina *L.*

CAMPANULACEÆ
Campanula Rapunculus *L.*

ERICACEÆ
Pyrola media *Swartz.*

GENTIANACEÆ
Cicendia filiformis *Delarb.*

SCROPHULARIACEÆ
Verbascum pulverulentum *Vill.*

LABIATÆ
Melittis Melissophyllum *L.*

BORAGINACEÆ
Anchusa sempervirens L.
Myosotis sylvatica *Hoffm.*

PINGUICULACEÆ
Utricularia minor *L.*
U. intermedia *Hayne*

EUPHORBIACEÆ
Euphorbia coralloides L.

AMENTIFERÆ
Salix ambigua v. spathulata *Ehrh.*

CYPERACEÆ
Scirpus carinatus *Sm.*
S. triqueter *L.*
Carex elongata *L.*
C. teretiuscula *Good.*

GRAMINEÆ
Calamagrostis lanceolata *Roth.*
Leersia oryzoides *Swartz*

FILICES
Lastræa Thelypteris *Presl.*

CHARACEÆ
Nitella gracilis *Agardh.*
N. mucronata *A. Braun.*
N. translucens *Agardh.*
N. flexilis *Agardh.*

III. THE ADUR

The confines of this district are the Arun boundary from the sea to Plummer's Plain, and thence the Ouse boundary to Rottingdean and the sea a little east of Brighton. It is drained by the Adur, whose eastern and western waters coalesce about a mile and a half west of Henfield, and by its numerous tributaries ; also by the Wellesbourne, a small independent stream which rises near Patcham, and passing by Preston reaches the sea at Brighton.

To the north of the Downs we have that part of the Weald in which Borrer made his researches, and in which most of his herbarium specimens were collected. The plants of the

BOTANY

chalk, especially in the neighbourhood of Brighton, have been already referred to. To the west of Brighton the Adur flows into the sea at Shoreham. Some low cliffs in the vicinity, composed of sand, gravel, and comminuted shells, afford many interesting species, while the ballast along Shoreham Harbour is the abode of several varieties.

Among the rarer plants we have :—

CRUCIFERÆ
Sisymbrium Sophia *L.*
Matthiola incana *R. Br.*

CARYOPHYLLACEÆ
Silene *noctiflora *L.*
S. *italica *Pers.*

TILIACEÆ
Tilia grandiflora Ehrh.

GERANIACEÆ
Geranium lucidum *L.*
Erodium maritimum *Sm.*

LEGUMINIFERÆ
Trifolium stellatum L.
T. glomeratum *L.*
Vicia lutea *L.*
V. *bithynica *L.*
Lathyrus aphaca *L.*
Anthyllis Vulneraria v. Dillenii *Schultz.*

ROSACEÆ
Rubus affinis *W. & N.*
R. incurvatus *Bab.*
R. thyrsoidens *Wimm.*
R. Grabowskii *Weihe*
R. villicaulis *W. & N.*
R. Hystrix *Bab.*
R. echinatus *Lind.*
R. fusco-ater *Weihe*
R. diversifolius *Lindl.*
R. Guntheri *Weihe*
R. althæifolius *Host.*
Rosa Sabini *Woods*
R. Doniana „

ONAGRACEÆ
Epilobium lanceolatum *Schrs.*
Isnardia *palustris *L.*

HALORAGIACEÆ
Callitriche obtusangula *Le Gal.*

UMBELLIFERÆ
Caucalis daucoides *L.*

RUBIACEÆ
Galium sylvestre *Poll.*

COMPOSITÆ
Crepis fœtida *L.*

SCROPHULARIACEÆ
Melampyrum arvense *L.*
Limosella aquatica *L.*

POLYGONACEÆ
Rumex palustris *Sm.*

AMENTIFERÆ
Salix pentranda *L.*
S. purpurea v. Helix *L.*
S. rubra *Huds.*
S. triandra v. amygdalina *L.*
S. Smithiana *Wild.*
S. cinerea v. oleifolia *Sm.*
S. ambigua *Ehrh.*

CHENOPODIACEÆ
Atriplex rosea *L.*

POLYGONACEÆ
Rumex palustris *Sm.*

CYPERACEÆ
Carex elongata *L.*

CHARACEÆ
Chara vulgaris v. longibracteata *Kuetz.*
Tolypella glomerata *Leonh.*
T. prolifera *Leonh.*

IV. THE OUSE

The limits of this district may be thus defined : We take first the Cuckmere boundary to Cross-in-Hand, and thence follow the East Rother boundary to Castle Hill, near Rotherfield. We then turn westward across the ridge of the Weald to Sand Hill, Stone Cross, Crowboro' Gate, Duddleswell Gate, Sweet Mine Pits, Nutley Hill, Charlwood, Charlwood Gate, Wych Cross, Cold Harbour, Tyne's Cross, West Hoathly, Turner's Hill, Half Smock, across Balcombe Down and Highbeech Warren to Hand Cross, thence on to Plummer's Plain, turning south-east, past Eastland's Farm, Slut House Farm, Warninglid, Slough Green and Whiteman's Green to Cuckfield, Butler's Green, over the tunnel at Hayward's Heath, taking the road to Wivelsfield by way of Westwood to Ditchling and Westmeston, striking the Downs east of Ditchling Beacon to Falmer, Newmarket Hill and Rottingdean. This district is drained by the Ouse, which has a larger catchment basin than any other in the county, and by its tributaries, the Uckfield, the Black-brook and the Ritch. Mr. J. H. A. Jenner of Lewes, who has given more attention to this district than any other observer, in his *Notes on the Flora of the South Downs*, states that the chalk hills of that neighbourhood are remarkably free from wood, with some few exceptions on the northern slope, and thus differ much from the downs of West Sussex and Kent. There are also cultivated tracts which have been lately much on the increase. On the open Downs the bulk of the turf consists of *Festuca ovina* and *Bromus erectus*, with here and there an admixture of *Kœleria cristata*, and on the northern slopes the very conspicuous *Brachypodium pinnatum*. On the broken declivities and ridges of cultivated ground grow *Rosa micrantha*, *Rosa rubiginosa*, rarely *Rosa spinosissima* and *Rosa sepium*, the last named being very local. *Juniperus communis* is extremely rare here, and only grows to the height of a few inches. The wooded parts are chiefly composed of beech and ash ; oak only occasionally occurs. *Taxus baccata* is invariably planted.

RANUNCULACEÆ
Eranthis hyemale Salisb.
Ranunculus Lingua *L.*
Delphinium Ajacis Reich.

CRUCIFERÆ
Nasturtium amphibium *Br.*
Thlaspi perfoliatum *L.*

CARYOPHYLLACEÆ
Silene noctiflora *L.*

HYPERICACEÆ
Hypericum montanum *L.*

LEGUMINIFERÆ
Trifolium maritimum *Huds.*
Vicia lathyroides *L.*
Anthyllis vulneraria v. Dillenii.

ROSACEÆ
Rosa sepium *Thuil.*
R. tomentosa v. subglobosa *Sm.*
R. canina v. lutetiana *Leman*
　　　　v. sphærica *Grem.*
　　　　v. urbica *Leman*
　　　　v. arvatica *Bak.*
　　　　v. tomentella *Leman*

UMBELLIFERÆ
Seseli Libanotis *Koch.*

GENTIANACEÆ
Gentiania campestris *L.*
Limnanthemum peltatum *Link.*

LABIATÆ
Melittis Melissophyllum *L.*

POLYGONACEÆ
Rumex maximus *Schreb.*

EUPHORBIACEÆ
Euphorbia pilosa *L.*

UMENTIFERÆ
Salix pentandra *L.*

ORCHIDACEÆ
Orchis ustulata *L.*
Habenaria albida *Br.*
Ophrys aranifera *Huds.*
Herminium monorchis *Br.*

AMARYLLIDACEÆ
Leucojum æstivum *L.*

NAIADACEÆ
Potamogeton Friesii *Rupr.*

CHARACEÆ
Chara fragilis v. Hedwigii *Desv.*
Nitella translucens *Agardh.*

V. THE CUCKMERE

In tracing the limits of this district we take the East Rother boundary to Cross-in-Hand, and then turn west of Passingworth Woods to Hawkhurst Common, East Hoathly, Stone Cross (to the west of Vert Woods), across the Dicker to Berwick, Alfriston and Climping, thence to the signal house on the coast west of Cuckmere Haven. The drainage of the western and largest part of this district is effected by the Cuckmere, which has two principal streams uniting at Hellingly. An independent stream, the Ashburn, drains the eastern portion and reaches the sea near the Red House at Pevensey. The outfall of the Cuckmere at Cuckmere Haven is bounded on the east and west by chalk cliffs, and is frequently blocked up by the shingle, which the set of the tide under the action of a south-west wind accumulates, and affords a favourable locality for marine plants. The highest points in this district are the South Downs, on the south-west, which rise to 536 feet at the noble promontory of Beachy Head.

The Wealden beds here are to a great extent brought under cultivation, and the woodlands are comparatively few. There is one large plantation however of about 1,000 acres, which chiefly consists of oak ; this includes Abbot's Wood, Wilmington Wood, Folkington Wood, and Gnat Wood, which latter has been thoroughly explored, and affords many interesting species. The Pevensey Levels, consisting of alluvium, form an extensive flat extending for nearly seven miles along the shore, and running for about six miles inland ; bordering this is a shingle beach about a mile in width at Langley, and forming thence a narrow belt from Pevensey to Bexhill. Here, although an unpromising place, a list of 152 plants was made some time ago, and this has since been extended.

BOTANY

RANUNCULACEÆ
Ranunculus intermedius *Hiern.*

CRUCIFERÆ
Raphanus maritimus *Sm.*

VIOLACEÆ
Viola lactea *Sm.*

MALVACEÆ
Malva borealis *Walton*

LEGUMINIFERÆ
Trifolium suffocatum *L.*
Medicago minima *Lam.*
Lotus angustissimus *L.*

ROSACEÆ
Pyrus torminalis *Ehrh.*
Rubus Schlectendalii *W. & N.*
R. horridus *Schultz*
R. althæifolius *Host.*
Rosa Canina v. Collina *Jacq.*
v. Koscindana *Bess.*
v. verticillicantha *Merat*
v. senticosa *Ach.*
v. vinacea *Bak.*
v. frondosa *Stev.*
v. andagavensis *Bast.*
v. cæsia *Sm.*
v. subcristata *Bak.*

HALORAGIACEÆ
Callitriche hamulata *Kirtz*

UMBELLIFERÆ
Seseli Libanotis *Koch*
Bupleurum aristatum *Bartl.*
Daucus gummifer *Lam.*
Pimpinella magna *L.*

COMPOSITÆ
Senecio campestris *DC.*
Crepis fœtida *L.*
Solidago canadensis L.
Lactuca saligna *L.*

CAMPANULACEÆ
Phyteuma spicatum *L.*

GENTIANACEÆ
Erythræa capitata var. sphærocephala *Towns.*

SCROPHULARIACEÆ
Scrophularia Ehrhartii *Stev.*
Sibthorpia Europæa *L.*
Bartsia viscosa *L.*

CERATOPHYLLACEÆ
Ceratophyllum submersum *L.*

NAIADACEÆ
Potamogeton plantagineus *Du Croz.*
P. acutifolius *Link.*
Zannichellia palustris var. pedicellata *Fries*

CYPERACEÆ
Scirpus uniglumis *Link.*

GRAMINEÆ
Agrostis setacea *Curt.*

CHARACEÆ
Chara aspera *Wild.*
Nitella opaca *Agardh.*

VI. THE EAST ROTHER

The confines of this district are as follows : We start from the coast and take the Kent boundary to Tunbridge Wells. Thence we proceed by the road skirting Eridge Park and Blackthorn Hill to Rotherfield and go on to Butcher's Cross and Five Ash Down to Cross-in-Hand. We next take the main road to Burwash as far as east side of Heathfield Park, through Cade Street, Punnett's Town, Turner's Green, Dallington, Netherfield Green, thence to Battle by the high road dividing High Wood, between Beauport and Crowhurst Parks, and through Hollington to the east of St. Leonards. The district is drained by the East Rother and two small independent streams, the Tillingham and the Brede, flowing from the westward, which meet the estuary of the East Rother near Rye.

The southern portion of this division is situated almost wholly on the Wealden formation, the cliffs of which rising sometimes to a height of nearly 300 feet from the coast-line, stretch from Cliff End Fairlight to St. Leonards, and from Bulverhythe to Bexhill. The remainder of the coast-line is occupied by marsh land, which contains in many places comparatively recent marine deposits. The country is undulated with hills of the ' Hastings Sands' division of the Wealden, which culminate in the Fairlight Downs, and much of it is thickly wooded.

Among the rarer plants are :—

CRUCIFERÆ
Dentaria bulbifera *L.*

LEGUMINIFERÆ
Trifolium suffocatum *L.*
T. glomeratum *L.*
Lotus angustissimus *L.*

ROSACEÆ
Rubus thyrsoidens *Wimm.*
Rosa canina v. dumalis *Bechst.*
v. obtusifolia *Lem.*

COMPOSITÆ
Senecio viscosus *L.*
Hypochæris glabra *L.*
Crepis biennis *L.*
Centaurea *Jacea *L.*

ELEAGNACEÆ
Hippophae Rhamnoides *L.*

CHENOPODIACEÆ
Atriplex Babingtonii *Woods*

EUPHORBIACEÆ
Euphorbia platyphyllos *L.*

POLYGONACEÆ
Polygonum Raii *Bab.*

AMENTIFERÆ
Salix laurina *Forst.*

NAIADACEÆ
Potamogeton rufescens *Schrad.*
P. rutilus *Wolf.*

CYPERACEÆ
Scirpus acicularis *L.*

GRAMINEÆ
Poa compressa *L.*
Festuca ambigua *Le Gall.*
F. sylvatica *Vill.*

FILICES
Asplenium marinum L.

VII. THE MEDWAY

This comparatively small district is bounded by Surrey and Kent on the north, and on the east by the Rother. Its southern boundary is formed by the Cuckmere and the Ouse. We leave the Ouse district at Handcross and bear westward across the Forest to Colgate and Stone Lodge. We then bear north-east to Roughey Street and east of Rusper to the Surrey boundary. This district is drained by the Medway, which originating in Sussex from a number of little streams becomes the boundary between Kent and Sussex, and runs into the German Ocean; and by the Mole, an independent river, which has its principal sources on the north side of the Forest Ridge, and which passing into Surrey joins the Thames at Hampton Court. This district differs from the rest in having no seaboard. It includes Waterdown Forest and a great part of the neighbourhood of Tunbridge Wells, and has an argillaceous soil more or less mixed with calcareous grit and sandstone rocks in parallel ridges. Damp hollows, rocky ravines and occasionally patches of bog are frequent. Several lists of its plants are extant. Observers however have not always been careful to separate Sussex species from those occurring beyond the Kentish border.

Its rarer plants are these :—

FUMARIACEÆ
Fumaria confusa *Jord.*

CRUCIFERÆ
Cardamine amara *L.*
Teesdalia nudicaulis *Br.*

CARYOPHYLLACEÆ
Sagina subulata *Wimm.*

ELATINACEÆ
Elatine hexandra *DC.*

LEGUMINIFERÆ
Genista pilosa *L.*
Trifolium ochroleucum *L.*

ROSACEÆ
Alchemilla vulgaris *Scop.*
Rubus pygmæus *Weihe*
R. affinis *W. & N.*
R. carpinifolius *W. & N.*
Rosa Borreri *Woods*
R. canina v. surculosa *Borr.*

UMBELLIFERÆ
Bupleurum rotundifolium *L.*

ARISTOLOCHIACEÆ
Aristolochia Clematitis L.

GENTIANEÆ
Cicendia filiformis Delarb.

COMPOSITÆ
Cnicus Forsteri *Sm.*

POLYGONACEÆ
Polygonum mite *Schrank*

NAIADACEÆ
Potamogeton obtusifolius *M. & K.*

GRAMINEÆ
Festuca sylvatica *Vill.*

FILICES
Asplenium lanceolatum *Sm.*
Hymenophyllum Tunbridgense *Sm.*

THE MOSSES (*Musci*)

The swamps in the Sussex forests, the bogs at the foot of the downs, the chalk itself and the flints upon it, the sand rocks, old walls, and the trunks of trees, especially their north sides, and even the boulders on the shore, will afford plenty of interesting resorts to the bryologist. The mosses delight chiefly in damp and shady situations, though they are by no means exclusively confined to such places, and the soil or substance on which they grow is sometimes remarkable. One curious little plant, says Hooker, is found only on the perpendicular faces of the pure white chalk pits that abound in Kent and Sussex, while *Fumaria hygrometrica*, common in our country, is almost sure to spring up where anything has been burned on the ground. Of mosses characteristic of the chalk we have of course many, while the arboreal species are numerous, especially in the Weald, which is the most humid part of the county.

The mosses of Sussex have had unusual attention paid them. Borrer, Davies, Jenner, Roper, Bloomfield, Mitten and Unwin have severally given us the results of their investigations concerning them. In 1870 Mr. C. P. Smith, in his *Moss Flora of Sussex*, published by the Brighton and Sussex Natural History Society, issued a compendium of them, with the names of their discoverers and the localities in which they occur. In this excellent little work too is recorded the stations noted by previous observers. From it I chiefly quote those subsequently given.

In 1878 Mr. W. C. Unwin of Lewes published his beautiful *Illustrations and Dissections of the Genera of British Mosses*, and in a Supplement, which he kindly sent me, gave the following account of two local species found only in Sussex : ' *Seligeria calcicola*, Mitten. Not uncommon on chalk nodules on the sides of disused and turfy banks, on the northern slopes of the downs round Lewes. Frequently observed on isolated pieces of chalk in and around Hanmer Park, also on Wolstonbury Hill. As a British plant it is only found in Sussex. Not noticed in Wilson's *Bryologia*. *Acaulon triquetrum*, Spruce, occurs on the cliffs between Brighton and Rottingdean and between Rottingdean and Newhaven, frequently associated with *Pottia cavifolia*. It is a minute periodical plant, occurring only in some years. First discovered by Borrer in 1844. Since found occasionally by other Sussex bryologists and by Mr. Mitten, in various parts of the Sussex coast.'

The following species have been considered peculiar to the county also : *Ephemerum tenerum, Astomum Mittenii, Anacalypta cæspitosa, Funaria microstoma, Bryum canariense, Brachthecium campestre*, all detected by Mr. Mitten of Hurstpierpoint, with *Acaulon triquetrum* found by Borrer, *Barbula canescens* by Jenner, and *Barbula vahliana* and *Eurhynchium Vaucheri* discovered by Davies.

According to Mr. C. P. Smith we have in Sussex 305 mosses, and additions have since been made. The following list is a selection of the more notable, and is arranged according to Hobkirk's *Synopsis of British Mosses*.

SPHAGNACEÆ

Sphagnum fimbriatum, Wils. *Henfield*
— Mongeotii, Nees. *Ashdown Forest*
— auriculatum, Schpr. *Hayward's Heath*
— subsecundum, Nees. *Bexhill*
— cuspidatum, Wils. *Blackdown*

BRYACEÆ

ACROCARPI
Archidium phascoides, Brid. *Wet heaths*
Ephemerum tenerum, Hampe. *Weald*
— sessile, B. & S. *Henfield*
Acaulon triquetrum, Spruce. *Rottingdean*

Acrocarpi (*continued*)—
Leucobryum glaucum, Hedw. *Chailey*
Phascum curvicolle, Dicks. *Downs*
Astomum Mittenii, Schpr. *Hurst*
— multicapsulare, Sm. *Weald*
Gymnostomum tenue, Schrad. *Ardingly*
Weissia verticillata, Brid. *Ardingly*
Dichodontium squarrosum, Hedw. *Danny*
Dicranella crispa, Hedw. *Tunbridge Wells*
Dicranum funescens, Turn. „ „
— scottianum, Turn. *Ardingly*
— spurium, Brid. *Wych Cross*
Campylopus brevipilus, B. & S. *Pressridge Warren*
Fissidens exilis, Brid. *Near Hurst*
Schistostega osmundacea, W. & M. *Bolney*
Brachyodus trichoides, N. & H. *Blackdown*
Anacalypta cæspitosa, Rohl. *Wolstonbury*
Didymodon flexifolius, Hedw. *Blackdown*
Pottia cavifolia, Ehr. *Rottingdean*
Trichostomum rigidulum, Hedw. *Hurst*
Barbula vahliana, Schultz. *Angmering*
— canescens, Bruch. *Hastings*
— latifolia, B. & S. *Weald*
— rigida, Schultz. *New timber*
— sumosa, Wils. *Arundel*
— squarrosa, De Not. *Littlehampton*
— insulana, De Not. *Weald*
— cuneifolia, Dicks. *Maresfield*
— marginata, B. & S. *Hayward's Heath*
— Brebissonii, Schpr. *Weald*
Tetraphis pellucida, Hedw. *Sand rocks*
Tetrodontium Brownianum, B. & S. *Ardingly*
Eucalypta streptocarpus, Hedw. *Uckfield*
Zygodon Stirtoni, Schpr. *Willingdon*
Ulota Ludwigii, Spreng. *Danny*
— Hutchinsiæ, Sm. *Trees on the Downs*
— crispula, Bruch. *Tunbridge Wells*
— phyllantha, B. & S. *Trees, Downs and coast*
Orthotrichum tenellum, B. & S. *Ash trees on the Downs*
— speciosum, Nees. *Henfield*
— rivulare, Turn. *Weald*
— pulchellum, Sm. *Hastings*
— sprucei, Mont. *Weald*
Racomitrium fasciculare, Hedw. *Balcombe*
— lanuginosum, Hedw. *Henfield*
Cinclidotus fontinaloides, P. Beauv. *By the Arun*
Splachnum ampullaceum, L. *Tilgate*
Physcomitrium fasciculare, Hedw. *Pyecombe*
Funaria calcarea, Brid. *Clayton Downs*
— microstoma, B. & S. *Maresfield*

Acrocarpi (*continued*)—
Orthodontium gracile, Schwpr. *Sand rocks*
Bryum bimum, Schreb. *Henfield*
— torquescens, B. & S. *Tunbridge Wells*
— canariense, Shwgr. *Wolstonbury*
— turbinatum, Hedw. *Albourne*
— alpinum, L. *Forests*
Mnium serratum, L. *Blackdown*
— rostratum, Schwgr. *Arundel*
— riparium, Mitt. *Weald*
— cuspidatum, Hedw. *Danny*
Bartramia stricta, Brid. *Maresfield*
Diphyscium foliosum, W. & M. *Eridge*

Pleurocarpi
Neckera complanata v. obtusa, Hedw. *Malling*
Cylindrothecium concinnum, B. & S. *Sedlescomb*
Climacium dendroides, W. & M. *Amberley*
Antitrichia curtipendula, Brid. *Bignor Hill*
Thuidium hystricosum, Mitten. *Houghton Downs*
— delicatulum, Hedw. *Wolstonbury*
Plagiothecium latebricola, Wils. *Weald*
— elegans, Hooker. *Ardingly*
Rhyncostegium depressum, Bruch. *Arundel*
— murale, L. *Uckfield*
Eurhynchium circinnatum, Brid. *Clayton*
— striatulum, B. & S. *Arundel*
— hians, Hedw. *Near Hurst*
— crassinervium, Tayl. *Wolstonbury*
— speciosum, Brid. *Albourne*
— piliferum, Schreb. *Maresfield*
— Vaucheri, Schp. *Downs*
Hyocomium flagellare, L. *Tilgate*
Brachythecium populeum, Sw. *Ardingly*
— campestre, Bruch. *Weald*
— mildeanum, Schpr. *Downs*
Scleropodium illecebrum, L. *Weald*
— cæspitosum, Wils. *Weald*
Amblystegium radicule, P. de B. *Shoreham*
Limnobium palustre, Schpr. *Near Hurst*
Hypnum Sommerfeldtii, Myr. *Wolstonbury*
— polygamum, B. & S. *Weald*
— revolvens, Sw. *Amberley*
— exannulatum, B. & S. *Ashdown*
— Kneifii, Schpr. *Hayward's Heath*
— commutatum, L. *Bignor*
— scorpioides, L. *Amberley*
— stramineum, L. *Ashdown*
— cordifolium, L. *Amberley*
— Schreberi, L. *Sand rocks*
Hylocomium brevirostrum, Ehr. *Wych Cross*
— loreum, L. *Blackdown*

BOTANY

THE LIVERWORTS (*Hepaticæ*)

When we consider the elegance of form, variety of hue, and curious structure of many of the Hepatics, classified by the botanists of the last century with the mosses to which they are nearly allied, one wonders at first why they have not been more studied. The chief reason perhaps is the difficulty of finding them in fruit, a circumstance which I have frequently experienced. They occur chiefly on damp soil, in bogs or on old trunks of trees. Hence those who knew best our Sussex forests have given them most attention. This group comprises Marchantia, Jungermannia, Riccia and Anthoceros, all of which are represented in Sussex. In this county they have been most fully examined by the Rev. E. N. Bloomfield, of Guestling, whose list with a few additions I here subjoin. The list is arranged according to Dr. Cooke's *Handbook of the British Hepaticæ*, 1894.

JUNGERMANNIACEÆ
Frullania dilata, L. *Eastbourne*
— tamarisci, Mich. *Pett*
Lejeunia minutissima, Sm. *St. Leonards*
— serpyllifolia, Mich. *Guestling*
Radula complanata, L.   „
Porella platyphylla, L. *Winchelsea*
Lepidozia reptans, L. *Guestling*
— setacea, Mitt. *Bexhill*
Cephalozia divaricata, Sm. *Guestling*
— connivens, Dick. *Bexhill*
— sphagni, Dick. *Eridge*
Chiloscyphus polyanthus, L. *Eastbourne*
Trichocolea tomentella, Ehr. *Dallington*
Plagiochila asplenoides, N. & M. *Eastbourne*
— decipiens, Mitt. *Polegate*
Scapania undulata, Ditt. *Fairlight*
— resupinata, Dumort. *Eridge*
— irrigna, Nees. *Guestling*
— curta, Dum. *Ardingly*
Plagiochila asplenioides, L. *Guestling*
Aplozia sphærocarpa, Hook. *Eastbourne*
Jungermannia crenulata, Sm. *Dallington*

Jungermannia ventricosa, Dick. *Fairlight*
— capitata, Hook. *Guestling*
— bicuspidata, L.   „
— incisa, Schrd. *Bexhill*
Nardia adusta, N. Carr. *Blackdown*
— Funckii, W. & M. Carr. *Tilgate*
Fossombronia pusilla, Nees. *Guestling*
Pellia calycina, Tayl.   „
Harpanthus scutatus, Spruce. *Tunbridge Wells*
Pallavicinia Lyellii, Lindb. *Chiltington*

MARCHANTIACEÆ
Reboulia hemispherica, Raddi. *Rusthall*
Dumortiera hirsuta, Sw. *Guestling*

RICCIACEÆ
Riccia glauca, L. *Guestling*
Ricciella fluitans, L.   „

ANTHOCERATACEÆ
Anthoceros lævis, Dill. *Guestling*
— punctatus, L.   „

FRESHWATER ALGÆ

Although considerable attention has been paid to the Sussex fresh-water algæ in several of the districts, the county with respect to them has been by no means thoroughly explored. In his *Flora of Tunbridge Wells and the Surrounding Country*, Mr. E. Jenner has given a list of those which occur in the Medway district, with their localities, and as these include Ashdown Forest, Waterdown Forest and the commons, bogs, streams and ponds therein, it is very useful for reference. *Zygnema Hasseli* and *Z. Jenneri* are first recorded from this county, the latter at Mark Cross. In his *Flora of Hastings*, the Rev. E. N. Bloomfield published a list of those in the East Rother district, which includes divers

61

of the rarer kinds, and Mr. Roper examined those of the Cuckmere. Of the Desmideæ, *D. Swartzii*, Ag., was discovered near Rotherfield by Borrer. Doubtless our rivers contain many unrecorded species. In the Ems I have noticed *Batrachospermum* in abundance. It comes to maturity both in spring and autumn. From our estuaries, just above the influence of the tide, additions to our lists are still to be made. Of the Diatomaceæ about 150 have been recorded.

This list is arranged according to Harvey's *Manual*.

CYANOPHYCEÆ

CHROOCOCCACEÆ
Protococcus irridis, Ag. *Hastings*
— pluvialis „ „
NOSTOCACEÆ
Nostoc cæruleum, Lyngb. *Hastings*
— variegatum, Moore. „
OSCILLATORIACEÆ
Oscillatoria limosa, Vauch. *Hastings*
— autumnalis, Ag. *Eastbourne*
Lyngbya muralis, Ag. *Hastings*
— ferruginea, Ag. *Brighton*
RIVULARIACEÆ
Rivularia nitida, Ag. *Brighton*

CHLOROPHYLLOPHYCEÆ

PALMELLACEÆ
Palmella cruenta, Ag. *Hastings*

ZOOSPOREÆ

CONFERVACEÆ
Cladophora glomerata, L. *Hastings*
— crispata, Ag. „
Conferva crassa, Ag. „

CONJUGATEÆ

Zygnema curvatum, Ag. *Henfield*
— quininum, Ag. *Hastings*

OOSPOREÆ

VAUCHERIACEÆ
Vaucheria sessilis, De C. *Hastings*
CARPOSPOREÆ
Drapurnaldia plumosa, Ag. *Hastings*
Batrachospermum moniliforme, Ag. *Hast.*
— atrum, Borr. *Brighton*

MARINE ALGÆ

The marine algæ do not abound on the Sussex coast as on the shores of our western counties. We meet with comparatively few seaweeds as we proceed eastward until we approach Brighton and Beachy Head, where they become more numerous, as well as at St. Leonards and Hastings further on. We have lists of them by some of our societies and an excellent account by Mrs. Merrifield in her *Natural History of Brighton and its Vicinity*, but a good monograph of the Sussex algæ is still a desideratum, and in such should be differentiated those growing within tide marks from waifs and strays. The occurrence of algæ in certain localities seems in some cases to be periodical, and as instances Mrs. Merrifield states that in 1849 the rare and beautiful *Griffithsia barbata, Delesseria hypoglossum, Halymema ligulata, Ginannia furcellata*, the lovely *Naccaria Wiggii* and the *Dudresnaia coccinea*, usually considered so rare, were found at Brighton abundantly, and again in 1858 says: 'During this present year the collectors of seaweeds have had an abundant harvest, no less choice in quality than prolific in species. Among the rarer algæ I picked up *Arthrocladia villosa, Sporochnus pedunculatus, Cutleria multifida* and *Taonia atomaria*, the seaweed which resembles a peacock's tail; but the greatest rarities in this district were *Griffithsia barbata, Seirospora Griffithsiana* and *Callithamnion plumula*, neither of which were previously found at Brighton. *Dudresnaia coccinea* was

BOTANY

also abundant.' Stormy weather from the south-west considerably affects the growth of algæ in Sussex, and brings occasionally such strangers as *Sargassum vulgare* to our coast.

The Melanospermeæ are numerous and include the largest seaweeds, or 'forest trees of the deep,' many of which grow on our shore. They are mostly common, but as exceptions we have *Sphacelaria plumosa*, Lyng, first discovered by Borrer at Beachy Head ; *Asperococcus Turneri*, Hook ; *Stilophora rhizoides*, J. Ag. ; *Striaria attenuata*, Grev. ; and *Litosiphon pusillus*, Carm., on old fronds of *Chorda filum*.

The Rhodospermeæ have the most beautiful hues, rose-red, pink, purple, and red-brown when growing in deep water, while in shallower they degenerate to a greenish or yellowish colour. They are also exquisite in form. These contain more than a moiety of the British species. Among the rarer which we possess are *Rhodomela lycopodioides* D. Ag. ; *Bonnemaisonia asperagoides*, C. Ag. ; *Dasya arbuscula*, C. Ag. ; *Polysiphonia Brodiæi*, Grev. ; *Gracillaria erecta*, Grev. ; *Griffithsia Devoniensis*, Harv. ; and the handsome *Calithamnion Borreri*, so named in honour of Borrer.

The Chlorospermeæ are well represented. The rare and curious *Codium bursa*, Ag., is occasionally thrown up at Brighton after a storm, and fourteen species of *Cladophora* have been found there. *Conferva melagonium*, Web., grows at Shoreham. Among the Ulvaceæ, *Enteromorpha erecta*, Hook, occurs at Eastbourne, and *Ulva linza* at Brighton.

The following list is arranged according to Dr. Harvey's *Synopsis*.

MELANOSPERMEÆ

FUCACEÆ
Cystoseira granulata, Ag. *Brighton*
— fœniculata, Ag. *Brighton*
— ericoides, Ag. *Brighton*
Pycnophycus tuberculatus, Kutz. *Hastings*
Fucus ceranoides, L. *Eastbourne*

SPOROCHNACEÆ
Desmarestia ligulata, Lamour. *Brighton*
— vividis, Lamour. *Brighton*
Arthrocladia villosa, Duby. *Brighton*
Sporochnus pedunculatus, Ag. *Hastings*

LAMINARIACEÆ
Laminaria Phyllitis, Lam. *Hastings*
— fascia, Ag. *Brighton*

DICTYOTACEÆ
Cutleria multifida, Grev. *Shoreham*
Asperococcus echinatus, Grev. *Brighton*
Litosiphon pusillus, Carm. *Brighton*

CHORDARIACEÆ
Mesogloia Griffithsiana, Grev. *Brighton*
Leathesia tuberiformis, Gray. *Hastings*
Myrionema punctiforme, Harv. „

ECTOCARPACEÆ
Sphacelaria scoparia, Lyng. *Brighton*
— sertularia, Lyng. *Hastings*
Ectocarpus fasciculatus, Harv. *Hastings*
— brachiatus, Harv. *Hastings*
— pusillus, Griffiths. „

RHODOSPERMEÆ

RHODOMELACEÆ
Rhodomela lycopodioides, Ag. *Brighton*
— scorpioides, Ag. *Shoreham*
Polysiphonia spinulosa, Grev. *Brighton*
— Brodiœi, Grev. *Brighton*
— furcellata, Harv. „
— fibrillosa, Grev. *Shoreham*
— elongella, Harv. *Brighton*
— atronitens, Grev. *Hastings*
— byssoides „ „
Dasya coccinea, Ag. *Seaford*
— venusta, Harv. *Brighton*
— arbuscula, Ag. „

LAURENCIACEÆ
Bonnemaisonia asparagoides, Ag. *Brighton*
Laurencia tenuissima, Grev. „
Chrysimenia clavellosa, Ag. *Hastings*
Chylocladia reflexa, Cham. *Brighton*

CORALLINACEÆ
Corallina squamata, Ellis. *Hastings*
Jania corniculata, Lam. *Eastbourne*

DELESSERIACEÆ
Delesseria sanguinea, Lam. *Bognor*
— hypoglossum, Lam. *Hastings*
— ruscifolia, Lam. *Hastings*
Nitophyllum punctatum, Grev. *Brighton*
— Gmelini, Grev. *Hastings*
Plocamium coccineum, Lyng. *Hastings*

63

RHODOMENIACEÆ
  Rhodymenia Palmetta, Grev. *Hastings*
  Sphærococcus coronifolius, Ag. „
  Gracilaria erecta, Grev. *Hastings*
CRYPTONEMIACEÆ
  Gigartina acicularis, Lam. *Hastings*
  Chondrus Norvegicus, Lam. *Brighton*
  Gymnogongrus Griffithsia, Mart. „
  Phyllophora palmettoides, J. Ag. *Hastings*
  Halymenia ligulata, Ag. *Hastings*
  Ginannia furcellata, Mart. „
  Crouania attenuata, J. Ag. „
  Naccaria Wiggii, Fries. *Brighton*
  Gloiosiphonia capillaris, Carm. *Brighton*
  Nemaleon purpureum, Harv. „
  Dudresnaia coccinea, Bonnem. „
CERAMIACEÆ
  Ceramium botryocarpum, Grev. *Hastings*
  — Deslongchampsii, Cham. *Eastbourne*
  — diaphanum, Ag. *Brighton*
  — gracillimum, Grev. *Hastings*
  — echionotum, Ag. „
  Griffithsia equisetifolia, Ag. *Seaford*
  — barbata, Ag. *Brighton*
  — Devoniensis, Harv. *Brighton*
  Wrangelia multifida, J. Ag. *Hastings*
  Seirospora Griffithsiana, Harv. *Brighton*
  Callithamnion plumula, Lyng. „
  — cruciatum, Ag. *Brighton*
  — roseum, Lyng. „

CERAMIACEÆ (*continued*)—
  Callithamnion byssoideum, Arnott. *Brighton*
  — Turneri, Ag. „
  — polyspermum, Ag. „
  — Borreri, Ag. „
  — floridulum, Ag. „
  — Hookeri, Ag. *Eastbourne*
  — thyoideum, Ag. *Hastings*

CHLOROSPERMEÆ

SIPHONACEÆ
  Codium bursa, Ag. *Brighton*
  Bryopsis plumosa, Lam. *Eastbourne*
CONFERVACEÆ
  Cladophora rupestris, Kutz. *Eastbourne*
  — gracilis, Griffiths. *Hastings*
  — Rudolphiana, Kutz. „
  — albida, Kutz. *Shoreham*
  — lanosa „ *Brighton*
  — glaucescens, Harv. *Brighton*
  Conferva arenicola, Berk. *Hastings*
  — melagonium, Web. *Shoreham*
  — ærea, Dill. *Brighton*
ULVACEÆ
  Enteromorphe erecta, Hooker. *Hastings*
  Ulva linza, L. *Brighton*
  Bangia fusco-purpurea, Lyng. *Brighton*
OSCILLATORIACEÆ
  Calothrix confervicola, Ag. *Brighton*
  Oscillatoria subsalsa, Ag. „

THE LICHENS (*Lichenes*)

Among the Cryptogams the lichens are perennial plants composed of cells so arranged as to form a foliaceous, woody, scaly, crustaceous or leprous thallus, or fusion of root, stem and leaves into a general mass. They like bright sunshine and fresh air, and die in an impure atmosphere. They occur under very varied conditions, on rocks, on the chalk downs, in bogs, on the bark of old trees, on old barn doors, and on the flints and boulders along the coast. Although studied but by a few of our botanists, Sussex has not been neglected in this respect, and although not possessing a knowledge of them myself, I have accompanied rambles in search of them with pleasure. Borrer, who published little under his own name, in conjunction with his friend Dawson Turner, wrote *An Attempt at a History of the British Lichens.* This had a private circulation only, but in its dedication a belief was expressed that it would be a monument of his industry, ability and profound knowledge of our lichens. In east Sussex we have lists made by Roper and Bloomfield, from which I quote, and from west Sussex one by Mr. W. C. Cooke, brother of Dr. Cooke, the well-known cryptogamist. This catalogue made by him for the Chichester Society I have now before me, and from this I give many of the habitats of our Sussex lichens.

The following list is arranged according to Leighton's *Lichen Flora of Great Britain.*

BOTANY

COLLEMACRI
Collema crispum, Huds. *Damp walls*
— pulposum, Bernh. *Chichester*
— microphyllum. *West Stoke*
— nigrescens. *Eastbourne*
Leptogium tenuissimum, Dicks. *By sandy roads*

CALICEI
Calcium hyperellum, Ach. *On oaks*

BÆOMYCEI
Bæomyces rufus, DC. *Chichester*
— roseus, Pers. *Broadwater*

CLAYDONIEI
Claydonia pyxidata, Fr. *Eastbourne*
— rangiferina Hoffm. *Commons*
— gracilis, Hoffm. *Heaths*
— alcicornis, Flk. *Camber*
— squamosa, Hffm. *Fairlight*
— furcata, Hffm. *Eastbourne*
— sylvatica var. alpestris, L. *Pett*

USNEEI
Usnea barbata var. articulata, Arch. *Fairlight*
    „ florida, L. *Valdoe*
    „ rubiginea, Ach. *Trees*

RAMALINEI
Evernia prunastri, L. *Trees and rails*
Ramalina calicaris, Fr. *Eastbourne*
— farinacea, L. *Woodcote*
— fraxinea, L. *Eastbourne*
— fastigiata, Pers. *Trees*
— pollinaria, Ach. *Barn doors*

CETRARIEI
Cetraria aculeata, Fr. *Camber*
Platysma sepincola, Ehr. *Rawmere*

PELTIGEREI
Peltigera canina, L. *Chichester*
— polydactyla, Hoff. *Eastbourne*

PARMELIEI
Sticta pulmonacea, Ach. *West Stoke*
Parmelia physodes, L. *Trees*
— perlata, L. *Trees*
— olivacea, Ach. *Eridge*
— caperata, L. *Ashling*
— saxatilis, L. *Trees and rocks*
— Borreri, Turn. *Tunbridge Wells*
Physcia flavicans, Sw. *Hastings*
— parietina, L. *Walls*
— stellaris, L. *Eastbourne*
— pulverulenta, Schreb. *Trees*
— „ var. pityrea, Ach. „
— obscura, Ehr. *Eastbourne*
— „ var. chloantha, Ach. *Eastbourne*

LECANOREI
Squamaria saxicola, Poll. *The Downs*
Placodium murorum, Hoffm. *Eastbourne*
— candicans, Dick. *Fairlight*
— callopismum, Ach. *Dell Quay*
Pannaria nigra, Huds. *Eastbourne*

LECANOREI (*continued*)—
Lecanora vitellina, Hoffm. *Eastbourne*
— subfusca, L. *Chichester*
— „ var. allophana, Ach. *Trees*
— „ „ atrynea, Ach. *Walls*
— parella, L. *The Downs*
— „ var. pallescens, L. *West Stoke*
— albella, Pers. *Trees*
— ferruginea, Huds. *Eastbourne*
— „ var. festiva, Ach. *Fairlight*
— rupestris, Scop. *On flints*
— calcarea, L. *Eastbourne*
— sophodes, Ach. *Uckfield*
— pyracea, Ach. *Eastbourne*
— „ var. ulmicola, DC. *Elm trees*
— aurantiaca, Light. *Trees*
— Mongeotioides, Schær. *Eastbourne*
— epixantha, Ach. „
Urceolaria scruposa, L. *Sandy banks*
Pertusaria multipuncta, Turn. „ „
— communis, DC. *Trees*
— leioplaca, Ach. *Eastbourne*
— fallax, Pers. „
— globulifera, Turn. *Guestling*
Phlyctis agelæa, Ach. *Eastbourne*

THELOTREMEI
Thelotrema lepadinum, Ach. *Guestling*

LECIDEINEI
Lecidea lucida, Ach. *Eastbourne*
— fusco atra, Ach. *Ecclesbourne*
— dubia, Borr. *Old railings*
— minuta, Schœr. *Eastbourne*
— parasema, Ach. *Hungershall*
— contigua, Fr. *Fairlight*
— calcivora, Ehr. *On flints*
— canescens, Dicks. *Trees*
— Lightfootii, Sm. *Broadwater*
— quernea, Dicks. *Oak trees*
— myriocarpa, DC. *Pine trees*
— aromatica, Sm. *Eastbourne*
— viridescens, Schrad. *Maresfield*
— lutea, Dicks. *Eridge*
— rubella, Ehrh. *Eastbourne*
— exanthematica, Sm. „
— Turneri, Leight. „
— concentrica, Fr. *Fairlight*
— sphæroides, L. *Goodwood*

GRAPHIDIEI
Graphis scripta, Ach. *Eastbourne*
— „ var. serpentina, Ach. *Eastbourne*
— „ „ tremulans, Leight. *Eastbourne*
— inusta, Ach. „
— dendritica, Ach. *Trees*
— sophistica, Nyl. *Eastbourne*
Opegrapha atra, Pers. *Trees*
— lyncea, Sm. *Hastings*

GRAPHIDIEI (*continued*)—
  Opegrapha Turneri, Leight. *Eastbourne*
  — herpetica, Ach. *Hastings*
  —   ,,   var. rufescens, Pers. *Hastings*
  — inusta, Ach. *Eastbourne*
  — dendritica, Ach. *Trees*
  Stigmatidium crassum, Dub. *Eastbourne*
  Arthonia astroidea, Ach. *Trees*
  — cinnabarina, Wallr. *On oaks*
  — pruinosa, Ach. *Eastbourne*

PYRENOCARPEI
  Verrucaria irridula, Schrad. *Eastbourne*
  — mauroides, Schœr. *On flints*
  — biformis, Borr. *Eastbourne*
  — nitida, Weig. *On trees*
  —   ,,   var. nitidella, Flk. ,,
  — gemmata, Ach.   ,,
  — epidermidis, Ach.   ,,
  — olivacea, Borr. *Eastbourne*

FUNGI

Since Sussex abounds in woodlands, parklands and copses, these together with its commons and downs render it rich with respect to the fungi, and of late years much attention has been paid to this very interesting division of our cryptogams. Both the West and the East Sussex Natural History Societies have engaged their members in what have been named 'fungus forays' with excellent results. While some fungi are poisonous and beautiful others are esculent and delicious. I have eaten about twenty species, and among these may be commended *Lactarius deliciosus, Hydnum repandum, Boletus edulis, Cantharellus cibarius* and *Helvella crispa. Lycoperdon giganteum* was, I was told by Mr. W. Cooke of Chichester, one of the best of the fungi he knew. In east Sussex *Agaricus procerus, Fistulina hepatica* and *Coprinus crispus* have been well spoken of with *Agaricus gambosus*; but the last species I have heard of as productive of violent pains. Indeed great care should be taken with respect to certain kinds represented by Badham and others as good for food. Of the rarer species, *Entoloma jubatus* has been mentioned as occurring near Goudhurst, and *Clitophilus popinalis* at Worthing, while *Sphæria fraxinicola* has been found near Lewes, and *S. triglochinicola* near Ringmer. Lists of the epiphyllous fungi have been published by the Chichester, the Eastbourne and the Hastings Natural History Societies.

The morell, *Morchella esculenta*, is one of the most delicious of our Sussex species. It grows above ground and is plentiful in many of our beech woods and hangers. I have eaten none better than those from Sutton and Stansted. Somewhat similar in flavour is the truffle (*Tuber cibarium*), which also loves the shadows of the beech and the chalky soil of our downs; they grow entirely underground. Patching was noted for its abundance of truffles. The Sussex truffler I am told trains his dog, a cross between a poodle and a terrier, by habituating it to their scent, and carries an ash staff with a pointed head at one end to dig up the truffle, and a two-pronged fork at the other to clear away the ground. The time for hunting for them is from September to December, and some of the best are got when the dead leaves are rotting at the tree roots.

The most extraordinary of our esculent species is the crisped sparassis (*Sparassis crispa*), cream-coloured and of a delightful fragrance. It has been known to attain a diameter of eighteen inches and resembles

BOTANY

a large cauliflower. It is by no means common in the county, but has been several times met with at Lavington and Harting.

In the following abbreviated list I mention most of the wholesome species which occur in the county, and such only of the larger kinds as are in other respects noteworthy. The indication of precise localities is generally to be avoided, since fungi are in their places of growth both evanescent and capricious.

The list is arranged according to Cooke's *Handbook of British Fungi*.

SPORIFERA

HYMENOMYCETES

Amanita muscarius, L. *Oakwood*
— rubescens, P. *Woods*
Armillaria mucidus, Fries. *Hastings*
Clitocybe infundibuliformis, Schæff. *Oakwood*
— geotropus, Bull. *Woods*
— nebularis, Bate. „
Tricholoma terreus, Schæff. *Fairlight*
Pleurotus ostreatus, Jacq. *On trees*
Hebeloma rimosus, Bull. *Hastings*
Coprinus comatus, Fr. *St. Leonards*
— atramentarius, Fr. *Fishbourne*
— plicatilis, Fr. *Pastures*
Cortinarus evernius, Fr. *Woods*
Lepista nuda, Bull. *Hastings*
— personata, Fr. *Pastures*
Paxillus involutus, Fr. *Hastings*
Hygrophorus conicus, Fr. *Eastbourne*
— psittacinus, Fr. *Westbourne*
— virgineus, Fr. *Commons*
Gomphidius viscidus, Fr. *Fairlight*
Lactarius torminosus, Fr. *Hastings*
Cantharellus tubæformis, Fr. *Fairlight*
Nyctalis asterophora, Fr. *Guestling*
Marasmius peronatus, Fr. *Woods*
— oreades, Fr. *Pastures*
Panus stypticus, Fr. *On stumps*
Lenzites betulina, Fr. „

POLYPOREI

Boletus scaber, Fr. *Woods*
Polyporus squamosus, Fr. *On ash*
— sulfureus, Fr. *Hastings*

POLYPOREI (*continued*)—
Polyporus betulinus, Fr. *Harting*
— fraxineus, Fr. *Harting*

HYDNEI

Hydnum ferruginosum, Fr. *Eastbourne*
— zonatum, Batsch. *Pett*

AURICULARINI

Craterellus cornucopiodes, Fr. *In woods*

CLAVARIEI

Clavaria cristata, Holmsk. *Oakwood*
— fastigiata, DC. *Pastures*

TREMELLINI

Exidia glandulosa, Fr. *On oak*
Hirneola Auricula-Judæ, Best. *On elm*

GASTEROMYCETES

PHALLOIDEI

Phallus impudicus, L. *Woods*

TRICHOGASTRES

Geaster rufescens, Fr. *Withyham*
Bovista plumbea, P. *Pastures*

MYXOGASTRES

Stemonitis fusca, Roth. *On wood*

NIDULARIACEÆ

Cyathus vernicosus, DC. *Stubble fields*

SPORIDIFERA (ASCOMYCETES)

ELVELLACEI

Morchella esculenta, Pers. *Woods*
— crassipes, Pers. *Eastbourne*
— semilibera, DC. *Hastings*
Peziza aurantia, Fr. *Oakwood*
— coccinea, Jacq. *On sticks*
— væruginosa, Fr. *Harting*

THE BRAMBLES (*Rubi*)

The distribution of the Sussex brambles is still only imperfectly ascertained. If we except the neighbourhood of such places as St. Leonards, Eastbourne and Brighton on the coast, the country round a few centres like Uckfield and Horsham towards the north, and the extreme north-west corner of the county bordering Surrey and Hampshire, the work of exploration for Rubi has still to be done.

The results already achieved are however full of interest to the students of this genus. Thus while Sussex brambles are proving on the whole, as was to be expected, most like those of Surrey and Kent, they are found to include two of our rarest species, which are so far unknown in those counties and are apparently endemic in England. These are *Rubus Salteri* (which is locally abundant to the east of St. Leonards) and *R. thyrsiger* (which has been discovered in Starvecrow Wood near Carter's Corner), both their localities being in East Sussex. *R. thyrsiger*, Bab. should be looked for elsewhere in the county, as Starvecrow Wood is its only known English locality away from the extreme south-west, where it grows in good quantity in widely separated districts of Cornwall, Devon and West Somerset. It is a very hairy and glandular bramble, with leaves chiefly ternate and a strikingly handsome open nearly naked panicle with many long few-flowered branches. *R. Salteri*, Bab. has long been known to occur in one Isle of Wight locality, and it has recently been added to the Bucks flora ; but its other nearest stations are in the counties of Hereford, Warwick and Leicester. It is nearly or quite eglandular, and may usually be readily distinguished from its allies in the *Silvatici* group by its clasping fruit-sepals.

Other rare species and sub-species already found in the county are the following :—

1. In both East and West Sussex.

Rubus holerythros, Focke. Several localities — erythrinus, Genev. *Linchmere to Fernhurst, West Sussex ; Worth Forest, East Sussex*

Rubus thyrsoideus, Wimm. *Hailsham to Hempstead* and near *Ditton's Wood, West Sussex* ; near *St. Leonards, East Sussex* — subinermis, Rogers. Abundant

2. In West Sussex only.

Rubus leucandrus, Focke. *Shottermill Common* — Gelertii, Frider. *Stanmer Park to Newick*

Rubus mutabilis, Genev. *Rudgwick* and near *Worthing*

3. In East Sussex only.

Rubus imbricatus, Hort. *Bexhill* and *St. Leonards*

Rubus cinerosus, Rogers. *Fairhazel Brooks, Uckfield* — hostilis, Muell. & Wirtg. *Battle*

To these may be added the following as being, if less rare for Britain as a whole, still decidedly local or otherwise especially interesting :—

Rubus dumnoniensis, Bab. In several localities between *Brighton* and *Eastbourne* — micans, Gren. & Godr. Near *Crawley, West Sussex ; Budlett's Common, Uckfield, East Sussex* — Babingtonii, Bell Salt. Fairly frequent

Rubus ericetorum, Lefv. Fairly frequent — cognatus, N. E. Br. *St. Leonards Forest* and *Holmbush, West Sussex* — Marshalli, Focke & Rogers. *Colegate, West Sussex.* An East Sussex specimen has also been seen

The total number of bramble forms now known for the county is seventy-five, consisting of fifty-four species and twenty-one subordinate forms (sub-species or varieties). Of these seventy-five forms forty occur in West Sussex, while East Sussex has as many as fifty-four—twenty-seven only of the whole number being common to both divisions of the county.

BOTANY

The only widely or moderately distributed British forms still undiscovered in Sussex are *R. Rogersii*, *R. nitidus*, *R. villicaulis* (type), *R. Selmeri*, *R. gratus*, *R. silvaticus*, *R. mucronatus*, *R. infestus*, *R. scaber*, *R. infecundus* and *R. viridis*. Most of these, together with a few rarer unrecorded species, will probably yet be found in some of the unexplored parts of the county.

ZOOLOGY

MARINE ZOOLOGY

UPON inquiring into the subject of the marine zoology of the Sussex coast, one is struck with the fact how few systematic and published records exist on that subject.

Natural history societies, more or less organized, appear to have done very little hitherto in recording and publishing the local fauna and flora, and it has devolved upon individuals with sufficient enthusiasm and love of the subject to undertake the task. In the case of the Hastings district, however, one is fortunate in finding a good and solid foundation laid for future investigators in *The Natural History of Hastings and St. Leonards and the Vicinity*, with its three supplements issued at various periods, edited by the Rev. E. N. Bloomfield, M.A., F.E.S., rector of Guestling, and Mr. E. A. Butler, B.A., B.Sc. The former gentleman kindly affords the information that Mr. Butler edited the fauna of the original number and of the first supplement, and that the two later supplements were edited by himself.

As regards the individual workers in the domain of marine zoology who have supplied the data upon which the publication was to some extent founded, may be mentioned the late Dr. Bowerbank, who, as is well known, worked out the sponges, a great proportion of which were obtained from the Diamond Ground off Hastings. The list of sponges in the original number of the Hastings Natural History was apparently compiled by the Rev. Mr. Bloomfield from Bowerbank's *Monographs of the British Spongiadæ*, and afterwards revised by Bowerbank shortly before his death.

Of the Hydrozoa, Mr. Tumanowicz appears to have left a legacy from *Hastings past and present*, and Miss Jelly and Mr. R. Hope, F.Z.S., apparently amplified the list in the original number, the latter also contributing to the second supplement.

For the Vermes Mr. Butler appears to be mainly responsible. The Polyzoa of the original list and most of the first supplement are attributable to Miss Jelly, and those of the later supplement, in the main, to Mr. R. Hope. In the sphere of the Mollusca Mr. A. H. Langdon contributes the list in the original number and in the first and second supplements.

In the ensuing lists of marine animals which appear in this paper, all those species which are quoted from the Hastings Natural History above referred to are distinguished by an asterisk thus (*)

Another source, whence a considerable and substantial addition to the present list of the fauna of this coast has been made, is a publication entitled *The Natural History of Brighton*, by Mrs. Merrifield. Some time has elapsed since the appearance of this book, but there is no reason to suppose that the fauna has since undergone much alteration in character. The whole of the species quoted in the following lists as occurring at Brighton (unless otherwise stated) which have been derived from this little work are distinguished by a dagger mark thus (†)

Only those species which have come within the personal ken of the present writer have received descriptive accounts.

A great proportion of the specimens referred to hereafter have been obtained from the Diamond Ground off Hastings, a considerable area of which consists of sand, but some parts of it are rough ground. Masses of rock, each weighing several hundredweight, are frequently brought up in the trawl. These blocks of stone are the hard, resisting residue left from the demolition of the Wealden rocks, which constitute the coast line between the chalk downs of Eastbourne on the west and those of Folkestone on the east. The softer clays and sandstones being readily disintegrated, leave the hard ironstones to continue a longer existence. Nearer the downs on either hand are found masses of Cherty Green-sand and large flints derived from the Chalk.

A section of the Channel, due south of Hastings, shows a gradual slope attaining to a depth, at fifteen miles from shore, of twenty fathoms, rapidly deepening to thirty fathoms, which depth is maintained for about ten miles ; after that there is a slight and gradual rise toward mid-channel.

The Diamond Ground, from the fisherman's point of view, commences at about the twenty-five fathom line, up to which point the ground is of a more or less rough description, and beyond this line it appears to extend for a somewhat unlimited distance. To the westward of Beachy Head, or the West Diamond Ground, as it is called, the ground is rough.

Off Rye and Dungeness there is mainly sand, but some six or seven miles from shore there is a deep deposit of mud extending in an easterly and westerly direction, called by the fishermen the Trail, and much frequented by certain kinds of fish. Still further on, rocky ground is met with, known as the East Shoal or Gringer Shoal. From the above short description therefore it will be inferred that the diversified character of the sea-bottom off Hastings affords a suitable ground for the varied and rich fauna which it possesses.

In the preparation of the present article, recourse has been had amongst other works to the following ; and in the case of the Hydroid Zoophytes and the Polyzoa the nomenclature of Hincks has been adopted, whilst in the Mollusca the list of the Conchological Society has been followed.

MARINE ZOOLOGY

FORAMINIFERA.—*On the Recent Foraminifera of Great Britain*, W. C. Williamson, Ray Society; 'Report on the Foraminifera' (*Challenger Expedition*), H. B. Brady.

SPONGES.—Article upon 'Sponges' in the *Encyclopedia Britannica*, W. J. Sollas; *A Monograph of the British Spongiadæ*, J. S. Bowerbank, Ray Society.

CŒLENTERA.—*A History of the British Hydroid Zoophytes*, Thomas Hincks; *A History of the British Sea Anemones and Corals*, P. H. Gosse; *Die Ctenophoren des Golfes von Neapel und der Angrenzenden Meeres-Abschnitte*, Dr. Carl Chun.

VERMES.—*A Catalogue of the British Non-parasitic Worms in the Collection of the British Museum*, George Johnston.

POLYZOA.—*A History of the British Marine Polyzoa*, Thomas Hincks.

ECHINODERMATA.—*A Catalogue of the British Echinoderms in the British Museum* (*Nat. Hist.*), F. Jeffrey Bell.

MOLLUSCA AND TUNICATA.—*A History of the British Mollusca*, Forbes and Hanley; *A Monograph of the British Nudibranchiate Mollusca*, Alder and Hancock, Ray Society; 'Report on the Tunicata' (*Challenger Expedition*), William A. Herdman.

GENERAL.—*A Manual of Marine Zoology for the British Isles*, P. H. Gosse.

A summary of the species detailed in the following lists will be found as follows :—

Protozoa	7 species
Porifera	58 ,,
Cœlentera	77 ,,
Vermes	31 ,,
Polyzoa	109 ,,
Echinoderma	25 ,,
Brachiopoda	1 ,,
Mollusca	192 ,,
Tunicata	14 ,,
Total	514 ,,

PROTOZOA
RHIZOPODA
FORAMINIFERA

1. *Nonionina crassula*, Walker.

Shell nautiloid, umbilicated, having eight or nine segments. Colour, a dull crystalline. Upon corallines, polyzoa, etc. Not uncommon. Hastings.

2. *Polystomella crispa*, Linnæus.*

Not uncommon. Hastings.

3. *Polystomella umbilicatula*, Walker.*

Common. Hastings.

4. *Rotalina beccarii*, Linnæus.*

Hastings.

5. *Miliolina seminulum*, Linnæus.

Shell ovate, milkwhite, with two segments to a volution; aperture alternately facing opposite ways. Common upon corallines. Hastings.

6. *Halyphysema tumanowiczii*, Bowerbank.

A species occurring upon seaweed and corallines. It is somewhat club-shaped, curved, tapering downwards to an expanded disc-like base. The test, more particularly the distal end, bristles with attached sponge spicules, arranged radially; grains of sand are also attached.

Under the above title this species appears described by Bowerbank among the Porifera in his *Monograph of British Spongiadæ*. It has since however been definitely referred to the Foraminifera (fam. Astrorhizidæ). Somewhat common. Hastings.

INFUSORIA
FLAGELLATA

7. *Noctiluca miliaris*.

The phosphorescence of the sea water is often due to these minute globular creatures. They are about the size of a pin's head, and emit the light more particularly when the water is agitated. In countless numbers. Hastings.

PORIFERA
CALCISPONGIÆ

1. *Leucosolenia (Ascon) botryoides*, Bowerbank.

This sponge occurs in little groups upon

corallines. When examined under the microscope it seems hardly to resemble bunches of grapes as the specific name would imply, but rather the fingers and shallow palm of an irregular glove, more particularly if we may suppose the fingers to give off other fingers, the ends being open to represent the oscula. The simple sponge is cylindrical, slightly swollen towards the end, with a wide paragaster and osculum. From moderately deep water. Rare. Hastings.

2. *Leucosolenia (Ascon) lacunosa*, Bowerbank.

Sponge white, fig-shaped, compressed, with a short stem, and with large oval orifices occurring over the whole surface. Bowerbank describes this as a very rare sponge. The form of the Hastings specimen is somewhat intermediate between Bowerbank's two figures.

The dimensions are : Height of stem, 1·5 mm. ; body, 6·5 mm. ; greatest width, 6 mm.; lesser diameter, 3 mm.

A single specimen only taken ; growing upon an Eudendrium. From moderately shallow water. Very rare. Hastings.

3. *Grantia (Sycon) ciliata*, Fleming.

This is a simple sponge consisting of a small white cylinder, the surface bristling with defensive spicules which project in minute tufts over the blind ends of the radial canals. Around the terminal osculum there is a fringe of spicules which suggest the specific name. Specimens taken from the rocks at low water are fully double the size of those found upon corallines, etc., from deeper water, and are of a more attenuated form, and have the oscular spicules more conspicuous. Not uncommon, but small. Hastings.

4. *Grantia (Sycon) compressa*, Fleming.

This species forms little grey or tan coloured sacks, cylindrical to ovate in form, generally with a single osculum. Hastings specimens do not exceed 1½ inches in height. Upon rocks at low tide ; not noted from deeper water. Not uncommon. Hastings.

PLETHOSPONGIÆ

Rhagon

5. *Ecionemia ponderosa*, Bowerbank.*
Hastings.

6. *Ciocalypta penicillus*, Bowerbank.*
Hastings.

7. *Ciocalypta*, sp.

A specimen taken from the rocks at low water. Mr. R. Kirkpatrick, of the British Museum of Natural History, who very kindly examined the specimen, expressed the opinion that it might possibly be a strongly marked variety in the young condition of *C. penicillus*, though it showed much divergence from the typical adult sponge. The specimen is in the South Kensington Museum. Rare. Hastings.

8. *Tethya lyncurium*, Johnston.

Sponge hemispherical, about ¾ inch in diameter ; surface warty-looking ; colour when fresh, orange. Upon rock from the Diamond Ground. Somewhat rare. Hastings.

9. *Raspailia cristata*, Montague.
Dictyocylindrus ramosus, Bowerbank.

Sponge 4 or 5 inches in height ; brown, branching, and hispid with defensive spicules. The shoots before branching are often palmate. From moderately shallow water. Common. Hastings.

10. *Raspailia ramosa*, Montague.

Not to be confounded with *Dictyocylindrus ramosus* of Bowerbank, the present species branching in the same plane, the branches being somewhat flattened. From the Diamond Ground. Rather rare. Hastings.

11. *Dictyocylindrus hispidus*, Bowerbank.

Sponge, light brown, hispid, dichotomously branching, the branches being in the same plane and curving inwards towards the ends. A fine specimen measures 12 inches in height. From the Diamond Ground. Somewhat rare. Hastings.

12. *Dictyocylindrus fascicularis*, Bowerbank.

Specimens a little over 5 inches in height, of a pale yellow colour, dichotomously branching, the branches being slender and curving inwards towards the upper parts. A dried specimen might be readily mistaken for a dead twig. From the Diamond Ground. Somewhat rare. Hastings.

13. *Dictyocylindrus radiosus*, Bowerbank.

Specimen 3½ inches in height, resembling to some extent *D. hispida*. The branching is dichotomous, and in the same plane, the branches being rather flattened and hispid, and instead of curving inwards, as in the last mentioned species, they expand in a radiating manner. From moderately deep water. Rare. Hastings.

14. *Dictyocylindrus aculeatus* (?), Bowerbank.

The Hastings specimens are in the dried condition, and present little grey feathery tufts about 2 inches in height, closely resembling the illustration of the Northumberland specimen figured by Bowerbank, but of twice the height. The writer learns that similar forms to the present in the British Museum are labelled by Bowerbank *D. ramosus*, Bk., but that Carter labels similar specimens *Raspailia aculeata* (? Bk. sp.). The present specimens were cast up on the beach after a storm, and similar forms have not been since noticed. Hastings.

15. *Microciona fictitia*, Bowerbank.*
Hastings.

16. *Microciona fallax*, Bowerbank.*
Hastings.

17. *Microciona plumosa*, Bowerbank.*
Hastings.

18. *Microciona atrasanquinea*, Bowerbank.*
Hastings.

19. *Microciona spinarcha*, Carter.*
Hastings.

20. *Hymeraphia stellifera*, Bowerbank.*
Hastings.

21. *Raphiodesma sordida*, Bowerbank.*
Hastings.

22. *Hymeniacidon lactea*, Bowerbank.*
Hastings.

23. *Hymeniacidon (Suberites) denuencula*, Olivi.
Sponge white, smooth, rounded and compressed, very solid, no pores or oscula apparent. Size 2 inches by 3 inches by ¾ inch in thickness. The specimen has been apparently attached to a rock. From moderately shallow water. Rare. Hastings.

24. *Hymeniacidon caruncula*, Bowerbank.*
Hastings.

25. *Hymeniacidon mammeata*, Bowerbank.*
Hastings.

26. *Hymeniacidon crustula*, Bowerbank.
Sponge somewhat cylindrical with rounded ends, smooth, orange coloured. Length, 4 inches by 1¼ inches in diameter. The specimen envelops the stems of a coralline. From moderately shallow water; rather rare. Hastings.

27. *Hymeniacidon suberea*, Bowerbank.*
Hastings.

28. *Hymeniacidon (Clione) celata*, Bowerbank.*
The species is dark brown in colour, and is found boring into shells and rock. It frequently bores through the valves of the scallop, obliging the animal to barricade itself within by fresh excretions of shelly matter. From the Diamond Ground ; common. Hastings.

29. *Hymeniacidon pannicea*, Johnston.
Sponge green, drying almost white. It incrusts the rocks at low water in considerable masses, often forming ridges of volcano-like vents. Finer specimens are obtained from deeper water, often upon tubularian stems and other hydroids. The deep water specimens are not so characterized by the ridges of vents, but are smoother. Very common. Hastings.

30. *Hymeniacidon glabra*, Bowerbank.*
Hastings.

31. *Hymeniacidon distorta*, Bowerbank.
Sponge rather low and branching ; colour, grey-brown. Before branching the shoots are palmate, giving off others in a plane at a right angle. Texture of sponge somewhat velvet-like. Scattered here and there over the surface are stellate oscula. From moderately shallow water; rather rare. Hastings.

32. *Hymeniacidon corrugata*, Bowerbank.*
Hastings.

33. *Hymeniacidon incrustans*, Johnston.*
Hastings.

34. *Hymeniacidon irregularis*, Bowerbank.*
Hastings.

35. *Hymeniacidon nigricans*, Bowerbank.*
Hastings.

36. *Hymeniacidon pattersoni*, Bowerbank.*
Hastings.

37. *Hymeniacidon ingalli*, Bowerbank.*
Hastings.

38. *Hymeniacidon farinaria*, Bowerbank.
Forming a pale buff-coloured coating of fine texture upon shell of *Pecten opercularis*, from the Diamond Ground off Hastings.

39. *Isodictya cinerea*, Bowerbank.*
Hastings.

40. *Isodictya indistincta*, Bowerbank.*
Hastings.

41. *Isodictya pallida*, Bowerbank.*
Hastings.

42. *Isodictya hyndmani*, Bowerbank.*
Hastings.

43. *Isodictya mammeata*, Bowerbank.*
Hastings.

44. *Isodictya simulans*, Johnston.
Sponge rather low and straggling, branching, the branches cylindrical or slightly compressed and anastomosing. Oscula distinct and upon one side only of the branches. Texture, fine; colour, ash-grey to brown. From moderately shallow water; somewhat rare. Hastings.

45. *Isodictya dichotoma*, Bowerbank.*
Hastings.

46. *Isodictya fucorum*, Bowerbank.*
Hastings.

47. *Isodictya rugosa*, Bowerbank.*
Hastings.

48. *Isodictya obscura*, Bowerbank.*
Hastings.

49. *Desmacidon fruticosa*, Bowerbank.
Sponge extensive, low, spreading, coarse in texture, grey, and giving off short wide funnel-like branches with wide terminal orifice, which also extends partly down the side. Growing rather insecurely upon two or three stones. From the Diamond Ground; somewhat rare. Hastings.

50. *Desmacidon ægagropila*, Bowerbank.*
Hastings.

51. *Desmacidon copiosa*, Bowerbank.*
Hastings.

52. *Desmacidon rotalis*, Bowerbank.*
Hastings.

53. *Raphyrus griffithsii*, Bowerbank.
Sponge bark brown, forming rounded masses upon stones, etc., the whole surface being closely pitted. From moderately deep water; somewhat rare. Hastings.

54. *Chalina occulata*, Bowerbank.
Sponge with a pedicel. Branches close and compact, and given off somewhat in the same plane. In a general way the oscula are arranged upon two opposite sides of the branches, but this order is by no means constant. A fine specimen measures 12 inches high. From the Diamond Ground; common. Hastings.

55. *Chalina montaguii*, Bowerbank.*
Hastings.

56. *Chalina gracilenta*, Bowerbank.*
Hastings.

57. *Dysidea fragilis*, Bowerbank.
Sponge forming somewhat shapeless or lobed masses, growing upon rock, etc. The fibres are cored with sand grains, and the sponge when dried is extremely fragile. Spicules are practically absent in this genus. Trawled in moderately shallow water; not uncommon. Hastings.

58. *Dysidea coriacea*, Bowerbank.*
Hastings.

CŒLENTERA
HYDROZOA
HYDROIDA
ATHECATA
CLAVIDÆ

1. *Clava multicornis*, Forskäl.
Polypite naked, spindle-shaped, semiopaque white; tentacles many and long, distributed irregularly over the body; gonophores round and borne below the tentacles. Upon shells and under stones at low water. Colonies small; somewhat rare. Hastings.

HYDRACTINIIDÆ

2. *Hydractinia echinata*, Fleming.
Colonies incrusting various shells occupied by the hermit crab, more particularly those of the whelk, natica and nassa; also noted upon claw of lobster.
This zoophyte is peculiar for the specialization of its members and the form of its polypary. The alimentary polypite is naked, columnar, tapering downwards, and with a single circlet of tentacles. The pink gonophores are borne on modified polypites, giving to the colony when very prolific a delicate rose colour. There are two other kinds of Zoöids, one forming coils and ostensibly a modified polypite and the other long and very contractile with bilobed 'head.' The functions of these two members are problematical. Sections of the crust show superimposed reticulating galleries formed of chitine and traversed by coenosarcal threads. Comparison may be made with advantage with sections of the polyparies of *Coppinia arcta*, *Antennularia ramosa* and other species. Very common upon the shore in warm weather; upon the approach however of cold weather the crab retires to deeper water. Hastings.

CORYNIDÆ

3. *Coryne van-benedenii*, Hincks.
Polypite small, club-shaped, with knob-

bed tentacles, the latter being dispersed over the body and numbering about nineteen. Colour semi-translucent white with opaque white dots. The polypary expands over the base of the polypite, below which it is plain or very slightly undulatory, and throughout the lower three-fourths of the stem it is lightly annulated. The polypary is colourless or of a faint buff shade. Upon *Tubularia indivisa*. Hastings.

4. *Coryne vaginata*, Hincks.

Zoophite 3 inches high, in form resembling a spruce fir tree; polypite naked, rose-coloured, with tentacles scattered as in *Clava*, but short and knobbed at the ends ; gonophores oval and borne amongst the tentacles. Common in rock pools, often densely covered with confervæ. Hastings.

EUDENDRIIDÆ

5. *Eudendrium rameum*, Pallas.

Polypite naked, tentacles forming a ring. This zoophyte has been aptly compared to a stunted and weather-beaten tree. The stem and main branches are compound, and when covered with the round and orange-coloured gonophores the colony might be likened to a shrub laden with berries. The gonophores are generally borne upon the cænosarc. Common in the trawl from the Diamond Ground and moderately deep water. Hastings.

6. *Eudendrium ramosum*, Linnæus.

This species suggests a collection of branching twigs. The stem is formed of a single tube, both it and the branches being of a straight and straggling character and of a glossy brown colour. No gonophores observed. Common upon scallops and rock from deep water. Hastings.

7. *Perigonimus repens*, Wright.

Polypite with a single circle of tentacles distant from the mouth ; polypary rather coarse, of a red-brown colour, and expanded over the base of polypite to form a rough cup. Taken upon shell of *Nucula nucleus*, in association with *Lovenella clausa*. Coralline zone ; rare. Hastings.

8. *Garveia nutans*, Wright.

This species requires more than a passing notice. The only localities given for it by Hincks are Inchgarvie, Firth of Forth, and Shetland. It has been taken some three or four times off shore at Hastings, upon all occasions climbing over Hydrallmania and throwing up short branches,

and not as figured by Hincks from northern specimens with erect and compound stem. The polypites have a single circle of tentacles and there is a gradual expansion of the polypary over the base of the polypite. Branches flexuous. The polypites themselves are conspicuous by their colour, which is orange or carrot colour, and which also extends to the cœnosarc. The gonophores are likewise orange coloured and are given off from the creeping stolon, emerging from an expansion of the polypary. The Hastings specimens agree fairly well with Hincks' description, but differ in the matter of the compound and erect stem, and in the fact that the polypites were not noticed to nod, from which peculiarity the species takes its name. Somewhat rare. Hastings.

TUBULARIIDÆ

9. *Tubularia indivisa*, Linnæus.

Polypite naked with two crowns of tentacles, the one oral and the other ab-oral, or midway down the body. Among the latter are borne the gonophores in grape-like bunches. The empty polyparium tubes much resemble tufts of stubble. Not a shore species; the finest specimens are obtained from moderately deep water. Common off Hastings.

10. *Tubularia larynx*, Ellis and Solander.

Except as regards size and habitat there seems little to distinguish this species from *T. coronata*. The Hastings specimens are very faintly annulated, and little or no branching can be detected. The polypites are naked, transparent, very finely spangled with opaque white ; gonophores round to oval and borne upon short branched peduncles. The gonophores and manubrium are rose-coloured, and the former have from not any to four tubercles at their distal ends. The gonozooid or extrusion is oval, constricted at the basal end, with twelve long ab-oral tentacles, sometimes less, clubbed at the ends and alternately raised and lowered, by which means this star-like creature stalks about, as upon stilts. At the oral end there are invariably four short thick tentacles, curved inwards. The creature having no bell seems awkward and sluggish, and is apparently intermediate between the fixed and freed forms. This species only visits Hastings in occasional years. In 1897 it appeared in great profusion upon rocks and stones from mid to low tide. Hastings.

A HISTORY OF SUSSEX

THECAPHORA

CAMPANULARIIDÆ

11. *Clytia johnstoni*, Alder.

Colonies trailing over most objects, seaweed, stones, shells, wood, etc., throwing up delicate partly-ringed stems terminating in calycles with dentate margins. The capsules are annulated and nearly always borne upon the stolon ; gonozoöid medusiform, minutely spotted with opaque white. Very common, ranging from the beach to moderately deep water. Hastings.

12. *Obelia geniculata*, Linnæus.

This very common little species throws up a zig-zag stem from a trailing stolon, giving off at each bend a short branch ending in a plain-rimmed calycle. Capsules borne in the axils. The gonozoöids of *Obelia* have the peculiar habit of often turning the swimming-bell inside out. Common upon weed, stones, shells, etc., upon the beach, and in deeper water. Hastings.

13. *Obelia gelatinosa*, Pallas.

A very beautiful zoophyte suggestive of a young and graceful birch tree. The stem is compound and the branches are usually given off in regular whorls. The calycles are said by Hincks to be dentate, but they are very difficult to define under the microscope, the margin usually appearing folded inwards. The capsules are deep and vase-like and are formed in the axils. A large and common species often growing in very exposed positions on the shore. From imperfect specimens preserved the impression is gained that this species may also occur with simple stolonic stem, overrunning other zoophyte stems. Hastings.

14. *Obelia longissima*, Pallas.

A species sometimes over a foot in length, branching and tapering gradually to the summit. The calycles are squarely dentate ; capsules a little deeper than wide. Amongst the trawlers' rubbish it may be readily mistaken for a tangle of hair. Common in the trawl from deep water. Hastings.

15. *Obelia dichotoma*, Linnæus.*
Hastings.

16. *Campanularia integra*, McGillivray.*
Hastings.

17. *Campanularia verticillata*, Linnæus.
Stem and main branches compound.

Around the axis are given off simple, partly-ringed branches, rather long and of equal length terminating in dentate calycles. The capsules are long and narrow-necked, and occur on the compound parts of the axis. Not uncommon in the trawl from moderately deep water. Hastings.

18. *Campanularia flexuosa*, Hincks.

The notes and sketches at hand of this species only allow of the remarks that the calycles have a plain margin and are borne upon rather long and well-ringed footstalks, and that the capsules are an elongate oval in form. Hastings.

19. *Campanularia neglecta*, Alder.*
Hastings.

20. *Lovénella clausa*, Lovén.

A minute species throwing up long slender stems ringed at the top, undulating elsewhere, with deep elegant calycles of which the scalloped margins are prolonged into pointed segments which meet overhead, closing the aperture. The chitine appears to be of some thickness at the bottom of the calycle, gradually thinning out towards the top ; polypite with from twelve to fourteen tentacles ; no capsules observed. A single specimen associated with *Perigonimus repens* upon *Nucula nucleus*. Coralline zone. Hastings.

21. *Gonothyrea gracilis*, Sars.

This zoophyte at first glance with the hand-glass may be mistaken for *Clytia johnstoni*, but the calycles are much deeper, the teeth of the margin longer and sharper, and inclining inwards rather than outwards. The stem just below the calycle has four or five rings and again at the base is ringed. Branches bearing a terminal polypite are given off at about two-thirds of the distance up the stems. Upon *Tubularia indivisa* ; rare. Hastings.

CAMPANULINIDÆ

22. *Opercularella lacerata*, Johnston.

Zoophyte of very slender habit. It occurs wound like fine thread around the polyzoan *Anguinella palmata*, throwing up short branching stems much annulated. The calycles on short ringed footstalks have the plain margin cut into segments which meet over the centre, forming an operculum. The polypite stretches out of its calycle fully to the extent of the length of the calycle. The species also occurs upon sponges ; not general. Hastings.

78

LAFOËIDÆ

23. *Lafoëa dumosa*, Fleming.

This species occurs in two forms, either with simple stem over-running other coral-lines and giving off, without footstalks, tubular calycles narrowed and slightly twisted at the base; or it is found with compound branching stem giving off around the axis the closely arranged calycles, the whole suggesting perhaps a very prickly bramble in miniature. Both forms common in the coralline zone. Hastings.

24. *Lafoëa pocillum*, Hincks.

Upon *Diphasia rosacea*, *Eudendrium rameum*, etc. The creeping stem gives off short, ringed peduncles with tubular but shapeable calycles, some of which appear to approach to the more tubular form *pygmæa*. In the Hastings specimens the peduncle has from four to six rings, whereas Hincks gives from five to eight for this species, and two or three to Alder's species *pygmæa*. Somewhat rare. Hastings.

25. *Lafoëa pygmæa* (?), Alder MS.

Some years ago this species was recorded from Hastings, but in the absence of notes and specimens mislaid, a query is here appended.

26. *Calycella syringa*, Linnæus.

Over-running the polyzoan *Anguinella palmata* together with *Opercularella lacerata*, already noticed. The calycles are borne upon short, three-ringed footstalks given off from the creeping unringed stem. They rather resemble those of *O. lacerata*, but are longer and not so swollen in the middle. Some of the smaller calycles which have the operculum introverted, and so not seen, bear a resemblance also to the calycles of *Lafoëa pocillum* and *pygmæa*. Common upon *Anguinella* at low tide. Hastings.

27. *Filillum serpens*, Hassall.

Stem nearly always creeping over other hydroids, but in one instance upon a scallop shell. It gives off ovate tubular calycles without footstalk, the lower half being adnate, and the upper half curved upwards, showing a slightly trumpet-shaped aperture. Calycles transversely lined.

There is a remarkable form in which apparently this species occurs, not mentioned by another author, so far as the writer is aware, and which merits notice. Upon old shells covered with incrusting polyzoa, the zoœcia of the latter will often be found to contain hydroid calycles peeping out of the apertures and bearing nearest resemblance to the present species. The calycles are always black and glassy, possibly discoloured by sulphuretted hydrogen; sometimes they are long and tubular, at others ovate in the lower, and tubular in the upper half, and always with very trumpet-shaped apertures. There is generally one calycle in each zoœcium, but occasionally there are two. On dissolving the zoœcia in acid, only imperfect calycles are obtained, showing no connection with a stem. It is possible that these may be the primary zoœcia of the present species which are prevented from freely budding by reason of their limited surroundings. The type form is common, and the other form described is not uncommon. From deep water. Hastings.

COPPINIIDÆ

28. *Coppinia arcta*, Dalyell.

A peculiar zoophyte, usually found surrounding in short masses the stem of *Hydrallmania*. A cross-section of the dry polypary shows a chitinous layer enveloping the stem, tunnelled with passages, one above the other. From these passages arise, at a little distance apart, tubular calycles bent in the upper portion at about a right angle. The calycles at half their height are cemented together by a floor of chitine. In the intervening spaces of this floor are seen slightly-tubular orifices, apparently subserving the escape of the planules. Not uncommon. Hastings.

HALECIIDÆ

29. *Halecium halicinum*, Linnæus.

Rather a coarse looking zoophyte. Stem and main branches compound; branches given off pinnately; the footstalks bearing the calycles are telescopic in appearance, the latter resembling in shape a drinking-tumbler. It is important to note in the female gonophores of this genus, as Hincks has pointed out, that the gonozoöid-bearing polypites are not atrophied as in all the rest of the *Thecaphora*, but are perfectly recognizable polypites, protruding from one side of the capsule. From moderate to deep water; common. Hastings.

30. *Halecium beanii*, Johnston.

A species of much more delicate and flexible habit than the last. In the female gonophore there is a lobe which projects considerably in front of the aperture. From deep or moderately deep water; not uncommon. Hastings.

31. *Sertularella polyzonias*, Linnæus.

A little, straggling species with stem and branches of the same thickness throughout. The calycles are somewhat oval and arranged alternately on either side of the axis into which they appear to be sunk. The capsules are large and wrinkled. Often found growing upon annelid tubes, flustra, etc. Common in the trawl. Hastings.

32. *Sertularella gayi*, Lamouroux.

This species resembles in type *S. polyzonias*, but it is larger and of stouter build. The stem is compound with calycles alternate, short, stout and turned well outward, and having four slight denticles to the margin. The polypary is brown, the margins of the calycles appearing somewhat lighter. Not uncommon in the trawl. Hastings.

33. *Sertularella rugosa*, Linnæus.

A small species often over-running flustra, and throwing up short branches with clusters of alternate wrinkled and oval calycles. The capsules resemble the calycles, but are much larger and contracted at the base. Common. Hastings.

34. *Sertularella tenella*, Alder.

Hastings specimens appear to link together as nearly as possible Alder's species *tenella* and Hincks' species *fusiformis*. The branches are about ⅛ inch in height, arising from the stem creeping over flustra. Calycles smooth, intermediate in slenderness, aperture with four denticles. The stem is bent at a right angle immediately above each calycle in a strongly zigzag manner. Capsules large, ringed and with four denticles. These points agree therefore with *tenella*, except in the calycles being smooth, not quite so slender, and in the capsules being toothed, in which respects the specimens resemble *fusiformis*. Hastings.

35. *Diphasia rosacea*, Linnæus.

A very delicate and graceful species, the laterally branched stems being flexible and plume-like. The calycles are tubular, bilateral, opposite, and bent straight outwards. The female capsule is thrown into vertical folds producing at the top a crown of spines of which two, one on either side, project, the others being curved over the centre. Habitat, upon other zoophyte stems, sponges, etc., from moderately deep water. Not uncommon. Hastings.

36. *Diphasia attenuata*, Hincks.

A species very like *rosacea* and difficult to determine in the absence of the capsules, which are certainly the best specific guide. In this species the height of the stem joint above the offshoot of the calycles below is not so great as in *rosacea*, and the stem between each pair of calycles is not so attenuated. The calycles are also a trifle longer and narrower. The male capsule has a crown of spines directed horizontally outwards, and one central and vertical spine. Very common from the coralline zone, and from moderately deep water. Hastings.

37. ? *Diphasia fallax*, Johnston.

The species is recorded with a query in the Natural History of Hastings before quoted. Although specimens are not at hand, the record appears well founded. Hastings.

38. *Sertularia pumila*, Linnæus.

This hydroid covers densely the bladder-wrack at low tide. The stem is only about ½ inch in height, and little branched. The calycles are tubular, short, bent outwards and arranged in pairs, oppositely. Capsules ovate. Very common. Hastings.

39. *Sertularia gracilis*, Hassall.

Of very similar growth to the last species but smaller, denser, and altogether more refined. Erect stems, not observed to branch. The calycle margin is thrown into two sharp points. Capsules ovate. This species over-runs other hydroid stems. Not very common. Hastings.

40. *Sertularia operculata*, Linnæus.

This is a rich and luxuriant species and has been termed 'seahair.' It affects mussel shells and *Laminarian* stems. The stems are long, fine, wavy, branching and of equal thickness throughout. The colour might be almost called a dull golden. The calycles are arranged in pairs, oppositely, and the margins of the apertures are thrown into sharp points. Capsules balloon-shaped. Occasionally colonies of this zoophyte might almost be said to rival in the number of its members the population of London. Very common from moderate to deep water. Hastings.

41. *Sertularia filicula*, Ellis and Solander.*
Hastings.

42. *Sertularia abietina*, Linnæus.

The erect stems are about 6 inches in

height, pinnately branched, stout, and with calycles lateral and opposite, to alternate. They are ovately tubular and bent slightly outwards. The capsules are oval and wrinkled. Common upon scallop shells, etc., from moderately deep water. Hastings.

43. *Sertularia argentea*, Ellis and Solander.

Stems of considerable length, gyratory, giving off around the axis short branches in a palmate manner. Calycles sub-opposite; apertures sharply pointed. Capsules shield-shaped. From moderate to deep water; not uncommon. Hastings.

44. *Sertularia cupressina*, Linnæus.

Stems very long, branches short and palmate, the zoophyte as a whole tapering to a point in a somewhat snake-like manner. The calycles are sub-opposite, diverge very little from the stem and have sharply-pointed margins. Capsules narrowly shield-shaped. Hastings specimens are rather inferior in size and condition. Common from moderate to deep water. Hastings.

45. *Hydrallmania falcata*, Linnæus.

Stems long and gyratory, giving off around the axis pinnate branches. The calycles are ovately tubular, borne crowded upon the upper sides of the branches, and almost in the same straight line. Their apertures are turned alternately to the right and left. Capsules ovate; very common from the coralline zone. Hastings.

PLUMULARIIDÆ

46. *Antennularia antennina*, Linnæus.

Stems simple, long and straight, from which are given off radiately at frequent nodes along the axis, short delicate sprays of equal length. The calycles which are cup-like are borne in a single line upon the upper sides of these sprays, and with them are associated the peculiar organs called nematophores. The capsules are ovate. Hincks gives 8 or 10 inches as the height of this species, but the writer has obtained it 18 inches in length from the Diamond Ground, where it is common. This zoophyte is much frequented by the Nudibranch molluscs *Doto coronata* and *D. pinnatifida*, which attach their egg-bands to its stem. Hastings.

47. *Antennularia ramosa*, Lamarck.

The most striking feature of this species is that it branches and rebranches. The stem is compound, a cross-section of it showing a large central tube with many minor ones, varying in size and overlying one another, running parallel with it, the whole being welded together. The tubes communicate one with the other, thus indicating the continuity of the cœnosarc. The calycles and nematophores closely resemble those of the last species, as do also the capsules, but the latter taper towards the base and are curved. Common upon scallops and rock from the Diamond Ground. Hastings.

48. *Aglaophenia pluma*, Linnæus.

This species envelops the stem of *Halidrys siliquosa* in a loose stolonic mesh, giving off beautiful plume-like branches with irregularly toothed calycles arranged in single line upon the upper surfaces of the pinnæ. Associated with the calycles are three nematophores, two lateral and one median. The capsules are ribbed, the ribs being armed with nematophores. Plentiful upon the beach, after rough weather. Hastings.

49. *Plumularia pinnata*, Linnæus.

A very delicate and beautiful species growing in tufts of plume-like stems. The calycles are shallow and cup-like, and arranged singly upon the upper sides of the pinnæ. There are two nematophores, one above and one below each calycle, and one generally situated in the axils of the pinnæ. The gonophores are conspicuously and closely set upon each side of the stem. Hincks observes that the calycles are only separated by a single joint. This does not always appear to hold good with Hastings shore forms, in which there are sometimes two joints. The form from deeper water is much larger but not of frequent occurrence at Hastings, where the shore form is always in profusion on rocks, stones, shells, sponges, etc., at low water. Hastings.

50. *Plumularia setacea*, Ellis.

A most delicate species, almost escaping detection. Readily distinguished from *P. pinnata* by the long drawn out, narrow-necked capsules, when present, or by the difference in the character and number of the nematophores. Taken upon *Antennularia* from deep water; rare. Hastings.

51. *Plumularia obliqua*, Saunders.*
Hastings.

52. *Plumularia similis*, Hincks.*
Hastings.

SIPHONOPHORA

PHYSOPHORIDÆ

53. *Physalia*, sp.

This record is made for Brighton upon the authority of Mr. W. Wells, superintendent of the Aquarium, Brighton.

LUCERNARIDA

ACRASPEDA

54. *Aurelia aurita.*

In this common jellyfish the umbrella is large and transparent ; the radial canals are of a delicate pale mauve colour, and the tentacles around the margin are many and short. Conspicuous through the umbrella are the opaque-white gonads in quarters. Oral arms short. Common. Hastings.

55. *Chrysaora cyclonota.*

The upper surface of the umbrella is marked around the centre with a brown circular ring, a short distance from which arise brown, V-shaped rays extending to a little distance short of the margin, the surface generally being finely speckled with brown. The marginal lappets are also of a dark brown. Intermediate in position between these are long streaming tentacles. Oral arms long and frilled. Common. Hastings.

56. *Cyanæa lamarckii.*

Looked at from above, the inner surface of the umbrella appears of a pale heliotrope colour, slightly marbled, and around the centre and not far from the margin there is a circular band or coronet of some depth, of a dark heliotrope colour, and sending off rays to the marginal lobes ; these are large, and veined with the branching canals. The tentacles are collected together in knots between the lobes. The surface bordering upon these is strongly cancellated with muscular tissue. This species grows to a large size. Common. Hastings.

ACTINOZOA

ZOANTHARIA

ACTINIARIA

SAGARTIIDÆ

57. *Actinoloba dianthus*, Ellis.

The disc of this anemone is thrown out into plume-like marginal lobes, covered and fringed with rather small and short tentacles. The column is tall and smooth. The colours are of the most delicate shades, running through every grade of white, pink, red, yellow, salmon, orange, grey

and brown. It is obtained from the Diamond Ground, and may occasionally be met with upon the shore at low tide, but specimens so found have probably been thrown overboard by fishermen. Common. Hastings.

58. *Sagartia bellis*, Ellis and Solander.*
Hastings.

59. *Sagartia miniata*, Gosse.

Animal dark red, as broad as high. Margin of disc thrown into unequal, ragged-looking lobes. Taken once or twice upon trawled rock. Rare. Hastings.

60. *Sagartia rosea*, Gosse.

The tentacles of this species vary in colour from rose-red to crimson-lake or lilac. A most lovely anemone. It is usually found anchored down to some stone or mussel shell below the surface. Not very common. Hastings.

61. *Sagartia sphyrodeta*, Gosse.*
Hastings.

62. *Sagartia troglodytes*, Johnston.

This species occurs at Hastings in great variety, a favourite haunt being a mussel-bed with shingle beneath, the whole being covered with a thin layer of mud or sand. Here the anemones can attach themselves to the shingle or the mussel shells and withdraw instantly, or push their way upwards to expand on the surface. The species is nearly always known by the 'B' mark at the base of the tentacles, upon the inner face. Very common. Hastings.

63. *Sagartia viduata*, Müller.*
Hastings.

64. *Sagartia parasitica*, Couch.*
Brighton.

65. *Adamsia palliata*, Bohadsch.

Specimens of the form *rhodopis*, Gosse, have been taken upon shell of whelk and *Natica* from somewhat shallow water, and the variety *crinopis*, Gosse, upon shell of *Scaphander lignarius*. The *Acontia* are of a beautiful mauve colour and readily attract attention. Rare. Hastings.

ANTHEIDÆ

66. *Anthea cereus*, Ellis and Solander.

This beautiful species with low wide column and long, green, worm-like tentacles tipped with magenta occurs along the beach at Brighton. Upon the authority of Mr. Wells, of the Brighton Aquarium, the variety *rustica* is also a resident there. The species is certainly not known at Hastings, and the fact may indicate a difference of temperature of the water between these localities.

ACTINIIDÆ

67. *Actinia mesembryanthemum*, Ellis and Solander.

Characteristic of this species are the vivid blue dart-charged spherules around the margin of the disc, outside the tentacles. It occurs at Hastings in several varieties of colours, viz. vars. *a, β, ζ, ι* and *λ* of Gosse, the colours being respectively liver-brown, dark crimson, dark olive-green with broken lines of light green, and liver-coloured with green spots. Very common at low water. Hastings.

BUNODIDÆ

68. *Bunodes gemmacea*, Ellis and Solander.†
Brighton.

69. *Bunodes clavata*, Thompson.†
Brighton.

70. *Tealia crassicornis*, Müller.

A large and handsome anemone with wide and low column, the outer surface of which is provided with suckers. By these means the animal attaches to itself grains of sand and shell, covering itself to such an extent that it has often the appearance of a piece of stucco. The tentacles are short and thick, and generally barred with pink and white. The tentacles are occasionally found budding, the buds being produced from all sides. Common at low tide and from deeper water. Hastings.

ILYANTHIDÆ

71. *Ilyanthus mitchellii*, Gosse.

A rare species, and as such deserving fuller notice. A dozen specimens were obtained on one occasion from a trawler. Length of a specimen, 1½ inches. The colouring of the column varied as follows : In one instance it was wholly of an orange or light tomato-colour ; in others, and more generally, there was below the tentacles a flesh-coloured band, then a narrow or broad zone of tomato-colour extending to a quarter or half the length of the column, followed by a broad band of flesh-colour and another of tomato-colour of about equal depth, extending to the base. In one specimen the whole of the column was of a pale flesh tint, with the exception of two zones of a very pale tomato-shade.

The disc and tentacles were coloured as follows : Lip, opaque white, with an outer ring of brownish purple, then a wider zone of cream-colour and the space extending to the tentacles of brown-purple. The tentacles were in two rows ; the core of tentacle was of a light golden or straw colour, with bars upon the inner face of purple-brown, or in some of the outer tentacles of dark-grey ; the outer face of the tentacles appeared grey or curry-coloured. Around the base and upon each side of the tentacles swerved a cream-coloured line, not however uniting upon the outer side. Gonidial radii cream-coloured ; stomach a light tomato, with a line of deep orange-colour running down each ridge of the folds. The specimens were taken at the beginning of the year, and the white or salmon-coloured ova were clustered like grapes upon the mesenteries. Locality, 25 miles off Beachy Head.

ZOANTHIDÆ

72. *Zoanthus*, sp.

Upon scallop shells. Not uncommon. Hastings.

ALCYONARIA

ALCYONIDÆ

73. *Alcyonium digitatum*.

The only common coral upon the Sussex coast. It forms lobed, rounded masses upon rocks at low water and upon shells and rock from deeper water. The skeleton is spicular, and the polyps are white, with eight tentacles, fringed laterally with papillæ. The colour of the colonies is milk-white or orange. Common. Hastings.

CTENOPHORA

74. *Pleurobranchia pileus*.

Animal almost spherical, barely ½ inch in diameter, with eight longitudinal rows of swimming paddles, beneath each of which runs a circulatory canal terminating blindly at either extremity. The flash of the irridescent paddles in the sun as the little balloon-like body ascends in the water is a sight well worth seeing. Very common during most years, in the summer, at Hastings.

75. (?) *Pleurobranchia rhodopis*, Chun.

A large species of about the size and shape of a walnut, and of similar structure to the foregoing species. It was taken in the trawl in profusion a few years ago. The specimens were examined at the time, but for want of reference were left undetermined. Judging from memory however they corresponded precisely with Chun's figure of *P. rhodopis*, and cannot be referred to the balloon-shaped *Hormiphora plumosa*. Length, about $1\frac{1}{4}$ inches. Hastings.

76. (?) *Hormiphora plumosa*.

Specimens resembling this genus in shape and somewhat larger than *Pleurobranchia pileus* have been taken at Hastings, but were not examined sufficiently for identification. Hastings.

77. *Beroë ovata*, Eschscholtz.

This species is filbert-shaped, and has been taken in the immature condition. Specimen transparent, colourless, $\frac{3}{4}$ inch in length. In this genus the circulatory canals unite at the aboral pole, and in the region of the pores there are ciliated tentaculoid processes, lobed and branched. Hastings.

VERMES

CEPHYREA

1. *Sipunculus*, Pallasii.†
Brighton.

ANNELIDA

HIRUDINEA

2. *Pontobdella muricata*.

This species has suckers at both extremities; there are neither feet nor bristles. The rings are strongly marked, and are studded the whole way round with conical warts, each ring somewhat resembling a well-armed dog collar. Colour, a dull buff with spots of brown at regular intervals. Trawled; rare. Hastings.

POLYCHÆTA

AURICOMIDÆ

3. *Pectinaria belgica*.

This species forms beautifully made sand tubes, the sand grains being cemented together by an excretion, the structure resembling mosaic work. The tubes are straight, conical, and very regular. Common. Hastings.

4. *Pectinaria arenaria*.†
Brighton.

5. *Sabellaria crassissima*, Link.*
Very common. Hastings.

6. (?) *Sabellaria alveolata*.*
Common. Hastings.

7. *Siphonostoma*, sp.

Specimen about $2\frac{1}{2}$ inches in length, greyish-brown in colour; much enlarged towards the head. The setæ become very long in the region of the mouth and project in front. The body is covered with small papillæ. Trawled. Hastings.

TEREBELLIDÆ

8. *Terebella littoralis*, Dal.

This species, in the adult state, forms membranous tubes with agglutinated particles of sand and shell. The tubes are of considerable length and have a fringe of smaller branching tubes arranged in a radiating manner around the anterior end. Very common upon the shore. Hastings.

9. *Terebella maculata*.*
Hastings.

10. *Terebella conchilega*.†
Brighton.

SABELLIDÆ

11. *Sabella penicillus*.*
Hastings.

12. *Sabella tubularia*.*
Hastings.

13. *Myxicola infundibulum*.

Animal white, $1\frac{1}{4}$ inches long, tapering to the posterior end, and with a slight depressed line running down the dorsal and ventrical sides. Setæ minute. The pectinated plume-like gills are arranged around the mouth, and curve gracefully over towards the centre. Trawled; rare. Hastings.

SERPULIDÆ

14. *Serpula contortuplicata*.

Annelid forming a calcareous tube, circular in section, much twisted and often aggregating together in involved masses. Animal with a flat-topped operculum. Very common upon shells and rock. Hastings.

15. *Serpula triquetra*.

This species inhabits a calcareous, serpentine tube cemented to shells and stone. Running down the back of the tube is a ridge or keel, and the base of attachment is spread out, so that a section would be somewhat triangular in form. The operculum is conical and generally furnished with two or three spines. Very common. Hastings.

16. *Spirorbis nautiloides*, Link.

A minute species with coiled tube, the coils being arranged in the same plane. Attached to weed, corallines, and many other objects. Very common. Hastings.

17. *Spirorbis lucidus*, Montagu.*
Common. Hastings.

18. *Spirorbis communis.* †
Brighton.

19. *Filograna implexa.*

Animal secreting a long filiform, calcareous tube. The individuals are social, the associated tubes being packed together parallel-wise in considerable masses. Trawled ; not very common. Hastings.

ARENICOLIDÆ

20. *Arenicola piscatorum.*

The 'fisherman's worm' is about 6 inches long, brown, and with a large head which is covered with spiny tubercles. The dendriform gills are arranged along each side of the middle portion of the body. Very common upon the sand shore, where it burrows deeply. Hastings.

CIRRATULIDÆ

21. *Cirratula*, sp.
Hastings.

CHÆTOPTERIDÆ

22. *Chætopterus insignis*, Baird.

This species forms a tough parchment-like tube, 12 inches in length, by $\frac{3}{4}$ inch in diameter. The tubes are trawled upon the Diamond Ground, but so far as the writer has observed are always empty. Not uncommon. Hastings.

23. *Nereis margaritacea.*

Animal about 4 inches long, of a pearly lustre, and flattened dorsally and ventrally. It is nearly always found inhabiting the same shell with the trawled hermit crab ; this however is not the case with the smaller, shore-frequenting hermit crab. Common. Hastings.

24. *Nereis fimbriata*, Müller.*
Bexhill.

25. *Nereis brevimanus.* †
Brighton.

26. *Nereis longissima.* †
Brighton.

27. *Nereis bilineata.* †
Brighton.

28. *Nephthys*, sp.
Hastings.

29. *Phyllodoce viridis.* *
Common. Hastings.

AMPHINOMIDÆ

30. *Euphrosyne foliosa.*
Not uncommon. Hastings.

APHRODITIDÆ

31. *Aphrodite aculeata.*
Common. Hastings.

POLYZOA
ECTOPROCTA
GYMNOLÆMATA
CHEILOSTOMATA

ÆTEIDÆ

1. *Ætea anguina*, Linnæus.

A minute species with zoarium of ivory whiteness, usually found trailing over seaweed, and giving off from enlargements of the creeping stem or stolon, short tubular zoœcia, curved and expanded in the upper part, and with aperture terminal. The zoœcium bears some fancied resemblance to the arched head and neck of the hooded cobra. From moderately deep water. Not uncommon. Hastings.

2. *Ætea recta*, Hincks.

Resembling *Æ. anguina* but with zoœcium straight, and with longer aperture. Common upon rock and shells from the Diamond Ground and deep water. Hastings.

EUCRATIIDÆ

3. *Eucratea chelata*, Linnæus.

This dainty little species might well receive the popular appellation of the little glass slipper, for the zoœcia strikingly resemble a series of semi-transparent little slippers united together toe and heel by short prolongations. A free form, long, and rather tubular in the lower part of the zoœcium also occurs at Hastings, but is comparatively rare. Type, upon weed and coralline stems ; somewhat rare. Hastings.

4. *Gemellaria loricata*, Linnæus.

Colonies some 7 inches in height, seaweed-like and of a dull buff or grey colour. Stems formed of matted fibres, and the branches of zoœcia somewhat ovate, but tapering downwards, and arranged back to back. Not uncommon. Hastings.

CELLULARIIDÆ

5. *Scrupocellaria scruposa*, Linnæus.

Growing in little white branching tufts upon rock, etc. The branches consist of two rows of alternating zoœcia, both rows facing in the same direction. The zoœcia are ovately tubular, but taper downwards slightly, and the apertures are armed above with three or four spines. Upon the outer side of each zoœcium is a prominent avicularium with beak upturned. No operculum. From moderate to deep water. Common. Hastings.

6. *Scrupocellaria scrupea*, Busk.

Similar to the last species, but with a non-foliated operculum, and with a flagellate chamber situated between and rather behind the zoœcia. Upon sponges, etc. From moderate depth. Hastings.

7. *Scrupocellaria reptans*, Linnæus.

A species of prostrate, straggling habit, and of a dull buff or grey colour. Around the upper margin of the aperture there are three or four spines, and guarding the opening there is a foliated operculum. An avicularium is situated sometimes in front, and sometimes there is a smaller one behind the spines upon the outer side. Not uncommon upon *flustra*, etc. Hastings.

BICELLARIIDÆ

8. *Bicellaria ciliata*, Linnæus.

Colonies form plumose tufts of about 1 inch in height, of a dull grey colour, and hang pendent, like little tassels, upon the sides of the rocks, at low water. The stem and branches consist of biserial, alternating, glassy zoœcia, with many and long spines around the apertures, below and rather on the outer sides of which is situated a highly formed avicularium. The zoarium is a very beautiful object under the microscope. Common. Hastings.

9. *Bugula avicularia*, Linnæus.

Stem about 2 inches in height, giving off branches forming a delicate and beautiful spiral. The zoœcia are biserial and have a spine at the outer and upper corner, but only a very rudimentary one at the inner corner. The avicularia are longer than in *B. turbinata*, but not so prolonged as in Hincks' figures, and are placed midway down the aperture. Not uncommon upon rocks at low tide. Hastings.

10. *Bugula turbinata*, Alder.

Growth very much resembling the above species, but there are from two to five zoœcia abreast in a division, with a large spine at each of the upper corners of the aperture, and the aperture extends to the zoœcium below. The avicularia are shorter and wider than in *B. avicularia* and are placed just below the spines. Washed ashore. Hastings.

11. *Bugula flabellata*, Thompson.

A short, brown, truncate-looking growth. In some parts the zoœcia number seven in a row. There are two spines at each of the upper corners of the zoœcia, and often there is an avicularium half way down the side of the aperture. Common upon *Flustra foliacea*. Hastings.

12. *Bugula calathus*, Norman.

This species resembles very closely *B. flabellata*, but the habit is more compact and shorter. There are five or more zoœcia in a row, and in many cases three, but generally two spines in each of the upper corners. Hincks calls attention to the difference in colour between this species and the last. His observations hold good as regards the Hastings specimens, they being of a very pale buff colour. Washed ashore. Hastings.

13. *Bugula plumosa*, Pallas.*

Not uncommon. Hastings.

14. *Beania mirabilis*, Johnson.

A minute and delicate species creeping over rock, etc. The zoœcia are somewhat spoon-shaped, laterally compressed, with numerous spines around the margin, and connected together by prolongations from the preceding zoœcia. Common upon rock from the Diamond Ground. Hastings.

NOTAMIIDÆ

15. *Notamia bursaria*, Linnæus.

This exquisite little species throws up plume-like stems, much curled, and branching. The zoœcia are arranged in biserial and opposite order. Above each of these there projects from the stem a pedunculated avicularium. Upon weed; rather rare. Hastings.

CELLARIIDÆ

16. *Cellaria fistulosa*, Linnæus.

Zoœcia lozenge-shaped, arranged around a branching, jointed axis. The zoarium is white, and often occurs in dense bush-like masses. From moderate to deep water; rather common. Hastings.

17. *Cellaria sinuosa*, Hassal.

A much stouter species than the last, and consequently there are a greater number of zoœcia in the circumference. The upper margins of the zoœcia are curved, not straight as in *C. fistulosa*, and the segments of the stem are much longer. The colour is a light buff. From deep water ; rare. Hastings.

FLUSTRIDÆ

18. *Flustra foliacea*, Linnæus.

Colonies forming long, flat, branching expansions, of a horny consistence, and with zoœcia arranged in lines and covering both surfaces. The zoœcia are coffin-shaped and carry two spines at either of the upper corners. The whole face of the zoœcium is membraneous. Very common upon shells, rock, etc. Hastings.

19. *Flustra papyracea*, Ellis and Solander.

This species occurs in the form of rather close tufts or rosettes about 2 inches in height. Zoœcia oblong, with only one spine at either upper corner. Colour buff ; not uncommon. Hastings.

MEMBRANIPORIDÆ

20. *Membranipora lacroixii*, Audouin.

Aperture of zoœcia oval, margin more or less beaded. It occurs upon rocks and stones at low tide, also upon shells, in three forms, viz. one producing considerable and uniform patches of stone ; secondly, it forms dendritic, and rather radiating patterns ; and, thirdly, there is a form with spines around the apertures, and producing colonies of a more or less close outline. Common. Hastings.

21. *Membranipora monostachys*, Busk.

Aperture of zoœcium oval, not occupying the whole width ; generally with one short and stout spine at the bottom, and often one or more on either side in the upper part ; occasionally there are none. The form of the colony is characteristic and might be expressed as erratically dendritic. Upon rock along the beach. Not very common. Hastings.

22. *Membranipora catenularia*, Jameson.

Zoœcia in single series, branches being given off at an open angle and uniting with others, thus forming reticulated patterns. The zoœcia are pear-shaped with oval and moderate sized apertures. Upon old shell of *Cardium norvegicum* from deep water. Rare. Hastings.

23. *Membranipora pilosa*, Linnæus.

Zoœcia glassy, perforated, with oval aperture occupying the full width of zoœcium, and armed with spines of which one at the bottom is very long and of a horny nature. Very common upon almost every object.

Membranipora pilosa var. *dentata*, having a short spine instead of a long one at the bottom of the aperture, is also common. Ranging from shore to deep water. Hastings.

24. *Membranipora membranacea*, Linnæus.

Covering rock and weed at low tide. Zoœcium coffin-shaped, brown, leathery, wrinkled, with a long spine upon the upper margin on either side, and occasionally one between them. Common. Hastings.

25. *Membranipora spinifera*, Johnston.* Hastings.

26. *Membranipora dumerillii*, Audouin.

Zoœcia form pearly patches upon rocks and stones at low water, also upon shells. They are oval to sub-triangular, with two spines on either side of aperture ; in some specimens the spines are abnormally long. Common. Hastings.

27. *Membranipora solidula*, Alder and Hincks.* Hastings.

28. *Membranipora aurita*, Hincks.

Forming patches upon stone at low tide. Zoœcium ovately oblong ; margin finely beaded, with a spine upon one side only, below the aperture. Not uncommon. Hastings.

29. *Membranipora flemingii*, Busk.

Zoœcium ovate, aperture sub-triangular and occupying rather more than half the front area, the other portion forming a calcareous wall. There are three spines upon either side of the upper half of the aperture. Upon scallop shells ; rather rare. Hastings.

30. *Membranipora rosselii*, Audouin.

Zoœcium coffin-shaped, margin strongly beaded, aperture sub-triangular and occupying barely half the length of the zoœcium ; colonies forming patches upon rock and shells. From moderately deep water ; rather rare. Hastings.

31. *Membranipora savartii*, Audouin.

Forming considerable patches upon old shells of oyster, *Lutraria*, etc. The zoœcia are arranged in lines and arched above and below; the front is closed in to the extent of one-fourth or one-third, leaving an aperture oval to sub-rectangular, with a few irregular projections around the edge. There is a raised and crenulated margin to the zoœcium, and the space between this and the aperture is also crenulated in the upper part. New to Britain. From deep water; rather rare. Hastings.

MICROPORIDÆ

32. *Micropora coriacia*, Esper.

Forming small rounded patches upon old shells. Zoœcia coffin-shaped; front wall finely perforated; margin with a tubercle at each corner of the aperture; aperture semicircular. Upon *Pecten opercularis* from deep water; somewhat rare. Hastings.

CRIBRILINIDÆ

33. *Cribrilina radiata*, Moll.

Occurring in various forms, encrusting old shells. Zoœcium oval, aperture semicircular and usually armed with five spines. The front wall is radiately ribbed, the extremities of the ribs often developing into blunt erect spines. Beneath the aperture there is generally more or less of a boss or umbo. Upon oyster and other shells from rather deep water; common. Hastings.

34. *Cribrilina punctata*, Hassall.

This species also occurs in several forms, producing patches upon old shells. The front wall is radiately punctured, and the aperture is semicircular with two spines upon the upper margin, the lower margin being thickened. In another form there are five spines to the upper margin and an avicularium at each corner. Not uncommon upon oyster, scallop shells, etc., from rather deep water. Hastings.

35. *Cribrilina figularis*, Johnston.

Zoœcia forming strongly marked patches upon old shells. They are ovate with subsquare apertures, the lower margin having a shallow sinus. Upon the front wall there is an inner oval area radiately punctured, the outer margin being plain. Avicularia very large. From rather deep water; somewhat rare. Hastings.

36. *Membraniporella nitida*, Johnston.

Zoœcia oval, of crystalline brightness, forming round patches. Aperture nearly semicircular; front wall formed of radiating ribs. Occurring upon *Lepralia foliacea* from deep water; rare. Hastings.

37. *Membraniporella melolontha*, Busk.

Forming glistening, more or less foliated or branching patches upon old shells. The species resembles *nitida*, but there is a spine at either corner of the aperture and a plain margin around the ribbed area. Quite characteristic however is the spinous process at the bottom of this area, and very suggestive of a little tail. Upon old oyster and other shells; rather rare. Hastings.

MICROPORELLIDÆ

38. *Microporella ciliata*, Pallas.

Forming nacreous patches upon shells, weed, etc. Zoœcium ovate; aperture with five spines, sometimes six, around the upper margin, and with a raised pore beneath the lower margin. Upon one side there is usually an avicularium with a mandible of extreme length, although not as yet of the vibraculoid type. From moderately deep water; very common. Hastings.

39. *Microporella malusii*, Audouin.

A very handsome species. Zoœcia ovately lozenge-shaped; aperture semicircular with three spines upon the upper margin. Beneath the lower margin there is a crescentic pore, and smaller dimpled pores occur over the front wall. This species forms white patches upon old shells, stones, etc. From moderate to deep water; common. Hastings.

40. *Microporella impressa*, Audouin.

Zoœcia coffin-shaped, rather long, the lower half pointed; aperture somewhat more deeply arched than a semicircle. Beneath it there is situated a pore, other minor ones being distributed over the front wall, more particularly around the margin. Colonies have a beautiful satin-like lustre. Upon weed from moderately deep water; not uncommon. Hastings.

41. *Microporella violacea*, Johnston.

Colonies rather extensive, of a violet lustre, encrusting old shells; the zoœcia are coffin-shaped, aperture semicircular to ob-ovate. In the middle of the front wall is a depression with a characteristic pore in the centre. Around the margin are radial vacancies unfilled in with shelly matter. Very common upon shells and stones from deep water. Hastings.

42. *Chorizopora brongniarti*, Audouin.

Forming delicate pearly patches upon old shells, stones, etc. Zoœcia ovate but tapering rather below, transversely wrin-

MARINE ZOOLOGY

kled, with aperture approximately semi-circular and a more or less pronounced prominence underneath. The connection with adjacent zoœcia is not continuous, but vacant spaces occur at intervals around the margin. Common upon scallop shells, etc., from deep water. Hastings.

PORINIDÆ

43. *Porina tubulosa*, Norman.

Zoœcia ovate in the lower half, the upper part narrowed and curving upwards, with a circular aperture. A little below this there is a tubular pore, and elsewhere the wall is pitted with pores. Upon old shell of *Cardium norvegicum*; rare. Hastings.

44. *Lagenipora socialis*, Hincks.*

Hastings (Miss Jelly).

MYRIOZOIDÆ

45. *Schizoporella unicornis*, Johnston.

Encrusts rock at low tide; zoœcia rather large, square to sexagonal; aperture semi-circular with sinus in the lower lip. Beneath there is usually a short blunt spine, and in either or both upper corners an avicularium. In one instance noted, an avicularian zoöid had usurped the position of an ordinary zoöid, the aperture of the latter appearing as a minute pore immediately above the mandibular apparatus of the former, the zoœcium remaining of the normal size but with partial obliteration of outline. Common. Hastings.

46. *Schizoporella vulgaris*, Moll.*

Hastings.

47. *Schizoporella simplex*, Johnston.

Encrusting old shells. Zoœcia ovate; aperture elevated and with a sinus to the primitive orifice, the matured one being circular. Beneath the aperture, and generally confluent with it, is a blunt prominence. Oœcia with a few irregular spiny protuberances. Not very common; from moderate to deep water. Hastings.

48. *Schizoporella linearis*, Hassall.

Encrusting old shells. Zoœcia oblong, arranged in lines; aperture round, with a small sinus in the lower margin; front wall with pores. Upon one or both sides of the aperture, and a little below, is placed an avicularium pointing towards it. Common. Hastings.

49. *Schizoporella bi-aperta*, Michelin.

Zoœcia more or less oblong; aperture round with a sharp sinus below; front wall plain. Upon one or both sides of the aperture there is a considerable prominence surmounted by an avicularium. Upon *Pecten opercularis*, etc. From moderately deep water; rather rare. Hastings.

50. *Schizoporella auriculata*, Hassall.

Forming round patches upon shells, stones, etc. Zoœcia square to oblong; primary aperture round with a sharp sinus in the lower margin; secondary margin forming a wide loop below, enclosing a short tubular pore (? avicularium). Beneath the aperture is a strong prominence. Oœcium sometimes crescentic, sometimes orbicular. Not uncommon. Hastings.

51. *Schizoporella discoidea*, Busk.

Zoœcia angular, rather short, and with the front wall slightly pitted. Primary aperture has five spines and a narrow sinus; mature orifice circular and raised, but not with an angular or pointed lip as shown in Hincks' figures. Just below, and to the right or left of the aperture, there is a small round avicularium. The oœcia greatly overlap the zoœcia. Rather rare. Hastings.

52. *Schizoporella hyalina*, Linnæus.

Encrusting seaweed. Zoœcia with a satin-like gloss, ovate but tapering and curved below. The aperture is round and has a small sinus in the lower lip, beneath which there is a slight umbo. Not uncommon. Hastings.

53. *Schizoporella venusta*, Norman.

Upon dead shells. Zoœcia glistening, lozenge-shaped to sexagonal; aperture subovate, slightly disjunct, below which there is a prominence. From moderate to deep water; rather rare. Hastings.

54. *Mastigophora hyndmanni*, Johnston.

Zoœcium ovate; aperture sub-circular with a narrow sinus; upon either side is situated a considerably modified avicularium, of which the chamber outline is often preserved. The mandible is greatly elongated, even more so than in *Microporella ciliata*, and has now more the appearance of a tapering stick or whip, and is termed by Hincks a vibraculum. Encrusting an old scallop shell from deep water; rare. Hastings.

55. *Schizotheca fissa*, Busk.

Zoœcia ovate, small, short; aperture elevated, with six spines and a narrow sinus in the lower lip; oœcium sub-crescentic or with a wedge-shaped fissure in the middle. Upon an old scallop shell from deep water; rare. Hastings.

56. *Hippothoa divaricata*, Lamouroux.

Colonies composed of oval zoœcia arranged in single sequence and connected together by tubular prolongations. Lateral branches are given off at an open angle and unite with others; the aperture is circular but with a narrow sinus below; beneath the aperture runs a thickened, longitudinal, median ridge. Common upon shells and stones from moderately deep water. Hastings.

57. *Hippothoa flagellum*, Manzoni.

Similar in habit to the last species, but the zoœcia are farther apart, the interval being usually equal in length to two zoœcia, whereas in *divaricata* it is usually equal to the length of one. The aperture is egg-shaped, and there is no median ridge. Common. Hastings.

58. *Rhyncopora bi-spinosa*, Johnston.

A species encrusting old shells, and one subject to several modifications in the region of the aperture, the margin of which is sometimes produced into two lateral and vertical processes; at others, one of these may be bent across the aperture, or may become central. A fairly constant feature is a more or less spinous mucro rising from beneath the aperture. There is often too a large avicularium mounted upon a broad pedestal, taking the place of this mucro, and generally placed rather laterally. One specimen obtained is found enveloping a colony of the hydroid *Hydractinia echinata*, itself encrusting the shell of a *Nassa*. The oœcia upon this specimen are particularly plentiful. Trawled; rather rare. Hastings.

Escharidæ

59. *Lepralia pollasiana*, Moll.

A hardy looking species encrusting rocks at low tide. Aperture large, more deeply arched than a semicircle; front wall pitted. Common. Hastings.

60. *Lepralia foliacea*, Ellis and Solander.

This species forms large masses of foliated and anastomosing laminæ, the zoœcia being disposed on both sides of the laminæ. The zoœcia are ovate, and have large pores over the front wall. Aperture horse-shoe-shaped, with sometimes a slight prominence beneath. Habitat, rather deep water. Somewhat scarce. Hastings.

61. *Lepralia pertusa*, Esper.

Encrusting old shells. Zoœcia oval, with a circular aperture, of which the lower margin is slightly disjunct; beneath is a process, tri-radiate in form; wall of zoœcium poriferous. It may be noted that young zoœcia of *Smittia cheilostoma* before the development of the sinus closely resemble the zoœcia of this species. From moderately deep water; rather rare. Hastings.

62. *Lepralia adpressa*, Busk.

Colonies encrusting small shells, e.g. whelk, *Natica*, *Trochus*. The zoœcia are ovate, pitted, and have a boss at either or both corners of the aperture. The latter is horseshoe shaped, the sides being slightly indented; from moderately deep water; somewhat rare. Hastings.

63. *Lepralia nitidula*, Hincks, MS.
Hastings.

64. *Porella concinna*, Busk.

A species encrusting shells and stones and showing much variation. The zoœcia are coffin-shaped, or various in form, and has an opalescent lustre. The margin is often deeply sinuous, almost dove-tailed, and is perforated along the border. Aperture horseshoe shaped, with two spines in marginal zoœcia and a prominence below. Very common. From moderate to deep water. Hastings.

65. *Smittia lanasborovii*, Johnston.

Zoœcia crystalline, oblong or coffin-shaped, with perforations in the front wall. Aperture nearly round and raised into a collar, with a small avicularium upon the lower lip. Not uncommon upon rock from deep water. Hastings.

66. *Smittia reticulata*, McGillivray.

In this species there is a deep sinus in the lower lip, and instead of an avicularium there, as in the last species, there is a larger one below, pointing downwards and looking like a pendant from a neck. Above the aperture there are either two or three spines, and the margin of the zoœcia is bordered with pits or vacancies. Hincks remarks upon an instance where two zoœcia side by side have a single wide oœcium

MARINE ZOOLOGY

in common. The writer has observed nearly the same phenomenon, and in a specimen before him the union of two oœcia is seen in different phases of completeness. The cause is evidently overcrowding, the zoœcia in which it occurs being extremely narrow. Associated with the last species ; not uncommon. Hastings.

67. *Smittia cheilostoma*, Manzoni.

Occurring as light red patches upon old shells and stones. Zoœcia coffin-shaped, rather pointed below ; front wall perforated ; aperture raised, sub-circular, but with a large sinus in the lower margin ; within is seen a flat-topped process. As already stated elsewhere, the immature zoœcia of this species resemble nearly the zoœcia of *Lepralia pertusa*. Common from deep water. Hastings.

68. *Smittia trispinosa*, Johnston.

Forming large buff-coloured patches upon old shells, stones, etc. Aperture raised, sharp, with a sinus in the lower lip, and in some cases four spines above. Below the aperture on one side, and pointing towards it, is an avicularium ; and around the margin of the zoœcium are a series of pits or perforations. From moderate to deep water ; very common. Hastings.

69. *Phylactella labrosa*, Busk.

Upon shells. Zoœcia ovate, short, perforated, and arranged in single divergent lines. The aperture is round, raised and expanded, and shows a small denticle within. From deep water ; somewhat rare. Hastings.

70. *Phylactella collaris*, Norman.

Colonies more compact than in the last species. The front wall is plain, and there is no denticle upon the lower lip of the aperture, which is sometimes slightly pointed. Upon old shells. From moderate to deep water ; not very common. Hastings.

71. *Mucronella peachii*, Johnston.

Encrusting dead shells, stones, etc. Zoœcia ovate to lozenge-shaped ; aperture round, with six spines around the upper margin ; upon the lower lip, within, is a double-pointed denticle, and upon the outer lip a small conical tooth. The area below the aperture is rather swollen. Common from moderate to deep water. Hastings.

72. *Mucronella ventricosa*, Hassall.

This species much resembles the last, but comparison, by the aid of a handglass only, will show colonies to be of coarser grain, or composed of larger zoœcia. These are ventricose, the aperture has four instead of two spines, and there is a tongue-like process projecting from immediately below the lower lip. Common upon shells from deep water. Hastings.

73. *Mucronella variolosa*, Johnston.

Colonies encrusting dead shells. When in good condition they have a strong violet lustre. The zoœcia are coffin-shaped and pitted around the margin ; aperture, round to subquadrate, with two long spines upon the upper rim, and a small process or tooth upon the lower one ; behind which is seen a flat-topped process. Common from moderate to deep water. Hastings.

74. *Mucronella coccinea*.

A very handsome species of a violet lustre. The zoœcia are rather short, wide, and with marbled markings. The aperture in marginal zoœcia is circular, with six spines upon the upper rim and a pointed process upon the lower lip. Upon both the right and left side of the aperture is a formidable-looking avicularium, one of them sometimes being very large. Not uncommon upon rock and other objects from deep water. Hastings.

Mucronella coccinea var. *mammilata*, answering exactly to Hincks' description, occurs also at Hastings. Upon shell of *Pectunculus glycymeris*.

75. *Palmicellaria skenei*, Ellis and Solander.*
Hastings.

CELLEPORIDÆ
76. *Cellepora pumicosa*, Linnæus.

This species by successive layers of zoœcia forms rounded masses of a few inches in diameter, upon scallop and other shells. The zoœcia are oval, upright, with circular aperture, and a long, pointed rostrum arising from beneath it, and carrying a small avicularium. Common from deep water. Hastings.

77. *Cellepora avicularis*, Hincks.*
Hastings.

78. *Cellepora costazii*, Audouin.*
Hastings.

Cellepora costazii var. *tubulosa*, Hincks.*
Hastings.

91

79. *Cellepora ramulosa*, Linnæus.

Partially encases the stems of corallines. The zoœcia are ovate to tubular, with a stout prominence beneath the aperture but not so vertical as in *C. pumicosa*, and with a rather large avicularium at the base, and upon the inner surface. Very common from the coralline zone. Hastings.

CYCLOSTOMATA

Crisiidæ

80. *Crisia cornuta*, Linnæus.

Colonies forming erect, feather-like growths upon seaweed and corallines. The zoœcia are tubular and curved, giving off other zoœcia from behind in single series. Near the base of each zoœcium there is a horny joint ; and in many cases at the side, and a little way below the aperture, there occurs a long, tapering, curved spine also having horny joints. Common from moderately deep water. Hastings.

A variety without spines, but not of Hincks' *geniculata* type, also occurs somewhat rarely at Hastings.

81. *Crisia eburnea*, Linnæus.

Of similar habit to the last species. The zoœcia are biserial and alternate with only the ends free. Horny joints occur at intervals along the stem and branches, but always at the commencement of each branch. The oœcia are pear-shaped, and occupy the position of a zoœcium.

Crisia eburnea var. *aculeata*, Hassall, with a long jointed spine upon the off-side of the aperture, also occurs, together with the type, at Hastings, both being rather common.

82. *Crisia denticulata*, Lamarck.

Much like the last species, but the zoœcia are more compact, not so elongated, apertures not so distant, more opposite, and the space between the two lines of zoœcia is greater ; the habit moreover is straighter. Not very common. Hastings.

Tubuliporidæ

83. *Stomatopora granulata*, Milne-Edwards.*
Hastings.

84. *Stomatopora major*, Johnson.

A species forming little straggling, irregularly-branching colonies upon rock, shells, etc. The zoœcia are tubular and number in the widest part as many as seven abreast, the number increasing with the length of the branch. The anterior ends of the zoœcia curve upwards and are free,

showing a circular aperture. This occurs either irregularly or, as is often the case, in rows. Not uncommon from moderately deep water. Hastings.

85. *Entolophora clavata*, Busk.*
Hastings.

86. *Tubulipora lobulata*, Hassall.

Encrusting shells, and forming somewhat radiatingly lobed or branching colonies, of a mauve colour. The tubular zoœcia are enlarged in the upper part, but contract toward the aperture which is upturned and free. The primary tubes multiply rapidly, producing fan-like expansion of the lobes. From deep water ; somewhat rare. Hastings.

87. *Tubulipora flabellaris*, Fabricius.

Forming thin, flat, fan-like colonies upon scallop and other shells. Apertures slightly enlarged and raised. The oœcia are seen as oval expansions occupying the width of three or four zoœcia. From deep water; common. Hastings.

88. *Idmonea serpens*, Linnæus.

Exquisite, mauve or purple coloured colonies, upon corallines, flustra, etc. The upturned anterior ends of the tubular zoœcia occur mainly in rows, upon either side of a central parting. Colonies branch by dividing. Not uncommon from moderately deep water. Hastings.

89. *Diastopora patina*, Lamarck.

Colonies forming little white discs of radiating tubular zoœcia, upon stone, corallines, etc. Occasionally colonies take a concave form. Around a small area in the centre the anterior ends of the zoœcia are erect and free, but outside remain horizontal and do not rise above the common matrix. Around the edge of the colony is seen the white border of a fine calcareous carpet, spread around for the due reception of the dainty polypides. Rather common from moderate to deep water. Hastings.

90. *Diastopora obelia*, Johnston.

Encrusting shells, etc. The zoœcia radiate from a centre, the apertures being barely elevated above the colonial crust. Lines forming the boundary between the adjacent rows of zoœcia, sinuous and distinctly marked. Dotted here and there between the apertures are small tubular orifices, reproducing in miniature the zoœcial apertures. Very common from deep water. Hastings.

91. *Diastopora sarniensis*, Norman.

Forming encrusting patches upon shells and rocks. The zoœcia radiate from a centre, the anterior ends curving upwards and being free. The apertures are elliptical and alternate, and in many cases closed, except as regards a small tubular orifice which projects from the operculum. There is a plain white basal border surrounding the colony. Common from deep water. Hastings.

92. *Diastopora sub-orbicularis.*

Colonies forming circular crusts upon dead shells. The zoœcia radiate from a centre, the apertures being elliptical, alternate, and only occasionally raised. Zoœcia and opercula minutely perforated. From deep water ; not very common. Hastings.

Lichenoporidæ

93. *Lichenopora hispida*, Fleming.

This species forms little mounds consisting of tubular zoœcia arranged radially, the free ends projecting beyond the common matrix ; the apertures are thrown into several sharp points. Colonies also occur in compound form of greater extent, the surface appearing dimpled. There is a wide border of the basal layer displayed around the colonies. Very common upon shells from deep water. Hastings.

CTENOSTOMATA

Alcyonidiidæ

94. *Alcyonidium gelatinosum*, Linnæus.

Colonies consisting of zoöids embedded in irregularly lobed masses of a gelatinous matrix. Specimens from deep water are often very large and intricately lobed. Colonies are smooth and of a light buff or brown-green colour. Common. Hastings.

95. *Alcyonidium hirsutum*, Fleming.

In occasional years this species is found covering weed at low tide in profuse masses. The surface of colonies is mammilated and the colour a buff-brown. Hastings.

96. *Alcyonidium parasiticum*, Fleming.

Forming inconsiderable colonies upon coralline stems ; colour, grey-brown. When the zoöids are withdrawn the surface is thrown somewhat into wrinkles. From the coralline zone ; not common. Hastings.

97. *Alcyonidium mytili*, Dalyell.*
Hastings.

Flustrellidæ

98. *Flustrella hispida*, Fabricius.*
Somewhat rare. Hastings.

Vesiculariidæ

99. *Vesicularia spinosa*, Linnæus.

This species forms erect, horny, branching growths of fine texture, and when dry resembles in colour and appearance so many strands of tow. The main stems are bent in zig-zag manner, giving off branches at each bend, but they are concealed by a number of finer, climbing tubes which also branch. The zoœcia are ovately cylindrical and are arranged uniserially and equidistantly upon the branches. Not uncommon from moderate to deep water. Hastings.

100. *Amathea londigera*, Linnæus.

Forms little intricate masses, consisting of horny, branching stems bearing at regular intervals linear groups of about eight zoœcia, resembling in imagination so many little sacks stacked together. The stems repeatedly divide, the division taking place immediately after each group of zoœcia Upon weed, etc., from moderately deep water. Not uncommon. Hastings.

101. *Bowerbankia imbricata*, Adams.†
Brighton.

102. *Bowerbankia pustulosa*, Ellis and Solander.

Little shrub-like growths of about $1\frac{1}{2}$ inches in height. Zoarium horny, brown in the lower parts, and branching at an angle of about 30°. The zoœcia are ovately cylindrical and occur in biserial and slightly spiral order at the end of each branch, or immediately before re-branching takes place. Upon trawled rock ; rare. Hastings.

103. *Farrella repens*, Farre.*
Hastings.

Farrella repens var. *elongata.**
Hastings.

Buskiidæ

104. *Buskia nitens*, Alder.*
Hastings.

Cylindrœciidæ

105. *Anguinella palmata*, Van Beneden.

Occurring in pendent, mud-coloured clusters upon rocks at low tide. Length from 3 to 4 inches. The stems, with their short and palmate branches, are rather catkin-like. The zoœcia are long and tubular, and do not differ in appearance from the axis. Colonies in texture are rather india-rubber-like. Common. Hastings.

VALKERIIDÆ

106. *Valkeria uva*, Linnæus.

Favourite habitat, over-running *Corallina afficinalis*. Zoœcia ovately cylindrical, slightly narrowing towards the aperture. Rather common. Hastings.

Valkeria uva var. *cuscuta*.*
Hastings.

ENTOPROCTA

PEDICELLINEA

PEDICELLINIDÆ

107. *Pedicellina cernua*, Pallas.

Species over-running *Corallina officinalis*, throwing up short pedicels, each bearing a polypide and a zoœcium at the top. The pedicel is spinous, and as in the other members of this genus, flexible, which is demonstrated by the zoöid making a motion as of bowing or nodding. In this species the pedicel tapers slightly towards the top, but is not constricted at the apex, as in *P. nutans*; and further the zoöid is greatly more protuberant upon the anal than upon the oral side.

Pedicellina cernua var. *glabra*, having a smooth pedicel, also occurs at Hastings together with the type. Both are common.

108. *Pedicellina nutans*, Dalyell.*
Hastings.

109. *Pedicellina gracilis*, Sars.*
Hastings.

ECHINODERMA

HOLOTHUROIDEA

1. *Synapta inhærens*, O. F. Müller.

Specimens wormlike, of a pale flesh colour; about 2 inches in length and $\frac{1}{8}$ inch in diameter. The body has no podia; the tentacles are twelve in number and bi-laterally lobed. Spicules occur in the form of anchors and perforated plates; the latter are egg-shaped in outline, and both are devoid of serrations. On some occasions the fishermen's nets are choked with these creatures. Rare generally. Hastings.

2. *Cucumaria pentactes*, Forbes.†
Brighton.

3. *Cucumaria lactea*, Forbes and Goodsir.

Animal about $1\frac{1}{4}$ inches in length, of a light chocolate-brown colour. Podia alternate, in five rows; discs of suckers, white. There are ten dendriform tentacles which, together with the disc, are of a light buff colour freckled with brown, the tentacles becoming quite pale towards the tips. The spicules are nodulated, perforated plates. A single specimen trawled half a mile from shore. Rare. Hastings.

4. *Thyone fusus*, O. F. Müller.

Specimens about 3 inches in length, flesh-coloured to pink; test rather delicate. The podia are numerous and scattered generally over the body, but in some cases show a tendency to longitudinal arrangement. The tentacles are dendroidal, and ten in number, two of them being smaller than the others and having red cores; these two tentacles are constantly applied to the mouth. The tentacles and disc are powdered with brown over the pink ground, and the mouth is of a dark brown. The spicules are sub-rectangular tables with two-legged central pieces. From the Diamond Ground; rare. Hastings.

5. *Thyone fusus* (?), O. F. Müller.

Specimens white, barely $\frac{1}{2}$ inch in length, probably immature. The podia are plentiful and scattered, displaying however some longitudinal arrangement. The spicules are perforated tables with two-legged central pieces, the immature ones being somewhat lozenge-shaped, and the mature ones ovate to sub-quadrangular. There is some little variation between the tables of these specimens and those of the last species, but they are probably referable to the same species. Associated with scallops. Shoreham.

6. *Phyllophorus drummondi*, Thompson.

Specimens white, about 5 inches in length, tapering below; test rather tough. The podia are scattered rather thinly, and occur to some extent along longitudinal lines. Tentacles seventeen in number, dendroidal, alternating in size; stems of tentacles rather brown, mouth of a dark brown. Spicular tables rather large, circular to sub-quadrangular in outline. From the Diamond Ground; rare. Hastings.

7. *Holothuria nigra*, Kinahan.†
Brighton.

ASTEROIDEA

ASTERINIDÆ

8. *Palmipes placenta*, Penn.

Species with five arms connected by a

web. Not uncommon in the trawl. Hastings.

SOLASTERIDÆ

9. *Solaster papposus*, Fabricius.

The 'sun' starfish, usually having thirteen rays and covered with spinous papillæ. Colour, purplish red. Not uncommon in the trawl. Hastings.

ECHINASTERIDÆ

10. *Henricia sanguinolenta*, O. F. Müller.* Hastings.

ASTERIIDÆ

11. *Asterias rubens*, Linnæus.

The common five-fingered starfish. Very common. Hastings.

12. *Asterias hispida*, Penn.† Brighton.

13. *Asterias aurantiaca*.† Brighton.

OPHIUROIDEA

OPHIOLEPIDIDÆ

14. *Ophiura ciliaris*, Linnæus.

This species has five arms, smooth and snake-like, and is of a grey-buff colour. Common in the trawl. Hastings.

15. *Ophiura albida*, Forbes.† Brighton.

OPHIOTHRYCIDÆ

16. *Ophiothrix fragilis*, Abilg.

Species with five very spiny arms, and one in which the variation in colouring is absolutely infinite. The most usual colours are white, salmon, pink, red, sage-green, grey, brown, etc. When handled alive they readily detach fragments of the arms, so that it is almost impossible to secure a complete specimen. When however the fishermen's nets are hung up to dry and the brittle stars are allowed to dry unhandled they may be taken in perfect condition, the arms displaying every possible curve and contortion. They are known by the fishermen as 'castle cats.' Not a shore species. Hastings.

AMPHIURIDÆ

17. *Amphiura elegans*, Leach.

A small species, common upon the rocks at low water. Hastings.

18. *Ophiocnida brachiata*, Montague.

A species with five very long arms. Rare. Hastings.

ECHINOIDEA

ECHINIDÆ

19. *Echinus esculentus*, Linnæus.
(?) Hastings.* Brighton.†

20. *Echinus miliaris*, Gmel.

Test circular, mouth central, anus apical; colour purple. Very common in the trawl and sometimes met with at extreme low tide. Hastings.

21. *Strongylocentrotus lividus*, Lamarck.† Brighton.

22. *Strongylocentrotus drœbachiensis*, O. F. Müller.† Brighton.

CLYPEASTRIDÆ

23. *Echinocyamus pusillus*, O. F. Müller.

A small depressed, heart-shaped species, measuring about $\frac{1}{4}$ inch in length ; colour, green ; mouth, central ; vent, midway between the mouth and margin. Trawled ; not uncommon. Hastings.

SPATANGIDÆ

24. *Spatangus purpureus*, O. F. Müller.

A large heart-shaped, purple species. The mouth is situated midway between the centre and the margin ; the spines upon the under surface are a favourite habitat of the minute bivalve mollusc *Montacuta substriata*. Trawled in rather deep water ; somewhat rare. Hastings.

25. *Echinocardium cordatum*, Penn.

Species heart-shaped, with rather fine spines ; colour, grey ; test, mouse-like ; mouth midway between the centre and the margin. Rather common in the trawl, and occasionally cast on shore. Hastings.

BRACHIOPODA
INARTICULATA

CRANIIDÆ

1. *Crania anomala*.† Brighton.

MOLLUSCA
AMPHINEURA
POLYPLACOPHORA

CHITONIDÆ

1. *Tonicella ruber*, Lowe.† Brighton.

2. *Callochiton lævis*, Montague.† Brighton.

A HISTORY OF SUSSEX

3. *Craspedochilus onyx*, Spengler.

Trawled upon rock from rather deep water ; common.   Hastings.

4. *Craspedochilus albus*, Linnæus.†
Brighton.

5. *Craspedochilus cinereus*, Linnæus.

Upon rocks near low water ; not uncommon.   Hastings.

6. *Acanthochiets fascicularis*, Linnæus.

Common upon rocks at low tide.   Hastings.

PELECYPODA

PROTOBRANCHIA

NUCULIDÆ

7. *Nucula nucleus*, Linnæus.

Common from the coralline zone.   Hastings.

8. *Nucula nitida*, Sowerby.*
Somewhat rare.   Hastings.

9. *Nuculana minuta* var. *brevirostris*, Jeffreys.

Rare.   Rye Bay.

FILIBRANCHIA

ANOMIACEA

ANOMIIDÆ

10. *Anomia ephippium*, Linnæus.

Not uncommon upon trawled rock, etc. Hastings.

Anomia ephippium var. *aculeata*, Müller.
Small ; rare.   Hastings.

11. *Anomia patelliformis*, Linnæus.

Often within or upon other dead bivalve shells.   Not uncommon ; trawled.   Hastings.

ARCACEA

ARCIDÆ

12. *Glycymeris glycymeris*, Linnæus.
Common upon the Diamond Ground. Hastings.

Glycymeris glycymeris var. *pilosa*, Linnæus.
Common.   Hastings.

Glycymeris glycymeris (?) var. *globosa*, Jeffreys.
Hastings.

13. *Barbatia lactea*, Linnæus.
Rather rare.   Hastings.

MYTILACEA

MYTILIDÆ

14. *Mytilus edulis*, Linnæus.
Very common.   Hastings.

Mytilus edulis var. *pellucida*, Pennant.
Somewhat rare.   Hastings.

15. *Volsella modiola*, Linnæus.
Not uncommon.   Hastings.

16. *Volsella barbata*, Linnæus.

Upon trawled rock and shells ; common.   Hastings.

17. *Volsella adriatica*, Lamarck.*
Very rare.   Hastings.

18. *Modiolaria marmorata*, Forbes.

Harboured within the tests of *Tunicates*, and amongst the root fibres of the hydroid *Antennularia*.   Not very common.   Hastings.

19. *Modiolaria discors*, Linnæus.†
Brighton.

PSEUDOLAMELLIBRANCHIA

OSTREIDÆ

20. *Ostrea edulis*, Linnæus.
Common.   Hastings.

PECTINIDÆ

21. *Pecten maximus*, Linnæus.

The scallops from the English side of the Channel are much covered with animal growth ; those from the French side are much cleaner and more variegated in colour. The winter of 1895–6 was so severe that the cold killed off all the scallops from the Hastings grounds, and the beds have not as yet been replenished, only one or two being occasionally taken.   Hastings.

22. *Hinnites pusio*, Linnæus.

Upon trawled rock, etc.   Rather rare. Hastings.

23. *Chlamys varius*, Linnæus.

A shell running through many most delicate shades of yellow, orange, puce and brown.   Moored by the byssus to rocks, dead shells, etc. ; trawled.   Hastings.

24. *Æquipecten opercularis*, Linnæus.

Shell displaying every shade of colour between white, yellow, orange, brown and purple, with combinations of these colours.

96

Æquipecten opercularis var. *lineata*, da Costa.

Shell with lines of a darker colour than the ground running down each rib. Both forms common. Hastings.

LIMIDÆ

25. *Lima subauriculata*, Montague.*
Hastings.

26. *Lima loscombi*, Sowerby.†
Brighton.

27. *Lima hians*, Gmelin.†
Brighton.

EULAMELLIBRANCHIA
SUBMYTILACEA

CYPRINIDÆ

28. *Cyprina islandica*, Linnæus.
Rather rare. Hastings.

LUCINIDÆ

29. *Lucina borealis*, Linnæus.
Rather rare. Hastings.

30. *Montacuta substriata*, Montague.

Habitat upon the spines of the underside of the sea-urchin, *Spatangus purpureus*. From the Diamond Ground, off Hastings.

LEPTONIDÆ

31. *Kellia suborbicularis*, Montague.*
Rare. Hastings.

TELLINACEA

SCROBICULARIIDÆ

32. *Syndosmya prismatica*, Montague.
Rather rare. Hastings.

33. *Syndosmya alba*, Wood.
Common. Hastings.

34. *Scrobicularia plana*, da Costa.

Occurring at the mouth of the Rother and in the channels leading into it. Common. Rye Harbour.

TELLINIDÆ

35. *Tellina crassa*, Gmelin.

From the Diamond Ground. Not uncommon. Hastings.

36. *Tellina tenuis*, da Costa.

A delicate little shell of various colours: white, yellow, pink, buff. Common. Hastings.

37. *Tellina fabula*, Gronovius.

Shell in appearance somewhat like that of the last species, but not so large, and the right valve is lined with diagonal striations. Common. Hastings.

38. *Macoma balthica*, Linnæus.

A small, strong shell; colour, white, yellow, or red. Common. Hastings.

DONACIDÆ

39. *Donax vittatus*, da Costa.

At low water this species may be detected in large communities by the little mounds of sand which they cast up in digging into the sand with the foot. Very common. Hastings.

MACTRIDÆ

40. *Mactra stultorum*, Linnæus.

Very common upon the sand shore. Hastings.

Mactra stultorum var. *cinerea*, Montague.
Not uncommon. Hastings.

41. *Spisula solida*, Linnæus.
Rare. Hastings.

42. *Spisula elliptica*, Brown.
Trawled; somewhat rare. Hastings.

43. *Spisula subtruncata*, da Costa.

Shell triangular, thick in the umbonal region; rather rare. Hastings.

44. *Lutraria elliptica*, Lamarck.

Trawled upon the Diamond Ground; not uncommon. Hastings.

45. *Lutraria oblonga*, Chemnitz.

Single valves only taken, and those in a very deteriorated condition. Trawled; rather rare. Hastings.

VENERACEA

VENERIDÆ

46. *Lucinopsis undata*, Pennant.
Trawled; rather rare. Hastings.

47. *Dosinia exoleta*, Linnæus.*
Rare. Hastings.

48. *Dosinia lupina* (*lincta*), Linnæus.
Rather rare. Hastings.

49. *Venus fasciata*, da Costa.
Brighton.

50. *Venus casina*, Linnæus.

Shell pale in colour; ornamented with concentric ribs or lamellæ; rare. Hastings.

51. *Venus verrucosa*, Linnæus.

Ornamentation resembling that of the last species, but the ribs are less pronounced except in front and behind, where they are interrupted and form folds. Not uncommon. Hastings.

52. *Venus ovata*, Pennant.

Shell small, radiately ribbed, and with fine concentric lines; rather rare. Hastings.

53. *Venus gallina*, Linnæus.*

Very rare. Hastings.

54. *Tapes virgineus*, Linnæus.

Shell laterally compressed, polished. Colour more or less in rays, undulatory. Trawled; common. Hastings.

55. *Tapes pullastra*, Montague.

Very common. Hastings.

Tapes pullastra var. *perforans*, Montague.

Shell rather smaller than the type; not so deep from umbo to margin; common. Hastings.

56. *Tapes decussatus*, Linnæus.

Shell somewhat quadrangular, strongly cancellated with radial and concentric lines; somewhat scarce. Hastings.

CARDIACEA
CARDIIDÆ

57. *Cardium echinatum*, Linnæus.

Common. Hastings.

58. *Cardium exiguum*, Gmelin.*

Very rare. Hastings.

59. *Cardium nodosum*, Turton.

A single valve only; rare. Hastings.

60. *Cardium edule*, Linnæus.

Common. Rye.

61. *Cardium norvegicum*, Spengler.

Common in the trawl. Hastings.

MYACEA
GARIDÆ

62. *Gari ferrœnsis* (Chemnitz).

Brighton.

MYIDÆ

63. *Mya truncata*, Linnæus.

A coarse shell, mainly conspicuous by the membranous, siphonal sheath; common. Hastings.

64. *Mya arenaria*, Linnæus.

A single valve only taken, and that of an immature specimen; rare. Hastings.

65. *Sphenia binghami*, Turton.*

Rare. Hastings.

SOLENIDÆ

66. *Solecurtus scopula*, Turton, var. *oblonga*, Jeffreys.

Shell proportionately not so deep from

umbo to margin as in the type. Trawled about 25 miles off Beachy Head; rare. Hastings.

67. *Cultellus pellucidus*, Pennant.†

Brighton.

68. *Ensis ensis*, Linnæus.

Shell curved, small; very common. Hastings.

69. *Ensis siliqua*, Linnæus.

Shell nearly straight; somewhat common. Hastings.

70. *Solen vagina*, Linnæus.

Shell short and straight.

SAXICAVIDÆ

71. *Saxicava rugosa*, Linnæus.

This little ugly deformed shell is found boring into the hardest rock. Not uncommon. Hastings.

GASTROCHÆNIDÆ

72. *Gastrochæna dubia*, Pennant.†

Brighton.

PHOLADACEA
PHOLADIDÆ

73. *Pholas dactylus*, Linnæus.

Shell large, delicate and white. Animal with boring propensities; common. Hastings.

74. *Barnea candida*, Linnæus.

Common. Hastings.

75. *Barnea parva*, Pennant.*

Somewhat rare. Hastings.

76. *Zirfæa crispata*, Linnæus.

Shell short and deep; not uncommon. Hastings.

TEREDINIDÆ

77. *Teredo navalis*, Linnæus.†

Brighton.

ANATINACEA
PANDORIDÆ

78. *Pandora inæquivalvis*, Linnæus.

Shell with the left valve flat, and the right one convex; rather rare. Hastings.

Pandora inæquivalvis var. *pinna*, Montague.

Shell not so produced in front as in the type; rather rare. Hastings.

LYONSIIDÆ

79. *Lyonsia norvegica* (Chemnitz)†

Brighton.

MARINE ZOOLOGY

ANATINIDÆ

80. *Thracia fragilis*, Pennant.
Rare. Rye Harbour.

Thracia fragilis var. *villosiuscula*, MacGillivray.
Brighton.†

SEPTIBRANCHIA

CUSPIDARIIDÆ

81. *Cuspidaria cuspidata* (Olivi) †
Brighton.

SCAPHOPODA

DENTALIIDÆ

82. *Dentalium vulgare*, da Costa.
Very common. Hastings.

83. *Dentalium entalis*, Linnæus.†
Brighton.

GASTROPODA
PROSOBRANCHIA
ASPIDOBRANCHIA

PATELLIDÆ

84. *Patella vulgata*, Linnæus.
The limpet; very common. Hastings.

Patella vulgata var. *depressa*.
Brighton.†

85. *Helcion pellucidum*, Linnæus.
A specimen shows alternate rays of blue and brown upon a dull orange ground; rare. Hastings.

ACMÆIDÆ

86. *Acmæa virginea* (Müller)
Shell pink, with interrupted lines of colour; rare. Hastings.

FISSURELLIDÆ

87. *Emarginula fissura*, Linnæus.
Shell depressed, with a marginal slit in front; rare. Hastings.

88. *Emarginula conica*, Schumacher.
Shell more conical than that of the last species; not uncommon upon trawled rock. Hastings.

89. *Fissurella græca*, Linnæus.
The 'key-hole' limpet. Shell cancellated with radial and concentric ribs, and having an apical perforation; somewhat rare. Hastings.

TROCHIDÆ

90. *Gibbula magus*, Linnæus.
Shell depressed, with large umbilicus; common. Hastings.

91. *Gibbula tumida*, Montague.*
Rare. Hastings.

92. *Gibbula cineraria*, Linnæus.
Shell slightly turreted; common. Hastings.

93. *Gibbula umbilicata*, Montague.
Shell conical, sides slightly convex; common. Hastings.

94. *Calliostoma montagui*, Wood.
Shell rather high in the spire, with spiral ridges, and fine striæ crossing the intervening furrows; rare. Hastings.

95. *Calliostoma exasperatum*, Pennant.†
Brighton.

96. *Calliostoma granulatum* (Born)
Shell acutely conical, granulated; sides slightly concave; not uncommon. Hastings.

Calliostoma granulatum var. *lactea*, Jeffreys.
Similar to the type, but white; rather rare. Hastings.

97. *Calliostoma zizyphinus*, Linnæus.
Shell acutely conical, sides straight, whorls spirally lined; common. Hastings.

Calliostoma zizyphinus var. *lyonsi*, Leach.
Shell white and nearly smooth; rather uncommon. Hastings.

TURBINIDÆ

98. *Phasianella pulla*.
Shell small, conical, and with lines of red running diagonally across the whorls; very rare. Hastings.

PECTINIBRANCHIA

LITTORINIDÆ

99. *Lacuna crassior*, Montague.
Periostracum horny-looking, wrinkled concentrically; rare. Hastings.

100. *Lacuna divaricata* (Fabricius)
Brighton.

101. *Lacuna parva* (da Costa)
Brighton.

102. *Lacuna pallidula* (da Costa)
Brighton.

103. *Littorina obtusata*, Linnæus.
Shell with low spire. Colour, canary or orange; common. Hastings.

104. *Littorina littorea*, Linnæus.
The edible periwinkle; very common. Hastings.

105. *Littorina rudis* (Maton)†
Brighton.

Littorina rudis var. *saxatilis*, Johnston.
Brighton.†

Littorina rudis var. *tenebrosa*, Montague.
Brighton.†

106. '*Littorina canaliculatus.*' †
(Recorded thus) Brighton.

107. '*Littorina lichina.*' †
(Recorded thus) Brighton.

RISSOIIDÆ

108. *Rissoa parva*, da Costa.*
Hastings.

Rissoia parva var. *interrupta*, Adams.
Hastings.

109. *Rissoia inconspicua* var. *ventrosa*,
Jeffreys.†
Brighton.

110. *Rissoia violacea*, Desmarest.†
Brighton.

111. *Alvania lactea* (Michaud)
Hastings.

112. *Manzonia costata* (J. Adams) †
Brighton.

113. *Zippora membranacea* var. *labiosa*,
Montague †
Brighton.

114. *Onoba striata* (J. Adams) *
Hastings.

115. *Cingula semistriata*, Montague.*
Hastings.

PALUDESTRINIDÆ

116. *Paludestrina stagnalis* (Basterot)
Shell conical; whorls smooth and nearly
flat; common. Rye.

Paludestrina stagnalis var. *octona*, Linnæus.
Whorls rather convex; common.
Hastings.

TRUNCATELLIDÆ

117. *Truncatella truncata* (Montague) †
This species is recorded as *T. montagui*.
Brighton.

CYPRÆIDÆ

118. *Trivia europæa*, Montague.*
The only British species; common.
Hastings.

NATICIDÆ

119. *Natica catena* (da Costa)
Shell rather globular, whorls convex,
suture distinct; common. Hastings.

120. *Natica alderi*, Forbes.
Shell half the size of the last species,
very glossy; whorls not so convex, suture
not so deep; common. Hastings.

LAMELLARIIDÆ

121. *Velutina lævigata*, Pennant.
Spire depressed; body-whorl large; rare.
Rye Harbour.

122. *Velutella flexilis*, Montague.†
Brighton.

CERITHIIDÆ

123. *Bittium reticulatum* (da Costa) *
Rare. Hastings.

124. *Cerithiopsis tubercularis*, Montague.*
Hastings.

SCALIDÆ

125. *Scala clathrus*, Linnæus.
Shell spiral; whorls furnished with concentric ribs and mauve coloured spiral lines;
somewhat rare. Hastings.

126. *Scala clathratula*, Adams.*
Rare. Hastings.

127. *Aclis minor*, Brown.*
Very rare. Hastings.

PYRAMIDELLIDÆ

128. *Brachystomia ambigua* (Maton &
Rackett) *
Hastings.

129. *Pyrgulina interstincta* (?) (Montague) *
Hastings.

130. *Pyrgulina clathrata*, Jeffreys.
Brighton.

131. *Spiralinella spiralis*, Montague *
Hastings.

132. *Turbonilla lactea* (Linnæus) *
Hastings.

EULIMIDÆ

133. *Eulima polita*, Linnæus.
Shell white, polished, with long spire
and flattened whorls; rare. Hastings.

TURRITELLIDÆ

134. *Turritella communis*, Lamarck.*
Hastings.

APORRHAIDÆ

135. *Aporrhais pes-pelecani*, Linnæus.*
Hastings.

BUCCINIDÆ

136. *Buccinum undatum*, Linnæus.
The whelk; common. Hastings.
The left-handed monstrosity, the keeled monstrosity and the acuminate form * also occur at Hastings, but are rare.

137. *Donovania minima*, Montague.*
Hastings.

138. *Neptunea antiqua*, Linnæus.*
This species is recorded as 'Fusus antiquus,' Linnæus, and may be received with a little caution, since the animal is often imported into the town with the common whelk, as food, the shells being thrown upon the beach. Hastings.

139. *Tritonofusus gracilis* (Costa)
Shell with the spire not quite in a straight line; somewhat rare. Hastings.

MURICIDÆ

140. *Ocinebra erinacea*, Linnæus.
Common. Hastings.

141. *Ocinebra corallina*, Scacchi.†
Brighton.

142. *Trophon clathratus*, Linnæus.†
(?) British species. Brighton.

143. *Purpura lapillus*, Linnæus.
This species occurs in great variety of colouring, mainly white, yellow, orange or brown. Very common. Hastings.

NASSIDÆ

144. *Nassa reticulata*, Linnæus.
Both this species and the following one are frequenters of the lobster 'pots.' Very common. Hastings.

145. *Nassa incrassata* (Ström)
Very common. Hastings.

146. *Nassa pygmæa*, Lamarck.*
Rare. Hastings.

PLEUROTOMIDÆ

147. *Bela turricula*, Montague.
Common in the trawl, dead shells only having been taken. Hastings.
Bela turricula var. *rosea*, M. Sars.
Rare. Hastings.

148. *Bela rufa*, Montague.*
Somewhat rare. Hastings.

149. *Mangilia costata* (Donovan)
Very rare. Hastings.

150. *Mangilia rugulosa* (Philippi)
Rare. Hastings.

151. *Mangilia nebula* (Montague)†
Brighton.

152. *Clathurella linearis*, Montague.*
Very rare. Hastings.

153. *Clathurella reticulata*, Renier.*
Very rare. Hastings.

OPISTHOBRANCHIA
TECTIBRANCHIA

ACTÆONIDÆ

154. *Actæon tornatilis*, Linnæus.
Rare. Hastings.

SCAPHANDRIDÆ

155. *Scaphander lignarius*, Linnæus.
Rare. Hastings.

156. *Bullinella cylindracea* (Pennant) †
Brighton.

PHILINIDÆ

157. *Philine aperta*, Linnæus.
Rather local; plentiful in Rye Bay. Hastings.

CAVOLINIIDÆ

158. *Cavolinia trispinosa*, Rang.
Very rare. Hastings.

NUDIBRANCHIA

HERMÆIDÆ

159. *Hermæa dendritica*.
Species a little over $\frac{1}{4}$ inch in length, the general colour varying from seaweed green to orange. There is only one pair of tentacles, and they are characteristic of the genus, being folded lengthwise. The papillæ are rather long and overhang the sides and middle of the back, giving to the animal a shaggy appearance. Further characteristic of the species is the dentritic veining, of a deeper colour, which runs down each side of the back supplying offshoots to the tentacles and papillæ, the veins being more or less reticulated. The animal has a habit of contracting the head and tail, and in that condition much resembles a young specimen of the anemone *Actinia mesembryanthemum*, the papillæ representing the tentacles of the anemone. This species is decidedly rare. It occurred at Hastings during a rather hot summer, upon rocks at low spring tides, but has not been observed since. It is very difficult to detect. Hastings.

EOLIDIDÆ

160. *Eolis papillosa*, Linnæus.

A fine species, and one that is always in summer to be found on our coast. Length, about 2 inches. The body is flesh-coloured, powdered with opaque white; the papillæ, which well clothe the sides, are somewhat lanceolate in form and are usually of a seaweed green finely speckled with opaque white. The colours however run through many gradations, as is seen in years of great abundance, when all shades of grey, green, orange, brown and brown-purple make their appearance. Habitat, along the shore under stones and crawling upon mud and sand. Common. Hastings.

161. *Æolidella alderi*, (?) Cocks (? *glauca*).

A single specimen taken upon *Lepralia foliacea* from moderately deep water appears almost intermediate in character between this species and *Æolidella glauca*. In form perhaps the specimen approaches nearer to *Æ. alderi*, but in colouring, size and habitat approximates to *Æ. glauca*. Length of specimen 1 inch, extending when crawling to $1\frac{1}{4}$ inches. The papillæ are neither 'vermicular' nor 'clavate,' but are thickest at about the middle, slightly conical at the apex, where there is in many cases a small pimple-like inflation of the outer membrane. Under magnification the internal gland is of a seaweed green-brown, the sheath and apex being pellucid white superficially and indefinedly banded with opaque sage-green paling to white, with a glow of orange upon the upper portions. The papillæ of the front row are semi-transparent white. The oral tentacles are a little longer than the dorsal ones, and are lightly tinged with orange; the latter are linear and obtuse at the apex and of a bright orange colour tipped with white. The tail is short and not very pointed. From the veil, and extending midway down the back, the colour is a bright orange, paling towards the middle of the back. Hastings.

162. *Cuthona aurantiaca*, Alder and Hancock.

Animal $\frac{1}{3}$ inch in length. The papillæ are rather long; gland of a rosy orange colour finely granulated with red. The apex and sheath are semi-opaque blue-white; below the apex and internally is a zone of opaque white granules; above this zone and overlapping it somewhat is a surface colouring of orange, toning down to yellow. Of the oral tentacles, the sheath is transparent, colourless, and the core semi-opaque white, rather defined. This species bears some resemblance to the following species, but may be distinguished by the absence of foot processes, and by the presence of an orange-coloured zone near the apex of the papillæ. Upon water-logged timber; trawled; rare. Hastings.

163. *Cratena concinna*, Alder and Hancock.

Length of specimen $\frac{1}{2}$ inch. The papillæ are often carried bent; they have a sheath of blue-green or bottle-green, the gland being orange coloured, or brownish-orange speckled with dark brown; but very characteristic is a crown around the apex, formed of linear opaque white granules, arranged perpendicularly to the surface. These are generally very strongly marked, but are occasionally absent, or nearly so. The foot has two blunt processes. Rare. Hastings.

164. *Tergipes despectus*, Johnston.

This little species is barely $\frac{1}{4}$ inch in length, and when met with cannot be confounded with any other. The body is semi-transparent white, with a tinge of red in front of and behind the dorsal tentacles. Upon either side of the back and arising from a central vessel are three or four club-shaped papillæ, with glands of a mottled seaweed-green colour, and apices of opaque white. The only habitat is upon shore hydroids, particularly *Obelia gelatinosa* and *O. geniculata*, where it will probably be first detected by the little globular masses containing the eggs which are deposited upon the stems. It may be noted that the papillæ of this little creature, when gliding over the stems of the hydroid, bear a striking resemblance to the egg capsules of the latter, and hence may reap some immunity from danger. During some years this species is very plentiful. Hastings.

165. *Galvina cingulata*, Alder and Hancock.

Animal $\frac{1}{3}$ inch in length, long and slender and with very tapering tail. The character of the papillæ in this species has very faithfully suggested a comparison to the quills of the 'fretful porcupine.' In the Hastings specimens there are eight rows of papillæ, each papilla having three surface bands of a marbled seaweed-green colour; above these is one of opaque white.

The gland is foliated and of an opaque whitish yellow, and somewhat granular. The papillæ when observed were slightly contracted, and in that condition, which appeared to be more or less normal, they became slightly constricted at each band, thus giving an undulating outline to the papillæ ; the reason for this lay in the fact that the internal gland was narrower at those points. The dorsal tentacles are almost twice the length of the oral ones ; they are long and linear and with obtuse tips, the latter being transparent white with a band of opaque white below, and about midway down there is a patch of seaweed-green colour. In 1900 about half a dozen specimens were taken upon *Plumularia pinnata*, to which had been attached about a dozen of their egg-bands. In the next year two more specimens, together with *Doto coronata*, were taken at low water, upon *Obelia longissima*. In the former instance the resemblance of the papillæ to the egg capsules of the hydroid was rather striking. Rare. Hastings.

166. *Galvina tricolor*, Forbes.

Length of specimen 1 inch. General appearance : animal of a pale orange or buff colour ; papillæ inflated and pointed, those in the front half or two-thirds of the body being tipped with orange ; the hinder papillæ also being orange-tipped, and in addition speckled with dark brown. The dorsal tentacles are colourless and have obscure internal lines of opaque white running down each, to bulbous bases and the eyes. Tail colourless. Closer examination of a papilla shows a constriction near the end, the end portion being divided into three zones of colour ; that nearest the constriction is opaque white with brown-black spots, the next is of orange or pale yellow, and the one at the apex colourless and transparent ; the lower portion of the papilla is semi-opaque white, a deeply lobed gland of a pale straw colour being occasionally seen, which sends a single straight stem-like lobe to the apex. A single specimen trawled from moderately deep water. Rare. Hastings.

167. *Coryphella rufibranchialis*, Johnston.
Eolis pellucida, Alder and Hancock.
Eolis gracilis, Alder and Hancock.

Length of animal, 1¼ inches ; body semi-transparent white. The papillæ are rather long and linear, the apex is pellucid white, below which is nearly always a ring of opaque white, of a granular character, and internal. The sheath is transparent colourless, and the gland of a bright orange-red or coral colour, uneven in outline, squared at the top and leaving only a small margin of the sheath showing. The dorsal tentacles are wrinkled and have a faint tinge of orange, the tips being granulated with opaque white ; they are a little longer than the oral ones, which are also tipped with opaque white granules upon the inner and upper side ; the foot processes are long. In March 1897 an abnormally coloured specimen was obtained from the coralline zone. In this specimen the veil, both pairs of tentacles, and the upper side of the end of the tail were coloured a beautiful mauve violet, excepting the apices of the tentacles which were opaque white. Some of the papillæ also partook somewhat of the mauve colour. Since the above date another specimen taken upon the shore (not its usual habitat) showed the same tendency towards mauve colouring. The deep-water form is much longer, and has papillæ more filamentous than the variety from shallower water. Habitat from moderately shallow water to the coralline zone. Occasionally plentiful. Hastings.

168. *Coryphella landsburgi*, Alder and Hancock.

The length of this beautiful little creature is not much more than $\frac{1}{12}$ inch. Animal in part colourless, semi-transparent, but coloured along the sides of the body, the papillæ and their bases, and over the head and hinder part of the body, with light violet or mauve. Looked at more closely, the central gland is orange, the sheath of a light violet, and there is a band or patch of opaque white near the apex. Both pairs of tentacles are violet for one-third of the way up them, the upper part being transparent white, with a slight patch of opaque white at the apex ; foot processes moderately long. Trawled half a mile from shore upon flustra, where it was only detected by its colour. Rare. Hastings.

169. *Facelina coronata*, Forbes and Goodsir.

In summer this gorgeously coloured species is always more or less with us. The length is 1¼ inches ; the body is pellucid grey slightly speckled with blue. In the papillæ, which are tapering, the core varies in colour from light to dark orange or red-brown ; the sheath is pellucid grey, with an irregular splash of very vivid blue about the centre, and a ring of opaque white around the apex, with spots of opaque white scattered below. The dorsal tentacles are ringed, and are of a pale buff or orange colour, the oral ones being long and sweeping. Habitat, under stones and upon rocks at low tide. Common. Hastings.

170. *Facelina drummondi*, Thompson.

Animal ⅔ inch in length ; body translucent, of a faint rose colour ; back, pale salmon. The dorsal tentacles have from twenty to thirty laminæ, are blunt at the apex which is of a pale orange tint, the tentacle itself being rose-orange and having in front a narrow patch of granular, opalescent white, extending one third of the way down ; there are also spots of a similar character between and in front of the tentacles. The oral tentacles are a trifle longer and more pointed than the dorsal ones, and somewhat similarly coloured. As regards papillæ, notes are unfortunately deficient. Obtained from shrimp trawler. Rare. Hastings.

171. *Antiopa cristata*, delle Chiaje.

An immature specimen barely ¼ inch in length. Body transparent, colourless, or with a slight tinge of buff. The papillæ are inflated, or club-shaped with pointed tips, the foremost three upon either side projecting greatly in advance of the tentacles and appearing to act somewhat as tactile organs, contracting at every contact with any object ; their tips form a broad line in advance of the animal ; the hinder papillæ are large and project considerably beyond the tail. The gland of the papillæ is very narrow and linear, enlarging or dividing near the apex and coloured purplish-brown or greenish-brown, the outer portion being transparent, but of the same hue. The apex is opaque white and where this meets the colour below, the result is a metallic blue. The dorsal tentacles are laminated and are short and blunt, with an opaque white spot at the apex ; between them is a raised and warty frontal piece, coloured buff. A single specimen taken upon weed in a rock pool at low water. Rare. Hastings.

DOTONIDÆ

172. *Doto coronata*, Gmelin.

Animal a little over ½ inch in length, of a pale orange colour, except as regards the foot which is colourless. There is a single pair of tentacles having characteristic

trumpet-mouthed sheaths. Along either side of the body are arranged eight club-shaped papillæ, each one being encircled with about eight equidistant rings of large tubercles, each tubercle having at its apex a distinct black spot ; internally there are opaque white egg-like bodies.

This species is common upon the coralline *Antennularia* to which it attaches its egg-band ; also taken upon *Obelia longissima*. Hastings.

173. *Doto pinnatifida*, Montague.

Animal very similar to the last species, but with a more or less interrupted band down the back of brownish-green ; and along each side of the cloak are from one to three rows of tubercles set alternately, each tubercle containing an opaque white body and in some cases a black speck also. Similar tubercules with like contents occur irregularly down the back, the black specks being conspicuous. These black specks are of peculiar interest since it has been surmised that they may be organs of vision. They also occur around the rim of the tentacle-sheath and on lobular processes arising from the latter. Common upon *Antennularia* from the Diamond Ground. Hastings.

DENDRONOTIDÆ

174. *Dendronotus frondosus*, Ascanius.

Animal mottled light and dark brown, or buff, sometimes almost golden ; in some cases the colour is uniform. Along either side of the back are from six to eight branching, tree-like gills. The tentacles are ringed and arise from a sheath the rim of which also gives off branching processes. Specimens obtained only a little distance from shore are small, that is from 1 to 2 inches in length, but some trawled upon the Diamond Ground must have measured close upon 5 inches. Rather rare. Hastings.

TRITONIIDÆ

175. *Tritonia hombergi*, Cuvier.

Animal fully 3 inches in length ; back warty, and slate coloured. Around the margin of the cloak are arranged rather closely a number of dendriform gills. The tentacles have sheaths and near the apex branched processes are given off. This creature is not prepossessing, being in the preserved condition rather toad-like. Not uncommon from the Diamond Ground. Hastings.

DORIDIDÆ

176. *Archidoris tuberculata*, Cuvier.*

Rather rare ; upon rocks at low water. Hastings.

177. *Jorunna johnstoni*, Alder and Hancock.

A large orange coloured species, nearly smooth. Taken two or three times upon rocks at low spring tides. Rather rare. Hastings.

POLYCERIDÆ

178. *Ægirus punctilucens*, d'Orbigny.†
Brighton.

179. *Palio lessoni*, d'Orbigny.

A single specimen obtained of this species agrees with Alder and Hancock's description in having short tentacles with ten or twelve laminæ, but the body is more ocellated, and the frill across the snout is as in var. *ocellata*. The body is more tuberculated perhaps than in the variety and has the line of tubercles along the head, but there are others also. The animal has the habit of spinning a thread of mucus at the tail and thereby mooring itself to some object ; it is also fond of screwing up the tail end of the foot into a regular disc, and suspending itself by it, from the surface of the water.

Palio lessoni, var. *ocellata*, Alder and Hancock.

Animal of a seaweed-green colour, covered with white or greenish white spots and tubercles. There is a single pair of tentacles which are laminated and of a green colour, in the upper part. The gills consist of three branching plumes facing backwards, and anal aperture being in the centre. Running along each side of the body from the front of the head, and terminating behind the gills in free processes is a pretty little frill. From this point, a line of white spiny tubercles runs down the centre of the tail, and similar tubercles occur generally distributed over the upper portion of the body. This variety during some years is rather plentiful upon rocks and under stones at low water, but in others it appears to be practically absent. Hastings.

180. *Polycera quadrilineata*, Müller.

This species has much the character of the foregoing species. The body is transparent white, with orange spots and spiny tubercles of the same colour down the centre of the back and tail, in the latter part of which they merge to form a streak of orange. Another line of tubercles runs down each side of the body commencing in front of the head, where they form four rather long points or processes projecting forward, and running backwards as far as the side of the gills where they terminate as free processes. There is a single pair of tentacles which are laminated in the upper part. The gills are plume-like and form an incomplete rosette situated about midway down the back. Taken a few times in the trawl a mile or so distant from shore. Rather rare. Hastings.

181. *Acanthodoris pilosa*, Müller.

Animal nearly 1 inch in length, of a pale yellow or white colour. Cloak covered with rather long and conical tubercles. Not uncommon upon rocks from mid to low tide. Hastings.

182. *Lamellidoris bilamellata*, Linnæus.

The cloak is of a pale, or rich brown colour, and is tuberculated, the tubercles being white. The branchiæ form a double rosette of plumes in the form of the letter Omega inverted ; tentacles laminated. Very common upon rocks from mid to low tide, often congregating in groups. Hastings.

183. *Lamellidoris diaphana*, Alder and Hancock.†
Brighton.

184. *Goniodoris nodosa*, Montague.

Animal ¾ inch in length, of a pale yellow colour, excepting the back which is flesh-coloured. There are two oral tentacles, and the dorsal ones are laminated behind in the upper half. The free margin of the cloak is very prettily frilled and turned up and may or may not unite behind the gills which form a rosette of plumes at the end of the back. The whole upper portion of the animal is more or less dotted with opaque white, and down the centre of the back there is a keel, and upon either side a few small tubercles are arranged in line and coloured opaque white ; down the centre of the tail there is an opaque saffron-coloured ridge. This is a mud-loving species and is therefore rather local. Hastings.

185. *Ancula cristata*, Alder.

Animal fully ½ inch in length ; transparent white. The gills which occupy the centre of the body are formed of three branching plumes which face backwards.

Upon either side of these and arising from the body are four or five erect, linear processes. The dorsal tentacles are laminated in the upper half, that portion being bent backwards. From near the base of each tentacle are given off two narrow arms directed forwards ; and upon either side of the lip there is a tentacular process. All of these appendages are more or less tipped with orange or yellow, besides which there is a line down the tail of the same colour. This species is very beautiful when under full sail in its proper element, but when seen upon the rocks at low tide it appears like a little shapeless ball of jelly quite unlikely to attract attention. It is usually found in moderate profusion. Hastings.

PULMONATA

AURICULIDÆ

186. *Alexia myosotis* (Draparnand)

Somewhat rare. Rye.

CEPHALOPODA

DIRBRANCHIATA

DECAPODA

OMMASTREPHIDÆ

187. *Todarodes sagittatus*, Lamarck.*

Very rare. Hastings.

LOLIGINIDÆ

188. *Loligo vulgaris*, Lamarck.

The 'Squid.' Common. Hastings.

SEPIIDÆ

189. *Sepia officinalis*, Linnæus.

The cuttle-fish. Common. Hastings.

SEPIOLIDÆ

190. *Sepiola scandica*, Steenstrup.

Common. Hastings.

OCTOPODA

POLYPODIDÆ

191. *Polypus vulgaris*, Lamarck.

Not uncommon during unusually warm summers. Hastings.

192. *Moschites cirrosa*, Lamarck.

Upon the authority of Mr. W. Wells of the Brighton Aquarium this species occurs off that town. It is peculiar for having a single row of suckers along each arm.

CHORDATA

UROCHORDATA

ASCIDIACEA

ASCIDEÆ SIMPLICES

ASCIDIADÆ

1. *Ascidia mentula*, O. F. Müller.

Test semi-opaque, rather coarse, of a faint yellowish flesh colour ; height, about 2 inches. Branchial aperture with eight lobes, and both apertures coloured bright crimson or with bright red spots. The test often has embedded in its exterior coralline stems, polyzoa, etc., and internally harbours the mollusc *Modiolaria marmorata*. Common in the trawl and sometimes cast ashore. Hastings.

2. *Ascidia virginea*, O. F. Müller.

Test transparent, smooth, colourless ; height 1¼ inches. Specimens often enfolded in the branches of corallines, the test sometimes extending a short way up the stems. Branchial aperture eight-lobed. Often harbours *Modiolaria marmorata*. Not uncommon ; trawled. Hastings.

3. *Ascidia vitrea*.†

Brighton.

4. *Ascidia*, sp.

Upon the shore at extreme low water, are often found extensive beds of an Ascidia, packed closely together. The test is coated with sand and is oblong to sub-globular in form ; length of a specimen about ¾ inch. Branchial orifice appears to be four-lobed, but the lobes are probably subdivided ; about four short tentacles are seen. Common. Hastings.

5. *Ascidia*, sp.

There is a species, somewhat resembling the last mentioned, occurring upon corallines. It is smaller, measuring about ¼ inch in diameter, rather depressed, and coated with sand. Lobes of the branchial orifice as in the foregoing species. Common. Hastings.

6. (?) *Molgula arenosa*, Alder and Hancock.

Animal nearly globular, barely ¾ inch in diameter ; coated with fine sand ; branchial orifice six-lobed. Specimen has been apparently slightly attached. Tubular character of orifice non-apparent. Hastings.

7. *Cynthia morus*, Forbes.

Animal barely ½ inch in width, wider than high, warty, attached by a wide base ; colour, magenta crimson ; branchial orifice with four pale lobes. A specimen preserved for some years in formalin has successfully retained its colour. Somewhat rare ; trawled. Hastings.

ASCIDIÆ COMPOSITÆ

BOTRYLLIDÆ

8. *Botryllus schlosseri*.†
Brighton.

9. *Botryllus polycyclus*.†
Brighton.

10. *Botryllus bivittatus*.†
Brighton.

11. *Leptoclinum listerianum*.†
Brighton.

12. *Distoma rubrum*.†
Brighton.

13. *Amaroecium*, sp.

Specimen consists of a little flat gelatinous mass, ¼ inch in thickness, and 1½ inches in length, lobed around the edge, and with the margin folded over upwards and inwards, like a clenched fist. One or two delicate algæ pass up through the centre. The mass is translucent, colourless, and the zoöids are of an opaque grey-buff, and are seen here and there in well defined oblong systems. In other portions the systems become indistinct, and in parts, there is no arrangement at all. There is no common aperture. The zoöid has a six-lobed branchial orifice, a long atrial languet, a long post-abdomen, which terminates in a flattened rounded lobe, with another lobe more or less well formed on either side. Anus, from lateral view, is bilobed ? Embedded in the gelatinous matrix is a little sand. The specimen does not appear to correspond with either of the species *proliferum*, *nordmanni*, or *argus* but bears some resemblance in the lobed character of the specimen to *Aplidium fallax*. In combining the two characters of systemic and non-systemic arrangement of the zoöids the specimen bears a resemblance to *A. irregulare* var. *concinnum*, Herdman, from different latitudes. Rare. Hastings.

14. *Amaroecium argus*.†
Brighton.

MOLLUSCS

The soil and climate of Sussex, as well as its diversified physical features, are favourable to molluscan life. The chalky south downs swarm with some species, which it is even claimed are the cause of the excellent flavour of the mutton grown in that district ; the woody copses and remnants of the Wealden forest shelter others ; while, though there are no very large rivers, the numerous streams, especially of the Pevensey Level, yield a great number of aquatic forms.

Out of the 139 species known to inhabit the British Islands, no less than 105 have been recorded as occurring in the county. Among these we have not reckoned the Roman snail (*Helix pomatia*) because the sole evidence of its presence depends on a single dead shell found in the Lady Holt covers near Harting, and though an attempt was subsequently made to establish a colony there it did not succeed. Why this species, so abundant on the north downs, should be absent from such an apparently equally favourable situation as the south downs is a mystery. A few other absentees, such as *Vitrea glabra,* some of the Vertigos and of the slugs, may yet be discovered.

The assemblage is of the average British type with the addition of two forms of interest, viz., *Helicella cartusiana* and the cheese snail (*Helicodonta obvoluta*), which last local species has been traced by Mr. Clement Reid, F.R.S., along the northern escarpment of the south downs, in ancient beech woods, from Harting to the river Arun, with a few colonies in the middle of the downs towards West Dean and Singleton.

The literature of the subject is very scattered, but the more important papers are those by Mr. J. E. Harting[1] and Mr. J. H. A. Jenner,[2] the latter which deals with East Sussex including the work of all previous writers.

A. GASTROPODA

I. PULMONATA

a. STYLOMMATOPHORA

Testacella scutulum, Sby. Lewes. (Specimens from Newport, Isle of Wight, have been turned loose at Chichester)
Limax maximus, Linn.
— *flavus,* Linn.
— *arborum,* Bouch.-Chant. West Sussex

Agriolimax agrestis (Linn.)
— *lævis* (Müll.)
Amalia sowerbii (Fér.)
— *gagates* (Drap.) Hastings
Vitrina pellucida (Müll.)
Vitrea crystallina (Müll.)
— *alliaria* (Miller)
— *cellaria* (Müll.)
— *nitidula* (Drap.)

[1] *Zoologist,* 1878, pp. 84, 122, 161.
[2] *Trans. Eastbourne Nat. Hist. Soc.* vol. viii. (1884) p. 44 ; and supplement *Journ. Conch.* vol. VI. (1891) p. 361, to which a few more species have been added by Mr. W. Whitwell, ibid. vol. X. (1901) p. 86.

MOLLUSCS

Vitrea pura (Ald.)
— *radiatula* (Ald.)
— *excavata* (Bean). St. Leonards Forest ; Midhurst ; near Piplye
— *nitida* (Müll.)
— *fulva* (Müll.)
Arion ater (Linn.)
— *hortensis*, Fér.
— *circumscriptus*, John. ⎫
— *subfuscus* (Drap.) ⎬ West Sussex
Punctum pygmæum (Drap.)
Pyramidula rupestris (Drap.)
— *rotundata* (Müll.)
Helicella virgata (Da C.)
— *itala* (Linn.)
— *caperata* (Mont.)
— *barbara* (Linn.) Rare ; it was found at Eastbourne on a spot now built over
— *cantiana* (Mont.)
— *cartusiana* (Müll.)
Hygromia fusca (Mont.) Warrengrove and Warrinson Wood, near Lewes
— *granulata* (Ald.)
— *hispida* (Linn.)
— *rufescens* (Penn.)
Acanthinula aculeata (Müll.)
Vallonia pulchella (Müll.)
Helicodonta obvoluta (Müll.) Up Park ; Graffham ; Storington ; Dunston ; Singleton, etc.
Helicigona lapicida (Linn.)
— *arbustorum* (Linn.)
Helix aspersa, Müll.
— *nemoralis*, Linn.
— *hortensis*, Müll.
Buliminus obscurus (Müll.)
Cochlicopa lubrica (Müll.)
Azeca tridens (Pult.)
Cæcilianella acicula (Müll.)
Pupa secale, Drap.
— *cylindracea* (Da C.)
— *muscorum* (Linn.)
Sphyradium edentulum (Drap.)
Vertigo antivertigo (Drap.) Lewes levels ; Eastbourne
— *pygmæa* (Drap.)
Balea perversa (Linn.)
Clausilia laminata (Mont.)
— *bidentata* (Ström.)

Clausilia rolphii, Gray
Succinea putris (Linn.)
— *elegans*, Risso.

b. BASOMMATOPHORA

Carychium minimum, Müll.
Melampus denticulatus (Mont.) Newhaven
Alexia myosotis (Drap.) Hastings; Newhaven ; Shoreham
Ancylus fluviatilis, Müll.
Velletia lacustris (Linn.)
Limnæa auricularia (Linn.)
— *pereger* (Müll.)
— *palustris* (Müll.)
— *truncatula* (Müll.)
— *stagnalis* (Linn.)
— *glabra* (Müll.) Near Malling ; Hastings ; near Brighton ; Horsted Keynes
Planorbis corneus (Linn.)
— *albus*, Müll.
— *glaber*, Jeff. West Sussex
— *nautileus* (Linn.)
— *carinatus*, Müll.
— *marginatus*, Drap.
— *vortex* (Linn.)
— *spirorbis*, Müll.
— *contortus* (Linn.)
— *fontanus* (Lightf.)
— *lineatus* (Walker)
Physa fontinalis (Linn.)
— *hypnorum* (Linn.)

II. PROSOBRANCHIATA

Paludestrina jenkinsi (Smith). Near Lewes
— *stagnalis* (Bast.) Hastings
Bithynia tentaculata (Linn.) The type is common ; but near Pevensey Mr. P. Rufford has obtained an interesting variety which is prettily marked with raised longitudinal brown stripes or bars
— *leachii* (Shepp.) Pevensey level ; river Arun
Vivipara vivipara (Linn.)
Valvata piscinalis (Müll.)
— *cristata*, Müll.
Pomatias elegans (Müll.)
Acicula lineata (Drap.) Fairlight Glen ; Coghurst Wood
Neritina fluviatilis (Linn.)

B. PELECYPODA

Unio pictorum (Linn.)
— *tumidus*, Retz.
Anodonta cygnæa (Linn.)
Sphærium rivicola (Leach). Near Hastings, dead shells only
— *corneum* (Linn.)
— *ovale* (Fér.) Near Lewes, one specimen.
— *lacustre* (Müll.)

Pisidium amnicum (Müll.)
— *pusillum* (Gmel.)
— *nitidum*, Jenyns. Near Lewes ; Hastings ; Guestling ; Chidham
— *fontinale* (Drap.) In addition to the type the variety *P. henslowianum* occurs at Pevensey Marsh
— *milium* (Held.) Hastings

INSECTS[1]

Sussex is one of the largest of the English counties, and with the exception of Hampshire, Kent, and possibly Norfolk, probably contains a larger number of species of insecta than any other English county.

The richness of its insect fauna[2] may be accounted for by its varied geological formations, its long coast line, its large extent of common or waste land, amounting to nearly 24,000 acres, and its numerous and extensive woodlands.

Although the great forests have during the last few hundred years been almost destroyed a large extent of moor and woodland still exists in the northern part of the county in Ashdown Forest, Tilgate Forest, Worth Forest, and St. Leonards Forest between Three Bridges and Horsham, making up with the other woods and plantations of the county, nearly 114,000 acres.

ORTHOPTERA

Earwigs, Cockroaches, Grasshoppers and Crickets

The Orthoptera have been so little collected in Sussex that the list is very meagre, and observation will without doubt add to the number of species known to occur in the county. Hampshire and Kent are two of our richest counties from the point of view of the orthopterist, and so Sussex, situated between them, should at least possess some of the more uncommon forms that have been found in them. *Labidura riparia*, Pall., has yet to be recorded for the Sussex coast, but has been taken both in Hampshire and in Kent ; *Apterygida albipennis*, Meg. (= *media*, Hagenb.), an earwig very rare in England, has been taken in Kent, and will very likely be discovered one day in Sussex. It should be sought for by sweeping among shrubs and flowers, especially in marshy places or by the side of streams. *Mecostethus grossus*, L., our finest grasshopper, is quite common in some boggy places in the neighbouring county of Hampshire, and might well be found also in Sussex. A common and widely distributed grasshopper, *Tettix subulatus*, L., has not been actually

[1] The sequence of the orders here followed is that adopted by Dr. D. Sharp, F.R.S., in the *Cambridge Natural History*, 1889–92.—H.G.

[2] We have to express our cordial thanks for valuable assistance received to Mr. R. Adkin, F.E.S. ; Mr. Joseph Anderson, F.E.S. ; the Rev. C. D. Ash, M.A. ; Mr. C. G. Barrett, F.E.S. ; the Rev. E. N. Bloomfield, M.A., F.E.S. ; Mr. Malcolm Burr, B.A., F.L.S. ; Mr. E. A. Butler, B.A., B.Sc. ; Mr. W. M. Christy, M.A., F.L.S. ; Mr. D. A. Edgell ; Mr. W. H. B. Fletcher, M.A., F.Z.S. ; the Rev. Canon Fowler, M.A., D.Sc., F.L.S. ; Mr. J. H. A. Jenner, F.E.S. ; Mr. A. Lloyd, F.C.S. ; Mr. W. J. Lucas, B.A., F.E.S. ; Prof. Raphael Meldola, F.R.S. ; Mr. Claude Morley, F.E.S. ; Mr. Edward Saunders, F.R.S. ; Captain Savile Reid, R.E., F.Z.S. ; and Mr. A. C. Vine.—H.A.D and H.G.

INSECTS

recorded, but is almost certain to occur, as we have notices of its capture all round the borders of the county. The rare 'Wartbiter,' *Decticus verrucivorus*, L., has been taken in Hampshire and in Kent, and so should be looked for in Sussex ; it is one of our finest British insects, and would form a handsome addition to the local fauna.

Of the more interesting species which are on the list, we may mention *Forficula lesnei*, Finot., an earwig apparently widely distributed in the southern counties of England and in the corresponding parts of northern France. Two native cockroaches, *Ectobia lapponica*, L., and *E. livida*, Fabr., have been taken in several localities, but *E. panzeri*, Steph., has only been noticed once. Two of the less abundant grasshoppers, *Stenobothrus lineatus*, Panz., and *S. elegans*, Charp., appear to be fairly widely distributed, as also *Gomphocerus rufus*, L., which is far from a common species. Two or three migratory locusts, which are occasional accidental visitors to our shores, are on record. A curious and very pretty little long-horned grasshopper, *Xiphidium dorsale*, Latr., is one of the most interesting on the list ; it is a species very locally distributed and nowhere common ; it should be sought for by sweeping among reeds. Finally the well known Mole Cricket (*Gryllotalpa gryllotalpa*) is only recorded once, and collectors should keep a sharp look-out for so interesting an insect.

To two gentlemen, Mr. H. L. F. Guermonprez of Bognor, and the Rev. E. N. Bloomfield of Guestling, we are indebted for most of the localities, and their records are marked respectively by (G) and (B). Where no authority is quoted, the captures are my own or are well known records in the magazines.

FORFICULARIA
Earwigs

Labia minor, L. The Lesser Earwig is fairly common in the early summer. It has been taken in Sussex (B), at Bognor (G), and by Mr. Claude Morley at Brighton and Polegate. *Forficula auricularia*, L. The Common Earwig is abundant everywhere. *Forficula lesnei*, Finot. This earwig has been taken in some numbers in different parts of Kent, Surrey, Hampshire, Berkshire and Dorsetshire. In Sussex it has been taken at Selsea (4, vi. 97, G.) and at Pagham (31, viii. 01, G.), always by sweeping.

BLATTODEA
Cockroaches

Ectobiidæ. *Ectobia lapponica*, L. Beaten from trees at Slindon, also Cocking Down and Dane Wood, Eartham (G). *E. livida*, Fabr. This species occurs in several places in Sussex ; Itchenor, Bognor, Slindon, Eartham, Charlton Forest, Fair Mile, Dane Wood, and Cocking (G) ; Hastings district (B). *E. panzeri*, Steph. Camber (B).

111

Phyllodromiidæ. *Phyllodromia germanica*, L., Hastings (B), Bognor (G), and Eastbourne. Common in storehouses and restaurants in most English towns.

Periplanetidæ. *Blatta orientalis*, L. The only too familiar black-beetle (which is neither black, nor a beetle) is too abundant in many places.

Panchloridæ. *Leucophæa surinamensis*, L. This cockroach is distributed throughout the tropical regions, and can only live in warm climates. Two, probably imported in bananas from Madeira, were once taken at Bognor (G). It is hardly likely to establish itself in this country, as the two previously mentioned species have done.

ACRIDIODEA

Short-horned Grasshoppers and Locusts

Truxalidæ. *Stenobothrus lineatus*, Panz. This is not a common species; in Sussex it has been taken at Selsea, Goodwood and Cocking (G). *S. viridulus*, L. This is common, especially on downs and grassy uplands. It has been taken at Ewhurst (B), and Goodwood and Cocking (G), and Forest Row and East Grinstead. *S. rufipes*, Zett. This is less common than the above; it has been taken at Guestling (B). *S. bicolor*, Charp., and *S. parallelus*, Zett. These are our two commonest and most widely distributed grasshoppers. In the later summer months they are to be found on almost any patch of grass or turf throughout the county. *S. elegans*, Charp. This is a somewhat local species. In Sussex it has been taken at Ewhurst (B) and Pagham Marsh (G). *Gomphocerus rufus*, L. Goodwood and Eartham (G); a locally distributed species. *G. maculatus*, Thunb. This is one of our smallest and prettiest grasshoppers; it has been taken at Dallington (B), Eartham, Cocking and Pagham (G), Forest Row and in Ashdown Forest.

Œdipodidæ. *Pachytylus danicus*, L., and *P. migratorius*, L. These two migratory locusts are generally confused. The former is the commoner and more widely distributed throughout the Old World, whereas the latter is confined to eastern Europe and the neighbouring parts of Asia. One specimen of each species has been taken at Fairlight, one of the former at Ore, Aug. 1901 (B), and one supposed to be *P. migratorius* has been recorded in the *West Sussex Gazette* by Mr. E. V. Bond, from Lower Beeding. Mr. Denison Roebuck mentions two *P. migratorius* at Battle and three at Newhaven. In the Hope Museum, Oxford, there is one from Littlehampton, dated ' 1846,' with Westwood's initials.

Tettigidæ. *Tettix bipunctatus*, L. This little grasshopper is common enough everywhere, especially in dry sandy places; it has been taken at Guestling (B), Dale Park (G), and Forest Row and Ashdown Forest. *T. subulatus*, L. I can find no actual record of this species, though I have taken it on the Surrey side of the border near East Grinstead, but it is a fairly common insect, and certain to occur in Sussex.

INSECTS

LOCUSTODEA

Long-horned Grasshoppers

Phaneropteridæ. *Leptophyes punctatissima*, Bosc. This is not an uncommon form, but frequents high trees, and so is not often seen ; the immature forms are common in hedges and thickets earlier in the summer ; it is recorded from Guestling, where it is probably not uncommon (B), Bognor, Slindon (G), and Polegate (Eland Shaw).

Meconemidæ. *Meconema varium*, Fabr. This is another species that is far commoner than is generally supposed ; it is to be found on oaks and limes late into the autumn, and is often taken 'at sugar.' In Sussex it has been recorded from Guestling (B), Bognor, Slindon, Dale Park and Old Park near Bosham (G).

Conocephalidæ. *Xiphidium dorsale*, Latr. This is one of our most locally distributed British Orthoptera. It is noted from Guestling (B) and Pagham Marsh (G), where it is to be taken by sweeping.

Locustidæ. *Locusta viridissima*, L. The familiar Great Green Grasshopper is common along the south coast. In Sussex we have it noted from Hastings Cemetery Ground (B) and Bognor (G), and Denison Roebuck mentions one taken two miles from Chichester, wrongly recorded as *Pachytylus migratorius* !

Decticidæ. *Thamnotrizon cinereus*, L. This is another species that is far commoner than is generally supposed. In Sussex it is on record from Guestling (B), also Bognor and Slindon (G) and East Grinstead ; a female was taken in October at Aldwich, in the act of laying its eggs in an elm tree, with the ovipositor firmly fixed into the trunk (G). *Platycleis grisea*, Fabr. Hastings (on Castle Hill) (B), and Mr. Claude Morley has taken it on Southwick Beach. It is to be found on chalky hills. *P. brachyptera*, Linn. This is a locally distributed form, which has been taken in Sussex at Bexhill (B), on Hastings Cliffs (G).

GRYLLODEA

Crickets

Gryllidæ. *Gryllus campestris*, L. The Field Cricket. One was taken at Pett near the sea (B), and recorded in the *Entomologist*. It is rare in England, but probably to be found in many more localities ; it frequents sandy places. *G. domesticus*, L. The House Cricket is not uncommon in old houses (B), and is found at Bognor (G). It especially frequents bakers' shops, in which it is known to be abundant at East Grinstead.

Gryllotalpidæ. *Gryllotalpa gryllotalpa*, L. The Mole Cricket. This very remarkable insect is familiar to most people in appearance, though it is not often captured. In Sussex Mr. J. Anderson has taken it by the Chichester Canal.

NEUROPTERA

Psocids, Stone-flies, May-flies, Dragonflies, Lacewings and Caddis-flies

Thanks to the exertions of the veteran entomologist, the Rev. E. N.

Bloomfield, in searching out and obtaining lists of captures from various naturalists who have interested themselves in the insects of Sussex, we are able to give for the county a moderately complete review of the much neglected order Neuroptera, using the word in the comprehensive sense adopted by most authors. The Trichoptera and Odonata are of course the groups that have been most attended to, and in connection with the latter good work has been done, for only some four possible species remain to be discovered. But even for these groups the localities examined cover only a very small part of the county, and plenty of room is left for further work. Situated as the county is with its sea-front facing France, collectors should be on the look-out for immigrants. One such is recorded—the striking *Gomphus flavipes*, Charp.—taken near Hastings by J. F. Stephens, 5 August, 1818, and still to be seen in good condition amongst the poor collection of British dragonflies in the British Museum.[1]

PSOCIDIA

Psocids

Of the *Psocidia*,[2] generally so very much neglected a group, we have amongst the wingless forms *Atropos divinitoria*, Müll.; *Clothilla pulsatoria*, Linn., *C. inquilina*, Heyd., and *C. sericea*, Kolbe (= *C. picea*, Mots.), occurring in houses; and *Hyperetes guestfalicus*, Kolbe, from Bognor. Coming to the winged species, of the eleven members of the genus *Psocus* seven have been noticed: *P. longicornis*, Fabr., at Hastings, Goodwood and Eartham; *P. nebulosus*, Steph., at Slindon, Eartham and Singleton; *P. variegatus*, Fabr., at Bognor, Welberton and Slindon; *P. fasciatus*, Fabr., at Hastings, St. Leonards, Charlton Forest and Cissbury; *P. bifasciatus*, Latr., at Ore and Bognor; *P. quadrimaculatus*, Latr., at Bognor; and *P. morio* at Bognor, Felpham and Bersted. *Stenopsocus immaculatus*, Steph., and *S. cruciatus*, Linn., are both common, as also are *Cæcilius pedicularius*, Linn., and *C. flavidus*, Steph. (Guermonprez). *C. obsoletus*, Steph., is recorded from Bognor (1 Aug. 1892); *C. dalii*, McLach., from Bognor, Aldwick and Felpham; and *C. vittatus*, Latr., from Aldwick, Slindon, Arundel, Hastings and Fairlight. *Peripsocus phæopterus*, Steph., occurs at Bognor and Fairlight. *Elipsocus unipunctatus*, Müll., is a common insect (Guermonprez); *E. westwoodii*, McLach., is recorded from Hastings, Bognor, Aldwick and Slindon; and *E. hyalinus*, Steph., from Bognor. *Ectopsocus briggsi*, McLach., was taken on 1 November, 1902, by Mr. Guermonprez in his garden at Bognor.

PERLIDIA

Stone-flies

As is usually the case very few of the *Perlidia* (stone-flies) have been

---

[1] In the following notes most of the species from Hastings district were taken by **Mr.** Butler and those from Guestling by the Rev. E. N. Bloomfield, and they were identified or confirmed by Mr. McLachlan. Mr. Guermonprez's list was rich in *Psocidia*. McLachlan's nomenclature is used in all groups except *Odonata*, in which group my *British Dragonflies* is the authority.—W.J.L.

[2] I am indebted to Messrs. Bloomfield and Guermonprez alone for information about the groups *Psocidia*, *Perlidia* and *Ephemeridia*.—W.J.L.

INSECTS

noticed. They are but three : *Isopteryx tripunctata*, Scop., Midhurst (30 May, 1894) and Hollington ; *Tæniopteryx trifasciata*, Pict., at Guestling ; and the common *Nemoura variegata*, Oliv.

EPHEMERIDIA
May-flies

Of the *Ephemeridia* (May-flies) also but few have been recorded. *Ephemera vulgata*, Linn., is of course common, and *E. danica*, Müll., has been taken at Ewhurst and Hollington ; *Leptophlebia submarginata*, Steph., at Hollington and Robertsbridge ; *Habrophlebia fusca*, Cur., at Slindon ; and *Cloeon simile*, Eaton, at Robertsbridge. *C. dipterum*, Linn., is common (Guermonprez). *Centroptilum luteolum*, Müll., has been taken at Midhurst and Hastings, and *Heptagenia venosa*, Fabr., at Guestling.

ODONATA
Dragonflies

Of Sussex *Odonata* we have a fair record, but to complete the possible list *Orthetrum cærulescens*, Fabr., should be looked for on boggy heaths, *Æschna juncea*, Linn., around ponds, especially in fir woods, and *Erythromma naias*, Hansem., over sluggish water, where they no doubt await discovery ; while it is quite possible that the little *Agrion mercuriale*, Charp., may be hiding its charms amongst the rank herbage of some boggy stream. *Sympetrum striolatum*, Charp., has been recorded from near Lewes, very common (W. C. Unwin), Eastbourne and Hailsham, common (G. T. Porritt), Hastings district, common (Bloomfield). *S. sanguineum*, Müll., Horsham (H. J. Turner), Kingston near Lewes, 1851 (Unwin), Hollington (Butler), Guestling (Bloomfield), near Rye (Lieut.-Col. Irby), Hastings district (E. Connold), near sea at Middleton (Guermonprez). *S. scoticum*, Don., near Liphook (Turner), near Hastings (Butler). *Libellula depressa*, Linn., Hailsham, Abbots Wood and near, abundant ; common in woods and lanes in east Sussex (Porritt), Worthing (S. A. Blencarn), plentiful on downs (Unwin), rather common in Hastings district (Bloomfield). *L. quadrimaculata*, Linn., Hailsham, east Sussex, Abbots Wood common (Porritt), near Liphook (Lucas), rare on downs (Unwin), Bopeep (Butler), rare at Guestling (Bloomfield), one, Bognor, 6 June, 1901 (Guermonprez); var. *prænubila*, Abbots Wood (Porritt). *L. fulva*, Müll., one on the downs (Unwin). *Orthetrum cancellatum*, Linn., near Liphook (Lucas). *Cordulia ænea*, Linn., one near Horsham, June, 1846 (Unwin), once in Hastings district (Connold). *Gomphus valgatissimus*, Linn., one on downs, 1846 (Unwin), one at Lewes, 1851 (Unwin). *G. flavipes*, Charp., one near Hastings, 5 August, 1818 (Stephens). *Cordulegaster annulatus*, Latr., Brighton district, rare (Unwin), Hastings, once (E. W. Andrews), one near Bexhill (Connold). *Anax imperator*, Leach, near Liphook (Lucas), Guestling (Connold), Hastings district (Connold), once near Uckfield (Unwin), seen at Abbots Wood (F. M. B. Carr). *Brachytron pratense*, Müll., Abbots Wood and near, east Sussex (Porritt), frequent near Lewes (Unwin), Ore (R. M. Sotheby), locally common at Bexhill (Connold), Hastings district (Connold), Guestling (Bloomfield). *Æschna mixta*, Latr., Worthing (F. C. Summerson), one on Camber Sands, 22 October (Connold); Guestling (Bloomfield). *Æ. cyanea*, Müll., Battle (Porritt), Worthing (Summerson), Uckfield and Newick (Unwin), common in Hastings district (Bloomfield). *Æ. grandis*, Linn., not uncommon near Lewes (Unwin), Guestling (Bloomfield), not common in the Hastings district (Butler). *Calopteryx virgo*, Linn., Midhurst (Guermonprez), Horsham (Turner), Ouse, etc., near Barcombe Mill, very common (Unwin), Hollington (Butler), Guestling (Bloomfield), Sedlescombe, common (Connold) locally, common at Battle and Crowhurst (Sotheby), Hastings district (Connold). *C. splendens*, Harr., Midhurst (Guermonprez), Ouse near Barcombe Mill (Unwin), banks of Cut (Unwin), Rother at Bodiam (Bloomfield), Hastings district (Connold), Ashburnham (Connold), Guestling (Bloomfield). *Lestes sponsa*, Hansem., Winchelsea Marshes (Lucas), Shoreham (Turner), Brighton district (Unwin), near Rye (Irby), Pett (Bloomfield), Hastings district (Connold). *Platycnemis pennipes*, Pall., once on downs near Lewes (Unwin). *Pyrrhosoma nymphula*, Sulz., Polegate (Guermonprez), near Liphook (Turner), Hailsham (Porritt), common in east Sussex (Porritt), Abbots Wood (Porritt), Shoreham (Turner), abundant near Lewes (Unwin), St. Leonards (Butler), common at Guestling (Bloomfield). *P. tenellum*, Vill., near Liphook (Lucas). *Ischnura pumilio*, Charp., Abbots Wood, July, 1900 (Blencarn). *I. elegans*, Lind., common at Bellagio (M. Burr), near Liphook (Lucas), very common near Lewes (Unwin), Guestling and Pett (Bloomfield), Hastings district (Connold) ; var. *rufescens*, Steph., Kingston and Landport near Lewes (Unwin). *Agrion pulchellum*, Lind., Hastings district (Connold), frequent near the Winterbourne and elsewhere round Lewes (Unwin). *A. puella*, Linn., east Sussex, common in woods and lanes (Porritt), near Liphook (Lucas), Worthing (Blencarn), very common in Lewes levels (Unwin), common in Hastings district (Bloomfield). *Enallagma cyathigerum*, Charp., scarce in Sussex (Bloomfield), near Liphook (Lucas), rare in Brighton district (Unwin), Ashburnham (Connold).

PLANIPENNIA

Lacewings, etc.

Next follow the *Planipennia*,[1] which are rather well represented. *Sialis lutaria*, Linn., is of course common, and *S. fuliginosa*, Pict., has been taken at St. Leonards and Guestling. The only *Raphidia* is *R. notata* (?), Fabr., recorded by Mr. Guermonprez from Heyshott. That fine insect *Osmylus maculatus*, Fabr., has been taken between Battle and Sedlescombe (Connold) and rarely at Hastings. *Sisyra fuscata*, Fabr., is recorded from Midhurst ; *Micromus variegatus*, Fabr., from the Hastings district and Aldwick ; *M. aphidivorus*, Schr., from Hazel Slindon ; and *M. paganus*, Linn., from Hastings, Fairlight, Guestling and Middleton. Of the genus *Heme-*

---

[1] For our knowledge of the members of this and the next sub-orders of the Sussex Neuroptera we are indebted almost entirely to Messrs. Bloomfield, Butler and Guermonprez.—W.J.L.

INSECTS

robius we have *H. micans*, Oliv., from Guestling and Singleton ; *H. humuli*, Linn., from Hastings, Hollington, Fairlight, Guestling and a garden at Bognor ; *H. stigma*, Steph. (= *limbatus*, Wesm.), from Fairlight ; *H. subnebulosus*, Steph., from Hastings and Fairlight and at a lamp at Bognor ; *H. nervosus*, Fabr., from Hastings and Aldwick ; *H. concinnus*, Steph., from Avisford. *Drepanopteryx phalænoides*, Linn., has once occurred at Hastings. The lacewings or golden-eyes (genus *Chrysopa*) are represented by *C. flava*, Scop., from Guestling and Felpham ; *C. vittata*, Wesm., somewhat common at Hastings ; *C. alba*, Linn., from Guestling and Cocking ; *C. flavifrons*, Brauer, from Hollington; *C. vulgaris*, Schn., from Guestling and Bognor ; *C. septempunctata*, Wesm., from Guestling commonly ; *C. ventralis*, Curt., from Guestling ; *C. perla*, Linn., from Guestling commonly, Hollington and Avisford ; *Coniopteryx psociformis*, Curt., taken at Felpham, Aldwick and Ewhurst, is the only representative of this genus of aphis-like insects. Of the three British scorpion-flies *Panorpa communis*, Linn., is recorded for Hastings and is common at Guestling, while the somewhat smaller but similar insect, *P. germanica*, Linn., is also recorded for the same two localities.

TRICHOPTERA
Caddis-flies

As regards the concluding sub-order *Trichoptera*,[1] the county seems to have been fairly worked, at any rate in a few localities. Of the *Phryganidæ* we have *Phryganea grandis*, Linn., at Ewhurst (Connold), common under loose bark on old willows round a pond at Hailsham (Porritt), and at Bognor ; *P. varia*, Fabr., at Guestling ; and *P. minor*, Curt., also at Guestling. The *Limnophilidæ* recorded are *Colpotaulius incisus*, Curt., at Itchenor and Slindon ; *Glyphotælius pellucidus*, Oliv., at Guestling, Dane's Wood and Bognor ; *Limnophilus flavicornis*, Fabr., at Pett, Guestling and Bognor ; *L. marmoratus*, Curt., at Guestling and Pagham Marsh ; *L. lunatus*, Curt., at Hastings, Bexhill and Felpham ; *L. ignavus*, McLach., at Battle ; *L. centralis*, Curt., at Abbots Wood (Porritt), Hastings, Ore, Guestling and Aldwick ; *L. vittatus*, Fabr., in Alexandra Park, Hastings (W. Esam), at Guestling and near Bognor ; *L. affinis*, Curt., at Ewhurst (Esam), Winchelsea, Guestling, Hailsham, Bognor and Pagham ; *L. hirsutus*, Pict., at Bognor ; *L. sparsus*, Curt., at Hastings and Aldwick ; *Anabolia nervosa*, Leach, at Pagham Marsh and Bognor ; *Stenophylax permistus*, McLach., somewhat common at Guestling ; *S. vibex*, Curt., at Hastings and Bognor ; *Micropterna sequax*, McLach., in the Hastings district ; *M. lateralis*, Steph., common at Hailsham, and abundant at 'sugar' in Abbots Wood (Porritt) and at Hastings ; *Hallesus radiatus*, Curt., taken off a lamp on 2 November, 1893, in St. Helen's Road, Hastings (Esam) ; and *Apatania muliebris*, McLach., at Arundel Park (McLachlan). Of the *Sericostomidæ* there are but three—*Sericostoma personatum*, Spence, at Guestling ;

[1] Almost all the Trichoptera were determined at one time or another by Mr. McLachlan.—E.N.B.

Silo pallipes, Fabr., at Fairlight and Guestling; and *Crunæcia irrorata*, Curt., at Fairlight and Binstead. The *Leptoceridæ* are *Beræa pullata*, Curt., Hastings; *Leptocerus aterrimus*, Steph., Guestling; *Mystacides nigra*, Linn., Hastings and Bersted; *M. longicornis*, Linn., Hastings; *Triænodes bicolor*, Curt., Hastings district; *Œcetis furva*, Ramb., Winchelsea; and *Œ. lacustris*, Pict., Bersted. Of the *Hydropsychidæ* we have *Hydropsyche pellucidula*, Curt., from Guestling; *Diplectrona felix*, McLach., from Fairlight; *Wormaldia occipitalis*, Pict., from Fairlight; *Plectrocnemia conspersa*, Curt., from Hastings; *Polycentropus flavo-maculatus*, Pict., from Bodiam; *Holocentropus dubius*, Ramb., from the Hastings district; *H. picicornis*, Steph., from Pett; *Tinodes assimilis*, McLach., from Fairlight and Bognor; and *T. wæneri* from Chichester. The list concludes with three *Rhyacophilidæ* —*Rhyacophila dorsalis*, Curt., from Fairlight; *Agapetus fuscipes*, Curt., from Bognor; and *A. comatus*, Pict., from Midhurst. The last family—the *Hydroptilidæ*—are at present unrepresented in the county list.

RESULT

Sub-orders		Sussex			British
Psocidia		24	out of about		44
Perlidia		3	,,	,,	25
Ephemeridia		8	,,	,,	39
Odonata		26	,,	,,	40
Planipennia		26	,,	,,	55
Trichoptera		43	,,	,,	156
		130			359

HYMENOPTERA

PHYTOPHAGA

TENTHREDINIDÆ

Sawflies

The sawflies are very little known to the general public, and even among entomologists there are not many who have paid much attention to them. Very few attract notice either in the larval or imago state, though some are at times very destructive.

The larva of *Hoplocampa testudinea* destroys our apples, devouring the interior and causing them to fall when about the size of walnuts. About fifty years ago the larva of *Athalia spinarum* was very destructive to young turnips, clearing whole fields in a very short time, but little has been heard of it of late years; while *Nematus ribesii*, the very common gooseberry pest, devours the leaves, leaving the branches bare, and thus injures the fruit.

Yet the Tenthredinidæ are very interesting on many accounts; the saws with which they are furnished and which they use to provide a nidus for their eggs are interesting structures and of very varied forms. The sawflies also afford very curious examples of complete or partial parthenogenesis. In some species the males and females occur in almost equal numbers, in others the males are very rare compared with the females, while there are other species, of which no male has ever been detected, though perhaps the females abound. Thus we have more or less perfect parthenogenesis. Yet here again there is a difference ; the offspring of some of these parthenogenetic females are almost all males, while in others, such as those in which no male is known, the offspring are all or nearly all females.

No one in Sussex has, I think, systematically collected the Tenthredinidæ, but through the occasional collecting by Messrs. E. A. Butler, E. W. Andrews, W. Bennett, etc., I am able to give a very fair list of the species of the Hastings district. Those from the neighbourhood of Lewes are on the authority of Mr. J. H. A. Jenner, while for the west of the county I have a short list of species met with by Miss Ethel Chawner at Storrington and another from Mr. Guermonprez of Bognor. Of those met with by him in that district almost all have been determined or confirmed by the Rev. F. Morice, who has also helped in many ways.

I have employed as far as possible the nomenclature of Konow, but as this seems in a very unsettled state I have generally given as synonyms the names under which these insects are described in Cameron's *British Phytophagous Hymenoptera*.

LYDINI

Neurotoma flaviventris, Retz. Near *Midhurst*, 30 May, 1895

Pamphilius sylvaticus, L. *Guestling*, 21 May, 1889

— hortorum, Klug. *Guestling*, 23 May, 1889 ; *Hastings* ; *Laughton*, 2 May, 1892

— balteatus, Fall. (cingulatus) *Heyshott Common*, 24 May, 1893

— depressus, Schr. *Guestling*

CEPHINI

Cephus pallipes, Klug. (phthisicus) *Hastings* district

— pygmæus L. Common

Macrocephus cynosbati, L. (femoratus). *Hastings* district ; *Guestling*, 22 May, 1902

— linearis, Schr. *Ore (Cam.* iii. 117), *St. Leonards, Guestling, Lewes*

— satyrus, Pz. *Lewes*

SIRICINI

Sirex juvencus, L. *Hastings* ; *Guestling*, 2 October, 1900 ; *Storrington, Bognor*, etc. ; taken 10 or 12 yearly at *Dale Park* and *Slindon* (E. Sandford)

— gigas, L. *Hastings, Storrington, Arundel, Emsworth*. Taken fairly plentifully to the extent of 20 or 30 yearly in woods round *Dale Park* and *Slindon* (E. Sandford)

ORYSSINI

Oryssus abietinus, Scop. *Hastings* district (E. Collett)

CIMBICINI

Cimbex connata, Schr. *Sussex (Cam.* iii. 112)

Trichiosoma lucorum, L. *Hastings* district, *Lewes*

Abia fasciata, L. *Hollington* ; *Walberton*, 20 July, 1900 ; Unwin's collection,

— sericea, L. *Hastings* district, *Lewes, Storrington*

— nigricornis, Leach. *Storrington*, a larva (Miss Chawner)

ARGINI

Arge enodis, L. *St. Leonards, Laughton*

— ustulata, L. *Guestling*, May and June ; *Slindon*, 21 May, 1896

— fuscipes, Fall. *Abbots Wood*, 29 September, 1892

— cyanella, Klug. *Storrington, Laughton* ; *Cocking*, 12 May, 1895

— cyanocrocea, Forst. *Hastings, Guestling* ; not uncommon

— rosæ, L. *Bognor*, 10 June, 1895

Lophyrus pini, L. *Bexhill*, 18 April, 1894 ; *Slindon*, 25 May, 1895

NEMATINA

Cladius pectinicornis, Fourc. *Guestling, Storrington, Bognor*

Trichiocampus viminalis, Fall. *Hastings* district (E. W. Andrews) ; *Bognor*, many specimens

NEMATINA (*continued*)

Trichiocampus ulmi, L. (rufipes) *Hastings* district ; *Bognor*, May, 1899

— drewseni, Thoms. *Guestling*

— eradiatus, Htg. *Hastings, Hollington*

Priophorus padi, L. Common

Leptocircus (Camponiscus) (?) luridiventris, Fall. *Guestling, Fairlight* ; larvæ only

Hemichroa alni, L. *Hastings, Guestling*

— rufa, L. *Guestling, Hastings, Laughton, Storrington*

Dineura nigricans, Christ. (virididorsata) *Guestling, Storrington, Slindon*

— stilata, Klug. *Peppering Ponds Battle, Bognor, Selsey*

Cryptocampus medullarius, Htg. (pentandræ) Bred from swollen sallow twigs (E. Connold)

Pontania leucosticta, Htg. *Hastings* district

— vallisnierii, Htg. (gallicola) The galls are very common.

Pteronus pavidus, Lep. *Storrington*

— miliaris, Pz. (croceus) *Bognor*, 11 September, 1900

— microcercus, Thoms. (miliaris). *Guestling*

— curtispina, Thoms. *Fairlight, Guestling, Bognor*

— melanaspis, Htg. (lacteus) *Storrington ; Bognor*, many on poplars

— myosotidis, F. *Battle, Guestling, Felpham, Arundel*

— ribesii, Scop. An abundant pest

— salicis, L. *Guestling*, (?) *Lavant*

Amauronematus amplus, Knw. *Bognor*, May, 1896

Crœsus septentrionalis, L. *Camber, Guestling, Laughton, Storrington*

Holcocneme cæruleocarpa, Htg. *Hastings* district, *Abbots Wood*

— lucida, Pz. *Guestling*, 31 May, 1889 ; *Eastham, Felpham*

Nematus abdominalis, Pz. *Hastings, Guestling, Tilgate*

— luteus, Pz. (ruficapillus) *Bognor*, 15 June, 1897

— bilineatus, Klug. *Bexhill*, 26 May, 1902

Pachynematus capreæ, Pz. Common

— rumicis, Fall. *Guestling*

— obductus, Htg. *Guestling, St. Leonards*

Lygæonematus compressicornis, F. *Fairlight ; Bognor*, August, 1902

Pristiphora pallidiventris, Fall. *Fairlight, Guestling, Bexhill*

— pallipes, Lep. (appendiculata) *Guestling, Bognor*

— puncticeps, Thoms. *Guestling*

NEMATINA (*continued*)

Pristiphora crassicornis, Htg. (Fletcheri) *Bersted*, July, 1898 ; *Guestling*

— ruficornis, Ol. *Hastings*

— betulæ, Retz. *Storrington*

TENTHREDINA

Phyllotoma vagans, Fall. *Fairlight*

Eriocampoides testaceipes, Cam. *Guestling*

— æthiops, F. (rosæ) *Guestling*, common on roses in garden

— varipes, Klug. ⎫ *Guestling, Storring-*
— annulipes, Klug. ⎬ *ton* ; doubtless
— limacina, Retz. ⎭ common

Hoplocampa cratægi, Klug. *Guestling, Westergate, Horndean*

— pectoralis, Thoms. *Guestling*, 22 June, 1888 ; *Hollington*. This species and the preceding are generally found on May bloom

— testudinea, Klug. *Guestling*, 1901. The larvæ eat out irregular cavities in the apples attacked by them

Mesoneura opaca, F. (verna) *Hastings ; Guestling*, 18 May, 1888 and 27 May, 1889

Periclista melanocephala, F. *Guestling*, larvæ

Phymatocera aterrima, Klug. *Fairlight*, 1893

Tomostethus fuliginosus, Schr. *Hastings, Fairlight, Guestling*

— dubius, Gmel. (ephippium) Common

— fuscipennis, Fall. *Fairlight, Guestling, Abbots Wood*

Blennocampa pusilla, Klug. *Guestling*

— affinis, Fall. (assimilis) *Bognor*, 9 March, 1894

— subcana, Zadd. *Lewes*

Scolioneura betuleti, Klug. *Guestling*, 5 September, 1888

— nana, Klug. *Guestling*

Monophadnus geniculatus, Htg. *Lewes*

— ruficruris, Brull. *Bexhill*, 26 May, 1902

— albipes, Gmel. *Hollington, Guestling, Felpham*

Kaliosysphinga pumila, Klug. *Hastings, Guestling*

— melanopoda, Cam. *Guestling*, probably common

Fenusa pygmæa, Klug. *Guestling, Woolbeding*

Harpiphorus lepidus, Klug. *Peppering*

Athalia glabricollis, Thoms. *Hastings, Lewes* ; probably common

— spinarum, F. *Guestling*, larvæ only

— lineolata, Lep. (rosæ) Very common

Selandria serva, F. Common

TENTHREDINA (continued)

Selandria sixii, Voll. (?) Hastings ; Storrington (Miss Chawner)

— flavens, Klug. Harting, 24 August, 1899 ; Beaumont

— stramineipes, Klug. Common

— morio, F. Guestling, 1899 ; Dallington, 5 August, 1891

Thrinax contigua, Knw. (mixta) Landport

Stromboceros delicatulus, Fall. Guestling, 22 June, 1891, 3 June, 1892

Strongylogaster cingulatus, F. Somewhat common

Eriocampa ovata, L. Guestling, Peppering, Tilgate, Laughton

Pœcilosoma pulverata, Retz. Guestling, 1888 and 1889 ; Peppering

— luteola, Klug. Bexhill, August, 1888 (E. A. Butler)

— klugi, Steph. (submutica) Ore, Guestling, Oxsettle, Bepton Down

— excisa, Thoms. Guestling, 23 May, 1889

Emphytus succinctus, Klug. (togatus) Ore, Storrington

— cinctus, L. Guestling, Hastings ; Dallington, 5 August, 1891 ; Lewes

— rufocinctus, Retz. Guestling, once

— calceatus, Klug. Hastings

— tibialis, Klug. Guestling, not scarce ; Dallington, Rewel Wood near Slindon

— serotinus, Klug. Hastings

— grossulariæ, Klug. Harting, 17 August, 1899

— carpini, Htg. Fairlight

— tener, Fall. Hastings district

Taxonus glabratus, Fall. Guestling, Lewes, Bognor

— equiseti, Fall. Guestling

Dolerus pratensis, Fall. (fulviventris) common

— palustris, Klug. Hastings, Fairlight, Ashdown Forest

— liogaster, Thoms. Bognor, several

— madidus, Klug. (lateritius) Bexhill

— gonager, F. Hastings, Guestling, Lewes, Shiffness

— picipes, Klug. (intermedius) Hastings district, Lewes, Bepton Down, 7 July, 1892

— nigratus, Mull. (fissus) St. Leonards, Guestling, Lewes, Bognor

— coruscans, Knw. Eartham, Bognor, not uncommon

— hæmatodes, Schr. Hastings, Lewes, Rewell Wood, 2 April, 1894

— niger, L. Cocking Down, 24 May, 1893

— æneus, Htg. Common

TENTHREDINA (continued)

Sciopteryx costalis, Klug. Near Lewes

— consobrinus, Klug. Guestling, 3 April, 1893. This species has not been taken elsewhere in Britain

Rhogogastera picta, Klug. Guestling, May and June, locally common ; Polegate

— viridis, L. Common

— punctulata, Klug. Hastings, Guestling, Lewes, Storrington

— fulvipes, Scop. (lateralis) St. Leonards

— aucupariæ, Klug. (gibbosa) Hastings, Guestling, Bognor, etc.

Tenthredopsis litterata, Geoff. (cordata ♀, etc.) Guestling, Lewes var. microcephala, Lep. Bognor, 18 June, 1902

— tiliæ, Pz. (nassata ♀). Somewhat common

— campestris, L. (scutellaris) Heyshott, 14 June, 1893

— coqueberti, F. (nigricollis) Guestling, etc. ; not uncommon

— dorsalis, Lep. Slindon, 30 June, 1902 ; Bepton Down, 7 July, 1902

Pachyprotasis variegata, Klug. Hastings district (E. W. Andrews)

— antennata, Klug. Guestling, 1892, Lewes (J. H. A. Jenner)

— rapæ, L. Common

Macrophya rustica, L. St. Leonards, Ninfield

— ribis, Schr. Hastings district (Theobald)

— 12-punctata, L. Hastings district (E. Connold)

— annulata, Geoff. (neglecta) St. Leonards, Hastings ; Guestling, May and June

Allantus maculatus, Fourc. Rare ; Ore, Abbots Wood

— vespa, Retz. (tricinctus) St. Leonards, Guestling, Barcombe

— scrophulariæ, L. Guestling, Peppering

— temulus, Scop. (bicincta) Common

— amænus, Grav. (cingulum) Guestling, July and August, 1887–8–9 ; two pairs were taken 27 July, 1888. A scarce species

— schäfferi, Klug. Guestling, 1883–9 and 1892 (E. N. Bloomfield) ; Hastings (E. A. Butler), Lewes (J. H. A. Jenner)

— arcuatus, Forst. Common

Tenthredo rufiventris, F. Guestling, May and June ; Dallington

— moniliata, Klug. Guestling, once

— atra, L. Hastings, Guestling, Landport var. dispar, Klug. Ninfield, 1898

TENTHREDINA (*continued*)
Tenthredo (?) colon, Klug. *Hastings* district (E. W. Andrews)
— livida, L. *Guestling, Storrington*, etc.; common

TENTHREDINA (*continued*)
Tenthredo fagi, Pz. (solitaria) *Guestling*, 15 June, 1892, *Ninfield, Abbots Wood, Laughton*
— mesomelæna, L. Common

CYNIPIDÆ
Gallflies

The Cynipidæ are seldom seen by the ordinary observer, though the galls made by some of them are very generally known ; such are the oak apple, the artichoke gall, the cherry gall and the spangle galls. The Cynips galls are also worthy of note as differing so extremely in form and position : some are conspicuous, such as those mentioned above, while others are small and well concealed ; they are found on the leaves, the twigs, the stems, and even the roots.

The economy of the gall makers is very curious ; we have here, in many cases, not only perfect parthenogenesis but alternations of generations. One generation then consists both of males and females, while the next generation are all females ; and so different are the insects in these alternate generations that they have been considered to belong to distinct genera, while the galls made by them are also quite different. I have therefore retained both names and have given a brief description of the galls.

I have been unable to obtain any information respecting the Sussex Cynips galls, except those which occur in the neighbourhood of Hastings, but of these I have a very good list. Mr. E. Connold has rendered much assistance, as he has assiduously collected these as well as other kinds of galls and thus has added many species.

Any one who is interested in this subject would do well to refer to the monograph of the *British Phytophagous Hymenoptera* by P. Cameron (vol. iv.), in which all these galls are figured and described, and to *Alternating Generations*, by Hermann Adler, translated and edited by C. R. Straton. In this latter work the oak galls alone are given, but the figures are good and there is much interesting information. The arrangement and nomenclature which I have used are those of the above mentioned monograph.

Rhodites eglanteriæ, Htg. Forms pea-shaped galls on the leaves of wild roses ; not uncommon
— rosæ, L. The well known bedeguar ; common
— nervosus, Curt. (rosarum). Galls like those of R. eglanteriæ but with several stout and sharp spines. *Guestling, Hastings*, etc.
Aulax glechomæ, Htg. Galls large, green or reddish, on the leaves of Glechoma hederacea. *Guestling, Pett, Crowhurst*
— hypochæridis, Kief. Spindle-shaped galls on the peduncles of Hypochæris radicata. *Fairlight, St. Helens, Ore* (E. Connold)
Aulax papaveris, Perr. The galls are formed within the seed vessels of poppies. Railway bank at *Crowhurst* (E. Connold)
— hieracii, Bouché. Swellings on the stems of Hieracia. *Guestling, Fairlight* ; scarce
Xestophanes potentillæ, De Vill. Irregular swellings on the stems and leaf stalks of Potentilla reptans. *Fairlight* ; *Battle* (E. Connold)

Xestophanes brevitarsis, Thoms. Similar swellings on the stems of P. tormentilla. *Guestling, Hollington, Hastings*

Periclistus caninæ, Htg. Distorts and enlarges galls of R. eglanteriæ. *Guestling*

Diastrophus rubi, Htg. Spindle-shaped polythalamous swellings on the stems of Rubi. *Guestling, Fairlight, Beauport Park*

All the following galls are found on the oak :—

Andricus glandium, Gir. Forms a number of galls within the acorn. *Beauport Park* on Turkey oak (Quercus cerris), *Hollington* on common oak (Q. robur)

— ostreus, Gir. The oyster gall ; small, breaking out from the ribs of the leaf ; common

— fecundatrix, Htg. The artichoke gall ; the true gall is hidden in the greatly developed leaf buds ; common

— *pilosus, Adler. Very small, hairy galls on the catkins

— globuli, Htg. Green globular bud gall. *Guestling, St. Helens*

— inflator, Htg. Gall concealed in the greatly thickened and shortened shoots; not uncommon

— radicis, F. Large polythalamous swellings on the lower part of the trunk. *Hastings, Guestling,* etc.

— trilineatus, Htg. Galls concealed in the twigs ; not common

— sieboldii, Htg. Gregarious conical galls on the twigs, red when young, brown and striate when old. *Bexhill, Guestling, Crowhurst,* etc.

— testaceipes, Htg. Small elongate galls on the mid-rib or petiole. *Hastings, Hollington*

— corticis, Htg. Galls on the thick roots or on the trunk where the bark has been injured. *St. Helens, Hollington*

— *gemmatus, Adler. A very small and inconspicuous gall on the adventitious buds

— *collaris, Htg. A small bud gall almost concealed in the bud scales

— curvator, Thoms. Irregular bladder-like swellings containing a small gall ; common

— quadrilineatus, Htg. Longitudinally furrowed galls on the catkins. *Guestling, Hastings,* etc. ; not uncommon

— cirratus, Adler. Oval galls on the catkins with woolly hairs at the apex

— callidoma, Thoms. A leaf bud gall on a long peduncle. *St. Helens, Hollington*

Andricus albopunctata, Mayr. A bud gall, green spotted with white. *Fairlight, Hollington,* etc.

— glandulæ, Schenck. A bud gall sometimes like an acorn and cup, at other times truncated. *Guestling, St. Helens, Hollington*

— solitarius, Fonsc. A pointed and spindle-shaped bud gall covered with ferruginous hair. *Guestling, St. Helens,* etc.

Cynips kollari, Htg. The marble gall ; on the twigs ; common

Trigonaspis megaptera, Pz. Small reddish galls on the adventitious buds; not uncommon

— renum, Gir. Small kidney-shaped galls on the veins of the leaves ; not uncommon

Biorhiza terminalis, F. The well known oak apple ; common

— aptera, F. Small galls on the roots

Dryophanta folii, Htg. The cherry gall ; on the mid rib of the leaf ; common

— taschenbergi, Schl. Small oval velvety galls on the adventitious buds. *Hollington*

— longiventris, Htg. Gall like that of D. folii, but smaller and striped. *Guestling, Hastings*

— *similis, Adler. Gall very like taschenbergi

— agama, Htg. Globular leaf galls with large central cavity. *Guestling*

— divisa, Htg. Galls smooth with small central cavity. *Guestling*

— *verrucosa, Schl. Oval greenish or yellowish galls

— disticha, Htg. Gall like a flattened orange. *Guestling, Hollington*

Neuroterus lenticularis, Oliv. The common spangle ; very abundant

— baccarum, L. The currant gall; on leaves and catkins ; common

— fumipennis, Htg. Like the common spangle, but smaller ; not uncommon

— tricolor, Htg. Small and whitish covered with glistening white hairs ; not uncommon

— læviusculus, Schenck. The smooth spangle ; very common

— albipes, Schenck. Galls small, indenting the edge of the leaf. *Guestling, Hastings*

— numismatis, Oliv. The silk button gall; common

— vesicatrix, Schl. Gall embedded in the leaf marked with rays from the centre. *Guestling, Hastings*

— aprilinus, Gir. A pea-like bud gall maturing very quickly. *Battle Great Wood*

* Not yet observed in the district, but must occur.

A HISTORY OF SUSSEX

ENTOMOPHAGA

ICHNEUMONIDÆ

Ichneumon flies

It is not necessary in a general work like the present to give voluminous notes regarding the economy of the species here treated; suffice it to say that all Ichneumonidæ are parasitic, some of them hyperparasitic, living during their larval condition entomophagously amid the adipose tissues of the caterpillars and chrysalides of Lepidoptera, Diptera, Coleoptera and Tenthredinidæ, a few even preying upon spiders and their egg-sacs. The Ichneumonides and Ophionides attack, almost exclusively, butterflies and moths; the Homalopi group of the Tryphonides destroy large numbers of injurious sawflies; the Schizodontes group lay their eggs in dipterous larvæ, e.g. Syrphus, etc.; the Pimplides play most havoc amongst the Coleoptera, especially the Longicornia; and the Cryptides appear to distribute their parasitism, which often extends to fellow-members of their own family.

It appears strange that we should have no more recent British catalogue of these conspicuous insects than that compiled by Rev. T. A. Marshall in 1872; but, since such is the case, it is perhaps preferable to follow the nomenclature there adopted (based upon that of Holmgren, Taschenberg and Wesmael) than to classify the species according to modern continental and American systems, which would throw British readers with a slight knowledge of the subject into hopeless confusion, since the synonymy has undergone numerous rectifications, the genera have been subdivided and greatly augmented, and even the subfamilies and tribes have often been redistributed.

The bulk of the material at my disposal was collected by the authors of the *Natural History of Hastings* and named for them by Messrs. Bridgman, Fitch and Bignell. The majority of these specimens were most generously presented to me by Rev. E. N. Bloomfield in 1898, though a few are in Mr. Bridgman's collection in the Norwich Museum. I have consequently been enabled to carefully examine these Sussex examples and to correct such errors as had crept into the local records. Since the publication in 1898 of the third supplement to the above history a very few species have been added by Messrs. Bennett, Esam, Theobald and myself. From other parts of the county there is a great paucity of information concerning this little-known family. Mr. Alfred Beaumont has collected a few species at Harting, Pevensey and Horsley; Mr. E. A. Elliott a few at Littlehampton; Mr. Esam at Eastbourne; and Mr. W. H. B. Fletcher has bred some from Sussex hosts at Worthing.

It is doubtful whether the species in the Hastings Museum are from Sussex.

Marshall represents 1,186 species as British, and up to the present time an additional 533 have been recorded, bringing the total number of indigenous species to 1,719; but I anticipate that nearly 2,500 occur with us. Only 280 have been noticed in Sussex.

INSECTS

ICHNEUMONIDES

Chasmodes motatorius, Fab. *Hastings, Guestling, Mountfield, Brede, Beaufort Park*; in tufts of Aira cæspitosa; doubtless common during the winter

Ichneumon bilineatus, Gmel. *Hastings*
— lineator, Fab. *Fairlight* in 1884
— impressor, Zett. A female at *Guestling* in August, 1886
— castaneiventris, Grav. *Guestling*
— scutellator, Grav. *Hastings* district
— computatorius, Müll. *Battle, Guestling, Hastings*
— sarcitorius, L. (vaginatorius, L.) *Littlehampton* (Elliott), *Shipley* (Gorham), *Guestling, Hastings*; on flowers in August; doubtless common
— xanthorius, Forst. *Hollington*
— confusorius, Grav. *Hastings* district; *Brede, Battle*, etc., in March (Morley)
— gracilentus, Wesm. *Hastings* district
— bisignatus, Grav. Mr. Bignell has named this as taken at Hastings by L. B. Hall
— extensorius, L. (luctatorius, L.). *Guestling*; *Hastings* (Esam); common at roots of grass about *Hastings* in April (Morley)
— latrator, Fab. *Hastings, Fairlight, Battle, Brede*, etc.; abundant. I have taken the brachypterous variety *means* at *Peppering* (Morley)
— gracilicornis, Grav. *Guestling* in 1889
— quadrialbatus, Grav. *Guestling*
— analis, Grav. A female at *Battle* in grass tufts in March, 1900 (Morley)
— saturatorius, L. *Hastings*
— nigritarius, Grav. *Guestling* in 1888; it occurs in woods in May
— fabricator, Fab. *Battle* and several times at *Guestling*; a common species; I. maculifrons, Ste., is the male of this species
— annulator, Fab. (curvinervis, Holmgr.) *Guestling* in 1880 and 1891
— coruscator, L. *Guestling*
— luteiventris, Grav. *Hollington* (Theobald)
— lanius, Grav. *Hastings*; occurs among oaks in May
— albilarvatus, Grav. *Hastings* district
— vacillatorius, Grav. Not uncommon at *Guestling*
— dumeticola, Grav. *Hollington*; *Hastings* in 1897
— leucomelas, Gmel. *Hastings*; probably not uncommon
— sanguinator, Rossi (discrepator, Wesm.) *Ecclesbourne* (Theobald), *Hastings* district (Bennett); said to occur in ants' nests in winter

Ichnuemon albicinctus, Grav. *Fairlight, Guestling*; *Brede* in March (Morley); a common species

Exophanes hilaris, Grav. (exulans, Grav.) *Hastings* in 1887 (Bennett)

Amblyteles palliatorius, Grav. *Hollington*; *Hastings* (Connold); an abundant species in August
— armatorius, Forst. *Hastings* (Collett and Connold); *Hollington, Guestling*; a somewhat common species in the neighbourhood of *Bodiam* (Esam)
— oratorius, Fab. Powder Mill Ponds near *Battle*. I. cingulipes, Ste., is a variety of this species which Mr. Connold has taken at *Hastings*
— flavocinctus, Desv. *Hastings* district
— quadripunctorius, Müll. (notatorius, Trentep.)
— subsericans, Grav. *Guestling*, probably common; *Hastings* in August (Beaumont)
— gravenhorsti, Wesm. *Guestling*
— castigator, Fab. *St. Leonards*
— fuscipennis, Wesm. (fusorius, Brit. Cat.) Both sexes bred from larvæ of Chærocampa porcellus. *Beachy Head*, 1892 (Esam); also bred from *Rye*

Probolus alticola, Grav. Several females at *Hastings* (Esam)

Trogus lutorius, Fab. An example, *perhaps not from Sussex*, in the *Hastings* Museum

Platylabus pumilio, Holmgr. *Hastings* district
— dimidiatus, Grav. *Hastings* district

Colpognathus celerator, Grav. *Harting* (Beaumont); *Battle*, and common at *Brede* in March (Morley)

Dicœlotus pumilus, Grav. *Fairlight*
— pusillator, Grav. *Hastings* district

Phæogenes semivulpinus, Grav. *Guestling* in 1888
— planifrons, Wesm. A doubtful example at *Guestling* in 1877
— melanogonus, Gmel. *Guestling*
— stimulator, Grav. *Hastings*
— fulvitarsis, Wesm. *Hastings* district
— cephalotes, Wesm. *Dallington*
— jucundus, Wesm. *Hastings*
— trepidus, Wesm. *Hastings* district
— impiger, Wesm. " "

Alomyia debellator, Fab. *Eastbourne, Hastings* (Esam); *Guestling*; doubtless common in the autumn

CRYPTIDES

Stilpnus gagates, Grav. *Fairlight*
— deplanatus, Grav. "

Phygadeuon fumator, Grav. *Battle, Westfield, Brede*, etc.; doubtless common

— jejunator, Grav.

— rusticellæ, Bridge. Both sexes bred by Mr. W. H. B. Fletcher from old birds' nests at *Bognor* (Bridgman)

— larvatus, Grav. *Battle*

— vagabundus, Grav. *Guestling*; doubtless abundant on Heracleum sphondylium flowers in July

— quadrispinus, Grav. One female in tuft of Aira cæspitosa at *Brede* in March, 1900 (Morley)

— abdominator, Grav. Probably common

— jucundus, Grav. *Hastings* district

— lacteator, Grav. A doubtful example at *Battle*

— sperator, Müll. *Guestling* in 1880

— erythrinus, Grav. *Hastings* district (Connold)

— hercynicus, Grav. *Guestling*

Cryptus viduatorius, Fab. Probably not uncommon

— tarsoleucus, Schr. *Hastings*

— bivinctus, Grav. *Guestling* in 1889 (*Nat. Hist. Hast.* 3rd Suppl. p. 14, bicinctus in error)

— titillator, Grav. *Guestling* in 1877

— obfuscator, Vill. *Hastings* district

— obscurus, Grav. Several times at *Guestling*; probably common

— perspicillator, Grav. *Guestling*

— porrectorius, Fab. *Hastings, Guestling*

— analis, Grav. *Polegate* early in May, 1896 (Morley)

— leucotarsus, Grav. *Guestling* in 1887

— peregrinator, L. *Guestling*

— cimbicis, Tschek. Several females with the cocoon of the Trichiosoma, upon which they are parasitic, in the *Hastings* Museum

— ornatus, Grav. *Guestling* in 1891; said to prey upon wasps

— migrator, Fab. *Hastings, Guestling*

Mesostenus obnoxius, Grav. *Fairlight* in 1880

— ligator, Grav. A female taken at *Hastings* (Connold)

Hemiteles furcatus, Tasch. Doubtfully recorded in first supplement

— micator, Grav. Probably quite common

— bicolorinus, Grav. *Hollington, Ore, Fairlight*; common

— minutus, Bridg. Bred by Mr. W. H. B. Fletcher from spiders' nests at *Worthing* (Bridgman)

— areator, Panz. *Harting* in August and September, 1899 (Beaumont); *Hastings, Ore*

— castaneus, Tasch. Doubtfully recorded from the *Hastings* district

Hemiteles cingulator, Grav. *Hastings* district

Orthopelma luteolator, Grav. Bred from galls of Rhodites, *Hastings*, 1880 (Collett)

Catalytus fulveolatus, Grav. *Battle*

Agrothereutes hopei, Grav. *Hastings, Peppering Powder Mills*

— batavus, Voll. A female in a sand-pit at *Guestling* in September (cf. *E.M.M.* 1881, p. 258)

Aptesis nigrocincta, Grav. *St. Helens Wood, Hastings*, in grass-tuft (Morley); several times at *Guestling*

— stenoptera, Marsh. In sand-pit at *Guestling* (cf. *E.M.M.* 1881, p. 258)

Theroscopus pedestris, Fab. *Pevensey, Harting* (Beaumont); *Hastings*

Hemimachus rufocinctus, Grav. (P. instabilis, Först) *Pevensey, Harting* (Beaumont); *Hastings*

— fasciatus, Fab. *Fairlight, Dallington, Peppering*, etc.; doubtless common

Pezomachus ratzeburgi, Först. *Hastings* district

— tener, Först. *Battle*

— zonatus, Först. *Brede*, in grass-tufts in April (Morley); *Hastings, Guestling*, etc.

— bellicosus, Först. *Harting* (Beaumont), *Netherfield, Guestling*

— rufulus, Först. *Battle*

— ochraceus, Först. *Hastings* district

— corruptor, Först. *Harting* (Beaumont), *Guestling, Battle*

— agilis, Först. A male at *Harting* (Beaumont)

— transfuga, Först. *Battle*

— gracilis, Först. *Hastings*

— anguinus, Först. *Bopeep, St. Leonards*

— linearis, Först. *Hastings*

— costatus, Bridg. *Camber* (Bennett)

— micrurus, Först. *Battle*

— geochares, Först. *Harting* (Beaumont)

— faunus, Först. *Guestling, Hollington* (= dubitator et analis of 1st suppl.; cf. *Trans. Ent. Soc.* 1886, p. 341)

— fraudulentus, Först. Two doubtful examples at *Dallington* in 1882 (in col. Butler)

— intermedius, Först. *Hastings* by Mr. Butler (Bridgman)

OPHIONIDES

Henicospilus ramidulus, L. *Harting* in September, 1899 (Beaumont)

Ophion obscurus, Fab. One of our commonest British Ichneumonids

— luteus, L. *Hollington, Guestling, Hastings*, etc., abundant; often attracted to light at night

INSECTS

Ophion minutus, Kriechb. First taken in Britain at *Fairlight* in 1880 (cf. Savage, *E.M.M.* 1881, p. 236)

Schizoloma amicta, Fab. A female, perhaps not from Sussex, in the Hastings Museum

Anomalon ruficorne, Grav. *Guestling*
— bellicosum, Wesm. *Guestling* in 1888
— clandestinum, Grav. *Dallington*

Agrypon flaveolatum, Grav. *Guestling* in 1888
— tenuicorne, Grav. *Guestling* in 1880

Trichomma enecator, Rossi. *Guestling* in 1889

Opheltes glaucopterus, L. An example, without locality, in Hastings Museum ; preys upon sawflies

Paniscus cephalotes, Holmgr. Bred from Dicranura vinula at *Guestling*
— virgatus, Fourc. *Guestling*, etc. ; probably common
— testaceus, Grav. *Hastings*, *Fairlight*, etc.
— fuscicornis, Holmgr. *Guestling*, *Fairlight* (Bennett)
— latungula, Thoms. First taken in Britain near *Hastings*

Campoplex pugillator, L. *Hastings*, *Ore*
— cultrator, Grav. *Hastings* district
— rugulosus, Först. *Guestling* in 1889
— femorator, Bridg. „ „ „
— foveolatus, Först. „ „ 1890
— angustatus, Thoms. „ „ 1888
— erythrogaster, Först. „ „ 1889

Cymodusa leucocera, Holmgr. *Hollington*
— cruentata, Grav. *Hastings* district

Casinaria orbitalis, Grav. *Hastings*
— vidua, Grav. *Ore* ; doubtless abundant ; it preys upon Abraxas grossulariata
— tenuiventris, Grav. *Fairlight*

Limneria annulata, Grav. *Hastings* district
— difformis, Gmel. „ „
— erucator, Zett. *Pett*, *Fairlight*
— distincta, Bridg. Bred by Mr. W. H. B. Fletcher from Gelechia lentiginosella, *Abbots Wood* (Bridgman)
— fenestralis, Holmgr. *Fairlight*
— majalis, Grav. *Hastings*
— mutabilis, Holmgr. *Fairlight*
— nana, Grav. A doubtful specimen at *Hastings*
— obscurella, Holmgr. *Hastings*
— rapax, Grav. *Hastings* district
— rufipes, Grav. An example, queried by Bridgman, at *Guestling*
— tristis, Grav. *Battle*
— brischkei, Bridg. *Hastings* district
— cursitans, Holmgr. *Ecclesbourne*
— dumeticola, Holmgr. *Hastings* district
— kriechbaumeri, Bridg. *Hollington* (Esam)
— lugubrina, Holmgr. A specimen, of which Fitch was doubtful, in the *Hastings* district

Limneria ovata, Brisch.
— volubilis, Holmgr. *Battle*

Nemeritis macrocentra, Grav. Fitch could not quite determine an example from *Peppering Powder Mills*

Atractodes gravidus, Grav. *Hastings* district

Exolytus lævigatus, Grav. *Harting* (Beaumont), *Guestling*

Mesochorus confusus, Holmgr. *Hastings*
— pectoralis, Ratz. *Ore*
— pictilis, Holmgr. All the species of this genus are hyperparasitic
— tetricus, Holmgr. Two at *Harting* in August by Beaumont (fide Marshall)

Plectiscus zonatus, Grav. *Hastings* district

Collyria calcitrator, Grav. *Hastings* and *St. Leonards* in June, 1900 (Esam) ; *Guestling*

Exetastes osculatorius, Fab. *Hastings* (Bennett), *Guestling* ; doubtless common
— guttatorius, Grav. *Horsley* in August (Beaumont), *Guestling*
— illusor, Grav. A doubtful specimen taken near *Hastings* by Bennett
— albitarsus, Grav. *Guestling* in 1889

Banchus variegator, Fab. „ „ 1887
— falcator, Fab. *St. Leonards*

TRYPHONIDES

Mesoleptus melanocephalus, Grav. *Guestling*
— testaceus, Fab. *Guestling* in 1889
— typhæ, Grav. „ „ 1879, etc.
— sulphuratus, Grav. *Hastings* district

Catoglyptus fuscicornis, Gmel. *Guestling* in 1879

Euryproctus geniculosus, Grav. *Guestling* in 1880
— notatus, Grav. The only British record is that of a doubtful example at *Fairlight*

Perilissus filicornis, Grav. *Guestling*, etc. ; probably common
— prærogator, Grav. Abundant throughout Britain on Heracleum flowers in autumn
— bucculentus, Holmgr. The only British example was taken at *Peppering Powder Mills*

Megastylus erythrostomus, Grav. *Fairlight*

Mesoleius aulicus, Grav. *Hastings*
— sanguinicollis, Grav. *Guestling* in 1891
— sylvestris, Grav. *Guestling* in 1880
— armillatorius, Grav. A doubtful example at *Guestling* in 1889
— formosus, Grav. *Guestling*
— multicolor, Grav. *Guestling* in 1879
— semicaligatus, Grav. *Fairlight*

Mesoleius insolens, Grav. *Guestling*; probably common

Trematopygus vellicans, Grav. One (queried by Fitch) at *Guestling*

Tryphon elongator, Fab. Always common

— trochanteratus, Holmgr. *Peppering Powder Mills* and several times at *Guestling*

— consobrinus, Holmgr. *Guestling* in 1886

— signator, Grav. *Guestling* in 1876 and

— 1888

— ephippium, Holmgr. *Guestling*

Polyblastus varitarsus, Grav. „ in 1878

Acrotomus lucidulus, Grav. „

Cteniscus apiarius, Grav. „ in 1880

Exyston cinctulum, Grav. *Hastings*

Exochus prosopius, Grav. *Hastings* district

— erythronotus, Holmgr. „ „

— procerus, Holmgr. *Guestling* (in col. Bridg.)

Chorinæus asper, Grav. *Hastings*

— cristator, Grav. *Hastings, Guestling*; *Harting* (Beaumont)

Bassus lætatorius, Fab. *Littlehampton* in August (Elliott); common everywhere

— nemoralis, Holmgr. A common species; *Hastings* (Esam)

— multicolor, Grav. *Guestling*

— pectoratorius, Grav. *Hastings* district

— biguttatus, Grav. „ „

— exsultans, Grav. „ „

— insignis, Grav. A doubtful example at *Fairlight*

— pictus, Grav. *Guestling* in 1887

— fissorius, Grav. *Hastings*

— strigator, Fab. „

— nigritarsus, Grav. *Hastings* district

— pulchellus, Holmgr. „ „

— cognatus, Holmgr. „ „

— obscuripes, Holmgr. „ „

— holmgreni, Bridg. „ „

Metopius dentatus, Fab. A specimen, probably of this species, captured at *Pett*

PIMPLIDES

Ephialtes carbonarius, Christ. Two or three species of this genus are in the Hastings Museum

Perithous mediator, Fab. *Guestling*

— varius, Grav. Members of this genus are parasitic upon Fossores

— divinator, Rossi. *Guestling* in 1887

Pimpla instigator, Fab. *Littlehampton* in August (Elliott), *Hastings* (Esam); doubtless common

— examinator, Fab. *Guestling* in 1890

— turionellæ, L. *Hastings, Guestling*

— rufata, Gmel. *Hastings* district

— scanica, Vill. *Hastings* (Connold), *Hollington Church Wood* on yew in March (Morley)

Pimpla oculatoria, Fab. *Pevensey* in September (Beaumont), *Hastings*, etc.

— graminellæ, Schr. *St. Leonards*

— stercorator, Fab. *Hastings, Fairlight*

— brevicornis, Grav. *Hastings*

— nucum, Ratz. „

— detrita, Holmgr. A doubtful example at *Ecclesbourne*

Ischnoceros rusticus, Fourc. *Fairlight*, in May, 1889; named by Capron

Glypta monoceros, Grav. *Harting* in August, 1899 (Beaumont)

— fronticornis, Grav. *St. Leonards*

— elongata, Holmgr. Bred from larvæ of Bactra lanceolana, *Worthing* (Bridgman)

— ceratites, Grav. *Peppering Powder Mills, Guestling*

— teres, Grav. *Hastings* district

— lugubrina, Holmgr. *Guestling, St. Leonards*

— mensurator, Fab. *Guestling* in 1879

— bifoveolata, Grav. *Fairlight*

— trochanterata, Bridg. *Hastings* district

— similis, Bridg. Bred by Mr. W. H. B. Fletcher from Ephippiphora scutellana, *Worthing* (Bridgman)

— cicatricosa, Ratz. First taken in Britain at *Guestling* (cf. *E.M.M.* 1890, p. 208)

— flavolineata, Grav. *Guestling* in 1889

Lampronota caligata, Grav. „ „ 1888

Lissonota parallela, Grav. *Hastings* district

— rufomedia, Bridg. Bred at *Worthing* by Fletcher from Crambus contaminellus and Eudorea mercurella (Bridgman)

— bellator, Grav. *Peppering, Guestling*, etc.; doubtless abundant on Angelica in August

— commixta, Holmgr. *Peppering Powder Mills*

— cylindrator, Vill. *Hastings*; probably common

— verberans, Grav. *Camber*

— segmentator, Fab. *Hastings* district

— sulphurifera, Grav. *Hastings* (Esam); *Hollington*, etc., common

— carbonaria, Holmgr. Bred by Fletcher from Tortrix pupa at *Abbots Wood*, Sussex (Bridgman)

— leucogona, Grav. First taken in Britain in a sand-pit at *Guestling* (cf. *E.M.M.* 1881, p. 258)

— errabunda, Holmgr., nec Grav. Near *Guestling* by Mr. Bennett (Bridgman)

Meniscus murinus, Grav. *Guestling, Hastings*, etc.; probably common in May

Phytodietus segmentator, Grav. *Guestling* in 1880

— coryphæus, Grav. *Hastings, Guestling*

— vetulus, Grav. *Guestling*; probably abundant in woods in spring

Œdemopsis scabriculus, Grav. *Hastings*

Xylonomus pilicornis, Grav. „

INSECTS

BRACONIDÆ [1]

Bracon minutator, F. *Battle*
— fuscicoxis, Wesm. *Harting*
Colastes hariolator, Hal. ,,
Oncophanes lanceolator, Nees. *Hastings*
Spathius exarator, L. *Hurst Green, Harting*; parasitic on Anobium domesticum
Rhogas circumscriptus, Nees. *Hastings* district
Chelonus pusio, Marsh. *Worthing*; bred from Elachista atricomella by Mr. W. B. Fletcher
Ascogaster instabilis, Wesm. *Hastings*
— variipes, Wesm. *Hastings* district
— quadridentatus, Wesm. *Hastings* (Fitch)
Accœlius subfasciatus, Hal. *Harting*
Apanteles ruficrus, Hal. *Hastings* district
— glomeratus, L. ,, ,,
— spurius, Wesm. *Ore*
— difficilis, Nees. *Ore*; bred from Selenia bilunaria, by Mr. E. A. Butler
— obscurus, Nees. *Harting*
— albipennis, Nees. ,,
— fraternus, Reinh. ,,
— lateralis, Hal. ,,
— fulvipes, Hal. ,,
Microplites sordipes, Nees. *Harting*
Microgaster subcompletus, Nees. *Hastings*
— (?) globatus, L. *St. Leonards*
Agathes nigra, Nees. *Hastings*; *St. Leonards*
Orgilus obscurator, Nees. Bred by Mr. Fletcher
Microdus clausthalianus, Ratz. *Hastings*, bred from Ephippiphora scutellana
— brevicaudis, Reinh. *Guestling*, bred from Coleophora troglodytella, by Mr. Fletcher
— tumidulus, Nees. *Hastings* district
Meteorus albiditarsis, Curt. *Guestling*. An abundant parasite on Noctuæ larvæ (Morley)
— ictericus, Nees. *Guestling, Ore*
— punctiventris, Ruthe. *Worthing*, bred from Scoparia lineola by Mr. Fletcher
— caligatus, Hal. *Abbots Wood*, bred from Eupithecia expallidata by Mr. Fletcher
— rubens, Nees. *Guestling*
— fragilis, Wesm. *Hastings*
Eubadizon extensor, L. *Hastings* district

Blacus ruficornis, Nees. *Battle, Harting, Seddlescombe*, etc.
Helcon annulicornis, Nees. *Guestling*. A very rare species
Macrocentrus abdominalis var. pallipes, Nees. *Battle, Hastings*
— marginator, Nees. *Guestling*
— infirmus, Nees. *Harting*
— collaris, Spin. ,,
Zele testaceator, Curt. *Ore, Guestling*
— chlorophthalma, Nees. *Hastings* district
Opius apiculator, Nees. *Fairlight*
Allœa contracta, Hal. *Harting*
Chasmodon apterus, Nees. *Fairlight*
Alysia manducator, Panz. *Guestling, Ewhurst*
Phænocarpa ruficeps, Nees. *Harting*
Anisocyrta venusta.
Chænon anceps, Curt. *Hastings* district

EVANIIDÆ

Fœnus jaculator, L. *Guestling*

OXYURA

Proctotrypes ater, Nees. *Hastings* district
— calcar, Hal. ,, ,,
— buccatus, Thoms. *Harting*
Codrus apterogynus, Hal. *Battle*
Lagynodes pallidus, Boh. *Battle, Guestling*
Megaspilus halteratus, Boh. *Battle, Hollington*
— rufipes, Nees. *Guestling*
Perisemus triareolatus, Forst. *Hastings, Fairlight, Battle*
Gonatopus pedestris, Dalm. *Dallington*
— nigriventris, Nees. *Battle*
Chelogynus fuscicornis, Dalm. *Hastings*
Belyta dorsalis, Thoms. *Hastings* district
Aclista brachyptera, Thoms. *Bexhill, Guestling*
— fuscata, Thoms. *Battle*
Cinetus gracilipes, Curt. *Hastings*
Aneurrhynchus pentatomus, Thoms. *Hastings* district
Paramesius brachypterus, Thoms. *Hastings*
Diapria conica, F. *Guestling, Westfield, Crowhurst*
— carinata, Thoms. *Hastings*
— verticillata, Latr. *Guestling, Hurst Green*

CHRYSIDIDÆ

This interesting family is but poorly represented in Sussex as far as our records are concerned. They are very brilliant insects parasitic in the larval state on other Hymenoptera and may often be seen searching

---

[1] The nomenclature and arrangement are those of Marshall's monograph in the *Entomological Society's Transactions*.

on walls, rocks, etc., for the burrows of their hosts. Some species seem very restricted in their choice of a prey, as for instance *Chrysis neglecta* and *C. viridula* which prey on *Odynerus spinipes*, while others, as *Chrysis ignita*, attack a good many species apparently without much preference. This latter species is excessively variable in size ; probably this may be due to the size of the grub which has been its victim. We are indebted to the Rev. F. D. Morice for the following particulars : ' *Chrysis cyanea* seems to be chiefly attached to wood-boring Hymenoptera, it is often found on palings, very seldom on sand banks ; *C. fulgida* seems to have the same habits, as I have always found it on posts or wooden buildings ; whereas *C. succincta* preys on sand burrowing species. *Elampus auratus* is common on bramble stems with small Pemphredons and Trypoxylons. The *Hedychrums* and *Hedychridiums* are I believe mainly parasitic on sand-wasps, they occur in sandy places frequented by Astata, Tachysphex, etc. *Notozus panzeri*, as I have, I think, made out for certain, infests Mimesa, while *Cleptes* infests (teste Lepelletier) the Nemati.'

The Sussex recorded species are as follows :—

Cleptes pallipes, Lep. *Guestling* (E.N.B.) *Bognor* (G.)

Elampus violaceus, Scop. (cæruleus, Dhb.) *Hastings*

— auratus, L. *Hastings* district, bred from bramble stems ; *Bognor* (G.), bred from peach wood

Hedychridium ardens, Coq. *Hastings* district, bred from bramble stems

Chrysis neglecta, Schuck. *St. Leonards*

— cyanea, L. *Guestling* (E.N.B.), *Bognor* (G.)

— ignita, L. Common

HYMENOPTERA

ACULEATA

Bees, Wasps, Ants, etc.

The list of the Aculeata of this county hardly compares well with that of either Surrey or Kent. The reason for this appears to be that although the coast has been visited and worked by numerous entomologists, the centre and north, judging from the paucity of records, have been much neglected. When these latter have had due attention paid to them no doubt the comparison with those of the neighbouring counties will be favourable. Thanks to the energies of the Rev. E. N. Bloomfield of Guestling and his co-workers the neighbourhood of Hastings has been especially well worked, and nearly two-thirds of the British species of this section of the Hymenoptera have been recorded in the local lists published under his supervision. Two species captured by Mr. Bloomfield at Guestling have not been recorded from any other county, viz. *Sphecodes niger*, v. Hag., and *Rophites 5-spinosus*, Spin. The former of these is a very small inconspicuous insect and might easily be overlooked, but the latter could hardly be missed by any one on the look out for it ; only two specimens were taken and these as far back as 1878. It has been repeatedly sought for since without success. Altogether **266** species are recorded.

INSECTS

HETEROGYNA

FORMICIDÆ

Formica, Linn.
— rufa, Linn. *Brighton*, 'common' (Unwin); *Hastings* district, common
— sanguinea, Ltr. Near *Hove, Brighton*, 'rare' (Unwin)
— fusca, Linn. *Hastings* district, scarce; *Burpham, Slindon* (Guermonprez)
   r. cunicularia, Ltr. *Hastings* district

Lasius, Fab.
— fuliginosus, Ltr. *Hastings* district, *Bersted* (Guermonprez); *Brighton*, 'common' (Unwin)
— niger, Linn. Common and generally distributed
   r. alienus, Först. *Hastings*
— umbratus, Nyl. *Guestling* near *Hastings, Bognor* (Guermonprez); *Brighton* (Unwin)
— flavus, De Geer. Common and generally distributed

PONERIDÆ

Ponera, Ltr.
— contracta, Ltr. *Brighton* (Power)

MYRMICIDÆ

Myrmecina, Curt.
— latreillei, Curt. *Worthing* (Saunders)

Tetramorium, Mayr.
— cæspitum, Linn. *Hastings* district

Leptothorax, Mayr.
— acervorum, Fab. *Guestling* near *Hastings, Bexhill* (Frisby)
— tuberum, Fab.
   r. unifasciata, Ltr. *Fairlight* near *Hastings*

Myrmica, Ltr.
— rubra, Linn.
   r. ruginodis, Nyl. *Hastings* district, scarce; *Brighton* (Unwin)
   r. lævinodis, Nyl. *Hastings* district, common; *Bognor* (Guermonprez)
   r. scabrinodis, Nyl. *Hastings* district, common; *Brighton* (Unwin)

FOSSORES

MUTILLIDÆ

Mutilla, Linn.
— europæa, Linn. *Hastings*, 'rare'; *Brighton*, 'rare' (Unwin), *Camber*

Myrmosa, Ltr.
— melanocephala, Fab. *Hastings, Bexhill, Littlehampton* (Saunders); *Bognor* (Guermonprez)

Methoca, Ltr.
— ichneumonides, Ltr. *Bexhill* (Rothney)

TIPHIIDÆ

Tiphia, Fab.
— minuta, V. d. L. *Hollington* near *Hastings*

SAPYGIDÆ

Sapyga, Ltr.
— quinque-punctata, Fab. *Guestling* near *Hastings* (Frisby), *Brighton* (Unwin)

SPHEGIDÆ

Pompilus, Fab.
— plumbeus, Fab. *Hastings* district; *Littlehampton* (Saunders)
— niger, Fab. *Guestling* near *Hastings*; *Brighton* (Unwin)
— viaticus, Linn. *Hastings* district
— consobrinus, Dahlb. *Hastings*
— spissus, Schiödte. *Guestling* near *Hastings*
— chalybeatus, Schiödte. *Camber* (Frisby), *Worthing* (W. W. Saunders)
— gibbus, Fab. *Hastings* district; *Brighton* (Unwin)
— unguicularis, Thoms. *Hayward's Heath* (Morice)
— pectinipes, V. d. L. *Hastings*

Salius, Fab.
— fuscus, Linn. *Hastings* (Frisby), *Bexhill* (Saunders)
— exaltatus, Fab. *Hastings* district; *Worthing, Littlehampton* (Saunders)
— notatulus, Saund. *Littlehampton* (Smith)
— obtusiventris, Schiödte. *Bexhill*
— pusillus, Schiödte. *Hastings* district; *Bognor* (Guermonprez)

Calicurgus, Lep.
— hyalinatus, Fab. *Hastings* (Frisby)

PSEUDAGENIA
— carbonaria, Scop. *Hastings* (Frisby)

Ceropales, Ltr.
— maculata, Fab. *Hollington* near *Hastings*; *Worthing* (Saunders)

Astatus, Ltr.
— boops, Schr. *Hastings, Bexhill* (Frisby)
— stigma, Pz. *Littlehampton* (Saunders), *Rye Sandhills* (Sladen)

Tachytes, Pz.
— unicolor, Pz. *Littlehampton* (Saunders)
— pectinipes, Linn. *Hastings* district; *Hayward's Heath* (Morice)

Trypoxylon, Ltr.
— figulus, L. *Hastings* district; *Hayward's Heath* (Morice)
— clavicerum, Lep. *Hastings* district
— attenuatum, Smith. „ „

Ammophila, Kirb.
— sabulosa, Linn. *Bexhill*
— lutaria, Fab. *Littlehampton* (Saunders)

Stigmus, Jur.
— solskyi, Moraw. *Guestling* near *Hastings*

Pemphredon, Ltr.
— lugubris, Ltr. *Hastings* district; *Bognor* (Guermonprez)

PSEUDAGENIA (continued)

Pemphredon shuckardi, Moraw. *Hastings* district ; *Brighton* (Unwin)
— lethifer, Shuck. *Hastings* district ; *Bognor* (Guermonprez), *Brighton* (Unwin)

Diodontus, Curt.
— minutus, Fab. *Hastings* district
— tristis, v. d. L.　　　　,,　　　,,

Passalœcus, Shuck.
— corniger, Shuck. *Guestling* near *Hastings*
— insignis, v. d. L. *Hollington* near *Hastings* ; *Tilgate* (W. W. Saunders), *Bognor* (Guermonprez)
— gracilis, Curt. *Guestling* near *Hastings*
— monilicornis, Dhlb. *Hastings*

Psen, Ltr.
— pallipes, Pz. *Hastings* district, *Bognor* (Guermonprez)

Gorytes, Ltr.
— tumidus, Pz. *Guestling, Camber*
— mystaceus, Linn. *Hastings* district ; *Brighton* (Unwin)
— bicinctus, Rossi. *Hastings*
— quadrifasciatus, Fabr. ,,

Nysson, Ltr.
— spinosus, Fab. *Hastings* district ; *Brighton* (Unwin)
— dimidiatus, Jur. *Hastings* district ; *Littlehampton* (Saunders)

Didineis, Wesm.
— lunicornis, Fabr. *Battle* (Butler), *Worthing* (W. W. Saunders)

Mellinus, Fab.
— arvensis, Linn. *Hastings* district, scarce ; *Harting* (Beaumont)

Cerceris, Ltr.
— arenaria, Linn. *Hastings* district ; *Brighton*, 'rare' (Unwin)
— ornata, Schæff. *Hastings* district ; *Brighton*, 'rare' (Unwin)

Oxybelus, Ltr.
— uniglumis, Linn. *Hastings* district ; *Hayworth's Heath* (Morice)

Crabro, Fabr.
— clavipes, Linn. *Hastings*
— tibialis, Fabr. *Brighton* (Unwin)
— leucostomus, Linn. *Guestling* near *Hastings* ; *Bognor* (Guermonprez), *Brighton* (Unwin)
— podagricus, v. d. L. *St. Leonards* ; *Brighton* (Unwin), *Horsham* (Morice)
— palmipes, Linn. *Bexhill*
— wesmaeli, v. d. L. *Hastings* district
— elongatulus, v. d. L. *Hastings* district ; *Bognor* (Guermonprez)
— 4-maculatus, Dhlb. *Hastings* district ; *Hayward's Heath* (Morice)

PSEUDAGENIA (continued)

Crabro dimidiatus, Fabr. *Hastings* district ; *Hayward's Heath* (Morice)
— signatus, Pz. *Tilgate Forest* (T. N. Hoey, Aug. 1876)
— vagabundus, Pz. *Hastings* district ; *Brighton* (Unwin)
— cephalotes, Pz. *Hastings* district, scarce ; *Bognor* (Guermonprez)
— chrysostomus, Lep. *Hastings* district ; *Harting* (Beaumont)
— vagus, Linn. *Guestling* near *Hastings* ; *Brighton* (Unwin)
— cribrarius, Linn. *Hastings* district, *Brighton* (Unwin) ; *Harting* (Beaumont)
— interruptus, De Geer. *Bognor* (Guermonprez)
— albilabris, Fab. *Hastings* district, common ; *Hayward's Heath* (Morice)

Entomognathus, Dhlb.
— brevis, v. d. L. *Hastings* (Saunders), *Hayward's Heath* (Morice)

DIPLOPTERA

VESPIDÆ

Vespa, Linn.
— crabro, Linn. *Hastings* district, rare
— vulgaris, Linn. Generally distributed
— germanica, Fabr.　　　,,　　　,,
— rufa, Linn.　　　,,　　　,,
— sylvestris, Scop.　　　,,　　　,,
— norvegica, Fabr. *Normanhurst* near *Battle, Ore, Guestling* (Bloomfield); *Bognor* (Guermonprez)

EUMENIDÆ

Odynerus, Ltr.
— spinipes, Linn. *Hastings* district
— melanocephalus, Gmel. *Hastings* district
— lævipes, Shuck. *Hollington* near *Hastings* ; *Hayward's Heath* (Morice)
— callosus, Thoms. *Hastings* district
— parietum, Linn. *Hastings* district, common ; *Bognor* (Guermonprez), *Brighton* (Unwin)
— pictus, Curt. *Hastings* district ; *Brighton*, 'rare' (Unwin)
— trimarginatus, Zett. *Hastings* ; *Littlehampton* (Saunders)
— trifasciatus, Oliv. *Hastings* ; *Brighton*, 'rare' (Unwin)
— parietinus, Linn. *Hastings* district ; *Bognor* (Guermonprez)
— gracilis, Brullé. *Guestling* near *Hastings* (Frisby)
— sinuatus, Fab. *Hastings* district

INSECTS

ANTHOPHILA

COLLETIDÆ

Colletes, Ltr.
— succinctus, Linn. *Hastings* district
— fodiens, Kirb. *Fairlight* near *Hastings*; *Littlehampton* (Saunders)
— picistigma, Thoms. *Fairlight* near *Hastings* (Saunders)
— daviesanus, Smith. *Hastings* district; *Hayward's Heath* (Morice)

Prosopis, Fab.
— cornuta, Smith. *Hollington* near *Hastings* (Saunders), *Hastings* (Bennett), *Hayward's Heath* (Morice)
— masoni, Saund. *Hastings*
— dilatata, Kirb. *Arundel* (Stevens), *Brighton* (Unwin), *Hayward's Heath* (Morice)
— communis, Nyl. *Hastings* district; *Brighton* (Unwin), *Hayward's Heath, Horsham* (Morice)
— signata, Pz. *Hastings* (Saunders); *Brighton, Lewes* (Unwin); *Hayward's Heath* (Morice)
— hyalinata, Smith. *Hastings* district, *Bognor* (Guermonprez); *Worthing, Littlehampton* (Saunders); *Hayward's Heath* (Morice)
— confusa, Nyl. *Hastings* district; *Hayward's Heath, Horsham* (Morice)
— genalis, Thoms. *Hollington* near *Hastings*
— brevicornis, Nyl. *Hastings* district; *Hayward's Heath* (Morice)
— pictipes, Nyl. *Hastings* district; *Bognor* (Guermonprez)

ANDRENIDÆ

Sphecodes, Ltr.
— gibbus, Linn. *Hastings* district, *Littlehampton* (Saunders); *Brighton* (Unwin)
— subquadratus, Smith. *Hastings* district, *Littlehampton* (Saunders)
— reticulatus, Thoms. *Harting* (Beaumont)
— rubicundus, v. Hag. *Littlehampton* (Saunders)
— puncticeps, Thoms. *Worthing* (Saunders), *Hastings, Hayward's Heath* (Morice)
— longulus, v. Hag. *Stopham* (Guermonprez), *Hayward's Heath* (Morice)
— niger, v. Hag. *Guestling* near *Hastings* (Bloomfield). The only British record
— pilifrons, Thoms. *Hastings* district
— similis, Wesm. *Hastings* district; *Littlehampton, Worthing* (Saunders)
— variegatus, v. Hag. *Hastings, Seaford* (Ramsden); *Worthing* (Saunders)

ANDRENIDÆ (*continued*)
Sphecodes affinis, v. Hag. *Hastings*; *Worthing* (Saunders)
— dimidiatus, v. Hag. *Worthing* (Saunders)

Halictus, Ltr.
— rubicundus, Chr. *Hastings* district; *Bognor* (Guermonprez), *Brighton* (Unwin)
— quadricinctus, Fab. *Brighton Downs* near *Falmer* (S. S. Saunders), *Seaford* (Ramsden)
— maculatus, Smith. Near *Fairlight* in 1879 (Saunders)
— xanthopus, Kirb. *Hastings, Brighton, Lewes, Arundel, Littlehampton*
— leucozonius, Schr. Generally distributed
— zonulus, Smith. *Hastings* district; *Horsham* (Morice)
— quadrinotatus, Kirb. *Hastings* district; *Bognor* (Guermonprez), *Glynde, Lewes, Brighton* (Unwin); *Harting* (Beaumont)
— lævigatus, Kirb. *Ewhurst* (Butler), *Shipley* (Gorham), *Brighton, Lewes* (Unwin), *Horsham* (Morice)
— cylindricus, Fab. Generally distributed
— longulus, Smith. *Brighton* (Unwin)
— albipes, Kirb. *Brighton* (Unwin), *Horsham* (Morice), *Guestling*, etc.
— subfasciatus, Kirb. *Burpham* (Guermonprez)
— pauxillus, Schk. *Hastings*; *Hayward's Heath, Horsham* (Morice)
— villosulus, Kirb. Generally distributed
— puncticollis, Saund. *Hastings*
— breviceps, Saund. „
— punctatissimus, Schk. *Hastings* district
— nitidiusculus, Kirb. *Hastings* district; *Bognor* (Guermonprez), *Hayward's Heath* (Morice), *Brighton* (Unwin)
— minutus, Kirb. *Ewhurst* (Butler), *Lewes, Seaford, Eastbourne*; *Brighton* (Unwin)
— minutissimus, Kirb. *Hastings* district; *Worthing* (Saunders), *Bognor* (Guermonprez), *Brighton* (Unwin)
— tumulorum, Linn. Generally distributed
— smeathmanellus, Kirb. *Brighton* (Unwin), *Eastbourne* (Morley), *Hastings* district; *Littlehampton* (Saunders), *Hayward's Heath* (Morice), *Bognor* (Guermonprez)
— morio, Fab. *Hastings* district; *Worthing* (Saunders); *Bognor* (Guermonprez), *Hayward's Heath* (Morice), *Brighton* (Unwin)
— leucopus, Kirb. *Bognor* (Guermonprez), *Lewes, Brighton* (Unwin)

ANDRENIDÆ (*continued*)

Andrena, Fab.

— albicans, Kirb. Generally distributed
— pilipes, Fab. *Hastings* district ; *Brighton* (Unwin)
— tibialis, Kirb. *Hastings* ; *Brighton* (Unwin)
— bimaculata, Kirb. *Bognor* (Guermonprez)
— rosæ, Panz. *Hastings* district ; *Brighton* (Unwin), *Hayward's Heath* (Morice)
— florea, Fab. *Bexhill* (Frisby)
— thoracica, Fab. *Hastings* district ; *Newhaven, Seaford, Brighton, Eastbourne* (Unwin)
— nitida, Fourc. *Hastings* district ; *Bognor* (Guermonprez), *Brighton* (Unwin)
— cineraria, Linn. *Peasemarsh* near *Hastings* ; *Brighton, Eastbourne* (Unwin)
— fulva, Schr. *Hastings* district ; *Bognor* (Guermonprez) ; *Brighton* (Unwin)
— clarkella, Kirb. *Hastings* district ; *Bognor* (Guermonprez), *Brighton* (Unwin)
— nigroænea, Kirb. *Hastings* district ; *Bognor* (Guermonprez), *Brighton* (Unwin), *Hayward's Heath* (Morice)
— gwynana, Kirb. *Hastings* district ; *Bognor* (Guermonprez), *Brighton* (Unwin), *Hayward's Heath* (Morice)
— angustior, Kirb. *Hastings* district ; *Bexhill* (Saunders)
— apicata, Smith. *Hastings* district
— præcox, Scop. *Hastings* district ; *Brighton* (Unwin)
— varians, Rossi. *Hastings* district ; *Bognor* (Guermonprez), *Brighton* (Unwin)
— helvola, Linn. *Brighton* (Unwin)
— fucata, Smith. *Hastings* district ; *Slindon* (Guermonprez)
— nigriceps, Kirb. *Bexhill* (Saunders)
— fuscipes, Kirb. *St. Leonards*
— denticulata, Kirb. *Hastings* district
— fulvicrus, Kirb. *Hastings* district ; *Brighton* (Unwin)
— fasciata, Nyl. *Croft* near *Hastings*
— ferox, Smith. *Guestling* (Bloomfield)
— cetii, Schr. *Dallington Forest, Lewes, Brighton*, 'rare' (Unwin)
— cingulata, Fab. *Guestling* ; *Brighton* (Unwin)
— albicrus, Kirb. *Hastings* district
— chrysosceles, Kirb. *Hollington* ; *Worthing* (Saunders), *Brighton* (Unwin)
— analis, Pz. *St. Leonards*

ANDRENIDÆ (*continued*)

Andrena coitana, Kirb. *Hastings* district, *Littlehampton* (Saunders)
— lucens, Imh. *Shipley* (Gorham)
— fulvago, Chr. *Hastings*
— humilis, Imh. *Guestling*
— labialis, Kirb. *Hastings* district ; *Brighton* (Unwin), *Worthing* (Saunders), *Bognor* (Guermonprez)
— minutula, Kirb. *Hastings* district ; *Amberley* (Guermonprez), *Brighton* (Unwin)
— nana, Kirb. *Hastings* district ; *Worthing, Bognor* (Saunders) ; *Horsham* (Morice)
— niveata, Friese. *Worthing, Bognor* (Saunders) ; *Seaford* (Crawshay)
— proxima, Kirb. *Ecclesbourne* near *Hastings*
— wilkella, Kirb. *Hastings* district
— afzeliella, Kirb. *Brighton* (Unwin)

Cilissa, Leach.

— leporina, Panz. *Hastings* district, *Littlehampton, Bognor* (Guermonprez)

Dasypoda, Ltr.

— hirtipes, Ltr. *Camber*

Panurgus, Panz.

— calcaratus, Scop. *Guestling*
— ursinus, Gmel. *Fairlight, Brighton* (Unwin)

Rophites, Spin.

— 5-spinosus, Spin. *Guestling* (Bloomfield) ; the only British record

Nomada, Fabr.

— solidaginis, Panz. *Hastings* district
— fucata, Panz. *Hastings* district ; *Brighton* (Unwin)
— sexfasciata, Panz. *Hastings* district ; *Brighton*, 'rare' (Unwin)
— succincta, Panz. Generally distributed
— lineola, Panz. *Hollington*
— alternata, Kirb. Generally distributed
— jacobææ, Panz. *Hollington, Littlehampton* (Smith)
— ruficornis, Linn. Generally distributed
— bifida, Thoms. *Hastings* district (Esam)
— borealis, Zett. *Hastings* district
— ochrostoma, Kirb. *Fairlight, Worthing* (Saunders)
— argentata, H.S. *Arundel* (Smith)
— fabriciana, Linn. *Hastings* district ; *Brighton* (Unwin)
— flavoguttata, Kirb. *Hastings* district
— furva, Panz. *Hastings* district ; *Brighton* (Unwin)

APIDÆ

Epeolus, Ltr.

— productus, Thoms. *Guestling*

Chelostoma

— florisomne, Linn. *St. Leonards* ; *Brighton* (Unwin)

INSECTS

APIDÆ (*continued*)

Chelostoma campanularum, Kirb. *Worthing* (Saunders), *Hayward's Heath* (Morice)

Cœlioxys, Ltr.
— quadridentata, Linn. *Slindon* (Guermonprez)
— rufescens, Lep. *Hollington* near *Hastings*; *Brighton* (Unwin)
— elongata, Lep. *Hastings*; *Littlehampton* (Saunders)
— acuminata, Nyl. *Hastings*; *Bognor* (Guermonprez)

Megachile, Ltr.
— maritima, Kirb. *Rye Harbour* (Sladen), *Hastings* district; *Bognor* (Guermonprez)
— willughbiella, Kirb. *Hastings, Bognor* (Guermonprez), *Brighton* (Unwin)
— circumcincta, Lep. „ „
— ligniseca, Kirb. *St. Leonards*; *Felpham* (Guermonprez), *Brighton* (Unwin), *Bognor* (Guermonprez)
— centuncularis, Linn. *Hastings* district, *Littlehampton* (Saunders)
— argentata, Fab. *Rye Harbour* (Sladen), *Hastings, Littlehampton* (Saunders)

Osmia, Panz.
— rufa, Linn. *Hastings* district; *Bexhill* (Saunders), *Bognor* (Guermonprez), *Brighton* (Unwin)
— pilicornis, Smith. *Hastings* district; *Abbots Wood* near *Polegate* (Morley)
— xanthomelana, Kirb. *Eastbourne* (Smith)
— cærulescens, Linn. *Hastings* district, *Bognor* (Guermonprez); *Brighton* (Unwin)
— fulviventris, Panz. *Ore*; *Bognor* (Guermonprez); *Brighton* (Unwin)
— bicolor, Schr. *Bognor* (Guermonprez), *Brighton* (Unwin)
— aurulenta, Panz. *Bexhill, Bognor, Littlehampton* (Saunders); *Brighton* (Unwin)
— leucomelana, Kirb. *Ecclesbourne, Hastings* (Saunders); *Hayward's Heath* (Morice)
— spinulosa, Kirb. *Ore*

Stelis, Panz.
— aterrima, Panz. *Hastings, Bognor* (Guermonprez); *Brighton* (Unwin)

Anthidium, Fab.
— manicatum, Linn. *Hastings* district; *Bognor* (Guermonprez), *Brighton* (Unwin), *Hayward's Heath* (Morice)

Eucera, Scop.
— longicornis, Linn. *Hastings* district; *Felpham* (Guermonprez), *Brighton* (Unwin)

APIDÆ (*continued*)

Melecta, Ltr.
— luctuosa, Scop. *Brighton* (Unwin)
— armata, Panz. *Hastings* district; *Bognor* (Guermonprez), *Brighton* (Unwin)

Anthophora, Ltr.
— retusa, Linn. *Guestling, Worthing* (Saunders); *Brighton* (Unwin)
— pilipes, Fab. *Hastings* district; *Bognor* (Guermonprez), *Brighton* (Unwin)
— furcata, Panz. *Guestling, Hastings, Littlehampton* (Saunders); *Bognor* (Guermonprez), *Brighton* (Unwin)
— 4-maculata, Pz. *Brighton* (Unwin)

Saropoda, Ltr.
— bimaculata, Panz. *Hastings* district

Psithyrus, Lep.
— rupestris, Fab. *Guestling, Pett*; *Brighton* (Unwin)
— vestalis, Fourc. *Guestling, Bognor* (Guermonprez); *Brighton* (Unwin)
— barbutellus, Kirb. *Guestling, Fairlight*; *Brighton* (Unwin)
— campestris, Panz. *Hastings* district; *Brighton* (Unwin)
— quadricolor, Lep. *Hastings* district

Bombus, Ltr.
— smithianus, White. Between *Rye* and *Lydd* (Sladen), *Seaford* (Saunders)
— venustus, Smith. *Hastings* district; *Bognor* (Guermonprez), *Brighton* (Unwin)
— agrorum, Fab. *Hastings* district; *Bognor* (Guermonprez), *Brighton* (Unwin)
— hortorum, Linn. *Hastings* district; *Hayward's Heath* (Morice), *Bognor* (Guermonprez), *Brighton* (Unwin)
— latreillellus, Kirb. *Hastings* district; *Brighton* (Unwin); *Eastbourne* (Morley)
— sylvarum, Linn. *Hastings* district; *Bognor* (Guermonprez), *Hayward's Heath* (Morice), *Brighton* (Unwin)
— derhamellus, Kirb. *Hastings* district; *Hayward's Heath* (Morice), *Brighton* (Unwin)
— lapidarius, Linn. Generally distributed
— jonellus, Kirb. *Hollington* near *Hastings*
— pratorum, Fabr. *Hastings* district; *Bognor* (Guermonprez), *Brighton* (Unwin), *Hayward's Heath* (Morice)
— cullumanus, Kirb. *Brighton Downs* (Smith)
— soroensis, Fabr. *Brighton Downs* (S. S. Saunders)
— terrestris, Linn. Generally distributed

Apis, Linn.
— mellifica, Linn. Generally distributed

A HISTORY OF SUSSEX
COLEOPTERA
Beetles

The county of Sussex is rich in Coleoptera, and the number of beetles already recorded is a very large one ; but it is probable that more species will be found, as a considerable portion of the county has not yet been properly worked : in fact some districts that are sure to yield good insects have hardly been touched. It will be noticed that the chief localities quoted below are in the neighbourhood of Hastings, Brighton and Lewes, and that the western part of the county has been comparatively neglected. There is no reason to believe that the fauna of this part of Sussex differs much from the remainder, but the wooded districts of the county, with one or two exceptions, have not been worked like the coast localities, and it is probable that the country round Arundel and Petworth will supply many fresh records. In the course of a walk one afternoon through Arundel Park, on the only occasion in which I have been in the neighbourhood, I took *Epitrix atropæ* in abundance, and this remains the sole record for the county.

The chief source of our knowledge of the Sussex Coleoptera is the list of Hastings Coleoptera which forms the First Supplement of *The Natural History of Hastings and St. Leonards and the Vicinity*. This was published in 1883, and has since been largely added to by the Second Supplement published in 1888, and the Third Supplement published in 1898. For these excellent lists the Rev. E. N. Bloomfield of Guestling and Mr. E. A. Butler of Hastings have been largely responsible, and I am much indebted to them for their kind help on various occasions. I must also express my thanks to Mr. J. H. A. Jenner of Lewes for allowing me the use of his records of the beetles taken in his district. The chief collectors in the Hastings district besides those already mentioned have been Mr. W. H. Bennett, Mr. Collett and Mr. Ford, while a large number of the Lewes records are due to Mr. C. Morris. The Brighton localities are in part taken from Mrs. Merrifield's *History of Brighton*, published many years ago ; but the chief species have been taken at Holm Bush near Brighton by Dr. Power, who has also collected very successfully at Littlington, Cowfold, Amberley and Seaford. The Rev. H. S. Gorham has worked the Horsham district, and I am indebted to him for many valuable notes.

Four species at least have been recorded as British from Sussex only, viz. *Homalota consanguinea, Bruchus viciæ, Cassida chloris* and *Apion opeticum.* We might perhaps add *Stenus oscillator*, which was described by Mr. E. C. Rye as a new species on a single specimen taken by Dr. Power at Holm Bush, near Poynings ; but, as no more specimens have been found, it has been thought that it is a hybrid between *S. paganus* and *S. latifrons*, or it may perhaps be an extreme form of one of these insects. Among the rarer species we may note the following : *Calosoma sycophanta* (a casual visitant and not indigenous), *Cafius cicatricosus, Lathrobium pallidum, Medon ripicola, Scydmænus poweri, Eumicrus rufus, Oxylæmus variolosus, Crypto-*

phagus fumatus, Odontæus mobilicornis, Prionocyphon serricornis, Thyamis agilis, Lixus algirus, Bagous nodulosus, Ceuthorrhynchidius hepaticus and *C. pulvinatus.* No less than sixty species of Apion have been found in the county. The list of Scolytidæ is comparatively a short one, but will probably receive considerable additions in the future.

CICINDELIDÆ

Cicindela campestris, L.

CARABIDÆ

Cychrus rostratus, L. *Hastings* district, rare ; *Abbots Wood, Brighton*

Carabus catenulatus, Scop.

— nemoralis, Müll.

— violaceus, L.

— auratus, L. One specimen found in *Hastings* fruit market 23 April, 1902 ; evidently an importation

— granulatus, L.

— monilis, F.
  var. consitus, Panz. *Ewhurst*

Calosoma sycophanta, L. *Hastings*, very rare ; probably not indigenous

Notiophilus biguttatus, F.

— substriatus, Wat.

— quadripunctatus, Dej. *Bexhill, Battle, Netherfield*

— aquaticus, L.

— palustris, Duft.

— rufipes, Curt. Rare ; *Hastings*

Leistus spinibarbis, F.

— fulvibarbis, Dej.

— ferrugineus, L.

— rufescens, F.

Nebria brevicollis, F.

Blethisa multipunctata, L. *Camber*

Elaphrus riparius, L.

— cupreus, Duft.

Loricera pilicornis, F.

Clivina fossor, L.

Dyschirius thoracicus, Rossi

— nitidus, Dej. *Shoreham*

— extensus, Putz. Very rare ; *Shoreham, Lancing*

— salinus, Schaum. *Hastings, Seaford, Newhaven*

— æneus, Dej. *Camber*

— globosus, Herbst

Broscus cephalotes, L.

Panagæus crux-major, L. *Hastings, Rye, Winchelsea*

— quadripustulatus. *Lewes*

Badister unipustulatus, Bon. *Winchelsea, Rye*

— bipustulatus, F.

— sodalis, Duft. *Hastings, Brighton*

— peltatus, Panz. *Shipley* near *Horsham, Rye, Winchelsea, Balcombe, Hayward's Heath*

Licinus silphoides, F. *Lewes*

CARABIDÆ (*continued*)

Licinus depressus, Payk. *Lewes, Worthing, Eastbourne*

Chlænius vestitus, Payk. *Hastings, Brighton*

— schrankii, Duft. Very rare ; one specimen taken by Dr. Power at *Kemp Town, Brighton*

— nigricornis, F. *Hastings, Brighton, Barcombe*

Oodes helopioides, F. *Rusper* near *Horsham, Winchelsea, Barcombe*

Stenolophus teutonus, Schr. *Guestling*

— skrimshiranus, Steph. *Hastings, Rye, Lewes*

— vespertinus, Panz. *Shipley* near *Horsham, Guestling*

Acupalpus dorsalis, F. *Camber*

— exiguus, Dej. *Hastings, Barcombe*
  var. luridus, Dej. *Hastings* district

— meridianus, L.

— consputus, Duft. *Guestling, Rye, Camber, Barcombe*

Bradycellus placidus, Gyll. *Eastbourne*, rare

— distinctus, Dej.

— verbasci, Duft.

— harpalinus, Dej.

— similis, Dej.

Harpalus sabulicola, Panz. Not common ; *Brighton, Hastings, Lewes*

— rotundicollis, Fairm.

— punctatulus, Duft. *Brighton*

— azureus, F. *Brighton*

— cordatus, Duft. Rare ; *Camber*

— rupicola, Sturm. *Hastings, Shipley*

— puncticollis, Payk.

— rufibarbis, F.

— parallelus, Dej. *Eastbourne*

— ruficornis, F.

— æneus, F.

— consentaneus, Dej. *Hastings, Brighton, Eastbourne*

— tenebrosus, Dej. Rare ; *Eastbourne* (A. C. Horner); *Kemp Town, Brighton*

— rubripes, Duft.

— latus, L.

— melancholicus, Dej. Rare ; *Hastings*

— tardus, Panz. Rare ; *Hastings*

— servus, Duft. Rare ; *Camber*

— anxius, Duft. *Camber, Brighton* ; not common

CARABIDÆ (*continued*)

Harpalus serripes, Schön. Rare ; *Camber, Brighton*

Dichirotrichus obsoletus, Dej.

— pubescens, Payk.

Anisodactylus binotatus, F. *Hastings, Camber, Bishopstone*

Diachromus germanus, Er. Very rare ; a few specimens have been taken running on the pathways at *St. Leonards* and *Hastings*

Zabrus gibbus, F. *Hastings, Worthing*

Stomis pumicatus, Panz. *Hastings, Brighton, Barcombe, Lewes*

Platyderus ruficollis, Marsh. *Hastings, Brighton* district, *Lewes*

Pterostichus cupreus, L.

— versicolor, Sturm

— madidus, F.

— niger, Schall.

— vulgaris, L.

— anthracinus, Ill. *Shipley* near *Horsham, Hastings*

— nigrita, F.

— gracilis, Dej. *Battle, Bexhill*

— minor, Gyll. *Dallington, Ewhurst, Bexhill, Ashburnham*

— strenuus, Panz.

— diligens, Sturm

— picimanus, Duft. *Hastings* and *Lewes* districts

— inæqualis, Marsh. *Hastings, Brighton, Barcombe, Bishopstone*

— vernalis, Gyll.

— striola, F.

Amara fulva, DeG.

— apricaria, Sturm

— consularis, Duft. *Lewes*

— aulica, Panz.

— convexiuscula, Marsh.

— rufocincta, Dej. *Camber*

— livida, F. (bifrons, Gyll.) *Camber, Lewes*

— fusca, Dej. Very rare ; *Bopeep* near *Hastings*

— ovata, F. *Guestling, Lewes, Barcombe flood*

— similata, Gyll. *Guestling, Brighton*

— acuminata, Payk. Apparently very rare ; one at *Brighton*, 1862 (Sharp)

— tibialis, Payk.

— lunicollis, Schiodte. *Hastings* district

— curta, Dej. Rare ; *Lewes, Brighton* district

— spreta, Dej. *Camber*

— familiaris, Duft.

— lucida, Duft. *Hastings, Camber, Rye, Newhaven*

— trivialis, Gyll.

— communis, Panz.

CARABIDÆ (*continued*)

Amara plebeia, Gyll. *Hastings, Brighton, Lewes*

Calathus cisteloides, Panz.

— fuscus, F. Not common ; *Camber*

— flavipes, Fourc. Rare ; *Camber*

— mollis, Marsh.

— melanocephalus, L.

— piceus, Marsh. Rare. *Fairlight*

Taphria nivalis, Panz. *Hastings, Lewes, Barcombe*

Pristonychus terricola, Herbst

Sphodrus leucophthalmus, L. *Hastings, Lewes*

Anchomenus angusticollis, F.

— dorsalis, Müll.

— albipes, F.

— oblongus, Sturm. *Peppering, Guestling, Barcombe*

— livens, Gyll. Rare ; *Shipley, Tilgate Forest, Brighton* district, *Peppering, Guestling, Battle* (in sphagnum), *Abbots Wood, Masher Wood, Malling, Lewes*

— marginatus, L.

— parumpunctatus, F.

— viduus, Panz. *Guestling, Barcombe, Lewes*

var. mæstus, Duft.

— versutus, Gyll. *Shipley*

— fuliginosus, Panz.

— gracilis, Gyll. *Hastings* district, *Barcombe, Lewes*

— piceus, L. *Guestling, Brighton, Barcombe*

— thoreyi, Dej. *Guestling, Brighton, Lewes*

— puellus, Dej. *Rye*

Olisthopus rotundatus, Payk.

Tachys scutellaris, Germ. *Hastings* district

— bistriatus, Duft. *Hastings* district

Lymnæum nigropiceum, Marsh. Rare ; *Hastings* district, *Newhaven*

Cillenus lateralis, Sam. *Rye*

Bembidium rufescens, Guér. *Guestling, Brighton, Barcombe flood*

— quinquestriatum, Gyll. *Hastings, Brighton, Abbots Wood, Lewes*

— obtusum, Sturm

— guttula, F.

— mannerheimi, Sahl. *Battle, Ore, Camber, Barcombe flood*

— biguttatum, F.

— riparium, Ol. *Hastings* list

— æneum, Germ.

— fumigatum, Duft. *Camber*

— assimile, Gyll. *Hastings* and *Lewes* districts

— clarki, Daws. *Shipley*

— articulatum, Panz.

INSECTS

CARABIDÆ (*continued*)
Bembidium minimum, F.
— normannum, Dej.
— gilvipes, Sturm. *Bopeep, Lewes, Brighton*
— lampros, Herbst
— tibiale, Duft.
— nitidulum, Marsh.
— affine, Steph. *Hastings* district, *Brighton*
— quadriguttatum, F.
— quadripustulatum, Dej. Very rare; taken by the Rev. H. S. Gorham at *Rusper* near *Horsham*
— quadrimaculatum, Gyll.
— testaceum, Duft. Rare; *Sussex* (A. C. Horner)
— femoratum, Sturm. *Hollington, Brighton, Shoreham*
— bruxellense, Wesm. *Pett* near *Hastings*
— saxatile, Gyll. *Rye, Lewes*
— littorale, Ol.
— fluviatile, Dej. *Newhaven* (Morris)
— bipunctatum, L.
— prasinum, Duft. Rare; *Bulverhythe* near *Hastings*
— ephippium, Marsh. *Hastings, Shoreham*
— flammulatum, Clairv.
— varium, Ol. Rare; *Hastings*
— adustum, Schaum. Rare; *Hastings*
— obliquum, Sturm. This very local and usually rare species has been taken at *St. Leonards* in some numbers by the Rev. H. S. Gorham; it has also occurred at *Brighton*
Tachypus flavipes, L.
Aëpus robinii, Lat. *Newhaven* (Morice); rare
Trechus discus, F. *Hastings* district
— micros, Herbst. *Horsham, Hastings* district, *Barcombe*
— lapidosus, Daws. *Hastings* and *Brighton* districts, *Bishopstone*
— minutus, F.
— obtusus, Er.
— secalis, Payk. *Dallington Forest*
Patrobus excavatus, Payk.
Pogonus luridipennis, Germ. *Shoreham, Bulverhythe* near *Hastings*
— littoralis, Duft. *Bulverhythe, Newhaven*
— chalceus, Marsh.
Masoreus wetterhalii, Gyll. Rare; *Camber*
Cymindis axillaris, F. *Lewes*, Downs; *Offham*, chalk pit
Odacantha melanura, Payk. *Balcombe, Shipley*

CARABIDÆ (*continued*)
Lebia chlorocephala, Hoff. *Hastings* district, not common; *Lewes, Abbots Wood*
— crux-minor, L. Several specimens of this extremely rare beetle were taken by Dr. Power at *Holm Bush* near *Brighton* in May, 1857
— turcica, F. One specimen has been taken by Mr. Bennett at *Guestling* near *Hastings* out of a birch stump
Demetrias atricapillus, L.
Dromius linearis, Ol.
— meridionalis, Dej.
— quadrimaculatus, L.
— quadrinotatus, Panz.
— quadrisignatus, Dej. Rare; *Guestling, Rusper* near *Horsham*
— melanocephalus, Dej.
— nigriventris, Thoms.
— vectensis, Rye. Rare; *Fairlight*
Blechrus maurus, Sturm.
Metabletus foveola, Gyll.
— truncatellus, L. Rare; *Bopeep* near *Hastings*
— obscuro-guttatus, Duft. *Hollington, Bopeep, Barcombe, Lewes*
Polystichus vittatus, Brullé. Rare; *Bopeep*, near *Winchelsea, Brighton* district, *Lewes*
Drypta dentata, Rossi. Very rare; *Bulverhythe* near *Hastings*
Brachinus crepitans, L.
[— sclopeta, F. '*Hastings*, locality doubtful' (Stephens), evidently in error]

HALIPLIDÆ
Brychius elevatus, Panz. *Lewes*
Haliplus obliquus, Er. *Hastings, Lewes*
— confinis, Steph. *Pett, Bopeep, Brighton*
— mucronatus, Steph. Very rare; *Holm Bush, Brighton* (Power); ditches, *Lewes* (Jenner); *The Rise, Lewes* (Morris)
— flavicollis, Sturm. *Fairlight*, rare; *Lewes*
— fulvus, F. *Hastings*, rare; *Lewes*, common
— variegatus, Sturm. *Winchelsea*, rare; *Lewes*
— cinereus, Aubé. *Pett, Ashburnham*
— ruficollis, De G.
— fluviatilis, Aubé
— lineatocollis, Marsh.
Cnemidotus impressus, F. *Hastings* district, *Leighside* and *The Rise, Lewes*
PELOBIIDÆ
Pelobius tardus, Herbst. *Hastings* district, *Brighton, Lewes*

139

Dytiscidæ

Noterus clavicornis, De G. *Brighton Marshes*, not common
— sparsus, Marsh. *Brighton, Lewes*
Laccophilus interruptus, Panz.
— obscurus, Panz.
— variegatus, Germ. *Bulverhythe, Lewes, Pevensey*
Bidessus unistriatus, Schr. Rare ; *Camber*
Hyphydrus ovatus, L.
Cœlambus versicolor, Schall. *Guestling*, not common
— inæqualis, F. *Bopeep, Brighton, Lewes*
— decoratus, Gyll. *Brighton*, rare
— confluens, F. *Hastings, Brighton, Lewes*
— parallelogrammus, Ahr. *Hastings, Brighton, Lewes*
— impressopunctatus, Schall. *Camber*
Deronectes latus, Steph. Very local ; *Hollington* near *Hastings, Guestling, Bodle Street*, near *Ashburnham* (Butler) ; *Tilgate Forest* (Power)
— depressus, F.
— duodecim-pustulatus, F.
Hydroporus pictus, F.
— dorsalis, F. *Hastings, Abbots Wood, Lewes*
— lineatus, F.
— angustatus, Sturm. *Winchelsea*
— gyllenhali, Schiödte. *Battle, Abbots Wood*
— morio, Dej. *Hollington* near *Hastings*, scarce
— vittula, Er. *Guestling*
— palustris, L.
— erythrocephalus, L.
— longulus, Muls. *Hastings, Tilgate Forest*
— memnonius, Nic. *Ore, Rye, Bopeep, Abbots Wood, Lewes*
— obscurus, Sturm. *Laughton, Lewes*
— nigrita, F. *Guestling, Laughton, Lewes*
— discretus, Fairm. Rare ; *Battle* (Butler)
— pubescens, Gyll.
— planus, F.
— lituratus, F. *Guestling, Abbots Wood, Laughton, Lewes*
— marginatus, Duft. Rare ; *Winchelsea*
— ferrugineus, Steph. Rare ; *Hastings, Fairlight*
Agabus guttatus, Payk. *St. Leonards, Battle, Lewes*
— paludosus, F. *Hastings, Winterbourne* near *Lewes*
— uliginosus, L. *Brighton* district
— didymus, Ol. *Hastings*, rare ; *Lewes, Winterbourne*, etc.

Dytiscidæ (*continued*)

Agabus nebulosus, Forst. *Hastings* and *Lewes* districts
— conspersus, Marsh. *Camber, Bopeep, Brighton*
— sturmii, Gyll. *Hastings, Stoneham, Lewes*
— chalconotus, Panz. *Hollington, Bexhill, Abbots Wood, Laughton, Brighton*
— bipustulatus, L.
Platambus maculatus, L. Rare ; *Hastings*
Ilybius fuliginosus, F.
— ater, De G. Rare ; *Guestling, Barcombe*
— obscurus, Marsh.
Copelatus agilis, F. Scarce ; *Bopeep, Abbots Wood, Lewes*
Rhantus pulverosus, Steph. Rare ; *Hastings, Lewes*
— bistriatus, Berg. Rare
Colymbetes fuscus, L.
Dytiscus punctulatus, F. *St. Leonards*, scarce ; *Abbots Wood, Lewes*
— marginalis, L.
— circumflexus, F. *St. Leonards, Rye*
— circumcinctus, Ahr. Rare ; *Eastbourne*
Hydaticus seminiger, De G. Rare ; *Guestling*
Acilius sulcatus, L. *Hastings, Abbots Wood, Laughton, Lewes, Brighton*

Gyrinidæ

Gyrinus urinator, L. Very local ; *Ewhurst, Staplehurst*
— elongatus, Aubé. *Bopeep* near *Hastings, Brighton, Lewes*
— bicolor, Payk. *Hastings* and *Brighton* districts
— natator, Scop.
— suffriani, Scriba. *Ewhurst, Bopeep, Winchelsea*
— marinus, Gyll.
Orectochilus villosus, Müll. *Guestling, Catsfield, Bodle Street* near *Ashburnham*

Hydrophilidæ

Hydrophilus piceus, L. Rare ; *Hastings* district, *Lewes, Brighton*
Hydrobius fuscipes, L.
— oblongus, Herbst. Rare ; *Guestling, Lewes*
Philhydrus testaceus, F. *Hastings, Lewes*
— maritimus, Thoms. *Newhaven, Brighton*
— nigricans, Zett. *Camber, Ore*
— melanocephalus, Ol. *Ore, Pett, Lewes, Brighton, Newhaven*
— coarctatus, Gredl. *Hastings* district, *Robertsbridge, Barcombe*

INSECTS

Cymbiodyta ovalis, Thoms. *Camber*

Enochrus bicolor, Gyll. *Winchelsea, Rye, Lewes*

Paracymus nigroæneus, Sahl. *Lewes*

Anacæna globulus, Payk.

— limbata, F.

Helochares lividus, Forst. *Hastings, Rye, Lewes, Brighton*

— punctatus, Sharp. *Lewes, Newhaven*

Laccobius sinuatus, Mots.

— alutaceus, Thoms. Near *Winchelsea*

— minutus, L.

— bipunctatus, F. Near *Winchelsea*

Berosus spinosus, Stev. Rare ; *Bopeep, Rye, Brighton, Eastbourne, Seaford*

— signaticollis, Charp. *Bexhill*

— luridus, L. *Hastings, Brighton*

— affinis, Brullé. *Hastings* and *Lewes* districts

Limnebius truncatellus, Thoms.

— papposus, Muls. Rare ; *Guestling*

— nitidus, Marsh. *Hastings* district, *Lewes* ; local

Chætarthria seminulum, Herbst

Helophorus rugosus, Ol.

— nubilus, F.

— intermedius, Muls. *Winchelsea, Barcombe, Brighton*

— aquaticus, L.
var. æqualis, Thoms.

— dorsalis, Marsh. *Guestling, Lewes, Holm Bush, Brighton*

— æneipennis, Thoms.

— mulsanti, Rye. *Bopeep*

— affinis, Marsh.

— brevipalpis, Bedel.

— nanus, Sturm. Rare ; *Ore* ; *Guestling* (Butler), *Lewes*

Hydrochus elongatus, Schall. *Pett* near *Hastings*

— angustatus, Germ. *Hastings, Abbots Wood, Laughton Wood*

Henicocerus exsculptus, Germ. *Dallington Forest*

Octhebius exaratus, Muls. *Rye, Camber, Lewes, Brighton*

— margipallens, Latr. *Bognor, Rye, Camber, Brighton*

— marinus, Payk. *Bopeep, Rye, Brighton*

— pygmæus, F. Generally distributed

— bicolon, Germ. *Bopeep, Brighton, Lewes*

— rufimarginatus, Steph. *Rye, Camber, Shoreham*

— nanus, Steph. *Winchelsea, Rye, Hastings, Shoreham, Brighton, Lewes*

Octhebius punctatus, Steph. *Rye, Brighton*

Hydræna testacea, Curt. *Battle, Holm Bush, Brighton*

— riparia, Kug. *Hastings, Brighton, Lewes*

— nigrita, Germ. *Hastings, Holm Bush, Brighton*

— gracilis, Germ. *Dallington Forest* (recorded 1898)*

— pulchella, Germ. *Ashburnham* (recorded 1898)*

Cyclonotum orbiculare, F.

Sphæridium scarabæoides, F.

— bipustulatum, Fab.
var. marginatum, F. *St. Leonards*, scarce ; *Lewes*, common

Cercyon littoralis, Gyll. *Camber*

— depressus, Steph. *Newhaven* (Morris)

— hæmorrhous, Gyll. *Hastings*, not common ; *Lewes*

— hæmorrhoidalis, Herbst. *Hastings, Brighton, Lewes*, etc.

— obsoletus, Gyll. *Hastings, Brighton, Lewes*

— aquaticus, Muls. *Robertsbridge* near *Hastings*

— flavipes, F.

— lateralis, Marsh.

— melanocephalus, L.

— unipunctatus, L.

— quisquilius, L.

— nigriceps, Marsh. *Hastings* district

— pygmæus, Ill. *Hastings, Lewes*

— terminatus, Marsh. *Hastings*, not common

— analis, Payk.

— lugubris, Payk. *Guestling*, rare

— granarius, Thoms.

Megasternum boletophagum, Marsh.

Cryptopleurum atomarium, Muls.

STAPHYLINIDÆ

Homœusa acuminata, Märk. *Tilgate Forest, Guestling*

Aleochara ruficornis, Grav. Rare ; *Shipley* near *Horsham*

— fuscipes, F.

— lata, Grav.

— brevipennis, Grav. *Battle, Camber, Brighton*

— tristis, Grav. *Hastings, Laughton, Shoreham*

— bipunctata, Ol. *Guestling, Lewes*

* These are the only records from the south of England, and are interesting as bearing out what I have before said (*Brit. Col.* i. 251), viz. that as several of these species are found in France they have probably been overlooked by collectors in the south.

STAPHYLINIDÆ (*continued*)

Aleochara cuniculorum, Kr. *Guestling* near *Hastings*, rare
— lanuginosa, Grav.
— mœsta, Grav. *Camber, Barcombe*
— mycetophaga, Kr. Rare ; *Tilgate Forest, Petworth, Peppering*
— nitida, Grav.
— morion, Grav. *Camber, Lewes*
— grisea, Kr. *Camber*
— algarum, Fauv. *Camber*, rare
— obscurella, Er. „ „

Microglossa suturalis, Mann. *St. Leonards, Landport, Ranscombe* near *Lewes*
— pulla, Gyll. *Tilgate Forest*
— nidicola, Fairm. *St. Leonards*

Oxypoda spectabilis, Märk. *Guestling*, rare
— lividipennis, Mannh. *Guestling, Barcombe*
— vittata, Märk. Rare ; *Hastings, Battle*
— opaca, Grav. *Hastings, Barcombe*
— alternans, Grav. *Guestling, Netherfield, Lewes*
— umbrata, Grav. *Winterbourne, Lewes, Barcombe, Newhaven*
— pectita, Sharp. *Littlehampton*
— nigrina, Wat. *Barcombe*
— longiuscula, Grav. *Battle, Barcombe, Lewes*
— formiceticola, Märk. *Guestling*
— recondita, Kr. *Malling, Lewes*
— hæmorrhoa, Mannh. *Guestling, Barcombe*
— annularis, Sahlb. var. pallidula, Sahlb. *Guestling*
— brachyptera, Steph. *St. Leonards, Brighton*

Thiasophila angulata, Er. *Guestling*
— inquilina. *Tilgate Forest, Guestling*

Ischnoglossa prolixa, Grav. *Hastings*, under oak bark
— corticina, Er. *Guestling*

Ocyusa maura, Er. *Camber, Netherfield*
— picina, Aubé. *Balcombe, Hayward's Heath*

Phlœopora reptans, Grav. *Guestling, Battle*
— corticalis, Grav. *Fairlight, Holm Bush, Brighton*

Ocalea castanea, Er. *Hastings, Lewes*
— badia, Er. *Bopeep, Rye, Lewes*

Ilyobates nigricollis, Payk. Rare ; *Amberley, Shipley, Guestling*
— propinquus, Aubé. Very rare ; *Littlehampton, Fairlight*, near *Hastings, Barcombe*

Calodera æthiops, Grav. *Lewes*
— umbrosa, Er. *Lewes*

STAPHYLINIDÆ (*continued*)

Chilopora longitarsis, Er. *Camber*
Dinarda märkeli, Kies. *Guestling*
Atemeles emarginatus, Grav. *Hollington*
Myrmedonia limbata, Payk. *Hastings, St. Leonards, Bopeep, Battle*
— funesta, Grav. *Hastings, Battle*
— humeralis, Grav. *Hollington, Guestling*
— cognata, Märk. *Tilgate Forest*
— lugens, Grav. *Tilgate Forest, Battle*
— laticollis, Märk. *Tilgate Forest, Shipley, Rusper, Hastings*

Astilbus canaliculatus, F.
Callicerus obscurus, Grav. *Hastings, Bopeep, Brighton, Lewes*
— rigidicornis, Er. *Hastings* district

Thamiaræa cinnamomea, Grav. *Hastings*
Notothecta flavipes, Grav. *Guestling*
— confusa, Märk. *Tilgate Forest*
— anceps, Er. *Guestling*

Alianta incana, Er. *Camber, Winchelsea*
— plumbea, Wat. *Shoreham*

Homalota languida, Er. Rare. *Worthing* (E. Saunders)
— pavens, Er. *Brighton*
— gregaria, Er.
— littorea, Sharp. *Worthing, Littlehampton, Brighton*
— imbecilla, Wat. *Hastings, Shoreham, Littlehampton, Brighton*
— luridipennis, Mannh.
— gyllenhali, Thoms. *Pebsham, Barcombe*
— elongatula, Grav.
— volans, Scriba.
— vestita, Grav. *Newhaven, Shoreham*
— silvicola, Fuss. *Hastings*
— vicina, Steph.
— graminicola, Gyll.
— halobrectha, Sharp. *Shoreham*
— fungivora, Thoms. *Lewes*
— æquata, Er. *Tilgate Forest*
— angustula, Gyll. *Hastings*
— linearis, Grav. *Plashett*, near *Lewes*
— pilicornis, Thoms. Rare ; *Tilgate Forest*
— debilis, Er. *Barcombe flood*
— cæsula, Er. *Camber*
— circellaris, Grav.
— elegantula, Bris. Rare ; *Amberley*
— ægra, Heer. Rare ; *Brighton*
— cuspidata, Er. *Hastings, Guestling, Bexhill*
— laticeps, Thoms. Very rare ; *Arundel*
— analis, Grav.
— depressa, Gyll. *Guestling, Lewes*
— exarata, Sharp. Very rare ; in nests of Formica fuliginosa ; *Tilgate Forest* (Power & Brewer)
— aquatica, Thoms. *Hastings, Barcombe, Lewes*

INSECTS

STAPHYLINIDÆ (*continued*)

Homalota æneicollis, Sharp. *Guestling, Lewes*
— xanthoptera, Steph. *Guestling*
— euryptera, Steph. (succicola, Thoms.) *Hastings* district
— trinotata, Kr.
— xanthopus, Thoms. *Abbots Wood* (Morris)
— triangulum, Kr. *Guestling*
— fungicola, Thoms. *Hastings*
— ignobilis, Sharp. „
— coriaria, Kr. *Littlington, Hurst*
— gagatina, Baudi. *Hastings*
— divisa, Märk. *Hastings* district, *Tilgate Forest*
— ravilla, Er. *Guestling, Tilgate Forest*
— scapularis, Sahlb. *Hastings, Rye, Brighton*
— testaceipes, Heer. Rare ; *Littlington*
— oblita, Er. „ „
— indubia, Sharp. Rare ; *St. Leonards, Hastings*
— mortuorum, Thoms. Rare ; *Littlington*
— inquinula, Er. *Cowfold* near *Horsham*
— nigra, Kr. *Battle, Lewes*
— sordidula, Er. *Lewes*
— cauta, Er. (parva, auct.)
— villosula, Kr. *Littlington*
— setigera, Sharp. *Guestling*
— lævana, Muls. *Brighton*
— cinnamoptera, Thoms. *Guestling, Hollington*
— atramentaria, Gyll. *Battle* and *Lewes* districts
— longicornis, Grav. *Guestling, Barcombe, Lewes*
— consanguinea, Eppl. Very rare; *Hollington* near *Hastings*, 1871 (E. Saunders) ; the only British record
— sordida, Marsh. *Hastings, Guestling, St. Leonards*
— testudinea, Er.
— aterrima, Grav. *Lewes*
— laticollis, Steph. *Hastings* district, *Pebsham*
— subsinuata, Er. *Littlington*, not common
— montivagans, Woll. *Littlington*, rare
— orbata, Er. *Camber*, rare
— fungi, Grav.
   var. dubia, Sharp.
— orphana, Er. Very rare ; *Holm Bush* near *Brighton* (Power)
Gnypeta labilis, Er. *Hastings, Battle, Barcombe*
Tachyusa constricta, Er. *Hastings, Netherfield*
— coarctata, Er. Very rare ; *Netherfield* near *Hastings* (E. A. Butler)
— flavitarsis, Sahlb. *Netherfield, Lewes*

STAPHYLINIDÆ (*continued*)

Tachyusa umbratica, Er. *Hastings, Shipley*
Xenusa uvida, Er. *Newhaven*
Falagria sulcata, Payk.
— sulcatula, Grav. *Shipley*
— thoracica, Curt. *Tilgate Forest*
— obscura, Grav.
Autalia impressa, Ol. *Hastings* district, *Abbots Wood*
— rivularis, Grav. *Hastings, Battle, Barcombe, Lewes*
Encephalus complicans, Westw. *Hastings* district
Gyrophæna pulchella, Heer. *Lewes*
— poweri, Crotch. Rare ; *Guestling*
— gentilis, Er. *Guestling*
— fasciata, Marsh. *Tilgate Forest*
— minima, Er. *Guestling*
— lævipennis, Kr. *Hastings* district
— lucidula, Er. *Guestling*
— manca, Er. *Littlington*
Placusa pumilio, Grav. *Tilgate Forest*
Silusa rubiginosa, Er. *Hastings*, rare
Leptusa fumida, Er. *Ecclesbourne*, not common
Sipalia ruficollis, Er. *Hastings* district, not common ; *Lewes*
Bolitochara bella, Märk. *Guestling, Abbots Wood, Winterbourne, Lewes*
— obliqua, Er. *Bognor*
Phytosus spinifer, Curt. *Bognor*
— balticus, Kr. *Camber*
Hygronoma dimidiata, Grav. *Netherfield, Lewes*
Oligota inflata, Mannh. *St. Leonards, Peppering, Lewes*
— parva, Kr. *Guestling*
— atomaria, Er. *Hollington, Littlington, Barcombe, Malling, Lewes*
— punctulata, Heer. *Guestling, Malling*
— granaria, Er. *Ecclesbourne*, rare
Myllæna dubia, Grav. *Barcombe, Tilgate, Hastings*
— intermedia, Er. *Barcombe, Lewes, Ecclesbourne*
— minuta, Grav. *Camber*
— kraatzii, Sharp. *Hastings*
— elongata, Matth. „
— brevicornis, Matth. *Lewes*
Deinopsis erosa, Steph. *Battle, Tilgate Forest, Hastings*
Hypocyptus longicornis, Payk. *Hastings* district, *Lewes*
— seminulum, Er. *Fairlight* near *Hastings, Lewes*
— discoideus, Er. *Battle*
Conosoma littoreum, L. *Guestling, Glynd* near *Lewes*
— pubescens, Grav.

STAPHYLINIDÆ (*continued*)

Conosoma immaculatum, Steph. *Hastings* district, *Bishopstone, Barcombe, Lewes*
— pedicularium, Grav. *Amberley* near *Arundel*
— lividum, Er. *Lewes, Newhaven*
Tachyporus obtusus, L.
— formosus, Matth. *Battle, Hollington, Barcombe, Lewes*
— solutus, Er. *Hastings*
— chrysomelinus, L.
— humerosus, Er.
— hypnorum, F.
— pusillus, Grav.
— brunneus, F.
Lamprinus saginatus, Grav. Rare; *Hastings* district
Cilea silphoides, L. *Hastings, St. Leonards, Guestling, Lewes*
—Tachinus humeralis, Grav.
— rufipes, L.
— subterraneus, L.
— marginellus, F.
— laticollis, Grav. *Guestling*, not common
— elongatus, Gyll. Rare; *Hastings, Battle*
Megacronus cingulatus, Mannh. *Ore* near *Hastings*
— analis, F. *Hastings* district, *Lewes*
— inclinans, Grav. Rare; *Hastings, Guestling*
Bolitobius lunulatus, L.
— trinotatus, Er.
— exoletus, Er.
— pygmæus, F.
Mycetoporus lucidus, Er. *Guestling*
— splendens, Marsh. *Lewes*
— lepidus, Grav. *Hastings* and *Lewes* districts
— longulus, Mannh. *Hastings* district
— nanus, Er. Rare; *Rye*
— reyi, Pand. *Hastings, Fairlight*
— clavicornis, Steph. *Guestling, Battle*
— splendidus, Grav. *Battle, Barcombe, Newhaven*
— longicornis, Kr. Rare; *Littlington*
Habrocerus capillaricornis, Grav. *Ecclesbourne*
Trichophya pilicornis, Gyll. *Horsham*
Euryporus picipes, Payk. Very rare; *Guestling, Holm Bush, Brighton*
Heterothops binotata, Er. *Battle*
— dissimilis, Grav. *Hastings, Lewes, Worthing*
— quadripunctula, Gyll. Rare; *Worthing*
Quedius lateralis, Grav. *Hastings*
— mesomelinus, Marsh.
— fulgidus, F.
— cruentus, Ol. Rare; *Guestling, Hastings, Ecclesbourne*

STAPHYLINIDÆ (*continued*)

Quedius cinctus, Payk. *Hastings* district, not common; *Lewes*
— brevis, Er. *Guestling*
— fuliginosus, Grav.
— tristis, Grav.
— molochinus, Grav.
— picipes, Mann. *Hurst Green, Fairlight, Guestling, Lewes*
— nigriceps, Kr. *Battle*
— fumatus, Steph. (peltatus, Er.) *Ecclesbourne, Hurst Green*; scarce
— umbrinus, Er. *Ecclesbourne, Camber*; scarce
— suturalis, Kies. *Hastings, Littlington*
— scintillans, Grav. *Littlington, Hove* near *Brighton, Lewes, Hastings*
— rufipes, Grav. *Hastings*, scarce
— attenuatus, Gyll. *Hastings* district
— semiæneus, Steph. *Camber, Battle, Peppering, Horsham*
— boops, Grav.
Creophilus maxillosus, L.
Leistotrophus nebulosus, F. *Hastings* and *Lewes* districts
— murinus, L. *Hastings* and *Lewes* districts
Staphylinus pubescens, De G. *Guestling, Hastings, Fairlight, Barcombe, Lewes*
— stercorarius, Ol. *Battle, Guestling, Lewes*
— latebricola, Grav. Rare; *Netherfield* near *Hastings*
— cæsareus, Ceder. *Guestling, Fairlight, Ore, Lewes*
Ocypus olens, Müll.
— similis, F. *St. Leonards, Brighton, Shoreham*
— brunnipes, F. *Hastings* and *Lewes* districts
— fuscatus, Grav. *Hastings, Lewes*
— cupreus, Rossi. „ „
— pedator, Grav. Rare; *Brighton*
— ater, Grav. *Hastings, Eastbourne, Newhaven, Lewes*
— morio, Grav. *Hastings, Lewes*
— compressus, Marsh. *Tilgate, Eastbourne*
Philonthus splendens, F. *Guestling*, scarce; *Lewes*, common
— intermedius, Boisd. *Hastings*, scarce; *Lewes*
— laminatus, Creutz. *Hastings, Lewes*
— æneus, Rossi
— proximus, Kr. (succicola, Thoms.). *Hastings*, scarce; *Lewes*
— addendus, Sharp. *Hastings* district (Butler)
— carbonarius, Gyll.
— decorus, Grav. *Hastings, Guestling*; not common

INSECTS

STAPHYLINIDÆ (*continued*)

Philonthus politus, F.
— varius, Gyll.
— marginatus, F.
— albipes, Grav. *Tilgate Forest, Hastings, Rye*
— umbratilis, Grav. *Guestling*
— cephalotes, Grav. *Hastings, Newhaven*
— fimetarius, Grav. *Hastings*, not common ; *Barcombe, Lewes*
— sordidus, Grav. *Hastings, Barcombe, Lewes*
— ebeninus, Er. *Hastings*, not common ; *Barcombe*
— corvinus, Er. *Shoreham* (Gorham)
— fumigatus, Er. *Littlington, Lewes, Barcombe flood*
— sanguinolentus, Grav. *Hastings, Camber, Lewes*
— cruentatus, Gmel. (bipustulatus, Panz.) *Bopeep, Netherfield, Camber*
— longicornis, Steph. *Battle, Hurst Green, Lewes*
— varians, Payk.
— ventralis, Grav. *Guestling, Lewes*
— discoideus, Grav. *Hastings* and *Lewes* districts
— quisquiliarius, Gyll. *Rye, Camber*
  var. dimidiatus, Er. *Littlington, Rye, Camber*
— thermarum, Aubé. *Guestling*, rare ; *Lewes*
— nigrita, Nord. *Battle*
— fumarius, Grav. *Rye, Brighton, Lewes, Eastbourne*
— micans, Grav. *Hastings, Lewes*
— trossulus, Nord.
— fulvipes, F. Rare ; *Faygate* (Power)
— punctus, Grav. Rare ; *Rye*
Cafius cicatricosus, Er. Very local ; *Shoreham, Worthing*
— fucicola, Curtis. *Rottingdean, Brighton*
— xantholoma, Grav.
— sericeus, Holme. *Bognor, Littlehampton*
Actobius cinerascens, Grav. *Battle, Lewes*
— signaticornis, Rey. *Rye*
— villosulus, Steph. Rare ; *Battle, Barcombe flood*
— procerulus, Grav. *Battle*
Xantholinus fulgidus, F. *Littlington*
— glabratus, Grav.
— punctulatus, Payk.
— ochraceus, Gyll.
— atratus, Heer. *Guestling, Hurst* (recorded doubtfully)
— glaber, Nord. Rare ; *Hastings* district
— tricolor, F. *Fairlight, Camber*
— linearis, Ol.
— longiventris, Heer

STAPHYLINIDÆ (*continued*)

Leptacinus parumpunctatus, Gyll. *Lewes, Shoreham*
— batychrus, Gyll. *Barcombe, Lewes*
— linearis, Grav. *Hastings, Lewes*
— formicetorum, Märk. *Hastings, Tilgate Forest, Landport, Lewes*
Baptolinus alternans, Grav. *Ashburnham*
Othius fulvipennis, F.
— læviusculus, Steph. *Battle, Peppering, Camber, Lewes*
— melanocephalus, Grav.
— myrmecophilus, Kies. *Hastings* district, rare
Lathrobium elongatum, L.
— fulvipenne, Grav.
— brunnipes, F.
— longulum. *Guestling, Hastings, Barcombe, Lewes*
— filiforme, Grav. Rare ; *Amberley*
— quadratum, Payk. *Shipley* near *Horsham*
— terminatum, Grav. *Battle, Rye, Barcombe*
  var. immaculatum, Fowler. *Battle*
— pallidum, Nord. As a rule very rare, but it has been taken in numbers at *Shipley* near *Horsham* by Mr. Gorham, and it has also occurred at *Amberley*
— multipunctum, Grav. *Hastings* and *Lewes* districts
Achenium depressum, Grav. *Bognor, Shipley, Hastings, Lewes, Newhaven*
— humile, Nic. *Bopeep, Brighton, Shipley* (in numbers), *Barcombe flood, Holm Bush*
Cryptobium glaberrimum, Herbst. *Rye, Dallington Forest*
Stilicus rufipes, Germ. *Hastings, Lewes*
— orbiculatus, Er. *Guestling, Battle* ; rare
— subtilis, Er. *Peppering* and *Dallington Forest*, not common ; *Lewes*, common
— affinis, Er. *Hastings, Lewes*
Scopæus sulcicollis, Steph. (minutus, Er.). *Hastings* district, *Lewes, Kemp Town, Brighton*
Medon pocofer, Peyr. *Shoreham, Worthing*
— brunneus, Er. *Bognor, Battle, Faygate, Lewes*
— fusculus, Mann. *Eastbourne, Brighton, Hastings*
— ripicola, Kr. *Pett* near *Hastings*, very rare
— propinquus, Bris.
— melanocephalus, F.
— obsoletus, Nord. *Littlington, Landport, Lewes*

A HISTORY OF SUSSEX

STAPHYLINIDÆ (continued)
Lithocharis ochracea, Grav.
Sunius filiformis, Latr. Usually rare ;
    Kemp Town, Brighton in some num-
    bers (Power) ; *Camber*
— intermedius, Er. Very local ; *Guestling,
    Brighton*
— diversus, Aubé. *Cowfold, Malling,
    Lewes*
— angustatus, Payk.
Pæderus littoralis, Grav.
— riparius, L. *Peppering, Barcombe flood*
— fuscipes, Curt. *Hastings, Eastbourne*
Evæsthetus scaber, Thoms. *Hastings,
    Lewes, Newhaven, Holm Bush,
    Brighton*
— ruficapillus, Lac. *Ore* near *Hastings*
— læviusculus, Mann. *Ore* near *Hastings*
    (W. H. Bennett)
Dianous cœrulescens, Gyll. *Fairlight*
Stenus biguttatus, L. *Battle, Hurst Green,
    Laughton, Lewes*
— bipunctatus, Er. *Hastings* district
— guttula, Müll. *Hastings, Hurst Green,
    Ecclesbourne, Shoreham*
— bimaculatus, Gyll.
— juno, F.
— ater, Mann. *Hastings* and *Brighton*
    districts
— longitarsis, Thoms. Rare ; *Rye,* near
    Winchelsea
— guynemeri, Duv. *Hastings* district
— speculator, Lac.
— providus, Er., var. rogeri, Kr.
— buphthalmus, Grav. *Hastings, Bar-
    combe*
— melanopus, Marsh. *Battle, Barcombe,
    Lewes*
— incrassatus, Er. *Rye, Camber, Bar-
    combe, Brighton*
— melanarius, Steph. Rare ; *Battle*
— morio, Grav. Very rare ; *Shipley* near
    Horsham (Gorham)
— atratulus, Er. Rare ; *Lewes, Barcombe*
— canaliculatus, Gyll. *Fairlight, Eccles-
    bourne, Barcombe, Brighton*
— pusillus, Steph. *Hastings* district
— exiguus, Er. *Hurst Green, Camber,
    Guestling, Holm Bush, Brighton*
— fuscipes, Grav. *Barcombe flood*
— declaratus, Er. *Hastings* and *Lewes*
    districts
— crassus, Steph. Very local ; *Amberley,
    Brighton, Lewes*
— carbonarius, Gyll. Rare ; *Amberley*
— argus, Grav. *Barcombe*
— nigritulus, Gyll. *Amberley, Lewes,
    Brighton, Rye*
— brunnipes, Steph.
— subæneus, Er. *Hastings, Lewes*

STAPHYLINIDÆ (continued)
Stenus ossium, Steph. *Hastings, Barcombe*
— fuscicornis, Er. *Lewes*
— impressus, Germ.
— ærosus, Er. *Lewes*
— erichsoni, Rye. *Eastbourne*
— pallipes, Grav. *Battle, Hurst Green,
    Holm Bush, Brighton*
— flavipes, Steph. *Hastings, Lewes, Brigh-
    ton*
— pubescens, Steph. *Winchelsea, Barcombe*
— binotatus, Ljungh. *Hastings, Brighton,
    Lewes*
— canescens, Rosh. (major, Rey). By
    ditches in levels, *Lewes* (Jenner)
— pallitarsis, Steph. *Hastings, Tilgate,
    Brighton, Barcombe*
— nitidiusculus, Steph. *Rye*
— bifoveolatus, Gyll. *Lewes* district
— picipennis, Steph. *Barcombe*
— picipes, Steph. *Hastings* and *Lewes*
    districts
— cicindeloides, Grav.
— similis, Herbst
— solutus, Er. *Barcombe, Hastings*
— paganus, Er. *Battle, Barcombe, Brighton*
— latifrons, Er. *Lewes, Hastings*
— oscillator, Rye. *Holm Bush, Brighton,*
    one specimen (Power)
— fornicatus, Steph. Rare ; *Netherfield*
    near *Hastings*
Oxyporus rufus, L. Not common ; *Pep-
    pering, Guestling, Fairlight, Lewes*
Bledius spectabilis, Kr. *Newhaven*
— tricornis, Herbst. *Rye, Shoreham, Cam-
    ber, Newhaven, Seaford*
— unicornis, Germ. *Camber, Shoreham*
— bicornis, Germ. *Seaford*
— pallipes, Grav. *Fairlight* near *Hastings*
— opacus, Block. *Hastings, Eastbourne,
    Brighton, Shoreham*
— atricapillus, Germ. *Bexhill*
— crassicollis, Lac. *Rye, Camber*
Platystethus arenarius, Fourc.
— cornutus, Gyll.
— nodifrons, Sahlb. *Rye, Hastings,
    Littlington*
— nitens, Sahlb. *Landport, Lewes*
Oxytelus rugosus, Grav.
— insecatus, Grav. *Hastings, Lewes*
— sculptus, Grav.
— laqueatus, Marsh. *Camber,* not com-
    mon ; *Barcombe*
— inustus, Grav. *Hastings,* not common ;
    Lewes, common
— sculpturatus, Grav. *Hastings, Battle,*
    not common ; *Barcombe*
— nitidulus, Grav.
— complanatus, Er. *Hastings, Battle,* not
    common ; *Lewes*

146

INSECTS

STAPHYLINIDÆ (continued)

Oxytelus clypeonitens, Pand. Rare ; *Hastings* district

— tetracarinatus, Block.

Haploderus cœlatus, Grav. *Hastings* and *Lewes* districts

Ancyrophorus omalinus, Er. *Guestling* (Bennett)

— aureus, Fauv. *Fairlight* (Phillips)

Trogophlœus bilineatus, Steph. *Hastings, Lewes, Shoreham, Newhaven*

— rivularis, Mots. *Battle, Barcombe*

— elongatulus, Er. *Hastings* district

— fuliginosus, Grav. *Guestling, Lewes*

— foveolatus, Sahlb. *Rye*

— corticinus, Grav. *Hastings* district, *Barcombe*

— halophilus, Kies. *Hastings, Shoreham*

— pusillus, Grav. *Hastings, St. Leonards, Guestling, Shoreham*

Thinobius brevipennis, Kies. *Hastings,* rare ; somewhat doubtfully recorded as this species

Syntomium æneum, Müll. *Battle, Guestling*

Coprophilus striatulus, F. *Hastings, Guestling, Barcombe, Lewes*

Deleaster dichrous, Grav. Very rare ; *Hastings ;* various localities round *Lewes,* singly

Lesteva longelytrata, Goeze.

— pubescens, Mann. *Fairlight,* rare

— sicula, Er. *Peppering, Barcombe, Lewes*

Acidota cruentata, Mann. Rare ; *Hastings, Guestling*

Olophrum piceum, Gyll. Not common ; *Hastings* list

Lathrimæum atrocephalum, Gyll. *Coombe Plantation, Lewes*

— unicolor, Steph. *Hastings,* rare ; *Lewes* district, *Newhaven*

Micralymma brevipenne, Gyll. *Ecclesbourne, Fairlight*

Philorhinum sordidum, Steph. *Bopeep, Guestling, Lewes*

Coryphium angusticolle, Steph. *Hastings* district, *Lewes*

Homalium rivulare, Payk.

— riparium, Thoms. *Camber, Bishopstone*

— exiguum, Gyll. Rare ; *Hastings* district, *Barcombe, Lewes*

— oxyacanthæ, Grav. *Guestling, Ore, Camber, Ashburnham*

— excavatum, Steph.

— cæsum, Grav. *Hastings, Lewes*

— nigriceps, Kies. *Camber, Guestling, Littlington*

— pusillum, Grav. *Hastings, Battle*

— punctipenne, Thoms. *Fairlight, Guestling*

STAPHYLINIDÆ (continued)

Homalium rufipes, Fourc. (florale, Payk.)

— salicis, Gyll. Very rare ; *Littlington* (Power)

— vile, Er. *Hastings,* rare ; *Bishopstone, Lewes*

— brevicorne, Er. Rare ; *Ecclesbourne, Guestling*

— gracilicorne, Fairm. Very rare ; *Guestling*

— iopterum, Steph. *Winchelsea*

— concinnum, Marsh. *Ecclesbourne,* rare ; *Lewes*

— deplanatum, Gyll. *Hastings, Guestling,* rare ; *Littlington*

— striatum, Grav. *Peppering,* rare ; *Lewes*

Hapalaræa pygmæa, Gyll. Rare ; *Cowfold* near *Horsham* (Power)

Eusphalerum primulæ, Steph. *Battle, Ringmer, Lewes*

Anthobium minutum, F. *North Banks ; Lewes,* once

— ophthalmicum, Payk.

— torquatum, Marsh.

— sorbi, Gyll. *Hastings, Lewes*

Proteinus ovalis, Steph.

— brachypterus, F. *Hastings,* common ; *Lewes,* once (Morris)

— macropterus, Gyll. *Guestling ; Lewes,* once (Morris)

— atomarius, Er. *Ore ; Lewes,* once (Morris)

Megarthrus denticollis, Beck. *Barcombe, Lewes*

— affinis, Mill. *Guestling, Littlington, Lewes*

— depressus, Lac. *Hollington, Barcombe, Lewes*

— sinuatocollis, Lac. *Hastings, Guestling*

— hemipterus, Ill. Local ; *Hastings, Abbots Wood*

Phlœobium clypeatum, Müll. *Camber, Abbots Wood, Lewes, Newhaven*

Phœocharis subtilissima, Mann. *Hastings* district

Pseudopsis sulcata, Newm. Rare ; *Fairlight* near *Hastings*

Prognatha quadricornis, Lac. Rare ; *Lewes*

LEPTINIDÆ

Leptinus testaceus, Müll. Rare ; *Guestling.* In a nest of Formica fuliginosa, *Tilgate Forest* (Champion), *Laughton*

SILPHIDÆ

Calyptomerus dubius, Marsh. *Hurst Green, Abbots Wood, Glynde* near *Lewes*

Clambus pubescens, Redt. *Hurst Green, St. Leonards*

— armadillo, De G. *Hastings* district, not common ; *Lewes,* common

SILPHIDÆ (*continued*)

Agathidium atrum, Payk. *Coombe Plantation, Hastings* district
— seminulum, L. *Abbots Wood, St. Leonards Forest*
— lævigatum, Er. *Peppering* near *Hastings*
— marginatum, Sturm. *Fairlight, Bexhill, Barcombe, Newhaven*
— varians, Beck. *Lewes* district
— globosum, Muls. *Guestling*
— rotundatum, Gyll. *Guestling, Ecclesbourne*
— nigrinum, Sturm. *Fairlight*
Amphicyllis globus, F. *Guestling, Abbots Wood, Laughton*
Liodes humeralis, Kug. *Peppering, Ecclesbourne, Laughton, Abbots Wood*
— orbicularis, Herbst. *Hastings, Lewes*
Cyrtusa pauxilla, Schmidt
Anisotoma cinnamomea, Panz. Rare; *Amberley, Lewes*
— oblonga, Er. Rare; *Hastings, Guestling, Maplehurst Wood*
— dubia, Kug. *Abbots Wood, Landport*
— badia, Sturm. *Hastings* district, *Lewes*
— ovalis, Schmidt. *Hastings* district, *Camber*
— punctulata, Gyll. *Hastings* district
— calcarata, Er. *Hastings, Hellingly, Lewes*
— nigrita, Schmidt. *Hastings* district
— lunicollis, Rye. Very rare; *Guestling*
— parvula, Sahlb. *Hastings* district
— ciliaris, Schmidt. Very rare; *Rye*
Colenis dentipes, Gyll. *Hollington, Peppering, Ore*
Agaricophagus cephalotes, Schmidt. Rare; *Hastings* district, *Tilgate, Rusper*
— conformis, Er. Very rare; *Cowfold* near *Horsham* (Power)
Hydnobius punctatissimus, Steph. *Rye, Lewes*
— punctatus, Sturm. *Bopeep* near *Hastings*
— strigosus, Schmidt. *Hastings, Shipley, Bognor*
Necrophorus germanicus, L. *Fairlight* near *Hastings*, doubtfully indigenous
— humator, Goeze
— mortuorum, F.
— vestigator, Hersch.
— ruspator, Er. *Hastings, Lewes, Barcombe, Alciston*, etc.
— interruptus, Steph. *Hastings, Lewes, Tilgate Forest*
— vespillo, L.
Necrodes littoralis, L.
Silpha tristis, Ill. Very rarely found; *Guestling, Brighton*
— obscura, L.
— quadripunctata, L. Rare; *Laughton, Brighton*

SILPHIDÆ (*continued*)

Silpha thoracica, L. *Hastings, Tilgate, Brighton*
— rugosa, L.
— sinudta, F.
— lævigata, F. Scarce; *Camber, Lewes*
— atrata, L.
Choleva angustata, F. *Guestling*
— cisteloides, Frohl. *Hastings, Laughton, Lewes*
— intermedia, Kr. *Guestling*, rare
— spadicea, Sturm. Rare; *Fairlight Holm Bush* near *Brighton*
— agilis, Ill. *Hastings* district
— velox, Spence. *Hollington Guestling, Lewes*
— wilkini, Spence. *Hastings* district
— anisotomoides, Spence. *Hastings* and *Lewes* districts
— nigricans, Spence. *Ecclesbourne, Guestling, Lewes*
— morio, F. *Guestling, Fairlight, Barcombe*
— grandicollis, Er. *Peppering, Guestling*,
— nigrita, Er. *Guestling*
— tristis, Panz. *Battle, Lewes*
— kirbyi, Spence. *Guestling*
— chrysomeloides, Panz. *Hastings* and *Lewes* districts
— fumata, Spence. *Hastings* districts
— watsoni, Spence. *Guestling Abbots Wood, Barcombe, Laughton*
Catops sericeus, F.
Colon viennense, Herbst. Very rare; *Hastings*
— serripes, Sahlb. Rare; *Guestling Ore*
— dentipes, Sahlb. Rare; *Battle*
   var. zebei, Kr. Very rare; *Hastings*
— brunneum, Latr. *Hastings* district
— latum, Kr. Rare; *Guestling*

SCYDMÆNIDÆ

Neuraphes elongatulus, Mull. *Hastings* district
— rubicundus, Mots. Very rare; *Fairlight*
— sparshalli, Den. *Hastings* district
   var. minutus, Chaud. (= Scydmænus pumilio, Schaum.) *Littlington*
— longicollis, Mots. *Guestling, Lewes*
Scydmænus scutellaris, Mull. *Hastings* and *Lewes* districts
— collaris, Müll. *Battle, Guestling*; not common
— pusillus, Müll. Rare; *Hastings, Guestling, Bexhill*
— poweri, Fowler. Very Rare; *Guestling*
— exilis, Er. Rare; *Guestling, Hurst Green*

INSECTS

SCYDMÆNIDÆ (*continued*)

Euconnus denticornis, Müll. *Hollington, Guestling*

— hirticollis, Ill. *St. Leonards, Guestling, Barcombe, Newhaven*

— fimetarius, Chaud. *Lewes* district

Eumicrus tarsatus, Müll.

— rufus, Mull. Very rare ; *Hurst Green* (E. A. Butler)

Euthia schaumi, Kies. Very rare ; *Guestling*

— plieata, Gyll. Rare ; *Hastings* district

Cephennium thoracicum, Müll. *Hastings Barcombe*

CLAVIGERIDÆ

Claviger testaceus, Preyss. *Lewes* district, *Seaford*

PSELAPHIDÆ

Tychus niger, Payk.

Bythinus glabratus, Rye. Very rare ; *Seaford Downs*, in a mossy hollow in company with a small yellow *Myrmica* (F. H. and E. A. Waterhouse, 1865)

— puncticollis, Denny

— bulbifer, Reich.

— curtisi, Denny. *Amberley, Hastings, Lewes*

— securiger, Reich. *Hastings, Lewes*

— burrelli, Denny. *Amberley*

Rybaxis sanguinea, L. *Guestling*

Bryaxis waterhousei, Rye. Rare ; *Rye, Newhaven, Shoreham*

— fossulata, Reich. *Hastings* and *Lewes* districts

— helferi, Schmidt. *Hastings, Shoreham, Newhaven*

— hæmatica, Reich. *Battle, Guestling, Camber, Barcombe*

— juncorum, Leach. *Hastings* and *Lewes* districts

Trichonyx märkeli, Aubè. Rare ; *Guestling, Eastbourne, Seaford*

Euplectus karsteni, Reich. *Hastings*

— signatus, Reich. *St. Leonards, Lewes*

— sanguineus, Denny. „ „

— piceus, Mots. *Peppering, Guestling*

— ambiguus, Reich. Rare ; *Guestling, Lewes*

TRICHOPTERYGIDÆ

Ptinella denticollis, Fairm. *Hastings* district

Trichopteryx atomaria, De G.

— anthracina, Matth. *Guestling, Lewes*

— grandicollis, Mann.

— lata, Mots.

— fascicularis, Herbst

— sericans, Heer

— picicornis, Mann. Very rare ; *Guestling*

Ptilium spencei, All. *Hastings* district

— affine, Er. Very rare ; *North Banks, Lewes*

TRICHOPTERYGIDÆ (*continued*)

Millidium trisulcatum, Aubè. *Landport, Lewes, Hastings* district

Nossidium pilosellum. *Littlington* (Power)

Ptenidium punctatum, Gyll. *Bognor, Shoreham, Littlehampton*

— nitidum, Heer

— evanescens, Marsh.

— atomaroides, Mots. *Winchelsea*

— wankowiezii, Matth. *Camber*

— formicetorum, Kr. *Tilgate, Hastings*

CORYLOPHIDÆ

Orthoperus kluki, Wank. (brunnipes, Brit. Cat.)

— atomus, Gyll. *Glynde, Malling, Lewes*

Corylophus cassidioides, Marsh. *Rye, Brighton*

— sublævipennis, Duv. *Hastings, Lewes*

Sericoderus lateralis, Gyll. *Guestling, Barcombe, Lewes*

SPHÆRIIDÆ

Sphærius acaroides, Waltl. *Glynde* near *Hastings*

PHALACRIDÆ

Phalacrus corruscus, Payk.

— brisouti, Rye. *Lewes, Newhaven*

— caricis, Sturm. *Shipley* near *Horsham*

Olibrus corticalis, Panz. *Battle*, rare

— æneus, F. *Battle, Guestling*

— liquidus, Er. *Camber*

— (?) particeps, Muls.

— pygmæus, Sturm. *Lewes*

Stilbus testaceus, Panz.

— oblongus, Er. *Camber*

COCCINELLIDÆ

Subcoccinella 24-punctata, L.

Hippodamia 13-punctata, L. Rare ; *Hastings* district, *Lewes*

— variegata, Goeze. *Lewes, Brighton*

Anisosticta 19-punctata, L. *Hastings, Lewes, Brighton*

Adalia obliterata, L.

— bipunctata, L.

Mysia oblongoguttata, L. *Peppering, Bexhill*

Anatis ocellata, L. *Peppering, Netherfield* ; not common

Coccinella 10-punctata, L.

— hieroglyphica, L.

— 11-punctata, L. *Hastings*, not common ; *Lewes, Brighton, Newhaven*

— 7-punctata, L.

— distincta, Fald. (labilis, Muls.) Rare ; *Guestling, Abbots Wood* ; sometimes common about nests of Formica rufa

Halyzia 16-guttata, L. *Hastings* district, rare ; *Brighton*, common ; *Lewes*, sometimes common

— 14-guttata, L. *Hastings* and *Lewes* districts

COCCINELLIDÆ (*continued*)

Halyzia 18-guttata, L.
— conglobata, L.
— 22-punctata, L.
Micraspis 16-punctata, L.
Hyperaspis reppensis, Herbst. *Camber, Abbots Wood, Lewes, Seaford, Brighton*
Scymnus nigrinus, Kug. *Hastings, Laughton, Lewes*
— pygmæus, Fourc. *Hastings, Fairlight, Bexhill, Lewes*
— frontalis, F. *Hastings* district, *Lewes, Newhaven*
— suturalis, Thunb. *Hastings* and *Lewes* districts
    var. limbatus, Steph. *Hastings* district
— testaceus, Mots. *Seaford, Lewes, Newhaven, Shoreham*
— hæmorrhoidalis, Herbst. *Hastings* and *Lewes* districts
— capitatus, F. *Hastings, Ore, Laughton*
— minimus, Rossi. *Littlington, Abbots Wood, Holm Bush, Brighton*
Platynaspis luteorubra, Goeze. *Hastings, Seaford*
Chilocorus similis, Rossi. *Hastings, Abbots Wood, Brighton, Lewes*
— bipustulatus, L. *Netherfield, Dallington Forest*; not common
Exochomus quadripustulatus, L. *Hastings* district, scarce; *Lewes*
Rhizobius litura, F.
Coccidula rufa, Herbst
— scutellata, Herbst. *Hastings, Lewes*

ENDOMYCHIDÆ

Mycetæa hirta, Marsh. *Hastings*, scarce; *Winterbourne, Lewes*
Alexia pilifera, Müll. *Battle, Guestling*, rare; *Glynde, Lewes*
Lycoperdina bovistæ, F. *Rusper, Shipley, Hastings*
Endomychus coccineus, L. *Hollington, Hastings, Lewes*

EROTYLIDÆ

Dacne humeralis, F. *Winchelsea*
— rufifrons, F. „
Cyrtotriplax bipustulata, F. „ *Guestling, St. Leonards Forest, Abbots Wood, Laughton*

COLYDIIDÆ

Oxylæmus variolosus, Duft. Very rare; *Holm Bush, Brighton* (Power)
Orthocerus muticus, L. *Hastings*
Ditoma crenata, F. *St. Leonards Forest*
Synchita juglandis, F. „ „
Cerylon histeroides, F.
— fagi, Bris. *Tilgate*

HISTERIDÆ

Hister unicolor, L.

HISTERIDÆ (*continued*)

Hister merdarius, Hoff. Very rare; *Brightling, Lewes*
— cadaverinus, Hoff.
— marginatus, Er. Very rare; *Guestling*
— carbonarius, Ill.
— 12-striatus, Sch. *Hastings, Barcombe, Lewes*
— bimaculatus, L. *Guestling, Lewes*
Carcinops minima, Aubé. *Bognor, Hurstpierpoint, Hastings, Barcombe, Bishopstone*
Dendrophilus punctatus, Ill. *Barcombe flood* (Morris)
Gnathoncus nannetensis, Mars. *Hastings*
Saprinus nitidulus, Payk.
— æneus, F. *Hastings* district, *Abbots Wood*
— immundus, Gyll. *Camber*, rather common
— virescens, Payk. Rare; *Lewes* and district
— metallicus, Herbst. *Camber Sandhills*, not uncommon; usually a very scarce species
— rugifrons, Payk. *Hastings* district
— maritimus, Steph. *Camber*
Abræus globosus, Hoff. *Barcombe flood*
Acritus minutus, Herbst. *Hastings* and *Lewes* districts
Onthophilus striatus, F. *Hastings*, not uncommon; *Barcombe flood*

MICROPEPLIDÆ

Micropeplus porcatus, Payk. *Fairlight*, rare
— staphylinoides, Marsh. *Fairlight*, rare
— margaritæ, Duv. *Hastings* district, common; *Lewes*

NITIDULIDÆ

Brachypterus pubescens, Er.
— urticæ, F.
Cercus pedicularius, L. *Hollington, Battle, Barcombe*
— bipustulatus, Payk. *Landport, Lewes*
— rufilabris, Latr.
Epuræa decemguttata, F. Rare; *Hastings*
— diffusa, Bris. Rare; *Ore* near *Hastings*
— æstiva, L.
— melina, Er. *Hastings, St. Leonards, Abbots Wood, Lewes, Brighton*
— longula, Er. *Tilgate Forest, Hollington*
— florea, Er.
— immunda, Er. Rare; *Hollington*[1]
— parvula, Sturm. *Hastings* district

---

[1] I do not feel sure whether this species may not have been confused with the common *E. deleta*, Er., to which it is allied; the latter has not been recorded from Sussex as far as I know. *E. immunda* has only occurred in Scotland and near Scarborough.

INSECTS

NITIDULIDÆ (continued)

Epuræa obsoleta, F. *Hastings, Abbots Wood, Lewes*

— pusilla, Herbst. *Hastings* and *Lewes*

Omosiphora limbata, F. *Laughton*

Micrurula melanocephala, Marsh. *Amberley, Lewes*

Nitidula bipustulata, L.

— quadripustulata, F. *Camber*

— rufipes, L. *Abbots Wood*

Soronia punctatissima, Ill. *Hastings* and *Brighton*, not common

— grisea, L. *Hastings, Fairlight, Ore*, not common ; *Abbots Wood, Lewes*

Amphotis marginata, Er. Rare ; *Tilgate Forest*

Omosita depressa, L. *Guestling*, not common ; *Laughton, Abbots Wood*

— colon, L.

— discoidea, F.

Thalycra sericea, Sturm. Rare ; *Tilgate Forest, Balcombe*

Pocadius ferrugineus, F. *Hastings* and *Lewes* districts

Pria dulcamaræ, Scop. *Hastings, Eastbourne*

Meligethes rufipes, Gyll.

— lumbaris, Sturm. *Lewes*

— fulvipes, Bris. *Fairlight*

— æneus, F.

— viridescens, F.

— difficilis, Heer. *Amberley*

— memnonius, Er. *Worthing*

— ochropus, Sturm. Rare ; *Rusper* near *Horsham*, on Stachys sylvatica (Gorham)

— brunnicornis, Sturm.

— pedicularius, Gyll (Mr. Jenner's list)

— bidens, Bris. *Amberley, Littlington*

— umbrosus, Sturm. *Rusper, Guestling*

— ovatus, Sturm. *Amberley, Hastings*

— flavipes, Sturm. *Eastbourne, Hastings*

— picipes, Sturm

— rotundicollis, Bris. *Hastings, Brighton*

— symphyti, Heer. Rare ; *Amberley* (J. J. Walker)

— serripes, Gyll. *Eastbourne*

— murinus, Er. *Hastings* district

— lugubris, Sturm. *Amberley*

— obscurus, Er. *Amberley, Hastings*

— erythropus, Gyll. *St. Leonards, Hastings*

— solidus, Sturm. *Amberley, Hastings*

Cychramus luteus, F.

— fungicola, Heer.

Cryptarcha strigata, F. *Hastings*, rare

— imperialis, F. *Guestling*, rare

Ips quadripunctata, Herbst. Rare ; *Barcombe*

— quadripustulata, F. Rare ; *Hastings*

NITIDULIDÆ (continued)

Pityophagus ferrugineus, F. *Barcombe*

Rhizophagus cribratus, Gyll. *Tilgate*

— depressus, F. *Battle*

— perforatus, Er. *Hastings* district

— parallelocollis, Er. *Hastings* district

— ferrugineus, Payk. *Lewes*

— bipustulatus, F.

TROGOSITIDÆ

Tenebrionides mauritanicus, L. *St. Leonards*

Thymalus limbatus, F. Rare ; *Guestling*

MONOTOMIDÆ

Monotoma conicicollis, Aubé. *Guestling*

— formicetorum, Thoms. *Hastings*

— spinicollis, Aubé. *Hastings* and *Lewes* districts

— brevicollis, Aubé. *Lewes*

— picipes, Payk.

— quadricollis, Aubé. *St. Leonards, Barcombe, Lewes*

— rufa, Redt. *Hastings* and *Lewes*

— longicollis, Gyll.

LATHRIDIIDÆ

Lathridius lardarius, De G.

— angulatus, Humm. *Battle, Fairlight, Eastbourne*

Coninomus nodifer, Westw.

— carinatus, Gyll. Rare ; *Brightling, Tilgate Forest, Littlington*

Enicmus minutus, L.

— transversus, Ol.

— testaceus. Steph. *Hastings* district

Cartodere ruficollis, Marsh.

— elongata, Curt. *Hastings* district

Corticaria pubescens, Gyll. *Bopeep, Battle, Barcombe*

— crenulata, Gyll. *Hastings* district, *Shoreham*

— denticulata, Gyll. *Hastings, Barcombe, Lewes, Newhaven*

— serrata, Payk. *Hastings* district

— fulva, Com. *Lewes* district

— elongata, Humm.

Melanophthalma gibbosa, Herbst

— fuscula, Humm.

— fulvipes, Com. *Hastings, Brighton, Newhaven, Seaford*

CUCUJIDÆ

Læmophlœus duplicatus, Waltl. Rare ; *Balcombe* ; *Holm Bush, Brighton*

— ferrugineus, Steph. *Tilgate*

Psammœchus bipunctatus, F. *Peppering, Guestling*

Nausibius dentatus, Marsh. *Hastings*

Silvanus surinamensis, L. *St. Leonards*

— unidentatus, F. *Hastings* (Bennett)

BYTURIDÆ

Byturus sambuci, Scop.

— tomentosus, F.

CRYPTOPHAGIDÆ

Diphyllus lunatus, F. *Winchelsea, Lewes*

Telmatophilus sparganii, Ahr. Rare ; *Pett near Hastings*

— caricis, Ol. *Hastings, Lewes*

— typhæ, Fall. *Ashburnham*

— schönherri, Gyll. *Winchelsea*

— brevicollis, Aubé. Rare ; *Rye*

Antherophagus nigricornis, F. *Hastings district, Abbots Wood, Lewes*

— pallens, Gyll. *Littlington, Hastings, Lewes*

Cryptophagus lycoperdi, Herbst. *Guestling, Fairlight, Battle*

— setulosus, Sturm. *Guestling*

— populi, Payk. *Guestling*

— saginatus, Sturm. *Hastings district*

— scanicus, L. *Guestling, Peppering, Lewes*

— badius, Sturm. *St. Leonards*, rare

— dentatus, Herbst. *Guestling, Camber, Hastings, Lewes*

— distinguendus, Sturm. *Hastings district, Malling, Lewes*

— acutangulus, Gyll. *Hastings district, Lewes*

— fumatus, Gyll. Very rare ; *Shipley* (Gorham), *Cowfold* (Power)

— cellaris, Scop. Generally distributed ; *Hastings* and *Lewes* districts

— affinis, Sturm. *Guestling, Bopeep*

— pubescens, Sturm. Rare ; *St. Leonards*

— bicolor, Sturm. *St. Leonards*, rare

Micrambe vini, Panz.

Paramecosoma melanocephala, Herbst. Scarce ; *Barcombe flood*

Cœnoscelis ferruginea, Sahl. Very rare ; *Lewes*

Atomaria fimetarii, Herbst. *Lewes*

— fumata, Er. *Bexhill*

— nigriventris, Steph. *Hastings* and *Lewes* districts

— umbrina, Er. *Holm Bush, Brighton*

— linearis, Steph. *Hastings*, not common ; *Lewes*

— elongatula, Er. *Hastings district*

— fuscipes, Gyll. *Camber, Lewes*

— peltata, Kr. (Doubtfully recorded from *Guestling*)

— nigripennis, Payk. *Guestling*

— munda, Er. *Lewes*

— fuscata, Sch. *Hastings* and *Lewes* districts ; general

— atra, Herbst. *Battle*, rare

— pusilla, Payk. *Battle, Fairlight, Barcombe, Lewes*

— atricapilla, Steph.

— berolinensis, Kr. *Hastings, Peppering, Camber*

— basalis, Er. *Battle, Peppering, Barcombe, Lewes*

CRYPTOPHAGIDÆ (*continued*)

Atomaria rhenana, Kr. Very rare ; *Bognor, Brighton* ; marsh between *Shoreham* and *Lancing*

— mesomelas, Herbst. *Peppering, Abbots Wood, Lewes*

— gutta, Steph. *Battle, Lewes*

— apicalis, Er. *Hastings district, Lewes*

— analis, Er. *Hastings* and *Lewes* districts

— ruficornis, Marsh. *Hastings, Battle*

— versicolor, Er. *Hastings district*

Ephistemus globosus, Waltl. *Barcombe flood* ; *Holm Bush, Brighton*

— gyrinoides, Marsh.

SCAPHIDIIDÆ

Scaphidium quadrimaculatum, Ol. *Hastings district, Abbots Wood*

Scaphisoma agaricinum, L. *Hastings* and *Lewes* districts

— boleti, Panz. *Battle, Lewes*

MYCETOPHAGIDÆ

Typhæa fumata, L.

Triphyllus punctatus, F. *Guestling*, not common

Mycetophagus piceus, F. *Guestling, Fairlight*

— atomarius, F. *Brightling*

— quadriguttatus, Müll. *Shipley*

DERMESTIDÆ

Dermestes murinus, L.

— undulatus, Brahm. *Hastings, Shoreham, Brighton*

— lardarius, L.

Attagenus pellio, L.

Anthrenus musæorum, L.

— claviger, Er. *Abbots Wood, Lewes*

BYRRHIDÆ

Syncalypta spinosa, Rossi. *Guestling, Lewes, Newhaven*

— hirsuta, Sharp. *Camber, Seaford, Newhaven*

Byrrhus pilula, L.

var. dennyi, Steph. Rare ; *St. Leonards, Littlington* (Power)

— dorsalis, F. *Hastings district*

Cytilus varius, F. *Hastings* and *Lewes* districts

Simplocaria semistriata, F.

Limnichus pygmæus, Sturm. *Hastings district*

Aspidiphorus orbiculatus, Gyll. *Hastings*

GEORYSSIDÆ

Georyssus pygmæus, F. *Rye*

PARNIDÆ

Elmis æneus, Müll. *Guestling, Lewes*

— volkmari, Panz. *Guestling, Crowhurst, Tilgate*

Limnius tuberculatus, Müll. *Crowhurst, Lewes*

PARNIDÆ (*continued*)

Potaminus substriatus, Müll. *Bodle Street* near *Ashburnham* (Bennett)

Parnus prolifericornis, F. *Battle, Lewes*

HETEROCERIDÆ

Heterocerus rectus, Wat. *Camber*, somewhat doubtful

— flexuosus, Steph. *Rye, Bishopstone, Shoreham, Brighton*

— obsoletus, Curt. *Rye*

— marginatus, F. *Hastings*

— lævigatus, Panz. *Hastings, Fairlight*

— britannicus, Kuw. (sericans, *Brit. Cat.*). *Rye, Camber, Shoreham*

LUCANIDÆ

Lucanus cervus, L. *Arundel, Barcombe, Brighton*

Dorcus parallelopipedus, L. *Winchelsea, Barcombe, Lewes, Brighton*

Sinodendron cylindricum, L. *Lewes, Brighton*

SCARABÆIDÆ

Copris lunaris, L. *Shoreham ; Lewes*, once

Onthophagus ovatus, L. *Hastings, Camber*, scarce ; *Lewes, Brighton*

— cœnobita, Herbst. *Hastings* district, scarce ; *Lewes, Brighton*

— vacca, L. *St. Leonards*, rare ; *Abbots Wood, Laughton*

— fracticornis, Payk. *Hastings* and *Lewes* districts

— nuchicornis, L. *Hastings, Abbots Wood, Laughton, Lewes*

Aphodius erraticus, L. *Hastings, Brighton* and *Lewes* districts

— subterraneus, L. *Hastings*, not common ; *Lewes*

— fossor, L.

— hæmorrhoidalis, L. *Hastings* district, scarce ; *Lewes*, common

— fœtens, F. Scarce ; *Hastings, St. Leonards, Southerham* near *Lewes, Brighton*

— fimetarius, L.

— scybalarius, F. Scarce ; *Rye, Camber*

— ater, De G. *Hastings* district, scarce ; *Lewes*, common

— granarius, L. *Hastings, Lewes*, and *Brighton* districts

— nitidulus, F. *Hastings* district, *Eastbourne* ; *Offham Hill, Lewes* ; *Brighton*

— sordidus, F. *Brighton*

— rufescens, F. *Hastings, Lewes*, scarce

— putridus, Sturm. *Eastbourne*

— plagiatus, L. *Rye, Guestling*

— lividus, Ol. *Lewes*

— porcus, F. *Hastings, Lewes*

— pusillus, Herbst. *Guestling*, rare ; *Lewes*, common

— merdarius, F. *Hastings* district, scarce ; *Brighton* and *Lewes*, common

SCARABÆIDÆ (*continued*)

Aphodius tessulatus, Payk. *Brighton, Lewes*

— sticticus, Panz. *Abbots Wood, Lewes*

— consputus, Cr. *Rye*

— punctato-sulcatus, Sturm

— prodromus, Brahm

— contaminatus, Herbst. *Hastings*, scarce ; *Lewes*

— obliteratus, Panz. *Amberley, Hastings, Lewes*

— luridus, F. *Peppering*, scarce ; *Lewes*

— rufipes, L.

Plagiogonus arenarius, Ol. *Shipley* near *Horsham, Abbots Wood, Lewes, Eastbourne, Amberley*

Heptaulacus sus, Herbst. *Camber*, scarce ; *Brighton*

— testudinarius, F. *Lewes*

— villosus, Gyll. Downs near *Lewes*

Oxyomus porcatus, F. *Brighton, Hastings, Lewes*

Ægialia arenaria, F.

Odontæus mobilicornis, F. Very rare ; *Hollington, Guestling, Hastings*

Geotrupes typhæus, L. *Hastings, Battle, Seaford, Hayward's Heath*

— spiniger, Marsh.

— stercorarius, L.

— mutator, Marsh. *Peppering, Lewes*

— vernalis, L. *Brighton*

— sylvaticus, Panz.

— pyrenæus, Charp. *Lewes*

Trox sabulosus, L. *Guestling*

— scaber, L. *Hastings, Guestling, Tilgate, Lewes*

Hoplia philanthus, Fuss. *Camber, Hollington*

Homaloplia ruricola, F. *Sussex* (Stephens), *Brighton*, downs near *Lewes* ; scarce

Serica brunnea, L. *Hastings* district, rather common ; *Brighton* and *Lewes*, scarce

Rhizotrogus solstitialis, L.

Melolontha vulgaris, F.

[Polyphylla fullo, F. A specimen of this insect was taken at *St. Leonards* on 29 July, 1902]

Phyllopertha horticola, L. *St. Leonards*, rare ; *Lewes*, formerly, not seen for some years ; *Brighton*, common in gardens some years ago.[1]

Cetonia aurata, L. *Hastings* district, 'very rare' ; *Lewes* and *Brighton*, common

---

[1] This insect appears to be one which only at certain times and under certain conditions becomes a pest and does a great deal of damage ; the chief instance of such beetles is perhaps the Colorado beetle (*Doryphora decem-lineata*).

SCARABÆIDÆ (continued)

[Oxytherea stictica, L. This species was recorded by Stephens from *Chichester*, but it has been for a long time erased from the British list as not indigenous]

BUPRESTIDÆ

Agrilus laticornis, Ill. *Balcombe*

— angustulus, Ill. *Guestling, Abbots Wood, Hellingly, Tilgate, Rotherfield*

— viridis, L. *Hayward's Heath*

Aphanisticus pusillus, Ol. *Arundel*

Trachys minuta, L. *Hastings, Abbots Wood*

— troglodytes, Gyll. Rare; *Guestling; Holm Bush, Brighton* (Power)

THROSCIDÆ

Throscus dermestoides, L. *Hastings*

— carinifrons, Bonv. *Tilgate*

— obtusus, Curt. *Rye, Hollington, Abbots Wood, Lewes*

EUCNEMIDÆ

Melasis buprestoides. *Guestling*

Microrrhagus pygmæus, F. *Battle*

ELATERIDÆ

Lacon murinus, L.

Elater elongatulus, F. '*Nuthurst, Sussex*' (Stephens)

— balteatus, L. *Dallington*

Melanotus rufipes, Herbst. *Hastings, Lewes*

Athous niger, L.

— longicollis, Ol. *Hastings, Lewes*

— difformis, Lac. *Hastings, St. Leonards, Guestling, Fairlight*

— hæmorrhoidalis, F.

— vittatus, F.

Limonius minutus, L. Downs near *Lewes, Offham*

Adrastus limbatus, F.

Agriotes sputator, L.

— obscurus, L. *Hastings* district, scarce; *Barcombe, Brighton, Lewes*

— lineatus, L.

— sobrinus, Kies.

— pallidulus, Ill.

Dolopius marginatus, L. *Guestling, Battle,* scarce; *Laughton*

Corymbites quercus, Gyll. *Rotherfield*

— holosericeus, F. *Lewes*

— metallicus, Payk. Rare; *Rye*

— bipustulatus, L. Scarce; *Hollington, Abbots Wood, Lewes*

Campylus linearis, L. Scarce; *Hastings* district, *Abbots Wood, Plashet Wood, Laughton, Lewes*

DASCILLIDÆ

Dascillus cervinus, L. *Brighton,* on thistles

Helodes minuta, L.

— marginata, F. *Hastings* district

Microcara livida, F. *Guestling,* rare; *Laughton, Lewes*

DASCILLIDÆ (continued)

Cyphon coarctatus, Payk.

— nitidulus, Thoms. *Peppering,* scarce

— variabilis, Thunb.

— pallidulus, Boh. *Guestling, Ore, Bopeep*

— padi, L. *Battle, Plashet Wood, Lewes*

Prionocyphon serricornis, Müll. Very rare; *Littlington*

Hydrocyphon deflexicollis, Müll. *St. Leonards*

Scirtes hemisphæricus, L. *Hastings* district, scarce; *Lewes,* common

— orbicularis, Panz. *Lewes*

Eubria palustris, Germ. Rare; *Fairlight* near *Hastings*

LYCIDÆ

Platycis minutus, F. Rare; *Arundel*

LAMPYRIDÆ

Lampyris noctiluca, L. Generally distributed

Phosphænus hemipterus, Geoff. *Hastings,* very rare; *Lewes,* in some numbers

TELEPHORIDÆ

Podabrus alpinus, Payk. *Hollington,* rare

Telephorus fuscus, L. *Hastings* district, *Shipley, Barcombe, Lewes, Isfield*

— rusticus, F.

— lividus, L.

var. dispar, F. *Hastings* district

— pellucidus, F.

— nigricans, Müll.

var. discoideus, Steph. *Hastings*

— lituratus, Fall.

— figuratus var. scoticus, Sharp. *Lewes* (Morris)

— bicolor, F.

— hæmorrhoidalis, F. *Hastings* district, scarce; *Lewes,* common

— oralis, Germ. (lateralis, L.) *Fairlight, Lewes, Brighton*

— flavilabris, Fall.

— thoracicus, Ol. *Guestling, Lewes*

Rhagonycha unicolor, Curt. *Guestling, Shipley*

— fuscicornis, Ol. *Bopeep,* rare; *Laughton, Lewes*

— fulva, Scop.

— testacea, L.

— limbata, Thoms.

— pallida, F.

Malthinus punctatus, Fourc.

— fasciatus, Ol. } *Hastings* and *Lewes*

— balteatus, Suff. } districts

— frontalis, Marsh. *Battle, Dallington*

Malthodes marginatus, Latr. *Hastings, Abbots Wood, Lewes*

— dispar, Germ. *Hastings* district

— pellucidus, Kies. *Tilgate* and *Dallington Forests*

— minimus, L. (sanguinolentus, Fall.)

— atomus, Thoms. *Battle*

INSECTS

MELYRIDÆ

Malachius æneus, L. *Tilgate, St. Leonards, Lewes, Isfield*
— bipustulatus, L.
— viridis, F. *Camber,* common ; *Lewes, Brighton*
— marginellus, Ol. *Camber,* rare ; *Eastbourne, Brighton*
Axinotarsus pulicarius, F. *Rye, Winchelsea* ; rare
— ruficollis, Ol. *Rye, Guestling,* rare ; *Lewes*
Anthocomus fasciatus, L.
Dasytes flavipes, F. *Brighton, St. Leonards, Guestling*
— oculatus, Kies. *Lewes*
— ærosus, Kies. *Battle, Guestling, Abbots Wood, Lewes, Laughton*
Psilothrix nobilis, Ill.
Haplocnemus nigricornis, F. *Hastings,* rare
Phlœophilus edwardsi, Steph. *Hastings* district, not common

CLERIDÆ

Opilo mollis, L. *Hastings,* rare ; *Brighton*
Thanasimus formicarius, L. *Fairlight*
Necrobia ruficollis, F. *Hastings,* scarce
— violacea, L. *Fairlight, Hurst Green* ; scarce
— rufipes, De G. *Hastings, Ewhurst*
Corynetes cœruleus, De G. *Guestling,* scarce

DRILIDÆ

Drilus flavescens, Rossi. Male local, female very rare ; male not uncommon near *Lewes* ; the female is recorded from ' the *Sussex Downs* '

PTINIDÆ

Ptinus germanus, F. Rare ; *Rye*
— fur, L.
— subpilosus, Müll. Rare ; *Tilgate Forest,* in ants' nests (Brewer)
[— pilosus, Müll. Said to have been taken in *Tilgate Forest,* but perhaps confused with the preceding]
Niptus hololeucus, Fabr.
Hedobia imperialis, L. *Hastings* district, *Barcombe, Lewes*
Gibbium scotias, Scop. *Hastings*

ANOBIIDÆ

Dryophilus pusillus, Gyll. *Laughton, Tilgate*
— anobioides, Chevr. Very rare ; *Laughton* (Morris)
Priobium castaneum, F. *Hastings, Abbots Wood, Barcombe, Lewes*
Anobium domesticum, Fourc.
— fulvicorne, Sturm. *Hastings, Lewes*
— paniceum, L.
Xestobium tessellatum, F. *Hastings, Battle, Lewes, Arundel*[1]

[1] Part of the roof of Arundel Church was destroyed by this insect some years ago.

ANOBIIDÆ (*continued*)

Ernobius mollis, L. *Hastings, Lewes* and *Newhaven* districts
Ptilinus pectinicornis, L. *St. Leonards, Guestling, Hastings* ; rare
Ochina hederæ, Müll. *St. Leonards, Hollington,* rare ; *Landport, Lewes*
Xyletinus ater, Panz. Rare ; *Shipley, Rusper*
Cœnocara bovistæ, Hoff. *Rye*
Dorcatoma flavicornis, F. *Hurst Green* (Butler)
Anitys rubens, Thoms. *Netherfield*
Rhizopertha pusilla, F. *Hastings*

CISSIDÆ

Cis boleti, Scop.
— villosulus, Marsh. *Hastings* district
— micans, Herbst. *Guestling*
— hispidus, Payk. *Guestling* ; *Broomham Grove, Lewes*
— bidentatus, Ol. *Hastings* district
— alni, Gyll. " "
— nitidus, Herbst. *Guestling, Lewes*
— pygmæus, Marsh. *Hastings* district
— festivus, Panz. " "
— fuscatus, Mel. " "
Ennearthron affine, Gyll. *Hastings, St. Leonards Forest*
— cornutum, Gyll. *Hastings, St. Leonards Forest, Hurst Green*
Octotemnus glabriculus, Gyll.

PRIONIDÆ

Prionus coriarius, L. Rare ; *Hollington, Buxted Park, Goodwood, Hayward's Heath*

CERAMBYCIDÆ

Callidium violaceum, L. *Hastings, Laughton, Hayward's Heath*
— variabile, L. *Ore* near *Hastings*
— alni, L. *Hastings* district, *Brighton, Abbots Wood, Crowhurst, Laughton, Rotherfield* near *Lewes*
Clytus arietis, L.
Gracilia minuta, F. *Hastings* district
Obrium cantharinum, L. ' *Brighton* ' (Stephens)
Rhagium inquisitor, F.
— bifasciatum, F.
Pachyta collaris, L. *Brighton* district, woods, rare
Toxotus meridianus, Panz.
Leptura livida, F.
[— rufa, Brullé. A single male recorded from *Holm Bush, Brighton* ; doubtfully indigenous]
Strangalia aurulenta, F. Very rare ; *Arundel* (S. Stevens)
— quadrifasciata, L. *Hastings* district, not uncommon ; *Abbots Wood, Laughton, Hayward's Heath*

CERAMBYCIDÆ (*continued*)
Strangalia armata, Herbst
— nigra, L. *Shipley* near *Horsham, Hayward's Heath, Laughton, Fletching, Plashet Wood*
— melanura, L.
Grammoptera tabacicolor, De G.
— ruficornis, F.

LAMIIDÆ
Acanthocinus ædilis, L. *Hastings* district, probably introduced
Leiopus nebulosus, Serv. *Hastings* district, *Plashet Wood, Hayward's Heath*
Pogonochærus bidentatus, Thoms. *Guestling, Abbots Wood, Lewes*
— dentatus, Fourc. *Hastings* district, *Lewes*
Lamia textor, L. Rare ; *Fairlight*
Saperda populnea, L. *Hollington, Abbots Wood, Laughton, Hayward's Heath*
Tetrops præusta, L. *Battle, Abbots Wood, Lewes*
Phytœcia cylindrica, L. Rare ; *Cowfold* near *Horsham* (Power) ; *Southerham, Ranscombe, Lewes* (Morris)

BRUCHIDÆ
Bruchus cisti, F. Chalk downs, *Lewes* and *Brighton*
— canus, Germ. *Brighton* (Power)
— rufimanus, Boh. *Fairlight, Laughton, Lewes, Brighton*
— atomarius, L. *Hastings, Faygate, Holm Bush* near *Brighton, Abbots Wood*
— luteicornis, Ill. *Guestling, Abbots Wood, Laughton, Lewes*
— rufipes, Herbst. Very rare ; *Laughton, Lewes*
— viciæ, Ol. Very rare ; two specimens only have occurred in Britain, both taken by Dr. Power ; one at *Hurst* and one at the *Devil's Dyke, Brighton*
— loti, Payk. *Hastings, Brighton, Lewes*
— villosus, F. (ater, Marsh.) *Hastings, St. Leonards Forest, Hurst Green, Laughton*

EUPODA
Orsodacna lineola, Panz. Rare ; *Plashet Wood, Laughton*
Donacia dentata, Hoppe. *Rye, Shipley, Arundel, Lewes*
— versicolorea, Brahm. (bidens, Ol.) *Hastings* district
— dentipes, F. *Faygate, Hastings, Lewes, Brighton*
— limbata, Panz. (lemnæ, F.) *Hastings, Barcombe, Lewes*
— bicolora, Zsch. (sagittariæ, F.) Rare ; *Hastings, Brighton*
— obscura, Gyll. Rare ; *Arundel* (S. Stevens)

EUPODA (*continued*)
Donacia thalassina, Germ. *Faygate, Hastings, Lewes*
— impressa, Payk. *Faygate, Hastings, Barcombe flood*
— simplex, F. (linearis, Hoppe.)
— vulgaris, Zsch. (typhæ, Ahr.) Scarce ; *Tilgate, Faygate, Hastings* district, *Lewes*
— clavipes, F. (menyanthidis, Gyll.) *Hastings, Arundel*
— semicuprea, Panz. *Hastings* district, *Barcombe*
— cinerea, Herbst (hypochæridis, F.) *Winchelsea, Faygate*
— sericea, L. *Hastings* district, common ; *Barcombe flood*
— braccata, Scop. (nigra, F.) *Winchelsea, Bopeep*
— affinis, Kunze. *Barcombe flood, Landport, Lewes*
Zeugophora subspinosa, F. Rare ; *Sedlescombe, Abbots Wood, Laughton*
Lema cyanella, L. *Hastings* district, *Hurst Green, Blackford, Abbots Wood, Lewes*
— lichenis, Voet.[1]
— erichsoni, Suffr. Very rare ; *Rye*
— melanopa, L.
Crioceris asparagi, L. *Brighton*, rare ; *Lewes*, common ; not recorded from the *Hastings* district

CAMPTOSOMATA
Labidostomis tridentata, L. Very rare ; *Laughton*
Clythra quadripunctata, L. *Hastings, Laughton, Abbots Wood, Hayward's Heath, Brighton*
Cryptocephalus sexpunctatus. Rare ; *Hollington* near *Hastings, Abbots Wood*
— bipunctatus, L., var. lineola, Scop. *Bexhill*
— aureolus, Suffr. *Horsham, Laughton*
— punctiger, Payk. Very rare ; *Rotherfield* (Jenner)
— decemmaculatus, L. Very rare ; *Abbots Wood* (Morris)
— parvulus, Müll. (flavilabris, F.) *Guestling, Bexhill, Plashet Wood*
— moræi, L. *Hastings, Arundel, Abbots Wood, Lewes*
— bilineatus, L. *Eastbourne, Arundel, Hastings, Lewes*
— fulvus, Goeze.
— pusillus, F.
— labiatus, L.
— frontalis. *Rusper* near *Horsham, Camber*

[1] A black variety of this species is found rarely in the Hastings district.

INSECTS

CYCLICA

Lamprosoma concolor, Sturm. *Hastings, Abbots Wood, Hellingly, Barcombe*
Timarcha tenebricosa, F. (lævigata, Duft.)
— violaceo-nigra, De G.
Chrysomela marginalis, Duft. *Cowfold near Horsham*
— marginata, L. Rare ; *Lewes*
— banksi, F. Scarce ; *Hastings* and *Brighton* districts
— staphylæa, L.
— polita, L.
— varians, Schall. *Guestling, Holm Bush near Brighton, Lewes*
— fastuosa, Scop. Rare ; *Guestling*
— didymata, Scriba. *Hastings* district
— hyperici, Forst. *Hastings* district, *Abbots Wood, Tilgate, Lewes*
Melasoma populi, L. *Hastings* district
— longicolle, Suffr. *St. Leonards, Netherfield, Abbots Wood*
Phytodecta rufipes, De G. Scarce ; *Battle, Laughton, Abbots Wood*
— viminalis, L. *Laughton, Abbots Wood*
— olivacea, Forst. *Hastings* and *Brighton* districts, *Abbots Wood*
— pallida, L. *Tilgate Forest*
Gastroidea polygoni, L.
Phædon tumidulus, Germ.
— armoraciæ, L. (betulæ, Küst.)
— cochleariæ, F.
Phyllodecta vulgatissima, L. *Abbots Wood,* apparently rare
— cavifrons, Thoms. *Hastings, Barcombe, Laughton*
— vitellinæ, L.
Hydrothassa aucta, F. *Hastings, Lewes* and *Brighton* districts
— marginella, L. *Brighton, Lewes*
Prasocuris junci, Brahm. *Barcombe, Winterbourne, Lewes* ; not recorded from the *Hastings* district
— phellandrii, L. Common ; *Hastings* and *Lewes* districts
Luperus nigrofasciatus, Goeze. *Hastings* district, scarce
— rufipes, Scop. *Hastings* district, rare
Lochmæa capreæ, L. *Peppering, Abbots Wood, Laughton*
— suturalis, Thoms. *Hastings* district, *Laughton*
— cratægi, Forst. Generally distributed
Galerucella viburni, Payk. *Hastings* district
— nymphææ, L. *Peppering, Barcombe, Lewes*
— sagittariæ, Gyll. *Lewes*
— lineola, F. *Peppering, Abbots Wood*
— calmariensis, L. *Guestling, Etchingham, Abbots Wood, Lewes*

CYCLICA (*continued*)

Galerucella tenella, L. *Hastings* district, *Abbots Wood*
Adimonia tanaceti, L. *Fairlight, Lewes*
Sermyla halensis, L. *Lewes*, common
Longitarsus pulex, Schrank. *Battle*
— anchusæ, Payk. *Bognor*
— holsaticus, L. *Dallington Forest*
— luridus, Scop.
— brunneus, Duft. *Lewes*
— fusculus, Kuts. Very rare ; *Littlington* (Power)
— agilis, Rye. Rare ; *Hollington* near *Hastings*
— suturellus, Duft., var. fuscicollis, Steph. *Hastings, Lewes*
— atricillus, L. *Hastings* district, *Littlington, Lewes*
— patruelis, All. *Hastings* district
— melanocephalus, All.
— suturalis, Marsh. *Lewes*
— nasturtii, F. *Cowfold* near *Horsham*
— piciceps, Steph. „ „
— lycopi, Foudr. *Hastings, Lewes*
— membranaceus, Foudr. (teucrii, All.) *Hastings* district
— flavicornis, Steph. *Fairlight, Bopeep*
— exoletus, L. *Rye, Eastbourne, Brighton, Lewes*
— pusillus, Gyll.
— reichei, All. *Littlington* (Power)
— tabidus, F. (verbasci, Panz.) *Amberley*
— jacobææ, Wat.
— rutilus, Ill. *Hastings* district, common[1]
— ochroleucus, Marsh. *Hastings* district
— gracilis, Kuts. „ „
— lævis, Duft. *Hastings, St. Leonards Forest, Eastbourne, Lewes*
Haltica ericeti, All. *Hastings* district
— oleracea, L. (pusilia, All.) *Lewes*
— pusilla, Duft. (helianthemi, All.) *Hollington, Peppering*[2]
Hermæophaga mercurialis, F. *Hastings* district, *Warrengore Wood* near *Lewes*
Phyllotreta nodicornis, Marsh. *Hastings, Bexhill*
— nigripes, F. (lepidii, Koch) *Hastings, Bexhill, Barcombe, Lewes*
— consobrina, Curt. (melæna, Ill.) *Hastings, Hollington*
— punctulata, Marsh. Rare ; *Brightling*
— atra, Payk. *Hastings, Battle, Lewes*
— cruciferæ, Goeze. *Rye, Bishopstone*

[1] I am inclined to think that there may be some mistake as to this record. The true *L. rutilus* is very scarce.
[2] *H. coryli* is recorded from Sedlescombe, Hastings, but I have not seen the specimens and cannot tell to which of our British species they should be referred (v. *Brit. Col.* iv. 358).

157

Cyclica (*continued*)

Phyllotreta vittula, Redt.
— undulata, Kuts.
— nemorum, L.
— flexuosa, Ill. *Lewes* (Morris)
— ochripes, Curt. *Battle, Lewes*
— sinuata, Steph. *Abbots Wood, Hellingly, Barcombe flood*
— tetrastigma, Com. *Hastings* and *Lewes* districts
— exclamationis, Thunb. *Hastings* district, scarce ; *Lewes*, common

Aphthona lutescens, Gyll. *Holm Bush, Brighton, Offham* ; osier beds, *Lewes*
— nigriceps, Redt. *Cowfold* (Power)
— nonstriata, Goeze.
— venustula, Kuts. *Hastings, Abbots Wood, Laughton, Lewes*
— atro-coerulea, Steph. *Hastings, Bishopstone, Lewes*
— virescens, Foudr. *Bopeep, Fairlight*
— atratula, All. *Malling, Lewes* (Morris)

Batophila rubi, Payk. *Hastings, Lewes*
— ærata, Marsh. *Lewes* district ; not recorded from *Hastings*

Sphæroderma testaceum, F.
— cardui, Gyll.

Apteropeda orbiculata, Marsh.
— globosa, Ill. *Hollington* near *Hastings*

Mniophila muscorum, Koch. *Ore, Barcombe, Lewes*

Podagrica fuscipes, L.
— fuscicornis, L.

Mantura rustica, L.
— obtusata, Gyll. *Battle, Catsfield*
— matthewsi, Curt. *Lewes* (Morris)

Ochrosis salicariæ, Payk. *Battle, Laughton, Lewes*

Crepidodera transversa, Marsh.
— ferruginea, Scop.
— rufipes, L. *Hastings*, scarce ; *Abbots Wood*
— ventralis, Ill. *Hollington*
— nitidula, L. *Littlington* (Power), *Barcombe flood* (Morris)
— helxines, L. *Hastings* district, scarce ; *Abbots Wood, Laughton*
— chloris, Foudr. *Rye*
— aurata, Marsh.

Hippuriphila modeeri, L. *Hastings, Barcombe, Lewes*

Epitrix pubescens, Koch. Extremely local in *Britain* ; *Shipley* near *Horsham*, abundant (Gorham) ; *Cowfold*, end of May, 1873 (Power)
— atropæ, Foudr. Very local ; *Arundel Park*, abundant, September, 1879 (W.W.F.)

Chætocnema subcoerulea, Kuts. *Balcombe, Cowfold, Hastings*

Cyclica (*continued*)

Chætocnema confusa, Boh. *Tilgate Forest, Shipley*
— hortensis, Fourc.

Plectroscelis concinna, Marsh.

Psylliodes attenuata, Koch. *Guestling, Hollington, Battle, Barcombe, Lewes*
— chrysocephala, L.
— napi, Koch. *Hastings* district, rare ; *Laughton, Barcombe*
— cuprea, Koch. Scarce ; *Hastings, Lewes*
— affinis, Payk. Scarce ; *Hollington, Peppering, Barcombe, Lewes*
— marcida, Ill. *Camber*
— dulcamaræ, Koch. *Hastings, Lewes*
— chalcomera, Ill. *Battle, Hurst Green*
— picina, Marsh. *Littlington*

Cryptostomata

Cassida murræa, L. *Holm Bush, Brighton* (Power)
— fastuosa, Schall. Very rare ; *Peppering, Rye*
— vibex, F. *Hastings* district, *Abbots Wood, Laughton*
— sanguinolenta, F. *Hastings* district, *Lewes* (Morris)
— chloris, Suffr. Very rare ; *Shipley*, two specimens (Gorham)
— nobilis, L. *Hollington, Guestling*, rare ; *Lewes*, common
— flaveola, Thunb. *Hastings* district, *Abbots Wood, Lewes*
— equestris, F. *Peppering, Guestling, Lewes*
— viridis, F.
— hemisphærica, Herbst. *Hastings* district, *Hollington, Fairlight, Dallington*

Tenebrionidæ

Blaps mucronata, Latr.
— similis, Latr. *Ore, Lewes, Brighton*

Crypticus quisquilius, L. *Camber*

Opatrum sabulosum, Gyll. Scarce ; *Hastings, Brighton*

Microzoum tibiale, F. Scarce ; *Rye*

Phaleria cadaverina, F. *Camber*

Diaperis boleti, L. 'Near *Hastings*' (Stephens)

Scaphidema metallicum, F. *Guestling, Stoneham, Lewes* district

Tenebrio molitor, L.
— obscurus, F. *Hastings, Beddingham* near *Lewes*

Gnathocerus cornutus, F. Rare ; *Hastings*

Tribolium ferrugineum, F.
— confusum, Duv. Rare ; *Hastings*

Helops coeruleus, L. *Hastings*
— pallidus, Curtis. *Camber*
— striatus, Fourc.

Lagriidæ

Lagria hirta, L.

INSECTS

CISTELIDÆ
Cistela luperus, Herbst.   Rare ; *Hollington*
— murina, L.   *Hastings*, scarce ; *Lewes*,
   common
Eryx atra, F.   Rare ; *Guestling*
Cteniopus sulphureus, L.   *Camber, Seaford*

MELANDRYIDÆ
Tetratoma fungorum, F.   Rare ; *Guestling,*
   Cowfold
— ancora, F.   Rare ; *Guestling, Newhurst,*
   Netherfield, Abbots Wood
Orchesia micans, Panz.   Rare ; *Coombe*
   Plantation, Lewes
Clinocara tetratoma,   Thoms.   (Orchesia
   minor, Walk.)   Rare ; *Fairlight*
Conopalpus testaceus, Ol.   Rare ; *Hastings,*
   Laughton, Lewes
Melandrya caraboides, L.   *Hollington, Abbots*
   Wood, Holm Bush, Brighton
Abdera bifasciata, Marsh.   Rare ; *Guestling*
— quadrifasciata, Steph.   Very   rare ;
   Northbanks, Lewes (Morris)
Phlœotrya rufipes, Gyll.   Very rare ; *Cam-*
   ber
Hypulus quercinus, Quens.   Very   rare ;
   Rusper (Gorham)

PYTHIDÆ
Salpingus castaneus, Panz.   *Peppering, Hurst*
   Green, Laughton
— æratus, Muls.   *Hastings, Fairlight, Lewes*
Lissodema quadripustulata, Marsh.   *West-*
   field, Lewes
Rhinosimus ruficollis, L.   Not common ;
   Guestling
— viridipennis, Steph.   Not   common ;
   Guestling, Lewes
— planirostris, F.

ŒDEMERIDÆ
Œdemera nobilis, Scop.   *Hastings* district,
   Lewes
— lurida, Marsh.   *Hollington, Lewes*
Oncomera femorata, F.   *Hastings, Arundel,*
   Shipley, Lewes
Nacerdes melanura, Schmidt.   *Camber,*
   Lewes

PYROCHROIDÆ
Pyrochroa coccinea, L.   *Abbots Wood*
   (Jenner)
— serraticornis, Scop.

MORDELLIDÆ
Mordella fasciata, F.   *Hollington, Battle,*
   Abbots Wood, Lewes
Mordellistena abdominalis, F.   *Hollington,*
   Guestling, Cowfold, Barcombe
— brunnea, F.   *Bexhill*
— pumila, Gyll.   *Fairlight, Bopeep, Abbots*
   Wood
— brevicauda, Boh.   *Eastbourne*
— parvula, Gyll., var. inæqualis, Muls.
   Lewes

MORDELLIDÆ (*continued*)
Anaspis frontalis, L.
— pulicaria, Costa
— rufilabris, Gyll.   *Guestling*
— geoffroyi, Müll.   *Guestling, Lewes*
— ruficollis, F.
— flava, L., var. thoracica, L.   *Hurst*
   Green
— subtestacea, Steph.   *Hastings, Lewes*
— maculata, Fourc.

RHIPIDOPHORIDÆ
Metœcus paradoxus, L.   *Hastings* district,
   Hayward's Heath (Crallan)

ANTHICIDÆ
Notoxus monoceros, L.
Anthicus humilis, Germ.   *Pett, Camber,*
   Bishopstone
— floralis, L.
— instabilis, Schmidt.   *Camber*
— angustatus, Curt.   *Hurst Green*
— antherinus, L.

XYLOPHILIDÆ
Xylophilus populneus, F.   *Guestling*
— brevicornis, Perris.   *Brightling*

MELOÏDÆ
Meloë proscarabæus, L.

PLATYRRHINIDÆ
Macrocephalus (Anthribus)   albinus,   L.
   Very rare ; *Guestling, Lewes, Laugh-*
   ton (Jenner), *Abbots Wood, Hayward's*
   Heath (Crallan)
Choragus sheppardi, Kirby.   *Guestling,*
   Fairlight,   Ewhurst,   St.   Leonards,
   Winchelsea, Littlington (Power)

CURCULIONIDÆ
Apoderus coryli, L.   *Hastings* district, *Abbots*
   Wood, Laughton, Hayward's Heath
Attelabus curculionoides,   L.   *Guestling,*
   Dallington,   Abbots   Wood,   Rotherfield,
   Hayward's Heath
Byctiscus betuleti,   F.   *Hollington, Guestling,*
   Laughton
— populi, L.   *Guestling,   Abbots   Wood,*
   Laughton
Rhynchites cupreus, L.   *Dallington Forest,*
   Hastings
— æquatus, L.   *Lewes*, common ; not re-
   corded from the *Hastings* district
— æneovirens, Marsh.   *Guestling, Abbots*
   Wood, Bexhill
— cœruleus, De G.   *Hastings* district,
   Littlington
— minutus, Herbst.   *Hastings, Abbots Wood,*
   Lewes
— interpunctatus, Steph.   (Mr. Jenner's
   list)
— pauxillus, Germ.   *Littlington* (Power)
— nanus, Payk.   *St. Leonards Forest,*
   Laughton, Abbots Wood
— pubescens, F.   *Guestling, Abbots Wood*

A HISTORY OF SUSSEX

CURCULIONIDÆ (*continued*)

Deporaüs megacephalus, Germ. *Guestling, Abbots Wood, Faygate*

— betulæ, L.

Apion pomonæ, F. *Hastings, Bexhill, Abbots Wood, Laughton, Lewes*

— opeticum, Bach. Two specimens only have occurred in *Britain*, taken by Dr. Power on Lotus corniculatus, growing on a railway bank at *Bopeep* near *Hastings*

— craccæ, L. *Bopeep* near *Hastings*

— subulatum, Kirby. *Bopeep, Abbots Wood*

— ulicis, Forst

— urticarium, Herbst. *Camber*

— miniatum, Germ.

— cruentatum, Walt. *Fairlight, Arundel, Barcombe flood, Lewes*

— hæmatodes, Kirby (frumentarium, Herbst)

— rubens, Steph. *St. Leonards*

— pallipes, Kirby. *Arundel, Hastings* district

— rufirostre, F.

— viciæ, Payk. *Hastings* district, *Rusper, Eastbourne*

— difforme, Germ. *Bopeep, Seaford, Arundel, Littlington*

— dissimile, Germ. *Seaford, Arundel*

— varipes, Germ. *Bopeep, Glynde, Lewes, Eastbourne, Arundel*

— lævicolle, Kirby. *Bopeep, Seaford, Eastbourne, Arundel*

— schonherri, Boh. *Eastbourne* (Waterhouse), *Seaford* (Rye)

— apricans, Herbst

— bohemani, Thoms. *Fairlight, Lewes, Shipley*

— trifolii, L. *Hastings, Bishopstone*

— dichroum, Bedel. (flavipes, *Brit. Cat.*) *Hollington, Lewes*

— nigritarse, Kirby. *Guestling, Barcombe, Lewes*

— confluens, Kirby. *Guestling, Fairlight, Arundel, Brighton*

— stolidum, Germ. *Hollington* near *Hastings*

— sorbi, F. Rare ; *Shoreham* (Matthews), *Bury Hill* near *Arundel* (S. Stevens), *Hastings*

— hookeri, Kirby. *Bopeep, Bishopstone, Shipley, Bognor, Worthing*

— æneum, F.

— radiolus, Kirby

— onopordi, Kirby

— carduorum, Kirby

— flavimanum, Gyll. *Arundel, Lewes*

— annulipes, Wenck. Very rare; *Lewes*, (Morris)

— atomarium, Kirby. *Arundel, Lewes*

CURCULIONIDÆ (*continued*)

Apion virens, Herbst

— astragali, Payk. Rare ; *Guestling*

— punctigerum, Payk. *Hastings* district, *Abbots Wood*

— pisi, F.

— æthiops, Herbst

— ebeninum, Kirby. *Hastings* district, *Abbots Wood, Littlington*

— filirostre, Kirby. Rare ; *Rusper, Arundel, Brighton*

— striatum, Kirby

— immune, Kirby. *Hastings*

— ononis, Kirby. *Fairlight, Lewes*

— spencei, Kirby. *Bopeep*

— ervi, Kirby. *Bopeep, Abbots Wood, Laughton*

— vorax, Herbst. *Guestling, Barcombe, Lewes*

— meliloti, Kirby. *Arundel, Lewes*

— scutellare, Kirby. *Guestling, Lewes*

— livescerum, Gyll. *Littlington*

— waltoni, Steph. *Brighton, Glynde* near *Lewes*

— loti, Kirby

— seniculum, Kirby

— tenue, Kirby. *Bopeep, Bishopstone*

— pubescens, Kirby. *Hastings, Seaford, Lewes, Arundel*

— curtisi, Walt. *Fairlight, Seaford, St. Leonards, Littlehampton, Arundel, Shipley, Brighton*

— sedi, Germ. *Camber*

— marchicum, Herbst. *Hastings* district

— violaceum, Kirby

— hydrolapathi, Kirby. *Hollington*

— humile, Germ.

Otiorrhynchus tenebricosus, Herbst. *Lewes*, apparently very scarce

— scabrosus, Marsh. *Guestling, Abbots Wood, Lewes*

— ligneus, Ol. *Hastings, Lewes*

— picipes, F.

— sulcatus, F.

— rugifrons, Gyll. *Hastings*

— ovatus, L. *Hastings*, not common

Trachyphlœus myrmecophilus, Seidl. *Hastings*

— aristatus, Gyll. *Hastings* and *Lewes* districts

— squamulatus, Ol. *Hastings, Seaford, Bishopstone, Lewes*

— scaber, L. *Hastings* district

— scabriculus, L. *Hastings, Lewes*

— spinimanus, Germ. *Arundel*

— alternans, Gyll. *Hastings* district, *Arundel*

Cœnopsis fissirostris, Walt. Rare ; *St. Leonards, Peppering, Guestling, Bexhill*

INSECTS

CURCULIONIDÆ (*continued*)

Cœnopsis waltoni, Schön. *Peppering, Guestling, Bexhill*
Strophosomus coryli, F.
— capitatus, De G. (obesus, Marsh.)
— retusus, Marsh.
— faber, Herbst. *Guestling, Lewes*
Exomias araneiformis, Schr.
Brachysomus hirtus, Boh. Very rare ; *Arundel,* in moss, February, 1842 (S. Stevens)
Sciaphilus muricatus, F.
Tropiphorus carinatus, Müll.[1] *Hastings*
Liophlœus nubilus, F.
Polydrusus tereticollis, De G. (undatus, F.)
— pterygomalis, Boh.
— flavipes, De G. *Holm Bush, Brighton*
— cervinus, L.
— chrysomela, Ol. *Camber* ; rare
— confluens, Steph. *Hastings, Brighton*
Phyllobius oblongus, L.
— calcaratus, F. *Peppering, Laughton*
— urticæ, De G. (alneti, F.)
— pyri, L.
— argentatus, L.
— maculicornis, Germ. *Malling, Lewes*
— pomonæ, Ol. *Fairlight,* not common
— viridiæris, Laich (uniformis, Marsh.)
Tanymecus palliatus, F. *Hastings, Battle, Guestling, Shipley, Abbots Wood*
Philopedon geminatus, F.
Atactogenus exaratus, Marsh. *Hastings* district
Barynotus obscurus, F. *Fairlight, Barcombe, Lewes*
— elevatus, Marsh. *Littlington*
Alophus triguttatus, F.
Sitones cambricus, Steph. *Hastings* district ; *Pebsham* (Morris)
— regensteinensis, Herbst
— waterhousei, Walt. *Fairlight,* rare ; *Seaford*
— crinitus, Herbst. *Littlington, Lewes*
— tibialis, Herbst
— hispidulus, F.
— humeralis, Steph.
— flavescens, Marsh. *Peppering, Lewes*
— puncticollis, Steph.
— suturalis, Steph.
— lineatus, L.
— sulcifrons, Thunb.
Gronops lunatus, L. *Hollington, Peppering, Bulverhythe, Bishopstone*
Hypera punctata, F.
— rumicis, L.

CURCULIONIDÆ (*continued*)

Hypera pollux, F.[2] *Guestling, Rye*
— alternans,[2] Steph. *Rye, Winchelsea, Camber*
— polygoni, L.
— variabilis, Herbst
— murina, F. *Arundel*
— plantaginis, De G.
— trilineata, Marsh.
— nigrirostris, F.
Rhinocyllus latirostris, Latr. *Shipley* near *Horsham* (Gorham)
Cleonus sulcirostris, L. *Fairlight, Newhaven*
Lixus algirus, L. Rare ; *Fairlight* near *Hastings* (Power, S. Stevens, etc.), *Shoreham* (Stephens), *Faygate* near *Rusper* (Gore)
Larinus carlinæ, Ol. *Rye*
Liosoma ovatulum, Clairv.
    var. collaris, Rye. *Hastings* list
— oblongulum, Boh. *Guestling*
— troglodytes, Rye. „
Curculio abietis, L.
Plinthus caliginosus, F. *Hastings* district, generally distributed, but rare ; *Malling, Lewes, Barcombe flood*
Trachodes hispidus, L. *Guestling, St. Leonards Forest* (Power)
Orchestes quercus, L.
— alni, L.
    var. ferrugineus, Marsh. *Guestling, Hollington*
— ilicis, F.
— avellanæ, Don. *Peppering, Hurst Green, Arundel, Eastbourne*
— fagi, L.
— pratensis, Germ. *Battle, Brighton, Abbots Wood*
— rusci, Herbst
— iota, F. (Mr. Jenner's list)
— stigma, Germ. *Hastings, Abbots Wood, Laughton*
— salicis, L. *Hastings, Abbots Wood, Laughton, Plashet*
Rhamphus flavicornis, Clairv.
Orthocætes setiger, Beck. *Guestling, Lewes, Brighton*
Procas armillatus, F. Very rare ; *Brighton* (Mr. S. Stevens records one specimen as taken by Mr. Hemming, and Mr. Morris has taken the species once at *North Banks, Lewes*)
Grypidius equiseti, F. *Fairlight, Battle, Lewes*

[1] The record of *Tropiphorus mercurialis,* Boh., found in the first supplement of the *Natural History of Hastings and St. Leonards,* p. 17, is erroneous and must therefore be cancelled.

[2] These two species, *Hypera pollux* and *H. alternans,* have been taken *in cop* by Mr. W. H. Bennett at Rye, and by Mr. F. Jennings in the Lee valley, Kent ; it has been doubted before this whether the species are really distinct.

CURCULIONIDÆ (*continued*)

Erirrhinus scirpi, F. *Peppering, Guestling, Faygate*
— acridulus, L.
Thryogenes festucæ, Herbst. *Hastings*, rare
— nereis, Payk. *Guestling, Pett Level, Barcombe, Lewes*
— scirrhosus, Gyll. *Bopeep*
Dorytomus vorax, F. *Abbots Wood, Plashet*
— tortrix, L. *Ore, Netherfield*
— maculatus, Marsh.
    var. cortirostris, Gyll. *Ore, Battle*
— melanophthalmus, Payk., var. agnathus, Boh. *Hastings*
— pectoralis, Gyll. *Rusper* near *Horsham*
Smicronyx reichei, Gyll. *Arundel Park*
— jungermanniæ, Reich. *Ashburnham*
Tanysphyrus lemnæ, F. *Hastings* and *Lewes* districts
Bagous alismatis, Marsh. *Peppering, Guestling, Lewes, Arundel*
— cylindrus, Payk. *Pett Marshes, Hastings* (Ford); *Pevensey* (Esam)
— binodulus, Herbst. *Arundel*, one specimen (Hamlet Clark); *The Rise, Lewes* (Morris)
— nodulosus, Gyll. Very rare; *Pevensey* (Donisthorpe and Bennett), *Arundel*
— limosus, Gyll. *Camber*
— tempestivus, Herbst. *Hastings, Camber*
— lutulosus, Gyll. *Guestling*
— frit, Herbst. *Rye, Camber*
— claudicans, Boh. (subcarinatus, *Brit. Cat.*) *Rye, Camber*
— glabrirostris, Herbst. *Hastings, Rye, Camber, Peasemarsh*
Anoplus plantaris, Naez.
Elleschus bipunctatus, L. *Fairlight, Battle, Tilgate, Abbots Wood*
Tychius quinquepunctatus, L. *Guestling, Abbots Wood*
— venustus, F. *Guestling* (Bennett)
— squamulatus, Gyll. *Hastings*
— schneideri, Herbst.   „
— meliloti, Steph. *Hastings* district, *Lewes*
— lineatulus, Steph. *Bopeep, Lewes*
— junceus, Reich. *Hastings*
— tomentosus, Herbst. *Hastings, Guestling, North Banks, Lewes*
— tibialis, Boh. *Bopeep, Bishopstone*
— pygmæus, Bris. *Fairlight, Bopeep, Guestling, Lewes*
Miccotrogus picirostris, F. *Hastings* and *Lewes* districts
Sibinia potentillæ, Germ. *Brighton, Ninfield*
— arenariæ, Steph. *Hastings* district, *Bishopstone*

CURCULIONIDÆ (*continued*)

Sibinia primita, Herbst. *Fairlight, Bopeep, Lewes*
Miarus campanulæ, L. *Arundel*
— graminis, Gyll. *Arundel* (S. Stevens)
— plantarum, Germ. *Littlington* (Power)
Gymnetron villosulus, Gyll. *Rye, Arundel*
— beccabungæ, L. *Hastings* district, *Lewes, Arundel*
— melanarius, Germ. *Guestling*
— rostellum, Herbst. *Hastings* district, *Laughton, Lewes*
— pascuorum, Gyll. *Hastings, Barcombe, Lewes*
— labilis, Herbst. *Hollington, Abbots Wood, Arundel, Littlington, Holm Bush, Brighton*
— antirrhini, Payk. (noctis, *Brit. Cat.*) *Bopeep, Brighton, Guestling, Lewes*
Mecinus pyraster, Herbst
— circulatus, Marsh. *Amberley, Arundel Park, Littlehampton*
Anthonomus ulmi, De G. *Fairlight*
— rosinæ, Des Gozis. *Hastings* and *Lewes* districts
— pedicularius, L.
— pomorum, L. *Guestling, Abbots Wood*
— rubi, Herbst
Nanophyes lythri, F.
— gracilis, Redt. Rare; *Balcombe*
Cionus scrophulariæ, L. *Hastings* district
— tuberculosus, Scop. Rare; *Hollington*
— hortulanus, Marsh. *Hastings, Lewes, Abbots Wood*, etc.
— blattariæ, F. *Hastings* and *Lewes* districts
— pulchellus, Herbst. *Guestling, Abbots Wood, Lewes*
Orobitis cyaneus, L. *Guestling, Peppering, Lewes, Arundel, Brighton*
Cryptorrhynchus lapathi, L.
Acalles roboris, Curt. *Hastings, Arundel, Plashet Wood*
— ptinoides, Marsh. Not common; *St. Leonards Forest, Guestling, Bexhill*
— turbatus, Boh. Not common. *Guestling, Hollington*
Cœliodes rubicundus, Herbst. *Hastings* district, *Brighton, Plashet Wood*
— quercus, F. *Hastings, Bexhill, Abbots* and *Plashet Woods*
— erythroleucus, Gmel. *Hastings, Abbots Wood, Plashet, Laughton*
— cardui, Herbst. *Hastings, Camber, Bexhill, Lewes*; scarce
— quadrimaculatus, L.
— exiguus, Ol. *Rye, Eastbourne, Arundel*
Poophagus sisymbrii, F. *Camber, Lewes*
Ceuthorrhynchus assimilis, Payk.
— constrictus, Marsh. *Hastings* district

INSECTS

CURCULIONIDÆ (*continued*)

Ceuthorrhynchus cochleariæ, Gyll.
— ericæ, Gyll.
— erysimi, F.
— contractus, Marsh.
— cyanipennis, Germ. *Hastings, Fairlight*
— chalybæus, Germ. *Hastings* district
— quadridens, Panz. *Hastings* district, *Lewes*
— geographicus, Goeze. *Hastings, Amberley*
— pollinarius, Forst.
— picitarsis, Gyll. *Rye*
— pleurostigma, Marsh.
— verrucatus, Gyll. *Bopeep*
— resedæ, Marsh. *Arundel, Eastbourne*
— marginatus, Payk. *Hastings* district
— urticæ, Boh. *Amberley* near *Arundel*
— rugulosus, Herbst. *Hastings, Eastbourne, Brighton, Worthing*
— melanostictus, Marsh. *Hastings, Arundel*
— asperifoliarum, Gyll. *Hollington, Lewes*
— chrysanthemi, Germ. *Cowfold, Rusper*
— litura, F. *Fairlight*, common; *Abbots Wood, Blackford, Lewes*
— trimaculatus, F. *Fairlight, Hollington*; rare

Ceuthorrhynchidius floralis, Payk.
— hepaticus, Gyll. Very rare; *Seaford* (Waterhouse), *Littlington, Hurstpierpoint* (Power)
— pyrrhorhynchus, Marsh.
— pulvinatus, Gyll. Very rare; *Hastings*, August, 1867 (Power)
— nigrinus, Marsh. *Littlington, Brighton*
— melanarius, Steph. *Arundel*
— posthumus, Germ. *Bishopstone* (Morris)
— terminatus, Herbst. *Hastings, Amberley, Worthing*
— horridus, F. Rare; *Bopeep, Lewes*
— quercicola, Payk. *Brighton*
— troglodytes, F.
— chevrolati, Bris. *Bopeep*
— rufulus, Duft. (frontalis, Bris.) *Rye, Bishopstone, Lewes*
— dawsoni, Bris. *Hastings* (Phillips)

Amalus hæmorrhous, Herbst. *Ecclesbourne, Arundel, Lewes*

Rhinoncus pericarpius, L.
— gramineus, F. *Rye, Ewhurst, Amberley, Faygate*
— perpendicularis, Reich. *Hastings* district, *Abbots Wood*
— castor, F. *Bopeep, Lewes*
— denticollis, Gyll. Rare; *Guestling, Netherfield, Holm Bush, Brighton*

Eubrychius velatus, Beck. *Rye, Arundel*

Litodactylus leucogaster, Marsh. *Hastings, Lewes*

CURCULIONIDÆ (*continued*)

Phytobius comari, Herbst. *Arundel*
— waltoni, Boh. *Peppering*
— quadrituberculatus, F.
— quadrinodosus, Gyll. Rare; *Bexhill* (Butler)

Limnobaris T-album, L. *Hastings, St. Leonards, Amberley*

Baris laticollis, Marsh. *Rye*
— lepidii, Germ. *Battle, Bopeep, Barcombe, Lewes, Rusper, Amberley*

Balaninus venosus, Grav. *Hastings, Abbots Wood, Laughton*
— nucum, L. *Hastings* district, *Abbots Wood, Laughton*
— turbatus, Gyll. *Camber, Ecclesbourne, Abbots Wood*
— villosus, F. *Hastings, Rusper, Abbots Wood, Laughton,* etc.
— salicivorus, Payk.
— pyrrhoceras, Marsh.

Calandra granaria, L.
— oryzæ, L.

Pentarthrum huttoni. Rare; *Hastings*

Rhopalomesites tardyi, Curt. *Fairlight* near *Hastings*

Rhyncholus lignarius, Marsh. *Guestling, Lewes*

Caulotrypis æneopiceus, Boh. *Hastings*

Codiosoma spadix, Herbst. *Camber, Bishopstone* (Jenner)

Magdalis armigera, Fourc. *Guestling, Laughton, Lewes*
— cerasi, L. *Hastings, Abbots* and *Plashet Woods, Laughton*
— pruni, L. *Guestling, Bexhill, Lewes*
— barbicornis, Latr. Rare; *Guestling, Plashet Wood*

SCOLYTIDÆ

Scolytus destructor, Ol. *Hastings*, rare; *Lewes*
— intricatus, Ratz. *Hastings*, rare

Hylastes ater, Payk. *Hastings, Barcombe*
— opacus, Er. *Faygate, St. Leonards Forest, Arundel*
— angustatus, Herbst. Very rare; one specimen taken at *Holm Bush, Brighton*, by Mr. E. C. Rye
— palliatus, Gyll. *Hastings, Faygate, Barcombe*
— cunicularius, Er. *Brighton*

Hylastinus obscurus, Marsh. *Fairlight, Eastbourne*

Hylesinus crenatus, F. *Hastings, Lewes*
— oleiperda, F. *Littlington, Lewes*
— fraxini, Panz.

Myelophilus piniperda, L. *Ore* near *Hastings*

Cissophagus hederæ, Schmidt. *Hastings* and *Horsham* districts, *Laughton*

163

SCOLYTIDÆ (*continued*)

Phlœophthorus rhododactylus, Marsh. *Hastings* district, *Rusper, Eastbourne*

Cryphalus abietis, Ratz. *Cowfold, Shipley, Laughton* ; rare

— fagi, Nord. *Guestling*, rare

Pityophthorus pubescens, Marsh. *Peppering*

Xylocleptes bispinus, **Duft.** *Eastbourne, Lewes*

Dryocætes villosus, **F.** *Hastings* district

Tomicus laricis, **F.** *Midhurst, Lewes*

SCOLYTIDÆ (*continued*)

Pityogenes bidentatus, Herbst. *Hastings* district

Trypodendron domesticum, L. *Hastings, Lewes*

Xyleborus dispar, **F.** *Ashburnham*

— saxeseni, Ratz. *Hastings* district

Platypus cylindrus, **F.** *Shipley* near *Horsham* (Gorham)

STYLOPIDÆ

Stylops melittæ, Kirby. Common on *Andrenæ* in the *Hastings* district

LEPIDOPTERA

RHOPALOCERA AND HETEROCERA

Butterflies and Moths

Sussex with its numerous forests and woodlands, moors and marshes, its chalk downs, and its extensive coast line, is almost as rich in species of Insecta as Kent or Hampshire. As in the adjoining counties last mentioned the numbers of species and specimens are, and have been for some years past, decreasing with the destruction of old forests and other woods, and the increase of cultivation and buildings. The county however still contains a number of interesting and local species, though there are fewer immigrants from the continent than in Kent. As in other English counties the Black-veined White butterfly (*Aporia cratægi*, L.), which was formerly abundant, has long disappeared, and that beautiful moth the Kentish Glory (*Endromis versicolor*, L.), so plentiful thirty or forty years ago in Tilgate Forest near Balcombe, and in St. Leonards Forest, between Three Bridges and Horsham, has been long extinct.

RHOPALOCERA

Butterflies[1]

The Wood White (*Leucophasia sinapis*, L.) was formerly plentiful near Faygate and elsewhere in St. Leonards Forest in the north of the county. I have taken it in Abbots Wood and in the adjoining woods near Hailsham years ago, but I have not seen it in the county since 1877 or 1878. It has been recorded from Bolney Wood, Frenchlands Woods, Ashington, Tilgate Forest, Denne Park, Rotherfield, from near Cocking and elsewhere in the county. The Black-veined White (*Aporia cratægi*, L.) was formerly common in many parts of the county, but it has been extinct for more than thirty years. The late

---

[1] The Swallow Tail (*Papilio machaon*, L.) is said to have been formerly common near Pulborough ; but if it ever occurred there it has been long extinct as a resident species in the county. Mr. W. H. B. Fletcher of Bognor says that ' the single specimens occasionally seen in the county have probably escaped from captivity. Those recorded as having occurred in Dorsetshire, Kent, Surrey, Sussex and Guernsey in 1900 (*Ent.* xxxiii. 267, 303 ; *Ent. Rec.* xii. 273) may possibly have been immigrants, as may also have been those found in 1876 and 1877 near Brighton and Lewes (*Ent.* ix. 230, x. 285).'

At the present day the species in a truly wild condition in this country is confined to Wicken Fen, Cambridgeshire, and to the fens in the Norfolk Broads.—H. G.

INSECTS

Mr. Jenner Weir informed me that this species was formerly abundant near Keymer and elsewhere in the county. Mr. Stainton in his *Manual* mentions Lewes as a locality, and it has been recorded from Firle, Henfield, the Holm Bush near Poynings, Horsham, and Abbots Wood[1] near Hailsham. The Large Cabbage White (*Pieris brassicæ*, L.), the Small Cabbage White (*P. rapæ*, L.) and the Green-veined White (*P. napi*, L.) are generally distributed, and are more or less abundant according to the season. That rare butterfly the Bath White (*P. daplidice*, L.) has been frequently taken in the county. Its capture has been recorded from Bognor, Eastbourne, Hastings, the Holmbush, Lewes, Brighton[2] and Polegate. The Orange Tip (*Anthocaris cardamines*, L.) is generally distributed and usually abundant by roadsides, and in lanes and woods, but it does not occur so commonly on the south side of the downs or near the coast. The Brimstone (*Gonepteryx rhamni*, L.) is generally common throughout the county, but less so near the coast where its food plant, the buckthorn, is scarce or altogether absent. It is very plentiful in Abbots Wood,[3] Wilmington Wood, Folkington Wood and elsewhere near Hailsham and Hellingly.

The Clouded Yellow (*Colias edusa*, Fb.) is very abundant in some seasons in clover and lucerne fields, and also on the downs and railway banks and in other localities. It occurred in great profusion in 1868, 1869 and 1870, and again in 1877 and 1892, appearing in lesser numbers in 1893 and the following years. In the south of Europe there appears to be a succession of broods following one another throughout the year. The white variety of the female (var. *helice*) is generally found with the type, more or less commonly. It occurred freely in 1868, 1869, 1870 and 1877. I have taken it in some numbers during the last thirty years near Brighton, Lewes and Eastbourne, and it was common in the county in 1892. The Pale Clouded Yellow (*C. hyale*, L.) is in some years abundant in clover and lucerne fields. It was plentiful near Brighton, Portslade, Rottingdean, Eastbourne and other parts of the county in 1868 and 1888. Mr. Fletcher states that it occurred again in 1900 all over the county and that a few specimens were taken near Worthing in 1902.

The Silver-washed Fritillary (*Argynnis paphia*, L.) is not uncommon in some woods in the county, though far less abundant than in the New Forest in Hampshire or in the Forest of Dean, Gloucestershire. I have taken it in Abbots Wood, Wilmington Wood and Folkington Wood near Hailsham, and it occurs in Ashdown Forest, Tilgate Forest, St. Leonards Forest and Charlton Forest. It has also been recorded from Bosham, Hayward's Heath, Midhurst, Sheffield Park, Slindon Woods,

[1] I have worked the neighbourhood of Poynings and Abbots Wood since 1868, but I never met with this species in Sussex.—H.G.
[2] A specimen taken by Mr. H. Gorringe at Bevingdean near Brighton in August, 1871, was brought to me alive and is in my collection.—H.G.
[3] I took a gynandromorphous specimen in Abbots Wood in July, 1874. The right wings are those of the female and the left wings those of a male, but I have not examined the sexual organs.—H.G.

and from near Watergate Emsworth. I am not aware that the melanic variety of the female (var. *valezina*[1]) occurs regularly in the county, but a specimen of it was shown to me many years ago by The O'Reilly, who stated that he had taken it in Ashdown Forest. The Dark Green Fritillary (*A. aglaia*, L.) is locally abundant, especially on the chalk downs between Brighton and Lewes, about Eastbourne, Seaford, Goodwood, Cocking, Sompting, Pyecombe, Sheffield Park and Hastings. It has also been taken in Tilgate Forest, Abbots Wood, and near Hayward's Heath. The High Brown Fritillary (*A. adippe*, L.) is common in many woods in the county, such as Abbots Wood and other woods near Hailsham, near Battle, in Charlton Forest, near Hayward's Heath, Slindon Woods, Steyning, and in Tilgate, Worth and St. Leonards Forests. In my experience it is far more plentiful in the East Sussex woods than *A. paphia* or *A. aglaia*, though the latter is a much commoner species on the chalk downs. The Queen of Spain Fritillary (*A. lathonia*, L.), though very rare in this country, is a common continental species. It has been occasionally taken in the county near Glynde, Hastings and Brighton. The Pearl-bordered Fritillary (*A. euphrosyne*, L.) is very common in Tilgate Forest, St. Leonards Forest, Charlton Forest, Abbots Wood, Goring Woods, Newtimber Copse near Poynings, and in nearly all the woods in the county. The Small Pearl-bordered Fritillary (*A. selene*, Schiff.) is far more local than the last species, but I have found it in abundance in Tilgate Forest and Abbots Wood, and it has been recorded from Charlton Forest, Hurston Warren and Slindon Common. That very local species the Greasy Fritillary (*Melitæa aurinia*, Rott.) occurred formerly in profusion in certain places in Tilgate Forest and near Wych Cross. I found it commonly in wet meadows about a mile south-east of East Grinstead in 1868, 1869 and 1870. I have also taken it near Forest Row and near Three Bridges. I am informed that it was also very abundant some thirty or forty years ago in certain fields near Poynings, but that it was exterminated by Brighton dealers and other collectors. The late Mr. Buckler recorded it from Foxborough Marsh, and Mr. Fletcher says that it is reported as having occurred at Heyshott, Laughton and Ringmer. The late Mr. Jenner Weir informed me that it was formerly abundant near Chailey, but I have not seen it in Sussex[2] for many years, and in this county, as in many other counties, it is apparently dying out. The Pearl-bordered Likeness or Heath Fritillary (*M. athalia*, Rott.), although extremely local, is in some years very abundant in Abbots Wood, Wilmington Wood, Folkington Wood and other woods and the adjoining fields near Hailsham and Hellingly. It occurred in great numbers in June, 1897, in a small wood to the east side of the road leading from Polegate to Hailsham. Captain Savile Reid, R.E., informs me that he found the species commonly in 1897

---

[1] Probably the same specimen referred to by Mr. Vine as having been taken in Ashdown Forest by The O'Reilly.—H.G.

[2] The late Mr. Tugwell found one or two specimens in a marsh in the middle of Abbots Wood near Hailsham some thirty years ago.—H.G.

INSECTS

in Hempstead Wood to the north-west of Hailsham. It has also been recorded from the neighbourhood of Battle. A black variety was taken by Mr. H. Gorringe of Brighton in Abbots Wood some thirty-five years ago and was acquired by the late Mr. F. Bond. The Small Tortoiseshell (*Vanessa urticæ*, L.) is common throughout the county. The Large Tortoiseshell (*V. polychloros*, L.) is generally distributed in the county, and Mr. Fletcher says that though for some years it was less common than formerly, it is now greatly increasing in numbers. He observed more hybernated specimens in the spring of 1902 than he had seen for many years. The species has been reported from Abbots Wood Hailsham, Battle, Bognor, Brighton, Catsfield, Cocking, Hastings, Horsham, Hayward's Heath, Hurstpierpoint, Lewes, Midhurst, Slindon, Stoughton and Worthing. The rare Camberwell Beauty (*V. antiopa*, L.)[1] has not unfrequently been taken in the county. A fine specimen was brought to me alive in September, 1873, by a Brighton bird-catcher who had taken it at Hassock's Gate. It was in such fine condition that it must have been bred in this country. A second specimen was brought to me about two years afterwards by some boys who had caught it near Burgess Hill. Mr. Fletcher[2] reports the capture of a specimen near Burwash in 1900. The Painted Lady (*V. cardui*, L.)[3] is irregular in appearance, but occurs in some years in the greatest profusion in clover and lucerne fields, especially near the coast. The Red Admiral (*V. atalanta*, L.) is common and generally distributed. The Peacock (*V. io*, L.) is generally distributed and sometimes abundant though less common than formerly. The White Admiral (*Limenitis sybilla*, L.) like many other butterflies is reported to be decreasing in numbers.[4] It has been reported from a few woods in east Sussex near Battle, Northiam and Hollington. The captures of single specimens have also been recorded from Abbots Wood, Hayward's Heath and Plashet Wood near Lewes. Mr. W. M. Christy says that it is not uncommon in some of the woods in west Sussex between Chichester and the western boundary of the county. The Purple Emperor (*Apatura iris*, L.) used to be common in some seasons in Abbots Wood, Wilmington Wood and Gnat Wood. I have seen it flying round the oaks and sitting in the muddy ruts in the road dividing Abbots Wood and Wilmington Wood on the west from Gnat Wood and Folkington Wood on the east, and possess specimens from the district.

Note.—The Glanville Fritillary (*Melitæa cinxia*, L.) was, according to Mr. Fletcher, included in the Fauna and Flora of Eastbourne, but this was undoubtedly an error.—H.G.

[1] See *Ent. Mo. Mag.* x. 139 (1873–4).—H.G.

[2] Mr. Fletcher remarks : 'Very rare ; an occasional immigrant appearing in some numbers in Great Britain at uncertain intervals, but does not seem able to establish itself as a resident even for a short period.'—H.G.

[3] The Comma Butterfly (*Vanessa c-album*, L.), which is a midland and west of England species, does not occur regularly in the county, but, as in Kent, immigrants have occasionally been found. Mr. J. H. A. Jenner reports it as having been taken singly at Southover, Horndean and Lewes. Mr. Edgell records the capture of a specimen at Firle in 1887, and another specimen was recorded by Mr. Vine as being taken between Bramber and Shoreham in April, 1887. Mr. Fletcher states that the species has also occurred singly near Horsham, in Tilgate Forest, and near Guestling.—H.G.

[4] I have collected in the woods of east and north Sussex since I was ten years of age, but I never saw the species in the county.—H.G.

Many specimens have been taken on the south-eastern edge of Gnat
Wood by 'sugaring' the tree stems. Dr. Hodgson (formerly of Brighton)
told me that a few years ago he found eight or nine larvæ of this species
on one sallow bush in Abbots Wood. The species occurs in most of
the oak woods in the Weald. It is reported from Ashburnham, Battle,
Buxted, Isfield, the Holmbush and Tilgate Forest. From west Sussex it
has been recorded from the neighbourhood of Bosham, Harting and the
Hundred of Manhood, also from St. Leonards Forest near Horsham,
and from Ticehurst. The Marbled White (*Arge galathea*, L.[1]) although
local is abundant in many localities, especially along the coast between
Eastbourne and Seaford. It also occurs in profusion in Abbots Wood
and the adjoining woods and fields near Hailsham. It has also been
recorded from Firle, Sompting, Tilgate Forest, Horsham and Charlton
Forest. The Wood Argus (*Satyrus egeria*, L.) is generally distributed
in woods and lanes, but is less common than formerly, Mr. Jenner
says it is disappearing from many localities. It is reported as being
generally common in west Sussex, as near Cocking, Bury, Charlton
Forest, Midhurst and in the Slindon Woods. The Wall Butterfly
(*S. megæra*, L.) is generally distributed and often abundant. The Gray-
ling (*S. semele*, L.) is common both on the sandy heaths and on the
chalk downs. The Meadow Brown (*S. ianira*, L.)[2] is abundant everywhere in meadows and on hillsides, and the Large Heath (*S. tithonus*,
L.) is common everywhere throughout the county by hedgerows, roadsides and in woods. The Ringlet (*S. hyperanthus*, L.[3]) is not so generally distributed as its congeners, but is locally common in woods in
both east and west Sussex. I have found it in abundance in the
woods near Hailsham, and Mr. W. M. Christy has reported the occurrence of the variety *arete* near Stoughton. The Small Heath (*Chorto-
bius pamphillus*, L.) is everywhere common in fields, woods and on
heaths and hillsides. The Green Hairstreak (*Thecla rubi*, L.) is not
uncommon in rough pastures, woods, and along hedgerows. Mr. Fletcher
says it is especially common where *Genista tinctoria* abounds. It used
to be abundant amongst the whitethorn bushes on the east side of Gnat
Wood near Polegate. The Purple Hairstreak (*T. quercus*, L.) is not
uncommon in oak woods in both east and west Sussex. I have seen
it swarming in Abbots Wood around the tops of oaks. The White
Letter Hairstreak (*T. w-album*, Knoch.) is said to be at the present day

[1] *Danais plexippus*, L. has been occasionally taken in the county. Mr. Fletcher says of it : 'A
very rare immigrant. At Hayward's Heath in 1876 (*Ent.* ix. 265) ; at Keymer in the same year (*Ent.*
x. 73) ; at Worthing two seen and one taken in August, 1887 ; one seen at Eastbourne in 1890.'
(Tutt. *Brit. Butterflies*, 370).—H.G.
[2] Mr. Fletcher says that there appears to be a partial second brood on the wing in the late summer
and early autumn. Specimens with irregular whitish patches on the wings are reported from Polegate,
the neighbourhood of Emsworth, and from Charlton Forest.—H.G.
[3] The Marsh Ringlet (*Cænonympha typhon* [*davus*], Rott.) was formerly recorded as having occurred
in Ashdown Forest. This is doubtless an error. The species is confined in the United Kingdom to
some parts of Scotland, Ireland, north Wales, Cumberland, Westmorland, north Lancashire, Cheshire,
Durham, Yorkshire and north Staffordshire.—H.G.

local and rare in the county. It was formerly[1] common in Frenchlands Wood, and has also been recorded from Abbots Wood. The Brown Hairstreak (*T. betulæ*, L.[2]) is reported to be local and not common in the county. It has been recorded from Charlton Forest by Mr. Edgell, from East Marden by Mr. Christy, from the Holmbush by Mr. Vine, from Eartham by Mr. Fletcher, and also from Horsham, Partridge Green, Slinfold, Henfield and Newick. The Small Copper (*Polyommatus phlæas*,[3] L.) is common and generally distributed all over the country, in fields, meadows and on hillsides, and in the rides of woods. The Silver Studded Blue (*Lycæna*[4] *ægon*, Schiff.), although local, is abundant on some of the heaths of the county, as in Ashdown Forest, Tilgate Forest and St. Leonards Forest. Chailey, Hayward's Heath, Goodwood Park, Hurston Warren, Lewes and Upmarden have also been named as localities. The Brown Argus (*L. agestis*, Hb.) is common in many places on the chalk, as between Brighton and Lewes, about Pyecombe and the Devil's Dyke, Cocking, Eastbourne, Beachy Head, Hastings, Slindon and on the downs near Emsworth. The Common Blue (*L. icarus*, Rott.) is generally distributed throughout the county on chalk, sand and clay, and is often plentiful. The Adonis or Clifden Blue (*L. adonis*, Fb., or *bellargus*, Rott.) is locally common on the chalk. I have found it in abundance in Hollingbury Combe, between Brighton and Lewes, in Bible Bottom and on Cliff Hill near Lewes, and between Eastbourne and Beachy Head. It is also recorded from Repton Down, Broadwater, Hastings and from near Shoreham. The Chalk Hill Blue (*L. corydon*, Fb.) is much less local than the last-named species and is generally abundant on the chalk. The Mazarine Blue (*L. acis*, Fb., or *L. semiargus*, Rott.) has been long extinct, if it ever was a resident species. Mr. Fletcher states that two specimens were taken many years ago near Chailey[5] and were in the collection of the late Mr. Unwin of Lewes, and that another specimen was taken in Abbots Wood[6] in July, 1881. The Small Blue (*L. alsus*, Fb., or *L. minima*, Fuers) is locally abundant on the chalk downs, and sometimes on the shingle beaches of the coast. It used to be

---

[1] Mr. Fletcher says : ' Local and rare, if not extinct. The localities given by Newman (*Brit. Butt.* p. 110) are Frenchlands Woods, abundant ; Abbots Wood and in Sussex, generally.' Barrett says, 1893 (*Brit. Lep.* i. 47) : ' Scarce though formerly more common in Sussex.'
    I have never taken or seen the species in the county, but having regard to the vast increase in its numbers during the last four or five years in Essex, Herts, Gloucestershire and Surrey there can be little doubt of its occurrence in Sussex at the present time.—H.G.

[2] This species is often common in the larval state without being observed in the perfect state. The larvæ can be obtained in numbers in the New Forest, but the butterflies are rarely seen on the wing. I have bred many dozens of specimens from New Forest larvæ, but never saw the butterfly there, though I have seen it commonly on bramble blossoms near Liss and Petersfield, Hants.—H.G.

[3] *Polyommatus virgaureæ* has been recorded as having been captured in the county near Burling Gap on 4 August, 1891.—H.G.

[4] *Lycæna bætica*, L., is not established in the county, but is an occasional immigrant. Mr. Fletcher says that 'a specimen was taken at Brighton by Mr. McArthur on 4 August, 1859, and another at Bognor in 1880' (Tutt. *Brit. Butterflies*, p. 194). Another specimen was reported from Brighton in 1890 (*Ent.* xx. 1901, p. 361) and two more near Hastings in August and September, 1893 (*Ent.* xx. 1901, pp. 301–27).—H.G.

[5] Jenner in *Proc. Eastbourne Nat. Hist. Soc.* 1885–6.

[6] *Entomologist*, xvi. 135.—H.G.

especially plentiful on waste ground, in old chalk pits and on banks by the left side of the London Road leading from Brighton to Clayton near the mouth of the Patcham Tunnel. The Holly Blue (*L. argiolus*, L.) is widely distributed and often abundant in gardens, woods and hedgerows. It has in Sussex, as in Surrey and other metropolitan counties, greatly increased in numbers of late years. The Duke of Burgundy (*Nemeobius lucina*, L.) is very local, but abundant in Newtimber Copse near Poynings. It has also been reported from the Holm Bush, from Horsham, Laughton, Plashet Wood, Slindon, and from St. Leonards Forest and Tilgate Forest. The Grizzled Skipper (*Syrichthus alveolus*, Hb.) is generally distributed in woods and other suitable localities, but is not often met with on the chalk hills. The Dingy Skipper (*Thanaos tages*, L.) is generally distributed throughout the county and is sometimes abundant on the chalk hills. The Small Skipper (*Hesperia linea*, Fb.) and the Large Skipper (*H. sylvanus*, Esp.) are both generally distributed and common. The Silver Spotted Skipper (*H. comma*, L.) is very local, but is abundant in Hollingbury Combe between Brighton and Lewes, in Bible Bottom, on Cliffe Hill and in other localities near Lewes, and in several places between Eastbourne and Seaford. It is also reported from Arundel Park, Cocking Down, Kingley Vale and West Stoke. *H. lineola*,[1] Ochs., which is chiefly an Essex species, has also been recorded from Kent and Sussex. I have only taken it near Thorpe and Walton-on-the-Naze in east Essex.

It is much to be regretted that owing to the claims of other subjects no detailed account in narrative form of the moths of the county can be found space for. The following list of species has been compiled by Mr. Fletcher and Mr. J. H. A. Jenner partly from their own knowledge, partly from records already published and from notes supplied to them by myself, by Mr. Robert Adkin, F.E.S., Mr. Joseph Anderson, F.E.S., the Rev. C. D. Ash, M.A., Mr. C. G. Barrett, F.E.S., the Rev. E. N. Bloomfield, M.A., F.E.S., Mr. W. M. Christy, M.A., F.L.S., Mr. D. A. Edgell, Mr. A. Lloyd, F.C.S., Mr. A. C. Vine and others.

HETEROCERA
Moths

SPHINGES

The Death's-Head Hawk (Acherontia atropos, Linn.) is somewhat sporadic in appearance. In some years large numbers of larvæ and pupæ are found in potato fields and gardens. The imago is much less commonly observed at large.

The Convolvulus Hawk (Sphinx convolvuli, Linn.) Like the preceding is somewhat sporadic in appearance. Occurs throughout the county. In some years considerable numbers of the moth are caught while hovering round flowers, especially those of the petunia and white tobacco (Nicotiana affinis). The larvæ and pupæ are not often observed, but several were found by potato diggers in the county in the early autumn of 1901.

The Privet Hawk (S. ligustri, Linn.) Common in most places

[The Spurge Hawk (Deilephila euphorbiæ, Linn.) Mr. Jenner reports (Barrett,

[1] Mr. Fletcher cites Meyrick's *Brit. Lep.* p. 358, and Barrett's *Brit. Lep.* i. 282 as to the occurrence of the species in Sussex.—H.G.

Brit. Lep. ii. 41) that Mr. J. Cosmo Melville obtained two specimens from a working man, who stated that he bred them from larvæ found at *Ecclesbourne* in 1871

The Bedstraw Hawk (D. galii, Rott.) Not uncommon near *Brighton* and *Lewes* in some seasons. Mr. Goss states that he has frequently found the larvæ feeding by night on Galium verum by the side of the roads between *Brighton* and *Ditchling* and between *Brighton* and the *Dyke*. Specimens have also been recorded from *Eastbourne*, where it has been taken at the electric lamps. It has also been recorded from *Hassocks, Hastings, Lewes*

The Striped Hawk (D. lineata, Fb.) Rare, probably always an immigrant. Specimens have been taken singly from time to time at *Brighton, Cuckfield* (Merrifield), *Guestling* (Bloomfield), *Firle, Hastings, Horsham, Lewes,*[1] *Ringmer, Slindon*

Chœrocampa celerio, Linn. *Brighton*, often captured in gardens attracted by the flowers of petunia and verbena (Vine); also recorded from *Ashling* (Rev. J. C. Parson), *Catsfield, Chichester* (Anderson); *Firle* in 1885–6 (Edgell); *Hastings, Hayward's Heath, Lewes* several times. Larvæ have been found in *Sussex* (Barrett, *Brit. Lep.* ii. 54)

The Small Elephant (C. porcellus, Linn.) is not uncommon, occurring chiefly on the downs and coast ; *Arundel Park, Brighton, Eastbourne,* near *Emsworth, Glynde, Guestling, Horsham, Lewes, Portslade, Shoreham* [2]

The Large Elephant (C. elpenor, Linn.) Not uncommon. The moth is often seen at 'sugar' (Vine) and the larvæ may sometimes be found in some numbers in wet places on Epilobium,[3] and occasionally in gardens on fuchsia. Has occurred at *Brighton, Bognor, Chichester,* near *Emsworth, Eastbourne, Glynde, Lewes, Hastings, Horsham, Henfield, Hayward's Heath, Shoreham*

— nerii, Linn. A rare immigrant, stated by Mr. Barrett (*Brit. Lep.* ii. 65) to be 'quite the most rare of our hawk-moths.' A very large proportion of the recorded British specimens seems to have been taken in *Sussex*. Mr. Barrett records (loc. cit.) the following : One at *Brighton* in each of the years 1852, 1857 and 1886 (the last was taken by Mr. T. Langley on 7 September; it is a male in good condition and passed into Mr. Fletcher's collection); two larvæ in 1859 and a moth in 1884 at *Eastbourne* ; a moth at *Lewes* on 3 September, 1874, seen alive by Mr. Jenner; one at *St. Leonards* in 1862 and another in 1868. A further specimen, a male, was taken on one of the lamps on the Marine Parade, *Brighton*, on 12 September, 1901 ; it was brought while still alive. to Messrs. Pratt & Sons, the well known naturalists, and is now in Mr. Fletcher's collection

The Eyed Hawk (Smerinthus ocellatus, Linn.)
The Poplar Hawk (S. populi, Linn.) } Seem generally common in the county.

The Lime Hawk (S. tiliæ, Linn.) Rare in *East Sussex* ; *Brighton, Hayward's Heath, Horsham* (Jenner) ; seems fairly common in *West Sussex*)Fletcher)

The Humming Bird Hawk (Macroglossa[4] stellatarum, Linn.) Occasionally common, but uncertain in appearance, sometimes on the wing during the greater part of the year, hibernated specimens appearing on the first warm days of March and April and belated ones in October and November. Recorded from all parts of the county.

— fuciformis, Linn. Woods, local, but widely distributed, and common in places ; *Abbots Wood, Battle, Charlton Forest, Hayward's Heath, Hastings, Horsham, Holm Bush, Laughton, Lewes, Midhurst, Poynings, Slindon, Tilgate Forest*

— scabiosæ, Z. Rare ; *Abbots Wood, Battle, Charlton Forest, Horsham, Laughton, Lewes, Midhurst*

Trochilium apiformis, Clerck. Uncommon ; *Hailsham, Lewes, Ringmer, Tilgate Forest*

---

[1] I possess a specimen taken at Brighton some thirty years ago.—H.G.

[2] It used to be abundant at dusk on the shore at Copperas Gap between Brighton and Shoreham flying over the flowers of *Echium vulgare.*—H. G.

[3] The larvæ of this species are very abundant near Byfleet and Weybridge in Surrey, feeding on wild balsam (*Impatiens fulva*), an American plant which has been naturalized on the Weybridge canal and on the Thames. The larvæ having been accustomed to balsam will not eat Epilobium.—H. G.

[4] The larvæ are in some years abundant, on *Galium verum*, near Brighton, Eastbourne and elsewhere on the Chalk.—H.G.

Trochilium crabroniformis, Lewin. *Brighton, Fairlight, Guestling, Hayward's Heath, Lewes, Tilgate Forest* and woods near *Worthing*

Sciopteron tabaniformis, Rott. A specimen taken in the *Brighton* Cemetery in 1868 was sold at the sale of the late Mr. S. Stevens' collection in March, 1900 (lot 155), with another specimen for £1

Sesia spheciformis, Gerning. Not uncommon in *Tilgate Forest*; Mr. Adkin takes it commonly there

— tipuliformis, Cl. A not uncommon garden insect

— vespiformis, Linn. (cynipiformis) Not uncommon in oak woods; *Abbots Wood, Black Brook Wood, Guestling, Hayward's Heath, Laughton, Lewes, Tilgate Forest*

— myopæformis, Bkh. Rare; *Abbots Wood*, occasionally in gardens at *Lewes* among apple

— culiciformis, Linn. Not uncommon in woods among birch; *Abbots Wood, Battle, Glynde, Laughton, Lewes, Tilgate Forest.* Mr. Meek and Mr. Tester took it in plenty in *Tilgate Forest*

— formicæformis, Esp. Rare and very local; occasionally near *Lewes* in osier beds

— ichneumoniformis, Fb. Local but abundant among Anthyllis vulneraria and Lotus corniculatus, especially on the coast and on railway banks; near *Brighton, Lewes* (singly), *Eastbourne, Hastings* on the cliffs, shingle near *Shoreham*, railway banks in *Tilgate Forest*

— chrysidiformis, Esp. Very rare and local; *Eastbourne*, 'one, worn,' G. P. Shearwood (*Ent.* 1874, p. 224). Is it possible that this specimen should be referred to S. ichneumoniformis, which occurs not uncommonly on the slopes between *Eastbourne* and *Beachy Head*?—W.H.B.F.

ZYGÆNIDÆ

Ino globulariæ, Hb. Very local but abundant where it occurs; *Bevingdean, Hollingbury* and *Moules Combe* near *Brighton, Bible Bottom* and downs near *Lewes*

— statices, Linn. Very local; *Abbots Wood*, downs near *Brighton* and *Lewes, Eartham* (Edgell), *Hayward's Heath, Tilgate Forest*

— geryon, Hb. Abundant in a few localities; on the downs and in valleys near *Brighton* and *Lewes*

Naclia ancilla, Linn. A specimen is recorded as captured at *Worthing* by Mr. Wildman in 1867 (*Ent. Ann.* 1868, p. 104). Mr. Meyrick remarks of the record

that it is 'extremely dubious' (*Brit. Lep.* p. 23)

Zygæna trifolii, Esp. Widely distributed; downs and wet commons; *Abbots Wood, Battle, Brighton, Chailey, Ditchling Common*, downs near *Emsworth* (in this last locality Mr. Christy took a large number of the yellow [1] form in 1893 and following years), *Eartham, Hayward's Heath, Hurston Warren, Tilgate*

— loniceræ, Scheven. Reported from *Brighton, Hayward's Heath* and *Cuckmere* district. I have never seen a Sussex specimen (W.H.B.F.)

— filipendulæ, Linn. Abundant and widely distributed, especially on the coast and downs. The breeding of a specimen of the very rare ab. chrysanthemi,[2] Bork., by Mr. Leslie at *St. Leonards* is recorded (*E.M.M.* i. 143)

Sarothripus revayana, Scop. *Abbots Wood, Chailey, Brighton, Battle, Guestling, Hayward's Heath, Roost Hole Horsham, Tilgate Forest, Warningcamp*

Earias chlorana, Linn. Not uncommon in osier beds; *Berwick, Brighton, Eastbourne, Heene, Guestling, Isfield, Lewes, Uckfield*

Hylophila prasinana, Linn. Generally common in oak woods

— bicolorana, Fues. Less common than the preceding; *Abbots Wood, Ashdown Forest, Hastings, Guestling, Plashet Wood*

Nola cucullatella, Linn. Everywhere common among hawthorn

— strigula, Schiff. *Abbots Wood*, plentiful in some years; woods near *Brighton* and *Lewes, Battle, Guestling*

— confusalis, H.S. Widely distributed and not uncommon; *Abbots Wood, Battle, Bognor, Brighton, Fernhurst, Guestling, Hastings, Lewes, Worthing*

— centonalis, Hb. Very rare; taken at *Hastings* in 1891

— albulalis, Hb. Very rare. A single specimen taken in *Abbots Wood* by Mr. T. Salvage in 1901 is now in Mr. Fletcher's collection

Nudaria senex, Hb. Not uncommon in wet places. *Henfield Common, Hurston Warren, Lewes* (formerly), *Shoreham, Tilgate Forest*

— mundana, Linn. Widely distributed and not uncommon. *Brighton, Bognor, Chichester*, near *Emsworth, Guestling, Lewes, Worthing*

[1] I have received specimens of this form from Mr. Christy—H.G.

[2] I took a specimen of the *ab. chrysanthemi* in the New Forest in July, 1900.—H.G.

INSECTS

Sentina irrorella, Clerck. Very abundant[1] on the beach between *Shoreham* and *Copperas Gap* ; has also occurred rarely at *Hastings, Newhaven* and *Southwater*

Calligenia miniata, Forst. Not uncommon in woods and plantations. A form with the red ground colour replaced by yellow has occurred once at *Battle*

Lithosia mesomella, Linn. Woods and heaths ; rather common

— sororcula, Hufn. In woods ; *Abbots Wood* (some years very common), *Battle, Brighton, Hayward's Heath, Horsham, Lewes, Laughton*

— griseola, Hb. Generally common, the variety stramineola, Dbl. occurring occasionally with the type

— deplana, Esp. Rare ; perhaps sometimes overlooked. Woods between *Arundel* and *Slindon, St. Leonards Forest* (Price)

— lurideola, Zinck. Generally common

— complana, Linn. Woods and heaths. *Abbots Wood, Battle, Brighton, Chichester Cissbury, Eastbourne,* near *Emsworth, Hastings, Hayward's Heath, Laughton* and *Lewes*

[— caniola, Hb. Near *Rye*, but the record requires confirmation.—W.H.B.F.]

Gnophria quadra, Linn. Generally rare, but in 1872 or 1874 it was so abundant in *Abbots Wood* that Mr. H. Gorringe took 105[2] specimens at ' sugar ' in one night ; *Abbots Wood, Ashburnham,* near *Emsworth, Guestling, Hastings, Hayward's Heath, Lewes, St. Leonards Forest* ; hedges between *Lancing* and *Shoreham*

— rubricollis, Linn. Woods; apparently somewhat local. *Abbots Wood,* sometimes in swarms about oak trees,[3] near *Emsworth, Fernhurst, Hayward's Heath, Hastings, Lewes, Worthing* (*Manual,* i. 140)

Deiopeia pulchella, Linn. Scarce and somewhat sporadic in appearance. Specimens have been taken from time to time at the following places : *Bexhill, Brighton,*[4] *Bognor, Eastbourne, Hastings, Littlehampton, Ringmer, Worthing*

Euchelia jacobææ, Linn. Common and generally distributed ; taken in *Chichester.* Mr. Anderson has two specimens in which the crimson of the wings is replaced by yellow

Callimorpha dominula, Linn. Rare, if not extinct in the county. *Tilgate Forest* ; old lists record it from the neighbourhood of *Eastbourne* and *Lewes,* from which it has disappeared. Mr. Fletcher took a specimen some twenty years ago in a garden at Worthing. It is recorded also from *Chichester* by Mr. Anderson

Nemeophila russula, Linn. Probably occurs on most of the heaths throughout the county. Very common formerly in *Tilgate Forest* and *St. Leonards Forest*

— plantaginis, Linn. Rather common in woods in *East Sussex* ; seems less so in the western division. Mr. Stainton records it as having occurred at *Worthing,* but not annually (*Manual,* i. 146). Formerly abundant in *Abbots Wood*

Arctia caja, Linn. Generally distributed, though less common than formerly

— villica, Linn. Widely distributed, though apparently less abundant than formerly. The larvæ used to be plentiful near Portslade

Spilosoma fuliginosa, Linn. Not common. *Abbots Wood, Bell Vale, Brighton, Battle, Hayward's Heath,* near *Emsworth, Lewes, Tilgate Forest, Slindon*

— mendica, Clerck. Widely distributed but not common. *Abbots Wood, Battle, Brighton, Chichester,* near *Emsworth, Fernhurst, Horsham, Hastings, Lewes, Tilgate Forest*

— lubricipeda, Linn. Generally common

— menthastri, Esp.   „   „

— urticæ, Esp. Local and rare ; near the *Arun* at *Horsham, Lewes* marshes, *Shoreham*

Hepialus humuli, Linn. Very common

— sylvanus, Linn. Not very abundant ; *Brighton, Eastbourne, Hastings, Hayward's Heath, Lewes, Shoreham, Upmarden, Worthing*

— fusconebulosa, De Geer. Local and scarce ; *Denne Park, Horsham, Upmarden.* The variety gallicus, Ld., also occurs at the latter locality (*Christy*)

— lupulinus, Linn. Abundant everywhere

— hectus, Linn. Common in woods

Cossus cossus, Linn. Common and generally distributed

Zeuzera pyrina, Linn. Not common but widely distributed

Heterogenea limacodes, Hufn. Somewhat rare ; *Abbots Wood, Battle, Brighton, Goring Woods, Guestling, Hayward's Heath, Plashet Wood, Upmarden*

---

[1] It was so in the ' seventies ' and may be still.—H.G.

[2] I saw all the specimens unset.—H.G.

[3] I have seen it swarming around oak trees in Abbots Wood.—H.G.

[4] Three specimens were brought to me alive in Brighton between 1872 and 1875.—H.G.

Heterogenea asella, Schiff. Very rare; once at *Abbots Wood*, *Rewel Wood* near *Slindon*, *Wakehurst*

Porthesia chrysorrhœa, Linn. Not uncommon and generally distributed. Mr. Anderson writes of this species: 'Larvæ very abundant on whitethorn hedges by canal, *Chichester*, 1877. After that date completely disappeared until 1900, when a single specimen (δ) was taken on a gas lamp.' This quite tallies with Mr. Fletcher's experience. The species seems to have been abundant at *Arlington* in 1901

— similis, Fues. Very common

Leucoma salicis, Linn. Common and generally distributed, especially where poplars are extensively planted in streets and gardens

Psilura monacha, Linn. Woods; *Abbots Wood* (common), *Battle, Brighton,* near *Emsworth, Fletching, Hastings, Hayward's Heath, Horsham, Henley Hill* (Barrett), *Lewes, Tilgate Forest, West Itchenor*

Dasychira fascelina, Linn. Occurred in the *White Field, Abbots Wood,* in 1882 (Jenner)

— pudibunda, Linn. Generally common

Orgyia antiqua, Linn. Common everywhere

Trichiura cratægi, Linn. Somewhat uncommon; *Abbots Wood, Chichester, Horsham, Lewes, Ringmer, Stoughton, Tilgate Forest, West Itchenor*

Pœcilocampa populi, Linn. Generally distributed and not uncommon

Eriogaster lanestris, Linn. Generally distributed

Bombyx neustria, Linn. Usually extremely abundant

— rubi, Linn. Generally common, especially on downs, heaths and commons

— quercus, Linn. Generally common

— trifolii, Esp. Rare and local; *Crowhurst, Eastbourne*

Odonestis potatoria, Linn. Generally common. Mr. Goss has obtained from *Brighton* the form in which the male is wholly of the pale yellowish buff colour usually distinctive of the female. On the other hand Mr. Fletcher has bred from larvæ from *Arlington* males entirely, or nearly so, of a rich purplish chocolate colour, some of the females even from this locality being similarly though less richly coloured

Lasiocampa quercifolia, Linn. Seems generally distributed over the county but nowhere abundant

Endromis versicolor, Linn. Probably now extinct; formerly common in *St. Leonards* and *Tilgate Forests.* Once seen flying in *Fernhurst* parish (Barrett). Mr. Goss writes: 'Mr. W. Borrer of Hurstpierpoint told me that his cousin in one day assembled with the aid of two bred females one hundred and twenty-five males in *Tilgate Forest.* I possess a fine series taken in *Tilgate Forest* about 1857 or 1858 by a Brighton florist; but the species had become extinct or very rare before I was old enough to collect'

Saturnia pavonia,[1] Linn. (carpini) Generally distributed and not uncommon in heathy places

Drepana lacertinaria, Linn. Common and generally distributed among birch

— falcataria, Linn. Not uncommon among alder and birch

— binaria, Hufn. Widely distributed in oak woods; *Abbots Wood, Blackdown, Brighton, Guestling, Hayward's Heath, Lewes, St. Leonards* and *Tilgate Forests*

— cultraria, Fb. Sometimes abundant in beech woods but does not seem generally common; *Eastbourne, Falmer,* near *Harting* and *Hastings, Lewes, St. Leonards Forest*

Cilix glaucata, Scop. Common everywhere

Dicranura bicuspis, Bork. Very rare; *Ashdown* (Vine), *St. Leonards* and *Tilgate Forests.* The larva has been found on alder to the north of *Three Bridges* (Fletcher). The old cocoons which endure for some years are not uncommon on old birch trunks in *St. Leonards Forest*

— furcula, Linn. Not common; *Abbots Wood, Ashdown Forest, Brighton, Hayward's Heath, Laughton, Lewes, Pett, Tilgate Forest*

— bifida, Hb. Not uncommon among poplars; *Bognor, Brighton, Cuckfield, Guestling, Horsham, Lewes, Tilgate, Worthing*

— vinula, Linn. Common among poplars

Stauropus fagi, Linn. Rare; *Abbots Wood* (Vine); *Battle, Brighton,* near *Emsworth* (Christy); *Hastings, Lewes, Rye* (Bloomfield); *Slindon* (Edgell); *St. Leonards Forest*

Ptilophora plumigera, Esp. *Watergate, Emsworth.* Mr. Christy writes to the effect that he has taken several in his moth-trap and that it is probably not uncommon in the neighbourhood

[1] I have assembled many dozens of males in Tilgate Forest by the aid of bred virgin females.—H.G.

INSECTS

Pterostoma palpina, Linn. Not uncommon ; *Abbots Wood, Ashdown Forest, Battle, Brighton,* near *Emsworth, Hastings, Hayward's Heath, Horsham, Lewes, Tilgate Forest*

Lophopteryx camelina, Linn. Rather common and generally distributed

— cuculla, Esp. Very rare ; taken at *Hayward's Heath* by the Rev. T. E. Crallan

— carmelita, Esp. Rare ; *Ashdown Forest* (Vine), *Blackdown Wooas* (Barrett), *Hayward's Heath* (Jenner's list), *Tilgate Forest* (Goss and Vine)

Notodonta dictæa, Linn. Widely distributed throughout the county among poplars

— dictæoides, Esp. Not common but widely distributed ; *Blackdown Woods* (Barrett), *Brighton,* near *Emsworth* (Christy), *Faygate, St. Leonards Forest, Hastings, Horsham, Slindon* (Edgell), *Tilgate Forest* (Vine)

— dromedarius, Linn. Scarce ; *Bexhill* (once), *Brighton,* near *Emsworth* (Christy), *Faygate* and *Tilgate Forests, Hayward's Heath*

— ziczac, Linn. Widely distributed ; *Abbots Wood, Brighton,* near *Emsworth, Guestling, Hailsham, Holm Bush, Horsham, Ringmer, Slindon, Tilgate Forest, Worthing*

— trepida, Esp. *Abbots Wood, Brighton,* near *Emsworth, Hayward's Heath, Horsham, Tilgate Forest*

— chaonia, Hb. Not common ; *Abbots Wood,* near *Emsworth, Horsham, Tilgate Forest, Westmeston, Guestling*

— trimacula, Esp. Rare ; *Battle, Brighton,* near *Emsworth, Horsham, Lewes, Tilgate Forest*

Phalera bucephala, Linn. Everywhere common

Pygæra curtula, Linn. Not common ; *Abbots Wood, Guestling, Horsham, Lewes, Tilgate*

— anachoreta, Fb. Miss Edwards records the finding in August, 1893, of eggs of this species on sallow at *Bulverhythe* and the subsequent rearing of the moths (*Ent.* xxvi. 361, xxvii. 176 ; see also Barrett, *Brit. Lep.* iii. 172)

— pigra, Hufn. Not an abundant species ; *Abbots Wood, Brighton, Burgess Hill, Guestling* (once), *Hassocks, Hayward's Heath, Tilgate Forest*

NOCTUÆ

Thyatira derasa, Linn. Generally common in woods in *East Sussex* ; in the western division recorded from near *Emsworth* and *Holmbush*

Thyatira batis, Linn. Generally common in *East Sussex* woods ; in *West Sussex* occurs near *Emsworth* and is generally distributed in the *Fernhurst* district

— Cymatophora octogesima, Hb. Very rare ; was taken at *Hayward's Heath* by the late Rev. T. E. Crallan

— or, Fb. Comes freely to 'sugar' in *Abbots Wood* ; taken also at *Battle, Blackdown Woods, Brighton,* near *Emsworth, Guestling, Hayward's Heath, Tilgate Forest*

— fluctuosa,[1] Hb. Rare ; *Abbots Wood, Battle, Brighton, Bell Woods, Guestling, Hayward's Heath, Tilgate Forest*

— duplaris, Linn. Generally common in woods

Asphalia diluta, Fb. Common in woods

— flavicornis, Linn. Locally common among birch ; *Abbots Wood, Battle, Brighton,* near *Emsworth, Frant, Hastings, Horsham, Tilgate Forest*

— ridens, Fb. In woods, rare ; *Abbots Wood, Brighton,* near *Emsworth, Guestling, Lewes, St. Leonards Forest*

Bryophila muralis, Forst. / — perla, Fb. } Generally common on lichen-covered walls. The moths come freely to 'light'

Moma (Diphthera) orion, Esp.[2] In oak woods, rather rare, but in some seasons very common at 'sugar' in *Abbots* and *Wilmington Woods* ; *Battle,* near *Emsworth, Guestling, Hollington, Plashet Wood, St. Leonards Forest*

Demas coryli, Linn. Not uncommon ; *Abbots Wood, Eastbourne,* near *Emsworth, Falmer, Guestling, Horsham, Lewes*

Acronycta tridens, Schiff. } — psi, Linn. } Common and generally distributed

— leporina, Linn. Widely distributed in the county ; *Abbots Wood, Battle, Bell Hanger, Bognor,* near *Emsworth, Hastings, Horsham, Ringmer, Tilgate Forest, Worthing*

— aceris, Linn. Generally common

— megacephala, Fb. Generally distributed and not uncommon

— alni, Linn. Very rare though widely distributed, usually taken singly and in the larval state ; has occurred at *Abbots Wood, Ashdown Forest,*[3] *Cuckfield,* near *Emsworth, Groombridge, Hayward's Heath, Holmbush,* where two specimens

[1] I have taken four or five in one evening at 'sugar' in Abbots Wood.—H.G.

[2] Abundant at 'sugar' in Wilmington Wood and adjoining woods about 1877 and 1880.—H.G.

[3] I possess a specimen from Ashdown Forest taken by Mr. Pratt nearly thirty years ago.—H.G.

were taken at 'sugar' by the late Mr. Thorncroft of Brighton some years ago, *Horsham, Petworth, Plashet Wood, Tilgate Forest, Westfield*

Acronycta ligustri, Fb. Generally distributed in *East Sussex*; in *West Sussex* has occurred near *Emsworth* and in the *Slindon Woods*

— rumicis, Linn. Widely distributed but apparently not so abundant as in some other counties

— auricoma, Fb. Very local, perhaps now extinct. Mr. Goss says it 'used to be common at " sugar " in *Abbots Wood* and adjoining woods,' and Mr. Vine states, ' Used to be taken very freely but now rare; my last capture was made April 17th, 1880.' Mr. Fletcher took a larva off bramble in *Abbots Wood* in June, 1884. The species has also occurred at *Battle* and *Guestling* where several came to light

Diloba cæruleocephala, Linn. Everywhere common.

Synia musculosa, Hb. Very rare and perhaps only an occasional immigrant. *Brighton* : ' Several specimens were taken at *Brighton* about the years 1856–60' (Jenner's East Sussex List). Mr. Vine writes : ' The late Messrs. Flowse, M'Arthur, Thorncroft and Tidy took about twenty specimens between them.' Mr. Henry Cooke was also among the fortunate captors in August, 1856 (*Substitute*, p. 28). 'Some specimens recently sold at Stevens' Rooms were labelled *Bexhill*' (Jenner's East Sussex List). More information about these would be interesting

Leucania conigera, Fb. Generally common.

— vitellina, Hb. Several specimens of this rare species, which was added to the British list by Mr. Henry Cooke (*Substitute*, p. 28), have been taken near *Brighton, Lewes* and *Shoreham* from time to time. Mr. Vine took three at *Shoreham* in September, 1875, and two at ' sugar ' on the *Brighton Downs* in September, 1900, in which month also Professor Meldola captured two at ' sugar ' at *Bognor*

— turca, Linn. Very local and perhaps extinct in some localities ; *Chesworth*, one near *Emsworth* (W. M. Christy), wood near *Lewes*, *St. Leonards Forest*

— lithargyria, Esp. Common in the county

— albipuncta, Fb. Rare ; one specimen at *Chichester* (J. Anderson) ; near *Rye* in 1900, 1901 (Rev. E. N. Bloomfield) ; several at *Shoreham* (A. C. Vine) ; also

has occurred at *Lewes* and *St. Leonards* (J. H. A. Jenner)

Leucania unipuncta, Hw. A very rare immigrant. A specimen taken by Dr. Allchin near *Lewes* on 9 September, 1859, was exhibited by him at the meeting of the Entomological Society on 3 October, 1859 (*Trans. Ent. Soc.* new. ser. v. 79)

— impudens, Hb. Very local. *Brighton* (Stainton, *Manual*, i. 189) ; *Camber Sandhills, Rye* (Rev. E. N. Bloomfield) ; *Holmbush* (A. C. Vine), *Tilgate Forest* (M. S. Blaker) and *St. Leonards Forest*

— loreyi, Dup. 'One of the most rare of British insects' (Barrett, *Brit. Lep.* v. 163). Mr. Doubleday (*Zoologist*, 1863, p. 8407) records the capture of two specimens, females, by Mr. Thorncroft near *Brighton* on 14 October, 1862. Mr. Barrett (loc. cit.) brings the history of these specimens up to date

— comma, Linn. Generally common

— straminea, Tr. Not common ; singly at *Eastbourne, Lewes* and *Pett*; has occurred also near *Brighton, Eastbourne, Horsham* near *Rye* (Rev. E. N. Bloomfield). Mr. Vine states that it comes freely to flowers of rushes near *Shoreham*

— impura, Hb. } Both very common
— pallens, Linn. }

Cœnobia rufa, Hw. Very local; has occurred near *Hastings*, and is very abundant on *Henfield Common* among Juncus articulatus, Linn.

Tapinostola fulva, Hb. Not common, but seems widely distributed. *Abbots Wood, Brighton, Fernhurst, Fairlight, Hayward's Heath, Horsham, Lewes, Shoreham* (where Mr. Vine writes it may be found freely by searching grass by ditches) and *Tilgate*

Nonagria cannæ, O. Of this species Mr. Barrett says (*Brit. Lep.* v. 80) : 'Its principle haunts are now the fens of *Norfolk* and *Suffolk*, whence all the more recent specimens have been obtained ; but a few are occasionally found about ponds in the middle of *Sussex*.' Its name does not occur in any of the local lists sent to me (W.H.B.F.)

— typhæ, Thnbg. Larvæ and pupæ may be found commonly in Typha angustifolia and latifolia near *Shoreham*, but the species does not seem to be generally abundant in the county. It has been taken at *Brighton, Lewes, Hastings, Tilgate*

— geminipuncta, Hatchett. Marshes near *Bognor, Brighton, Lewes* and *Shoreham*. The larvæ and pupæ are not uncommon in ' stems ' of reeds

Calamia lutosa, Hb. Occasionally near *Hastings*, *Horsham* and *Lewes*; appears to be fairly common at *Bognor* and *Shoreham*

Gortyna ochracea, Hb. Widely distributed; recorded from near *Emsworth, Hastings, Hayward's Heath, Horsham, Tilgate Forest, Worthing*

Hydrœcia nictitans, Bkh. Common and widely distributed. The form paludis, Tutt, is abundant near *Clymping* and on the salt marshes at *Lancing*; it occurs also on the banks of the Arun, and Mr. Christy has met with it on *Thorney Marsh*

Hydrœcia micacea, Esp. Common and widely distributed

Axylia putris, Linn. Generally common

Xylophasia rurea, Fb. Common

— lithoxylea, Fb. „

— sublustris, Esp. Locally common; *Abbots Wood, Brighton, Eastbourne,* near *Emsworth, Horsham, Lewes, St. Leonards, Tilgate*

— monoglypha, Hufn. Everywhere abundant

— hepatica, Hb. Generally common

— scolopacina, Esp. Very local; *Arundel Park, Horsham*

Dipterygia scabriuscula, Linn. Rare though widely distributed. *Ashdown Forest, Brighton,* near *Emsworth, Fernhurst, Hayward's Heath, Horsham, Lewes, Tilgate Forest*

Aporophyla australis, Bdv. Locally abundant on the downs near *Brighton, Lewes* and *Shoreham*

Lamphygma exigua, Hb. Very rare. Mr. Vine reports the capture of three specimens at *Brighton,* one on a gas-lamp, two on the racecourse and three at 'sugar' at *Shoreham.* Other specimens have been taken singly at *Brighton* and *Lewes.* (Mr. Jenner), and Mr. Stainton (*Manual,* i. 203) gives *Worthing* as another locality in which the species has occurred

Neuria reticulata, Vill. Not generally abundant, though Mr. Christy records it as having been quite common at *Stoughton* in 1885. It has occurred at *Brighton, Eastbourne* and *Lewes* and rarely at *Guestling* and *Tilgate*

Neuronia popularis, Fb. Common

Charæas graminis, L. Occasionally common near *Brighton* and *Lewes*; has occurred also near *Emsworth, Hastings, Shoreham, Worthing*

Cerigo matura, Hufn. Not uncommon, especially on the downs

Luperina testacea, Hb. Very abundant

— dumerilii, Dup. A very rare immigrant; 'Sussex' (Meyrick, *Handbook,* p. 113). In a list of Lepidoptera captured and bred in 1859, Dr. Allchin writes: 'L. dumerilii ? Took one at *Brighton* in September' (*Ent. Weekly Intell.* vii. 203). I do not know if the doubt as to the identity of the specimen expressed by the note of interrogation was ever removed, nor do I know of any record of the capture of any other specimen in the county (W.H.B.F.)

— cespitis, Fb. Not often captured but is probably not uncommon on the downs. It has occurred near *Brighton, Chichester, Emsworth, Guestling, Hayward's Heath, Horsham, Lewes* and *Worthing*

Mamestra abjecta, Hb. Not common, and confined to the neighbourhood of the salt marshes near the coast. In *East Sussex* has occurred near *Brighton* and *Lewes,* and in the western division near *Shoreham,* and *Lancing* and in *Thorney*

— sordida, Bork. Not uncommon

— furva, Hb. 'Usually a northern and western species, but it has been taken rarely in *Sussex*' (Barrett, *Lep. Brit.* iv. 354). Once near *Lewes*; no recent record (J. H. A. Jenner)

— brassicæ, Linn. ⎫
— persicariæ, Linn. ⎬ All very common
Apamea basilinea, Fb. ⎭

— gemina, Hb. Common in some parts of the county but appears not to be so generally. Reported from *Bognor, Brighton, Fernhurst, Hailsham, Horsham, Hayward's Heath, Hastings, Lewes, Stoughton, Tilgate Forest, Uckfield,* etc.

— unanimis, Tr. *Shoreham*; reported as being rather common, but seems rare elsewhere; has occurred at *Abbots Wood, Brighton, Guestling, Hayward's Heath, Lewes, St. Leonards* and *Tilgate Forests*

— ophiogramma, Esp. Rare; has been taken at *Hollington, Horsham, Shoreham*

— leucostigma, Hb. Very rare; *Brighton, Guestling* (once in 1870), *Shoreham, Slaugham*

— secalis, L. (didyma, Esp.) Abundant everywhere

Miana strigilis, Clerck. Generally common

— fasciuncula, Hw. „ „

— literosa, Hw. Probably not uncommon near the coast but rare elsewhere; *Ashdown Forest, Blackdown Woods, Brighton, Chichester, Clymping, Cocking, Hayward's Heath, Hastings, Lewes, Shoreham, Thorney*

Miana bicoloria, Vill. Everywhere common
— arcuosa, Hw. Marshy places, not common; *Abbots Wood, Brighton, Hastings, Horsham, Hayward's Heath, Lewes*; rough ground near *Castle Goring*

Celæna haworthii, Curt. Rare; recorded as taken at *Brighton* formerly, at *Bexhill* recently, *Horsham*

Grammesia trigrammica, Hufn. Generally common

Stilbia anomala, Hw. Rare and very local; *Fernhurst, Hastings*, near *Horsham*, near *Lewes*, once; *Tilgate Forest*

Caradrina morpheus, Hufn. ⎫
— alsines, Brahm. ⎬ Common in the
— taraxaci, Hb. ⎭ county
— ambigua, Fb. A few specimens have been taken by Mr. Vine on *Brighton Racecourse* and near *Shoreham*; one was taken at 'sugar' by Professor Meldola at *Pagham* in 1900
— quadripuncta, Fb. Common

Rusina umbratica, Goeze. ,,

Agrotis vestigialis, Rott. Very local; probably confined to the coast; has been taken on the *Camber* and *Clymping* sandhills
— puta, Hb. Not uncommon and generally distributed
— ypsilon, Rott. Generally common
— saucia, Hb. Periodically common and generally distributed
— segetum, Schiff. Very abundant
— exclamationis, Linn. ,, ,,
— corticea, Hb. Not uncommon
— cinerea, Hb. Not taken in great numbers but widely distributed on the chalk; downs near *Brighton, Clayton, Goring, Lewes, Steyning, Polegate*
— ripæ, Hb. Very local, confined to the coast sandhills. At *Pagham*, where the larvæ may sometimes be taken in large numbers, the imago is rarely seen. Has occurred also on the *Camber* and *Clymping* sandhills
— nigricans, Linn. Not uncommon
— tritici, Linn. Common on the downs at *Brighton*, appears to be less so elsewhere; reported also from *Clymping, Eastbourne, Horsham* in gardens, *Lewes, Pett, Thorney*
— aquilina, Hb. Scarce; perhaps occurs more on the downs and less on the coast than the last; *Brighton, Lewes, Shoreham*
— obelisca, Hb. Not rare at *Shoreham* (A. C. Vine) but seems so elsewhere; Dr. Allchin took one at *Brighton* in 1859 (*Ent. Weekly Intell.* vii. 204), and Mr. W. E. Nicholson has met with the species at *Lewes*

Agrotis agathina, Dup. The larvæ are reported as being common in *Tilgate Forest* and would probably be found to be so generally on Erica cinerea (bell heather), if that plant were searched or swept for them in late spring; recorded also from *Ashdown Forest, Fernhurst, St. Leonards Forest*
— strigula, Thnb. Common among ling, calluna, throughout the county

Noctua glareosa, Esp. Not common; *Abbots Wood, Brighton, Fernhurst, Guestling, Hassocks, Holmbush, Lewes*
— augur, Fb. Very local; *Brighton*, woods near *Horsham*, and marshes near *Lewes*
— plecta, Linn. ⎫ Common and gener-
— c-nigrum, Linn. ⎬ ally distributed
— ditrapezium, Bork. Very local; may be taken freely in the larval state from birch and sallow in *Tilgate Forest*; also recorded from *Cowfold*, near *Emsworth* (2), *Fernhurst, Hayward's Heath, Horsham*
— triangulum, Hufn. Common, especially in woods
— stigmatica, Hb. Seems generally rare in the county, but is reported by Mr. Christy as not uncommon lately at *Stoughton*; rare in *Charlton Forest* (the Rev. C. D. Ash); also reported as having occurred at *Hayward's Heath*, and once near *Lewes*
— brunnea, Fb. ⎫ Common, especially in
— primulæ, Esp. ⎬ woods
— dahlii, Hb. Locally common in woods; *Abbots Wood, Battle, Brighton*, near *Emsworth, Guestling, Horsham, Lewes*
— rubi, View. Common and widely distributed
— umbrosa, Hb. Not uncommon
— baja, Fb. ,, ,,
— castanea, Esp. Very local; *Cocking*, near *Hastings, Laughton*. Mr. Vine states that the larvæ may be taken freely in *Tilgate Forest*. This would most likely be the case in most of the heathy places in the county. The fact that many of these are not easily worked by entomologists after dark probably accounts for many moths being observed less frequently than would otherwise be the case
— xanthographa, Fb. Common everywhere

Triphæna janthina, Esp. Generally common
— fimbria, Linn. Not uncommon, especially in woods; *Abbots Wood, Battle, Brighton, Chichester, Cocking, Hastings, Hayward's Heath, Horsham, Laughton, Lewes, Worthing*

Triphæna interjecta, Hb. Generally distributed but not abundant; *Bognor, Brighton, Chichester, Cocking, Eastbourne, Fernhurst, Hastings, Horsham, Hayward's Heath, Lewes, Worthing*

— orbona, Hufn. Very scarce; Mr. E. K. Robinson records having bred a specimen from a larva found in *Hollington Wood* near *Hastings* (*Ent.* 1877, p. 299), and Mr. Christy has taken a few on the extreme west of the county near *Emsworth*

— comes, Hb. Abundant everywhere

— pronuba, Linn. „ „

Amphipyra pyramidea, Linn. } Generally
— tragopogonis, Linn. } abundant

Mania typica, Linn. Generally common, especially in marshy places

— maura, Linn. Generally common

Panolis griseovariegata, Goeze. Local and somewhat scarce; *Bexhill, Brighton,* near *Emsworth, Fernhurst, Frant, Horsham, Isfield, Lewes, Ringmer, Tilgate Forest, Worthing, Wych Cross*

Pachnobia leucographa, Hb. Rare; *Battle, Cocking, Emsworth, East Grinstead, Groombridge, Horsham, Lewes, Tilgate Forest, Ticehurst*

— rubricosa, Fb. Common at sallow bloom

Mesogona acetosellæ, Fb. A single specimen was taken by Mr. T. Salvage at 'sugar' in his garden at *Arlington* on 26 October, 1895 (see article by Mr. R. Adkin, *Ent.* xxviii. 317)

Tæmiocampa gothica, Linn. } Common at sal-
— incerta, Hufn. } low bloom

— opima, Hb. Local and scarce; *Abbots Wood, Horsham, Hayward's Heath, Laughton, Tilgate Forest*

— populeti, Tr. Not common; *Abbots Wood, Guestling, Hayward's Heath, Horsham, Laughton, Lewes, Worthing*

— stabilis, View. Common at sallow bloom

— gracilis, Fb. „ „ „

— miniosa, Fb. Common; the larvæ are sometimes very abundant on oak growing in hedgerows and woods

— munda, Esp. Mr. Jenner notes this species as being rather scarce in *East Sussex,* occurring at *Abbots Wood, Brighton, Battle, Frant, Hastings, Hayward's Heath, Laughton, Lewes;* it seems quite common in *West Sussex,* the larva being more often observed perhaps than the imago

— pulverulenta, Esp. Common in woods

Orthosia suspecta, Hb. Very local; *Tilgate Forest*

— fissipuncta, Hw. Locally common, especially in marshy places; the larvæ

may be found abundantly under the bark of large willows (the Rev. C. D. Ash)

Orthosia lota, Clerck. Generally common
— macilenta, Hb. „ „
Anchocelis helvola, Linn. „ „
— pistacina, Fb. „ „
— lunosa, Hw. „ „
— litura, Linn. Reported by Mr. Jenner as scarce in *East Sussex,* but common in the western division; *Abbots Wood, Ashdown Forest, Brighton, Cocking, Emsworth, Fernhurst, Guestling, Hayward's Heath, Horsham, Laughton, Lewes*

Cerastis vaccinii, } Both generally common
Linn. } and the latter very vari-
— ligula, Esp. } able

— erythrocephala, Fb. Very rare and local; the first British specimen was taken near *Brighton* by Mr. H. Cooke in November, 1847. Subsequently specimens were taken by the late Mr. S. Stevens under the South Downs between *Brighton* and *Eastbourne* (Barrett, *Brit. Lep.* vi. 11). Mr. Jenner records that between 1857 and 1874 several were taken by himself and others near *Lewes,* the variety glabra occurring with the type. None appear to have been taken in the county since 1874

Scopelosoma satellitia, Linn. Generally common

— rubiginea, Fb. Very rare; has occurred near *Brighton* (J. H. A. Jenner), in the grounds attached to *Bramber Castle* at ivy bloom (A. C. Vine) and at *Denne Park, Horsham,* at sallow bloom

Hoporina croceago, Fb. Seems more abundant in the eastern than in the western division of the county, being not uncommon in the former in oak woods; *Abbots Wood, Battle, Brighton, Guestling, Hayward's Heath, Horsham, Laughton, Lewes, Tilgate Forest, West Stoke* (a single specimen taken by Mr. Arnold Shaw)

Xanthia citrago, Linn. Very local; *Abbots Wood, Hassocks, Horsham, Northiam*

— fulvago, Linn. Generally common; the form flavescens, Esp., occurring with, but less abundantly than, the type

— lutea, Ström. Generally common

— aurago, Fb. Sometimes abundant in beech woods; *Bramber, Charlton Forest, Cocking,* near *Emsworth, Falmer, Horsham, Isfield, Lewes*

— gilvago, Esp. Apparently very uncommon; has occurred near *Brighton,* where specimens of a 'bright orange-yellow with the markings reduced and broken up into spots and shades of rich purple red' have been taken (Barrett, *Brit. Lep.* v. 374). The species has also been met with at *Chichester, Horsham, Shoreham*

Xanthia circellaris, Hufn. Generally common

— ocellaris, Bkh. Although recorded in error as British so long ago as 1857 the yellow form of X. gilvago having been mistaken for it, this species was only identified as having occurred in Britain in 1893, in which year a few specimens were taken in Surrey. In October of the following year one was taken at 'light' in *Bognor* by Mr. Guermonprez, this specimen was identified by Mr. Barrett and recorded (*Brit. Lep.* v. 379)

Cirrhœdia xerampelina, Hb. Generally scarce, though Mr. Vine states that the larvæ are often common on ash trunks in the early spring. Has occurred at *Hassocks, Horsham, Lewes, Withdean*

Tethea subtusa, Fb. Very local ; the larvæ may sometimes be found very abundantly between the leaves of Populus nigra and doubtless of other species of poplar. Recorded from *Brighton, Guestling, Holm Bush, Lewes, Worthing*

— retusa, Linn. Like the preceding very local, but the larvæ may sometimes be beaten freely from Salix aurita and other sallows at dusk ; *Abbots Wood, Battle, Bodiam, Brighton, Guestling, Hayward's Heath, Hassocks, Lewes, Tilgate*

Calymnia trapezina, Linn. Generally common

— pyralina, View. Very rare ; *Bognor* (three specimens taken at 'light' in 1881 by Mr. Lloyd), *Chichester, Cocking, Brighton, Horsham, Lewes, Shoreham* (two specimens taken at 'sugar' by Mr. Vine)

— diffinis, Linn. Both this and the next species seem rather local, though sometimes common where they occur. *Brighton, Chichester, Cocking, Horsham, Lewes, Poling, Shoreham, Worthing*

— affinis, Linn. *Brighton, Chichester,* near *Emsworth, Horsham, Hastings, Lewes Poling, Worthing*

Eremobia ochroleuca, Esp. Common on the downs, where the larvæ may be swept freely from Avena elatior (false oat grass), and the moths found resting on the flower heads of Centaurea scabiosa ; *Brighton,* near *Emsworth, Falmer, Lewes, St. Leonards* once, *Worthing*

Dianthœcia nana, Rott. Locally abundant on the downs among Silene inflata ; *Brighton, Eastbourne,* near *Emsworth, Lewes, Portslade, West Dean Park, Worthing*

— capsincola, Hb. Not uncommon, especially in the southern portion of the county, where the larvæ may be found freely in the capsules of various species of Lychnis growing on the downs, in hedgerows and gardens

— cucubali, Fuessl. Locally common among Silene inflata and S. maritima on the coast and downs

— carpophaga, Bkh. Very abundant on the coast and downs among Silene inflata and S. maritima ; recorded from *Horsham* also

Hecatera chrysozona, Bkh. Rare in the county ; reported from *Brighton, Chichester, Hayward's Heath*

— serena, Fb. Locally abundant

Polia chi, Linn. Mr. Jenner records it as having been once bred from a larva found near *Lewes* (*Macro-Lep. of East Sussex,* p. 12). Devon and Dorset are the only southern counties in which this species is recorded as occurring (Barrett, *Brit. Lep.* iv. 308)

— flavicincta, Fb. Seems somewhat rare in the county generally, though the moths may be found not uncommonly sitting on gate pillars and walls near *Worthing,* and the caterpillars are somewhat abundant in gardens there ; recorded also from *Brighton, Horsham* (once), *Lewes* (once), *Shoreham*

Epunda lichenea, Hb. Very rare ; 'Scarce even in *Sussex*' (Barrett, *Brit. Lep.* iv. 288) ; 'Reported from *Abbots Wood*' (Jenner, *Macro-Lep. of East Sussex,* p. 13)

Aporophyla lutulenta, Bkh. Rare, occurring chiefly in woods ; *Abbots Wood, Brighton, Hayward's Heath, Lewes, Shoreham, Warnham*

— nigra, Hw. Very rare ; reported from *Abbots Wood, Brighton, Lewes, Ringmer*

— viminalis, Fb. Common and generally distributed, especially in woods

Miselia oxyacanthæ, Linn. Common and generally distributed

Agriopis aprilina, Linn. Common in oak woods

Euplexia lucipara, Linn. Generally common

Phlogophora meticulosa, Linn. Very common

Trigonophora flammea, Esp. Always local, apparently now extinct. First met with at *Brighton* in 1855 by Mr. Win ter and Mr. Eagles (*Ent. Ann.* 1856, p. 30). Both Mr. Goss and Mr. Vine state that the species was formerly common in the grounds attached to Bramber Castle, while Mr. Jenner and other entomologists used to take it freely in the neighbourhood of *Lewes*. It has also been taken at *Arundel*, *Battle*, *Findon* and near *Newhaven*.

Aplecta prasina, Fb. Somewhat scarce but widely distributed. Mr. Goss has found it common at 'sugar' in *Abbots Wood* and neighbouring woods. Reported also from *Battle*, *Brighton*, *Charlton Forest*, near *Emsworth*, *Fernhurst*, *Holm Bush*, *Hastings*, *Horsham*, *Laughton*, *Lewes*

— occulta, Linn. Very rare; once at *Battle* (J.H.A.J.), near *Emsworth* (W. M. Christy), *Brighton Racecourse* (A. C. Vine), *Lewes* (Stainton, *Manual*, i. 272), *St. Leonards* (once)

— nebulosa, Hufn. Common in woods

— tincta, Brahm. In woods, not generally abundant; *Abbots Wood*, where Mr. Goss has met with the moth not uncommonly at 'sugar'; *Brighton*, near *Emsworth* (W. M. Christy), *Hastings*, *Horsham*, *Laughton*, *Lewes*, *Tilgate Forest*, where the larvæ may be taken freely from birches in May

— advena, Fb. Rare; once at *Battle* (J. H. A. J.), *Brighton*, near *Emsworth* (W. M. Christy), *Faygate* (once), *Guestling*, *Hayward's Heath*

Hadena adusta, Esp. Not common; *Abbots Wood*, *Ashdown Forest*, downs near *Clayton*, near *Emsworth*, *Hayward's Heath*, *Horsham*, *Lewes*

— protea, Bkh. Common in woods at 'sugar' and ivy bloom

— peregrina, Tr. The following statement appears in *E.M.M.* v. 150: 'Hadena peregrina at *Lewes*—A Noctua which proves to be H. peregrina was taken on the downs at the back of my house by one of my school children—Martha Meek, Lewes, September, 1868.' See also Barrett, *Brit. Lep.* iv. 181

— dentina, Esp. Generally common

— trifolii, Rott. Common in rough places on and near the sea shore, where the larvæ may be found freely among Atriplex and Chenopodium; elsewhere rare; *Bognor*, *Brighton*, *Hastings*, *Hayward's Heath*, *Lewes*, *Pagham*, *Worthing*

— dissimilis, Knoch. Rare; seems almost confined to the neighbourhood of the coast; *Appledram* (J. Anderson), *Brighton*, *Guestling* (once), *Pagham* (D. A.

Edgell), *St. Leonards Forest*, *Thorney* (W. M. Christy)

Hadena oleracea, Linn. Common, especially in gardens

— pisi, Linn. Locally abundant, especially among Genista tinctoria, but rare in many parts of the county; *Abbots Wood*, *Brighton*, *Ditchling Common*, near *Emsworth*, *Fernhurst*, *Guestling*, *Horsham*, *Hayward's Heath*, *Laughton*, *Lewes*, *Midhurst*, woods near *Slindon*

— thalassina, Rott. Generally common in woods

— contigua, Vill. Rare; *Brighton*, near *Emsworth*, *Holm Bush*, *Lewes*, *Tilgate Forest*

— genistæ, Bkh. Not common; *Abbots Wood*, *Brighton*, *Battle*, *Charlton Forest*, near *Emsworth*, *Guestling*, *Horsham*, *Lewes*, *Shoreham*, *St. Leonards Forest*

— areola, Esp. Fairly common and generally distributed

Xylomiges conspicillaris, Linn. Very rare; 'One or two in greenhouses' are stated to have occurred at *Horsham*

Calocampa vetusta, Hb. Apparently scarce; *Brighton*, *Guestling*, *Hayward's Heath*, *Horsham*, *Lewes*, *Pagham*

— exoleta, Linn. Not uncommon and generally distributed

Xylina ornithopus, Rott. Somewhat common and widely distributed

— semibrunnea, Hw. Rare, but widely distributed; *Bramber*, *Chichester*, *Cocking*, *Hastings*, *Hayward's Heath*, *Holm Bush*, *Horsham*, *Lewes*, *Shoreham*, *Tilgate*

— socia, Rott. Widely distributed and common at times at ivy bloom and 'sugar'

— sphinx, Hufn. Generally distributed and probably not uncommon in woods. The moth is rarely taken except at street lamps, and owing to the pertinacity with which the larvæ cling to their food plant they are only beaten in small numbers

Cucullia verbasci, Linn. Common; the larvæ may generally be found in abundance wherever Verbascum occurs

— scrophulariæ, Capieux. Reported from *Brighton*, but perhaps an error; specimens of C. verbasci bred from Scrophularia and of C. lychnitis sometimes do duty in collections for C. scrophulariæ

— lychnitis, Ramb. First noticed in this country by the late Mr. Samuel Stevens, who found the larvæ near *Arundel* about the year 1842 (Barrett, *Brit. Lep.* vi. 75). The larvæ are still found freely from time to time in the district lying between *Arundel* and the western boundary of the county. It has been reported from *Hayward's Heath* and *Horsham*; no station however is recorded in Arnold's *Flora of Sussex* near either of these towns for the food plant of this species (Verbascum nigrum)

Cucullia asteris, Schiff. Not uncommon in woods and on heaths, probably occurring wherever its food plant, golden rod (Solidago virgaurea), is abundant; generally taken in the larval state

— gnaphalii, Hb. Very rare; *Abbots Wood, Hayward's Heath, Tilgate Forest*

— chamomillæ, Schiff. Not uncommon along the coast; apparently rare inland. The moth is sometimes found sitting on gate-posts and palings, and the larvæ may be found tolerably freely on the scentless mayweed (Pyrethrum inodorum); *Appledram, Bognor, Brighton, Battle, Chichester, Eastbourne, Hayward's Heath, Horsham, Lewes, Thorney, Tilgate Forest, Worthing*

— umbratica, Linn. Common and generally distributed

— libatrix, Linn. Generally common

Abrostola tripartita, Hufn. Local; common at *Brighton* and *Lewes*, rare at *Hastings*; occurs also at *Bognor, Chichester*, near *Emsworth, Fernhurst, Horsham, Worthing*

— triplasia, Linn. Apparently rare in *East Sussex*, being only recorded from *Guestling*. In *West Sussex* seems quite common, far more so than the preceding species. The larvæ may be obtained freely in nettle beds, preferring those at the base of a wall or building. *Bury, Chichester, Bognor, Horsham, Worthing*

Plusia chryson, Esp. Very rare; taken by Mr. Robinson near *Hastings* (Hastings list), *Tilgate Forest* (J. H. A. Jenner, *Macro-Lep. of East Sussex*). The late Mr. W. Buckler met with the larvæ near *Emsworth*, but Mr. Christy, who is familiar with its habits in the Cambridgeshire fens, has not succeeded in finding it in Sussex; as however, in addition to Mr. Buckler's experience, Mr. Robinson records the capture of two moths near *Petersfield*, it is not improbable that the species may yet be found more freely in Sussex

— chrysitis, Linn. Locally common

— festucæ, Linn. Very local; occasionally at *Hastings* and *Lewes*, sometimes not uncommon at *Shoreham*; met with by Professor Meldola at *Pagham* in 1900; also recorded from *Horsham*

Plusia iota, Linn. Occurs occasionally in *Ashdown Forest*, at *Bognor, Brighton, Charlton Forest, Cocking*, near *Emsworth, Hastings, Horsham, Hayward's Heath, Linchmere, Lewes, Pagham*

— pulchrina, Hw. Not common; *Ashdown Forest, Brighton, Charlton Forest*, near *Emsworth, Fernhurst, Hastings, Horsham, Hayward's Heath, Lewes*

— gamma, Linn. Generally abundant

— interrogationis, Linn. Mr. J. H. A. Jenner states (*Macro-Lep. of East Sussex*, p. 14): 'I took one specimen at *Battle* in 1872.' This most remarkable capture is referred to *Ent. Ann.* 1872, p. 110, and Barrett, *Brit. Lep.* vi. 133. In the latter the date is given as 1870

— moneta, Fb. This recent addition to the British list was first taken in this county on 2 July, 1890, by Mr. W. M. Christy in a wood near his residence near *Emsworth* (*Ent.* 1890, pp. 254, 344). Mr. Christy has bred other specimens from larvæ found on Aconitum napellus. The species has also since occurred at *Chichester, Lodsworth, Hastings, Uckfield* and other places in the county. It seems to be not uncommon at *Tunbridge Wells*, which is partly in Kent and partly in Sussex

Anarta myrtilli, Linn. Common in all the heathy districts of the county

Heliaca tenebrata, Scop. Widely distributed in the county; *Abbots Wood, Chichester, Battle, Brighton*, near *Emsworth, Fernhurst, Hastings, Hayward's Heath, Horsham, Lewes, Ringmer*

Heliothis peltigera, Schiff. Local and rare generally, though the larvæ are not at times uncommon on restharrow (Ononis arvensis) near *Brighton*; has occurred also at *Bognor, Hastings, Lewes*

— armigera, Hb. Very rare and irregular in appearance. Mr. Vine writes that specimens are occasionally taken at rest on walls; has occurred at *Bognor, Brighton, Chichester, Hastings, Lewes, Worthing, Guestling*

Chariclea umbra, Hufn. Probably occurs wherever restharrow (Ononis arvensis) grows

Acontia luctuosa, Esp. Rare and local; has been taken at *Brighton, Eastbourne, Lewes, Ovingdean*

— lucida, Hufn. Very rare; probably an occasional immigrant. A specimen was taken in a clover field at *Brighton* on 25 August, 1859 (*Ent. Ann.* 1860, p. 131). It passed into the collection of the Rev. Henry Burney, thence at the sale of his collection in November, 1893, into that of Mr. C. A. Briggs, and when the latter collection was dispersed in November, 1896, into that of Mr. E. R. Bankes. Another specimen was taken by Mr. Rolfe at *Eastbourne* in 1880 (J. H. A. Jenner, *Macro-Lep. of East Sussex*, p. 14)

Erastia venustula, Hb. Very local; has been taken in some numbers in *St. Leonards Forest*[1]

— fasciana, L. Not uncommon in woods; *Abbots Wood, Battle, Brighton*, near *Emsworth, Fernhurst, Hastings, Hayward's Heath, Horsham, Plashet Wood*

Phytometra viridaria, Clerck. Generally common

Euclidia mi, Clerck. Generally common, especially on the downs

— glyphica, Linn. Rather local but widely distributed. *Abbots Wood, Brighton, Charlton Forest, Cocking, Cuckmere, Hayward's Heath, Horsham, Laughton, Lewes, Slindon*

Ophiodes lunaris, Schiff. A great rarity; one was taken by Mr. M. S. Blaker near *Lewes* on 17 June, 1873, at 'sugar' (*Ent.* vi. 458); a second was taken near *Brighton* on 20 June, 1874, by Mr. F. Trangmar, also at 'sugar' (*Ent.* vii. 164); a third was taken by a friend of the late Mr. W. H. Tugwell while collecting with him in *Abbots Wood* as it flew up from the undergrowth in May, 1875 (*Ent.* viii. 164); and Mr. Vine states that another specimen was taken at 'sugar' on *Brighton* racecourse by Mr. T. Salvage of Arlington

Catephia alchymista, Schiff. Very rare and probably an immigrant. A female specimen was taken in *Abbots Wood* by Mr. W. Borrer when collecting with Mr. H. Goss on 4 June, 1875 (*Ent.* viii. 164; Barrett, *Brit. Lep.* vi. 232); a second specimen was taken by Mr. Saunders, jun., at *St. Leonards* on 24 June, 1888 (*E.M.M.* xxv. 96 and Barrett, *Brit. Lep.* vi. 232); and a third, a male, now in Mr. Fletcher's collection, was taken in *Abbots Wood* by Mr. T. Salvage on 2 July, 1898. All these were taken at 'sugar'

Catocala fraxini, L. Rare; specimens have been taken from time to time in

different parts of the county; *Arundel, Brighton, Eastbourne, Hastings, Lewes, Winchelsea*

Catocala nupta, L. Common and generally distributed

— sponsa, L. Rare; recorded from *Lewes* (Stainton, *Manual*, i. 316), but no recent captures are known to have been made; taken singly at *Ewhurst* and *Winchelsea* (Barrett, *Brit. Lep.* vi. 262), in *St. Leonards Forest, West Marden*

— promissa, Esp. Rare; *Abbots Wood* (once), *Plashet Wood* (formerly), *Shoreham* (A. C. Vine), *West Marden* one in 1880 (W. M. Christy)

— electa, Bkh. A specimen was taken at 'sugar' at *Shoreham* on 24 September, 1875, by Mr. A. C. Vine. The only other specimen known to have been taken in *Britain* is one taken by Mr. E. Bankes at Corfe Castle, *Dorsetshire*, on 12 September, 1892

Aventia flexula, Schiff. Widely distributed but not common; *Abbots Wood, Battle, Bognor, Broadwater, Brighton, Chichester, Cocking, Horsham, Lewes, Poynings, Ringmer, Uckfield*

Toxocampa pastinum, Tr. Scarce; *Brighton, Cocking, Hassocks* on railway banks, *Hastings, Lewes*, near *Emsworth*

Rivula sericealis, Sc. Generally common

Zanthlognatha grisealis, Hb. Common

— tarsipennalis, Tr. „

— emortualis, Schiff. Mr. Henry Cooke records the capture of a specimen at *Brighton* on 18 June, 1858, by Mr. Pocock (*Ent. Intell.* v. 123)

Herminia cribralis, Hb. Near *Brighton* (Stainton, *Manual*, ii. 132), in *Sussex* (Barrett, *Brit. Lep.* vi. 303)

— derivalis, Hb. Oak woods, local but sometimes abundant; *Abbots Wood, Battle, Guestling, Lewes, Laughton*

Pechipogon barbalis, Clerck. Common in woods

Madopa salicalis, Schiff. Mr. Barrett says of this species: 'Its range with us seems therefore to be limited to *Kent, Surrey, Sussex* and possibly *Hants*' (*Brit. Lep.* vi. 286). He records (loc. cit.) its occurrence at *Petersfield* on the borders of *Sussex* and *Hants*, and also his own captures of specimens at *Haslemere, Surrey*

Bomolocha fontis, Thnb. Very rare; has been taken near *Horsham*

Hypena rostralis, Linn.⎫ Generally common
— proboscidalis, Linn.⎭

Hypenodes tænialis, Hb. Local; sometimes abundant in *Abbots Wood*; taken also at *Brighton, Guestling, Laughton, Lewes*

[1] Very abundant in St. Leonards Forest in June, 1876, 1877.—H. G.

Hypenodes costæstrigalis, Stephen. Local; *Ashdown Forest, Fairlight, Shoreham, Tilgate Forest*

Tholomiges turfosalis, Uck. Very abundant on *Hurston Warren*; occurs also at *Shoreham*

Brephos parthenias, Linn. Somewhat common in the forest district among birch; *Abbots Wood, Battle, Brighton, Cocking, Hastings, Horsham, Plashet Wood, Tilgate Forest*

— notha, Hb. Sometimes common in *Abbots Wood*; has also occurred near *Brighton* and *Battle*

GEOMETRÆ

Urapteryx sambucaria, Linn. Generally common

Epione parallelaria, Schiff. The capture of a specimen at *Arundel* on 29 August, 1879, by himself is recorded by Mr. Sidney Olliff (*Ent.* xiii. 311). It is difficult to account for the occurrence of this specimen of this extremely local insect in a locality which does not seem to be a station for its food-plant, Salix repens

— apiciaria, Schiff. Not uncommon

— advenaria, Hb. Local; *Abbots Wood, Battle, Bepton Down, Charlton Forest, Fernhurst, Hastings,* near *Lewes, St. Leonards Forest, Tortington Woods*

Rumia luteolata, Linn. Generally abundant

Venilia macularia, Linn. Common in woods

Angerona prunaria, Linn. Common in woods in *East Sussex* and in *Charlton Forest* in the western division.

Metrocampa margaritata, Linn. Common in woods

Ellopia prosapiaria, Linn. Among Scotch firs; *Brighton, Battle, Fernhurst, Hayward's Heath, Horsham, Midhurst, Stedham, Tilgate Forest*

Eurymene dolabraria, Linn. In woods; generally distributed

Pericallia syringaria, Linn. Generally distributed but not abundant

Selenia bilunaria, Esp. Generally common

— lunaria, Schiff. Not common; *Abbots Wood, Battle, Brighton, Bury Hill, Guestling, Hayward's Heath, Horsham, Tilgate Forest*

— tetralunaria, Hufn. Not common; *Bognor, Brighton, Horsham, Hastings, Hayward's Heath, Tilgate Forest*

Odontoptera bidentata, Clerck. ⎱ Generally
Crocallis elinguaria, Linn. ⎰ common

Eugonia autumnaria, Wernb. Rare; the first specimen taken in the county was taken at *Brighton* by Mr. Winter (*Ent.*

Ann. 1856, p. 47) on 15 September, 1855; another was taken there in 1862 (Barrett, *Brit. Lep.* vii. 60). A few specimens have been taken during the last few years at *Chichester* by Mr. Anderson and eggs obtained, and others at *Bognor* by Professor Meldola and Messrs. Guermonprez and Fletcher

— alniaria, Linn. Widely distributed and not uncommon at street lamps; *Abbots Wood, Bognor, Brighton, Battle, Chichester, Guestling, Horsham, Hayward's Heath, Lewes, Tilgate Forest*

— fuscantaria, Hw. Widely distributed; *Abbots Wood, Battle, Brighton, Bognor, Chichester, Eastbourne, Guestling, Hayward's Heath, Horsham, Lewes*

— erosaria, Hb. *Abbots Wood, Brighton, Charlton Forest, Guestling, Hayward's Heath, Horsham, Linchmere, Lewes, Worthing*

— quercinaria, Hufn. Everywhere common

Himera pennaria, Linn. ⎱ Common and gene-
Phigalia pedaria, Fb. ⎰ rally distributed

Nyssia hispidaria, Fb. Scarce; *Abbots Wood, Horsham, Ringmer, Tilgate*

Biston hirtaria, Clerck. Scarce; reported from *Brighton* and *Tilgate Forest*

Amphidasys strataria, Hufn. Not uncommon, especially at street lamps

— betularia, Linn. ⎱ Common and gene-
Hemerophila abruptaria, Thnb. ⎰ rally distributed

Cleora angularia, Thnb. Very rare if not extinct in the county; *Brighton* (Stainton, *Manual,* ii. 24); the late Mr. William Tester used to take it in *Tilgate Forest,* and Mr. Merrifield met with it some years ago at *Holm Bush* near *Henfield*

— jubata, Thnb. Taken but not commonly in *Charlton Forest* by the Rev. C. D. Ash

— lichenaria, Hufn. Common and generally distributed

Boarmia repandata, Linn. Generally common; the variety conversaria, Hb., has occurred at *Battle* and *Lewes*

— gemmaria, Brahm. Generally common

— ribeata, Clerck. Very local; *Charlton Forest,* larvæ beaten from young spruce firs by the Rev. C. D. Ash; occurs also at *Stoughton* and *Tilgate Forest*

— cinctaria, Schiff. Local and rare; *Brighton, Battle, Tilgate Forest* (Barrett, *Brit. Lep.* vii. 207)

— roboraria, Schiff. In oak woods, rare; *Abbots Wood, Charlton Forest, Hayward's Heath, Holm Bush, Laughton, St. Leonards Forest, Westfield*

Boarmia consortaria, Fb. Not uncommon in woods

Tephrosia consonaria, Hb. In woods, local ; *Ashdown Forest, Abbots Wood, Battle, Brighton, Charlton Forest, Falmer, Fernhurst, Guestling, Hayward's Heath, Tilgate Forest*

— crepuscularia, Hb.⎱ Common and widely
— biundularia, Esp. ⎰ distributed

— luridata, Bkh. Not uncommon in woods in *East Sussex* ; taken by Mr. Barrett at *Fernhurst* in the western division

— punctularia, Hb. Rather common and generally distributed in woods among birch

Gnophos obscuraria, Hb. Locally abundant. The form on the chalk is much lighter in colour than that found on the clay or sand, and a still lighter form (var. calceata, Stgr.) is found somewhat rarely at *Lewes. Brighton, Crowborough, Eastbourne, Fernhurst, Hastings, Lewes, Storrington, Tilgate Forest*

Pseudoterpna pruinata, Hufn. Common and generally distributed

Geometra papilionaria, Linn. Widely distributed ; *Ashdown Forest, Abbots Wood, Battle, Bosham, Brighton, Cocking, Chichester, Guestling, Hastings, Hayward's Heath, Horsham, Linchmere, Plashet Wood, Tilgate Forest*

— vernaria, Hb. Common on the chalk among Clematis vitalba

Phorodesma bajularia, Hufn. Not rare in *Abbots Wood* ; occurs also at *Battle, Brighton, Guestling, Hayward's Heath, Horsham, Lewes, Worthing*

Thalera fimbrialis, Scop. The capture of a specimen by his son on a slope near *Beachy Head* on 7 August 1902 is recorded by Mr. Charles Capper (*E.M.M.* xxxix. 216)

Iodis lactearia, Linn. ⎱ Generally com-
Hemithea strigata, Müll. ⎰ mon

Zonosoma porata, Fb.⎱ Not uncommon in
— punctaria, Linn. ⎰ oak woods

— linearia, Hb. In beech woods ; local, but widely distributed

— annulata, Schulze. Common among maple (Acer campestre)

— orbicularia, Hb. Occasionally at *Abbots Wood, Battle, Brighton, Guestling, Hayward's Heath, Holme Bush, Lewes, St. Leonards* and *Tilgate Forests*

— pendularia, Clerck. Generally distributed and rather common among birch

Hyria muricata, Hufn. Rare and local ; *St. Leonards* and *Tilgate Forests*

Asthena luteata, Schiff. *Abbots Wood, Battle, Bramber, Cocking, Fernhurst, Guestling,* *Hayward's Heath, Horsham, Laughton, Lewes, Tilgate Forest*

Asthena candidata, Schiff. Generally common in woods

— testaceata, Don. Not uncommon in woods and widely distributed

Eupisteria obliterata, Hufn. Not uncommon among alders

Acidalia rubiginata, Hufn. One specimen taken at 'light' by the Rev. E. N. Bloomfield on 3 August, 1872 (*E.M.M.* ix. 218)

— dimidiata, Hufn. Generally common

— bisetata, Hufn.   „   „

— trigeminata, Hw. Not common ; *Abbots Wood, Charlton Forest, Horsham, Tilgate Forest*

— rusticata, Fb. Very local ; recorded from *Brighton* and *Lewes*

— dilutaria, Hb. Locally abundant ; *Eastbourne, Fernhurst, Hailsham, Hastings, Lewes, Worthing*

— virgularia, Hb. Common and generally distributed

— ornata, Scop. Very rare, near *Hastings* and *Tilgate*

— marginepunctata, Göze. Locally abundant, especially on the chalk ; *Arundel, Brighton, Bognor, Clymping, Eastbourne, Hastings, Horsham, Lewes, St. Leonards*

— straminata, Tr. Very rare ; one at *Eastbourne, St. Leonards Forest*

— subsericeata, Hw. Local ; *Abbots Wood, Battle, Clymping Sandhills, Ditchling Common, Guestling, Laughton, Plashet Wood*

— immutata, L. In damp places, very local ; *Hurston Warren, Rackham, St. Leonards Forest, Rye*

— remutaria, Hb. Very common in woods

— immorata, L. Very local ; found near *Lewes* in 1887 by Mr. C. H. Morris and taken there by him and others every year since. A specimen had been met with many years before by Mr. Desvignes and passed into Mr. S. Stevens' collection, being regarded as a variety of Strenia clathrata (Barrett, *Brit. Lep.* viii. 51). No other British locality is known

— strigilaria, Hb. *Hastings* once

— imitaria, Hb. Locally common ; *Abbots Wood, Battle, Bognor, Brighton, Chichester, Fernhurst, Horsham, Hastings, Lewes, Tilgate Forest*

— emutaria, Hb. Probably occurs in wet places in all the marshes near the coast ; *Bognor, Clymping, Lewes, Shoreham, Thorney*

Acidalia aversata, Linn. Generally abundant
— inornata, Hw. Not common; *Abbots Wood, Brighton, Hastings, Laughton, Lewes, Uckfield*
— emarginata, Linn. Locally common; *Abbots Wood, Battle, Brighton, Chichester, Cocking, Guestling, Rackham, Shoreham*
Timandra amata, Linn. Common
Cabera pusaria, Linn. Generally common; the form rotundaria, Hw., has occurred at *Brighton, Hastings, Tilgate* and *Uckfield*. It is generally bred in captivity from collected larvæ
— exanthemata, Scop. Generally common
Bapta temerata, Hb. Generally distributed
— bimaculata, Fb. Not common; *Brighton, Charlton Forest, Cocking, Fernhurst, Hastings, Hayward's Heath, Horsham, Lewes, Worthing*
Aleucis pictaria, Curt. Local and rare; *Bepton Down, Horsham, Lewes* formerly (Stainton, *Manual*, ii. 53), *Tilgate Forest*
Macaria alternaria, Hb. Very rare; *Fairlight, Tilgate Forest*
— notata, L. Woods, scarce; *Abbots Wood, Battle, Brighton, Hastings, Hayward's Heath, Heathfield, St. Leonards* and *Tilgate Forests*
— liturata, Clerck. Among Scotch fir, not common; *Ashdown Forest, Brighton, Bexhill, Fairlight, Fernhurst, Hayward's Heath, Horsham, Laughton, Tilgate Forest*
Halias wavaria, Linn. A not uncommon garden insect
Strenia clathrata, Linn. Locally common
Panagra petraria, Hb. Common among bracken in heathy places
Numeria pulveraria, Linn. Not uncommon in woods
Scodiona fagaria, Thnb. *Black Down*, near *Fernhurst, Hurston Warren* near *Amberley*
Ematurga atomaria, Linn. Generally common on heaths and in woods
Bupalus piniarius, Linn. Common in woods among Scotch fir
Minoa murinata, Scop. Local and rare; near *Brighton, Charlton Forest* in open coppices, *Hastings, Lewes*
Scoria lineata, Scop. Mr. Herbert Goss, who is familiar with this species in its well-known Kentish localities, took a specimen in a small wood between *Hailsham* and *Polegate* on 25 June, 1875
Sterrha sacraria, Linn. Very rare, probably only an occasional immigrant; specimens have been taken at *Brighton, Lewes* and *Shoreham*

Aspilates strigillaria, Hb. Local; *Abbots Wood, Bexhill, Brighton, Cocking, Hayward's Heath, Laughton, St. Leonards* and *Tilgate Forests*
— ochrearia, Rossi. Local but sometimes not uncommon near the coast and on the downs; *Bepton* and *Levin Downs*, near *Cuckmere Haven, Eastbourne, Lewes Downs, Ovingdean Slopes*, coast and downs near *Shoreham*
— gilvaria, Fb. Rare and local; *Brighton, Horsham*, near *Polegate, Shoreham*
Abraxas grossulariata, Linn. Abundant everywhere. Both in Cambridge and Sussex this species has taken to feeding on the evergreen Euonymus so common in gardens
— sylvata, Scop. Very local but sometimes abundant where it occurs; *Chichester, West Dean, Fairlight* once, near *Lewes, Withdean*
Ligdia adustata, Schiff. Generally common among spindle (Euonymus europæus)
Lomaspilis marginata, L. Very common in lanes and woods
Pachycnemia hippocastania, Hb. Locally abundant on heaths; *Brighton, Fernhurst, Hastings, Linchmere, St. Leonards* and *Tilgate Forests*
Hybernia rupicapraria, Hb. Abundant everywhere
— leucophearia, Schiff. Locally abundant in oak woods in both *East* and *West Sussex*
— aurantiaria, Esp. Generally distributed and not uncommon
— marginaria, Bkh. Generally common
— defoliaria, Clerck.   ,,   ,,
Anisopteryx æscularia, Schiff. Generally common
Cheimatobia brumata, Linn. Everywhere common
— boreata, Hb. Local; not uncommon in *Tilgate Forest*; *Brighton* and *Lewes*, rare
Aporabia dilutata, Bkh. Generally common
Larentia didymata   ,,   ,,
— multistrigaria, Hw. Common on the downs; *Brighton, Cocking, Fernhurst, Horsham, Lewes, Shoreham*
— viridaria, Fb. Abundant
Emmelesia affinitata, Steph. Common and widely distributed
— alchemillata, Linn. Locally abundant; near *Amberley, Abbots Wood, Bognor, Brighton, Charlton Forest, Fernhurst, Hastings, Horsham, Shoreham, Tilgate Forest*
— albulata, Schiff. Not generally common; *Barcombe, Bognor, Horsham, Hailsham, Mundham, Shoreham*

INSECTS

Emmelesia flavofasciata, Thnb. Somewhat common in woods and hedgerows ; *Battle, Brighton, Cocking, Chichester, Fernhurst, Flansham, Hailsham, Hastings, Hayward's Heath, Lewes, Tilgate Forest*

— unifasciata, Hw. Locally abundant on the downs among Bartsia odontites, from the capsules of which the larvæ may be obtained in great numbers ; *Berwick, Brighton, Crowhurst, Cuckmere, Eastbourne, Guestling* (once), *Lewes, Sompting*

— adæquata, Bkh. The Rev. C. D. Ash records the capture of two specimens in 1878 on the borders of *Charlton Forest* (*Trans. Chichester and West Sussex Nat. Hist. Soc.* 1886–7, p. 75). The only English counties given by Mr. Barrett as habitats for this species are Cumberland and Durham (*Brit. Lep.* viii. 243)

Eupithecia venosata, Fb. Locally abundant on the downs among Silene inflata ; *Brighton, Chichester, Cocking, Lewes, Shoreham, Worthing*

— insigniata, Hb. Recorded by Mr. Stainton (*Manual*, ii. 84) as having occurred at *Lewes* ; *Rye* in 1901

— linariata, Fb. Local, larvæ sometimes common on Linaria vulgaris ; *Amberley, Brighton, Fernhurst, Hastings, Hayward's Heath, Horsham, Lewes, Shoreham*

— pulchellata, Stph. Not uncommon among foxglove (Digitalis purpurea) ; *Abbots Wood, Brighton, Charlton Forest, Crowborough, Eastbourne, Fernhurst, Guestling, Horsham, Laughton, Tilgate Forest*

— oblongata, Thnbg. Generally common

— succenturiata, Linn. Rare ; *Brighton, Chichester, Guestling, Hayward's Heath, Lewes*

— subfulvata, Hw. Not common ; *Bognor, Cocking, Ditchling Common, Guestling, Lewes, Worthing*

— scabiosata, Bkh. Local ; *Arundel Park, Horsham*, on the coast near *Lancing*

— plumbeolata, Hw. Common in woods among cow wheat (Melampyrum pratense)

— isogrammaria, H.S. Common on the downs among Clematis vitalba ; *Bognor, Brighton, Cocking, Goring, Lewes*

— satyrata, Hb. Very local ; *Abbots Wood, Brighton, Cocking, Guestling, Laughton.* At the last named locality Mr. Jenner records the occurrence of the heath or northern form

— castigata, Hb. Generally common

Eupithecia trisignaria, H.S. Woods between *Arundel* and *Slindon*

— virgaureata, Dbld. Rare ; *Abbots Wood, Hastings, Horsham*

— fraxinata, Crewe. Local and scarce ; sometimes found resting on palings near ash trees ; *Bognor, Brighton, Fernhurst, Guestling, Lewes*

— pimpinellata, Hb. Common and generally distributed, especially on the downs, among burnet saxifrage (Pimpinella saxifraga)

— valerianata, Hb. *Clapham Woods* and probably elsewhere among wild valerian

— pusillata, Fb. Local ; *Horsham, Laughton, St. Leonards* and *Tilgate Forests* ; among larch

— irriguata, Hb. Rare and local ; *Abbots Wood, Brighton, Burgess Hill, Fernhurst, Guestling, Laughton, St. Leonards Forest*

— denotata, Hb. Very local, but common where it occurs among Campanula trachelium ; *Lewes, South Stoke* near *Arundel*

— indigata, Hb. Very local ; *Brighton, Highwood, Bexhill, Fernhurst, Tilgate Forest*

— distinctaria, H.S. Rare ; *Brighton, Lewes, Wolstonbury*

— nanata, Hb. Common on heaths throughout the county

— subnotata, Hb. Local, but not uncommon in waste places along the shore ; *Bognor, Brighton, Horsham, Laughton, Lewes, Pett, Shoreham*

— vulgata, Hw. Abundant everywhere

— albipunctata, Hw. Not uncommon in woods among wild angelica ; *Abbots Wood, Goring Woods, Guestling, Hastings, Laughton, Lewes, Warrengore*

— expallidata, Gn. Not generally common, though the larvæ are sometimes very abundant in *Abbots Wood* on golden rod ; reported also from *Brighton, Fairlight, Lewes, Tilgate Forest*

— absinthiata, Clerck. This usually abundant insect seems to be rather local in its distribution in *Sussex* ; It is reported from *Bognor, Cocking, Ditchling Common, Ford, Guestling, Lewes, Tilgate*

— minutata, Hb. On heaths ; local ; *Fernhurst, Hayward's Heath, Lewes, Midhurst Common*

— assimilata, Gn. Common among currants and hops

— tenuiata, Hb. Apparently rare ; *Guestling, Slindon Common, Tarring*

— inturbata, Hb. Very local ; abundant in *Arundel Park*, and occurs also near *Lewes* among maple

Eupithecia lariciata, Frr. Not uncommon among larch ; *Ashburnham, Charlton Forest, Horsham, Laughton, Lewes, Slindon Common, Tilgate Forest, Wych Cross*

— abbreviata, Stph. Widely distributed in oak woods ; *Abbots Wood, Brighton, Fernhurst, Guestling, Horsham, Laughton, Lewes, Slindon*

— dodoneata, Gn. In woods and lanes ; not common ; *Abbots Wood, Bognor* among evergreen oak (Quercus ilex), *Guestling.* See also *E.M.M.* xxxviii. 231

— exiguata, Hb. Common and generally distributed

— sobrinata, Hb. Very abundant on *Cissbury* and *Salvington Downs* and doubtless elsewhere in *West Sussex*, where its food plant is very plentiful. East of *Brighton* the juniper is very rare and consequently the moth, which is recorded from *Brighton* and *Guestling*

— togata, Hb. Met with by the late Mr. W. H. Tugwell in *Tilgate Forest.* Fallen cones eaten by larvæ which may have been of this species have been noticed in a wood near *Slindon*

— pumilata, Hb. Common and widely distributed

— coronata, Hb. Common and widely distributed, especially on the downs, among clematis, hemp agrimony and other plants

— rectangulata, Linn. Common among apple in gardens and elsewhere

— debiliata, Hb. Rare and local ; reported by Mr. Price as occurring near *Horsham*

Lobophora sexalisata, Hb. Rare ; *Abbots Wood, Battle, Brighton, Fernhurst, Holm Bush, Guestling, Laughton, Linchmere*

— halterata, Hufn. Local and rare ; *Abbots Wood, Brighton, Chichester, Cocking, Fernhurst, Lewes, Linchmere, Tilgate Forest*

— viretata, Hb. Local and rare ; *Bognor, Brighton, Ecclesbourne, Fernhurst, Hastings, Lewes, Worthing*

— carpinata, Bkh. Not uncommon ; *Abbots Wood, Brighton, Fernhurst, Frant, Hastings, Hayward's Heath, Horsham, Isfield, Laughton, Lewes, Linchmere, Tilgate Forest*

— polycommata, Hb. Local but often abundant where it does occur. The larvæ may be found plentifully by searching for leaves of privet with ovate pieces eaten from their edges ; *Brighton, Emsworth, Findon, Lewes, Polegate*

Thera juniperata, Linn. Very abundant on *Cocking Downs, Cissbury* and *Salvington Downs,* and no doubt elsewhere in *West Sussex,* where juniper is abundant ; not recorded from the eastern division, where its food plant is very rare

— cognata, Thnb. Recorded from *Brighton, Hayward's Heath* and *Tilgate Forest,* but the records are doubtful. The simulata of Mrs. Merrifield's list (*Nat. Hist. Brighton,* p. 208) marked as abundant in the Weald is possibly the species now known as T. variata, Schiff.

— variata, Schiff. Generally common among Scotch fir

— firmata, Hb. Rare ; *Brighton, Bognor, Fernhurst, Hastings, Horsham*

— ruberata, Frr. Found by Mr. A. C. Vine in lanes and by roadsides near Poynings

— autumnalis, Ström. Rather rare ; *Abbots Wood, Brighton, Guestling, Horsham, Tilgate Forest*

— sordidata, Fb. Generally common

Melanthia bicolorata, Hufn. Local but not uncommon ; *Abbots Wood, Battle, Bognor, Donnington, Guestling, Hayward's Heath, Horsham, Lewes, Poynings*

— ocellata, Linn. Generally common

— albicillata, Linn. Not uncommon in woods in *East Sussex* ; occurs in *Abbots Wood* and *Charlton Forest,* also at *Fernhurst* and *Withdean*

Melanippe hastata, Linn. In woods, local ; formerly very abundant in *Abbots Wood* and the neighbouring woods (H.G.), but very scarce of late years ; recorded also from *Battle, Fernhurst, Hastings, Hayward's Heath, Laughton, Lewes, Tilgate Forest*

— tristata, L. Very rare ; reported from *Horsham,* 'gardens very scarce,' a somewhat curious habitat for an insect which occurs ' usually on heaths in mountain districts, but occasionally in fir woods and in the north flitting about the borders of farms' (Barrett, *Brit. Lep.* viii. 97)

— procellata, Fb. Abundant and widely distributed among traveller's joy (Clematis vitalba), especially on and near the downs

— unangulata, Hw. Widely distributed and not uncommon ; *Abbots Wood, Battle, Brighton, Chichester, Cocking, Fernhurst, Falmer, Guestling, Hayward's Heath, Horsham, Piltdown, Rackham, Tilgate Forest, Uckfield*

— rivata, Hb. Locally common ; *Abbots Wood, Bognor, Brighton, Cocking, East-*

bourne, *Goring, Hastings, Hayward's Heath, Horsham, Lewes*

Melanippe sociata, Bkh.   Generally common

— montanata, Schiff.   „   „

— galiata, Hb. Local but not uncommon in chalk pits ; *Brighton, Cocking, Eastbourne, Goring, Hastings, Hayward's Heath, Lewes*

— fluctuata, Linn.   Very abundant

Anticlea cucullata, Hufn.   Very local near *Amberley, Chichester, Eastbourne, Emsworth* and *West Dean.*   The pretty and somewhat conspicuous larvæ may be found in the middle of August in the daytime extended bridge-like between the branchlets of the inflorescence of Galium mullugo growing in hedgerows

— rubidata, Fb.   Locally common ; *Bognor, Bramber, Brighton, Chichester, Cocking, Fairlight, Horsham, Lewes*

— badiata, Hb.   Common among wild rose

— nigrofasciata, Goeze.   Widely distributed but not common ; *Abbots Wood, Brighton, Cocking, Fernhurst, Hastings, Hayward's Heath, Horsham, Lewes, Uckfield*

Coremia designata, Rott.   Generally common, especially in woods

— ferrugata, Cl.   ⎱ Common and generally
— unidentaria, Hw. ⎰ distributed

Camptogramma bilineata, L.   Abundant everywhere

— fluviata, Hb.   Rare ; occasionally taken at *Blatchington, Brighton, Battle, Guestling, Goring, St. Leonards*

Phibalapteryx tersata, Hb.   Locally common among traveller's joy (Clematis vitalba) ; *Battle, Brighton, Chichester, Cocking, Guestling, Goring, Lewes*

— vittata, Bkh.   Very local ; *Amberley, Hastings, Hayward's Heath, Horsham, Lewes*

— vitalbata, Hb.   Local but sometimes not uncommon among traveller's joy (Clematis vitalba) ; *Abbots Wood, Bognor, Brighton, Chichester, Cocking, Goring, Hastings, Lewes, North Stoke*

Triphosa dubitata, Linn.   Local, but the larvæ may sometimes be found abundantly where the buckthorn occurs; *Abbots Wood, Brighton, Cocking, Chichester, Hastings, Horsham, Lewes, Salvington Down*

Scotosia certata, Hb.   Very rare ; Mr. Vine took three specimens at *Hailsham* some few years ago, and it is also recorded from *Tilgate Forest*

— undulata, Linn. In woods, scarce ; *Ashdown Forest, Abbots Wood, Battle, Brighton, Bosham, Charlton Forest, Guestling,*

Holm Bush, *Hayward's Heath, Horsham, Lewes*

Scotosia vetulata, Schiff.   Locally common among buckthorn ; *Brighton, Lewes, Salvington Down, Tilgate Forest*

— rhamnata, Schiff.   Occurs among buckthorn in the same localities as the last species

Cidaria psittacata, Hufn.   Not common ; *Abbots Wood, Brighton, Fernhurst, Frant, Horsham, Lewes, Tilgate Forest*

— miata, L.   Generally common

— picata, Hb.   Woods, rather scarce ; *Abbots Wood, Ashdown Forest, Battle, Brighton, Charlton Forest, Guestling, Horsham, Tilgate Forest*

— corylata, Thnbg.   Generally common in woods

— truncata, Hufn.   Generally common

— immanata, Hw.   „   „

— suffumata, Hb.   Widely distributed but not common

— silaceata, Hb.   Locally common ; *Battle, Brighton, Charlton Forest, Clapham Woods, Fernhurst, Guestling, Horsham, Lewes, Poling, Tilgate Forest*

— prunata, Linn.   Common in gardens

— testata, Linn.   Generally common

— populata, Linn.   *Brighton* (Stainton's *Manual*, ii. 114), *Shoreham* (A. C. Vine)

— fulvata, Forst.   Generally common

— dotata, L.   Generally distributed, but not common

— associata, Bkh.   Local and not common ; *Abbots Wood, Bognor, Brighton, Guestling, Horsham, Lewes, Shoreham, Tilgate Forest, Worthing*

Pelurga comitata, Linn.   Common and generally distributed near the coast, seems less so inland ; *Bognor, Brighton, Chichester, Hastings, Horsham, Lewes, Worthing*

Eubolia cervinata, Schiff.   Not uncommon among mallow ; *Bognor, Brighton, Bramber, Chichester, Clymping, Eastbourne, Hastings, Horsham, Lewes*

— mœniata, Sc.   A specimen is recorded to have been taken 11 August, 1873, near *East Grinstead*, by Mr. W. Thomas (*Ent.* vi. 516).   Very few specimens have been recorded as captured in the British Isles, and supposing no errors in identification have occurred they are probably but chance immigrants

— limitata, Sc.   Generally common

— plumbaria, Fb.   Locally common, especially on heaths

— bipunctaria, Schiff. Abundant on the chalk

Mesotype virgata, Rott.   Locally abundant on the downs and coast sandhills

Anaitis plagiata, Linn. Generally common among St. John's wort

Chesias spartiata, Fuesl. Probably not uncommon where its food-plant, broom, grows freely ; *Brighton, Guestling, Hastings, Horsham, Isfield*

— rufata, Fb. Very local among broom (Cytisus scoparius) and dyer's greenweed (Genista tinctoria) ; *Battle, Brighton, Ditchling Common, Hayward's Heath, Horsham*

Tanagra atrata, Linn. Very local, but abundant where it does occur ; *Abbots Wood, Brighton, Hayward's Heath, Slaugham*

PYRALIDES

Cledeobia angustalis, Schiff. Locally abundant on commons, downs, and on sandhills and shingles near the coast

Aglossa pinguinalis, Linn. Common in stables and similar buildings

Pyralis costalis, Fb. Generally distributed and sometimes very abundant

— glaucinalis, Linn. Occurs at *Bognor, Brighton, Battle,* near *Emsworth, Hastings, Lewes, Shoreham* ; being occasionally taken at 'light' and at 'sugar'

— farinalis, Linn. Generally distributed, especially in stables and similar buildings

Scoparia ambigualis, Tr. Generally common

— basistrigalis, Knaggs. Probably widely distributed especially in beech woods on the chalk ; *Henley Hill* near *Fernhurst* (Barrett) ; woods near *Arundel* and *Slindon* ; *Wolstonbury,* not uncommon on beech trunks (Vine)

— cembræ, Hw. *Arundel, Battle, Hastings, Houghton* chalk-pit, *Lewes, Salvington,* on the shingles near *Southwick*

— dubitalis, Hb. Very abundant, especially on the downs and near the coast. In Mr. South's collection were some specimens of the form ingratella, Knaggs, from Eastbourne

— murana, Curt. *Lewes* (Jenner)

— lineola, Curt. *Bognor, Eastbourne, Lewes* (*Manual,* ii. 163) ; *Worthing,* where the larvæ may be found in great abundance feeding on lichens growing in old hedges and post and rail fences

— frequentella, St. Common and generally distributed

— cratægella, Hb. Sometimes abundant in *Arundel Park* ; occurs also on *Rackham Common*

— resinea, Hw. *Arundel Park, Lewes* (*Manual,* ii. 162), *Flansham* near *Bognor* ; *Shoreham,* where it comes freely to 'sugar' and is often very abundant and variable

— truncicolella, St. Very abundant near *Amberley* and *Storrington,* where the larvæ and pupæ may be found in moss on old thatch

Scoparia angustea, Stph. Apparently rather local ; *Amberley, Arundel Park, Hastings, Camber Sandhills, Rye, Sompting*

— pallida, Stph. Locally abundant in damp places, ditch by side of *Arun* near *Ford, Henfield Common, Lewes,* coast near *Southwick, Shoreham*

Nomophila noctuella, Schiff. Generally common and in some years very abundant

Odontia dentalis, Schiff. Widely distributed along the coast and in some places abundant ; *Brighton, Eastbourne, Hastings, St. Leonards, Pagham Harbour, Southwick, Shoreham* ; formerly common at *Copperas Gap* near *Portslade* (H.G.)

Pyrausta aurata, Sc. Common and widely distributed on the downs among Origanum vulgare

— purpuralis, Linn. Widely distributed and not uncommon among Prunella vulgaris

— ostrinalis, Hb. *Abbots Wood, Arundel, Brighton, Falmer, Lewes, St. Leonards*

Herbula cespitalis, Schiff. Generally distributed and abundant

Ennychia cingulata, Linn. Abundant at *Moulescombe Pit* near *Brighton* ; occurs also on downs near *Eastbourne* and *Lewes*

— nigrata, Sc. Locally common on the downs among Asperula cynanchica ; *Arundel Park, Brighton, Cocking,* near *Emsworth, Lewes, Slindon*

— funebris, Ström. Very local ; *Brighton, Lewes* (*Manual,* ii. 140). Sometimes abundant in *Abbots Wood* ; also recorded from *Battle, Guestling, Laughton, Plashet Wood*

Agrotera nemoralis, Sc. Rare and very local ; formerly common in *Abbots Wood* (abundant in the 'seventies'—H.G.) now very rare there if not extinct ; has occurrred also at *Battle, Guestling,* and *Holm Bush* near *Henfield* (*Manual,* ii. 141)

Endotricha flammealis, Schiff. Common in woods and locally so on the coast ; *Abbots Wood, Battle, Bognor, Clymping Common, Eastbourne,* near *Emsworth, Hastings, Laughton, Plashet Wood, Rackham, Slindon Woods,* coast near *Southwick*

Eurrhypara urticata, Linn. Everywhere common among nettles

Scopula lutealis, Hb. Recorded from *Hastings* doubtfully, and *Lewes,* but apparently rare in the eastern division of the county, in the western widely distributed in the chalk district ; *Botolphs, Cissbury, Cocking, Salvington, Shoreham*

Scopula olivalis, Schiff. Everywhere common
— prunalis, Schiff. „ „
— ferrugalis, Hb. Fairly common and double brooded ; *Bognor, Brighton, Eastbourne, Fernhurst, Hastings, Lewes, Worthing*

Mecyna polygonalis, Hb. Probably an immigrant. A specimen taken in October, 1855, by Mr. Mitten at *Hurstpierpoint* was included in the sale of the late Mr. S. Stevens' collection in March, 1900, and is now in the collection of Mr. E. R. Bankes of Corfe Castle, Dorsetshire

Botys pandalis, Hb. Widely distributed in woods ; *Abbots Wood, Battle, Brighton,* near *Emsworth, Eartham, Hastings, Lewes*
— flavalis, Schiff. Abundant on the chalk near *Brighton, Eastbourne* and *Lewes* (Goss) ; a single specimen on the *Clymping sandhills* in 1889 (Fletcher)
— hyalinalis, Hb. Very local ; *Abbots Wood,* near *Emsworth*
— ruralis, Scop. Everywhere common
— fuscalis, Schiff. Locally abundant among Melampyrum, Pedicularis and Rhinanthus
— asinalis, Hb. ' *Sussex* to *Devon* and *Pembroke* ' (Meyrick, *Handbook*, p. 417), *Eastbourne* (Shearwood)

Ebulea erocealis, Hb. Widely distributed among Conyza squarrosa and Inula dysenterica and not uncommon
— verbascalis, Schiff. Rare ; reported only from *St. Leonards*
— sambucalis, Schiff. Everywhere common
— stachydalis, Germ. Locally abundant among Stachys sylvatica ; *Brighton, Bramber,* near *Emsworth, High Down* near *Goring, Hastings*

Spilodes stiticalis, Linn. *Brighton* (*Manual,* ii. 153), *Cissbury,* one specimen (Fletcher), *Eastbourne*
— palealis, Schiff. Coast near *Brighton, Bevendean Slopes, Cissbury, Eastbourne* (*Shearwood*), *Hastings, Worthing*
— verticalis, Linn. Apparently not common ; *Brighton* (*Manual,* ii. 153), *Eastbourne*

Pionea forficalis, Linn. Everywhere common

Orobena straminalis, Hb. Apparently scarce ; *Arundel Park, Brighton* commonly (*Manual,* ii. 152), *Bramber, Battle, Eastbourne, Guestling*

Perinephele lancealis, Schiff. Not common ; *Abbots Wood, Brighton* (*Manual,* ii. 149), *Emsworth, Battle, Guestling*

Margarodes unionalis, Hb. An occasional immigrant. A specimen taken at *Brighton* was in the late Mr. Stevens' collection, and at the sale thereof passed into the possession of Mr. Sydney Webb. Another, a male, was taken in *Bognor* in 1895 by Mr. Guermonprez

Diasemia litterata, Sc. The late Mr. Samuel Stevens on more than one occasion told me that many years ago he met with this species on *Bury Hill* near *Arundel.* I know of no recent captures in *West Sussex* (W.H.B.F.) ; *Eastbourne* (R. Adkin)
— ramburialis, Dup. Probably an occasional immigrant. Once at *Landport* near *Lewes* (G. H. Verrall)

Stenia punctalis, Schiff. Very local ; *Eastbourne, Falmer, Hastings, Lewes*

Cataclysta lemnata, Linn. Very common, flying over ponds and ditches ; may be bred from old flower stems of Alisma plantago collected in May

Paraponyx stratiotata, Linn. Locally abundant at *Lewes* and *North Mundham,* and occurs also at *Eastbourne* and *Hastings*

Hydrocampa nympheata, Linn. Common and widely distributed, especially in marshy districts
— stagnata, Don. Locally common ; *Arundel Park,* near *Emsworth, Hastings, Lewes, Shoreham*

Acentropus niveus, Olivier. Rare ; *Hastings, Guestling* once taken at ' light '

PTEROPHORI

Agdistis bennetii, Curt. *Thorney Island* and doubtless in other places round *Chichester Harbour* where Statice limonium grows. The moth is also very abundant on the shores of *Hayling Island*

Platyptilia ochrodactyla, Hb. *Brighton* ; not uncommon among Achillæa millefolium (Vine) and along the bank of the river near *Petworth* among Tanacetum vulgare ; occurs also in the *Fernhurst* district
— bertrami, Rössl. Not common ; recorded from *Brighton, Lewes, Hastings*
— gonodactyla, Schiff. Among Tussilago farfara at *Burgess Hill, Hastings, Lewes, Steyning*

Amblyptilia acanthodactyla, Hb. Common and generally distributed
— cosmodactyla, Hb. Apparently very local ; *Brighton, Falmer Downs, Shoreham* (Vine)

Oxyptilus teucrii, Jordan. Not uncommon in *Tilgate Forest* (Vine)
— parvidactylus, Hw. Widely distributed and not uncommon, especially on the downs. *Arundel Park, Clapham Down, Ditchling Common,* downs near *Shoreham*

Mimæscoptilus phæodactyla, Hb. *Brighton Downs* (Vine)

— bipunctidactylus, Hw. Generally distributed and common

— zophodactyla, Dup. Apparently not common. A specimen taken in *Abbots Wood*, and capsules of Erythræa centaurium found in *Clapham Wood* mined as though by the larva of this species (Fletcher)

— pterodactyla, Linn. Abundant among Veronica chamædrys

Œdematophorus lithodactylus, Tr. Locally abundant among Conyza squarrosa and Inula dysenterica ; *Goring, Hastings, Lewes*

Pterophorus monodactylus, Linn. Generally distributed and common

Leioptilus tephradactylus, Hb. Locally common among Solidago virgaurea ; *Abbots Wood, Battle, Ditchling Common, Hastings, Lewes*

— osteodactylus, Z. Abundant in *Abbots Wood* among Solidago virgaurea

— microdactylus, Hb. Abundant in chalk pits near *Arundel* and *Goring* among Eupatorium cannabinum ; found also at *Hastings, Lewes*

Aciptilia galactodactyla, Hb. *Brighton, Hastings* (rare) ; common in the *Goring, Clapham* and *Arundel Woods* among Arctium lappa

— spilodactyla, Curt. A single specimen bred from a pupa found on Marrubium vulgare on *Cissbury* several years ago (Fletcher). A large number of bred specimens of the moth from *Freshwater* were let loose in another locality in the county a few years back, but it is unknown if they established a colony (id.)

— baliodactyla, Z. *Bevendean Slopes, Lewes* (*Manual*, ii. 444), abundant in a rough field near *Slindon* among Origanum vulgare

— tetradactyla, Linn. Locally common on the downs ; *Arundel Park, Clapham* and *Lewes Downs*

— pentadactyla, Linn. Everywhere abundant

— paludum, Z. In a boggy spot on a heath near *Pulborough*. The moths fly like gnats over the bog for about an hour before dusk, the first brood sparingly in June and the second brood much more abundantly on still warm evenings early in September. The larvæ from the latter hatch in October and seem disposed to hibernate in a small state, but the food plant does not appear to be known (Fletcher)

Alucita hexadactyla, Linn. Generally common among honeysuckle

CRAMBI

Chilo phragmitellus, Hb. Apparently very uncommon in the county ; *Hastings*, very rare ; *Lewes* (*Manual*, ii. 186) ; *Shoreham*, three or four specimens (Vine)

— forficellus, Thnb. *Henfield Common, Lewes, St. Leonards, Worthing* (*Manual*, ii. 185)

— mucronellus, Schiff. One specimen at *Shoreham* (Vine)

— gigantellus, Schiff. *Shoreham*, not rare (Vine)

Platytes cerusellus, Schiff. Very abundant on the downs and on the sandhills and shingles near the coast

Crambus alpinellus, Hb. Not uncommon on the *Clymping* sandhills, flying at dusk in July and August, especially when a thunderstorm is brewing

— falsellus, Schiff. *Lewes*, occasionally ; once found very abundantly over an old thatch. *Hastings*, rare ; in *West Sussex* common and generally distributed ; may be bred freely from moss off old walls

— verellus, Znk. A very fine male specimen was taken at *The Dome, Bognor*, by Mr. Alfred Lloyd, F.E.S., in July, 1890

— pratellus, Linn. Common and generally distributed

— dumetellus, Hb. Very local ; abundant in a rough meadow in *Abbots Wood* ; a specimen in cabinet labelled *Worthing* (Fletcher) ; *Hastings*, rare

— hamellus, Thnb. *Shoreham*, one specimen (Vine) ; near *St. Leonards*, rare

— pascuellus, Linn. Common, especially in wet places ; *Arundel Park, Ditchling Common, Fernhurst, Henfield Common, Hastings, Hurston Warren, Lewes, Slindon*

— uliginosellus, Z. Abundant on *Henfield Common* and *Hurston Warren* ; occurs also at *Clymping* and near *Shoreham*

— pinellus, Linn. Widely distributed, but seems not common ; *Ashdown Forest, Abbots Wood, Battle, Hastings, Lewes, Plashet Wood, Slindon, Tilgate Forest*

— latistrius. *Abbots Wood*, common in the ridings (Vine) ; a single specimen on a heath near *Storrington* (Fletcher)

— perlellus, Sc. Widely distributed and common

— selasellus, Hb. Locally abundant ; *Hastings* ; grassy places near the coast, *Lancing* ; banks of the *Arun* below *Ford*

— tristellus, Fb. Generally common

INSECTS

Crambus inquinatellus, Schiff. *Lewes, Hastings,* rare ; widely distributed and abundant in *West Sussex*

— contaminellus, Hb. *Hastings,* rare

— salinellus, Tutt. Abundant on the coast at *Lancing* ; also met with at *Bognor* by Mr. Guermonprez. Probably occurs in all localities in the county where its food-plant, Glyceria (Poa) maritima, grows

— geniculeus, Hw. Abundant and widely distributed

— culmellus, Linn. Everywhere common

— chrysonuchellus, Sc. Very abundant on the chalk downs ; *Arundel, Lewes, Shoreham, Worthing*

— craterellus, Sc., var. cassentiniellus, Z. Mr. Douglas exhibited a specimen taken by Mr. J. Hemmings on the downs near *Brighton* at the meeting of the Entomological Society of London on 2 October, 1854 (*Proc. Ent. Soc.* new ser. iii. 1854–6, p. 27). Mr. Stainton stated (*Ent. Ann.* 1855, p. 43) that it was taken 'a few years back'

— hortuellus, Hb. Common everywhere

Anerastia lotella, Hb. Reported as rare from *Hastings,* occurs also on the coast at *Clymping* and *Southwick*

Homœosoma sinuella, Fb. *Eastbourne, Hastings,* somewhat rare ; abundant on the coast at *Clymping, Lancing* and *Southwick*

— nimbella, L. Locally abundant. The larvæ may be found abundantly on the coast between *Hove* and *Shoreham* in the flowers of Pyrethrum inodorum, near *Amberley* station in those of Senecio jacobæa, and in *Thorney Island* in those of Artemisia maritima

— binævella, Hb. Locally common ; *Brighton, Cissbury, Eastbourne, Hastings, Lewes, Shoreham*

Ephestia elutella, Hb. Occurs at *Worthing* in houses and stables, and is probably generally distributed throughout the county in stores and similar places

— kuchniella, Z. This species, which may be expected to occur in mills and other places where flour is stored, has been found at *Hastings*

Euzophora pinguis, Hw. *Hastings, Lewes* on ash trunks

Cryptoblabes bistriga, Hw. *Abbots Wood, Ashdown Forest, Hastings, Fernhurst*

Gymnancyla canella, Hb. On the *Camber* sandhills among Salsola kali ; occurs also at *Pagham*

Phycis betulæ, Göze. Not uncommon in *Tilgate Forest* ; found also at *Battle* and *Hastings*

Phycis fusca, Hw. Not uncommon in *Ashdown* and *Tilgate Forests* ; has been met with on *Hurston Warren* and near *St. Leonards*

— dilutella, Hb. Common among wild thyme on the downs and coast shingles

Dioryctria abietella, Fb. (decuriella, Hb.) A single larva found on a Scotch fir on *Slindon Common* in 1888, from which a moth was reared (Fletcher)

Nephopteryx spissicella, Fb. Abundant in *Abbots Wood* and occurs at *Hastings* and in the *Rewel Wood, Arundel*

— rhenella, Zk. Very abundant among heather in *Ashdown Forest* on *Hurston Warren,* and on *Blackdown, Fernhurst*

Rhodophæa formosa, Hw. *Charmandean* near *Worthing*

— consociella, Hb. Abundant in *Abbots Wood, Hastings, Lewes* and *Worthing* (*Manual,* ii. 171)

— advenella, Zk. *Hastings,* somewhat rare ; *High Down* near *Goring, Lewes* and *Worthing* (*Manual,* ii. 173)

— marmorea, Hw. Not uncommon among stunted sloe bushes on the downs and commons ; *Bury Hill, Charmandean, Eastbourne, Lewes, Milton Hide* near *Hailsham, Shoreham*

— suavella, Zk. *Bury Down, Milton Hide*

— zelleri, Rag. *Lewes* and *Worthing* (*Manual,* ii. 171) ; abundant in *Abbots Wood* ; *Guestling*

— tumidana, Schiff. Apparently rare. One at 'sugar' at *Shoreham* on 28 August, 1895, and another on 31 August, 1896 (Vine) ; one on a paling at *Charmandean* (Fletcher)

Oncocera ahenella, Hb. Very generally distributed over the chalk downs, but seems nowhere common ; *Guestling*

Galleria mellonella, L. Reported from *Hastings*

Aphomia sociella, L. Generally distributed and somewhat common

Achroia grisella, Hb. Common in beehives

TORTRICES

Tortrix podana, Sc. Common and widely distributed

— piceana, Linn. *Tilgate Forest* (W. H. Tugwell, *Proc. S. Lond. Ent. Soc.* 1890, p. 55)

— cratægana, Hb. Local and not common ; *Abbots Wood, Fernhurst, Hastings* district, *Lewes*

— xylosteana, Linn. Widely distributed and abundant ; *Abbots Wood, Burgess Hill, Fernhurst, Guestling, Lewes, Slindon*

— sorbiana, Hb. Common at *Guestling* and occurs also near *Lewes*

Tortrix rosana, Linn. Common and generally distributed

— dumetana, Tr. Local but probably widely distributed on the downs; *Bramber, Charmandean, Eastbourne*. The full-grown larvæ may be found freely at the end of June and beginning of July feeding on the leaves of Knautia arvensis, Centaurea nigra and scabiosa, and of Malva sylvestris

— cinnamomeana, Tr. Common in *Ashdown Forest* near fir plantations; occurs also in *Bell Hanger, Fernhurst* and in *Tilgate Forest*

— heparana, Schiff. ⎫
— ribeana, Hb. ⎪ Common and gener-
— corylana, Fb. ⎬ ally distributed
— unifasciana, Dup. ⎭

— costana, Fb. *Brighton, Lewes, Hastings, North Mundham*. At the latter place the moth occurs along the Portsmouth and Arun canal, the form being the typical one which occurs in the fens, and not the pale salt-marsh one which is found on the coast of *Hayling* and the *Isle of Wight*; occurs also at *Shoreham*

— viburnana, Fb. *Ashdown Forest, Gritham Common*

— palleana, Hb. Common in *Ashdown Forest* and reported from *Hastings*

— viridana, Linn. ⎫
— ministrana, Linn. ⎬ Common and very widely distributed
— fosterana, Fb. ⎭

Dichelia grotiana, Fb. Abundant in *Abbots Wood*; somewhat rare at *Guestling*; occurs at *Henley Hill* near *Midhurst* and in the *Rewel Wood, Arundel*

Leptogramma literana, Linn. *Abbots Wood, Dallington, Fernhurst, Guestling, Lewes*

Peronea sponsana, Fb. Generally abundant among beech and in *Abbots Wood* among hornbeam

— mixtana, Hb. *Chailey Common, Fernhurst, Hastings, Lewes, Linchmere, Tilgate Forest*, and probably on all the large heaths

— schalleriana, Fb. Generally distributed; the var. latifasciana, Hw., occurs in *Abbots Wood*

— comparana, Hb. Abundant in *Abbots Wood*, and occurs also at *Fernhurst, Hollington* and *Uckfield*

— permutana, Dup. *Eastbourne* downs between *Brighton* and *Lewes*; believed also to occur on those near *Clapham*

— variegana, Schiff. Everywhere common

— cristana, Fb. *Arundel Park*, where the larvæ feed on the flowers and young fruits of Pyrus aria, and doubtless also on those of the hawthorn there and in

many other places on the downs. It is reported also from *Fairlight* (rare), *Lewes* and *Uckfield*

Peronea hastiana, Linn. Widely distributed among sallows; *Abbots Wood, Fernhurst, Guestling, Shoreham, Uckfield*

— umbrana, Hb. *Lewes*, very rare

— ferrugana, Tr. *Abbots Wood, Fernhurst, Guestling; Rewel Wood, Arundel*; probably abundant in all woodlands among birch

— caledoniana, Stph. A specimen (♂) taken at *Cinderbank, Tilgate Forest*, in August, 1891 (Fletcher). Possibly the larva may feed on Potentilla tormentilla, but see *E.M.M.* xxii. 112

— logiana, Schiff. Abundant near *Berwick, Clapham, Guestling, Lewes, Steyning*, and probably generally so in hedgerows on the chalk among Viburnum lantana

— aspersana, Hb. Very abundant, especially on the chalk, the larvæ feeding on Helianthemum vulgare, Potentilla tormentilla, Comarum palustre, Spiræa filipendula, Poterium sanguisorba and Helianthemum vulgare

Rhacodia emargana, Fb. *Abbots Wood, Balcombe, Battle, Fernhurst, Guestling, Rackham, Warningcamp*

Teras contaminana, Hb. Everywhere common

Dictyopteryx lœflingiana, Linn. Abundant in woods; *Abbots Wood, Fernhurst, Guestling, Lewes; Rewel Wood, Arundel*

— holmiana, Linn. ⎫
— bergmanniana, Linn. ⎪ Abundant and
— forskaleana, Linn. ⎬ widely distributed
Argyrotoxa conwayana, Fb. ⎭

Ptycholoma lecheana, Linn. Abundant in *Abbots Wood*; occurs also at *Binsted, Fernhurst, Guestling, Worthing*

Ditula scriptana, Hb. *Clapham, Guestling*; rare

— semifasciana, Hw. Not rare in *Abbots Wood*, and occurs also in the *Rewel Wood, Arundel*

Penthina corticana, Hb. *Abbots Wood, Bell Woods, Fernhurst, Guestling, Tilgate Forest*

— betulætana, Hw. Abundant in *Tilgate Forest*, and occurs in woods near *Slindon, Guestling*

— capræana, Hb. *Abbots Wood, Chailey, Lewes, Hastings, Tilgate Forest*

— sororculana, Zett. Common in *Abbots Wood* (Vine). A specimen from *Slindon* is in Mr. Guermonprez's collection

— pruniana, Hb. Everywhere common

— ochroleucana, Hb. Not uncommon at *Worthing, Guestling*

— variegana, Hb. Everywhere abundant

INSECTS

Penthina dimidiana, Sodof. Abundant in *Abbots Wood*, the larvæ feeding on birch in the autumn ; occurs also at *Guestling*, and possibly in the *Rewel Wood, Arundel*

— gentiana, Hb. Widely distributed and not uncommon among teazle

— oblongana, Hw. *Abbots Wood, Ditchling Common* ; abundant among Betonica officinalis

— sellana, Gn. *Arundel, Slindon, Steyning, Worthing* ; not uncommon

— fuligana, Hb. Widely distributed, but seems nowhere abundant ; *Abbots Wood, Ditchling Common, Guestling, Tilgate Forest*

Antithesia salicella, Linn. *Guestling*, not common ; *Tarring*, the larvæ feeding on black poplar

Hedya ocellana, Fb. Abundant everywhere

— lariciana, Hein. Abundant at *Blatchington* and on *Slindon Common* ; flies in the afternoon round the tops of larches

— aceriana, Dup. *Abbots Wood, Hastings, Worthing*

— incarnana, Hw. Generally common

— neglectana, Dup. Abundant in *Abbots Wood, Hastings*

— servillana, Dup. *Abbots Wood* and *Holm Bush* ; the larvæ may sometimes be found not uncommonly in swollen twigs of sallow

— simplana, Fisch. *Abbots Wood*, not uncommon among aspen

Spilonota incarnatana, Hb. *Clapham Downs, Milton Hide* near *Hailsham*, and probably in other places in the county in which Rosa spinosissima occurs

— suffusana, Z. *Hastings, Worthing* ; not uncommon

— rosæcolana, Dbld. *Fernhurst, Guestling, Worthing* ; not uncommon

— roborana, Tr. *Fernhurst, Guestling, Rewel Wood* near *Arundel, Worthing*

Pardia tripunctana, Fb. ⎱ Common and
— uddmanniana, Linn. ⎰ widely distributed

Sideria achatana, Fb. *Abbots Wood, Bell Woods Fernhurst, Hastings, Hassocks* ; somewhat uncommon

Sericoris latifasciana, Hw. This very local species has been taken somewhat freely in *Abbots Wood* by Mr. Vine

— euphorbiana, Frr. Locally abundant ; *Arundel*

— littoralis, Curt. Very local, apparently much less widely distributed than its food-plant ; *Clymping Common, Hastings, Pett*

— cespitana, Hb. Locally common on the coast and downs ; *Abbots Wood, Clymping Common, Lancing Ring*, shingles near Chemical Works, *Shoreham*

Sericoris rivulana, Sc. Rather local ; *Charmandean, Slindon*, the larvæ feeding on Origanum ; *Tilgate Forest*

— urticana, Hb. Generally abundant and widely distributed

— lacunana, Dup. Abundant everywhere

Roxana arcuella, Cl. Locally abundant in woods ; *Abbots Wood, Battle, Guestling, Lewes*

Euchromia rufana var. purpurana, **Hw.** Locally abundant on the shingles near *Lancing* and *Southwick*, the larvæ feeding on Sonchus arvensis and Taraxacum densleonis ; occurs also at *Hastings*

Orthotælia antiquana, Hw. *Shoreham* (Vine)

— striana, Schiff. Not uncommon locally ; pupæ sometimes collected with those of E. rufana ; *Arundel Park, Bognor, Abbots Wood, Findon, Hastings* district, shingles near *Lancing* and *Southwick*

— ericetana, Westw. A single specimen in a 'hanger' on the outskirts of *Clapham Woods* (Fletcher)

Eriopsela fractifasciana, Hw. Local, but often excessively abundant where it occurs, the larvæ on the radical leaves (flower heads, Meyrick, *Handbook*, p. 486) of Scabiosa ; *Arundel Park, Abbots Wood, Ewhurst* ; *High Down, Goring* ; *Sompting*

— quadrana, Hb. Abundant in *Abbots Wood* among Teucrium, on which perhaps the larvæ may feed ; has been also taken at *Lewes* and once at *Guestling*

Phtheochroa rugosana, Hb. Seems to occur abundantly round *Worthing* wherever Bryonia dioica grows

Cnephasia politana, Hw. *Abbots Wood, Brighton, Chailey, Tilgate Forest, Uckfield*

— musculana, Hb. Generally common in woods

Sciaphila nubilana, Hb. *Hastings*, extremely abundant in a hawthorn hedge at *Broadwater*, and doubtless in many similar places in the county

— conspersana, Dougl. *Hastings*

— incertana, Tr. ⎫
— wahlbomiana, Linn., var. ⎬ Common
    virgaureana, Tr. ⎭ everywhere
— pasivana, Hb.

— chrysantheana, Dup. Occurs freely on the park paling at *Charmandean* with several of its congeners ; *Eastbourne*

— sinuana, Stph. *Guestling, Wolstonbury* ; larvæ not rare on Scilla nutans

— hybridana, Hb. Abundant and widely distributed

Sphaleroptera longana, Hw. *Hastings*, locally abundant on the downs near *Worthing*

Capua favillaceana, Hb. Very abundant in *Abbots Wood* among hornbeam and nut; occurs at *Fernhurst* and is common at *Guestling*

Clepsis rusticana, Tr. Plentiful on *Ditchling Common* and occurs in *Tilgate Forest*

Bactra lanceolana, Hb. The small double-brooded rush-feeding form is very abundant among rushes, the large form feeding in Scirpus maritimus, which seems to be single-brooded and may be a distinct species, occurs freely in ditches near the shore at *Shoreham, Lancing* and *Clymping*

Phoxopteryx siculana, Hb. *Chailey, Fernhurst, Guestling, Tilgate Forest*

— unguicella, Linn. *Abbots Wood, Hurston Warren, Tilgate Forest*; abundant in heathy places

— uncana, Hb. *Abbots Wood, Fernhurst, Guestling, Hurston Warren*

— biarcuana, Steph. *Hurston Warren, Tilgate Forest*; probably widely distributed among sallows

— inornatana, H.S. *Guestling*

— comptana, Fröl. Abundant in *Abbots Wood* and on the downs, where the larva feeds on Poterium sanguisorba

— myrtillana, Tr. *Hastings, Fernhurst*

— lundana, Fb. Widely distributed and abundant in woody districts among wild vetches

— derasana, Hb. *Abbots Wood, Bury Hill, Fernhurst, Salvington Down*; seems abundant wherever Rhamnus catharticus grows

— diminutana, Hw. Not uncommon in *Abbots Wood*; occurs also at *Fernhurst, Guestling* and in *Tilgate Forest*

— mitterbacheriana, Schiff. *Abbots Wood, Fernhurst, Guestling, Tortington Wood*

— upupana, Tr. A specimen from *Charlton Forest* is in Mr. Guermonprez' collection; recorded from *Guestling* as rare

— lactana, Fb. Abundant in *Abbots Wood* and *Tilgate Forest*; occurs also in *Goring Woods*

Grapholitha ramella, Linn. Widely distributed and not uncommon; *Abbots Wood, Arundel Park, Guestling, Lewes, Lancing Ring, Tilgate Forest*

— nisella, Clerck. Abundant at *Burgess Hill*; occurs also at *Guestling* and in the *Rewel Wood* near *Arundel*

— cinerana, Hw. Occurs at *Ore*; is perhaps a form of the last species

— nigromaculana, Hw. Widely distributed and not uncommon among Senecio erucæfolia, in the flower-heads of which

the larvæ feed; *Broadwater, Cissbury, Hurston Warren, Pett*

Grapholitha subocellana, Don. Generally common among sallows

— trimaculana, Don. Very abundant among elm near *Bognor* and *Worthing*; occurs also at *Fernhurst* and *Ecclesbourne* near *Hastings*

— penkleriana, Fisch. Generally common in woods

— obtusana, Hw. Not uncommon in woods; *Abbots Wood, Binsted, Fernhurst, Guestling, Goring Woods, St. Leonards Forest*

— nævana, Hb. Apparently everywhere common

— geminana, Stph. Possibly a form of the last species, attached to Vaccinium; occurs in *Ashdown Forest* and the *Hastings* district

— tetraquetrana, Hw. Generally abundant among birch

— immundana, Fisch. In woods, widely distributed and not uncommon; *Fairlight, Rewel Wood* near *Arundel*, St. *Leonards* and *Tilgate Forests*

— demarniana, Fisch. 'Sussex' (Meyrick, Handbook, p. 493)

Hypermœcia cruciana, Linn. *Abbots Wood, Clapham Common, Fernhurst, Guestling, Hassocks, Rewel Wood* near *Arundel*

Batodes angustiorana, Hw. Very abundant at *Bognor* and *Worthing* among evergreen oak and yew; occurs also at *Abbots Wood, Arundel Park, Guestling, Isfield*

Pædisca bilunana, Hw. *Broadwater, Fairlight*; St. *Leonards Forest*, abundant

— oppressana, Tr. Common at *Burgess Hill* on palings near poplar trees (Vine)

— ratzeburghiana, Rtzb. Abundant among spruce firs in the *Rewel Wood*; recorded also by Mr. Vine as common at *Blatchington* among larch

— corticana, Hb. ⎫ Generally common in
— profundana, Fb. ⎭ oak woods

— ophthalmicana, Hb. *Abbots Wood*, not common (Vine); *Lewes*

— diniana, Gn. *Brighton, Hastings*

— solandriana, Linn. Not uncommon in woods among birch; *Abbots Wood, Ashdown Forest, Fernhurst, Guestling, Rewel Wood*

— semifuscana, Stph. *Brighton, Felpham, Fernhurst, Fairlight*; *Worthing*, locally abundant

— sordidana, Hb. *North Ambersham*; *Tilgate Forest*, abundant

Ephippiphora similana, Hb. Locally abundant; *Abbots Wood, Amberley, Fernhurst, Guestling, Lewes*

INSECTS

Ephippiphora pflugiana, Hw. Widely distributed and abundant, the larvæ feeding in stems of thistles ; *Abbots Wood, Cissbury, Fernhurst, Tilgate Forest*

— luctuosana, Dup. Apparently less abundant than the preceding, the larvæ feeding in stems of Centaurea scabiosa ; canal bank between *Barnham* and *Chichester*, railway bank between *Polegate* and *Hailsham, Pagham*

— brunnichiana, Fröl. Locally abundant among coltsfoot ; *Brighton, Eastbourne, Lewes, Steyning*

— inopiana, Hw. Abundant in and near *Goring Woods*, and doubtless in many other places in the county among Inula dysenterica

— fœnella, Linn. Locally abundant at *Broadwater* and *Lancing* among Artemisia vulgaris

— nigricostana, Hw. Not uncommon among Stachys sylvatica ; *Abbots Wood, Bramber, High Down* near *Goring*

— signatana, Dgl. Very local ; *Abbots Wood, Lewes*

— trigeminana, Stph. *High Down* near *Goring, Hastings, Lewes, Tilgate Forest*

— tetragonana, Stph. *Abbots Wood*, where it may be found flying freely among Rosa arvensis at the end of July and beginning of August ; occurs also at *Guestling* and in *Tilgate Forest*

— populana, Fb. *Abbots Wood, Fernhurst, Uckfield*

— gallicolana, Z. *Guestling, Tilgate Forest*

Olindia ulmana, Hb. Generally distributed in the *Fernhurst* district (Barrett), *Ore, Tilgate Forest* not common (Vine)

Semasia spiniana, Dup. *Abbots Wood, Bury Down, Hassocks*

— janthinana, Dup. *Arundel Park, Broadwater, Burgess Hill, Hastings*

— gallicana, Gn. Generally common near the coast among Daucus carota; on the downs near *Shoreham* the larvæ feed on Pastinaca sativa, and on *Slindon Common* on Silaus pratensis

— wœberiana, Schiff. *Worthing*, and doubtless elsewhere among old fruit trees

Coccyx cosmophorana, Tr. *Rewel Wood* ; the moths may be reared from the fallen cones of spruce collected in early spring

— scopariana, H.S. *Ditchling Common* among Genista tinctoria

— strobilella, Linn. *Rewel Wood*, the larvæ feeding in fallen cones of spruce

— splendidulana, Gn. *Fernhurst, Guestling, Goring Woods, Offington* ; probably generally common in oak woods

Coccyx argyrana, Hb. *Goring Woods, Guestling*

— tedella, Clerck. Generally very abundant among spruce firs

— distinctana, Hein. One specimen taken in *St. Leonards Forest* 7 June, 1890 (Fletcher)

— nanana, Tr. *Rewel Wood* and *Tilgate Forest*, abundant among spruce

Heusimene fimbriana, Hw. *Abbots Wood, Hastings*

Retinia buoliana, Schiff. Common among Scotch fir ; *Blachington, Fairlight, Preston, Slindon Common*

— pinicolana, Dbld. *Hastings, Tilgate Forest, Uckfield*

— turionana, Hb. Very abundant on *Slindon Common, Uckfield*

— pinivorana, Z. *Bexhill, Slindon Common, Uckfield*

Carpocapsa splendidana, Hb. *Abbots Wood, Guestling, Rewel Wood, Worthing*

— grossana, Hw. *Arundel Park, Bognor ; Falmer Woods*, abundant ; *Hastings*

— pomonella, Linn. Everywhere abundant among apples

— funebrana, Tr. *Bognor* among damson trees (Fletcher) ; Mr. Vine has bred the moths from plums supposed to have been grown in *Sussex; Guestling*

Endopisa nigricana, Stph. Generally distributed and not uncommon

Stigononota obscurana, Stph. Rare and local ; *Tilgate Forest*

— perlepidana, Hw. *Abbots Wood*, abundant ; *Tilgate Forest*

— pallifrontana, Z. Abundant near *Bury* ; flies at the beginning of July in the sunshine from 2–4 p.m. along hedgerows in which Astragalus glycyphyllos grows

— compositella, Fb. Common among clover on the downs and in meadows

— nitidana, Fb. *Abbots Wood, Fernhurst, Guestling, St. Leonards Forest*; among oak

— flexana, Z. In beach woods ; *Falmer, Guestling, Houghton Forest*

— regiana, Z. Sometimes very common among sycamores even in towns ; the larvæ and pupæ may be found freely under the loose bark on the trunks; *Bognor, Hastings, Lewes, Worthing*

— roseticolana, Z. Not uncommon among wild roses ; *Abbots Wood, Lancing, Thorney Island*

— germarana, Hb. *Abbots Wood, Fernhurst, Hastings, Lewes*

Dichrorampha alpinana, Tr. Locally abundant among yarrow ; *Eastbourne, Ford, Guestling*, between *Lancing* and *Worthing*

Dichrorampha quæstionana, Z. Locally abundant among tansy in gardens and elsewhere; *Brighton, Hastings*, river bank near *Petworth*

— sequana, Hb. Not uncommon among yarrow; *Burpham, Charmandean, Durrington, Shoreham Shingles, Slindon Common, Worthing*

— petiverella, Linn.
— plumbana, Sc. } Generally abundant among yarrow
— plumbagana, Tr.

— acuminatana, Z. *Burpham, High Down* near *Goring, Houghton* among Chrysanthemum leucanthemum

— simpliciana, Hw. *Broadwater, Lancing, Lewes, Petworth* among Artemisia vulgaris

— consortana, Wilk. On the downs near Sompting and by the roadside between *Bramber* and *Shoreham*

Pyrodes rheediella, Clerck. Common among hawthorn and whitebeam

Catoptria albersana, Hb. Locally abundant among honeysuckle; *Abbots Wood, Fernhurst, Guestling, St. Leonards Forest*

— succedana, Frölich. Everywhere abundant among Genista, Ulex, etc.

— juliana, Curt. *Hastings*; the form herrichiana, Hein., occurs in *Abbots Wood* (Fletcher)

— hypericana, Hb. *Fernhurst, Hastings, Lewes, Worthing*; probably generally distributed and abundant among Hypericum

— cana, Hw. Widely distributed and abundant among Arctium, Carduus and Centaurea

— fulvana, Stph. Abundant in the *Worthing* district among Centaurea scabiosa

— candidulana, Nolck. Abundant among Artemisia maritima; banks of *Arun* and *Cuckmere, Rye*

— scopoliana, Hw. Generally abundant among Centaurea; the small form, parvulana, Wlk., is abundant in *Abbots Wood* among Serratula tinctoria, and on the downs near *Sompting* among Centaurea nigra

— cæcimaculana, Hb. Apparently rather local and uncommon; *Abbots Wood, Arundel Park, Polegate*

— æmulana, Schläg. Locally abundant among golden rod; *Abbots Wood, Hastings, Rewel Wood, Arundel*

— expallidana, Hw. Local, among Sonchus; *Hastings*, near coast between *Shoreham* and *Worthing, Withdean*

— citrana, Hb. Not uncommon locally on the downs near *Brighton* and on the coast between that place and *Worthing, Hastings*

Trycheris aurana, Fb. Abundant on the downs in the neighbourhood of *Steyning* and *Worthing* among Heracleum sphondylium; occurs also at *Hastings*

Choreutes bjerkandrella, Thnbg. '*Hurst, Sussex*' (*Manual*, ii. 159). The late Mr. S. Stevens showed me a specimen that he had taken at *Poling* on Inula bloom, and I think stated that he had met with another at *Holmbush* (Fletcher)

— myllerana, Fb. Locally abundant; *Abbots Wood, Chailey Common, Henfield Common, Plashet Wood*

— pariana, Clerck. *Felpham* (Guermonprez), near *Uckfield* (Jenner)

— fabriciana, Linn. Very abundant among nettles

Eupœcilia nana, Hw. Somewhat abundant locally among birch; *Guestling, St. Leonards* and *Tilgate Forests*

— dubitana, Hb. Locally abundant in rough places among Crepis virens; *Brighton, Hove, Hastings, Worthing*

— atricapitana, Stph. Not uncommon locally among Senecio jacobæa; *Brighton, Fairlight*, on both sides of basin at *Portslade*

— maculosana, Hw. Abundant in woods among Scilla nutans; *Abbots Wood, Clapham Wood, Guestling, Linchmere*

— sodaliana, Hw. Not uncommon on the downs round *Worthing* where Rhamnus catharticus grows

— hybridella, Hb. Very local; *Houghton* chalk pit, *Pett*, coast near *Southwick*

— angustana, Hb. Generally distributed and abundant among heather and on grassy places, especially on the downs, among plantain

— ambiguella, Hb. Local and perhaps not often observed except in the earlier stages; *Fernhurst* (Barrett), *Tilgate Forest* (Jenner)

— curvistrigana, Wilk. Locally abundant in woods among golden rod (Solidago virgaurea); *Abbots Wood, Guestling, Rewel Wood* near *Arundel*

— affinitana, Dgl. Abundant by the estuary of the Adur at *Shoreham* and probably wherever the food plant, Aster tripolium, is common

— vectisana, Westw. Abundant by the riverside at *Shoreham* among Triglochin maritimum, in the crowns of which the larvæ feed

— udana, Gn. Ditches near *Lancing* and *Shoreham* among Alisma plantago

— notulana, Z. Lanes and roadsides at *St. John's Common* (Vine); larvæ probably of this species have been observed in stems of Lycopus europæus in *Abbots Wood* and at *Mundham* (Fletcher)

INSECTS

Eupœcilia manniana, Fisch. *Guestling*, rare
— rupicola, Curt. Abundant in chalk pits near *Arundel* and *Goring* among Eupatorium cannabinum; *Guestling*, somewhat rare
— roseana, Hw. *Arundel, Pett*; abundant among Dipsacus sylvestris
— subroseana, Hw. *Abbots Wood*, abundant among Solidago virgaurea
— implicitana, Wck. Very abundant on both sides of the basin near *Southwick* among Matricaria inodora, *Guestling*
Xanthosetia zœgana, Linn. ⎫ Widely distributed on
— hamana, Linn. ⎭ the downs, near the coast, etc.
Chrosis alcella, Schulze. Widely distributed and very abundant on the downs and coast shingles, also at *Abbots Wood, Fernhurst, St. Leonards Forest*, etc.
— bifasciana, Hb. Not rare in the ridings in *Abbots Wood*; rare at *Guestling*; has occurred at *Lewes* once and also is found in *Tilgate Forest*
Lobesia permixtana, Hb. *Abbots Wood* and woods between *Binsted* and *Tortington*
Argyrolepia hartmanniana, Clerck. *Abbots Wood* and *Ditchling Common*; in the latter locality abundant and very variable; occurs also at *Battle, Lewes, Laughton, Hastings, Tilgate Forest*, though possibly some of these localities may appertain to the following species
— subbaummaniana, Wlk. *Burpham* and *Houghton* chalk pits
— zephyrana, Tr. Abundant on the downs and coast among Daucus carota; reported also from *Ewhurst*
— maritimana, Gn. On the *Camber Sandhills* among Eryngium maritimum
— badiana, Hb. *Bramber, Guestling*; apparently not abundant
— cnicana, Dbld. *Abbots Wood, Guestling, Fairlight, Hurston Warren*; scarce
Conchylis dipoltella, Hb. *Brighton Downs*, not uncommon
— francillana, Fb. *Brighton, Eastbourne, Hastings, Lewes, Shoreham*
— dilucidana, Stph. *Abbots Wood, Eastbourne*; very abundant on downs near *Worthing*
— smeathmanniana, Fb. Local; not uncommon on the *Brighton Downs*, occurs also at *Hollington* and *Worthing*
— straminea, Hw. *Broadwater, Eastbourne, Guestling, High Down* near *Goring*
Aphelia osseana, Scop. Abundant on the chalk
Tortricodes tortricella, Schiff. Abundant in woods

TINEÆ

Lemnatophila phryganella, Hb. Abundant in woods

Dasystoma salicella, Hb. *Abbots Wood*; common in lanes near *Bury*, the larvæ abundant in August and September on leaves of Cornus sanguinea; *Guestling*
Diurnea fagella, Fb. Abundant everywhere
Semioscopis avellanella, Hb. *Tilgate Forest*, abundant
Epigraphia steinkellneriana, Schiff. *Fernhurst, Guestling, Salvington Down*
Narycia monilifera, Geoff. *Bognor*, the larvæ not uncommon on tree trunks
Diplodoma herminata, Geof. *Abbots Wood, Broadwater, Guestling, Selsey*
Solenobia inconspicuella, Stainton. *Eastbourne, St. Leonards Forest*
— lichenella, Linn. Locally abundant on park palings; *Angmering, Horsham*
Talæporia tubulosa, Retz. Generally distributed and abundant; the full-grown larvæ and pupæ may be collected from palings and tree trunks
Luffia ferchaultella, Stph. Widely distributed and very abundant among powdery lichens on trees and palings; *Arundel, Horsham*, shingles near *Shoreham*
Fumea casta, Pallas. *Abbots Wood, Guestling, Rackham Common, Washington*
Whittleia reticella, Newman. *Cuckmere estuary* near *Exceat Bridge*; flies in the afternoon sunshine somewhat abundantly
Epichnopteryx pulla, Esp. *Brighton* district (Cooke) (Tutt, *Lep. Brit.* ii. 365)
[Acanthopsyche villosella, O. ? *Sussex, Brighton* district (Cooke) (tom. cit. p. 395)]
Psychoides verhuellella, St. *Felpham, Tarring*; not uncommon among Scolopendrium vulgare in hedgerows
Ochsenheimeria birdella, Curt. *Fairlight, Lancing, Rackham, Rewel Wood*
— bisontella, Z. Abundant on *Ditchling Common* among bracken; a single specimen in a rough field, *Slindon*
Scardia boleti, Fb. *Arundel*; the larvæ may be found not uncommonly in fungi on oak trees
— corticella, Curt. *Tilgate Forest* (Vine)
— parasitella, Hb. *Fernhurst* (Barrett)
— granella, Linn. *Burgess Hill*
— cloacella. *Arundel Park, Broadwater, Burgess Hill, Guestling*; may be reared freely from fungi growing on trees
— arcella, Fb. *Clayton, Fairmile Bottom, Guestling, Rewel Wood, Sullington, Worthing*; abundant in lanes
— imella, Hb. Shingles and slopes between *Brighton* and *Shoreham*
— ferruginella, Hb. *Arlington, Broadwater, Fernhurst, Pett*; lanes and hedgerows, not common

199

Scardia rusticella, Hb. Generally abundant; may be bred freely from old birds' nests

— spilotella, Tengström. Apparently not uncommon in *Abbots Wood*. Birds' nests from that district yielded S. rusticella abundantly, but no spilotella (Fletcher)

Tinea fulvimitrella, Sodof. *Abbots Wood, Cissbury, Fairlight, Guestling*

— tapetzella, Linn. *Fernhurst, Guestling*

— albipunctella, Hw. *Arlington, Burpham, Chailey, Falmer*; rather scarce

— caprimulgella, H.S. *Arundel*, in hollow trunks of ash

— misella, Z. Abundantly in an old barn in *Winding Bottom* near *Sompting*, and doubtless in similar places elsewhere

— pellionella, Linn. Abundant in houses and outbuildings

— fuscipunctella, Hw. Abundant in stables and outbuildings, where the cases of the larvæ may be found on the roofs and walls

— argentimaculella, Stt. *Bognor, Broadwater, Horsham,* near *Petworth, Washington*; the silken tubes of the larvæ abundant among powdery lichens on dry banks, old walls and tree trunks

— pallescentella, Stt. Not uncommon in a house in *Worthing*

— lapella, Hb. May be bred freely from old birds' nests

— nigripunctella, Hw. Not uncommon in a cottage and stables attached to a house in *Worthing*

— semifulvella, Hw. *Broadwater, Fernhurst, Guestling; Preston*, common on palings; *Wiggonholt*

Phylloporia bistrigella, Hw. *Abbots Wood, Chailey, Guestling, Linchmere, Rackham*; not rare among birch

Tineola biselliella, Hummel. Common generally in houses

Lampronia morosa, Z. *Sompting*, among wild rose

— luzella, Hb. *Fernhurst, Goring Woods, Guestling*

— prælatella, Schiff. *Abbots Wood, Binsted Woods, Goring Woods, Guestling*

— rubiella, Bjerk. *Fernhurst, Hastings, North Ambersham, Wolstonbury*

Incurvaria muscalella, Fb. *Abbots Wood, Fernhurst, Guestling, Tortington, Worthing*; abundant

— pectinea, Hw. *Abbots Wood, Fernhurst*

— tenuicornis, Stt. *Guestling*, rare (Bloomfield)

— œhlmanniella, Tr. *Abbots Wood, Fernhurst, Guestling*

— capitella, Cl. *Guestling*, rare; *Wolstonbury*

Micropteryx calthella, Linn. Widely distributed and very abundant

— aruncella, Sc. *North Ambersham* (Barrett)

— seppella, Fb. *Clapham Woods, Cissbury, Fernhurst*; locally very abundant

— mansuetella, Z. Not rare in moist meadows round *Abbots Wood* (Vine)

— aureatella, Sc. *Tilgate Forest* (Vine)

— thunbergella, Fb. *Bury Hill, Fernhurst, Guestling, Goring Woods, Houghton Forest, Tortington Woods*; locally abundant

— subpurpurella, Hw. Common in oak woods

— purpurella, Hw.
— semipurpurella, Stph. } Generally abundant among birch
— unimaculella, Zett.

— sangii, Wood. *Chailey, Clapham* and *Goring Woods*; abundant

— kaltenbachii, Wood. *Balcombe, Chailey, Hassocks*

— salopiella, Stt. *Abbots Wood, Clapham Woods, Fernhurst*

— sparmannella, Boze. *Abbots Wood, Fernhurst, Guestling, Rewel Wood*

Nemophora swammerdammella, Linn. *Fernhurst, Guestling, Worthing*

— schwarziella, Z. *Fernhurst, Guestling, Houghton Forest, Tortington*; common

— metaxella, Hb. *Abbots Wood, Binsted Woods, Fernhurst, Falmer Woods, Guestling*; locally abundant

Adela fibulella, Fb. *Bury, Clapham Wood, Binsted, Fernhurst, Guestling, Houghton* chalk pit; abundant

— rufimitrella, Sc. *Abbots Wood*, canal near *Aldingbourne Bridge*; locally abundant

— cræsella, Sc. *Durrington, Fernhurst, Hastings, Worthing*; apparently uncommon

— degeerella, Linn. *Abbots Wood, Binsted Woods, Guestling, Linchmere*; usually very abundant in its localities

— viridella, Sc. Generally abundant in woods

— cuprella, Thnbg. *Fairlight* (Bloomfield)

Nematois metallicus, Poda. Local and rare; *Hastings*, chalk pit near *Bramber*

— cupriacellus, Hb. Locally abundant; hedgerows between *Berwick* and *Arlington, Moulescombe* pit

— minimellus, Z. Abundant in *Abbots Wood*; occurs also on *Ditchling Common*

Swammerdamia combinella, Hb. Generally distributed in hedgerows

— cæsiella, Hb. Abundant and generally distributed among blackthorn

— heroldella, Hb. *Abbots Wood*, abundant among birch; *Guestling*

INSECTS

Swammerdamia lutarea, Hw. *Arundel Park, Worthing* ; abundant among hawthorn
— pyrella, Vill. Generally abundant among fruit trees in gardens and among hawthorn in hedgerows
Scythropia cratægella, Linn. *Abbots Wood, Burgess Hill* ; abundant
Hyponomeuta vigintipunctatus, Retz. A single specimen near the Royal Oak, *Avisford*, in 1887 (Fletcher)
— plumbellus, Schiff. *Clapham Woods, Hastings* ; common among spindle on the downs round *Worthing*
— padellus, Linn. Very abundant among apple, blackthorn and hawthorn
— cognatellus, Hb. Generally abundant where spindle occurs and sometimes found in shrubberies among Euonymus japonica
— decemguttella, Hb. Near *Shoreham*, abundant ; once at *Bognor*
Prays curtisellus, Don., and var. rustica, Hw. Widely distributed and not uncommon among ash
Eidophasia messingiella, Fisch. Hedgerows between *Berwick* and *Arlington, Burgess Hill, Guestling*
Plutella maculipennis, Curt. Everywhere abundant
— porrectella, Linn. *Bramber, Guestling, Worthing* ; not uncommon in gardens
— sequella, Cl. *Arundel Park* and *Rewel Wood*, abundant ; *St. John's Common*, by roadside hedgerows
— radiatella, Don. Very abundant in oak woods
— parenthesella, Linn. Common in woods
— sylvella, Linn. *Abbots Wood, Arundel Park, Hassocks*
— alpella, Schiff. *Guestling, Worthing*
— lucella, Fb. *Abbots Wood, Guestling*. The female is common in collections, but the male is very rare. Mr. Farren's collection contained two specimens. Standinger and Rebel's Catalogue states '($\male$ ignot)'
— horridella, Tr. *Abbots Wood*
Harpipteryx nemorella, Linn. *Broadwater, Ore, Rewel Wood* near *Arundel, Sompting*
— xylostella, Linn. Generally distributed among honeysuckle
Theristis mucronella, Sc. *Fernhurst, Polegate* ; abundant on the downs round *Worthing* among spindle
Enicostoma lobella, Schiff. Abundant among blackthorn in hedgerows round *High Down* near *Goring*
Phibalocera quercana, Fb. Everywhere abundant

Depressaria costosa, Hw. Abundant and generally distributed among gorse
— flavella, Hb. Abundant and generally distributed
— pallorella, Z. Abundant on the *Steyning Downs*
— umbellana, Stph. *Ashburnham*, downs near *Bramber, Fernhurst, Fairlight*
— assimilella, Tr. *Abbots Wood, Fernhurst, Guestling, Tilgate Forest*
— nanatella, Stt. *Chailey* (Vine)
— scopariella, Hein. *Ditchling Common* (Vine), *Hastings*
— atomella, Hb. *Ditchling Common* (Fletcher)
— arenella, Schiff. Generally distributed
— propinquella, Tr. *Clapham Woods, Fernhurst*
— subpropinquella, Stt. *Fairlight, Shoreham, Worthing*
— alstrœmeriana, Cl. *Brighton Downs, Fernhurst, Guestling*, hangers near *Shoreham*
— purpurea, Hw. *Fernhurst, Guestling, Hardham*
— liturella, Hb. *Guestling* ; abundant round *Worthing*
— conterminella, Z. *Hassocks*, abundant
— angelicella, Hb. *Goring Woods, Guestling*
— cnicella, Tr. *Camber* and *Clymping* sandhills
— carduella, Hb. *Clapham Woods, Fairlight, Tarring*
— ocellana, Fb. *Burgess Hill, Ditchling Common, Fernhurst, Guestling*
— yeatiana, Fb. *Clapham Common, Guestling* ; *Shoreham*, abundant
— applana, Fb. Everywhere abundant
— ciliella, Stt. *Abbots Wood, Brighton* coast, *Fernhurst, Goring, Guestling, Hardham*
— zephyrella, Hb. *Steyning Downs* (Griffith, Vine)
— rotundella, Dgl. *Eastbourne, Fairlight, Steyning Downs*
— albipunctella, Hb. *Fernhurst*
— discipunctella, H.S. *Felpham* (Guermonprez), *Guestling* (Bloomfield)
— pulcherrimella, Stt. *Burpham, Cissbury, Bramber, Ditchling, Salvington* ; common among Bunium flexuosum
— douglasella, Stt. *Fairlight, Shoreham*
— weirella, Stt. *Broadwater, Cissbury* ; larvæ on Chærophyllum temulentum and Peucedanum sativum
— chærophylli, Z. *Fernhurst, Guestling, Worthing*
— ultimella, Stt. *Lewes* (Vine)
— nervosa, Hw. *Burgess Hill, Fernhurst, Guestling, Hardham* ; locally abundant
— badiella, Hb. *Arundel Park, Cissbury, Hastings, Salvington Down* ; not uncommon

I 201 26

Depressaria heracliana, De Geer. Abundant and generally distributed

Psoricoptera gibbosella, Z. *Abbots Wood, Ewhurst, Henley Hill* near *Midhurst*

Gelechia vilella, Z. *Tarring*, the larvæ feeding in fruits of mallow growing at base of walls

— malvella, Hb. Banks of the *Arun* near *Ford*; the larvæ in fruits of Althæa officinalis

— lentiginosella, Z. *Ditchling Common, North Mundham*; abundant among Genista tinctoria

— velocella, Dup. *Hurston Warren*, not common

— fumatella, Dgl. Not uncommon on the *Clymping* sandhills in July and August. It may be turned out of the tufts of coarse grasses by blowing into them. This species is sunk as synonymous with distinctella, Z., by Standinger and Rebel. It is however abundantly distinct and may probably be oppletella (H.S., fig. 382) or perhaps nigricans (Hein., p. 205). Until the question of identity has been decided it is as well to keep alive Douglas' name (Fletcher)

— ericetella, Hb. Abundant and generally distributed among ling on heaths and in woods

— mulinella, Z. Everywhere common among gorse

— sororculella, Hb. *Abbots Wood, Burgess Hill, Chailey*; *Goring Wood, Worthing*, not uncommon among sallows

— virgella, Thnb. *Ashdown* and *Tilgate Forests* (Vine)

— diffinis, Hw. *Pett*; very abundant on the shingles near *Shoreham*

— rhombella, Schiff. *Abbots Wood*

— distinctella, Z. Very abundant on the sandhills at *Clymping* in June and July; recorded also from the *Hastings* district

— celerella, Stt. Probably ♀ of the preceding species

— mouffetella, Schiff. Generally distributed among honeysuckle in hedgerows

Bryotropha terrella, Hb. Everywhere abundant in grassy places

— desertella, Dgl. Extremely abundant on the *Clymping* sandhills, *Camber* sandhills, a single specimen on *Hurston Warren*

— senectella, Z. Very abundant on the *Clymping* sandhills and on the shingles near *Shoreham* and *Southwick*, occurs also sparingly on a park paling at *Broadwater* and in a brickpit at *Burgess Hill*

Bryotropha mundella, Dgl. Very abundant on the sandhills at *Clymping*

— similis, Stt. Abundant on old walls at *Bury, Ewhurst*

— affinis, Dgl. Near the fort, *Clymping*; abundant on bank just east or entrance to *Shoreham Harbour*

— umbrosella, Z. Very abundant on the sandhills at *Clymping*; portlandicella, Richardson, which appears to be a form of the ♀ of this species rather than of mundella, to which it is attributed in Standinger and Rebel's *Catalogue*, occurs not unfrequently with the typical form. On *Hurston Warren* a form occurs abundantly in sandpits which differs from the coast insect in being rather larger, much blacker and more shiny-looking; it occurs also on *Gritham Common*

— basaltinella, Z. On an old barn at *Bury, Fernhurst*

— domestica, Hw. Widely distributed and abundant among moss on old walls

Lita acuminatella, Sircom. *Arundel Park, Cissbury, Salvington Down*; abundant

— artemisiella, Tr. Abundant among wild thyme on the downs near *Bramber*

— costella, Westw. *Arundel, Bognor, Bramber*, shingles near *Shoreham, Worthing*; abundant among Solanum

— maculea, Hw. *Abbots Wood, Cissbury, Burgess Hill, Fernhurst, Guestling, Rewel Wood* near *Arundel*

— tricolorella, Hw. *Abbots Wood, Burgess Hill, Durrington, Fernhurst, Guestling*

— semidecandrella, Threlfall. Very abundant on the sandhills, *Clymping*; also occurs near the mouth of *Shoreham Harbour*

— leucomelanella, Z. Abundant on the shingles near *Eastbourne* and between *Brighton* and *Lancing* among Silene maritima

— knaggsiella, Stt. *Fernhurst, Guestling* (Barrett)

— marmorea, Hw. Very abundant on *Clymping Common*, occurs also at *Pett*

— obsoletella, Fisch. Abundant on the shingles of the coast; the larvæ feeding in fruit and stems of Atriplex hastata, *Clymping, Eastbourne, Worthing*

— instabilella, Dgl. Very abundant at *Shoreham* and *Lancing* among Atriplex portulacoides, and no doubt in all other localities where the food plant abounds

— salicorniæ, Hering. Abundant at *Lancing*, the larvæ feeding on Salicornia, Suæda and Spergularia

— plantaginella, Stt. *Lancing* and *Shoreham* among Plantago coronopus and maritimus

Teleia proximella, Hb. *Abbots Wood, Guestling, St. Leonards Forest*

— notatella, Hb. *Hastings*

— vulgella, Hb. *Abbots Wood, Worthing*

— luculella, Hb. Abundant in *Abbots Wood, Hastings*

— scriptella, Hb. *Arlington*, common in lanes and roadside hedges ; *Hastings*

— fugitivella, Linn. *Arundel*; *Bognor*, very abundant among elms ; *Brighton, Fairlight*

— sequax, Hw. *Arundel Park* and *Brighton Downs*, abundant among Helianthemum vulgare

— dodecella, Linn. *Brighton, Broadwater, Guestling, Wolstonbury*

— triparella, Z. *Abbots Wood*, abundant among oak ; *Guestling*

Recurvaria nanella, Hb. *Brighton* (Vine)

Pœcilia gemmella, Linn. *Abbots Wood*, sometimes very abundant ; *Rewel Wood*

— albiceps, Z. *Worthing*

Argyritis tarquiniella, Stt. *Clymping Common*, apparently scarce

Nannodia stipella, Hb. *Worthing*

Apodia bifractella, Dgl. *Arlington, Ditchling Common, Guestling, Rewel Wood* ; abundant among Conyza squarrosa and Inula dysenterica

Ptocheuusa inopella, Z. *Guestling, Goring Woods, Slindon* ; abundant among Inula dysenterica

— subocellea, Stph. Down near *Bramber* among Origanum

Ergatis brizella, Tr. Very abundant on the shingles near *Shoreham* among Statice armeria, *Pett*

— ericinella, Dup. *Fernhurst, Hurston Warren, Tilgate Forest*

Doryophora suffusella, Dgl. A form similar to that occurring in Dorsetshire and smaller than the fen form is abundant in June on *Hurston Warren*

— lutulentella, Z. Not uncommon on *Ditchling Common* in June and July

Monochroa tenebrella, Hb. *Bognor, Eastbourne, Fernhurst, Slindon Common, Shoreham Shingles* ; probably very widely distributed among Rumex acetosa and acetosella

— unicolorella, Dup. Not uncommon in rides in *Abbots Wood* and in a chalk pit near *Steyning* in June and July

Lamprotes atrella, Hw. *Abbots Wood, Cissbury, Clapham Woods, Ditchling Common, Eastbourne, Guestling, Slindon Common* ; among St. John's wort

Anacampsis albipalpella, H.S. Abundant on *Ditchling Common* among Genista tinctoria

Anacampsis vinella, Bnks. *Ditchling Common* among Genista tinctoria

— ligulella, Z. Local, not common ; *Guestling, Goring Wood*, 1 ♂, a few on a rough meadow near *Ditchling Common* (Fletcher)

— vorticella, Sc. Much more abundant than the preceding ; *Abbots Wood*, bred from Lotus major ; *Ditchling Common* among Lotus corniculatus, *Hurston Warren, Wiggonholt*

— tæniolella, Z. *Abbots Wood, Brighton Downs, Ditchling Common, Hurston Warren*, downs and shingles near *Worthing* ; very abundant

— anthyllidella, Hb. *Fairlight*, very abundant on shingles near *Shoreham* and on the downs round *Worthing*

Acanthophila alacella, Dup. *Rewel Wood* near *Arundel*

Tachyptilia populella, Cl. *Clapham, Fernhurst, Guestling, Heene, Rewel Wood*

Brachycrossata cinerella, Cl. *Arundel Park*, abundant ; *Cissbury*

Ceratophora rufescens. *Guestling, Goring, Worthing*

Cladodes gerronella, Z. *Brighton Downs, Broadwater, Fernhurst, Hastings, Hurston Warren, Henfield Common, Rewel Wood, Worthing*

Parasia lappella, Linn. Abundant near *Shoreham* among Arctium lappa

— metzneriella, Stt. *Abbots Wood* where a small form occurs feeding in the larval state in the heads of Serratula tinctoria ; *Brighton, Ditchling Common, High Down*

— carlinella, Stt. *Abbots Wood*, where a small form occurs feeding in fruits of Solidago virgaurea ; abundant on the downs near *Lewes* and *Shoreham* among Carlina vulgaris, *Pett*

— neuropterella, Z. Downs near *Lewes* ; the larvæ may be collected abundantly about the middle of October in the heads of Carduus acaulis and much more sparingly in those of Centaurea nigra

Cleodora cytisella, Curt. *Abbots Wood, Ditchling Common, Hastings, Rewel Wood* near *Arundel* ; bred by Mr. Connold from larvæ feeding on the pinnules of bracken

— striatella, Hb. Extremely scarce ; *Brighton* (*Manual*, ii. 349)

Chelaria hübnerella, Don. Widely distributed among birch in woods, *Abbots Wood, Fernhurst, Hastings, Poling, Rackham, Rewel Wood*

Anarsia spartiella, Schrk. Downs near *Bramber, Hastings, Clymping*

Anarsia genistæ, Stt. *Ditchling Common* ; the larva feeding on Genista tinctoria

Hypsolophus fasciellus, Hb. *Abbots Wood, Poynings, Shaves Wood* ; very local and not abundant

— schmidiellus, Heyd. *Arundel, Slindon* ; abundant among Origanum

— marginellus, Fb. Abundant on the downs round *Worthing* among juniper

Sophronia parenthesella, Linn. *Arundel Park, Cissbury, Ditchling Common, Guestling* ; locally abundant especially on the downs

Pleurota bicostella, Cl. *Ashdown Forest, Fernhurst, Guestling, Hurston Warren* ; abundant on heaths

Harpella geoffrella, Linn. *Guestling, Fernhurst, Worthing* ; abundant in hedgerows

Dasycera sulphurella, Fb. Generally abundant about dead trees and sticks

— oliviella, Fb. Among dead wood, local ; *Abbots Wood, Chichester, Guestling*

Œcophora minutella, Linn. *Bognor* reared from birds' nests, *Guestling* ; *St. Leonards Forest*, beaten from thatch

— fulviguttella, Z. *Fernhurst, Goring Woods*, among Angelica sylvestris ; *Hastings, Slindon Common*, reared from Silaus pratensis

— tripuncta, Hw. *Abbots Wood, Arlington, Burgess Hill, Guestling, Wolstonbury* ; not rare

— augustella, Hb. *Hurstpierpoint* ; not uncommon on oak trunks

— lunaris, Hw. *Bognor* on tree trunks, *Burgess Hill* on palings

— lambdella, Don. *Fairlight*

— tinctella, Hb. *Abbots Wood, Broadwater* ; not abundant

— panzerella, Stph. *Abbots Wood, Binsted Wood, Fernhurst, Guestling*

— unitella, Hb. A single specimen on a park paling, *Broadwater* (Fletcher)

— flavifrontella, Hb. *Abbots Wood, Fernhurst, Guestling, Houghton Forest, Rewel Wood*

— fuscescens, Hw. *Bognor*, reared from larvæ feeding on dead leaves ; *Fernhurst*, abundant in thatch ; *Guestling*

— pseudospretella, Stt. Everywhere abundant

Œgoconia quadripuncta, Hw. *Bramber, Bognor, Hastings, Worthing*

Endrosis lacteella, Schiff. Everywhere abundant

Butalis grandipennis, Hw. *Abbots Wood, Bexhill, Ditchling Common, Fairlight, Hurston Warren*, downs near *Sompting* ; abundant among gorse

Butalis senescens, Stt. *Arundel Park, Clymping, Clapham Down, High Down* ; abundant among Lotus and Thymus

— fuscocuprea, Hw. *Arundel Park* and *High Down* with the preceding; abundant

— laminella, H.S. Abundant in *Arundel Park*, the larvæ feeding on Helianthemum

Pancalia leuwenhoekella, Linn. *Cissbury, Clapham Down* ; abundant among Viola hirta, on which the larva feeds

— latreillella, Curt. *Brighton Downs*

Acrolepia granitella, Tr. *Abbots Wood, Goring Woods, Guestling* ; abundant among Inula dysenterica

— pygmæana, Hw. *Abbots Wood, Bognor, Bramber, Broadwater* ; abundant among Solanum

Roeslerstammia erxlebella, Fb. *Abbots Wood, Fernhurst, Hastings, Rewel Wood* near *Arundel*

Glyphipteryx fuscoviridella, Hw. Abundant everywhere in grassy places

— thrasonella, Sc. Abundant generally among rushes, the variety cladiella, Stt., occurring in many localities with the type

— equitella, Sc. *Worthing* ; abundant in a garden among Sedum, perhaps imported with S. acre from the shingles near *Shoreham*

— fosterella, Fb. *Goring Woods* ; not uncommon among Carices, the larvæ feeding in the fruit-spikes

— fischeriella, Z. Widely distributed and generally abundant

Æchmia dentella, Z. Not uncommon near *Arundel*, among Chærophyllum temulentum ; also recorded from *Hastings*

Perittia obscurepunctella, Stt. *Botolphs, Broadwater, Ditchling Common, Fernhurst, Guestling, North Ambersham, Slindon*

Heliozela sericiella, Hw. Oak woods, generally abundant

— hammoniella, Sorgh. Two moths swept off birch on *Hurston Warren* in June, 1890 ; mines of the larvæ in birch leaves have been noticed abundantly in that locality, also at *Rackham* and in woods between *Arundel* and *Slindon* (Fletcher)

— stanneella, Fisch. *Chailey* (Vine)

— resplendella, Stt. *Abbots Wood* ; empty mines have been noticed in abundance in alder leaves in *Tilgate Forest*

Douglasia ocnerostomella, Stt. *Pett*, shingles near *Selsey* and *Shoreham* ; very abundant among Echium

INSECTS

Argyresthia ephippella, Fb. *Hastings, Rewel Wood, Salvington, Worthing*; abundant among garden and wild cherries
— nitidella, Fb. Generally abundant among hawthorn
— semitestacella, Curt. *Arundel Park, Fernhurst, Preston, Rewel Wood*; abundant among beech
— albistria, Hw. Generally abundant among sloe
— conjugella, Z. *Fernhurst, Guestling*
— semifusca, Hw. *Fairmile Bottom, Preston*, common on palings, *Rackham*, believed also to occur at *Guestling*
— mendica, Hw. Generally abundant among sloe
— glaucinella, Z. *Abbots Wood*
— retinella, Z. *Abbots Wood, Arundel Park, Fernhurst, Guestling, Rackham*; abundant among birch
— dilectella, Z. *Cissbury*, downs near *Steyning*; abundant among juniper
— andereggiella, Dup. *Wiggonholt Common*
— cornella, Fb. *Guestling, Wiggonholt*
— pymæella, Hb. *Abbots Wood, Fernhurst, Goring Woods, Guestling, Worthinig*
— gœdartella, Linn. *Abbots Wood, Broadwater, Guestling, Rackham*
— brockeella, Hb. *Abbots Wood, Arundel Park, Guestling*
— arceuthina, Z. ⎱ *Cissbury*, abundant
— aurulentella, Stt. ⎰ among juniper
Cedestis farinatella, Dup. *Arundel Park, Fernhurst*
Ocnerostoma piniariella, Z. *Broadwater, Fernhurst, Tilgate Forest*
Zelleria hepariella, Stt. *Rewel Wood, Tilgate Forest*
Gracilaria alchimiella, Sc. *Binsted Woods, Fernhurst, Guestling, Tortington*; abundant in oak woods
— stigmatella, Fb. *Abbots Wood, Guestling, Salvington*; probably occurs everywhere among sallows and willows
— falconipennella, Hb. *Abbots Wood*, rare (Vine)
— semifascia, Hw. *Arundel Park*, among maple
— populetorum, Z. *Abbots Wood* (Vine), *Lewes* and *Worthing* (*Manual*, ii. 377)
— elongella, Linn. *Abbots Wood, Fernhurst, Guestling, Hardham, Sullington*; probably common, generally among alder. The variety stramineella, Stt. occurs with the type in *Abbots Wood*
— tringipennella, Z. Widely distributed and abundant among Plantago lanceolata
— syringella, Fb. Everywhere abundant among ash, lilac, privet and allied plants

Gracilaria omissella, Stt. Locally abundant among Artemisia vulgaris. *Broadwater, Hurston Warren, Sompting*
— phasianipennella, Hb. *Fernhurst* (Barrett)
— auroguttella, Stph. *Abbots Wood, Eastbourne, Guestling, Worthing*; very abundant among Hypericum
— ononidis, Z. *Arundel Park, Ditchling Common*, downs near *Bramber* and *Sompting, Slindon*; not uncommon among red clover
Coriscium brongniardellum, Fb. *Abbots Wood, Coldwaltham, Fernhurst, Guestling*, near *Steyning*
— cuculipennellum, Hb. *Fernhurst, Rewel Wood*, larvæ from which imagines have been bred abundant on ash and privet; also on *Slindon Common*
— sulphurellum, Hw. *Abbots Wood, Guestling, Rewel Wood*
Ornix avellanella, Stt. Everywhere abundant among hazel
— anglicella, Stt. Everywhere abundant among hawthorn
— betulæ, Stt. *Abbots Wood, Fernhurst, Guestling*; doubtless generally abundant among birch
— torquillella, Z. Widely distributed and abundant among sloe
— scoticella, Stt. *Arundel Park, Bognor, Fernhurst, Worthing*; the larvæ on leaves of Pyrus aria, malus, Cotoneaster affinis, etc.
— guttea, Hw. *Bognor, Guestling, Mundham, Worthing*; abundant in gardens among apple trees
Goniodoma limoniella, Stt. Larvæ found in September, 1889, in *Thorney Island*, and the moths bred in 1890 (Fletcher)
Coleophora spissicornis, Hw. *Arundel Park, Ditchling Common, Lancing, Shoreham, Wolstonbury*; the larvæ feeding on fruits of Trifolium repens
— deauratella, Z. *Burgess Hill* (Vine)
— fuscocuprella, H.S. *Abbots Wood*; larvæ sometimes abundant on hazel; *Guestling*
— alcyonipennella, Koll. *Arundel, Guestling, Salvington Down*
— paripennella, Z. Near *Castle Goring*; the larvæ feeding on bramble; *Guestling* (?)
— ahenella, Hein. *Fernhurst* (Barrett)
— potentillæ, Elisha. *Cissbury, Guestling* (?), *Horsham, Hurston Warren*, downs near *Bramber*; the larvæ feed on leaves of Potentilla, Poterium, Rubus, Spiræa, and even on those of stray elm suckers growing among their more usual food plants

Coleophora wockeella, Z. *Abbots Wood*; abundant among Stachys betonica in a rough meadow; *Guestling*, very rare

— ochrea, Hw. *Arundel Park*, among Helianthemum

— salicorniæ, Hein-Wck. Abundant among Salicornia on the mudlands between *Shoreham* and *Worthing*; *Pett*

— lixella, Z. Not uncommon on the downs near *Worthing, Arundel Park, Cissbury, Clapham Down, High Down,* shingles near *Shoreham*

— vibicella, Hb. *Ditchling Common* among Genista tinctoria

— pyrrhulipennella, Z. *Brighton Downs, Chailey, Hurston Warren, Leechpool, Pett*

— albicosta, Hw. Widely distributed among gorse

— anatipennella, Hb. *Guestling, Hurston Warren, Portslade*

— palliatella, Zk. *Abbots Wood, Guestling, Hurston Warren*; not abundant

— ardeæpennella, Scott. *Burgess Hill*

— currucipennella, Z. *Abbots Wood, Cissbury, Guestling*

— niveicostella, Z. *Arundel Park, Clapham Down, High Down*; among wild thyme

— discordella, Z. Generally abundant among Lotus

— genistæ, Stt. *Ditchling Common*; abundant among Genista anglica

— bilineatella, Z. *Ditchling Common*; abundant among Genista tinctoria; has also occurred at *North Mundham*

— onosmella, Brahm. *Pett*; abundant among Echium near *Shoreham*

— conyzæ, Z. Brickpits near *Ditchling Common* on Inula (Griffith)

— nutantella, Mhlg. Abundant near *Steyning* among Silene inflata

— therinella, Tgstr. *Cissbury*, downs near *Bramber*; not uncommon

— troglodytella, Dup. *Goring*, downs between *Bramber* and *Shoreham*; *Pett*

— lineola, Hw. *Brighton Downs, Guestling, Pett*; abundant round *Worthing* among Ballota nigra and Stachys sylvatica

— murinipennella, Dup. Widely distributed and generally abundant in grassy places among Luzula campestris; *Abbots Wood, Bognor, Clapham Wood, High Down, Tortington,* etc.

[— sylvaticella, Wood. *Guestling* (?); Mr. Bloomfield took larvæ early in the year on Luzula sylvatica

— alticolella, Z. Widely distributed and abundant in damp places among Juncus articulatus, and its sub-species; *Arundel*

Park, Berwick, Henfield Common, Hurston Warren, Lancing, Mundham

Coleophora glaucicolella, Wood. *Shoreham* and doubtless in many other localities among Juncus glaucus, articulatus, etc.

— cæspititiella, Z. Everywhere abundant among Juncus communis, etc. This species and the preceding are often mingled in collections

— adjunctella, Hodgk. Very abundant in the salt marshes between *Shoreham* and *Worthing,* and doubtless elsewhere along the coast among Juncus compressus

— laripennella, Zett. Generally abundant on the downs, shingles and on dry waste land among Atriplex and Chenopodium

— mæniacella, Stt. Very abundant near *Shoreham* among Atriplex portulacoides and doubtless occurs wherever the plant is abundant

— flavaginella, Z. Abundant on the coast at *Lancing* among Suæda maritima

— salinella, Stt. Local, but abundant near *Shoreham* among Atriplex portulacoides

— apicella, Stt. Widely distributed and abundant among Stellaria graminea

— argentula, Z. Generally abundant among Achillea millefolium

— tripoliella, Hdgk. Abundant among Aster tripolium near *Ford, Rye* and *Shoreham*

— virgaureæ, Stt. *Abbots Wood, Balcombe, Faygate, Fernhurst, Guestling, North Ambersham, Rewel Wood*

— juncicolella, Stt. *Falmer Downs*, not rare among Calluna vulgaris; *Pett*

— laricella, Hb. *Tilgate Forest*; probably generally abundant among larch

— albitarsella, Z. *Durrington, Pett, Sompting*; among Glechoma hederacea

— nigricella, Stph. Generally abundant among apple, hawthorn, pear and whitebeam

— fuscedinella, Z. Generally abundant among alder, birch and elm

— orbitella, Z. *Abbots Wood*, the larvæ common on birch in the autumn (Vine)

— gryphipennella, Bouché. Abundant among wild roses

— siccifolia, Stt. *Arundel*

— bicolorella, Stt. *Goring Woods, Pagham*; locally abundant among nut on which the larva feeds. A larva with a similar case to that of the nut-feeder occurs on birch on *Hurston Warren* and in *Tilgate Forest* and may be of the same species (*Conf. Ent. Ann.* 1861, p. 89, and *Trans. Ent. Soc. Lond.* new ser. v. 410)

INSECTS

Coleophora viminetella, Z. *Brighton, Guestling, Shoreham* ; among sallow

— olivaceella, Stt. *Abbots Wood*

— solitariella, Z. *Clapham Wood, Guestling, Salvington*

— lutipennella, Z. *Abbots Wood, Guestling, Fernhurst* ; abundant

— limosipennella, Dup. *Abbots Wood, Fernhurst, Hurston Warren, Rewel Wood* ; abundant on birch

Bedellia somnulentella, Z. *Clymping, Lancing, Shoreham* ; sometimes abundant among Convolvulus arvensis

Stathmopoda pedella, L. *Guestling* ; very local

Cosmopteryx schmidiella, Frey. Locally abundant in lanes near *Amberley*

Batrachedra præangusta, Hw. *Bognor, Burgess Hill, Worthing*

— pinicolella, Dup. *Burgess Hill,* resting on palings near fir-trees ; *Wiggonholt*

Oinophila v-flavum, Hw. *Brighton, Worthing* ; occasionally occurring in houses

Chauliodus illigerellus, Hb. *Goring Woods, Hastings*

— insecurellus, Stt. *Arundel Park* among Thesium humifusum ; scarce, may be expected to occur more freely in localities in *East Sussex,* where the food plant is abundant

— daucellus, Peyer. A single specimen in *Arundel Park* ; identification confirmed by the late Mr. Stainton

— chærophyllellus, Goeze. *Goring,* abundant among Heracleum spondylium ; *Hastings* ; *Seaford,* a specimen bred from Seseli libanotis

Laverna propinquella, Stt. *Goring Woods, Hurston Warren* ; *Mundham,* abundant among Epilobium

— lacteella, Stph. *Goring Woods, Poling* ; larvæ feeding in leaves of Epilobium montanum

— miscella, Schiff. Very abundant in *Arundel Park,* and on the downs near *Worthing* among Helianthemum vulgare

— conturbatella, Hb. Abundant near *Coombes* and in the *Rewel Wood* among Epilobium angustifolium

— raschkiella, Z. Near *Coombes* and in the *Rewel Wood* ; abundant

— fulvescens, Hw. Generally abundant among Epilobium hirsutum

— ochraceella, Curt. *Goring Woods*

— phragmitella, Stt. *Guestling* ; old millpond near *Cophall*

— decorella, Stph. *Abbots Wood, Fernhurst, Guestling, Goring, Rewel Wood* ; widely distributed but not abundant

— subbistrigella, Hw. *Fernhurst, Goring Woods, Poling*

Laverna vinolentella, H.S. *Brighton,* abundant in gardens, the larvæ feeding under bark of apple twigs ; *Guestling*

— hellerella, Dup. *Arundel Park, Fernhurst, Guestling,* downs near *Salvington*

— rhamniella, Z. *Bell Woods, Fernhurst*

Chrysoclista schrankella, Hb. *Fernhurst, Henfield Common*

— aurifrontella, Hb. *Falmer Woods, Fernhurst, Guestling, Tarring*

Asychna modestella, Dup. *Fernhurst, Guestling, High Down* near *Goring, Slindon*

— æratella, Z. In fields at *Aldrington, Blatchington, Steyning, Withdean,* not common ; larvæ in very great abundance in August, 1893 and 1895, on the headland of a field to the north of *Old Shoreham,* from which a very thin crop of oats had been harvested

— terminella, Westw. *Tilgate Forest* ; the larvæ abundant in leaves of Circæa lutetiana, *Fairlight*

Antispila pfeiferella, Hb. *High Down, Houghton Forest, Slindon*

— treitschkiella, Fish. *Falmer, Sompting* ; abundant

Stephensia brunnichiella, Linn. *Rackham, Slindon* ; downs round *Worthing,* abundant among Calamintha clinopodium

Chrysocoris festaliella, Hb. Generally distributed among bramble

Elachista gleichenella, Fb. *Abbots Wood,* abundant ; *Ditchling Common*

— magnificella, Tgstr. *Abbots Wood*

— albifrontella, Hb. Widely distributed and abundant

— atricomella, Stt. *Cissbury* ; *Steyning Downs,* abundant

— luticomella, Z. *Broadwater, Fernhurst, High Down*

— cinereopunctella, Hw. Very abundant on *Cissbury,* also recorded from *Fernhurst, Hastings*

— stabilella, Frey. *Arundel Park, High Down* ; very abundant

— subnigrella, Dgl. *Arundel Park, Sompting*

— humilis, Z. Abundant in *Arundel Park, Clapham Down,* and other places on the downs ; *Fernhurst*

— bedellella, Sircom. Generally abundant on the chalk ; *Hastings*

— zonariella, Tgstr. *Abbots Wood*

— tæniatella, Stt. Very abundant in hedgerows, hangers and chalk pits on the downs near *Bramber, Goring* and *Worthing,* among Brachypodium sylvaticum

— megerlella, Stt. *Fernhurst* ; *Worthing,* abundant by roadside hedgerows

Elachista cerusella, Hb. *Hastings* ; *Houghton,* by the side of the river

— albidella, Tgstr. *Hurston Warren,* very abundant

— scirpi, Stt. Salt marshes at *Clymping, Lancing, Shoreham* ; among Scirpus maritimus, etc.

— paludum, Frey. *Hurston Warren,* near *Rackham*

— biatomella, Stt. *Fernhurst* ; abundant on the downs generally

— serricornis, Stt. Locally abundant ; *Hurston Warren* in May and June, may be swept from the herbage on sunny afternoons

— triatomea, Hw. Widely spread on the downs but not abundant ; *Arundel Park, High Down, Sompting, Steyning,* also in salt marshes near *Old Shoreham*

— disertella, H.S. *Arundel Park, High Down*

— rufocinerea, Hw. *Fernhurst, Guestling, Worthing*

— argentella, Cl. Generally abundant

Tischeria complanella, Hb. *Abbots Wood, Fernhurst, Guestling* ; probably abundant in oak woods throughout the county

— dodonæa, Stt. *Holm Bush, Hurstpierpoint*

— marginea, Hw. Generally abundant among brambles

Lithocolletis roboris, Z. *Abbots Wood, Battle, Hassocks* ; not common

— lantanella, Schrk. *Berwick, Clapham, Sompting* ; abundant among Viburnum lantana

— quinqueguttella, Stt. *Chailey Common, Ditchling Common, Hurston Warren* ; among Salix fusca

— irradiella, Scott. *St. John's Common* ; plentiful by roadside hedges

— lautella, Z. *Abbots Wood, Fernhurst, Guestling*

— anderidæ, Fletcher. *Abbots Wood* ; *Tilgate Forest,* among birch

— cavella, Z. *Abbots Wood, Fernhurst, Slindon Common*

— concomitella, Bnks. Near *Pulborough, Tilgate Forest* and other localities in the county ; abundant among crabapple in woods and hedgerows

— blancardella, Fb. *Abbots Wood,* near *Pulborough, Tilgate Forest, Wiggonholt* ; very abundant among crab-apple

— oxyacanthæ, Frey. Generally abundant among hawthorn

— pyrivorella, Bnks. In gardens among pear, apparently very scarce ; *Bognor, Worthing*

Lithocolletis mespilella, Hb. The species which occurs in *Abbots Wood* on Pyrus torminalis as well as that on Pyrus aucuparia at *Burgess Hill* and *Wiggonholt* should probably be referred to this species

— coryli, Nicelli. Everywhere abundant among hazel

— spinicolella, Z. Generally abundant among sloe

— faginella, Z. Abundant among beech

— salicicolella, Sircom. Generally abundant among Salix cinerea

— viminetorum, Stt. *Arundel* ; larvæ in leaves of Salix viminalis in osier beds

— carpinicolella, Stt. *Abbots Wood, Arundel Park, Burgess Hill, Chailey, Guestling* ; abundant among hornbeam

— ulmifoliella, Hb. Generally abundant among birch

— spinolella, Dup. *Balcombe, Goring Woods, Hassocks* ; among Salix capræa

— quercifoliella, Z. Generally abundant among oak

— messaniella, Z. Abundant among oak, both deciduous and evergreen species

— corylifoliella, Hw. Widely distributed but apparently not abundant among apple, hawthorn, pear and whitebeam ; *Arundel, Bognor, Hastings, Worthing*

— viminiella, Stt. Canal between *Barnham* and *Chichester, Burpham, Coombes* ; among Salix alba

— ulicicolella, Stt. *Clymping, Leechpool, Moulescombe Pit* ; abundant among gorse

— alniella, Z. *Abbots Wood, Hassocks, Parham* ; among alder

— heegeriella, Z. ⎰ Generally abundant
— cramerella, Fb. ⎱ in oak woods

— tenella, Z. *Abbots Wood, Burgess Hill, Guestling* ; among hornbeam

— sylvella, Hw. *Eastbourne, Fairlight, Guestling,* between *Shoreham* and *Coombes*

— emberizæpennella, Bouché. *Eastbourne, Fernhurst, Pevensey, Tilgate Forest*

— nicellii, Stt. *Abbots Wood, Goring Woods, Hastings* ; among hazel

— schreberella, Fb. Generally abundant among elm in hedgerows

— tristrigella, Hw. *Falmer* ; *Henfield,* among elm, locally abundant

— trifasciella, Hw. Abundant generally among honeysuckle

Lyonetia clerkella, Linn. Generally distributed and often abundant, the larvæ feeding in leaves of birch, sallow, cherry, apple and hawthorn

— prunifoliella, Hb. In September, 1893, the larvæ of this species were abundant in leaves of apple in the Infirmary garden, *Worthing*, and a few were found feeding also in those of Prunus sinensis in another garden in the same town (Fletcher)

Phyllocnistis suffusella, Z. Abundant at *Bognor* and *Worthing* among Populus nigra ; rare at *Guestling, North Ambersham*

— saligna, Z. Abundant in the *Arun Valley* between *North Stoke* and *Warningcamp*, rare at *Guestling, Fernhurst*

Cemiostoma spartifoliella, Hb. *Burgess Hill, Hastings* ; among broom

— laburnella, Stt. Extremely abundant, generally in gardens among laburnum

— scitella, Z. *Broadwater, Hastings*

— wailesella, Stt. *Ditchling Common, Mundham* ; abundant among Genista tinctoria

— lotella, Stt. *Tilgate Forest* near *Cinderford*

Opostega salaciella, Tr. *Fernhurst, Gritham Common, Rewel Wood, Tilgate Forest* ; has been bred from Rumex acetosella (Meyrick, *Handbook*, p. 729), and has been observed to lay its eggs on the leaves of that plant

— crepusculella, Z. *Fairlight* (Bloomfield)

Bucculatrix nigricomella, Z., ab. aurimaculella, Stt. *Bramber, Ditchling Common, Guestling, High Down* near *Goring*

— cidarella, Z. *Abbots Wood; Tilgate Forest*, abundant among alder

— ulmella, Z. *Goring Woods, Rewel Wood*

— cratægi, Z. *Abbots Wood* among hawthorn and Pyrus torminalis, *Burgess Hill*

— demaryella, Dup. *Abbots Wood, Fernhurst*. A few larvæ cocoons and cocoonets found on birch in the *Rewel Wood* must no doubt be referred to this species

— maritima, Stt. Very abundant in the salt marshes between *Shoreham* and *Worthing*

— boyerella, Dup. *Broadwater*

— frangulella, Goeze. *Fernhurst, Findon, Parham, Storrington*

— cristatella, Z. *Arundel Park, Clapham Down, Clymping, Ditchling Common, Lancing* ; not uncommon among yarrow

— thoracella, Thnbg. *Horsham*, among lime trees

Nepticula atricapitella, Hw. } Generally distributed and abundant among oak
— ruficapitella, Hw. }

— basiguttella, Heeri. *Abbots Wood*, scarce

— anomalella, Goeze. Generally abundant among garden and wild roses

Nepticula fletcheri, Tutt. Widely distributed among Rosa arvensis ; *Balcombe, Bramber, Clapham, Parham, Slindon*

— pygmæella, Hw. *Arundel Park, Portslade, Worthing* ; very abundant among hawthorn

— pomella, Vaughan. *Bognor, Mundham, Worthing* ; abundant among apples in gardens

— oxyacanthella, Stt. Generally abundant, the larvæ feeding in leaves of Cratægus, Cotoneaster and Pyrus

— minusculella, H.S. *Worthing*, sometimes abundant among pear in gardens

— viscerella, Stt. *Bramber, Goring, Willingdon* ; among elm

— catharticella, Stt. *Arundel Park, Salvington Down* ; among Rhamnus catharticus

— septembrella, Stt. *Arundel, Abbots Wood, Eastbourne, High Down* near *Goring* ; among Hypericum sp.

— cryptella, Stt. *Arundel Park, Erringham, High Down, Shingles* near *Shoreham, Steyning*

— intimella, Z. *Abbots Wood, Hassocks* ; among Salix sp., scarce

— headleyella, Stt. Not uncommon in *Arundel Park* ; among Prunella vulgaris

— subbimaculella, Hw. *Abbots Wood, Fernhurst, Goring Woods* ; abundant among oak

— argyropeza, Z. *Abbots Wood, Falmer Woods* ; not uncommon among Populus tremula

— trimaculella, Hw. *Bognor, Worthing* ; abundant in gardens and plantations among Populus nigra. Larvæ observed in leaves of P. balsamifera near *Amberley* and *Bramber* railway stations are probably of this species

— assimilella, Z. *Abbots Wood*, larvæ in leaves of Populus tremula ; mines probably of this species have been observed in *Tilgate Forest*

— sericopeza, Z. *Arundel Park* ; larvæ not rare in fruits of Acer campestre

— floslactella, Hw. Everywhere abundant among hazel and hornbeam

— lapponica, Wck. } *Chailey, Falmer Woods*
— confusella, Wood } (Vine)

— salicis, Stt. Generally abundant among Salix cinerea, etc.

— vimineticola. Frey. *Abbots Wood*, valleys of the *Adur* and *Arun* ; not uncommon among Salix alba, in the leaves of which the larvæ feed

— microtheriella, Stt. Generally abundant among hazel

Nepticula poterii, Stt. *Cissbury*, larvæ not uncommon in leaves of Poterium sanguisorba

— betulicola, Stt. *Abbots Wood, Fernhurst, Tilgate Forest*

— ignobilella, Stt. *Brighton* (Vine)

— argentipedella, Z. *Abbots Wood*, abundant among birch

— acetosæ, Stt. Locally abundant. *Newmarket* and racecourse hills near *Brighton, Cissbury, Hurston Warren*

— plagicolella, Stt. Generally abundant among sloe in hedgerows and various species of Prunus in gardens

— prunetorum, Stt. *Abbots Wood, Goring*; locally abundant

— turicella, H.S. *Arundel Park, Abbots Wood, Slindon*

— basalella, H.S. *Abbots Wood, Houghton Forest, Preston.* Both this and the preceding species are doubtless generally abundant among beech

— angulifasciella, Stt. *Arundel, Sompting*; abundant among wild rose

— rubivora, Wck. *Arundel, Amberley, Slindon*; locally very abundant, the larvæ feeding in leaves of Rubus cæsius, especially in damp shady places or when the leaves are more or less buried among grass and other herbage

— agrimoniæ, Frey. *Abbots Wood*, among Agrimonia eupatoria

— atricollis, Stt. *Arundel Park*, abundant

— arcuatella, H.S. *Clapham Woods*, abundant among wild strawberry

— gratiosella, Stt. *Brighton* (Vine)

— ulmivora, Fologne. *Bramber*, the larvæ not uncommon in leaves of common elm

— marginicolella, Stt. Generally abundant among common elm in hedgerows

— alnetella, Stt. *Hassocks, Tilgate Forest*

— glutinosæ, Stt. *Hassocks*

— continuella, Stt. *Abbots Wood* (Vine)

— serella, Stt. *Chailey Common* (Vine). Mines found on *Ditchling Common* and

in *Tilgate Forest* in leaves of Potentilla tormentilla are no doubt the work of larvæ of this species, its ally N. tormentillella not having been found thus far in Great Britain

Nepticula æneofasciella, Stt. *Abbots Wood, Arundel, Cissbury, Poling, Slindon*; larvæ in Agrimonia eupatoria, Potentilla anserina (rarely), reptans and tormentilla

— centifoliella, Z. *Cissbury*, larvæ in leaves of Rosa rubiginosa sub-sp. micrantha, near *Seaford* in those of R. spinosissima

— filipendulæ, Wck. Downs near *Brighton, Eastbourne, Steyning, Worthing*; larvæ not uncommon in leaves of Spiræa filipendula

— fragariella, Heyd. *Arundel* and *Clapham Woods*, larvæ in Fragaria vesca; *Balcombe*, in Agrimonia eupatoria (see Tutt, *Lep. Brit.* i. 237)

— gei, Wck. *Arundel, Bramber, Polegate, Worthing*; widely distributed and not uncommon, the larvæ feeding in leaves of Geum urbanum and Rubus sp., especially cæsius and corylifolius

— aurella, Fb. Generally abundant, the larvæ feeding in leaves of Rubus fruticosus

— splendidissimella, H.S. Locally abundant, the larvæ feeding in leaves of Rubus cæsius; *Arundel, Filching, Goring, Polegate*

— luteella, Stt. *Abbots Wood, Tilgate Forest*

— lapponica, Wck. *Falmer Woods* and *Chailey* (Vine)

— regiella, H.S. *Arundel Park*, apparently; very scarce

Trifurcula immundella, Z. *Abbots Wood, Burgess Hill*; among broom

— pallidella, Z. *Ditchling Common*

— pulverosella, Stt. Mines of the larvæ seem abundant in crab-apple generally in the county; they have been observed at the following among other localities: *Arundel, Ditchling Common, Wiggonholt*

DIPTERA

Flies

This list contains about 950 species out of the 3,000 odd species of Diptera at present known to be British. This is as large a list as any county at present gives. This satisfactory result is owing to the county having been worked at times by Mr. G. H. Verrall, the well known authority on British Diptera. It is through his friendship that I have been enabled myself to add many species to the list. The eastern part of the district has been well worked by the Rev. E. N. Bloomfield,

INSECTS

whose records have mostly been embodied in the publications of the Hastings Natural History Society.

Collectors whose names frequently recur are indicated as follows:—

G.H.V. = Mr. G. H. Verrall. His various publications, notes and verb. com.

J. = J. H. A. Jenner—in most instances captures confirmed by Mr. Verrall

E.N.B. = Rev. E. N. Bloomfield, Guestling

    The Hastings district insects were in most cases determined or confirmed by Mr. Verrall, but a good many *Tachinidæ* and *Anthomyidæ* by Dr. Meade

H. List = The published lists of the Hastings and St. Leonards Natural History Society

C.M. = Mr. Claude Morley

U. = The late Mr. W. C. Unwin of Lewes

Mrs. M. = The list by Mr. Unwin in Mrs. Merrifield's *Natural History of Brighton*

G. = Mr. Guermonprez, Bognor

E.C. = Mr. Edward Connold, who has added very much to our knowledge of the Sussex Gall-making Diptera

E.A.B. = Mr. E. A. Butler

ORTHORRHAPHA

NEMATOCERA

PULICIDÆ

Pulex irritans, L. Everywhere on man
— canis, Curt. On dogs and cats
— felis, Bouché. On cats
— erinacei, Bouché. On hedgehogs
— goniocephalus, Tasch. Generally on rabbits ; on Arvicola amphibia (G.)

Trichopsylla fasciatus, Bosc. On Mus sylvaticus (G.) ; on field vole (H. List)
— sciurorum, Bouché. *Guestling* (H. List)
— gallinæ, Schrk. On fowls ; bred from sparrows' nest (G.)

Typhlopsylla agystes, Heller. On field vole (H. List)
— gracilis, Tasch. *Bognor* (G.)

Ctenopsyllus musculi, Dugés. On Mus musculus ; *Lewes* (J.H.A.J.), *Bognor* (G.)

Hystrichopsylla, talpæ, Curt. *Guestling, Ore* (H. List)

Ceratopsyllus elongatus, Curt. *Guestling,* on serotine bat (E.N.B.)

CECIDOMYIDÆ

Lasioptera rubi, Schrk. From stems of Rubi (E.N.B.) ; *Guestling*

Asphondylia pimpinellæ, F. From Daucus carota, *Guestling* (E.N.B.)
— sarothamni, Lw. *Ore* near *Hastings* (E.N.B., E.C.)
— ulicis, Traill. Flower buds of Ulex, *Hastings* district (E.N.B.)

Cecidomyia acrophila, Winn. *Guestling,* rare (E.C.)
— betulæ, Winn. *Hastings* (E.N.B.), in catkins of Betula alba

CECIDOMYIDÆ (*continued*)

Cecidomyia bursaria, Bremi. *Hastings* (E.N.B.), *Lewes* (J.), from Glechoma hederacea
— cardaminis, Winn. *Hastings* (E.N.B.), in flower buds of Cardamine pratensis
— cratægi, Winn. *Lewes* (J.), *Hastings* (E.N.B.) ; from Cratægus oxyacantha
— filicina, Kief. *Hastings* (E.N.B.), from Pteris aquilina
— galii, Lw. *Hastings* (E.N.B.), galls on Galium aparine
— lathyri, Frfld. *Hastings* (E.N.B.), leaves of Lathyrus pratensis
— marginemtorquens, Bremi. *Hastings* (E.N.B.), from Salix viminalis
— persicariæ, L. From Polygonum amphibium ; *Guestling, Ashburnham* (H. List)
— ranunculi, Brem. *Hastings* (E.N.B.), from Ranunculus repens
— rosaria, Lw. *Hastings* (E.N.B.) ; forms terminal rosettes on Salix
— rosarum, Hardy. *Hastings* (E.N.B.), in folded leaves of Rosa
— salicis, Schrk. From Salix ; *Hastings* (E.N.B.)
— sisymbrii, Schrk. *Lewes* (J.), *Crowhurst* (J.), *Hastings* (E.C.)
— taxi, Inch. *Hastings* (E.N.B.), *Crowhurst* (E.C.), *Lewes* (J.)
— tiliæ, Schrk. *Hastings* (E.N.B.), galls on Tilia europæa
— ulmariæ, Bremi. *Lewes* (J.), from Spiræa ulmaria ; *Hastings* (E.N.B.)
— urticæ, Perris. From Urtica dioica ; *Lewes* (J.), *Hastings* (E.N.B.)
— veronicæ, Vallot. *Lewes* (J.), *Hastings* (E.N.B.) ; from galls on Veronica chamædrys ; very common

A HISTORY OF SUSSEX

CECIDOMYIDÆ (*continued*)

Cecidomyida violæ, F. *Hastings* (E.N.B.), *Lewes* (J.)

Diplosis botularia,Winn. *Guestling*(E.N.B.), on Fraxinus excelsior

— dryobia, F. Lw. *Hastings* (E.N.B.)

— loti, Deg. „

— pyrivora, Riley. *Guestling* (E.N.B.); the 'pear gnat'

— tremulæ, Winn. *Hastings* (E.N.B.)

— tritici, Kirby. *Lewes* (J.), *Guestling* (E.N.B.)

Hormomyia annulipes, Hart. Galls on Fagus sylvatica, *Guestling* (E.N.B.)

— capreæ, Winn. *Guestling* (E.C.)

— millefolii, Lw. *Guestling* (E.C.), *Fairlight, Ore*; scarce

MYCETOPHILIDÆ

Sciara thomæ, Linn. Generally common

Mycetophila punctata, Mg. *Guestling* (H. List), *Bexhill* (C.M.)

— lineola, Mg. *Lewes* (G.H.V.)

— vittipes, Ztt. *Three Bridges* (G.H.V.)

— cingulum, Mg. *Guestling* (H. List)

Brachycampta serena, Winn. *Three Bridges* (G.H.V.)

Glaphyroptera fascipennis, Mg. *Guestling* (H. List)

— subfasciata, Mg. *Guestling* (H. List)

Anaclinia nemoralis, Mg. *Warrengore, Lewes* (G.H.V.)

Boletina trivittata, Mg. *Eridge* (G.H.V.)

Leptomorphus walkeri, Curt. *Guestling*, rare (H. List)

Lasiosoma hirtum, Mg. *Lewes* (G.H.V.)

Sciophila fasciata, Ztt. *Bognor* (G.)

Asindulum flavum, Winn. *Guestling* (H. List)

Platyura marginata,Mg. *Guestling*(E.N.B.), *Charlton Forest, Eartham* (G.)

— nana, Mcq. *Three Bridges* (G.H.V.)

Macrocera fasciata, Mg. *Guestling* (H. List), *Abbots Wood* (G.H.V.)

— lutea, Mg. *Guestling* (H. List)

— centralis, Mg. „ „

— angulata, Mg. *Guestling* (H. List), *Abbots Wood* (G.H.V.)

— stigma, Curt. *Guestling* (H. List), *Frant, Eridge* (G.H.V.)

— phalerata, Mg. *Guestling* (H. List)

BIBIONIDÆ

Scatopse notata, Linn. Generally common

— geniculata, Ztt. *Malling, Plashet Wood* (G.H.V.)

— scutellata, Lw. *Barcombe* (G.H.V.)

— flavicollis, Mg. *Barcombe, Ranscombe, Malling* near *Lewes* (G.H.V.)

— infumata, Hal. *Plashet Wood* (G.H.V.)

— albitarsis, Ztt. *Barcombe* (G.H.V.)

BIBIONIDÆ (*continued*)

Scatopse inermis, Ruth. *Warrengore, Ringmer, Plashet Wood* (G.H.V.)

— halterata, Mg. *Seaford, Warrengore,* etc. (G.H.V.)

— platyscelis, Lw. *Landport, Lewes* (20 June, 1867, G.H.V.); very rare

— clavipes, Lw. *Rotherfield, Ranscombe, Malling* near *Lewes* (G.H.V.)

— minutissima, Ver. Near *Pagham* before the harbour was reclaimed (G.H.V. 22 June, 1876)

— recurva, Lw. *Malling* near *Lewes* (G.H.V.)

Dilophus febrilis, Linn. Generally common

— albipennis, Mg. *Worth* (J.), *Guestling* (H. List), *Lewes* (G.H.V.), *Bognor* (G.)

Bibio pomonæ, F. *Crowborough* (J.), *St. Leonards* (H. List), *Eartham* (G.)

— marci, Linn. Generally common

— leucopterus, Mg. *Guestling* (H. List), *Laughton* (J.), *Abbots Wood* (G.H.V.), *Cocking* (G.)

— hortulanus, Linn. *Lewes* (J., H. List), *Bognor* (G.)

— anglicus, Ver. Common near *Lewes* (J.)

— venosus, Mg. *Guestling* (H. List), *Itchenor* (G.)

— reticulatus, Lw. *Lewes* (J.), *Abbots Wood, Plashet* (G.H.V.); *Hastings* (H. List)

— nigriventris, Hal. *Cooksbridge, Frant* (G.H.V.); *Bognor* (G.)

— varipes, Mg. *Guestling* (H. List), *Cocking* (G.)

— laniger, Mg. „ „

— johannis, Linn. Generally common

— lacteipennis, Ztt. *Worth* (J. & G.H.V.), *Guestling* (H. List)

— lepidus, Lw. *Guestling* (H. List)

— clavipes, Mg. *Plashet Wood, Lewes* (J. & G.H.V.); *Arundel, Aldwick* (G.)

SIMULIDÆ

Simulium ornatum, Mg. } *Hastings* district

— maculatum, Mg. } (G.H.V.)

CHIRONOMIDÆ

Chironomus plumosus, Linn. *Lewes* (J.), *Hastings*, etc. (H. List)

— riparius, Mg. (E.N.B.)

— dorsalis, Mg. *Three Bridges* (G.H.V.)

— pedellus, Deg. *Lewes*, abundant (J.); *Three Bridges* (G.H.V.)

— nubeculosus, Mg. *Three Bridges* (G.H.V.)

Orthocladius stercorarius, Deg. *Lewes* (G.H.V.)

— minutus, Ztt. *Three Bridges* (G.H.V.)

212

INSECTS

CHIRONOMIDÆ (continued)

Tanytarsus flavipes, Mg. *Lewes* (G.H.V.)

Diamesa obscurimanus, Mg. „ „

Tanypus nebulosus, Mg. *Plashet, Handcross* (G.H.V.)

— choreus, Mg. *Three Bridges* (G.H.V.)

— varius, F. *Bognor* (G.)

— carneus, F. *Landport, Lewes* (G.H.V.)

Clunio marinus, Hal. *Hastings* (Mr. C. Dale), *Brighton* (Mr. Unwin's list in Mrs. Merrifield's *History of Brighton*)

Ceratopogon pulicaris, Linn. *Bexhill* (H. List); bites sharply

— serripes, Mg. *Three Bridges* (G.H.V.)

— fasciatus, Mg. *Guestling, Ewhurst* (H. List)

— rubiginosus, Winn. *Three Bridges* (G.H.V.)

— albipes, Winn. *Lewes* (G.H.V.)

— solstitialis, Winn. *Three Bridges* (G.H.V.)

PSYCHODIDÆ

Pericoma palustris, Mg. *Hastings* (H. List)

— compta, Eat. *Sussex* (G.H.V. fide Eaton)

— fusca, Mcq. *Three Bridges* (J. & G.H.V.), *Frant* (G.H.V.)

— soleata, Hal. *Three Bridges* (G.H.V. fide Eaton)

Psychoda albipennis, Ztt. *Abbots Wood* (G.H.V.)

— sexpunctata, Curt. *Lewes* (G.H.V. & J., H. List)

— phalænoides, Linn. *Lewes* (G.H.V., J.), *Bognor* (G., H. List); common

— humeralis, Mg. *Lewes*; bred from decaying snails (J.)

CULICIDÆ

Corethra culiciformis, Mg. Near *Tunbridge Wells* (G.H.V.)

— plumicornis, F. (H. List). Near *Tunbridge Wells* (G.H.V.)

Anopheles bifurcatus, Linn. *Plashet, Barcombe* (G.H.V.)

— maculipennis, Mg. *Malling, Lewes* (G.H.V.); *Guestling* (H. List)

Culex annulatus, Schrk. *Lewes* (J., G.H.V.), *Guestling* (H. List)

— cantans, Mg. (H. List), near *Tunbridge Wells* (G.H.V.)

— nemorosus, Mg. *Abbots Wood*, near *Tunbridge Wells* (G.H.V.)

— pipiens, Linn. *Lewes* (J.), *Rotherfield, Eridge* (G.H.V.); very common

DIXIDÆ

Dixa æstivalis, Mg. *Lewes, Landport, Three Bridges*, near *Tunbridge Wells* (G.H.V.)

PTYCHOPTERIDÆ

Ptychoptera contaminata, L. *Guestling* (H. List), *Lewes* (J.), *Arundel* (G.)

— paludosa, Mg. *Guestling* (H. List), near *Tunbridge Wells* (G.H.V.)

— lacustris, Mg. *Eridge, Frant* (G.H.V.)

— albimana, F. *Icklesham* (H. List), *Battle, Lewes* (J.); near *Tunbridge Wells* (G.H.V.), *West Sussex* (G.)

LIMNOBIDÆ

Limnobia bifasciata, Schrk. *Laughton* (J.), *Guestling* (E.N.B.), *Five-mile Bottom* (G.), *Hastings* (Stephens)

— quadrinotata, Mg. *Guestling* (H. List), *Three Bridges, Frant, Crawley* (G.H.V.)

— nubeculosa, Mg. *Guestling* (H. List), *Lewes* (J.), near *Tunbridge Wells* (G.H.V.), *Rewell Wood* (G.)

— flavipes, F. *Guestling* (H. List), *Lewes* (G.H.V.)

— nigropunctata, Schum. *Lewes, Laughton, Abbots Wood* (J.); *Charlton Forest* (G.), *Guestling* (H. List)

— tripunctata, F. *Guestling* (H. List), *Landport* (G.H.V.), *Lewes* (J.)

— trivittata, Schum. *Guestling* (H. List)

— macrostigma, Schum. *Frant, Wadhurst* (G.H.V.)

Dicranomyia pilipennis, Egg. *Sussex* (G.H.V., E.M.M. xii. 1886)

— lutea, Mg. *Eridge, Frant, Landport, Rotherfield* (G.H.V.)

— chorea, Mg. *Hollington, Guestling* (H. List); *Lewes, Eridge* (G.H.V.); *Bognor* (G.)

— sericata, Mg. *Lewes*, near *Tunbridge Wells* (G.H.V.); *Laughton* (G.H.V.)

— didyma, Mg. *Guestling* (H. List), near *Tunbridge Wells, Eridge* (G.H.V.)

— dumetorum, Mg. *Guestling* (H. List), *Eridge, Frant, Three Bridges, Abbots Wood* (G.H.V.)

— morio, F. Near *Uckfield* (G.H.V.)

Rhipidia maculata, Mg. *Guestling* (H. List), *Three Bridges* (J.), *Frant* (G.H.V.)

Rhamphidia longirostris, Mg. *Eridge*, near *Tunbridge Wells* (G.H.V.)

Empeda flava, Schum. *Lewes* (J.), near *Tunbridge Wells* (G.H.V.)

— nubila, Schum. *Three Bridges, Eridge* (G.H.V.)

Goniomyia lateralis, Mcq. *Eridge* (G.H.V.)

Acyphona maculata, Mg. *Landport, Three Bridges*, near *Tunbridge Wells* (G.H.V.); *Woolbeding* (G.), *Guestling* (H. List)

Molophilus appendiculatus, Stæg. *Eridge, Frant* (G.H.V.)

LIMNOBIDÆ (*continued*)

Molophilus propinquus, Egg. *Sussex* (G. H.V.)

Rhypholophus nodulosus, Mcq. *Three Bridges, Frant* (G.H.V.)

— pentagonalis, Lw. *Frant* (G.H.V.)

— similis, Stæg. *Landport, Plashet* near *Lewes* (G.H.V.)

Erioptera flavescens, Mg. *Guestling* (H. List), *Three Bridges* (G.H.V.), *Lewes* (J.)

— macropthalma, Lw. *Frant,* near *Tunbridge Wells* (G.H.V.)

— tænionota, Mg. *Landport, Lewes, Frant* (G.H.V.)

— fuscipennis, Mg. *Eridge* (G.H.V.)

— trivialis, Mg. *Lewes, Frant, Wadhurst* (G.H.V.)

Symplecta punctipennis, Mg. *Guestling* (H. List), near *Tunbridge Wells* (G.H.V.)

— stictica, Mg. *Barcombe, Seaford* (G.H.V.) ; *Lewes* (J.)

Lipsothrix errans, Wlk. *Rotherfield, Wadhurst* (G.H.V.)

Ephelia submarmorata, Verr. *Guestling* (H. List), rare ; *Frant* (G.H.V.)

— marmorata, Mg. *Frant* (G.H.V.), *Faygate* (Bond)

Pæcilostola punctata, Schrk. *Guestling* (H. List), *Reedpond, Plumpton* (G.H.V.) ; *Pagham* (G.)

— pictipennis, Mg. *Lewes* (J.)

Epiphragma picta, F. *Guestling,* rare (H. List)

Limnophila dispar, Mg. *Guestling* (H. List), *Frant, Abbots Wood* (G.H.V.)

— lineola, Mg. *Guestling* (H. List), *Plumpton, Lewes, Wadhurst* (G.H.V.)

— lineolella, Verr. *Frant* (G.H.V.)

— aperta, Verr. „ „

— ferruginea, Mg. *Guestling* (H. List), *Plumpton, Frant, Eridge, Crawley* (G.H.V.)

— ochracea, Mg. *Guestling* (H. List), *Eridge* (G.H.V.)

— fuscipennis, Mg. *Frant* (G.H.V.)

— discicollis, Mg. *Guestling* (H. List), *Eridge, Frant* (G.H.V.)

— subtincta, Ztt. *Landport, Lewes* (J.)

— lucorum, Mg. *Eridge* (G.H.V.)

— sepium, Verr. *Frant* (G.H.V.)

— nemoralis, Mg. *Hastings* (H. List), *Frant* (G.H.V.)

— filata, Wlk. *Frant, Eridge* (G.H.V.)

Adelphomyia senilis, Hal. *Eridge, Frant* (G.H.V.)

Trichocera annulata, Mg. *Landport, Lewes* (G.H.V.) ; *Aldwick* (G.)

— hiemalis, Deg. *Hastings* (H. List),

LIMNOBIDÆ (*continued*)

Landport, Lewes (G.H.V.) ; *Bognor* (G.)

Trichocera fuscata, Mg. *Malling, Landport, Lewes* (G.H.V.)

— regelationis, L. *Hastings* (H. List), *Bramber, Handcross, Lewes* (J., G.H.V.)

Ula pilosa, Schum. *Guestling* (H. List), *Handcross* (G.H.V.)

Dicranota pavida, Hal. *Eridge, Wadhurst, Frant* (G.H.V.)

Amalopis immaculata, Mg. Near *Tunbridge Wells* (G.H.V.)

— unicolor, Schum. *Rotherfield* (G.H.V.)

— clavipennis, Verr. *Frant* (G.H.V.)

— littoralis, Mg. *Hastings, Hollington* (H. List) ; *Wadhurst, Frant, Eridge* (G.H.V.)

Pedicia rivosa, L. *Tilgate Forest, Three Bridges, Frant* (G.H.V.) ; *Hastings, Guestling,* rare (H. List)

Liogma glabrata, Mg. *Landport, Lewes* (G.H.V.)

Phalacrocera replicata, L. *Landport, Lewes* ; bred from aquatic pupa (J.)

TIPULIDÆ

Dolichopeza sylvicola, Curt. *Guestling,* rare (H. List) ; near *Tunbridge Wells* (G.H.V.)

Pachyrrhina imperialis, Mg. *Hastings, Guestling* (H. List) ; *Three Bridges, Eridge* (G.H.V.)

— scurra, Mg. *Hastings* (H. List)

— histrio, F. *Guestling* (H. List), *Lewes* (J.), *Brighton* (C. Morley), *Bognor* (G.)

— maculosa, Mg. *Guestling* (H. List), *Landport, Lewes, Rotherfield* (G.H.V.), *Bognor* (G.)

— guestfalica, Westh. *Sussex* (G.H.V.)

— quadrifaria, Mg. Common (H. List), *Landport, Lewes, Eridge* (G.H.V.), *Bognor* (G.)

— annulicornis, Mg. *Guestling,* rare (H. List) ; *Frant* (G.H.V.)

Tipula nigra, L. *Lewes* (J. & G.H.V.)

— pagana, Mg. *Guestling* (H. List), *Plashet, Lewes* (G.H.V.)

— obsoleta, Mg. *Landport, Ranscombe, Lewes* (G.H.V.)

— signata, Stæg. *Frant, Rotherfield* (G.H.V.)

— confusa, v. d. Wulp. *Guestling* (H. List)

— marmorata, Mg. Near *Lewes* (J. & G.H.V.)

— rufina, Mg. *Hastings* (Theobald)

— longicornis, Schum. *Guestling* (H. List), *Rotherfield* (J.), *Eridge, Wadhurst* (G.H.V.)

Tɪᴘᴜʟɪᴅᴀ (*continued*)

Tipula pabulina, Mg. *Lewes* (G.H.V.), *Rotherfield* (J.)

— hortulana, Mg. *Guestling* (H. List)

— varipennis, Mg. *Guestling*, etc. (H. List), *Rotherfield* (G.H.V.)

— scripta, Mg. *Guestling* (H. List), near *Tunbridge Wells* (G.H.V.)

— pruinosa, W. *Eridge* (G.H.V.), *Lewes* (J.)

— flavolineata, Mg. *Guestling*, rare (H. List), *Rotherfield* (G.H.V.)

— lunata, L. *Guestling* (H. List), *Rotherfield* (G.H.V.)

— lateralis, Mg. *Guestling* (H. List), *Landport, Warrengore, Lewes* (J. & G.H.V.)

— vernalis, Mg. Generally common

— vittata, Mg. *Guestling*, rare (E.N.B.), *Slindon* (G.)

— gigantea, Schrk. *Guestling* (H. List), *Lewes, Abbots Wood, Laughton, Crowborough* (J.); *Avisford* (G.)

— lutescens, F. *Guestling* (H. List), *Eridge* (G.H.V.), *Rotherfield* (J.)

— oleracea, Linn. Generally abundant

— paludosa, Mg. *Guestling* (H. List), *Frant* (G.H.V.), *Lewes* (J.)

— fascipennis, Mg. *Guestling* (E.N.B.), *Hastings* (Theobald), *Lewes* (J.), *Eridge* (G.H.V.)

— ochracea, Mg. *Abbots Wood*, etc. (G.H.V.), *Guestling* (H. List), *Lewes* (J.)

Dictenidia bimaculata, L. *Guestling*, rare (E.N.B.)

Ctenophora flaveolata, F. *Sussex* (Carrington)

Rʜʏᴘʜɪᴅᴀ

Rhyphus fenestralis, Scop. Generally common

— punctatus, F. *Lewes* (J.), near *Tunbridge Wells* (G.H.V.), *Guestling* (H. List)

BRACHYCERA

Sᴛʀᴀᴛɪᴏᴍʏɪᴅᴀ

Nemotelus pantherinus, Linn. *Rye* (H. List), *Lewes* (J.), *Brighton* (U.)

— uliginosus, Linn. *Rye* (H. List), *Bognor, Worthing* (G.H.V.), *Lewes, Pevensey* (W.)

— notatus, Ztt. *Sussex* (?) (H. List), *Selsea* (G.)

— nigrinus, Fln. *Hollington* (H. List), *Bognor, Selsea* (G.)

Oxycera formosa, Mg. *Guestling*, rare (H. list); *Plumpton* (G.H.V.)

— pulchella, Mg. *Rye* (H. List)

— trilineata, F. *Rye* (H. List), *Lewes* (J. & U.), *Hastings* (Theobald)

Sᴛʀᴀᴛɪᴏᴍʏɪᴅᴀ (*continued*)

Stratiomys potamida, Mg. *Guestling* (H. List), *Battle* (Connold), *Lewes* (J.), *Brighton* (U.)

— riparia, Mg. *Seaford* (J.)

— furcata, F. *Rye* (W. Esam, H. List), *Felpham* (G.)

— longicornis, Scop. *Guestling* (H. List), various localities near *Lewes*; rare (J.)

Odontomyia argentata, F. Near *Seaford* (U.), *Brighton* coast (Mrs. M.)

— ornata, Mg. *Guestling* (H. List), *Abbots Wood* (G.H.V.), *Lewes*, bred from aquatic pupæ (J.)

— tigrina, F. *Rye, Pett* (E.N.B.); *Lewes Marshes* (J.), *Malling* (G.H.V.), *Bognor* (G.H.V.)

— viridula, F. Locally common

Chrysonotus bipunctatus, Scop. *Iford* near *Lewes*, once in 1855 (U.)

Sargus flavipes, Mg. *Guestling* (H. List)

— cuprarius, Linn. *Hastings* (H. List), *Lewes* (J.), *Brighton* (Mrs. M.), *West Sussex* (G.)

— iridatus, Scop. *Rye, Guestling* (E.N.B.), *Lewes* (J.)

Chloromyia formosa, Scop. Generally common

Microchrysa polita, Linn. Common

— flavicornis, Mg. *Guestling, Rye* (H. List), *Lewes* (J.)

Beris vallata, Forst. *Guestling* (H. List), *Lewes* (J.), *West Sussex* (G.)

— clavipes, Linn. *Lewes* (U.), *Felpham* (G.)

— chalybeata, Forst. *Guestling* (H. List), *Uckfield* (G.H.V.), *Lewes* (J.), *West Sussex* (G.)

— morrisii, Dale. *Guestling*, rare (H. List)

Chorisops tibialis, Mg. *Guestling* (E.N.B.)

Tᴀʙᴀɴɪᴅᴀ

Hæmatopota pluvialis, Linn. Generally common

— crassicornis, Whlbg. *Guestling*, rare (E.N.B.), *Blackboys* (G.H.V.)

Therioplectes tropicus, Mg. var. bisignatus, Jæn. *Guestling*, rare (H. List)

— solstitialis, Mg. *Guestling* (H. List), *Lewes* (U.)

Atylotus rusticus, F. *Lewes* (J.)

— fulvus, Mg. *Ashdown Forest*, bred from pupa in Sphagnum (J.), *Lewes* district (U.)

Tabanus bovinus, Linn. *Hastings*, very rare (H. List), *Rottingdean, Kingston* (U.); occasional (G.)

— autumnalis, Linn. Generally common

— bromius, Linn. *Guestling* (H. List), *Lewes* (J.)

TABANIDÆ (*continued*)

Chrysops cæcutiens, Linn. *Lewes* (J.), *Three Bridges* (G.H.V.), *Slindon* (G.), common (H. List)

— quadrata, Mg. *Guestling* (H. List), *Abbots Wood* (G.H.V.)

— relicta, Mg. *Lewes* (J.), *Hastings* (H. List), *Bognor* (G.H.V.)

LEPTIDÆ

Leptis scolopacea, Linn. *Battle* (J.), *Lewes, Laughton* (J.); *Abbots Wood, Guestling,* etc. (H. List)

— tringaria, Linn. *Guestling,* etc. (H. List), *Lewes* (J.), *Brighton* (U.), *Slindon* (G.)

— lineola, F. Somewhat common (H. List), *Lewes* (W.), *West Sussex* (G.)

Chrysopilus aureus, Mg. *Lewes* (J.), *Hollington,* rare (H. List), *Felpham* (G.)

— auratus, F. Somewhat common ; *East Sussex, Cocking* (G.)

Atherix ibis, F. *Brighton,* local (Mrs. M.), no recent record for *East Sussex, Woolbeding* (G.)

— crassipes, Meig. *Ticehurst* (H. W. Andrews, 1900, *E.M.M.* 1901, p. 10)

Ptiolina wodzickii, Frfld. *Seaford* (J. & G.H.V.)

ASILIDÆ

Leptogaster cylindrica, Deg. Generally distributed

Dioctria œlandica, Linn. *Ninfield* (Connold), *Laughton* (J.)

— atricapilla, Mg. *Sussex* (?)

— rufipes, Deg. *St. Leonards; Guestling* (H. List), *Lewes* (J.), *Brighton* (U.), *Slindon, Felpham* (G.)

— baumhaueri, Mg. *Guestling* (H. List)

— flavipes, Mg. *Guestling* (H. List), *Plashet* (G.H.V.)

Isopogon brevirostris, Mg. *Warrengore, Lewes* (J.) ; *Bunkers Hill, Lewes* (G.H.V.) ; *Pevensey* (L. B. Hall), *Cocking* (G.)

Laphria marginata, Linn. *Guestling,* rare (H. List), *Plashet, Abbots Wood* (G.H.V.)

Asilus crabroniformis, Linn. *Lewes* (J.), *Battle* (J.), *Hastings, Guestling* (H. List), *Goodwood Park* (G.)

Philonicus albiceps, Mg. *Guestling,* rare (H. List), *Camber* (Connold)

Epitriptus cingulatus, F. *Guestling,* rare (H. List), *Cliffe Hill, Lewes* (J.), *Bognor* (G.)

Neoitamus cyanurus, O. Sack. *Guestling* (H. List), *Laughton* (J.), *Lewes* (U.), *Goodwood* (G.)

ASILIDÆ (*continued*)

Machimus atricapillus, Fln. *Guestling* (H. List), *Goodwood* (G.H.V.)

Dysmachus trigonus, Mg. *Guestling,* rare (H. List), *Cliffe Hill, Lewes* (J.)

Anthrax paniscus, Rossi. *Camber,* Aug. 1902 (E. A. Butler)

Bombylius discolor, Mik. Generally common ; bred from pupæ in banks ; *Ranscombe, Lewes,* 1888 (J.)

— major, Linn. Generally distributed in woods

THEREVIDÆ

Thereva nobilitata, F. *Guestling* (H. List), *Bognor* (G.)

— bipunctata, Mg. *Guestling* (H. List), *Lewes* (U.)

— annulata, F. *Fairlight, Camber* (H. List), *Newhaven* (U.)

Scenopinus fenestralis, Linn. *Lewes* (J.), frequent (U.)

CYRTIDÆ

Acrocera globulus, Pz. Very rare ; once, *Heathfield* (J.)

EMPIDÆ

Hybos grossipes, Linn. *Guestling* (H. List), *Lewes* (J.), *Abbots Wood* (G.H.V.)

— femoratus, Mull. *Hastings* (H. List)

Rhamphomyia nigripes, F. *Laughton* (J.)

— sulcata, Fln. *Guestling* (H. List), *Lewes* (J.)

— albosegmentata, Ztt. *Abbots Wood* (G.H.V.)

— costata, Ztt. *Three Bridges* (G.H.V.)

— simplex, Ztt. *Southerham, Lewes, Cuckmere* (G.H.V.)

— gibba, Fln. *Three Bridges* (G.H.V.)

— variabilis, Fln. *Dallington* (H. List)

— æthiops, Ztt. *Guestling* (H. List)

Empis tessellata, F. Abundant generally

— livida, Linn. Generally common

— stercorea, Linn. *Guestling,* rare (H. List), *Lewes* (J.), *Bognor, Bersted* (G.)

— trigramma, Mg. *Guestling* (H. List), *Lewes* (J.), *Abbots Wood* (G.H.V.)

— punctata, Mg. *Bersted* (G.)

— lutea, Mg. *Guestling* (H. List), *Malling, Lewes* (G.H.V.)

— scutellata, Curt. *Hastings* district (H. List), *Blackboys, Abbots Wood* (G.H.V.), *Cocking* (G.)

— pennipes, L. *Ninfield* (H. List), *Bersted* (G.)

— vernalis, Mg. *Warrengore, Lewes* (G.H.V.)

— caudatula, Lw. *Landport, Lewes* (G.H.V.)

— vitripennis, Mg. *Rotherfield, Three Bridges* (G.H.V.), *Brighton* (U.)

INSECTS

EMPIDÆ (*continued*)

Empis grisea, Fln. *Three Bridges, Abbots Wood* (G.H.V.)

Pachymeria femorata, F. *Fairlight* (H. List), *Lewes* (J.), *Brighton* (U.), *Slindon* (G.)

Ragas unica, Wlk. *Faygate* (G.H.V.)

Hilara interstincta, Fln. *Guestling* (H. List)

— maura, F. *Guestling* (H. List), *Lewes* (J.)

— quadrivittata, Mg. *Brighton* (U.) (?)

— cornicula, Lw. *Three Bridges* (G.H.V.)

— litorea, Fln. *Guestling* (H. List)

Oreogeton flavipes, Mg. *Guestling* (H. List)

Heleodromia stagnalis, Hal. *Landport, Lewes* (G.H.V.), *Brighton* (U.)

— fontinalis, Hal. *Guestling* (H. List), *Lewes* (G.H.V.)

Hemerodromia precatoria, Fln. *Lewes* (J.), *Battle, Hollington* (H. List)

Ardoptera irrorata, Fln. *Three Bridges* (G.H.V.)

Lepidomyia melanocephala, F. *Guestling* (H. List), *Abbots Wood* (G.H.V.)

Thamnodromia albiseta, Ztt. *Three Bridges* (G.H.V.)

— vocatoria, Fln. *Guestling* (H. List)

Drapetis assimilis, Fln. *Barcombe* (G.H.V.)

— exilis, Mg. *Lewes* (G.H.V.)

Tachypeza nubila, Mg. *Abbots Wood* (G.H.V.)

Tachista arrogans, Linn. *Lewes, Seaford* (G.H.V.), *Felpham, Bognor* (G.)

DOLICHOPODIDÆ

Psilopus platypterus, F. *Hollington* (H. List), *Malling, Lewes* (G.H.V.)

— wiedemanni, Fln. *Sussex* (G.H.V.)

— longulus, Fln. *Worthing* (G.H.V.)

Neurigona suturalis, Fln. *Ewhurst* (W. Esam, H. List)

Eutarsus aulicus, Mg. *Lewes, Cooksbridge, Three Bridges, Pagham* (G.H.V.)

Hygroceleuthus diadema, Hal. *Lewes* (J.)

Dolichopus atripes, Mg. *Guestling* (H. List)

— vitripennis, Mg. *Blackboys, Framfield* (G.H.V.)

— atratus, Mg. *Framfield* (G.H.V.), *Lewes* (J.)

— campestris, Mg. *Seaford, Malling, Lewes* (G.H.V.); *Itchenor* (G.)

— nubilus, Mg. *Seaford* (G.H.V.)

— latelimbatus, Mcq. *Three Bridges* (G.H.V.)

— discifer, Stan. *Lewes* (J.)

— plumipes, Scop. *Guestling* (H. List), *Lewes* (J.), *Seaford, Three Bridges* (G.H.V.)

DOLICHOPODIDÆ (*continued*)

Dolichopus wahlbergi, Ztt. *Abbots Wood, Plashet, Three Bridge* (G.H.V.)

— popularis, W. *Buxted* (G.H.V.)

— griseipennis, Stan. *Guestling* (H. List), *Lewes* (J.), *Three Bridges, Seaford* (G.H.V.)

— virgultorum, Hal. *Plashet, Lewes* (G.H.V.)

— festivus, Hal. *Guestling* (H. List), *Lewes, Plashet, Three Bridges* (G.H.V.)

— trivialis, Hal. Generally common

— brevipennis, Mg. *Malling, Lewes* (G.H.V.)

— æneus, Deg. Generally common

Pœcilobothrus nobilitatus, Linn. Generally common

— ducalis, Lw. *Seaford* (J. & G.H.V.)

— principalis, Lw. „ „

Hercostomus chærophylli, Mg. „ *Malling, Landport, Lewes* (G.H.V.)

— nigripennis, Fln. *Guestling* (H. List), *Blackboys* (G.H.V.)

— nanus, Mcq. *Three Bridges* (G.H.V.)

— parvilamellatus, Mcq. *Blackboys* (G.H.V.)

Hypophyllus obscurellus, Fln. *Three Bridges, Rotherfield, Buxted* (G.H.V.)

Orthochile nigrocærulea, Ltr. *Guestling* (E.N.B.)

Gymnopternus cupreus, Fln. *Pett* (H. List), *Blackboys* (G.H.V.)

— celer, Mg. *Three Bridges, Blackboys* (G.H.V.)

— metallicus, Stan. *Plashet, Three Bridges, Abbots Wood* (G.H.V.)

— ærosus, Fln. *Three Bridges* (G.H.V.)

— assimilis, Stæg „ „ „

Chrysotus neglectus, W. *Malling, Lewes, Blackboys* (G.H.V.)

— cilipes, Mg. *Seaford* (G.H.V.)

— cupreus, Mcq. *Guestling* (H. List), *Laughton, Blackboys, Faygate* (G.H.V.)

— læsus, W. *Guestling* (H. List), *Buxted* (G.H.V.)

— palustris, Verr. *Seaford* (G.H.V.)

— gramineus, Fln. *Three Bridges, Laughton, Plumpton* (G.H.V.)

Diaphorus oculatus, Fln. *Abbots Wood, Three Bridges* (G.H.V.)

— winthemi, Mg. *Plashet, Three Bridges* (G.H.V.)

Argyra diaphana, F. *Guestling* (H. List), *Three Bridges* (G.H.V.), *Woolbeding* (G.)

— argentina, Mg. *Guestling* (H. List), *Lewes, Three Bridges* (G.H.V.)

— leucocephala, Mg. *Guestling* (H. List), *Three Bridges* (G.H.V.), *Lewes, Barcombe, Abbots Wood* (G.H.V.)

DOLICHOPODIDÆ (continued)

Leucostola vestita, W. *Pagham* (G.H.V.)

Thrypticus bellus, Lw. *Bishopstone, Warrengore, Lewes* (G.H.V.)

Porphyrops spinicoxa, Lw. *Three Bridges, Faygate, Uckfield, Abbots Wood* (G.H.V.)

— nemorum, Mg. } *Landport, Lewes,*
Syntormon zelleri, Lw. } (G.H.V.)

— pumilus, Mg. *Lewes* (G.H.V.)

— monilis, Wlk. *Framfield* (G.H.V.)

— pallipes, F. *Lewes, Seaford, Bognor* (G.H.V.)

Machærium maritimæ, Hal. *Bishopstone* (G.H.V.)

Xiphandrium caliginosum, Mg. *Lewes, Glynde, Plumpton* (G.H.V.)

— appendiculatum, Ztt. *Three Bridges, Plashet, Uckfield, Lewes* (G.H.V.)

Achalcus cinereus, Wlk. *Rotherfield* (G.H.V.)

— flavicollis, Mg. *Three Bridges* (G.H.V.)

Medeterus micaceus, Mg. *Worthing* (G.H.V.)

— jaculus, Mg. *Barcombe* (G.H.V.)

— truncorum, Mg. *Guestling* (H. List), *Plashet* (G.H.V.)

Scellus notatus, F. *Guestling* (E.N.B.), *Pett* (H. List), *Laughton* (G.H.V.), *Lewes* (J.)

Hydrophorus bipunctatus, Lehm. *Barcombe* (G.H.V.)

— balticus, Mg. *Lewes* (G.H.V.)

— litoreus, Flu. „ „

— præcox, Lehm. *Pett* (H. List), *Seaford, Pagham* (G.H.V.)

— bisetus, Lw. *Goring* (G.H.V.)

Liancalus virens, Scop. *Brighton*, rare (U., Mrs. M.)

Allæoneurus lacustris, Scop. Near *Hastings* (C. W. Dale), *Malling, Lewes* (G.H.V.)

Campsicnemus scambus, Fln. *Three Bridges* (G.H.V.)

— curvipes, Fln. *Guestling* (H. List), *Lewes, Three Bridges, Rotherfield* (G.H.V.)

— loripes, Hal. *Three Bridges* (G.H.V.)

Teuchophorus pectinifer, Kow. *Three Bridges* (G.H.V.)

Sympycnus annulipes, Mg. *Plashet, Lewes* (G.H.V.)

Lamprochromus elegans, Mg. *Landport, Lewes* (G.H.V.)

Bathycranium bicolorellus, Ztt. *Plashet, Lewes* (G.H.V.)

Thinophilus ruficornis, Hal. *Sussex* (?)

Schœnophilus versutus, Wlk. *Seaford* (G.H.V.)

Micromorphus albipes, Ztt. *Bognor* (G.H.V.)

LONCHOPTERIDÆ

Lonchoptera punctum, Mg. *Brighton* (Mrs. M.)

— flavicauda, Mg. *Guestling* (H. List)

CYCLORRHAPHA

PROBOSCIDEA

PLATYPEZIDÆ

Callimyia amæna, Mg. *Sussex* (G.H.V.)

Agathomyia antennata, Ztt. „ „

Platypeza fasciata, Mg. Near *Hastings* (H. List, Dale)

PIPUNCULIDÆ

Chalarus spurius, Fln. *Sussex* (G.H.V.), *Cocking* (G.)

Verrallia pilosa, Ztt. *Guestling* (H. List)

— villosa, v. Ros. *Guestling* (H. List.), *Eridge* (G.H.V.)

Pipunculus furcatus, Egg. *Guestling* (H. List)

— zonatus, Ztt. *Guestling* (H. List)

— fuscipes, Ztt. „ „

— ruralis, Mg. *Blackboys* (G.H.V.)

— unicolor, Ztt. *Sussex* (G.H.V.)

— terminalis, Thoms. *Three Bridges* (G.H.V.)

— varipes, Mg. *Guestling* (H. List)

— campestris, Latr. „ „

— flavipes, Mg. *Three Bridges* (G.H.V.)

— strobli, Verr. „ „

— xanthopus, Thoms. *Abbots Wood* (G.H.V.)

— geniculatus, Mg. *Dale Park* (G.)

— sylvaticus, Mg. *Sussex* (G.H.V.)

SYRPHIDÆ

Paragus tibialis, Fln. *Abbots Wood, Seaford* (G.H.V.)

— bicolor, F., var. lacerus, Lw. *Seaford*, once (J.)

Pipizella virens, F. *Guestling, St. Leonards, Hollington* (H. List); *Plashet* (G.H.V.), *Landport, Lewes* (U.); *Bognor* (G.)

Pipiza quadrimaculata, Pz. *Hastings* (H. List)

— noctiluca, Linn. *Guestling* (H. List), *Plashet, Abbots Wood* (G.H.V.); *Laughton* (J.)

— fenestrata, Mg. *Lewes* (U.)

— signata, Mg. *Battle* (J.)

— notata, Mg. *Abbots Wood, Tilgate* (G.H.V.); *Lewes* (U.)

Orthoneura nobilis, Fln. *Dallington* (H. List)

— elegans, Mg. *Landport, Lewes* (J.)

Liogaster metallina, F. *Guestling* (H. List), *Chailey* (G.H.V.), *Eastbourne* (Billups)

Chrysogaster splendens, Mg. *Guestling* (H. List)

— hirtella, Lw. *Guestling* (H. List)

INSECTS

SYRPHIDÆ (*continued*)

Chrysogaster chalybeata, Mg. *Plashet* (G.H.V.), *Lewes* (U.)

— solstitialis, Fln. *Guestling, St. Leonards* (H. List), *Rotherfield* (G.H.V.), *Lewes* (S.H.V., J.)

Chilosia maculata, Fln. *Sussex* (G.H.V.)

— sparsa, Lw. *Guestling* (H. List)

— antiqua, Mg. *Hollington* (H. List), *Frant* (G.H.V.), *Laughton* (J.)

— longula, Ztt. *Three Bridges* (G.H.V.)

— scutellata, Fln. *Guestling* (H. List), *Abbots Wood* (G.H.V.)

— pulchripes, Lw. *Guestling* (H. List), *Three Bridges* (G.H.V.), *Lewes* (U.)

— variabilis, Pz. Generally distributed

— illustrata, Haw. *Guestling* (H. List), *Laughton, Abbots Wood* (J.) ; *Knepp* (G.H.V.), *Plashet* (U.)

— grossa, Fln. *Hastings*, very rare (H. List), *Hailsham* (J.)

— albipila, Mg. *Guestling* (H. List), *Laughton, Battle* (J.)

— nebulosa, Verr. *Battle* (J.), *Guestling* (E. N. B.), *Warrengore, Plashet* (G.H.V.)

— albitarsis, Mg. Generally common

— fraterna, Mg. Not uncommon in many localities

— præcox, Ztt. Once, *Lewes* (U.)

— mutabilis, Fln. *Eridge* (G.H.V.)

— vernalis, Fln. *Guestling* (H. List), *Abbots Wood* (J.), *Chailey, Lewes, Three Bridges* (G.H.V.)

Platychirus manicatus, Mg. *Guestling* (H. List), *Plumpton* (G.H.V.), common (U.), *Bognor* (G.)

— discimanus, Lw. *Tilgate Forest*, 1886 (J.)

— peltatus, Mg. Common (H. List), *Seaford* (G.H.V.), *Pevensey, Eastbourne* (U.)

— scutatus, Mg. *Hastings* (H. List), *Bognor* (G.)

— albimanus, F. *St. Leonards, Hastings, Guestling* (H. List) ; *Lewes* (J.), *Bognor* (G.)

— immarginatus, Ztt. *Landport, Lewes* (G.H.V.)

— clypeatus, Mg. *Landport, Lewes* (G.H.V.) ; *Guestling* (H. List), *Bognor* (G.)

— angustatus, Ztt. *Guestling* (H. List), *Framfield* (G.H.V.)

Pyrophæna granditarsa, Forst. *Pett* (H. List), *Lewes* (J.) ; scarce

— rosarum, F. *Chailey* (G.H.V.)

Melanostoma ambiguum, Fln. *Warrengore, Plashet, Plumpton* (G.H.V.)

— mellinum, Linn. Generally common

SYRPHIDÆ (*continued*)

Melanostoma scalare, F. Generally common

Xanthandrus comtus, Haw. *Stanmer Park* near *Lewes* (J.), rare ; *Bognor* (G.)

Leucozona lucorum, Linn. Generally distributed

Ischyrosyrphus laternarius, Müll. *Guestling* (H. List), *Laughton, Abbots Wood* (J.), *Pevensey* (U.) ; scarce

Catabomba pyrastri, Linn. Common in some seasons

— selenitica, Mg. Garden, *Bognor* (G.)

Syrphus albostriatus, Fln. *Guestling* (H. List), *Chailey* (G.H.V.), *Tilgate, Lewes* (J.) ; *Bognor* (G.)

— tricinctus, Fln. *Pett*, rare (H. List), *Laughton* (J.), *Plashet, Firle* (U.) ; rare

— venustus, Mg. *Guestling* (H. List)

— lunulatus, Mg. Generally distributed

— nigricornis, Verr. *Guestling* (H. List), *Frant* (G.H.V.)

— torvus, O.S. *Plashet Wood*, 1867 (G.H.V.)

— annulatus, Ztt. *Frant* (G.H.V.), *Three Bridges* (J.)

— vittiger, Ztt. *Sussex* (G.H.V.)

— grossulariæ, Mg. *Firle* (U.), *Three Bridges* (J.)

— ribesii, Linn. Generally common

— vitripennis, Mg. „ „

— latifasciatus, Mcq. *Guestling*, rare (H. List), *Pagham* (G.H.V.), *Lewes* (J.); periodical

— nitidicollis, Mg. *Guestling* (H. List), *Battle, Laughton* (J.); *Abbots Wood* (G.H.V.)

— nitens, Ztt. *Plashet Wood*, 1867 (G.H.V.)

— corollæ, F. Abundant

— luniger, Mg. *Hastings* (H. List), *Bognor* (G.), *Plashet Wood* (U.)

— bifasciatus, F. Generally common

— balteatus, Deg. Abundant

— cinctellus, Ztt. Generally distributed

— auricollis, Mg., var. maculicornis, Ztt. *Aldwick* (G.), *Guestling* (E.N.B.), *Lewes* (J.)

— euchromus, Kow. *Three Bridges* (G.H.V.)

— punctulatus, Verr. *Plashet Wood* (G.H.V.)

— umbellatarum, F. *Sussex* (G. H. V.), *Guestling*, rare (H. List)

— lasiopthalmus, Ztt. *Battle* (J., H. List), *Plashet Wood, Warrengore* (J.)

Sphærophoria scripta, Linn. *Guestling* (H. List), *Lewes*, common (U), *Bognor* (G.)

var. dispar, Lw. Common (H. List), *Lewes*

SYRPHIDÆ (*continued*)

Sphærophoria menthastri, Linn. *Guestling* (H. List), *Lewes*, common (U.)
    var. picta, Mg. *Hastings* district (E.N.B.)
— flavicauda, Ztt. *Lewes* (J.), *Bognor* (G.)

Xanthogramma ornatum, Mg. *St. Leonards, Guestling*, rare (H. List); *Battle* (J.), *Lewes* (J.), *Uckfield, Pagham, Abbots Wood* (G.H.V.); *Ringmer, Newhaven* (U.)
— citrofasciatum, Deg. Downs, *Lewes* (J.), *Abbots Wood* (G.H.V.), *Guestling*, rare (H. List), *Firle, Brighton* (U.); *Bognor, Cocking* (G.)

Baccha elongata, F. *Guestling*, rare (H. List), *Laughton* (J.), *Lewes, Frant, Abbots Wood* (G.H.V.)
— obscuripennis, Mg. *Bognor* (G.)

Sphegina clunipes, Fln. *Frant, Three Bridges* (G.H.V.)

Ascia podagrica, F. Very common generally
— dispar, Mg. *Bognor, Yapton* (G.)
— floralis, Mg. *Plumpton* (G.H.V.), *Ewhurst* (W. Esam)

Brachyopa bicolor, Fln. *Guestling*, rare (E.N.B.), *Laughton*, occasionally common at sap (J.)

Rhingia campestris, Mg. Generally common

Volucella bombylans, Linn. Generally common
— inanis, Linn. *Guestling*, rare (H. List), *Three Bridges* (G.H.V.)
— inflata, F. *St. Leonards, Guestling*, rare (H. List); *Laughton, Battle* (J.); *Abbots Wood* (G.H.V.), *Plashet Wood* (U.), *Dale Park* (G.)
— pellucens, Linn. *Guestling*, etc. (H List), *Lewes, Abbots Wood, Battle* (J.); *Plashet Wood* (U.).

Eristalis sepulchralis, Linn. *Pett* (H. List), *Lewes* (G.H.V.), *Seaford* (J.), *Bognor, Middleton* (G.)
— æneus, Scop. *Seaford* (J. & G.H.V.), *Pevensey* (U.), *Bognor* (G.)
— cryptarum, F. *St. Leonards* (Mr. Dale, H. List)
— tenax, Linn. Generally abundant
— intricarius, Linn. Generally distributed
— arbustorum, Linn. Abundant
— nemorum, Linn. *Hastings, Guestling* (H. List), *Rotherfield, Plashet, Abbots Wood* (G.H.V.)
— pertinax, Scop. Generally common
— horticola, Deg. *Guestling* (H. List), *Plashet Wood* (G.H.V.), *Laughton* (J.), woods near *Lewes* (U.), *Danes Wood, Walberton* (G.)

SYRPHIDÆ (*continued*)

Myiatropa florea, Linn. Generally distributed

Helophilus trivittatus, F. *Guestling, Rye* (H. List), *Seaford* (J., G.H.V.), *Lewes* (J.), periodical ; *Bognor* (G.)
— hybridus, Lw. *Guestling, Pett*, rare (H. List); *Seaford, Lewes* (J.)
— pendulus, Linn. Generally common
— versicolor, F. Rare ; *Ashdown Forest* (J.)
— transfugus, Linn. *Winchelsea* (W. Esam, H. List)
— lineatus, F. Near *Tunbridge Wells* (G.H.V.), *Stoneham* near *Lewes* (J.), *Firle* (U.); rare
— vittatus, Mg. *Winchelsea* (Hall, H. List), *Seaford* (J.) very rare

Tropidia scita, Haw. *Hastings* district (H. List), *Lewes* (J.), *Goring* (G.H.V.)

Criorrhina ranunculi, Pz. Once at *Battle* (J.)
— berberina, F. *Guestling*, rare (E.N.B.), *Laughton, Tilgate* (J.)
— oxyacanthæ, Mg. *St. Leonards, Guestling* (H. List); *Three Bridges, Abbots Wood* (G.H.V.); *Laughton* (J.), *Plashet* (U.), *Bognor* (G.)
— floccosa, Mg. *Lewes*, (G.H.V.) *Glynde, Tilgate* (J.)
— asilica, Fln. *Guestling* (H. List), *Abbots Wood*, (G.H.V.), *Three Bridges, Laughton* (J.)

Xylota segnis, Linn. *Guestling, Hastings* (H. List) ; woods round *Lewes* (U.), *Abbots Wood, Laughton* (J.) ; *Walberton* (G.)
— tarda, Mg. *Three Bridges* (G.H.V.)
— sylvarum, Linn. *Guestling, St. Leonards* (H. List); *Battle* (J.), *Abbots Wood* (G.H.V.), woods, *Lewes* (U.), *Walberton* (G.)
— abiens, W. *Abbots Wood* (G.H.V.)

Syritta pipiens, Linn. Abundant everywhere

Eumerus ornatus, Mg. *Plashet Wood, Three Bridges* (G.H.V.)

Chrysochlamys cuprea, Scop. *Guestling* (E.N.B.), *Laughton, Battle* (J.) ; *Abbots Wood, Three Bridges, Uckfield* (G.H.V.)

Sericomyia borealis, Fln. *Guestling, Dallington* (H. List) ; *Battle, Abbots Wood* (J.)

Chrysotoxum cautum, Haw. *Guestling* (H. List), *Battle, Abbots Wood* (J.) ; *Frant, Eridge* (G.H.V.) ; *Firle* (U.), *Bognor* (G.)
— elegans, Lw. *Guestling*, rare (H. List), *Battle, Abbots Wood, Laughton* (J.) ; *Plashet* (U.)

INSECTS

SYRPHIDÆ (*continued*)

Chrysotoxum festivum, Linn. *Guestling* ('Theobald), *Tilgate* (J. & G.H.V.)

— bicinctum, Linn. *St. Leonards, Guestling* (H. List); *Abbots Wood* (G.H.V.), *Laughton* (J.)

Callicera ænea, F. *Guestling*, once (E.N.B., *E.M.M.* xxv. 238)

CONOPIDÆ

Conops vesicularis, Linn. *Tilgate Forest*, once (J.)

— quadrifasciata, Deg. *Hastings* (E.N.B.), woods near *Lewes* (U.)

— flavipes, Linn. *Guestling* (E.N.B.), *Lewes, Abbots Wood, Eridge* (G.H.V.)

Physocephala rufipes, F. *Guestling* (H. List), woods near *Lewes* (U.)

Oncomyia atra, F. *Guestling*, rare (H. List)

— pusilla, Mg. *Lewes* (G.H.V.), *Guestling* (E.N.B.)

Sicus ferrugineus, Linn. *Guestling, Hastings* (H. List); *Abbots Wood* (G.H.V.)

Myopa buccata, Linn. *Guestling* (E.N.B.), *Laughton* (J.), *Bognor* (G.)

— testacea, Linn. *Plashet, Chiddingly* (G.H.V.), *Lewes* (J.)

— polystigma, Rnd. *Guestling* (E.N.B.), *Hastings* (W. Esam)

ŒSTRIDÆ

Gastrophilus equi, F. *Guestling* (E.N.B.), *Lewes* (J.)

— nasalis, Linn. *Firle* (U.)

Hypoderma lineatum, Vill. *St. Leonards* (specimen in British Museum)

Œstrus ovis, Linn. *Guestling* (H. List), *Battle* (J.); rare

TACHINIDÆ

Exorista fimbriata, Mg. Near *Hastings* (H. List)

— notabilis, Mg. *Bognor* (G.)

— perturbans, Ztt. *Hastings* (H. List)

— jucunda, Mg. *Ewhurst* (W. Esam)

Epicampocera succincta, Mg. *Guestling* (H. List)

— ambulans, Mg. *Abbots Wood* (G.H.V.)

Blepharidea vulgaris, Fln. *Guestling* (H. List), *Eastbourne* (C. Morley)

Myxexorista macrops, B. & B. *Hollington* (W. Esam), *Abbots Wood* (G.H.V.)

Phorocera serriventris, Rnd. Near *Hastings* (H. List)

— cilipeda, Rnd. Near *Hastings* (H. List), *Bognor* (G.)

— pumicata, Mg. *Guestling* (H. List)

Bothria assimilis, Fln. „ „

— cæsifrons, Mcq. Near *Hastings* (H. List)

Blepharipoda ? atropivora, Rnd. *Hastings* district

TACHINIDÆ (*continued*)

Chætolyga amæna, Mg. *Guestling* (H. List)

Tachina larvarum, Linn. „ „

Gonia fasciata, Mg. *Hastings* district

— divisa, Mg. *Eastbourne* (W. Esam)

Thelymorpha vertiginosa, Fln. *Guestling* (E.N.B.)

Monochæta leucophæa, Mg. *Guestling* (H. List)

Aporomyia dubia, Fln. *Guestling, Pett* (E.N.B.)

Somolia rebaptizata, Rnd. *Pevensey* (L. B. Hall)

Mintho præceps, Scop. *Bognor* (G.)

Melanota volvulus, F. *Guestling* (H. List)

Macquartia tenebricosa, Mg. „ „

Ptilops chalybeata, Mg. „ „

Anthracomyia nana, Mg. *Hastings* district (E.N.B.)

— anthracina, Mg. *Guestling, Hastings* district (E.N.B.)

Degeeria ornata, Mg. *Guestling* (Meade), *Polegate* (C. Morley)

Thelaira leucozona, Pz. *Guestling* (H. List)

Demoticus plebeius, Fln. Near *Hastings* (W. Esam)

Olivieria lateralis, F. Generally common

Micropalpus vulpinus, Fln. *Isfield* (G.H.V.), *Hastings* district

Erigone radicum, F. *Guestling* (H. List)

— vagans, Mg. *Hastings* district, *Ewhurst*

Echinomyia grossa, Linn. *Abbots Wood* (J.), near *Lewes* (Unwin)

— fera, Linn. Not uncommon

Fabricia ferox, Linn. *Lewes* (J.), *Bognor* (G.)

Servillia lurida, F. *Guestling*, rare (H. List)

— ursina, Mg. *Guestling* (H. List)

Plagia ruralis, Fln. *Bexhill* (H. List)

Anachætopsis ocypterina, Ztt. *Guestling* (E.N.B.), *Ore* (E. A. Butler)

Phorichæta lugens, Mg. *Hastings* district

— carbonaria, Pz. *Littlehampton* (E. Saunders)

— tricincta, Rnd. *Hastings* district

Ræselia antiqua, Fln. „ „

Thryptocera pilipennis, Mg. „ *Guestling* (E.N.B.)

— crassicornis, Mg. *Guestling* (H. List)

— bicolor, Mg. „ „

— minutissima, Ztt. „ „

Siphona geniculata, Deg. *Guestling* (E.N.B.), *Lewes* (Unwin), *Bognor* (G.)

Gymnosoma rotundatum, Linn. *Abbots Wood* (J.), *Guestling*, very rare (E.N.B.); very rare in England

Cercomyia curvicauda, Fln. *Guestling* (E.N.B.)

TACHINIDÆ (*continued*)

Psalida simplex, Fln. *Guestling* (H. List)

Alophora pusilla, Mg. „ „

— hemiptera, F. *Walberton*; *Felpham*, bred from Bombyx neustria (G.)

Fortisia fœda, Mg. *Guestling* (H. List)

Melanophora roralis, Linn. „ „

— atra, Meg. *Guestling* (E.N.B.), *Middleton* (G.)

Rhinophora atramentaria, Mg. *Guestling* (E.N.B.)

Brachycoma devia, Fln. *Guestling* (H. List)

Clista lepida, Mg. *Guestling* (E.N.B.)

Cynomyia mortuorum, Linn. Once, *Cliffe Hill, Lewes* (G.H.V.)

Onesia sepulchralis, Linn. *Guestling* (H. List)

— cognata, Mg. *Pevensey* (L. B. Hall)

Sarcophaga carnaria, Linn. Generally common

— albiceps, Mg. *Hastings* district

— atropos, Mg. „ „

— agricola, Mg. *Guestling* (H. List)

— laticornis, Mg. *Ore* (H. List)

— nigriventris, Mg. *Hastings, Guestling* (H. List); *Littlehampton* (Saunders)

— hæmorrhoidalis, Mg. *Hastings* district, *Bognor* (G.)

— hæmatodes, Mg. *Pett* (L. B. Hall)

— hæmorrhoa, Mg. *Guestling* (H. List)

Nyctia halterata, Pz. *Guestling, Ore, Pett*

Miltogramma punctatum, Mg. *Guestling* (E.N.B.)

Metopia argyrocephala, Mg. *Guestling* (H. List)

— leucocephala, Rossi. *Guestling*, rare (E.N.B.)

— amabilis, Mg. *Hollington* (H. List)

Macronychia agrestis, Fln. *Guestling* (E.N.B.)

Dexiosoma caninum, F. *Guestling* (H. List)

Myiostoma cristatum, Rnd. *Plashet* (G.H.V.)

Dexia vacua, Fln. *Guestling* (E.N.B.)

MUSCIDÆ

Stomoxys calcitrans, Linn. Generally common

Hæmatobia stimulans, Mg. *Abbots Wood* (G.H.V.)

Pollenia vespillo, F. *Guestling* (H. List), *Battle* (J.)

— rudis, F. Common generally

Myiospila meditabunda, F. *Lewes, Guesting, Pett*, etc.

Graphomyia maculata, Scop. Common generally

Musca domestica, Linn. Abundant

— corvina, F. *Lewes, Guestling, Framfield*; very common at times

MUSCIDÆ (*continued*)

Cyrtoneura stabulans, Fln. *Guestling* (H. List), *Lewes* (J.)

— pabulorum, Fln. *Guestling* (H. List)

— pascuorum, Mg. „ „

— cæsia, Mg. *Hastings* district „

Morellia simplex, Lw. *Guestling* (H. List)

— hortorum, Fln. Common generally

— curvipes, Mcq. *Guestling* (H. List)

Mesembrina meridiana, Linn. Generally distributed

Pyrellia lasiopthalma, Mcq. *Ranscombe, Lewes* (G.H.V.)

— eriopthalma, Mcq. *Guestling* (H. List)

Protocalliphora azurea, Fln. *Guestling*, rare (E.N.B.), *Glynde* (J.), *Abbots Wood* (G.H.V.)

Calliphora erythrocephala, Mg. Abundant everywhere

— vomitoria, Linn. *Guestling*, somewhat rare (E.N.B.), *Lewes* (J.)

Euphoria cornicina, F. *Guestling* (E.N.B.), *Lewes* (J.)

Lucilia cæsar, L. Abundant everywhere

— sylvarum, Mg. *Guestling*, once (E.N.B.)

— sericata, Mg. Common (H. List), *Bognor* (G.)

ANTHOMYIDÆ

Polietes lardaria, F. Generally common

— albolineata, Fln. *Guestling* (H. List), *Abbots Wood* (J.)

Hyetodesia incana, W. *Hastings* district (H. List), *Malling* (G.H.V.)

— lucorum, Fln. *Hastings* district, *Lewes* (G.H.V.), *Bognor* (G.)

— goberti, Mik. *Fairlight* (H. List)

— obscurata, Mg. *Lewes* (G.H.V.), *Pevensey* (Hall)

— umbratica, Mg. *Hastings* district, *Lewes, Abbots Wood*

— semicinerea, W. *Chauctonbury, Faygate* (G.H.V.)

— signata, Mg. *Hollington, Guestling, Pevensey, Lewes, Goodwood*

— lasiopthalma, Mcq. *Abbots Wood, Uckfield* (G.H.V.); *Guestling* (E.N.B.)

— erratica, Fln. *Hollington* (H. List), *Lewes* (J.), *Brighton* (C. Morley)

— basalis, Ztt. *Guestling* (H. List)

— scutellaris, Fln. *Guestling* (E.N.B.), *Laughton* (J.), *Bognor* (G.)

— populi, Mg. *Guestling* (E.N.B.), *Abbots Wood* (G.H.V.)

— pallida, F. *Hastings, Guestling* (H. List)

Allœostylus flaveola, Fln. *Hastings* district

Mydæa vespertina, Fln. *Guestling* (H. List)

— allotalla, Mg. *Guestling* (H. List), *Plashet* (G.H.V.)

INSECTS

Mydæa urbana, Mg. Common generally
— tincta, Ztt. *Guestling* (H. List)
— pagana, F. *Hastings* (H. List)
— impuncta, Fln. *Lewes, Abbots Wood* (G.H.V.), *Bognor* (G.), *Guestling* (E.N.B.)
Sphecolyma inanis, Fln. *Guestling* and *Hastings* (H. List)
Spilogaster maculosa, Mg. *Three Bridges, Shipley* (G.H.V.)
— duplicata, Mg. *Hastings* district, *Brighton* (C. Morley)
— communis, Dsv. *Pett, Guestling* (H. List)
— quadrum, F. *Guestling* (H. List), *Bognor* (G.)
— depuncta, Fln. *Guestling* (H. List), *Lewes, Abbots Wood* (G.H.V.)
— protuberans, Ztt. *Hastings* district
— uliginosa, Fln. *Guestling* (H. List), *Brighton* (C. Morley)
— trigonalis, Mg. *Three Bridges* (G.H.V.)
— consimilis, Fln. *Faygate* (G.H.V.)
Hydrotæa ciliata, F. *Lewes, Three Bridges, Goodwood* (G.H.V.)
— occulta, Mg. *Shipley* (G.H.V.)
— irritans, Fln. Common generally
— dentipes, F. *Guestling* (H. List), *Lewes*
— armipes, F. *Guestling* (H. List), *Eastbourne* (C. Morley)
— albipuncta, Ztt. *Chiddingly, Abbots Wood, Seaford* (G.H.V.)
Ophyra leucostoma, W. *Guestling* (H. List), *Lewes* (G.H.V.), *Bognor* (G.)
Trichopticus cunctans, Mg. *Hastings* district
Hydrophoria divisa, Mg. *Pett* (H. List)
— conica, W. Common ; *Guestling* (H. List), *Abbots Wood* (G.H.V.)
— anthomyica, Rnd. *Blackboys, Three Bridges* (G.H.V.)
Hylemyia variata, Fln. Common generally
— lasciva, Ztt. *Guestling* (H. List)
— seticrura, Rnd. *Pett* (H. List), *Shipley* (G.H.V.)
— cardui, Mg. *Guestling* (H. List), *Eastbourne* (C. Morley)
— pullula, Ztt. *Guestling* (H. List), *Seaford, Lewes, Shipley* (G.H.V.)
— strigosa, F. Common generally
— puella, Mg. *Guestling* (H. List)
— coarctata, Fln. *Warrengore, Lewes* (G.H.V.)
Eustalomyia festiva, Ztt. *Guestling* (H. List)
Lasiops rœderi, Kow. *Abbots Wood* (G.H.V.)
— meadii, Kow. *Bexhill* (C. Morley)

Anthomyia pluvialis, L. Common generally
— albicincta, Fln. *Hastings* district, once ; very rare
— pratincola, Pz. *Guestling* (H. List)
— radicum, L. *Guestling* (H. List), *Lewes* (G.H.V.), *Bognor* (G.)
— sulciventris, Ztt. *Guestling* (H. List)
Chortophila buccata, Fln. *Guestling* (H. List), *Littlehampton* (E. Saunders)
— striolata, Fln. *Lewes* (G.H.V.)
— cinerea, Fln. *Guestling* (H. List)
— sepia, Mg. ,, ,,
Phorbia floccosa, Mcq. *Hastings* district, *Chiddingly* (G.H.V.)
— discreta, Mg. *Lewes* (G.H.V.)
— pudica, Rnd. *Hastings* district
— muscaria, Mg. *Plashet* (G.H.V.)
— cilicrura, Rnd. *Hastings* district
— trichodactyla, Rnd. *Abbots Wood* (G.H.V.)
— ignota, Rnd. *Hastings* district
Pegomyia betæ, Curt. *Guestling, Fairlight* (H. List)
— latitarsis, Ztt. *Hastings* district
— bicolor, W. *Guestling* (H. List)
— nigritarsis, Ztt. ,, ,,
— flavipes, Fln. *Guestling* (H. List), *Abbots Wood, Three Bridges* (G.H.V.)
— vittigera, Ztt. *Hastings* district
Homalomyia hamata, Mcq. *Ewhurst* (W. Esam, H. List), *Abbots Wood, Shipley* (G.H.V.)
— pretiosa, Schin. *Guestling* (H. List), *Rotherfield, Three Bridges* (G.H.V.)
— manicata, Mg. *Glynde* (G.H.V.)
— monilis, Hal. *Hastings* district
— scalaris, F. Common generally
— canicularis, L. Very common in houses
— armata, Mg. *Guestling* (E.N.B.), *Abbots Wood, Shipley, Three Bridges* (G.H.V.)
— coracina, Lw. *Guestling* (H. List), *Shipley, Three Bridges* (G.H.V.)
— serena, Fln. *Laughton* (G.H.V.), *Hastings* district
— polychæta, Stein. *Guestling* (H. List)
— incisurata, Ztt. *Hastings* district (H. List), *Shipley, Three Bridges* (G.H.V.)
— mutica, Ztt. *Hastings* district (H. List)
Piezura pardalina, Rnd. *Shipley* (G.H.V.)
Azelia macquarti, Stæg. *Guestling* (H. List), *Ewhurst* (W. Esam)
— cilipes, Hal. *Guestling* (H. List), *Three Bridges* (G.H.V.)
— triquetra, W. *Abbots Wood, Faygate* (G.H.V.)
— zetterstedti, Rnd. *Plashet* (G.H.V.)
Caricea tigrina, F. Common generally

ANTHOMYIDÆ (*continued*)

Caricea intermedia, Fln. *Abbots Wood* (G.H.V.)

Cænosia elegantula, Rnd. *Guestling* (H. List)

— sexnotata, Mg. *Guestling* (H. List), *Lavant* (G.)

Lispe tentaculata, Deg. *Guestling* (H. List), *Lewes* (J.), *Isfield, Abbots Wood* (G.H.V.)

— gemina, v.d. Wulp. *Worthing* (G.H.V.)

Fucellia fucorum, Fln. *St. Leonards* (H. List)

CORDYLURIDÆ

Cordylura pubera, F. *Winchelsea, Pett* (H. List)

— umbrosa, Mg. *Lewes* (G.H.V.)

Parallelomma albipes, Fln. *Guestling* (H. List)

Norellia spinimana, Fln. *Battle* (H. List)

Scatophaga lutaria, F. *Guestling* (H. List)

— stercoraria, L. Abundant everywhere

— litorea, F. *Hastings* district (H. List)

— suilla, F. *Guestling*, rare (H. List)

PHYCODROMIDÆ

Orygma luctuosum, Mg. *Bognor* (G.)

HELOMYZIDÆ

Helomyza rufa, Fln. *Guestling* (H. List), *Bognor* (G.)

— pectoralis, Lw. *Guestling* (H. List)

— flava, Mg. ,, ,,

— zetterstedtii, Lw. ,, ,,

— pallida, Fln. ,, ,,

Blepharoptera serrata, L. *Lewes, Guestling*; frequents windows

Tephrochlamys rufiventris, Mg. *Guestling* (E.N.B.), *Bexhill* (C. Morley)

SCIOMYZIDÆ

Dryomyza flaveola, F. *Guestling* (H. List), *Lewes* (J.), *Bognor* (G.)

Neuroctena analis, Fln. *Hastings* district (H. List)

Neottiophilum præustum, Mg. *Bognor* (G.); bred from birds' nest

Sciomyza pallida, Fln. *Frant, Three Bridges* (G.H.V.)

— schœnherri, Fln. *Pett* (H. List), *Polegate* (Hall), *Pagham, Bognor* (G.)

— albocostata, Fln. *Guestling* (H. List)

Phæomyia fuscipennis, Mg. *Hastings* district (H. List)

Tetanocera elata, F. *Guestling, Pett* (H. List)

— lævifrons, Lw. *Plashet, Lewes* (G.H.V.)

— ferruginea, Fln. *Hastings* district (H. List), *Cocking* (G.)

— punctata, F. *Pett* (H. List), *Pevensey*

— coryleti, Scop. *Pett* (H. List), *Three Bridges* (G.H.V.), *Pagham* (G.)

— punctulata, Scop. *Guestling, Ore* (H. List); *Lewes* (Unwin), *Bognor* (G.)

SCIOMYZIDÆ (*continued*)

Limnia marginata, F. *Hastings* district (H. List), *Bersted* (G.)

— unguicornis, Scop. *Guestling* (H. List), *Bersted* (G.)

Elgiva albiseta, Scop. *Hastings* district (H. List), *Bersted* (G.)

— dorsalis, F. *Guestling* (H. List)

— rufa, Pz. *Guestling, Bopeep, Pett* (H. List); *Plashet* (G.H.V.), *Bognor* (G.)

— cucularia, L. *Pett* (H. List), *Lewes* (J.)

Sepedon sphegeus, F. *Guestling, Winchelsea, Battle, Pett* (H. List); *Lewes* (J.), *Pagham* (G.)

— spinipes, Scop. *Guestling, Pett* (H. List); *Selsea, Pagham* (G.)

PSILIDÆ

Psila fimetaria, L. *Hastings* district (H. List)

— nigricornis, Mg. *Guestling* (H. List)

— villosula, Mg. *Hastings* district (H. List)

Loxocera aristata, Pz. *Dallington* (H. List), *Three Bridges, Uckfield, Abbots Wood* (G.H.V.); *Arundel* (G.)

— albiseta, Schrk. *Hastings* district (H. List), *Lewes, Seaford* (G.H.V.)

— fulviventris, Mg. *Guestling* (H. List)

MICROPEZIDÆ

Micropeza corrigiolata, L. *Guestling, Robertsbridge* (H. List)

Calobata cibaria, L. *Guestling* (H. List)

— cothurnata, Pz. *Hastings* district (H. List)

ORTALIDÆ

Ptilonota centralis, F. *Cocking* (G.)

Pteropæctria afflicta, Mg. *Ewhurst* (H. List), *Seaford, Plashet* (G.H.V.)

— nigrina, Mg. *Lewes, Plashet, Abbots Wood* (G.H.V.), *Hastings* district (H. List), *Lynch Down* (G.)

— palustris, Mg. *Ewhurst, Guestling* (H. List), *Plashet, Abbots Wood* (G.H.V.)

— frondescentiæ, L. *Warrengore, Faygate* (G.H.V.), *Bishopstone* (J.)

Ceroxys crassipennis, F. *Hastings* district (H. List), *Worthing* (G.H.V.), *Itchenor* (G.)

— pictus, Mg. *Worthing* (G.H.V.), *Itchenor, Felpham* (G.)

Platystoma seminationis, F. *Winchelsea* (H. List), *Lewes* (J.), *Brighton* (Unwin), *Bognor* (G.)

Rivellia syngenesiæ, F. *Guestling* (H. List)

Seoptera vibrans, L. *Guestling* (H. List), *Lewes* (J.), *Bognor* (G.)

Ulidia erythropthalma, Mg. *Fairlight* (H. List), *Lewes* (J.)

Chrysomyza demandata, F. *Guestling* (E.N.B.)

INSECTS

CHLOROPIDÆ

Lipara lucens, Mg. *Bexhill, Pevensey* (E.A.B.), *Bognor* (G.); bred from tops of reed, Arundo phragmites,

Platycephala planifrons, F. *Pett, Pevensey* (E.A.B.)

Meromyza pratorum, Mg. (H. List), *Camber*, etc. (E.A.B.)

— læta, Mg. *Lewes* (G.H.V.)

Anthracophaga strigula, F. *Guestling* (H. List)

Haplegis divergens, Lw. *Warrengore, Lewes* (G.H.V.)

Chloropisca ornata, Mg. *Hastings* district (H. List)

AGROMYZIDÆ

Agromyza pusilla, Mg. *Hastings* district (H. List)

PHYTOMYZIDÆ

Phytomyza nigricans, Mcq. *Guestling* (H. List)

Chromatomyia affinis, Mg. *Hastings* district (H. List)

PHYTOMYZIDÆ (*continued*)

Chromatomyia albiceps, Mg. *Guestling* (H. List)

BORBORIDÆ

Borborus nitidus, Mg. *Hastings* district (H. List)

— roseri, Rnd. *Bexhill* (C. Morley)

— pedestris, Mg. *Lewes*, in moss, etc. (J.)

— equinus, Fln. Generally common

Sphærocera subsultans, F. Generally common

Limosina limosa, Fln. *Lewes* (Unwin)

Phora abdominalis, Fln. *Ewhurst* (H. List)

— rufipes, Mg. *Ore* (C. Morley)

HIPPOBOSCIDÆ

Ornithomyia avicularia, Linn. *Guestling* (H. List); *Battle*, on pigeons (J.); *Lewes*, on rooks (J.)

Stenopteryx hirundinis, Linn. *Hastings* district (H. List), *Bognor* (G.)

Melophagus ovinus, Linn. *Pett* (H. List); *Lewes* (J.), common on sheep; *Bognor* (G.)

NOTE.—Since the above was in type the following interesting species have been added by Mr. Guermonprez: Cœlopa pilipes, Hal.; *Felpham*. Actora æstuum, Mg.; *Pagham*. Sciomyza cinerella, Fln.; *Goodwood Park*. Chyliza leptogaster, Pz.; *Cocking*. Palloptera umbellatarum, F.; *Bognor*. Sapromyza notata, Fln.; *Felpham*. Sepsis violacea, Mg.; *Elmer*.

HEMIPTERA HETEROPTERA

Bugs

In the following list 298 species of Heteroptera are recorded as having occurred in Sussex. This is equivalent to nearly 66 per cent of the known British species. Only two are peculiar to the county, viz. *Peritrechus gracilicornis*, which is recorded by Mr. J. W. Douglas from Hastings, and *Monanthia angustata*, which Mr. E. Saunders discovered at Cissbury near Worthing. The localities given lie almost wholly in the extreme east and the south-west of Sussex; the meagreness of the records from the central parts is accounted for by the paucity of workers in this order. Where the Hastings *district* is quoted, it is implied that the species referred to is generally distributed in that part of the county which lies south of a line joining Etchingham and Heathfield, and east of a line from Heathfield to the coast midway between Bexhill and Pevensey. Similarly, the Bognor district means the south-western corner from Chichester to Littlehampton, and thence northward to Burpham, Madehurst and Cocking. By the great extension of some of the coast towns in recent years, several localities, which were once well stocked with insects, are now either built upon or cultivated, and the distribution of some local species has been modified accordingly. For example, *Henestaris laticeps* was, not many years ago, abundant all along the top of the cliff to the west of what was then the village of Bexhill. Its haunt has been destroyed by the foundation of the esplanade of this rapidly developing seaside resort, and one small colony farther to the west is now all that remains of the once abundant Hemipteron. Similarly *Salda littoralis* seems to have been exterminated altogether from the same neighbourhood, as the marsh in which it occurred has been drained and converted into pleasure gardens. The locality referred to as Camber consists of the waste land at the mouth of the river Rother, and especially the sandhills on its eastern border. As these latter are now a favourite resort of golfers, insects are scarcer than formerly.

Of the Homoptera, 156 species are recorded, belonging to the sections Cicadina and Psyllina. This represents over 47 per cent of the British species of these groups, a proportion which is perhaps as large as was to be expected, considering that the records are mainly the work of two collectors. Some of these species are amongst our most abundant insects, and only one is at present recorded from no other county. This is *Limotettix stactogala*, which was discovered in 1901 by Mr. H. L. F. Guermonprez on tamarisk bushes at Pagham, and which I have since found in abundance in the Hastings district. The solitary bush of *Hippophaë rhamnoides* on the Camber sandhills, which was the only recorded locality in the county for *Psylla hippophaës*, has been removed and with it of course the insect has disappeared.

GYMNOCERATA

PENTATOMIDÆ

Eurygaster, Lap.
— maura, Linn. *Dallington Forest* (Butler)
Podops, Lap.
— inuncta, Fab. *Guestling, Fairlight, Hastings, Bexhill* (Butler); *Holm Bush* (Wollaston), *Bognor* (Guermonprez), *Worthing* (Saunders)
Sehirus, Am. S.
— dubius, Scop. *Eartham* (Guermonprez)
— biguttatus, Linn. *Guestling, Battle, Hurst Green* (Butler)
Gnathoconus, Fieb.
— albomarginatus, Fab. *Guestling, Hastings, Bexhill* (Butler); *Avisford* (Guermonprez)
Ælia, Fab.
— acuminata, Linn. *Camber* (Bennett), *Guestling* (Morley), *Hastings* (Champion), *Slindon* (Guermonprez)
Neottiglossa, Curt.
— inflexa, Wolff. *Hastings* (Collett), *Battle, Dallington Forest* (Butler)
Peribalus, M. & R.
— vernalis, Wolff. *Slindon* (Guermonprez)
Pentatoma, Oliv.
— baccarum, Linn. *Camber, Hastings, Hollington* (Butler); *Slindon* (Guermonprez)
— prasina, Linn. *Guestling, Hastings, Hollington, Battle, Eastbourne, Laughton* (Butler); *Slindon* (Guermonprez)

PENTATOMIDÆ (*continued*)
Strachia, Hahn.
— festiva, Linn. *Battle, Netherfield, Ashburnham, Dallington Forest* (Butler)
— oleracea, Linn. Near *Hastings* (Bennett)
Piezodorus, Fieb.
— lituratus, Fab. *Hastings, Battle, Hurst Green, Dallington Forest* (Butler); *Slindon, Selsea* (Guermonprez)
Tropicoris, Hahn.
— rufipes, Linn. *Hastings, Battle* (Butler); *Slindon, Bognor* (Guermonprez)
Picromerus, Am. S.
— bidens, Linn. *Battle, Netherfield, Dallington Forest* (Butler); *Handcross* (Newbery)
Asopus, Burm.
— punctatus, Linn. *Hastings* (Collett), *Eastbourne* (Butler), *Holm Bush* (Fenn)
Podisus, H.S.
— luridus, Fab. *Battle* (Butler), *Slindon Bognor, Goodwood* (Guermonprez)
Zicrona, Am. S.
— cærulea, Linn. *Battle, Netherfield, Dallington Forest, Frant* (Butler); *Worthing, Goodwood* (Guermonprez)
Acanthosoma, Curt.
— hæmorrhoidale, Linn. *Hastings, Battle* (Butler); *Burpham, Slindon, Eartham, Bognor* (Guermonprez)
— dentatum, De G. *Guestling* (Bloomfield), *Hastings, Dallington Forest* (Butler); *Binstead* (Guermonprez)

PENTATOMIDÆ (*continued*)

Acanthosoma interstinctum, Linn. *Guestling* (Bloomfield), *Battle, Dallington Forest* Butler) ; *Colgate* (Newbery), *Slindon* (Guermonprez)

— tristriatum, Linn. *Cissbury* (Saunders), *Worthing* (Guermonprez)

COREIDÆ

Enoplops, Am. S.

— scapha, Fab. *Fairlight* (Hall)

Syromastes, Latr.

— marginatus, Linn. *Hastings* (Butler), *Slindon* (Guermonprez)

Ceraleptus, Cost.

— lividus, Stein. *Camber* (Collett)

Coreus, Fab.

— denticulatus, Scop. *Hastings, Hollington, Bexhill* (Butler) ; *Avisford* (Guermonprez)

Stenocephalus, Latr.

— agilis, Scop. *Hollington* (Collett), *Bognor* (Guermonprez)

Therapha, Am. S.

— hyoscyami, Linn. *Bognor* (Guermonprez)

Corizus, Fall.

— maculatus, Fieb. *Dallington Forest* (Collett), *Handcross* (Newbery), *Harting* (Beaumont)

— capitatus, Fab. *Battle* (Collett), *Slindon* (Guermonprez)

— parumpunctatus, Schill. *Camber* (Butler), *Ashdown Forest* (Champion)

Myrmus, Hahn.

— miriformis, Fall. *Hastings* district (Butler), *Handcross* (Newbery), *Goodwood* (Guermonprez)

Chorosoma, Curt.

— schillingi, Schml. *Camber* (Butler)

BERYTIDÆ

Berytus, Fab.

— crassipes, H.S. *Fairlight* (Butler), *Hastings* (Champion)

— minor, H.S. *Camber, Pett, Hastings, Hollington, Hurst Green, Lewes* (Butler) ; *Bersted* (Guermonprez)

— signoreti, Fieb. *Fairlight, Hastings, Bexhill, Hurst Green* (Butler)

— montivagus, Fieb. *Worthing* (Saunders)

Metatropis, Fieb.

— rufescens, H.S. *Battle* (Butler)

Metacanthus, Cost.

— punctipes, Germ. *Fairlight* (Butler), *Avisford* (Guermonprez)

LYGÆIDÆ

Nysius, Dall.

— thymi, Wolff. *Camber, Pett, Bexhill* (Butler) ; *Hastings* (Collett), *Littlehampton* (Saunders), *Pagham* (Guermonprez)

LYGÆIDÆ (*continued*)

Cymus, Hahn.

— glandicolor, Hahn. *Hastings, Battle, Ashburnham, Dallington* (Butler)

— melanocephalus, Fieb. *Harting* (Beaumont)

— claviculus, Fall. *Guestling, Fairlight, Hastings, Battle, Dallington Forest* (Butler) ; *Handcross* (Newbery)

Ischnorhynchus, Fieb.

— resedæ, Panz. *Hastings* (Butler), *Slindon* (Guermonprez)

— geminatus, Fieb. Generally distributed on heaths

Henestaris, Spin.

— laticeps, Curt. *Bulverhythe, Bexhill* (Butler) ; *Seaford* (Douglas), *Pagham* (Guermonprez)

Chilacis, Fieb.

— typhæ, Perr. *Guestling, Ashburnham* (Collett) ; *Dallington* (Butler)

Heterogaster, Schill.

— artemisiæ, Schill. *Linch Down* (Guermonprez)

— urticæ, Fab. *Rye* (Butler)

Plociomerus, Say.

— fracticollis, Schill. *Harting* (Beaumont)

Rhyparochromus, Curt.

— dilatatus, H.S. *Hastings, Battle* (Butler)

— chiragra, Fab. *Camber, Bexhill* (Butler) ; *Bognor* (Guermonprez) var. sabulicola, Thoms. *Camber* (Butler)

— antennatus, Schill. *Battle* (Morley)

— prætextatus, H.S. *Camber* (Butler)

Ischnocoris, Fieb.

— angustulus, Boh. *Bexhill* (Morley), *Dallington Forest* (Butler)

Macrodema, Fieb.

— micropterum, Curt. *Bexhill, Netherfield* (Butler) ; *St. Leonards Forest* (Newbery) ; macropterous form, *Netherfield* (Butler)

Plinthisus, Fieb.

— brevipennis, Latr. *Camber, Bexhill* (Butler), *Littlehampton* (Saunders), *Selsea* (Guermonprez)

Stygnus, Fieb.

— rusticus, Fall. *Hastings* district (Butler), *Colgate* (Newbery)

— pedestris, Fall. *Hastings* district (Butler) ; *Colgate, Handcross, St. Leonards Forest* (Newbery) ; *Slindon* (Guermonprez)

— arenarius, Hahn. *Hastings* district (Butler), *Bognor, Selsea* (Guermonprez)

INSECTS

LYGÆIDÆ (*continued*)
Peritrechus, Fieb.
— geniculatus, Hahn. *Hastings* (Somerville) ; *Sedlescombe* (Morley) ; *Battle, Bexhill* (Butler) ; *Ashdown Forest* (Billups)
— gracilicornis, Put. *Hastings* (Douglas)
— nubilus, Fall. *Ashdown Forest* (Billups)
— luniger, Schill. *Hastings, Hollington, Battle* (Butler); *Sedlescombe* (Morley); *Bognor* (Guermonprez)
Trapezonotus, Fieb.
— distinguendus, Flor. *Shoreham* (Champion), *Worthing* (Saunders)
— agrestis, Panz. *Camber, Fairlight, Hastings, Battle, Bexhill* (Butler) ; *Littlehampton* (Saunders)
Aphanus, Lap.
— lynceus, Fab. *Camber* (Collett)
— pini, Linn. *Ashdown Forest* (Billups), *East Grinstead* (Champion)
Drymus, Fieb.
— sylvaticus, Fab. Generally distributed
— brunneus, Sahlb. *Hurst Green* (Butler), *Bexhill* (Morley), *Colgate, St. Leonards Forest* (Newbery)
Notochilus, Fieb.
— contractus, H.S. Generally distributed
Scolopostethus, Fieb.
— puberulus, Horv. *Bexhill* (Butler)
— affinis, Schill. *Rye, Hastings, Hollington, Battle* (Butler), *Felpham, Bognor* (Guermonprez)
— grandis, Horv. Near *Hastings* (Bennett)
— neglectus, Edw. *Hastings, Hollington* (Butler) ; *Felpham, Bognor* (Guermonprez)
— decoratus, Hahn. Generally distributed on heaths
Gastrodes, Westw.
— ferrugineus, Linn. *Battle, Hurst Green, Dallington Forest* (Butler)
TINGIDIDÆ
Piesma, Lap.
— quadrata, Fieb. *Camber* (Collett), *Fairlight, Hastings, Bexhill* (Butler) ; *Hove* (Douglas & Scott), *Bognor* (Guermonprez)
— capitata, Wolff. *Fairlight, Hastings, Hollington, Battle, Ashburnham* (Butler) ; *St. Leonards Forest* (Newbery)
Serenthia, Spin.
— læta, Fall. *Fairlight* (Butler)
Orthostira, Fieb.
— brunnea, Germ. *Hurst Green* (Butler)
— cervina, Germ. *Guestling* (Collett), *Fairlight, Hollington* (Butler)
— parvula, Fall. *Hastings* district (Butler), *Colgate* (Newbery), *Felpham, Cocking* (Guermonprez)

TINGIDIDÆ (*continued*)
Dictyonota, Curt.
— crassicornis, Fall. *Hastings* district (Butler), *Colgate* (Newbery), *Bognor* (Curtis), *Pagham* (Guermonprez)
Dictyonota strichnocera, Fieb. *Battle, Netherfield, Hurst Green* (Butler)
Derephysia, Spin.
— foliacea, Fall. *Fairlight, Bexhill, Dallington Forest* (Butler) ; *St. Leonards Forest* (Newbery), *Aldwick* (Guermonprez)
Monanthia, Lep.
— ampliata, Fieb. *Fairlight, Hastings, Battle, Bexhill* (Butler) ; *Tilgate* (Champion), *Handcross* (Newbery), *Selsea* (Guermonprez)
— cardui, Linn. Generally distributed
— angustata, H.S. *Cissbury* (Saunders)
— ciliata, Fieb. *Tilgate* (Champion)
— costata, Fieb. *Hastings* (Ford)
— dumetorum, H.S. *Pett* (Butler), *Slindon, Itchenor* (Guermonprez)
— humuli, Fab. *Hastings, Battle, Dallington Forest, Pevensey* (Butler) ; *Tilgate* (Champion), *Handcross* (Newbery), *Pagham* (Guermonprez)
ARADIDÆ
Aradus, Fab.
— depressus, Fab. *Guestling, Hastings, Battle* (Butler) ; *St. Leonards Forest* (Newbery), *Slindon, Madehurst* (Guermonprez)
Aneurus, Curt.
— lævis, Fab. *Guestling, Hollington* (Collett); *Fairlight* (Butler), *Bognor* (Guermonprez)
HEBRIDÆ
Hebrus, Curt.
— pusillus, Fall. *Pevensey* (Butler)
HYDROMETRIDÆ
Mesovelia, M. & R.
— furcata, M. & R. *Ashburnham, Dallington* (Butler)
Hydrometra, Latr.
— stagnorum, Linn. *Hastings* district (Butler), *Bognor* district (Guermonprez)
Microvelia, West.
— pygmæa, Duf. *Rye, Winchelsea, Pett Level, Dallington* (Butler)
Velia, Latr.
— currens, Fab. Generally distributed ; macropterous form, *Bexhill, Dallington Forest* (Butler) ; *East Grinstead* (Burr)
Gerris, Fab.
— rufoscutellata, Latr. *Guestling* (Collett)
— paludum, Fab. *Hastings, Battle, Ashburnham* (Butler)

HYDROMETRIDÆ (*continued*)

Gerris najas, De G. *Hastings* (Butler), *Crowhurst* (Collett)

— thoracica, Schum. *Guestling* (Bloomfield), *Hastings, Hollington* (Butler); *Bognor* district (Guermonprez)

— gibbifera, Schum. *Guestling, Hastings, Dallington* (Butler); *Faygate* (Newbery)

— lacustris, Schum. Generally distributed

— odontogaster, Zett. *Guestling* (Bloomfield)

— argentata, Schum. *Guestling* (Bloomfield), *Battle* (Butler)

REDUVIIDÆ

Ploiaria, Scop.

— vagabunda, Linn. *Battle* (Butler), *Slindon, Bognor, Aldwick* (Guermonprez)

— culiciformis, De G. *Hastings* (Collett)

Reduvius, Fab.

— personatus, Linn. *Rusper* (Newbery)

Coranus, Curt.

— subapterus, De G. *Camber* (Collett), *Battle* (Butler)

Nabis, Latr.

— brevipennis, Hahn. *Battle* (Butler)

— lativentris, Boh. *Hastings* district, *Lewes* (Butler); *Handcross* (Newbery), *Bognor* district (Guermonprez)

— major, Cost. Generally distributed

— flavomarginatus, Scholtz. *Guestling* (Collett), *Pett, Fairlight, Pevensey* (Butler); *Handcross* (Newbery), *Pagham* (Guermonprez)

— limbatus, Dahlb. Generally distributed

— lineatus, Dahlb. *Camber* (Collett), *Pevensey* (Butler), *Pagham* (Guermonprez)

— ferus, Linn. Generally distributed

— rugosus, Linn. „ „

— ericetorum, Scholtz. Generally distributed on heaths

SALDIDÆ

Salda, Fab.

— saltatoria, Linn. *Battle* (Butler), *Handcross* (Newbery), *Bognor* (Guermonprez)

— pallipes, Fab. *Hastings* (Butler), *Worthing, Littlehampton* (Saunders)

— pilosella, Thoms. *Rye* (Butler), *Hastings, Worthing* (Saunders)

— orthochila, Fieb. *Colgate* (Newbery)

— littoralis, Linn. *Rye* (Collett), *Bexhill* (Butler)

— lateralis, Fall. *Rye* (Collett), *Worthing* (Saunders)

— cincta, H.S. *Hastings* (C. W. Dale), *Pett, Battle, Pevensey* (Butler); *Hand-*

SALDIDÆ (*continued*)

cross, Faygate (Newbery); *Worthing* (Saunders)

Salda cocksii, Curt. *Battle, Frant* (Butler)

CIMICIDÆ

Ceratocombus, Sign

— coleoptratus, Zett. *Hurst Green, Battle, Bexhill* (Butler)

Cimex, Linn.

— lectularius, Linn. Generally distributed

Lyctocoris, Hahn.

— campestris, Fab. Generally distributed

Piezostethus, Fieb.

— galactinus, Fieb. *Hastings, Battle, Hurst Green* (Butler)

— cursitans, Fall. *Hastings* (Collett), *East Grinstead* (Champion)

Temnostethus, Fieb.

— pusillus, H.S. Generally distributed

Anthocoris, Fall.

— confusus, Reut. Generally distributed

— nemoralis, Fab. „ „

— gallarum-ulmi, De G. *Hollington* (Butler)

— sarothamni, D. & S. *Guestling* (Collett)

— sylvaticus, Linn. Generally distributed

Tetraphleps, Fieb.

— vittata, Fieb. *Slindon* (Guermonprez)

Acompocoris, Reut.

— pygmæus, Fall. *Hastings, Hollington, Battle, Hurst Green* (Butler); *Colgate* (Newbery)

— alpinus, Reut. *Hollington, Battle, Hurst Green* (Butler)

Triphleps, Fieb.

— nigra, Wolff. *Battle* (Butler), *Colgate* (Newbery), *Slindon* (Guermonprez)

— majuscula, Reut. Generally distributed

— minuta, Linn. *Pett, Hastings* (Butler)

Xylocoris, Duf.

— ater, Duf. *Battle* (Collett)

Microphysa, Westw.

— pselaphiformis, Curt. *Hollington, Hurst Green* (Butler); *St. Leonards Forest* (Newbery)

— elegantula, Baer. *Fairlight, Battle, Hurst Green* (Butler); *Hollington* (Collett), *Bognor* (Guermonprez)

Myrmedobia, Baer.

— tenella, Zett. *Battle* (Butler)

— inconspicua, D. & S. *Camber* (Butler)

CAPSIDÆ

Pithanus, Fieb.

— mærkeli, H.S. *Hastings* district, *Pevensey* (Butler); *Bognor* (Guermonprez), macropterous form, *Fairlight* (Collett)

INSECTS

CAPSIDÆ (*continued*)

Acetropis, Fieb.
— gimmerthalii, Flor. *Fairlight* (Collett)

Miris, Fab.
— calcaratus, Fall. Generally distributed
— lævigatus, Linn. „ „
— holsatus, Fab. *Guestling, Hastings, Dallington Forest* (Butler); *Handcross* (Newbery), *Cocking* (Guermonprez)

Megaloceræa, Fieb.
— erratica, Linn. Generally distributed
— longicornis, Fall. *Fairlight* (Collett), *Hastings* (Saunders), *Hurst Green* (Butler)
— ruficornis, Fab. Generally distributed

Teratocoris, Fieb.
— antennatus, Boh. *Camber* (Butler)

Leptopterna, Fieb.
— ferrugata, Fall. Generally distributed
— dolobrata, Fall. „ „

Monalocoris, Dahlb.
— filicis, Linn. *Hastings* district (Butler), *Colgate* (Newbery), *Slindon* (Guermonprez)

Bryocoris, Fall.
— pteridis, Fall. *Battle* (Butler)

Pantilius, Curt.
— tunicatus, Fab. Near *Hastings* (Ford), *Slindon* (Guermonprez)

Lopus, Hahn.
— gothicus, Linn. *Guestling, Fairlight* (Collett); *Hastings* (Saunders), *Bexhill* (Butler), *Handcross* (Newbery), *Slindon* (Guermonprez)
— sulcatus, Fieb. *Selsea* (Guermonprez)

Miridius, Fieb.
— quadrivirgatus, Cost. *Pett, Guestling, Fairlight, Hollington, Robertsbridge, Hurst Green, Bexhill* (Butler); *Hastings, Worthing* (Saunders)

Phytocoris, Fall.
— populi, Linn. *Bognor* district (Guermonprez)
— tiliæ, Fab. *Hastings, Battle, Netherfield, Hurst Green* (Butler); *Bognor* district (Guermonprez)
— longipennis, Flor. *Hastings* district (Butler), *Bognor* district (Guermonprez)
— dimidiatus, Kb. *Tilgate Forest* (Newbery), *Slindon* (Guermonprez)
— reuteri, Saund. *Hollington, Westfield* (Butler)
— varipes, Boh. Generally distributed
— ulmi, Linn. „ „

Calocoris, Fieb.
— striatellus, Fab. *Guestling, Hastings, Battle, Hurstmonceux, Pevensey, Eastbourne* (Butler); *Bognor* district (Guermonprez)

CAPSIDÆ (*continued*)

Calocoris fulvomaculatus, De G. *Guestling, Hastings* (Collett); *Battle* (Butler), *Burpham, Avisford* (Guermonprez)
— bipunctatus, Fab. Generally distributed
— chenopodii, Fall. *Hastings* district, *Lewes* (Butler); *Bognor* district (Guermonprez)
— roseomaculatus, De G. *Guestling, Hastings, Bexhill, Dallington Forest* (Butler); *Colgate* (Newbery), *Linch Down* (Guermonprez)
— infusus, H.S. *Hastings, Battle* (Butler)
— striatus, Linn. *Guestling* (Collett), *Abbots Wood* (Butler), *Eartham, Cocking* (Guermonprez)

Oncognathus, Fieb.
— binotatus, Fab. Generally distributed

Dichrooscytus, Fieb.
— rufipennis, Fall. *Hastings* (Hall)

Plesiocoris, Fieb.
— rugicollis, Fall. *Battle, Bexhill* (Butler)

Lygus, Hahn.
— pratensis, Fab. Generally distributed
— rubricatus, Fall. *Hollington, Battle, Hurst Green, Bexhill* (Butler); *Littlehampton* (Champion)
— contaminatus, Fall. *Hollington* (Power), *Dallington Forest* (Butler), *Burpham* (Guermonprez)
— viridis, Fall. *Hollington* (Saunders)
— lucorum, Mey. *Hastings* district, *Pevensey* (Butler); *Singleton* (Guermonprez)
— spinolæ, Mey. *Hastings, Hollington, Lewes* (Butler); *Tilgate* (Champion)
— pabulinus, Linn. Generally distributed
— pastinacæ, Fall. *Hollington, Battle* (Butler); *Bognor* district (Guermonprez)
— cervinus, H.S. *Hastings, Battle* (Butler); *Bognor* district (Guermonprez)
— kalmii, Linn. *Rye, Hastings, Bexhill, Lewes* (Butler); *Slindon* (Guermonprez)

Zygimus, Fieb.
— pinastri, Fall. *Bexhill, Hurst Green* (Butler)

Pœciloscytus, Fieb.
— gyllenhalii, Fall. *Guestling, Hastings, Hollington, Battle* (Butler)
— unifasciatus, Fab. *Camber* (Collett), *Lewes* (Butler)

Liocoris, Fieb.
— tripustulatus, Fab. Generally distributed

Capsus, Fab.
— laniarius, Linn. *Rye, Hastings, Dallington Forest* (Butler)

CAPSIDÆ (*continued*)
Bothynotus, Fieb.
— pilosus, Boh. One macropterous, *Hastings* (Collett); two brachypterous, *Guestling* (Bloomfield)
Rhopalotomus, Fieb.
— ater, Linn. *Guestling, Fairlight, Hastings* (Butler); *Felpham* (Guermonprez)
Pilophorus, Hahn.
— perplexus, Scott. *Hastings, Hollington* (Butler)
— clavatus, Linn. *Tilgate* (Champion)
Systellonotus, Fieb.
— triguttatus, Linn. *Camber* (Butler), *Littlehampton* (Saunders)
Halticus, Hahn.
— luteicollis, Panz. *Guestling, Westfield, Hollington, Battle* (Butler); *Hastings* (Saunders), *Tilgate* (Champion)
— apterus, Linn. *Hollington, Battle, Hurst Green* (Butler); *Tilgate* (Champion)
Strongylocoris, Cost.
— leucocephalus, Linn. *Bepton Down* (Guermonprez)
Labops, Burm.
— saltator, Hahn. *Fairlight, Hastings, Hollington, Bexhill, Hurst Green* (Butler); *Bognor* (Guermonprez)
— mutabilis, Fall. *Hollington, Bexhill, Hurst Green* (Butler); *Handcross* (Newbery)
Macrolophus, Fieb.
— nubilus, H.S. *Hollington, Battle* (Butler)
Dicyphus, Fieb.
— constrictus, Boh. *Battle, Ashburnham* (Butler)
— epilobii, Reut. Generally distributed
— errans, Wolff. *Fairlight, Hastings, Hollington, Catsfield* (Butler); *Bognor* (Guermonprez)
— stachydis, Reut. *Hastings* (Saunders)
— pallidicornis, Fieb. *Guestling, Hurst Green, Netherfield* (Butler)
— globulifer, Fall. *Hastings* (Billups), *Hollington, Battle, Ashburnham, Dallington Forest* (Butler); *Slindon* (Guermonprez)
Campyloneura, Fieb.
— virgula, H.S. Generally distributed
Cyllocoris, Hahn.
— histrionicus, Linn. *Fairlight* (Collett), *Hastings, Bexhill* (Butler); *Bognor* district (Guermonprez)
— flavonotatus, Boh. *Guestling, Hastings* (Butler); *Slindon* (Guermonprez)
Ætorhinus, Fieb.
— angulatus, Fall. Generally distributed

CAPSIDÆ (*continued*)
Globiceps, Latr.
— flavomaculatus, Fab. *Fairlight, Hurst Green* (Butler)
— cruciatus, Reut. *Hastings* (Saunders), *Hollington, Hurst Green* (Butler)
Mecomma, Fieb.
— ambulans, Fall. *Guestling, Hastings, Battle, Dallington* (Butler); *Colgate* (Newbery)
Cyrtorrhinus, Fieb.
— caricis, Fall. *Eridge* (Butler), *Handcross* (Newbery), *Slindon* (Guermonprez)
— pygmæus, Zett. *Pett, Pevensey* (Butler)
Orthotylus, Fieb.
— bilineatus, Fall. *Bexhill* (Butler)
— flavinervis, Kb. *Hastings* (Saunders)
— marginalis, Reut. *Hastings, Hollington, Battle, Hurst Green, Frant, Pevensey* (Butler); *Itchenor* (Guermonprez)
— nassatus, Fab. *Hurst Green* (Butler)
— prasinus, Fall. *Hollington* (Butler)
— scotti, Reut. *Hastings, Hollington* (Butler)
— ochrotrichus, D. & S. *Pett, Hollington, Pevensey* (Butler)
— diaphanus, Kb. *Hastings, Bexhill* (Butler)
— flavosparsus, Sahl. *Hastings, Littlehampton* (Saunders); *Pett, Bexhill* (Butler); *Bognor* (Guermonprez)
— chloropterus, Kb. *Hastings* district (Butler)
— adenocarpi, Perr. *Hollington* (Butler)
— rubidus, Put. *Rye* (Butler), *Worthing* (Saunders)
— ericetorum, Fall. Generally distributed on heaths
Hypsitylus, Fieb.
— bicolor, D. & S. *Hastings, Hollington, Battle, Hurst Green* (Butler); *Slindon* (Guermonprez)
Loxops, Fieb.
— coccinea, Mey. *Winchelsea* (Butler), *Hastings* (Saunders), *Hollington* (Collett)
Heterotoma, Latr.
— merioptera, Scop. Generally distributed
Heterocordylus, Fieb.
— genistæ, Scop. *Fairlight, Hollington, Hurst Green* (Butler); *Hastings* (Saunders), *Tilgate* (Champion)
— tibialis, Hahn. *Guestling, Hollington, Battle* (Butler); *Hastings* (Collett)
Malacocoris, Fieb.
— chlorizans, Fall. Generally distributed
Onychumenus, Reut.
— decolor, Fall. *Hastings* district, *Eridge* (Butler), *Tilgate* (Champion), *Colgate* (Newbery), *Goodwood* (Guermonprez)

INSECTS

CAPSIDÆ (*continued*)
Oncotylus, Fieb.
— viridiflavus, Goeze. *Hastings, Battle, Crowhurst, Hurst Green, Dallington Forest* (Butler), *Tilgate* (Champion), *Rusper* (Newbery)
Macrotylus, Fieb.
— paykulli, Fall. *Fairlight* (Butler)
— solitarius, Mey. *Hurst Green* (Butler)
Macrocoleus, Fieb.
— hortulanus, Mey. *Bepton Down* (Guermonprez)
— molliculus, Fall. *Hastings* district, *Lewes* (Butler)
Amblytylus, Fieb.
— affinis, Fieb. *Battle, Hurst Green* (Butler)
Harpocera, Curt.
— thoracica, Fall. *Hastings, Hollington, Battle* (Butler) ; *Bognor* district (Guermonprez)
Byrsoptera, Spin.
— rufifrons, Fall. Generally distributed
Phylus, Hahn.
— palliceps, Fieb. *Hastings* (Collett)
— melanocephalus, Linn. *Guestling, Fairlight, Hastings* (Butler) ; *Bognor* district (Guermonprez)
— coryli, Linn. *Guestling, Hastings, Hollington, Battle, Bexhill* (Butler) ; *Bognor* district (Guermonprez)
Atractotomus, Fieb.
— magnicornis, Fall. *Hollington, Catsfield, Hurst Green* (Butler) ; *Colgate* (Newbery)
Psallus, Fieb.
— ambiguus, Fall. *Hastings, Battle* (Butler) ; *Bognor* district (Guermonprez)
— betuleti, Fall. *Hastings* (?), *Colgate* (Newbery), *Bognor* district (Guermonprez)
— obscurellus, Fall. *Hollington, Battle, Hurst Green* (Butler)
— variabilis, Fall. *Hastings* (Butler), *Bognor* district (Guermonprez)
— quercûs, Kb. *Hastings* (Saunders), *Cocking* (Guermonprez)
— lepidus, Fieb. *Hastings, Hollington, Frant* (Butler)
— alnicola, D. & S. *Hollington, Hurst Green* (Butler) ; *Avisford, Rewel Wood, Singleton, Itchenor* (Guermonprez)
— fallenii, Reut. *Battle, Dallington Forest* (Butler)
— varians, H.S. Generally distributed
— diminutus, Kb. *Hastings* (Butler)
— sanguineus, Fab. *Hastings* district (Butler)

CAPSIDÆ (*continued*)
Psallus salicellus, Mey. *Hastings* district (Butler), *Tilgate* (Champion), *Slindon* (Guermonprez)
Plagiognathus, Fieb.
— albipennis, Fall. *Rye* (Collett)
— viridulus, Fall. Generally distributed
— arbustorum, Fab. „ „
— pulicarius, Fall. *Camber* (Butler), *Hastings* (Collett)
— saltitans, Fall. *Camber, Hastings* (Butler)
Asciodema, Reut.
— obsoletum, D. & S. *Hastings, Hollington, Hurst Green, Bexhill* (Butler)

CRYPTOCERATA

NAUCORIDÆ
Naucoris, Geoffr.
— cimicoides, Linn. Generally distributed
NEPIDÆ
Nepa, Linn.
— cinerea, Linn. Generally distributed
Ranatra, Fab.
— linearis, Linn. *Pett Level* (Butler), *Guestling, Hastings* (Collett) ; *Bognor* (Guermonprez)
NOTONECTIDÆ
Notonecta, Linn.
— glauca, Linn. Generally distributed
Plea, Leach
— minutissima, Fab. *Rye, Winchelsea, Pett Level, Hastings, Pevensey* (Butler) ; *Rusper* (Newbery)
CORIXIDÆ
Corixa, Geoffr.
— geoffroyi, Leach. Generally distributed
— atomaria, Ill. *Rye* (Butler), *Bognor* district (Guermonprez)
— lugubris, Fieb. *Winchelsea, Pett Level, Guestling, Hastings* (Butler) ; *Felpham* (Guermonprez)
— hieroglyphica, Duf. *Winchelsea, Guestling* (Butler) ; *Felpham* (Guermonprez)
— sahlbergi, Fieb. *Pett Level, Guestling, Fairlight, Hastings* (Butler) ; *Rusper* (Newbery), *Aldwick* (Guermonprez)
— linnæi, Fieb. *Rye, Pett Level, Hastings* (Butler)
— limitata, Fieb. *Tilgate* (Champion), *Felpham* (Guermonprez)
— semistriata, Fieb. *Lagness* (Guermonprez)
— striata, Linn. *Rye, Pett Level, Fairlight, Hastings* (Butler) ; *Amberley, Lagness* (Guermonprez)
— fallenii, Fieb. *Hastings, Ashburnham* (Butler) ; *Amberley, Lagness* (Guermonprez)

CORIXIDÆ (*continued*)
Corixa distincta, Fieb. *Ashburnham* (But-ler)
— fossarum, Leach. *Pett Level* (Butler), *Guestling* (Bloomfield)
— mœsta, Fieb. *Winchelsea, Pett Level* (Butler) ; *Faygate, Colgate* (New-bery)
— fabricii, Fieb. *Fairlight, Hastings, Ash-*

CORIXIDÆ (*continued*)
burnham (Butler) ; *Faygate* (New-bery), *Middleton* (Guermonprez)
— coleoptrata, Fab. *Winchelsea* (Butler)
Sigara, Fab.
— minutissima, Linn. *Pett Level* (Collett)
— scholtzii, Fieb. *Guestling* (Butler), *St. Leonards Forest* (Saunders), *Little-hampton* (Billups)

HEMIPTERA HOMOPTERA

Cicadas, Fiend-flies, Lantern-flies, Frog-hoppers, Aphides, etc.

CICADINA

MEMBRACIDÆ
Centrotus, Fab.
— cornutus, Linn. *Guestling, Hastings* (Butler) ; *Cocking* (Guermonprez)
ISSIDÆ
Issus, Fab.
— coleoptratus, Geoffr. *Hastings* district (Butler), *Slindon* (Guermonprez)
CIXIIDÆ
Oliarus, Stål.
— panzeri, Löw. *Hollington, Pevensey* (Butler)
Cixius, Latr.
— pilosus, Ol. Generally distributed
— cunicularius, Linn. *Guestling* (Butler), *Slindon* (Guermonprez)
— nervosus, Linn. Generally distributed
— brachycranus, Fieb. *Dale Park* (Guer-monprez)
— similis, Kb. *Hastings* (Edwards)
DELPHACIDÆ
Delphax, Fab.
— pulchella, Curt. *Pett, Bexhill, Pevensey* (Butler)
Liburnia, Stål.
— lineola, Germ. *Fairlight* (Butler), *Bognor* district (Guermonprez)
— fuscovittata, Stål. *Dallington Forest* (Butler)
— vittipennis, J. Sahl. *Hurst Green, Dallington Forest* (Butler)
— prasinula, Fieb. *Pevensey* (Butler)
— glaucescens, Fieb. *Pett* (Butler), *Itchenor* (Guermonprez)
— capnodes, Scott. *Chichester* (Buckton)
— leptosoma, Flor. *Handcross* (Newbery)
— pellucida, Fab. *Hastings* (Butler), *Bersted* (Guermonprez)
— discolor, Boh. *Hastings, Battle* (But-ler)
— denticauda, Boh. *Guestling* (Capron)
— exigua, Boh. *Hollington, Catsfield* (But-ler)
— aubei, Perr. *Camber* (Butler)

DELPHACIDÆ (*continued*)
Liburnia fairmairei, Perr. *Felpham* (Guer-monprez)
— limbata, Fab. Generally distributed
Dicranotropis, Fieb.
— hamata. *Camber, Hastings, Battle, Hurst Green, Bexhill* (Butler) ; *Felp-ham* (Guermonprez)
Stiroma, Fieb.
— albomarginata, Curt. *Bexhill* (Butler)
— pteridis, Boh. *Battle, Pevensey* (Butler)
— nigrolineata, Scott. *Elmer* (Guermon-prez)
CERCOPIDÆ
Triecphora, A. & S.
— vulnerata, Ill. *Hastings, Hollington, Netherfield, Eastbourne* (Butler) ; *East Grinstead* (Kirkaldy), *Cocking* (Guer-monprez)
Aphrophora, Germ.
— alni, Fall. Generally distributed
— salicis, De G. *Hurst Green* (Butler)
Philænus, Stål.
— spumarius, Linn. Generally distri-buted
— campestris, Fall. *Hastings* district (Butler), *Bepton Down* (Guermon-prez)
— exclamationis, Thunb. *Eridge* (Butler), *Seaford* (Douglas & Scott), *Dale Park, Bepton Down* (Guermonprez)
— lineatus, Linn. Generally distributed
LEDRIDÆ
Ledra, Fab.
— aurita, Linn. *Hastings* (Collett), *Slin-don, Selsea* (Guermonprez)
ULOPIDÆ
Ulopa, Fall.
— reticulata, Fab. *Rye, Guestling, Battle, Netherfield, Dallington Forest* (But-ler) ; *Pagham* (Guermonprez)
— trivia, Germ. *Camber* (Butler)
PAROPIIDÆ
Megophthalmus, Curt.
— scanicus, Fall. Generally distributed

INSECTS

BYTHOSCOPIDÆ

Macropsis, Lewis

— microcephala, H.S. *Goodwood* (Guermonprez)

— lanio, Linn. *Hastings, Dallington Forest* (Butler) ; *Bognor* district (Guermonprez)

Bythoscopus, Germ.

— alni, Schr. *Guestling* (Butler)

— rufusculus, Fieb. *Guestling* (Collett), *Hollington, Battle, Dallington Forest, Heathfield* (Butler) ; *Slindon* (Guermonprez)

— flavicollis, Linn. *Hastings* district, *Frant* (Butler) ; *Bognor* district (Guermonprez)

Pediopsis, Burm.

— scutellatus, Boh. *Hollington, Crowhurst* (Butler) ; *Slindon, Bersted* (Guermonprez)

— tibialis, Scott. *Battle* (Butler)

— fuscinervis, Boh. *Bexhill* (Butler)

— cereus, Germ. *Battle* (Butler)

— virescens, Fab. *Fairlight, Battle, Hurst Green, Bexhill* (Butler)

Idiocerus, Lewis

— adustus, H.S. *Battle* (Butler), *Bognor* (Guermonprez)

— tremulæ, Estl. *Battle* (Butler)

— elegans, Flor. „ „

— laminatus, Flor. „ „

— lituratus, Fall. *Fairlight, Hurst Green, Dallington Forest, Frant, Pevensey* (Butler) ; *Bognor* (Guermonprez)

— populi, Linn. *Fairlight, Hastings, Battle, Bexhill* (Butler) ; *Bognor* (Guermonprez)

— confusus, Flor. *Fairlight, Hastings, Bexhill, Hurst Green, Dallington Forest* (Butler) ; *Bognor* (Guermonprez

— albicans, Kb. *Bognor* (Guermonprez)

Agallia, Curt.

— puncticeps, Germ. *Colgate* (Newbery)

— venosa, Fall. *Camber, Pett, Hollington* (Butler) ; *Pagham* (Guermonprez)

TETTIGONIDÆ

Evacanthus, L. & S.

— interruptus, Linn. *Hastings* (Butler), *Slindon* (Guermonprez)

— acuminatus, Fab. *Hastings, Netherfield, Bexhill* (Butler) ; *Rusper* (Newbery), *Slindon* (Guermonprez)

Tettigonia, Geoffr.

— viridis, Linn. *Pett, Battle, Pevensey* (Butler) ; *Arundel, Bersted* (Guermonprez)

ACOCEPHALIDÆ

Strongylocephalus, Flor.

— agrestis, Fall. *Pett* (Butler)

ACOCEPHALIDÆ (*continued*)

Acocephalus, Germ.

— nervosus, Schr. Generally distributed

— bifasciatus, Linn. *Battle* (Butler)

— albifrons, Linn. Generally distributed

— brunneo-bifasciatus, Geoffr. *Pett, Hastings, Hollington* (Butler)

— histrionicus, Fab. *Camber* (Butler)

Eupelix, Germ.

— cuspidata, Fab. *Camber, Hastings, Battle, Bexhill, Dallington Forest* (Butler) ; *Goodwood, Selsea* (Guermonprez)

Doratura, J. Sahl.

— stylata, Boh. *Hollington, Battle, Eridge* (Butler)

Paramesus, Fieb.

— nervosus, Fall. *Pett, Bexhill* (Butler) ; *Pagham* (Guermonprez)

Glyptocephalus, Edw.

— proceps, Kb. *Catsfield, Bexhill, Eridge* (Butler)

JASSIDÆ

Stictocoris, Thoms.

— preyssleri, H.S. *Cissbury Hill, Arundel Park* (Piffard)

Athysanus, Burm.

— brevipennis, Kb. *Hastings, Dallington Forest* (Butler) ; *Bognor* (Guermonprez)

— sordidus, Zett. *Fairlight, Bexhill, Hurst Green, Pevensey* (Butler) ; *Bognor, Pagham* (Guermonprez)

— communis, J. Sahl. Generally distributed

— obscurellus, Kb. Generally distributed

— obsoletus, Kb. *Dallington Forest* (Butler), *Slindon* (Guermonprez)

var. piceus, Scott. *Eridge* (Butler)

Deltocephalus, Burm.

— striifrons, Kb. *Felpham* (Guermonprez)

— pascuellus, Fall. *Pett, Battle, Pevensey* (Butler) ; *Bersted* (Guermonprez)

— ocellaris, Fall. *Hastings, Battle, Bexhill* (Butler)

— flori, Fieb. *Battle, Hurst Green* (Butler)

— linnæi, Fieb. *Battle* (Butler)

— socialis, Flor. *Fairlight* (Butler)

— sabulicola, Curt. *Camber* (Butler)

— striatus, Linn. Generally distributed

— argus, Marsh. *Dallington Forest* (Butler)

— pulicaris, Fall. *Battle, Hurst Green* (Butler) ; *Colgate* (Newbery), *Bognor* (Guermonprez)

Allygus, Fieb.

— mixtus, Fab. *Battle, Bexhill, Dallington Forest* (Butler) ; *Arundel* (Guermonprez)

235

A HISTORY OF SUSSEX

JASSIDÆ (*continued*)
Thamnotettix, Zett.
— prasina, Fall. *Dallington Forest* (Butler), *Aldwick* (Guermonprez)
— dilutior, Kb. *Hastings, Battle, Bexhill* (Butler)
— subfuscula, Fall. *Guestling, Hastings, Battle* (Butler) ; *Slindon, Cocking, Daneswood* (Guermonprez)
— striatula, Fall. *Battle* (Butler)
— cruentata, Panz. *Dallington Forest* (Butler)
— torneella, Zett. *Slindon* (Guermonprez)
— splendidula, Fab. *Fairlight, Battle, Bexhill* (Butler) ; *Aldwick* (Guermonprez)
— crocea, H.S. *Rye, Fairlight, Hastings, Battle* (Butler) ; *Bognor, Pagham* (Guermonprez)
— attenuata, Germ. *Rye, Hastings* (Butler)
Limotettix, J. Sahl.
— stactogala, Am. *Winchelsea, Pett, Hastings, Bexhill* (Butler) ; *Pagham* (Guermonprez)
— striola, Fall. *Pagham* (Guermonprez)
— antennata, Boh. *Battle, Ashburnham* (Butler) ; *Colgate* (Newbery)
— quadrinotata, Fab. *Pett, Hastings* (Butler) ; *Cocking* (Guermonprez)
— aurantipes, Edw. *Handcross* (Newbery)
— sulphurella, Zett. *Hollington, Battle* (Butler)
Cicadula, Fieb.
— septemnotata, Fall. *Battle* (Butler)
— variata, Fall. *Dallington Forest* (Butler)
— sexnotata, Fall. *Battle, Hurst Green* (Butler) ; *Tilgate Forest* (Newbery), *Felpham* (Guermonprez)
— cyanæ, Boh. *Ashburnham, Dallington* (Butler)
TYPHLOCYBIDÆ
Alebra, Fieb.
— albostriella, Fall. *Guestling, Hollington, Battle, Hurst Green, Dallington Forest* (Butler)
Dicraneura, Hardy
— flavipennis, Zett. *Battle.* (Butler)
— citrinella, Zett. *Hurst Green* (Butler), *Aldwick* (Guermonprez)
— similis, Edw. *Battle* (Butler)
Kybos, Fieb.
— smaragdula, Fall. *Hastings, Battle, Dallington Forest, Pevensey* (Butler) ; *Bersted* (Guermonprez)
Chlorita, Fieb.
— flavescens, Fab. *Hollington, Hastings,* (Butler)

TYPHLOCYBIDÆ (*continued*)
Chlorita viridula, Fall. *Hastings, Hurst Green* (Butler) ; *Boxgrove* (Guermonprez)
Eupteryx, Curt.
— vittatus, Linn. *Battle, Hurst Green* (Butler) ; *Bognor* (Guermonprez)
— notatus, Curt. *Hurst Green* (Butler)
— urticæ, Fab. *Hastings* (Butler), *Aldwick* (Guermonprez)
— stachydearum, Hardy. *Battle* (?), *Felpham* (Guermonprez)
— collinus, Flor. *Bognor* (Guermonprez)
— melissæ, Curt. *Winchelsea, Battle* (Butler) ; *Bognor* (Guermonprez)
— auratus, Linn. *Hastings* (Butler), *Felpham* (Guermonprez)
— atropunctata, Goeze. *Hastings, Battle* (Butler) ; *Felpham* (Guermonprez)
— germari, Zett. *Battle, Hurst Green* (Butler) ; *Bersted, Boxgrove* (Guermonprez)
— pulchellus, Fall. *Guestling, Hollington, Bexhill, Dallington Forest* (Butler) ; *Binsted, Felpham* (Guermonprez)
— concinna, Germ. *Battle, Dallington Forest* (Butler) ; *Itchenor* (Guermonprez)
Typhlocyba, Germ.
— jucunda, H.S. *Fairlight, Battle, Hurst Green* (Butler)
— sexpunctata, Fall. *Fairlight, Battle* (Butler) ; *Dale Park* (Guermonprez)
— ulmi, Linn. *Hollington* (Butler), *Bognor* district (Guermonprez)
— tenerrima, H.S. *Hastings* (Butler), *Felpham,* (Guermonprez)
— douglasi, Edw. *Eartham* (Guermonprez)
— gratiosa, Boh. *Hollington, Battle* (Butler)
— rosæ, Linn. *Hastings, Battle* (Butler)
— quercûs, Fab. *Hollington, Dallington Forest* (Butler) ; *Bognor* (Guermonprez)
— nitidula, Fab. *Dallington Forest* (Butler) ; *Aldwick* (Guermonprez)
— geometrica, Schr. *Hastings* (Butler)
Zygina, Fieb.
— alneti, Dahlb. *Hurst Green* (Butler)
— flammigera, Geoffr. *Fairlight, Hastings* (Butler) ; *Aldwick* (Guermonprez)
— scutellaris, H.S. *Pett, Bexhill* (Butler) ; *Colgate* (Newbery)

PSYLLINA

LIVIIDÆ
Livia, Latr.
— juncorum, Latr. *Hastings* (Butler)

INSECTS

APHIDES

As far as I am aware, very few aphides have been recorded from Sussex. Among these are some of the well known pests, such as *Siphonophora rosæ* on roses, *Phorodon humuli* on the hop, *Myzus cerasi* on cherry, *M. ribis* on currant, etc. But there are others of more interest. *Thelaxes betulina*, a species of a very small genus, has, I believe, only been recorded from Guestling. The fine aphis *Lachnus longipes* is not so remarkable for its long legs as for its very long wings, which exceed those of any other British aphis ; it has been sent from Ewhurst. *Dryobius roboris*, from Guestling and Ore, has conspicuously mottled wings.

Some of the aphides cause galls ; thus *Pemphigus spirothecæ* forms spiral galls on the petioles of the leaves of poplar. *Tetraneura ulmi* lives in erect, often pedunculated galls on the upper surface of elm leaves. *Schizoneura ulmi*, also on elm, causes the leaves to become distorted, pale and bladdery. *Chermes abietis* inhabits conelike galls on the spruce fir, while *Phylloxera punctata*, which is common, causes yellow spots on the leaves of the oak and is nearly allied to *P. vastatrix*, the dreaded pest of the vine.

ARACHNIDA

Spiders, etc.

No great research has been made in connection with members of this order in the county of Sussex, so that it is not possible to consider the following account of the spider-fauna of the district under consideration in any respect complete.

It will doubtless prove as rich a locality when thoroughly well worked as others of similar physical characters and geological formation. One is however unable to point particularly to any one locality as more likely to repay research than another, though the country districts, with river banks and meadows, firwoods and oak and hazel plantations will be found to provide abundant species in suitable seasons.

As a rule, wild uncultivated areas are much more fertile in spider forms than those that are highly cultivated. Yet even in the latter case, where isolated districts of wild growth and forest land occur, with cultivated land on all sides, the former are often found to be more prolific than even large tracts of untilled forest.

Of the 118 species of spiders recorded none are peculiar to the district, though several are worthy of special mention : *Atypus affinis*, *Dysdera crocota*, *Cœlotes atropos*, *Thanatus formicinus* and *Metopobactrus prominulus*.

The greater part of the species recorded were collected by Mr. F. P. Smith of Islington ; others by Rev. O. Pickard-Cambridge and Rev. J. Harvey-Bloom.

In cases where the generic or specific name quoted is not that under which the spider has usually been recognized in the works of English authors, a note has been added calling attention to the fact.

ARANEÆ

MYGALOMORPHÆ

ATYPIDÆ

Spiders with eight eyes, four lung books, and three tarsal claws.

1. *Atypus affinis*, Eichwald
   Hastings (F.P.S.)

Adult in May, June and October.

This is the only example of the *Mygalomorphæ* found in the British Islands. Though belonging to the same sub-order as the well-known trap-door spiders of the south of Europe and other tropical and sub-tropical regions, distinguished from the *Arachnomorphæ* by the possession of two pairs of pulmonary organs, or lung books, and by the vertical movement of the mandibles, these spiders make no trap-door at all.

The retreat consists of a long tunnel, half an inch in diameter and from seven to nine inches long, burrowed in the soil, and lined throughout with white silk, terminating at the lower end in a slightly enlarged cell, where the egg-sac is formed and the young are hatched, and tended by the female. The upper end of the silk lining is prolonged for about three inches beyond the extremity of the burrow, forming a loose tube, closed at the end, and either lying on the surface of the soil, woven amongst the roots of heather and herbage, or hanging down free, according to the nature of the surroundings.

Mr. Enock reports that the spider does not leave this retreat in search of prey, but waits in the slack portion of the tube lying outside the burrow until some insect sets foot upon this silken, purse-like structure. Instantly the fangs of the spider's mandibles are struck through the walls of the tube, the insect seized and dragged into the burrow through a

SPIDERS

rent in the silk, which is afterwards mended from within. The male is smaller, almost black, and may sometimes be found moving slowly about in the sunshine in the neighbourhood of the colony. The spider has also been recorded under the names *A. sulzeri* and *A. piceus* by English authors.

2. *Atypus beckii*, O. P.-Cambridge
  Hastings (R. Beck)

This species is that which has been, by continental authors, referred to as *A. piceus*, Sultzer. It is very doubtful whether this species has ever been taken in this country; but has probably been recorded for Sussex by mistake.

ARACHNOMORPHÆ
DYSDERIDÆ

Spiders with six eyes and two pairs of stigmatic openings, situated close together on the genital rima; the anterior pair communicating with lung books, the posterior with tracheal tubes. Tarsal claws, two in *Dysdera*, three in *Harpactes* and *Segestria*.

3. *Dysdera cambridgii*, Thorell
  Sussex (O.P.-C.)

Not uncommon under stones and bark of trees, where it lurks within a tubular retreat. The spider is easily recognizable by its elongate form, orange legs, dark mahogany carapace and pale clay-yellow abdomen. The palpal bulb of the male has no cross-piece at the apex.

This spider is also known as *D. erythrina*, Blackwall.

4. *Dysdera crocota*, C. L. Koch
  Hastings (F.P.S.); Shoreham (J.H.B.)

Larger than the last species, with a deep orange-pink carapace, orange legs, and abdomen with a delicate rosy-pink flush. The palpal bulb of the male has a cross-piece at the apex.

This spider is also known as *D. rubicunda*, Blackwall.

4A. *Oonops pulcher*, Templeton
  Hastings (F.P.S.)

5. *Harpactes hombergii* (Scopoli)
  Hastings (F.P.S.)

Common on heaths, also to be met with under bark of trees, and recognizable by its ant-like linear form, black carapace and pale abdomen, and its three tarsal claws.

DRASSIDÆ

Spiders with eight eyes, situated in two transverse rows. The tracheal openings lie just in front of the spinners. The tarsal claws are two in number, the anterior pair of spinners are set wide apart at the base, and the maxillæ are more or less impressed across the middle.

6. *Drassodes lapidosus* (Walckenaer)
  Hastings (F.P.S.) Shoreham (J.H.B.)

Usually common beneath stones in every locality.

7. *Drassodes cupreus* (Blackwall)
  Brighton

This is a darker spider than the last. The mandibles of the male are less developed and the tibia of the palpus is shorter and broader. The central tongue of the vulva of the female is not so much dilate behind. It may be considered a sub-species.

8. *Drassodes sylvestris* (Blackwall)
  Hastings (F.P.S.)

Not uncommon amongst dead leaves in woods.

9. *Scotophæus blackwallii* (Thorell)
  Brighton

A dark elongate mouse-grey spider, often found wandering about the walls of dwellings and outhouses at night.

10. *Prosthesima pedestris* (C. Koch)
  Folkestone (O.P.-C.); Hastings (F.P.S.)

10A. *Gnaphosa lugubris*, C. L. Koch
  Worthing (O.P.-C.)

CLUBIONIDÆ

Spiders with eight eyes, situated in two transverse rows. The tracheal openings lie immediately in front of the spinners. The tarsal claws are two in number, but the anterior pair of spinners are set close together at the base, and the maxillæ are convex, not impressed across the middle.

11. *Micaria pulicaria* (Sundevall)
  Hastings (F.P.S.)

A small dark spider, iridescent and shining, with a white cincture round the middle of

the anterior half of the abdomen. Known also as *Drassus nitens*, Blackwall.

12. *Phrurolithus festivus*, C. L. Koch
  Hastings (F.P.S.)

13. *Agrœca brunnea* (Blackwall)
Hastings (F.P.S.)

The egg-cocoon of this species is a familiar object to the field naturalist ; a white silken sac shaped like an inverted wine-glass and hung by the stem to the stalks of rushes, heather, etc. The spider subsequently covers the silk with a layer of mud.

13A. *Agrœca striata*, Kulczynski
Shoreham (O.P.-C.)

14. *Zora spinimana* (Sundevall)
Brighton

Common everywhere amongst herbage.

15. *Clubiona phragmitis*, C. L. Koch
Hastings (F.P.S.)

16. *Clubiona pallidula* (Clerck)
Hastings (F.P.S.)

17. *Clubiona stagnatilis*, Kulczynski
Hastings (F.P.S.)

18. *Clubiona reclusa*, O. P.-Cambridge
Hastings (F.P.S.)

19. *Clubiona terrestris*, Westring
Hastings (F.P.S.)

20. *Clubiona compta*, C. L. Koch
Hastings (F.P.S.)

21. *Chiracanthium erraticum* (Walckenaer)
Hastings (F.P.S.)

Common on the roadsides among bramble leaves. This spider is also known as *C. carnifex.*

21A. *Micromata virescens* (Clerck)
Hastings (F.P.S.)

ANYPHÆNIDÆ

The spiders of this family resemble those of the *Clubionidæ* in most respects, except that the tracheal stigmatic openings beneath the abdomen are situated about midway between the genital rima and the spinners, and not as in the last family immediately in front of the spinners. One species only is indigenous to Great Britain, and is very common amongst the foliage of trees in May and June.

22. *Anyphæna accentuata* (Walckenaer)
Hastings (F.P.S.)

THOMISIDÆ

Spiders with eight eyes, situated in two transverse rows, two tarsal claws, and anterior spinners close together at their base. Maxillæ not impressed. The crab-like shape and side-long movements of these spiders are the chief characteristic which enable them to be distinguished from the more elongate *Drassidæ* and *Clubionidæ*.

23. *Philodromus dispar*, Walckenaer
Hastings (F.P.S.)

24. *Philodromus aureolus* (Clerck)
Brighton

25. *Tibellus oblongus* (Walckenaer)
Brighton

Common amongst dry coarse grass on sand-hills and also amongst the rich vegetation in swamps, where the species is as a rule much larger.

26. *Thanatus formicinus*, C. L. Koch
East Grinstead (Rev. T. R. Stebbing)

A rare species, taken only in the New Forest previously.

27. *Xysticus cristatus* (Clerck)
Hastings (F.P.S.)

28. *Xysticus pini* (Hahn)
East Grinstead (F.P.S.)

29. *Oxyptila praticola* (C. L. Koch)
Hastings (F.P.S.)

30. *Oxyptila simplex*, O. P.-Cambridge
Hastings (F.P.S.)

ATTIDÆ

The spiders of this family may be recognized in a general way by their mode of progression, consisting of a series of leaps, when alarmed. More particularly they may be known by the square shape of the cephalic region and the fact that the eyes are arranged in three rows of 4, 2, 2 ; the centrals of the anterior row being much the largest and usually iridescent. Otherwise these spiders are simply specialized *Clubionids*, with two tarsal claws and other minor characters possessed in common with members of this latter family. The commonest,

SPIDERS

Salticus scenicus, will be well known to all observers, running and leaping on the walls of houses in the bright sunshine.

31. *Euophrys frontalis* (Walckenaer)
Brighton

32. *Heliophanus flavipes* (C. L. Koch)
Brighton (O.P.-C.)
Abundant in most districts.

33. *Heliophanus cupreus* (Clerck)
Hastings (F.P.S.)

34. *Salticus scenicus* (Clerck)
Hastings (F.P.S.)
This spider is also known as *Epiblemum scenicum*

35. *Marpissa muscosa* (Clerck)
Hastings (F.P.S.)
One of the largest and most beautiful of our *Attidæ*, often abundant under the bark of old wooden palings, or among the loose stones of walls, such as those which cross the downlands.

36. *Ergane falcata* (Clerck)
East Grinstead (F.P.S.)

37. *Euophrys æquipes*, O. P.-Cambridge
Brighton (O.P.-C.)

37A. *Attus mancus*, Thorell
Worthing (O.P.-C.)

PISAURIDÆ

Spiders with eight eyes in three rows, and three tarsal claws. The first row of eyes consists of four small eyes which are sometimes in a straight line, sometimes recurved and sometimes procurved. Those of the other two rows are situated in the form of a rectangle of various proportions. *Pisaura* runs freely over the herbage, carrying its egg-sac beneath its sternum, while *Dolomedes* is a dweller in marshes and swamps.

38. *Pisaura mirabilis* (Clerck)
Hastings (F.P.S.)
Known also as *Dolomedes*, or *Ocyale*, *mirabilis*.

39. *Dolomedes fimbriatus*, Walckenaer
East Grinstead (F.P.S.)

LYCOSIDÆ

The members of this family also have eight eyes, similarly situated to those of the *Pisauridæ*, but the first row is straight. Tarsal claws three. The spiders are to be found running freely on the ground and carrying their egg-sac attached to the spinners. Many of the larger species make a short burrow in the soil and there keep guard over the egg-sac.

40. *Lycosa ruricola* (De Geer)
Hastings (F.P.S.) ; Shoreham (J.H.B.)
A very common species. This male has a claw at the end of the palpus.

41. *Lycosa accentuata*, Latreille
Hastings (F.P.S.)
Known also as *Tarentula* or *Lycosa andrenivora*.

41A. *Lycosa pulverulenta* (Clerck)
Lancing (J.H.B.)

41B. *Lycosa terricola*, Thorell
Brighton (F.P.S.)

42. *Pardosa lugubris* (Walckenaer)
Brighton

43. *Pardosa amentata* (Clerck)
Hastings (F.P.S.) ; Lancing (J.H.B.)

44. *Pardosa pullata* (Clerck)
Hastings (F.P.S.)

45. *Pardosa palustris* (Linn.)
Hastings (F.P.S.)

46. *Pardosa annulata* (Thorell)
Hastings (F.P.S.)

47. *Pardosa proxima* (C. L. Koch)
Hastings (F.P.S.)

48. *Pirata piraticus* (Clerck)
Hastings (F.P.S.)

AGELENIDÆ

Spiders with eight eyes situated in two straight or more or less curved transverse rows. Tarsal claws three. The species of this family spin a large sheet-like web, and construct a tubular retreat at the back of it, which leads to some crevice among the rocks or the herbage, or the chinks in the walls of outhouses, wherever the various species may happen to be found. The habits of *Argyroneta* are however different.

49. *Tegenaria derhami* (Scopoli)
Hastings (F.P.S.)

50. *Tegenaria atrica* (C. L. Koch)
Hastings (F.P.S.)

51. *Tegenaria silvestris*, L. Koch
Hastings (F.P.S.)

52. *Agelena labyrinthica* (Clerck)
Hastings (F.P.S.)

A very common spider, making a sheet-like web on the herbage with a funnel-shaped tubular retreat.

53. *Hahnia nava* (Blackwall)
Hastings (F.P.S.)

54. *Cœlotes atropos*, Walckenaer
Hastings (F.P.S.)

55. *Textrix denticulata* (Olivier)
Hastings (F.P.S.)

ARGIOPIDÆ

The spiders included in this family have eight eyes, situated in two rows, the lateral eyes of both rows being usually adjacent if not in actual contact, while the central eyes form a quadrangle. The tarsal claws are three, often with other supernumerary claws. The web is either an orbicular snare or consists of a sheet of webbing, beneath which the spiders hang and capture the prey as it falls upon the sheet. This immense family includes those usually separated under the names *Epeiridæ*, *Linyphiidæ*, etc.

56. *Meta segmentata* (Clerck)
Hastings (F.P.S.)

57. *Meta merianæ* (Scopoli)
Brighton

58. *Tetragnatha solandri* (Scopoli)
Hastings (F.P.S.)

59. *Pachygnatha clerckii*, Sundevall
Brighton

60. *Pachygnatha degeerii*, Sundevall
Hastings, Brighton

61. *Zilla* × -*notata* (Clerck)
Hastings (F.P.S.)

62. *Zilla atrica*, C. L. Koch
Hastings (F.P.S.)

63. *Araneus cucurbitinus*, Clerck
Hastings (F.P.S.)

This and the following three species are also known under the generic name *Epeira*.

64. *Araneus diadematus*, Clerck
Hastings (F.P.S.)

65. *Araneus cornutus*, Clerck
Brighton
Known also as *Epeira apoclisa*.

66. *Araneus umbraticus*, Clerck
Hastings (F.P.S.)

67. *Linyphia clathrata*, Sundevall
Hastings (F.P.S.)
Known also as *Neriene marginata*, Blackwall.

68. *Lepthyphantes tenuis* (Blackwall)
Hastings (F.P.S.) ; Shoreham (J.H.B.)

This and the following species included in this and the next genus are usually known under the name *Linyphia*.

69. *Lepthyphantes ericæus* (Blackwall)
Hastings (F.P.S.)

69A. *Lepthyphantes minutus* (Blackwall)
Hastings (F.P.S.)

70. *Bathyphantes dorsalis* (Wider)
Hastings (F.P.S.)

71. *Bathyphantes concolor* (Wider)
Hastings (F.P.S.)

72. *Macrargus rufus* (Wider)
Hastings (F.P.S.)

73. *Centromerus bicolor* (Blackwall)
Hastings (F.P.S.)

74. *Pœciloneta variegata* (Blackwall)
Hastings (F.P.S.)

75. *Microneta conigera* (O. P.-Cambridge)
Brighton (O.P.-C.)

76. *Erigone promiscua* (O.P.-Cambridge)
Brighton, Worthing (O.P.-C.)

77. *Erigone dentipalpis* (Wider)
Hastings (F.P.S.)

78. *Metopobactrus prominulus* (O. P.-Cambridge)
Newhaven (O.P.-C.)

79. *Tiso vagans* (Blackwall)
Hastings (F.P.S.)

80. *Gonatium rubens* (Blackwall)
Hastings (F.P.S.)
This and the next species are known also under the name of *Neriene*.

81. *Gonatium isabellinum* (C. L. Koch)
Brighton

82. *Trachygnatha dentata* (Wider)
Hastings (F.P.S.) ; Shoreham (J.H.B.)

83. *Kulczynskiellum fuscum* (Blackwall)
Hastings (F.P.S.)

84. *Kulczynskiellum agreste* (Blackwall)
Hastings (F.P.S.)

SPIDERS

85. *Viderius anticus* (Wider)
    Hastings (F.P.S.)

86. *Cornicularia unicornis* (O. P.-Cambridge)
    Hastings (F.P.S.)

87. *Arrecerus accuminatus* (Blackwall)
    Hastings (F.P.S.)

88. *Prosoponcus cristatus* (Blackwall)
    Hastings (F.P.S.)

89. *Plæsiocrærus fuscipes* (Blackwall)
    Hastings (F.P.S.)

90. *Lophocarenum parallelum* (Wider)
    Hastings (F.P.S.)

MIMETIDÆ

Spiders of this family are similar in general respects to the *Theridiidæ*, having eight eyes and three tarsal claws. The species of *Ero* construct a small brown pear-shaped or cylindrical egg-cocoon suspended on a fine silken stalk. The legs are very spinose.

91. *Ero furcata* (Villers)
    Brighton

THERIDIIDÆ

The members of this family have eight eyes, situated in very much the same position as those of the *Argiopidæ* ; but the mandibles are usually weak, the maxillæ are inclined over the labium, and the posterior legs have a comb of stiff curved spines beneath the tarsi. The web consists of a tangle of crossing lines, and the spider often constructs a tent-like retreat wherein the egg-sac is hung up. Tarsal claws, three. The legs are devoid of spines.

92. *Theridion tepidariorum*, C. L. Koch
    Brighton

One of the commonest spiders in our hot-houses, and often venturing to endeavour to acclimatize itself out of doors in the gardens.

93. *Theridion sisyphium* (Clerck)
    Hastings (F.P.S.)

94. *Theridion varians*, Hahn
    Brighton

95. *Theridion denticulatum*, Walckenaer
    Brighton

96. *Theridion bimaculatum* (Linn.)
    Hastings (F.P.S.)

97. *Theridion ovatum* (Clerck)
    Brighton

This spider is also known as *T. lineatum*, or under the generic name *Phyllonethis*.

97A. *Theridion pallens*, Blackwall
    Brighton (F.P.S.)

98. *Pholcomma gibbum*, Westring
    Hastings (F.P.S.)

99. *Steatoda bipunctata* (Linn.)
    Brighton

100. *Steatoda guttata* (Wider)
    Hastings (F.P.S.)

101. *Steatoda sticta* (O. P.-Cambridge)
    Worthing (O.P.-C.)

102. *Laseola prona* (Menge)
    Newhaven (O.P.-C.)

PHOLCIDÆ

103. *Pholcus phalangioides* (Fuesslin)
    Brighton

DICTYNIDÆ

The species belonging to this family possess eight eyes, situated in two transverse almost parallel rows, the laterals being in contact. The calamistrum and cribellum are present, and there are three tarsal claws. They construct a tubular retreat with an outer sheet of webbing, which is covered with a flocculent silk made with the calamistrum and threads from the cribellum.

104. *Amaurobius fenestralis* (Stroem)
    Hastings (F.P.S.)

105. *Amaurobius similis* (Blackwall)
    Hastings (F.P.S.) ; abundant everywhere

106. *Amaurobius ferox* (Walckenaer)
    Hastings (F.P.S.)

107. *Dictyna uncinata*, Thorell
    Hastings (F.P.S.)

108. *Dictyna pusilla*, Westring
    Hastings (F.P.S.)

109. *Protadia patula* (E. Simon)
    Newhaven (O.P.-C.)

CHERNETES

CHELIFERIDÆ

Out of twenty species of false scorpions hitherto recorded as indigenous to Great Britain only two have been taken in this county. The various species can usually be found amongst moss and dead leaves, or beneath stones and the bark of trees. They are unmistakable on account of their possession of a pair of forcipated palpi, like those of the true scorpion.

110. *Chelifer latreillii*, Leach
Hastings (E. A. Butler)

111. *Obisium muscorum* (Leach)
Hastings (E. A. Butler)

CRUSTACEANS

'Crabs and lobsters come from Bognor,' according to Frank Buckland, writing in 1875.[1] In 1877 he and Spencer Walpole agreed in naming Sussex as one of eight counties that own the chief fisheries for crabs and lobsters in England and Wales.[2] From their combined wisdom also the following statements are derived : 'Crabs and lobsters form the most important species of the stalk-eyed crustacea. The principal crab eaten in this country is the *Cancer pagurus*. Only one species of lobster, the *Homarus vulgaris*, is found off the coasts of Great Britain. In using the word "crab," then, we shall always in this report refer to the *Cancer pagurus*. The word "lobster," in the following pages, similarly refers to the *Homarus vulgaris* alone.'[3] The commissioners in these remarks are naturally alluding not to the scientific but to the economic importance of the species, and they supply the homely detail that the creels for catching them are baited with fish, 'fresh fish being preferred for crabs and stinking fish for lobsters.'[4] Bell, in his *History of British Stalk-eyed Crustacea*, had however earlier pointed out that crabs cannot be over-particular, since he had often seen them taken together 'with lobsters in pots in which the bait was far from sweet.' Bell observes that *Cancer pagurus* (Linn.) prefers those parts of the coast which are rocky. 'Its usual retreats are amongst the holes in the rocks, where it generally retires when not engaged in seeking its food. It is often seen in such situations even when the tide has retreated sufficiently to render the rocks accessible, as for instance among those on the shore at Hastings, where I have often seen them in the pools and caverns left by the receding tide. These are however always small individuals rarely more than 3 inches in breadth ; the larger ones remain farther at sea among the rocks in deep water ; and they also bury themselves in the sand, but always in the immediate neighbourhood of the rocks.'[5]

The predominance of the eatable crab and the common lobster in English markets has probably had a retarding effect on the study of crustacea among us by producing a vague but very prevalent impression of its extremely limited scope. Even commissioners chosen for special capacity and attainments can, as we have seen, have the audacity to tell

[1] *Report on the Fisheries of Norfolk . . . ordered by the House of Commons to be printed*, p. 72.
[2] *Report on the Crab and Lobster Fisheries of England and Wales*, p. i.
[3] Loc. cit. p. iii.   [4] Loc. cit. p. vi.
[5] *History of British Stalk-eyed Crustacea* (1853), pp. 61, 62.

the House of Commons that only one species of lobster is found off the coasts of Great Britain, as though they had never heard of the rock lobster, *Palinurus vulgaris*, or of *Nephrops norwegicus*, the Norway lobster. But the consideration of lobsters, with their kith and kin, must be deferred till the numerous crabs of Sussex have been discussed. Though crabs and lobsters are alike Decapods, or ten-footed stalk-eyed Malacostraca, the crabs form a great division apart known as Brachyura or short-tails. In these the insignificant abdomen, tail, or pleon, is so folded against the breast as often to escape altogether the notice of the unobservant. This is especially the case with the male. In the female the tail, though not thick, is usually broad, the more effectually to take its part in holding together the eggs. These are often so multitudinous that they force the tail far out from the breast or sternal plastron by their swollen mass and make it conspicuous. The Brachyura are divided into five great sections. The one that includes the eatable crab bears the title Cyclometopa, not because the front is like a wheel or cycle, but only because it is more or less arcuate. Twelve Sussex species belong to various families of this section. The family Cancridæ is represented by *Cancer pagurus*, the family Xanthidæ by *Pirimela denticulata* (Montagu) and *Pilumnus hirtellus* (Linn.). This latter is not uncommon. Adam White records a specimen of it from Sussex, presented to the British Museum by J. E. Gray, Esq.,[1] and Bell says, ' the finest specimens I ever saw I procured from prawn and lobster pots at Bognor in September, 1842. It is worthy of remark that amongst twenty or thirty specimens I found only one female, a dried and mutilated one.'[2] This shaggy little species is the only one that our waters produce out of an extensive genus, and according to Bell it can be readily distinguished from all its foreign brethren by the absence of spines from the upper margin of the orbit. On the other hand it will be found to have a rather pretty feature in the orbit's denticulate lower margin. There is a marked inequality in the size of the two chelipeds, the larger being developed impartially on the right side or the left. *Pirimela denticulata* is a small species, but attracting attention by the dentation and prominence of its front, the ridges on the back of its carapace, and the characters of its outer maxillipeds. It is perhaps nowhere very common. Mr. Guermonprez informs me that he has taken a single specimen at Bognor.

To the family Portunidæ belongs *Carcinus mænas* (Pennant), the shore crab. This, like *Cancer pagurus*, is eatable and is eaten, but though thousands and myriads have fallen victims to man's appetite their martyrdom has never won them much respect. Bell speaks of the flavour being very delicate and sweet,[3] without apparently influencing gastronomers, who perhaps seldom study his book. Apart however from any value it may have for the epicure, this bold and defiant tenant of the shore has had its day of popularity. At one time a controversy was rife between naturalists who affirmed and others who denied that metamor-

[1] *List of the Specimens of British Animals in the British Museum* (1850), pt. iv. p. 11.
[2] *British Stalk-eyed Crustacea*, p. 70.   [3] Loc. cit. p. 78.

CRUSTACEANS

phoses are undergone by crustacea between the egg and the adult condition. Then it was that the common shore crab became of service just because of its commonness and the intrepidity which made it so very easy to catch. Moreover the tenacity of life which the parent exhibits was found to be so far inherited by the offspring that they could with comparative facility be reared in an aquarium. Accordingly it was soon proved that here at least very remarkable changes of form are undergone in the juvenile period. Adam White refers this species to 'British coast, everywhere,' and also states that the British Museum possesses a variety from Brighton, presented by Mr. W. Wing.[1] It is also recorded as very common in the special district of Sussex explored by the observers to whom we are indebted for the *Natural History of Hastings and St. Leonards and the Vicinity.*[2] In regard to the valuable catalogues contained in this work and its three supplements, the Rev. E. N. Bloomfield of Guestling Rectory, Hastings, has kindly informed me that the lists of crustacea in the first issue and the first supplement may be attributed to Mr. E. A. Butler, the Entomostraca of the second supplement to Mr. H. Langdon, and the few additions in the third supplement to Mr. P. Rufford. For the nomenclature of the stalk-eyed crustaceans these authorities adopted the names used by Bell, which are by no means remarkable for conforming to the rules of priority, although, as we shall later have occasion to notice, the principle of those rules was accepted by Bell himself. The coastline included in the Hastings district may be described as extending from Rye to Bexhill; and the introduction to the *Natural History* explains that cliffs of the Wealden formation, rising sometimes to a height of nearly 300 feet, form this line from Cliff End, Fairlight, to St. Leonards, and from Bulverhythe to Bexhill, the remainder being occupied by marsh land which contains in many places comparatively recent marine deposits and remains of a submarine forest. 'A few miles to the south-east of Hastings there is a Shoal known as the "Diamond"; it is much frequented by fishermen and forms an excellent hunting ground for the Naturalist.'[3] The authors add that many of the marine animals in their lists have been found only on this shoal, but without indicating which these are.

Portumnus latipes (Pennant) is recorded as common in the Hastings district[4] under the name *P. variegatus* given it by Leach and Bell. Both those authors expressly recognize that Pennant had much earlier called it *latipes*. This name of 'broadfoot' it owes to the flattened middle joints of its ambulatory legs and the rather broadly lanceolate form of the terminal joints in the last pair. Leach, who speaks of it as one of the most beautiful of our malacostracous animals,[5] may have called it 'variegated' for two reasons, being partly influenced by its pale purplish white colour mottled with a darker hue, and partly by the descriptive title, *Cancer latipes variegatus*, used by Plancus.[6] But that

---

[1] *List Brit. Mus.* p. 12.   [2] *Nat. Hist. Hastings* (1878), p. 41.   [3] Loc. cit. p. 4.
[4] Loc. cit. p. 41.   [5] *Malacostraca Podophthalmata Britanniæ*, pt. 2 (1815), text to pl. 4.
[6] *De Conchis minus notis* (1739, ed. 2, 1760), p. 34.

conchologist, whose own name in its Italian dress was Bianchi, though anterior to Pennant, had given no definite name to the species, and as Pennant for that purpose chose the first of his descriptive epithets, it was no longer admissible for Leach to substitute the second.

The genus *Portunus*, Fabricius, is represented by four species in Sussex. They have in common the character that the last two joints of the hindmost legs are notably flattened out to a greater breadth than the preceding joint. Leach says of them: 'The *Portuni*, which are commonly named by our fishermen *flying* or *flat-footed crabs*, have the power of swimming in the ocean; they effect this by means of their flat hinder legs, which serve the purpose of fins.'[1] *Portunus puber* (Linn.), the downy or velvet crab, when dry and faded in the cabinet is not greatly admired, but alive and seen glistening in water, with its eyes and a few other points bright red, and having its carapace and limbs all picked out with peacock blue, it is a delightful object. Bell quotes the following note upon its occurrence from Mr. Hailstone: 'In July, 1834, several dozens were taken off Hastings to the astonishment of the fishermen, who had rarely seen them here; and since that influx they have quite disappeared: this advance and retreat is of frequent occurrence.'[2] The *Hastings Natural History* records the species as not uncommon.[3] *P. depurator* (Linn.), the cleanser crab, is said by Leach to be 'by far the most common species that inhabits the British coast.'[4] Bell understands this to mean the most common species of the genus, and without some such qualification it would certainly contradict modern experience. Bell himself had not found it on the coast of Sussex, where he had found other species in great plenty; but he adds, 'Mr. Hailstone however states that it is frequently caught at Hastings in the shrimping net.'[5] White by some accident has overlooked it in his *Popular History of British Crustacea*, though incidentally quoting the name from Bell.[6]

On crabs of the species *P. arcuatus*, Leach, Bell remarks: 'They are gregarious, like most of their congeners; and I found them extremely abundant at Bognor, where they constantly infest the prawn pots, and, as the fishermen believe, keep the prawns from the bait.'[7] The front, that is the margin of the carapace between the eyes, is granulated, evenly arched, and fringed with rather long hair. Leach first described a female specimen with a slight depression in the middle of the front, and this evidently suggested the specific name *emarginatus*. He then described a male specimen with the front normally arched, and this he named *arcuatus*. In three successive works, from 1813 to 1816, he always placed *emarginatus* in front of *arcuatus*, so that under ordinary circumstances the former name ought to prevail. But here the circumstances are rather complicated, for after saying that except for its arcuated front his second species is exactly like the first he adds a curious paragraph about it:

[1] *Malacostraca Podophthalmata Britanniæ*, pt. 10 (1816), text to pl. 6.
[2] *British Stalk-eyed Crustacea*, p. 92.   [3] p. 41.
[4] *Malacostraca Podophthalmata Britanniæ*, pt. 11 (1816), text to pl. 9, fig. 1.
[5] *British Stalk-eyed Crustacea*, pp. 103, 104.   [6] p. 51.   [7] p. 99.

CRUSTACEANS

'Mr. Montagu considers this as the male of *P. emarginatus*. Mr. Leach thinks that *emarginatus* may prove to be an accidental variety of this species, but considers the distinctions as too strong for usual sexual distinction.'[1] Since the Mr. Leach referred to was the writer himself who had instituted both species, and since by his own confession the strong distinctions between them concerned only a single particular, the character and constancy of that solitary difference become important. Leach himself suspected that the emargination in his female specimen might be an accidental variety, and as it does not appear to have been again observed the name founded upon it has been set aside by general consent in favour of the more appropriate and contemporary name *arcuatus*. The same species was named *rondeletii* by Risso in 1816, and Bell with justice criticizes Milne-Edwards[2] because he has 'kept Risso's name against the law of priority of description.'[3] By inadvertence later in his work however he himself uses the repudiated name, where, speaking of a particular season, he says: 'At Bognor I found multitudes of *Portunus rondeletii*, which absolutely swarmed in the prawn and lobster pots, but not a specimen of any other species was obtained there.'[4]

Of *P. marmoreus*, Leach, Bell says: 'At Hastings I procured a single specimen which I found in a shop where shells, crustacea and other marine productions were sold, but it was certainly native at that place.'[5] The *Natural History of Hastings* records it as not uncommon. On the other hand that catalogue enters the *P. holsatus* of Fabricius with a query, which 'indicates that there is some doubt whether the specimen referred to was really of the species named.'[6] Leach instituted a species *P. lividus*. Bell, following Milne-Edwards, identifies this with the earlier *holsatus*, but he is further persuaded that *P. marmoreus*, Leach, is only a variety of the same. Still he has not quite the courage of his conviction, for he describes *marmoreus* and *holsatus* as if they were two distinct species. Of the 'marbled swimming crab' he says: 'The colours of this species are exceedingly varied and beautiful, particularly in the males. Buff, light-brown, deeper brown and brownish-red are arranged over the carapace in varied but always exactly symmetrical patterns. The only way in which these beautiful markings can be preserved is by raising the carapace, taking out the soft parts and drying the specimens in a shady place in a brisk current of air. If they are put into spirit the whole of the beauty of the colour is lost.'[7] Elsewhere he suggests that faded specimens of *P. marmoreus* might easily be mistaken for *P. holsatus*.[8] Apart from distinction of colour the points chiefly relied on for separating the latter species from the former are that the middle tooth of the front is slightly more prominent, and that the last joint of the hindmost leg has the apical point projecting from an otherwise more broadly rounded terminal

---

[1] *Edinburgh Encyclopædia* (1813), vii. 390.
[2] *Histoire Naturelle des Crustacés* (1834) i. 444.   [3] *British Stalk-eyed Crustacea*, p. 98.
[4] Loc. cit. p. 107.   [5] Loc. cit. p. 107.
[6] Loc. cit. p. 41 compared with p. 5.   [7] Loc. cit. p. 106.   [8] Loc. cit. p. 111.

margin. These differences, assuming them to be constant, are too in-definite and elusive to bestow specific rank on *P. marmoreus*. One may well suppose also that the one or two specimens which Leach differentiated as *lividus* or livid were in a faded condition. Of the three names then *holsatus*, being the earliest, is alone entitled to stand.

The species *Portunus corrugatus* (Pennant) may now be added to the crustacean fauna of Sussex. This crab is distinguished by the 'numerous raised serrato-granular, hairy, transverse lines' on the carapace, and by having the ' terminal joint of the posterior feet, with a raised median and marginal line, lanceolate and mucronate.'[1] Its rarity in this locality may be inferred not only from the absence of any earlier report, but from the circumstance that so indefatigable a collector as Mr. H. L. F. Guermonprez, to whom this record of it is due, has only met with a single specimen.

The last of our Sussex Portunidæ is *Polybius henslowii*, Leach. It was obtained by Bell at Hastings, and he received it at the hands of his friend Mr. Dixon from Worthing.[2] In this handsome species the last joint of the hindmost leg forms an oval rather exceptionally broad, tend-ing to increase the swimming capacity. Bell speaks of it as 'very local in its distribution, and probably existing nowhere in great numbers.'[3] This may be true of our own coasts, but for general application must be qualified, since the Prince of Monaco writes to the following effect: ' One day on the coast of Spain the dredge came up loaded with crabs (*Polybius Henslowi* Leach) as large as mice. The cubage of this mass made it clear to us that it contained about *five thousand* individuals, and the dredge, being burst in several places, must have lost a good number during the forty-five minutes that it took to come up from the bottom of the sea. This crustacean wields nippers as sharp as the claws of a cat, and the mischievous use that it makes of them is perfectly malignant. Swarming over the deck, crawling everywhere, from one end of the ship to the other, our *Polybius* visitors hooked themselves on to the bare feet of the sailors or clung to their fingers.'[4]

Corystes cassivelaunus (Pennant) was obtained by Bell at Hastings, where, he says, ' the late Mr. Hailstone also mentions having seen it caught by the trawlers.'[5] In the *Natural History of Hastings* it is marked not uncommon.[6] This sand-burrowing species, remarkable for its long second antennæ, and in the male for the great elongation of the cheli-peds, has been the subject of much scientific observation. It belongs to the family Corystidæ, which are regarded as the lowest of the Cyclome-topa. In contrast to what is usual in that section the carapace of this species is considerably longer than broad, in which respect it is very unlike *Cancer pagurus*, for there the carapace is conspicuously broader than long, and has moreover the anterior part of each lateral margin divided into nine lobes. The other species we have been discussing have their margins divided into only five lobes or teeth, our *Corystes*

---

[1] *British Stalk-eyed Crustacea*, p. 94.   [2] Loc. cit. p. 118.   [3] Loc. cit. p. 117.
[4] *Bulletin Soc. de Géographie de Paris* (1887), p. 539.   [5] *British Stalk-eyed Crustacea*, p. 161.   [6] p. 41.

alone differing by having only three teeth and a tubercle on the front half of its long side margin and a little tooth close to the hinder extremity of it.

The section Catometopa, or crabs with a downward bent front, to judge by existing records, has only two representatives in Sussex. Of these *Goneplax angulata* (Pennant) is marked rare in the *Natural History of Hastings*.[1] This species resembles *Corystes cassivelaunus* in the great length of its chelipeds, but its second antennæ are short and its carapace is broader than long. Its name by interpretation is a plaque or tablet with angular corners. The hind corners however of the carapace are rounded, but the front ones, against which the long eye-stalks fold down, are exceedingly sharp. The family Goneplacidæ is spoken of as showing a close resemblance to the Cyclometopa, being an instance of those transitions which make classification difficult and the study of nature interesting. Among the Pinnotheridæ, *Pinnotheres pisum* (Linn.), which, in contrast to the preceding species, is a little short-armed, round button of a crab, is noted by the *Natural History of Hastings* as common,[2] and this may very well be, since its well known habit of taking lodgings with a mussel, an oyster, or some other obliging mollusc, gives it a kind of freedom to be found in all waters where its hosts foregather.

With species of the section Oxyrrhyncha the county is fairly well supplied. In these the front is usually more or less sharply produced, and ' the beak' is often divided into two acute horns.

The family Inachidæ contains seven of the species here requiring notice. *Macropodia rostrata* (Linn.) was obtained from Sussex by Bell, who calls it *Stenorynchus phalangium* (Pennant), although by his own confession these are not its earliest names. He quotes from Mr. Hailstone the statement that ' it is very common at Hastings, both among the rocks on the shore, and in deep water, and is occasionally caught in the trawl-net in vast numbers : of sixty-eight specimens brought up at once the proportion of males to females was as two to one.'[3] *Macropodia tenuirostris* (Leach) was taken by Bell in prawn pots at Bognor. He says, ' this elegant species may be readily distinguished from the former by the long attenuated rostrum, by the existence of a small spine on the epistome immediately behind the basal joint of the external antennæ, and by a series of minute spines on the inner part of the arm: the body is altogether more elongated, and the spines more acute, but in other respects the characters are nearly the same.'[4] For comprehending these distinctions it is necessary to remember that the so-called ' arm' of the chelipeds is the long joint which immediately precedes the three terminal joints called wrist, hand and finger. The fixed thumb of the hand and the movable finger form the chela or nippers of a crustacean. The epistome or over-mouth is to be found on the under side of the crab, just above that important 'buccal area' which is more or less closed in by the external maxillipeds. The species *M. tenuirostris* was long identified with *Inachus longirostris*, Fabricius, but Miss M. J. Rathbun

[1] *Nat. Hist. Hastings*, p. 41. [2] p. 41. [3] p. 4. [4] p. 6.

in 1897, from examination of the type specimen, was enabled to identify the *longirostris* of Fabricius with *M. rostrata*, thereby reinstating Leach's *tenuirostris* as a valid specific name.

In this family two species, *Macropodia egyptia* (Milne-Edwards) and *Achæus cranchii*, Leach, have been added to the fauna of the county by Mr. Guermonprez. The former is actually reported as abundant, although in Bell's *British Stalk-eyed Crustacea* it is not even mentioned. It has however been named by more recent writers as occurring in south British waters. From the other two species of the same genus *M. egyptia* can be separated by the rostrum, which is nearly as long as the peduncle of the second antennæ, while in *M. rostrata* it is much shorter, and in *M. tenuirostris* decidedly longer than that peduncle. Milne-Edwards remarks that in *M. egyptia* the two anterior tubercles of the gastric region of the carapace nearly touch one another.[1] These little tubercles are very distinctly shown in Savigny's figure of the species,[2] and are quite clear in the male but not in the female specimen which Mr. Guermonprez has kindly sent me from the shore at Felpham. Of the little *Achæus cranchii*, Leach, he has met with only one specimen in the course of his researches at Bognor. It represents a genus very closely allied to *Macropodia*. E. J. Miers says : 'It is in fact only distinguished from it by the absence of rostral spines, the rostrum in *Achæus* being composed merely of two small acute or subacute lobes.' He further points out that the fourth joint of the outer maxillipeds in certain species, and among them in the typical *A. cranchii*, is shorter than in *Macropodia*, and distally truncated.[3]

The species of *Inachus* are at first sight not very different from those of *Macropodia*, but in the latter the bifid rostrum is long and has its two horns contiguous and the eyes are not retractile, whereas in *Inachus* the apices of the short rostrum are separate, and the eyes can be drawn back into the shelter of the hinder part of the orbit. *I. dorsettensis* (Pennant) was obtained by Bell at Hastings.[4] *I. dorynchus*, Leach, a less globose species than the preceding, was found by Hailstone at Hastings and by Bell at Hastings and Bognor. As to the latter collecting place Bell remarks that several small specimens, taken among the refuse of prawn and lobster pots, were of a lighter colour than most which he had observed from other localities, and this he thinks may have arisen from their being young.[5] *I. leptochirus*, Leach, the largest of the three, has relatively the slenderest chelipeds, to which allusion is made in the specific name, meaning thin-handed. The *Natural History of Hastings*, the only authority for its occurrence in this county, marks it as rare,[6] while Bell, speaking for Great Britain in general, calls it extremely rare. On the other hand Professors Alphonse Milne-Edwards and Bouvier, reporting on crustacea resulting from the scientific campaigns of the Prince of Monaco, say that, though this

---

[1] *Histoire Naturelle des Crustacés*, i. 280.   [2] *Crustacea of Egypt*, pl. 6, fig. 6.
[3] *Challenger Reports*, vol. xvii. 'Brachyura,' p. 8.
[4] *British Stalk-eyed Crustacea*, p. 15.   [5] p. 17.   [6] p. 41.

species is rare on the coasts of England and France, it is abundant more to the south as far as the coasts of the Sahara, and refer to its having been taken on various occasions at the Azores.[1]

In the family Maiidæ the county is credited with five species. *Maia squinado* (Herbst) is mentioned in the *Natural History of Hastings* as not uncommon.[2] Mr. Guermonprez incorporates it in his list as common at Bognor. It is a large species with the outside prickly, the inside good for food. Among its hairs and thorns other crustaceans often find lodgment for their small bodies, making the Maia a sort of curiosity shop for the microscopist. *Hyas araneus* (Linn.) was received from Worthing by Bell, who states that it occurs in considerable abundance at Hastings and that he had himself obtained it there.[3] It grows to a large size, though its body is never comparable in bulk with that of *Maia squinado*. *Hyas coarctatus*, Leach, was also procured by Bell at Hastings and received by him from Worthing.[4] The lateral constriction of the carapace, which has suggested the name *coarctatus*, is almost the only character for distinguishing this species from the larger *H. araneus*. The smaller form is said to frequent the greater depths, but they occur so frequently in the same localities that some suspicion of their specific distinctness may be permitted. Fine specimens are found in arctic waters as well as in our own. Mr. Hailstone allowed himself to suggest a third species, under the name *H. serratus*, for specimens a quarter of an inch long,[5] which are almost undoubtedly only the fry of the earlier named species, whether the word 'species' be applied in the singular or the plural. *Blastus tetraodon* (Pennant), better known as *Pisa tetraodon*, the four-horned spider-crab, is recorded by Leach from Brighton, and Bell says: ' The habits of this species, so far as I have had an opportunity of observing them, are curious. They are found concealed under the long hanging fuci which clothe the rocks at some distance from the shore, in which situation I have taken them among the Bognor rocks. They congregate in vast numbers at the place I have just mentioned in the prawn and lobster pots. I have seen probably thirty among the refuse of one of these, attracted no doubt by the garbage which is placed in them as bait. These were much larger and finer than any I have seen elsewhere.'[6] *Blastus tribulus* (Linn.), under the name of *Pisa gibbsii*, Leach, is recorded by Bell from Hastings.[7] In it the rostrum is longer, with the component horns of it much less divergent, than in the preceding species. This genus is distinguished from *Hyas* by having the last joint in the walking legs fringed with a comb of denticles, of which *Hyas* is devoid.

Eurynome aspera (Pennant) represents the long-armed and often rugged family of the Parthenopidæ, wherein the walking legs are notably shorter than the chelipeds. Hailstone describes from the Sussex coast

[1] *Résultats des Campagnes Scientifiques*, fasc. 7 ; *Crustacés Décapodes* (1894), p. 7.   [2] p. 41.
[3] *British Stalk-eyed Crustacea*, p. 33.   [4] p. 36.
[5] *Loudon's Magazine of Natural History*, viii. 549.
[6] *British Stalk-eyed Crustacea*, p. 24.   [7] Loc. cit. p. 29.

'Eurynome [Leach] ? spinòsa [Hailstone] ? áspera in a young state. Female.'[1] But his experience was evidently at the time not such as to justify him in suggesting a new species, so that the alternative he offers of regarding his *spinosa* as the young of *aspera* has been accepted with general acquiescence. The readiness of all the spider-crabs to array themselves in borrowed plumes, and the nice adaptation of their own limbs and armature to the ingenious devices not of vanity but of self-concealment, are now well understood in principle. They still offer tempting opportunities for more detailed explanation or corroborative evidence on the part of patient and skilful observers.

Outside of the genuine Brachyura is a section known as the primitive or anomalous Brachyura, sometimes called the Dromiacea. In it the oviducts of the female open not on the sternal plastron but on the first joint in the legs of the third pair. One species of this section, known as *Dromia vulgaris*, Milne-Edwards, though possibly only an occasional visitant, has a fairly good claim to be included in the fauna of the county. Bell says: 'In the *Zoologist*, 1848, p. 2325, occurs a notice of no fewer than nine full-sized specimens having been dredged on the coast of Sussex. Mr. Newman gives the details of its occurrence, and a figure of the species, having received it from Mr. George Ingall. About the same time my lamented friend Mr. Dixon, of Worthing, sent me three specimens which had been procured off Selsey Bill.'[2] Adam White, who gives the same reference to the *Zoologist*, speaks of the species as 'found at Beachy Head, Sussex, by G. Ingall, Esq., 1848.'[3] White calls it the sponge-crab, obviously in allusion to the fact that this hairy ball of a crustacean often becomes covered with sponge. Of the legs not only the first pair are chelipeds, but also the fourth and fifth pairs, which are small and turned back over the carapace, have a minutely chelate ending. The species seems very closely related to *D. rumphii*, Fabricius, which ranges from the Red Sea to Japan. In the family Dromiidæ, to which these species belong, there are two little lateral plates between the sixth and seventh segments of the pleon, a feature not very easy to observe in these hirsute animals, and one that when observed might by many be passed over as unimportant. It is however of considerable significance, for while the true Brachyura have no appendages to the sixth pleon segment, in the Macrura these appendages attain a high development. We may note then that the two little plates in *Dromia*, on the supposition that they are vestigial appendages, supply a link between these two great contrasted groups of the decapod crustaceans.

The anomalous Macrura are represented in Sussex by seven well known species, belonging to three families, the crab-like Porcellanidæ, the lobster-like Galatheidæ, and the Paguridæ, known as hermit-crabs, though they are far from crab-like in nature or appearance. *Porcellana longicornis* (Linn.), the 'minute porcelain crab,' is reported in the

[1] *Loudon's Magazine Nat. Hist.* viii. 549.   [2] *British Stalk-eyed Crustacea*, p. 371.
[3] *List of British Animals in British Museum*, p. 23.

CRUSTACEANS

Natural History of Hastings as common, and the larger but not large *P. platycheles*, the flat-clawed ' hairy porcelain crab ' as not uncommon.[1] Here the thin but rather broad pleon is flexed against the breast as in the Brachyura, but the sixth segment of it carries well developed appendages, and the seventh segment is peculiarly sutured, as if it were composed of a segment with coalesced appendages. A species found by Mr. Hailstone in Sussex was at first determined by Westwood as a new species, *P. minuta*, and afterwards referred by Mr. Hailstone himself to *P. linneana*, Leach, which is in fact a synonym of *P. longicornis*.[2]

Of *Galathea squamifera*, Leach, Bell says, ' The largest I have seen were procured by myself at Bognor, where they are often taken in considerable numbers in prawn and lobster pots.'[3] *G. nexa*, Embleton, and *G. strigosa* (Linn.) are both recorded as rare by the *Natural History of Hastings*,[4] but by Mr. Guermonprez the last is reported as 'frequent' at Bognor. In this genus the pleon is in some respects similar to that of *Porcellana*, but it is thicker and far less completely inflexed. For discriminating the three species above mentioned it is useful to remember that the first two have, and the third is without, epipods on the chelipeds and two following pairs of legs. The epipod is the secondary branch attached to the first joint of a malacostracan appendage. In *G. nexa* the third maxillipeds have the third joint as long as the fourth, whereas it is shorter than the fourth in *G. squamifera*.[5] The surface markings, spines, and colours in this genus are almost always artistically effective, and will attract some observers more than the minutiæ, which must be inspected for distinguishing the several species.

Eupagurus bernhardus (Linn.) is noted as very common by the *Natural History of Hastings*, and *Eupagurus prideaux* (Leach) as rare.[6] The former is on the shore the commonest of English ' hermits ' ; the second is admired for the persistence with which it claims the companionship of the sea-anemone, *Adamsia palliata*, perched like a sentinel outside the hermit's cell. Mr. Guermonprez, writing to me from Bognor, expresses some doubt as to the occurrence of this species on the Sussex coast, questioning whether the specimens may not probably be brought from near the French coast by the scallop fishers. To the Sussex fauna he himself adds the little *Eupagurus cuanensis* (Thompson), in which the eye-stalks are relatively much longer than in *E. bernhardus*, and the front of the carapace is not as in the latter species excavate to receive them.

Of the genuine Macrura some tribes are rather sparsely represented in these waters. Thus of the Thalassinidea only one family, the Callianassidæ, can be claimed, and that only on the strength of a single species, *Upogebia stellata* (Montagu), which Mr. Guermonprez has found at Bognor occasionally. He informs me by letter that it makes long burrows in the ground occupied by the sea-grass, *Zostera marina*, below

[1] *Nat. Hist. Hastings*, p. 41.   [2] *Loudon's Magazine*, viii. 395.
[3] *British Stalk-eyed Crustacea*, p. 198.   [4] p. 41.
[5] Bonnier, *Bulletin Scientifique de la France et de la Belgique* (1888), sér. 3, i. 43.   [6] p. 41.

and at low-water mark. He himself has only dug out one specimen, having taken others 'stupefied by the cold after frosts at the March spring-tides, washed out at low-water mark.' He suggests that the accompanying form, which was described by Leach as *U. deltaura*, is the female of *U. stellata*. Bell also believes that the two forms belong to a single species. The hairy pinched-in front and spreading tail-fan of this crustacean, and its imperfectly chelate claws, are noticeable characters. Of another tribe, the Scyllaridea, one family, the Palinuridæ, is likewise represented here by a single species, since Mr. Guermonprez is able to record the occasional capture at Bognor of the common craw-fish, *Palinurus vulgaris*, Latreille.

In the tribe Astacidea the family Nephropsidæ must not be over-looked, since it comprises a very prominent Sussex crustacean, *Astacus gammarus* (Linn.). Upon this, which is better known as the common lobster, Messrs. Buckland and Walpole supply several interesting observations. Buckland in 1875 says, 'A great many small lobsters are sent up [to London] from Bognor, in Sussex, and a few large ones come from Bognor. These smaller kind of Bognor lobsters are in great demand during the season for breakfast and luncheon.'[1] He was informed that the Bognor lobster fishery begins about March and ends at Christmas, or earlier in a very cold season. 'When first caught in the early part of the year, the lobster appears sandy and covered with sea-weed and slime ; as the sun gets stronger this comes off, and towards August and September they appear quite clean.'[2] The close season of two or three months is ex-plained as being the time needed by the fishermen for mending their lobster pots. In the evidence given before Buckland and Walpole, John Richards, a fisherman of Bognor, says, 'At the bottom of the sea, close in to shore, there are grass banks with holes like rat or rabbit holes, in which the lobsters live. These banks extend for 20 miles from Selsea to Shoreham in patches. The grass weed grows on mud banks. These mud banks form a breeding ground.'[3] The grass intended is clearly the sea-grass, *Zostera marina*. The commissioners themselves say, 'Bognor, on the coast of Sussex, in some respects resembles Budleigh Salterton. There are some rocks called the Owers, 12 miles out to sea, where there is a considerable fishery, and there are no indications of failure on these rocks. But the inshore fishery is in a different condition. The bottom of the sea is a warm plateau of mud and sand covered with weed, which is apparently a nursery for small crustacea. The smallest lobsters in England are caught on this plateau, and very small crabs are also taken in the immediate neighbourhood off Selsea. The fishermen consider that the lobsters come here from other places for the purpose of repro-duction, and they assert that there are no indications of any diminution in the number of these crustacea. It is universally admitted, however, that the crab fishery at Selsea is declining in importance, and that there are not one third as many crabs as there used to be. It ought to be

[1] *Report on the Fisheries of Norfolk*, p. 73. [2] Loc. cit. p. 74.
[3] *Report on the Crab and Lobster Fisheries of England and Wales*, p. 65.

added that Bognor is more dependent on its prawn fishery than on either lobsters or crabs, and that the little lobsters are taken with the prawns in the prawn pots.'[1] Mr. Guermonprez in 1902 reports the lobster at Bognor as still abundant. Whether in this same tribe the family Potamobiidæ is represented in Sussex by the widely distributed *Potamobius pallipes*, the river crayfish, I have not been able to ascertain. It is at least highly probable that the species will be found in some of the streams.

Of prawns the incidental mention has already been frequent, and one could wish that the subject were as simple as the name is familiar. But the words prawn and shrimp, being unscientific terms, have often been applied interchangeably and without method, those who use them being guided by differences of size and colour rather than by the structural features and relationships of the animals. Most of them fall to some one of the many families of the tribe Caridea. In the family Palæmonidæ is included our best known English prawn, *Leander serratus* (Pennant), of which Bell says, 'I found that at Bognor the fishermen consider them, when young, as a distinct species, and assert that, at certain seasons, they drive the true *prawns* from their ordinary place of resort. The probability is that at the season when the young ones have arrived at a certain age, they separate themselves from the older ones, which at that period of the year retire further from the shore.'[2] There are indeed few households of living creatures in which nature does not exercise a centrifugal force of one kind or another, so as to check unwholesome concentration. *Leander squilla* (Linn.), a species very similar to *L. serratus*, but smaller, is recorded by White from 'Sussex (Little Hampton).'[3] In the market place this species shares with some others the colloquial names of white shrimps and cup shrimps. *Palæmonetes varians* (Leach), which I have myself taken at Lancing, and which is recorded by the *Natural History of Hastings* as common,[4] has the peculiarity of making itself at home in fresh and brackish waters, whereas the other two species are strictly marine. In all three it is only the first two pairs of legs that are furnished with pincers, and it is the second pair that is the longer, a different arrangement from that in the lobster, which has an enormous first pair of chelipeds, followed by two pairs that are minutely chelate. In the family Processidæ the second pair of legs, though longer than the first, are not so strong, and are tipped with tiny nippers. *Processa canaliculata*, Leach, has a front pair of legs that are not properly a pair, since only one of them is chelate, the other being simple, that is devoid of a chela. Adam White records this species in the British Museum collection from 'Bognor. Presented by Prof. Bell.'[5] We may assume that this is a boiled example, since Bell, speaking of specimens, says, 'That from which my figure and the above description are given was accidentally found by myself in a dish of boiled prawns, on which I was about to breakfast, at Bognor, in the year

[1] *Report on the Crab and Lobster Fisheries of England and Wales*, p. xii.
[2] *British Stalk-eyed Crustacea*, p. 303.   [3] *List of British Animals in British Museum*, p. 42.
[4] p. 40.   [5] *List of British Animals*, p. 39.

1842.'[1] Both White and Bell use the designation *Nika edulis*, Risso, White calling the species ' Risso's shrimp,' and explaining that ' the name here adopted is prior to Dr. Leach's, and is given to it from the species being eaten on the coasts of the Mediterranean, as the Shrimp is eaten here.'[2] But on the question of priority he is mistaken, since Risso's genus and species were published in 1816, while the fourth part of Leach's *Malacostraca Podophthalmata Britanniæ*, containing, in plate 41 and its accompanying text, the figures and description of *Processa canaliculata*, was published on July 1, 1815. Of the Pandalidæ *Pandalus montagui*, Leach, is reported by Mr. Guermonprez as occurring often at Bognor. The only other species at present claiming to rank among Sussex prawns, as distinguished from shrimps, is involved in much obscurity. In 1798 Fabricius established the genus *Alpheus* for species in which the first pair of chelipeds are enormously larger than the second and are composed of two unequal and dissimilar limbs, though both are strongly chelate, while, instead of the long serrate horn with which our ordinary prawns are armed, in *Alpheus* the rostrum is minute and the carapace is produced over the eyes, thus protecting them by a more or less pellucid shield. In evident allusion to this last character the eccentric naturalist Rafinesque in 1814, probably unaware of the Fabrician genus, named a new one *Cryptophthalmus*, meaning ' eyes under cover,' for a Mediterranean species which he called *C. ruber*. In 1835 S. Hailstone, jun., Esq., while apparently still a tyro in the subject, investigated several crustaceans from the Sussex coast, and then submitted his descriptions, figures and specimens to the distinguished and afterwards celebrated entomologist, J. O. Westwood. The latter published a report upon them which in some respects was far from giving satisfaction to Mr. Hailstone. The point here needing mention is that one of the species was entitled ' *Hippolyte rubra*, Westwood,' and this the discoverer of the specimen claimed a right to call ' *H. macrocheles*, Hailstone.' Westwood himself was undecided both as to the genus and the species, for he suggested that it might be proper to call the object examined *Cryptophthalmus ruber*. Subsequently he formed a new genus for it, *Dienecia*, with ' *Hippolyte ? rubra* ' for the type.[3] In 1837 Milne-Edwards, knowing nothing of this insular dispute, called a species *Alpheus ruber*, which goes by his name as author, although he explains in a footnote that it appears to him to be the same as Rafinesque's species.[4] In 1854 Mr. Guise described a species as *A. affinis*, and in 1857 Adam White, accepting this as distinct from *A. ruber* of Milne-Edwards, gives the description, and in a footnote says, ' Mr. Guise thinks this may be the *Hippolyte rubra* of Hailstone, on which Mr. Westwood founded the genus *Dienecia*.'[5] But if *Alpheus affinis*, Guise, be distinct from *A. ruber* (Rafinesque) and identical with *A. ruber* (Westwood), then

---

[1] *British Stalk-eyed Crustacea*, p. 277.   [2] *Popular History of British Crustacea*, p. 114.
[3] *Loudon's Magazine of Natural History*, viii. 274, 395, 552.   [4] *Hist. Nat. Crustacés*, ii. 351.
[5] *Popular History of British Crustacea*, p. 112, with reference to ' *Ann. and Mag. Nat. Hist.* (1854), p. 278, fig. p. 280.'

CRUSTACEANS

Westwood's name would lapse as preoccupied, and Hailstone's *megacheles* would hold the field as prior to Guise's *affinis*. Spence Bate thought that Hailstone's *megacheles* was the same as *A. edwardsii* (Andouin), and if that could be proved Hailstone would once more have the nominal glory snatched from between his teeth. *A. ruber* has the movable finger of the greater claw not so long as the immovable one, sometimes called the thumb, whereas in *edwardsii* and *affinis* the movable is not shorter than the immovable finger. To prove the difference constant would need a comparison of numerous specimens. White, who had Hailstone's species at command in the British Museum,[1] ventures no independent judgment, the state of preservation perhaps precluding any.

Of the true Hippolytidæ Mr. Guermonprez reports *Hippolyte varians*, Leach, as common at Bognor. It has indeed a very extensive distribution, as well as a great capacity for adapting its colour to its environment. Of *Hippolyte fascigera*, Gosse, the same diligent recorder mentions a solitary specimen. In 1899 grave doubt was thrown by Mr. A. O. Walker, F.L.S., on the validity of this species. It is certainly the case that those tufts or fascicles of hairs on the body to which the specific name is due are ready to fall off at the slightest provocation, after which there appears to be nothing left by which this form can be distinguished from *H. varians*. Mr. Guermonprez states that *H. cranchii*, Leach, occurs at Bognor now and then. This should probably be referred to Bate's genus *Spirontocaris*.[2]

In the family *Crangonidæ* three species are attributed to Sussex. On *Crangon vulgaris* (Linn.) Bell quotes from Hailstone's MS. Notes on the Crustacea of Hastings.[3] From the same writer's researches two species were published in 1835 as *Pontophilus trispinosus*, Hailstone, and *P. bispinosus*, Westwood, though Westwood, while using the generic name *Pontophilus*, Leach, expressed his opinion that French authors had rightly made it a synonym of *Crangon*.[4] To this genus the two species were for some time referred, until Kinahan in 1862 placed them under a new generic name *Cheraphilus*, which he on insufficient grounds substituted for *Pontophilus*.[5] Some of his species fall therefore to that genus, but the Sussex species become *Philocheras trispinosus* (Hailstone) and *Philocheras nanus* (Kröyer).[6]

The important group of the Schizopoda has not hitherto made a good figure in this county. Only Mysis sp., from Ecclesbourne, is recorded in the *Natural History of Hastings*,[7] under the Stomapoda, an old arrangement now relinquished, which combined the schizopods with the entirely different Squillidæ. Now however Mr. Guermonprez has removed to some extent the stigma of poverty by cataloguing five species. For these he uses generally the nomenclature adopted in Bell's *British Stalk-eyed Crustacea*, calling the species *Mysis chamæleon*, *M. vulgaris*,

---

[1] *List of British Animals in British Museum*, p. 41. [2] Stebbing, *History of Crustacea*, pp. 234, 236.
[3] *British Stalk-eyed Crustacea*, p. 258. [4] *Loudon's Magazine*, viii. 261, 265, 395.
[5] *Proc. Royal Irish Acad.* (1862), pt. 1, viii. 7. [6] Stebbing, *South African Crustacea* (1900), p. 47.
[7] First Supplement (1883), p. 45.

M. griffithsiæ, Cynthilia flemingii, Themisto brevispinosa. For the first three of these the names should now rather be respectively *Praunus flexuosus*, Leach, *Neomysis vulgaris* (Vaughan Thompson), *Siriella armata* (Milne-Edwards). Goodsir's *Cynthia flemingii* is supposed to be the same as *Leptomysis lingvura*, Sars. The generic names *Cynthia* and *Cynthilia* are withdrawn from it as contravening existing rules, but the specific name *flemingii* has the priority, if the identity of the species with *lingvura* can be considered well established. *Themisto brevispinosa*, Goodsir, probably belongs to the genus *Mysis*. *Themisto* in any case cannot be used for its generic name, as it is preoccupied.[1]

The Stomatopoda, as they are now by preference called, are in modern classification limited to the one family Squillidæ. White notes the species *Squilla desmarestii*, Risso, as having been taken off Brighton, and consigned to the British Museum from Dr. Mantell's collection.[2] These 'mantis-shrimps' differ greatly from all the preceding sets of crustacea, by having the second maxillipeds transformed into powerful claws in which the two last joints close together like a clasp knife, and even more by having the breathing organs on the appendages of the pleon instead of on those of the front body. White says that Risso's Squilla 'is of a yellowish colour dotted with brown, but is sometimes of a delicate rosy hue; length about 4 inches.'[3] A well preserved specimen of this pretty species sent me from Bognor by Mr. Guermonprez fully agrees with the characters which have been assigned to it. The eyes are small, triangular. The finger of the great claws has only five spines. The first five segments of the pleon are devoid of submedian carinæ. The Rev. E. N. Bloomfield, in a letter dated July 30, 1902, reports this species also from Hastings, found there by Miss H. F. Davies.

Of the sessile-eyed Malacostraca species are recorded in sufficient variety to indicate that Sussex would be well worth exploring for more members of this copious division. Of the Isopoda anomala or cheliferous isopods Mr. Guermonprez reports the occurrence on floating wood of the species long known as *Tanais vittatus* (Rathke), but now, according to M. Dollfus, more properly designated by the earlier name *Tanais cavolinii*, Milne-Edwards.[4] Among the Isopoda genuina may first be mentioned the small but peculiar family of the Gnathiidæ, for among the specimens from the Sussex coast which Hailstone submitted to Westwood was one which the latter authority determined as *Gnathia maxillaris* (Montagu), adding, 'It has been said that this is the male of the genus Praniza, of which I have published an account in the *Annales des Sciences Naturelles*. Is this so?'[5] It is interesting to know that Dr. Leach, when establishing the genus *Gnathia* in 1813, expressed the opinion that the animal afterwards referred to a genus *Praniza* was the female of *Gnathia maxillaris*. But it was not till 1855 that M. Eugène

---

[1] On this group see Norman in *Ann. Nat. Hist.* (1892), and Stebbing, *History of Crustacea* (1893).
[2] *List of British Animals in British Museum*, p. 46, and *Popular History*, p. 155.
[3] *Popular History*, p. 155.
[4] *Bulletin Soc. Zool. de France*, xxi. 207 (1897).   [5] *Loudon's Magazine*, viii. 273.

Hesse succeeded in persuading a tolerably large fraction of his scientific brethren that this was indisputably the case. For a long time Leach's *Gnathia* was in general ignored in favour of *Anceus*, Risso, 1816, and while the husband was assigned to a family Anceidæ, the wife and children were placed in a quite distinct family, Pranizidæ. The adult male is square-headed, with strangely projecting mandibles, while the adult female has a subtriangular head, with no effective mandibles at all. The young ones are blood-sucking parasites, with appropriate stilets for procuring the juices of fish. On consideration of all the changing characters it will not be thought that the naturalists who went astray about the relationships of these voracious little animals were wholly without excuse. The Ægidæ are another family fond of fish. Under the description of what they call *Æga bicarinata*, Leach, it is said by Bate and Westwood that 'specimens from St. Leonards are in the Hopeian collection at Oxford.'[1] But Schiödte and Meinert point out that Leach's species is a synonym of the earlier *Æ. rosacea* (Risso), and that Bate and Westwood have in their account mixed up two species, Risso's *rosacea* and the still larger *Æ. strömii*, Lütken, which sometimes attains a length of just upon 2 inches.[2] With which of the two species Sussex is to be credited awaits determination until the specimens in the Hope Museum have been reinspected. In the Cirolanidæ the little *Eurydice achata* (Slabber), better known as *E. pulchra*, Leach, occurs in the sands of Sussex. It is praised for the beautiful markings of its surface, and blamed for the biting propensities of its equally beautiful mouth-organs.[3] The timber-destroying 'gribble,' *Limnoria lignorum* (J. Rathke), which gives its name to the family Limnoriidæ, is mentioned by Mr. Guermonprez as common. From the parasitic family Bopyridæ, *Bopyrus squillarum*, Latreille, is reported by the *Natural History of Hastings*,[4] and in fact wherever the prawn *Leander serratus* abounds this companion is likely to be found nestling in a compact little family group under the carapace of one specimen or another. *Gyge galatheæ*, Bate and Westwood, is recorded by Mr. Guermonprez. Of the Idoteidæ the *Natural History* records *Idotea linearis* (Linn.) and the exceedingly common *I. tricuspidata*, for which the more correct name appears to be *I. balthica* (Pallas).[5] Mr. Guermonprez' list contains both of these, and also *I. pelagica*, Leach. Mr. Henry Scherren, F.Z.S., has sent me *I. viridis* (Slabber) from Seaford. This is a family of narrow species. The Sphæromidæ, on the other hand, are of such a shape that they can roll up into a more or less perfect ball. Of these the *Natural History of Hastings* records *Sphæroma serratum* (Fabricius) from Fairlight and Pett Level, the marshes and beach between Cliff End and Winchelsea,[6] in addition to two species of which the occurrence was previously known. Of *S. hookeri*, Leach, Bate and Westwood say : 'We have received specimens of this species from Mr. Slade, who found them at Bexhill, near St.

[1] *British Sessile-eyed Crustacea*, ii. 280.   [2] *Naturhistorisk Tidsskrift* (1879), ser. 3, xii. 353.
[3] Stebbing, *Annals and Magazine Nat. Hist.* (1875), ser. 4, xv. 78.   [4] p. 41.   [5] p. 41.
[6] First Supplement, p. 45.

Leonards, in brackish water affected by land drainage.'[1] *S. rugicauda*, Leach, distinguished from the preceding by a pair of longitudinal ridges on the pleon, I have myself found in company with it in marshy ground near the sea at Worthing. *Dynamene viridis*, Leach, from Fairlight,[2] has the distinction of being very common and very obscure, no one as yet having arrived at any certainty as to its proper generic or specific name. In another family, Asellidæ, the freshwater *Asellus aquaticus* (Linn.) is reported common,[3] and so it is probably in all our counties. From the neighbouring family Janiridæ, Mr. Guermonprez notes also as common the marine species *Janira maculosa*, Leach, and *Jæra albifrons*, Leach, the latter of which has recently been identified by Sars with the form named *Oniscus marinus* by Otho Fabricius in the *Fauna grönlandica*, so that it must now be called *Jæra marina* (O. Fabricius).

Of the terrestrial Isopoda, or woodlice, the often quoted *Natural History* gives under the heading Oniscidæ the species *Lygia oceanica*, rare ; *Philoscia muscorum*, very common ; *Platyarthrus hoffmannseggii*, not uncommon ; *Oniscus asellus*, common ; *Porcellio scaber*, common ; *Armadillo vulgaris*, very common ;[4] with the addition in the First Supplement of *Philougria riparia*, Koch, from Hastings.[5] A more precise classification would give the earlier *Trichoniscus pusillus*, Brandt, in place of *P. riparia*, assigning this to the family Trichoniscidæ, and *Ligia oceanica* (Linn.) to the Ligiidæ, allotting *Armadillidium vulgare* (Latreille) to the Armadillidiidæ, and leaving in the Oniscidæ *Porcellio scaber*, Latreille, *Philoscia muscorum* (Scopoli), *Oniscus asellus*, auctorum, and *Platyarthrus hoffmannseggii*, Brandt. This last little pallid frequenter of ants' nests I have found at Cissbury Camp near Worthing. Mr. Guermonprez informs me that *Porcellio dilatatus*, Brandt, is also found in Sussex.

Concerning the Amphipoda, a group abounding in species, exuberant in individuals, and distributed in endless diversity over all seas, there is little occasion to speak here at length. They have not yet attracted interest on the Sussex coast. After mentioning the freshwater *Gammarus pulex* (Linn.) and *Corophium longicorne* from the Cuckmere district as local and very common,[6] the *Natural History of Hastings* adds nothing to its catalogue in this department till its Third Supplementary List in 1898, the accretion in twenty years being limited to *Caprella linearis* (de Geer), noted as somewhat rare.[7] *Corophium longicorne*, a mud burrowing species, with the second antennæ much longer than the first, and a habit of revolving in its burrow, should rather be called *Corophium volutator* (Pallas). *Caprella linearis* is one of the linear skeleton shrimps, of which the specific name should preferably be backed by some details of the structure, for, struck by the filiform aspect of these curious objects, each fresh observer is apt to take for granted that the species before him must be *C. linearis*, although there are several linear species besides that. Of these, *Phtisica marina*, Slabber, is now reported by Miss H. F. Davies from

[1] *British Sessile-eyed Crustacea*, ii. 411.
[2] *The Nat. Hist. of Hastings*, First Supplement, p. 45. [3] Loc. cit. p. 45.
[4] p. 41. [5] p. 45. [6] p. 41. [7] p. 22.

CRUSTACEANS

Hastings. In the year 1874 I myself, together with a friend, made search for sand-burrowing species in the sands which stretch for about fourteen miles from Lancing by Worthing and Goring and on past Littlehampton. Unless where here and there weeds and stones afforded a shelter, these extensive sands at that particular time rewarded our efforts with no amphipods except a species of the genus *Bathyporeia*, Lindström, and a single specimen of the genus *Urothoe*, Dana. The latter, since then destroyed by an accident, was at the time wrongly referred to Slabber's genus *Haustorius*, then known as *Sulcator*, Bate. The former was described as *Bathyporeia pilosa*, Lindström. But Professor G. O. Sars, writing in 1891 on a species which ' occurs along the whole coast of Norway,' says : ' The redescription of the British form of Bathyporeia by the Rev. Mr. Stebbing has enabled me to identify this species with *B. pelagica* Sp. Bate.' From *B. pilosa*, he says, it is ' easily known by the bright red ocular pigment, and by the much more slender form of the 2 posterior pairs of pereiopoda.'[1] This elegant little creature, which is less than a quarter of an inch long, ' could have been taken in thousands' in the Sussex district above mentioned. ' Its presence beneath the sand is betrayed by a small furrow, sometimes short and nearly straight, ending in a little pit, at others twisting and meandering about and occasionally zigzagged. The mothers with young look as if their bodies were tinted with a delicate blue ; but this is due partly to a double stripe upon each ovum, the colouring of which is seen through the pellucid sides of the parent, and partly perhaps to the contents of the alimentary canal.'[2] Greatly elongated second antennæ distinguish the adult male from females and young ones of either sex. To these rather scanty records Mr. Guermonprez contributes some valuable additions. His list comprises *Talitrus locusta* (Pallas), the sandhopper, *Orchestia gammarellus* (Pallas), the shore hopper, *Gammarus locusta* (Linn.) and *G. marinus*, Leach, two species which closely resemble the freshwater *G. pulex*, and along with these stands *Amathilla sabini* (Leach), of which perhaps the generic and certainly the specific name requires to be changed, with the result of transforming the designation into *Gammarellus homari* (J. C. Fabricius). Mention is also made of the wood-boring species *Chelura terebrans*, Philippi, as found on floating timber, and of *Hyperia galba* (Montagu) found so commonly in medusæ. Of two or three other species procured the names have not been decisively ascertained.

At this point may conveniently be mentioned *Nebalia bipes* (O. Fabricius), of which Mr. Guermonprez has met with a single specimen on the coast of Sussex. It has the particular interest of hovering between the two principal sections of the Crustacea, some authors thinking that it has a right to be classed with the Malacostraca, to which all the hitherto mentioned species belong, while others would place it in the following group. So embarrassing is the situation that the very restricted

[1] *Crustacea of Norway*, pt. 6, i. 130.
[2] Stebbing, *Annals and Magazine Nat. Hist.* ser. 4, xv. 78, pl. 3.

family of the Nebaliidæ is sometimes thought worthy of being placed by itself in a separate section called the Leptostraca.

The Entomostraca, whether of the sea or of the fresh water, have not yet been subjected to any extensive or elaborate investigation for this county. In the gymnophyllous division of the Phyllopoda, that is in the peculiar group which have their leaf-like limbs not covered by a carapace, the graceful fairy shrimp, *Chirocephalus diaphanus*, Prevost, was recorded by Dr. Baird in 1850 as taken near Brighton by C. Ager.[1] Recently the species has been again discovered in Sussex by G. H. Maxwell-Lefroy, Esq., a student at the Cambridge zoological laboratory, and now Government Entomologist in the West India Province. In sending me specimens, my friend Mr. J. J. Lister, F.R.S., writes : ' The locality is recorded in Harmer's Museum records as a small pond on " High and Over " (one of the downs, I take it) to the right of the Alfrestone Road, rather more than one mile out of Seaford. The pond is said to be dry from April to September, and the specimens most abundant in March and early April ; but these were collected in December, 1899.' It is a pleasant experiment to take soil from the dried-up floor of such a pond, and pour water over it in a finger-bowl, for the excellent chance of being able in two or three weeks' time to watch the development and growth of fairy shrimps, or, failing them, of other interesting entomostracans.

Of the Cladocera Brady mentions taking *Daphnia obtusa*, Kurz, in a pond at Burpham, Sussex, and *D. propinqua*, Sars, in ponds at Arundel and Angmering of the same county. But he agrees with M. Jules Richard in regarding *D. propinqua* as only a variety of *D. obtusa*, and he practically agrees with Sars and with Lilljeborg in considering that *D. obtusa* with the short apical process can scarcely be distinguished from the common *D. pulex*, which sometimes though not always has a long one.[2] The *Natural History of Hastings* in 1888 records under ' Daphniadæ ' '*D. magna*, Strauss ; *D. vetula*, Müll., common'; and under 'Lynceidæ' *Chydorus sphæricus*, Müll., common.[3] Of the Daphniidæ *Daphnia magna*, Straus, in 1898 was transferred by Brady to a new genus, *Dactylura*, which Lilljeborg in 1901 rejects as not needed. Lilljeborg points out that *Daphnia pennata*, O. F. Müller, 1785, includes *D. magna* along with *D. pulex*, but because of this confusion he rejects Müller's earlier name.[4] *D. vetula* is now known as *Simocephalus vetulus* (O. F. Müller). *Chydorus sphæricus* (O. F. Müller) should be referred not to the Lynceidæ, a family name required elsewhere, but to the Chydoridæ.

Of Ostracoda the *Hastings Natural History* records *Cypris tristriata*, Baird, and '*C. ? fusca*, Strauss.'[5] Brady and Norman make the former a synonym of *C. virens* (Jurine), ' one of the commonest and most widely distributed of British fresh-water species,'[6] and by the latter is

---

[1] *British Entomostraca*, Ray Society, p. 54.
[2] *Nat. Hist. Trans. Northumberland*, pt. 2, xiii. 224, 226.
[3] Second Supplement (1888), p. 16. [4] *Cladocera Suciæ*, p. 71.
[5] *Nat. Hist. Hastings*, Second Supplement, p. 16. [6] *Trans. Roy. Dublin Soc.* ser. 2, iv. 74.

probably intended *C. fuscata*, Jurine, 'one of the most abundant British species.'[1]

Of the Copepoda the species recorded are entered as follows : Cyclopidæ, comprising *Cyclops quadricornis*, very common ;[2] *C. signatus*, Koch, from Ore, including St. Helens and Coghurst ; *C. strenuus*, Fischer, from Bopeep, the flat marshy ground known as the Salts, extending from Bopeep station to Bulverhythe ; *C. gigas*, Claus, common ; *C. æquoreus*, Fischer, from Bexhill ; Calanidæ, represented by *Temora longicornis*, Müller, from Bopeep ; Harpacticidæ, comprising *Tachidius brevicornis*, Müller, from Bopeep ; *Canthocamptus minutus*, Müller, common ; *C. ? palustris*, Brady, from Bopeep ; and *Thalestris longimana*, Claus, from Ecclesbourne.[3] The indefinite *Cyclops quadricornis* may be reckoned as a synonym of *C. signatus*. *C. gigas* is now considered to be a synonym of *C. viridis* (Jurine). Of the parasitic Copepoda the *Hastings Natural History* records in the Caligidæ *Caligus diaphanus*, Nordmann ; in the Chondracanthidæ *Lernentoma lophii*, Johnston ; in the Lernæidæ *Lernæenicus spratta*, Baird ;[4] and Adam White notes that the British Museum possesses *Cecrops latreillii*, Leach, of the family Cecropidæ, from 'Selsey Bill, near Bognor, Sussex : presented by G. Newport, Esq.'[5] This well known parasite of the sunfish, *Orthagoriscus mola*, is placed by Bassett-Smith in the Caligidæ, under the heading Division II. Pandarinæ. The same author displaces Baird's *Lernentoma lophii* in favour of the name *Chondracanthus lophii* given it earlier by Johnston, and follows Olsson and Richiardi in referring *Lerneonema spratta* to an older genus founded by Lesueur,[6] so that its proper title will be *Lernæenicus spratta* (Sowerby). This slender species attaches itself, as might be guessed, to the sprat, while the preceding one is parasitic on *Lophius piscatorius*, known in English by titles of varying elegance, as the angler, the fishing frog, and the sea devil.

The Thyrostraca, Cirripedia, or barnacles, are represented in Sussex, according to the record so often quoted, by *Balanus balanoides* (Linn.), very common, and *B. porcatus*, da Costa, these being in the sessile family Balanidæ, while the pedunculate Lepadidæ afford *Lepas anatifera*, Linn., *L. fascicularis*, Ellis and Solander, and *Scalpellum vulgare*, Leach, somewhat rare.[7] To the names of the species I have added the names of the authors to whom they are by the courtesy of science attributed, and although a simple catalogue gives us no means of judging whether the species themselves have been rightly determined, there is no real room for doubting that all the barnacles named in this particular list are to be found on the coast of Sussex.

It should be mentioned in conclusion that the results of Mr. Guermonprez' careful and energetic researches were not at my disposal till this chapter in its earlier form was already in print. Otherwise

[1] *Trans. Roy. Dublin Soc.* ser. 2, iv. 73.   [2] *Nat. Hist. Hastings*, p. 41.
[3] Loc. cit. Second Supplement, p. 16.   [4] Second Supplement, p. 16, and Third, p. 22.
[5] *List of British Animals in British Museum*, p. 123.
[6] *Proc. Zool. Soc. London* (1899), pp. 464, 484, 494.   [7] *Nat. Hist. of Hastings*, p. 41.

the name of this valued contributor might have been appended as guaranteeing almost all the records of decapod species. On the other hand, it would be improper to conceal the doubt which he has expressed to me by letter as to the occurrence at Hastings of *Goneplax angulata*, *Galathea nexa* and *Eupagurus prideaux*, 'in view of the fact that the Hastings boats go far afield to the French coast and Channel Islands for their fishing.' Great weight must be attached to the opinion of so experienced an observer, but as all these species are known from our south-west coast, it is not absolutely improbable that they should be found also within a reasonable distance of the Sussex shore.

Though the species here reviewed have been on the whole rather numerous, they form but a small fraction of all the English crustacea, and almost certainly they will eventually prove to form only a small fraction of the crustacea of this county, but that will not be until the more minute forms, and especially the marine and freshwater entomostracans, have been made the subject of the same assiduous pursuit as that of late so advantageously bestowed upon the higher groups.

FISHES

It is a regrettable fact that salmon and sea-trout are now almost extinct in those rivers of Sussex in which they were formerly not uncommon. I have however been able to ascertain that a considerable number of sea-trout, grilse and sometimes salmon are occasionally sent to fishmongers in Brighton from the lower part of the Ouse. The fishermen have been left entirely to themselves for many years, and of course net the river in illegal ways. The only attempt hitherto to stop this illegal fishing was made in May, 1901, by a private body, the Ouse Preservation Society, who, with the sanction of the Board of Conservators, obtained a conviction against two fishermen.

It is a fact not generally known that the trout in some of the rivers in Sussex visit the sea in considerable numbers. I have seen trout with all the markings of brown trout caught in nets at some miles distant from the mouth of any river. This habit of the trout has been noticed many times.

There is apparently good evidence to show that dace are not indigenous to some at any rate of the rivers in Sussex where they are now very numerous. This is notably the case with the Ouse. The only way in which their presence can be accounted for is that the Ouse was formerly celebrated for pike fishing, and attracted a considerable number of fishermen from London, who brought live dace with them as baits. Some of these must have been turned loose at the end of the day's fishing and have bred freely. Men who fished the Ouse between thirty and forty years ago all agree that there were then no dace in the river. At the present time they swarm there.

TELEOSTEANS

ACANTHOPTERYGII

*1. Perch. *Perca fluviatilis*, Linn.

This fish is common in most of the rivers and ponds fed by streams. As a rule specimens do not reach a size of more than half a pound, though sometimes heavier are recorded. The largest which has come under my personal observation weighed just over three pounds, and was caught at Horsted Keynes.

*2. Pope or Ruff. *Acerina cernua*, Linn.

This species is common in some localities only.

**3. Bass or Sea Bass. *Morone labrax*, Linn.

Large shoals of small bass travel some distance up the rivers in the summer months. This is particularly noticeable in the Cuckmere River, where they sometimes go up as high as Alfriston. The common people in some localities call the fish 'white salmon.'

4. Maigre. *Sciæna aquila*, Cuv. et Val.

A specimen from Hastings is recorded in 1867 and one from Brighton in 1868. Since then many have been recorded from the Sussex coast.

NOTE.—A single asterisk (*) accompanies the names of such species as are found only in fresh water. Two asterisks (**) distinguish such species as may be taken in either fresh or salt water.

5. Black Bream. *Cantharus lineatus*, Thompson.

This species is probably commoner off the Sussex coast than anywhere else in the British Isles.

6. Common Sea Bream. *Pagellus centrodontus*, Delaroche.

This bream is also very common off the Sussex coast. The young, which the fishermen call 'chad,' form a very favourite bait for other fish.

7. Red Mullet. *Mullus barbatus*, Linn.

This species is numerous on the Sussex coast, particularly towards the west. The local fishermen adhere to the existence of two species, the striped and the plain.

8. Striped Wrass. *Labrus mixtus*, Linn.

9. Ballan Wrass. *Labrus maculatus*, Bloch.

10. Connor or Gilt-head. *Crenilabrus melops*, Linn.

*11. Miller's Thumb. *Cottus gobio*, Linn.

12. Sea Scorpion. *Cottus scorpius*, Linn.

13. Father-lasher. *Cottus bubalis*, Linn.

14. Four-horned Cottus. *Cottus quadricornis*, Linn.

15. Grey Gurnard. *Trigla gurnardus*, Linn.

The gurnards are as a rule called 'gurnets' by the fisher folk in Sussex.

16. Red Gurnard. *Trigla cuculus*, Linn.

17. Sapphirine Gurnard. *Trigla hirundo*, Linn.

18. Pogge. *Agonus cataphractus*, Linn.

19. Lump Sucker. *Cyclopterus lumpus*, Linn.

This species is not common though specimens are occasionally obtained.

20. Sea Snail. *Liparis vulgaris*, Flem.

21. Diminutive Sea Snail. *Liparis montagui*, Donovan.

22. Rock Goby. *Gobius niger*, Linn.

23. Spotted Goby. *Gobius minutus*, Linn.

24. Paganellus. *Gobius paganellus*, Gmel.

25. John Dory. *Zeus faber*, Linn.

26. Boar Fish. *Capros aper*, Lacép.

[Pilot Fish. *Naucrates ductor*, Cuv. et Val.
Several specimens of this fish, said to have been caught off the Sussex coast, have been shown at the Brighton Aquarium during the past ten years. It is however possible that the fishermen obtained them from a greater distance.]

27. Scad. *Caranx trachurus*, Linn.

28. Mackerel. *Scomber scombrus*, Linn.

The mackerel caught off the Sussex coast are uniformly small in comparison with those from the North Sea and the Atlantic.

29. Great Weever. *Trachinus draco*, Linn.

30. Lesser Weever. *Trachinus vipera*, Cuv.

31. Dragonet. *Callionymus lyra*, Linn.

The female of this fish is sometimes called the 'dusky skulpin,' or fox.

32. Angler Fish. *Lophius piscatorius*, Linn.

Though by no means common, specimens of this fish are sometimes caught by the fishermen and carried round different watering places on a barrow for show. I have twice had photographs sent to me from seaside towns in Sussex, asking me to identify the fish.

33. Shanny. *Blennius pholis*, Linn.

34. Gattorugine. *Blennius gattorugine*, Bl.

35. Gunnel or Butter Fish. *Centronellus gunnellus*, Linn.

ANACANTHINI

36. Cod. *Gadus morrhua*, Linn.

37. Whiting. *Gadus merlangus*, Linn.

38. Pout or Whiting Pout. *Gadus luscus*, Linn.

39. Pollack. *Gadus pollachius*, Linn.

40. Poor Cod. *Gadus minutus*, Linn.

41. Hake. *Merluccius vulgaris*, Fleming.

42. Five-bearded Rockling. *Motella mustela*, Linn.

43. Three-bearded Rockling. *Motella tricirrata*, Bl.

44. Turbot. *Rhombus maximus*, Linn.

45. Brill. *Rhombus lœvis*, Linn.

46. Common Topknot. *Zeugopterus punctatus*, Bloch.

47. Plaice. *Pleuronectes platessa*, Linn.

48. Dab. *Pleuronectes limanda*, Linn.

49. Lemon Dab. *Pleuronectes microcephalus*, Donovan.

FISHES

50. Pole Dab. *Pleuronectes cygnoglossus*, Linn.

**51. Flounder. *Pleuronectes flesus*, Linn.

52. Sole. *Solea vulgaris*, Quens.

53. Variegated Sole or Thick Back. *Solea variegata*, Donovan.

PLECTOGNATHI

54. File-Fish. *Balistes capriscus*, Linn.

A specimen was taken off Brighton in 1901 (*Zoologist*, 1901, p. 225).

55. Short Sun-Fish. *Orthagoriscus mola*, Linn.

One or two specimens are generally brought in during the year by the fishing boats, but it is by no means certain that they are caught off the Sussex coast.

PERCESOCES

56. Atherine. *Atherina presbyter*, Jen.

This species is very numerous on the Sussex coast, where it is called sand smelt or smelt.

**57. Thin-lipped Grey Mullet. *Mugil capito*, Cuv.

**58. Thick-lipped Grey Mullet. *Mugil chelo*, Cuv.

Both species are numerous on the Sussex coast. They visit the mouths of the rivers, and ascend a considerable distance up into the fresh water during the summer months.

59. Larger Launce. *Ammodytes lanceolatus*, Lesauv.

60. Lesser Launce. *Ammodytes tobianus*, Linn.

The two preceding species are known to the fisher people as large and small sand eels.

61. Gar Fish. *Belone vulgaris*, Fleming.

62. Saury Pike. *Scombresox saurus*, Linn.

HEMIBRANCHII

**63. Three-spined Stickleback. *Gastrosteus aculeatus*, Linn.

*64. Ten-spined Stickleback. *Gastrosteus pungitius*, Linn.

65. Fifteen-spined Stickleback. *Gastrosteus spinachia*, Linn.

LOPHOBRANCHII

66. Greater Pipe Fish. *Syngnathus acus*, Linn.

67. Lesser Pipe Fish, or Broad-nosed Pipe Fish. *Siphonostoma typhle*, Linn.

68. Snake Pipe Fish. *Nerophis ophidion*, Linn.

HAPLOMI

*69. Pike. *Esox lucius*, Linn.

OSTARIOPHYSI

*70. Carp. *Cyprinus carpio*, Linn.

*71. Crucian Carp. *Cyprinus carassius*, Linn.

Gold fish and Prussian carp have become domesticated in ponds in many parts of the county. I have seen several ponds where they have increased in numbers in a most marvellous manner. The gold fish variety grows to a considerable size in a wild state in some of these ponds. I have seen one caught which weighed nearly a pound and a half.

*72. Gudgeon. *Gobio fluviatilis*, Linn.

*73. Roach. *Leuciscus rutilus*, Linn.

*74. Rudd. *Leuciscus erythrophthalmus*, Linn.

This species does not seem to be indigenous to the county, as there is a history of artificial introduction in most cases where it occurs, and is exceedingly localized in its distribution.

*75. Chub. *Leuciscus cephalus*, Linn.

*76. Dace. *Leuciscus dobula*, Linn.
See introduction.

*77. Minnow. *Leuciscus phoxinus*, Linn.

*78. Tench. *Tinca vulgaris*, Cuv.

*79. Bream. *Abramis brama*, Linn.

*80. Loach. *Nemachilus barbatulus*, Linn.

MALACOPTERYGII

**81. Salmon. *Salmo salar*, Linn.

**82. Sea Trout. *Salmo trutta*, Linn.

*83. Trout. *Salmo fario*, Linn.

[The rainbow trout (*Salmo irideus*) from the Pacific coast of America has been introduced into many of the waters in Sussex, and seems likely to become acclimatized.]

**84. Freshwater Herring. *Coregonus oxyrhynchus*, Linn.

Day records one taken near Chichester.

85. Herring. *Clupea harengus*, Linn.

The herrings of Sussex, like the mackerel, are much smaller than those of the North Sea and Atlantic.

86. Sprat. *Clupea sprattus*, Linn.

87. Pilchard. *Clupea pilchardus*, Linn.

**88. Allis Shad. *Clupea alosa*, Linn.

**89. Thwait. *Clupea finta*, Cuv.

APODES

**90. Common Eel. *Anguilla vulgaris*, Turt.

91. Conger. *Conger vulgaris*, Cuv.

GANOIDS

**92. Sturgeon. *Acipenser sturio*.

Specimens are occasionally captured off the coast. Three have been brought alive to the Brighton Aquarium during the past twenty years by the Brighton beach boats.

CHONDROPTERYGIANS

93. Row Hound. *Scyllium canicula*, Linn.

94. Nurse Hound. *Scyllium stellare*, Linn.

95. Smooth Hound. *Mustelus lævis*, Cuv.

96. Tope. *Galeus vulgaris*, Flem.

97. Porbeagle. *Lamna cornubica*, Gmelin.

98. Blue Shark. *Carcharias glaucus*, Linn.

99. Thresher Shark. *Alopias vulpes*, Linn.

Two living specimens have been brought into the Brighton Aquarium during the past ten years, which the fishermen stated were caught off the Sussex coast.

100. Basking Shark. *Selache maxima*, Gunn.

A specimen was caught off Bognor in 1896.

101. Spur Dog. *Acanthias vulgaris*, Risso.

102. Monk or Angel Fish. *Rhina squatina*, Linn.

103. Common Skate. *Raia batis*, Linn.

104. Sharp-nosed Skate. *Raia alba*, Lacép.

105. Long-nosed Skate. *Raia vomer*, Fries.

106. Homelyn. *Raia maculata*, Montagu.

107. Thornback. *Raia clavata*, Linn.

108. Sting Ray. *Trygon pastinaca*, Linn.

CYCLOSTOMES

**109. Sea Lamprey. *Petromyzon marinus*, Linn.

*110. Lampern. *Petromyzon fluviatilis*, Linn.

REPTILES
AND BATRACHIANS

The chief interest of the present article lies in the announcement —it is believed for the first time in print—of the occurrence of the sand lizard and the smooth snake in Sussex. The evidence will be found in the account of these species. The natter-jack has been recorded from all the adjacent counties, and its recognition in this was therefore not unexpected; although it appears to be a very local species throughout its range. The webbed newt has been much overlooked, and will probably prove to be common enough in most places.

Judging from the records in Natural History journals the herpetological fauna of the county does not seem to have attracted much attention, and this accounts for the paucity of records for the rarer species. The writer would be glad if the present necessarily brief notice led to a closer study of these 'scandalized' creatures by Sussex naturalists. A sufficient description has been added to the accounts of the rarer species to lead to their identification.

REPTILES

LACERTILIA

1. Common Lizard. *Lacerta vivipara*, Jacq.

Commonly distributed in suitable localities throughout the county.

2. Sand Lizard. *Lacerta agilis*, Linn.

On May 27, 1892, Mr. Michael J. Nicoll of St. Leonards caught a lizard of this species in the disused brickfields near West St. Leonards station. Since that date some others have been caught in the same locality.

This is a larger and more stoutly built lizard than the last species, some reach 8 inches in length. 'A typically coloured male during the breeding season is grass-green on the sides and suffused with green on the under parts; the sides are dotted with black, with whitish eye-spots. The under parts are spotted with black. The adult female is brown or grey above, with large dark brown, white-centred spots, which are arranged in three rows on each side. The under parts are cream-coloured, with or without black specks' (Gadow, *Amphib. and Rept.* p. 554).

3. Slow-worm or Blind-worm. *Anguis fragilis*, Linn.

The slow-worm is locally common throughout the county.

OPHIDIA

4. Ringed or Grass Snake. *Tropidonotus natrix*, Linn.

(*Natrix torquata*, Bell.)

Generally distributed and common. The grass snake feeds largely upon frogs, and is therefore most often found in damp meadows. It swims well and is also able to climb low bushes.

5. Smooth Snake. *Coronella austriaca*, Laur.

On June 12, 1898, Mr. W. J. Lewis Abbott, F.G.S., of St. Leonards, found a snake which he assigns to this rare and local species, in the churchyard of St. John's, Hollington. This specimen was in Mr. Abbott's possession for some time, and he remarked the large shields on the head and the round pupil. I feel little hesitation in accepting the identification. Moreover I have recently had the satisfaction of finding a second specimen. This I picked up dead on July 9, 1901, about a mile from the place where the former occurred. The animal was much mutilated and had probably been killed by means of a stick.

This species may be distinguished from the viper (which it sometimes approaches in general colouration) by the circumstance that the dorsal scales are smooth, whereas in the latter they have an elevated keel down the middle. The dorsal scales in the grass snake also are carinated. Full-grown examples are about 17 (rarely more) inches in length.

6. Viper. *Vipera berus*, Linn.

Generally distributed but more local and less common than the grass snake. John Perris, who has caught snakes in the neighbourhood of Hastings for more than thirty years, tells me that the largest viper he ever caught measured 23½ inches. The old man states that he has been bitten six times. It is known that he has been medically treated for snake-bite on two occasions, and I think his statement may be accepted. On July 22, 1900, I received from Mr. B. Parratt of Fairlight, Hastings, a female example of the form known as the black adder, which had been killed at Fairlight the same day by a member of the coastguard service. In this the ground colour is so dark as to obscure the zigzag dorsal fascia. Mr. Sayer-Milward's gamekeeper at Fairlight, to whom I showed the specimen, saw a similar viper 'a few years ago.'

BATRACHIANS

ECAUDATA

1. Common Frog. *Rana temporaria*, Linn.

Abundantly distributed throughout the county.

2. Toad. *Bufo vulgaris*, Laur.

Generally distributed and common.

3. Natter-jack Toad. *Bufo calamita*, Laur.

This species has been recognized in one locality only in Sussex up to the present, namely, on the confines of Hampshire, in the neighbourhood of Petersfield, where it is not uncommon (Rev. H. Marmaduke Langdale *in lit.*).

The natter-jack is remarkable for its loud croak and short hind limbs. It is readily distinguished from the common toad by the presence of a yellowish stripe down the back.

CAUDATA

4. Great Crested Newt. *Molge cristata*, Laur.

Locally (Hastings), Jack Effet.

Plentiful in most parts of the county.

The breeding male is distinguished by the presence of an elevated membranous dorsal crest, which in the female is entirely absent.

5. Common Smooth Newt. *Molge vulgaris*, Linn.

(*Lissotriton punctatus*, Bell.)
Locally, Effet.

Generally distributed and common. This is much smaller, and the crest is festooned and not deeply serrated as in the last species.

6. Palmated or Webbed Newt. *Molge palmata*, Schneid.

(*Lissotriton palmipes*, Bell.)

Recorded from Eastbourne by C. Foran (*Science Gossip*, 1879, p. 186).

I have taken this species from ponds near St. Leonards (Hollington, Silverhill, Bopeep), Crowhurst, Battle, Ore, Bodiam, Sedlescombe, and Hurstmonceaux. In some ponds I have found almost all the newts to be of this species.

The webbed newt may be distinguished from the common smooth newt 'at all stages of life and at all seasons by the absence of every trace of pigment on the throat, which is of a transparent flesh colour' (Boulenger). In the smooth newt the nuptial crest of the male is regularly crenate, but in this species it is low and straight at the edge.

BIRDS[1]

Notwithstanding the great alterations that agriculture and railroads have brought about to the detriment and in many cases the extermination of certain resident birds, the county of Sussex still contains a variety of woodland, marsh and shore that is naturally attractive to bird life. Its great swamps that formerly sheltered the bittern, the ruff and many other interesting waterfowl are gone for ever, and many of the quiet mud-flats and bogs along the coast, where flocks of the rarer waders paddled in the shallows in peace and security, are now the favoured haunt of the sham negro minstrel and the German band.

Still the land remains the same in its attraction to most of the smaller perching birds, and the county can boast that it is more favourably situated to receive wanderers from the south and spring migrants than any other in England, as it is the first landing place for all that come to spend the summer.

The whole of the county, with the exception of the downs and river levels, is well wooded, chiefly with the oak *Quercus pedunculata*, which is considered indigenous.

In these woodland tracts and their surrounding rough commons we have probably lost but few species of birds that were once resident or summer visitors to Sussex. Although still nesting with us at the beginning of the nineteenth century the honey-buzzard, the three harriers, the kite and many other perching birds have ceased to be recorded except as rare visitors, whilst the most serious losses to the ornithology of the county within this period are the great bustard, which probably did not nest later than 1815, and blackgame, which cannot be considered as a resident later than 1860, although one or two greyhens have bred since that date.

The Dartford warbler may also be mentioned as an interesting species which is diminishing in numbers, and they are certainly not nearly so common along the south coast as they were ten years ago. In the large plantations and the edges of the forests tits are very numerous and golden-crested wrens are common, as are also nuthatches in the large oaks and elms of the Weald, whilst all three species of woodpecker

[1] My thanks are especially due to Mrs. and Miss Borrer for the facilities which they have afforded me in viewing the collections at Cowfold formed by the late Mr. W. Borrer and inspecting papers left by that admirable naturalist. Also to Mrs. Eversfield for allowing me to peruse the Markwick MS. at Denne Park, and to Mr. Ruskin Butterfield for a few excellent notes on the birds of east Sussex.

are constantly seen by those who know their haunts and habits. In certain seasons too, such as the winters of 1895–6, the county is visited in winter by immense flocks of migratory wood-pigeons, which settle in some districts where acorns have been unusually abundant and do not leave till the following spring.

The coast line of Sussex from Brighton to Eastbourne consists of cliffs rising to various heights and attaining their greatest elevation at Beachy Head (600 feet). Here the cliffs terminate, and Pevensey Level stretches to beyond Hastings. There are sandy cliffs about the latter place, and these gradually fall to the levels of Rye and Winchelsea. West of Brighton the coast is somewhat flat and continues so until the borders of Hants.

In such a varied coast line of mud-flat, pebbly beach, sandy shore and chalk cliff the southern littoral of Sussex is naturally a favourite winter resort and resting place at all seasons of a large number of species of water birds. That the coast attractions have suffered during the past century from the birds point of view it is hardly necessary to point out ; for the growth of sea traffic and the extension of seaside resorts have brought with them crowds of visitors who, if not actual destroyers, are nevertheless constant disturbers of birds, and serve to drive them from their haunts. About the year 1881 things had reached their worst, for with the introduction of the Wild Birds Protection Act a new era arrived when the terns could nest in comparative peace and the flocks of waders, gulls and other sea birds were not subject to harassment all the year round. Now in certain sheltered bays that are well known to the few one may any May morning lie on the shore and watch with pleasure small flocks of several of the rarer waders in their beautiful summer dress, a treat denied the ornithologist in almost every other county in England except Norfolk.

No very great change has taken place in the riparian character of the Sussex rivers except in the case of the Arun, which flows through the Weald. Till 1820 all the open meadowlands now reclaimed and stretching from Pulborough to the South Downs were described by Knox as 'covered with dense woods, where the adventurous sportsman delighted to contend with the tangled brushwood, and wade, knee deep, through the marshy jungles that extended for miles on either side of the river, affording shelter and sustenance at all seasons to various tribes of water fowl which haunted its recesses.' From these wild swamps the bittern and the ruff have gone for ever, and only a small remnant of the original fen remains to-day in the wild marsh by the ruins of Amberley Castle.

But while we have lost a few of the most interesting of the once resident species there are indications that in the near future protection will have had its full reward, and that we shall induce other species to take their place.

Already in the neighbouring counties and in other parts of England and Scotland ornithologists are noting with pleasure the extension in the breeding range of the ducks, and at no distant date we may reasonably hope to name the wigeon, the gadwall, the pintail, the shoveler, the pochard and perhaps even the garganey as resident within the county. The great crested grebe too has greatly increased as a summer bird in the southern counties, and why he has so far avoided Sussex during the nesting season is somewhat of a mystery, as so many sheets of water are especially suited to his habits.

In all we can include in the birds of the county 302 species which are either resident, summer or winter visitors, or rare stragglers.

In the following list brackets placed round the name of the original describer of a species indicate that he did not employ the generic named which is now adopted.

1. Missel-Thrush. *Turdus viscivorus*, Linn.

A very common resident and a species that is evidently largely on the increase.

2. Song-Thrush. *Turdus musicus*, Linn.

Very abundant during the summer and autumn months, the majority remaining throughout the winter unless severe weather sets in.

3. Redwing. *Turdus iliacus*, Linn.

A few redwings commence to arrive in September, being joined by larger flocks as winter advances. They associate in numbers with the next species, a few missel-thrushes joining them in mild weather. Redwings stay every year in west Sussex till the end of April.

4. Fieldfare. *Turdus pilaris*, Linn.

The number of fieldfares that visit Sussex during the winter months seems to be principally regulated by the mildness or severity of the season. In hard weather, when they come in large numbers, field-fares become much tamer than redwings or missel-thrushes, even waiting to pick off the haws within a few feet of the passer-by, whilst the two other species will hardly permit an approach within gunshot.

5. Black-throated Thrush. *Turdus atrigularis*, Temminck.

Yarrell in his *British Birds* mentions that a young male of this species was shot near Lewes on December 23, 1868, and passed into the collection of the late Mr. T. J. Monk of that town.

6. Blackbird. *Turdus merula*, Linn.

Very abundant and less migratory than other thrushes. As an instance of the conservative habits and smallness of range of the blackbird I may mention that a pied cock blackbird has lived regularly in one garden at Horsham for the past six years, and so far as I know has never been seen two fields away.

7. Ring-Ouzel. *Turdus torquatus*, Linn.

A somewhat rare spring and autumn migrant. Mr. Booth was of opinion that the species had nested in the South Downs in 1865.

8. Wheatear. *Saxicola œnanthe* (Linn.)

The first spring migrant after the wagtails, a few only stopping to nest.

9. Whinchat. *Pratincola rubetra* (Linn.)

A fairly common migrant.

10. Stonechat. *Pratincola rubicola* (Linn.)

More numerous than the last species and breeding on the commons where furze and heath are found. Stonechats also frequently stay with us through the winter, and in east Sussex Mr. Butterfield considers that they are equally common at all seasons.

11. Redstart. *Ruticilla phœnicurus* (Linn.)

Of all the spring visitors there is no bird so local as the redstart. I have only once observed the species near Horsham, viz. in Denne Park in 1899, whilst I have frequently seen it near the coast. Very few apparently breed in Sussex.

12. Black Redstart. *Ruticilla titys* (Scopoli).

A regular autumnal visitor, arriving in October in small numbers. The black redstart often stays with us throughout the winter, and I have a beautiful old male in full breeding dress that was killed near Brighton in the spring of 1880. The species seems fond of frequenting market gardens; individuals were seen by Mr. A. H. M. Cox in the same allotments in 1900 and 1901, two of which in the latter year were taken by Mr. M. J. Nicoll.

13. Bluethroat. *Cyanecula suecica* (Linn.)

A female of this species is recorded by Yarrell as having been killed near Worthing May 2, 1853, and there is a most beautiful old male in the Borrer collection at Cowfold, which was caught by a boy between Stanmore Park and Brighton on October, 1862. I have lately seen a bluethroat in the hands of Mr. Wells of Worthing that was undoubtedly killed in Sussex some years ago, although particulars of its capture are wanting.

14. Redbreast. *Erithacus rubecula* (Linn.)

Very common. In the autumn the males fight desperately with others of their own species coming on to their own beat, and I have even caught a pair in my hand who were thus wrangling on the ground.

15. Nightingale. *Daulias luscinia* (Linn.)

A fairly common summer visitor to east and west Sussex. Though found in places along the edge of St. Leonards Forest it seldom penetrates far into the less frequented parts, rather preferring the long strips of coppice and the pits near some path or thoroughfare.

16. Whitethroat. *Sylvia cinerea* (Bechstein).

A very abundant summer visitor.

17. Lesser Whitethroat. *Sylvia curruca* (Linn.)

Though not a common species the lesser whitethroat is more abundant in Sussex than in any other county. It is easily recognized by its song, and is very tame on its first arrival in summer.

18. Blackcap. *Sylvia atricapilla* (Linn.)

Rather a scarce summer visitor to west Sussex and in no part of the county very common, except about St. Leonards.

19. Garden-Warbler. *Sylvia hortensis* (Bechstein).

A somewhat scarce and local visitor, and is the last warbler to arrive.

20. Dartford Warbler. *Sylvia undata* (Boddaert).

Found locally in small numbers along the South Downs. It is to be feared that this interesting little resident must be classed amongst the diminishing species. Mr. Wells, the Worthing naturalist, states that he has not seen a specimen near that town for twenty years. Mr. Butterfield also informs me that Mr. Thomas Sorrell of Hastings used to find the nest regularly near that town until the year 1886, so that the rapid diminution in the numbers of Dartford warblers must have commenced about that date.

21. Goldcrest. *Regulus cristatus*, Koch.

Common throughout the year and, in the winter months, associating with flocks of tits. In 1899 the nest of a goldcrest in the garden at Denne Park was so placed on the trailing branches of some honeysuckle that the hats of passers-by brushed against it without disturbing the female bird, who successfully hatched out her numerous progeny.

22. Firecrest. *Regulus ignicapillus* (Brehm.)

Probably an irregular visitor. Two males were shot by Mr. R. Butterfield on February 24, 1901, at St. Helen's, Hastings.

23. Chiffchaff. *Phylloscopus rufus* (Bechstein).

The first warbler to arrive in Sussex, nesting in small numbers throughout the county.

24. Willow-Warbler. *Phylloscopus trochilus* (Linn.)

The most numerous of the common warblers.

25. Wood-Warbler. *Phylloscopus sibilatrix* (Bechstein).

This species, which is one of the last to arrive and to depart, is common in all the large beech and oak groves of St. Leonards Forest. Its beautiful wild song is the most noticeable of bird sounds which one hears on a summer day's ramble in the forest. The wood-warbler is far more difficult to approach than the willow-warbler or the chiffchaff. In east Sussex this bird is very local.

26. Rufous Warbler. *Aëdon galactodes* (Temminck).

The first example of this species obtained in England was shot by Mr. Swaysland at Plumpton Besthill near Brighton on September 16, 1854. It was a male preparing to moult (Borrer). A note in Mr. Borrer's handwriting occurs in his book, 'Rufous warbler on downs, September, 1899.'

27. Icterine Warbler. *Hypolais icterina* (Vieillot).

Although this little warbler is common on the continent to the south and also in Norway, where I have seen many even within the arctic circle, it has rarely visited our shores. Only one example has been obtained in Sussex. The specimen, a female, was shot at Burwash on April 30, 1897, and was

BIRDS

exhibited by Mr. N. F. Ticehurst at the British Ornithologists' Club on May 19 of that year.

28. Melodious Warbler. *Hypolais polyglotta* (Vieillot).

In the *Zoologist* for July, 1897, Mr. N. Ticehurst mentioned the occurrence of a small warbler which had been taken on April 30 of that year at Burwash, and which he suggested might belong to this species. The bird itself was afterwards sent by Mr. G. Bristow, the owner, to Mr. Howard Saunders, who corroborated Mr. Ticehurst's view and identified it as belonging to this species. A second specimen, a male, was shot at Ninfield on May 11, 1900, and identified by Mr. Butterfield. This bird has also been examined by Mr. H. Saunders (*Ibis*, 1900, p. 569).

29. Reed-Warbler. *Acrocephalus streperus* (Vieillot).

Common in suitable localities where large reed and willow beds are to be found.

30. Great Reed-Warbler. *Acrocephalus turdoïdes* (Meyer).

Mr. Borrer includes this species amongst the birds of Sussex on the authority of Mr. Jeffery, who states that he saw one in Ratham garden on July 26, 1885.

31. Sedge-Warbler. *Acrocephalus phragmitis* (Bechstein).

Very common in the summer months. Like several of the reed-warblers it sings throughout the night, and is an excellent mimic.

32. Aquatic Warbler. *Acrocephalus aquaticus* (J. F. Gmelin).

The first example of this warbler which occurred in England was one obtained by Mr. Pratt of Brighton at Hove on October 19, 1853. It passed into the collection of Mr. Borrer, where I have lately seen it.

33. Grasshopper-Warbler. *Locustella nævia* (Boddaert).

A somewhat uncommon but regular migrant to Sussex. I have seen this species twice in six years, both times near Rusper. It is however fairly numerous on the commons south of Pulborough.

34. Hedge-Sparrow. *Accentor modularis* (Linn.)

Locally, Hedge Mike, Hedge Betty (M. J. Nicoll).

Very common everywhere.

35. Alpine Accentor. *Accentor collaris* (Scopoli).

Two specimens of the Alpine accentor are recorded in Yarrell as having been shot near Hailsham on December 26, 1857, and Borrer also states that he watched one for some time on his lawn at Cowfold.

36. Dipper. *Cinclus aquaticus*, Bechstein.

A rare visitor.

37. Bearded Reedling. *Panurus biarmicus* (Linn.)

Formerly this beautiful species was resident and breeding within the county, and Borrer mentions that bearded tits had bred near Amberley about 1844, and that it also nested regularly near Lancing. Now it has departed with the great reed beds and rarely occurs even as a straggler. Mr. Meade-Waldo saw a small flock near East Grinstead in 1892.

38. Long-tailed Tit. *Acredula caudata* (Linn.)

Common and resident.

39. Great Tit. *Parus major*, Linn.

Very abundant.

40. Coal-Tit. *Parus ater*, Linn.

Very common in all the fir woods of the county.

41. Marsh-Tit. *Parus palustris*, Linn.

Although this species is not supposed to love the neighbourhood of marshes and its title is considered by many to be somewhat a misnomer, yet it is indubitably more common in the swampy places of St. Leonards Forest than in any other part of Sussex. It prefers to go about in pairs, though occasionally hanging on to the outskirts of a winter flock of longtail, great, coal and blue tits.

On a recent visit to Mr. Ernst Hartert at Tring, that excellent naturalist showed me some marsh-tits shot by Mr. Butterfield near St. Leonards whose heads were suffused by a slight brown tinge and without gloss, and which he has since identified as a new British species under the name of the willow-tit (*Parus montanus kleinschmidti*).[1]

[1] Even if the birds are to be distinguished as a slight local variety I entirely fail to see that a slight brown tinge on the black crown of a bird is sufficient to entitle them to especial recognition. The world of naturalists is now made up of those who would condense and those who would multiply names and species *ad infinitum*, but if we are to acccept *Parus montanus kleinschmidti*, how can we possibly fail to name the forty-two different types

277

42. Blue Tit. *Parus cæruleus*, Linn.

Very common throughout the year and destructive to fruit trees in the spring.

43. Nuthatch. *Sitta cæsia*, Wolf.

Though a fairly common species it is not nearly so abundant as in the neighbouring counties of Surrey and Kent.

44. Wren. *Troglodytes parvulus*, K. L. Koch.

Abundant everywhere.

45. Tree-Creeper. *Certhia familiaris*, Linn.

Fairly common throughout the year, and associating in the winter with flocks of tits.

46. Wall-Creeper. *Tichodroma muraria* (Linn.)

Mr. Ruskin Butterfield has recorded an adult in breeding plumage which was shot some years ago near Winchelsea by Mr. W. Mitchell (*Zoologist*, 1896, p. 302). The specimen is now in the possession of Canon Tristram.

47. Pied Wagtail. *Motacilla lugubris*, Temminck.

A few remain throughout the year, but the greater number return to us in February and March, many of the males being then in their full breeding plumage.

48. White Wagtail. *Motacilla alba*, Linn.

White wagtails appear to stop for a few days in the spring on their northward migration. They come about the second week in April and then probably follow the south coast of England eastwards before turning northward to Scandinavia and Iceland, as no specimens have been taken in Sussex north of the South Downs. Mr. Wells states that they have bred in Sussex.

49. Grey Wagtail. *Motacilla melanope*, Pallas.

A scarce though regular winter visitor. As there are few clear pebbly streams in Sussex such as the species love they do not stop to nest with us. I have noticed every winter one or more grey wagtails frequent a roadside ditch close to the village of Roffey.

50. Blue-headed Wagtail. *Motacilla flava*, Linn.

A scarce though regular spring visitor to the

of goldfinches found inhabiting England, France, Algeria, Germany, Russia, China and Siberia, all and every one differing slightly and confined to small areas except when on migration. Personally I cannot see that the difference between this very slight local form and other British marsh-tits is sufficient to entitle it to a separate name.

sea coast. Mr. Booth was of opinion that the blue-headed wagtail had nested on several occasions in Sussex. Certainly this species is occasionally seen throughout the summer. Mr. Butterfield informs me that a nest of this species with both parent birds were recently taken near Winchelsea by Mr. G. Bristow.[1]

51. Yellow Wagtail. *Motacilla raii* (Bonaparte).

A somewhat scarce summer visitor.

52. Tree-Pipit. *Anthus trivialis* (Linn.)

A common summer visitor, breeding throughout the county.

53. Meadow-Pipit. *Anthus pratensis* (Linn.).

More numerous in the autumn and spring, but breeding in fair numbers wherever open uncultivated land is to be found.

54. Red-throated Pipit. *Anthus cervinus* (Pallas).

Mr. J. H. Gurney recorded the first instance of the capture of this pipit in Sussex (*Zoologist*, 1884, p. 192). It was caught near Brighton on March 13, 1884, and afterwards passed into the collection of Mr. Monk of Lewes. A second example, in winter plumage, was shot near St. Leonards on November 13, 1895, and examined by Mr. R. Butterfield. It was exhibited by Dr. R. Bowdler Sharpe at a meeting of the British Ornithologists' Club on December 30 of that year.

55. Tawny Pipit. *Anthus campestris* (Linn.)

Nearly all the instances of the occurrence of this rare pipit have taken place near Brighton. The first was captured near Shoreham on August 15, 1858, and another at Rottingdean in 1862. These two specimens were examined by Mr. Rowley, who identified them as *Anthus campestris* and he recorded them in the *Ibis*, 1863. Several others have been taken near Brighton since then, and have passed through the hands of Mr. Swaysland and Mr. Pratt.

56. Richard's Pipit. *Anthus richardi*, Vieillot.

One Sunday morning in the month of April, 1898, I saw a bird near the lodge gates of Warnham Court which I feel certain not only on account of its size but by its loud note was a bird of this species. It remained sitting quietly on the top of an oak paling till

[1] Mr. H. E. Dresser, who has examined these specimens, is of opinion that they come nearest to the sub-species *Motacilla beema* (Sykes). There is also a specimen, probably referable to the same form, in the Tring Museum, shot near Brighton.

BIRDS

I approached to within a few yards and then flew away in a northerly direction. Two or three Richard's pipits have been taken within the county.

57. Water-Pipit. *Anthus spipoletta* (Linn.)

The water-pipit is a scarce spring and autumn migrant to the Sussex littoral. I have seen specimens in the hands of the Brighton naturalists, and there are examples in my own and the late Mr. Borrer's collection taken on the south coast.

58. Rock-Pipit. *Anthus obscurus* (Latham).

Resident along the coast where rocks are to be found. Sometimes a rarer form or sub-species known as the Scandinavian rock-pipit, *Anthus rupestris*, is occasionally obtained on the coast in the autumn and spring.

59. Golden Oriole. *Oriolus galbula*, Linn.

A rare summer visitor. One or two specimens are seen almost annually in the south of the county. A fine adult male was killed at Denne Park in 1880, and is now in the possession of Miss Pigott. Mr. Borrer once had the good fortune to see fourteen of these beautiful birds as they were sunning themselves on a low bush on Henfield Common.

60. Great Grey Shrike. *Lanius excubitor*, Linn.

A somewhat rare though regular late autumn and winter visitor to Sussex. As a stranger it exhibits the same shy and watchful nature that is characteristic of its ways even in its summer home.

61. Red-backed Shrike. *Lanius collurio*, Linn.

The butcher bird is distinctly local and sparingly distributed throughout the county in the summer months. I am inclined to think that nearer to the coast they are more numerous than further inland; certainly I have seen many more in the neighbourhood of Lancing and Worthing than towards the Surrey border. Butcher birds will return year after year and nest in the same thorn bush if their nest is undisturbed.

62. Woodchat. *Lanius pomeranus*, Sparrman.

An adult male of this species was taken near Brighton on May 11, 1856 (Borrer). In Mr. Borrer's notes, written by himself, in his copy of *The Birds of Sussex*, is the following: 'Woodchat, adult male, 25th July, 1892 : shot near Fairlight Church.' This specimen is now in the collection at Cowfold, where I have recently seen it. A male was seen by Mr. M. J. Nicoll at St. Leonards on April 29, 1898, and was afterwards shot on May 1 in the same year. It passed through the hands of Mr. G. Bristow.

63. Waxwing. *Ampelis garrulus*, Linn.

A rare winter visitor, occurring sometimes in large flocks. The first mention I find of the occurrence of this chatterer in Sussex is in Markwick's MS. (now at Denne Park), where he alludes to the capture of a specimen near Catsfield in February, 1801.

64. Pied Flycatcher. *Muscicapa atricapilla*, Linn.

A rare spring and autumn migrant. Mr. R. Butterfield informs me that he has several shot by himself at both seasons near St. Leonards.

65. Spotted Flycatcher. *Muscicapa grisola*, Linn.

Only a few pairs remain to breed in west Sussex, but this species is very common in all other parts of the county.

66. Swallow. *Hirundo rustica*, Linn.

The swallow arrives regularly in Sussex immediately after the sand-martin and some time before the house-martin, whose advent is often delayed. I have seen it as early as March 20 and as late as December 10. A pure albino swallow was killed on Warnham pond by the late Mr. F. M. Lucas in the year 1883.

67. House-Martin. *Chelidon urbica* (Linn.)

Of late years, owing to the increase of the common sparrow, the house-martins in Sussex have had to submit to almost constant persecution. In one row of houses with which I am acquainted six martins' nests were built, and of these all were seized by the robber sparrows. The martins then again commenced their house building and four completed their nests : from three of these again the rightful owners were evicted, while the fourth pair eventually deserted their nest. The two following years the martins were subjected to the same inhospitable treatment, and now they have wisely deserted the spot. Certainly this species suffers more than any other bird from the plague of sparrows. Large numbers of house-martins breed annually in Scotland at a late date, and their young work south and reach Sussex in numbers about November 10. These young birds are generally the stragglers of the main body that have departed, and should a night frost occur before they leave numbers of them will be found lying dead beneath the houses where they have roosted.

68. Sand-Martin. *Cotile riparia* (Linn.)

Whilst both swallows and house-martins appear to vary in numbers and date of arrival according to the season, the sand-martins always seem to be numerous and regular in their appearance in spring.

69. Greenfinch. *Ligurinus chloris* (Linn.)

Abundant everywhere, although not so common as in Wiltshire.

70. Hawfinch. *Coccothraustes vulgaris*, Pallas.

The hawfinch is fairly common locally, but in some years they desert certain districts completely, and generally at the beginning of the nesting season. I have seen as many as ten freshly made hawfinches' nests at Denne Park which have been deserted. In the next year four nests only were built and one tenanted, from which young were brought out. With great regularity family parties of hawfinches appear in our gardens and attack the ripe peas, a somewhat bold move for birds which are generally so shy.

71. Goldfinch. *Carduelis elegans*, Stephens.

The goldfinch is undoubtedly far scarcer than formerly, but its numbers are certainly not now on the decrease. Though large numbers of this beautiful little bird were, and are, annually caught on the downs near Brighton, I think with Mr. Meade-Waldo that its present scarcity is due rather to the disappearance of its favourite fallows and pastures. Somewhat large flocks of migratory goldfinches are to be occasionally seen in the autumn. As an instance of the abundance of this species near Brighton in former times, Mr. Booth states that a bird-catcher once took at one pull of his net eleven dozen goldfinches, and Mr. Hussey (*Zoologist*, 1860, p. 7144) put the annual capture of this species near Worthing at about 1,154 dozen.

72. Siskin. *Carduelis spinus* (Linn.)

A regular winter visitor, and generally found in small flocks feeding on the alders.

73. Serin. *Serinus hortulanus*, K. L. Koch.

I have no doubt that the serin visits Sussex in the spring far more frequently than is generally supposed, though specimens have rarely been taken. One year, 1884, the Brighton bird-catchers captured three of these birds, one of which, a beautiful adult male, was kept alive for a short time by the late Mr. Henry Seebohm, who on its death kindly presented it to me.

74. House-Sparrow. *Passer domesticus* (Linn.)

Quite a plague, especially at harvest time.

75. Tree-Sparrow. *Passer montanus* (Linn.)

Rare as a breeding species but fairly common in winter, when it may readily be distinguished by its high-pitched note. Mr. Butterfield says that a colony breed and reside at Camber Castle near Rye.

76. Chaffinch. *Fringilla cœlebs*, Linn.
Locally, Cavenger (M. J. Nicoll).

Abundant throughout the year. In the autumn when a large number of migratory chaffinches pass through Sussex the sexes keep apart. For some days males only are seen, and then for a while the other sex will be in evidence. In the spring again a migration of the males to the north comes first.

77. Brambling. *Fringilla montifringilla*, Linn.
A regular winter visitor.

78. Linnet. *Linota cannabina* (Linn.)
Common and resident.

79. Mealy Redpoll. *Linota linaria* (Linn.)
A rare winter visitor.

80. Lesser Redpoll. *Linota rufescens* (Vieillot).

The lesser redpoll generally arrives and associates with the siskins during its short winter stay. A few have been known to remain and nest.

81. Twite. *Linota flavirostris* (Linn.)

A somewhat unusual winter visitor to west Sussex but occurs annually in east Sussex; it is generally found in small flocks near the coast.

82. Bullfinch. *Pyrrhula europæa*, Vieillot.

Bullfinches are certainly far commoner than they were a few years ago. One now sees large numbers in the woods when covert shooting is going on.

83. Scarlet Grosbeak. *Pyrrhula erythrina* (Pallas).

There is only one instance of the occurrence of this species in Sussex, a specimen having been caught on the downs near Brighton in September, 1869 (Yarrell).

84. Pine-Grosbeak. *Pyrrhula enucleator* (Linn.)

The pine-grosbeak is said to have occurred twice in Sussex.

85. Crossbill. *Loxia curvirostra*, Linn.

Large numbers of crossbills visit us in certain seasons, arriving in September and often staying throughout the whole winter. They are particularly fond of the west end of St. Leonards Forest, where in 1899 I got close to a flock of over a hundred. All the visitors are apparently of the smaller species, in fact I have never seen the big form known as the 'parrot-crossbill' south of the Scottish border. Mr. Borrer however records two specimens of the large form captured within the county.

86. Two-barred Crossbill. *Loxia bifasciata* (C. L. Brehm).

A beautiful male was shot between Westfield and Sedlescombe on February 23, 1899, and exhibited by Mr. Norman Ticehurst at a meeting of the British Ornithologists' Club held on July 4, 1899.

87. Black-headed Bunting. *Emberiza melanocephala*, Scopoli.

An old female of this species, the first British example, was shot about November 3, 1868, on Brighton racecourse (Gould, *Ibis*, 1869, p. 128). Another was picked up on the railway near Bexhill on November 23, 1894 (*Zoologist*, 1897, p. 273).

88. Corn-Bunting. *Emberiza miliaria*, Linn.

A very local species, being common near the coast and rare in north and west Sussex, the country in these parts being probably too heavily timbered to suit its tastes.

89. Yellow Hammer. *Emberiza citrinella*, Linn.

A common resident.

90. Cirl Bunting. *Emberiza cirlus*, Linn.

A local species generally found near the coast about Brighton, Worthing and Bognor. The cirl bunting rarely visits the Weald. It nests regularly near St. Leonards, Winchelsea and Worthing.

91. Ortolan Bunting. *Emberiza hortulana*, Linn.

The ortolan bunting was considered to be at one time a regular spring and summer visitor to the fig gardens near Lancing, and before the days of the Wild Birds Protection Act a few were certainly taken near there by the bird-catchers. Now it is only a rare summer visitor. I have a specimen in my collection which was captured near Brighton, and which I obtained from the late Mr. Swaysland, who had kept it alive for a short time. Mr. Borrer records some six instances of its capture, and Mr. Pratt says he received two in 1896 respectively from Rottingdean and Eastbourne.

92. Rustic Bunting. *Emberiza rustica*, Pallas.

The first example of the rustic bunting

known to have occurred in England was caught near Brighton on October 23, 1867. It is now in the collection of Mr. T. G. Monk of Lewes.

93. Little Bunting. *Emberiza pusilla*, Pallas.

The only British example of the little bunting was taken alive near Brighton and brought to Mr. Swaysland on November 2, 1864. It is now in Mr. Monk's collection.

94. Reed-Bunting. *Emberiza schœniclus*, Linn.

Resident by the rivers and marshes, but in no part of Sussex very plentiful.

95. Snow-Bunting. *Plectrophenax nivalis* (Linn.)

A winter visitor, arriving with the snow, and in cold seasons numerous, especially near the coast. The snow-bunting has a very sweet song. In the barren wastes of Iceland, where the stillness is seldom broken except by the melancholy calls of the whimbrel and the golden plover, the notes of this little bird are singularly effective.

96. Lapland Bunting. *Calcarius lapponicus* (Linn).

A rare autumn or winter visitor. A specimen in my collection was caught in the winter of 1878 and kept alive until it had completely assumed its full summer plumage. I consider this bunting a far more regular visitor than it is generally supposed to be. I have known one lark-catcher to take as many as four in two years.

[Red-winged Starling. *Agelæus phœniceus* (Pallas).

This rare visitor, so common in America, is said to have occurred twice within the county (Borrer), but it is very doubtful whether the species should be included in the birds of Great Britain.]

97. Starling. *Sturnus vulgaris*, Linn.

Next to the sparrow the commonest of birds and still increasing in number. Formerly the starling generally nested either in houses or in old trees in their immediate vicinity, but now they will even repair to the lonely depths of the forest and evict the woodpeckers.

98. Rose-coloured Pastor. *Pastor roseus* (Linn.)

The rose-coloured pastor has occurred several times in Sussex, notably of late years. There is a beautiful adult male in the Borrer collection shot near Brighton on August 20, 1870.

99. Chough. *Pyrrhocorax graculus* (Linn.)

In the Markwick MS., written in the first years of the nineteenth century, that observer says, 'I have seen them (choughs) at Beachy Head near Eastbourne,' and he further infers that they were breeding there at that time. Also Gilbert White states that they were breeding there in 1773. They seem to have nested on Beachy Head till 1821, after which date they appear to have soon become extinct.

100. Nutcracker. *Nucifraga caryocatactes* (Linn.)

The first Sussex example of the nutcracker was shot on September 26, 1844, at Littlington. It was an adult bird, though the sex was not ascertained (Borrer). A second was shot near Chichester November 3, 1893 (*Zoologist*, ser. 3, p. 310), and a third is recorded by the Rev. Marmaduke Langdale. This specimen was shot at Chilgrove by Mr. J. Woods on December 21, 1900. All the above specimens are assignable to the thin-billed Siberian form.

101. Jay. *Garrulus glandarius* (Linn.)

Common and certainly not decreasing, in spite of the war waged against the species.

102. Magpie. *Pica rustica* (Scopoli).

Now a scarce bird.

103. Jackdaw. *Corvus monedula*, Linn.

Abundant everywhere.

104. Raven. *Corvus corax*, Linn.

There is little doubt that a pair or more of ravens still nest annually on the chalk cliffs bordering the Channel, but as a breeding species in the interior of the county it has disappeared. Formerly ravens nested annually until 1840 at Hurstpierpoint, but forsook this place for a clump of firs on the South Downs near Wolstanbury Hill, where they were subjected to constant persecution and so soon left the neighbourhood. They also nested irregularly at both Burton and Parham, as well as at Petworth in the high mound covered with firs which stands in the middle of the park. Knox records their breeding there in 1843 and 1844, and the late Bishop Wilberforce, writing in September, 1849, in the *Quarterly Review*, says that the ravens had again returned to their old nesting site at Petworth but left it again without rearing their young. Since that date there is no record of the ravens having returned to Petworth, and on a recent visit the keeper told me that the two trees in which they used to nest had both been blown down. I saw a pair of ravens flying high over the beach at Shoreham in the spring of 1896.

105. Carrion-Crow. *Corvus corone*, Linn.

Now somewhat scarce owing to constant persecution. Mr. Butterfield says that the carrion-crow has almost completely disappeared from east Sussex.

106. Hooded Crow. *Corvus cornix*, Linn.

A regular winter visitor, being particularly common near the coast.

107. Rook. *Corvus frugilegus*, Linn.

The rook seems to be increasing in Sussex. Certainly there are more rookeries in the western portion of the county than formerly, whilst few of the old haunts are deserted. In the south of England it is now not uncommon to notice that certain rooks from every rookery have become more or less carnivorous as well as adept egg-stealers. These birds with 'criminal' instinct are not numerous as yet in the south of England, although persistent young bird-slayers and egg-stealers have long been recognized in Scotland, and so the depredations of one or two individuals, who in the summer time prefer a flesh and egg diet, are generally attributed to the whole community. One particular rook from Horsham Park used regularly to hunt every morning in May and June for two years all the small gardens near my house, and I believe that he entirely cleared the place of small birds' eggs, except when the owners had built in very dense undergrowth. A common lark which built its nest within fifteen feet of my dining-room window was robbed of her treasures, and on again laying in the same nest was subjected to a second visitation. So cunning was this particular marauder that I never once obtained a shot at him, although twice I witnessed his depredations. Rooks frequently retain the feathered nostril until the second year, and breed in what was formerly considered to be an immature plumage.

108. Sky-Lark. *Alauda arvensis*, Linn.

Abundant, especially in winter, when immense numbers come in from the north.

109. Wood-Lark. *Alauda arborea*, Linn.

A rare bird in Sussex, but resident in a few places. Sometimes it occurs in small flocks in the winter.

110. Crested Lark. *Alauda cristata*, Linn.

A rare autumn visitor which has occurred three times within the county (Borrer). Besides these examples, I have in my collection a fine adult male which was shot near Worthing. This I procured from Mr. Swaysland in the spring of 1879, and the feet of the bird were quite soft and pliant, showing that, as he stated, it had just been taken. It is curious that this lark does not come to us more frequently. I have seen many in summer in the north of Normandy, where the species is common.

111. Short-toed Lark. *Alauda brachydactyla*, Leisler.

This lark has occurred three times in Sussex (Borrer).

112. White-winged Lark. *Alauda sibirica*, J. F. Gmelin.

The only British specimen of this rare lark was taken in a net at Brighton and exhibited by Mr. Rowley at a meeting of the Zoological Society, January 27, 1870. The specimen is now in Mr. Monk's collection.

113. Shore-Lark. *Otocorys alpestris* (Linn.)

A somewhat rare winter visitor, occurring in small numbers on the coast.

114. Swift. *Cypselus apus* (Linn.)
Locally, Anchor bird (M. J. Nicoll).

A regular summer visitor, arriving after the swallows and departing before them.

115. Alpine Swift. *Cypselus melba* (Linn.)

It is stated in the *Zoologist* (p. 3330) that a specimen of the Alpine swift was captured at St. Leonards-on-Sea in October, 1851. It is said to have passed into the hands of a Mr. Johnson, chemist, of that place. The specimen does not seem to be now forthcoming, for nothing is known of its existence in that town.

116. Nightjar. *Caprimulgus europæus*, Linn.

A regular summer visitor to the districts of forest, fern-bank and heath. I think that the species is much scarcer than it used to be.

117. Wryneck. *Iÿnx torquilla*, Linn.

A regular spring migrant, nesting throughout the county in small numbers.

118. Green Woodpecker. *Gecinus viridis* (Linn.)
Locally, Galley bird (M. J. Nicoll).

Fairly well distributed throughout the county and even common in the big oak district of the north and west. In the late summer and autumn the green woodpecker may frequently be seen searching for insects on the ground.

119. Great Spotted Woodpecker. *Dendrocopus major* (Linn.)

The least common of the three species of woodpecker. Where natural conditions prevail in the form of large oaks, elms and beeches the great spotted woodpecker is not rare, but its shy and retiring disposition causes it to be frequently overlooked.

120. Lesser Spotted Woodpecker. *Dendrocopus minor* (Linn.)

Although the 'yaffle' is considered the commonest of the woodpeckers in Sussex, I am inclined to think that in west Sussex the lesser spotted woodpecker is far the most numerous (in east Sussex the larger bird is considered the commoner species). If this little bird fancies that danger is to be apprehended, it will remain quite still on the reverse side of a bough away from the observer, and there lie 'perdu' for half an hour without a move.

121. Kingfisher. *Alcedo ispida*, Linn.

Resident and found by nearly every stream and lake. In the winter many repair to the ditches of the Weald and even to tidal waters.

122. Roller. *Coracias garrulus*, Linn.

The earliest record of this species in Sussex is that of Hill (*Hist. Anim.* p. 369), who states that he saw one in Charlton Forest in 1752. Markwick says in his catalogue read before the Linnæan Society (1795), 'A bird of this species was killed in this neighbourhood,' and in the Denne MS. I find that the specimen was shot near Crowhurst Church on September 22, 1790. Since that date several have been obtained at rare intervals throughout the past century.

123. Bee-eater. *Merops apiaster*, Linn.

Like the last named species a rare straggler.

124. Hoopoe. *Upupa epops*, Linn.

Every year a few hoopoes make their way north and arrive in Sussex about the end of April or beginning of May. Its brilliant plumage and graceful flight are only too attractive, and so the man with the gun finds it irresistible in spite of acts prohibiting its slaughter. I must plead guilty to having shot one many years ago at Angmering near Worthing, a locality regularly visited by the hoopoe. The hoopoe sometimes rests in Sussex on the autumn migration.

125. Cuckoo. *Cuculus canorus*, Linn.

An abundant summer visitor.

126. White or Barn-Owl. *Strix flammea*, Linn.

Still fairly numerous in spite of the senseless and even harmful warfare waged against it. Mr. Butterfield informs me that a very beautiful chocolate specimen has passed through the hands of Mr. G. Bristow.

127. Long-eared Owl. *Asio otus* (Linn.)

Irregularly distributed and generally frequenting plantations of fir and larch.

128. Short-eared Owl. *Asio accipitrinus* (Pallas).

A late autumn and winter visitor. It seems to prefer the open lands in the neighbourhood of the sea, and may be seen hunting for food during the day.

129. Tawny Owl. *Syrnium aluco* (Linn.)

The most abundant species of owl in west Sussex. In the east of the county it is considered somewhat rare. I have seen both the snowy owl and the tawny owl hunting for fish by day. In the case of the snowy owl the bird descended upon its quarry exactly like an osprey, with wings held straight up.

130. Little Owl. *Athene noctua* (Scopoli).

Of late years several little owls have been let out by various naturalists, and these and their progeny figure occasionally in the columns of the *Field* and elsewhere.

131. Scops-Owl. *Scops giu* (Scopoli).

A specimen of this owl was killed at Shillingbee, the seat of the Earl of Winterton, about the year 1850 (Knox).

132. Eagle-Owl. *Bubo ignavus*, T. Forster.

Montagu, Yarrell and Jenyns give an instance of the occurrence of this species in Sussex, and although this record was possibly that of a wild bird, it is more than likely that most of the subsequent captures of the eagle-owl which have been recorded are those of tame birds which gentlemen like Mr. Meade Waldo have in a generous spirit endeavoured to acclimatize.

Formerly many eagle-owls were kept in a considerable space formed by the walls of the donjon keep at Arundel. There they bred and reared several young ones every year.

133. Marsh-Harrier. *Circus æruginosus* (Linn.)

There is little doubt that at the beginning of the nineteenth century the marsh-harrier was still common in Sussex, yet by the year 1850, owing to the drainage of its principal hunting grounds, it was considered a rare bird, a fact that is proved by there being no Sussex specimen in Mr. Borrer's collection. The species is now a very scarce autumn visitor.

134. Hen-Harrier. *Circus cyaneus* (Linn.)

The most commonly met with of the three species of harrier formerly resident. Now a regular but somewhat rare winter visitor.

135. Montagu's Harrier. *Circus cineraceus* (Montagu).

Formerly resident and breeding in the county till 1850. Specimens have been killed at Wiversfield (1874), Arundel (1844), Hollycombe and Oafham (1842) (Charles Knox). Now only a rare spring visitor, and it would undoubtedly breed again with us, as it has recently done so in several of the southern counties, were any protection afforded. The most recent capture of this species is that of an adult female which was shot at Patcham near Brighton on June 16, 1891 (Pratt). Mr. Butterfield tells me that a solitary individual frequented the hills near Fairlight, Hastings, during the spring and summer of 1901. Mr. M. J. Nicoll informs me that this bird was afterwards shot, and that he also received a male from Burwash which had been killed by a keeper on July 28, 1899.

136. Common Buzzard. *Buteo vulgaris*, Leach.

Now only a rare autumn migrant in the county where he was once common and resident. Certainly far rarer than the rough-legged or the honey-buzzard.

137. Rough-legged Buzzard. *Buteo lagopus* (J. F. Gmelin).

A scarce autumn visitor. In November, 1896, I saw a bird of this species when partridge shooting near Horsham, and another the same week near Cowfold.

138. White-tailed Eagle. *Haliaëtus albicilla* (Linn.)

One or two white-tailed eagles, generally young birds, find their way to Sussex every winter. They come in the vain hope of gaining a living on our coasts, but generally fall a victim to the gamekeeper, the farmer or the shore-shooter. Markwick evidently confused this bird with the golden eagle, and it is curious that he made no allusion to the sea-eagle in his 'Catalogue of the Birds of Sussex' (published in the Linnæan *Transactions*, 1795), for in his day the species was probably of more frequent occurrence than in our times. Knox gives five instances of its capture.

139. Sparrow-Hawk. *Accipiter nisus* (Linn.)

Common and resident in spite of constant persecution.

140. Kite. *Milvus ictinus*, Savigny.

Formerly well known and breeding in the Weald. After 1830 it was considered a rare bird in the county, and Knox mentions only two instances of its occurrence—once near Brighton and once at Sidlesham between the years 1840-50.

141. Honey-Buzzard. *Pernis apivorus* (Linn.)

There is no record of the honey-buzzard having ever bred in the county, though it is highly probable that it has done so. Till recently it regularly nested in the neighbouring county of Hants as well as in other southern counties. Coming to us generally when the woods are in full leaf, and frequenting for the most part densely wooded tracts, the species is both inconspicuous, silent and shy in its ways, so that it may even escape the notice of the most watchful keeper. Knox gives several instances of its capture, and also charmingly describes the appearance of a honey-buzzard which he saw in Charlton Forest in the act of tearing out a wasps' nest. There are two fine examples in the collection of the late Mr. William Borrer. One of these, killed at Poyning's Common, September, 1845, is of the creamy breasted type. I once had the good fortune to obtain alive a bird of this species, and must confess that it was by far the most interesting pet I have ever possessed. Only the very point of the wing was injured when I shot it at Frostendon in Suffolk, so I determined to try and save its life. For more than a week it refused all food, so that I feared it would soon die of starvation. Little birds, frogs and insects were offered in vain, and only as an experiment did I force a French plum down its throat, for that was the nearest approach to honey at hand. To my surprise the bird picked up and swallowed the next plum with avidity, and from that moment I had no trouble with the menu.[1] From this date he lived on French plums and their juice for a month, when I managed to procure heather honey regularly from Scotland, and principally on this diet, varied with the contents of an occasional wasps' nest, I kept him till the end of winter. He was of a most amiable and even gentle disposition, giving a loud and long peevish scream as one approached, and

[1] As an instance of the extraordinary tastes of this mild raptorial, it may be mentioned that the late Lord Lilford fed his specimen for a long time on rice pudding.

would fly down and rest on my hand as I carried him about the garden looking for bees and wasps. These he would capture with remarkable grace and certainty, his powers of flight being soon quite restored. If I sat reading a book under a tree he would never go far away, but soon came flying back uttering his peevish, whistling cry. I shall never forget the first time we went to attack a wasps' nest to which a farm boy was guiding me. 'Where is it?' I said to the boy, but before he gave answer the honey-buzzard suddenly stretched his neck, and intently watching a wasp that flew by cast itself into the air and with great rapidity flew low and straight to the 'bike,' about a hundred yards distant and situated in a high bank. In a moment the bird was suddenly transformed from a listless, apathetic dullard to the most energetic and business-like excavator. He used his beak occasionally to pull aside a root or other obstruction, but most of the work of unearthing the nest was done with his feet. Meanwhile the wasps in access of fury swarmed all over him, and of these little tormentors he seemed not to take the smallest notice, a circumstance explained, as I afterwards found out, by the fact that though the wasps entered his plumage with their heads and could even reach the skin, they nevertheless found it impossible to screw round their meta-thorax and sting the bird owing to the way in which he held his feathers and to the strength and elasticity of the down. The honey-buzzard swallowed grubs, comb and full-grown wasps during his meal, and for three days afterwards wasps still remained in the plumage of the bird. This seemed to cause the buzzard no inconvenience but rather a pleasant source of supply, for I constantly saw him during this time searching his plumage and abstract a wasp, which he at once nipped and swallowed.

142. Greenland Falcon. *Falco candicans*, J. F. Gmelin.

A female bird of this species was shot on September 26, 1882, at Bullock's Hill, Balsdean near Lewes. It is now in Mr. Monk's collection at Lewes (Gurney, *Zoologist*, 1883, p. 80).

143. Gyr-Falcon. *Falco gyrfalco*, Linn.

There is a fine adult specimen of the gyr-falcon in the Borrer collection. It is the only Sussex specimen recorded, and was shot in January, 1845, at Mayfield.

144. Peregrine Falcon. *Falco peregrinus*, Tunstall.

A regular visitor, appearing in almost every

month of the year, and but for the scarcity of suitable nesting sites no doubt more would stay and breed with us. Since time immemorial peregrines have bred on Beachy Head and in the Newhaven Cliff to the west, and there is little doubt that they have not yet abandoned their favourite seaside residence on the Sussex coast. In the winter the wandering peregrine, generally an old bird, will often take up his abode by some lake such as exists at Burton Park, and here live on the wildfowl for the season. The peregrine is known in Sussex, as well as in America, as the duckhawk.

145. Hobby. *Falco subbuteo*, Linn.

Formerly a regular summer visitor to the Weald and breeding there, but now only occurring at long intervals in the summer and autumn.

146. Merlin. *Falco æsalon*, Tunstall.

A regular winter visitor. Inland it preys principally on larks, and on the coast the dunlin is its favourite food.

147. Red-legged Falcon. *Falco vespertinus* Linn.

One of these birds was shot by Mr. Howard Saunders at Rottingdean in 1851 (Dresser, *Birds of Europe*). Mr. Rowley has also recorded (*Field*, May 24, 1873) a second specimen taken near Brighton. An adult male was killed at Pett on June 3, 1901.

148. Kestrel. *Falco tinnunculus*, Linn.

The forests in the north and west of Sussex are a great harbour for this interesting and practically harmless little falcon. There many nest in comparative security, so the species well holds its own and is by far the commonest bird of prey in spite of constant persecution.

149. Osprey. *Pandion haliaëtus* (Linn.)

Almost every spring and autumn ospreys, generally immature birds, visit Sussex. Borrer and Knox both cite numerous instances of its occurrence and capture. At one time the rising tide on the river Arun forced its way up from the sea to some distance above the ruins of Amberley Castle, and with it came in summer time the grey mullet, a favourite food of the osprey, and there are many instances in the writings of past authors of the appearance of the 'mullet-hawk,' as the osprey was called, with the spring running of the fish. Knox records an instance of the capture of an osprey by a shepherd boy, who observed it alight heavily on the cliffs of Rottingdean. The unfortunate bird was both

unable to rise or to free itself from its intended victim, a large fish.

150. Common Cormorant. *Phalacrocorax carbo* (Linn.)

Sparsely distributed along the coast line during the winter months. At the present time the species only breeds on Seaford Head. It is however fairly common in spring in the estuary north of Thorney Island.

151. Shag. *Phalacrocorax graculus* (Linn.)

Occasionally an immature shag has appeared of late years on the Sussex coast, but the species though formerly breeding on the Isle of Wight may now only be considered a rare winter visitor.

152. Gannet. *Sula bassana* (Linn.)

A regular winter visitor to the English Channel, occurring in some numbers and generally keeping well out to sea. After severe gales specimens are sometimes found inland in a helpless condition.

153. Heron. *Ardea cinerea*, Linn.

Sussex is well favoured in the preference shown to it by this splendid bird. There are several well established heronries in the county, notably at Windmill Hill Place near Hailsham and at Parham, where the number of birds is undoubtedly decreasing owing to the increase of the rooks. There is also a small heronry at Molecomb near Goodwood. At Parham all the nests are built in fir trees and mixed up with the rooks making it difficult to count them, but this year (1901) there were certainly thirty nests there. The heronry at Brede, where formerly there were about 200 nests, is now deserted.

154. Purple Heron. *Ardea purpurea*, Linn.

Two examples of this rare heron have occurred in Sussex. The first mentioned by Knox was shot on September 28, 1848, at Worthing and 'is now in the museum of the Cambridge Philosophical Society.' Another was killed in October, 1851, at Catsfield and preserved by a Lewes bird-stuffer (Borrer).

155. Squacco Heron. *Ardea ralloides*, Scopoli.

This heron occurs at rare intervals on migration. Borrer records two Sussex specimens, the first a completely adult bird which was killed at Wick Pond in the parish of Albourne in the summer of 1828. The second was shot at Warnham Pond near Horsham in the summer of 1849, and was first recorded by Mr. Knox as a little egret. Its possessor, Sir Percy Shelley, gave it to the

Hon. Grantley Berkeley, who in turn presented it to Mr. Hart for his museum at Christchurch, where I have seen it. Mr. M. J. Nicoll informs me that two immatures were shot at Pett on October 16 and 25, 1901.

There is a fine specimen of this heron in the late Mr. Borrer's house, and in a collection so strictly British and so carefully kept it is somewhat remarkable to find no label attached or reference to it in his book.

156. Night-Heron. *Nycticorax griseus* (Linn.)

Two examples of the night heron are recorded as having occurred in Sussex—one at Alfriston, November, 1839 (Borrer), and another at Cuckmere Haven, 1851 (Knox).

157. Little Bittern. *Ardetta minuta* (Linn.)

A rare summer visitor. Of recent occurrences one was obtained at Hove, September, 1894, and is now in the Booth Museum. Another, an adult female, which I examined in the flesh, was found dead near Billingshurst May 6, 1901. I also have two in my collection that were obtained near Petworth in the spring of 1889.

158. Common Bittern. *Botaurus stellaris* (Linn.)

A few bitterns still come to us regularly every winter. Formerly it used to breed in some numbers in the great marsh known as the Wildbrook that existed near Amberley and is now drained.

159. American Bittern. *Botaurus lentiginosus* (Montagu).

Has twice occurred in the county. One of these, a fine adult, was killed on November 30, 1879, in the Amberley Wildbrook, and is now preserved in the collection of the late Mr. William Borrer.

160. White Stork. *Ciconia alba*, Bechstein.

A rare visitor, which has occurred on several occasions in spring and autumn. The latest capture is that of an adult male taken on Broadwater Down, August, 1899.

161. Glossy Ibis. *Plegadis falcinellus* (Linn.)

There is a fine adult specimen of the glossy ibis in the late Mr. Borrer's collection which was shot at Piddinghoe near Newhaven on May 25, 1850. The species is only a rare straggler from south-eastern Europe and has occurred in the county but three times.

162. Spoonbill. *Platalea leucorodia*, Linn.

Mr. J. E. Harting has shown that the spoonbill formerly nested in Sussex at Eskden near Goodwood; now it is only a rare spring and autumn visitor, having occurred within the county on about twenty occasions.

163. Grey Lag-Goose. *Anser cinereus*, Meyer.

A rare winter visitor.

164. White-fronted Goose. *Anser albifrons* (Scopoli).

With the brent the most common of the wild geese that visit the Channel during the winter. Within the memory of man this goose was quite common in winter time on the marshes of Pevensey Level.

165. Bean-Goose. *Anser segetum* (J. F. Gmelin).

An irregular winter visitor, sometimes passing in big flocks.

166. Pink-footed Goose. *Anser brachyrhynchus*, Baillon.

Although this goose is considered very rare within the county, a fact to a certain extent borne out by there being no Sussex specimens in the late Mr. Borrer's collection, yet I cannot believe that it does not visit us with the big packs of passing bean-geese and grey lags. In Scotland, where I have had a close acquaintance for many years with all the foregoing species of wild geese, I have invariably found that the pink-foot is by far the commonest, and whilst keeping for the most part in flocks of their own kind they unite for safety in one great flock with both grey lags and bean-geese. When therefore the two last species move south through stress of weather or other causes it is more than likely that a certain number of the pink-foots go with them. Certainly this is the case in Norfolk, where the present species is common throughout the winter, so that it is more likely that the species has been overlooked than that it is of uncommon rarity.

167. Barnacle-Goose. *Bernicla leucopsis* (Bechstein).

A rare winter straggler.

168. Brent Goose. *Bernicla brenta* (Pallas).

The 'black' goose is certainly the commonest of the genus that visits us in winter, sometimes appearing in considerable packs where the *Zostera marina*, their favourite food, grows. It is however not nearly so abundant as formerly. On the south coast of England the 'black' form of this goose is practically the only form, whereas in the north of Scotland when out shooting with the big gun I have generally killed equal proportions of the 'black' and the 'white' form. The dark birds are all supposed to come from the north-eastern Arctic, whilst the more beautiful light-breasted birds hail from the north-western coasts of the Atlantic.

169. Canada Goose. *Bernicla canadensis*, Pallas.

There is little doubt that considerable flocks of this splendid goose visited England and Scotland during the winters of 1868–9, although Mr. Howard Saunders is either unaware of or does not accept this evidence in his *Manual of British Birds*. Certainly many stayed in Scotland and afterwards bred on the waters of Loch Leven and have since spread throughout the kingdom. Nowadays many owners of lakes in Sussex keep these fine birds, and as they nest freely their progeny wander and are shot. A specimen in my collection was shot at Pagham in 1885 and given to me by the late Mr. Henry Seebohm. The Canada goose will, I hope, be considered a bona fide British bird in the near future.

170. Whooper Swan. *Cygnus musicus*, Bechstein.

A regular visitor in flocks during hard winters. I found whoopers during the breeding season in Iceland to be just as shy as during the winter months on our coasts. Whoopers have stayed the whole winter at Knepp Castle lake, where they are always protected.

171. Bewick's Swan. *Cygnus bewicki*, Yarrell.

A somewhat rare winter visitor, its appearance being due to severe weather in the north.

172. Mute Swan. *Cygnus olor* (J. F. Gmelin).

As the old birds of this species drive off their young in the spring time from the sheets of water where they intend to nest the mute swan becomes generally distributed and is now ranked as a wild bird. As many as fifty swans, nearly all strangers, have been counted of late years at Knepp, but not more than three or four pairs stay to breed. Another favourite swan resort is Warnham Pond.

173. Sheld-duck. *Tadorna cornuta* (S. G. Gmelin).

This handsome duck does not now breed on the Sussex coast; it is only a somewhat scarce winter visitor coming to us in small parties. These are generally immatures.

174. Ruddy Sheld-duck. *Tadorna casarca* (Linn.)

Of late years pinioned birds of this species have bred in Sussex, so that recent examples of its capture in a wild state do not necessarily mean genuinely wild birds. The Sussex specimen now in the Booth Museum and mentioned by Borrer as having been shot at Harting September 3, 1890, may or may not have been a wanderer from the south.

175. Mallard. *Anas boscas*, Linn.

Abundant in winter and resident in fair numbers.

176. Gadwall. *Anas strepera*, Linn.

A rare winter visitor; there is no record of its having nested within the county. The gadwall as well as the wigeon is an increasing species on the inland waters during winter, and we may yet hope at no distant date to see this species together with the wigeon, the pintail, the shoveler and the tufted duck all nesting and resident on our inland lakes and ponds, as they are now quite established in parts of England and Scotland.

177. Shoveler. *Spatula clypeata* (Linn.)

A regular winter visitor, increasing in numbers every year. At present it is not known to have nested in the county.

178. Pintail. *Dafila acuta* (Linn.)

A regular winter visitor to the coast in October and remaining through the winter. The pintail is a bird that only the professional wildfowler sees much of. The birds remain far out to sea during the hours of daylight and only come at night to feed on the mudflats. My experience of the species is that it is by far the shyest of the ducks, whether diving or surface feeding. Even in the breeding season in Iceland I have had no little difficulty in shooting a couple of drakes.

179. Teal. *Nettion crecca* (Linn.)

The teal is resident and breeds in small numbers throughout the county. In the winter large numbers come in as early as September and stay all the winter, frequently remaining as late as April.

180. Garganey. *Querquedula circia* (Linn.)

A rare summer visitor which has not been known to breed in the county. In nearly every work on British birds this species is referred to amongst the ducks which are increasing in our islands. This is certainly not my experience, for in Norfolk, where it formerly used to nest in some numbers, it now barely holds its own; so far as I could gather from thoroughly reliable sources there were only about thirteen nests discovered in the whole of that county in the season of 1900. Of late years however it has nested in Hampshire, and it may form a new home there.

BIRDS

181. Wigeon. *Mareca penelope* (Linn.)

The wigeon arrives in numbers about the end of September, and the main flocks continue to add to their numbers throughout the winter. By the end of March most of them have departed to the breeding grounds. The wigeon in a wild state stayed and bred on one of the Hammer Ponds at Coolhurst during 1853-4 (Borrer). Of late years pinioned birds have bred at Leonardslee and South Lodge near Horsham.

182. Red-crested Pochard. *Netta rufina* (Pallas).

A rare winter visitor. There are two specimens, an adult and an immature male, in the late Mr. Borrer's collection, evidently recently killed and stuffed from the flesh. They are probably Sussex specimens killed since Mr. Borrer wrote *The Birds of Sussex*, for there is no reference to the species in the pages of that work.

183. Common Pochard. *Fuligula ferina* (Linn.)

The commonest of the diving ducks that visit us. The nest of the pochard has once been taken within the county, namely by Borrer at the Lower Mill pond at Bolney.

184. Ferruginous or White-Eyed Duck. *Fuligula nyroca* (Güldenstädt).

A rare straggler. It has occurred twice in Sussex (Borrer).

185. Tufted Duck. *Fuligula cristata* (Leach).

A fairly common winter visitor. It has bred several times within the county and will doubtless increase in numbers as a resident.

186. Scaup-Duck. *Fuligula marila* (Linn.)

This sea-frequenting species visits the coasts in some numbers every winter, its affection for certain spots being due to the presence of mussel banks. It is plentiful about Eastbourne in certain seasons.

187. Goldeneye. *Clangula glaucion* (Linn.)

Small parties and single goldeneyes visit Sussex every winter. Most of these are immature, adult males being rare.

188. Long-tailed Duck. *Harelda glacialis* (Linn.)

A scarce winter visitor. Nearly all the long-tailed ducks that visit the British Islands south of the Firth of Tay are immatures. There seems to be a sharp line of limitation fixed by the birds themselves at this estuary I have named, and where I have seen hundreds of adults nearly every winter. Seven miles south in St. Andrews Bay hardly an adult is to be seen, whilst in the Forth only immatures are noticed, and so on right down the east and west coast of England.

189. Eider Duck. *Somateria mollissima* (Linn.)

A regular winter visitor in small numbers.

190. Common Scoter. *Œdemia nigra* (Linn.)

A regular winter visitor in large numbers to the Channel. I have noticed that single birds can be observed in almost every month in the year. This is somewhat curious, as these birds are as often adult as otherwise. I have noticed the same disposition to remain through the summer in the case of the velvet-scoter.

191. Velvet-Scoter. *Œdemia fusca* (Linn.)

A somewhat scarce and local species appearing in small flocks in winter. A regular visitor to Rye and St. Leonards, where in some seasons it is almost as often seen as the common scoter.

192. Goosander. *Mergus merganser*, Linn.

A scarce winter visitor generally found on inland lakes.

193. Red-breasted Merganser. *Mergus serrator*, Linn.

More common than the last species and preferring tidal waters.

194. Smew. *Mergus albellus*, Linn.

A regular visitor, being common in severe winters. Adult males are scarce, females and young males being the most numerous.

195. Hooded Merganser. *Mergus cucullatus* (Linn.)

Mr. J. E. Harting informs me that there was a bird of this species in the collection of Sir A. Biddulph, which was said to have been killed at Burton Park.

196. Wood-Pigeon. *Columba palumbus*, Linn.

Immense flights of wood-pigeons visit us succeeding a heavy acorn or beech mast year. These great flocks, which as it were settle down on a particular district and 'eat it out,' are always composed of migratory birds which arrive in November. As a resident the species is also abundant.

197. Stock-Dove. *Columba œnas*, Linn.

Though less numerous than the wood-pigeon the stock-dove is nevertheless abundant as a resident, and evidently their number is fast increasing.

198. Rock - Dove. *Columba livia,* J. F. Gmelin.

Evidently a very rare bird in its purely wild state. Our cliffs being unsuited to its habits it is not known to have bred within the county.

199. Turtle-Dove. *Turtur communis,* Selby.

A very common and increasing species. I doubt if there is any place in England where this beautiful little dove is so common as in the neighbourhood of Horsham. In the summer of 1899, a friend from Scotland being anxious to take a nest of this species, we entered a small cover at Warnham for this purpose, and in an hour had discovered seventeen nests. The same year I counted over one hundred together in a small patch of buckwheat.

200. Pallas's Sand-Grouse. *Syrrhaptes paradoxus* (Pallas).

This straggler from the Eastern steppes was first observed and obtained in Sussex during the invasion of these birds to England in 1863. In the second great arrival of these birds in England and Scotland in 1888 they were seen in the county as elsewhere in considerable flocks, and many specimens were shot along the coast. Some few even stayed through the winter and were captured in 1889. The bird during this immigration is recorded only to have nested in Scotland.

201. Black Grouse. *Tetrao tetrix,* Linn.

Although stragglers still appear at intervals, blackgame as a resident and breeding species may be said to have become extinct about 1845. Mr. Padwick of Horsham says that about the year 1840 his father shot as many as six brace in a morning at Combe Bottom, St. Leonards Forest. Though still seen and killed annually about Leith Hill, Crowborough and Hindhead near the Sussex border until the year 1870, blackgame have since become practically extinct, and I cannot ascertain that any person has actually seen them since 1890. Two attempts to reintroduce this fine bird have met with no success. It is generally the case that when indigenous and breeding species are stamped out, new importations, unless tried on a most extensive scale, are failures.

202. Pheasant. *Phasianus colchicus,* Linn.

Borrer, quoting from the *Sussex Archæological Collections,* tells us that the pheasant was known in Sussex as early as 1245, for 'the custos of the bishopric of Chichester was ordered to send to the king for his use at Easter amongst other game twenty-four pheasants.' More covers are every year devoted to pheasants, and certainly the sport of shooting them is not diminishing in favour. Sussex is a 'pheasant' county, though not so good as either Cambridgeshire, Hertfordshire or Norfolk.

203. Partridge. *Perdix cinerea,* Latham.

Although partridges are well and generally distributed throughout the county Sussex cannot properly be called a 'partridge county.' Bags of fifty brace in a day are rare and only made in an exceptionally good year.

204. Red-legged Partridge. *Caccabis rufa* (Linn.)

Knox mentions that two coveys of these birds were hatched and reared under domestic hens and turned down at Kirdford near Petworth in July, 1841. Since that date they have rapidly spread over the whole of the Weald and certainly in west Sussex are an increasing species. Formerly an open ground loving species and by nature a dweller in the fields and rough pastures, the red-legged partridge will now readily take to and live almost entirely in the woods when his safety depends on it.

205. Quail. *Coturnix communis,* Bonnaterre.

A scarce spring visitor, breeding occasionally on the South Downs and more rarely in the Weald.

206. Landrail. *Crex pratensis,* Bechstein.

A regular summer visitor, breeding with us and leaving in September. Occasionally a straggler remains throughout the winter.

207. Spotted Crake. *Porzana maruetta* (Leach).

A scarce summer visitor, its habits resembling the last named species but showing an especial taste for the edge of marshes. It has also occurred in the winter.

208. Little Crake. *Porzana parva* (Scopoli).

Mr. J. E. Harting has made known the first instance of the occurrence of this rare crake in Sussex. He found on reference to an unpublished manuscript by Markwick, now in the library of the Linnæan Society, that the coloured figure and description therein attributed to the spotted gallinule was in fact a bird of this species. There are two good specimens in the Borrer collection taken respectively at Beeding chalk-pit near Shoreham, October, 1855, and at Eastbourne in April, 1869. Five other examples taken within the county are mentioned by Mr. Borrer.

BIRDS

209. Baillon's Crake. *Porzana bailloni* (Vieillot).

The first example of Baillon's crake that has occurred in Sussex is recorded in the *Zoologist* (p. 4159) by Captain Clark Kennedy as having been captured at Eastbourne on August 6, 1874. Another has since been obtained, September, 1894, near Brighton and is now in the Booth's Museum.

210. Water-Rail. *Rallus aquaticus*, Linn.

Generally distributed and found frequenting the coarse herbage that grows along streams and ditches. The water-rail seems to neglect its safety somewhat during frosty weather, for it may be seen sitting in the open, huddled up with cold and almost fearless of man.

211. Moor-hen. *Gallinula chloropus* (Linn.)

Abundant and resident.

212. Coot. *Fulica atra*, Linn.

A common and resident bird in suitable ponds and lakes. I have noticed that the coots on Warnham Pond near my house will sit on the ice for three days when the lake is frozen over; if the frost continues they then repair to a grass field contiguous to the pond for one day or more, and then should there be no chance of a thaw they leave for the estuaries or the sea and do not return till April.

213. Crane. *Grus communis*, Bechstein.

Two are recorded, the first from Pevensey Level, May, 1849, and the second being killed at Pagham, October 18, 1854 (Borrer).

214. Great Bustard. *Otis tarda*, Linn.

Formerly this magnificent bird was common in Sussex, and small parties of them were seen as late as 1810. Gilbert White writing to his friend, Daines Barrington, in October, 1770, says, 'There are bustards on the wide downs near Brighthelmstone.' It was formerly a favourite sport of the Sussex country gentlemen to course the young birds of this species with greyhounds. There is an account of the capture of one of these birds mentioned in Yarrell's *British Birds*, when a female was shot on the downs near Eastbourne January 14, 1876. A very large bird appeared in a field near Horsham in April, 1899, and from the description given to me by the farmer and one of his labourers I have little doubt that it was a bird of this species. A female great bustard was shot by Charles Cooke, a watcher on Pett level, on January 6, 1891 (*Zoologist*, 1891, p. 104).

215. Little Bustard. *Otis tetrax*, Linn.

There are four instances on record of the occurrence of the little bustard in Sussex. Specimens have been shot at Cuckmere, October, 1846, and at Bosham near Chichester (Borrer), whilst in the *Zoologist* two others are mentioned, the first having been killed at Eastbourne December 11, 1879, and the second at Clymping near Arundel in October, 1887. It seems that the little bustard only visits us as a rare straggler in winter. A little bustard was killed in December, 1900, by the Hon. John Ashburnham while partridge shooting at Ashburnham. Another has since been seen in the same neighbourhood.

216. Stone-Curlew. *Œdicnemus scolopax* (S. G. Gmelin).

Arriving in April and departing as a rule in September the stone-curlew still visits the county in small numbers especially in the neighbourhood of the South Downs and on their southern slope. Many instances have occurred of specimens being seen and taken in the winter.

217. Dotterel. *Eudromias morinellus* (Linn.)

The South Down about Brighton and Seaford is one of the first landing places touched by this beautiful plover on its northward migration in spring. The birds come in small flocks of from six to a dozen and do not stay for many days, and fewer trips visit us every year. So far as I have been able to ascertain, after leaving us the dotterel pursue a north-easterly course, resting in some numbers on the Gog Magog Hills in Cambridge and again in Yorkshire, whence they move on directly to the Grampians and Aberdeenshire hills, where a few still breed.

218. Ringed Plover. *Ægialitis hiaticula* (Linn.)

Common and resident along the coast. They are partially migratory in spring and autumn.

219. Little Ringed Plover. *Ægialitis curonica* (J. F. Gmelin).

A very rare visitor. Two are recorded by Borrer. The first killed at West Wittering, May (no date given), is in the Borrer collection. The second was shot by Mr. Dennis at Tide Mills Creek, Bishopstone, on August 28, 1865. In the *Zoologist* (p. 3279) Mr. Ellman states that he obtained a specimen of this bird in Sussex during the latter part of September, 1851.

220. Kentish Plover. *Ægialitis cantiana* (Latham).

The Kentish plover exists in small numbers about the shingly beaches of the eastern coast of Sussex. Here in the neighbourhood of Rye Harbour and Winchelsea it breeds occasionally. It is a migratory species, arriving in April and departing in September.

221. Golden Plover. *Charadrius pluvialis,* Linn.

A regular winter visitor, sometimes in large flocks, to the open lands of Sussex. I have noticed golden plovers return year after year to the same ground in the Weald of Sussex. There they have their resting field and two regular feeding grounds, to which they adhere closely for two or three months unless repeatedly disturbed. In hard weather they leave for the coast.

222. Grey Plover. *Squatarola helvetica* (Linn.)

The grey plover, which is far more maritime in its habits than the golden plover, regularly visits the coast of the county in spring and autumn. Some years they stay at Lancing and Pagham till the end of May, when the fine summer plumage has been completely assumed. There is a fine case of summer specimens killed in Sussex by the late Mr. Booth in the Dyke Road museum, Brighton, and I have a perfectly black-breasted male that was killed at Lancing in May, 1880, and another shot at Worthing about the same time.

223. Lapwing. *Vanellus vulgaris,* Bechstein.

Abundant and resident. I think that the peewit is again increasing as a breeding species.

224. Turnstone. *Strepsilas interpres* (Linn.)

Fairly common along the coast in spring and autumn. A few remain throughout the year.

225. Oyster-catcher. *Hæmatopus ostralegus,* Linn.

This inappropriately named bird, which never catches oysters, is locally common on the coast, especially about Shoreham and Rye, where I have recently seen large flocks. Locally this species is known by the curious name of 'olive.'

226. Avocet. *Recurvirostra avocetta,* Linn.

Formerly breeding in the marshes of the county, the avocet is now only a very rare straggler in the spring. Markwick states that is was not uncommon in his days, and says that he had found a young one, just hatched, near Rye.

227. Black-winged Stilt. *Himantopus candidus,* Bonnaterre.

A very rare visitor. There are two instances of its capture in Sussex, the first at Bosham by Mr. A. Cheeseman, December, 1855, and the second on a small pond near the junction of Midhurst and Bepton Commons, May 17, 1859 (*Ibis,* 1859, p. 395). Mr. Clark Kennedy also records (*Zoologist,* 1880, p. 300) having seen a specimen near Eastbourne on May 6, 1880.

228. Grey Phalarope. *Phalaropus fulicarius* (Linn.)

An irregular autumn visitor. In some years, such as 1869, this little bird visited the coast of Sussex in considerable numbers. They as well as the following species are always exceedingly tame, and on this occasion scores of grey phalaropes fell victims to sticks and stones.

229. Red-necked Phalarope. *Phalaropus hyperboreus* (Linn.)

This species has occurred on several occasions, generally during the autumn migration, on the coast of the county; it is however much rarer than the grey phalarope. In Scotland it is now considered rare as a breeding species, but I know of one marsh, the shooting of which I rented in 1899–1900, where at least thirty pairs had bred. The tameness of this little bird is quite remarkable; near the Myvatn Lake in Iceland a female red-necked phalarope actually came and fed her young ones in some rough grass at my feet. I could certainly have touched her had I wished to do so. There are Sussex killed specimens in the possession of Mr. G. W. Bradshaw of Reading, Mr. Gilbert Knight of St. Leonards, and Mr. E. P. Overton of Hastings.

230. Woodcock. *Scolopax rusticula,* Linn.

The woodcock is resident in Sussex, and we can now claim it as a species that breeds regularly with us in small but increasing numbers. During the autumnal migration a fair number of birds visit us, especially in west Sussex about the wet ground of St. Leonards Forest. Here I have seen as many as seven woodcocks moved in a few minutes from an acre patch of birch and bracken. Of late seasons however woodcocks have not come in well during the winter months, and it is some years since we had what is known as a ' woodcock year.' Woodcocks frequently nest twice in the season, and they are amongst the earliest as well as the latest breeders. I have seen young ones able to fly in April, and once came across a family party of three still in half-down at Marthly in Scotland on August 11. Mr. Monk of Lewes, a well known collector of British birds, took the trouble to ascertain how many woodcocks remained to breed in the eastern division of Sussex, and the conclusion he arrived at was that in seven districts of east Sussex, comprising twenty-two parishes, there were annually on an average from 150 to 200 nests of this bird (*Zoologist*, 1879, p. 434).

231. Great Snipe. *Gallinago major* (J. F. Gmelin).

A rare autumn visitor. Markwick was the first to notice the occurrence of this bird in Sussex. The specimen was killed near Horsham on October 1, 1793. Since that date there are a good many instances of its capture.

232. Common Snipe. *Gallinago cœlestis* (Frenzel).

The common snipe breeds in Sussex in small numbers, and although most of their chief winter resorts are now reclaimed for agriculture fair snipe shooting is still to be had about Pulborough and Amberley. There is one instance of the occurrence of the dark variety known as Sabine's snipe. This bird was shot at Appledram Common, and purchased by Mr. Knox from Mr. Smith, a Chichester bird-stuffer, for £5 (Knox).

233. Jack Snipe. *Gallinago gallinula* (Linn.)

Fairly common in winter but as elsewhere not nearly so numerous as the last-named species.

234. Broad-billed Sandpiper. *Limicola platyrhyncha* (Temminck).

The late Mr. Borrer gives an interesting account in his book of how one day in the latter part of October, 1845, he met a boy near the west end of Brighton carrying a bunch of dunlins and amongst them one of these rare strangers, which his experienced eye had instantly detected. The ornithologist purchased the treasure for sixpence. This is the first Sussex example of this rare visitor and one of the very few that have occurred in our islands. Mr. Butterfield says that two others killed on the Sussex coast are in the possession of Mr. Boyd Alexander of Cranbrook, Kent.

235. Pectoral Sandpiper. *Tringa maculata*, Vieillot.

The only occurrence of this accidental visitor from North America is recorded by Mr. J. E. Harting in his *Handbook of British Birds* (p. 141), as having been obtained at Eastbourne in September, 1870.

236. Baird's Sandpiper. *Tringa bairdii* (Vieillot).

This sandpiper, which is fairly common in the interior of North America, has only once paid a visit to the British Islands, or in fact to Europe, and on the particular occasion on which it came Rye Harbour in Sussex was the chosen locality. Here the bird, an immature female, was shot by Mr. M. J. Nicoll on October 11, 1900. It was forwarded to Mr. Hartert of the Tring Museum, who identified it as Baird's sandpiper and showed it subsequently at one of the evening meetings of the British Ornithologists' Club.

237. Bonaparte's Sandpiper. *Tringa fuscicollis*, Vieillot.

This little sandpiper, which is very common on the east coast of North America, has occurred twice in Sussex. The first example was obtained by Mr. Kent near the village of Bexhill in a flooded meadow on October 8, 1857 (*Zoologist*, pp. 673-7). The second specimen was taken at Eastbourne on November 12, 1870, and was afterwards purchased by Mr. J. H. Gurney, who recorded its capture in the *Zoologist* (p. 2442).

238. Dunlin. *Tringa alpina*, Linn.

The most abundant of all the waders that visit our coast line.

239. Little Stint. *Tringa minuta*, Leisler.

A regular summer and autumn visitor to the coast, especially about Rye and Pagham. There are fine examples in the full breeding plumage in the collection formed by the late Mr. Booth, and I have a perfect specimen killed in June, 1860, near Chichester. I purchased the bird from the late Mr. Swaysland. In the months of August and September small parties of young birds remain for a short time on the shores. Associating as it does with flocks of dunlins, and being similar to them in its habits, it is curious that this little wader seems only very rarely to pass the winter with us.

240. Temminck's Stint. *Tringa temmincki*, Leisler.

This straggler, which does not visit us regularly, as it probably does the county of

Norfolk, comes occasionally in small parties to the mud-flats and estuaries of our tidal rivers. Usually it arrives in August, but one was shot by the late Mr. Booth on July 25, 1878, at Shoreham.

241. Curlew-Sandpiper. *Tringa subarquata* (Güldenstädt).

This sandpiper often arrives as early as May and is then in full breeding plumage, but it is not in any sense numerous till August and September, when young birds with a few old ones arrive from the arctic circle and stay till the beginning of October.

242. Purple Sandpiper. *Tringa striata*, Linn.

An autumn and winter visitor in small numbers, preferring the rocky parts of the coast. Like the phalaropes it is always remarkably tame. I have seen oyster-catchers, redshanks and purple sandpipers swim without fear from an isolated rock to the shore.

243. Knot. *Tringa canutus*, Linn.

A common autumn and winter visitor. Many knots arrive in May, and after spending a month or so on the coast they move northward to the breeding grounds, only a few staying throughout the year.

244. Sanderling. *Calidris arenaria* (Linn.)

The appearance of the sanderling on the coast is more or less coincidental with the last named species. Parties of sanderlings are very tame on their first arrival in autumn.

245. Ruff. *Machetes pugnax* (Linn.)

Formerly the ruff used to breed in small numbers on Pevensey levels, but it has long ceased to visit us except as a rare visitor in autumn.

246. Buff-breasted Sandpiper. *Tringites rufescens* (Vieillot).

In the *Zoologist* for 1843 the late Mr. Bond, in a note dated March 28, stated that a specimen of the buff-breasted sandpiper, obtained on the Sussex coast, had lately come into his possession (Borrer). This seems to be a most unusual date for this American sandpiper to have visited our shores, and I cannot help thinking that there was some mistake as to the identification of the bird.

247. Bartram's Sandpiper. *Bartramia longicauda* (Bechstein).

In the *Zoologist*, p. 9118, is recorded by Mr. Dalton of Eastbourne that he purchased at the sale of birds belonging to the late Mr. Wille of Lewes a specimen of Bartram's sandpiper shot at Newhaven some time between 1836 and 1840.

248. Common Sandpiper. *Totanus hypoleucus* (Linn.)

A regular spring and autumn visitor. Though often remaining throughout the summer, it has not been known to breed within the limits of the county.

249. Spotted Sandpiper. *Totanus macularius* (Linn.)

Two specimens of the American sandpiper were shot at the Crumbles Pond near Eastbourne in October, 1866 (Borrer).

250. Green Sandpiper. *Totanus ochropus* (Linn.)

A regular migrant in spring and autumn, but so erratic are the visits of this sandpiper that in suitable places it may be seen in any month of the year.

251. Wood-Sandpiper. *Totanus glareola* (J. F. Gmelin).

A rare autumn migrant.

252. Redshank. *Totanus calidris* (Linn.)

A resident which still breeds sparingly in Sussex. It is common on migration.

253. Spotted Redshank. *Totanus fuscus* (Linn.)

A scarce autumn migrant.

254. Greenshank. *Totanus canescens* (J. F. Gmelin).

The greenshank arrives in May on the coast but soon passes on to the northern breeding grounds. In August a few, mostly young birds, appear, and these are reinforced by others throughout September. A greenshank is seldom seen after October 18. I observed two greenshanks on Warnham Pond on July 25, 1901.

255. Bar-tailed Godwit. *Limosa lapponica* (Linn.)

So well is the summer arrival of this species known to the coast men that May 12 is known as 'Godwit day.' Like most of the summer arrivals amongst the waders it goes elsewhere to nest, but returns to us in considerable numbers in August.

256. Black-tailed Godwit. *Limosa belgica* (J. F. Gmelin).

A rare visitor on migration.

257. Curlew. *Numenius arquata* (Linn.)

A very common species in spring and autumn. It is no longer known to nest with us.

BIRDS

258. Whimbrel. *Numenius phæopus* (Linn.)

The whimbrel passes our coast in considerable numbers in May. A few also, mostly single birds, spend a short time on the Sussex coast on their way south in August and September. In north Iceland the whimbrel is so common in the nesting season that for two months, whether by day or night, the traveller is never out of hearing of their long-drawn bubbling cry. As he goes along the rough track a pair of whimbrels fly round about, each uttering their monotonous and ceaseless call. A pair of birds escort the intruder for a mile or less and then hand him over to the next pair, who in turn pass him on indefinitely.

259. Black Tern. *Hydrochelidon nigra* (Linn.)

A rare visitor in autumn. In April, 1899, I saw two of these terns flying over Warnham Pond near Horsham. Formerly the black tern bred in the Rye marshes and in the Pevensey levels.

260. White-winged Black Tern. *Hydrochelidon leucoptera* (Schinz).

Two examples of this rare tern are recorded as having been taken in Sussex. The first was killed at South Weighton near Newhaven in May, 1873 (*Field*), and the second is recorded in the same paper by Mr. Clark Kennedy, who states that one was killed some years previous to 1875 near Eastbourne.

Recently I identified a specimen of this rare tern in the small collection of birds belonging to Mr. Eardley Hall at Henfield. It was changing into winter plumage and was killed many years ago at Warnham Pond near Horsham.

261. Gull-billed Tern. *Sterna anglica,* Montagu.

The type specimen of this tern was killed in Sussex by the ornithologist Montagu, who however did not give the precise locality and date of his capture. The late Mr. Borrer and Mr. Knox each records the occurrence of this species, and there is another specimen in the Chichester Museum which was obtained at Selsey on March 31, 1852.

262. Sandwich Tern. *Sterna cantiaca,* J. F. Gmelin.

Formerly the sandwich tern bred on the sandy beaches about Rye and Winchelsea, but now a few only appear in spring and summer and pass away northward and westward to breed.

263. Roseate Tern. *Sterna dougalli,* Montagu.

This is the most graceful as well as the rarest of the terns that used to breed in small colonies on one of the Scilly Isles and on the Farnes, and it is more than likely that a pair or two still nest annually in the islands off the coast of Northumberland. A specimen lately in the collection of Mr. Rising is said to have been taken about the year 1848 near Eastbourne (*Zoologist,* 1885, p. 481).

264. Common Tern. *Sterna fluviatilis,* Naumann.

A common summer visitor to the Channel. Formerly the species bred in some numbers on the shingly beach from Rye to beyond Winchelsea, but now only a few pairs nest there in company with some lesser terns.

265. Arctic Tern. *Sterna macrura,* Naumann.

A regular summer visitor, but not in such numbers as the last named species. Formerly the arctic tern nested in colonies at Pevensey (Knox).

266. Little Tern. *Sterna minuta,* Linn.

A somewhat sparsely distributed summer visitor which arrives in May and breeds near Rye and one or two other places. In east Sussex the little tern outnumbers the common species (R. Butterfield).

267. Sabine's Gull. *Xema sabinii* (J. Sabine).

The capture of an immature specimen of this rare gull at Tide Mill near Newhaven in December, 1853, was recorded by the late Mr. W. Borrer in the *Zoologist* (p. 4408), and another was picked up at Hove in September, 1871, and is now in the collection formed by the same ornithologist. Three other specimens are also known to have occurred.

268. Bonaparte's Gull. *Larus philadelphia,* Ord.

The late Mr. Cecil Smith, a well known Somersetshire naturalist, noticed an example of this rare gull in the collection of Mr. F. Persehouse of Torquay. The owner stated that he shot the bird, an immature, at St. Leonards-on-Sea early in November, 1870 (*Zoologist,* 1883, p. 120).

269. Little Gull. *Larus minutus,* Pallas.

A rare autumn and winter visitor to the English Channel and the coast of Sussex. On the eastern side of England it is a far more frequent visitor.

270. Brown-headed Gull. *Larus ridibundus*, Linn.

This abundant and resident species is seen at all times of the year but is most common in winter. Great extremes in the variety of types are noticeable both in the young in down and the eggs of this species. During one day at the Bog of the Ring, Tullamore, Ireland, by far the largest breeding station in the British Islands, I picked up and handled some hundreds of nestlings, and out of these I kept one almost entirely yellow with hardly a dark patch and another so dark that there was hardly any yellow noticeable.

271. Common Gull. *Larus canus*, Linn.

A common winter visitor.

272. Herring-Gull. *Larus argentatus*, J. F. Gmelin.

A very common resident which breeds in small numbers on the cliff near Newhaven and at the cliff to the westward of Belle Tout Lighthouse, Eastbourne (Borrer).

273. Lesser Black-backed Gull. *Larus fuscus*, Linn.

A few adult lesser black-backs visit the coast of Sussex every spring and remain throughout the summer, whilst in the autumn immatures take their place and occasionally spend the winter with us. It is doubtful whether it breeds nearer to the Sussex coast than the Isle of Wight.

274. Great Black-backed Gull. *Larus marinus*, Linn.

A regular winter visitor in small numbers. These are generally immatures.

275. Glaucous Gull. *Larus glaucus*, Fabricius.

A rare winter visitor, appearing as a rule after continuous and heavy gales from the north. Although I went regularly to the Orkney Islands for the purpose of shooting this and the next named species I only once was so fortunate as to see and capture specimens. This was in the severe winter of 1884, and following a week of the severest snowstorms I can remember.

276. Iceland Gull. *Larus leucopterus*, Faber.

Rarer and more irregular in its appearance than the last named species.

277. Kittiwake. *Rissa tridactyla* (Linn.)

The kittiwake is found off the Sussex coast, generally at some distance from land, at all seasons, but it is most common in winter. It does not now breed in Sussex.

278. Ivory Gull. *Pagophila eburnea* (Phipps).

The late Mr. Knox stated that the ivory gull had been obtained twice within the county, and that he had seen a specimen which had been found in a dying state at St. Leonards-on-Sea. Two other examples are supposed to have occurred (Borrer).

279. Great Skua. *Megalestris catarrhactes* (Linn.)

A rare winter visitor. In confinement this fine bird makes a very tame and agreeable pet. One that I kept for some time would follow me about like a dog. It was a most voracious feeder and would swallow a squirrel whole without any apparent inconvenience.

280. Pomatorhine Skua. *Stercorarius pomatorhinus* (Temminck).

A scarce and irregular winter visitor.

281. Richardson's Skua. *Stercorarius crepidatus* (J. F. Gmelin).

A late autumn and winter visitor. I once had a fine view of the migration of this interesting bird whilst passing Cape Finisterre in Spain. As the ship in which I sailed turned northward and towards the English Channel we met large flocks of Richardson's skua flying in a southerly direction. Most of the groups were composed of some twenty individuals, but sometimes there were as many as fifty, the light and dark forms being apparently equally numerous. Now and again I noticed what was apparently a perfectly black bird without any of the golden feathers at the back of the head. The skuas seemed to fly slowly and easily and kept a considerable interval between each member of the parties. Altogether quite eight or nine hundred adult birds of this species passed close to the ship in the space of two hours, and I saw no immatures. This occurred on November 10, 1893.

282. Buffon's Skua. *Stercorarius parasiticus* (Linn.)

The late Mr. Borrer records two instances of the occurrence of this, the rarest of the skuas, in Sussex, and also states that Mr. Booth secured several in adult plumage in the spring of 1875.

283. Razorbill. *Alca torda*, Linn.

The razorbill is very common at some distance from the coast at all seasons of the year. Only a very few breed on the Sussex cliffs.

BIRDS

284. Common Guillemot. *Uria troile* (Linn.)

Common and resident like the last named species. Only a few pairs of guillemots now breed on Beachy Head.

285. Black Guillemot. *Uria grylle* (Linn.)

A rare winter straggler.

286. Little Auk. *Mergulus alle* (Linn.)

Sometimes a considerable number of little auks find their way to the south coast and are picked up dead on the seashore. Although I have not seen the subject mentioned elsewhere, I feel sure that the great number of little auks which in severe winters are driven south to the Orkneys and Shetlands never return to northern latitudes. I remember once seeing over one hundred little auks in one bay on the south coast of Pomona, and the following week the majority of them were lying on the beach. The cause of this mortality is probably due to the difficulty of obtaining food after a long storm-tossed voyage in deep water.

287. Puffin. *Fratercula arctica* (Linn.)

Adult puffins are not often seen off the Sussex coast, and those that are noticed are probably far going fishers from the Isle of Wight, where a few breed. Many immatures are washed ashore in the autumn, and like the little auk the puffin is occasionally blown inland.

288. Great Northern Diver. *Colymbus glacialis*, Linn.

There is a regular spring visitation of the adult great northern diver to the sea off the Sussex shores. Most of these however pass on early in May. In the winter again young birds come and stay from October till March.

289. Black-throated Diver. *Colymbus arcticus*, Linn.

The rarest of the three divers, occurring generally in the immature state. Adults in full summer plumage have been taken in spring (Borrer).

290. Red-throated Diver. *Colymbus septentrionalis*, Linn.

Abundant throughout the winter and departing in April. A few however stay throughout the year.

291. Great Crested Grebe. *Podicipes cristatus* (Linn.)

This beautiful bird is now steadily on the increase throughout south and central England, but Sussex is not one of its favourite counties as a breeding resort, and so far there is no record of its nest being taken within the county. The species is a regular winter visitor to the coast, and it is occasionally seen on such favourite sheets of water as Burton, Knepp and Warnham Pond.

292. Red-necked Grebe. *Podicipes griseigena* (Boddaert).

A rare winter visitor.

293. Slavonian Grebe. *Podicipes auritus* (Linn.)

A regular winter visitor, leaving the coast in March.

294. Eared Grebe. *Podicipes nigricollis* (Brehm.)

By far the rarest of the grebes that come to visit us. The late Mr. Borrer was fortunate enough to secure an adult in full summer plumage on the Salts Farm near Lancing in April, 1854. Mr. Booth too tells us that on December 10, 1879, he obtained specimens of this grebe between Worthing and Shoreham, and adds that others have been obtained of late years by local gunners.

295. Little Grebe. *Podicipes fluviatilis* (Tunstall).

Locally (at Rye), Spider Diver.

A common resident.

296. Storm-Petrel. *Procellaria pelagica*, Linn.

At times considerable numbers of this little petrel are seen in the Channel generally far from land.

297. Fork-tailed Petrel. *Oceanodroma leucorrhoa* (Vieillot).

Occasionally examples of this species are driven ashore and picked up after winter gales.

298. Wilson's Petrel. *Oceanites oceanicus* (Kuhl).

Mr. Borrer has recorded (*Zoologist*, p. 148) the only occurrence of this rare petrel on the Sussex coast.

299. Sooty Shearwater. *Puffinus griseus* (J. F. Gmelin).

It seems a curious fact that this shearwater, which is not known to breed north of New Zealand, should come all the way to Europe to spend the summer and then return south in the nesting season, and also that it should be fairly common off the central Norwegian coast, where I have seen numbers, and so rare in its visits to us. It has occurred twice on the shore of the county (Borrer).

300. Manx Shearwater.   *Puffinus anglorum* (Temminck).

A scarce visitor to the eastern part of the English Channel.

301. Little Dusky Shearwater.   *Puffinus assimilis*, Gould.

An example of this small shearwater was picked up on the beach near Bexhill during a severe gale on December 28, 1900. It is now in the possession of Sir Vauncey Crewe, and its occurrence was first recorded by Mr. Ruskin Butterfield in a note read by Mr. Hartert before the British Ornithologists' Club on February 13, 1901.

302. Fulmar.   *Fulmarus glacialis* (Linn.)

A rare winter visitor.

MAMMALS

The mammalian fauna of Sussex compares favourably with that of other English counties of which an account has been published, both with respect to the number of species and the abundance of individuals.

The circumstance that the present is the first account of Sussex mammals as a whole, and that the records relating thereto in zoological journals have been very scarce, will explain the imperfect treatment of the marine forms.

Of the bats admitted by general consent into the British list the only species hitherto unrecognized in Sussex are the lesser horseshoe bat, *Rhinolophus hipposiderus* ; the parti-coloured bat, *Vespertilio murinus* ; and the hairy-armed bat, *Pipistrellus leisleri.* The greater horseshoe and Bechstein's bat are only known to have occurred on one occasion each ; but on the other hand some species usually regarded as rare—such as the serotine, Natterer's, and the whiskered bat—are shown to be by no means infrequent.

No more need be said here of the Insectivora than that the lesser shrew appears to be common, especially in the eastern division of the county.

We may remark upon the pleasing circumstance that the badger fully holds its own in many parts. In the neighbourhood of Hastings there is hardly a parish unrepresented. This animal is in general so unobtrusive and harmless that its presence may be hardly suspected even on an estate where it is fairly numerous. After diligent inquiries we have failed to ascertain that a single Sussex polecat is preserved in any collection. With respect to the marine Carnivora the common seal is the only species included.

Coming to the Rodentia we have been able to include the yellow-necked mouse, a subspecies of the long-tailed field mouse recognized as British since 1894. The bank vole is often mistaken for the field vole, and like the latter it is subject to much variation in numbers from time to time. The black rat has disappeared, leaving behind practically no evidence of its former abundance.

In conclusion we may remark that much remains to be done, and especially in regard to the occurrence of the marine forms and the distribution of the smaller terrestrial forms. In the case of the former, examples caught near or stranded upon the shore should be photographed unless they belong to well known species. The absence of such means of identification renders useless the numerous notices of the capture of cetaceans and seals contained in the columns of local newspapers.

A HISTORY OF SUSSEX

CHEIROPTERA

1. Greater Horseshoe Bat. *Rhinolophus ferrum-equinum*, Schreber.

Like most of the rarer bats this species appears to be very restricted in its range. The greater horseshoe bat is not known as a resident within the county, and we have only been able to ascertain the capture of a single specimen, which was found hiding in the sail of a lugger on Brighton beach in January, 1890. It was sent in the flesh to Mr. Eardley Hall at Henfield, where we have recently seen it.

2. Long-eared Bat. *Plecotus auritus*, Linn.

The long-eared bat is generally distributed and common throughout the county. Mr. Borrer has recorded a 'snow-white' specimen taken in May, 1872, at Horsham; a similar specimen from the same premises was in the possession of the late Mr. Frederick Bond (*Zoologist*, 1874, p. 4128). The large ears, by which the species may easily be identified, are laid backwards along the shoulders when the animal is at rest. This bat is generally described as an inhabitant of the open country, but we have found it frequently in wooded districts, and hibernating in the same cave with Bechstein's, Natterer's and Daubenton's bats. All these species even in January will soon shake off their torpidity and fly about a room.

3. Barbastelle. *Barbastella barbastellus*, Schr. Bell [1]—*Barbastellus daubentonii*.

The only recorded instance of the barbastelle for Sussex is the statement by Mr. C. W. Brazenor that in 1886 he received a specimen from his brother, which was shot by the latter at Horsham (*Zoologist*, 1887, p. 151). On a recent visit however to Mr. Eardley Hall he showed us a beautiful specimen of this rare bat which he had taken with two others from an old summer house in his garden at Henfield in the spring of 1880. The barbastelle is easily recognized by its rich dark coat interspersed with white hair on the back. Mr. Hall, who has made a special study of the British bats and knew of the existence of this family party, says that they invariably fly by day.

4. Serotine. *Vespertilio serotinus*, Schr. Bell—*Scotophilus serotinus*.

In 1851 the late Mr. W. Borrer turned out at Cowfold fifteen specimens of this species which he had brought from Dover Castle, Kent. In the following year they were seen at Cowfold, after which they disappeared; but in 1870 or 1871 Mr. Borrer found this bat common at Henfield, and formed the opinion that his specimens had probably migrated to that place (*Zoologist*, 1874, p. 4126). There is a colony of about twenty individuals established beneath the eaves of the rectory at Guestling, Hastings. The Rev. E. N. Bloomfield writes that he first noticed them about the year 1888. They first appear about the middle of April, and are last seen towards the end of October. They are usually preceded in their vespertinal flight by the smaller species, *Plecotus auritus* and *Pipistrellus pipistrellus*. Examples of both sexes and of the young have been taken from outhouses on the estate of Mr. W. Lucas-Shadwell at Fairlight, Hastings (Ruskin Butterfield). Mr. Eardley Hall discovered a colony at the Vicarage house, Burpham, Arundel, on April 27, 1893. He noticed eighteen in all, and was so severely bitten that blood was drawn (*Zoologist*, 1893, pp. 223, 224). In the following year he also noticed a colony in Arundel church. The same observer states that the serotines are still numerous at Henfield, and that they do not fly at a high elevation like the noctule, but often close to the ground. Two bats assigned to this species by Mr. W. B. Ellis were obtained in the roof of the parish church at Arundel, October 5, 1893. Next day he received a third 'killed four miles away' (*Zoologist*, 1893, p. 458).

5. Noctule or Great Bat. *Pipistrellus noctula*, Schr.

Bell—*Scotophilus noctula*.

This species, the *Vespertilio altivolans* of Gilbert White,[2] 'from it's manner of feeding high in the air,' is common in most parts of Sussex. The late Professor T. Bell considered that the noctule was rarely seen abroad much later than July, but it may frequently be seen in August and September, and Mr. William Borrer shot one at Cowfold on November 3, 1862. The number of young produced at a birth is stated by some authorities to be two, but we have never taken more than one embryo from the same parent.

6. Pipistrelle. *Pipistrellus pipistrellus*, Schr.

Bell—*Scotophilus pipistrellus*.

[1] *A History of British Quadrupeds*, ed. 2 (1874), p. 81.

[2] *Nat. Hist. Selborne*, Letter xxxvi. to Pennant, orig. ed. p. 93.

The 'flittermouse'[1] is abundant and generally distributed in the county. In some districts it is the commonest of the bats, but in others this distinction belongs to the long-eared bat. With the exception of January we have seen bats of this species on the wing during every month of the year, and they may often be seen during bright sunshine. The pipistrelle is fond of hibernating in the summer blinds that protect the windows of Warnham Court, and we have seen a perfect shower of these bats when they were lowered in the spring time. This bat may be easily caught by attracting it with a looking-glass or reflector. Both *P. pipistrellus* and *Plecotus auritus* will take moths and insects from flowers, alighting upon them to do so, and we have known both species to settle by day on cowdung and pick off the red flies.

7. Bechstein's Bat. *Myotis bechsteini*, Leisl.
Bell—*Vespertilio bechsteinii.*

An old male of this species was shot by Mr. Ruskin Butterfield near Normanhurst, Battle, on July 28, 1896, and its identification was confirmed by the late Sir William H. Flower. The specimen is now in the Hastings Museum, and is the only one hitherto recognized in Sussex. The true position and shape of the ears of this rare species was the subject of a paper by Mr. J. G. Millais read before the Zoological Society, June, 1901. The ears of *M. bechsteini* are very large, and in life stand up perpendicularly, and not at an angle of 70° as in Bell's figure. Another noticeable feature is the great width of the gape. Two bats belonging to the late F. Bond were caught at Preston near Brighton, 1860, and were described (*Zoologist*, 1888, p. 260) as Bechstein's bats. A recent inspection, however, of the two specimens proves them to be undoubtedly assignable to *M. nattereri*.

8. Natterer's Bat. *Myotis nattereri*, Kuhl.
Bell—*Vespertilio nattereri.*

This bat is generally distributed in the county, but apparently more numerous in the western than in the eastern portion. Mr. J. E. Harting has given the following localities for Sussex in his article on the species (*Zoologist*, 1889, p. 241): Cowfold, Henfield, St. Leonards Forest (W. Borrer); Balcombe, Three Bridges (F. Bond); Poynings (Oxford Museum); Midhurst, Nigh Woods, Rogate, West Grinstead and Hellingly (Harting). Mr.

Millais has also seen several and taken specimens in the neighbourhood of Hawkins's Pond, St. Leonards Forest. In east Sussex Mr. Ruskin Butterfield has taken examples at Battle, May 13, 1898; Rye (two young ones from the walls of an old gateway), July 17, 1898; and Guestling (from a hollow tree), August 1, 1900.

Natterer's bat may be recognized by the presence of hairs upon the feet, and by the bristly margin to the interfemoral membrane towards the tip. The fur on the underparts is sometimes quite white, and when flying it is not difficult to recognize on this account. In west Sussex the species is sometimes known as the 'forest bat,' but it shows a great partiality for hawking above ponds and lakes like *M. daubentoni*, though performing its flight at a much greater elevation.

9. Daubenton's Bat. *Myotis daubentoni*, Leisl.
Bell—*Vespertilio daubentonii.*

The late Mr. W. Borrer examined specimens taken near Preston, Brighton (*Zoologist*, 1889, p. 162), and these seem to be the only bats of the species recorded for Sussex. One was taken from a hollow tree near the powder-mill ponds at Battle on May 21, 1901, and the same evening three others were observed flying over the surface of the ponds (Ruskin Butterfield). This bat may be easily distinguished on the wing by its persistent backward and forward flight close to the surface of ponds and streams, whence it will pick the insects. In the hand it may be recognized, as was pointed out by Mr. W. E. de Winton, by the circumstance that the 'spur' runs three-quarters of the distance to the tail, and there is always a notch at the end.

The species is probably more local than rare in the county. Specimens of Daubenton's bat taken by Mr. J. G. Millais were found to be infested by a very large red parasite which he did not notice as affecting bats of other species found in the same cave.

10. Whiskered Bat. *Myotis mystacinus*, Leisl.
Bell—*Vespertilio mystacinus.*

This species is probably generally distributed and not uncommon in the county, although it does not seem to have been noticed by many observers. An adult skin in the British Museum is marked 'Hastings' (*Brit. Mus. Cat. Chiroptera*, p. 315), and Mr. Borrer has recorded others from Cowfold and Lindfield (*Zoologist*, 1874, p. 4128); also Mr. Pratt received several from Horsham in

---

[1] Other Sussex names for bats are said to be 'fluttermouse' and 'flindermouse' (cf. W. D. Cooper, *Provincialisms of Sussex*, p. 19).

1895. In east Sussex this bat has been obtained in the following places : St. Leonards, Hastings, Hollington, Battle, Rye, Guestling, Catsfield, Bexhill, Udimore and Brede.

Like most of this genus the whiskered bat shows a partiality for the neighbourhood of water, but it may also be found flying in and out of trees and searching for insects close to the foliage. In flight it closely resembles the pipistrelle.

INSECTIVORA

11. Hedgehog. *Erinaceus europæus*, Linn.
Common.

12. Mole. *Talpa europæa*, Linn.
Abundant.

13. Common Shrew. *Sorex araneus*, Linn.
Common and generally distributed.

14. Pigmy Shrew. *Sorex minutus*, Pallas.
Bell—*Sorex pygmæus*.

The pigmy shrew seems to be generally distributed in east Sussex. It was first noticed near St. Leonards June 16, 1898, and afterwards taken at St. Helens, Bexhill, Hollington, Catsfield, Brede, Udimore and Lewes. In west Sussex it appears to be rare, Mr. Pratt of Brighton having only received one specimen in twenty years, yet it is probably common locally. The lesser shrew is fond of making its runs under ivied walls and is easily trapped.

15. Water Shrew. *Neomys fodiens*, Pallas.
Bell—*Sorex fodiens*.

This species is fairly numerous in suitable localities throughout the county. An albino was caught near Pevensey April 11, 1900 (Mr. Daniel Francis *in lit.*)

CARNIVORA

16. Fox. *Vulpes vulpes*, Linn.
Bell—*Vulpes vulgaris*.

Generally distributed. As an instance of the great distances these animals will travel and their homing instincts, a dog fox, half of whose brush had been removed by a gin trap, was recently hunted from Graylands, Horsham, to the South Downs, after a run which in the windings cannot have been less than forty miles. Early next morning it was found dead outside its earth at Graylands.

17. Pine Marten. *Mustela martes*, Linn.
Bell—*Martes abietum*.

'About the year 1841 a marten was caught in a rabbit-wire by one of the Duke of Norfolk's keepers at Clapham Wood near Findon ; and about the same time another and a finer one was killed at Wadhurst by Mr. Gill of Applesham. On that gentleman's death and sale of his collection this specimen was purchased by Mr. R. D. Drewitt of 53, Holland Park, Kensington, who furnished this information. A third, killed about the same time, was taken in a rabbit-wire in Michelgrove Woods, Arundel, and was for a long time in the possession of one of the Duke of Norfolk's gamekeepers. It turned up at a sale at Pettering near Arundel on August 26, 1891, but who became the purchaser I have not ascertained. The last marten believed to have been seen in the county was killed by the Crawley and Horsham foxhounds at Holmbush near Crawley five - and - twenty years ago. It was stuffed by Leadbeater of Brewer Street, London, for Mr. Borrer of Cowfold, in whose collection I have seen it. . . . It was subsequently however destroyed by moth, and only the skull is now preserved ' (Harting, *Zoologist*, 1891, pp. 457, 458). In Mr. Borrer's collection there is another marten which has all the appearance of having been mounted early in the last century. This may possibly be the other specimen which is referred to in the collector's notes as follows : ' Nov. 30, 1850. This day Thos. Broadwood, Esq., most kindly presented me with a stuffed specimen of the marten shot at the back of his house, Holmbush, Horsham, in the year 1825. This is the last I have heard of killed in Sussex. I think it is immature.' This stuffed specimen has no birdstuffer's name on the back of the case. It is certainly immature ; and it cannot be the same as the specimen previously noticed, because Mr. Borrer himself acknowledges receiving the mounted specimen in its case.

18. Polecat. *Putorius putorius*, Linn.
Bell—*Mustela putorius*.

A polecat was killed at Udimore, Rye, in October, 1848, by the gamekeeper to Mr. F. Langford (J. B. Ellman, *Zoologist*, p. 2406).

The late Sir Anchitel Ashburnham told Mr. Ruskin Butterfield in 1897 that he recollected a very fine polecat being trapped at Broomham, Hastings, ' about thirty years since.' Major Sir Archibald Lamb writes that one was caught at Beauport, Battle, when he was a boy. The Rev. E. N. Bloomfield has information of another said to have been seen at Ecclesbourne near Hastings about sixteen years ago. There is little doubt that the polecat has been extinct for many years in Sussex, most of those now figuring in the naturalist's shop being escaped tame ones.

19. Stoat. *Putorius ermineus*, Linn.
Bell—*Mustela erminea.*

Common and generally distributed. Examples in the perfect winter dress are rarely met with, there being almost always some of the ordinary colour remaining about the head ; but every year individuals are trapped which have partially assumed the winter pelage. One day whilst sitting under a tree in Denne Park, Horsham, Mr. Millais observed a large stoat emerge from a small rabbit warren close at hand. There were about fifty rabbits round about and none of these betrayed the slightest alarm at the presence of the stoat. After running about for a few minutes the stoat made a rush at a young rabbit and knocked it over as if in play, and then commenced mauling it about the neck and pretending to worry it. The rabbit meanwhile crouched down and evidently was not very frightened, as it commenced feeding again as soon as its persecutor left it. The stoat then went up to two other rabbits and repeated the same performance, every movement of which could be distinctly seen through a powerful telescope. It was then apparently satisfied, and retired to one of the holes, into which it presently disappeared. There is not the least doubt that this cunning fellow was making his home amongst the rabbits on whose young he lived, and that this daily play was practised so as to accustom his nervous neighbours to the presence of the murderer.

20. Weasel. *Putorius nivalis*, Linn.
Bell—*Mustela vulgaris.*

Common and generally distributed. On more than one occasion individuals have been caught on the sea-front at St. Leonards. It is a pity that gamekeepers are so relentless in their persecution of this graceful little animal. The damage it does to game is more than outweighed by its services in keeping down the numbers of voles and rats which unquestionably constitute its chief prey. The tenacity with which the weasel will stick to its prey is remarkable. Recently when shooting with Mr. Fletcher at Dale Park, Arundel, we saw a weasel chase and seize a half-grown rat on the side of a steep down. The pursuer had not a very good hold, so that the victim could make some resistance, and both came rolling down the hill, a distance of nearly a hundred yards, and landed almost at our feet without separating.

21. Badger. *Meles meles*, Linn.
Bell—*Meles taxus.*

The badger is by no means uncommon in east Sussex, and at present there is little danger of any serious diminution, as in many parts the animal is protected. There are at the present time colonies of greater or less extent at the following places, viz. Ashburnham, Battle, Beauport, Catsfield, Crowhurst Park, Fairlight, Guestling (Broomham Park), Hollington, Pett, Sedlescombe, Udimore, Westfield, Winchelsea (Wickham Cliff).

Sir Archibald Lamb, Bart., of Beauport writes that some time since a terrier belonging to Colonel Lamb went to ground after the badgers and had to be dug out. During the operation a litter of recently-born badgers was disturbed, and Colonel Lamb is certain that there were six, if not seven, in the litter. In 1893—a great wasp year—the badgers at Beauport devoured between thirty and forty wasp nests during two ensuing nights. Mr. George Bristow, jun., to whom we are indebted for many particulars of Sussex mammals, has weighed several badgers which have scaled over 30 lb.

In west Sussex the badger continues to hold its own in nearly all the heavily wooded districts, and we know of one protected spot within three miles of Brighton where they are always to be found. In a wood with which we are acquainted foxes and badgers have made earths together, and have lived for some years in comparative harmony. Occasionally however there are squabbles, and when these occur the latter invariably get the best of it, young foxes having been found dead at the mouth of the badger hole.

22. Otter. *Lutra lutra*, Linn.
Bell—*Lutra vulgaris.*

Otters have been met with in most of the larger streams of the eastern part of the county. Specimens have been killed at Rye, Pett, Brede, Ninfield, Sedlescombe, Ashburnham and Pevensey. In the west there are always a few resident on the Adur and the Arun, whilst a season seldom passes without individuals being seen or their tracks noted on the lakes in St. Leonards Forest. The ponds at Knepp Castle and Burton Park are other favourite places, and in 1891 a pair of otters stayed the whole season at Warnham Pond and successfully reared a litter there.

23. Common Seal. *Phoca vitulina*, Linn.

A not infrequent visitant to Sussex waters, but unfortunately it seems to have been no one's business to place on permanent record precise particulars of the occurrences. A specimen was shot in the river Arun about seven miles from the sea, and examined by Mr. Percy E. Coombe (*Zoologist*, 1897, p. 571). A fine specimen was shot by Mr. Chas. Cook on Pett Levels, January 11, 1901, and brought to the Hastings fishmarket to be sold by Mr. W. M. Adams. Whilst bathing one day near Brighton Mr. E. Molyneux of St. Leonards found a large seal, presumably of this species, floating in an exhausted condition. He took it to the Brighton Aquarium, but it only survived for a few days.

RODENTIA

24. Squirrel. *Sciurus leucourus*, Kerr.
  Bell—*Sciurus vulgaris*.

Abundant throughout the county, especially where the various species of firs are cultivated.

25. Dormouse. *Muscardinus avellanarius*, Linn.
  Bell—*Myoxus avellanarius*.

Although perhaps nowhere very common, the dormouse is pretty generally distributed in Sussex. Holes in banks or in trees are mostly selected as *hybernacula*, but the period of torpidity is sometimes passed in a nest built in a bush like the ordinary summer nest.

26. Brown Rat. *Mus decumanus*, Pallas.

In the autumn of 1900 a great migration of brown rats took place into north-west Sussex. All the banks in the neighbourhood of Rusper, Horsham, Slinfold and Southwater were riddled with the roadways of these pests, and they are still in such numbers that they will come forth into the open fields to feed in broad daylight. Apparently they have not as yet invaded the buildings in force, and will probably move on to new grounds as soon as the food supply becomes scarce. A male killed at Warnham Court in 1900 was measured by Mr. Millais. It taped $19\frac{1}{2}$ inches, and is the largest specimen we have ever seen.

Albinos are extremely rare, but pied varieties are comparatively common. The late Mr. William Borrer has recorded an adult female and two young of the 'black variety' of *M. decumanus* taken early in May, 1877, near Rottingdean (*Zoologist*, 1877, p. 292).

27. Black Rat. *Mus rattus*, Linn.

Mr. R. M. Christy found a black rat lying dead on the mud at Shoreham Harbour in April, 1880, and about two months later another under similar circumstances nearer to Brighton (Harting, *Essays on Sport and Natural History*, p. 161). Upon investigation it does not appear that the species survives in any part of the county.

[Examples of the form *M. alexandrinus* (readily distinguished from the common brown rat by its large ears and very long tail) are sometimes caught near the harbour at Shoreham. Two of these caught in 1898 are in the possession of Mr. Daniel Francis. These rats have probably been brought into the harbour by ships.]

28. House Mouse. *Mus musculus*, Linn.
Abundant.

29. Long-tailed Field Mouse. *Mus sylvaticus*, Linn.
Abundant.

30. Yellow-necked Mouse. *Mus flavicollis*, Melchior.

This mouse, first recognized as British in 1894 by Mr. W. E. de Winton,[1] will probably prove to be by no means infrequent in the county. Specimens have been trapped by Mr. Ruskin Butterfield on the railway embankment near Crowhurst, June 13, 1899, and April 8, 1901. Through the kindness of Mr. de Winton these have been compared with a specimen from Herefordshire. Others have also been taken in 1900 at Balcombe, and two of these were sent to Mr. Millais by Mr. de Winton. Mr. Millais has also trapped in his garden at Horsham a specimen with a pale yellow throat, and there is little doubt that *M. flavicollis* interbreeds with true *M. sylvaticus*. In fact the dentition of the two forms is similar and their habits identical.

31. Harvest Mouse. *Mus minutus*, Pallas.

Apparently the harvest mouse always had a somewhat restricted range in Sussex, seldom being found further east than Brighton, west of Worthing or north of Henfield and Pulborough. Fifty years ago it was extremely plentiful both in the corn and grass fields between Henfield and Brighton, and Knox mentions having often found remains in the pellets and crops of the kestrel ; but it is now a scarce

---

[1] *Zoologist*, 1894, p. 441.

animal, and has left its old breeding haunts in the long stubbles and rears its young in stacks of both hay and corn. Its diminutive size causes it to escape notice, but locally it is still common to the north-west of Brighton. In east Sussex the harvest mouse occurs near Westfield, as we are informed by Mr. Michael J. Nicoll of St. Leonards.

32. Water Vole. *Microtus amphibius*, Linn.
Bell—*Arvicola amphibius*.

The water vole is common in suitable haunts throughout the county. Examples in the dark 'phase' have been met with near Pevensey and Chichester. Mr. W. Jeffery, jun., in a note to *The Zoologist* (July, 1865, p. 9706) records that he shot a full grown specimen near Ratham on May 21, 1863, and a second near the same place on May 22, 1865. It remains to add that an albino was obtained near Hurstpierpoint in April or May, 1874 (*Zoologist*, ser. 2, p. 4074).

33. Field Vole. *Microtus agrestis*, Linn.
Bell—*Arvicola agrestis*.

Abundant and widely distributed. A pure white specimen with *black* eyes was brought to Mr. G. Bristow, jun., from Hollington on July 13, 1893. It was kept for some time alive, but on the appearance of a few dark hairs its owner killed it.

34. Bank Vole. *Evotomys glareolus*, Schr.
Bell—*Arvicola glareolus*.

Common and generally distributed throughout Sussex.

35. Common Hare. *Lepus europæus*, Pallas.
Bell—*Lepus timidus*.

In the north and west of the county hares have undergone sad diminution of late years, but are still abundant on all the large estates near the South Downs. We have seen numbers at Petworth, Arundel and Dale Park.

36. Rabbit. *Lepus cuniculus*, Linn.
Very abundant.

UNGULATA

37. Red Deer. *Cervus elaphus*, Linn.

Red deer were from the earliest times indigenous to the wooded districts of England, and amongst the first records of history we learn that the Saxon kings hunted deer in the forests of Sussex.[1] A new era may be said to have arrived after the Norman Conquest, when William, his barons and dependants, hunted for sport as well as for the primary consideration of fresh meat, and there is more than one mention in ancient archives that the king himself loved to hunt the stag in the great forests of oak and beech that stretched from Kent to Hants and from the South Downs to London and its immediate environs. So popular indeed was the pastime that enclosed spaces of forest land in which the chase could be enjoyed were set apart, and these were the origin of our parks. The increase of parks continued until the time of the Commonwealth, when the Roundheads with their desire to make all things equal ruthlessly tore down the fences and allowed the deer to escape. Up to this date a constant destruction of timber had been in progress, the trees being felled for the purposes of iron smelting, and also for glass making and salterns; and consequently the wild creatures found their haunts more and more curtailed as time went

on. At the restoration of Charles II. however the squires were once more in the ascendant, and immediately began again to form their deer parks, and many of our best known enclosures have their origin from this date, although some survived the general destruction and were maintained unimpaired throughout these troublous times. It may be mentioned that owing to the destruction of forest trees Charles II. issued an order that the whole of the forest now known as St. Leonards should be afforested and made into a deer park, a somewhat questionable method of saving the young timber, as all growing copse wood was at once destroyed by the deer that speedily began to increase. But little now remains of the ancient forest of Anderida except the small portions known as the forests of St. Leonards, Tilgate and Ashdown,[1] whilst a smaller woodland known as Charlton Forest is also generally supposed to have formed a part of it.

Queens Mary and Elizabeth both hunted wild deer in Sussex, and there is little doubt that a few existed at the end of the eighteenth century in the forest of St. Leonards, which even at that late date was of so wild a character and bore such an evil reputation that travellers to Brighton preferred to make the journey from London by way of Kent, but it is not certain when the last wild red deer were killed. Nowadays the few that are scattered through

---

[1] The ancient forest of Anderida is thus described by the Venerable Bede, who lived about the year 731: 'It is thick and inaccessible . . . and a place of shelter for large herds of deer and swine, as well as wolves.'

[1] Now only a forest in name. The country about Ashdown is mostly moorland.

the forests of St. Leonards and Tilgate are usually hinds that have escaped from the Surrey or Warnham staghounds and have no chance of perpetuating their species, as no uncut stags are hunted nowadays.

The following parks in Sussex contain red deer, the number in each enclosure being compiled either from Mr. Whitaker's *Deer Parks and Paddocks of England* or from the result of recent visits made by Mr. Millais:—

Arundel (owner, the Duke of Norfolk, K.G.) . 40
Ashburnham (owner, the Earl of Ashburnham) 15
Brickwall (owner, Edward Frewen, Esq.). . 60
Buckhurst (owner, the Earl De La Warr and
    Buckhurst) 300
Eridge (owner, the Marquess of Abergavenny,
    K.G.) 100
Warnham Court (owner, Charles Lucas, Esq.) 157

Formerly red deer were also kept at Denne, Ladyholt and Petworth. The red deer of Eridge are remarkably fine, whilst those of Warnham Court have no superior in England. A stag which was killed in this park in 1894 carried 45 points, and some of his dropped antlers of the previous years were even larger—1888, 29 points, $9\frac{1}{2}$ lb.; 1889, 34 points, $12\frac{1}{2}$ lb.; 1890, 34 points, $13\frac{1}{2}$ lb.; 1891, 37 points, 16 lb.; 1892, 47 points, 17 lb.; 1893, 45 points, $16\frac{1}{2}$ lb.

At present (1901) there are three remarkable stags alive in this park, carrying respectively 22, 24, 27 points, the weight of horns shed in March of the last named being $15\frac{1}{2}$ lb. Park lands for deer can be greatly improved by dressing every third season with a preparation of bone dust, lime and phosphates.

38. Fallow Deer. *Cervus dama*, Linn.

Although many naturalists accept the theory that fallow deer were introduced by the Romans either from Asia Minor or the Isles of Greece there is really no contradictory evidence to prevent the supposition that they were not as perfectly indigenous to Great Britain as the red deer and roe, owing their descent direct from what is called *Cervus browni*, an animal whose form must have been identical with our present species. *C. browni* was certainly a finer animal, and his remains have recently been found in some quantity amongst the brick earths of the Thames valley, and though there appears to be a certain gap between this and the historic period, a gap filled up in the case of the red deer and the roe, we really see no reason why our animal should not have been directly descended from native stock. From the date of the Norman Conquest the history of the fallow deer in Sussex is practically the same as his larger

relation. They were hunted in a wild state and kept in parks, and were on the whole always more popular in a general sense owing to their prolificness and superior venison.

Nowadays there are always a few fallow deer living in comparative security and a wild state in the forest of Tilgate and the woods about Kingsfold, and in both of these places we have seen them when shooting. They owe their freedom to having escaped from the parks, and there are now no wild fallow deer in Sussex in the true sense of the word.

Fallow deer are kept in the following parks :—

Arundel (owner, the Duke of Norfolk, K.G.) 600
Ashburnham (owner, the Earl of Ashburn-
    ham). 200
Brickwall (owner, Edward Frewen, Esq.) . 80
Brightling (owner, Henry J. Nicoll, Esq.) . 11
Buckhurst (owner, the Earl De La Warr and
    Buckhurst) 300
Burton (owner, Anthony John Biddulph,
    Esq.). 150
Buxted (owner, Lord Portman) 250
Cowdray (owner, the Earl of Egmont) . . 350
Cuckfield (owner, Captain Sergison) . . . 140
Denne (owner, Mrs. Eversfield) 250
Eridge (owner, the Marquess of Aberga-
    venny, K.G.), about 450
Parham (owner, Lord Zouche) 250
Petworth (owner, the Lord Leconfield) . . 900
Saint Hill (owner, Edgar March Crook-
    shank, Esq.). 40
Up (owner, Miss Fetherstonhaugh) . . . 1,000
Warnham Court (owner, Charles Lucas, Esq.) 52
West Grinstead (owner, Sir Meyrick Burrell,
    Bart.) 350
Wiston (owner, the Rev. John Goring) . . 300

The fallow deer of Sussex are second to none both in size and the superiority of their venison, and those now at Petworth are certainly the finest in Great Britain. The heads of those that have been 'fatted' grow to a very large size, and Mr. Millais has one whose horns and upper part of the skull weigh 8 lb. 1 oz.

39. Roe Deer. *Capreolus capreolus*, Linn.
Bell—*Capreolus caprea*.

Very few prehistoric roe horns have been unearthed in Sussex, but there is good reason to believe that the species was numerous and even abundant in Pleistocene times owing to the great numbers which undoubtedly existed close at hand along the southern bank of the Thames. It is not known at what period roe became extinct within the county, but their disappearance certainly took place at an earlier date than in the western counties and probably within historic times.

At present roe deer are only found within

MAMMALS

the boundaries of the fine old walled park at Petworth, and cannot be considered as a purely feral animal as their range is restricted. The date of their introduction to this enclosure is not known to Lord Leconfield, who has kindly sent the following note : 'I have been quite unable to find any records to show when the roe were imported or how they got into the park at Petworth. The portion which they inhabit was originally a wild and rough bit of ground where red deer were kept. These were destroyed by my grandfather and this part of the park was ploughed up. The roe deer which were there at the time were however preserved and are there still. It is, I fear, impossible to correctly estimate their

numbers. Some years ago, within my recollection, there were only seven left when my father introduced a change of blood from Scotland and once more put them on their legs again, and there are now quite a good stock.' About six or seven bucks are killed annually. Sir Edmund Loder, Bart., has on more than one occasion tried roe at Leonardslee, but they have never thriven well there in spite of the excellent natural protection and wild ground apparently so well suited to their habits. The last buck died at Leonardslee in 1897. It is not improbable that at some future date wandering roe may find their way from Hampshire where they are now increasing.

CETACEA

40. **Common Rorqual.** *Balænoptera musculus,* Linn. *B. physalus* (Linn.). True.

This cetacean may fairly claim a place amongst the Sussex mammals as it is the commonest whale that visits the Channel.[1] It has been frequently seen by those qualified to give an opinion, although there is no actual record of its capture unless we accept the following note taken from Mrs. Merrifield's *A Sketch of the Natural History of Brighton,* 1860, p. 114 : 'About the year 1833 or 1834 a large whale 70 feet in length and 35 feet in circumference was stranded on the shore near Roe-dean turnpike gate. The blubber was melted down into oil, and the enormous skeleton, after being cleaned, was again put together and exhibited on the level as a show. The jaw bones were set up in

[1] Old records show that the 'Oyl fish' industry was at one time largely carried on in the Channel. The object of the chase was probably the members of this species, which seems to have been common.

Mr. Bass's garden.' Mr. Lydekker says that specimens of this whale are 'stranded on the British coasts, more especially those of the southern parts of England.'

41. **Porpoise.** *Phocæna communis,* Lesson.

A common and regular summer visitor to the Channel.

42. **Risso's Grampus.** *Grampus griseus,* Cuv.

A young male assigned to this species was captured at Siddlesham in west Sussex in July, 1875, and kept alive for some hours at the Brighton Aquarium.

[**Common Dolphin.** *Delphinus delphis,* Linn.

A probable visitor. In the Second Supplement (1888) to *The Natural History of Hastings and St. Leonards and the Vicinity* the dolphin is added to the list of cetaceans, but no particulars are given of the alleged occurrence.]

REFERENCE

— Palæolithic Implements

✻ Miscellaneous Finds, *Neolithic implements, coins, &c.*

✕ Bronze Implements

Scale of Miles

0   2   4   6   8   10

The Edinburgh Geographical Institute

J.G. Bartholomew

EARLY MAN

THE prehistoric antiquities of Sussex are very important and numerous, and entitle the county to a position second only to Kent among the counties of the south-east of England. Every sub-division of the prehistoric period is represented by the contents of the museums at Lewes, Chichester, Brighton, Hastings and Eastbourne, and by other objects found in Sussex which are in the British Museum and in various private collections. To attempt to describe in detail all these antiquities would be impossible within the scope of the present article. A topographical list of discoveries at the end of this article, and a map marked so as to show the distribution of prehistoric antiquities of various kinds throughout the county, will, it is hoped, make it easy to form an idea of the evidences upon which the earliest part of the story of Sussex is founded.

The prehistoric era, commencing with the first appearance of man and ending with the Roman occupation of Britain, is usually divided into the following sections or ages : (1) Palæolithic Age, (2) Neolithic Age, (3) Bronze Age, and (4) Prehistoric Iron Age. It is proposed to follow this arrangement in dealing with the subject of Early Man in Sussex, but at the very beginning it may be well to explain that these several ages must be regarded, not as indicating particular periods of time, but as representing successive stages in culture.

As far as Sussex and Britain generally are concerned there is reason to believe that the first appearance of man is associated with the Palæolithic Age, when stone tools were shaped by chipping and when the grinding or polishing of stone was an unknown art. The 'Eolithic Age,' as it has been called, which by some is supposed to have preceded the Palæolithic, and to be represented by tools of immensely ruder types, is not universally accepted, and further evidence must be produced before the suspiciously irregular forms of what have been called 'eolithic implements' can be acknowledged to have been formed by man.

THE PALÆOLITHIC AGE

It is usual to consider this the earlier of the two ages of stone, and there can be no question that such was the case, but the use of the term 'Stone Age' is perhaps open to the objection that it seems to imply that stone alone was used for tools, weapons, and other articles. If the term 'Pre-metallic Age' could be substituted it would perhaps prevent the possibility of this form of misconception. In the Palæolithic Age not only was stone employed, but weapons and tools were made of bone, horn, wood, and doubtless other substances. In the working of flint, however, man does not seem to have discovered the art of shaping it by grinding. Chipping in bold, skilful fashion, so as to detach large fragments by each blow, was characteristic of the palæolithic tool-maker.

Comparatively few palæolithic remains have been found in Sussex. Sir John Evans, however, records the discovery of implements at Bell's Farm, Friston, near Eastbourne ; at East Dean ; and in the so-called Elephant-bed near Brighton.

In 1893 a small ovate implement, about 3 in. by $2\frac{1}{4}$ in., was found on high ground at Midhurst, which is now in the possession of Mr. R. C. Fisher.

In 1897 Mr. William Hayden of Chichester found a well-made palæolithic implement at Appledram. It is of somewhat ovoid form at present, but its shape has been considerably modified by injuries. The edge particularly has been broken, and the owner has repaired the damage, not quite satisfactorily, by restoration in putty. It measures $5\frac{1}{2}$ in. by $3\frac{1}{4}$ in., but has clearly been somewhat larger in its complete state.

Another distinctly palæolithic implement, about $3\frac{1}{2}$ in. by $2\frac{1}{2}$ in., believed to have been obtained in the Broadwater district, is now in the possession of Mr. Frank Lasham of Guildford.

The discovery of a fine boldly-struck flake of palæolithic character at Wiggonholt, in 1904, by Mr. W. Paley Baildon, F.S.A., suggested to Mr. R. Garraway Rice, F.S.A., the advisability of putting upon record all the available details of palæolithic implements already found in Sussex. It induced him, moreover, to make careful examinations for further specimens, particularly in the river-gravels of the Arun and the western Rother in and around the Pulborough district. The result of Mr. Rice's researches has been to add three more palæolithic sites to Sussex, viz. Coates, Fittleworth and Greatham. The implements from Fittleworth much resemble those already mentioned as having been discovered at Midhurst and in the Broadwater district ; whilst the large and somewhat roughly shaped implement found at Coates measures rather over $5\frac{1}{2}$ in. in length and is of a distinct type. Mr. Rice communicated, 2 February 1905, to the Society of Antiquaries of London a minute account of these various Sussex discoveries, and his paper will be found in *Proceedings*, vol. xx. pt. 2.

THE NEOLITHIC AGE

This age, in England at any rate, is believed to have been separated from the Palæolithic Age by something more than an advance in culture. It is probable that important physical changes took place, during which, what we now know as the British Isles was separated from the continent of Europe. On the continent, probably, there was continuity of human life, but it seems improbable that this was the case within these islands.

objects to every one who knows this coast. Their weather-worn fissures extend for considerable distances into the rock, and generally speaking are sufficiently broad to serve as galleries along which one can walk. In a few places they are wide enough to accommodate several people. It is remarkable that the suitability of such a place as this for a primitive rock-shelter should not long ago have occurred to the minds of archæologists ; but the general impression seems to have been that the weathering and disintegration of the sandstone of which the rocks are composed advanced at a much greater speed than has actually been shown to have been the case, and that as a consequence the deep ravines, fissures, and channels as we now see them could never have served as shelters for prehistoric man. About the year 1878, however, Mr. R. Garraway Rice found among the loose sand at the bottoms of the fissures numerous flint implements of a neolithic character and fragments of pottery. From that time onward both he and other antiquaries, particularly Mr. W. J. Lewis Abbott, F.G.S., have continued to find evidences of an extensive neolithic population at this point. A little before the year 1895 the latter gentleman made a careful exploration of the ground just round Castle Hill. Upon removing the superficial layer of washed or blown-sand, about a foot thick, ' the middens,' writes Mr. Abbott,[1] ' are reached ; probably about nine-tenths of the material is dirt, the rest, relics of man's occupation, which therefore occur in bushels. They embraced the whole paraphernalia of the life of the period, and consisted chiefly of shells of molluscs, bones of animals, birds and fishes, stone and bone implements and pottery.'

It is noteworthy that the bones of such animals as the small ox (*Bos longifrons*) and the wild boar (*Sus scrofa*), which were found in all sizes, had always been split open for the sake of the marrow, and in two cases Mr. Abbott found a flint wedge still fixed in the bone as it had been left by prehistoric man. It would be difficult to find a more convincing proof of the neolithic age of this site than is afforded by the use of flint wedges for a purpose for which metal implements, had they been obtainable, would have served so much better. The other bones found consisted of those of the sheep or goat (in abundance), the roe, the fox, the badger, three kinds of birds, about six species of fish, and shells of many kinds of shell fish.

The flint implements which have been found in great numbers are divisible, in Mr. Abbott's[2] opinion, into three groups. First, there was a minor group of the ordinary neolithic forms, such as are found practically all over the country. Secondly, there was a large group containing forms identical both in general appearance and detail of secondary work with those found in the French caves. Thirdly, there was a group of minute and highly specialized forms. The last group includes some very small fragments of delicately chipped flint, possibly intended for the barbs of fish-hooks, and other purposes.

[1] *Journal of the Anthropological Institute*, xxv. 124.   [2] Ibid. p. 126.

EARLY MAN

The Neolithic Age is well represented in Sussex by a large number of antiquities, such as stone implements and earthworks. Sussex, like Kent, has had the advantage of much research and observation at the hands of competent archæologists, and discoveries have been recorded from practically every part of the county. The distribution of the neolithic remains, however, is so instructive that it seems desirable to devote a few words to that subject before proceeding to deal with the more important antiquities discovered.

The chalk hills extending from Beachy Head westward across the southern part of Sussex at a distance of from 3 to 8 miles from the sea-shore, and generally known as the South Downs, form what is unquestionably the most prominent of the physical features of the county. On the surface of these Downs, particularly on the southern slopes, numerous flint implements, mostly scrapers, simple flakes and cores, have been discovered, pointing perhaps to the temporary rather than the settled presence of neolithic man.

It is abundantly proved that the chief population of Sussex in neolithic times was in the more immediate neighbourhood of the sea-coast or rivers. Indeed, the preference for waterside situations usually shown by early man is well illustrated in the case of Sussex, where a long sea-coast and numerous and circuitous rivers offered suitable conditions for residence. The simple fact is that until the art of well-boring was introduced or the alternative of dew-ponds discovered, it was practically impossible for any considerable number of people to live far away from the banks of the rivers or the sea-coast. Fish in the rivers and in the sea would furnish a reliable form of food which could hardly fail to attract the greater part of the inhabitants of the district. One has only to note the traces of the various neolithic settlements round the coast of Sussex in order to realize the truth of this.

Earthworks in the form of hill-top camps, enclosing the highest points of the South Downs, are comparatively abundant in Sussex, and many are probably as old as the neolithic period, although some at any rate show traces of having been occupied by later races. In the absence of any sufficiently definite and precise evidence as to the period to which these remains belong, however, it has been considered best to describe all the Sussex earthworks together in a separate section, dealing with them with reference to their forms and plans rather than on theoretical grounds as to their chronological sequence.

Barrows or sepulchral mounds are well represented among the pre-historic earthworks of Sussex, but they belong for the most part to the Bronze Age. At Seaford, however, and possibly elsewhere, there has been found evidence of neolithic interments.[1]

The traces of a neolithic population on the Sussex sea-coast are abundant and important. Commencing at the eastern end of the county the Hastings kitchen middens call for special notice. The rocks on the cliff between the castle and the sea are very familiar

[1] A list of barrows and tumuli in Sussex will be found in the article on Ancient Earthworks.

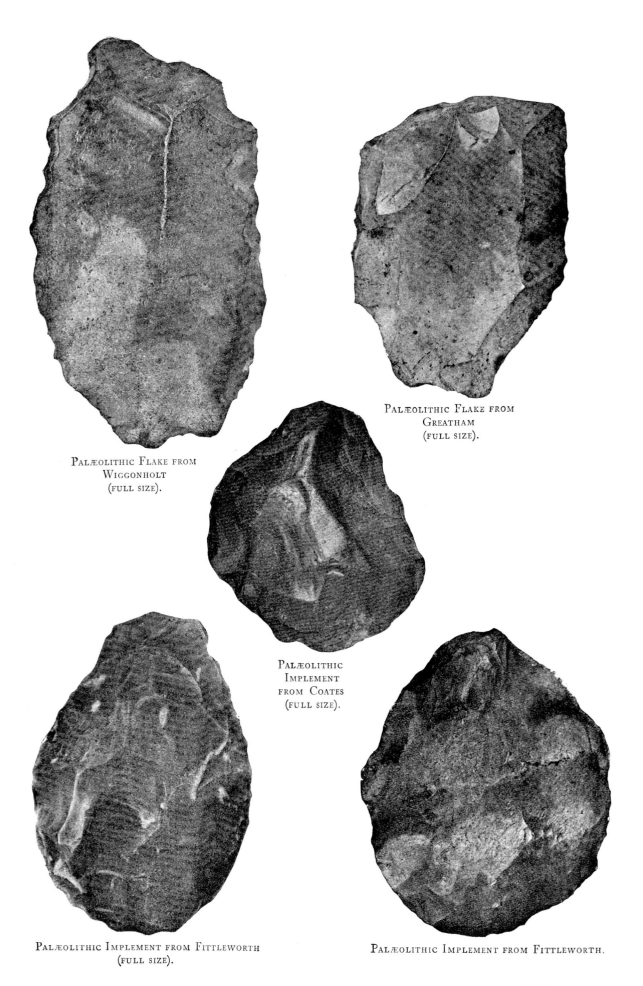

PALÆOLITHIC FLAKE FROM
WIGGONHOLT
(FULL SIZE).

PALÆOLITHIC FLAKE FROM
GREATHAM
(FULL SIZE).

PALÆOLITHIC
IMPLEMENT
FROM COATES
(FULL SIZE).

PALÆOLITHIC IMPLEMENT FROM FITTLEWORTH
(FULL SIZE).

PALÆOLITHIC IMPLEMENT FROM FITTLEWORTH.

To face p. 310.

PALÆOLITHIC IMPLEMENT FROM THE BROADWATER
DISTRICT (FULL SIZE).

PALÆOLITHIC IMPLEMENT FROM MIDHURST
(FULL SIZE).

PALÆOLITHIC IMPLEMENT FROM APPLEDRAM
(FULL SIZE).

PALÆOLITHIC IMPLEMENT FROM COATES
(FULL SIZE).

To face p. 312.

It has been suggested that these last types of instruments belong to the latter end of the neolithic period.

The pottery, judging from the specimens which have been examined by the present writer, points to a period extending from the Bronze Age to the Romano-British period ; and its association with flint implements suggests a survival of neolithic forms in stone implements extending down to the period of the Roman occupation, rather than that the pottery is itself of the neolithic period.

Pevensey Castle marks the site of another neolithic quarter where flint implements were produced in large numbers.

Evidences of neolithic man in the neighbourhood of Beachy Head and Eastbourne have been found in great abundance, by far the larger number of implements having been found by Mr. Stephen Blackmore of East Dean, a shepherd. His collection, which has been made whilst tending sheep on the downs and in the fields, contains some very beautiful examples of chipped and ground implements. It is said to be one of the finest collections of neolithic flint implements in private hands in England.[1] Selections of implements found in this district are exhibited in the museums at Lewes, Brighton, and the Brassey Institute, Hastings, but by far the best specimens remain in the possession of the finder.

The whole district around Eastbourne and Beachy Head must have once had a large neolithic population, and characteristic implements of flint and also hammer-stones formed of a species of slaty stone procured from the sea-beach, have been found and are still to be found scattered over practically the entire surface. Implements are specially abundant at some points, and Mr. H. S. Toms, of the Brighton Museum, has been good enough to indicate to the writer three such spots in the Beachy Head district, viz.—(1) the northern slope of Crapham Hill, (2) Pea Down, and (3) a place called the Peak, a spur of the Downs.

Along the whole extent of the southern slope of the South Downs neolithic implements, flakes and chips are abundant. It may suffice to mention a few places where they have been specially noted : (1) Near Black Rock, Brighton ; (2) near the Booth Museum, Dyke Road, Brighton ; (3) half-way between the Clock Tower, Brighton, and the Devil's Dyke ; (4) Lychpole Hill; (5) another point about 400 yards to the east of it ; and (6) still another point on a spur of the Downs, the last three places being near Cissbury Hill, which is more or less covered by flint chips, flakes, and implements. At Appledram, about $1\frac{1}{2}$ miles to the south-west of Chichester, there are evidences of a somewhat extensive factory where large numbers of implements, particularly of small types, have been made. Flakes, cores, and waste chips of flint lie plentifully scattered on the eastern foreshore of the most eastern arm of Chichester Harbour, especially at a point near Appledram Church. Mr. W. Hayden of Chichester, who discovered this deposit and who has collected a large number of flint implements and fragments, kindly pointed out the site to the present writer. There appears to be a well-

[1] *Sussex Arch. Coll.* xxxix. 97.

defined layer of chips and implements, doubtless representing the surface of the ground in neolithic times. This layer where exposed, lies at a level about 4 feet below that of the surrounding marsh meadows, but of course the layer can be seen only where the tides, in consequence of changes at the mouth of the harbour, are washing away the silty deposit.

The flakes have for the most part been well made out of selected flint ; some of them bear evidence of secondary work ; and some of the better and straighter specimens have been broken obliquely across, apparently in order to procure arrow-heads or teeth for sickles. They resemble the flint flakes of similar character found some years ago at Millfield, Keston, Kent.[1]

The flint mines at Cissbury Hill form a very important piece of evidence as to the condition of the neolithic inhabitants of Sussex, and they point to a very high degree of civilization. The camp itself will be dealt with in the section relating to earthworks. On the western side of that enclosure there are numerous pits from 10 ft. to 70 ft. in diameter, and from 5 ft. to 7 ft. deep. In and around them numerous flint flakes and implements, as well as waste chips, a few bones, land shells, charcoal, and fragments of coarse pottery have been discovered, and they possibly mark the sites of rude neolithic huts. Close examination of some of these pits, however, has proved that they really cover deeper excavations leading to galleries which have been made in order to reach a band of flints of a particularly suitable kind for the manufacture of implements. Mr. E. H. Willett,[2] who conducted some explorations on the site subsequently to General Pitt-Rivers's investigations, discovered many important traces of prehistoric workings for flint, and much of the same character as those investigated by Canon Greenwell at Grimes' Graves.

Sir John Evans draws attention in his book on stone implements[3] to the most remarkable characteristics of the Cissbury implements. He writes : ' Looking at a series of the worked flints from Cissbury, exclusive of flakes and mere rough blocks, the general facies is such as to show that the ordinary forms of celts, or hatchets, were those at which in the main the workmen aimed. A small proportion of these are highly finished specimens, not improbably hidden away in the loose chalk when chipped out and accidentally left there. Others are broken ; not, I think, in use, but in the process of manufacture. A great proportion are very rude, and ill adapted for being ground. They are, in fact, such as may be regarded, if not as wasters, yet, at all events, as unmarketable ; for it seems probable that at Cissbury, as well as at other manufactories of flint implements, they were produced, not for immediate use by those who made them, but to be bartered away for some other commodities.'

The general character of the flint implements found at Cissbury

---

[1] *Proc. Soc. Antiq.* (ser. 2), xvii. 219.   [2] *Arch.* xlv. 337–48.
[3] Evans. *Stone Implements* (ed. 2), pp. 79–80.

entitles them to rank as a distinct type. There is a freedom, a boldness, almost a roughness of chipping which suggests the methods of palæolithic work rather than that of neolithic implements. But they are types of a class of which examples have been found at several other

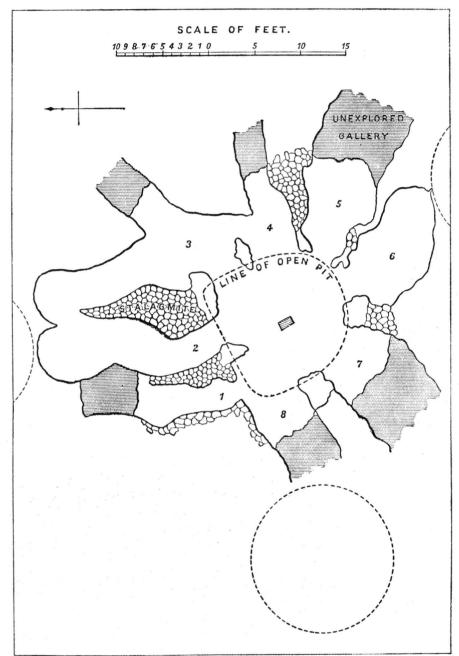

SCALE OF FEET.

PLAN OF FLINT MINES AT CISSBURY HILL.

localities. Such flints, for instance, have been found in some numbers on the Downs near Lewes, and by the writer at Riddlesdown, Surrey, at West Wickham, and at Broadstairs, Kent. No one who has closely studied these implements can doubt that they belong to an early part of the Neolithic Age. They have been compared by some writers with the simply chipped flakes, etc., found in abundance at Lough Neagh, Ireland. An interesting group of such flakes was found by the writer on the side of one of the mounds at Cissbury, left practically as they had been chipped off by their neolithic maker long ago. The removal of the earth by which they had so long been covered was caused by the burrowing of rabbits, which are working so much damage to what is unquestionably the finest camp in Sussex. The position of the flint flakes and chips upon the mound proves that the earthworks were completed during the Neolithic Age.

A collection of typical Cissbury implements together with mining tools, such as rude picks made of antlers of the red deer; blade bones of ox, probably used as shovels; and lamp made of hollowed-out mass of chalk, may now be seen in the British Museum. Numerous other examples of stone implements from the flint mines at Cissbury have been placed in the museums at Lewes and Brighton, and others are in private collections. The large numbers of implements found, point to extensive and long-continued operations, and there is reason to believe that the combined flint-mining and implement-making industries carried on at Cissbury were of equal importance to those at Grimes' Graves, Weeting, Norfolk.

Details of individual finds as far as possible will be given in the index at the end of this article, but attention may be directed to the following more remarkable features of neolithic antiquities in Sussex: (1) A group of eight chipped celts found in 1803 at Clayton Hill; (2) a chipped celt fixed in its wooden handle discovered at Mitchdean, East Dean; (3) minute implements of flint found in association with other implements of regular neolithic character and later pottery, at the rock-shelters at Hastings; (4) numerous roughly chipped celts or agricultural tools found in various parts of the county and now placed in the museums at Lewes, Brighton, Hastings, etc.; (5) numerous hollow or concave scrapers found near Brighton and Eastbourne; (6) numerous celts which have been thoroughly rounded by grinding, found in the Eastbourne and Beachy Head district; and (7) the large number of varieties of stone employed for implement making, including Sussex iron-stone, granite, quartzite and diorite.

The megalithic remains of Sussex appear to be very scanty. There is said once to have been a circle of stones at Goldstone Bottom, near the Brighton Waterworks, which has since been destroyed, and other remains, possibly of the Neolithic Age, are mentioned in the section on Ancient Earthworks.

THE BRONZE AGE

The introduction of metal for the purposes of every-day life marks a very important and decided step in prehistoric progress and culture. The available evidence goes to show that there was not here, as in some parts of the European continent, an age of copper. We seem rather to have passed from the Stone Age to the Bronze Age direct. It may be inferred that the art of working metal was not introduced into Britain until the secret of producing a comparatively hard combination of tin and copper had been discovered. This combination of metals which we call bronze involved the knowledge of working two very dissimilar metals, and, from remains which have been found, we know that gold also was used during the Bronze Age. A primitive race holding the secret of working three distinct metals must have possessed immense advantages over a race which was still in its stone age, and when the Goidelic branch of the great Celtic race first brought this valuable knowledge to Britain, a new era in civilization was inaugurated. The new race was probably welcomed by the neolithic inhabitants of Britain, and both seem to have lived together in some degree of harmony for a considerable period. This is indicated generally in Britain by the characteristic interments of the two peoples. The neolithic races buried their dead by the process known as inhumation, without first partially consuming them by fire, and usually in a contracted position. The bronze-using race, the Celts, on the other hand, seem always to have practised cremation. It is by the association of these two forms of burial, often side by side, on the one hand, and by certain anthropological evidence in the actual remains of man himself on the other, that the mixture of the two races is indicated.

The pottery of the Bronze Age shows a great advance on that of the Neolithic Age, and although the wheel does not appear to have been used in its production, a development in forms and the skilful use of ornament are manifest.

The distribution of population during the Bronze Age, as far as it is represented by the various discoveries of bronze celts and other typical weapons and implements of the time, is clearly shown by the archæological map which accompanies this paper. It will there be seen that a much greater proportion of antiquities of this period have been found on and near the sea-coast than in the more central regions. It is not difficult indeed to identify distinct centres of population at Brighton, Lewes, Eastbourne, etc., by the groups of X-shaped symbols on the map. The distribution of isolated finds is equally suggestive, and points clearly to the preference which the Bronze Age people exhibited for the sea-side and the country bordering it as a place of residence.

The following are brief particulars of the more important discoveries, a full list of every discovery being given as far as possible in the topographical list at the end of the article.

In Brighton itself a socketed celt of Gaulish type, and a palstave with broad and well-curved cutting edge were found many years ago ; but the more important finds have been made a little outside Brighton. Thus at Hove a very important Bronze Age sepulchral deposit[1] was uncovered during some building operations in 1856. The remains comprised a rude oaken coffin containing pieces of charcoal, fragments of partially decayed bone, an amber cup of hemispherical form and furnished with a handle, a bronze knife or dagger blade, a whetstone

[1] *Sussex Arch. Coll.* ix. 119-24.

drilled with a hole for suspension, and a perforated stone axe with one cutting edge and one slightly blunted end. A sepulchral mound of earth, or barrow had been thrown up over the interment, and the coffin was found nine feet below the surface of that mound. It is unfortunate that no very precise notes or photographs were taken when the discovery was made, but the objects found have been carefully preserved and are now in the Brighton Borough Museum. The discovery is one of the most important ever made in the county, and it is of special value as showing the association of objects of different characters in one receptacle. Had they been found in or near one spot merely, the juxtaposition might have been considered the result of chance or accident. The amber cup, which is probably unique, in this country at any rate, has been shaped with great pains and some skill. Its capacity is rather more than half a pint. It is $3\frac{1}{2}$ in. in external diameter, $2\frac{1}{2}$ in. high, and about $\frac{1}{10}$ of an inch thick. The regularity of form and of the parallel lines running round as an ornament on the outside, and the general smoothness of the surface are points which clearly indicate that the vessel was shaped, at least in part, on the lathe. Whether it was actually produced in this country or imported is uncertain, but a good many vessels turned in Kimmeridge shale and probably of Bronze Age, or Prehistoric Iron Age, workmanship have been found in Britain, and they point pretty clearly to native manufacture and the use of the lathe prior to the Roman period.

The occurrence of a perforated stone axe-head in a Bronze Age burial, and associated with a bronze knife-dagger, is also important. It has, of course, long been recognized that the highly-finished and perforated axe-heads and hammer-heads of stone, with which one is familiar in various collections in Britain, must have considerably overlapped the age of metal; but it has remained for a recent writer[1] to point out the numerous instances in which such forms of stone implements have been found in connection with Bronze Age sepulchral deposits. Yorkshire, Wiltshire and Derbyshire seem to have furnished the largest numbers of such discoveries. The cult of the axe was pretty generally diffused among the Neolithic and Bronze Age races. In Brittany and Denmark stone axes are more frequently associated with Stone Age burials, but in Great Britain they are more often found with those of the Bronze Age. Mr. J. Romilly Allen suggests three reasons why stone axes should be so often found with burials, namely, (1) that they were objects prized by the deceased during his lifetime; (2) that he would require weapons in a future state of existence; and (3) that the axe was a symbol associated with the worship of some deity. To whatever reason the presence of the perforated axe in the Hove burial may be attributed, it can hardly be questioned that the grave marked the resting-place of a personage of considerable consequence, whilst the presence of a bronze knife-dagger

---

[1] Mr. J. Romilly Allen, F.S.A., 'Note on a perforated stone axe-hammer found in Pembrokeshire,' in *Arch. Cambr.* (ser. 6), iii. 224–38. A list of such objects found in barrows in Great Britain is given in Mr. Allen's paper.

FLINT KNIFE FROM SOUTHBOURNE, NEAR EASTBOURNE (6 INCHES LONG.)

OBJECT MADE OF ANTLER OF RED DEER FROM BULVERHYTHE

AMBER CUP FROM HOVE (3½ INS. DIAM.), NOW IN THE CORPORATION MUSEUM, BRIGHTON.

(From a Photograph taken by the kind permission of the Museum Authorities.)

To face p. 318.

of the regular Bronze Age type makes it equally impossible to doubt that the burial belonged to the period of bronze. A fourth object, a shaped and perforated piece of stone, evidently intended for a whetstone, is interesting as pointing to the sharpening of metal edges.

Another remarkable series of Bronze Age antiquities was found in 1825 at Hollingbury Hill, an eminence of nearly 600 ft. situated $2\frac{1}{2}$ miles north of Brighton. The series included four massive objects of bronze curved in a form approaching a circle, and considered by some[1] to be bracelets. These were placed regularly on the outside of a handsome torques, also of bronze, without hooks, twisted, and ornamented with spiral rings of bronze. A broken palstave was placed within the circle of the torques. These objects, arranged in their original relative position, are now exhibited in the British Museum. The regularity of this deposit of bronze articles and the fact that two of the number had been broken, apparently with a special purpose, suggests that this was a votive or funereal offering.

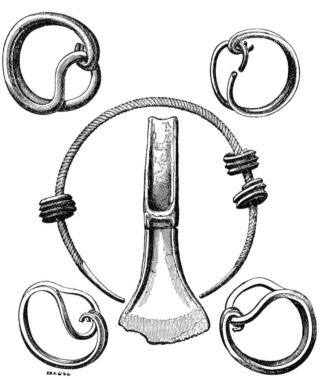

OBJECTS OF THE BRONZE AGE FOUND AT HOLLINGBURY HILL, BRIGHTON.

The great weight and generally unsuitable shape of two of the four articles referred to seem opposed to the idea that they can ever have been intended to serve as bracelets. The extremely limited range of the distribution of the heavier type of these objects is another difficulty; because, whilst such articles have not been found out of Sussex (with one doubtful exception), several examples have been found in the Brighton district.[2] It seems clear that an adequate and satisfactory explanation of their purpose has yet to be found. Bracelets of similar character, but much thinner and lighter, have however been found in more northern parts of England and in Wales. Both the lighter and heavier types of these articles were shaped in the same way. Each is formed of a long bar of bronze, square or circular in section, which is bent double, leaving a rather open loop at the bent end. The two free ends are then to-

[1] Mr. Martin F. Tupper quaintly suggested that they were ' meant to steady the wrists of the young druidess, or other sacred damsel,' etc. (*Sussex Arch. Coll.* ii. 266 ff.)

[2] *Proc. Soc. Antiq.* (ser. 2), xviii. 409–11.

gether brought round and hooked over the open loop in a manner which will be easily seen from the accompanying engraving, but is difficult to describe.

A hoard of bronze implements, deposited in a coarse earthen pot, was found near Worthing in 1877. The hoard, which comprised nearly thirty examples of looped palstaves, some socketed celts, and some lumps of metal, is now in the collection of Sir John Evans, K.C.B.

Other minor articles of bronze found in what may be called the Brighton district are a palstave and disc found at Wolstanbury Hill, a prominent point on the South Downs 7 or 8 miles nearly north of Brighton ; a winged celt found at Clayton Hill ; and looped palstaves and spear-heads discovered at Hangleton Downs.

The Bronze Age antiquities in the Lewes district, apart from earthworks such as tumuli and camps, comprise a very charming example of a decorated flanged celt ; a spear-head now in the British Museum said to have been found in a tumulus ;[1] a long pin of bronze found in a barrow near Lewes ;[2] and a pin with a long oval ring-like head found between Lewes and Brighton.[3]

About midway between Lewes and Eastbourne, where the present village of Wilmington lies under the shoulder of the South Downs, an interesting hoard of Bronze Age antiquities was found in 1861. The objects, which, as in the case of the Worthing hoard, were deposited in a pot of coarse earthenware, comprised thirty-three bronze articles, mainly socketed and looped celts and looped palstaves. The implements were mostly worn or broken when buried, but when found they had not suffered from oxidation in any material degree, and they are now preserved in the Lewes Museum. Unfortunately the earthen pot was destroyed by the workmen.

In the year 1807 a collection of extremely important antiquities obtained from the sea-shore at Beachy Head, Eastbourne,[4] was exhibited by Mr. Holt at a meeting of the Society of Antiquaries of London. They comprised (1) four bracelets of pure gold ranging in weight from 3 oz. 1 dwt. to 16 dwt. 4 gr., and of elegant form without ornamentation ; (2) the base of a bronze sword blade pierced with seven holes for fastening to the handle ; (3) three palstaves ; (4) two socketed celts ; and (5) three lumps of pure copper. All these are now in the British Museum. Perhaps one of the most significant things about this discovery is the occurrence of gold ornaments for personal wear in association with implements of baser metal but of characteristic Bronze Age forms, an association which forms another proof of the knowledge of gold in the Bronze Age.

The celebrated hoard of gold ornaments found at Mountfield was probably of the Prehistoric Iron Age, and will therefore be mentioned under that section of this article.

Sussex possesses many barrows or sepulchral mounds of the Bronze

---

[1] *Horæ Ferales*, pl. vi. fig. 28.
[2] *Sussex Arch. Coll.* ii. 260.
[3] Ibid. ii. 265.
[4] *Arch.* xvi. 363, pl. 68.

EARLY MAN

Age. There are several in the neighbourhood of Eastbourne, Lewes, near the Devil's Dyke, Brighton, and north of Chichester. Some have never yet been properly examined, but remains of actual burials, pottery, etc., have been recorded from barrows at Alfriston, Beddingham, East Blatchington, Hove, Lewes, Rottingdean, Storrington, etc. There are several pieces of sepulchral pottery in the Lewes and Brighton Museums. In the Lewes Museum are some very interesting sepulchral urns found at Mount Harry near Lewes.[1]

In the British Museum are two Bronze Age palstaves and one socketed celt found in Sussex, but the exact locality is unknown.

THE PREHISTORIC IRON AGE

The period beginning with the introduction of iron and ending with the appearance of the Romans in Britain is in some respects the most interesting of all the prehistoric past. Although the antiquities are less numerous than those of two of the earlier periods, they bear witness to a higher degree of culture. The pottery assumes elegant and delicate shapes ; the metals are elaborately worked ; and an extremely beautiful form of conventional decoration makes its appearance. Among other clear evidences of advance in culture are the establishment of a system of metallic currency, the development of the art of enamelling, the institution of kingly government, and the introduction of a form of religious faith.

The antiquities of this age found in Sussex illustrate all these phases of culture in a more or less complete manner. Commencing with metallic objects, attention may be drawn to what is supposed to be a gold toe ring ploughed up on land at Bormer near Lewes, and now in the British Museum. It is formed of two bars of gold, square or rectangular in section, and thick in the middle with diminishing ends. These bars are twisted in the way one usually finds torques are twisted, and the four ends are amalgamated at the thinnest part of the ring. The ring may possibly be as late as the Roman period, but the style of manufacture is certainly earlier.

A celebrated discovery of gold ornaments was made in January 1863, at Mountfield,[2] a parish situated 4 miles north from Battle. A ploughman in the course of his ordinary work turned up a long piece of metal twisted in three grooves, about a yard long, and with trumpet-like terminations. He also found a great number of rings, some of larger size than the others. The larger kind were round and not completely closed. Altogether the man found about 11 lbs. avoirdupois of metal, which he, supposing it to be merely old brass, sold for the sum of 5s. 6d. Finally the metal passed into the hands of Messrs. Brown, the refiners in Cheapside, they purchasing it as Barbary gold for the sum of £529. The deposit turned up by the plough at Mountfield

[1] See list of barrows, etc., in the article on Ancient Earthworks.
[2] *Proc. Soc. Antiq.* Lond. (ser. 2), ii. 247-8.

was in fact a collection of prehistoric gold ornaments, comprising a fine example of a torques with the familiar trumpet-shaped ends, a number of penannular rings, and an armlet of flinted work with lines of punctured dots in the hollows. It may be that there were other articles found, but it is hardly likely that more information will now be obtained upon the point, because with the exception of three fragments the whole of the gold ornaments found were melted down.

It seems pretty clear that the ploughs have in passing through the soil encountered the deposit of gold ornaments, tearing the torques from its hiding-place, and straightening it in the process. The penannular rings were apparently ring money of similar character to those found at Streatham, near Ely, in 1850.

In Horsfield's *Antiquities of Lewes*[1] there is figured an object which is evidently a bronze harness ring. Horsfield describes it as 'a green porcelain pendant amulet,' but the form is much like that of the bronze horse-trappings, often enriched with enamel, which have been found at many different parts of the country, and which indeed may be regarded as among the characteristic antiquities of the Late Celtic period. Another good example of a Late Celtic harness ring with enamelling in

LATE CELTIC HARNESS RING FROM ALFRISTON.

colour on the bronze of which it is composed was found at Alfriston, and is now in the British Museum.[2]

Several antiquities in iron of very great interest were discovered at Mount Caburn[3] during the excavations carried out by General Pitt-Rivers. These comprise a hammer (probably part of an adze), two spear-heads, a small plough-share, spud, knives, sickle, bill-hook, fragment of armour, and numerous minor pieces of iron, together with horn combs for weaving or combing flax, pottery and many other antiquities. The iron objects are of special interest from the fact that they were possibly manufactured from Sussex iron, for there seems reason to believe that the iron industry in the Weald was commenced before the Roman period. The bill-hook again, with its curved cutting edge and imperfectly formed socket for the handle, is noteworthy. It is a form of implement which was certainly known as early as the prehistoric age of iron, yet it still survives in many rural districts. The pottery found at Mount Caburn was in some cases ornamented with

---

[1] Pl. iii. fig. 3, p. 47.　　[2] *Horæ Ferales*, p. 196, plate xx. fig. 2.
[3] *Arch.* xlvi. 423-95.

delicate curves resembling the conventional forms often given to the vine, in others with a species of punctured festoon, and in another case we find an ornament made up of irregular lozenges. The shapes of two of the pots which were capable of restoration are curious. They may be said to resemble a handle-less saucepan with a somewhat greater development of the rim.

Another example of this kind of pot decorated with an ornament which approaches the returned spiral ornament even more closely than does the ornament from Mount Caburn, was found quite recently at Elm Grove, Brighton. This has a slightly fuller rim than the Mount Caburn pots, but otherwise it is strikingly like them in form. It is clearly a special form of pot, and perhaps it may be a purely Sussex type. In the Caldecott Museum at Eastbourne there are three specimens of Late Celtic pottery, one of which found at Seaford has a

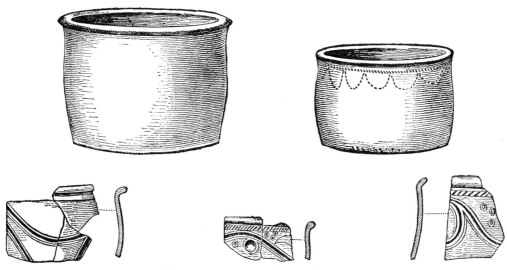

POTTERY FOUND AT MOUNT CABURN.

pedestal and is decorated with cordons in a way that reminds one of the Aylesford and Essex Late Celtic forms.

In the Long Man of Wilmington,[1] a gigantic human figure cut out on the hillside, Sussex possesses an ancient monument comparable with the Giant at Cerne Abbas, Dorset, and the various White Horses to be found in different parts of the country.[2] The figure is that of a man 240 feet in height, and may be well seen from the railway near Polegate. Originally it was cut out rather slightly in the ground, but the outlines have been in recent years clearly defined in white brick, and the Long Man may now be seen from considerable distances. He holds two staves, each 230 feet long. An attempt has been made by some writers to show that these hillside figures were associated with

[1] *Sussex Arch. Coll.* iv. 63-4, and xxvi. 97-112

[2] Mr. Charles Dawson, F.S.A., informs the writer that on a steep part of the Downs near the Cuckmere Valley below Hinover, there is a very rough cutting or outline resembling a horse, which was periodically 'scoured' by the country folk until a few generations ago.

religious rites and beliefs, an explanation which seems feasible, especially in view of the phallic character of the Cerne Abbas Giant. One writer, Dr. J. S. Phené, F.S.A.,[1] makes the ingenious suggestion that their purpose was sacrificial, and that they may be the actual figures described by Cæsar, formed of osiers and filled with living men, the whole structure and contents being then destroyed by fire.

The grounds upon which this gigantic figure can be assigned even approximately to any period are, it must be confessed, of a somewhat indefinite and unsatisfactory character. It is pretty certain, however, that it is not modern, and the general character of the form must be pronounced more in accordance with the art of the early than the middle ages. If, however, we may compare these enormous human figures with the gigantic figures of horses (which clearly have a likeness to the figures on ancient British coins), the balance of probability is in favour of referring the Long Men of Wilmington and of Cerne Abbas to the period immediately preceding the appearance of the Romans in Britain.

COINS OF THE ANCIENT BRITONS

The ancient British coins found in Sussex are of considerable importance both with regard to their numbers and their variety. They are of gold, silver, copper-gilt, and tin, and it will be convenient to divide them into two groups, viz., (1) those which are uninscribed, and (2) those which are inscribed.

(1) *Uninscribed coins.*—These are of various types, among which are several degraded forms of the horse copied and re-copied from the well-known pieces struck by Philip of Macedon in the fourth century B.C. On the obverse of the Macedonian prototype was a laureate head of Apollo, or possibly of the youthful Hercules. This head and the horses, biga, and charioteer of the reverse, have been converted by unskilled artists into the large number of grotesque forms we now find on uninscribed British coins.

The small group of tin coins found at Mount Caburn near Lewes are specially interesting from this point of view, because they are of native British manufacture, they belong to the Late Celtic period of culture, and exhibit very feebly drawn representations of what are supposed to be intended for a head (possibly helmeted) and an animal, perhaps a bull. The attenuated body of the bull may be compared with the White Horse at Uffington. Uninscribed British coins have been found in upwards of twenty different parishes in Sussex.

(2) *Inscribed coins.*—The use of an inscribed coinage in Britain is believed to date from about the year 30 B.C., and from that time we are able to trace in the more or less abbreviated inscriptions on the coins the names of those princes or kings who ruled different parts of the land about the time of the coming of the Romans.

[1] *Roy. Instit. Brit. Archit. Trans.* 1872, pp. 191-2.

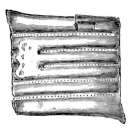

LATE CELTIC URN FROM ELM GROVE, BRIGHTON (7 IN. DIAM.)
NOW IN BRIGHTON MUSEUM.
(From a Photograph taken by permission of the Museum Authorities.)

FRAGMENTS OF GOLD FROM
THE MOUNTFIELD FIND.

THREE CINERARY URNS FROM SEAFORD.

To face p. 322.

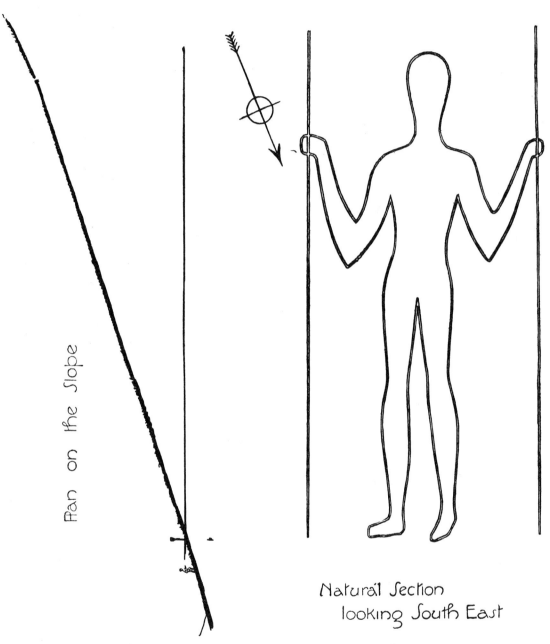

Plan on the Slope

Natural Section
looking South East

THE WILMINGTON GIANT, SUSSEX

Scale of 10 0 10 20 30 40 50 60 70 80 90 100 Feet

One important personage at that period reigning over a part of Britain was Commios. He appears to have had three sons, viz., Tincommios, who was king of the Regni, a tract practically answering to the present county of Sussex ; Verica, whose sway was over the eastern part of the Attrebates ; and Eppillos, who ruled over Kent. Tincommios was king of the Regni about the time of Julius Cæsar, and from the number of his coins found in Sussex it may be inferred that he was a very important king. Examples have been found at Aldwick, Alfriston, Bognor, Bramber, East Wittering, Lancing Downs, Pallant, and Steyning. Coins of Verica have been obtained from Bognor, East and West Wittering, Lancing Downs, Pagham, Shoreham, Steyning.

Other important discoveries were a coin inscribed Commios found at Hastings about the year 1872, and a gold-plated copper coin inscribed TFSC (doubtless a shortened form of Tasciovannus) found at Brighton and now in the collection of Mr. Henry Willett.

Important hoards of British coins have been found at Ashdown Forest, Battle, Bognor, and Lancing Downs ; whilst along the sea-shore at Selsey large numbers of coins have been picked up, the collection of the late Mr. E. H. Willett alone comprising nearly three hundred examples from this district.

For further details respecting the ancient British coins found in Sussex, the reader may be referred to the papers on the subject by Mr. E. H. Willett in the *Sussex Archæological Collections*, vols. XXIX. and XXX. ; Sir John Evans's well-known work on the *Coins of the Ancient Britons*, and *Supplement*, and some of the volumes of the *Numismatic Chronicle*.

MISCELLANEOUS ANTIQUITIES

In addition to the various objects already mentioned, which it is possible to assign to a more or less definite period in prehistoric times, there are one or two antiquities which may perhaps be most conveniently treated in a separate group under what may be termed miscellaneous antiquities. Some or all of them may possibly belong to a pre-Roman period, but the evidence does not seem sufficiently strong to assign them definitely to such an early time. On the other hand, it would be impossible, on the available data, to place them even approximately within the historic period.

The artificial caverns in the chalk at Hayes Down, Lavant, which were examined in 1893–4 by Messrs. Charles Dawson[1] and John Lewis, are of considerable extent, and present many curious points of interest. The excavations are of irregular form, but the accompanying plan, which was made by Mr. Lewis, will show that whilst the supporting pillars occupy a comparatively small space, the galleries, or chambers, are large, indicating that the excavation was made for the sake of the chalk or flint. The whole excavations are believed to cover an extent

---

[1] A paper on the subject was read by Mr. Dawson at a meeting of the Sussex Archæological Society at Chichester in 1893 (see *Sussex Daily News*, 12 Aug. 1893).

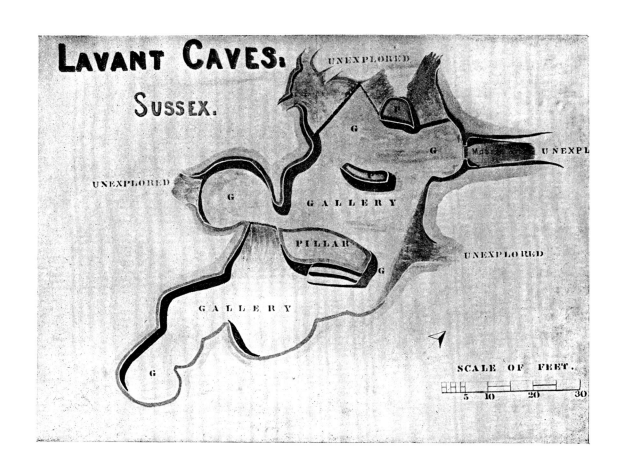

LAVANT CAVES.
SUSSEX.

UNEXPLORED

P

G

G

Mas

UNEXPL

UNEXPLORED

G

GALLERY

UNEXPLORED

PILLAR

G

GALLERY

G

SCALE OF FEET.

5   10   20   30

To face page 326.

of nearly an acre. The objects found in the chambers during the careful examination by Messrs. Dawson and Lewis are of a remarkable and miscellaneous character. They include neolithic implements, cores, etc., Romano-British pottery and some metallic objects of the Roman and subsequent periods; also a portion of an antler of the red deer, fragments of human teeth, and charred wheat. It must be explained that the floor of the chambers was covered by two layers; the lower layer, in which these objects were found, consisted of finely broken chalk nearly 3 ft. thick, and the upper, made up of large loose fragments of chalk, was of various thicknesses at different parts. As some of the objects in this lower level, such as leaden seals or badges, were of seventeenth century date, it follows that the caves were open and this part of the floor was being built up at least as late as that period. The pieces of Roman pottery, etc., seem sufficiently numerous to point to the conclusion that the excavation is as old as the Roman times. Generally speaking, however, the evidence which has so far been produced does not seem to be very convincing. There is a curious mixture of objects which suggests contact with external influences; and the only thing that can at present be made out is that the excavations are of considerable age and were constructed for some economic purpose. Probably they have been put to the secondary purpose of hiding-places.

The extensive caves near Hastings Castle known as St. Clement's Caves are doubtless to a very large extent and in their origin the result of natural forces. The large fissures in the rock are too extensive to have been produced by artificial means. But it is clear that the passages and chambers have undergone considerable modification at the hand of man. The local tradition that these subterranean chambers have been used as hiding-places for smuggled goods lacks confirmation. Much of the sand removed from the caves has been dug for the purpose of sanding floors in Hastings. Without a systematic examination of the caves, however, it seems useless to speculate as to the period to which they should be assigned.

Ancient boats, possibly of British age, have been discovered buried in the soil at Bexhill, Burpham, and North Stoke.

In the Dawson Loan Collection exhibited at the Brassey Institute, Hastings, are several local discoveries of Neolithic and Bronze Age antiquities of considerable interest. Among them are two articles, the period of which appears to be somewhat uncertain. They comprise (1) a socketed piece of bronze evidently only a part of a larger implement and ending in a kind of reversed shield found at St. Leonards Marina, and (2) a piece of stag-horn 11 inches long, pierced in the middle by a nearly square hole. This object is described on its label as a hammer, for which purpose it does not seem to be particularly fitted, and it is said to have been found in the submarine forest at Bulverhythe, half-way between St. Leonards and Bexhill. It seems rather closely related to those objects made of the tines and beams of the red deer antlers which, it has been suggested,

were used as the cheek-pieces of bridle bits, and of which examples
have been found in the river Thames; in Heathery Burn Cave, Durham; and in the Bronze Age lake dwellings of Switzerland. There are
certain difficulties as to this explanation of their use, and if the Bulverhythe example really is one of the same group, it increases, rather than
diminishes, the difficulty, because it is clearly too long for such a purpose.

TOPOGRAPHICAL LIST OF PREHISTORIC ANTIQUITIES IN SUSSEX

ALDRINGTON.—Neolithic implements found here, and now preserved in Brighton Museum.

ALDWICK.—British coins of Tincommios [Evans, *Coins of the Ancient Britons*, 500-1].

ALFRISTON.—Neolithic implements of rude character in Brit. Mus. Neolithic celts found in
Bronze Age sepulchral barrow [Evans, *Stone Implements*, 84, 148]. Bronze socketed celt
with one loop, square and elongated in general form: a typical celt of the southern
counties [Evans, *Bronze Implements*, 114-5]. Late Celtic enamelled bronze ring, part
of horse-harness, now in Brit. Mus. Several British coins, two being of Tincommios
[Evans, *Coins*, 64, 161, 164, 432].

WINDORE HILL.—Neolithic scraper of horse-shoe form found in a barrow [Evans, *Stone
Imp.* 308].

AMBERLEY.—Neolithic implements have recently been found at Stone Gate by Mr. R. Garraway Rice, F.S.A.

APPLEDRAM.—Palæolithic implement found here in 1897 by Mr. W. Hayden [*Proc. Suss. Arch.
Coll.* ser. 2, vol. xx. pt. ii.] Factory of neolithic implements.

ASHDOWN FOREST.—Uninscribed British coins [Evans, *Coins*, 92-3, 108].

BARNHAM.—Flanged bronze celt and palstave in Lewes Museum.

BATTLE.—Bronze leaf-shaped sword, 29½ inches long, with eleven rivet-holes, now in Brit.
Mus. [Evans, *Bronze Imp.* 280]. Bronze trumpet of Late Celtic type [ibid. 363; Grose,
Ancient Armour, pl. xiii.] Hoard of British coins [Evans, *Coins*, 361, 381, 397].

TELHAM FARM.—Neolithic celt of flint and another of basalt, now in Brit. Mus.

BEDDINGHAM.—Bronze Age urn with characteristic ornament, now in Lewes Museum.

BELTOUT.—Neolithic implements abundant [Evans, *Stone Imp.* 281].

BIGNOR, WESTBURTON HILL.—Bronze palstave with a projecting rib below the stop-ridge
and also in the recess above [Evans, *Bronze Imp.* 84].

BILLINGSHURST.—Small neolithic celt of greystone in Brit. Mus. Bronze palstave with central rib [ibid. 81].

BOGNOR.—Four winged celts of bronze [ibid. 80-1]. Hoard of British coins Tincommios,
Verica, etc. [Evans, *Coins*, 90, 92, 94-5, 97, 166].

BOLMER.—Neolithic implements now in Lewes Museum.

BORMER.—Late Celtic ring, now in Brit. Mus.

BOSHAM.—Neolithic implements.

BOW HILL.—See STOUGHTON.

BRACKLESHAM BAY.—Rapier-shaped bronze blade [Evans, *Bronze Imp.* 244]. Uninscribed
British coins [Evans, *Coins*, 89, 95].

BRAMBER.—British coin of Tincommios [ibid. 161].

BRIGHTON.—Ovate palæolithic implement found in the 'Elephant Bed' [Evans, *Stone Imp.*
622]. Bronze palstave [Evans, *Bronze Imp.* 80; *Suss. Arch. Coll.* ii. 268]. Bronze
socketed celt of Gaulish type [Evans, *Bronze Imp.* 115; *Suss. Arch. Coll.* ii. 268]. British
coins [Evans, *Coins*, 435, 437, 535].

GOLDSTONE BOTTOM.—Megalithic circle (?).

HOLLINGBURY HILL.—Numerous and important Bronze Age antiquities [Evans, *Bronze
Imp.* 76, 115, 378, 386, 390, 464].

BROADWATER.—Palæolithic implement found near Broadwater, now in the possession of Mr.
F. Lasham, of Guildford [*Proc. Soc. Antiq.* ser. 2, vol. xx. pl. ii.]

BULVERHYTHE.—Curious objects of deer-horn.

BUXTED.—Bronze socketed and looped celts and two looped palstaves in Lewes Museum.

CABURN, MOUNT.—Late Celtic fortress. Ancient British coins of tin [Evans, *Coins*, 485;
Arch. xlvi. pl. xxv. figs. 61, 62, 63].

EARLY MAN

CAKEHAM.—See WEST WITTERING.

CHAILEY.—Part of early Bronze Age celt, now in Lewes Museum.

CHICHESTER.—Bronze palstave with central rib [Evans, *Bronze Imp.* 81 ; *Proc. Soc. Antiq.* v. 38]. Ancient British coin of Tasciovanus [Evans, *Coins*, 90].

    PALLANT.—British coin of Tincommios [ibid. 500].

CHILGROVE.—Bronze bracelets (? of the Bronze Age) [*Proc. Soc. Antiq.* ser. 1, vol. i. p. 6].

CISSBURY HILL.—Numerous neolithic flint implements and excavations of the Neolithic Age made in the chalk for flint [Evans, *Stone Imp.* 32–3, 35, 72, 75, 78, 80–2, 248, 277, 281]. See pp. 314-6. Many of these antiquities are now in Brit. Mus.

CLAYTON.—Bronze winged celt with four vertical stripes [Evans, *Bronze Imp.* 80]. Eight neolithic celts chipped out of flint found together in 1803 [Evans, *Stone Imp.* 76].

CLIFFE.—Perforated hammer found in a barrow [ibid. 229]. Spindle-whorl of clay, now in Brit. Mus. Small Bronze Age urn found in a barrow, now in Brit. Mus.

COATES.—Palæolithic implements found in gravel by Mr. R. Garraway Rice, F.S.A. [*Proc. Soc. Antiq.* ser. 2, vol. xx. pt. ii.]

CRAWLEY.—Neolithic celt (ground) in Brit. Mus.

CROWBOROUGH.—Neolithic flint saw in the Dawson Loan Collection, Hastings. Pick-like bronze palstave in Dawson Loan Collection, Hastings.

CUCKMERE HAVEN.—Neolithic scraper [Evans, *Stone Imp.* 304]. Neolithic implements in Brighton Museum.

DEAN, EAST.—Pointed palæolithic implements [ibid. 622]. Chipped neolithic celt in wooden handle found here [*Suss. Arch. Coll.* xxxix. 97–8 ; Evans, *Stone Imp.* 153].

    RINGWOOD, GROVE FARM.—Chipped and ground neolithic celt [ibid. 94].

DIDLING.—Neolithic celt (ground) 6 $\frac{9}{16}$ inches long.

EASTBOURNE.—Numerous neolithic implements found by Stephen Blackwell [ibid. 76, 87, 126, 179, 357]. Bronze spear-head [Evans, *Bronze Imp.* 316]. Large urn, perhaps of the Bronze Age, now in Lewes Museum. Ancient British coins (uninscribed) [Evans, *Coins*, 95, 435, 485]. Bronze socketed spear-head 11 inches long, now in the Museum at Eastbourne.

    BEACHY HEAD.—Numerous neolithic implements, in Brit. Mus., also in the museums at Brighton and Lewes. Important hoard of gold and bronze antiquities of the Bronze Age [*Arch.* xvi. 363, pl. 68 ; Evans, *Bronze Imp.* 94, 283, 423, 467].

    BIRLING GAP.—Neolithic scrapers [Evans, *Stone Imp.* 301, 303, 305].

EAST HOATHLY.—Part of bronze palstave now in Lewes Museum.

EAST WITTERING.—Ancient British inscribed and uninscribed coins [Evans, *Coins*, 162, 176, 435, 457, 500, 512].

EDBURTON.—Neolithic implements, now in Brit. Mus.

FALMER.—Neolithic implements in Brighton Museum.

FERRING, HIGH DOWN HILL.—An ancient camp. Numerous worked flints [*Arch.* xlii. 74–6]. Bronze knife and chisel, gold ring, and stone mace [*Proc. Soc. Antiq.* ser. 2, xviii. 387–8].

FINDON.—Neolithic implements found at Church Hill, and now in Brighton Museum.

FIRLE.—Bronze pin found in barrow [Evans, *Bronze Imp.* 369 ; Horsefield, *Lewes*, i. 48, pl. iii. fig. 12]. Very small flat bronze celt of early type now in Lewes Museum.

FITTLEWORTH.—Palæolithic implements found here [*Proc. Soc. Antiq.* ser. 2, vol. xx. pt. ii.]

FRISTON.—Ovate palæolithic implements [Evans, *Stone Imp.* 622]. Neolithic implements in Brighton Museum.

FUNTINGTON.—Neolithic implements.

GOODWOOD.—Uninscribed British coins [Evans, *Coins*, 62].

GORING.—Neolithic celt found on beach, now in British Museum.

GREATHAM.—Palæolithic flake found here by Mr. R. Garraway Rice, F.S.A. [*Proc. Soc. Antiq.* ser. 2, vol. xx. pt. ii.]

HANGLETON DOWN.—Two looped bronze palstaves and a bronze spear-head with two loops [*Suss. Arch. Coll.* viii. 269 ; Evans, *Bronze Imp.* 87, 322].

HARDHAM.—Numerous neolithic implements [Evans, *Stone Imp.* 283]. Bronze Age urn found at Hardham, now in Brighton Museum.

HARTING SOUTH.—Neolithic implements in Brighton Museum.

HASTINGS.—Rock shelters (neolithic and later) on Castle Hill, and numerous flint implements. (See pp. 311-12) [*Suss. Arch. Coll.* xix. 53–60 ; Evans, *Stone Imp.* 71, 281, 309, 325, 389]. Ancient British coins [Evans, *Coins*, 433, 451, 450, 462, 499].

HEENE.—British uninscribed coin [ibid. 435].

HIGH DOWN.—See FERRING.

HORSHAM.—Flint arrow-heads (? neolithic) [Evans, *Stone Imp.* 389]. Neolithic flint saw, and perforated stone hammer [ibid. 229, 295].

HOVE.—Important Bronze Age interment [Evans, *Bronze Imp.* 243, 453, 486; *Suss. Arch. Coll.* ix. 120; *Arch. Journ.* xiii. 184]. Bronze palstave, 7½ inches long, now in Brighton Museum.

HURSTPIERPOINT.—Neolithic implements now in Lewes Museum.

IFORD.—Bronze palstave with a central rib on the blade [*Suss. Arch. Coll.* xxix. 134; Evans, *Bronze Imp.* 81].

LANCING.—Bronze Age 'incense cup' and three other small urns found in a barrow, now in Brit. Mus. Neolithic implements and bronze palstave 6¼ inches with loop, now in Brighton Museum. Numerous ancient British coins [Evans, *Coins*, 110, 169, 183].

LEWES.—Numerous neolithic implements all over the Lewes district. A bronze dagger with handle found at Lewes is now in Brit. Mus. Three Bronze Age palstaves (each with one loop) found at The Wallands, Lewes, in 1871, now in Lewes Museum.

MARESFIELD.—Neolithic implements in Lewes Museum.

MAYFIELD.—Neolithic celt (ground) in Jermyn Street Museum.

MIDHURST.—Palæolithic implement found at Hill Top, Midhurst, in 1893 [*Proc. Soc. Antiq.* ser. 2, vol. xx. pt. ii.]

MOUNTFIELD.—Important discovery of gold ornaments of Late Celtic types [ibid. ii. 247-8; *Arch.* xxxix. 507].

NEWHAVEN.—Neolithic flint flake and saw [Evans, *Stone Imp.* 278, 295]. Neolithic hoe found near [ibid. 71]. Some of these are now in the Lewes Museum. In a kitchen midden found here were many neolithic chips, flakes, etc.

OVING.—Neolithic hoe [ibid. 69].

PAGHAM.—British coins of Verica and uninscribed [Evans, *Coins*, 65, 95, 172].

PALLINGHAM.—Perforated hammer-head (Neolithic or Bronze Age) [Evans, *Stone Imp.* 229; *Suss. Arch. Coll.* ix. 118].

PEVENSEY.—Neolithic factory under walls of Roman castrum. British silver coin [Evans, *Coins*, 109].

PIDDINGHOE.—Numerous arrow-heads and neolithic implements found here, and now in Brighton Museum.

PLUMPTON.—Neolithic chipped celt in Lewes Museum. Bronze flanged celt and socketed celt of interesting form [Evans, *Bronze Imp.* 52, 110]. Looped bronze palstave in Lewes Museum.

POLEGATE.—Uninscribed British coin [Evans, *Coins*, 433].

POLING.—Uninscribed British coin [ibid. 435].

PORTSLADE.—Neolithic implements found here, and now in Brighton Museum.

POYNINGS.—Neolithic implements in Brighton Museum.

PULBOROUGH.—Pestle of grey granite (? neolithic) [Evans, *Stone Imp.* 254]. Bronze palstave (looped) [*Proc. Soc. Antiq.* ser. 2, iv. 442; Evans, *Bronze Imp.* 87]. Socketed celt with traces of vertical ribs [ibid. 119].

PYECOMBE.—Neolithic flint celt with expanding edge [Evans, *Stone Imp.* 93]. Bronze leaf-shaped spear-head [Evans, *Bronze Imp.* 318].

ROTTINGDEAN.—Numerous neolithic implements found here. A well chipped flint celt nearly 8 in. long is in Brighton Museum.

ST. LEONARDS FOREST.—Neolithic implements [*Suss. Arch. Coll.* xxvii. 177].

ST. LEONARDS-ON-SEA.—Bronze palstaves, whole and broken, found here. They are now in the possession of Mr. Charles Dawson, F.S.A., and are exhibited in the museum at the Brassey Institute at Hastings.

SEAFORD.—Numerous neolithic implements, some of them obtained from sepulchral barrows [Evans, *Stone Imp.* 71, 149, 249, 295, 309]. Some neolithic implements from Seaford are now in the Lewes Museum, and others are in the Brighton Museum. Three sepulchral urns showing late Celtic influence, now in the Museum at Eastbourne. Uninscribed British coin [Evans, *Coins*, 432].

SELSEY.—Numerous British coins [ibid. 66, 90, etc.].

SHIPLEY.—Uninscribed British coin [ibid. 435].

SHOREHAM.—British coin of Verica [ibid. 173].

SLAUGHAM HANDCROSS.—Bronze object known as a bracelet [Evans, *Bronze Imp.* 385]. See p. 319.

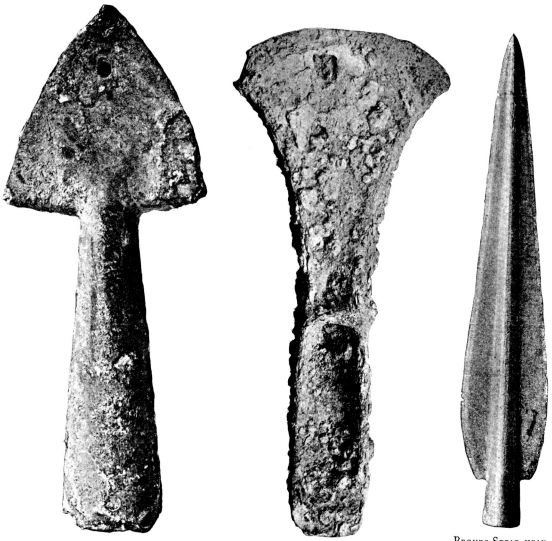

BRONZE SOCKETED OBJECT FROM THE
MARINA, ST. LEONARDS-ON-SEA.

BRONZE PALSTAVE FROM
ST. LEONARDS-ON-SEA (FULL SIZE).

BRONZE SPEAR-HEAD
FROM MEADS, EASTBOURNE
($11\frac{1}{2}$ INCHES LONG).

To face p. 330

SOUTHBOURNE.—Neolithic chipped knife, now in the Museum at Eastbourne.

STEYNING.—Ancient British coins of Tincommios and Verica [Evans, *Coins*, 161, 174].

STORRINGTON.—Small bronze awl found with a burnt interment [Evans, *Bronze Imp.* 190].

STOUGHTON, BOW HILL.—Whetstone of compact red sandstone found in a barrow [Evans, *Stone Imp.* 268].

TARRING.—Uninscribed British coins [Evans, *Coins*, 61, 67].

UCKFIELD : POSSINGWORTH MANOR.—Neolithic chips and flakes in Brit. Mus.; numerous implements [Evans, *Stone Imp.* 281 ; *Arch. Journ.* xxii. 68].

WALDRON.—Five bronze palstaves [*Suss. Arch. Coll.* 366 ; Evans, *Bronze Imp.* 91].

WARBLETON.—British coin of Verica [Evans, *Coins*, 511].

WARTLING.—Neolithic implements in Brighton Museum.

WEST STOKE.—Neolithic implements.

WEST WITTERING.—Neolithic implements. Ancient British coins [ibid. 434, 511].

CAKEHAM.—Ancient British coins [ibid. 435, 436].

WIGGONHOLT.—Palæolithic flake found here by Mr. W. Paley Baildon, F.S.A. [*Proc. Soc. Antiq.* ser. 2, vol. xx. pt. ii.]

WILMINGTON.—Important bronze hoard [*Suss. Arch. Coll.* xiv. 171 ; *Arch. Journ.* xx. 192 ; *Proc. Soc. Antiq.* ser. 2, v. 423 ; Evans, *Bronze Imp.* 87, 447, 468]. The hoard is now in the Lewes Museum.

WISTON.—Uninscribed British coin [Evans, *Coins*, 65].

WITHYHAM.—Neolithic celt (ground) in Brit. Mus.

WOLSTANBURY HILL. Bronze palstave and disc 5 in. in diameter [Evans, *Bronze Imp.* 84, 401].

WORTHING.—See also HEENE.—Neolithic celt of unusually large size [*Proc. Soc. Antiq.* ser. 2, xvii. 364]. Important bronze hoard now in Lewes Museum [Evans, *Bronze Imp.* 87, 423, 467]. Looped bronze palstave now in Lewes Museum. Ancient British uninscribed coin [Evans, *Coins*, 67].

ANGLO SAXON REMAINS

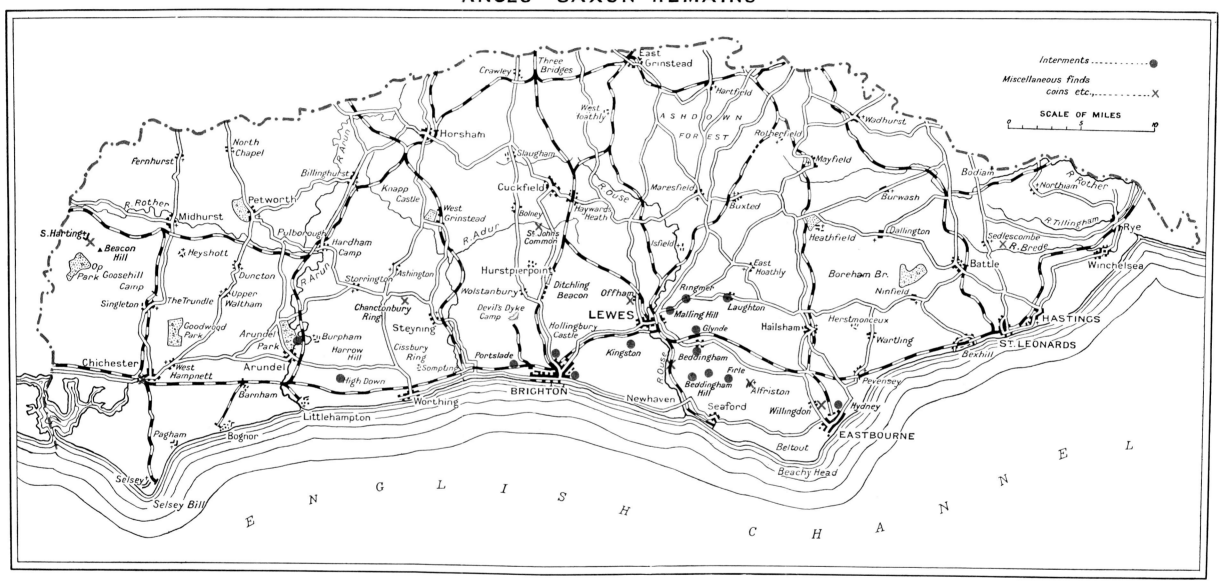

ANGLO-SAXON REMAINS

THERE are few districts in England where the nature and course of the Anglo-Saxon conquest should be more easily traced than in Sussex. About the derivation of the name there can be no doubt whatever, and the kingdom of the South Saxons implies other Saxon areas from which it had to be distinguished. Wessex, the country of the West Saxons, is still a recognized division of England, though its boundaries are somewhat vaguer than of old, and Essex has remained a political unit in the east, while the territory of the Middle Saxons to-day includes the capital of an empire.

To judge from the tribal name, the South Downs were evidently held in the post-Roman period by a population distinct from that of Kent, but related to the occupants of the district round the upper Thames and of a large area north of that river's lower reaches. Romney Marsh would in itself form a natural barrier on the east, and whatever the actual course of events in what is now Hampshire, it is recorded [1] that in 661 Wulthere of Mercia handed over Wight to his godson Ethelwald, King of the South Saxons. It was evidently about the same date that the Gospel was preached in these parts. From the time of their landing to the middle of the seventh century, we may therefore regard the South Saxons as a pagan community, and their cemeteries show that they lived and died on the southern slopes of the Downs or in the fertile strip of low-lying country along their base. Beyond the chalk escarpment stretched the forest of the Weald, not inhabited to any extent till after the eleventh century, as the Domesday map clearly shows.

At what date the Teutonic invaders first secured a footing on this part of the sea-board, cannot be precisely determined ; and it is the business of archaeology to throw some light on questions of this kind, by careful examination of such relics as may be assigned to the fifth and sixth centuries of our era. It must, however, be confessed at the outset that such discoveries have hardly fulfilled the expectations raised by the historical records. This is no doubt due in part to defective observation and inadequate descriptions of the explorations ; but with

[1] *Anglo-Saxon Chron.* (Rolls Ser.), i. 54.

the growth of interest in our national past, it may be possible to procure more precise and satisfactory evidence at no distant date.

The present survey of Anglo-Saxon discoveries in the county includes little but burials of an early date, some doubtless of pagan Saxons, others probably of Christian converts who died before the middle of the eighth century, when, by order of the Church, burial was no longer permitted in the open country, but confined to the consecrated ground of the churchyard. By that time also the practice of depositing ornaments and weapons in the grave was given up ; and the church-yards, even if disturbed, would yield but little evidence of service to archaeology.

The first entry in the *Anglo-Saxon Chronicle* relating to Sussex has certain suspicious features, but may well indicate the date at which the occupation began. It is under the year 477, and runs as follows : ' This year Aella and his three sons, Cymen, Wlencing and Cissa, came to the land of Britain with three ships at a place called Cymenesore, and there slew many Welsh, and some they drove in flight into the wood called Andredslea.'[1] Thirty-seven years later the West Saxons are said to have arrived in three ships at Cerdicsore, and in that same year Aella is said to have died. Much however seems to have happened in the course of his long reign, and a notable battle, which no doubt marked an important stage in the conquest but cannot now be located, is reported at the river called Mercrœdsburn in 485. Another six years dealt what was apparently the final blow to British independence in this region, and the fall of Anderida (perhaps Pevensey) has often been quoted as proof of the ruthless methods of the invading Saxon. This record however stands alone, and the fact that ' Aella and Cissa slew all that dwelt in Andredsceaster so that not a single Briton was there left ' may first have been recorded on account of its exceptional character. It had taken fourteen years to conquer what to-day is the southern half of Sussex, and according to Bede,[2] Aella was something more than King of Sussex, and was the first to hold the title of Bretwalda, which is generally translated Wielder of Britain. Whether this implied dominion over the native British population beyond the borders of Sussex is open to question ; but if the *Anglo-Saxon Chronicle* is to be trusted on such a point, the conquest of Kent had begun more than forty years before the siege of Anderida, and the predominance of Aella must be ascribed to his own exceptional prowess, as Ethelbert of Kent only came third in the list.

The rehearsal of these few scraps of history or tradition is a neces-sary preliminary to the investigation of the relics that undoubtedly belong to a Teutonic people or group of settlers from beyond the seas, during a period but vaguely defined but quite in accordance with the dates already mentioned. Further deductions as to race or chronology must be reserved till the discoveries have been presented ; and as the relative dates of the Saxon cemeteries of Sussex cannot at present be

[1] *Anglo-Saxon Chron.* (Rolls Ser.), i. 22.   [2] Bede, *Eccl. Hist.* ii. 5 (Plummer), i. 89.

accurately determined, it will be convenient to begin the series with those at the eastern extremity of the county and continue westward.

The promontory overlooking the old haven of Hydney near Eastbourne has been prolific in remains of the Britons and Saxons, but these have not always been recorded or investigated with sufficient care. Where the Grange now stands in the Mill Field, a large number of interments were discovered in 1877 and fully described by Mr. Herbert Spurrell. The graves were spaced with the utmost regularity, and were about 2 ft. from the surface. Knives, spears, shield-bosses, glass tumblers, a wooden bucket with mounts of silvered bronze, an armlet, stirrups and swords were found, one of which had the upper portion of the wooden scabbard bound with a gilt bronze rim bearing a triangle and interlaced pattern.[1]

A little nearer the town, on this same ridge, a grave was laid bare, containing an iron shield-boss on the chest of the skeleton, a spear-head, and a small wooden bucket about 6 inches high, the silvered (or tinned) bronze hoops of which were fastened by little screw-nuts. An iron sword was also found on the site with a silver-gilt mount; and a bracelet lay in position on the wrist bones of another skeleton.[2] There was no trace of mounds over the graves, but the Mill Field had been under cultivation for some time and any small barrows may have been obliterated. Fragments of Saxon pottery mixed with sherds of the Roman period are said to have been found in abundance all over the west slope of the hill, and further traces of the Saxons seem to have been met with when the road to Willingdon was lowered near the cemetery, several graves having been cut through in the course of the work.

In January 1843 a small Saxon cemetery was discovered by Mr. Coles Child on the South Downs about six miles east of Lewes. On this, the highest eminence in the county, was a cluster of more than a dozen depressed mounds, the largest not more than 9 ft. in diameter; and in each was a single skeleton laid in a cist about 3 ft. deep. In every case the feet were at the east end, and no spears or ornaments were found in the graves, though on the left side of one skeleton were seen traces of rust on the chalk, evidently the remains of the usual iron knife. This skeleton was the tallest in the group and was estimated at 6 ft. 4 in., belonging to a man between thirty-five and forty years of age at the time of death. His cranium showed a terrible sword-cut between 4 and 5 inches long, but the smoothness of the cut showed, in the opinion of Dr. Barnard Davis,[3] that he lingered a few days before dying of the wound. The skull is fully described and said to have a modern English appearance, being regular and ovoid; so much so that it is regarded as typical of one of the chief forms common among Anglo-Saxon skulls—a form that has evidently descended from pre-Norman

---

1 *Sussex Archaeological Collections*, vol. xxxvii. p. 112 ; *Proc. Soc. Antiq.* xv. 275.
2 *Trans. Eastbourne Nat. Hist. Soc.* vol. i. 1882, p. 30 ; 1884, p. 6.
3 Thurnam and Davis, *Crania Britannica*, pt. 2, pl. 29.

times to the English people of the present day. Subsequent discoveries in the same district gave almost identical results. In September 1849 John Yonge Akerman excavated three barrows of the Anglo-Saxon period on the Downs between Firle Beacon and Litlington, and found a perfect skeleton in each. The first was that of a boy about fourteen years of age ; the second of a young man, and the third of a man of advanced age. The perfect condition of the teeth was noticeable, though those of the old man were much worn. The only objects discovered were two knives of the usual pattern and presumably of iron, placed with the second and third burials. Some years before the same investigator had obtained similar results in the same locality, and concluded that these were the graves of a population in quiet possession of the district and of very primitive habits, in striking contrast to the discoveries of many weapons and ornaments when Malling Hill and others in the neighbourhood of Lewes were levelled.[1] The locality well illustrated the distinction between grave-mounds of the Anglo-Saxon and Bronze periods, the former being on the brow of the hill overlooking some hamlet evidently of Saxon origin, and the latter on the highest points of the range, often out of sight of the inhabitants of the valley. Dr. Davis described two skulls found on this occasion, not far from Firle Beacon. They belonged to male adults of different ages, but both exhibit the Anglo-Saxon characteristics in an eminent degree ; and it may be mentioned that the elder showed signs of decay in the teeth, a somewhat rare occurrence in skulls of this period. Like that described above, these were considered typical skulls, the particular oval form being regarded as an unquestionable indication of race. The absence of grave-furniture and the east-and-west position are both in favour of the view that all these were graves of Christian converts. They would in that case be later than the mission of Bishop Wilfrid (681–686) and before the transfer of burials to the churchyards about the middle of the eighth century.

In 1896 Rev. J. O. Bevan exhibited to the Anthropological Institute[2] a knife found in January of that year with eight skeletons during the erection of some fences in the parish of Alfriston, near Berwick, Sussex. The discovery was made near the summit of a hill overlooking the village. There were seven skeletons in a row, about 4 ft. apart, lying east and west (presumably with the head to the west) and another about 21 ft. south-east of the easternmost. They lay in the chalk, the mould being about 6 or 8 inches thick, the stratum immediately on the bodies being a mixture of soil and stones known locally as challice. In addition there was discovered a small piece of jet or amber, with two holes drilled half through ; and a small piece of glass, the upper edge being smooth and rounded. The ground in the vicinity was tested, but no other remains were ascertain-

[1] *Proc. Soc. Antiq.* 1st ser. ii. 47 ; *Crania Britannica*, pt. ii. plates 39, 40, and illustration of iron knife in text.
[2] *Journal*, vol. xxvi. p. 1 ; *Proc. Soc. Antiq.* xvi. 92.

able. Competent authorities declared at the time that the remains were of Saxon origin, and it may here be added that the piece of jet or amber was in all probability a specimen of the so-called ' pulley-beads,' which have been noticed in cremated burials at Castle Acre and Pensthorpe in Norfolk,[1] and in an unburnt burial at Sarre, Kent.[2] They may have been used in a game resembling the modern backgammon, dice having been found with them in Kent ; and the holes were possibly for fixing the rough material on the lathe centre.

Already in 1824 the distinction between the prehistoric and Anglo-Saxon barrows or sepulchral mounds in the vicinity of Lewes was clear to the local historian ; and it is a rare pleasure to quote a paragraph which well represents the present view : ' While the larger barrows (of the pre-Roman population) are more thinly scattered than the smaller ones and scarcely ever occur in groups of more than three or four, the small barrows are generally in large groups, but occasionally they are to be found separate. According to Dr. Douglas (the author of *Nenia Britannica*, 1793, and at one time vicar of Preston, Brighton), these owe their origin to the period included between the fifth and the latter part of the seventh centuries, after which time burial on the waste lands ceased, as cemeteries became connected with churches when the inhabitants were converted to Christianity. In these were occasionally discovered military weapons of iron, swords, spear-heads, and the bosses of shields. Graves of women and children contained beads of glass, amber and amethyst, brooches inlaid with garnets and other gems, gold and silver amulets, buckles and other curious relics ; and in barrows of this class were occasionally found coins of the Christian emperors, Valentinian, Anthemius (467–472), etc.'[3]

Very few Anglo-Saxon finds are, however, recorded by Horsfield, and essential details are generally wanting ; but there seems little doubt as to the nature of a barrow on the hill overlooking Glynde Bourne, a socketed spear-head of iron[4] being found on the right side of a skeleton. On the same hill among barrows containing urn-burials of earlier date, were found six or seven skeletons lying in separate excavations in the chalk but near each other. They had been carefully interred at a depth of 4 or 5 feet, and each had a knife[5] in the left hand, while most of them were surrounded by a circle of large flints, placed with great care around the body. An umbo (shield-boss) in good preservation is casually mentioned[6] as having been discovered at Hammond Place, near St. John's Common ; but more interest attaches to a find, now preserved in the British Museum. Three circular specimens are illustrated[7] of a considerable number of bronze brooches found in a barrow on Beddingham Hill, some being oblong though not further described ; but a buckle from the same barrow[8] is more determinate.

[1] *V.C.H. Norfolk*, i. p. 335. [2] *Arch. Cant.* vii. 308, grave 198.
[3] Rev. T. W. Horsfield, *History and Antiquities of Lewes*, p. 42.
[4] Op. cit. pl. iii. fig. 13 and p. 46. [5] Op. cit. pl. iv. fig. 3.
[6] Op. cit. p. 49, note 2. [7] Op. cit. p. 48, pl. v. figs. 10, 11, 12.
[8] Op. cit. pl. iii. fig. 3.

A HISTORY OF SUSSEX

In the year 1800 Lord Gage exhibited to the Society of Antiquaries of London [1] two swords and a knife, fragments of a stone bracelet and of a buckle which had been recently found with six human skeletons in a field which had been tilled for two centuries, in the parish of Beddingham, about five miles from Lewes. The skeletons lay about a foot below the surface, in different directions. Three males and one female lay east-and-west, with the head westward, and the female between the two others ; while one was north-and-south, with the head to the south, and another with the head to the north. A quantity of beads were also collected, which had probably been hung round the woman's neck.

The position of several graves above the chalk pit near Glynde railway station [2] was not marked in any way on the surface ; and it was only by the removal of the top-soil or by the fall of the underlying chalk that they were discernible. Bones were often observed on the lower level, but very seldom could they be traced to any grave above. Except for a small pottery vase [3] between 3 and 4 inches high found in 1870, nothing but the usual iron knives were found on the site, and the inference is natural that the community was a poor one. The graves, which were about 18 inches from the surface, were however all east-and-west, and the absence of grave-furniture may have been due to religious scruples. The only peculiarities noticed were that in some cases one leg was crossed over the other, and in one instance, in a grave 3 ft. deep, the head lay on the right side facing the south.

In 1879 Saxon interments were found by the side of the road leading from Glynde to Ringmer, through a spear-head projecting from the face of a cutting.[4] Eight burials were brought to light, and seven of these lay nearly parallel to each other with the head towards the south-west, the remaining one pointing almost due north. Between two of these graves were found seven urns of the ordinary black pottery imperfectly fired.[5] They had been placed on the chalk, which had been carefully smoothed to receive them, and were quite plain, containing bones in each case. The articles found with the unburnt burials consisted as usual of iron spear-heads and knives, and a shield-boss ; and there were also some rivets, a bronze buckle, and a Roman coin of the kind known as third brass, which was quite illegible through corrosion. Several balls of pyrites were found in the graves, but these do not appear to have been used for making fire. An interesting point was that the position of the large-headed iron nails, used to ornament the edge of the shield, showed that it was circular with a diameter of about $2\frac{1}{2}$ ft., and was made of wood.

On the north-western slope of the high ground east of Lewes a

---

[1] *Archaeologia*, xiv. 273.
[2] *Sussex Arch. Collns.* xxiii. p. 82.
[3] Figured full-size, *Sussex Arch. Collns.* xx. p. 54.
[4] *Sussex Arch. Collns.* vol. xxxiii. p. 129.
[5] These seem to have been Bronze age cinerary urns, but they were possibly Roman. Anglo-Saxon cremations have not been proved south of the Thames.

discovery was made in 1830 during the construction of the winding road which avoids the steep ascent of Malling Hill. At a point opposite the first mile-stone from the county town, upwards of twenty human skeletons were laid bare, associated with iron spear-heads, sword-blades, knives or daggers and shield-bosses. The greater number were destroyed, but Dr. Gideon Mantell[1] secured some swords, the longest 34 inches and 2 inches wide ; spear-heads from 8–12 inches long ; knives, bosses, iron buckles, two small pottery vases, and the green glass bracelet now in the British Museum, which still encircled the bones of the fore-arm, no doubt of a woman. These skeletons were very near the sur-face, the mounds (if any) which originally covered them having been levelled by the plough ; and as there were indications of similar remains many yards round the spot excavated, this may be included among the cemeteries of the South Saxons. It was noticed here as elsewhere that no coffins were used, and that the sword was on the left of the warrior, the spear on the right, though not necessarily in the same grave. The direction of the interments is unfortunately not recorded, but by analogy they were probably east-and-west.

Anglo-Saxon remains were discovered in 1891 while excavations were in progress for the foundations of a house called 'Saxonbury' and in the grounds adjoining. The site is in the parish of Kingston, near the west end of the parish of Southover, in a field at the rear of the Sussex Artillery Volunteer depôt, not far from the Brighton and Lewes railway line. The discoveries were spread over a period of some months and at first recorded by various members of the Sussex Archaeo-logical Society, a complete account being afterwards compiled by Mr. John Sawyer[2] ; and the objects recovered from the soil were presented to the Lewes Museum by the owner of the site, Mr. Aubrey Hillman. In all about thirty-two skeletons were found in an area of 130 ft. by 50 ft., and with few exceptions were lying east-and-west, the head being at the west end of the grave, and so facing the east. A few graves were quite empty, the bones having perished, while in several no relics of any kind were found with the skeletons. About the same number of graves contained no furniture beyond the common iron knife, but three swords were found along the left thigh, and several spear-heads of iron either on the right or left side of the head. Shields, or remains of them, were found in four or more cases, over the middle of the skeleton ; and brooches, some in pairs, were found in the graves of women. Of two pairs of shallow 'saucer' brooches, one had a diameter of $1\frac{1}{4}$ inches with concentric rings separated by short radiating lines ; and the other pair, slightly smaller, was decorated with the debased animal forms char-acteristic of the period. Half of a bronze-gilt clasp, probably for a bracelet, belongs to a type common in East Anglia, but quite out of place in Sussex ; and four beads, with part of a bronze dish not further described, practically complete the list of finds.

---

[1] *A Day's Ramble in and about Lewes*, p. 134.
[2] *Sussex Arch. Collns.* xxxviii. 177, with plan of the graves.

From the neighbourhood of Lewes we pass to Brighton. The elevated ground between Dyke Road, Stanford Road, Port Hall Road and the old Shoreham Road seems to be the site of a Saxon cemetery dating from pagan times.[1] A Roman villa and sundry graves had been found in the vicinity some years before, but it was in 1884 that the first traces of later interments were discovered. During excavations for the foundations of the school at the top of Hamilton Road some human bones were uncovered that were resting on the chalk subsoil about 3 ft. from the clay surface. The position of the skeleton was north-and-south, the head being to the south, and the grave contained a large iron spear-head, an iron dagger (or part of sword) and a knife. The second grave close by was found to be 5 ft. longer than the skeleton within it, though the latter was of large build. It contained a smaller spear-head and an iron shield-boss of the usual kind, which retained traces of the wood to which it had been fixed, while the finger-bones were still attached to the handle. A rivet from the shield was also recovered which is of interest as showing that the thickness of the wood was about $\frac{3}{4}$ in. The iron relics are preserved in the Brighton Museum, with three shield-bosses found with a sword in Stafford Road.

In the museum at Lewes Castle are a few spear-heads, a shield-boss and knives found with skeletons about $2\frac{1}{2}$ ft. from the surface near the junction of Church Road and St. Andrew's Road at Portslade-by-Sea.[2] The orientation of these graves suggested a Christian origin, and accords well with many cemeteries in the county which have yielded similar relics.

The discovery on High Down Hill of what may be regarded as a typical cemetery of the South Saxons has not only supplied material for the early history of the district, but has also proved a valuable addition to the archaeology of the period. The site is about two miles from the sea, behind the village of Ferring, a few hundred yards west of the well-known Miller's Tomb, and about 5 miles to the west of Worthing, the land between the down and the sea being a dead level of fertile soil. Within the ramparts of an ancient British camp,[3] the Saxon cemetery covers rather more than half the width of the enclosed area ; and was found to contain upwards of 86 interments, which were carefully excavated and fully described[4] by Mr. Chas. H. Read, the Secretary of the Society of Antiquaries. In the autumn of 1892 Mr. Edwin Henty, while planting trees on this site, came upon a number of graves which, from the character of the relics found in them, were readily determined to be of Saxon origin ; but it was found impossible to make an accurate record of the earliest discoveries. As soon as the nature of the find was determined, the owner readily undertook a thorough examination

[1] D. B. Friend's *Brighton Almanac*, 1885, p. 166.

[2] *Portslade-by-Sea Parish Magazine*, August 1898 and June 1899, kindly communicated by Rev. C. A. Marona.

[3] A plan and section of the earthwork is given in *Archaeologia*, vol. xlii. p. 27 ; and earlier excavations described in *Journ. Brit. Arch. Assoc.* xiii. 274.

[4] *Archaeologia*, liv. 369 ; lv. 203.

ANGLO-SAXON REMAINS

of this part of the camp. Various excavations had been made in former years within the intrenchments, but the existence of a Saxon cemetery had not hitherto been suspected ; and the discoveries made in 1893 and 1894 far surpassed in interest and value all previous results. The area excavated, which seems to include all the Saxon burials within the ramparts, extends northwards from about the middle of the southern side, and can only have been used as a cemetery during a limited period. The graves are of uniform construction, there being at most half-a-dozen exceptions to the rule that the body should lie stretched on the back, with the head at the west end of the grave. The depth varied from $2\frac{1}{2}$ to 5 ft. from the surface, the solid chalk forming the bottom of the grave ; and the filling in was, first, chalk rubble, above which was often found a layer of grey material, as if a kind of plaster had been made of the chalk. This grey layer sometimes extended to the upper soil, and when thus found was a sure indication of a grave beneath. Although there was no apparent design in the arrangement of the graves, yet there was never any overlapping of the various interments, nor in any case did two bodies lie in one grave. The limits of each burial were quite distinct, and though sometimes two were close together, there was no appearance of chance in the selection of the spot.

It may be concluded that here, as at Farthingdown, Surrey, and elsewhere, some kind of memorial of a more or less permanent character

IRON 'ANGON,' HIGH DOWN CEMETERY. ($\frac{1}{6}$)

had been placed above each grave, but no traces of such exist ; and it may safely be assumed that the surface of the ground within the ancient camp has, apart from natural causes, not been altered in any way since the cemetery was made. The skeletons presented no remarkable features, but the men were mostly of large build, the thigh bone indicating a height of about 6 feet, and none had the appearance of old age, if the state of the teeth may be taken as an indication. A curious parallel to an instance at Firle was noticed in the case of a young man who had a hole in his skull large enough to admit a finger, but death had not been instantaneous, for the opening had been originally twice as large, and the bone had therefore grown considerably since the wound was inflicted. The orderly arrangement of the cemetery and the care evidently bestowed on the interments are sufficient argument that here, as in so many other localities, the inhabitants were in peaceful possession of the land ; and it seems probable that the settlement in this case was on the lower land at Goring or Ferring, each about a mile distant from the hill, and, as the names imply, both of Saxon origin.

Details of all the graves are supplied in Mr. Read's two papers, and it will only be necessary to notice here the more remarkable relics recovered from the site. To deal first with weapons, a single example of the so-called 'angon' (see fig.) was unearthed, the characteristics of

341

this rare type of spear-head being the pair of barbs that usually lie along the shaft and the disproportionate length and slender make of the metal stem, which was provided with a socket for a wooden shaft, though itself 30 inches long. About one grave in every ten contained the ordinary iron spear-head which is usually considered the mark of the Saxon warrior, but no spear could be found in the grave which contained one of the two swords met with in the cemetery, a fact in support of the view that the thane wielded the sword on horseback while the ceorl fought on foot, armed with the spear. On the other hand it was observed that four of the thirteen graves known to have been those of men, contained no spear-head. Any distribution of the entire number of graves between the sexes cannot now be attempted, but about ten per cent. were the interments of children. An analysis of the relics does, however, indicate that men alone were buried with strike-a-lights, tweezers,[1] and vessels of glass, pottery or wood ; while beads and other ornaments were confined to the other sex.

POTTERY VASE, HIGH DOWN CEMETERY. ½

Special attention must be drawn to the vases, which occur in twenty-two graves. Only one bucket was found, and that had hoops of iron 6 inches in diameter, which lay at the right of the head. The more customary bucket with bronze mounts was not represented except by a solitary fragment in the grave of a woman. Pottery vases, to be distinguished from the cinerary urns found in cremation districts, were found in twelve graves, all of men or boys, and included a Roman 'thumb-pot' of New Forest ware like one found at Hassocks. In one grave two vases were discovered in association with a plain conical glass drinking horn, 5½ inches high, and three other glasses of this type were found in the cemetery, the decoration consisting of applied glass threads, either encircling the cup (fig. 8) or in vertical loops (fig. 9). Two cups of 'mammiform' type were recovered : one ornamented with threads, lay beneath a spear-head at the right shoulder, and the other, unfortunately shattered by the spade, had a bold quatrefoil design on the bottom, originally traced with applied threads. Of quite another pattern were the other three glasses, which brought the total up to nine. Two of these were of modern appearance, but were peculiar in having the foot hollow, while the third is at present without a parallel in this country.

[1] It is sometimes asserted that these implements were used in sewing, to draw the thread through holes made by a stiletto.

ANGLO-SAXON REMAINS

The accompanying illustration (fig. 2) renders a description of the shape unnecessary, but something must be said with regard to the remarkable inscription in Greek capitals below the lip. The letters, like the frieze of hare and hounds below, were lightly cut by means of the wheel, and are evidently a rendering of the common Latin phrase *utere felix*, an explanation first suggested by Mr. Haverfield. The Greek phrase, with a feminine participle, has indeed been found on a small gold hairpin in France,[1] and it may be regarded as a wish that good health may attend the use of the phial. Mr. Read points out that, while the Greek inscription suggests the south of Europe, Byzantium itself may well have been the place of origin, for such an artistic and valuable object could hardly have been produced in the Teutonic north at that time. While similar hunting scenes occur on a number of vases dating from late Roman times, the shape of the vessel is neither Roman nor Saxon, and there can be little doubt that the phial was imported, not perhaps in the ordinary course of trade, but possibly by some warrior who had shared the plunder of a highly civilized community.

Nothing further was found in the grave, at the west end of which the phial had been placed, so that it is now impossible to decide on the sex of the interred person. All the other vessels came from the graves of men, but a chemical analysis of the contents by Prof. Church renders it probable that the phial once contained a cosmetic, and the interment may thus be an exception to the rule observed in this cemetery.

Ornaments which usually mark a woman's grave, are exceptionally found associated with the spear or other symbols of the sterner sex : one particularly rich interment must be noticed. At the head lay the iron hoops of a bucket already mentioned, and elsewhere a pair of iron tweezers, an iron knife, buckle and ring, and a spiral ring of silver for the finger ; but the most interesting relics were a pair of bird-shaped brooches of bronze-gilt, inlaid with silver and set with garnets (fig. 6). These belong to an unmistakable type found in the Isle of Wight and Kent, and occasionally elsewhere in southern England, but also common in the contemporary graves of Normandy. The exact converse of the Saxon brooch is presented by a pair of iron brooches with pins of bronze : they are of a common late Roman form, but are rarely found in Anglo-Saxon graves.

The gilt buckle with its plate (fig. 1) as well as the small 'button' brooches (fig. 4) might have come from Kent or the Isle of Wight, but larger brooches on the same principle are known as saucer-brooches and are practically confined to the West Saxons. The High Down examples of this type are comparatively numerous, and except those from Saxonbury are the only specimens the county has produced : the ornament consists of an alternation of concentric rings and radiating strokes, or the continuous spiral, recalling the *Keilschnitt* of the 5th century. The latter style of incising bronze is also seen on the delicately chased orna-

---

[1] *Revue Archéologique*, xxxviii. (1879), 39-45.

ment for a girdle (fig. 3), which is strangely unlike Saxon work and bears a close resemblance to a specimen from Bishopstone, Bucks.[1] These were either imported from the Continent or were the work of some Romanized craftsmen, whose continued presence can hardly be inferred from the few articles of Roman character from the site. Besides the New Forest vase and iron brooches already mentioned, there were several melon-shaped beads, also single coins of Domitian (much worn and pierced), of Fausta (struck at Trèves about 329 and also pierced for suspension), and of Constan-

BRONZE HEAD OF FAUN, HIGH DOWN. (½)

tius II, who reigned 337–361. With this last was a barbaric copy of the head of a Faun (see fig.). The coins only show that the burials were later than the middle of the 4th century, and that Roman coins had become rare enough to be made into pendent ornaments.[2]

A few square-headed brooches (fig. 5) were found in pairs, and can be readily assigned to a well-defined class common in Kent and the Isle of Wight, the cruciform design on the foot having no special significance but being a constant feature. Other brooches from High Down are difficult to classify, but the more elaborate are akin to a rare Kentish type of which the best known example is from Sarre, Kent, and is now in the British Museum. The square form (fig. 7) is altogether unusual, and the ornamentation has none of the Saxon characteristics. One example of the penannular brooch seems of somewhat later date, and belongs to a small series found in various parts of England, Wales, and Ireland, perhaps of the early Viking period. One without a pin was found in an Anglo-Saxon cemetery at Bifrons,[3] near Canterbury, and the pattern may be a reminiscence of the small penannular brooch of Roman times. In any case they appear out of place in south-east England, and were probably worn by the pirates who frequented St. George's Channel.[4]

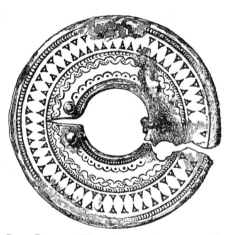

RING-BROOCH, HIGH DOWN CEMETERY. (¼)

More than one problem arising from the discoveries at High Down must here be left unnoticed, but for our present purpose it is essential to remark

---

[1] *V.C.H. Bucks*, i. 199.
[2] Examples from East Shefford, Berks, are in the National Collection.
[3] *Arch. Cant.* vol. x. p. 303.
[4] Two in the British Museum are from Abingdon (*V.C.H. Berks*, i.) and Dublin; other are known from Derbyshire, Anglesey and Kent, as well as from the Roman site of Caerwent, Mon.

C·PRÆTORIUS·F·S·A·

ANGLO SAXON ANTIQUITIES FROM SUSSEX

the uniform orientation of so many graves, and the entire absence of relics in twenty-five, or about thirty per cent. of the total excavated. This is by no means unprecedented, but supports the view that burials with the head to the south or south-west, of which there are a few examples at High Down, are earlier and pagan, while the change was due to Christian influences which cannot have been very strong among the Anglo-Saxon population till the second half of the 7th century.

The similarity between two flattened bronze tubes from graves at High Down and one found at Croydon, Surrey, was remarked upon ;[1] but besides these three peculiar and unexplained objects there are other particulars which point to some connexion between the early Teutonic settlers north and south of the Weald. At Croydon were found several relics of remarkable interest ; and though parallels have been found for all of them, some were of such rare and peculiar form as to warrant a further inquiry into their local distribution. The most striking instance perhaps, after the tubes already mentioned, is the glass vase standing on a foot[2] which has more than a family likeness to three found at High Down, and it is seldom even in Kent that glass of this period has anything but a rounded base, constituting a true tumbler.[3] The 'button' (or diminutive 'saucer') brooch which is rarely found outside the Jutish districts occurs both at High Down and at Croydon ;[4] and the ring-brooch, which is such a special feature of the High Down cemetery, is also represented at Croydon,[5] but hardly anywhere else, and it should be noticed that the angon occurs once on both sites. Another weapon of equal rarity in this country is the francisca, or battle-axe of peculiar type, and though it has not yet been found at High Down, specimens are known from Croydon,[6] and one from Lewes[7] is preserved in the museum of the Sussex Archaeological Society there. The orientation of the High Down graves is now established ; and, though not certain, it is probable that the Croydon burials were likewise east-and-west. According to the evidence available, this was the prevailing practice in both counties,[8] though it involves a problem that still awaits solution. That light will before long be thrown on the ethnological relations of the tribes that carved England out of Britain, is rendered highly probable by an examination of the important series from the cemetery of Herpes, Charente, about the centre of the west coast of France. Among the objects recently acquired for the British Museum are several square-headed brooches like fig. 5, buckles like fig. 1, conical glasses like figs. 8 and 9, and several with feet like that of fig. 2 ; also a button brooch like fig. 4, while bird-brooches like fig. 6 frequently occurred. Nor do the coincidences end here, for the angon and francisca were found, the latter in some quantity, and several rare brooch-forms were represented on both sites.

---

[1] *Archaeologia*, liv. 378.   [2] Illustrated in *V.C.H. Surrey*, p. 257, fig. 1.
[3] The delicate lobed vases are a distinct class.   [4] *V.C.H. Surrey*, fig. 8, and p. 261.
[5] Op. cit. p. 262.   [6] *Proc. Soc. Antiq.* xv. 331.
[7] *Proc. Soc. Antiq.* xviii. 28.   [8] *V.C.H. Surrey*, i. 269.

Some interesting deductions were made by Mr. Horton-Smith [1] from the examination of fourteen skulls from High Down, Sussex, presented to the Cambridge University Anatomical Museum by Mr. C. H. Read. The fact that many Saxon ornaments had been found with them leaves no doubt as to the age of the burials ; and comparison with West Saxon and other skulls shows that the Sussex specimens uniformly exhibit certain peculiarities which may throw some light on the character of the Teutonic conquest of this district. The craniological details which form the basis of his arguments were supplied by Mr. Horton-Smith himself ; and his results accord so well with the scanty but equally trustworthy evidence of archaeology, that no excuse is needed for introducing this factor in the elucidation of early Sussex.

Broadly speaking, the amount of Teutonic blood in a given subject varies directly in this country with the comparative length of the skull from back to front ; and it may be regarded as a leading principle in British craniology that the intermixture of Teutonic immigrants with the original occupants of the soil may be estimated by the variation of the skull from the average Anglo-Saxon type. By this method it appears that the South Saxons were of a purer type than their fellows of the west. While the sea-board of Wessex compared with the size of the kingdom was anything but extensive, intermarriage with the Romanized Britons would in all probability have proceeded rapidly and have left its mark in a modification of feature and skull form. Sussex on the other hand consisted in the early days of little more than the sea-coast, and was doubtless occupied by relays of Saxons, who must have intermarried to some extent with the natives, but retained the Teutonic type in comparative purity. The fusion of race is much more noticeable among the West Saxons, as Dr. Beddoe has also observed. According to that authority the Saxon type is very conspicuous about Chichester, the starting-point of the Conquest. Regular features, elliptic head and face, brows moderately arched, nose straight and often rounded or bulbous at the point, mouth well moulded, complexion fair and transparent, eyes well opened, the iris seldom large, of a beautiful clear blue, but sometimes brown or hazel, hair flaxen or brown of various shades, seldom bright, curly or abundant. [2]

A discovery further west has still to be noticed. In the neighbourhood of Arundel several Anglo-Saxon barrows were opened near a spot called ' Friday's Church ' on the Downs in 1893–4. Besides skeletons the only finds were two iron knives and a small bronze pin. The slightly raised mound called Friday's Church was found to consist of a rough platform of large flints embedded in clay. A small spring of water is at the foot of the hill, and it has been suggested that the spot was originally dedicated to Freya, the present name being a corruption. [3]

The discoveries so far described belong to a period before the

[1] *Journal of Anthropological Institute*, vol. xxvi. p. 82.
[2] *Races of Britain*, pp. 256–7.
[3] Communicated by Mr. H. C. Collyer, of Beddington.

restriction of burials to the consecrated ground of the churchyard. This change took place about the middle of the eighth century, and by that time Christianity had been professed by the South Saxons for about a century, they having been converted among the last in England. Some of the unfurnished graves with the Christian orientation may well belong to that century of transition, but the bulk must obviously date from the two hundred years preceding the conversion, if we accept the traditional date of the Teutonic conquest. It may some day be possible to make further subdivisions and to distinguish the earlier from the later pagan burials by an examination of the grave-goods, possibly in connexion with orientation. Though the entire sequence cannot yet be formulated, some points bearing on the subject may here be mentioned, in addition to the comments already made on the various cemeteries.

As might be expected in a district between two Jutish settlements, there are some examples in the county of Kentish work, or at least of work best represented among the Cantwara, for many of the relics may have been imported ready made from the Continent. And here the connexion is as much with the western coast as with the north of France. The rich and extensive cemetery of Herpes in the Charente includes most of the ornamental types found on High Down, while the bird brooch is found not only in the Visigothic cemetery but plentifully in Normandy and farther east. Such ornaments may indeed have been traded to these shores, but it is natural to suppose that some at least were brought by settlers from Gaul who would preserve and reproduce their traditional patterns in England. They would also adhere to their own burial practices, and it must be remembered that the Visigoths founded a kingdom in south-west France early in the fifth century, when they had been nominally Christians for a hundred years. Though nothing of an unmistakably religious character has been found in the early graves of Sussex, the east-and-west position of the majority corresponds to the almost invariable orientation of several large cemeteries abroad, in which Christian symbols are also remarkably scarce. Existing evidence is insufficient to determine the actual course of events ; and graves cut in other directions become increasingly difficult to explain if the east-and-west position is considered to have been the rule amongst the first Teutonic settlers of Sussex.

Influence from another quarter can be traced at High Down if nowhere else in the county, and the *Anglo-Saxon Chronicle* supplies a plausible explanation of West Saxon brooches in that cemetery.[1] In 607 Ceolwulf, King of Wessex, is recorded to have fought against the South Saxons ; and though Sussex was evidently under Mercian protection in 661, twenty years later the South Saxon king was slain by Caedwalla of Wessex ; and troubles began which culminated five years later in the wasting of Kent and the Isle of Wight by the unconverted West Saxon. The High Down graves are in all probability somewhat

[1] *Anglo-Saxon Chron.* (Rolls Ser.), i. 38.

earlier than the middle of the seventh century, and the warfare of 607 may have resulted in some permanent West Saxon settlement. Further, if the battle of 568 was really fought at Wimbledon, it is by no means impossible that Sussex as well as Surrey suffered from the prowess and ambition of Wessex in the latter half of the sixth century. Certain curious parallels in cemeteries north and south of the Weald have already been referred to.

An interesting relic[1] of later Anglo-Saxon times is figured in the first volume of the *Sussex Archaeological Collections*, and was found in 1847 at Willingdon, in cutting the branch railway from Polegate to Eastbourne. This is a casket of cast lead 12 inches long, with a breadth of 10 or 11 inches and a depth of 7 ; and the sockets of iron handles for lifting remain on two sides. On both the other and longer sides is a triangular device of interlaced work, including a cross ; and in addition to this the vessel is ornamented with a lozengy pattern of corded work, which was commonly employed on lead coffins of the Roman period. Though there is little to show the purpose for which it was made, there is every reason to agree with the date assigned to it by the owner, for the knot-work is characteristic of the tenth century.

All the finds that now remain to be noticed are of coins dating from the period between the full establishment of Christianity in Sussex, and the landing of another conqueror at Pevensey. Though such hoards have a value of their own, they do not at that comparatively late period throw much light on the origin or condition of the inhabitants, and may therefore be dealt with in a summary fashion.

The discovery of a single Saxon penny at Milton Street near Alfriston led in 1843 to the recovery of about sixty more in a field where two had been found some fifteen years before that date. Though this total was reached only by careful sifting of the earth, it is not unlikely that they formed part of a hoard which had been deposited in the days of Edward the Confessor (about 1060), for many varieties of his coinage are represented as well as twelve pennies of Cnut, two of Harold I. and one of Harthacnut. Four pieces are from Sussex mints : a Cnut from Chichester, an Edward from both Lewes and Hastings, and a Harthacnut from Hastings, struck by the same moneyer as the last, three of these being figured in the original account contributed to the first volume of the *Sussex Archaeological Collections* (p. 38).

What is generally known as the Chanctonbury hoard is of considerable importance. In 1868 Mr. J. C. Lucas wrote of the site as follows : 'The manor of Chancton, of which Chancton Farm was the demesne, is situated in the parish of Washington, about one mile north of Chanctonbury Ring. In the time of Edward the Confessor it belonged to Harold's brother, Gurth. The Old Manor House has long disappeared, and the farmhouse which stood on its site is remembered only traditionally. A barn, cattle-shed and yard marked the site until 1865, and on their removal the ground was planted, and a few coins of

[1] Illustrated in *Journ. Brit. Arch. Assoc.* iii. 160. It is now in Lewes Museum.

CASKET OF CAST LEAD FROM WILLINGDON

To face p. 348

the same period as those since discovered were found. In December 1866 this site was ploughed for the first time, and the jar in which the hoard had been deposited was disturbed and the contents scattered in all directions. A general scramble ensued and a large number of coins were dispersed, but 1,720 were delivered to the Treasury as treasure-trove.' All these coins, secreted probably by some tenant of Earl Gurth just before the arrival of the Normans, were silver pennies of Edward the Confessor and Harold II., struck at various mints, including four in Sussex, viz., Chichester, Hastings, Lewes and Steyning.[1]

About 17 miles east of Chancton is Offham, where in 1796 a small quantity of Anglo-Saxon coins was discovered.[2] It consisted chiefly of pennies of Edward the Confessor and Harold, which appeared as if they had come fresh from the mint, so that they were probably deposited at the same time and under the same circumstances as the famous Chancton hoard.

A coin of Offa found at Beddingham recalls the charter of Archbishop Wulfred, dated 825, in which Offa's previous connexion with the monastery[3] there is recorded ; and an allusion is also made to it in a charter, dated 801, of Coenwulf King of Mercia, one of whose coins is supposed to have been found in the neighbourhood.[4] A coin of Alfred is recorded from the West Gate, Chichester[5] ; and of five silver pennies of Ethelred II. found in digging for flints just below the turf on the south side of Harting Beacon four were struck in London, and one at Colchester.[6]

The village of Sedlescombe lies between two and three miles east of Battle Abbey, and in 1876 a labourer employed in draining found a metal vessel[7] containing a hoard of coins, perhaps once enclosed in a leather bag. They numbered between two and three thousand pieces, of which 1,136 were catalogued, and all belonged to the reign of Edward the Confessor (1042–66). They were minted at forty-four different cities and towns in England, from York to Dover and Exeter, but three-fifths were struck at Hastings itself ; and all belong to the middle of the reign.[8] By that time Norman influence was gaining strength, and the Anglo-Saxon race that had fought and conquered some six centuries before were soon to find a master on the fatal field of Senlac.

[1] *Sussex Arch. Collns.* xix. 189 ; xx. 212. *Numismatic Chronicle*, N.S. vii. (1867), 63.
[2] *Sussex Arch. Collns.* xxi. 219. Dallaway and Cartwright, *History of Rape of Arundel*, 222.
[3] *Sussex Arch. Collns.* xxi. 32. [4] Ibid. xxi. 219. [5] Ibid. xxiv. 298.
[6] Ibid. xxxix. 225. [7] Now in the Barbican at Lewes.
[8] *Sussex Arch. Collns.* xxvii. 227 ; xxxiii. 1, 20.

DOMESDAY SURVEY

THE county of Sussex having in its origin been a complete and self-contained kingdom, and having even after its conquest by Wessex remained for a considerable period semi-independent; being, moreover, cut off from Surrey on the north by the dense forest of Andredsweald and from Kent on the east by the same forest and the marshes of Rye and Romney; it is to be expected that we should find this county presenting certain features, if not unique, at least dissimilar to those of neighbouring counties. Such a distinctive feature is to be found in the existence of the rapes, which have greatly influenced the political history of Sussex from the time of the Conquest down to the present day.

At the time of the Domesday Survey Sussex was divided apparently into five portions, between which the boundaries ran, roughly, north and south. These five divisions were the rapes of Hastings, Pevensey, Lewes, Bramber (not actually so named in the Survey) and Arundel (which included what was afterwards the two rapes of Arundel and Chichester).[1] Each of these rapes consisted of a strip of country of varying size and value, containing one town or borough of maritime, military and commercial importance. These towns were Hastings,[2] Pevensey, Lewes, Steyning and Chichester. Each of these towns had a harbour and a market, and although genuine pre-Norman castles in England have been proved extremely rare, it is possible that each possessed fortifications of a kind, and it is certain that by 1086 the Norman lords had built in each a castle—except in the case of Steyning which, being in the hands of the abbey of Fécamp, had been supplanted for military purposes by the neighbouring position of Bramber.

Each rape was in the hands of a single tenant-in-chief, that of Hastings being held by Robert Count of Eu, Pevensey by the Count of Mortain, Lewes by William de Warenne, Bramber by William de Braose, and Arundel by Earl Roger Montgomery; and the rapes were so far identified with their lords that the scribe more often wrote 'the rape of the Count of Mortain' than 'the rape of Pevensey'; in fact 'the rape of William de Braose' appears only under that name and not

---

[1] The Rape of Arundel is mentioned twice *eo nomine*, but there is frequent mention of 'the rape of Earl Roger,' and, as he held the present rape of Chichester as well as that of Arundel, it would seem that, at least in his hands, they were treated as a single rape (J.H.R.)

[2] Rye and Winchelsea in this rape were probably already ports of some importance, and the latter appears to have had a mint for a short period as early as Edgar's reign (Hawkins, *Silver Coins of England* [ed. 3], 148).

as the rape of Bramber. Moreover each rape appears to have had its own sheriff. Mr. Round was the first to suggest that this was the case, and to point out that Robert fitz-Tetbald, a prominent undertenant of Earl Roger, was probably sheriff of Arundel.[1] Gilbert 'vicecomes' mentioned under the borough of Pevensey (fo. 20*b*) in the Survey was probably sheriff of Pevensey rape, as Walter de Richardiville was at a later date;[2] another sheriff of that rape being Ranulf, who is referred to by William Count of Mortain as 'vicecomes meus.' In the rape of Hastings Reinbert, who was one of the largest subtenants, appears in several charters to the collegiate church of Hastings as 'Reinbert the sheriff', while Henry Count of Eu granted to the same church tithes 'de vicecomitatu meo,' which must refer to the rape of Hastings. This last charter also contains mention of a gift of land made by William son of Wibert 'quia de vicecomitatu comitatus quem tenuit retinuit decimam', where we apparently have the shrievalty of the county opposed to that of the honour or rape; and a similar case is presented by the title with which Roger Hay attested a charter by Robert 'the butler', as 'vice-comes regis'. For the rape of Lewes, while Domesday gives us no hint of the identity or even existence of a sheriff, we have ample evidence of such an officer in the chartulary of Lewes priory.[3] William de Warenne IV. (?) confirmed a grant to the priory by Peter the sheriff, his charter being attested by Payn 'vicecomes de Lewes', who as plain 'vicecomes' also attested a charter in company with Seffrid, Bishop of Chichester, and Hamelin, Earl Warren, the date of which must be between 1180 and 1202. William de Warenne II. (?) also addressed two charters, one to Hugh 'vicecomes de Lewes' and the other 'Hugoni vicecomiti ceterisque suis villicis et omnibus suis hominibus'; this being probably Hugh de Plumpton who is alluded to by the same earl in another grant as 'tunc vicecomes meus'. Finally, Reginald de Warenne's concession of a merchant guild to the burgesses of Lewes c. 1148 is addressed 'vicecomiti de Lewiis et omnibus baronibus comitatus.'[4] In the case of the rape of Bramber two deeds of Philip de Braose confirming his father's grants to the abbey of Battle, dated about 1096, are attested by 'Buzeus vicecomes.'[5]

Having considered the nature of the rapes—apart from their fiscal aspect, which will be considered later—we have to deal with the question of their origin.

When we consider the uniqueness of the institution, which cannot be paralleled in either England or Normandy, it would seem more likely that they should have originated under the independent and isolated kings of the South Saxons than under the wide rule of the Conqueror.[6] Nor is the name 'rape' antagonistic to such an origin, for although it is usually held to be connected with the Icelandic terri-

[1] *Suss. Arch. Coll.* xlii. 86.   [2] Round, *Cal. of Doc. France*, p. 434.
[3] Cott. MSS. Vesp. F. xv.   [4] Ibid. Nero C. iii.
[5] Visc. Gage's MSS. (*Hist. MSS. Com. Rep.* iii. 223).
[6] The only similar territorial division is found, it is said, in Holland, where the name is supposed to have originated in the rope enclosing the open-air court of the district (J.H.R.)

torial division *hrepp*, it is at least as likely that it might be derived from the Saxon *rap*, a (measuring) rope,[1] or *reaps*, a space. It would seem improbable that the Conqueror should divide one county alone in England in this manner; but on the other hand, it must be remembered that Sussex was of unique importance to the Normans as the key of England, its ports being the shortest and most direct route between the two countries. It was therefore necessary for William to secure his lines of communication by placing them in the hands of men bound to him by the closest ties of blood and service, such as Robert of Mortain, his half-brother; the Count of Eu; the great Roger de Montgomery, his cousin and trusted officer; William de Warenne, whose wife seems to have been the Conqueror's step-daughter; and William de Braose. It was especially important to secure the fencible ports of Hastings, Pevensey, Lewes, Steyning, Arundel and Chichester, while the necessity of protecting the lines of communication from the coast to London and the midlands in the always possible event of one of the tenants-in-chief proving rebellious would favour the shaping of these fiefs or baronies into a series of parallel strips running north and south. Thus only by a most improbable political combination could the road from Normandy to London be blocked.

A further argument in favour of the Norman origin of the rape is to be found in the fact that, as will be shown later, the rapes appear to have been essentially geldable units and to have been granted by the Conqueror to their tenants at an arbitrary assessment of a round number of hides, which bore no such definite relation to the pre-Conquest assessment of the same districts as we should have expected had those districts enjoyed the same organization before as after the Conquest. Also the apparent application of the term rape[2] to the liberty of Battle Abbey (fo. 17*b*) which we know to have been formed by grant of William I. suggests that the other rapes must also have been of Norman formation.

Again, the far greater frequency with which the rapes are referred to by their possessorial than by their territorial titles suggests a recent institution, which is further borne out by the fact that the outlying portions of many manors were in the Confessor's time scattered through the county without regard to the boundaries of the rapes, though after the Conquest all such outlying portions were cut off from the parent manor and included in the body of the rape within which they lay. Finally, we may notice that the boundary between the rapes of William de Warenne and William de Braose cut through the two hundreds of Windham and Fishergate, and was therefore probably of more recent establishment than they; and it will be seen later that these hundreds were probably of no great antiquity.

[1] Lower (*Compendious Hist. of Suss.* i. p. vii.) quotes from a 'recent publication by an able French antiquary (Hericher)' the following passage :—'We shall find in Normandy a great number of the names of those chiefs to whom Rollo distributed Neustria by the cord—"suis fidelibus terram funiculo divisit."'

[2] But see below, p. 375.

So then there is some evidence in favour of a Norman origin for the rape ; but we have still to consider the cases in which the word occurs in conjunction with a verb in the past tense apparently implying a reference to the time of King Edward. For instance, Sedlescombe 'pro una hida et iii virgis foris rapum se defendebat' (fo. 20). Here the allusion is clearly to the period before the Conquest, but its wording implies a contradiction, as land *foris rapum* is shown in the section of this article dealing with the fiscal side of the survey to have been exempt from that payment of geld which is implied in the phrase *se defendebat*. A possible explanation is that *foris rapum* is used merely in its technical sense of exempt from geld and applies only to the virgates, the translation being ' was assessed for one hide and (there were) three virgates exempt.' The case of Shelvestrode, however, where the Count of Mortain ' hab(et) 1 hidam que jacuit in rapo de Lewes. Nunc extra rapum est. Non geldat. Alnod tenuit de rege E.' (fo. 22*b*) appears to be a distinct reference to the pre-Conquest existence of rapes, as does an entry concerning Sedlescombe, which sets out that one virgate held by Walter fitz Lambert ' nunquam geldavit et semper fuit foris rapum ' (fo. 20) ; while a puzzling phrase is found in connection with a manor in Lewes rape,—' Ipsi villani sunt in rapo comitis Moritonii sed semper fuerunt extra rapum ' (fo. 27*b*). When we further find in the ancient customs of the borough of Lewes that a payment was due from the purchaser of a man ' in whatever place he may buy him within the rape,' it seems at least highly probable that the rape was of pre-Conquest institution.[1]

But whatever was the origin of the rapes as *districts*, as *lordships* they owed their existence to the Norman Conquest alone. With the exception of the Church's holdings the whole of each rape was held by a single Norman lord. As the possessions of the English landowners had straggled over several rapes and were intermixed with one another, the new system revolutionized the whole tenure of the county. The lordship of land was now determined, not by the manor to which it had belonged, but by the rape in which it lay. So rigidly was this system enforced by the breaking up of those manors which lay in two or more rapes that Domesday notes, as if an exception, of Fécamp's estate at Steyning :—' In rapo de Harundel sunt xxxiii hidæ et dimidia et aliæ in rapo Willelmi de Braose, et *tamen* abbas tenet omnes modo.' For in the same column the church of Bosham, as an illustration of the rule, is recorded to have lost no less than forty-seven hides, which lay in the distant rape of William de Warenne.

The second remarkable feature of the Sussex survey is connected with the pre-Conquest manors in the county. The exact significance of the term ' manor ' as used in Domesday has been the subject of much debate and confusion, due in part at least to the endeavour to tie the

[1] The origin of the rapes was discussed in vol. i. of the *Archæological Review* ; Mr. F. E. Sawyer arguing for their introduction by the Normans (pp. 54–9), while Sir Henry Howorth and Mr. Round supported the opposite view (pp. 229–30).

Domesday scribe to a rigid consistency of language which the whole record shows to have been to a remarkable degree alien to his nature. Mr. Round has shown that the terms 'manerium' and 'terra' were often used indifferently as equating one another,[1] and the conclusion to be drawn from this is expressed by Professor Vinogradoff[2] when he says that 'we find the hall, the grange, and the berewick as constitutive elements and adjuncts of the manor, and this shows that the essence of the manor consisted in its economic organization—it was an estate to begin with, whatever other meanings and applications the term may have had.' The manor, alike in name and feudal significance, was a still young institution of Norman origin, probably partially introduced into England by the foreign favourites of the Confessor. The invaders on their arrival found a certain number of manors existing, formed many more themselves, and applied the term to any estate whose organization approximated, however loosely, to the condition of a manor. It is not unnatural that there should be the same confusion between a manor and an estate during the early childhood of the manorial system that we find when that system was moribund in the eighteenth century. At the same time the term had a certain significance, though vague and indeterminate, and it is necessary to examine what light is afforded by the portion of Domesday here under examination.

It is clear that the essential feature of the manor was its hall ; so far was this the case that the two were regarded as equivalent, and it was possible to write ' in his duabus terris nisi una halla' (fo. 26b), or the converse but similar phrase, 'tunc fuerunt ii hallæ modo in uno manerio' (fo. 27). This 'hall' appears in the concrete as an actual building—the manor-house or court—under 'Apedroc,' where a virgate is mentioned where the Count has his hall as Harold had before him (fo. 21b). In it Professor Maitland thought he saw the house at which the geld was paid,[3] a theory which derives some support from a phrase used of Westmeston—'non fuit ibi halla neque geldavit ut dicunt' (fo. 27), but which has been shown by Mr. Round[4] to be based on insufficient grounds, so far at least as certain counties are concerned. Another phrase which equates with hall is 'caput manerii', which occurs under Ditchling, where six copses are said to have belonged 'ad caput manerii' (fo. 25b), or again under 'Nerewelle,' where Robert 'the cook' is said to hold the 'caput manerii' (fo. 18) with two virgates. In this last phrase one is tempted to see the Saxon 'heafod-bodel' ; and indeed the *mansio* or *manerium* in its primitive sense of a manse is almost a translation of the *bodel*—the abode, and points us back to our former conclusion that the manor in its origin was an estate centering upon the house of the landlord or his representative. This seems as far as our evidence will safely carry us, and so far our conclusions are applicable to any county, but we have now to consider in what respects the manors of Sussex differed from those of other districts.

[1] *Engl. Hist. Rev.* xv. 293.   [2] *Growth of the Manor,* p. 301.
[3] *Domesday Book and Beyond,* p. 107.   [4] *Engl. Hist. Rev.* xv. 293–5.

In the Domesday Survey of many counties we find a large number of cases in which manors possessed outlying estates called berewicks, and in some counties also soc-land ; these members were usually at no great distance from the manor to which they belonged. But in Sussex, although the term berewick only occurs on three occasions,[1] and soc-land not at all, we have between sixty and seventy cases in which a manor had in King Edward's time one or more outlying estates intimately connected with it, though often as much as twenty or thirty miles distant from it.

The case of Aldrington to the west of Brighton throws light in various ways on the manorial problem. Before the Conquest we find it divided into two portions, of which one contained seven ploughlands and was assessed at $7\frac{1}{8}$ hides, while the other, though only containing four ploughlands,[2] was assessed at 9 hides. The former was an outlyer of the Crown manor of Beeding, and the latter of Wigod (of Wallingford)'s manor of Broadwater, both of which were in Bramber rape and therefore fell, at the Conquest, to the share of William de Braose. As Aldrington lay in Lewes rape, its two portions were severed from the manors to which they had belonged, and were both given by William de Warenne to Godfrey, one of his knights.[3] Domesday, however, surveys them separately, but adds the note : ' In his duabus terris nisi una aula,' implying that their joint tenure by Godfrey was making of them one manor. The details of the survey show that in 1086 only the (former) Broadwater portion had a demesne, while the Beeding portion, which had been held by villeins (' villani tenuerunt '), was still worked by villeins and bordars alone, having no demesne land.[4] At Brighton itself, on the same page, we have an interesting case for comparison in Widard's manor (5 ploughlands), which was 'in uno manerio' at the time of the survey, but which had been held by three ' aloarii,' of whom ' unus habuit aulam et villani tenuerunt partes aliorum duorum,' which implies that these two latter had no demesne.

Another interesting illustration is afforded by the case of Edburton, between Steyning and Poynings, on the border of the two rapes. Of its 1,250 acres about 700 are in its eastern half, the hamlet of Fulking, which is in the rape of Lewes, while the western half, in the rape of Bramber, contains Edburton village itself, the manor of Truleigh in the west of the parish, and the hamlet of Perching in the centre. Domesday, surveying the parish under Truleigh, Perching, and Fulking, assigns the first only to William of Braose and his rape of Bramber, and shows us Perching as divided, before the Conquest, into four portions. Two of these had been held by separate tenants of Azor, but were surveyed in one entry as a single manor, held of William de Warenne by William de Wateville.[5] A third was still held by its English owner, Osward,

---

[1] It is still found in the county as a place-name.

[2] It is noteworthy that in 1835 ' the whole of the parish' was described as ' divided into two farms, of very unequal size.'   [3] Probably Godfrey de Pierpoint.

[4] Similarly at Westmeston, an estate of Countess Gueda, we read ' sub ea tenebant villani ; non fuit ibi halla.'   [5] ' Tunc fuerunt duæ hallæ ; modo in uno manerio.'

but now under William de Warenne; and the fourth, which had belonged to Truleigh (in Bramber rape), was now severed therefrom, as being in Lewes rape, and given by William de Warenne to Tezelin, who also received from him the adjoining estate of Fulking, an outlyer of the distant Shipley in Bramber rape[1] and therefore now severed. Domesday observes of these two estates: 'Hæ duæ terræ Tezelini insimul sunt; valent et valuerunt semper 1 solidos.' This implies that, though separately surveyed, Tezelin was making of them one manor. Thus were the old combinations broken up at the Conquest, and fresh ones formed. And this one has an interest of its own; for we can trace the manor. Tezelin was a cook, and as a cook he held by a cooking service, among the king's serjeants at Addington in Surrey.[2] Consequently Addington and the estate in Edburton descended together, and the history of the latter (as 'Perching') can be traced throughout.[3]

When manors were thus dissolving and forming in the melting-pot of the new system, it is not surprising that Domesday's information on their pre-Conquest constituents is at times not only defective, but perhaps inexact. The 50-hide manor of Alciston, lying in Pevensey rape, had lost outlying members to the extent of $3\frac{1}{2}$ hides situate in Hastings rape and 2 hides in that of Lewes. But no indication of their whereabouts is given under these rapes, and we are left to discover their identity from a charter of Henry I. So also we read of Ham(sey) that it had lost eleven of its twenty-five hides 'quia aliæ sunt in rapo comitis Moritonii scilicet vii hidæ, et in rapo Rogerii comitis iiij hidæ dimidia virga minus.' But in the two rapes named the only estate mentioned as having formed part of Ham(sey) is one of four hides in Horsted (Keynes) in Pevensey rape, which had been held like Hamsey, by Wulfgifu ('Ulveva'). As her name only occurs twice elsewhere, in Sussex, one is tempted to guess that her seven hides at (East) Preston in Earl Roger's rape had been a constituent of Ham(sey), and that the scribe had actually transposed the names of the rapes in the passage quoted above.

Besides the instances already given, the most remarkable case of this association of scattered estates is to be found in a large group of manors in the rape of Pevensey, contained, roughly speaking, within a triangle whose points are at Eastbourne, Waldron and Beddingham. Almost every one of the manors in this group had one or more detached portions lying in Hastings rape in the hundreds of Hawksborough, Shoeswell, and Henhurst. As it has been assumed by several writers in the past that the group of holdings entered under the Count of Eu's lands in Hastings rape, but bearing the names of Pevensey manors, were actually situated within the bounds of Pevensey rape, but had been granted to the count in addition to his holdings in

---

[1] 'In Sepelei jacuit, quod tenet Willelmus de Braose.'   [2] *V.C.H. Surrey*, i. 328.

[3] See preface to Stapleton's *Liber de antiquis legibus* (Cam. Soc.), p. iv. where, however, that distinguished antiquary makes the strange mistake of identifying the manor of Perching, which descended with Addington as that which 'was held of him (W. de Warenne) by William de Watteville.' This destroys the point of the Domesday evidence.

Hastings rape, it may be as well to point out that the contrary can be shown to be the fact, by analogy with the cases in the other rapes—of which a few are quoted above—by the fact that the descendants of those who held most largely in the lands in question subsequently held in Hastings and not in Pevensey, and by a charter of Henry I., referred to below, which shows that portions of Alciston manor did actually lie at Borzell, Shoeswell, and other places in the eastern rape.

The origin of these scattered members can be explained in two ways, either by the simple grant of the lesser estate to the tenant of the greater, or by the settlement on waste lands of *coloni* from the manor for purposes of cultivation. The latter theory would suit well enough in the case of the densely wooded country in the rape of Hastings, but is improbable in most of the instances outside that rape, and especially in such a case as that of Bosham, where it is far more likely that Plumpton and Saddlescombe should have been granted to the richly endowed church than that they should have been waste or uncultivated. The manner in which the outlying estates are spoken of inclines one to believe that both such processes—grant and colonization—may have been at work. On the one hand we have definitely named estates apparently as complete in themselves as their parent manor ; on the other we have estates which, although now separate and self-contained, have as yet no name, but can only be referred to as having been ' in ' such a manor ; and finally we have two instances of transition in the ' manor which is called Hou '—now Howcourt in Lancing—formerly part of Hurst(pierpoint), and the other ' manor which is called Hou ' —now Hooe—which had belonged to Willingdon.

It is noteworthy that though all these outlying members had a potential assessment they were not paying geld at the end of the Confessor's reign ; as in each case it is either definitely asserted that the detached holding in question 'nunquam geldavit,' or else all mention of its assessment T.R.E. is omitted. Now before 1086 these outlying estates had all been cut off from their manors and formed into separate holdings attached to the rape in which they physically lay ; and in almost every case the geld assessment of the parent manor was reduced by an amount equal to that at which the lost member was potentially assessed.[1] This can only point to the geld having been assessed in Sussex at the end of King Edward's reign not by vills but by manors. In support of this theory may be advanced the phrase already quoted, ' non fuit ibi halla neque geldavit', and the most interesting phrase in connection with Washington, ' Lewin dedit geldum domino suo et dominus suus nihil dedit ' (fo. 28). To this latter instance we have a post-Conquest parallel in the liberty of Battle Abbey, which was exempt from payment of geld to the king, but which paid geld—as is shown by

---

[1] The few cases in which the assessment remained unchanged in spite of the loss of a member may be due to the reconstruction of manors, a new estate being absorbed in compensation for that lost—or by the fact that the assessment was arbitrary and not directly connected with the extent or even value of the holding.

the exception made in favour of the abbot's demesne—presumably to the abbot.

In dealing with the fiscal side of the survey in Sussex—and Domesday is of course essentially a fiscal record—one is met at once with an exceedingly remarkable difficulty. No axiom of Domesday research is more elementary than that four virgates make one hide, and yet in Sussex we are compelled to suspect and almost to assert that eight virgates went to the hide. The question has been debated by Professor Tait and the present writer in the *English Historical Review*,[1] and here it will be sufficient just to indicate the nature of the evidence on either side. Briefly, then, the existence of the eight-virgate hide is supported by : (i) a number of entries of holdings of 'half a hide and 2 virgates,' '4 hides and 5 virgates,' '3 hides less 2 virgates' ; and the case of Brightling which was assessed at one hide, and where 'of this hide Robert holds 4 virgates' ; all of which suggest a hide of more than four virgates : (ii) the clear statement of the chronicler of Battle Abbey[2] that 'eight virgates make one hide,' supported by the assessment of the liberty of Battle Abbey, which is stated in the chronicle[3] to be 6 hides and half a virgate, and is found to consist of $3\frac{1}{2}$ hides and $20\frac{1}{2}$ virgates : (iii) the case of 'Francwelle,' which is assessed at 2 hides, and was composed of 1 hide and 8 virgates ; also several other cases pointing in the same direction but not clear and indisputable. Against this must be set : (i) the cases of 'Werste,' where 4 hides and 3 virgates and 5 virgates appear to make 6 hides ; and Boxgrove, where 6 hides seem to be composed of $5\frac{1}{2}$ hides and 2 virgates : (ii) the probability that the fiscal units of hide and virgate would bear the same relation to one another in Sussex as in other counties. This last argument is indeed so strong that, although a good case can be made out for the 8-virgate hide, I hesitate to go further than to suggest its probable existence.[4] Professor Tait's suggestion that the difficulty may be due to 'beneficial hidation'—the total assessment of the manor being reduced but that of the subtenures retained—is strengthened by the evidence we have produced for the geld having been paid by manors and not by vills, and is further supported by the evidence of pre-Conquest 'beneficial hidation' which has now to be considered.

In the case of several midland counties—Cambridge, Northants, Bedfordshire—Mr. Round has, by means of some very pretty little addition sums, proved the existence of the 'five-hide unit' in the assessment of vills. No such unit is observable in Sussex [5]—nor indeed

---

[1] Sept. 1903; Jan. and July, 1904.   [2] Dugdale, *Mon.* iii. 242.

[3] Domesday Book says $6\frac{1}{2}$ hides.

[4] At the same time it is clear that the existence of a hide containing double the usual number of virgates would not cause any confusion in the collecting of the geld, as the assessors—working upon the unit of the hide—would assess the fractions of the hide at twice the usual number of virgates ; thus half a hide would equate with 4 virgates in Sussex instead of with 2 as in other counties, and so on.

[5] Mr. Round however holds that such assessments as those of Alciston (50), Lyminster (20), Malling (80), Stanmer (20), Pagham (50), Tangmere (10), Bishopstone (25), Henfield (25), Selsey (10), Preston (20), Donnington (5), Bexhill (20), Wilesham (15), and Sherrington (5), show distinct traces of the five-hide unit.

should we expect it during the period when the county was assessed by manors and not by vills—and, indeed, no system at all can at first be discerned in the geld figures even when they have been tabulated. The assessment of the hundreds T.R.E. varies from 265 hides (Steyning) to $1\frac{3}{4}$ ('Latille') and $1\frac{1}{2}$ ('Tifeld'), and practically the only point of resemblance between the various totals lies in their almost unanimous avoidance of any semblance of a round number. It is difficult to believe that such can have been the original condition of the hundreds, and it is worth noticing that it is possible to form the Domesday hundreds into groups strictly in accordance with their positions on the map, each of which groups is approximately a simple multiple of eighty hides—taking the figures given T.R.E.[1] Moreover the only hundred of which we can assert the antiquity with any degree of certainty is that of Malling, held entirely and for more than two centuries before the survey by the archbishop; and this was assessed at 80 hides. In view of the hundred being supposed to have originally contained one hundred hides this suggests a pre-Conquest reduction, or 'beneficial hidation,' of twenty per cent.; and this theory receives support from another important source. The total number of 80-hide units in Sussex is found to be forty-two and a half, which gives an original, unreduced assessment of 4,250 hides, which is in remarkably close agreement with the 4,350 hides attributed to Sussex in the early hidage roll known as the Burghal Hidage.[2]

Whether any such wholesale reduction did take place or not, it is clear that beneficial hidation was in progress before the end of the Confessor's reign, from a number of entries which state that there *were* so many hides in the manor, but they paid geld for a smaller number. Mr. Round has shown[3] that this refers to an earlier assessment and not to the existence of areal hides. A good instance is to be found in the first entry in the Sussex survey, where it is said of Godwin's manor of Bosham ' then there were $56\frac{1}{2}$ hides but it paid geld for 38 ' (fo. 16).

It is, however, in the Norman period that beneficial hidation becomes so pronounced a feature of the Sussex Domesday. At first sight the reduction of assessment appears most wild and arbitrary. Nothing could have much less appearance of method than the assessment of the archbishop's holdings, where Pagham is reduced from 50 hides to 34, Lavant from 18 to $9\frac{1}{2}$, Patching from 12 hides to 3 hides $3\frac{1}{2}$ virgates, and Tarring from 18 hides to 7 hides 1 virgate. It is not until we add up the totals and find that an assessment of 214 hides has been reduced to 160 hides $\frac{1}{2}$ virgate that we realize that the archbishop had obtained an abatement of twenty-five per cent. on his whole

---

[1] This is not the place for the elaboration of what is after all only a theory, but I may mention that I discovered this grouping by 80-hide units accidentally, while vainly endeavouring to re-constitute the Domesday hundreds into 100-hide groups; and that the groups, which vary from 3 units to half a unit, are usually less than two and never more than six per cent. at variance with the sum required on the 80-hide hypothesis. Whether it would be possible to re-constitute each of the original 80-hide units from its components I have not yet discovered.

[2] *Dom. Bk. and Beyond*, p. 502.   [3] *V.C.H. Hants*, i. 404.

fee. The slight reduction of the Bishop of Chichester's geld from 168 hides to 160 hides 1 virgate may possibly have been intended to place him on an equality with the archbishop. When we turn to the lay barons the same lack of apparent method in the reductions is noticeable, but when we find the assessment of the Count of Mortain reduced from 520 hides to 401, that of William de Warenne from 597 to 526, Earl Roger from 768 to 648, the Count of Eu from 190 to 172 and William de Braiose from 425 to about 132, it is scarcely overbold to assume that the rape of Pevensey was assessed at 400 hides, that of Lewes at 525, Earl Roger's holding at 650, Hastings rape at 175, and that of Bramber at probably 150 (the Braose figures are rather puzzling). For the geld from these round numbers of hides the sheriffs of the several rapes were no doubt responsible to the sheriff of the county, and naturally the assessment within each rape was so adjusted as to benefit the lord of that rape ; that is to say, instead of reducing the liability of each manor, vill or hundred, by an amount proportionate to its share of the whole, the two or three principal demesne manors of the tenant-in-chief had their liability very greatly reduced, while the remaining manors were left practically unaffected.[1] Thus Earl Roger's manors of Singleton and Harting were reduced respectively from $97\frac{1}{2}$ hides to 47 and from 80 to 48 ; in Lewes rape Iford was cut down from 58 to 36, Rodmell from 64 to 33, and Patcham from 60 to 40. The Count of Mortain did things on a still larger scale, reducing the 48 hides of Firle and the 50 hides of Willingdon to nothing. In the rape of Hastings the reductions are so slight as to be hardly worth notice, while in that of Bramber on the contrary almost every manor is more or less reduced, though here again the greatest fall is in the case of William de Braose's demesne manor of Washington, reduced from 59 hides to nothing.

An additional argument in favour of the rape having been a fiscal unit is the association in Domesday and contemporary records of the terms rape and geld, an association so intimate that *foris rapum* became a technical expression signifying exemption from geld, and it was possible to write either : ' *Tunc se defendebat* pro 41 hidis modo pro nichilo *quia nunquam geldavit*' (fo. 27), or ' Una virga est insuper que non geldat *quia est foris rapum* ' (fo. 26*b*). Here we have a double equation, *se defendebat* (was assessed) answering to *geldavit* (paid geld) and *foris rapum* to *non geldavit*.[2] A number of instances of the use of the phrase *foris rapum* occur in Domesday, and in the deeds of this period in the cartulary of Lewes Priory ; an especially good example is the grant by William Malfed of certain lands which ' owe no hidage or other service *quia sunt de forsrap*.'[3]

Before leaving the subject of the geld we may note the remarkable case of ' Esseswelle ' Hundred, which, as is stated both at the beginning

---

[1] Mr. Round drew attention to this arrangement in *Domesday Studies* (pp. 111, 113), and inferred that it involved the reduction being later than the process of sub-infeudation.

[2] The use of *nunquam* in the restricted sense of ' never since the Conquest' should be noted, and can be paralleled from several other passages.

[3] Cott. Vesp. F. xv. fo. 43.

and end of the return of that hundred, never paid geld (fo. 19) ; and also the mention—unique in Domesday—of 'herdigelt,' which is said to be paid by all the estate of Beeding (fo. 28).

Turning from the problem of the geld assessment to that of monetary values, we are met by the much debated question of the exact significance of the Domesday 'valet.' Here again the whole difficulty arises from the endeavour to restrict the scribe to a definite and unvarying use of the term, and yet it is sufficiently obvious that no article of the survey would be less likely to be consistent than this of the 'valet.' The 'value' of an estate as declared by its landlord, its tenant, a land valuer, and the local oracle will be found to vary considerably and may even fluctuate in the opinion of its owner according as he is appealing against an assessment or for compensation. Where we are told that an estate 'has always been worth 100 shillings,' or that it 'was worth 15 shillings and now 30 shillings,' we suspect a rough estimate by the jurors of the hundred, but when the value is given as being £6 11s. 8d., or we are told that the manor 'was worth 13 shillings and is now worth 63 pence,' it is clear that the reference is to the actual rents and other issues received. The identity of the 'valet' and issues is also evident in cases where, besides the value in money we hear of rents in kind—so many eels from the mills, so many thousand herrings, or so much honey—while in a number of cases on the other hand the two are carefully contrasted. Thus the value of Steyning is £100, but 'it is on lease (ad firmam) for £122'; in Bosham the bishop's share was worth £16 10s. 'et tamen habet de firma 20 solidos plus,' and Mauger whose share was worth £6 7s. had 50s. more. In the case of Earl Roger's manor of Singleton we are told that 'it is now valued (appreciatur) at £93 and 1 mark of gold, and yet it pays £120 and 1 mark of gold.' In all these instances it is clear that the hundred court considered that the sums obtained from the manors by the chief or mesne lords could only be wrung from the peasantry by extortion and grinding oppression, excessive even to the unsentimental mind of men used to the hard servile tenures of the time. And indeed in several instances we find that the grasping landlord had overreached himself and had been obliged to reduce his demands ; thus Shoreham, which was worth at most £35, had been leased at £50, 'but that could not be borne,' and the same words are used of Patching, a manor of the Archbishop of Canterbury, who was a great offender in this respect, as the jurors noted that his manor of Pagham which was worth £60 was paying £80— 'sed nimis grave est,' and his manor of Wooton which was worth only £4 had for a while paid £6, 'sed non potuit perdurare' ; the Bishop of Chichester also had tried to make £25 out of his manor of Preston 'but it could not pay so much.'

The valuation of a manor is given for three periods—the time of King Edward, the time when it passed into the hands of its present possessor, and the time of the survey. Speaking generally the most noticeable feature of these three valuations is a fall during the second period, usually accompanied by a rally in the third, bringing the last value up to or beyond the first. Of course there are many instances of values maintained, or even steadily rising, but as a rule the value immediately after the Conquest is less than it had been just previously. This is indeed what would be expected ; but, as far as western Sussex is concerned, it does not seem possible to draw any definite conclusions from the figures : adjacent lands suffered in very different degrees, and the personality of the Saxon tenant seems to have had no influence on the depreciation—contrary to what we find in some counties where the manors of Earl Godwin appear to have been ravaged and those of the queen spared. But in eastern Sussex we are able to see something of the desolating effect of the passage of an army through the country. The values for the second period are lacking in the case of the hundred of Pevensey, where William landed, but the fifty-two burgesses of Pevensey diminished to twenty-seven, and the manors of Bexhill, Wilting, and Filsham lying between Pevensey and Hastings are all returned as having been 'waste' in 1066, as were also Guestling and 'Ivet,' east of Hastings and probably ravaged while the troops were lying in the town, or in the expedition against the men of Romney. The southern portions of Herstmonceux and Hooe probably suffered during this march as their values had fallen respectively from £6 to £1 and from £25 to £6 ; Wartling in some unaccountable way escaped all injury, and neither 'Bolinton' nor Hollington were much affected. On their way to the field of battle the Normans passed through Crowhurst and left it waste, while of six manors within Netherfield Hundred where the battle took place three became waste, one was at the time of the survey valueless, another had fallen from 100 shillings to 20 shillings, and Mountfield had come off lightly with a fall from £3 to 20*s.* Ashburnham, Ninfield and Catsfield all suffered considerably, and 'waste' is written against them and against part of Saddlescombe, Salehurst and the neighbourhood of Ticehurst, but whether these more northern lands were desolated by Harold's army or William's, or by both, it would be rash to decide. Of the varying depreciation of values throughout the county some explanation might be sought in the different warmth with which the tenants responded to Harold's call for levies, and in the losses sustained by the several contingents, but speculation is an unsatisfactory substitute for knowledge, and more than has already been stated cannot safely be deduced from our figures. Although the immediate effects of the Conquest were thus disastrous to Sussex, the injury was but temporary, and by 1086 almost all the wasted manors had recovered, and many had surpassed their original values.[1]

Besides money rents there are three instances in the survey of the

---

[1] Mr. Round has shown that Prof. Freeman in writing on 'William's ravages in Sussex' has erred strangely in asserting that 'the lasting nature of the destruction wrought at this time is shown by the large number of places round about Hastings, which are returned in Domesday as waste,' and in speaking of 'the lasting damage which is implied in the lands being returned as "waste" twenty years after' (*Norman Conquest* [ed. 2], iii. 741) ; for Domesday on the contrary shows the recovery of the manors then laid waste.

survival in Sussex of the interesting and ancient rent in kind known as the ' Firma unius noctis ' or ' Firma unius diei.' The three are King Edward's manors of Eastbourne and Beddingham in east Sussex and Beeding in the west. In the case of the last named we are told that it was worth £95 5s. 6d., which is sufficiently near the £105 which Mr. Round has shown to be the usual value of the ' day's farm.' [1] The other two manors are unfortunately not valued, and there is no trace of any other manor or group of manors having originally rendered this ferm, though the curious valuation of Ditchling at £80 5s. 6d. suggests its former union with another estate valued at £15 which cannot however be traced with any degree of certainty. Nor is there any trace of the peculiarity which marked the royal manors which paid this ' day's farm ' in Hampshire—their not being hidated ;[2] with the exception of a piece of pasture land belonging to Stoughton and a piece of land in the suburb of Chichester, Sussex was completely assessed in hides.

When we turn from the consideration of manorial revenue to that of its sources it is natural to deal first with the most important of these —the arable land. This is estimated in Sussex by the number of ploughs which would be required to till the land of the manor, each plough team being reckoned, in other counties and therefore presumably in Sussex, as of eight oxen, for the use of horses in ploughing was in the eleventh century though not unknown yet quite unusual, and indeed on the Sussex Downs the ploughteam of magnificent black oxen is still a common and most picturesque sight. The ploughteams actually existing on the manor were divided into those on the demesne, or home farm, and those of the villeins,[3] and though usually corresponding to the estimated number were sometimes far fewer, as at Trotton where there were only five ploughs although there was employment for thirty-six, and sometimes in excess, the most notable instances being South Malling, where there were ninety-four ploughs though the number required was estimated at fifty, and Ditchling, where sixty ploughlands supported ninety-nine and a half ploughs. Nor did the ploughlands bear any definite relation to the hidage ; thus, South Malling rated at eighty hides had only fifty ploughlands, while Rotherfield with twenty-six ploughlands was rated at only three hides. For the whole county the number of hides and ploughlands is nearly equal, but their relative values were subject to great local variation ; thus the ratio of hides to ploughlands was in the rape of Hastings approximately one to two, in Pevensey one to one, in Lewes eight to seven, in Bramber three to two, and in Earl Roger's rape nine to eight—the hidage being here taken at its pre-Conquest figure.

---

[1] *V.C.H. Hants*, i. 402.   [2] Ibid.

[3] Mr. Round points out that the endowment of Lewes Priory affords remarkable evidence on this point. William de Warenne's foundation charter (now in the Bibliothèque Nationale, Paris) grants to the abbey of Cluni ' terram duarum carrucarum in proprio in Suamberga cum villanis ad eam pertinentibus . . . et villam Falemetam ubi sunt tres carruce proprie cum his omnibus que ad eam pertinent.' On turning to Domesday we find that the monks had two ploughlands on the demesne of their estate at Iford in Swanborough Hundred, and two on their demesne at Falmer, thus showing that the grant referred expressly to the *demesne*, to which the rest of the manor was looked on as appurtenant.

DOMESDAY SURVEY

The existence of ploughteams implies the existence of pasture, and of this a certain amount was always secured by the well-known three-field system of agriculture, but when much live stock was maintained this pasture would be insufficient, and we accordingly find considerable value set on the water-meadows,[1] of which the holdings varied from two or three acres in the wooded districts of east Sussex to one or two hundred acres in the neighbourhood of Lewes. There are also frequent entries of payments made by men of the manor for the use of the pasture, such payments being usually made in swine, of which large herds were kept and which formed practically the only meat of the poorer classes. The pig occurs very prominently in connection with the woodland. Sussex, for its size, has always been one of the most thickly wooded counties in England, and was especially so at the time of Domesday, and the quantity of woodland in each manor was expressed by the rent paid to the lord of the manor by the villeins for pannage, the right of pasturing their herds of swine in the woods, and this rent was almost invariably paid in swine.[2]

Three different phrases are employed to describe payments due in swine ; one of these, 'porci de gablo,' which is found at Beeding and at Plumpton, occurs, it would seem, nowhere else in Domesday ; another is 'de herbagio x porci,' and the third is, as at Washington, 'de pasnagio silvæ lx porc(i),' or, as in the entries preceding and succeeding, 'silva x porcorum' . . . 'silva de x porcis.' It is to be observed that Plumpton and Beeding have respectively 'silva de xx porcis' and 'silva lxx porcorum' in addition to their gafol-swine, this proving that the two dues were quite distinct in character. Again under Malling, the archbishop's manor, we read of 'silva ccc porcorum de pasnagio' as well as of 'ccclv porci' as part payment 'de herbagio,' which proves that the dues for 'mast' and for pasture were similarly distinct. Lastly an important entry found under the archbishop's manor of Pagham records that every villein who has seven swine must give one of them 'de herbagio,'[3] while a marginal note adds : 'Similiter per totum Sudsex.'[4] This last provision reminds one of the dues from a *gebur* at Tidenham (Glouc.) in earlier days : 'If he has seven swine he pays three, and so forth at that rate, and nevertheless gives mast-dues if there be mast.'[5]

[1] Mr. Round considers that the 'pratum' of Domesday affords a rough indication of rivers or streams, and he points out that the 7 acres at Brighton, 15 acres at Preston, and 84 at Patcham might be accounted for by the stream which once flowed down the London Road valley to the Steyne at Brighton. Also that the rich meadows of the Ouse valley, glorious in summer with green and gold, can be clearly discerned in Domesday, where we trace them through Southease (130 acres) and Rodmell (140) to Iford (208), Tarring Neville also having 50 and Bishopstone 40. At Lewes itself South Malling had 195 acres, and Hamsey above it 200.

[2] In the edition of the survey published by the Sussex Archæological Society in 1886 the translator fell into the unfortunate error of reading *silva de x porcis* as 'wood for x swine,' and in order to be consistent, translated *herbag' de vij porcis unum* as 'herbage for one of 7 hogs.'

[3] So also, under Ferring, 'silva iiii porcorum et pro herbagio unus porcus de vii.' So also at Elsted and Woolavington.

[4] A similar provision is found in Surrey at Malden ('De herbagio unus porcus de vii porcis') and Titsey ('pro pastura septimus porcus villanorum '), while at Battersea and Streatham the tenth pig was due. *V.C.H. Surrey,* i. 29 (J. H. R.)   [5] Seebohm, *English Village Community,* p. 155.

Possibly the payment for the use of the woods was proportionate to the number of swine kept, as in the case of the pasturage rent, but in the absence of evidence it is impossible to form any deductions as to the size of the herds from the rents paid, which vary from 1 to 150 swine.[1]

Though the swine thus formed the most important part of the 'exitus silvæ' referred to under Offham, there were other items, as for instance honey from the swarms of wild bees, mentioned under Beeding and Wappingthorne. Wood with which to make fences occurs in a few cases; a forest is mentioned in connection with Dallington; and the Count of Eu's park in Baldslow Hundred. At Rotherfield was a park which the king had first granted to the Bishop of Bayeux and subsequently taken into his own hands;[2] and land in Tortington and in Waltham had been imparked by Earl Roger, who had also a great park just across the Hampshire border,[3] though we merely hear of it incidentally, while that which William de Braose had formed at Bramber[4] is not mentioned at all.

Another important source of revenue was the water-mills—windmills were unknown in England in the eleventh century. Of these 157 are mentioned in Sussex, very unequally distributed, as only four were in Hastings rape, while Earl Roger had seventy-three, nine of these being in his manor of Harting and five in Cocking; the king had eight in his manor of Bosham and the archbishop the same number in South Malling. In Chiddingly there was a mill 'cum molinario,' meaning either a small mill or more probably the site of a mill; it has occasionally been rendered 'with a miller,' but this is not at all likely to be correct. Their value also was very variable, ranging from 20d. to 20s., the average being just over 8s. In addition to the monetary values there is not infrequent mention of a render of so many hundred eels from the mill pond, and the mill at Arundel made a yearly payment of ten bushels of wheat and as much of mixed grain (probably used for brewing), with four bushels extra (fo. 23). There is even one case of a swine-rent for four mills in Steyning, which paid 47s. and sixty-eight swine in addition (fo. 17).

Rents in kind were also sometimes paid from the fisheries, the payment here as in the case of the mills being made in eels. The entries of herring renders are important as implying that the herring fishery was then carried on from Brighton and from the Ouse, where herrings were received from the adjacent parishes of Southease, Rodmell, and Iford, if not from Lewes itself.[5] At Iford they formed part of the consideration for the pasture; at Brighton they appear to have represented rent (*gablum*). The largest payment of herrings was at South-

---

[1] In the case of 'Estone,' where the large number of 1,500 swine is given, it is possible that the formula should read 'wood for 1,500 swine,' but see note on p. 426.

[2] *Suss. Arch. Coll.* xli. 50.   [3] *V.C.H. Hants*, i. 405.

[4] Round, *Cal. of Docts. France*, p. 37.

[5] The Rodmell entry looks as if the herrings formed part of the rent due from appurtenant houses, but careful consideration of the entries as a whole favours the view that they were due from Rodmell.

ease, where the abbey of Hide wisely provided for fast days by a toll of 38,500 herrings, and this manor also paid a composition of £4 for porpoises (*marsuins*, or sea-pigs, the record calls them). The coast manors possessed a further source of revenue in their saltpans, of which the survey mentions 285, averaging 30*d.* in value. Of these no fewer than one hundred were on the abbot of Fécamp's manor of 'Rameslie' in the neighbourhood of Rye and Hastings ; and their importance is attested by an entry under Pevensey Hundred, showing that the Count of Mortain has retained in his own hands eleven saltpans belonging to the manor of Hailsham, and that he held, as a complete holding, four saltpans in Hooe.

Although the iron mines in Sussex had been worked at least as early as the time of the Romans, only one mine (*ferraria*) is mentioned in the survey, that being in the hundred of East Grinstead and formerly appurtenant to the royal manor of Ditchling. A quarry worth 9*s.* 4*d.* occurs under Iping and another at Stedham valued at 6*s.* 8*d.*, and a third worth 10*s.* 10*d.* under 'Greteham.' In Bignor there was a 'molaria' or quarry for mill-stones, valued at 4*s.* This completes the list of sources of manorial revenue given in the survey ; the special cases of the boroughs will be treated in the section on the Sussex boroughs at the end of this chapter.

On the condition of the population of Sussex, Domesday throws little light. Freemen occur only as pre-Conquest tenants and have no place in the Norman classification, being no doubt for the most part absorbed into the ranks of the villeins. Of the services of these last we learn nothing, though we have one glimpse of their organization in the mention of the reeve of Tangmere, who received 20*s.* from the issues of the manor which it was his duty to collect. Although the villeins in the eleventh century were absolutely at the disposal of their lord and were theoretically mere chattels they often had in practice an amount of liberty to which legally they had no claim. Thus they might even attain to such a measure of comparative independence as to farm the manor to which they belonged, or a portion of it.

As this point is of much importance, the Sussex evidence may here be summarized. Mr. Round has referred to it when dealing with the adjoining county of Hampshire,[1] where we read of two of St. Swithin's manors, that ' villeins held and hold ' Alverstoke, while at Millbrook ' villeins held it and hold it ; there is no hall there ' ; the Sussex instances are more numerous, and belong, as Mr. Round observed, to Brighton and its neighbourhood. At Brighton itself we have the three allodial owners, one of whom had a hall, while the shares of the others were held by villeins ; at Aldrington to the west ' villeins held ' the outlyer of Beeding T.R.E., and we also read that ' villeins held ' another outlyer of Beeding in Lewes rape. Bevendean to the east had been held by ' villeins of Keymer,' and of estates in Iford, adjoining it on the east, we read ' Has terras tenuerunt villani.' Bulmer had been

---

[1] *V.C.H. Hants,* i. 442.

A HISTORY OF SUSSEX

held by villeins, who 'belonged to Falmer'; of 'Felesmere' also we read that 'villeins held' it. Lastly at Westmeston, to the north of Brighton, lying at the foot of the South Downs, we have the noteworthy entry: 'Gueda comitissa tenuit, et sub ea tenebant villani; non fuit ibi halla.' Here we have the same absence of a 'hall' (i.e. demesne) as in the villein-held estates of Millbrook, Hants,[1] and of Willesden, Middlesex.[2] Between Sussex and Middlesex we have, in Surrey, two examples of estates held by villeins.[3]

Nor did the Conquest entirely put an end to this state of affairs, for under Ninfield 'a certain villein' is mentioned as one of the subtenants. It is just possible that in this last instance we may have the former English tenant reduced from freedom to villeinage and holding on sufferance a small portion of the manor of which he has previously held the whole.

Next below the villeins came the bordars, who are called by the equivalent name of cottars[4] in all the hundreds of Hastings rape except Ninfield and Staple[5] and in West Easwrith, Risberg,[6] Benestede, Bury and Bosgrave. About them nothing beyond their number is recorded, save for a single entry in the hundred of Hawksborough where Osbern had 'one cottar who pays twelve pence' (fo. 19). Nor can we learn anything of the lowest class—the serfs—who were not very numerous in this county, the largest number on any manor being twenty at Hastings; there were also seventeen on the royal manor of Bosham, but otherwise they in no case exceeded ten on any estate, being rarer than in Surrey. Burgesses occur several times, but will be considered under the boroughs; 'ten shepherds' are mentioned in Patcham, and 'a fowler' was fortunate enough to retain a small estate near Marden which he had held in King Edward's time, and Chetel 'the huntsman' was allowed to retain land in 'Lodesorde,' which, although surveyed under Surrey, is probably Lodsworth in Sussex.

A class that might in some ways be regarded as almost intermediate between the peasantry and the landowner was the priests, for while they were of course freemen they were yet, in their association with and dependence on their churches, almost 'adscripti glebæ.' Domesday not concerning itself with things ecclesiastical, we hear nothing of parishes, but find the priest spoken of as 'the priest of the manor'; nor is there any particular method in the mention or omission of the church and its minister; usually the church alone is mentioned, sometimes the church

---

[1] 'Non est ibi aula.'   [2] 'In dominio nil habetur.'

[3] *V.C.H. Surrey*, i. 290, 291.

[4] A similar phenomenon has been observed in Surrey, where in three hundreds 'the *cotarii* are nearly universal, to the exclusion of *bordarii*, while in the others the *bordarii* are nearly or quite universal, to the exclusion of the *cotarii*' (*Domesday Studies*, 469–70; *V.C.H. Surrey*, i. 292). It should be observed that these Sussex cottars are classed with the villeins in connexion with the ploughs, which is the regular position of the *bordarii* (J. H. R.)

[5] Under the abbey of Fécamp's manor of 'Rameslie' in Guestling Hundred we find bordars instead of cottars, but cottars are duly entered under the same abbey's manor of Bury.

[6] In the case of the holdings of the Archbishop and Bishop of Chichester in this hundred bordars are returned, but in that of the abbot of Westminster cottars.

368

and its priest, and in four instances the priest is set down without any definite mention of the church which his presence implies. Sometimes the priest is entered as holding the church and a certain amount of land —usually about half a hide, though the 'clerks of the church' of Boxgrove held one hide and the 'clerks of the church' of Singleton as much as 3 hides 1 virgate—at other times the priest's holding and the church are mentioned separately, and most often no land is assigned to the church, not, probably, because there was no endowment, but because the lands thus set apart were usually exempt from geld, as for instance in the case of 'Wilesham,' where 'Ulward the priest of this manor' held the church and one virgate of land, which did not form part of the 15 hides at which the manor was assessed and had never paid geld. Tithes worth 40s. are stated to have been held at Bosham by the clerks, and at Arundel also the clerks of St. Nicholas were in receipt of the tithes, while at Iping 'Circet' or Church-Scot of 30d. is mentioned. It is well recognized that no argument can be based on the omissions of Domesday, and this can be well demonstrated in the case of Sussex, where there is no allusion to the church of Selsey, although barely ten years had elapsed since the see had been transferred from that place, or to St. Dunstan's church of Mayfield, or to that of Worth, which displays so many features of pre-Conquest architecture, or to the nine churches of Lewes mentioned in contemporary charters. But, however many churches were omitted, the survey mentions ninety-eight besides nine 'ecclesiolæ' or chapels, and four priests whose presence implies a place of worship; there were also in Pevensey Hundred three small estates held 'in alms' by clerks, which would suggest the probable existence of chapels.[1] The monasteries and religious foundations which occur in the Domesday account form one of the divisions of the class of landowners with which we have now to deal.

In examining the distribution of the lands within the county previous to the advent of the Normans it is natural to consider first the royal demesne. King Edward had in his own hands the manors of Filsham, Eastbourne, Beddingham, Ditchling, Beeding, Steyning and Lyminster, yielding a total of 240 hides, to which may be added 34 hides held in Bury, Littlehampton and round Warbleton by his sister the Countess Goda,[2] and 91 hides in the hands of Queen Edith at Iford, Frog-Firle, etc., with possibly another 34 hides assigned in various places to 'Eddeva'; 400 hides in all, at most. The royal demesnes sink into insignificance when compared with the vast estate of the mighty house of Godwin, everywhere rich and powerful, but nowhere more so than in Sussex, which was possibly his native county.[3] At Bosham Harold had a manor house which is shown in the Bayeux tapestry, and from that port he set out on the fateful journey which ended

[1] See below, p. 376.

[2] Owing to the carelessness of the Domesday scribes it is difficult to distinguish this Countess Goda from Earl Godwine's wife, the Countess Gida.

[3] For a discussion of the identity of Godwin's father Wulfnoth with Wulfnoth the South Saxon, see Freeman, *Norman Conquest*, i. App. MM.

I   369   47

in his shipwreck on the Norman coast ; Lyminster was possibly connected with Swegen's downfall,[1] and Pevensey was the first scene in his murder of Biorn, which was accomplished at Bosham ; and the seizure by Harold of Steyning which the Confessor had granted to the abbey of Fécamp was one of the many excuses put forward by William to justify the invasion of which the first act saw the fall of Harold, Gurth and Leofwin on the field of Hastings. Altogether Sussex played a large part in the history of the house of Godwin, and if mainly the scene of their disasters was also the source of much of their wealth and influence. Earl Godwin is shown to have held in his own hands 348 hides in the important manors of Bosham, Singleton, Westbourne, Climping, Hurst-pierpoint, Laughton and Willingdon and elsewhere, besides 178 hides held of him by various tenants ; and some part of another 45 hides which are assigned to ' Godwin ' probably belonged to the earl. Harold[2] was, as we should expect, the next largest landowner with 297 hides in Findon, Steyning, Patcham, Rodmell, Ripe, Crowhurst and other manors, and another 41 hides held of him in different places. Next comes the Countess Gida, Earl Godwin's wife, who held $123\frac{1}{2}$ hides including the manors of Harting, Washington, Trotton and Binderton. Earl Leofwin is only given his title in connection with a small holding in ' Ellede ' in Hastings rape, but most if not all of the 70 hides attributed to ' Lewin ' in Sompting, Lancing, Street and elsewhere may be put to his share. Gurth is also only called Earl in connection with his manor (of 59 hides) of Washington, but also held 8 hides in Merston and 5 in ' Cumbe ' ; and Tostig held 6 hides in Fishbourne and half a hide belonging to Leofwin's manor of Sompting. Altogether the house of Godwin held over 1,100 hides, or more than a third of the county. How much of this was personal property and how much consisted of ' villæ comitales ' it is unfortunately impossible to estimate.

Mr. Round observes that the peculiar distribution of lands in Sussex by the Normans prevents our tracing, as in other counties, the English predecessors of the Domesday tenants by the succession to their lands. Of the lesser English landowners in Sussex Azor stands out prominently,[3] his scattered estates ranging from West Dean and Tarring Neville to Greatham, and including such considerable manors as Kingston-Bucy (21 hides), Keymer (14 hides), Cocking and Wiston (12 hides each), and yielding a total of 146 hides. A man of wider fame and more historic importance was Alnod ' cild,' who is elsewhere called Alnod of Kent, and has been shown to be identical with Ethelnoth of Canterbury, one of the hostages whom King William took with him to Normandy in 1067.[4] In Sussex he held the fifty-hide manor of Alciston and

---

[1] It is not quite certain whether the abbess whom he abducted belonged to this place or to Leominster in Hereford, though the latter is more probable.

[2] Mr. Round points out that the Sussex entries bring out acutely the difficulty caused in Domesday by the entries both of Godwine and of Harold as holding T.R.E. ; for T.R.E. is taken to mean the time of King Edward's death, and Godwine predeceased the King. It is difficult to understand why Harold is not given as the former holder in all cases if he had succeeded his father.

[3] It is, however, impossible to be certain that there was only one Azor.

[4] *V.C.H. Surr.* i. 283.

another 4 hides which passed with it into the hands of the Abbot of Battle, but it is not safe to assert that he is the 'Alnod' to whom another 37 hides are assigned, as the name was not uncommon. Ulmar 'cild' occurs at 'Sidenore,' and Brixi, who held at Itford, Stoke and Thakeham, was probably the Kentish noble Brixi 'cild' who also held at Stoke in Surrey.[1] To argue from similarity of names is dangerous, but as Mr. Round has shown that Carle who held Send in Surrey held also in Hampshire, Wiltshire and Somerset, it is allowable to suggest his identity with the Carle who appears at Hartfield, Fletching and Wappingthorn.

Norman, who had held Frankwell, Dallington, Wannock and Annington, and was possibly the Norman who held Camberwell and two manors in Kent,[2] was allowed to retain, as undertenant, half a hide of his manor of Frankwell; the same quantity of land at Cortesley was granted to Golduin the pre-Conquest lord of that manor. Other Englishmen were more fortunate; three nameless men were left in undisturbed possession of 'Glesham,' Bricmaer retained his land in 'Welesmere,' Alward at Heene, and Turchil in Stopham; Levenot lost several estates but kept Peathorne; Osward managed to save Portslade and Perching, and Alwin Wickham and 'Stoechestone.' Most fortunate of all, however, was Haiminc, who must have rendered active help to the invaders to have saved undiminished his manors of Sherrington, Exceat, Frog-Firle and Cholington, leaving them at his death to his son with the Norman name of Richard, who appears as a benefactor of Lewes Priory, and seems to have taken the name of 'de Essete' from his chief manor.[3] But all these now held under the Norman lords of their respective rapes instead of directly of the king.

Of the natives who held lands after the Conquest other than they had held of King Edward the most notable were Ode of Winchester and Eldred his brother, who held of the king in chief at Woolbeding and Iping. Of these two brothers and their possessions in Hampshire and elsewhere Mr. Round has given an account in his introduction to the Hampshire survey.[4] Amongst the subtenants occur such names as Alward, Alwin, Ednod, Alvric, Osward, Godwin, Siward and Wineman, but with one exception they are but names and merely serve to indicate that some few English were less unfortunate than the majority of their brethren. The exception referred to is Chetel, who held by the gift of King William in Stockbridge Hundred a ploughland which had never been assessed in hides (fo. 24). To the fortunate circumstance that this land subsequently passed into the hands of the Bishop of Chichester we are indebted for the preservation of two early charters of much interest. In 1254 the king laid claim to certain land in the suburbs of Chichester which was then held by the bishop, who claimed that it and three messuages in the city had been granted to the see by

---

[1] *V.C.H. Surr.* i. 283.

[2] Ibid. p. 281. The name, however, was not sufficiently uncommon to make this identification sure.

[3] See Mr. Round's paper in *Suss. Arch. Coll.* xl. 77.   [4] *V.C.H. Hants,* i. 427.

the Conqueror, producing in support the following charter[1] : ' W. Rex Angl' W. Epo. Cycestr' et O. fil' Aulg'i et Hoello et aliis ministris suis salm̃. Concedo eccle Cycestr' terram que fuit Chetelli ex[a] portam Cycestr' tenend' libere et honorifice cum soca et saca et infonghenthef. Teste Com. de Moulont apd. Brokehurst.' A point of great importance is that, if this transcript can be relied upon, this charter is addressed to Bishop William whose existence is only known from William of Malmesbury's statement that he succeeded Stigand and from the entry of his name in Bishop William Rede's *Cathalogus.*[2] As Stigand died in 1087 and Godfrey was consecrated Bishop of Chichester in 1087, William's episcopate has hitherto been ignored,[3] but this charter would enable us to restore him to his place amongst our bishops, while at the same time dating itself accurately as having been granted in 1087. Unfortunately, however, the version of this charter given by Dugdale,[4] from a Chichester chartulary which has now disappeared, makes the charter addressed ' R. Epo. Cycestriae,' thus assigning it to William II., Ralph (1091–1125) being the first bishop to whom it could be referred. This chartulary has been shown to be very inaccurate and unreliable as regards the Selsey charters,[5] so that the question of the date of this charter cannot be finally settled without further evidence than is yet forthcoming. A second charter—said to be ' ejusdem regis,' but possibly in reality of William II.—ran as follows :—' W. Rex Ang' Rog' Com' et oibz baronibz suis de Sussex saltm. Sciatis me dedisse eccle de Cycestr' carucatam t're qm. tenuit Ketellus Esterman in Sutsexa et domos q[s] ipse Ketellus habebat in civitate Cycestr'. Testibus Rodb. Bisp' et Rico. de Cuceyo'. The names of the witnesses are evidently corrupt ; probably Dugdale's rendering ' Rodeburto Dispensatore et Rico. de Curceye' is correct.

When we come to the consideration of the Norman holders of lands we find precedence given, as always, to King William ; but it is to his rank that this is due and not to the extent of his estates, which consisted solely of two manors. This is in striking contrast to what we find in other counties, where William normally retained for himself not only Edward's Crown demesne, but the bulk of Harold's manors as well. The manor of Bosham, originally assessed at $56\frac{1}{2}$ hides, but reduced before the Confessor's death to 38 hides—at which it remained rated under William—had been held by Earl Godwin, and had been one of the principal residences probably of himself and certainly of his son, the ill-fated Harold. Its appearance on the Bayeux tapestry has already been alluded to, and it is possible that sentiment may have suggested to William the retention of a place which was once the special seat of his fallen rival. Sentiment is a more important historic factor than many will admit, but whether that or some more prosaic reason influenced him, Bosham was the only Sussex manor which the Con-

---

[1] Curia Regis, 151, m. 38.   [2] *Suss. Arch. Coll.* xxviii. 14.
[3] By Stephens, *See of Chichester,* and Stubbs, *Reg. Sacr. Angl.* amongst others.
[4] *Mon.* vi. 1165.   [5] *Hist. MSS. Com. Rep.* (1901), 179.

queror retained in his own hands when he apportioned the county to his followers. At the time of the survey, however, he also held Rother-field, which had belonged to his unruly brother Odo, Bishop of Bayeux and Earl of Kent. This estate had also belonged to Earl Godwin, and although only assessed at 3 hides was of considerable extent and included a park, in which some writers[1] have seen the explan-ation of the king's seizure of this one item of Odo's great fee, which was otherwise intact in 1086, though the prelate himself was in dis-grace. The economic importance of the smallness of the Conqueror's estate in Sussex lay in the resulting fact that Bosham was the only manor of ' ancient demesne,' and that consequently when the villeins of Brede, Steyning, Laughton, and other manors attempted, as they did occasionally during the thirteenth and fourteenth centuries, to claim the special privileges which attached to manors of ' ancient demesne,' their claims ' scrutato libro de Domesdei ' always failed.

Next to the king came the ecclesiastical tenants-in-chief, beginning with the Archbishop of Canterbury, who held extensively in the county, his chief estate being the manor and hundred of South Malling, which formed a broad strip of land reaching north-east from Lewes to the borders of Kent. It had been rated at 80 hides, but 5 hides had been annexed by the Count of Mortain—who had also taken away $1\frac{1}{2}$ hides of the archbishop's manor of Wootton ;—it is said to have been leased to Godfrey[2] at £90, but as the value of the demesne thus leased was only £70 and had been as low as £30 previously, it is not surprising that the lease had terminated. Wootton, Stanmer, Patching and Tarring formed links carrying the chain of Canterbury manors into west Sussex, where the archbishop held East Lavant, Tangmere and Pagham ; to the latter was appurtenant the church of All Saints in Chichester, ' which pays 64 pence,' either from tithes, church scot, etc., or more probably from rents from houses in the peculiar of the Pallant in Chichester.

The Bishop of Chichester, who in or shortly after 1075 had trans-ferred his ' cathedra ' to that town from the village of Selsey, where it had first been established, held Selsey, Sidlesham, Wittering, Alding-bourne and Amberley in the west of the county, and Henfield, Preston and Bishopstone in Mid-Sussex, but had lost the two manors in Hastings rape which Alric his predecessor had held. Bexhill had been seized by the Count of Eu when he received the ' castelry ' of Hastings, but had been recovered by 1166 when Bishop Hilary made the return of his knights.[3] ' Haslesse ' in Ticehurst had also been lost, but as the Dean and Chapter held land in this parish in the thirteenth century it is possible that part at least of this estate was recovered. The only other loss recorded was four hides in Westbourne which Alric had held ' ad monasterium.' In view of the service of four knights by which the

[1] E.g. Mr. Round in *Suss. Arch. Coll.* xli. 50.
[2] Possibly Godfrey de Pierpoint.
[3] *Red Bk. of the Exch.* (Rolls Ser.), i. 200. Domesday records the hidation as 20 hides, but according to the 1166 return the bishop only claimed (and recovered) ten hides.

bishop in later times held his fee, it is of interest to notice that four 'milites'—Herald, Murdac,[1] Ansfrid and Lovel—occur as undertenants at Aldingbourne, but the application of the term 'miles' to William the subtenant of Henfield, as seemingly equivalent to 'homo' in the entries suggests caution in attaching a technical meaning to the term. The last entry of this fee is an interesting one, showing the canons of Chichester holding in common 16 hides, of which the situation is not stated.

Besides the bishopric two other Sussex religious establishments are entered as holding in chief, though the first of these occurs under the name of its possessor the Bishop of Exeter. At Bosham, where Wilfrid, the apostle of the South Saxons, had found the only glimmering of Christianity in the kingdom, in the humble cell of Dicul and his companions, there had grown up under the Saxon kings a collegiate church which, thanks to the munificence of benefactors whose memory has perished, was so richly endowed that its estate was rated at 112 hides and estimated to be worth £300. This valuable foundation was granted by the Confessor to his Norman chaplain and favourite Osbern,[2] who as Bishop of Exeter retained possession of it under the Conqueror and left it to descend to his successors as a peculiar, causing constant friction between the sees of Chichester and Exeter on points of jurisdiction and privilege. The lands of the church, however, at the time of the survey had been diminished by the loss of 47 hides in the neighbourhood of Lewes, of which Ralph de Chesney held 17 hides at Plumpton noted as formerly part of Bosham and as having been held of Earl Godwin by Godwin the priest. The other 30 hides, held by Hugh son of Ranulf, were evidently, as Mr. Round has pointed out,[3] at Saddlescombe, as here also the subtenant under Earl Godwin was Godwin the priest, who also occurs as the tenant of the church's manors of Woolavington and Farringdon (Hants), and was most probably the head of the college. It was not to Norman rule, however, that this spoliation was due, but to Earl Godwin's greed.[4]

The other Sussex foundation referred to was the Conqueror's great votive abbey of Battle. In accordance with his vow made before the momentous struggle which was to decide the fate of England, William, in gratitude for a victory which had added a kingdom to his Norman duchy, erected to the glory of God and the soldier Saint Martin a great monastery whose church rose where Harold fell. The spot where the battle was fought was wild, little cultivated, hardly inhabited, no village near, perhaps a few little farms and homesteads, but none large enough to give its name to the abbey, which was therefore called 'the Abbey of the Battle.' To this house William gave lands in many counties ; and first of all he gave all the land within a measured circle round the church of three miles radius. This circle constituted the

[1] Richard Murdac was one of the bishop's knights in 1166.
[2] Round, *Feudal England*, p. 320.
[3] *Suss. Arch. Soc. Coll.* xliv. 141.   [4] Ibid. 142.

DOMESDAY SURVEY

Lowy, or ' Leuga ' of Battle,[1] and all the lands within it were freed for ever from the payment of geld and other services. One result of thus drawing a circle was that the Liberty contained only one complete pre-Conquest manor or estate—' Bocheham '—and portions of twelve other manors, of which the main body was surveyed under the lands of the Count of Eu. These lands were assessed at 6 hides—with an extra unassessed half-hide according to the survey, or half-virgate according to the Abbey Chronicle, which in two cases complains that ' the king's book ' has attributed more to the monks than they really held. We have seen that the king exempted the lands of the Liberty from Danegeld and all other payments to the Crown, but as it is expressly stated in Domesday that the $2\frac{1}{2}$ hides which the abbot held in demesne ' have not paid geld in the rape,' it is clear that the remaining $3\frac{1}{2}$ hides must have paid it, in which case the only conclusion is that the abbot collected the geld but did not hand it over to the king. In addition to this grant of land round the site of the church the abbey also received the valuable manor of Alciston in Pevensey rape, which had been rated at 50 hides, but was now reduced to $44\frac{1}{2}$ hides, as outlying portions of the manor had been annexed to the rapes of Lewes and Hastings, in which they were situated. A charter of Henry I.[2] relates that the abbot and convent of Battle had complained that they were charged for 50 hides for their manor of Alciston, although 7 (sic) hides had been taken away from it; in granting relief the king states that these hides lay at Ovingdean, Codingele (Coding in Hooe), Betelesford (Batsford in Warbleton ?), Wivenham, Daningawurde, Scoweswelle (Shoyswell), Baresselle (Borzell), Wertesc, Brembreseboc and Seuredeswelle.

The abbey of Westminster held Parham by grant of King Edward, the abbey of Hyde,[3] Southease and Donnington, and the nuns of St. Edward of Shaftesbury held Felpham in west Sussex. Of Norman monasteries the only one that appears as tenant-in-chief is the abbey of Fécamp, to which the Confessor had given the two valuable manors of ' Rameslie ' in the extreme east of the county, including Rye and Winchelsea and at least part of Hastings, and Steyning. This latter in King Edward's time was worth £86, and had consequently attracted the attention of Harold, who seized it from the abbey and held it ' in fine Regis Edwardi.' William is said to have particularly pledged himself before setting out on the invasion of England to restore this manor to the abbey ; but while doing so he found it advisable to deprive the monks of certain tenements in Hastings—possibly including the site

[1] These lands are described in Domesday Book as held by the abbot ' in suo rapo,' but after careful consideration of all the evidence in and outside Domesday, Mr. Round is of opinion that these words need not imply a ' rape of Battle,' but may only mean ' in the rape of Hastings in which his abbey stands,' as opposed to the rape of Pevensey, in which the rest of the endowment lay.

[2] Harl. ch. 43 C. 12.

[3] Hyde Abbey also claimed Treyford, and the hundred court found that it had been held of the abbot by a tenant who had only held it for his life. A virgate in Riston Hundred had also belonged to Newminster, as the abbey was then called.

of the castle—and in order to compensate them for this loss gave them, in 1086, the manor of Bury.[1]

Turning to the monasteries which are entered amongst the subtenants we find that the wealthy abbey of Wilton had held the manor of Firle, worth £60, and that of Falmer, valued at £20, but had lost both. Sometimes a policy of robbing Peter to pay Paul appears to have prevailed, and land taken from one house was bestowed on another. Thus William de Warenne granted Falmer to his priory of St. Pancras at Lewes, and the Count of Mortain gave 'St. John's' manor of Frog-Firle to his Norman foundation of Grestain, with 2 hides at Beddingham and the manor of Wilmington, where a cell was established and continued until the suppression of the alien priories. In the same way half a virgate of the Abbess of Wilton's manor of Firle situated in Henhurst Hundred fell to the share of Tréport, which also held half the estate of 'Bolintun' in Bexhill. In West Sussex Earl Roger had converted the secular canons of St. Nicholas in Arundel into a priory subordinated to the abbey of St. Martin of Sées, re-granting to them, for the welfare of his brother-in-law, a monk of Sées, the church of Harting, which the seculars had held, and giving them also tithes of Arundel worth 24s., and the vills of Eastergate and Fishbourne; and after the death of his Countess Mabel in 1082 he divided his manor of Climping into two equal portions, giving one to Sées. The other half of Climping he bestowed on the abbey of Almenesches, of which his daughter was abbess, and from whence he had settled a colony of nuns on his estate at Lyminster. At Runcton and Waltham the abbey of Troarn had lands by grant of the earl, and 'a monk of St. Evroult' held one hide of the manor of Singleton. Finally, the monks of Mortain had eight burgages in Pevensey bringing in 5s. 6d. It is probable that they had also already received from the Count of Mortain lands in Withyham which were temporarily usurped by Walter de Richardiville when sheriff of the honour of Pevensey,[2] as these lands seem to have been included in 'Hertvel,' which was held by 'Walter' in 1086.

Some of the small ecclesiastical endowments are difficult to identify. In addition to the individual holdings of priest or clerk, monk or canon, we have canons of Malling holding lands, which shows that the church of South Malling was already collegiate, in addition to the canons of St. Michael, also mentioned under Malling, and doubtless identical with them. But the 'clerks' who held in common St. Michael's endowment in Horse Eye near Pevensey are less easy to identify.[3] The clerks of St. Nicholas (of Arundel) are mentioned under Harting, and the clerks of Boxgrove church held 1 hide. The 'clerks of St. Pancras' appear as holding 2½ hides in West Firle, possibly the endowment of that church of St. Pancras at Lewes which formed part of the original gift by William de Warenne to the monks of Cluni. It is possible that 'St. John,' otherwise unidentified, may be, like St. Pancras, a Lewes church, that of St. John-sub-castro. 'Holy Trinity,' which had held and lost $1\frac{1}{2}$ hides in 'Berchelie,' was then the name of the archbishop's monastery at Canterbury. This estate was an outlyer of his manor in Westmeston, which he held in trust for the monks. Domesday tells us that this manor's assessment had been reduced from 6 to $4\frac{1}{2}$ hides, 'quia aliud (*sic*) est in rapo comitis de Moritonio,' and the above $1\frac{1}{2}$ hides at 'Berchelie' are the 'aliud' spoken of.

The consideration of the lay tenants-in-chief and their lands need not detain us ; it was as 'rapes' rather than as 'honours' that their possessions affected the history of the county. The honours of Lewes and Bramber remained for centuries in the heirs of the families of Warren and Braose, while those of Earl Roger and the Count of Mortain were forfeited by their respective sons and became, one the honour of Arundel and the other, from its subsequent connection with the lords of Laigle (de Aquila), the honour of the Eagle, or of Aquila.

It is interesting to observe that—with the exception of Pevensey, with its rape, which fell, as 'the first fruits of the Conquest' to the Conqueror's half-brother, Count Robert of Mortain—East and West Sussex were respectively allotted to Norman lords east and west of the river Seine. Thus the most easterly of the rapes, that of Hastings, was assigned to the Count of Eu, a little port in the extreme northeast of Normandy, while Lewes was given to William de Warenne, the earthworks of whose stronghold on the Varenne (now the Arques) are still to be seen at Bellencombre to the south-west of Eu. Bramber, with its rape, was secured by William de Briouze ('Braose'), whose Norman lordship lay to the south-west of Falaise, while the western rapes of Chichester and Arundel were the portions of Roger de Montgomery, who raised in the latter a hill fortress such as that which he had left in Normandy, where its traces are still visible at St. Germain de Montgomery, south of Lisieux.

Of these magnates it was the Count of Eu who most certainly bestowed Sussex lands upon his own knights. Geoffrey de Floc, who is found in Domesday holding of him at Guestling, was named from Flocques adjoining Eu, while Robert de Cruel, his tenant at Ashburnham and in Bexhill, derived his name from Criel hard by on the coast. Another Bexhill tenant, Robert (de) St. Leger, came probably from St. Leger-aux-bois to the south-east of Eu, while yet another, William de 'Sept Mueles,' had his Norman home at Sept-Meules, which lies halfway between St. Leger and Eu. To these we may add the Freulleville family, who were knights of the count in Normandy, and who held land in Playden[1] ; Ricarville near Freulleville gave name to the sheriff of the rape of Pevensey.[2] The tenants of William de Warenne in his rape cannot be similarly traced to his own Norman district. In East Anglia, where his great fief was connected in some mysterious way with

---

[1] *Cal. of Doc. France*, p. 81.   [2] Walter de Ricarville, see above, p. 352.

the ' castle ' or ' castlery ' of Lewes,[1] a subsequent document enables us to detect a local follower in that William ' de Grinnosa villa ' who bestowed lands on Lewes Priory,[2] and who derived his name from Grigneuseville in the ' canton ' of Bellencombre. It is also only in Suffolk that Domesday mentions the full names of Godfrey and Robert de Pierpoint (' Petroponte '), who held of him in Sussex as Godfrey and Robert,[3] and who came from Pierrepont near Falaise in a distant part of Normandy. William de Wateville, his tenant at Brighton and elsewhere, derived his name from Watteville on the left bank of the Seine between Rouen and the sea ; and Ralf de ' Caisned,' who held of him at Plumpton, is believed to have been named from Quesnay between St. Lô and Caen. The tenants of William de Braose are hard to localize in Normandy, but if Morin of Thakeham was Morin de St. André,[4] he doubtless came from St. André-de-Briouze, near the *stammhaus* of his lord, while Pointel, from which was named the William de ' Pointel '[5] who witnesses a grant of Philip de ' Brausia,' actually adjoins Briouze. And the Bucy family, whose name is preserved in Kingston Bucey or Bowsey, may have been named from Boucé in the Cange valley some fourteen miles from Briouze. Not only in Sussex but in Northants the Count of Mortain had a great follower in that William de ' Cahainges,' as the Sussex Domesday terms him, whose name is preserved in Horsted Keynes, and who came from Cahagnes, between Vire and Bayeux, according to Mr. Stapleton, who asserts that he held there, as in England, under the Count de Mortain.[6]

In the western rape by far the most important tenant was Robert Fitz-Tetbald, the lord of what afterwards became the honour of Petworth. Of his bequest of the manor of Toddington to the abbey of Sées, Mr. Round says :[7]—

> One of the most interesting illustrations of Domesday is that afforded by the death-bed gift of Robert son of Tetbald, ' the sheriff,' to St. Martin of Sées. To Mr. Eyton belongs the credit of discovering the importance of this tenant of Earl Roger of Shrewsbury (*Hist. of Shrops.* ii. 266). He boldly claimed him as ' by far the greatest feoffee in the earl's Sussex fief, and as the Domesday lord of the honour of Petworth ; and he further suggested that it may have been Sussex of which he was the Norman sheriff. Mr. Eyton, however, was not acquainted with this instructive charter, which proves the identity of the Robert who held ' Totintune ' (Toddington in Lyminster) in Domesday with Robert son of Tetbald. It supplies not only the name of his wife (Emma), but the date of his own death (1087). This date is the more important because Mr. Eyton held that Robert was still living after 1108, and was not affected by his lord's catastrophe in 1102. But further, the last four witnesses to the charter are ' Robertus de Petehorda presbiter, Corbelinus, Hamelinus, et Turstinus de Petehorda.' We have clearly here the priest of Petworth, the ' Corbelinus ' who held under ' Robert ' in 1086 at Barlavington[8] the ' Hamelinus ' who held of him similarly at Burton, and probably also the ' Turstinus ' who held of him at Greatham. We may therefore identify him with the Robert who appears in Domesday Book as

[1] See its entry in Dom. Bk. *passim.* [2] *Anct. Charters* (Pipe Roll Soc.), p. 5.
[3] Ibid. p. 7. [4] *Cal. of Doc. France*, p. 401.
[5] Ibid. [6] *Rotuli Scacc. Norm.* ii. ccli.
[7] *Cal. of Doc. France*, pref. l.
[8] He held also at Marden, and Richard and Robert, sons of Corbelin, attested Earl Roger's confirmation of this grant of Robert's.

the tenant of these manors, and thus prove the correctness of Mr. Eyton's happy conjecture. Nor is this all that we learn from these documents of Robert, for we need not hesitate to say that he is the same as that Robert 'de Harundello' who gave land at Hardham ('Eringeham') to the Cluniac Priory of Lewes. Arundel, with which Domesday connects him, would be his official residence as sheriff, not as Mr. Eyton believed, of Sussex, but, we may infer, of 'the honour of Arundel.'

Robert, son of Tetbald, is mentioned in the survey under Arundel as having his toll, or dues, from 'hominibus extraneis,' by which is probably meant men outside the honour of Arundel. In a charter[1] of Earl Roger to St. Evroult, Robert, son of Tetbald, and Hugh his son sign as witnesses immediately after the earl and his sons, and it was probably through Hugh's adherence to Robert of Bellesme that the honour of Petworth came into the hands of Henry I., and was subsequently granted to Josceline, the queen's brother.

Another group of holdings which descended *en bloc* and also suffered forfeiture in 1102 was that held by 'William' in Halnaker, Boxgrove, Walberton, Barnham, etc., which subsequently became the honour of Halnaker. In four instances—at Tadeham, Bridham, Boxgrove, and East Hampnett—William had as subtenant a certain 'Nigel.'

It is probable that future research amongst monastic charters and other unpublished sources will throw further light on some of the undertenants. It has already been shown by Mr. Round that Oismelin and 'Aseius,' who bestowed tithes on Troarn, were the Domesday undertenants of Merston and Offham.[2]

The undertenants of William de Braose are few in number, and the solution of their identity is much assisted by a group of charters granted by William de Braose to the abbey of St. Florent de Saumur.[3] The first of these charters, conferring the manor of Annington on the monks, is witnessed by '. . . Robertus Silvaticus, Radulphus de Vivo Monastero, Willelmus Normanni filius, Willelmus Magni filius, and Radulfus de Boceio.' In the first of these, whose surname is merely a latinized variant of Savage, we recognize that 'Robert,' whose manors of Durrington, Worthing, Lancing, Ashington, and Buncton are in the thirteenth century found in the hands of the representatives of the Savage family. William, son of Norman, held in Coombes, Applesham, and Offington, and William 'filius Manne' in Wappingthorne; while Ralph de Boceio is the Ralph who held in Kingston and Shermanbury, which descended to the family of Bucy, and probably one of the two Ralphs who held lands in Lancing. As the estates of William son of Ranulf at Woodmancote, Morley and Sakeham are afterwards found in the hands of Simon le Comte he was probably the first of that line, one of whom, as 'Simon Comes,' witnessed a grant by Philip de Braose about 1096 in company with Hugh de Cumbes, possibly the successor of William son of Norman. 'Gislebertus de Cleopeham,' witness to another deed of about the same

[1] Ord. Vital. *Hist. Eccl.* (ed. Le Prevost) ii. 415. [2] *Suss. Arch. Coll.* xlii. 82. [3] *Cal. of Doc. France*, pp. 396-401.

date, is clearly the Gilbert who held at 'Clopeham,' or Clapham, in 1086 ; and possibly Morin de Sancto Andrea, who occurs in a charter of 1093, may be the Morin who is found at Thakeham and Muntham.

In Lewes 'Ralph,' by his grant of Brighton church to Lewes Priory, and by the descent of his manors of Saddlescombe, Street, and 'Hame' to the de Says, is shown to be Ralph 'de Caisned' or Chesney.[1] William de Wateville, who held lands in Brighton, Perching and Keymer, is noticeable from the appearance of his wife as tenant of Clayton in her own name ; and Mr. Round observes that 'Tosardus,' who held land in 1086 at Iford, gave it to Lewes Priory on becoming a monk there.[2]

Under the Count of Mortain one of the most important tenants was William de Cahannes, or Keynes, who occurs by name at Bevrington, Tilton, and Sherington, and can be discerned, with the help of the charters of Lewes Priory, to which his family were considerable benefactors, in the 'William' mentioned at Selmeston, 'Remecinges,' Langley, 'Litelforde,' Horsted(-Keynes) and Bunchgrove. Another man of wide estates was Ralph, who took the surname of de Dene from his manor of West Dean : a certain amount of light is thrown upon his fee by the charters of Otham Abbey, which was founded by his grandson and further endowed by the latter's heir, Ela de Sakeville ; the bulk of his lands passed eventually to Isabel de la Haye, one of the co-heiresses of 'Catherine de Monte Acuto.' With Ralph de Dene must be taken Ansfrid, whose long list of manors is almost entirely reproduced in the fee of Ralph's descendants, and who was therefore evidently connected in some way with Ralph.[3] Of the other men of the count, Boselin, who occurs under Pevensey, was Boselin de Dives, and his son William, who held of the archbishop in South Malling, is shown by the Lewes charters to be the William who held in Alfriston, and was probably also the William who was tenant at Eastbourne, Hailsham, and Bowley ; Rannulf, who appears at Ratton, Horsted, Alfriston, and elsewhere may be Rannulf the seneschal of the Count of Mortain, father of Robert de Haia, as a branch of the family of Haye was early settled in this neighbourhood ; and Alvred, of Eastbourne, Pevensey, and Claverham, is certainly the 'Alvred the butler' who held largely of the count in Somerset, Northants, and elsewhere, and was apparently the founder of the house of Montague, one branch of which continued in this part of Sussex until near the close of the thirteenth century.

In the rape of Hastings precedence must be given to Reinbert 'the sheriff,' not only by reason of his official position and extensive possessions, which included Salehurst, Mountfield, Ninfield, Udimore, Whatlington, Cortesley, and other estates, but from his having been the founder of the influential house of Etchingham, of which name the first was Simon son of Dru, which Dru was 'the heir of Reinbert,' as he is styled in a deed of about 1100, which also refers to Reinbert's two nephews, Richard

[1] Mr. Round, in *Suss. Arch. Coll.* xliv. 141, and *Genealogist*, July, 1901.
[2] *Suss. Arch. Coll.* xxix. 144.   [3] Ibid. xl. 68.

and Warmund.[1]   Another family of some importance was the Scotneys of Lamberhurst and Crowhurst, who succeeded Walter son of Lambert ; the descendants of Robert de Cruel (or Criol) continued at Ashburnham till the thirteenth century,[2] and those of Robert St. Leger at Fairlight and the neighbourhood of Bexhill.   In Gerald, who held at Hooe, we may see the count's steward, Gerald de Normanville, and Ingelran, who held in the same place and at Wilting, Filsham, and Baldslow is possibly the Ingleran ' vicecomes,' and Ingelran de Hastings who attests several charters of the Count of Eu,[3] and may possibly appear under the disguise of Ingelran ' de Escotengiis ' (i.e. Scotney) in 1106.[4]

The identification of place-names is dealt with in detail in notes to the text, and is rendered easier in this county by the unusual accuracy with which the hundredal headings are given throughout.   These headings are omitted in few cases and misplaced in still fewer, and the hundreds themselves have as a whole remained almost unaltered, though their names have in many cases changed ; thus, 'Risberg' became Poling, ' Benestede'Avisford, and ' Ediveherst'Shiplake. 'Wandelmestrei' formed the two later hundreds of Alciston and Longbridge, and 'Falmere' was divided between Whalesbone and Youngsmere, while 'Tifeld' and 'Auronhelle' both disappeared.   Even with this assistance some twenty names remain unidentified, and without it many more would have done so, as the vagaries in spelling of the Domesday scribes are even more eccentric than usual in Sussex ; thus, Netherfield appears both as Nedrefelle (fo. 18b) and Nirefeld (fo. 17b) ; Shelvestrode as Calvrestot (fo. 22) and Celrestius (ibid.) ; Easwrith as Isewerit (fo. 29), Isiwirde (fo. 17), Isiwiridi (fo. 24), and Eswende (fo. 17) ; and Eckington as Echentone (fo. 19), Eschintone (fo. 19b), Achinton (fo. 22), Achiltone (fo. 22), Alchitone (fo. 19b), and Hechestone (fo. 19).   In several cases inversion is a source of error, Rotherfield appearing as Reredfelle (fo. 16), Chalvington as Caveltone (fo. 19), and Runcton as Rochintone (fo. 25b).   Misreadings of letters are frequent, as Cloninctune for Donnington, Filleicham for Sidlesham ; n is often confused with u, Peneuesel (fo. 20b) being written for Pevenesel, and one place occurring both as 'Lodintone' and 'Lodivtone' (fo. 22).   There is also confusion between r and n, Binderton being written as Bertredtone (fo. 23), Ninfield as Nerewelle (fo. 18), and Easwrith as Eswende (for Esweride).   Of etymological interest is the use of G for W, as Garnecamp for Warningcamp and Gorde for Worth, and the variable value of Ch, which, though usually hard, is sometimes soft, East and West Chiltington occurring respectively as Childetune (fo. 27) and Cilletune (fo. 29), and Perching as both Percinges and Berchinges (fo. 27).   The initial H of Harundel (Arundel), Hovingedene (Ovingdean), and Herlintone (Arlington) points to the arbitrary use of that letter which still characterizes the Sussex dialect, and is very noticeable in the case of Antone

[1] Visc. Gage's MSS. (Hist. MSS. Com. Rep. iii. 223).   [2] Suss. Arch. Coll. xxiv. 3.
[3] Cal. of Doc. France, p. 81.   [4] Ibid. p. 134.

(East Hampnett) and Hentone (West Hampnett) (fo. 25*b*). Finally we may notice the introduction of *E* before the initial *S*, as in Esserintone (fo. 19) and Serintone (fo. 20*b*), Estorchestone (fo. 24) and Storgetune (fo. 29).

In dealing with the boroughs of Sussex we find their salient feature in the marked increase of wealth and population which the Conquest had brought them, and which was doubtless due partly to the impulse it gave to traffic with Normandy and partly to the settlement in their castles of Norman lords. At Pevensey itself, William's landing-place, the burgesses were reduced to twenty-seven when Robert of Mortain received it, but at the time of the survey their number had risen to sixty in the count's demense and fifty belonging to his tenants, 110 in all. At Chichester there were far more houses than there had been under King Edward, and even Steyning had increased. Lewes, it was reckoned, had increased in value thirty per cent. since the Conquest. It must be remembered that the vessels of the time were small and of shallow draught, while the Sussex rivers, probably, were larger then than now. Consequently Arundel, Steyning, and Lewes most of all, would be then ports of consequence. We have to deplore the omission in the survey of the city of Chichester—except for a brief statement that there had been 97$\frac{1}{2}$ haws, or closes, there on which the houses had now increased by sixty—and of Hastings. The loss of the latter is particularly regrettable in view of the position afterwards held by Hastings as head of the Cinque Ports. Nor is there any great amount of detail in the treatment of the other boroughs, though the customs of Lewes (fo. 26) are of considerable interest. Of these the first deals with the scypfyrd : ' If the king wished to send his men to guard the sea without going himself (the burgesses) collected from all the men whoever held the land 20 shillings, which money those had who were in charge of the arms in the ships.' Some light is thrown on this by the similar customs of Malmesbury,[1] where the burgesses were bound either to supply one man as the military service due from the 5 hides at which they were rated, or to pay 20*s*. towards the maintenance of the ' buzcarles.'[1] Reading these two entries together it seems probable that when the king led his forces in person Lewes had to provide one man, or possibly more, but that otherwise the service was commuted for a payment of 20*s*. Moreover, the ' buzcarles ' would seem to be equivalent to ' those who were in charge of the arms in the ships,' and these we may reasonably conjecture to have had some connection with the ' helm and hauberk ' which King Ethelred levied in 1008 from every 9 hides for the arming of the ships provided by the different counties.[2]

The second clause of the customs is, that ' he who sells a horse in the borough gives to the reeve one penny and the buyer (gives) another ; for an ox a halfpenny ; for a man four pence, in whatever place he buys

---

[1] Dom. Bk. fo. 64*b*.   [2] Freeman, *Norman Conquest*, i. App. LL.

within the rape.' This points to the importance of Lewes as a market town at this early date, and is also a grim reminder of the status of serfs.

The remaining customs refer to the payment of fines of 7*s.* 4*d.*[1] for bloodshed, 8*s.* 4*d.* (i.e. 100*d.*) for prison breaking, and the same for rape or adultery ; in the case of the last-named offence, the criminous man, or rather his fine, belonged to the king and the woman to the archbishop.[2] There was also a payment of 20*s.* due from each moneyer, ' cum moneta renovatur '—that is to say, when new dies were issued by the central authorities. Of all these occasional issues, or perquisites as they would be termed at a later date, two-thirds went to the king and the remainder (the well-known third penny so closely connected with earldoms) to the earl. Of the total fixed rents and issues which in King Edward's time amounted to £26, the king had received half, and the earl, to whom William de Warenne succeeded, the other half. The value had risen in 1086 to £34, with an additional 112*s.* ' de nova moneta,' which would seem to be the new farm paid for the mint, either by private moneyers or possibly by the burgesses.

Details of the fixed issues are not given in the case of Lewes, though we are told that in King Edward's time the 127 burgesses used to pay £6 4*s.* 1½*d.* for burgage rents (*de gablo*) and market dues (*de theloneo*). These two items recur in connection with Pevensey, where twenty-four burgesses had formerly paid 14*s.* 6*d.* in burgage rents, 20*s.* market dues, 35*s.* harbour dues, and 75*s.* 3*d.* for the use of the common pasture. As the burgesses at Pevensey had increased to the number of sixty in 1086, the first two of these items had risen respectively to 39*s.* and £4. Here also there was a mint paying 20*s.*, but it had been newly set up since the Conquest, unlike the ancient mint of Lewes,[3] or those of Hastings, Steyning, and Chichester, all of which are passed over unnoticed by the survey.

At Arundel again we have a glimpse of ancient customs, for we are told that in the time of King Edward ' Castle Arundel ' used to pay 40*s.* from a mill ' et de tribus conviviis xx solidos et de uno pasticio xx solidos.' The ' convivium ' appears to be the obligation of providing food and lodging for the lord of the manor once, or in this case three times, in the year ; it continued as an incident of feudal tenure in some parts as late at least as the thirteenth century, for in 1202 William of Billinghurst held half a hide of land from Henry Tregoze by service of the tenth part of a knight's fee and the render of ' unum convivium per annum ad summonicionem suam.'[4] The ' pasticium ' seems to have been a custom of similar nature, but

[1] Probably a scribal error for 8*s.* 4*d.*
[2] The appearance of the archbishop instead of the Bishop of Chichester (or rather Selsey) was probably due to the propinquity of his great manor and peculiar of South Malling, though it is just possible that these customs may carry us back as far as the early part of the eighth century, when there was no bishop's seat in the county.
[3] The early importance of Lewes is shown by the decree of Ethelstan, about 930, establishing two mints in the borough.
[4] *Cal. Feet of F.* (Suss. Rec. Soc.), No. 79.

evidently entailing greater expense : possibly it was a render of food which had to be sent to the lord wherever he might be. The whole render bears a considerable resemblance to the rent in kind paid by certain royal manors, and known as the 'farm of one day,' already referred to. The entry continues : 'Now, between the borough and the port of the river, and the ship-dues it pays 12 pounds, and yet it is worth 13 pounds.' There was also here, as at Pevensey and Lewes, a market, of which Robert son of Tetbald, as sheriff of the honour, had the dues 'from men outside the liberty (*de hominibus extraneis*).'

In all the boroughs there were besides the demesne burgesses, that is to say those whose payments were made to the lord of the borough, a greater or less number whose burgages while no doubt giving their share towards the common payments of the borough yet belonged to some other lord. Thus at Pevensey, where there had been in the Confessor's day only twenty-four demesne burgesses, the Bishop of Chichester had had five others, and the priests Edmer, Ormer and Doda twenty-three between them. At the time of the survey, when the Count of Mortain had sixty demesne burgesses, another fifty were in the hands of certain of his sub-tenants. The terms 'burgess,' 'burgage (*masura*)', and 'haw, or close (*haga*)' equate one another, and for the purposes of Domesday are equivalent to 'a rent '—which fluctuates but averages about 7*d*.—thus at Arundel the scribe with his love of variety writes : 'Morin has a customary payment of 12 pence from 2 burgesses ; Ernald has a burgess paying (*de*) 12 pence ; Ralph a haw of 12 pence ; Nigel 5 haws which do service.' The render of service or work by burgage tenants occurs again on a large scale in Steyning, where the only details given are that ' there were in the borough 118 burgages (*masure*) which used to pay 4 pounds and 2 shillings ; now there are 123 burgages, and they pay 100 shillings and 100 pence and have 1½ ploughs ; they used to perform works at the manor-court (*ad curiam operabantur*) like villeins in the time of king Edward.' Mr. Ballard points out that it is probable that all the non-demesne burgages, or at least most of them, were appurtenant to certain manors in the neighbourhood. This system of the attachment of a close within the borough to a manor in the same district is particularly noticeable in the case of Lewes and Chichester ; in the former thirty-five manors held between them 258 burgages in Lewes, the largest numbers being Iford and Patcham with twenty-six each, South Malling with twenty-one, and Barcombe with eighteen. In the city of Chichester 142 burgages were held by forty-three manors, the bishop's manors accounting for thirty-five, with an additional ten granted to him by the king from his manor of Bosham.[1] The possession of burgesses and houses appurtenant to various rural manors is, in Domesday, one of the features of a county town, and

[1] Ballard, *The Domesday Boroughs*, 19, 39.

suggests that Chichester and Lewes were then rivals for the headship of the county. Mr. Ballard has, however, shown that this peculiarity was not confined, in Sussex, to Lewes and Chichester; twenty burgesses are mentioned as appurtenant to the abbey of Tréport's manor of 'Bolintun,' and must clearly have been in Hastings, where also the abbey of Fécamp had four burgesses.[1] Arundel had seventeen houses—belonging, as he holds, to seven estates in the neighbourhood—and Pevensey fifty belonging to sixteen manors.[2] Here then we have circumstantial evidence of the quasi-independent character of the rapes, each of them with a local capital, as each had a sheriff.

It only remains for us to deal with the castles of Sussex mentioned in Domesday Book. It has often been asserted that Arundel castle was of Saxon foundation, and was already standing when the Normans came, this idea being based on the statement of Domesday : 'Castrum Harundel reddebat . . . T.R.E.'; but Mr. Round has shown[3] that this should be translated not 'the castle of Arundel' but 'Castle Arundel,' a place-name analogous to Newcastle or Castle Acre. Again, the castle mounds at Lewes have often been claimed as Saxon, but modern research shows this class of mound to be typically Norman, and very rarely, if ever, English. Lewes castle itself is not mentioned in the survey of Sussex, but in connection with some of William de Warenne's manors in Norfolk we find mention of the 'castellatio' of 'Lawes,' 'de Laquis' in its semi-Latinized shape, and finally by a bold piece of translation on the scribe's part 'castellatio Aquarum.' To Hastings castle also the only reference is under Bexhill, when the grant to the Count of Eu of the 'castelry of Hastings' is mentioned. Of the castle erected within the still strong Roman walls of Pevensey no direct mention is made, but under Eastbourne and Firle 'the warders of the Castle' occur as holding land, and it is clear that these are the 'vigiles de Pevensel' and 'de Monte Acuto,' who occur on the Pipe Rolls of Henry II. That part of this land was the fee in Southeye and Eastbourne subsequently held by Henry de Palerne and the family of Brade by service of guarding the outer gate of Pevensey castle seems probable, and there is an obvious connection with the 'vigiles de Monte Acuto' who occur on the Pipe Rolls for Somerset during the same period, and who are the successors of the 'duo portitores de Montegud' of the Somerset Domesday. Finally, we may refer to Bramber castle, which is spoken of as being situated on one hide of the manor of Washington.

Thus we conclude our study of the Sussex survey; some of the questions raised by it may be claimed as answered, on some light has been thrown, but to others we can at present only say, as the compilers of Domesday said about an estate at Hankham, 'Inde nullum responsum.'

---

[1] Fecamp had also in their manor of 'Rameslie' a 'new borough' with sixty-four burgesses; from other instances of the use of this term 'new borough' in Domesday—e.g. Norwich and Nottingham—it seems probable that this refers to a French settlement in Hastings, unless it was Winchelsea.

[2] Ibid. pp. 21–2, 39, 40.

[3] *Archæologia* lviii. 342.

NOTE

The reader should bear in mind that three periods are referred to in the Domesday Survey : (i.) 'The time of King Edward,' which is, nominally at least, the date of his death (Jan. 5, 1066); this period is also referred to simply as 'then.' (ii.) 'Afterwards' or 'when received,' being the time when the estate passed to its new holder. (iii.) 'Now,' that is to say, when the Survey was compiled, 1086. The unit of assessment was the 'hide,' which, it is most important to observe, in Sussex apparently contained 8 'virgates.' The 'ferdinc' or quarter of the 'virgate' also occurs. Manors held 'in demesne' were those retained by the tenant-in-chief in his own hands; but 'the demesne' of a manor is the portion which the holder worked as a home farm with the help of labour due from the peasants who held the rest from him. The arable, spoken of simply as 'land,' was calculated in terms of the ploughs which could be employed upon it, each plough being reckoned to have a team of eight oxen. The woodland was not measured in Sussex, but was valued at the number of swine, or their equivalent in money, paid by the villeins for the 'pannage,' or right of feeding swine in the woods. The three classes of the peasantry were, in descending order, villeins, bordars or cottars, and serfs.

It must be remembered that the manors, especially before the Conquest, were not always compact estates, and that consequently land 'in' any manor may be many miles from the place which gives its name to that manor. Thus in many cases portions of the thickly wooded wealden country in the north of the county appear to have been attached to manors on the coast, and this is particularly noticeable in the case of the manors in the neighbourhood of Shoreham. Also when Domesday speaks of A holding B, it does not necessarily mean that A held the whole of it.

In 1886 the Sussex Archæological Society issued a facsimile of the Sussex portion of Domesday, printed from the plates of the Ordnance Survey edition of 1862, with a translation and list of place-names and suggested identifications. The volume is not very accurate or reliable; references to it in my footnotes are made under the initials S.D.B.

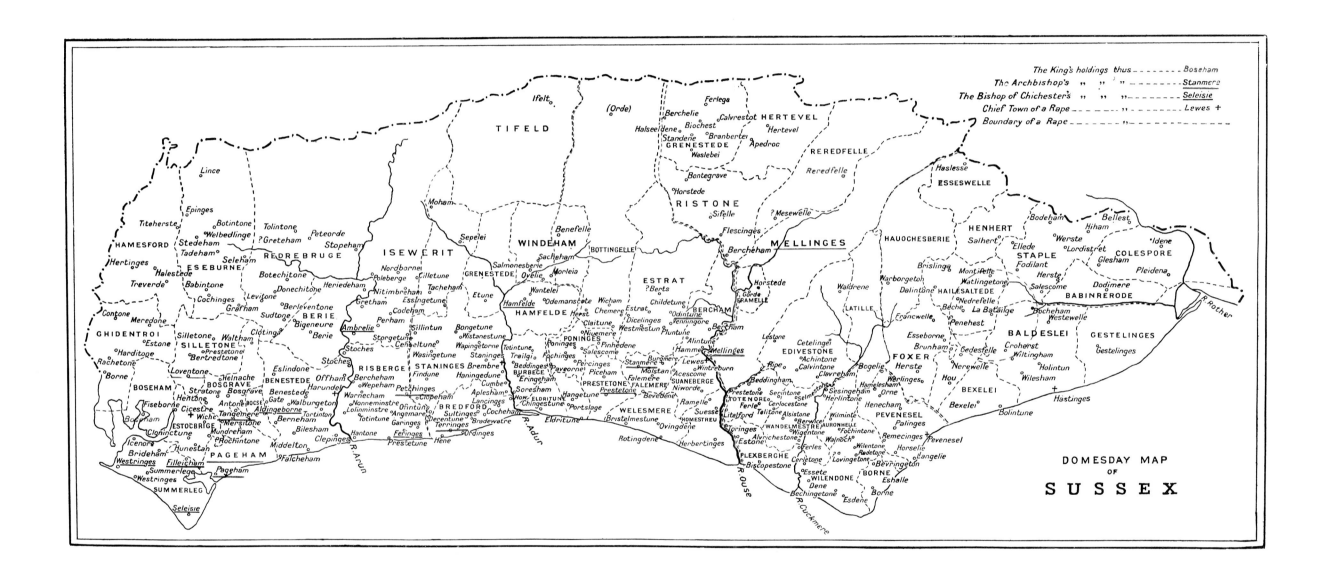

DOMESDAY MAP
OF
SUSSEX

The King's holdings thus ——————— Boseham
The Archbishop's ,, ,, ,, ——————— Stanmere
The Bishop of Chichester's ,, ,, ,, ——————— Seleisie
Chief Town of a Rape ——————— ,, Lewes +
Boundary of a Rape ——————— ,,

NOTES TO DOMESDAY MAP.

(Compiled by L. F. SALZMANN.)

IN this map those manors in which the King had an interest are printed in scarlet; a scarlet line denotes the Archbishop of Canterbury's estates, and a black line those of the Bishop of Chichester.

The boundaries of the Rapes—and of the Liberty of Battle Abbey—are indicated by broken scarlet lines, and those of the Hundreds by dotted black lines. In the northern portion of the county the boundaries of the Hundreds can be given only approximately, as at the time of the survey this district was densely wooded. The small size of many of the Hundreds should be observed.

Domesday often records a name in more than one form, but only one of the variants can be given on the map.

For the sake of uniformity and convenience of reference, the boundaries of the county are shown as they stand at the present time. For the same reason the names of rivers are given in their modern forms, though they do not occur in Domesday, and are mostly of quite recent origin.

SUDSEXE

HERE ARE ENTERED
THE HOLDERS OF LANDS
IN SUDSEXE

I KING WILLIAM
II The Archbishop of Canterbury
III The Bishop of Chichester
IV The abbey of Westminster
V The abbey of Fécamp (*Fiscannensis*)
VI Osbern Bishop of Exeter
VII The abbey of Winchester
VIII The abbey of Battle (*la batailge*)
IX The Count of Eu (*Ow*)
X The Count of Mortain
XI Earl Roger
XII William de Warenne
XIII William de Braiose
XIV Ode of Winchester (*Wincestre*)
XV Eldred

THE LAND OF THE KING

King WILLIAM holds in demesne BOSEHAM [Bosham]. Earl Godwin held it, and then there were 56½ (hides), and it paid geld for[1] 38 hides, and (does) now likewise. There is land   .[2] On the demesne are 6 ploughs, and 39 villeins with 50 bordars have 39 ploughs. There (is) a church,[3] and 17 serfs, and 8 mills yielding (*de*) 4 pounds all but (*minus*) 30 pence. There are 2 fisheries yielding (*de*) 8 shillings and 10 pence. Wood-(land) yielding (*de*) 6 swine.

To this manor were appurtenant 11 haws[4] in Cicestre [Chichester], which in the time of King Edward returned 7 shillings and 4 pence. Now the Bishop (of Chichester) has ten of them by the king's gift (*a rege*), and (so) there is now one belonging to (*in*) the manor. The whole manor in the time of King Edward,

and afterwards, was worth 40 pounds. Now likewise (it is worth) 40 pounds; yet it returns 50 pounds by weight of assayed money (*ad arsuram et pensum*), which are worth 65 pounds (by tale).

Of this manor Engeler[5] has 2 hides of the king, and there he has 1 plough and 1 bordar.

IN REREDFELLE [ROTHERFIELD] HUNDRED

King William holds in demesne REREDFELLE [Rotherfield] of the fee of the Bishop of Bayeux (*Baioc[ensis]*).[6] Earl Godwin held it, and then, as (*et*) now, it was assessed for 3 hides. There is land for 26 ploughs.[7] On the demesne are 4 ploughs, and 14 villeins with 6 bordars have 14 ploughs. There are 4 serfs, and wood(land) yielding (*de*) 80 swine from the pannage. There is a park.

In the time of King Edward it was worth 16 pounds, and afterwards 14 pounds. Now (it is worth) 12 pounds, and yet it returns 30 pounds.

---

[1] *Pro* interlined.
[2] A blank.
[3] Not the church of Bosham, which Bishop Osbern held; possibly the church of West Stoke is meant.
[4] These haws lay 'between the towergate and the crossgate in the West Street' (see Hay's *History of Chichester*, p. 200).

[5] Engeler de Bohun.
[6] Few of Odo's possessions are mentioned in Domesday as having been forfeited, though he had been disgraced four years.
[7] Note the disproportion of ploughlands to hides.

II. THE LAND OF THE ARCHBISHOP

IN MELLINGES [LOXFIELD] HUNDRED

ARCHBISHOP LANFRANC holds the manor of MELLINGES [South Malling],[1] and it is in the rape of Peneuesel [Pevensey] ; and in the time of King Edward it was assessed for 80 hides, but now the archbishop has only 75 hides, because the Count of Mortain has 5 hides outside (*extra*) the hundred.[2] The land of the whole manor (is sufficient) for 50 ploughs. On the demesne are 5 ploughs, and 219 villeins with 35 bordars have 73 ploughs and 43 crofts.

There are 5 mills yielding (*de*) 4 pounds and 10 shillings and 2,000 eels. There (are) 195 acres (200 *acre* 5 *minus*) of meadow, and wood-(land) (yielding) 300 swine from the pannage. From the pasturage (*de herbagio*) (come) 38 shillings and 6 pence and 355 swine for pasturage (*herbag*[*io*]). In the time of King Edward it was worth 40 pounds ; when received, 30 pounds ; now, 70 pounds. Godfrey held this manor to farm at (*pro*) 90 pounds.

Of this manor Bainiard holds of the archbishop 5 hides, and there he has on (his) demesne 2 ploughs, and 14 villeins with 2 bordars have 2 ploughs. There (are) 35 acres of meadow, and from the pasturage (*herbagio*) (come) 3 swine. (This) is worth 8 pounds.

Of the same manor the son of Boselin[3] holds of the archbishop 2 hides, and there he has on (his) demesne 1 plough, and 11 villeins with 2 bordars have 3 ploughs. There (are) 2 mills yielding (*de*) 10 shillings, and from the pasturage (*herbagio*) (come) 2 swine, and from the wood(land) 20 swine from the pannage. (This) is worth 60 shillings.

Of the self-same manor Godfrey holds 1 hide of the archbishop, and there he has 2 ploughs on (his) demesne, and (there are) 2 villeins with 3 bordars, and a mill yielding (*de*) 5 shillings. Wood(land) (yielding) 1 pig from the pannage. (This) is worth 50 shillings.

Of the same manor Walter holds of the archbishop two-thirds (2 *partes*) of half a hide, and there he has 2 ploughs on (his) demesne, and (there are) 1 villein and 1 bordar with 1 plough, and 3 acres of meadow, and wood-(land yielding) 3 swine from the pannage, and 1 pig (comes) from the pasturage (*herbagio*). (This) is worth 40 shillings.

fo. 16b

Of the selfsame manor moreover the canons of Saint Michael[4] hold 4 hides, and there is on (their) demesne 1 plough, and 4 villeins with 16 bordars have 2 ploughs, and (this) is worth 3 pounds.

William de Cahainges holds 1 virgate of this manor, and it is at (*ad*) Alsihorne [Alchorne[5]].

IN ESTREU [STREET] HUNDRED

The archbishop himself holds ODINTUNE [Wooton], (which is) appropriated to the clothing of the monks[6] (*de vestitu monachorum*). In the time of King Edward it was assessed for 6 hides, and now for 4½ hides, because the rest (*aliud*) is in the rape of the Count of Mortain.[7] There is land for 5 ploughs. On the demesne are 2 ploughs, and 10 villeins with 4 bordars have 3 ploughs. There (is) a mill yielding (*de*) 39 pence, and 22 acres of meadow, and wood(land) yielding (*de*) 2 swine.

In the time of King Edward it was worth 4 pounds, and afterwards 40 shillings ; now 4 pounds. Formerly it returned 6 pounds, but (that) could not be long continued (*perdurare*).

IN FALEMERE HUNDRED[8]

The canons of Mellinges [South Malling] hold of the archbishop STA(N)MERE [Stanmer]. In the time of King Edward, as (*et*) now, it was assessed for 20 hides. There is land for 20 ploughs. On the demesne are 4 ploughs, and 49 villeins with 10 bordars have 26 ploughs. Wood(land) yielding (*de*) 6 swine. In the time of King Edward, and afterwards, as (*et*) now, it was worth 15 pounds. To this manor belong (*adjacent*) 7 haws in Lewes [Lewes] which return 21 pence yearly.

The archbishop himself has in LEWES [Lewes] 21 haws, returning 8 shillings and 8 pence yearly, and they are appurtenant to Mellinges [South Malling] manor.[9]

IN PAGEHA(M) [ALDWICK] HUNDRED

The archbishop himself holds PAGEHAM [Pagham] in demesne. In the time of King Edward it was assessed for 50 hides, and now for 34. There is land for 30 ploughs. On

---

[1] The manor and hundred extended from Lewes to Wadhurst on the border of Kent.

[2] Possibly in Framelle Hundred (see note 3, p. 415).

[3] Probably William son of Boselin de Dives.

[4] The collegiate church of South Malling.

[5] A manor in Buxted and Rotherfield.

[6] Monks of Christ Church, Canterbury.

[7] Accounted for under Berchelie in East Grinstead Hundred (see note 1, p. 419).

[8] Stanmer now forms a detached portion of Ringmer Hundred ; the rest of the Domesday Hundred of Falemere is now Youngsmere.

[9] Part of Lewes is still in South Malling.

the demesne are 7 ploughs, and 74 villeins with 78 bordars (*cum quater xx[ti] bordariis ii[bus] minus*) have 23 ploughs. There is a mill yielding (*de*) 10 shillings,[1] and (there are) 80 acres of meadow, and a small wood (sufficient) for the fences (*ad clausuram*). From the pasturage (*herbagio*) 1 pig from every villein who has 7 swine. [In like manner (*similiter*) throughout all Sudsex].[2] In the time of King Edward and afterwards it was worth 40 pounds. Now (it is worth) 60 pounds, and yet it returns 80 pounds. But (that) is too heavy (*nimis grave*). There is a church there, and 1 church in Cicestre [Chichester] [3] (which) returns 64 pence.

Of this manor Oismelin holds 1 hide of the archbishop. There he has 2 bordars.

The archbishop himself holds in demesne TANGEMERE [Tangmere]. Clerks held it of the archbishop. In the time of King Edward it was assessed for 10 hides, now for 6 hides. There is land .[4] On the demesne are 2 ploughs, and 15 villeins with 15 bordars have 4 ploughs. There is a church.

In the time of King Edward it was worth 6 pounds, and afterwards 100 shillings. Now (it is worth) 6 pounds, and the reeve of the manor has 20 shillings thereof (*inde*).

To this manor are appurtenant 4 haws in Cicestre [Chichester] (which) return 22 pence.

IN SILLENTONE [SINGLETON] HUNDRED

The archbishop himself holds LOVENTONE [East Lavant] in demesne. In the time of King Edward it was assessed for 18 hides, now for 9½ hides. There is land .[5] On the demesne are 3 ploughs, and 14 villeins with 8 bordars have 4 ploughs. There is a mill yielding (*de*) 6 shillings, and 26 acres of meadow.

In the time of King Edward and afterwards it was worth 12 pounds; now 15 pounds.

Of this manor Ralph holds 3 hides of the archbishop, and there 1 villein with 3 bordars have 1 plough. (This) is worth 3 pounds.

IN RIEBERGE HUNDRED [6]

The archbishop himself holds PETCHINGES [Patching]; then as now (*semper*) it was ap-

propriated to the clothing of the monks. In the time of King Edward it was assessed for 12 hides, and now for 3 hides and 3½ virgates. There is land for 9 ploughs. On the demesne are 2 ploughs, and 22 villeins with 21 bordars have 6 ploughs. There is a church. Wood-(land yielding) 4 swine. In the time of King Edward it was worth 12 pounds, and afterwards 10 pounds; now 15 pounds. Lately it stood at (*fuit ad*) 20 pounds, but (that) could not be borne (*pati*).

IN BRADFOTA [BRIGHTFORD] HUNDRED

The archbishop himself holds TERRINGES [West Tarring], which then as now belonged to the minster [7] (*semper fuit in monasterio*). In the time of King Edward it was assessed for 18 hides, and now for 7 hides and 1 virgate. There is land for 14½ ploughs. On the demesne are 3 ploughs, and 27 villeins with 14 bordars have 10 ploughs. There are 2 churches, and woodland yielding (*de*) 6 swine.

In the time of King Edward it was worth 14 pounds and 4 shillings, and afterwards 10 pounds; now 15 pounds.

Of this manor William de Braiose holds 4 hides,[8] and there he has on (his) demesne 1 plough, and 4 villeins with 5 bordars have 1½ ploughs. There (are) 5 acres of meadow; from the wood(land) 10 pence; from the pannage 20 shillings and 2 swine. (This) is worth 70 shillings.

III. THE LAND OF THE BISHOP OF CHICHESTER (*CICESTRE*).

IN FLEXEBERG (FLEXBOROUGH) HUNDRED

The Bishop of Cicestre [Chichester] holds in demesne BISCOPESTONE [Bishopstone]. In the time of King Edward it was assessed for 25 hides, and now likewise. There is land .[9] On the demesne are 3 ploughs, and 30 villeins with 9 bordars have 30 ploughs. There (are) 40 acres of meadow. Wood(land) (yielding) 3 swine from the pannage, and from the pasturage (*herbagio*) 1 pig from (every) 3 [10] swine.

In the time of King Edward it was worth 26 pounds, and afterwards 11 pounds; now 20 pounds.

Of this manor Geoffrey holds 4 hides, and Harold 2 hides and Richard 3 hides. There (are) 6 ploughs on the demesne, and (there are) 13 bordars. The whole of this (*totum h.*) is worth 100 shillings and 10 shillings.

---

[1] Underlined for deletion.
[2] Marginal note. See Introduction, p. 365.
[3] All Saints in the Pallant.
[4] A blank.
[5] A blank.
[6] The parish of Patching is now a Hundred, but it was formerly part of Poling Hundred.

[7] Christ Church, Canterbury.
[8] A blank.   [9] A blank.
[10] Probably 3 is an error for either 6 or 7.

IN HAMFELDE [TIPNOAK] HUNDRED

The bishop himself holds in demesne HA(M)-FELDE [Henfield]. In the time of King Edward it was assessed for 15 hides, and now for 11 hides and 1 virgate. There is land for 20 ploughs. On the demesne are 2 ploughs, and 23 villeins with 15 bordars have 10 ploughs. There (is) a church, and 40 acres of meadow(land). A mill [1] and a fishery are wanting because they have been made over (*pro superfacto*) to William de Braiose.

Of these hides William holds of the bishop 3 hides; and there he has on (his) demesne 1 hide (*sic*), and 1 villein with 10 bordars have half a plough. Wood(land) yielding 3 swine. The whole manor in the time of King Edward was worth 10 pounds, and afterwards 7 pounds. Now what the bishop holds (is worth) 10 pounds; what the knight holds 40*s.*; and yet it was at farm for 18 pounds.

In Lewes are 3 burgesses appurtenant to this manor, returning 21 pence.

IN BOCSE [BOX] HUNDRED

The bishop himself holds in demesne ALDINGEBORNE [Aldingbourne]. In the time of King Edward, as (*et*) now, it was assessed for 36 hides. There is land for 20 ploughs. On the demesne are 2 ploughs, and 16 villeins with 13 bordars have 5 ploughs. There (is) a church, and 3 serfs, and 6 acres of meadow. Wood(land yielding) 3 swine from the pannage; and from the pasturage (*herbagio*) 1 pig of (every) 6 swine. To this manor are appurtenant 16 haws which return 7 shillings and 6 pence.

Of this manor the priest holds 1 hide, Robert 5 hides, Hugh 3 hides, Alward 1 hide; these 3 are clerks; the following (*hi*) 4 (are) knights; Herald (who holds) 3 hides, Murdac 3 hides, Ansfrid 1 hide, Lovel 1 hide. Between (them) all they have 6 ploughs on (their) demesne and 12 villeins and 25 bordars.

The whole manor in the time of King Edward was worth 15 pounds, and afterwards 10 pounds. Now what the bishop holds (is worth) 10 pounds; what the clerks (hold) 4 pounds; what the knights (hold) 4 pounds likewise.

IN RISBERG [POLING] HUNDRED

The bishop himself holds FERINGES [Ferring] in demesne. In the time of King Edward it was assessed for 12 hides, and now for 8 hides. There is land .[2] On the

demesne are 2 ploughs, and 15 villeins with 14 bordars have 5 ploughs. There (is) 1 serf, and 20 acres of meadow, and wood(land yielding) 4 swine; and for the pasturage (*herbagio*) 1 pig of (every) 7.

fo. 17a

Of this manor Ansfrid holds 2 hides, and he has on (his) demesne half a plough with 4 bordars.

In the time of King Edward it was worth 7 pounds, and afterwards 100 shillings; now 7 pounds. What Ansfrid holds is worth 20 shillings.

IN ESWENDE [WEST EASWRITH] HUNDRED

The bishop himself holds AMBRELIE [Amberley]. In the time of King Edward, as (*et*) now, it was assessed for 24 hides. There is land .[3] On the demesne are 2 ploughs, and 10 villeins with 13 bordars have 12 ploughs, and (there are) 30 acres of meadow, and wood(land yielding) 7 swine from the pannage.

Of this manor William the clerk holds 2 hides, and Aldred the priest 3 hides, Baldwin 2½ hides, Ralph 2 hides all but (*minus*) 1 virgate,[4] Tedric (*Teodericus*) 3 hides, Huscarle 2 hides.[5] Between (them) all they have 5 ploughs on (their) demesne, and 17 villeins (*villanos*) and 25 bordars, who have (*habentes*) 5 ploughs.

The whole manor in the time of King Edward was worth 20 pounds, and afterwards 15 pounds. Now what the bishop holds is worth 14 pounds; what the others hold of the bishop is worth 7 pounds.

IN SU(M)MERLEG [MANHOOD] HUNDRED

The bishop himself holds FILLEICHA(M) [Sidlesham [6]] in demesne. In the time of King Edward, as (*et*) now, it was assessed for 12 hides. There is land for 12 ploughs. On the demesne are 2 ploughs, and 16 villeins with 14 bordars have 7 ploughs. There (is) 1 acre of meadow, and wood (sufficient) for the fences (*ad clausuram*).

Of this manor Gilbert holds 3 hides, Rozelin 1 hide, Ulf 1 hide, and on (their) demesne they have 3 ploughs with 12 bordars.

The whole manor in the time of King Edward was worth 10 pounds, and afterwards

---

[1] Possibly the mill mentioned under Wantelei (see p. 446).
[2] A blank.
[3] A blank.
[4] *Una virga minus* interlined.
[5] *ii hidas* interlined.
[6] Sidlesham is the only important manor belonging to the bishopric not otherwise accounted for, and confusion between *s* and *f* is not infrequent; *ch* usually has the value of *k*, but compare Childetune = Chiltington.

8 pounds. Now what the bishop holds (is worth) 10 pounds; what the men (hold) 65 shillings.

The bishop himself holds SELEISIE [Selsey] in demesne. In the time of King Edward, as (*et*) now, it was assessed for 10 hides. There is land for 7 ploughs. On the demesne are 2 ploughs, and 16 villeins with 11 bordars have 5 ploughs. There (are) 2 serfs, and 6 haws in Cicestre [Chichester] yielding (*de*) 38 pence.

Of this manor Geoffrey holds 1 hide, and William half a hide and half a virgate, and they have 1½ ploughs with 1 bordar.

The whole manor in the time of King Edward was worth 12 pounds, and afterwards 10 pounds. Now the demesne of the bishop (is worth) 12 pounds, (that) of his men 40 shillings.

The bishop himself holds WESTRINGES [West Wittering] in demesne. In the time of King Edward, as (*et*) now, it was assessed for 14 hides. There is land for 8 ploughs. On the demesne are 2 (ploughs), and 15 villeins with 12 bordars have 5 ploughs. There (is) 1 mill yielding (*de*) 30 pence, and 13 haws yielding (*de*) 26 pence. (For the) pasturage (*herbag[io]*) one of (every) 7 swine.

Of this manor Ralph holds 1 hide, Herbert 3 hides, and they have on (their) demesne 2½ ploughs, and 2 villeins with 12 bordars and half a plough.

The whole manor in the time of King Edward and afterwards was worth 8 pounds. Now what the bishop has is worth the same sum (*tantumdem*), what his men (have is worth) 50 shillings.

(IN PRESTON HUNDRED [1])

The bishop himself holds PRESTETONE [Preston [2]], and then as now it belonged to the minster (*semper fuit in monasterio*). In the time of King Edward, as (*et*) now, it was assessed for 20 hides. There is land for 12 ploughs. On the demesne is 1 (plough) and a half, and 30 villeins with 20 bordars have 12 ploughs; and in Lewes (there are) 3 haws yielding (*de*) 18 pence. There (is) a church, and 15 acres of meadow, and wood(land) yielding (*de*) 2 swine from the pannage.

Of this manor Lovel holds 2 hides, and there he has 2 ploughs and 9 villeins (*villanos*) with 3 bordars who have (*habentibus*) 2 ploughs, and there (is) 1 mill. (This) is worth 40 shillings.

[1] The Hundredal heading is omitted.
[2] Sometimes called Bishop's Preston to distinguish it from the other Prestons in Sussex.

The whole manor in the time of King Edward was worth 18 pounds, and afterwards 10 pounds, now 18 pounds. Formerly it was at farm at 25 pounds (*olim fuit ad xxv* [3] *libras de firma*) but it could not return (so much).

The canons of Cicestre [Chichester] hold in common (*communiter*) 16 hides which have never paid geld, as (the jurors) say, and there they have 4 ploughs on (their) demesne. This is worth 8 pounds.

IV. THE LAND OF SAINT PETER OF WESTMINSTER

IN ISIWIRDE [WEST EASWRITH] HUNDRED

THE ABBOT OF SAINT PETER of Westminster (*Westmonasterio*) holds PARHAM [Parham] and held it of King Edward. Then it was assessed for 7 hides, now for 3. There is land for 4 ploughs. On the demesne is 1 (plough), and 8 villeins with 5 cottars have 2 ploughs. There (are) 9 acres of meadow. It is worth and was worth 1 pound.

V. THE LAND OF THE CHURCH OF FÉCAMP (*FISCANNENSIS*)

IN GHESTELINGES [GUESTLING] HUNDRED

THE ABBOT of Fécamp (*Fiscanno*) holds of the king RAMESLIE [[4]], and held it of King Edward, and then it was assessed for 20 hides, now for 17½ hides. There is land for 35 ploughs. On the demesne is 1 plough, and 99 villeins (*c villani uno minus*) have 43 ploughs. There (are) 5 churches returning 64 shillings. There (are) 100 saltpans yielding (*de*) 8 pounds and 15 shillings, and 7 acres of meadow, and wood(land yielding) 2 swine from the pannage.

In the same manor is a new borough,[5] and there (are) 64 burgesses returning 8 pounds all but (*minus*) 2 shillings. In Hastinges [Hastings] 4 burgesses and 14 bordars return 63 shillings.

Of this manor Robert of Hastings holds 2½ hides of the abbot, and Herolf half a hide. They have 4 villeins and 4 cottars and 2 ploughs.

The whole manor in the time of King Edward was worth 34 [6] pounds. Now the

[3] *v* interlined.
[4] This name has not yet been identified, but I have found mention of Rammeshorn in Fairlight early in the thirteenth century, which may be connected with it; it corresponded pretty closely to what was afterwards the manor of Brede.
[5] See Introduction, p. 375.
[6] *iiii* interlined.

abbot's demesne (is worth) 50 pounds, and (*vero*) (that) of the men 44 shillings.

IN STANINGES [STEYNING] HUNDRED

The abbot himself holds STANINGES [Steyning]. Harold (*Heraldus*) held it at the end (of the reign) of King Edward (*in fine regis E.*),[1] and then it was assessed at 81 hides, and (there were) moreover in addition (*insuper adhuc*) 18 hides and 7 acres outside (*foris*) the rape which have never paid geld.[2] Now (there are) 67 hides. In the rape of Harundel [Arundel] are $33\frac{1}{2}$ hides, and the others (are) in the rape of William de Braiose, and yet the abbot holds (them) all now.

The land of the whole manor (is sufficient for) 41 ploughs. On the demesne are 7 ploughs, and 178 villeins with 63 bordars have 48 ploughs. There (are) 2 churches,[3] 9 serfs and 4 mills yielding (*de*) 47 shillings and 68 swine in addition (*insuper*).[4] There (are) 113 acres of meadow. Wood(land yielding) 45 swine from the pannage.

In the borough there were 118 burgages (*masure*) (which) used to return 4 pounds and 2 shillings. Now there are 123 burgages (*masure*), and they return 100 shillings and 100 pence, and (the burgesses) have $1\frac{1}{2}$ ploughs. In the time of King Edward (the burgesses) used to do villein service at the court (*ad curiam operabantur sicut villani*).

In the time of King Edward it was worth 86 pounds, and afterwards 50 pounds. Now (it is worth) 100 pounds, and yet it is at farm for 122 pounds all but (*minus*) 2 shillings.

IN BERIE [BURY] HUNDRED

The abbot himself holds of the king BERIE [Bury].[5] Countess Goda held it of King Edward, and then it was assessed for 16 hides. Now for 12 hides. There is land for 16 ploughs. On the demesne are 2 ploughs, and 48 villeins with 22 cottars have 18 ploughs. There (is) a church, and 30 acres of meadow, and wood(land yielding) 40 swine, and 1 fishery.

---

[1] The manor of Steyning had been given to the abbey by King Edward, but Harold deprived them of it.

[2] This must refer to the 18 hides and 3 virgates which formed William de Braiose's manor of Staninges (see note 3, p. 445).

[3] The second church was probably Warminghurst.

[4] The only case of a swine rent for mills in Sussex.

[5] Given to the abbey by King William in exchange for tenements in Hastings (*Cal. of Docts. France*, 38).

In the time of King Edward, and afterwards, it was worth 12 pounds, now 24 pounds.

VI. THE LAND OF BISHOP OSBERN

Bishop OSBERN holds of the king the church of BOSEHAM [Bosham], and held it of King Edward. To this church used to belong (*pertinebant*) 112 hides; now 47 (hides) are outside (*foris*) (the manor, and of these) Hugh son of Rannulph holds 30 hides,[6] and Ralph de Quesnay (*caisned*) 17 hides.[7]

When Osbern received it the church was assessed for 65 hides, and now likewise. There is land .[8] On the demesne are 2 ploughs, and 21 villeins with 18 bordars have 8 ploughs. There (are) 3 mills yielding (*de*) 14 shillings, and 12 acres of meadow, and 1 saltpan yielding (*de*) 2 shillings, and 1 haw yielding (*de*) 8 pence.

Mauger (*Malgerus*) holds of the land of this church 12 hides as (*pro*) one manor; it is called Tornei [Thorney] and pays geld for 8 hides. There he has 32 villeins with 8 ploughs.

Of the same land of the church Ralph holds 1 hide, a certain clerk 1 hide, and 4 clerks 1 hide in common (*communiter*). These men (*ipsi*) have 3 ploughs on (their) demesne,

fo. 17b

and 3 villeins and 10 bordars who have 1 plough and a half; there (is) a church and a priest, and 2 serfs, and 1 haw yielding (*de*) 8 pence.

The whole (manor) in the time of King Edward was worth 300 pounds, and afterwards 50 pounds.

Now what the bishop holds (is worth) 16 pounds and 10 shillings, and yet he has 20 shillings more from the farm (*de firma*) (thereof). What Mauger (*Malgerus*) holds is worth 6 pounds, and yet he has 50 shillings more. What the others hold is worth 4 pounds and 15 shillings.

(The) clerks hold the tithe [9] of the church, and it is worth 40 shillings.

In the time of King Edward there used to belong (*pertinebat*) to this manor 1 hide in Icenore [Itchenor].[10] Now Warin, Earl Roger's man, holds it.

---

[6] At Plumpton (see note 10, p. 441).

[7] At Saddlescombe (see note 5, p. 440).

[8] A blank.

[9] The only mention, by name, of tithes in Sussex, but see note 4, p. 421.

[10] See note 1, p. 427.

IN HAMESFORD [DUMPFORD] HUNDRED

The bishop himself holds HALESTEDE [El-sted], and held it of King Edward, and then it was assessed for 13 hides, now for 5½ hides. There is land .[1] On the de-mesne are 2 ploughs, and 7 villeins with 23 bordars have 2 ploughs. There (are) 2 serfs, and 1 mill yielding (*de*) 4 shillings, and there (is) a church. Wood(land yielding) 10 swine. (For) the pasturage (*herbagium*) of (every) 7 swine 1 (pig).

Of this manor Richard holds 1 hide, Osbern the clerk half a hide, Ralph the priest 1 hide which is appurtenant to the church.

The whole manor in the time of King Edward and afterwards, as (*et*) now, was worth 15 pounds.

IN SILLETONE [SINGLETON] HUNDRED

Durand holds of the bishop PRESTETON [Preston in Binderton]. In the time of King Edward, as (*et*) now, it was assessed for 3 hides. There is land .[2] On the demesne is 1 plough and a half, and 3 villeins with 4 bordars have half a plough. There (are) 6 acres of meadow, and a small wood (sufficient) for the fences (*ad clausuram*).

In the time of King Edward it was worth 4 pounds, and afterwards, and now, 3 pounds.

IN REDREBRIGE [ROTHERBRIDGE] HUNDRED

Richard holds of the bishop LEVITONE [Woolavington]. Godwin the priest held it of King Edward in almoigne, and then, as (*et*) now, it was assessed for 6 hides. There is land .[3] On the demesne are 2 ploughs, and 11 villeins with 7 bordars have 4 ploughs.

There (is) a church, and in Cicestre [Chi-chester] 1 haw yielding (*de*) 3 pence, and 12 acres of meadow. Wood(land yielding) 10 swine, and (for the pasturage) of (every) 7 swine one.

In the time of King Edward it was worth 10 pounds, and afterwards 6 pounds; now 10 pounds.

All these estates (*terre*) belonged and do belong to the church of Boseha(m) [Bosham] in almoign.[4]

VII. THE LAND OF SAINT PETER OF WINCHESTER [5] (*WINTONIA*)

THE ABBOT OF SAINT PETER of Winchester

holds SUESSE [Southease].[6] Then as now it belonged to the minster (*semper fuit in monas-terio*). In the time of King Edward it was assessed for 28 hides, and now for 27 hides. There is land for 28 ploughs. On the de-mesne is 1 plough, and 46 villeins with 4 bordars have 21 ploughs. There (is) a church, and 130 acres of meadow.

In LEWES [Lewes] (there are) 10 burgesses yielding (*de*) 52 pence : and from villeins (come) 38 thousand and five hundred herrings. For porpoises (*marsuins*) 4 pounds. For tallage (*forisfactura*) of the villeins (he received) 9 pounds, and 3 seams (*summas*) of peas.

In all values in the time of King Edward and afterwards it was worth 20 pounds. Now it is appraised at just so much (*tantumdem*) but yet it returns 28 pounds.

IN ESTOCBRIGE [STOCKBRIDGE] HUNDRED

The abbot himself holds CLONINCTUNE [Donnington].[7] In the time of King Edward the abbey held it, and then, as (*et*) now, it was assessed for 5 hides. There is land .[8] On the demesne is 1 plough, and 15 villeins with 4 bordars have 6½ ploughs. There (are) 2 serfs, and 25 acres of meadow, and wood (sufficient) for the fences (*ad clau-suram*). In Cicestre [Chichester] (is) 1 haw yielding (*de*) 4 pence. From the pannage 1 pig and a half.

In the time of King Edward it was worth 4 pounds and 10 shillings and 7 pence;[9] now 6 pounds.

VIII. THE LAND OF THE CHURCH OF BATTLE (*LA BATAILGE*)

IN WANDELMESTREI [ALCISTON] HUNDRED[10]

The abbot of Saint Martin of Battle (*de la batailge*) holds ALSISTONE [Alciston] of the king. Alnod cild held it of King Edward, and then it was assessed for 50 hides, and now for 44½ hides. There is land for 28 ploughs.

Of these hides, 3½ hides belong to (*jacent*

---

[6] Including Telscombe, which is on the coast.

[7] For similar confusion between *cl* and *d* com-pare 'Dotone'=Clapton in Northants, and 'Adem'=Acle in Essex (*V.C.H. Essex*, i. 395).

[8] A blank.

[9] An unusually exact valuation ; in this case the 'value' must have been the amount actually re-ceived.

[10] Wandelmestrei was subsequently divided into the Hundreds of Alciston and Longbridge.

---

[1] A blank.   [2] A blank.
[3] A blank.   [4] See also p. 392.
[5] The abbey of Hyde.

in) the rape of Hastinges,[1] and 2 hides to the rape of Lewes,[2] as do (*et*) 7 burgesses.

On the demesne the abbot has 4 ploughs, and 65 villeins with 7 bordars have 21½ ploughs. There (are) 12 serfs, and 50 acres of meadow. Wood(land yielding) 4 swine from the pannage, and 6 swine from the pasturage (*herbagio*).

Of the above-mentioned 5 hides[3] Robert holds 1 hide and 3 virgates of the abbot, Reinbert 5 virgates, Geoffrey half a hide, Alvred 3 virgates. They (*ipsi*) have on (their) demesne 4 ploughs and 5 villeins and 1 bordar with 1½ ploughs.

The whole manor in the time of King Edward was worth 48 pounds, and afterwards 30 pounds. Now what the abbot holds (is worth) 36 pounds ; what his men (have) 4 pounds and 5 shillings.

In Totenore [Totnore] Hundred

The abbot himself holds of the king 4 hides. Alnod cild held them of King Edward and then, as (*et*) now, they were assessed for 4 hides. There the abbot has 6 villeins with 3 ploughs. (This) is appraised in another manor.

(In the Liberty of Battle[4])

The abbot himself has in his own rape[5] 6½ hides.[6] This land was assessed for 6 hides, and (the other) half (hide) was geld-free (*quieta*) because (it was) outside (*foris*) the rape.[7]

Of (*in*) these hides the same abbot holds in demesne Bocheha(m) [Buckhurst in Westfield]. Olbolt held it of Earl Godwin. Then, as (*et*) now, it was assessed for half a hide ; now 1 virgate is in the rape of the Count of Eu (*Ow*).[8] On the demesne the abbot has 1

plough, and (there are) 4 bordars with 1 plough. There (are) 3 acres of meadow, and wood (land yielding) 2 swine. In the time of King Edward, as (*et*) now, it was worth 20 shillings.

In Bece [Beech in Whatlington] which Osbern (holds) of the Count of Eu the abbot has 3 virgates of land, and there are 3 villeins with 1 plough. (This) is worth 6 shillings.

In Wasingate [[9]] which Reinbert holds the abbot has 1 virgate of land with 1 villein and half a plough. There (is) wood(land yielding) 2 swine. (This) is worth 4 shillings.

In Wilminte [Wilmington][10] which the Count of Mortain holds the abbot has 6 virgates of land, and there are 6 villeins with 4 ploughs ; and wood(land yielding) 2 swine. (This) is worth 15 shillings.

In Nirefeld [Netherfield] which the Count of Eu holds the abbot has 6 virgates of land, and there are 5 villeins and 1 bordar with 3 ploughs. (This) is worth 10 shillings.

In Penehest [Penhurst][11] which Osbern holds of the Count of Eu the abbot has half a hide, and there are 2 villeins with 2 ploughs, and 1 acre of meadow, and wood-(land yielding) 2 swine. (This) is worth 15 shillings.

In the manor of Hou [Hooe] which the Count of Eu holds the abbot has half a hide, and there are 2 villeins with 1 plough. (This) is worth 5 shillings.

---

[1] A charter of Henry I. (Harl. Ch. 43 C. 12) mentions 7 hides as separated from the 50 hides which belonged to Alciston, and says that they lay at Ovingedene (see note 10, p. 437), Codingele (Coding in Hooe), Betelesford (Batsford in Warbleton), Wivenham (? Witherenden near Burwash, see note 1, p. 402), Danigawurde, Scoweswelle (Shoyswell, see note 3, p. 403), Baresselle (Borzell, see note 2, p. 402), Wertesce, Brēbreseboc and Seuredeswelle (? Sores Wood in Etchingham, see note 7, p. 404).

[2] These 2 hides, and the 7 burgages, were at Ovingdene (see last note and note 10, p. 437).

[3] This must be a misreading for 50.

[4] No heading, but a line left blank.

[5] See Introduction, p. 375.

[6] According to the Battle Abbey Chronicle, 6 hides and half a virgate. See Introduction, p. 359.

[7] *Foris rapum* (see Introduction, p. 361).

[8] The Abbey Chronicle states that 1 virgate of

this land is now outside the 'Leuga,' and belongs to Crowhurst, having been exchanged with Walter Fitz-Lambert for a wood—possibly the wood mentioned at the end of the survey of the 'Leuga' as being outside the rape.

[9] Identified by the Abbey Chronicle with Bodherstgate, or Bathurst in Battle ; the Chronicle also asserts that the abbey has only half a virgate there.

[10] Here again the Chronicle asserts that the amount held by the abbey is 5 virgates and not 6. This land was part of the nameless manor in Hailesaltede Hundred held by Hugh (see note 1, p. 399), and had formerly belonged to the manor of Wilmington.

[11] This manor is not mentioned in the Count of Eu's rape ; it may possibly have gone with Bexhill, where Osbern held 10 hides (see note 1, p. 397 ; but see note 2, p. 399).

THE HOLDERS OF LANDS

In PILESHAM [Filsham][1] which the Count of EU holds the abbot has 1 virgate and 1 villein with 1 plough, and (there is) 1 acre of meadow. (This) is worth 4 shillings.

In CEDESFELD [Catsfield] which Werenc holds of the Count of EU the abbot has 3 virgates in demesne.[2]

In BOLLINTUN [Bollington in Bexhill] which the Count of EU holds the abbot has 2 hides all but (minus) 1 virgate,[3] and there are 7 villeins with 5 ploughs. (This) is worth 20 shillings.

In CROHERST [Crowhurst] which Walter holds of the Count of EU the abbot has 1 virgate of land.

In WITINGES [Wilting] which Ingelran holds of the count the abbot has 1 virgate of land,[4] (which is) waste (wastam).

In HOLINTUN [Hollington] which the Count of EU holds the abbot has 1 virgate of land, (which is) waste (wastam).

There is also (adhuc) 1 wood yielding (de) 5 swine outside (foris) the rape.

Of all this land the abbot has in demesne 2½ hides, and there (he has) 1 plough with 21 bordars and 2 mills unrented (sine censu). (This) is worth 40 shillings.

These hides have not paid geld in the rape.[5]

THE LAND OF SAINT EDWARD (OF SHAFTESBURY)

IN BENESTEDE [Avisford] HUNDRED

THE ABBEY OF SAINT EDWARD holds and did hold in the time of King Edward FALCHEHAM [Felpham]. Then it was assessed for 21 hides. Now for 15½ hides. There is land for 12 ploughs. On the demesne is 1 plough, and (there are) 48 villeins and 19 cottars with 15 ploughs. There (is) a church and a fishery yielding (de) 5 shillings. In Cicestre [Chichester] (are) 6 burgesses yielding (de) 7 shillings. There (are) 8 acres of

meadow. Wood(land) yielding (de) 30 swine. In the time of King Edward it was worth 10 pounds, now 20 pounds.

fo. 18a
IX. THE LAND OF THE COUNT OF EU (OW)

THE COUNT OF EU holds in demesne a manor which is called HOU [Hooe].[6] Earl Godwin held it, and in the time of King Edward, as (et) now, it was assessed for 12 hides. There is land for 44 ploughs. On the demesne are 2 ploughs, and 44 villeins with 12 bordars have 28 ploughs. There (is) a chapel (ecclesiola), and 1 mill yielding (de) 7 shillings, and 71 acres of meadow, and 30 saltpans yielding (de) 33 shillings. Wood(land yielding) 10 swine from the pannage. From the pasturage (herbagio) 7 swine.

Of the villein lands (terra villanorum) of this manor Reinbert holds half a hide, Robert 2½ virgates, Osbern 2 virgates, Alvred 2 virgates, Girald 2 virgates, Ingelran 2 virgates, Witbert 4½ virgates, Werelc 2 virgates, another Robert 2 virgates.

Between (them) all they have on (their) demesne 3½ ploughs, and 12 villeins and 3 bordars with 7 ploughs.

The whole manor in the time of King Edward was worth 25 pounds, and afterwards 6 pounds. Now the count's demesne (is worth) 14 pounds; (that) of his knights 7 pounds and 7 shillings.

Werenc holds of the count CEDESFELLE [Catsfield]. Elfelm held it of King Edward and could betake himself (ire) with his land whither he pleased. Then it was assessed for 1 hide and a half, now for 1 hide and 1 virgate.[7] There is land for 7 ploughs. On the demesne is 1 plough, and 11 villeins with 2 bordars have 8 ploughs. There (is) a chapel (ecclesiola), and 1 mill serving the hall (ad hallam serviens). There (are) 4 acres of meadow, and wood(land yielding) 3 swine, and pasturage (herbagium) (yielding) 5 swine. In the time of King Edward it was worth 50 shillings, and afterwards 20 shillings; now 60 shillings.

Wibert holds of the count MEDEHEI [   ].[8] Osward held it of King

---

[1] Called Philesham in the Chronicle; the manor is called Wilesham in the Count of Eu's rape (see p. 397).
[2] See note 7.
[3] See p. 397.
[4] See note 6, p. 398.
[5] All the lands within the Leuga of Battle abbey were exempt from payment of geld to the Crown, but from the expression 'in suo rapo' it seems that the lands not held in demesne paid geld to the abbey; but see Introduction, p. 358.

[6] This had formed part of the manor of Willingdon (see note 3, p. 411).
[7] Assessment reduced probably because 3 virgates were in the 'lowey' of Battle (see note 2).
[8] S.D.B.'s identification of this as Meads in Eastbourne is groundless and improbable. It was probably in the neighbourhood of Northye, Keeteye and Southeye.

A HISTORY OF SUSSEX

Edward, and could betake himself (*ire*) with his land whither he pleased, and then, as (*et*) now, it was assessed for 3 virgates. There is land for 4 ploughs. On the demesne is 1 plough, and (there are) 4 villeins with 4 ploughs, and (there are) 5 saltpans yielding (*de*) 64 pence, and 2½ acres of meadow, and wood(land yielding) 3 swine from the pannage.

In the time of King Edward it was worth 4 pounds, and afterwards 20 shillings; now 110 shillings.

Robert holds of the count NEREWELLE [Ninfield].[1] Blac held it of King Edward, and could betake himself (*ire*) with his land whither he pleased. Then it was assessed for 3 hides, now for 2½ hides. There is land for 12 ploughs. On the demesne Robert has 1 plough, and a church, and 1 bordar.

Of the land of this manor the Count of Eu himself holds 5 virgates in demesne, Osbern 3 virgates, Werenc 2 virgates, Reinbert 7 virgates. On (their) demesne they have 2 ploughs, and 8 villeins and 2 bordars have 6 ploughs.

The aforesaid Robert the cook (*coquus*) holds the seat (*caput*) of the manor, and he holds 2 virgates only, and a certain villein holds the others (*alias*).

The whole manor in the time of King Edward was worth 6 pounds, and afterwards 20 shillings. Now the whole (is worth) 105 shillings.

IN FOLSALRE [FOXEARLE] HUNDRED

Wibert holds of the count HERSTE [Herstmonceux]. Edmer the priest held it in the time of King Edward, and could betake himself (*ire*) with his land whither he pleased; and then, as (*et*) now, it was assessed for 5 hides. There is land for 12 ploughs. On the demesne are 3 ploughs, and 30 villeins with 12 cottars have 16 ploughs. There (is) a church, and 7 acres of meadow, and wood-(land yielding) 1 pig.

In the time of King Edward it was worth 6 pounds, and afterwards 20 shillings; now 10 pounds.

William holds of the count WERLINGES [Wartling]. Alnod held it of King Edward and could betake himself (*ire*) with his land whither he pleased, and then, as (*et*) now, it was assessed for 5 hides. There is land for 16 ploughs. On the demesne are 2 ploughs,

and 30 villeins with 10 cottars have 18 ploughs. There (are) 3 saltpans yielding (*de*) 7 shillings. Wood(land yielding) 30 swine, and 30 acres of meadow.

Of the land of this manor Girard holds 1 hide, Ralf 1 hide, Wennenc the priest 2 virgates. There (are) 12 villeins with 4 cottars with 9 ploughs, and 8 acres of meadow.

The whole manor in the time of King Edward and afterwards[2] was worth 10 pounds. Now what William holds (is worth) 10 pounds; what the knights (hold) 4 pounds.

Robert de Cruel holds of the count ESSEBORNE [Ashburnham]. Seward held it of King Edward, and then, as (*et*) now, it was assessed for 2½ hides. There is land for 12 ploughs. On the demesne is 1, and 21 villeins with 3 cottars have 14 ploughs. There (is) a church, and 3 saltpans yielding (*de*) 58 pence.

In the time of King Edward it was worth 6 pounds, and afterwards 20 shillings; now 9 pounds.

The count of Eu holds FRANCWELLE [Frankwell[3]], and 6 knights (hold it) of him. One of them, Norman, held it in the time of King Edward, and then, as (*et*) now, it was assessed for 1 hide and a half. There is land for 2 ploughs.

Of this land the same Norman has half a hide, Ralph 2 virgates, Hugh 2 virgates, Osbern 2 virgates, Wenenc 1 virgate, Girard 1 virgate. On the demesne (is) 1 plough, and (there are) 8 villeins and 1 cottar with 4 ploughs.

In the manor (are) 12 acres of meadow, and wood(land yielding) 2 swine.

The whole manor in the time of King Edward was worth 40 shillings, and afterwards 10 shillings; now 46 shillings.

Ingelran holds of the count 1 hide in the same hundred. Two free men held it in the time of King Edward, and could betake themselves (*ire*) with their land whither they pleased. Then, as (*et*) now, it was assessed for 1 hide. There is land for 4 ploughs. On the demesne is 1 (plough); and 6 villeins with 4 cottars have 4 ploughs.

In the time of King Edward it was worth 30 shillings, and afterwards 20 shillings; now 30 shillings.

Olaf holds of the count 1 virgate in the selfsame hundred. Hernetoc held it in the time of King Edward, and could betake him-

[1] The form Nerewelle suggests Netherfield, but unless it is entered out of place its position requires it to be Ninfield.

[2] *Et post* interlined.   [3] In Ashburnham.

396

self (*ire*) whither he would, and then, as (*et*) now, it was assessed for 1 virgate. There is land for 1 plough, and there it is on the demesne, with 1 villein and 2 cottars. It is and was worth 10 shillings.

IN BEXELEI [BEXHILL] HUNDRED

Osbern holds BEXELEI [Bexhill] of the count. In the time of King Edward Bishop Alric held it, because it belongs to (*est de*) the bishopric,[1] and afterwards he held it until King William gave the castelry of Hastings (*castellariam de Hastinges*) to the count. In the time of King Edward, as (*et*) now, it was assessed for 20 hides. There is land for 26 ploughs.

Of the land of this manor the count himself holds in demesne 3 hides, and there he has 1 plough, and (there are) 7 villeins with 4 ploughs.

Of the same land Osbern has 10 hides, Wenenc 1 hide, William de Sept Mueles 2½ hides all but (*minus*) half a virgate, Robert St. Leger 1 hide and half a virgate, Reinbert half a hide, Anschitil half a hide, Robert Cruel half a hide, Geoffrey and Roger, clerks, 1 hide as a benefice (*in prebenda*). There (are) 2 churches. On (their) demesne are 4 ploughs, and (there are) 46 villeins and 27 cottars with 28 ploughs. In the whole manor (are) 6 acres of meadow.

The whole manor in the time of King Edward was worth 20 pounds, and afterwards it was waste (*wasta*). Now (it is worth) 18 pounds and 10 shillings. Of this (*his*) the count's portion accounts for (*capit*) 40 shillings.

Osbern holds of the count 2 virgates of land in the same hundred, and they were assessed for 2 virgates then as now (*semper*). There he has 5 ploughing oxen (*boves in car[uca]*). (This) was worth 8 shillings, now 16 shillings.

Levenot held BOLINTUN [Bollington in Bexhill] of King Edward, and it was assessed for 5 hides both then and now. There is land for 5 ploughs.

Of this land the count holds in demesne 3 virgates; and there he has 20 burgesses[2] and 5 cottars with 2 ploughs.

The abbey of Tréport[3] (*Ultresport*) holds 3 hides all but (*minus*) 2 virgates, and for so much (this holding) is assessed. On the demesne is 1 plough, and 13 villeins with 13 cottars have 5 ploughs; (there are) 20 acres of meadow.

In the time of King Edward the whole manor was worth 6 pounds, and afterwards 50 shillings. Now the count has 43 shillings and the monks 4 pounds.

IN BALDESLEI [BALDSLOW] HUNDRED

King Edward held WILESHAM [Filsham] in demesne. There are 15 hides which do not pay geld and have not paid geld. There is land for 30 ploughs.

Of this land the count himself holds 8 hides and 1 virgate; and there he has 2

fo. 18b

ploughs, and 48 villeins with 7 cottars have 34 ploughs.

Of the land of the same manor Geoffrey holds 2 hides, Robert 1 hide and 1 virgate, William half a hide, Hugh the crossbowman 5 virgates, Ingelran 2 virgates, Robert the cook[4] half a hide, Walter 5 virgates, Sasward 1 virgate, Wenenc the priest 1 virgate, Osward 2 virgates, Roger Daniel half a hide.[5] On (their) demesne are 6½ ploughs, and 13 villeins and 17 cottars and 3 serfs with 7½ ploughs. In the manor (are) 30 acres of meadow, and wood(land yielding) 8 swine.

The whole manor in the time of King Edward was worth 14 pounds. Afterwards it was laid waste (*vastatum*).[6] Now (it is worth) 22 pounds. Of this (*his*) 14 pounds are assigned to the count's portion (*computantur in parte comitis*).

Ulward the priest of this manor holds a church with 1 virgate, but (that virgate) does not belong to the 15 hides. Ulmer held it of King Edward, and it did not then pay geld, nor does it (*nec facit*) now. (This) is worth 5 shillings.

---

[1] Bexhill was recovered by the Bishop of Chichester before 1166, when it was rated at 10 hides (*Red Book of the Exchequer* [Rolls Series] i. 200); the 10 hides held by Osbern may have formed a separate manor (see note 11, p. 394).

[2] It is difficult to account for the appearance of burgesses here and nowhere else in the Count of Eu's rape; their borough must have been Hast-

ings, and the land itself may have been at Bulwarhithe which was afterwards a member of Hastings.

[3] Robert Count of Eu gave 'Boniton' to the abbey of Tréport; it apparently included Pepplesham, as that was afterwards in the abbey's possession.

[4] *Coc(us)* interlined.

[5] The total amount of land here accounted for, including the 1 virgate attributed to Pilesham in the 'rape' of Battle, is 1 virgate short of 15 hides.

[6] The routes of the armies of William and Harold at the time of the invasion can be partly traced by these notices of devastated manors, but it is remarkable how completely they had recovered, and even increased, their value. See Introd. p. 363.

Godwin and Alestan held HORINTONE [Hollington] in the time of King Edward, and could betake themselves (*ire*) with their land whither they pleased. Then it was assessed for 4½ hides. Now for 3 hides and 2 virgates. There is land for 8 ploughs.

Of this land the count holds in demesne 1½ hides and 2 virgates, and there he has 1 plough and 12 villeins with 4 ploughs.

Of the selfsame land Reinbert has half a hide, William 1 hide, Hugh half a hide, Ulward 2 virgates.

On the demesne is 1 plough, and (there are) 3 villeins and 3 cottars with 3 ploughs. In the manor (are) 2 acres of meadow, and wood(land yielding) 2 swine.

The whole manor in the time of King Edward was worth 30 shillings, and afterwards 20 shillings; now 58 shillings.

Golduin held CROTESLEI [Cortesley[1]] in the time of King Edward, and could betake himself (*ire*) whither he pleased; and then, as (*et*) now, it was assessed for 6 hides. There is land for 8 ploughs.

Of this land ([2]) holds half a hide, and there is 1 villein with 1 plough.

Of the same land William holds 4½ hides and Godwin (holds them) of him, Reinbert half a hide, Hugh half a hide.

There they have 24 villeins and 2 cottars with 8 ploughs.

In the manor (are) 27 acres of meadow.

The whole manor in the time of King Edward, and afterwards,[3] was worth 100 shillings. Now 6 pounds and 7 shillings.

Wenestan held WESTEWELLE [Westfield] in the time of King Edward, and could betake himself (*ire*) whither he pleased. Then, as (*et*) now, it was assessed for 1 hide and 2 virgates. There is land for 3 ploughs. Wibert[4] holds (it) of the count, and has on (his) demesne 1½ ploughs and 7 villeins and 1 cottar with 3 ploughs.

In the time of King Edward it was worth 20 shillings, and afterwards 70 shillings; now 72 shillings.

Earl Harold held CROHEST [Crowhurst]. Then it was assessed for 6 hides. Now for 3 hides. There is land for 22 ploughs.

Walter son of Lambert[5] holds (it) of the count, and has 2 ploughs on the demesne, and 12 villeins and 6 cottars have 12 ploughs. There (are) 15 acres of meadow, and wood(land yielding) 4 swine.

A certain Walo holds half a hide and 2 virgates. There are 3 villeins with 1 plough.

In the time of King Edward it was worth 8 pounds. Now 100 shillings. It was laid waste (*vastatum fuit*).

Two free men held WILTINGHAM [Wilting] in the time of King Edward. Then, as (*et*) now, it was assessed for 4 hides. There is land for 9 ploughs.

Of this land Ingelran holds of the count 2 hides and 2 virgates, Reinbert half a hide and 2 virgates, Ralf half a hide, Robert 2 virgates. There (are) on the demesne 3 ploughs, and (there are) 9 villeins and 5 cottars with 6 ploughs. There (are) 16 acres of meadow. The whole manor in the time of King Edward was worth 100 shillings. Now 4 pounds. It was laid waste (*vastatum*). The count has 1 virgate of this manor in his park.[6]

In the same hundred Ingelran holds of the count 3 virgates, which 12 freemen held in the time of King Edward, but they have never returned geld. There (are) 3 villeins with 2 ploughs. (This) is worth 10 shillings.

IN HAILESALTEDE [NETHERFIELD] HUNDRED

Earl Harold held WATLINGETONE [Whatlington]. Then, as (*et*) now, it was assessed for half a hide. There is land for 6 ploughs. Reinbert holds (it) of the count, and there he has 2 ploughs, and 6 villeins and 3 cottars with 3 ploughs. There are 10 acres of meadow, and wood(land yielding) 6 swine.

In the time of King Edward, as (*et*) now, it was worth 50 shillings. It was laid waste (*vastatum*).

The same Reinbert[7] holds of the count MONTIFELLE [Mountfield]. God(a) held it in the time of King Edward, and could betake herself (*ire*) whither she pleased. Then, as (*et*) now, it was assessed for 1 hide. There

---

[1] A manor in Hollington and adjacent parishes.
[2] Name of tenant omitted.
[3] *Et post* interlined.
[4] Wening, by permission of William son of Wibert his lord, gave the church of Westfield to Battle Abbey, and Reinald de Anseville heir of William son of Wibert confirmed the gift. (Add. Ch. 20161.)

[5] Ancestor of the Scotneys of Crowhurst and Lamberhurst.
[6] The remaining virgate is accounted for under Witinges in the 'rape' of Battle (see p. 395).
[7] Reinbert the sheriff (of the rape of Hastings) gave the church of Mountfeld to the collegiate church of Hastings; he was one of the chief holders of lands in the rape, and was ancestor of the family of Echingham (see Introd. p. 380).

is land for 8 ploughs. On the demesne are 2 (ploughs), and 9 villeins with 2 cottars have 6 ploughs. There (are) 8 acres of meadow, and wood(land yielding) 10 swine. In the time of King Edward it was worth 3 pounds, and afterwards 20 shillings; now 4 pounds.

Herolf holds of the count NEDREFELLE [Netherfield]. Goda held it of King Edward. Then it was assessed for 1½ hides. Now for 1 only. There is land for 4 ploughs. On the demesne is 1 (plough), and 7 villeins have 3 ploughs. There are 8 saltpans yielding (*de*) 8 shillings, and wood(land yielding) 10 swine. In the time of King Edward it was worth 100 shillings; now 50 shillings. It was waste (*vastata*).

In this Hundred Hugh holds a manor[1] of the count, which Alnod held in the time of King Edward, and he could betake himself (*ire*) whither he would, and then it was assessed for 1 hide and a half. Now for 1 only. There is land for 4 ploughs. On the demesne is 1 plough, and (there are) 12 villeins with 5 ploughs. There (are) 5 acres of meadow, and wood(land yielding) 4 swine. In the time of King Edward it was worth 100 shillings, and afterwards 20 (shillings); now 50 shillings.

The same Osbern (*sic*)[2] holds 1 virgate of the count in BECHE [Beech]. Ulbald held it in the time of King Edward. Then (it was assessed) for 1 virgate, now for nothing. Then it was worth 2 shillings; now nothing.

Wenenc the priest holds of the count BRUNHA(M) [Broomham [3]]. Edith (*Eddid*) held it in the time of King Edward, and could betake herself (*ire*) whither she would, and it was assessed for half a hide then, as (*et*) now. There is land for 3 ploughs. On the demesne is 1 (plough), and (there are) 4 villeins and 2 cottars with 2 ploughs. (There is) 1 acre of meadow. Wood(land yielding) 2 swine. In the time of King Edward, as (*et*) now, (it was worth) 20 shillings. It was laid waste (*vastata*).

Hugh holds of the count 1 virgate in ESLEDE [Eyelid farm in Ewhurst [4]]. Lewin

held it of Earl Lewin.[5] It has never paid geld. There (is) 1 plough, and wood(land yielding) 3 swine. It was worth 5 shillings; now 12 shillings.

IN STAPLEHA(M) [STAPLE] HUNDRED

The same Hugh holds 2 virgates belonging to (*pertinentes in*) ELLEDE [Eyelid]. Earl Lewin held them, and they were assessed for 2 virgates then, as (*et*) now. There (is) 1 villein with 1 plough.

The Count himself holds 1 virgate belonging to (*pertinentem in*) ESLEDE [Eyelid]. Earl Lewin held it. It has never given geld. There is land for 1 plough, and there it is with 1 villein. Then (it was worth) 4 shillings; now 5 shillings.

In the same hundred Hugh holds of the count 1 virgate. Cane (*Can'*) held it in the time of King Edward. Then, as (*et*) now, it was assessed for 1 virgate. There is land for 1 plough. There (the plough) is, with 1 villein. (This) is, and was, worth 4 shillings.

(IN NETHERFIELD HUNDRED)[6]

The Count of Eu holds BRISLINGA [Brightling]. In the time of King Edward 2 brothers held it of the king. It was assessed for 1 hide then, as (*et*) now. On the demesne is 1 plough, and (there is) a church, and wood(land) yielding (*de*) 5 shillings.

Of this hide Robert holds 4 virgates of the count, and there he has 10 villeins with 2 cottars who have (*habentes*) 7 ploughs.

In the time of King Edward it was worth 100 shillings, and afterwards 10 shillings; now 42 shillings.

The Count of Eu holds DALINTONE [Dallington]. Norman held it in the time of King Edward, and could betake himself (*ire*) whither he would, and it was assessed for 1 hide, now for nothing. There is land .

Of this hide the count has a half as (*in*) forest, and it is worth 5 shillings.

William has the other half, and there he has 1 plough on (his) demesne, with 2 cottars.

The same William has 1 virgate and a half in FOXER [FOXEARLE] HUNDRED.[7] King Edward held it, and it has never paid geld. There 1 villein and 2 cottars have 1 plough.

---

[1] This was a detached portion of Alnod's manor of Wilmington (see note 8, p. 412), by which name it was still called (see note 10, p. 394).

[2] Possibly an entry relating to Penhurst, which Osbern held (see note 11, p. 394), preceded this in the original returns.

[3] A manor in Penhurst and the adjacent parishes.

[4] On the borders of Netherfield and Staple Hundreds.

[5] Leofwine brother of Harold killed at the battle of Hastings.

[6] No Hundredal heading to mark return from Staple Hundred to Netherfield.

[7] Part of Dallington is in Foxearle Hundred.

The whole in the time of King Edward was worth 45 [1] shillings; now 35 shillings.

IN HAUOCHESBERIE [HAWKSBOROUGH] HUNDRED [2]

Wibert holds of the count WARBORGETONE [Warbleton]. Countess Goda [3] held it. Then, as (*et*) now, it was assessed for 1 hide. There is land for 2 ploughs. On the demesne is 1 (plough), and 2 villeins with 6 cottars have 1 plough. It was worth 40 shillings; now 20 shillings.

In BELINGEHA(M) [? Beddingham] the count has 1 hide in demesne. Queen Edith (*Eddid*) held it. It has never paid geld. There is land for 3 ploughs. On the demesne is 1 (plough), and 3 villeins have 2 ploughs. In the time of King Edward it was worth 20 shillings, and afterwards 10 shillings;
fo. 19a
now 20 shillings.

The count himself has half a hide in BELINGHA(M) [? Beddingham [4]]. King Edward held it, and it has never paid geld. There are 2 villeins with 3 ploughs. It was and is worth 10 shillings.

Also in BELINGHA(M) [? Beddingham] the count holds 4 hides all but (*minus*) half a virgate. Countess Goda held (this), and it has never paid geld. There is land for 10 ploughs. There 18 villeins have 13 ploughs. In the time of King Edward it was worth 4 pounds, and afterwards 40 shillings; now 70 shillings.

The count himself holds in demesne 1½ hides and 1 virgate [5] of the manor of FERLA [West Firle]. In the time of King Edward the abbey of Wilton held (this). It has never paid geld. There is land for 6 ploughs. There 9 villeins have 8 ploughs. In the time of King Edward, as (*et*) now, it was worth 30 shillings.

The same count holds 1 virgate and a half of HERLINTONE [Arlington [6]]. The abbey of Wilton held it in the time of King Edward. It has never paid geld. There is land for 1 plough. There 5 villeins have 3 ploughs. In the time of King Edward, as (*et*) now, it was worth 7 shillings.

The same count has 1 virgate and a half of the manor of LESTONE [Laughton]. Countess Goda held it. It has never paid geld. There 3 villeins have 2 ploughs. In the time of King Edward, as (*et*) now, it was worth 8 shillings.

The same count holds 1 virgate of land belonging to (*pertinentem ad*) HECHESTONE [Eckington [7]] Agemund held it in the time of King Edward, and could betake himself (*ire*) whither he would. And it has not paid geld. There 2 villeins have 2 ploughs. In the time of King Edward, as (*et*) now, it was worth 4 shillings.

The same count holds half a hide and half a virgate of the manor of RIPE [Ripe]. Earl Harold held (this), and it has never paid geld. There 2 villeins have 1 plough. It is, and was, worth 5 shillings.

The same count holds 1 virgate in the manor of TELITONE [Tilton]. Earl Harold held it, and it has never paid geld. There 2 villeins have 1 plough. It is, and was, worth 5 shillings.

In the manor of ESDENE [East Dean] (the count has) 1 virgate and a half. Countess Goda held it; it has never paid geld. There 2 villeins have 1 plough. It is, and was, worth 3 shillings.

In the manor of WILLENDONE [Willingdon] Countess Goda held 1½ virgates, and it has never paid geld. There the count has 2 villeins with 2 ploughs. It is, and was, worth 5 shillings.

There Ulmer the priest held 1 virgate, [8] and could betake himself (*ire*) whither he would, and it has never paid geld. There the count has 1 villein with 1 plough. It is, and was, worth 3 shillings.

---

[1] The *v* of *xlv* is interlined.

[2] The Hundreds of Hauochesberie, Henhert and Esseswelle each consisted of a very small group of estates whose manorial hall was situated within the bounds of the Hundred, and a much larger group of estates which in King Edward's time had been attached to manors in the rape of Pevensey. See Introd. p. 357.

[3] Sister of King Edward.

[4] I think there can be little doubt that this is King Edward's manor of Beddingham. This group of lands held by the count lay round Burwash, which was afterwards the chief manor of the Counts of Eu.

[5] *Et* 1 *virgam* interlined.

[6] Arlington is not mentioned by name in Pevensey rape but was possibly included in the abbey of Wilton's manor of (West) Firle.

[7] The form Hechestone suggests Heighton, but Agemund's manor was Eckington (see note 10, p. 417).

[8] Probably this is the 'other virgate' mentioned under Chiddingly, which Ælmar (? a scribal error for Ulmar), held (see note 7, p. 418).

There Alwin held [1] I virgate and one [2] quarter of the manor of SASINGHA(M) [Sessingham] and could betake himself (ire) whither he would, and it has never paid geld. There the count has 2 villeins with 2 ploughs. It is, and was, worth 10 shillings.

Wibert holds of the count half a hide in RADINTONE [Ratton]. A certain freeman, Cane (Cana), held it, and it has never paid geld. There 3 villeins have 2 ploughs. It is, and was, worth 8 shillings.

In DENE [(? West) Dean] Countess Goda held I hide, and it has never paid geld. There Wibert has 2 villeins with 2 ploughs. It is, and was, worth 14 shillings.

In LESTONE [Laughton] Countess Goda held I hide, and it has never paid geld. There Wibert has 4 villeins with 3 ploughs. It is, and was, worth 13 shillings.

In BORTONE [Burton [3]] a certain free man, Ulmer, held half a hide, and it has never paid geld. There Wibert has I villein and I cottar with I plough. Then, as (et) now, (it was worth) 8 shillings.

Osbern son of Geoffrey holds of the Count 5 hides in LESTONE [Laughton]. Countess Goda held (this), and it has never paid geld. There is land for 10 ploughs. There 15 villeins have 15 ploughs. In the time of King Edward it was worth 4 pounds, and afterwards 40 shillings; now 4 pounds.

In STOCHINGHAM [[4]] Levenot held half a hide, and it has never paid geld. There Osbern has I cottar returning 12 pence. Then (it was worth) 3 shillings, now 2 shillings.

In ACHINGEWORDE [[5]] Brictuin a free man held half a hide, and it has never paid geld. There Osbern has on his demesne I plough, and I villein with I plough, and 2 acres of meadow. Then and afterwards, as (et) now, it was worth 10 shillings.

In ECHENTONE [Eckington] Agemund held I hide of King Edward, and it has never paid geld. There is land for 2 ploughs. There Osbern has 3 villeins with 3 ploughs. Then and afterwards, as (et) now, (it was worth) 14 shillings.

In FERLE [West Firle] the abbey of Wilton held I virgate of King Edward, and it has never paid geld. There Osbern has I villein with I plough. Then, as (et) now, it was worth 30 pence.

In PRESTITONE [Preston in Beddingham] Botiz a free man held half a hide, and it has never paid geld. There Osbern has 5 villeins with 3 ploughs. Then, as (et) now, (it was worth) 5 shillings.

In WALDERE [Waldron] Ælveva a free woman held half a virgate, and it has never paid geld. There Osbern has I villein with 5 oxen. It is worth 2 shillings.

In RIPE [Ripe] Earl Harold held I virgate. It has never paid geld. There Alwin a man of the Count of Eu has I plough on the demesne and I villein and I cottar with I plough. There (are) 3 acres of meadow, and wood(land yielding) 3 swine. Then and afterwards 4 shillings; now 10 shillings.

IN ESSESWELLE [SHOYSWELL] HUNDRED

THIS HUNDRED HAS NEVER PAID GELD

Walter son of Lambert holds of the count HASLESSE [Hazelhurst in Ticehurst [6]], Bishop Alric held it in fee of King Edward. Then, as (et) now, (there were) 4½ hides. There is land for 9 ploughs. There (are) on the demesne 2 ploughs, and 6 villeins and I cottar with 7 ploughs. There (is) a church, and wood(land yielding) 10 swine. Of this land Walo holds I hide, and there he has 4 villeins with 2 ploughs and I cottar. The whole manor in the time of King Edward was worth 114 shillings; now 7 pounds. It was laid waste (vastatum).

In CAVELTONE [Chalvington] 2 free men, Lewin and Edward, held I virgate. There the count has 2 villeins with I plough. Then, and afterwards, as (et) now, (it was worth) 40 pence.

---

[1] *Tenuit* interlined.

[2] *Unum* interlined; 1¼ virgates is probably intended.

[3] In the neighbourhood of Willingdon, possibly Burghton near Jevington (see note 1, p. 412).

[4] See note 4, p. 418.

[5] Etchingworth otherwise Hagingworth is a name found in the thirteenth century in connection with Waldron; possibly it is Etchingwood in Buxted; this seems to be the half hide belonging to Bristui's manor of Haingurge (see note 9, p. 413).

[6] The manor of 'Haslesse' passed to the Scotneys, descendants of Walter; but the church of Chichester appears to have recovered some part of it, as in the thirteenth century the dean and chapter held lands in Ticehurst.

In ESSERINTONE [Sherrington] Lewin, a free man, held 1 virgate. There the count has 2 villeins with 1 plough. Then and afterwards, as (*et*) now, (it was worth) 6 shillings.

In ALSITONE [Alciston][1] the abbey of Wilton held 1 virgate. There the count has 1 villein with 1 plough. Then and afterwards, as (*et*) now, (it was worth) 5 shillings.

Reinbert holds of the count 1 virgate in RADETONE [Ratton]. Ulf, a free man, held it. There (is) 1 plough on the demesne, and (there are) 15 acres of meadow, and 3 cottars return 2 shillings. Then and afterwards, as (*et*) now, (it was worth) 5 shillings.

In ALSITONE [Alciston[2]] the abbey of Wilton held 1 virgate. There Reinbert has 2 ploughs and 3 cottars, and wood(land yielding) 2 swine. Then and afterwards, as (*et*) now, 5 shillings.

In WIGENTONE [Winton ?[3]] Countess Goda held 1 virgate. There Reinbert had on the demesne 1 plough with 1 cottar. Then (it was worth) 5 shillings; now 10 shillings. It was laid waste (*vast[ata]*).

In WILENDONE [Willingdon] Countess Goda held half a virgate. There Reinbert has 1 cottar returning 12 pence. Then, as (*et*) now, (it was worth) 12 pence. It was laid waste (*vast[ata]*).

In RADETONE [Ratton] Countess Goda held 1 virgate. There Reinbert has 4 villeins with 3 ploughs. Then and afterwards, as (*et*) now, (it was worth) 10 shillings.

In RIPE [Ripe] Godwin, a free man, held 1 virgate. There Reinbert has 1 villein with 1 plough. Then and afterwards, as (*et*) now, (it was worth) 4 shillings.

[1] This and the two preceding entries, being held by the count, must have been in or near Burwash (see note 4, p. 400); and this portion of Alciston would be at Witherenden—if that may be identified with Wivenham (see note 1, p. 394), which however is at least doubtful.
[2] This was at Borzell (see note 1, p. 394), which was held by Reinbert's descendants the Etchinghams.
[3] Formerly Wingeton on the borders of Alfriston and Berwick; it is not mentioned in the Count of Mortain's rape, but as it subsequently went with the manor of Berwick it was probably

Osbern son of Geoffrey holds of the count half a hide in WILLEDONE [Willingdon]. Countess Goda held it. There (are) now 2 ploughs on the demesne with 1 cottar. Then and afterwards, as (*et*) now, (it was worth) 40 shillings.

In FERLE [West Firle] the abbey of Wilton held 1 virgate. There Osbern has 1 villein with 1 plough. Then and afterwards, as (*et*) now, (it was worth) 8 shillings.

In RADETONE [Ratton] Countess Goda held 1 virgate. There Eustace the clerk has on the demesne 1 plough with 1 villein. Then and afterwards (it was worth) 5 shillings; now 6 shillings.

In LOVINGETONE [[4]] Countess Goda held 1 virgate. There Hugh has of the count 1 villein with 1 plough. Then and afterwards, as (*et*) now, (it was worth) 5 shillings.

In RIPE [Ripe] Earl Harold held 1 hide. There Walter son of Lambert has on the demesne 2 ploughs, and 3 villeins with 2 ploughs, and 2 acres of meadow. Then and afterwards (it was worth) 20 shillings; now 30 shillings.

In FERLE [West Firle] the abbey of Wilton held 1 hide and 1 virgate and a half. There Walter has 9 villeins with 5 ploughs. There is land for 6 ploughs. In the time of King Edward and afterwards (this) was worth 3 pounds; now 4 pounds.

fo. 19b

In ESCHINTONE [Eckington] Agemund, a free man, held half a hide[5] and 1 virgate. There Walter has 3 villeins with 2 ploughs. Then and afterwards, as (*et*) now, (this was worth) 20 shillings.

In SIRINTONE [Sherrington] Alwin, a free man, held half a hide. There Walter has on the demesne 1 plough and 2 villeins with 1 plough. Then and afterwards this was worth 10 shillings; now 5 (shillings).

In LESTONE [Laughton] Goda held 1 virgate. Walter has nothing there except 2 shillings.

included with the latter in Beddingham (see note 7, p. 403). S.D.B.'s identification of Wigentone with Jevington is practically impossible.
[4] Possibly a misreading for Jevington (compare note 1, p. 409).
[5] *Dimidiam hidam* interlined.

THE HOLDERS OF LANDS

In BURGELSTALTONE [¹] Ulfi² held
1 virgate; he was a free man. There Walter
has 2 villeins with 1 plough. Then and
afterwards, as (et) now, (it was worth) 5 shillings.

In DENE [(? West) Dean] Goda held half
a hide. There Walter has on the demesne
2 ploughs with 3 cottars. Then and afterwards (it was worth) 10 shillings; now 20
shillings.

In ALSITONE [Alciston]³ the abbey of
Wilton held 1 virgate. There Walter has
3 villeins with 2 ploughs.

ESSEWELDE [SHOYSWELL] HUNDRED HAS NEVER
PAID (reddidit) GELD

IN HENHERT [HENHURST] HUNDRED

Reinbert holds of the count SALHERT [Sale-
hurst]. Countess Goda held it. Then, as
(et) now, it was assessed for half a hide.
There is land for 4 ploughs. On the demesne
is 1 (plough), and 7 villeins and 8 cottars with
6 ploughs. There (is) a church and 16 acres
of meadow. In the time of King Edward it
was worth 20 shillings, now 30 shillings. It
was laid waste (vastatum).

Alvric holds of the count DRISNESEL
[⁴]. A certain free man, Cane, held
it, and then, as (et) now, it was assessed for
3½ hides and 1 virgate.⁵ There is land for 8
ploughs. On the demesne are 2 (ploughs),
and 18 villeins and 6 cottars have 12 ploughs.
There (are) 10 acres of meadow, and wood-
(land yielding) 20 swine. In the time of King
Edward it was worth 3 pounds, now 4
pounds. It was laid waste (vastatum).

William holds of the count half a hide in
this hundred. Leveva held it in the time of
King Edward, and then, as (et) now, it was
assessed for half a hide. There is land   .⁶
On the demesne is 1 plough, and 6 acres of
meadow, and wood(land yielding) 6 swine.
In the time of King Edward, as (et) now, it
was worth 20 shillings, when received 10
shillings.

Reinbert holds of the count 1 hide in this
hundred. A certain free man, Cane, held it,
but it has not paid geld. There (are) now 8
villeins (and) 3 cottars with 6 ploughs. Then,
as (et) now, (it was worth) 30 shillings. It
was laid waste (vast[ata]).

In this hundred Norman held half a hide;
he was a free man. It has never paid geld.
There Reinbert has 1 plough with 1 cottar,
and (there is) 1 mill yielding (de) 2 shillings,
and 3 acres of meadow, and wood(land
yielding) 1 pig. Then, as (et) now, it was
worth 20 shillings.

In this hundred Azor, a free man, held 1
virgate, but it did not pay geld. There Reinbert has 1 plough on the demesne with 1
villein. There (are) 10 acres of meadow.
Then, as (et) now, (it was worth) 10 shillings,
when received 5 shillings.

In BURNE [Eastbourne] King Edward held
1 hide. It has never paid geld. There Reinbert has 4 villeins with 3 ploughs. Then and
afterwards, as (et) now, (it was worth) 20
shillings.

In BEREWICE [Berwick⁷] King Edward
held half a hide. It has never paid geld.
There Reinbert has 1 villein and 4 cottars
with 1 plough, and a mill yielding (de) 10
shillings, and 11 acres of meadow, and wood-
(land yielding) 6 swine, and 2 fisheries yielding (de) 6 pence. In the time of King Edward
it was worth 30 shillings and afterwards 10
shillings; now 35 shillings.

In BORNE [Eastbourne⁸] King Edward held
half a hide. It has never paid geld. There
Reinbert has on the demesne 3 ploughs with
5 cottars, and (there is) 1 fishery. There
is land for 2 ploughs. In the time of King
Edward it was worth 20 shillings and afterwards 10 shillings; now 45 shillings.

In the same hundred is half a hide and 1
virgate and a half. There is land for 3
ploughs. This land in the time of King
Edward belonged to (pertinuit) 3 manors,

¹ S.D.B. suggests Burghill in Chiddingly. It is
not mentioned in the Count of Mortain's rape,
but was probably included in Ulfon's manor of
Ratton (see note 10, p. 411).
² S.D.B. reads Ulsi.
³ At Shoyswell (see note 1, p. 402), which was
held by the Scotneys, descendants of Walter.
⁴ Not identified.
⁵ Et pro una virga inserted in margin.
⁶ A blank.

⁷ Berwick is not mentioned in the Count of
Mortain's rape, but as it was held by King Edward
it was possibly included in the royal manor of
Beddingham or that of Eastbourne. From the
mention of a mill and two fisheries this land would
seem to have been on the Rother.
⁸ There is a Bourne farm in Salehurst; it is
on a branch of the Rother, which may be the fishery
mentioned.

Ratendone [Ratton], Willendone [Willingdon], Ferle [Firle]. It has never paid (*reddidit*) geld. There Reinbert has 6 villeins with 3 ploughs. In the time of King Edward, as (*et*) now, (it was worth) 22 shillings.

In SIELMESTONE [Selmeston] Elfer held of King Edward half a hide. It has never paid geld. There Reinbert has 1 plough with 1 villein. There (are) 3 acres of meadow, and wood(land yielding) 1 pig. It is, and was, worth 10 shillings.

In BURGEHAM [1] Ulgar held of King Edward half a hide. It has never paid geld. There Reinbert has 2 villeins with 2 ploughs. In the time of King Edward, as (*et*) now, it was worth 12 shillings.

The same Reinbert holds of the count half a hide which belonged (*pertinuit*) in the time of King Edward to 2 manors, BERUICE [Berwick] and CLAVREHAM [Claverham]. The king held one (of these manors) and Osward held the other of King Edward.2 It has never paid geld. There (is) now 1 villein and 1 cottar. It was worth 5 shillings, now 7 shillings.

The same Reinbert holds 1 virgate3 which Cole held of King Edward. It has never paid geld. There (is) 1 villein with 1 plough. It is, and was, worth 5 shillings.

In WILENDONE [Willingdon] Goda held of the count (*sic*)4 half a hide. It has never paid geld. There is land for 2 ploughs. There Reinbert has 2 ploughs on the demesne, and 4 villeins and 2 cottars with 2 ploughs. There (are) 5 acres of meadow, and wood(land yielding) 2 swine, and 1 serf. In the time of King Edward it was worth 20 shillings, and afterwards 10 shillings; now 30 shillings.

In ALCHITONE [Eckington5] Azor, a free man, held 1 virgate. It has never paid geld. There Reinbert has 3 villeins with 1 plough and a half. Then, as (*et*) now, (it was worth) 6 shillings.

1 S.D.B. suggests Burghlow in Arlington. This holding lay probably at Burgham in Etchingham.
2 King Edward held Berwick (see note 7, p. 403), and Osward held Claverham (see p. 417).
3 Possibly attached to Lovringetone, which Cola held (see note 2, p. 411).
4 This should no doubt be 'of Earl Godwin,' who held Willingdon manor.
5 'Alchitone' by inversion from 'Achiltone,' which is Eckington (see p. 417).

In SEGNESCOME [6] Lewin, a free man, held half a hide. It has never paid geld. There the count has 2 villeins with 5 oxen, and 1 cottar. Then, as (*et*) now, (it was worth) 5 shillings.

In ALSITONE [Alciston7] Countess Goda held 2½ hides. They have never paid geld. There is land for 3 ploughs. There Robert has 4 villeins and 5 oxen (*et v bobus*). (This) was worth 30 shillings; now 20 (shillings).

In ALSISTONE [Alciston] Goda held half a virgate. It has never paid geld. There Hugh has of the count 1 villein. Then (it was worth) 5 shillings; now 2 shillings.

In WILENDONE [Willingdon] Goda held 1 virgate and a half. It has never paid geld. There Hugh has 2 villeins with 1 plough. In the time of King Edward and afterwards (it was worth) 10 shillings; now 5 shillings.

In FERLE [West Firle] the abbey of Wilton held half a virgate. It has never paid geld. There the monks of Tréport (*Ultresport8*) have 2 villeins and 2 cottars with 1 plough. Then and afterwards, as (*et*) now, (it was worth) 5 shillings.

IN BABINRERODE 9 [GOSTROW] HUNDRED
Rainer holds of the count CHECEHA(M) [10]. Edric held it in the time of King Edward; he was a free man. Then, as (*et*) now, it was assessed for half a hide. There is land for 1 plough, and there it is on the demesne, with 3 cottars, and (there are) 2 acres of meadow. In the time of King Edward and afterwards it was worth 10 shillings; now 20 (shillings).

Reinbert holds of the count DODIMERE [Udimore]. Algar held it of Earl Goduin. Then, as (*et*) now, it was assessed for 6 hides. There is land for 10 ploughs. On the demesne is 1 (plough), and 22 villeins have 15 ploughs. There (is) a church, and 2 acres of

6 Not identified.
7 If Seuredeswelle may be identified with Sores Wood (see note 1, p. 394), this portion of Alciston no doubt lay there.
8 As a fine of 42 Henry III. shows that the abbey of Tréport held land in Burhers [Burwash], this was no doubt in that parish.
9 Occurs as Babirote on the Pipe Roll of 31 Hen. I.
10 Possibly Kitchenham in Peasmarsh, which is however now in Goldspur Hundred. S.D.B.'s suggestion of Icklesham has nothing to support it, so far as I know.

meadow. In the time of King Edward, as (*et*) now, (it was worth) 8 pounds; when received 30 shillings.

In GESTELINGES [GUESTLING] HUNDRED

Geoffrey de Floc[1] holds of the count GESTELINGES [Guestling]. Ulbald held it of King Edward. Then, as (*et*) now, it was assessed for 4½ hides. There is land for 7 ploughs. On the demesne are 2 ploughs, and 12 villeins with 5 cottars have 4 ploughs. There (are) 5 acres of meadow.

Of this land Robert de Olecu(m)be holds 1 hide, and there he has 2 ploughs on (his) demesne, and 2 villeins and 2 cottars with 1 plough. In the time of King Edward, as (*et*) now, (the whole manor was worth) 100 shillings. It was waste (*vastatum*).

William de Septmuels holds IVET [[2]]. Levret held it of Earl Godwin. It is 1 hide.[3] It has never paid geld. There is land for 2 ploughs. On the demesne is 1 (plough), and 1 villein (*villanum*) and 3 cottars with 2 ploughs. There (are) 3 acres of meadow. In the time of King Edward, as (*et*) now, (it was worth) 19 (*ixx.*[4]) shillings. It was waste (*vastatum*).

In the same HUNDRED Robert holds of the count 1 furlong (*unum ferlang*)[5]. Ulmer held it of Earl Godwin. Then it was assessed for 6 hides, now for 2 hides. There is land for 12 ploughs. On the demesne are 4 ploughs, and 14 villeins and 5 cottars with 8 ploughs. There (is) a church. In the time of King Edward it was worth 100 shillings, and afterwards 40 shillings; now 6 pounds.

In COLESPORE [GOLDSPUR] HUNDRED

In EVEBENTONE [[6]] Earl Godwin held half a hide, and for so much it was assessed. There the count has 2 villeins with 1 plough and a half. Then, as (*et*) now, (it was worth) 12 shillings.

The count himself holds PLEIDENA(M) [Playden]. Siulf held it of King Edward.

fo. 20a

Then, as (*et*) now, it was assessed for 4 hides. There is land for 7 ploughs. This land (*hanc*) the following men hold of the count. Ednod 1 hide, Walter 1 hide, Reinir[7] 1 hide, Geoffrey half a hide, Tetbald the priest 3 virgates and 1 church, and 1 plough on the demesne.

Between (them) all they have 22 villeins and 15 cottars with 10½ ploughs, and on the demesne 1 plough. There (are) 5 acres of meadow. The whole manor in the time of King Edward was worth 6 pounds; now 112 shillings. The count has thereof (*inde*) what is worth 7 pounds and 3 shillings.

Geoffrey, (who holds) 1 virgate, and Lewin, (who holds) 2 virgates, hold of the count IDENE [Iden]. Ednod, a free man, held it in the time of King Edward, and then, as (*et*) now, it was assessed for 3 virgates. There is land for 2 ploughs, and there they are on the demesne, with 1 villein and 7 cottars. There (are) 6 acres of meadow. In the time of King Edward, as (*et*) now, (it was worth) 30 shillings.

Three men hold GLESHAM [Glossames in Beckley[8]] of the count, and they (*qui*) held it in the time of King Edward, and could betake themselves (*ire*) with the selfsame land whither they would. Then, as (*et*) now, it was assessed for 1 hide and a half. There is land for 2 ploughs. They (*ipsi*) have on the demesne 3 ploughs, and 1 villein and 2 cottars. There (are) 8 acres of meadow, and wood(land yielding) 10 swine. In the time of King Edward (it was worth) 40 shillings, and afterwards 20 shillings, now 30 shillings.

In the same HUNDRED Alwin holds of the count 1 virgate.[9] Edward, a free man, held it, and it was assessed for 1 virgate. There are 2 acres of meadow. Then and afterwards, as (*et*) now, (it was worth) 5 shillings.

In BADESLEI [BALDSLOW] HUNDRED

In IVET[10] Levric held 1 virgate; he was a free man. It has never paid geld. Then it was worth 3 shillings, now 12 pence. William holds it.

---

[1] Geoffrey de Floscis gave the church of Gestlinges to the collegiate church of Hastings.
[2] Printed Luet in S.D.B. and by Record Commission.
[3] *Est* interlined.
[4] Possibly 20 (*xx*) written over some other figure.
[5] As a furlong could hardly contain 12 ploughlands I think there can be little doubt that *unum ferlang* is a scribal error for Ferleg' [Fairlight], in which case the tenant is Robert St. Leger, as Fairlight was afterwards in that family.
[6] Not identified.

[7] S.D.B. reads Remir.
[8] Or Glasseye, formerly Gleseye, in the same parish.
[9] Probably attached to Sherrington manor (see note 4, p. 410).
[10] See note 2.

In CLAVESHAM [Claverham][1] Osward a free man held 2 virgates. It has never paid geld. There Reinbert has 1 villein and 1 cottar with 1 plough. Then (it was worth) 2 shillings ; now 4 shillings.

IN AILESALTEDE [NETHERFIELD] HUNDRED

In CALVINTONE [Chalvington] Godo, a free man, held 2 virgates. They have never paid geld. There Reinbert has 1 villein and 1 cottar with 1 plough. Then (this was worth) 2 shillings ; now 4 shillings.

In HECTONE [Heighton][2] Godwin, a free man, held 2 virgates. They have never paid geld. There Osbern has 2 villeins with 1 plough. Then, as (et) now, (this was worth) 4 shillings.

In HECTONE [Heighton] Godwin, a free man, held 1 virgate. It has never paid geld. There Hugh has 1 cottar. Then (it was worth) 2 shillings ; now 12 shillings.

In HECTONE [Heighton] Godwin held 1 virgate. It has never paid geld. There Hugh has 1 villein with 5 oxen. It is and was worth 2 shillings.

In the same HUNDRED Saswalo holds of the count 1 virgate. One free man held this. It has never paid geld. Then (it was worth) 15 pence ; now 12 pence.

IN STAPLE [STAPLE] HUNDRED

The count himself holds in demesne WERSTE [Ewhurst]. Ælfer held it of King Edward. Then it was assessed for 6 hides. Now for 4 hides and 3 virgates, and there are 5 virgates[3] withdrawn (from paying geld ; and the assessment is further reduced) because 1 hide is in the rape of the Count of Mortain.[4] There is land for 20 ploughs. On the demesne are 4 ploughs, and 12 villeins and 10 bordars with 6 ploughs. There (are) 4 serfs, and 12 acres of meadow, and wood(land yielding) 10 swine.

Of the land of this manor Osbern[5] holds 1 hide and 3 virgates in BODEHAM [Bodiam] ; then, as now, it belonged to (semper jacuit in) WERSTE [Ewhurst], and there was a hall (halla) there. Roger (holds) half a hide, Ralph 2 virgates. On (their) demesne is 1 plough and a half, and 7 villeins and 10 bordars with 3½ ploughs.

The whole manor in the time of King Edward was worth 10 pounds, and afterwards 6 pounds ; now 9 pounds.

The count himself holds HIHAM [Higham]. Earl Godwin held it. In the time of King Edward there were 2½ hides, but it was assessed for 2 hides, as (the jurors) say ; and now (it is assessed) for 2 hides. There is land for 16 ploughs. On the demesne is 1 (plough), and 30 villeins and 10 bordars with 19 ploughs. There (are) 6 acres of meadow, and wood(land yielding) 2 swine. In the time of King Edward it was worth 100 shillings ; now 6 pounds. It was waste (vastatum) (when received).

Walter son of Lambert holds of the count SALESCOME [Sedlescombe]. Lefsi held it of Countess Goda. It was assessed for 1 hide, and 3 virgates outside (foris) the rape,[6] and now for 1 hide.[7] There is land for 4 ploughs. On the demesne is 1 (plough), and 6 villeins with 2 bordars have 5 ploughs. There (are) 7 acres of meadow, and wood(land yielding) 6 swine. There (is) a chapel (ecclesiola). In the time of King Edward (it was worth) 60 shillings, and afterwards 20 shillings ; now 40 shillings.

Wibert holds of the count LORDISTRET [Lording Court].[8] Wenestan held it of Osward, and could not betake himself (ire) whither he would. Then, as (et) now, it was

---

[1] This probably lay at Claverham in Battle parish.

[2] This and the next two entries may possibly constitute the half hide referred to under 'Ferles' in Flexborough Hundred (see note 6, p. 413).

[3] V(irge) interlined.

[4] Modo pro iiii hidis et iii virgis et quinque virge sunt retro quia una hida est in rapo comitis de Morito-nie. This is a puzzling sentence and hard to translate ; I consider that quinque virge sunt retro is a parenthesis, quia referring back to pro iiii hidis et iii virgis ; the meaning is, that of the original 6 hides 1 is in the other rape, and the remainder pay geld for 4 hides and 3 virgates, 5 virgates being excused. (See Introd., and Eng. Hist. Rev. xix. 95.) The hide in the Count of Mortain's rape is probably that held by Alfec in Pevensey Hundred

(see note 7, p. 416) ; it is the only case of a manor in Hastings having a detached portion in Pevensey rape.

[5] The Osbern who held Bodiam is said in the Battle Abbey Chronicle to have been son of Hugh de Ow, and is therefore not identical with Osbern son of Geoffrey mentioned above, but may be the Osbern de Ow who occurs in Domesday in Surrey.

[6] Foris rapum must refer only to the 3 virgates and se defend(ebat) only to the 1 hide, as land 'outside the rape' was not 'assessed.'

[7] Et modo pro 1 hida interlined.

[8] In Ewhurst.

assessed for half[1] a hide. There is land for 3 ploughs. On the demesne is 1 (plough), and 4 villeins and 3 bordars with 2 ploughs. There (is) 1 acre of meadow and wood(land yielding) 1 pig. In the time of King Edward and afterwards (it was worth) 14 shillings ; now 20 (shillings).

In BELLEST [Bellhurst][2] Ældret held 2 virgates in parage (in paragio), and for so much it was assessed then, as (et) now. There William has on the demesne 1 plough and 1 villein with 1 plough. It is and was worth 7 shillings.

In SELESCOME [Sedlescombe] Walter son of Lambert holds 1 virgate. It has never paid geld and has always been outside the rape. There is land for 1 plough. There (the plough) is on the demesne, and (there are) 3 acres of meadow and wood(land yielding) 1 pig. Then and afterwards (it was worth) 10 shillings ; now 20 shillings.
There Geoffrey the canon holds half a hide. It belonged to (jacuit in) SELESCOME [Sedlescombe]. It is assessed for half a hide. There are 2 bordars with 1 plough, and wood-(land yielding) 3 swine. It is worth 10 shillings. It was waste (wasta).

The count himself holds on his demesne 1 villein, who belonged to (jacuit in) Selescome [Sedlescombe] ; and he holds 1 virgate outside (foris) the rape. It is worth 5 shillings.

In the same HUNDRED Wenestan held half a hide (at) FODILANT [Footland],[3] and could betake himself (ire) whither he would. It is assessed for 2 virgates. There Anschitil has 1 plough with 1 villein, and wood(land yield-ing) 4 swine. It is worth 10 shillings.

In HERSTE [Herst in Sedlescombe] Ulwin held half a hide. In the time of King Edward it was assessed for 2 virgates, and so it is now (et modo facit). There Ednod has on the demesne 1 plough, and 1 acre of meadow. It is and was worth 10 shillings.

Five men hold WALILAND [Welland in Ewhurst] of the count. (There) is 1 hide. Four brothers held this, and could betake themselves (ire) whither they pleased. There was only 1 hall (haula). In the time of King Edward, as (et) now, it was assessed for 1 hide.

Of this hide Alwold holds 2 virgates, An-schitil 3 virgates, Roger 5 virgates, Hugh 1 virgate, Osbern 2 virgates.[4] There is land .[5] On the demesne (is) 1 plough, and 7 villeins and 1 bordar have 4½ ploughs. There (are) 5 acres of meadow, and wood-(land yielding) 20 swine. In the time of King Edward, as (et) now, (it was worth) 66 shillings.

Osbern holds BASINGEHA(M) [   ][6] of the count. Alviet held it in parage (in paragio) ; then, as (et) now, it was assessed for 2 virgates. There is 1 villein. It is worth 8 shillings.

fo. 20b

X. THE LAND OF THE COUNT OF MORTAIN

In the BOROUGH OF PEVENESEL [Pevensey] in the time of King Edward there were 24 burgesses on the king's demesne, and they returned from the burgage-rents (de gablo) 14 shillings and 6 pence ; from the market-dues (de theoloneo) 20 shillings ; from the harbour-dues (de portu) 35 shillings ; from the pastur-age (de pastura) 7 shillings and 3 pence.
The Bishop of Chichester (Cicestre) had 5 burgesses, Edmer the priest 15, Ormer the priest 5, Doda the priest 3.
When the Count of Mortain received it (there were) only 27 burgesses.
Now he himself has on (his) demesne 60 burgesses, returning 39 shillings from the burgage-rents (de gablo). The market-dues (theoloneum) (yield) 4 pounds ; the mint (moneta) 20 shillings.[7]
The monks of Mortain (Moriton) (have) 8 burgesses yielding (de) 66 pence, Gilbert the sheriff[8] 1 burgess yielding 20 pence, William de Cahainges 2 burgesses yielding 2 shillings, Boselin[9] 5 yielding 2 shillings, William 4 yielding 2 shillings, Ansfrid[10] 4 yielding 2

---

[4] As this makes 1 hide contain 13 virgates there is evidently some error in the figures.
[5] A blank.   [6] Not identified.
[7] Pevensey and Lewes are the only two Sussex mints mentioned in Domesday ; others existed at Winchelsea, Hastings, Steyning and Chichester. As 20s. was the normal payment for each moneyer at this period it would seem that there was only one moneyer here : coins from this mint are very scarce (compare note 2, p. 435).
[8] Sheriff of the rape, no doubt (see Introd. p. 352).
[9] Boselin de Dives.
[10] Ansfrid held considerable estates in Pevensey rape, in all of which he was succeeded by the family of de Dene, so that he must have been a relation of Ralph de Dene (see Introd. p. 380).

[1] Una corrected to dimidia.
[2] In Beckley parish.
[3] In Sedlescombe.

shillings, Girold 2 yielding 6 shillings, Ansgot 3 yielding 12 pence, Bernard 2 yielding 7 pence, Ralph 2 yielding 12 pence, Alan 6 yielding 4 shillings, Ralph 3 yielding 53 pence, Azelin 3 yielding 4 shillings. This last (*ipse*) holds 1 house yielding 32 pence and a plot of land (*parum terre*) yielding 3 shillings. Walter (has) 2 burgesses yielding 16 pence, Roger 2 yielding 12 pence, Hugh 1 yielding 8 pence.

The count has 1 mill yielding (*de*) 20 shillings. Alvred[1] has from the pasturage (*herbagio*) 15 shillings and 4 pence.

IN BORNE [EASTBOURNE] HUNDRED

The Count of Mortain holds in demesne BORNE [Eastbourne]. King Edward held it. There were and are 46 hides. There is land for 28 ploughs. On the demesne are 4 ploughs, and (there are) 68 villeins and 3 bordars with 28 ploughs. There (is) 1 mill yielding (*de*) 5 shillings, and 16 saltpans yielding (*de*) 4 pounds and 40 shillings, and 25 acres of meadow. From the pasturage (*pastura*) (come) 6 pounds.

Of the land of this manor 2 hides and 1 virgate are in the rape of Hasting(s).[2]

Of the same land William holds 1 hide, Alvred 1 hide, the warders of the castle (of Pevensey) (*custodes castelli*) 2 hides,[3] Roger the clerk 3 virgates.

On the demesne is 1 plough and a half, and (there are) 2 villeins and 6 bordars with half a plough. In the time of King Edward it rendered one night's ferm. When the count received it (it rendered) 30 pounds. Now his demesne (renders) 40 pounds, that of his men 67 shillings.

IN TOTENORE [TOTNORE] HUNDRED

The count himself holds in demesne BED-DINGHA(M) [Beddingham]. King Edward held it. Then it was assessed for 52½ hides. Now for 50 hides. One hide and a half and half

a virgate are in the rape of Hasting(s)[4]. There is land for 33 ploughs. On the demesne are 4 ploughs, and (there are) 68 villeins and 6 bordars with 34 ploughs. There (are) 5 serfs, and 4 saltpans yielding (*de*) 40 pence, and 50 acres of meadow, and wood(land yielding) 30 swine from the pannage. From the pastur-age (*herbagio*) (come) 35 shillings.

Of the land of this manor Godfrey holds 4 hides, Gilbert 1 hide and a half. On (their) demesne they have 3½ ploughs, and 15 bordars with half a plough, and a mill yielding (*de*) 8 shillings.

In the time of King Edward it rendered one night's ferm (*firmam unius noctis*). When the count received it (it rendered) 20 pounds. Now what the count has (renders) 30 pounds, what the men (have) 6 pounds.

(IN EASTBOURNE HUNDRED)[5]

Walter holds of the count ESHALLE [East-hall[6]]. Two free men held it and could betake themselves (*ire*) whither they would. Then, as (*et*) now, it was assessed for 3 hides. There is land for 3 ploughs. On the de-mesne is 1 plough, with 1 villein and 8 bor-dars who have 1 plough. There (are) 2 acres of meadow. In the time of King Edward it was worth 50 shillings, and afterwards 30 (shillings); now 40 shillings.

The same Walter holds BEVRINGETONE [Beverington[7]]. Two men held it of King Edward and could betake themselves (*ire*) whither they pleased. It was assessed for 3 hides then, as (*et*) now. There is land for 3 ploughs. On the demesne are 2 (ploughs), and 2 bordars have half a plough. In the time of King Edward it was worth 50 shillings, and afterwards 30 shillings; now 40 shillings.

IN TOTENORE [TOTNORE] HUNDRED

Haiminc holds of the count CLOTINTONE [8] and he himself held it of King

---

[1] Alvred 'the butler' who held largely in several counties and appears to have been the ancestor of the family of Montague.

[2] Of this 1 hide and a half was in Henhurst Hundred (see p. 403); with this possibly went half a hide of Berwick (see note 7, p. 403) and 1 vir-gate of the half hide belonging to Berwick and Claverham (see p. 404).

[3] This is the '*terra vigilium de Pevenesel de Monte Acuto*' of the Pipe Rolls of Henry II. (compare note 10, p. 410); probably it is Montague in Pevensey Level. In the thirteenth century the family of Brade held lands in Eastbourne and Southeye by service of guarding the outer gate of Pevensey Castle, which was most likely the same land.

[4] One hide and a half 'in Belingeham' in Hawksborough Hundred (see note 4, p. 400).

[5] The two Hundreds of Eastbourne and Tot-nore are mixed together.

[6] This was one of the 'boroughs' of Eastbourne in the thirteenth century, and was near the present town-hall. (See article by Rev. W. Hudson, F.S.A. on, 'The Hundred of Eastbourne and its Boroughs,' in *Sussex Arch. Coll.* vol. 42.)

[7] Another of the Eastbourne 'boroughs,' on the borders of Eastbourne and Willingdon.

[8] If this had not immediately followed the fresh heading of Totnore I should have identified it with Cholington, a third of the Eastbourne

THE HOLDERS OF LANDS

Edward, and could betake himself (*ire*) whither he pleased. Then, as (*et*) now, it was assessed for 2 hides. There is land for 2 ploughs. On the demesne is 1 plough, and (there is) 1 villein and 5 bordars with 1 plough. In the time of King Edward it was worth 40 shillings, and afterwards 16 shillings and 8 pence ; now 30 shillings.

(IN EASTBOURNE HUNDRED)

William de Cahainges holds BEVRINGETONE [Beverington] and LOVRINGETONE [Yeverington[1]]. Two free[2] men held them of King Edward. Then, as (*et*) now, they were assessed for 2 hides. There is land for 3 ploughs. On the demesne is half a plough with 3 bordars, and (there are) 2 acres of meadow. In the time of King Edward they were worth 30 shillings, and afterwards 15 shillings ; now 24 shillings.

There Hugh and Morin hold 2½ hides. Cana and Frane (held them) of King Edward, and could betake themselves (*ire*) whither they would. There is land for 2 ploughs. There (the 2 ploughs) are, with 6 villeins and 1 bordar, and there (is) 1 acre of meadow. This land is appraised in the manor[3] of Willendone [Willingdon].

Ralph son of Gunfrid holds in ESHALLE [Easthall] 1 hide. Edmund held it of King Edward, and could betake himself (*ire*) whither he pleased. It was assessed for 1 hide then, as (*et*) now. In the time of King Edward it was worth 15 shillings ; afterwards and now 10 shillings.

In the same hundred Rannulf holds 1 virgate[4] of the count, and for so much it is assessed. Ulfer held it of King Edward. There is land for half a plough. There is 1 villein. Then, and afterwards, as (*et*) now, it was worth 4 shillings.

'boroughs,' and I am inclined to think that this is the correct identification and that the Hundredal heading is misplaced.

[1] Yeverington, in Eastbourne manor, occurs frequently in the thirteenth century in connection with Beverington, and rarely separate ; and the difference between Ievringetone and Lovringetone is sufficiently slight to make a scribal error not unlikely, so that I think this is a fair identification.

[2] *Liberi* interlined.

[3] Probably 'manor' should be 'Hundred,' as Hugh and Morin succeeded Cane and Frane in the manor of Ratton in Willingdon Hundred, but are not recorded as holding of Willingdon manor.

[4] Part of his manor of Little Horsted (see note 4, p. 415).

(IN TOTNORE HUNDRED)

William[5] holds LITELFORDE [? Itford] of the count. Brixi held it of King Edward, and could betake himself (*ire*) whither he pleased. Then, as (*et*) now, it was assessed for 4 hides. There is land for 4 ploughs. On the demesne are 2 (ploughs), and (there are) 4 villeins and 2 serfs with 1 plough, and 50 acres of meadow.

In the time of King Edward, as (*et*) now, it was worth 4 pounds ; when received 40 shillings.

Ralph[6] holds PRESTETONE [Preston in Beddingham] of the count. Cola held it of King Edward. Then, as (*et*) now, it was assessed for 4 hides. There is land for 3 ploughs. On the demesne is 1 (plough), and (there are) 5 villeins with 2 oxen. In the time of King Edward it was worth 4 pounds, and afterwards 30 shillings ; now 40 shillings.

In the same HUNDRED the count himself holds 8 hides, but they are appraised in another hundred.

The abbot of GRESTAIN holds of the count 2 hides in BEDINGHA(M) [Beddingham]. Ulnod the priest[7] held them of King Edward, and they were assessed for 2 hides then, as (*et*) now. There is land for 2 ploughs. On the demesne is 1 (plough), and (there are) 2 villeins and 2 bordars with 1 plough. In the time of King Edward, as (*et*) now, it was worth 40 shillings ; when received 30 (shillings).

Durand holds of the count in[8] CERLOCESTONE [Charlston in West Firle] 6 hides. Three free men held them of King Edward as (*pro*) 3 manors. Then, as (*et*) now, they were assessed for 6 hides. There is land for 5 ploughs. On the demesne (is) half a plough, and 1 villein and 1 bordar with 2 oxen.

Of this land Roger holds 2 hides, Gilbert 2 hides. These have on (their) demesne 2 ploughs and 2 villeins and 2 bordars with 1 plough.

In the time of King Edward (this) was worth 60 shillings, and afterwards 40 shil-

[5] William de Cahaignes, or Keynes ; Itford subsequently passed to the Leukenores by marriage with the heiress of the Keynes.

[6] Ralph de Dene ; Preston was held by Isabella de la Haye, his descendant.

[7] The Count of Mortain gave to Grestain Abbey land in Hestone [Heighton] which Alnod the priest held (Dugdale, *Mon.* vi. 1053).

[8] *In* interlined.

I 409 52

lings ; now 100 shillings for the whole (*inter totum*).

There Hubert holds of the count 2 hides. Alnod held them of King Edward, and could betake himself (*ire*) whither he pleased. There is land for half a plough. On the demesne is 1 plough, and (there are) 2 villeins and 2 bordars with 1 plough and a half. In the time of King Edward and afterwards (this) was worth 10 shillings ; now 20 shillings.

In TELENTONE [Tilton [1]] William de Cahanges holds 2 hides of the count. Elfer held them as (*pro*) 1 manor [2] of King Edward. There is land for 2 ploughs. Then, as (*et*) now, (this) was assessed for 2 hides. On the demesne is 1 plough, and (there are) 2 villeins with half a plough. Then and afterwards, as (*et*) now, (this was worth) 20 shillings.

The same William holds SERINTONE [Sherrington [3]] of the count. Edward held it of King Edward, and could betake himself (*ire*) whither he pleased. There is land for 5 ploughs. Then it was assessed for 5 hides ; now half a hide is in the rape of Hastings. [4] On the demesne is 1 plough, and (there are) 2 bordars.

In the time of King Edward it was worth 60 shillings, and afterwards 25 shillings ; now 40 shillings. For the half hide which is not there 20 shillings are deducted (*decidunt*).

fo. 21a

There Haminc holds of the count 5 hides, and he himself held them of King Edward. Then they were assessed for 5 hides ; now half a hide is in the rape of Hastings. [5] There is land for 4 ploughs. On the demesne (is) 1 plough and a half, and (there are) 2 villeins with half a plough and 3 bordars. In the time of King Edward (this) was worth 60 shillings, and afterwards 25 shillings ; now 40 shillings.

Osbern holds of the count 4 hides in TELENTONE [Tilton]. Godwin held them of King Edward as (*pro*) a manor. Then they were assessed for 4 hides ; now for 2 hides and 1 virgate. [6] There is land for 4

ploughs. There is nothing there now except 2 villeins and 4 acres of meadow. In the time of King Edward (this) was worth 70 shillings ; now 20 shillings.

There the count himself has 1 hide, William 1 hide, Ralph [7] 1 hide. Godwin held this land. There is land for 4 ploughs. It was worth 18 shillings ; now 15 shillings.

The count himself holds in demesne FERLE [West Firle]. The abbey of Wilton held it in the time of King Edward, and then it was assessed for 48 hides ; now for nothing. Of this land 7 hides are in the rape of Hastings. [8] There is land for 40 ploughs. On the demesne the count has 5 ploughs, and 80 villeins with 34 ploughs. There (are) 2 mills yielding (*de*) 30 shillings, and 72 acres of meadow, and wood(land yielding) 40 swine.

Of these hides the clerks of St. Pancras [9] have 2½ hides, Roger 1 mill, Gozelin 1 hide, William 1 hide, Gilbert 2 hides, the warders of the castle (of Pevensey) [10] (*custodes castelli*) 3 hides and 20 acres. On (their) demesne (are) 6 ploughs, and (there are) 3 villeins and 11 bordars with 4 ploughs. There (are) 7 acres of meadow. Also Gilbert holds 60 acres of waste land.

The whole manor in the time of King Edward was worth 60 pounds, and afterwards 30 pounds. Now what the count has (is worth) 40 pounds, what the other men (have) 4 pounds and 10 shillings.

In CONTONE [Compton [11]] the count himself holds 4 hides. Harold held them of King Edward. Then, as (*et*) now, they were assessed for 4 hides. This land is appraised in Lestone [Laughton].

IN WILENDONE [WILLINGDON] HUNDRED

Walter holds of the count in ESSETE [Exceat] 2½ hides. Doda held them of King

---

[1] A manor in Selmeston.
[2] *Pro uno manerio* interlined.
[3] A manor in Selmeston.
[4] One virgate of this is attributed to Esserintone in Esseswelle Hundred (see p. 402). Possibly the virgate in Gestelinges Hundred formerly held by Edward may have belonged to this manor (see note 9, p. 405).
[5] Under Sirintone in Esseswelle Hundred (see p. 402).
[6] One virgate was in Hawksborough Hundred, under Telitone (see p. 400).

[7] Ralph de Dene, whose descendants held Tilton.
[8] Of land attributed to Ferle in Hastings rape, in Shoyswell was 1 virgate (see p. 402) and 1 hide 1½ virgates (ibid.), in Henhurst half a virgate (see p. 404), in Hawksborough 1½ hides 1 virgate (see p. 400) and 1 virgate (see p. 401) ; the remainder of the 7 hides is to be found in the 4 hides less half virgate attributed to Belingham in Hawksborough (see p. 400).
[9] See Introduction, p. 376.
[10] This is the '*terra vigilium de Pevenesel de Hecton* [Heighton]' of the Pipe Rolls of Henry II. (compare note 3, p. 408).
[11] A manor in Berwick and Firle, sometimes called Compton St. John's, from its having been held by the Hospitallers.

Edward, and could betake himself (*ire*) whither he pleased. Then, as (*et*) now, they were assessed for 2½ hides. There is land for 2 ploughs. On the demesne is 1 (plough), and (there are) 7 bordars with 1 plough. In the time of King Edward, as (*et*) now, (this was worth) 40 shillings.

There William holds of the count 3 hides. Edward and Alwin held them of King Edward, and could betake themselves (*ire*) whither they pleased. Then, as (*et*) now, they were assessed for 3 hides. There is land for 3 ploughs. On the demesne is 1 plough, with 7 bordars.

In the time of King Edward (this) was worth 50 shillings, and afterwards 30 shillings ; now 40 shillings.

Ralph holds of the count 7½ hides in Lovringetone [Yeverington [1]]. Cola held them of King Edward as (*pro*) a manor. Then, as (*et*) now, they were assessed for 7 hides.[2] There is land for 14 ploughs. On the demesne is 1 plough, and 16 villeins with 5 bordars have 4 ploughs. There is 1 serf, and 1 mill yielding (*de*) 8 shillings.

In the time of King Edward (this) was worth 6 pounds, and afterwards 3 pounds ; now 4 pounds and 10 shillings.

The count himself holds in demesne Wilendone [Willingdon]. Earl Godwin held it. Then it was assessed for 50½ hides. Now for nothing. Of this land there are in the rape of Hastings 14½ hides.[3] There is land for 36 ploughs. On the demesne are 6 ploughs, and (there are) 75 villeins and 24 bordars with 26 ploughs. There (are) 60 acres of meadow, and 11 saltpans yielding (*de*) 35 shillings. There (is) 1 serf, and wood(land yielding) 3 swine.

Of this land Osbern holds of the count 4 hides, William 1 hide, Gozelin 2 hides, Gilbert 1 hide, Alwin 1 hide, Ansgot 2 hides, Godfrey the priest 1 hide and 1 virgate. On (their) demesne (are) 3½ ploughs, and (there are) 3 villeins and 4 bordars with 1 plough.

The whole manor in the time of King Edward was worth 60 pounds, and afterwards 30 pounds. Now what the count

holds (is worth) 40 pounds ; what the men (hold) 7 pounds.

The count himself holds in demesne Westbortone [West Burton [4]]. Alvric and Golvin held it of King Edward, and could betake themselves (*ire*) whither they pleased. Then it was assessed for 2 hides ; now for nothing.[5] There is land for 2 ploughs. There (are) 3 villeins with 1 plough and a half. It is worth 24 shillings.

Haminc [6] holds of the count Essete [Exceat]. He himself held it of King Edward. Then, as (*et*) now, it was assessed for 4½ hides. There is land for 4 ploughs. On the demesne (is) 1 plough and a half, and 3 villeins and 6 bordars have half a plough, and there (is) 1 serf. In the time of King Edward it was worth 4 pounds ; now 3 pounds.

Ralph [7] holds of the count Cerletone [Charlston in West Dean]. Ulvric held it of King Edward. Then it was assessed for 10 hides. Now 2½ hides are in the rape of Hastings.[8] There is land for 8 ploughs. On the demesne is 1 (plough) ; (there are) 6 villeins and 8 bordars with 4 ploughs. There (are) 3 serfs, and 3 saltpans yielding (*de*) 10 shillings and 4 pence, and 20 acres of meadow.

In the time of King Edward it was worth 9 pounds ; now 4 pounds and 10 shillings.

Gozelin holds of the count Radetone [Ratton [9]]. Ulfon held it of Earl Godwin. Then it was assessed for 6 hides, and now for 4 hides. In the rape of Hastings are 2 hides all but (*minus*) 1 virgate.[10] There is land for 7 ploughs. On the demesne (is) 1 plough,

---

[1] See note 1, p. 409.

[2] See note 3, p. 404.

[3] Of these hides 12 formed 'the manor called Hou [Hooe],' formerly held by Earl Godwin (see note 6, p. 395) ; attributed to Willingdon are : in Hawksborough 1½ virgates (see p. 400), in Shoyswell ½ virgate (see p. 402) ½ hide (ibid.), in Henhurst ½ hide, and 1½ virgates and ½ hide 1½ virgates attributed to Ralton, Willingdon and Firle (see p. 404).

[4] The situation of West Burton is not known ; there is a West Barton in Friston (S.D.B.) (see also note 3, p. 401).

[5] A space left after *tunc* for insertion of *et modo* ; and *modo pro nichilo* interlined ; the scribe was evidently uncertain about the present assessment when making the entry.

[6] He was succeeded by his son Richard, who was probably 'Richard de Essete.'

[7] Ralph de Dene ; Charlston passed to his descendant Isabel de la Haye.

[8] I cannot find any trace of these.

[9] A manor in Willingdon.

[10] In Shoyswell are 3 virgates attributed to Ratton, of which Ulf had held 1 and Countess Goda the other 2 (see p. 402) ; whether these latter belonged to this manor of Ratton is uncertain. With these may have gone 1 virgate in Burgelstaltone (see note 1, p. 403), which Ulfi held, and possibly the half hide in Dene held by Countess Goda and otherwise unaccounted for (see p. 403).

and (there are) 8 villeins and 5 bordars with 2½ ploughs. There (is) 1 mill yielding (*de*) 4 shillings, and 6 acres of meadow.

Of the land of this manor Azelin holds 1 hide in almoigne of the count, Rannulf half a hide, Ansfrid half a hide.

The whole manor in the time of King Edward was worth 6 pounds; now 4 pounds and 10 shillings.

Ralph holds of the count in the same hundred 1 manor, which Ulmar held of King Edward. Then it was assessed for 4½ hides. Now half a hide is in the rape of Hastings.[1] There is land for 6 ploughs. There is 1 villein, and 2 bordars, and 2 serfs. In the time of King Edward it was worth 4 pounds, and afterwards, as (*et*) now, 30 shillings.

Osbern holds of the count DENE [(? East) Dean]. Edwin held it of King (Edward) as (*pro*) a manor. Then, as (*et*) now, it was assessed for 2 hides. There is land for 1 plough and a half. There (are) 5 villeins and 3 bordars with 2 ploughs. In the time of King Edward it was worth 30 shillings, and afterwards, as (*et*) now, 20 shillings.

In DENE [(West) Dean] Ralph[2] holds of the count 8 hides. Azor held them of King Edward as (*pro*) a manor. Then, as (*et*) now, they were assessed for 8 hides. There is land for 8 ploughs. On the demesne are 2 ploughs, and (there are) 11 villeins and 3 bordars with 3 ploughs. There (are) 3 serfs, and 4 saltpans yielding (*de*) 8 shillings.

In the time of King Edward (this) was worth 7 pounds, afterwards 60 shillings; now 100 shillings.

IN WILEDENE [WILLINGDON] HUNDRED

Ralph holds of the count RADETONE [Ratton]. Osward held it of King Edward as (*pro*) a manor. Then it was assessed for 5 hides. Now 1 (hide) is in the rape of Hastings.[3] There is land for 5 ploughs. On the demesne are 2 (ploughs), and (there are) 4 villeins and 4 bordars with half a plough. There (are) 4 acres of meadow. Pasture yielding (*de*) 28 shillings. In the

time of King Edward it was worth 100 shillings; now 4 pounds.

In RADETONE [Ratton] Morin holds of the count 3 hides.[4] Cana held them of King Edward as (*pro*) a manor. Then they were assessed for 3 hides. Now half a hide is in the rape of Hastings.[5] There is land for 7 ploughs. On the demesne is 1 (plough), and (there are) 6 villeins and 3 bordars with 1 plough. There (are) 2 acres of meadow, and the fourth part of a saltpan yielding (*de*) 10 pence. In the time of King Edward (this) was worth 60 shillings, and afterwards 20 shillings; now 40 shillings.

In RADETONE [Ratton] Hugh holds of the count 3 hides. Frano held them of King Edward as (*pro*) a manor. Then they were assessed for 3 hides. Now half a hide is in the rape of Hastings. There is land for 7 ploughs. On the demesne is half a plough, and (there are) 5 villeins and 3 bordars with 2 ploughs. There (are) 2 acres of meadow, and the fourth part of a saltpan yielding (*de*) 10 pence. In the time of King Edward (this) was worth 60 shillings; now 40 shillings.

William holds of the count WALNOCH [Wannock]. Norman held it of King Edward as (*pro*) a manor. Then, as (*et*) now, it was assessed for 6 hides. There is land for 8 ploughs. On the demesne are 3 ploughs, and (there are) 3 villeins with 1 plough. There (are) 4 acres of meadow.

In the time of King Edward it was worth 110 shillings, and afterwards 40 shillings; now 4 pounds and 10 shillings.

IN AURONEHELLE[6] [LONGBRIDGE] HUNDRED
fo. 21b

The abbot of Grestain holds of the count WINELTONE [Wilmington[7]]. Alnod held it of Earl Godwin. Then, as (*et*) now, it was assessed for 8 hides. There is land for 9 ploughs. One of these hides lies in the rape of Hastings.[8]

There the same abbot holds 4 hides which Ulnod held of Earl Godwin. Then, as (*et*) now, they were assessed for 4 hides.

There the same abbot holds 2 hides of the count which Ulstan held of Earl Godwin. Then, as (*et*) now, they were assessed for 2 hides.

---

[1] This must be the half hide in Bortone which Ulmar held (see note 3, p. 401), in which case the tenant is Ralph de Dene, as his descendants held Burton.

[2] Ralph took the name of de Dene from this manor.

[3] Probably the hide in Hawksborough held by Countess Goda and attributed to Dene (see p. 403), which is otherwise unaccounted for (compare note 10, p. 411).

[4] *iii hidas* interlined.

[5] In Hawksborough Hundred (see p. 401).

[6] Alrehelle Hundred occurs on Pipe Roll 31 Hen. I.

[7] The Count of Mortain founded a priory at Wilmington as a cell to the Norman abbey of Grestain.

[8] In Netherfield Hundred and partly within the liberty of Battle (see note 1, p. 399).

On the demesne are 3 ploughs, and (there are) 16 villeins and 10 bordars with 6 ploughs. There (are) 3 serfs. In the time of King Edward, as (et) now, it was worth 13 pounds.

William holds FOCHINTONE [Folkington] of the count. Goda held it of King Edward, and could betake herself (ire) whither she pleased. Then, as (et) now, it was assessed for 6 hides. There is land for 5 ploughs. On the demesne are 3 ploughs, and (there are) 4 villeins and 6 bordars with a plough and a half.

In the time of King Edward it was worth 100 shillings, and afterwards 40 shillings; now 60 shillings.

IN FLEXEBERGE [FLEXBOROUGH] HUNDRED

The count himself holds in demesne TORINGES [Tarring[1]]. Azor held it of Earl Godwin. Then, as (et) now, it was assessed for 8 hides.[2] There is land for 5 ploughs. On the demesne are 2½ ploughs, and (there are) 11 villeins and 9 bordars with 3 ploughs. There (are) 3 serfs, and 50 acres of meadow. From the pasture come 40 pence.

In the time of King Edward it was worth 8 pounds, and afterwards 6 pounds; now 10 pounds.

The abbot of Grestain holds FERLES [Frog Firle[3]] of the count. Queen Edith (Eddid) held it, and gave it to Saint John[4] in the time of King Edward. Then it was assessed for 8 hides; now for 5 hides.

There the same abbot holds 1 hide which Earl Godwin held. There is land for 4 ploughs. On the demesne are 2 (ploughs), and (there are) 4 villeins with 2 ploughs, and 3 bordars. In the time of King Edward and afterwards it was worth 3 pounds; now 4 pounds.

There Haminc holds of the count 2 hides.[5] He himself held them of Earl Godwin. Then, as (et) now, they were assessed for 2 hides. There is land for 1 plough. There (is) 1 villein and 1 bordar with 1 plough. In the time of King Edward (this was worth) 30 shillings; now 20 shillings.

William holds ESTONE [(South) Heighton]

of the count. Gundulf held it of King Edward as (pro) 1 manor. Then, as (et) now, (it was assessed) for 2 hides. There is land for 2 ploughs. On the demesne is 1 (plough), and (there are) 2 villeins and 3 bordars with 2 oxen.

In the time of King Edward, as (et) now, (it was worth) 30 shillings; when received 20 shillings.

In the same hundred Durand holds of the count 1 hide. Alward held it of King Edward as (pro) 1 manor. Then, as (et) now, it was assessed for 1 hide. There is land for half a plough. There are 2 oxen with 1 bordar. Wood(land yielding) 1 pig. In the time of King Edward it was worth 20 shillings; now 10 shillings.

In FERLES [Frog Firle] Alan holds of the count 4 hides. Almer and Godwin held them of King Edward as (pro) 2 manors. Then, as (et) now, they were assessed for 4 hides. There is half a hide outside the rape which does not belong to these.[6] There is land for 4 ploughs. On the demesne are 2 ploughs, with 15 bordars.

In the time of King Edward, as (et) now, (this was worth) 60 shillings; afterwards 30 shillings.

IN LATILLE [DILL] HUNDRED

In PENGEST [[7]] the count has in demesne 1 virgate of land. Ulvied held it of King Edward, and could betake himself (ire) whither he pleased. Then, as (et) now, it was assessed for 1 virgate. There is land for 1 plough. There (is) 1 villein with half a plough.

In the time of King Edward, as (et) now, it was worth 25 pence.

In HAINGURGE [[8]] the count has 1 hide, but half is in the rape of Hastings,[9] and now it is assessed for half a hide. Bristui held it as an alod (in alodium). There is land for 2 ploughs. There (is) 1 villein with 2 ploughs, and wood(land yielding) 4 swine from the pannage. In the time of King Edward it was worth 20 shillings, and afterwards 10 shillings; now 15 shillings.

[1] Afterwards called Tarring Neville to distinguish it from West Tarring.
[2] With this went 1½ virgates in Standene (see p. 419).
[3] In Alfriston. This seems to have been part of the queen's manor of Iford (see note 6, p. 435).
[4] Compare note 2, p. 415.
[5] This had been part of Rottingdean manor (see note 8, p. 437).

[6] This possibly refers to the 4 virgates in Netherfield attributed to Hecton [(? South) Heighton] and held by Godwin (see note 2, p. 406).
[7] Not identified.
[8] Probably this name is arrived at by the scribe misreading Hanekrugge for Hauekrugge [Hawkrigge in Waldron] (for a somewhat similar case compare note 5, p. 437).
[9] See note 5, p. 401.

A HISTORY OF SUSSEX

In HENDENE [[1]] the count has half a hide, and for so much it is assessed. Almar held it as an alod (*in alodium*). There is land for 2 ploughs. There (is) 1 villein with 1 plough and 2 bordars. In the time of King Edward it was worth 9 shillings, and afterwards 4 shillings; now 5 shillings.

In WANDELMESTREI [LONGBRIDGE] HUNDRED

William [2] holds of the count SELMESTONE [Selmeston] and SIDENORE [[3]]. Alfer held them as an alod (*in alodium*). Then, as (*et*) now, they were assessed for 4½ hides. There is land for 7 ploughs. On the demesne are 3 ploughs, and (there are) 4 villeins and 3 bordars with 4 ploughs. There (is) a church, and a priest, and 5 serfs.

In the time of King Edward, as (*et*) now, (this) was worth 70 shillings; when received 40 shillings.

Ralph holds of the count 1 hide in SIDENORE [   ] and for so much it is assessed. Ulmar cild held it as an alod (*in alodium*). There is land for 1 plough, and there (the plough) is, with 1 villein. In the time of King Edward it was worth 8 shillings, and afterwards 6 shillings; now 10 shillings.

There Walter holds of the count half a hide, and for so much it is assessed. Godwin held it. There is land for half a plough, and there (the half plough) is, with 1 villein. It is and was worth 4 shillings.

Gerold holds of the count in SESINGEHA(M) [Sessingham] 1 hide. Half of it is in the rape of Hastinges.[4] Alwin held it as an alod (*sicut alodium*). There is land for 6 ploughs, and there they are with 16 villeins; and (there is) 1 mill yielding (*de*) 10 shillings and 500 eels. In the time of King Edward, as (*et*) now, it was worth 60 shillings; when received 20 shillings.

Gilbert holds to farm (*ad firmam*) of the count in ALVRICESTONE [Alfriston] 1 hide. Alvric held it as an alod (*sicut alodium*).

There is land for 1 plough. There (is) now 1 bordar. In the time of King Edward and afterwards, as (*et*) now, (it was worth) 8 shillings.

In the self same ALVRICESTONE [Alfriston] there hold of the count Rannulf 1 hide, Ralph [5] half a hide, William [6] half a hide, Ralph [5] 1 hide, Walter 2 hides. Altogether (*inter totum*) 5 hides, and for so much they are assessed. Lewin,[7] Alwold, Alnod and Godwin held this land as alods (*sicut alodia*). There is land for 5 ploughs. On the demesne now (are) 3½ ploughs, and 2 villeins and 6 bordars do half the ploughing (*arant ad medietatem*).[8] In the time of King Edward the whole was worth 20 shillings; now 54 shillings.

In HERTEVEL [9] [HARTFIELD] HUNDRED

The count himself holds in demesne WILDENE [[10]]. Earl Harold held it. Then, as (*et*) now, it was assessed for 2 hides. There is land for 7 ploughs. On the demesne are 2 (ploughs), and 7 villeins and 3 bordars have 5 ploughs. In the time of King Edward and afterwards it was worth 60 shillings; now 70 shillings.

In HERTEVEL [Hartfield] Walter holds of the count 1 hide and for so much it is assessed. Carle held it as an alod (*sicut alodium*). There is land for 3 ploughs. On the demesne is 1 plough and a half, and (there are) 6 villeins and 2 serfs with 1 plough and a half. There (is) 1 mill yielding (*de*) 4 shillings and 350 eels, and 3 acres of meadow, and wood(land yielding) 5 (*iiii*) swine from the pannage. In the time of King Edward, as (*et*) now, (it was worth) 40 shillings; when received 20 shillings.

In the same HUNDRED the count has 1 hide and a half outside the rape, and it is appurtenant to the manor of Ramelle [Rodmell].[11] Earl Godwin held it, and it has

[1] The family name of de Henden is found frequently in connection with Hellingly and Waldron in the thirteenth and following centuries, but the locality is unknown.

[2] William de Cahaignes; a fine of 4 Edw. I. shows that Richard de Keynes held the manor of Selmeston, and Lewes Chartulary mentions his gift of 2½ hides in Sidenoure.

[3] Sidenore is to be met with at least as late as 1350, but is now lost.

[4] One virgate and a quarter is accounted for in Hawksborough Hundred (see p. 401).

[5] One of these two Ralphs is Ralph de Dene, whose descendants held land here; the other may be Ralph nephew of Grento, the tithe of whose lands in Alfriston was held by Lewes Priory.

[6] William son of Boselin (de Dives) gave half a hide in Alfriston to Lewes Priory.

[7] Lewes Priory held the tithe of Lefsi brother of Lewine at Alfrichestune.

[8] I am inclined to read *arant al(iam) medietatem*, in which case the number of ploughs on the demesne ought to be 2½.

[9] Hertenel corrected to Hertevel.

[10] Not identified.

[11] See note 2, p. 436.

never paid geld. There is land for 6 ploughs. There are 7 villeins and 1 bordar with 5 ploughs. There (is) wood(land yielding) 40 swine.

In the time of King Edward, as (*et*) now, it was worth 40 shillings; when received 30 shillings.

In the same HUNDRED Ralph holds to farm of the count 1 hide outside the rape. Azor held it as an alod (*sicut alodium*), and it has never paid geld. There is land for 2 ploughs. There are 3 villeins with 2 ploughs. In the time of King Edward and afterwards, as (*et*) now, (it was worth) 10 shillings.

In APEDROC [Parrock [1]] the count himself holds half a hide. It has never paid geld. It is outside the rape. Queen Edith (*Eddid*) held it. There is land for 2 ploughs. There are 2 villeins with 1 plough and a half. Wood(land yielding) 40 swine and 12 shillings. There is 1 virgate where the count has his hall (*aulam*). In the same way Earl Harold had it, and he took it away from Saint John.[2]

In the time of King Edward and afterwards, as (*et*) now, (it was worth) 52 shillings.

In FRAMELLE [FRAMFIELD] HUNDRED [3]

There William holds of the count 1 virgate outside the rape. It has never paid geld. Lewin held it as an alod (*sicut alodium*). There is land for half a plough, and there (the half plough) is, with 3 bordars. Wood(land yielding) 1 pig from the pannage. In the time of King Edward (it was worth) 10 shillings; afterwards and now 5 shillings.

Ralph holds of the count in GORDE [Worth in Little Horsted] 1 hide and 1 virgate, and

fo. 22a

for so much they are assessed. Helghi held them of King Edward, and could betake himself (*ire*) whither he pleased. There is land for 6 ploughs. On the demesne is 1 plough and a half, and (there are) 8 villeins and 1 bordar with 2 ploughs. There (is) 1 mill yielding (*de*) 9 shillings, and 2 acres of meadow, and wood(land yielding) 6 swine.

In the time of King Edward, as (*et*) now, (this was worth) 50 shillings; when received 30 shillings.

Rannulf holds of the count in HORSTEDE [Little Horsted] 5 hides and 3 virgates, and for so much they are assessed.[4] Ulfer held them of King Edward, and could betake himself (*ire*) whither he pleased. There is land for $7\frac{1}{2}$ ploughs. On the demesne are 2 (ploughs), and (there are) 9 villeins and 6 bordars with $4\frac{1}{2}$ ploughs, and (there is) 1 mill yielding (*de*) 8 shillings.

Of this land 1 hide lies in the rape of Lewes, and Azelin holds another hide in Bechingetone [Bechington [5]], and Grento holds 1 virgate and a half.[6] They (*hi*) have 1 plough and a half on (their) demesne.

The whole in the time of King Edward was worth 100 shillings, and afterwards 50 shillings; now 60 shillings.

In PEVENSEL HUNDRED [THE LOWEY OF PEVENSEY]

The count himself holds at LODINTONE [[7]] $4\frac{1}{2}$ hides, and for so much they are assessed. Six thegns (*teigni*) held this land as an alod (*sicut alodium*). There is land for 5 ploughs. On the demesne are 2 ploughs, and (there are) 5 villeins with 5 ploughs, and 1 mill yielding (*de*) 20 shillings, and pasture yielding (*de*) 20 shillings, and 5 saltpans yielding (*de*) 41 shillings and 8 shillings (*sic*). In the time of King Edward (this) was worth 30 shillings; now 6 pounds and 11 shillings and 8 pence.

William [8] holds of the count at HAMELESHA(M) [Hailsham] 1 hide and a half, and for so much it is assessed. Alnod held it as an alod (*sicut alodium*). There is land for 4

---

[4] Another virgate which had probably belonged to this manor lay in Eastbourne Hundred (see note 4, p. 409).

[5] A manor in Friston. This is probably the hide held by Azelin in Willingdon Hundred as part of Ulfon's manor of Ratton (see p. 412).

[6] Grento gave to Lewes Priory land in Burgingehurst [Burghurst in Horsted].

[7] Possibly Doddington, or Duddington, on the borders of Hailsham and Folkington. For a similar confusion between *l* and *d* compare Belingeham (see note 4, p. 400). There is a small tributary of the Cuckmere in the immediate neighbourhood of Duddington on which the mill might have stood.

[8] Possibly William son of Boselin (de Dives), as Hugh de Dives about 1200 held land in that portion of Hailsham parish which is in Pevensey Lowey.

[1] About the thirteenth century this was always called la Parrock.

[2] See Introd. p. 377.

[3] The parish of Framfield is in Loxfield Hundred, and Little Horsted is a detached portion of Rushmonden. Framelle Hundred seems to have been carved out of the archbishop's holding of Mellinges (see note 2, p. 388).

ploughs. There are 4 bordars with 1 ox, and 2 saltpans yielding (*de*) 7 shillings. In the time of King Edward it was worth 110 shillings ; now 20 shillings.

In this manor the count has kept in his own hands (*retinuit*) 11 saltpans, which are worth 24 shillings and 6 pence.

Ansfrid holds of the count at CHENENOLLE [¹] 2 hides. There is land for 2 ploughs. Tochi held (this) as an alod (*sicut alodium*). On the demesne is half a plough, and (there is) 1 villein with half a plough, and 5 acres of meadow. In the time of King Edward (this) was worth 40 shillings ; now 15 shillings.

The same Ansfrid holds of the count in WILENDONE [Willingdon] half a hide, and for so much it is assessed. Leward held it as an alod (*sicut alodium*). There is land for half a plough. Then, as (*et*) now, it was worth 10 shillings.

Godfrey the clerk holds in almoigne in PALINGES [Peeling] 1 hide, and there he has 2 bordars who return 8 pence. It is and was worth 3 shillings.

Roger the clerk holds 1 hide at COONARE [Cudnor ²] in almoigne. There is land for 1 plough, and there (the plough) is on the demesne, with 1 bordar and 1 ox. Brictuin held it.

The same Roger holds at HORSELIE [Horseye] 1 hide in almoigne of Saint Michael.³ Clerks held it in common. There is land for 1 plough. There is 1 villein with 1 plough.

¹ This must be the land of Cnolla given by Robert de Dene, who inherited Ansfrid's possessions, to Lewes Priory, and is either Knolle near Chilley or Knolle in the Hailsham portion of the Lowey, both names being found in the sixteenth century.
² In Westham. S.D.B. suggests Crannor in Lamport manor, but even if this is within the Lowey, Cudnor is closer in form to Coonare and is historically much more important. I have never met with Crannor in any document, while Cudnor is of frequent occurrence.
³ In the time of Edward the Confessor these 2 hides, with the church of Eastbourne—in which place this same Roger the clerk held land—appear to have belonged to Fécamp Abbey. Whether the original church of Eastbourne was dedicated to St. Michael, or whether the reference is to the chapel which is known to have existed at a later date at Horseye, or to some other religious establishment, is uncertain (see Introd. p. 376).

These 2 hides then, as (*et*) now, were assessed for so much. Then (they were worth) 10 shillings ; now 22 shillings.

Walter holds of the count 1 hide, and for so much it is assessed. Brictuin held it at COONORE [Cudnor]. There is land for half a plough, and there (the half plough) is on the demesne. It is worth 5 shillings.

Ansfrid holds of the count at ORNE [Horns, near Pevensey] 2 hides, and for so much they were assessed. Three men held them as an alod (*sicut alodium*). There are 2 bordars and 8 acres of meadow. In the time of King Edward (this) was worth 25 shillings ; now 10 shillings.

Ranulf holds of the count at ORNE [Horns] 1 hide.   ⁴ There is land for 2 ploughs. There is 1 bordar. Then it was worth 13 shillings ; now 63 pence.

In HOU [Hooe] the count holds 4 saltpans in demesne, which are worth 20 shillings.

In REMECINGES [Renchyng Hill in Westham] William⁵ and Ralph⁶ and another Ralph hold of the count 2 hides, and for so much they are assessed. Two free men held them as an alod (*sicut alodium*). There is land for 4 ploughs. There (are) 2 villeins, and 1 bordar, and 2 ploughing oxen. In the time of King Edward (this) was worth 16 shillings ; now 15 shillings.

In PELLINGES [Peeling in Westham] Alan and Godfrey and Ansfrid and Roger hold 4 hides of the count, and for so much they are assessed. There is land for 4 ploughs. Alward and Algar held them of King Edward as (*pro*) 2 manors as alods (*in alodia*). There (is) now 1 villein and 1 bordar.

In LANGELIE [Langney] Rannulf holds of the count 1 hide, and for so much it is assessed. Lemar and Bricstan held it as an alod (*sicut alodium*). There are 2 bordars.

There William⁷ holds 1 hide, and for so

⁴ Half a line blank.
⁵ William de Cahaignes ; Hugh de Kahannes gave 60 acres here to Lewes Priory.
⁶ Ralph de Dene, whose granddaughter's husband, William Malfed, gave 120 acres here to Lewes Priory.
⁷ William de Cahaignes, who gave 1 hide in Langeney to Lewes Priory. This seems to be the hide belonging to Ewhurst (see note 4, p. 406).

much it is assessed. Alfec held it. There are 2 bordars. In the time of King Edward it was worth 16 shillings and 8 pence; now 10 shillings.

William holds of the count at HENECHA(M) [Hankham in Westham] 2 hides, which were part of (*jacuerunt in*) the manor of BORNE [Eastbourne]. There is land for 3 ploughs. There are 4 bordars. In the time of King Edward (this) was worth 15 shillings; now 8 shillings.

In HENECHA(M) [Hankham] the count has 1 hide and half a virgate. King Edward held (this). There is land for 1 plough. Of this holding no return has been made (*Inde nullum responsum*).

There Ansgot holds of the count half a hide which was part of (*jacuit in*) BURNE [Eastbourne]. It is worth 9 shillings.[1]

In BOGELIE [Bowley in Hailsham] William holds of the count half a hide. Earl Harold held it. There is land for 2 ploughs, and there they are with 2 villeins and 1 bordar, and 8 acres of meadow, and 4 saltpans yielding (*de*) 22 shillings and 4 pence. In the time of King Edward it was worth 15 shillings; now 30 shillings.

There Ansgot holds of the count half a hide, which belonged to (*jacuit in*) BORNE [Eastbourne]. It is worth 9 shillings.[2]

To (*In*) LODIUTONE [[3]] should be added (*mitti*) 13 shillings (arising) from pasture which the count has put into that manor (*dedit ei*).

IN EDIVESTONE [4] [SHIPLAKE] HUNDRED

The count himself holds RIPE [Ripe]. Earl Harold held it. Then, as (*et*) now, it was assessed for 22 hides. Of these (hides) 8 lie in the rape of Hastings.[5] There is land

for 10 ploughs. On the demesne are 2 ploughs, and (there are) 16 villeins and 8 bordars with 8 ploughs. There (are) 12 acres of meadow, and 8 saltpans yielding (*de*) 20 shillings. In the time of King Edward it was worth 12 pounds; now 8 pounds.

The count himself holds CLAVEHA(M) [Claverham [6]]. Osward held it of King Edward. Then, as (*et*) now, it was assessed for 4 hides. There is land for 4 ploughs. On the demesne is 1 plough, and there are 2 villeins and 2 bordars and 2 serfs with half a plough.

Of these 4 hides half a hide is in the rape of Hastinges,[7] and Alvred holds 1 hide and has there 1 villein.

The whole in the time of King Edward was worth 40 shillings; now 36 shillings.

In CLAVEHA(M) [Claverham] Morin [8] holds of the count 1 hide and 1 virgate, Hugh 3 hides all but (*minus*) 1 virgate. Cane and Frane held (this) as (*pro*) 2 manors of King Edward. Then, as (*et*) now, (this) was assessed for 4 hides. There is land for $3\frac{1}{2}$ ploughs. On the demesne is 1 plough and a half, and (there is) 1 villein and 5 bordars.

In the time of King Edward (this) was worth 45 shillings; now 40 shillings.

William holds ACHINTONE [Eckington [9]] of the count. Agemund held it of King Edward. Then it was assessed for 5 hides; now for 3, because 2 lie in the rape of Hastings.[10] There is land for 4 ploughs. On the demesne are 2 ploughs, and (there are) 7 bordars with 1 plough. There is wood(land) yielding (*de*) 10 swine.

Of this land a certain man of his (*unus homo ejus*) holds half a hide, and there he has 1 plough on (his) demesne.

In the time of King Edward it was worth 100 shillings; now 60 shillings.

In ACHILTONE [Eckington] and CALVINTONE [Chalvington] the count himself holds

---

[1] As this is repeated word for word in the margin opposite the next entry it is probably misplaced and should have been deleted.
[2] Written in the margin (see last note).
[3] See note 7, p. 415.
[4] The Record Com. edition reads Edlvestone, but Ediveherst hundred occurs on Pipe Roll of 31 Hen. I.
[5] The assessment remaining unchanged in spite of this loss can only be explained by the manor having increased its territory within the rape of Pevensey. Of the land attributed to Ripe, $\frac{1}{2}$ hide $\frac{1}{2}$ virgate (see p. 400) and 1 virgate (see p. 401) lay in Hawksborough, 1 virgate, and 1

hide (see p. 402) in Shoyswell; the remainder I cannot trace.
[6] In Arlington.
[7] Two virgates in Baldslow (see p. 406), and the remainder in Henhurst (see note 2, p. 404).
[8] *Morin* interlined.
[9] An important manor in Ripe.
[10] In Hawksborough, at Hechestone 1 virgate (see note 7, p. 400), and in Echentone 1 hide (see p. 401); in Shoyswell, in Eschintone $\frac{1}{2}$ hide 1 virgate (see p. 402); in Henhurst, in Alchitone 1 virgate (see note 5, p. 404).

in demesne 5 hides, and for so much they are assessed. Queen Edith (*Eddid*) held them as (*pro*) 2 manors. There is land for 6 ploughs. There are 7 villeins with 2 ploughs.

In the time of King Edward (this) was worth 40 shillings ; now 30 shillings.

In CALVINTONE [Chalvington] Ansfrid holds of the count 4 hides, and for so much they are assessed. Osward and Toti held them as (*pro*) 2 manors as an alod (*sicut alodium*). There is land for 1 plough and a half. On the demesne is 1 plough with 2 bordars and 2 serfs. Of this land half a hide lies in the rape of Hastings,[1] and Humphrey (*Hunfridus*) holds 1 hide, and there he has half a plough on (his) demesne. In the time of King Edward, as (*et*) now, this was worth 40 shillings.

In WALDRENE [Waldron] Ansfrid holds of the count 1 hide, and for so much it is assessed.[2] Ælveva held it of King Edward as an alod (*sicut alodium*). There is land for $3\frac{1}{2}$ ploughs. On the demesne is 1 plough with 1 villein. Then, as (*et*) now, (it was worth) 20 shillings.

The count himself holds in demesne LESTONE [Laughton]. Earl Godwin held it. Then it was assessed for 10 hides ; now for 6, because 4 lie in the rape of Hastings.[3]

fo. 22b

There is land for 16 ploughs. On the demesne are 3 ploughs, and (there are) 14 villeins and 3 bordars with $10\frac{1}{2}$ ploughs. There (are) 16 saltpans yielding (*de*) 25 shillings. In the time of King Edward it was worth 15 pounds ; now 10 pounds and 5 shillings.

The count himself holds ESTOCHINGEHA(M) [[4]]. Levenot held it of King Edward. Then, as (*et*) now, it was assessed for 10 hides. There is land for 8 ploughs. On the demesne is 1 plough, and (there are) 10 villeins

with $4\frac{1}{2}$ ploughs. From the pasturage (*herbagio*) (come) 12 swine. In the time of King Edward, as (*et*) now, it was worth 60 shillings.

In CETELINGEI [Chiddingly] Ralph[5] and Godwin hold of the count 1 virgate. Ælmar held it of King (Edward) as an alod (*sicut alodium*). Then, as (*et*) now, it was assessed for 1 virgate. There is land for 3 ploughs. On the demesne is 1 plough, and (there are) 2 villeins with 1 plough, and 1 mill with a small mill (*molinario*)[6] yielding (*de*) 4 shillings. Another virgate lies in the rape of Hastings.[7] In the time of King Edward it was worth 20 shillings ; now likewise.

In GRENESTEDE [EAST GRINSTEAD] HUNDRED

In CALVRESTOT [Shovelstrode[8]] the count has 1 hide, which lay in the rape of Lewes. Now it is outside the rape. It does not pay geld. Alnod held it of King Edward. There is land for 2 ploughs. There (the 2 ploughs) are, with 1 villein and 3 bordars. From the pasturage (*herbagio*) (come) 3 swine. From the wood(land) 5 (swine). In the time of King Edward, as (*et*) now, it was worth 20 shillings.

In CELRESTUIS [Shovelstrode] Ansfrid holds of the count 1 virgate outside the rape. It has never paid geld. Ælmar held it of King Edward. There is land for 1 plough. There (the plough) is, with 1 villein. Wood(land) and pasturage (*herbagium*) (yielding) 2 swine.

In the time of King Edward it was worth 5 shillings ; now 7 shillings.

In FELESMERE [? Falmer[9]] the count holds 1 hide and a half outside the rape. It has not paid geld. Villeins held it, and it is appraised in the manor.[10]

In BERCHELIE [Burgleigh[11]] William holds 1 hide and a half of the count. It is outside

---

[1] One virgate (see p. 401) in Shoyswell and 2 virgates (see p. 406) in Netherfield.

[2] Half a virgate was in Hawksborough Hundred (see p. 401).

[3] In Hawksborough $1\frac{1}{2}$ virgates (see p. 400), 1 hide and 5 hides (see p. 401) ; in Shoyswell 1 virgate (see p. 402). As this makes 2 hides $2\frac{1}{2}$ virgates in excess of the amount said to be in Hastings rape there must be some error in the figures, unless part of this went with the adjacent manor of Ripe (see note 5, p. 417).

[4] Not identified. S.D.B. suggests Stock farm in Beddingham, which is not in this Hundred and has no evidence to support it. Half a hide of this manor lay in Hawksborough (see note 4, p. 401).

[5] Ralph de Dene, whose descendants held land here.

[6] Or, a site for a mill. S.D.B. translates it 'with a miller,' a possible but unlikely reading.

[7] See note 8, p. 400.

[8] A manor in East Grinstead, sometimes called Shelvestrode.

[9] This was probably near Felbridge on the borders of Sussex and Surrey. As 3 hides belonging to Falmer were in this rape (see note 12, p. 436) it is possible that this belonged to that manor.

[10] It is not clear what manor is meant.

[11] On the borders of Worth and East Grinstead.

XI. THE LAND OF EARL ROGER

In CICESTRE [Chichester] city in the time of King Edward there were 97½ haws (*c hage ii et dimidia minus*), and 3 crofts, and they returned 49 shillings all but (*minus*) 1 penny. Now the city itself is in the hand of Earl Roger, and there are on the same burgages (*masuris*) 60 houses more than there were before, and there (is) 1 mill yielding (*de*) 5 shillings. It returned 15 pounds—to the king 10 pounds, to the earl 100 shillings. Now it is worth 25 pounds, and yet it returns 35 pounds.

Humphrey Fla(m)me has there 1 haw yielding (*de*) 10 shillings.

CASTLE HARUNDEL [Arundel] in the time of King Edward returned from a certain mill 40 shillings, and in composition for 3 entertainments (*de iii conviviis*[1]) 20 shillings, and for one day's procurage (*de uno pasticio*[2]) 20 shillings. Now, between the borough and the port of the river (*aque*) and ship-dues (*consuetudinem navium*) it returns 12 pounds, and yet it is worth 13 pounds.[3] Of this (money) Saint Nicholas has 24 shillings.[4] There (is) 1 fishery yielding (*de*) 5 shillings, and 1 mill returning 10 bushels (*modia*) of corn, and 10 bushels of mixed grain (*grosse annone*),[5] (and) in addition 4 bushels (*insuper iiii modia*). This is appraised at 14 pounds.

Robert son of Tetbald has 2 haws yielding (*de*) 2 shillings, and he has for his own the market dues (*theoloneum*) from men who are outside the liberty (*de hominibus extraneis*).

Morin has there a customary payment (*consuetudinem*) of 12 pence from 2 burgesses. Ernald (has) 1 burgess yielding (*de*) 12 pence, Saint Martin[6] 1 burgess yielding (*de*) 12 pence, Ralph 1 haw yielding (*de*) 12 pence, William 5 haws yielding (*de*) 5 shillings, Nigel 5 haws (whose tenants) do service.

IN SILLETONE [SINGLETON] HUNDRED

Earl Roger holds in demesne SILLETONE [Singleton]. Earl Godwin held it. Then it was assessed for 97½ hides (*c hidis ii*[ss] *et dim[idia] minus*). Now for 47 hides. There is land for 40 ploughs. On the demesne are 7 ploughs, and (there are) 86 villeins and 52 bordars with 33 ploughs. There (are) 17 serfs, and 2 mills yielding (*de*) 12 shillings and 7 pence, and 60 acres of meadow, and from the wood(land come) 150 swine. There (is) a church to which belong (*in qua jacent*) 3 hides and 1 virgate of this land. The clerks (of the church) have 2 ploughs and 5 bordars.

Of the land of this manor Pagen holds of the earl 1 hide, William 1 hide, Geoffrey 2 hides. On the demesne (is) 1 plough, and (there are) 3 villeins, and 1 bordar, and 3 serfs, with half a plough.

To this manor are appurtenant 9 haws in Chichester; they return 7 shillings and 4 pence, and (there is) 1 mill yielding (*de*) 40 pence, and from the pasturage (*herbagio*) (come) 15 shillings.

A monk of Saint Evroul (*S. Ebrulfo*[7]) holds 1 hide of the land of this manor. It is worth 10 shillings.

The whole manor in the time of King Edward was worth 89 pounds, and afterwards 57 pounds. Now what belongs to the earl is appraised at 93 pounds, and 1 mark of gold; yet it returns 120 pounds, and 1 mark of gold. What the clerks hold (is worth) 8 pounds, and yet they receive (*habent*) 10 pounds. What the knights have (is worth) 14 pounds.

The earl himself holds BERTREDTONE [Binderton]. Countess Gida[8] held it. Then it was assessed for 7 hides; now for 3 hides. There is land for 4 ploughs. On the demesne are 2 ploughs, and (there are) 8 villeins and 9 bordars with 2 ploughs. There (are) 4 acres of meadow. There (is) a church. In the time of King Edward it was worth 100 shillings, and afterwards 60 shillings; now 7 pounds.

Ivo[9] holds LOVENTONE [Mid-Lavant] of the earl. Godwin held it of Earl Godwin. Then, as (*et*) now, it was assessed for 9 hides. There is land for 5 ploughs. On the demesne are 2 (ploughs), and (there are) 10 villeins and 10 bordars with 3 ploughs. There (is) 1

---

[1] *Convivium* appears to have meant the obligation to supply food and entertainment for the lord of the manor and his suite once a year.

[2] *Pasticium* seems to be the lay form of 'procurage,' which was the obligation of the clergy to provide food and lodging for the bishop or his deputy when he was visiting their churches.

[3] The only case in which the return is said to be less than the value.

[4] That is to say, the tithe.

[5] Wheat mixed with rye.

[6] The abbey of Séez.

[7] The Lewes Chartulary contains an undated deed by which the abbot of St. Evroul grants to Lewes Priory 5 shillings of rent in the manor of Graffham, for which they are to celebrate the anniversary of Dom. Robert de Rouelent, brother of Dom. Ernald, monk of St. Evroul. Graffham adjoins Singleton.

[8] Wife of Earl Godwin.

[9] He was succeeded here, as at Racton, by Savaric Fitz-Kane, who gave the church of Mid-Lavant to Lewes Priory (*Suss. Arch. Coll.* xl. 61).

mill yielding (*de*) 7 shillings, and in Chichester 1 haw yielding (*de*) 5 pence. In the time of King Edward, as (*et*) now, (it was worth) 8 pounds.

There Wido holds 1 hide, and for so much it is assessed. Alwin held it of Earl Godwin as a manor. There is nothing there ; yet it is and was worth 20 shillings.

IN HAMESFORD [DUMPFORD] HUNDRED

The earl himself holds in demesne HERTINGES [Harting]. Countess Gida held it of King Edward. Then it was assessed for 80 hides ; now for 48 hides. There is land for 64 ploughs. On the demesne are 10 ploughs, and (there are) 128 villeins and 35 bordars with 51 ploughs. There (are) 20 serfs, and 9 mills yielding (*de*) 4 pounds and 18 pence. From the pasturage (*herbagio*) 18 shillings, and (there are) 30 acres of meadow. Wood(land yielding) 100 swine. In Chichester (are) 11 haws yielding (*de*) 15 shillings.

Of the land of this manor the clerks of Saint Nicholas[1] hold 6 hides, and there they have 6 villeins and 7 bordars with 3 ploughs, and so it was in the time of King Edward.

The whole manor in the time of King Edward was worth 80 pounds, and afterwards 60 pounds ; now 100 pounds.

The earl himself holds in demesne TRAITONE [Trotton]. Countess Gida held it of King Edward. Then it was assessed for 9 hides ; now for 3. There is land for 36 ploughs. On the demesne are 2 (ploughs), and (there are) 4 villeins and 10 bordars with 3 ploughs. There (is) a church, and 1 mill yielding (*de*) 12 shillings and 6 pence, and 5 acres of meadow, and from the wood(land) 10 swine.

In the time of King Edward it was worth 60 shillings, and afterwards 30 shillings ; now 100 shillings ; and yet these 2 manors, Hertinges and Traitone, return 120 pounds and 1 mark of gold.

Robert son of Tetbald[2] holds of the earl TREVERDE [Treyford]. Ælard held it of Earl Godwin. Then, as now, it was assessed for 11 hides. There is land for 6 ploughs. On the demesne are 2 ploughs, and (there are) 8 villeins and 8 bordars with 4 ploughs. There (are) 5 serfs, and 1 mill yielding (*de*) 30 pence, and 6½ acres of meadow, and wood(land yielding) 10 swine.

Of the land of this manor 2 hides belong to (*sunt in*) a prebend of the church[3] of Chichester. Robert holds them of the bishop. Offa held them of the bishop in fee as a manor. They were assessed for 2 hides then, as now. They are appraised at 8 shillings, and yet they return 15 shillings.

The whole manor in the time of King Edward, as now, was worth 100 shillings ; when received 60 shillings.

The abbey of Saint Peter of Winchester claims (*calumniatur*) this manor. The hundred (court) testifies that in the time of King Edward he who held it (*eum*) of the abbot, held it only for the term of his life.

Morin holds TITEHERSTE [Chithurst] of the earl. Almar held it of Earl Godwin as an alod (*in alodium*). Then, as (*et*) now, it was assessed for 4 hides. There is land for 2 ploughs. On the demesne is 1 (plough), and (there are) 6 villeins and 5 bordars with 2 ploughs. There (is) a chapel (*ecclesiola*), and 3 serfs, and 1 mill yielding (*de*) 8 shillings and 100 eels, and 5 acres of meadow, and from the wood(land) 3 swine. In Chichester (is) 1 haw yielding (*de*) 6 pence. In the time of King Edward it was worth 40 shillings, and afterwards 30 shillings ; now 60 shillings.

(IN EASEBOURNE HUNDRED)[4]

Robert holds of the earl STEDEHA(M) [Stedham]. Edith (*Eddiva*) held it of Earl Godwin. Then, as (*et*) now, it was assessed for 14 hides. There is land for 15 ploughs. On the demesne are 4 ploughs, and (there are) 23 villeins and 16 bordars with 10 ploughs. There (is) a church,[5] and 10 serfs, and 3 mills yielding (*de*) 30 shillings, and 4 acres of meadow, and wood(land yielding) 40 swine, a quarry yielding (*de*) 6 shillings and 8 pence, and in Chichester 1 haw yielding (*de*) 6 pence. Of this land 1 Frenchman (*francigena*) holds 1 hide and 4 acres. The whole manor in the time of King Edward was worth 15 pounds, and afterwards 8 pounds ; now 12 pounds.

The same Robert holds of the earl COCHINGES [Cocking]. Azor held it of King Edward. Then, as (*et*) now, it was assessed for 12 hides. There is land for 11½ ploughs. On the demesne are 2 (ploughs), and there are 18 villeins and 8 bordars with 9 ploughs. There (is) a church, and 6 serfs, and 5 mills yielding

---

[1] The church of Arundel.

[2] Sheriff of the rape of Arundel, and tenant of what was afterwards the Honor of Petworth ; most of the entries in Earl Roger's rape referred to Robert may be ascribed to him (see Introd. p. 378).

[3] *Ecclesie* interlined.

[4] Hundredal heading omitted.

[5] *Ecclesia et* interlined.

37 shillings and 6 pence. Of this land Tu-rald holds of Robert half a hide, and has half a plough there; and in Chichester is 1 haw of 12 pence.

In the time of King Edward, as (*et*) now, it was worth 15 pounds; when received 10 pounds.

The same Robert holds of the earl LINCE [Linch]. Ulvric held it of King Edward. Then as (*et*) now, it was assessed for 5 hides. There is land for 6 ploughs. On the demesne is 1 plough, and (there are) 7 villeins and 5 bordars with 2 ploughs. There (is) a church and 2 serfs, and 3 acres of meadow, and wood(land yielding) 10 swine. In Chichester (is) 1 haw of 10 pence. In the time of King Edward it was worth 8 pounds, and afterwards 4 pounds; now 100 shillings.

fo. 23b

The same Robert holds of the earl BOTIN-TONE [Buddington], and Ralph (holds it) of him. Edwin held it of Earl Godwin. Then, as (*et*) now, it was assessed for 1 hide. There is land for 3 ploughs. On the demesne is 1 (plough), and (there are) 5 villeins and 3 bordars with 2 ploughs. There are 2 serfs. In the time of King Edward it was worth 30 shillings, and afterwards, and now 20 shillings.

Robert holds of the earl SELEHA(M) [Sel-ham], and Fulk (*Fulcoius*) (holds it) of him. Codulf held it of Earl Godwin. Then, as (*et*) now, it was assessed for 4 hides. There is land for 3 ploughs. On the demesne is 1 (plough), and (there are) 2 villeins and 2 bordars with 1 plough. There (are) 2 serfs, and a mill yielding (*de*) 10 shillings and 100 eels, and 17 acres of meadow, and wood(land yielding) 10 swine. In Chichester (is) 1 haw yielding (*de*) 7 pence.

The whole manor in the time of King Edward was worth 4 pounds, and afterwards 30 shillings; now 54 shillings.

Geoffrey holds of the earl BABINTONE [Bepton]. Wigot held it of King Edward. Then, as (*et*) now, it was assessed for 4 hides. There is land for 4 ploughs. On the demesne is 1 plough, and (there are) 10 villeins and 10 bordars with 3 ploughs. There (is) a church, and 3 serfs. In Chichester (is) 1 haw yielding (*de*) 10 pence.

In the time of King Edward it was worth 4 pounds, and afterwards 40 shillings; now 100 shillings.

William holds of the earl TADEHA(M)

[Todham[1]]. Nigel holds it of him. Ulnod held it of Earl Godwin. Then, as (*et*) now, it was assessed for 4 hides. There is land for 3 ploughs. On the demesne is 1 (plough), and (there are) 8 villeins and 3 bordars with 1 plough, and the third part of a mill, yielding (*de*) 14 pence. There (are) 8 acres of meadow, and wood(land yielding) 3 swine.

In the time of King Edward, as (*et*) now, it was worth 40 shillings; when received 20 shillings.

Four Frenchmen (*iiii francigene*) hold GRAFHA(M) [Graffham] of the earl; Robert,[2] Ralph[3] 4 hides, Rolland 2½ hides, Ernald 2 hides. 6 thegns (*teigni*) held it in the time of King Edward as a manor as alods of their own (*pro m[anerio] in alodia sua*). Then, as (*et*) now, it was assessed for 10 hides. There is land .[4] On the demesne are 2½ ploughs, and (there are) 7 villeins and 6 bordars with 2 ploughs. There (is) a church, and from the wood(land come) 8 swine.

In the time of King Edward the whole manor was worth 8 pounds, and afterwards 7 pounds; now 8 pounds.

IN REDREBRUGE [ROTHERBRIDGE] HUNDRED

Robert holds of the earl PETEORDE [Pet-worth]. Edith (*Eddeva*) held it of King Edward as an alod (*in alodium*). Then, as (*et*) now, it was assessed for 9 hides. There is land for 12 ploughs. On the demesne are 2 (ploughs), and (there are) 22 villeins and 10 bordars with 8 ploughs. There (is) a church, and 9 serfs, and 1 mill yielding (*de*) 20 shillings and 180[5] eels, and 29 acres of meadow, and wood(land) yielding (*de*) 80 swine. In Chichester (are) 2 haws yielding (*de*) 16 pence. Of this land 2 Frenchmen (*francigene*) hold 2 hides, and there they have 3½ ploughs and 2 villeins and 1 bordar.

The whole manor in the time of King Edward was worth 18 pounds, and afterwards 10 pounds; now 18 pounds.

IN ESEBURNE [EASEBOURNE] HUNDRED[6]

Robert holds TOLINTONE [Tillington] of the earl. Edith (*Eddeva*) held it of King Edward. Then, as (*et*) now, it was assessed

---

[1] In Easebourne parish.
[2] *Robertus* interlined.
[3] Ralph de Caisned; Roger de Chaisnei gave the tithes of his land of Graffham to Lewes Priory.
[4] A blank.
[5] *ix^clxxx*; evidently *ix^xx* was first written and then altered to its equivalent *clxxx*.
[6] This heading is misplaced; Tillington is in Rotherbridge Hundred.

for 5 hides. There is land for 7 ploughs. On the demesne are 2 (ploughs), and (there are) 21 villeins and 11 bordars with 5 ploughs. There (are) 8 serfs, and 1 mill yielding (*de*) 20 shillings and 120 eels ; and in Chichester (is) 1 haw yielding (*de*) 8 pence, and (there are) 12 acres of meadow, and wood(land yielding) 20 swine. Of this land 2 Frenchmen (*francigene*) hold 1 virgate and a half, and there they have 5 bordars.

In the time of King Edward it was worth 8 pounds, and afterwards 100 shillings ; now 8 pounds and 6 shillings.

Robert holds of the earl GRETEHA(M) [? Gritt enham [1]]. Two thegns (*teigni*) held it of King Edward as an alod (*in alodium*) as 3 manors. Then, as (*et*) now, it was assessed for 4 hides and 1 virgate. There is land for 7 ploughs. On the demesne are 2 (ploughs), and (there are) 14 villeins and 9 bordars with 3 ploughs. There (are) 5 serfs, and 1 mill yielding (*de*) 10 shillings, and a quarry (*quadraria*) yielding (*de*) 10 shillings and 10 pence, and 20 acres of meadow, and wood(land yielding) 30 swine. Of this manor Turstin holds half a hide and 1 virgate, and there he has 2 ploughs with 3 villeins and 3 bordars.

In the time of King Edward it was worth 6 pounds, and afterwards 4 pounds, and now 6 pounds and 5 shillings.

IN REDREBRUGE [ROTHERBRIDGE] HUNDRED

Robert holds of the earl DONECHITONE [Duncton]. Lewin held it of King Edward as an alod (*in alodium*). Then, as (*et*) now, it was assessed for 5 hides. There is land for 5½ ploughs. On the demesne are 2 ploughs, and (there are) 15 villeins and 8 bordars with 3 ploughs. There (is) a church, and 2 serfs, and 4 mills yielding (*de*) 38 shillings, and 2 fisheries yielding (*de*) 360 eels, and 25 acres of meadow, and wood(land yielding) 15 swine, and in Chichester 1 haw yielding (*de*) 2 shillings.

Of this manor 4 Frenchmen (*francigene*) hold 1 hide and a half and 1 virgate and a half [2] and 10 acres of land, and there they have 6 bordars with half a plough.

The whole in the time of King Edward was worth 6 pounds, and afterwards 3 pounds ; now 7 pounds and 3 shillings.

The same Robert holds of the earl SUDTONE [Sutton], and 5 thegns (*teigni*) held it as a

manor as an alod (*in alodium*). Then, as (*et*) now, it was assessed for 8½ hides. There is land for 8½ ploughs. On the demesne are 2 (ploughs), and (there are) 17 villeins and 11 bordars with 4 ploughs. There (are) 5 serfs, and 3 mills yielding (*de*) 13 shillings and 9 pence, and 22 acres of meadow, and wood(land yielding) 30 swine. Of this manor 3 Frenchmen (*francigene*) hold 3 hides and 1 ferding, and there (is) 1 plough on (their) demesne, and (there are) 8 villeins and 7 bordars with 2 ploughs.

In the time of King Edward it was worth, as (*et*) now, 10 pounds, and when (Robert) received it [3] 6 pounds.

Robert holds BERLEVENTONE [Barlavington] of the earl, and Corbelin (holds it) of him. Frawin held it of King Edward as an alod (*in alodium*). Then, as (*et*) now, it was assessed for 5 hides. There is land for 6 ploughs. On the demesne are 2 (ploughs), and (there are) 8 villeins and 8 bordars with 3 ploughs. There (are) 4 serfs, and 2 mills , [4] and 7 acres of meadow, and wood(land yielding) 2 swine.

In the time of King Edward it was worth 100 shillings, and afterwards 60 shillings ; now 7 pounds.

Robert holds CLOTINGA(M) [Glatting [5]] of the earl, and Ralph (holds it) of him. Four free men held it as an alod. Then, as (*et*) now, it was assessed for 4 hides. There is land for 3 ploughs. On the demesne are 2 (ploughs), and (there are) 3 villeins and 2 bordars with 1 plough. There (are) 6 serfs.

In the time of King Edward it was worth 60 shillings, and afterwards 40 shillings ; now 4 pounds.

Robert holds STOPEHA(M) [Stopham] of the earl ; Ralph (holds it) of him. Five free men held it as an alod (*in alodium*). Then it was assessed for 5 hides ; now for 3 hides. There is land for 5 ploughs. On the demesne is 1 (plough), and (there are) 4 villeins and 4 bordars with 1 plough. There (is) 1 serf, and 8 acres of meadow, and 3 fisheries, and wood(land yielding) 10 swine, and in Chichester 1 haw yielding (*de*) 3 pence.

In the same Hundred Turchil holds of the earl 1 virgate, and he himself held it of

---

[1] A farm in Tillington. S.D.B. suggests Greatham, but that was in West Easwrith—a Hundred in which there are no bordars.

[2] *Et dimidiam* interlined.

[3] *Post* altered to *cum recepit*.

[4] A blank.

[5] A farm in Burton. Ralph, the under-tenant, was Ralph de Kaisneto (or Cheyney) who gave the tithe of Glottinges to Lewes Priory.

Harold, and it is (and was) assessed for 1 virgate. There is land for 1 plough, and there (the plough) is on the demesne, with 1 bordar and 1 mill. Then, as (et) now, it was worth 10 shillings.

Robert holds of the earl BOTECHITONE [Burton [1]], and Hamelin (holds it) of him. Ulmer held it of King Edward as 2 manors, as an alod (in alodium). Then, as (et) now, it was assessed for 5 hides. There is land for 5 ploughs. On the demesne are 2 (ploughs), and (there are) 8 villeins and 3 bordars with 2 ploughs. There (are) 2 serfs, and 1 mill yielding (de) 11 shillings, a fishery yielding (de) 280 (eels), and 4 acres of meadow, and wood(land yielding) 2 swine.

In the time of King Edward and afterwards it was worth 40 shillings ; now 100 shillings.

In the same Hundred Hamelin holds 1 hide and a half, and for so much it is assessed. Ulwin held it of King Edward as a manor. There is land for 1 plough, and there (the plough) is on the demesne, with 1 villein and 3 bordars, and 6 acres of meadow. In the time of King Edward, as (et) now, it was worth 20 shillings.

In the same Hundred Morin holds 1 manor of the earl. Edric held it of King Edward, as an alod (in alodium). Then, as (et) now, it was assessed for 1 hide. There is land for 2 ploughs, and they are there, with 3 villeins and 3 bordars and 2 serfs. In the time of King Edward, as (et) now, it was worth 20 shillings ; when received 10 shillings.

IN GHIDENTROI [WESTBOURNE] HUNDRED

The earl himself holds in demesne BORNE [Westbourne]. Earl Godwin held it. There (are) .36 hides, but it was assessed then, and (is) now, for 12 hides. There is land for 30 ploughs. On the demesne are 2 ploughs, and (there are) 27 villeins and 31 bordars with 15 ploughs. There (are) 7 serfs, and 4 mills yielding (de) 40 shillings, and a fishery yielding (de) 16 pence, and wood(land yielding) 3 swine. In Chichester (are) 6 haws yielding (de) 30 pence.

To this manor is appurtenant Warblitetone in Hantescire [Warblington in Hampshire]. In the time of King Edward it was assessed for 12 hides, now for 4 hides. There is land .[2] On the demesne are 2 ploughs,

[1] Formerly called Bodecton.
[2] A blank.

and (there are) 17 villeins and 12 bordars with 5 ploughs. There (are) 2 churches, and 6 serfs, and 1 mill yielding (de) 10 shillings.

Of this estate (terra) Pagan holds 4 hides. Alric held them as belonging to the minster (tenuit ad monasterium).[3] On the demesne is 1 plough, and (there are) 8 villeins and 5 bordars with 2 ploughs, and a mill yielding (de) 10 shillings, and 2 acres of meadow. In Chichester (is) 1 haw yielding (de) 12 pence. The whole manor in the time of King Edward was worth 30 pounds, and afterwards 10 pounds. Now what the earl holds (is worth) 40 pounds, and yet it returns 50 pounds. What Pagan holds is and was worth 60 shillings.

Robert holds MEREDONE [Marden], and Corbelin (holds it) of him. Alwin and Alvric held it as 2 manors, as an alod (in alodium). Then, as (et) now, it was assessed for 5 hides. There is land for 6 ploughs. On the demesne are 2 (ploughs), and (there are) 13 villeins and 2 bordars with 4 ploughs. There (are) 5 serfs, and in Chichester 1 haw yielding (de) 14 pence.

Fulk (Fulcoius) holds half a hide which is appurtenant to this manor. Alvric held it as an alod (in alodium).

The whole in the time of King Edward was worth 4 pounds and 10 shillings, and afterwards 45 shillings; now 115 shillings.

Ivo holds of the earl RACHETONE [Racton]. Fulk (Fulcoius) held it of King Edward. Then, as (et) now, it was assessed for 5 hides. There is land for 4 ploughs. On the demesne is 1 plough, and (there are) 8 villeins and 13 bordars with 2½ ploughs. There (are) 3 acres of meadow, and wood(land yielding) 4 swine. In Chichester (is) 1 haw yielding (de) 20 pence.

In the time of King Edward it was worth 60 shillings, and afterwards 40 shillings ; now 4 pounds.

Engeler holds of the earl MEREDONE [Up-Marden].[4] Lepsi held it of Countess Gida. Then, as (et) now, it was assessed for 3 hides. There is land for 3 ploughs. On the demesne is half a plough, and (there are) 2 villeins and 3 bordars with 2 oxen. In Chichester (is) 1 haw yielding (de) 1 penny.

[3] The bishopric of Chichester, or rather Selsey.
[4] It is difficult to distinguish the different Mardens, but the church of Up-Marden was afterwards given to Lewes Priory by Savaric Fitz-Kane, successor of Engeler.

In the time of King Edward it was worth 50 shillings, and afterwards 20 shillings; now 30 shillings.

Azo holds of the earl MEREDONE [Marden]. Alwin held it of King Edward as an alod (*in alodium*). Then, as (*et*) now, it was assessed for 4 hides. There is land for 4 ploughs. On the demesne are 2 (ploughs), and (there are) 6 villeins and 4 bordars with 1 plough. There (are) 3 serfs. In Chichester (are) 3 haws yielding (*de*) 21 pence. In the time of King Edward, as (*et*) now, (it was worth) 60 shillings, when received 30 shillings.

William holds of the earl HARDITONE [Lordington[1]]. Ulstan held it of King Edward as an alod (*in alodium*). Then, as (*et*) now, it was assessed for 4 hides. There is land for 4 ploughs. On the demesne is 1 plough, and (there are) 8 villeins and 7 bordars with 2 ploughs. There (are) 2 serfs, and a mill yielding (*de*) 30 pence, and wood(land yielding) 3 swine.

In the time of King Edward it was worth 50 shillings, and afterwards 30 shillings; now 70 shillings.

Geoffrey holds of the earl CONTONE [Compton].[2] Sbern held it of Earl Godwin. Then, as (*et*) now, it was assessed for 10 hides. There is land for 10 ploughs. On the demesne is 1 plough, and (there are) 18 villeins and 5 bordars with 5 ploughs. There (is) a church, and 4 serfs. In Chichester (are) 2 haws yielding (*de*) 2 shillings. The priest holds half a hide.

In the time of King Edward, as (*et*) now, it was worth 8 pounds; when received 100 shillings.

The earl himself holds in demesne ESTONE [Stoughton[3]]. Earl Godwin held it. There are 36 hides, but then, as (*et*) now, it was assessed for 15 hides. Of these (36 hides) 16 hides were temporarily attached (*misse*) to the manor of BURNE [Westbourne], now they are again part of (*sunt in*) Estone [Stoughton]. There is land for 26 ploughs. On the demesne are 3 ploughs, and (there are) 54 villeins and 35 bordars with 23 ploughs. There are 5 serfs, and 11 acres of meadow, and wood(land yielding) 100 swine. In Chichester

(are) 15 haws[4] yielding (*de*) 7 shillings and 8 pence. In this manor is a church to which belongs (*pertinet*) 1 hide and a half, and there the priest has half a plough. This is worth 4 pounds.

The whole manor in the time of King Edward was worth 40 pounds, and afterwards 30 pounds; now (it is worth) 40 pounds, and yet it returns 50 pounds.

Of this manor there is in the rape of William de Braiose 1 hide, and wood(land yielding) one thousand five hundred swine.[5]

Alwin holds of the earl MEREDONE [Marden]. Godwin held it as an alod (*in alodium*). Then, as (*et*) now, it was assessed for 2 hides. On the demesne is 1 (plough) with 6 bordars.

In the time of King Edward, as (*et*) now, it was worth 40 shillings; when received 20 shillings.

Near MEREDONE [Marden] a certain Falconer (*Accipitrarius*) holds half a hide of the earl. He himself held it as a manor, as an alod (*in alodium*).

IN ESTOCBRIGE [STOCKBRIDGE] HUNDRED

The church of St. Martin of Séez (*Sais*) holds of the earl FISEBORNE [Fishbourne]. Earl Tosti held it. Then, as (*et*) now, it was assessed for 6 hides. There is land for 6 ploughs. On the demesne are 2 (ploughs), and (there are) 6 villeins and 11 bordars with 2 ploughs. There (is) 1 serf, and 2 mills yielding (*de*) 40 shillings, and 27 acres of meadow. In Chichester (are) 2 haws yielding (*de*) 21 pence. In the time of King Edward it was worth 6 pounds, and afterwards 50 shillings; now 7 pounds.

Hugh holds of the earl WICHE [Rumboldswyke], and Warin (holds it) of him. Five free men held it for 5 manors. Then it was assessed for 9 hides; now for 6 hides. There is land for 9 ploughs. On the demesne is 1 plough, and (there are) 6 villeins and 2 bordars with 2 ploughs. There (is) 1 serf. Then, as (*et*) now, (it was worth) 100 shillings; when received 40 shillings.

Alcher holds of the earl MUNDREHA(M) [Mundham]. Countess Gida held it of Earl Godwin. Then it was assessed for 9 hides;

[1] In the thirteenth century it was called both Lerdington and Erdington.

[2] With this manor went 1 hide in Surrey (see p. 451).

[3] This seems the only possible identification; Estone may be an error for Estoctone—Stoctona being an early form of Stoughton.

[4] Some houses in the North Street of Chichester were till recently held of the manor of Stoughton.

[5] These figures must be wrong; I am inclined to think that the scribe misread '*silva M(anerii) quinq(ue) porcorum*,' as '*silva M(ille) quing(entorum) porcorum*.'

now for 6 hides. There is land for 6 ploughs. On the demesne are 2 (ploughs), and (there are) 14 villeins and 13 bordars with 2 ploughs. There (are) 2 serfs, and 1 mill and a half yielding (*de*) 6 shillings and 8 pence. There (is) a church to which belongs half a hide. The priest has half a plough. In the time of King Edward, as (*et*) now, it was worth 8 pounds; when received 100 shillings.

In the same Hundred Chetel holds land for (*ad*) 1 plough. It has never been assessed in hides (*nunquam hidata fuit*). King William granted this to him. There he has 1 mill yielding (*de*) 5 shillings, and 1 bordar, and 5 acres of meadow. It is worth 25 shillings.

William holds of the earl HUNESTAN [Hunston]. Six free men held it as an alod (*in alodium*). Then, as (*et*) now, it was assessed for 4 hides. There is land for 4 ploughs. On the demesne is 1 plough, and (there are) 5 villeins and 19 bordars with 2 ploughs. There (is) 1 mill yielding (*de*) 20 shillings, and 2 saltpans, and from 1 haw 6 pence.

In the time of King Edward it was worth 40 shillings, and afterwards 30 shillings; now 4 pounds.

IN WESTRINGES [MANHOOD] HUNDRED

The same William holds of the earl BRIDEHA(M) [Birdham], and Nigel (holds it) of him. Alnod held it as an alod (*in alodium*). Then, as (*et*) now, it was assessed for 3½ hides. There is land for 5 ploughs. On the demesne are 2 (ploughs), and there are 5 villeins and 8 bordars with 3 ploughs. There (is) 1 mill yielding (*de*) 20 shillings, and 2 fisheries, and 3 acres of meadow. From the wood(land) and pasturage (*herbagio*) (come) 5 swine.

Of this manor Anschitil holds 1 hide and a half, and he has there 1 plough, and 1 villein and 2 bordars.

The whole in the time of King Edward was worth 40 shillings, and afterwards 30 shillings; now 65 shillings.

Warin holds of the earl ICENORE [Itchenor].[1] Lewin held it of Earl Godwin. Then, as (*et*) now, it was assessed for 1 hide. There is land for 1 plough. On the demesne is 1 plough, and (there are) 3 villeins and 3 bordars with 1 plough. There (is) 1 acre of meadow. In the time of King Edward it was worth 20 shillings, and afterwards 15 shillings; now 22 shillings.

[1] Formerly part of Bosham manor (see p. 392).

Rainald holds of the earl SU(M)MERLEGE [Somerley]. Helghi held it of King Edward as an alod (*in alodium*). Then, as (*et*) now, it was assessed for 1 hide. There is land for 1 plough. On the demesne is 1 (plough), and (there are) 2 villeins and 3 bordars with 1 plough. There (is) 1 serf. In the time of King Edward, as (*et*) now, it was worth 20 shillings; when received 15 shillings.

Ralph holds of Robert, and Robert of the earl, WESTRINGES [East Wittering]. Two free men held it as 2 manors. Then, as (*et*) now, it was assessed for 1 hide. There is land for 1 plough. There are 4 villeins with 2 ploughs, and 1 haw yielding (*de*) 6 pence. In the time of King Edward and afterwards, as (*et*) now, it was worth 20 shillings.

IN ISIWIRIDI [WEST EASWRITH] HUNDRED

Robert holds of the earl ESTORCHETONE [Storrington], and Durand holds it of him. Then it was assessed for 6 hides; now for 5½ hides.[2] There is land for 3 ploughs. On the demesne are 2 ploughs, and there are 6 villeins and 7 cottars with 1 plough. There (is) a church, and 2 mills yielding (*de*) 11 shillings. In the time of King Edward, as (*et*) now, it was worth 4 pounds, and afterwards 40 shillings.

Robert holds of the earl STOECHESTONE[3] [ ], and Alwin (holds it) of him, and this latter himself (*istemet*) held it in the time of King Edward, and could betake himself (*ire*) whither he would. Then, as (*et*) now, (it was assessed) for 3 hides. There
fo. 24b
is land for 2 ploughs. On the demesne is 1 plough, with 1 villein and 5 cottars and 2 serfs, and a mill yielding (*de*) 5 shillings. In the time of King Edward, and afterwards, as (*et*) now, it was worth 30 shillings.

Robert holds CODEHA(M) [Cootham[4]] of the earl, and Aubrey (holds it) of him. Two free men held it in the time of King Edward. Then, as (*et*) now, it was assessed for 4 hides and 1 virgate. There is land for 3 ploughs. On the demesne are 2 (ploughs),

[2] Assessment probably reduced for loss of pasture now in William de Braiose's rape (see note 2, p. 450).
[3] S.D.B. reads this as Storchestone [Storrington], for which it may be an error; but the Assize Roll for 1288 mentions the vill of Stoketon in this Hundred, so I have thought it better to leave the identification open.
[4] A manor in Storrington.

and (there are) 4 villeins and 5 cottars with half a plough. In the time of King Edward and afterwards, as (*et*) now, it was worth 3 pounds.

Of (*in*) the same manor Robert holds of the earl 2 hides and 1 virgate, and for so much they are assessed. Two free men held them. There is land for 2 ploughs, and there they are on the demesne, with 1 villein and 1 cottar. In the time of King Edward and afterwards, as (*et*) now, (this) was worth 20 shillings.

Robert holds PERHAM [Parham] of the earl. A certain free man, Tovi, held it. Then, as (*et*) now, it was assessed for 3 hides. There is land for 2 ploughs. On the demesne is 1 (plough) and a half, and (there are) 2 villeins and 1 cottar with half a plough, and 1 mill yielding (*de*) 30 pence. In the time of King Edward and afterwards, as (*et*) now, it was worth 3 pounds.

The same Robert holds NORDBORNE [Nutbourne] of the earl; Warin (holds it) of him. Two free men held it in the time of King Edward. Then, as (*et*) now, it was assessed for 6 hides. There is land for 6 ploughs. On the demesne is 1 (plough), and (there are) 20 villeins and 4 cottars with 7 ploughs, and 2 mills yielding (*de*) 25 shillings. There (are) 7 acres of meadow, wood(land) yielding (*de*) 12 swine. In the time of King Edward, as (*et*) now, it was worth 7 pounds; when received 6 pounds.

Roger holds of the earl NITINBREHA(M) [Nyetimber in Pulborough], and Alward (holds it) of him. Lewin held it in the time of King Edward, and could betake himself (*ire*) whither he would. Then, as (*et*) now, it was assessed for 4 hides. There is land for 5 ploughs, and (there are) 16 villeins and 3 cottars with 4 ploughs, and 3 acres of meadow, and wood(land) yielding (*de*) 10 swine. In the time of King Edward and afterwards, as (*et*) now, it was worth 3 pounds.

Robert holds of the earl POLEBERGE [Pulborough]. Ulvric held it in the time of King Edward. Then, as (*et*) now, it was assessed for 16 hides. There is land for 18 ploughs. On the demesne are 4 ploughs, and (there are) 35 villeins and 15 cottars with 13 ploughs. There (are) 9 serfs, and 2 mills yielding (*de*) 11 shillings, and 30 acres of meadow, and wood(land) yielding (*de*) 25 swine, and 2 fisheries yielding (*de*) 3 shillings. There (are) 2 churches.

Of the land of this manor Tetbald and Ivo hold 2 hides and half a virgate, and there (is) on (their) demesne 1 plough, and 3 villeins and 4 cottars with 1 plough.

The whole manor in the time of King Edward was worth 16 pounds, and afterwards 16 pounds. Now Robert's demesne (is worth) 22 pounds, (that) of the men 35 shillings.

Ernucion holds GRETHA(M) [Greatham] of the earl. Azor held it of King Edward. Then it was assessed for 5 hides. Now 1 hide is in the rape of William de Braiose. There is land for 3 ploughs. On the demesne are 2 (ploughs), and (there are) 10 villeins and 7 cottars with 2 ploughs, and four fisheries yielding (*de*) 5 shillings. In the time of King Edward it was worth 6 pounds, and afterwards, as (*et*) now, 100 shillings.

Robert holds of the earl CILLETONE [West Chiltington], and Osulf (holds it) of him. Azor held it of King Edward. Then it was assessed for 6 hides; now 3 hides are in the rape of William de Braiose.[1] There is land for 3 ploughs. On the demesne is 1 plough, and there are 4 villeins and 2 cottars with 1 plough. There (is) a church. Then and afterwards, as (*et*) now, (it was worth) 30 shillings.

IN SILLINTONE [Sullington [2]] Robert holds 1 virgate. Ulward held it of King Edward. There is 1 villein with half a plough. It is and was worth 2 shillings.

IN RISBERG [POLING] HUNDRED

The earl himself holds in demesne LOLINMINSTRE [Lyminster]. King Edward held it in demesne. There are 20 hides. It has never paid geld. There is land for 44 ploughs. On the demesne are 4 ploughs, and (there are) 68 villeins and 43 cottars with 40 ploughs. There (is) a church, and a mill yielding (*de*) 5 shillings, and 2 saltpans yielding (*de*) 20 pence, and 8 acres of meadow, and wood(land yielding) 30 swine. In the time of King Edward and afterwards, as (*et*) now, it was worth 50 pounds.

There Robert holds 1 hide of the earl. Azor held it. It has never paid geld. There (are) 6 acres of meadow, and 60 acres of pasture. It is and was worth 10 shillings.

[1] In East Easewrith Hundred (see p. 449).
[2] In William de Braiose's rape (see note 6, p. 445).

Robert holds TOTINTUNE [Toddington[1]] of the earl. Azor held it of King Edward. Then, as (et) now, it was assessed for 4 hides. There is land for 4 ploughs. On the demesne are 2 ploughs, and there are 10 villeins and 11 cottars with 2 ploughs, and 6 acres of meadow, and 1 serf. In the time of King Edward and afterwards it was worth 60 shillings; now 70 shillings.

Nigel holds WARNECHA(M) [Warningcamp[2]]. Turgot held it of King Edward. Then, as (et) now, it was assessed for 4 hides. There is land for 3 ploughs. On the demesne is 1 plough, and (there are) 4 villeins and 3 cottars with 1 plough, and 8 acres of meadow.

Of this land Rafin holds of Nigel 3 hides, and there (is) 1 plough on (his) demesne, and (there are) 8 villeins and 3 cottars with 2 ploughs. There (are) 24 acres of meadow, and 2 fisheries yielding (de) 18 pence. Wood(land) yielding (de) 3 swine.

The whole manor in the time of King Edward was worth 60 shillings, and afterwards 20 shillings; now 50 shillings.

The abbey of Almanesches holds of the earl NONNEMINSTRE [Lyminster].[3] Esmund the priest held it of King Edward. Then, as (et) now, it was assessed for 13 hides. There is land for 12 ploughs. On the demesne are 3 ploughs, and (there are) 69 villeins and 12 cottars with 17 ploughs. There (is) a church, and 4 serfs, and 2 salt-pans yielding (de) 30 pence. Wood(land) yielding (de) 20 swine. In the time of King Edward it was worth 20 pounds, and afterwards 16 pounds; now 25 pounds.

There Roger holds of the same abbey 1 hide. Esmeld the priest held it, and it has never paid geld. There is land for 1 plough. There (the plough) is on the demesne, with 9 cottars, and (there are) 25 acres of meadow, and 1 fishery yielding (de) 2 shillings, and 60 acres of pasture.

And moreover Roger holds of the same abbey 1 hide. Alwin held it of King Edward.[4] There is land for 2 ploughs. It is assessed for 1 hide. There are 4 villeins and 6 cottars with 2 ploughs, and a mill yielding (de) 30 pence.

These 2 hides in the time of King Edward and afterwards, as (et) now, were worth 60 shillings.

Warin holds of the earl ANGEMARE [Angmering]. Earl Godwin held it. Then it was assessed for 5 hides. Now one of these hides is in the rape of William de Braiose. There is land for 2 ploughs. On the demesne is 1 (plough), and (there are) 6 villeins and 4 cottars with 1 plough. In the time of King Edward and afterwards, as (et) now, it was worth 40 shillings.

Geoffrey holds of the earl ANGEMARE [Angmering]. Three free men held it in the time of King Edward. Then it was assessed for 5 hides. Now one of these hides is in the rape of William de Braiose. There is land for 2 ploughs. On the demesne is 1 (plough), and (there are) 6 villeins and 2 cottars with 2 ploughs. There (are) 3 acres of meadow, and (woodland) yielding (de) 3 swine.

In the time of King Edward and afterwards it was worth 50 shillings; now 60 shillings.

Rainald holds of the earl STOCHES [North Stoke]. Brixi held it of King Edward. Then, as (et) now, it was assessed for 8 hides. There is land for 7 ploughs. On the demesne are 3 ploughs, and (there are) 16 villeins and 16 cottars with 4 ploughs. There (is) a church, and 5 serfs, and 2 fisheries yielding (de) 10 pence. In the time of King Edward and afterwards, as (et) now, it was worth 20 pounds.

Roger holds of the earl BERCHEHA(M) [Burpham], and Alward (holds it) of him. Lewin held it of King Edward. Then, as (et) now, it was assessed for 5 hides. There is land for 4 ploughs. On the demesne are 3 ploughs, and (there are) 8 villeins and 12 cottars with 3 ploughs. There (is) a church, and 10 serfs, and 8 acres of meadow, and wood(land yielding) 3 swine.

In the time of King Edward and afterwards it was worth 8 pounds, and (is) now, and yet it returns 10 pounds.

Robert holds of the earl PRESTETUNE [East Preston]. A certain free woman, Ulveva, held it in the time of King Edward. Then, as (et) now, it was assessed for 7 hides.[5] There is land for 4 ploughs. There are 14 villeins

---

[1] In Lyminster.   [2] In Lyminster.
[3] A nunnery was founded here by Earl Roger as a cell of Almanesches. The church of Lyminster is called Nummenistre in a papal bull of 1178, printed in Dugdale Mon. vi, 1032.
[4] This and the preceding hide were probably part of Clopeham (see note 8, p. 445).

[5] This was part of Ulveva's manor of Hamsey (see note 9, p. 442).

and 1 cottar with 4 ploughs, and 3 saltpans yielding (*de*) 30 pence. It is worth 4 pounds.

The same Robert holds of the earl GAR-INGES [Goring]. It was an outlying estate (*berewica*) of King Edward.[1] There (are) 6 hides. They have never paid geld. There is land for 7 ploughs. On the demesne are 2 ploughs, and (there are) 20 villeins and 12 cottars with 5 ploughs. It was worth, then as now (*semper*), 4 pounds.

Robert holds of the earl GARINGES [Goring]. Godwin, a free man, held it in the time of King Edward. Then it was assessed for 11 hides; now William de Braiose has 2 hides[2] in his rape. There is land for 4 ploughs. On the demesne are 2 ploughs, and (there are) 13 villeins and 8 cottars with

fo. 25a

2 ploughs. In the time of King Edward and afterwards, as (*et*) now, it was worth 100 shillings.

The same Robert holds of the earl GAR-INGES [Goring]. Gondrede held it of King Edward. Then it was assessed for 4 hides; now for 2½, because 1 hide and a half is in the rape of William de Braiose. There is land for 1 plough, and there (the plough) is on the demesne, with 2 villeins, and there (are) 3 acres of meadow. In the time of King Edward and afterwards, as (*et*) now, it was worth 20 shillings.

The same Robert holds of the earl GAR-INGES [Goring]. Three free men held it in the time of King Edward. Then it was assessed for 8 hides; now for 5½ hides; the remainder (*quod restat*) is in the rape of William de Braiose.[3] There is land for 3 ploughs. On the demesne are 2 ploughs, and (there are) 6 villeins and 3 cottars with 1 plough, and 2 acres of meadow. It is and was worth, then as now (*semper*), 40 shillings.

Picot holds of the earl WEPEHA(M) [Wepham]. Two free men held it in the time of King Edward. Then, as (*et*) now, it was assessed for 8 hides. There is land for 6 ploughs. On the demesne are 2 (ploughs), and a mill yielding (*de*) 30 pence, and 10 acres of meadow, wood(land) yielding (*de*) 3

swine, and 2 fisheries yielding (*de*) 3 shillings, and 18 villeins and 9 cottars with 4 ploughs.

In the time of King Edward it was worth 8 pounds, and afterwards 9 pounds; now 10 pounds.

(IN AVISFORD HUNDRED)

The abbey of Almanesches hold CLEPINGES [Climping] of the earl in almoigne.[4] Earl Godwin held it. Then, as now, it was assessed for 11 hides. There is land for 9 ploughs, and (there are) 26 villeins and 24 cottars with 7 ploughs. There (is) a church, and 12 acres of meadow. Wood(land yielding) 20 swine.

In the time of King Edward it was worth 20 pounds, and afterwards, as (*et*) now, 15 pounds.

Of (*In*) the same manor St. Martin of Séez (*sais*) holds of the earl in almoigne 11 hides, and for so much they were assessed in the time of King Edward, and (are) now. Earl Godwin held them. There is land for 9 ploughs. On the demesne are 2 ploughs, and (there are) 26 villeins and 24 cottars with 7 ploughs. There (is) a church,[5] and 12 acres of meadow, and wood(land yielding) 20 swine.

In the time of King Edward it was worth 20 pounds, and afterwards, as (*et*) now, 15 pounds.

In HANTONE [Littlehampton] William holds of the earl 1 hide. Countess Goda held it, and it is assessed for 1 hide. There is land for 1 plough, and there (the plough) is on the demesne, with 2 cottars, and 1 acre of meadow. It is and was worth, then as now (*semper*), 10 shillings.

IN BERIE [BURY] HUNDRED

Robert holds of the earl BIGENEURE [Bignor], and Ralph (holds it) of him. Three free men held it in the time of King Edward. Then, as (*et*) now, it was assessed for 4 hides. There is land for 3 ploughs. On the demesne are 2 ploughs, and (there are) 9 villeins and 5 cottars with 2 ploughs. There (is) a church, and 2 mills yielding (*de*) 28 shillings and a

[1] Part of King Edward's manor of Steyning (see note 4, p. 445).

[2] The 3½ hides mentioned in this and the next entry as being in William de Braiose's rape were in Sompting manor (see p. 448).

[3] This was no doubt the 'land for 3 ploughs' in Steyning Hundred (see p. 446).

[4] The exact equality of this and the next entry would seem to imply a recent division of the manor, and as a matter of fact the gift of half the manor of Climping to Séez was made by Earl Roger after the death of his countess in 1082, the gift to Almanesches being made presumably at the same time (*Cal. Doc. France*, 234).

[5] At Atherington, where the abbey of Séez established a cell or grange.

quarry for mill-stones (*molaria*) yielding (*de*) 4 shillings. There (are) 2 serfs, and 2 acres of meadow, and wood(land yielding) 3 swine.

In the time of King Edward it was worth 3 pounds, and afterwards 40 shillings; now 4 pounds.

Robert holds of the earl HERIEDEHA(M) [Hardham]. Godwin, a free man, (held it) in the time of King Edward. Then, as (*et*) now, it was assessed for 5 hides. There is land for 4 ploughs. On the demesne are 2 (ploughs), and (there are) 10 villeins and 4 cottars with 3 ploughs. There (are) 3 fisheries yielding (*de*) 6 shillings, and 15 acres of meadow. Wood(land yielding) 3 swine. Of this land Ivo holds of Robert 3 virgates of land, and there he has 1 villein.

In the time of King Edward it was worth 4 pounds, and afterwards 40 shillings; now 100 shillings.

IN BENESTEDE [AVISFORD] HUNDRED

Oismelin holds BENESTEDE [Binsted] of the earl. Three free men held it in the time of King Edward. Then, as (*et*) now, it was assessed for 4 hides. There is land for 2 ploughs. On the demesne are 2 ploughs, and (there are) 2 villeins with 6 cottars with half a plough. There (are) 8 acres of meadow, and wood(land) yielding (*de*) 6 swine.

In the time of King Edward it was worth 3 pounds, and afterwards 40 shillings; now 3 pounds.

William holds of the earl WALBURGETONE [Walberton]. Three free men held it in the time of King Edward. Then, as (*et*) now, it was assessed for 11 hides and 2 virgates.[1] There is land for 6 ploughs. On the demesne are 3 ploughs, and (there are) 19 villeins and 13 cottars with 5 ploughs. There (is) a church, and 6 serfs, and 14 acres of meadow, and wood(land) yielding (*de*) 4 swine.

In the time of King Edward it was worth 10 pounds, and afterwards 6 pounds; now 12 pounds.

Of this land Rolland holds 1 hide, all but (*minus*) 1 virgate which (*et hanc*) the earl himself has in his park, and there 2 villeins with 4 cottars have 1 plough. And Acard the priest has 2 virgates as a benefice (*in prebenda*), and there he has 1 villein.

All this is worth 20 shillings.

William holds BERNEHA(M) [Barnham] of the earl. Alnod, a free man, held it in the

time of King Edward. Then, as (*et*) now, it was assessed for 4 hides. There is land for 4 ploughs. On the demesne is 1 (plough), and (there are) 12 villeins and 12 cottars with 4 ploughs. There (is) a church, and 20 acres of meadow, and wood(land) yielding (*de*) 3 swine, and 1 mill.

In the time of King Edward and afterwards, as (*et*) now, it was worth 4 pounds.

William [2] holds MIDDELTONE [Middleton] of the earl. Five free men held it in the time of King Edward. Then, as (*et*) now, it was assessed for 5 hides and 2 virgates. There is land for 3 ploughs. There (is) a church,[3] and 2 villeins with half a plough.

Of the land of this manor 3 Frenchmen (*francigene*) hold 4 hides and 5 virgates of William, and there (is) on (their) demesne 1 plough, and (there are) 10 villeins and 4 cottars with 1 plough and a half.

The whole manor in the time of King Edward was worth 4 pounds.

Ernald holds of the earl STOCHES [South Stoke]. Ulnod, a free man, held it in the time of King Edward. Then, as (*et*) now, it was assessed for 4 hides. There is land for 2 ploughs. On the demesne is 1 plough, and (there are) 10 villeins and 4 cottars with 2 ploughs. There (is) a church, and 24 acres of meadow. In the time of King Edward and afterwards, as (*et*) now, (it was worth) 4 pounds.

Ernucion holds TORTINTON [Tortington] of the earl. Lewin, a free man, held it in the time of King Edward. Then it was assessed for 4 hides, now for 3 hides, because the earl has one in his park. There is land for 2 ploughs, and there they are on the demesne, and (there are) 6 villeins and 2 cottars. There (are) 30 acres of meadow, and wood(land) yielding (*de*) 6 swine.

In the time of King Edward it was worth 60 shillings, and afterwards 30 shillings; now 40 shillings.

Hugh holds BILESHAM [Bilsham [4]] of the earl. Godwin, a free man, held it in the time of King Edward. Then, as (*et*) now, it was assessed for 4 hides. There is land for 3 ploughs. On the demesne is 1 (plough), and (there are) 14 villeins with 2 ploughs, and 8 acres of meadow.

[2] The tithe of Middleton was given to Lewes Priory by William son of Reiner.
[3] The church, and most of the parish, has been washed away by the sea.
[4] A manor in Yapton.

[1] *Et ii virgis* interlined.

In the time of King Edward it was worth 4 pounds, and afterwards 40 shillings; now 50 shillings.

The same Hugh holds of the earl 3 hides, and Warin (holds them) of him. Three free men held them in the time of King Edward. Then, as (*et*) now, they were assessed for 3 hides. There is land for 2 ploughs. On the demesne is 1 plough, and (there are) 5 villeins and 5 cottars with 1 plough. There (are) 3 acres of meadow. In the time of King Edward, as (*et*) now, (this) was worth 30 shillings; when received 20 shillings.

The same Hugh holds of the earl ESLINDONE [Slindon]. A certain free man, Azor, held it in the time of King Edward. Then, as (*et*) now, it was assessed for 8 hides. There is land for 8 ploughs. On the demesne is 1 plough and a half, and (there are) 23 villeins and 12 cottars with 7 ploughs. There (is) a church.
In the time of King Edward it was worth 20 pounds, and afterwards, as (*et*) now, 16 pounds.

The same Hugh holds of the earl 8 hides.
.[1] Nine free men held them in the time of King Edward. Then they were assessed for 8 hides; now (for) 1 virgate less, which the earl holds and (which) does not pay geld.[2] There is land for 4 ploughs, and (there are) 16 villeins with 5 ploughs. There (are) 8 acres of meadow.
In the time of King Edward and afterwards, as (*et*) now, (this) was worth 3 pounds.

Morin holds of the earl BORHA(M) [
[3]]. A free man held it in the time of King Edward. Then, as (*et*) now, it was assessed for 1 virgate. There (are) 2 virgates.[4] There are 5 ploughing oxen with 1 cottar. In the time of King Edward, as (*et*) now, it was worth 20 shillings; when received 10 shillings.

In the same Hundred William holds of the earl 3 hides, and for so much they are assessed. Two free men held them in the time of King Edward. There is land for 3 ploughs. On the demesne is 1 (plough) and

a half, and (there are) 5 villeins and 5 cottars and 2 serfs with 2 ploughs. In the time ot King Edward, as (*et*) now, it was worth 4 pounds; when received 3 pounds.

Azo[5] holds of the earl OFFHA(M) [Offham in South Stoke]. Alwin a free man held it in the time of King Edward. Then, as (*et*) now, it was assessed for 4 hides. There is land for 2 ploughs. On the demesne is 1 (plough), and (there are) 8 villeins and 5 cottars with 2 ploughs. There (are) 5 serfs, and 48 acres of meadow, and a fishery yielding (*de*) 2 shillings. Wood(land) yielding (*de*) 3 swine.
The whole in the time of King Edward was worth 7 pounds, and afterwards 6 pounds; now 4 pounds.

There the earl has 2 mills, pasture and the issues (*exitum*) of the wood(land). (This) is worth 4 pounds and 10 shillings.

fo. 25b

St. Martin of Séez (*Sais*) holds GATE [Eastergate] in almoigne of the earl. Earl Harold held it. There (are) 3 hides, but then, as (*et*) now, it was assessed for[6] 2 hides. There is land for 4 ploughs. On the demesne are 2 ploughs, and (there are) 18 villeins and 10 cottars with 2 ploughs. There (is) a church, and 4 acres of meadow. Wood(land yielding) 5 swine. In the time of King Edward, as (*et*) now, it was worth 4 pounds; when received 3 pounds.

In this Hundred of BENESTEDE [Avisford] Warin holds of the earl half a hide. Azor a free man held it, and it has never paid geld. There is land for 1 plough, and there (the plough) is, with 2 villeins. It is and was worth 30 shillings.

Gondran holds of the earl in the same place 1 hide, and for so much it was assessed, then as now (*semper*). Herulf held it of Earl Godwin. There is land for 1 plough, and there (the plough) is on the demesne, with 1 villein and 4 cottars, and 2 acres of meadow, and wood(land yielding) 3 swine. Then as now (*semper*) (it was worth) 20 shillings.

In the same Hundred Acard holds of the earl 2½ hides. They were assessed for 2 hides all but (*minus*) half a virgate then, as (*et*) now. There is land for 2 ploughs. On the demesne

---

[1] A space left for the name of the manor in which these hides are.
[2] *Et n(on) geld(at)* interlined.
[3] Not identified. S.D.B. suggests Barnham, or Barham; but where the latter place may be I cannot ascertain.
[4] *Ibi due virge* interlined.

[5] Aseius gave the tithe of Offham to the abbey of Troarn (*Cal. of Docs. in France*, 167).
[6] *Se def(en)d(ebant)* interlined.

is 1 plough, and (there are) 6 villeins and 6 cottars with 1 plough. There (is) a church,[1] and wood(land yielding) 6 swine. Ansgot held it of Earl Godwin. Then, as (*et*) now, (this was worth) 40 shillings; when received 20 shillings.

In the same place Pagen holds of the earl 1 virgate, and for so much it was assessed then as now (*semper*). Ansgot held it of Earl Godwin. There is 1 cottar. Then as now (*semper*) it was worth 30 pence.

In the same Hundred William holds of the earl half a hide and 2 virgates, and for so much they were assessed then as now (*semper*). Two Englishmen held this of Earl Godwin. There is land for 1 plough. There are 4 villeins and 1 cottar with half a plough. (This) is and was worth 10 shillings.

In the same Hundred Hugh holds of the earl 5½ virgates, and for so much they were assessed then as now (*semper*). Azor a free man held them in the time of King Edward. There is land for 2 ploughs. There is 1 villein, and 1 cottar. Then and afterwards, as (*et*) now, (this) was worth 8 shillings.

In the selfsame Hundred Rolland holds of the earl 1 hide, and for so much it was assessed then as now (*semper*). Godwin a free man held it. There is land for 2 ploughs. On the demesne is 1 plough, and (there are) 2 villeins and 4 cottars with 1 plough. It is and was worth 20 shillings.

In the same Hundred Wineman holds of the earl 1 virgate and for so much it was assessed then as now (*semper*). Turchil held it; he was a free man. It is and was worth 5 shillings.

In Bosgrave [Box] Hundred

William holds of the earl Bosgrave [Boxgrove]. Two free men held it in the time of King Edward. Then, as (*et*) now, it was assessed for 6 hides. There is land for 4 ploughs. Of this land Humphrey (*Hunfridus*) holds 3 hides and 1 virgate, Nigel 1 hide and 1 virgate, William half a hide, the clerks of the church 1 hide. On the demesne are 2 ploughs, and 1 villein and 12 cottars with 1 plough.

The whole in the time of King Edward was worth 40 shillings, and likewise afterwards, and likewise now.

The same William holds of the earl Antone [East Hampnett], and Nigel (holds it) of him. Alward a free man held it. Then, as (*et*) now, it was assessed for 7 hides, and 8 villeins and 11 cottars with 3 ploughs are there. There is land for 4 ploughs. On the demesne are 2 ploughs, and (there are) 3 acres of meadow.

In the time of King Edward it was worth 60 shillings, and afterwards 40 shillings; now 50 shillings.

The same William holds Helnache [Halnaker] of the earl. Alward held it in the time of King Edward, and then, as (*et*) now, it was assessed for 9 hides. There is land for 5 ploughs. On the demesne are 2 ploughs, and (there are) 17 villeins and 12 cottars with 2 ploughs. There are 8 acres of meadow, and wood(land yielding) 9 swine. In Chichester[2] (are) 3 burgesses yielding (*de*) 5 shillings. In the time of King Edward and afterwards it was worth 4 pounds; now 100 shillings.

The same William holds of the earl Hentone [West Hampnett[3]]. Two free men held it of Earl Godwin. Then, as (*et*) now, it was assessed for 9 hides. There is land .[4] There William has 1 mill yielding (*de*) 5 shillings, and 12 cottars, and wood(land yielding) 6 swine, and in Chichester 1 haw.

Of this land William holds 1 hide, Restold 1 hide, Richard 3 virgates, Godfrey 1 virgate. On (their) demesne is 1 plough, and (there are) 4 cottars, and 1 church.

The whole in the time of King Edward was worth 60 shillings, and afterwards 40 shillings; now 60 shillings.

The same William holds of the earl 3 hides, and for so much they are assessed in the same Hundred. Two free men held them in the time of King Edward. There is land for 1 plough.

Of this land Richard holds 2 hides, Turgis 1 hide.

[1] As Acard was the priest of Walberton this may have been the adjacent parish of Yapton, where there is a church of possibly pre-Conquest origin.

[2] In St. Pancras are several houses holden under the manor of Halnaker to this day (Hay's *History of Chichester* p. 220).

[3] That this is *West* Hampnett is shown by the presence of a church, and also by the mill, for the river Lavant runs through this parish, whereas there is no stream near *East* Hampnett, which is in Boxgrove parish.

[4] A blank.

On the demesne (is) 1 plough, with 9 cottars, and 1 mill yielding (*de*) 3 shillings, and 2 haws yielding (*de*) 9 pence. In the time of King Edward (this) was worth 20 shillings, and afterwards 15 shillings; now 10 shillings.

The same William holds of the earl STRATONE [Strettington]. Four free men held it in the time of King Edward. Then, as (*et*) now, it was assessed for 10 hides. There is land for 6 ploughs. There are 6 villeins and 16 cottars with 2 ploughs. In Chichester (are) 3 haws yielding (*de*) 2 shillings. In the time of King Edward it was worth 6 pounds, and afterwards, and now 40 shillings.

Austin (*Augustinus*) holds of the earl STRATONE [Strettington]. Godwin, a free man, held it in the time of King Edward. Then, as (*et*) now, it was assessed for 3 hides. There is land for 1 plough, and there (the plough) is on the demesne, with 2 villeins and 2 cottars, and 1 haw yielding (*de*) 3 pence, and 2 serfs, and 1 acre of meadow. In the time of King Edward it was worth 20 shillings, and afterwards 10 shillings; now 30 shillings.

Of (*in*) the same manor Arnald holds of the earl 2 hides, and for so much they are assessed. Godwin a free man held them in the time of King Edward. There is land for 1 plough, and there (the plough) is on the demesne, with 2 cottars and 2 serfs, and 1 haw yielding (*de*) 8 pence.

In the time of King Edward (this) was worth 3 pounds, and afterwards and now 20 shillings.

Oismelin holds MERSITONE [Merston] of the earl. Gort held it of King Edward. Then it was assessed for 8 hides, now for 6 hides. There is land for 3 ploughs. On the demesne are 2 ploughs, and 10 villeins with 6 cottars have 3 ploughs, and (there are) 3 mills yielding (*de*) 7 shillings, and 2 haws yielding (*de*) 2 shillings, and 10 acres of meadow.

In the time of King Edward it was worth 5 pounds, and afterwards 4 pounds; now 6 pounds.

The abbey of Troarn (*Troard*) holds ROCHINTONE [Runcton][1] in almoigne of the earl. Two free men held it in the time of King Edward. Then it was assessed for 8 hides; now for 3 hides. There is land for 3

[1] In North Mundham.

ploughs. On the demesne are 2 ploughs, and (there are) 6 villeins and 15 cottars with 1 plough. There (are) 5 serfs, and 2 mills yielding (*de*) 12 shillings and 6 pence, and a fishery yielding (*de*) 6 pence, and 2 haws yielding (*de*) 18 pence.

In the time of King Edward it was worth 5 pounds, and afterwards 4 pounds; now 6 pounds.

Ernald holds of the earl WALTHAM [Up Waltham]. Godwin, a free man, held it. Then it was assessed for 6 hides, now for 4. Ernald has 2 hides, and there are 2 cottars and 1 serf. And the abbey of Troarn (*Troard*) has 2 hides, and there are 3 cottars, and 1 haw yielding (*de*) 16 pence; and from pasturage (*herbagio*) 2 shillings. And the earl has 2 hides in his park. There is land for 1 plough.

The whole in the time of King Edward was worth 40 shillings, and afterwards 20 shillings. (Now) what Ernald (has) is worth 10 shillings; the abbey's share 35 shillings.

Geoffrey holds of the earl WALTHAM [Up Waltham]. Two free men held it in the time of King Edward. Then it was assessed for 4 hides; now for 3, because the earl has 1 (hide) in his park. There is land for 4 ploughs. On the demesne is 1 (plough), with 5 cottars, and wood(land) yielding (*de*) 10 swine, and 1 haw yielding (*de*) 7 pence. The pasturage (*herbagium*) (yields) 2 shillings.

In the time of King Edward (it was worth) 30 shillings, and afterwards 10 shillings; now 20 shillings.

In the selfsame Hundred William holds of the earl 1 hide. Alward, a free man, held it, and it was assessed for 1 hide as part of (*in*) HELNECHE [Halnaker] then, as (*et*) now. Then (it was worth) 15 shillings, and afterwards 5; now 10 shillings.

In the selfsame Hundred Siward holds of the earl 1 hide, and for so much it was assessed then as now (*semper*). Siret held it; he was a free man. There is land for 1 plough. Then, as (*et*) now, (it was worth) 20 shillings.

In the selfsame Hundred Rainald holds of the earl half a hide, and for so much it is assessed. Helghin held it in the time of King Edward. Then (it was worth) 3 shillings, and afterwards 2 shillings; now 12 pence.

fo. 26a

XII. THE LAND OF WILLIAM DE WARENE

THE BOROUGH OF LEWES in the time of King Edward returned 6 pounds and 4 shillings and 3 halfpence from the burgage-rents (*de gablo*) and from the market-dues (*de theoloneo*). There King Edward had 127 burgesses in demesne. The customary service they rendered was (*eorum consuetudo erat*): If the king wished to send his men to patrol the sea without going himself, they collected from all the men, whosoever land it was, 20 shillings, and this money those had who were in charge of the arms in the ships.[1]

Whoever sells a horse in the borough gives to the reeve a penny (*nummum*) and the buyer (gives) another; for an ox a halfpenny; for a man, in whatever place he may buy him within the rape, 4 pence.

He who sheds blood pays a fine of (*emendat per*) 7 shillings and 4 pence.

A man who commits adultery or rape pays a fine of 8 shillings and 4 pence, and a woman the same. The king has the penalty from the adulterous man, the archbishop from the woman.

From a fugitive, if he be retaken, 8 shillings and 4 pence.

When the mint is renewed, each moneyer gives 20 shillings.[2]

Of all these (payments) two-thirds (*partes*) were[3] the king's and the third (was) the earl's.

Now the borough returns in all (*per omnia*) as much as it did then (*sicut tunc*) and 38 shillings in addition (*de superplus*).

[4] Belonging to (*de*) the rape of Pevenesel [Pevensey] (are) 39 burgages (*mansure*) in-

habited (*hospitate*) and 20 uninhabited (*inhospitate*), from which the king receives 26 shillings and 6 pence, and of this (money) William de Warene receives half.

In the time of King Edward the whole was worth 26 pounds. The king had (one) half and the earl the other. Now it is worth 34 pounds, and from the new mint 112 shillings. Of all this William has (one) half and the king the other.

In the rape of Pevenesel [Pevensey] William de Warene has 12 burgages (*mansuras*), 7 inhabited (*hospitatas*) and 5 not. (They belong) to (*in*) Lestun [Laughton] a manor of the count of Mortain.[5]

IN SONEBERGE [SWANBOROUGH] HUNDRED

William de Warene holds in demesne NIWORDE [Iford]. Queen Edith (*Eddid*) held it. In the time of King Edward it was assessed for 77½ hides. When William received it (there were) only 58 hides, because the others were within the rape of the Count of Mortain.[6] These 58 hides are assessed now for 36 hides. There is land for 52 ploughs. On the demesne are 5 ploughs, and 97 villeins (100 *villani* 3 *minus*) and 32 bordars have 34 ploughs. There (is) a church, and 6 serfs, and 2 mills yielding (*de*) 23 shillings, and 208 acres of meadow. Wood-(land yielding) 30 swine. In the borough of Lewes (are) 26 burgesses yielding (*de*) 13 shillings.[7] From the pasture (come) 15 shillings and 8 pence and 16 thousands of herrings.

Of this land the monks of St. Pancras[8] hold 6½ hides, and there they have on (their) demesne 2 ploughs and 10 villeins with 3 ploughs. These hides do not pay geld.

Of the same land Hugh[9] has 2 hides and

---

[1] *Si rex ad mare custodiendum sine se mittere suos voluisset, de omnibus hominibus cujuscunque terra fuisset colligebant xx solidos and hos habebant qui in navibus arma custodiebant.* (See Introd. p. 382.)

[2] This is rather a puzzling phrase; it may refer to the issue of new dies for the coinage, or, as seems more likely, to the (? annual) renewal of the licence to coin. The question is further complicated by the entry lower down of 112 shillings *de nova moneta*; this would seem to be the payment due from (? all, or each of) the moneyers in 1086, the other being the pre-Conquest payment. The use of the present tense in this and the preceding entries can be explained by their having been copied from some pre-Conquest document (compare next note).

[3] *Sunt* altered to *erant* (see last part of preceding note).

[4] This possibly refers to the suburb of Cliffe, which is separated from the remainder of the borough by the river, which also forms the division between the rapes.

[5] This also probably refers to Cliffe. Although this is the only case mentioned in Domesday of a manor in Pevensey rape having burgages, or haws, in Lewes it is possible that there were others, as an extent of West Firle, in the Burrell MSS., mentions a messuage in Cliffe as belonging to the manor.

[6] Of these 19½ hides, 8 were probably at Frog Firle (see note 3, p. 413), with which went half a hide in Parrock (see p. 415). As land of the manor of Beddingham in Hawksborough Hundred is said to have been held by Queen Edith (see p. 400) the other 11 hides may have been absorbed into Beddingham manor.

[7] The suburb of Westout in Swanborough Hundred.

[8] The priory of Lewes.

[9] Hugh fitz-Golde gave the church of Iford and tithes there to Lewes Priory.

Tosard[1] 1 hide and a half. On (their) demesne they have 2 ploughs, with 4 bordars. Villeins held these lands.

The whole manor in the time of King Edward was worth 50 pounds, and afterwards 20 pounds. Now William's demesne (is worth) 35 pounds; (that) of the monks 3 pounds; (that) of the men 75 shillings.

IN HOMESTREU [HOLMSTROW] HUNDRED

William himself holds in demesne RAMELLE [Rodmell]. Earl Harold held it. In the time of King Edward it was assessed for 79 hides. William received 64 hides, because the others (are) in the rape of the count (of Mortain)[2] and (in that) of William de Braiose.[3] These 64 hides are now assessed for 33 hides. There is land for 36 ploughs. On the demesne are 6 ploughs, and (there are) 107 villeins and 25 bordars with 34 ploughs. There (are) 11 saltpans yielding (de) 26 shillings, and 140 acres of meadow, and wood(land yielding) 23 swine. In the manor is a church.

In Lewes (are) 44 haws[4] yielding (de) 22 shillings and 4,000 herrings.

Of this land Norman[5] holds 2 hides of William, and there (is) 1 plough on (his) demesne, with 2 bordars and 1 serf. He who held this land could not betake himself elsewhere (recedere) with it.

The whole manor in the time of King Edward was worth 60 pounds, and afterwards 20 pounds, now 37 pounds.

IN PRESTETUNE [DEAN] HUNDRED

William himself holds PICEHAM [Patcham] in demesne. Earl Harold held it in the time of King Edward. Then it was assessed for 60 hides, and now for 40. There is land for 80 ploughs. On the demesne are 8 ploughs, and (there are) 163 villeins and 45 bordars with 82 ploughs. There (is) a church, and 6 serfs, and 10 shepherds (berquarii).[6] There are 84 acres of meadow and wood(land yielding) 100 swine.

In Lewes (are) 26 haws yielding (de) 13 shillings.

Of this land Richard (Ricoardus) holds 7 hides and a knight of his 1 hide and a half. On (their) demesne they have 2 ploughs, with 2 bordars.

In the time of King Edward the whole was worth 100 pounds, and afterwards 50 pounds; now 80 pounds.

IN SOANEERGE [SWANBOROUGH] HUNDRED[7]

William himself holds in demesne DIGELINGES[8] [Ditchling]. King Edward held it. It has never paid geld. In the time of King Edward it was assessed for 46 hides. When received (there were) only 42 hides; the others were in the rape of the Count of Mortain,[9] as were (et) 6 woods, which used to belong (pertinebant) to the seat (caput) of the manor. Now it is assessed for 33 hides. There is land for 60 ploughs. On the demesne are 8 ploughs, and 108 villeins and 40 bordars have 81 ploughs.[10] There (is) a church and 1 mill yielding (de) 30 pence, and 130 acres of meadow. Wood(land yielding) 80 swine. In Lewes (he has) 11 burgages (masuras) yielding (de) 12 shillings.

Of this land Gilbert holds 1 hide and a half, Hugh 2 hides, Alward 3 hides, Warin 3 hides, Richard 1 hide. On (their) demesne they have 7½ ploughs, with 29 bordars, and (there are) 3 villeins and 10 serfs with 3 ploughs. In Lewes (are) 6 burgesses yielding (de) 43 pence.

The whole manor in the time of King Edward was worth 80 pounds and 66 pence, and afterwards 25 pounds. Now William's demesne (is worth) 60 pounds, and that of the men 12 pounds and 10 shillings.

IN FALEMERE [YOUNGSMERE] HUNDRED

St. Pancras[11] holds of William FALEMERE [Falmer]. The abbey of Wilton held it in the time of King Edward, and was seised (thereof) on the day of his (death) (in die ejus). In the time of King Edward it was assessed for 21 hides, now for 18 hides; the others are in the rape of the Count of Mortain[12] and do not pay geld. There is land

[1] See Introd. p. 380.
[2] In Hartfield Hundred, 1½ hides ascribed to Rodmell, and probably the 1 hide in the next entry (see p. 414).
[3] In Burbeach Hundred, 8 hides (see p. 444).
[4] The suburb of Southover; it was afterwards formed into a Hundred, which extends from Lewes to Rodmell.
[5] Norman the hunter gave the tithe of his land in Horecumbe [Halcombe in Piddinghoe] to Lewes Priory.
[6] The only mention of this class.

[7] Ditchling is really in the Hundred of Street.
[8] S.D.B. reads Dicelinges.
[9] Two hides were in East Grenested Hundred, 1 virgate at Ferlega (see p. 419), the rest held by Ansfrid (ibid.).
[10] A remarkable excess of ploughs over ploughlands.
[11] The priory of Lewes.
[12] It is possible that the 1½ hides in Felesmere in East Grinstead belonged to this manor (see note 9, p. 418); the remainder was probably included in the abbey of Wilton's manor of West Firle.

for 15 ploughs. On the demesne are 2 ploughs, and (there are) 25 villeins and 7 bordars with 13 ploughs. There (is) a church and 1 serf. There (are) 4 acres of meadow and wood(land) yielding (*de*) 20 swine.

In the time of King Edward and afterwards, as (*et*) now, (it was worth) 20 pounds.

IN HOMESTREU [HOLMSTROW] HUNDRED

Godfrey[1] holds of William HERBERTINGES [Herpingden].[2] Alnod held it in the time of King Edward, and could betake himself (*ire*) whither he pleased. Then it was assessed for 10½ hides; now for 6 hides, but half a hide is in the rape of the Count of Mortain.[3] There is land for 4 ploughs. On the demesne are 2 ploughs, and there are 14 villeins and 6 bordars with 2 ploughs. There are 17 acres of meadow, and wood(land) yielding (*de*) 30 swine. In Lewes (are) 4 haws[4] yielding (*de*) 20 pence.

In the time of King Edward it was worth 40 shillings, and afterwards 50 shillings; now 60 shillings.

Nigel holds of the earl LANESWICE [? Orleswick].[5] Earl Godwin held it, and 7 alodial tenants (*aloarii*) (held it) of him. In the time of King Edward it was assessed for 6½ hides; now for 5 hides. There is land for 4 ploughs. On the demesne is 1 plough,

fo. 26b

and (there are) 11 villeins and 6 bordars with 2 ploughs. There (are) 2 serfs, and 17 acres of

meadow. In Lewes (are) 2 haws yielding (*de*) 10 shillings.

In the time of King Edward it was worth 30 shillings, and afterwards 40 shillings; now 60 shillings.

IN WELESMERE HUNDRED[6]

Hugh[7] holds of William ROTINGEDENE [Rottingdean]. Haminc held it of Earl Godwin. Then, as (*et*) now, it was assessed for 2 hides, and it was part of (*jacuit in*) Ferle [Frog Firle] which the Count of Mortain holds in his rape.[8] There is land for 2 ploughs. There (the ploughs) are on the demesne, with 10 bordars.

In the time of King Edward it was worth 40 shillings, and afterwards 20 shillings; now 60 shillings.

Godfrey[9] holds of William HOVINGEDENE [Ovingdean]. Alnod held it of King Edward and could betake himself (*ire*) whither he pleased. Then it was assessed for 5 hides.[10] In the same vill (*villa*) Edith (*Eddeva*) held 3 hides of the king in parage. When Godfrey received it, then he found it (all) as (*in*) 1 manor. But of these 8 hides the Count of Mortain has a hide and a half in his rape. What Godfrey (has) pays geld for 6 hides now. There is land for 4 ploughs. On the demesne are 2 ploughs, and (there are) 5 villeins and 5 bordars with 1 plough. There (is) a chapel (*ecclesiola*), and 4 serfs. In Lewes are 10 haws yielding (*de*) 5 shillings.

With these hides Godfrey holds 2 hides of a certain manor of William, his lord, which have never paid geld, and there he has nothing.

The whole in the time of King Edward was worth 6 pounds, and afterwards 4 pounds; now 7 pounds.

In the same vill Bricmaer holds of William 2 hides. He himself held them of Azor in

---

[1] The entires in this rape attributed to Godfrey are to be ascribed to Godfrey de Pierpoint. At ' Herbertinges' William de Herbertinges gave land to Lewes Priory by leave of William de Pierpoint his lord.

[2] A manor in Piddinghoe.

[3] There is a hamlet called Harebeating in the parish of Hailsham, and as the latter was a manor of Alnod's (see p. 416) this half hide probably lay there.

[4] A sixteenth century rental of Portslade manor shows that ' Harpetinge alias Harpingedene in Pedinghoo' then belonged to that manor, as did also certain tenements in Keere Street, Lewes, which are still held of the manor of Portslade; as no haws are recorded in Domesday as attached to the latter manor, it is probable that the houses in Keere Street are on the site of the haws belonging to Herbertinges.

[5] Nigel gave to Lewes Priory land in Orlaueswica, which is shown by the Lewes Chartulary to have been near Herbertinges, and must be identical with this Laneswice—*n* and *u* being often confused (compare note 8, p. 413). Orleswick is found in an eighteenth century rental of Swanborough manor, but the name is now lost.

[6] Of the places named under this heading Brighton is in Whalesbone Hundred, and the others are all in Youngsmere, which latter is also called in Domesday, Falemere Hundred. It is possible that part of Welesmere was formed into the Hundred of Whalesbone and the remainder united with Falemere to form Youngsmere. In the *Placita Corone* for 1248 ' Whallesbon' appears and Youngsmere is called both ' Iwonesmere' and ' Hywelesmere.'

[7] Hugh fitz-Golde gave the tithe of his land in Rottingdean to Lewes Priory.

[8] See note 5, p. 413.

[9] Godfrey de Pierpoint gave 1 hide in Ovingdean to Lewes Priory.

[10] This includes 2 hides of Alnod's manor of Alciston (see note 2, p. 394).

the time of King Edward, and then as (*et*) now, they were assessed for 2 hides. There he has 1 plough with 2 bordars. (This) is and was worth, then as now (*semper*), 20 shillings.

(IN WHALESBONE HUNDRED)

Ralph[1] holds of William BRISTELMESTUNE [Brighton]. Brictric held it by grant (*de dono*) of Earl Godwin. In the time of King Edward, as (*et*) now, it was assessed for 5½ hides. There is land for 3 ploughs. On the demesne is half a plough, and (there are) 18 villeins and 9 bordars with 3 ploughs and 1 serf. From gafol-rents (*de gablo*) 4,000 herrings.

In the time of King Edward it was worth 8 pounds and 12 shillings, and afterwards 100 shillings; now 12 pounds.

In the same vill Widard holds of William 6 hides and 1 virgate, and for so much they are assessed. Three alodial tenants (*aloarii*) held them of King Edward, and could betake themselves (*ire*) whither they would. One of them had a hall (*aulam*), and villeins held the shares of the other two. There is land for 5 ploughs, and it is (all) in one manor. On the demesne (is) 1 plough and a half, and (there are) 14 villeins and 21 bordars with 3½ ploughs. There (are) 7 acres of meadow, and wood(land yielding) 3 swine. In Lewes (are) 4 haws.

In the time of King Edward (this) was worth 10 pounds, and afterwards 8 pounds; now 12 pounds.

In the same place William de Watevile holds BRISTELMETUNE [Brighton] of William. Ulward held it of King Edward. Then, as (*et*) now, it was assessed for 5½ hides. There is land for 4 ploughs. On the demesne is 1 plough, and (there are) 13 villeins and 11 bordars with 1 plough. There (is) a church.

In the time of King Edward it was worth 10 pounds, and afterwards 8 pounds; now 12 pounds.

(IN YOUNGSMERE HUNDRED)

Goze[2] holds of William BURGEMERE [Balmer]. Villeins who belonged to (*jacuerunt in*) Falemere [Falmer] held it in the time of King Edward.[3] Then, as (*et*) now, it was

assessed for 4 hides. There is land for 2 ploughs. On the demesne is 1 with 1 villein and 2 bordars and 2 serfs. There is a chapel (*ecclesiola*) and wood(land) yielding (*de*) 4 swine.

In the time of King Edward it was worth 20 shillings, and afterwards, and now, 30 shillings.

Eustace[4] holds of William 1 hide in FALEMERE HUNDRED [Youngsmere]. One villein of Falemere [Falmer] held it. It is assessed for 1 hide. It is worth 6 shillings.

Walter holds of William BEVEDENE [Bevendean]. Azor held it of King (Edward). Then, as (*et*) now, it was assessed for 4 hides. There is 1 virgate in addition (*insuper*) which does not pay geld, because it is outside (*foris*) the rape.[5] There is land for 3 ploughs. On the demesne are 2 ploughs, and there are 2 villeins and 3 bordars with 1 plough. In Lewes (are) 2 haws yielding (*de*) 18 pence. In the time of King Edward it was worth 100 shillings, and afterwards 4 pounds; now 6 pounds. Villeins of Chemele [? Keymer][6] held this land.[7]

IN SUANEBERGE [SWANBOROUGH] HUNDRED

Eldeid holds of William WINTREBURNE [Winterbourne];[8] there is 1 hide, and for so much it is assessed. Edith (*Eddeva*) held it of King Edward. There is land for half a plough, and there (the half plough) is on the demesne, with 6 bordars, and 1 acre and a half of meadow. In Lewes[9] (are) 3 haws and the third part of 1 haw yielding (*de*) 18 pence. In the time of King Edward and afterwards it was worth 10 shillings; now 20 shillings.

---

[1] Ralph de Caisned (Cheyney), who gave the church of Brighton to Lewes Priory.

[2] William de Warenne II. confirmed to Lewes Priory '2 hides at Borgemere which Goze my foster-father (*nutricius*) held.'

[3] See Introd. p. 368.

[4] William de Warenne gave to Lewes Priory 1 nide in Burgemere which Eustace held.

[5] This may refer to the 1½ virgates of this manor at Standen in East Grinstead (see p. 419), though from the wording the virgate would appear to be still part of the manor.

[6] Keymer is called Chemere and was one of Azor's manors, and although it is some distance from Bevendean, there lies between the two a farm called Standean, which was also the name of the detached portion of the manor of Bevendean (see last note).

[7] See Introd. p. 368.

[8] Close to Lewes. It had probably been separated off from the queen's manor of Iford.

[9] Winterbourne appears to have been absorbed into the manor of Houndean, of which manor is held certain land on School Hill, in the parish of All Saints, Lewes.

THE HOLDERS OF LANDS

In the Half Hundred of Eldretune [Fishergate]

Godfrey[1] holds of William Eldretune [Aldrington]. It was part of (*jacuit in*) Beddinges [Beeding], a manor of King Edward, which (*et*) now William de Braiose holds in his rape. Godfrey holds 7 hides and half a virgate. There is land for 7 ploughs. It has not paid geld. Villeins held it in the time of King Edward. There are 41 villeins and 10 bordars with 7 ploughs. In the time of King Edward and afterwards it was worth 4 pounds; now 6 pounds.

In the same vill the same Godfrey holds of William 9 hides, and for so much they are assessed. Wigot held them of King Edward and they were part of (*jacuerunt in*) Bradewatre [Broadwater] which William de Braiose holds in his rape. There is land for 4 ploughs. On the demesne is 1 plough, and (there are) 10 villeins and 12 bordars with 2 ploughs.

In the time of King Edward and afterwards (this) was worth 4 pounds; now 100 shillings. In these two estates (*terris*) (there is) only 1 hall (*halla*).

Nigel holds of William Esmerewic [ ].[2] Azor held it of King Edward. Then, as (*et*) now, it was assessed for 1 hide and a half. There is land for 4 ploughs. On the demesne are 2 ploughs, and (there are) 4 villeins and 6 bordars with 2 ploughs.

In the time of King Edward it was worth 40 shillings, and afterwards 30 shillings; now 4 pounds.

William de Watevile holds of William Hangetone [Hangleton]. Azor held it of King Edward. Then it was assessed for 14 hides and 1 virgate. Now for 8½ hides. There is land for 8 ploughs. On the demesne are 2 ploughs, and (there are) 31 villeins and 13 bordars with 5 ploughs.

This estate (*terra*) was part of (*jacuit ad*) Chingestone [Kingston-Bucy], a manor of William de Braiose.

In the time of King Edward, as (*et*) now, it was worth 10 pounds; when received 8 pounds.

[1] Godfrey de Pierpoint gave 1 hide in Aldrington to Lewes Priory.

[2] Not identified. S.D.B. asserts that this is 'now Southwick,' but there appears to be no evidence for the assertion, and Southwick was in the rape of Bramber. As Ralph son of Nigel gave to Lewes Priory the tithe of his land in Hangleton, and as it had been held by Azor, it was no doubt part of the latter's estate of Hangleton, which in turn was part of his manor of Kingston.

Osward holds of William Porteslage [Portslade] half a hide. He himself held it in the time of King Edward, and it has not paid geld. This man could betake himself (*ire*) with his land whither he pleased. There is 1 villein. It is worth 6 shillings.

Albert holds half a hide in Porteslamhe [Portslade]. It has not paid geld. There is 1 villein with half a plough. It is and was worth 6 shillings.

In Poninges [Poynings] Hundred

Levenot holds of William Paveorne [Peathorne[3]]. He himself held it of King Edward, and could betake himself (*ire*) whither he would. Then it was assessed for 4 hides, now for 1 hide and a half, because the others are in the rape of William de Braiose. There is land for 1 plough, and there (the plough) is on the demesne, with 2 bordars.

In Lewes (are) 3 haws yielding (*de*) 18 pence. It is and was worth 30 shillings.

Osward holds of William Berchinges [Perching[4]]. He himself held it in the time of King Edward, and could betake himself (*ire*) whither he pleased. Then, as (*et*) now, it was assessed for 3 hides. There is land for 2½ ploughs. On the demesne is 1 (plough), and (there are) 2 villeins and 3 bordars with 1 plough, and half a mill yielding (*de*) 40 pence, and 7 acres of meadow, wood(land yielding) 2 swine. In Lewes (is) 1 haw and a half yielding (*de*) 9 pence. It is and was worth 40 shillings.

In the same vill Tezelin[5] holds of William 2 hides, and for so much they are assessed. They were part of (*jacuerunt in*) Trailgi [Truleigh] which William de Braiose holds. Bellinc held them of Earl Godwin. On the demesne is 1 plough, and (there are) 3 villeins and 2 bordars with half a plough. (There is) half a mill yielding (*de*) 13 shillings and 4 pence,[6] and 3 acres of meadow. Wood(land yielding) 2 swine. In Lewes half a haw (yielding) 2 pence.[7]

The same Tezelin holds of William Fochinges [Fulking]. It was part of (*jacuit*

[3] A manor in Fulking, a hamlet of Edburton.

[4] A manor in Fulking.

[5] At Perching Lewes Priory held the tithe of the land of William son of Techelin. (See Introd. p. 357.)

[6] Probably an error for 3 shillings and 4 pence, as the other half of the mill was worth 40 pence.

[7] The value of this estate is omitted,

fo. 27a

in) Sepelei [Shipley],[1] which William de Braiose holds. Harold held it in the time of King Edward. Then, as (*et*) now, it was assessed for 3 hides and 1 virgate. There are 6 villeins with 2 ploughs.

These two estates (*terre*) of Tezelin's go together (*insimul sunt*). They are and were worth, then as now (*semper*), 50 shillings.

William son of Rainald holds of William PONINGES [Poynings]. Cola held it of Earl Godwin, because he gave it to him. In the time of King Edward, as (*et*) now, (it was reckoned) at (*pro*) 8 hides, but it has never paid geld. There is land for 13 ploughs. On) the demesne are 2 ploughs, and (there are 25 villeins and 8 bordars with 15 ploughs. Three (is) a church, and 2 serfs, and 2 mills yielding (*de*) 12 shillings, and 50 acres of meadow. Wood(land) yielding (*de*) 40 swine. In the time of King Edward it was worth 12 pounds, and afterwards and now 10 pounds.

The same William holds of William PINHEDENE [Pangdean [2]]. Levfel held it of King Edward. Then, as (*et*) now, it was assessed for 10 hides. There is land for 11 ploughs. On the demesne is 1 plough, and (there are) 20 villeins and 8 bordars with 8 ploughs. There (is) wood(land) yielding (*de*) 2 swine. In Lewes (are) 2 haws yielding (*de*) 2 shillings, and (there is) 1 acre of meadow. In the time of King Edward, as (*et*) now, it was worth 100 shillings; when received 6 pounds.

The same William holds of William PINWEDENE [Pangdean]. Osward held it of King Edward, and could betake himself (*ire*) whither he pleased. Then, as (*et*) now, it was assessed for 9 hides. There is land for 10 ploughs. On the demesne is 1 (plough), and (there are) 15 villeins and 6 bordars with 6 ploughs. In Lewes (are) 2 haws yielding (*de*) 2 shillings. In the time of King Edward and afterwards it was worth 6 pounds; now 100 shillings.

Of the same land Roger and Walter hold of William 2 ploughs with 4 bordars. (This) is worth 30 shillings.

Ralph [3] holds of William SALESCOME

[Saddlescombe [4]]. Godwin the priest held it of Earl Godwin. It was part of (*jacebat in*) Boseha(m) [Bosham].[5] Then, as (*et*) now, it was assessed for 17 hides. There is land for 10 ploughs. On the demesne are 2 ploughs, and (there are) 24 villeins and 4 bordars with 7 ploughs. There (are) 13 acres of meadow. From salt (come) 15 pence. In Lewes (is) 1 haw. There was wood(land) yielding (*de*) 5 swine, but it (*que*) is now in the rape of William de Braiose.

Of this land Ralph holds 4 hides, and there he has on (his) demesne 1 plough and 3 villeins and 2 bordars with half a plough.

The whole in the time of King Edward was worth 15 pounds, and afterwards 10 pounds; now 11 pounds.

The same Ralph holds of William NIU-EMBRE [Newtimber]. Ælfech held it of King Edward, and could betake himself (*ire*) whither he pleased. Then, as (*et*) now, it was assessed for 10 hides. There is land for 7 ploughs. On the demesne are 2 ploughs, and there are 14 villeins and 7 bordars with 5 ploughs. There (is) 1 mill yielding (*de*) 20 pence, and 2 acres of meadow, and wood-(land yielding) 3 swine.

In the time of King Edward and afterwards it was worth 7 pounds; now 8 pounds.

William de Watevile holds P(ER)CINGES [Perching]. Azor held it of King Edward, and 2 men (held it) of Azor. It was assessed for 5½ hides then, as (*et*) now. Then there were 2 halls, now (it is all) in 1 manor. There is land for 5½ ploughs. On the demesne is 1 (plough), and (there are) 4 villeins and 3 bordars with 1 plough. There (are) 2 serfs, and 3 acres of meadow. Wood(land yielding) 3 swine, from pasture 6 pence.

In the time of King Edward it was worth 60 shillings, and afterwards 40 shillings; now 50 shillings.

IN BOTINGELLE [BUTTINGHILL] HUNDRED

Robert [6] holds of William HERST [Hurst-pierpoint]. Earl Godwin held it. Then it was assessed for 41 hides, now for nothing, because it has never paid geld.[7] When re-

---

[1] This manor is not mentioned in William de Braiose's rape. It may have been included in Thakeham, the largest of the adjacent manors.

[2] A manor in Piecombe.

[3] Ralph de Caisned (Cheyney), from whom it descended to Geoffrey de Say, who gave it to the Knights Templars.

[4] In Newtimber.

[5] See note 7, p. 392.

[6] Robert de Pierpoint.

[7] This is a contradiction of terms. The statement that land *se defendebat* implies that it did pay geld; probably the scribe carelessly expanded *n(on) geld(at)* into *nunq(uam) geldavit*; or else we must supply the words 'since Robert received it.'

ceived (there were) only 18½ hides. In the rape of the Count of Mortain are 3½ hides. In the rape of William de Braiose are 19 hides.[1] There is land for 25 ploughs. On the demesne are 2 ploughs, and (there are) 35 villeins and 8 bordars with 21½ ploughs. There (is) a church, and 8 serfs, and 3 mills yielding (de) 9 shillings, and 80 acres of meadow. Wood(land) yielding (de) 50 swine. Of this land William holds 3 hides, Gilbert 3½ hides. Villeins held (this).

The whole in the time of King Edward was worth 36 pounds, and afterwards 9 pounds ; now 12 pounds amongst the whole.

The wife of William de Watevile[2] holds of William CLAITUNE [Clayton]. Azor held it of King Edward. Then, as (et) now it was assessed for 7 hides. There is land for 12 ploughs. On the demesne are 2 ploughs, and there are 26 villeins and 5 bordars with 14 ploughs. There (is) a church, and 23 acres of meadow. Wood(land) yielding (de) 15 swine. In Lewes (are) 9 haws[3] yielding (de) 4 shillings and 7 pence. In the time of King Edward it was worth 10 pounds, and afterwards and now 8 pounds.

Alwin holds of the woman herself Wicham [Wickham[4]]. He himself held it of[5] Azor. Then, as (et) now, it was assessed for 3 hides. On the demesne is 1 plough, and (there are) 3 villeins with 1 plough ; and in Lewes (are) 3 quarters (partes) of 1 haw yielding (de) 15 pence.

William de Watevile holds of William CHEMERE [Keymer]. Azor held it of King Edward. Then, as (et) now, it was assessed for 14 hides. There is land for 25 ploughs. On the demesne are 2 ploughs, and (there are) 36 villeins and 11 bordars with 17 ploughs. There (is) a church,[6] and 3 serfs, and 40 acres of meadow, and 2 mills yielding (de) 12 shillings. In Lewes (are) 7 haws

yielding (de) 26 pence. In the time of King Edward and afterwards it was worth 14 pounds ; now 12 pounds.

IN ESTRAT [STREET] HUNDRED

Ralph[7] holds of William ESTRAT [Street]. Lewin held it of King Edward. Then it was assessed for 9 hides ; now for 8 hides. There is land for 16 ploughs. On the demesne are 3 ploughs, and (there are) 20 villeins and 12 bordars with 8 ploughs. There (are) 6 acres of meadow. From the wood(land come) 16 swine. In Lewes (are) 3 haws yielding (de) 18 pence.

Of this land a certain Ralph holds 1 hide, and there he has 1 plough with 1 villein.

There (are) 2 chapels (ecclesiole). In the time of King Edward and afterwards, as (et) now, it was worth 100 shillings.

Robert[8] holds of William in[9] WESTMESTUN [Westmeston] 12 hides. Countess Gueda held them, and villeins held (them) under her. There was no hall there, and it did not pay geld, so (the jurors) say. There is land for 9 ploughs. On the demesne is 1 plough, and (there are) 4 villeins and 12 bordars with 2 ploughs. There (are) 3 acres of meadow, and wood(land) yielding (de) 10 swine.

Of this land 1 knight holds 3 hides and 3 virgates, and there he has on (his) demesne 1 plough, and (there are) 2 villeins and 5 bordars. In Lewes (is) 1 haw returning nothing.

In the time of King Edward it was worth 7 pounds, and afterwards 5 shillings ; now 6 pounds.

Hugh son of Rannulf holds of William PLUNTUNE [Plumpton]. Godwin the priest held it of Earl Godwin.[10] Then it was assessed for 32 hides, now for 30. There is land for 24 ploughs. On the demesne are 3 ploughs, and (there are) 51 villeins and 6 bordars with 22 ploughs. There (is) a church, and 8 serfs, and 2 mills yielding (de) 20 shillings. Wood(land) yielding (de) 20 swine. From gafol-rent (de gablo) 17 swine ; meadow .[11] In Lewes (are) 9 haws[12] yielding (de) 4 shillings and 5 pence.

---

[1] At How in Lancing were 6 hides (see p. 449) ; another 6 hides probably in Burbeach Hundred (see note 1, p. 444).

[2] A remarkable instance of a married woman with an estate held independently of her husband.

[3] A sixteenth century rental of the Borough of Lewes shows that a portion of a croft on the north side of the castle was then held of the manor of Clayton.

[4] In Clayton.

[5] *Ipse de* interlined.

[6] The church of Keymer was given to Lewes Priory by Ralph de Caisned, who seems to have succeeded William de Watevile in most, if not in all, of his manors.

[7] Ralph de Caisned, whose descendant Geoffrey de Say held it.

[8] Probably Robert de Pierpoint.

[9] *In* interlined.

[10] See note 6, p. 392.

[11] A blank.

[12] Certain tenements in St. Anne's parish are still held of the manor of Plumpton.

In the time of King Edward, as (*et*) now, it was worth 25 pounds; when received 15 pounds.

Robert holds of William CHILDELTUNE [East Chiltington]. Fredri held it of King Edward, and could betake himself (*ire*) whither he pleased. Then it was assessed for 7 hides, now for 5 hides and 1 virgate,[1] the others are in the rape of the Count of Mortain. There is land for 6 ploughs. On the demesne is 1 plough, and (there are) 3 villeins with 1 plough. In Lewes (is) 1 haw yielding (*de*) 12 pence.

Of this land a certain knight holds 2½ hides, and there he has on (his) demesne 1 plough, and (there are) 6 villeins and 2 bordars with 1 plough, and half a mill yielding (*de*) 15 pence, and 1 haw and a half yielding (*de*) 8 pence.

In the time of King Edward it was worth 4 pounds, and afterwards (the same); now 100 shillings.

Godfrey holds of William CHILDE(N)TUNE [East Chiltington]. Godric held it of King Edward. Then it was assessed for 2 hides; now for 1 hide and a half, because a half is in the rape of the Count of Mortain. There is land for 2 ploughs. On the demesne is 1 plough, and (there are) 5 villeins and 3 bordars with 1 plough. There (are) 2 acres of meadow. Wood(land) yielding (*de*) 12 swine. In Lewes 1 burgess yielding (*de*) 6 pence.

fo. 27b

In the time of King Edward and afterwards it was worth 16 shillings; now 20 shillings.

Nigel holds of William 1 hide in ODINTUNE [Wooton in East Chiltington]. Godric held it of King Edward. It did not give geld. No one lives (*manet*) there. It is worth 12 shillings.[2]

Hugh holds of William VENNINGORE [Waningore[3]]. Four alodial tenants held it of King Edward, and could betake themselves (*ire*) whither they pleased with their lands. Then it was assessed for 3½ hides, now half (a hide) is in the rape of the Count of Mortain.[4] There is land for 3 ploughs. On the demesne are 3 ploughs, and (there are) 6 villeins and 5 bordars with 3 ploughs. .[5] Three haws yielding (*de*) 21 pence.

In the time of King Edward it was worth 40 shillings and afterwards 30 shillings; now 60 shillings.

The same Hugh holds of William 3 virgates in BEDINGES [Beeding], which (manor) William de Braiose holds. Villeins held them in the time of King Edward. They have never paid geld. On the demesne is 1 plough, and (there are) 15 villeins and 3 bordars with 5 ploughs. There is land for 5 ploughs. There (are) 3 acres of meadow. Wood(land) yielding (*de*) 10 swine.

In the time of King Edward and afterwards it was worth 15 shillings; now 30 shillings.

IN BERCHA(M) [BARCOMBE] HUNDRED

William de Watevile holds of William BERCHAM [Barcombe]. Azor held it of Earl Godwin. Then it was assessed for 13 hides; now for 10½ hides; the others are in the rape of the Count of Mortain.[6] They have never paid geld, so (the jurors) say. There is land for 20 ploughs. On the demesne are 2 ploughs, and (there are) 24 villeins and 2 bordars with 9 ploughs. There (is) a church,[7] and 3½ mills yielding (*de*) 20 shillings. In Lewes (are) 18 haws yielding (*de*) 8 shillings and 7 pence.

In the time of King Edward it was worth 12 pounds, and afterwards 6 pounds; now 8 pounds.

Ralph[3] holds of William HAME [Hamsey]. Ulveva held it of King Edward. Then it was assessed for 25 hides; now there are 14 (hides), because the others are in the rape of the Count of Mortain, namely 7 hides, and in the rape of Earl Roger 4 hides all but (*minus*) half a virgate.[9]

Now what Ralph has pays geld for 13 hides. There is land for 13 ploughs. On the demesne are 2 hides, and (there are) 16 villeins and 14 bordars with 10 ploughs. There (is) a church, and 200 acres of meadow. Wood(land) yielding (*de*) 10 swine. From the pasturage (*herbagio*) 13 shillings.

---

[1] *Et una virga* interlined.
[2] *Denarios* altered to *solidos*.
[3] In Chailey.
[4] At Brockhurst in East Grinstead (see p. 419).
[5] A space left.

[6] In Fletching (see notes 3 and 4, p. 420).
[7] The church was given to Lewes Priory by Ralph de Caisned (compare note 6, p. 441).
[8] Ralph de Caisned, from whose descendants, the family of de Say, the manor took its name of Hammes-Sey.
[9] The figures here seem to have been inverted; the 4 hides were in the Count of Mortain's rape at Horsted (see p. 419), and the 7 hides were presumably in Earl Roger's rape in Ulveva's manor of East Preston (see Introd. p. 357).

Of the same land Hugh holds 1 hide, Ralph half a hide.[1]

The whole in the time of King Edward was worth 20 pounds, and afterwards 10 pounds ; now 10 pounds.

The same Ralph holds of William ALINTUNE [Allington[2]]. Ulward held it of King Edward. Then, as (et) now, it was assessed for 6 hides. There is land for 6 ploughs. There are 8 villeins and 3 bordars with 2½ ploughs. In Lewes (is) 1 haw yielding (de) 6 pence.

Of this land Warner holds 1 hide, Osmund 1 hide.

The whole in the time of King Edward was worth 4 pounds and 2 shillings, and afterwards 62 shillings ; now 50 shillings.

In the same vill Hugh holds of William 2 hides. Edith (*Eddeva*) held them in the time of King Edward, and could betake herself (*ire*) whither she pleased. Then, as (et) now, they were assessed for 2 hides. There is land for 1 plough. On the demesne is half a plough, and (there are) 3 villeins and 2 bordars with 1 plough. In Lewes (are) 4 haws yielding 4 shillings. It is and was worth 20 shillings.

In the same place Nigel holds half a virgate, and for so much it pays geld. There a certain villein has half a plough. It is and was worth 10 shillings.

IN FALEMERE [YOUNGSMERE] HUNDRED

Gozelin holds of William 1 hide in MOLSTAN [Moulstone[3]]. Azor held it of King Edward as of (*ad*) the manor of Hoingesdene [Ovingdean]. It has not paid geld. On the demesne is 1 plough. It is and was worth 20 shillings.

IN WINGEHA(M) [WINDHAM] HUNDRED

Scolland[4] holds of William BENEFELLE [Benefield in Twineham]. Turgod held it of Cola, and Cola of King Edward. Then it was assessed for 2 hides ; now for nothing. There is land for 3 ploughs. On the demesne are 2 ploughs, and 5 villeins with 8 bordars have 2 ploughs.

In the time of King Edward it was worth 60 shillings, and afterwards likewise ; now 6 pounds.

Alfred[4] holds of William 1 hide in BENEFELLE [Benefield] and 1 virgate, and for so much it was assessed in the time of King Edward ; now for nothing. Lewin held it in parage. There is land for 1 plough, and there (the plough) is on the demesne, and (there are) 4 villeins with half a plough. There (are) 4 acres of meadow and wood(land) yielding (*de*) 3 swine.

In the time of King Edward and afterwards (this) was worth 10 shillings ; now 40 shillings.

IN SOANEBERGE [SWANBOROUGH] HUNDRED

William son of Reinald holds of William ACESCOME [Ashcombe[5]]. Cola held it in the time of King Edward. Then, as (et) now, it was assessed for 2 hides. On the demesne is 1 plough, and (there are) 5 villeins with 3 ploughs. The villeins themselves are in the rape of the Count of Mortain, but they have always been outside the rape.[6]

In the time of King Edward and afterwards, as (et) now, it was worth 26 shillings.

fo. 28a

XIII. THE LAND OF WILLIAM DE BRAIOSE

IN BURBECE [BURBEACH] HUNDRED

William de Braiose holds BEDDINGES [Beeding]. King Edward held it as part of (the sources of) his ferm (*in firmam suam*). Then it was assessed for 32 hides. It has not paid geld. Of these hides William de Warene has 10 hides in his rape.[7] William de Braiose holds the others. There is land for 28 ploughs. On the demesne are 4 ploughs, and (there are) 62 villeins and 48 bordars with 24 ploughs. There (are) 2 churches,[8] and 6 acres of meadow. Wood(land yielding) 70 swine, and 20 swine from the gafol-rent (*de gablo*), and 2 sestiers of honey.

of the hall which Scolland gave and the tithe of Alfred the earl's foster-father ' (*nutricius*).

[5] In the parish of Westout, Lewes.

[6] A very puzzling and obscure phrase.

[7] Of this, 7 hides ½ virgate were in Aldrington (see p. 439), and in Street Hundred were 3 virgates (see p. 442) ; I am inclined to think that the latter should be 3 hides—which would account for the 10 hides belonging to the manor—especially as the Street estate is said to have 5 ploughlands, which would be a very large allowance for 3 virgates.

[8] One of these was probably the church, or chapel, *de Veteri Ponte* on the old bridge between Bramber and Beeding ; the other being the church of Beeding.

[1] These are probably Ralph de Caisned's sons.

[2] In the parish of St. John-sub-Castro, Lewes.

[3] In Falmer, east of Stanmer Park ; occurs in 760 as Mulestana (Birch, *Cart. Sax.* i. 380). Ex inform. W. Renshaw, K. C.

[4] In Twineham Lewes Priory held ' the tithe

In the time of King Edward it rendered one day's ferm (*unum diem de firma*) and was worth 95 pounds 5 shillings and 6 pence, and afterwards it was worth 50 pounds; now 40 pounds. All this land renders Herdigelt.

William himself holds 8 hides which formed part of (*jacuerunt in*) REDMELLE [Rodmell] which William de Warene holds in his rape, and they are assessed for 5½ hides. There are 10 villeins who have 5½ ploughs, and 4 acres of meadow. In the time of King Edward and afterwards, as (*et*) now, (this) was worth 8 pounds.

The same William holds 7 hides which were part of (*jacuerunt in*) BERTS [Berth[1]] which William (de Warene) has in his rape. It was an outlying estate (*berewicha*). Now they are assessed for 1 hide and a half. On the demesne are 2 ploughs, and (there are) 3 villeins and 6 bordars with 2½ ploughs.

In the time of King Edward (this) was worth 6 pounds, and afterwards 55 shillings; now 4 pounds.

William himself holds ERINGEHA(M) [Erringham[2]]. Fredri held it of King Edward and could betake himself (*ire*) whither he pleased. Then it was assessed for 5 hides, now for half a hide. There (are) 2 villeins and 5 bordars who have nothing (*nil habentes*). In the time of King Edward, as (*et*) now, it was worth 40 shillings; when received 20 shillings.

William himself holds SORESHA(M) [Shoreham]. Azor held it of King Edward. Then it was assessed for 12 hides; now for 5 hides and half a virgate. There is land for 15 ploughs. On the demesne are 3 ploughs, and (there are) 26 villeins and 49 bordars with 12 ploughs. There (is) a church, and 6 acres of meadow, and wood(land) yielding (*de*) 40 swine.

In the time of King Edward it was worth 25 pounds, and afterwards 16 pounds; now 35 pounds, and yet it was farmed (*fuit ad firmam*) for 50 pounds, but that could not be borne (*pati*).

William a knight holds of William TRAILGI

[Truleigh[3]]. Bedling (held it) of Earl Godwin in the time of King Edward. Then it was assessed for 4 hides; now for nothing. There is land for 2½ ploughs. On the demesne (is) 1 plough, and (there are) 3 villeins and 6 bordars with half a plough,[4] and 2 mills yielding (*de*) 65 pence.

Of this land Ansfrid holds half a hide, and there he has half a plough.

The whole manor in the time of King Edward was worth 4 pounds, and afterwards 60 shillings; now 70 shillings.

William himself holds in demesne TOTINTUNE [Tottington[5]]. It was part of (*jacuit in*) Fintune [Findon]. An outlying estate (*berewicha*). Harold (*Hairaudus*) held it in the time of King Edward. Then it was assessed for 6 hides; now for 1 hide. There is land for 5 ploughs. On the demesne is 1 (plough), and (there are) 3 villeins and 7 bordars with 2 ploughs, and 4 acres of meadow.

Of this land a certain William holds 2 hides, and there he has 3 villeins with 1 plough and a half.

The whole in the time of King Edward and afterwards, as (*et*) now, was worth 6 pounds.

IN STANINGES [STEYNING] HUNDRED

William himself holds HANINGEDUNE [Annington]. Norman held it of King Edward. Then it was assessed for 12 hides; now for 6 hides. There is land for 5 ploughs. On the demesne is 1 (plough), and (there are) 15 villeins and 34 bordars with 4 ploughs. There (is) a church.[6] Wood(land yielding) 10 swine.

In the time of King Edward and afterwards it was worth 12 pounds; now 25 pounds.

William himself holds WASINGETUNE [Washington]. Earl Guerd[7] held it in the time of King Edward. Then it was assessed for 59 hides. Now it does not give geld. In one of these hides is situated (*sedet*) the castle of BRE(M)BRE [Bramber]. There is land for 34 ploughs. On the demesne are 5 ploughs, and (there are) 120 villeins and 25 bordars with 34 ploughs. There are 5 salt-pans yielding (*de*) 110 ambers of salt or 9

---

[1] A farm in Wivelsfield. This is the identification given in S.D.B. and seems probable; as the manor is not mentioned by name in William de Warene's rape it must have been included in some other manor, most likely that of Herst (see note 1, p. 441).

[2] A manor in Upper Beeding and Old Shoreham.

[3] A manor in Edburton. Two hides of this manor were in Perching (see p. 439).

[4] *Cum dimidia caruca* underlined for deletion.

[5] In Upper Beeding.

[6] The church of (St.) Botolphs, in which parish Annington lies.

[7] Brother of Harold.

THE HOLDERS OF LANDS

shillings and 2 pence,[1] and 4 acres of meadow. From the pannage of the wood(land come) 60 swine. There (are) 6 serfs.

Of this land Gilbert holds half a hide, Ralph 1 hide, William 3 virgates, Lewin half a hide, and he (*qui*) could betake himself elsewhere (*recedere*) with his land and gave geld to his lord and his lord gave nothing.[2] These men have 4 villeins and 2 bordars with 2½ ploughs, and 7 acres of meadow, and wood(land) yielding (*de*) 10 swine.

The whole manor in the time of King Edward was worth 50 pounds, and afterwards 50 pounds. Now William's demesne (is worth) 50 pounds and 5 shillings, (that) of the knights 50 shillings and 12 pence. Yet this manor was farmed for (*fuit ad firmam ad*) 100 pounds.

William himself holds STANINGES [Steyning[3]]. King Edward held it as part of (the sources of) his ferm (*ad suam firmam*). Then it was assessed for 18 hides and 3 virgates. It has never paid geld. Of these hides William has 12 hides, the others are in the rape of Earl Roger attached to (*in*) Garinges [Goring].[4] In the hides which William has there is land for 21 ploughs. On the demesne are 2 ploughs, and (there are) 45 villeins and 33 bordars with 18 ploughs. There (is) 1 mill unrented (*sine censu*), and 3 saltpans yielding (*de*) 30 pence, and 5 acres of meadow. Wood(land yielding) 20 swine from the pannage.

In the time of King Edward it was worth 28 pounds, and afterwards 20 pounds; now 25 pounds.

William himself holds FINDUNE [Findon]. Harold held it in the time of King Edward. Then it was assessed for 30½ hides. Of these 10 hides are in the rape of Earl Roger.[5] The others have not paid geld, except 3 hides. There is land for 17 ploughs. On the de-

mesne are 3 ploughs; and (there are) 27 villeins and 17 bordars with 17 ploughs. There (is) a church, and 6 serfs, and wood(land yielding) 20 swine.

Of this land a certain William holds 5 hides, and (there are) 2 ploughs on (his) demesne, and (there are) 2 villeins and 6 bordars with 1 plough.

The whole in the time of King Edward was worth 28 pounds, and afterwards 20 pounds; now 28 pounds and 10 shillings.

William himself holds SEMLINTUN [Sullington]. Ulward held it of King Edward. Then it was assessed for 9 hides; now for 4 hides. Of this land 3 virgates are in the rape of Arundel.[6] There is land for 7 ploughs. On the demesne are 3 ploughs, and (there are) 20 villeins and 14 bordars with 6 ploughs. There (is) 1 mill yielding (*de*) 6 shillings, and 6 acres of meadow. Wood(land yielding) 30 swine.

In the time of King Edward it was worth 9 pounds, and afterwards, and now, 8 pounds.

Ralph holds of William WISTANESTUN [Wiston]. Azor held it of Earl Godwin. Then it was assessed for 12 hides. Now for nothing. There is land for 8 ploughs. On the demesne are 2 ploughs, and (there are) 10 villeins and 24 bordars with 5 ploughs. There (is) a church, and 5 serfs, and 7 acres of meadow. Wood(land yielding) 30 swine. In the time of King Edward, as (*et*) now, it was worth 12 pounds; when received 4 pounds.

William son of Manna holds of William WAPINGETORNE [Wappingthorne[7]]. Carle held it of King Edward. Then it was assessed for 6 hides; now for 2 hides. There is land for 6 ploughs. On the demesne is 1 plough, and (there are) 7 villeins and 15 bordars with 4 ploughs. There (are) 7 acres of meadow. Wood(land) yielding (*de*) 5 pence. From salt 20 pence, and 1 sestier of honey.

In the time of King Edward it was worth 100 shillings, and afterwards 20 shillings; now 4 pounds.

Gilbert holds of William CLOPEHA(M) [Clapham]. Alwin held it of King Edward, and it was part of (*jacuit in*) Lolinminstre [Lyminster] which Earl Roger holds in his rape.[8] Then it was assessed for 8 hides, but

---

[1] As this shows the value of an amber of salt to be one penny it enables us to estimate the annual output of the saltpans throughout the county.

[2] This is a remarkable phrase, and has considerable importance in connection with the question of geld liability. (See Introd. p. 361.)

[3] See note 2, p. 392.

[4] These 6 hides were the 'berewick' of King Edward mentioned under Goring (see note 1, p. 430).

[5] These I cannot trace; but as the only mention of land held by Harold in Earl Roger's rape is in Avisford Hundred, where there are a number of nameless holdings, it is not unlikely that the 10 hides lay in that Hundred. Another 6 hides belonging to Findon now formed the manor of Tottington (see p. 444).

[6] One virgate is accounted for in West Easwrith Hundred (see note 2, p. 428).

[7] A manor in Steyning.

[8] See note 4, p. 429.

2 hides are in the rape of Earl Roger. What Gilbert holds has paid geld for 3 hides. There is land for 4 ploughs. On the demesne are 2 ploughs, and (there are) 5 villeins and 8 bordars with 2 ploughs.

In the time of King Edward it was worth 8 pounds, and afterwards 4 pounds ; now 6 pounds.

The same Gilbert holds of William land for 3 ploughs. This was part of (*jacuit in*) Garinges [Goring] which is in the rape of Earl Roger.[1] It is outside the rape and not assessed in hides (*extra numerum hidarum*). It has never paid geld. There are 6 villeins and 5 bordars with 3 ploughs.

In the time of King Edward and afterwards, as (*et*) now, it was worth 30 shillings.

Richard holds of William CENGELTUNE [Chancton[2]]. Essocher held it of Earl Godwin. Then it was assessed for 4 hides; now for nothing. There is land for 2 ploughs. On the demesne is 1 plough, with 5 bordars.

In the time of King Edward it was worth 4 pounds, and afterwards 40 shillings ; now 60 shillings.

fo. 28b

[3]Tetbert holds 1 hide in Cengeltune [Chancton] of William. Werun held it of Earl Godwin. [It paid geld for 1 hide; now for nothing.[4]] There is nothing there. It is worth 11 shillings.

William son of Norman holds CUMBE [Coombes] of William. Guert held it in the time of King Edward. Then it was assessed for 10 hides; now for 5 hides. There is land for 8 ploughs. On the demesne are 2 (ploughs), and (there are) 27 villeins and 4 bordars with 10 ploughs. There (is) a church, and 2 serfs, and from the saltpans 50 shillings and 5 pence. Wood(land) yielding (*de*) 4 swine.

In the time of King Edward it was worth 12 pounds, and afterwards 10 pounds ; now 13 pounds.

The same William holds of William APLESHAM [Applesham[5]]. Lewin held it of Earl Godwin. Then it was assessed for 7½ hides, now for nothing. There is land for 5

ploughs. On the demesne are 3 ploughs, and (there are) 7 villeins and 7 bordars with 2 ploughs. There (is) 1 serf, and 1 mill yielding (*de*) 6 shillings ; and 5 acres of meadow, and wood(land) yielding (*de*) 5 swine.

In the time of King Edward and afterwards, as (*et*) now, it was worth 6 pounds.

Two knights hold of this land 1 hide and a half, and there is 1 bordar, and 2 saltpans yielding (*de*) 5 shillings. (This) is worth 23 shillings and 4 pence.

The same William holds of William in OFINTUNE [Offington] 2 hides. They have not paid geld. Godwin held them. There is 1 plough on the demesne. Nothing more. It is and was worth 26 shillings.

IN HA(M)FELT [TIPNOAK] HUNDRED

William son of Rannulf[6] holds of William ODEMANSCOTE [Woodmancote]. Countess Guda held it. Then it was assessed for 3½ hides ; now for 2 hides. There is land for 9 ploughs. On the demesne is 1 plough, and (there are) 16 villeins and 4 bordars with 8 ploughs. There (is) a church, and 5 acres of meadow. Wood(land yielding) 13 swine.

Of this land a certain knight holds 1 hide, and there he has 1 plough, with 1 villein. In the time of King Edward and afterwards, as (*et*) now, (the whole) was worth 3 pounds and 10 shillings.

Ralph[7] holds of William WANTELEI [Wantley[8]]. Bricmar held it of Azor, and Azor of Harold. Then it was assessed for 4½ hides ; now for nothing. There is land for 2 ploughs. On the demesne is 1 (plough), and (there are) 2 villeins and 2 bordars with half a plough. There (are) 2 serfs, and 1 mill[9] yielding (*de*) 20 pence, and 10 acres of meadow.

In the time of King Edward and afterwards it was worth 40 shillings ; now 22 shillings.

WINDEHA(M) [WINDHAM] HUNDRED

The same Ralph holds of William in OVELEI [? Woolfly[10]] half a hide. Alwin held it of

---

[1] See note 3, p. 430.
[2] A manor in Washington.
[3] Tetbert gave to Battle Abbey 1 hide '*que vocatur hida Wulurun*' in Heregrave (near Worminghurst) (Burrell MSS.).
[4] Marginal note.
[5] A manor in Coombes.

[6] He appears to have been the ancestor of the family of le Counte, as all his estates in this rape are afterwards found in the possession of that family. (See Introd. p. 379.)
[7] Probably Ralph de Buci, as Hugh de Buscy afterwards quitclaimed certain lands in Wantele to Lewes Priory.
[8] In Henfield. [9] See note 1, p. 390.
[10] A farm in Henfield near Shermanbury. The similarity of the names and the suitability of the position make this identification almost certain.

Azor, and then it was assessed for half a hide, now for nothing. There is nothing there except 10 acres of meadow. It is worth 5 shillings.

The same Ralph holds of William Sal-monesberie [Shermanbury]. Azor held it of Harold. Then it was assessed for 2 hides; now for nothing. There is land for 2 ploughs. On the demesne is 1 plough, and (there is) 1 villein and 3 bordars with 1 plough. There (is) a chapel (*ecclesiola*), and 4 serfs.
In the time of King Edward and afterwards, as (*et*) now, it was worth 24 shillings.

William son of Rannulf holds of William half a hide in Morleia [Morley[1]]. Alward held it of Azor, and it was assessed for half a hide then, as (*et*) now. There is half a plough, with 2 bordars. In the time of King Edward and afterwards it was worth 10 shillings; now 5 shillings.

The same William holds of William Sacheha(m) [Sakeham[2]]. Brictuin held it of Azor. Then it was assessed for 2 hides; now for nothing. There is land for 2 ploughs. There (are) now only two oxen (*animalia*), and 1 villein and 2 bordars. Wood(land) yielding (*de*) 10 pence. In the time of King Edward and afterwards it was worth 10 shillings; now 5 shillings.

In Eldritune [Fishergate] Hundred

Ralph[3] holds of William Chingestune [Kingston-Bucy]. Azor held it of Harold. Then it was assessed for 21 hides. Of these 6 hides are in the rape of William de Warene.[4] What Ralph holds has paid geld for 6 hides. There is land for 8 ploughs. On the demesne are 2 ploughs, and (there are) 12 villeins and 20 bordars with 10 ploughs. There (is) a church, and 6 saltpans yielding (*de*) 20 shillings and 10 ambers of salt.
Of this land 3 knights hold 4½ hides, and there they have 2 ploughs and 2 villeins and 6 bordars.
The whole manor in the time of King Edward was worth 15 pounds. Now Ralph's

share (is worth) 11 pounds and 7 shillings and 6 pence. What the knights hold is worth 100 shillings.

In the same vill William son of Rannulf[5] holds of William 7 hides all but (*minus*) 1 virgate. Gunnild held them of Harold, and for so much they were assessed. There is land for 3 ploughs. On the demesne are 2 ploughs, and (there are) 4 villeins and 8 bordars with 1 plough. There (is) a church, and 1 serf, and 3 saltpans yielding (*de*) 22 pence. From pasture 16 shillings, and 4 acres of meadow.
In the time of King Edward, as (*et*) now, it was worth 7 pounds; when received 3 pounds.

In Bredford [Brightford] Hundred

Robert[6] holds of William Bradewatre [Broadwater]. Wigot held it of King Edward.[7] Then it was assessed for 29 hides. Of these 9 hides are in the rape of William de Warene,[8] and William de Braiose has 2 hides in demesne. What Robert holds has paid geld for 6 hides. There is land for 7 ploughs. On the demesne are 2 ploughs, and (there are) 30 villeins and 4 bordars with 10 ploughs. There (is) a church and 3 serfs, and 1 mill yielding (*de*) 7 shillings, and 60 acres of meadow. Wood(land yielding) 20 swine.

Of this land 1 knight holds 1 hide.
The whole in the time of King Edward and afterwards was worth[9] 15 pounds; now 14 pounds.

Ralph holds of William Hene [Heene]. Levret held it of Earl Godwin. Then, as (*et*) now, it was assessed for 2½ hides. On the demesne is 1 plough, and (there are) 3 villeins and 2 bordars with 1 plough, and 1 serf, and 3 acres of meadow. It is and was worth 40 shillings.

In the same vill Alward holds of William 2½ hides. He himself held it of King

[1] In Woodmancote.
[2] In Shermanbury.
[3] Ralph de Buci, from whom the manor took the name of Kingston-Bucy, now corrupted to Kingston-by-Sea.
[4] At Hangleton were 14 hides and 1 virgate ascribed to this manor (see p. 439), from which it would appear that 6 hides is an error due to confusion with Ralph's own 6 hides.

[5] As Simon le Counte (see note 6, p. 446) gave the church of Southwick to the Knights Templars this estate is probably Southwick.
[6] All the estates held by Robert in this rape are to be attributed to Robert 'Salvagius' and subsequently passed to Hawysa le Sauvage, who married John de Gatesden, from whom they went by marriage to the family of Camoys.
[7] Wigot appears to have made an exchange of part of this manor with Humphrey Visdelupo for 2 hides in Kingsclere Hundred in Hampshire (see *V.C.H. Hants,* i. 508).
[8] These 9 hides were at Aldrington (see p. 439).
[9] *Totum T.R.E.* [b]*valebat* [a]*et post.*

Edward. Then, as now, it was assessed for 2½ hides. [1] On the demesne is 1 plough, and (there are) 3 villeins and 5 bordars with 1 plough. It is and was worth 40 shillings.

Robert holds of William DERENTUNE [Durrington]. Ulward held it of Earl Harold. Then it was assessed for 4 hides, now for 1 hide. There is land for 2 ploughs. There are 2 villeins and 5 bordars with half a plough, and 4 acres of meadow. Wood(land yielding) 4 swine. Of this land 1 Frenchman (*francigena*) holds 1 hide and a half, and there (are) 2 bordars.

In the time of King Edward and afterwards it was worth 40 shillings; now 60 shillings.

The same Robert holds in the same place of William DERENTUNE [Durrington]. Edward held it of King Edward. Then it was assessed for 8 hides; now for 2 hides and 1 virgate. There is land for 6 ploughs. On the demesne is 1 plough, and (there are) 9 villeins and 9 bordars with 7 ploughs. There (is) a church, and 4 serfs, and 8 acres of meadow. Wood(land yielding) 10 swine.

In the time of King Edward and afterwards, as (*et*) now, it was worth 100 shillings.

The same Robert holds of William ORDINGES [Worthing]. Seven alodial tenants (*alodarii*) held it of Earl Godwin. Then it was assessed for 11 hides. Now Robert has 9 hides and they have paid geld for 2 hides. There is land for 3 ploughs. On the demesne are 2 ploughs, and (there are) 6 villeins and 9 bordars with 1 plough. There (is) 1 serf, and 7 acres of meadow.

In the time of King Edward and afterwards, as (*et*) now, it was worth 100 shillings.

Robert holds of William MORDINGES [Worthing]. There is 1 hide and a half. Lewin held it of King (Edward), and it has paid geld for half a hide. [2] There (is) 1 villein and 5 bordars, and half an acre of meadow. It is and was worth 12 shillings.

In the same vill Ralph holds half a hide. It was part of (*jacuit in*) Stultinges [Sompting]. Tosti held it of Lewin, and it was assessed for half a hide [3] then, as (*et*) now. There are 4 oxen, and 1 bordar, and 1 acre of meadow. It is worth 5 shillings, and was worth (so much).

Ralph holds of William SULTINGES [Sompting]. Lewin held it of King Edward. Then it was assessed for 17 hides. Of these 2 hides are in the rape of Earl Roger, attached to (*in*) Garinges [Goring]; and in other manors (*alibi*) are 3½ hides which other men hold. Ralph has in his own hand 11½ hides.
fo. 29a
Now they pay geld for 2 hides and 3 virgates. There is land for 5 ploughs. On the demesne are 2 ploughs, and (there are) 19 villeins and 16 bordars with 9 ploughs. There (is) a church, and 5 serfs, and 1 mill yielding (*de*) 3 shillings, and 8 saltpans yielding (*de*) 13 shillings, and 30 acres of meadow.

Of this land a knight holds 1 hide and a half, and has on (his) demesne 1 plough, and 2 villeins and 4 bordars, and 1 saltpan yielding (*de*) 2 shillings, and 2 acres of meadow.

The whole in the time of King Edward and afterwards was worth 8 pounds; now 7 pounds and 8 shillings.

Of the same manor another Ralph holds of William 2 hides, but they are additional to the hides assessed above (*super numerum hidarum superiorum*). Lewin held them of King Edward, and then they were assessed for 2 hides; now for 1½. There are 4 villeins and 1 bordar with half a plough, and 2 acres of meadow. There is land for 1 plough.

In the time of King Edward and afterwards (this) was worth 50 shillings; now 70 shillings.

Of the selfsame manor Robert holds of William 1 hide additional to the hides assessed above (*super numerum hidarum superiorum*).[4] Lewin held it, and then it was assessed for 1 hide; now for half [5] a virgate. There is 1 villein and 1 bordar, and 4 acres of meadow. It is worth 8 shillings and was worth (so much).

Ralph holds of William COCHEHA(M) [Cokeham[6]]. Grene held it of Earl Harold. Then it was assessed for 2 hides and 1 virgate; now for nothing. On the demesne is 1 plough with 5 bordars, and 8 acres of meadow. It is worth 55 shillings and always (was worth so much).

---

[1] A space left for the plough-lands.
[2] A space left for the plough-lands.
[3] *Tanto* altered to *dimidia hida*.
[4] This is probably the manor of Sompting-Weald, a detached portion of Sompting manor lying in Itchingfield, where the family of le Sauvage held land.
[5] *Una* altered to *dimidia*.
[6] A manor in Sompting.

The same Ralph holds of William DEN-
TUNE [¹]. Auti held it of Earl
Godwin. Then it was assessed for 5 hides;
now for 1 hide and 3 virgates. There is
land for 2 ploughs. Of this land William
holds 2 hides and 1 virgate, Robert 1 hide and
1 virgate, and another knight 1 hide and a
half. On the demesne is nothing save only
(*sed tantum*) 2 villeins and 3 bordars, and 10
acres of meadow.

The whole in the time of King Edward
and afterwards, as (*et*) now, (was worth) 72
shillings.

Robert holds of William LANCINGES [Lan-
cing]. Lewin held it of King Edward.
Then it was assessed for 16 hides and 1 virgate. Of these Robert himself has 12 hides
and 1 virgate, and they have paid geld for 5
hides and 1 virgate and a half. There is land
for 5 ploughs. On the demesne are 2½ ploughs,
and (there are) 13 villeins and 7 bordars with
2 ploughs. There (is) 1 mill yielding (*de*)
8 shillings, and 7 saltpans yielding (*de*) 20
shillings and 3 pence.

Of this land 2 knights hold 2½ hides and
half a virgate, and there they have on (their)
demesne 2 ploughs, and 11 saltpans yielding
(*de*) 12 shillings and 6 pence.

The whole in the time of King Edward
was worth 9 pounds, and afterwards 7 pounds;
now 14 pounds and 10 shillings.

In the same vill Ralph holds 3½ virgates,
and they are (part) of the abovesaid 16 hides,
and have paid geld for 1 virgate. There is
1 villein and 2 bordars. (This) is worth 5
shillings.

Of the self-same manor another Ralph
holds 3 hides and 1 virgate, and they are
likewise of the above 16 hides. This land of
Ralph's has paid geld for 3 virgates, and does
(*facit*) now. On the demesne is 1 plough,
and (there are) 2 villeins and 2 bordars with
half a plough. There (are) 5 saltpans yielding (*de*) 12 shillings and 6 pence. (This) is
and was worth 50 shillings.

And moreover Ralph holds 1 virgate which
was part of (*jacuit in*) Lancinges [Lancing]
and gave geld. One villein holds and held it.
It is and was worth 5 shillings.

Ralph son of Tedric holds of William
COOHEHA(M) ² [Cokeham]. Brismar held it

of Azor. Then, as (*et*) now, it was assessed
for 1 hide and a half. On the demesne is
half a plough, and (there is) 1 villein and 3
bordars with half a plough, a saltpan yielding
(*de*) 40 pence, and 2 acres of meadow. Wood-
(land yielding) 1 pig. It is worth 15 shillings, and was worth (so much).

William son of Bonard holds of William
an outlying estate which formed part of (*unam
berewicam que jacuit in*) HERST [Hurstpier-
point], a manor which William de Warene
holds.³ It is called How [How Court⁴].
Earl Godwin held it. Then it was assessed
for 6 hides; now for 2 hides all but (*minus*)
1 virgate. There is land for 6 ploughs. On
the demesne are 2 ploughs, and there are 14
villeins and 8 bordars with 4 ploughs. There
(are) 6 saltpans yielding (*de*) 7 shillings and 6
pence.

Of this land a knight holds 1 hide, and
there he has half a plough.

The whole in the time of King Edward
and afterwards was worth 4 pounds; now 6
pounds.

IN ISEWERIT [EAST ESEWRITH] HUNDRED

Robert holds of William ESSINGETUNE
[Ashington]. Two alodial tenants (*alodiarii*)
held it of Earl Godwin. Then it was assessed
for 2½ hides; now for nothing. It was part
of (*jacuit in*) Wasingetune [Washington].
There is land for 3 ploughs. On the demesne is 1 (plough), and (there are) 6 villeins
and 2 bordars with 1 plough and a half. It
is worth and always was worth 30 shillings.

Ralph ⁵ holds of William 3 hides belonging
to (*in*) Cilletune [West Chiltington], which
is in the rape of Earl Roger. They have
not paid geld. There is land for 6 ploughs.
On the demesne is half a plough, and (there
are) 18 villeins and 6 bordars with 3½ ploughs.
There (are) 6 acres of meadow, and wood-
(land yielding) 30 swine.

In the time of King Edward and afterwards, as (*et*) now, (this) was worth 60
shillings.

Morin holds of William TACEHA(M)
[Thakeham]. Brixi held it of King Edward.

---

¹ This name is now lost, but Mr. Round points
out that it is evidently identical with Dentunninga,
one of the boundary marks in a charter of King
Edwig in 956 (*Abingdon Chron.* [Rolls Series] i.
228).

² A clerical error for Cocheha(m).

³ See p. 441.

⁴ A manor in Lancing. It is rather curious
that this detached portion of Earl Godwin's manor
'is called How,' while a detached portion of
another of his manors became 'the manor which
is called Hou' in Hastings rape.

⁵ Ralph de Caisned gave land in 'Cylentona' to
Lewes Priory.

Then it was assessed for 20 hides and 3 virgates ; now for 5 hides. There is land for 14 ploughs. On the demesne are 2 ploughs, and (there are) 30 villeins and 12 bordars with 8 ploughs. There (is) a church and 1 mill yielding (*de*) 3 shillings, and 16 acres of meadow. Wood(land yielding) 60 swine.

Of this land a knight holds 1 hide. There he has 5 oxen with 1 bordar.

The whole in the time of King Edward, as (*et*) now, was worth 14 pounds ; when received 10 pounds.

The same Morin holds of William Moha(m) [Muntham[1]]. Osward held it of King Edward. Then it was assessed for 3 hides ; now for nothing. There is land for 2 ploughs. There are 5 villeins and 6 bordars with 2 ploughs. Wood(land yielding) 5 swine. In the time of King Edward it was worth 50 shillings, and afterwards 30 shillings ; now 70 shillings.

The same Morin holds of William 1 hide which was part of (*jacuit in*) Wasingetune [Washington]. Edwin held it of Earl Godwin. Then it was assessed for 1 hide ; now for nothing. There is 1 villein, and 1 mill yielding (*de*) 15 pence. It is worth 10 shillings and always (was worth so much).

Alviet holds of William land for 1 plough ; (it is part) of William's demesne and is not assessed in hides (*sine numero hide*). There is 1 plough, and 1 mill yielding (*de*) 3 shillings. It was part of (*jacuit in*) Storgetune [Storrington] as (*in*) pasture.[2] Now it has been lately brought under cultivation (*noviter est hospitata*).[3] It is worth 10 shillings.

In Grenestede [West Grinstead] Hundred

William son of Bonard holds of William Etune [Eatons[4]]. Turgod held it of Earl Godwin. Then it was assessed for 3½ hides ; now for 1 hide. It was part of (*jacuit in*) Garneca(m)po [Warningcamp] which is in the rape of Earl Roger. There is land for 2 ploughs. On the demesne is 1 (plough), and

[1] There are two manors of this name, one in Findon, Sullington and Washington, and the other, which is held of Thakeham manor, in Itchingfield; it is probable that at the time of the Domesday Survey the two were united.
[2] See note 2, p. 427.
[3] 'Farmed' in the modern agricultural sense of the word would be the best rendering of *hospitata*, as it implies occupation as well as cultivation.
[4] A farm in Ashurst.

(there are) 5 villeins and 3 bordars with 1 plough, and 6 acres of meadow. Wood(land) yielding (*de*) 5 pence. In the time of King Edward it was worth 20 shillings and afterwards 15 shillings ; now 40 shillings.

In Tifeld [Burbeach] Hundred

William son of Rannulf holds of William Ifelt [Ifield]. Alwi held it of King Edward. Then, as (*et*) now, it was assessed for 1 hide. On the demesne is nothing, and (there are) 5 villeins and 4 bordars with 1 plough, and 6 acres of meadow, and wood(land yielding) 6 swine. It is worth 20 shillings and was worth (so much).

The same William holds half a hide which was part of (*jacuit in*) Soreha(m) [Shoreham] which William de Braiose holds. This hide (*sic*) is exempt (*quieta*) from geld. There is 1 villein with half a plough. It is worth 6 shillings.

In Staninges [Steyning] Hundred

Robert holds of William Bongetune [Buncton[5]]. Lewin held it of King Edward. Then it was assessed for 4½ hides ; now for nothing. There is land for 5 ploughs. On the demesne is 1 plough, and (there are) 19 villeins and 7 bordars with 5 ploughs. There (are) 2 acres of meadow, wood(land yielding) 10 swine, and 1 mill yielding (*de*) 2 shillings. In the time of King Edward and afterwards (it was worth) 30 shillings ; now 40 shillings.

The same Robert has a small pasture with 2 bordars who return 5 shillings. This belongs to (*est in*) Langemare [? Angmering] which Earl Roger holds in his rape.

XIIII. THE LAND OF ODO AND ELDRED[6]

In Esborne [Easebourne] Hundred

Odo holds of the king Welbedlinge [Woolbeding]. Fulcui held it of King Edward (as) an alod (*alodium*). Then, as (*et*) now, it was assessed for 6 hides. There is land for 7 ploughs. On the demesne is 1 plough, and (there are) 14 villeins and 5 bordars with 6 ploughs. There (are) 5 serfs, and 1 mill yielding (*de*) 10 shillings, and 23 acres of meadow. Wood(land) yielding (*de*) 30 swine. There (is) a church.

In the time of King Edward, as (*et*) now, it was worth 6 pounds ; when received 4 pounds.

[5] A manor in Ashington.
[6] Eldred was brother to Ode of Winchester.

THE HOLDERS OF LANDS

Aldred holds of the king Epinges [Iping]. Oualet held it of King Edward. Then, as (*et*) now, it was assessed for 4 hides. There is land for 3 ploughs. On the demesne is 1 plough, and (there are) 8 villeins and 2 bordars with 2 ploughs. There (are) 5 serfs, and 1 mill yielding 3 shillings and 4 pence, and 4 acres of meadow; woodland yielding (*de*) 20 swine, and a quarry (*quadraria*) yielding (*de*) 9 shillings and 4 pence. One haw yielding (*de*) 20 pence. From circet[1] 40 pence.

In the time of King Edward, as (*et*) now, (it was worth) 4 pounds; when received 4 pounds.

IN SURREY

[2] In Wodetone [Wotton] Hundred

Earl Roger has of the king 1 hide, which belongs to (*jacet in*) Contone [Compton], his manor in Sudsexe [Sussex]. In the time of King Edward he who held Contone held this hide of the king. It was then assessed for 1 hide, now for nothing. There is in demesne 1 plough. In the time of King Edward it

[1] A payment of corn due to the priest of the parish.

[2] *V.C.H. Surrey*, i. 313.

was worth 20 shillings, and afterwards, and now, 15 shillings.

[3] In Cherchefelle [Reigate] Hundred

Siward holds of Richard (de Tonbridge) Orde [Worth in Sussex]. Oswol held it of King Edward. Then, and now, it (was and) is assessed for half a hide. There is 1 villein with half a plough. In the time of King Edward it was worth 30 shillings, and afterwards 2 shillings; now 20 shillings.

[4] In Wochinges [Woking] Hundred

Chetel the huntsman holds of the king Lodesorde [? Lodsworth in Sussex]. His father held it of King Edward. It was then assessed for 1 hide; now for half. The land is for 2 ploughs. In demesne there is 1, and (there are) 2 villeins and 5 bordars with 1 plough. There is a mill worth 2 shillings, and 4 acres of meadow. Wood worth 20 hogs. It is, and was, worth 50 shillings.

[3] Ibid. 316.
[4] Ibid. p. 328. But Woking Hundred does not seem likely to have contained Lodsworth, which is not near it.

EARTHWORKS

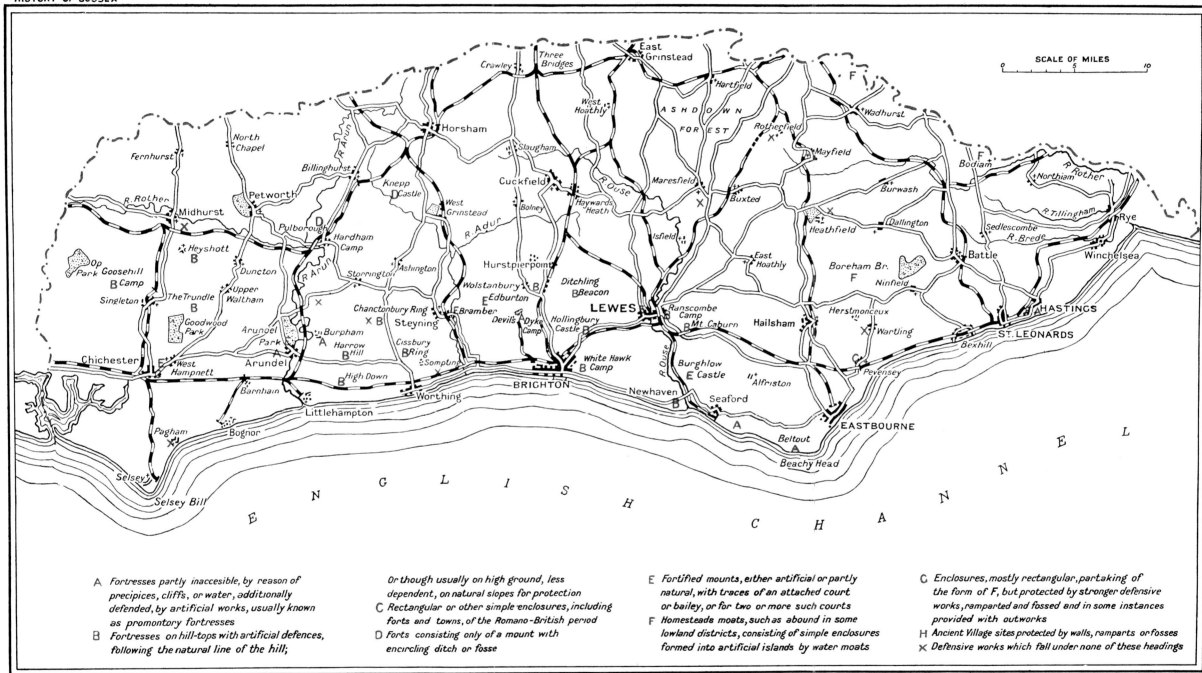

SCALE OF MILES

A Fortresses partly inaccessible, by reason of precipices, cliffs, or water, additionally defended, by artificial works, usually known as promontory fortresses

B Fortresses on hill-tops with artificial defences, following the natural line of the hill;

Or though usually on high ground, less dependent, on natural slopes for protection

C Rectangular or other simple enclosures, including forts and towns, of the Romano-British period

D Forts consisting only of a mount with encircling ditch or fosse

E Fortified mounts, either artificial or partly natural, with traces of an attached court or bailey, or for two or more such courts

F Homesteads moats, such as abound in some lowland districts, consisting of simple enclosures formed into artificial islands by water moats

G Enclosures, mostly rectangular, partaking of the form of F, but protected by stronger defensive works, ramparted and fossed and in some instances provided with outworks

H Ancient Village sites protected by walls, ramparts or fosses

X Defensive works which fall under none of these headings

ANCIENT EARTHWORKS

THE earthworks of Sussex are numerically and archæologically important. They present considerable variety of form, and are capable of definite classification.

In the present article it is proposed to deal with each of the earthworks in Sussex, and to illustrate by means of plans all the more important examples. It may be convenient to explain that the purpose is to record and describe each work, to give an account of its surroundings and strategic value, but not, except where sufficient and satisfactory evidence is available, to venture upon conjecture or speculation as to the period to which it belongs. The danger of assigning prehistoric and historic earthworks to definite dates or periods without a careful exploration and excavation on the site will be obvious to those who remember that several of the camps have been occupied at different periods, and that their defensive works may have been modified or extended by successive occupants. So little is known about objects which may lie below the surface, and the period they indicate, that the present state of archæological knowledge on the subject of British earthworks must be described as imperfect. In some cases probably nothing short of an elaborate investigation of the site will suffice to settle the question of age, but in the meanwhile the Congress of Archæological Societies has outlined an excellent scheme for recording ancient defensive earthworks and fortified enclosures. In the schedules contemplated by the Committee on Earthworks, with whom the scheme originated, it is suggested that 'though careful record should be made of any " finds " indicative of period of use of the forts, no effort need be made to assign a definite period of construction, excepting in those cases in which the age is beyond question, e.g. camps and fortified settlements of undoubted Roman origin, or enclosures of proved Neolithic, Bronze, or Iron Age.'

The following are the classes into which defensive works may be divided :—

'(A) Fortresses partly inaccessible, by reason of precipices, cliffs, or water, additionally defended by artificial banks or walls usually known as promontory fortresses.

(B) Fortresses on hill-tops with artificial defences, *following the natural line of the hill* ;

453

Or, though usually on high ground, less dependent on natural slopes for protection.

(C) Rectangular or other simple enclosures, including forts and towns of the Romano-British period.

(D) Forts consisting only of a mount with encircling ditch or fosse.

(E) Fortified mounts, either artificial or partly natural, with traces of an attached court or bailey, or of two or more such courts.

(F) Homestead moats, such as abound in some lowland districts, consisting of simple enclosures formed into artificial islands by water moats.

(G) Enclosures, mostly rectangular, partaking of the form of F, but protected by stronger defensive works, ramparted and fossed, and in some instances provided with outworks.

(H) Ancient village sites protected by walls, ramparts or fosses.

(X) Defensive works which fall under none of these headings.'

The above classification will be followed as closely as possible in the present article, but it will be necessary also for our purpose to deal briefly with sepulchral mounds, or barrows, and with other miscellaneous earthworks.

Before proceeding to deal with the earthworks in detail, a word or two may be conveniently written here as to the ground plans which are used as illustrations. These are in nearly every case founded upon the ordnance survey maps, tracings from those of the scale of 25 inches to the mile having been checked by a personal examination of each work. The plans of the Sussex earthworks as given on the ordnance survey maps can only be considered approximately correct, certain features having received detailed attention and others very little notice. Moreover, two very important points, viz. the contour of the surface of the interior of the camp, and the relation of the earthworks to the natural slopes in the vicinity, are not indicated.

In the plans given in the present article an attempt has been made to remedy these deficiencies by means of sketch sections where necessary.

It must be admitted that the officers responsible for the ordnance survey maps had no light task before them. Some of the camps have suffered considerably from weathering, the burrowings of rabbits, and accidental or intentional injury at the hand of man. In other cases considerable confusion has been caused by modifications and alterations of the earthworks at the hands of occupants at different periods.

PROMONTORY AND HILL FORTRESSES
[CLASSES A AND B]

The Sussex camps furnish examples of most of the classes just named. Those falling under classes A and B may, however, more conveniently be grouped together.

ANCIENT EARTHWORKS

The hill-top camps or earthworks of Sussex, which form a well-marked and interesting feature in the prehistoric archæology of the county, have been investigated by General Pitt-Rivers, and a memoir on the subject was read before the Society of Antiquaries of London[1] in 1868.

The following camps are essentially hill-top earthworks of the South Downs, commencing in the eastern part of Sussex.

BELTOUT.—This is an extensive work enclosing the highest part of a prominent hill close to the sea-shore and a little to the west of the new lighthouse at Beachy Head. In its present condition a space of about two-fifths of its circumference consists, not of rampart and ditch, but of dangerously steep sea-cliff, and the destruction of cliff and alteration of sea-coast at this point are proceeding at a rapid rate. The cliff, indeed, is practically perpendicular, and frequent falls of chalk testify to the rapidity with which the coast is being cut into by the action of the sea.

The question whether this earthwork was ever continuous round the top of the hill, enclosing the whole of the upper part of it, in the same way as Ditchling and Hollingbury, for example, is very difficult to settle. Judging from its present form, and the remains of the hill which the waves have spared, it seems not improbable that the ramparts may have extended originally entirely round the hill; but rapid as the waste of the chalk cliffs at this point is, the camp when first constructed can hardly have been far from the sea-shore, and it is by no means improbable that the steep, sheer cliffs may have furnished sufficient protection on one side, without requiring any special earthen defence of an artificial character. The great extent of the present works and the large area they enclose also point to such a possibility; yet the irregular and somewhat elongated shape offer almost equally clear evidence that a considerable part of the camp has been destroyed by the sea.

Allowing for only a moderate amount of waste, it is clear that Beltout must have been a very large and important work. It lies on a hill somewhat less than 300 ft. above the sea, and effectively overlooks the surrounding country. Its site, indeed, suggests that it was a valuable strategic point in the Beachy Head district. There is one weak point, however, which would be very serious from military point of view : there is no natural water supply. The obvious inference is that abundant as are neolithic implements in the neighbourhood, Beltout was only used as a temporary camp of refuge for families and cattle during periods of danger from marauding tribes. It is impossible to avoid being struck by the fact that this eminence would be well adapted for such a purpose.

The ramparts are slight, and were probably supplemented by palisading. As will be seen by the plan, there is a ditch, or fosse, on the outside, from which has been obtained the material for the construction of the rampart. Flint flakes, etc., are very abundant.

[1] *Arch.* xlii.

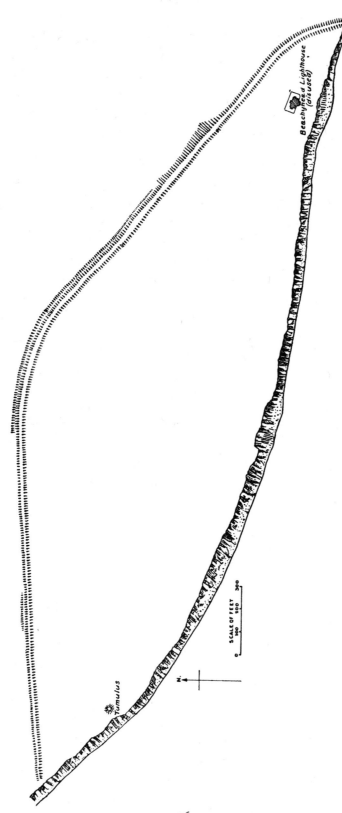

Tumulus

SCALE OF FEET

Beachyhead Lighthouse
(disused)

Beltout Camp, Beachy Head.

456

ANCIENT EARTHWORKS

SEAFORD.—This is a considerably smaller work than Beltout, although, like it, it occupies high ground and has been partly destroyed by the sea. It is marked as 'Roman' on some of the published maps, but apparently without the slightest evidence.

One of the peculiarities of Seaford Camp is the great height at which it stands above the surrounding country. On the sea side the cliff is precipitous, whilst the approach from Seaford, on the north-west, is difficult, and would be hazardous to an invading force. As the camp exists to-day it is roughly of triangular form with a somewhat convex side to the north-west, the shortest side being towards the east. What the original shape may have been, however, is somewhat doubtful, as it is clear that much of it has been destroyed by the inroads of the sea.

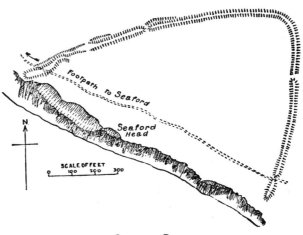

SEAFORD CAMP.

The north-west side of the camp conforms to the contour of the surface, and contains two entrances. The eastern side, however, which is straight, cuts across the plateau on that side, and has an entrance about the middle of its course. Water for the use of the camp may have been procured from a natural spring at the bottom of the slope to the north.

The position of the camp is such as to command a good deal of the district in which it is situated, and Beltout is visible on one hand and the site of the camp at Newhaven on the other.

Neolithic flakes and Roman remains have been found in and about Seaford Camp.

NEWHAVEN.—The earthwork known as Newhaven Castle was situated about three miles to the north-west of Seaford Camp. It has suffered so much from the erosion of the cliff, from the construction of modern defensive works, and from the decomposition and settlement of the plastic clay on which it was constructed, that little now remains. General Pitt-Rivers, writing in 1868, mentions that 'about 1,680 yards of the northern front still remain, and it appears to be arranged in a succession of re-entering curves and salient points. . . . This work, like that of Beltout, occupied the whole summit of the hill, and conformed to the outline of the brow.' The situation of Newhaven 'Castle' was high, commanding the whole of the surrounding country, but with certain limitations of the view to the north-west.

Following along the south coast of Sussex the next earthwork to be noted is—

I   457   58

A HISTORY OF SUSSEX

WHITE HAWK CAMP, an interesting work situated at the southern end of the Racecourse at Brighton. The construction of the racecourse has caused some destruction of the northern part, but enough remains to show that there has been a double vallum following a somewhat irregular circle. On one part of the east side, however, the vallum was single. There was probably once an outwork on the south side which has been destroyed. Chanctonbury Ring, and other prominent hill-top camps in the neighbourhood, are clearly visible from this point. Neolithic implements and flakes are abundant. White Hawk Camp is just about one mile to the north-east of Brighton Pavilion.

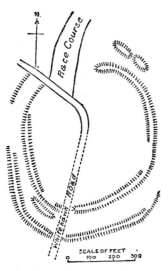

WHITE HAWK CAMP.

HOLLINGBURY, or HOLLINGBURY CASTLE, as it is sometimes called, lies less than three miles to the north of Brighton Pavilion. Although marked 'Roman' on the ordnance survey map, it possesses all the usual characteristics of a hill-top camp. In form it may be described as a very irregular circle with four rounded angles. It has a well-defined rampart with a fosse on the outer side. The inner level of the camp is higher than the outer level, and it is clear that the form of the defences has been determined by the contour of the surface, although there is no very pronounced natural slope except on the east side of the camp. Evidences of the manufacture of neolithic implements have been observed near this camp, whilst actually within its boundary a hoard of Bronze Age implements was discovered some years ago. There is at the south-west side of the camp an ancient hollow-way which was probably connected with one of the entrances.

Hollingbury 'Castle' has in recent years been acquired by the Corporation of Brighton, and every care is being taken to keep it intact.

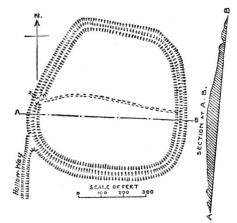

HOLLINGBURY CASTLE.

MOUNT CABURN.—On the detached spur of chalk downs immediately to the east of Lewes, there are two hill-top camps, one known as Mount Caburn, being of special importance. The eminence called Mount Caburn is a bold, conical, and regularly-shaped hill immediately to the north of the railway, half-way between Lewes and Glynde stations. The earthworks which occupy the highest point of the hill are visible from the railway. The earthwork, or camp proper, occupies a nearly perfectly circular space or platform at the top of the

458

hill, and consists of a well-pronounced rampart and outer fosse on the east, south, and west sides, and a more complicated and disturbed arrangement on the north side. The nearly circular form is due to the shape of the hill, and the works simply follow the line where more or less level tableland ends and steep slope commences ; whilst the more elaborate works on the northern side are obviously due to the more gentle slope and greater accessibility on that side. General Pitt-Rivers, in referring to the defensive works of this camp, writes : ' The ramparts of these intrenchments were intended not so much to give cover to the defenders or as an obstacle to the assailants, but rather to give the defenders a command over the outside of the work. It is probable that the defenders stood upon the banks and threw their darts and other missiles over a palisade or an *abatis* at the approaching enemy.

' On those sides where the natural slope of the hill gave all the command that could be desired, artificial banks of any great height were unnecessary, and the defence was probably limited to a stockade or an *abatis* on those sides. This is the only way of accounting for the total absence of earthworks in some points of a line of intrenchments, where a natural declivity presents itself, and where the line of fortification could not certainly have been regarded as complete or inaccessible without some additional defence.'

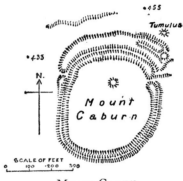

MOUNT CABURN.

The camp at Mount Caburn has two entrances. That on the north-east is strengthened by the rampart being thrown back on each side of the opening in a re-entering angle so as to command and flank the passage across the fosse which is over an embanked causeway. There are three circles, possibly the huts of an advanced guard, placed outside this opening, which were clearly intended to serve as part of the defence of the entrance. The other gateway or entrance to the camp was on the north-west side, leading in the direction of another earthwork, known as Ranscombe Camp, presently to be noticed. Within the camp at Mount Caburn there were traces of upwards of fifty pits, probably the sites of dwellings, but these are not now very distinct. They were perhaps destroyed during the explorations here, the results of which clearly proved that, whatever may have been the period of the first construction of the camp, it was a stronghold of considerable importance during the Late Celtic period. Neolithic chips of flint have been found in some abundance scattered in the vicinity of the camp, but outside rather than within its boundaries.

RANSCOMBE CAMP.—This interesting work is situated about 500 yards to the west of Mount Caburn. It cuts across the hill and faces Mount Caburn, having a ditch on its east side. Although it looks insignificant when mapped, and indeed shows but indifferently as an earthwork, when studied in connection with the neighbouring camp it presents many features of interest. At first sight it is impossible to avoid the impression that it is an outwork of Mount Caburn, because it cuts across the somewhat narrow ridge of land which stretches in a direction leading north-west from Mount Caburn. The

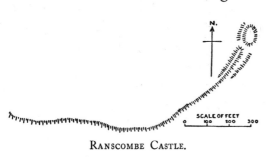

RANSCOMBE CASTLE.

difficulty which opposes itself to such an explanation of the purpose of Ranscombe Camp is, of course, the fact that the fosse is on the east. It is held by General Pitt-Rivers that this in itself would not be a sufficient objection to its having been an advanced work belonging to Caburn. 'But,' he adds, ' the southern end of the trench bends round to the west as if to cover the right flank of a force forcing towards Caburn ; and this makes it hardly possible to doubt that this work must either have been a line of rampart thrown up during an attack on that place, or that it may be the eastern face of another camp, the remaining sides of which have entirely perished.'

There is no necessity, of course, for supposing that the two works were erected at the same time, or that they were occupied by the same people.

Neolithic flakes and implements occur in considerable numbers both inside and outside the Ranscombe Camp.

From both Mount Caburn and Ranscombe the views over the surrounding country are remarkably fine and extensive.

The range of South Downs which stretches from Lewes in a western direction furnishes several excellent examples of hill-top camps, the first being—

DITCHLING BEACON, a camp which stands between 800 and 900 feet above sea-level. It is one of the important view points of Sussex, commanding a wide expanse of Wealden scenery to the east, north and west. Ditchling Beacon is about one mile to the south-west of Westmeston church, and slightly over two miles to the east of the main London and Brighton Railway. The earthworks, which are of irregular quadrilateral form, are not very prominently developed. The sides, like those of Hollingbury Castle, are slightly convex in shape. The north-eastern side of the camp has no earthen defence, the abrupt natural declivity of the hill down to the Weald having been considered sufficient protection.

At the north-west corner of the camp and on the outside of the ramparts is a shallow dish-like depression to which the rainwater which falls on the adjacent surface is conducted by a trench constructed for the purpose. The depression, which is now dry, resembles a dew-pond in general form, but is apparently simply a rainwater dish. There is a regular dew-pond on the east of the camp.

ANCIENT EARTHWORKS

It is open to doubt, perhaps, whether this dew-pond is of any great antiquity, but the rainwater pond probably is of the same age as the camp, because the ramparts have been modified so as to supply it with rainwater. This provision for the storage of water, taken in conjunction with the lowness of the ramparts, points possibly to this having been a refuge camp for the enclosure of cattle rather than a strictly military work. Strengthened by palisading the ramparts would probably be sufficient for such a purpose, whilst no amount of palisading would make them really formidable defences against a powerful foe.

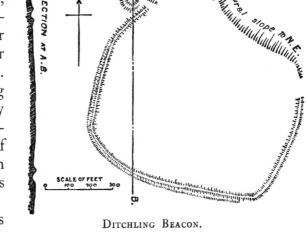

DITCHLING BEACON.

WOLSTANBURY.— This camp is situated on an outlying spur of the downs above Hurstpierpoint. It is essentially a hill-top camp, following the contour of the hill in such a way as to enclose the platform on the top of the hill and, at the same time, to utilize the steep slopes to their full extent as defensive features. The result is a more or less circular work about 250 yards in diameter.

The natural steepness of the sides of this hill rendered it possible to employ a method of fortification which is sometimes, but not often, employed for hill-top defences. Instead of throwing the earth dug from the fosse up the hill towards the interior of the camp, it was thrown downwards, the rampart being built up below or outside the fosse. We thus find that the fosse has been constructed within the rampart, a reasonable and sensible method of construction by which a great economy of labour was effected. This method of construction has been followed throughout, excepting in those parts to the north and east where the steep end of a natural ravine runs close up to the work and artificial defence is unnecessary.

There is an outwork running across the neck of land by which this spur is connected with the main chain of the downs.

Neolithic implements are found here in some numbers. To the west of the camp, and just outside the ramparts, are several shallow pits which may possibly have been the sites of huts or dwellings.

DEVIL'S DYKE.—This is a large, important and remarkable earthwork occupying the level top of a spur or section of the South Downs between five and six miles to the north-west of Brighton Pavilion. It occupies a prominent position and commands extensive and beautiful views. Indeed, it is the best known view-point on the Sussex Downs. It commands not only a large part of the Weald, but also is visible from some important camps, or signalling-posts, such as White Hawk, Edburton, Chanctonbury Ring, etc.

The natural steepness of the hillsides on the north-west, north-east, and south-east renders the site one of great strength, and has made it unnecessary to add much artificial work. Accordingly, although the line of fosse and rampart runs completely round the large irregularly shaped oblong enclosure, attention has chiefly been directed to the south-west and south-south-west sides, where the camp has been cut off from the adjacent level ground of the Downs ; the rampart has been

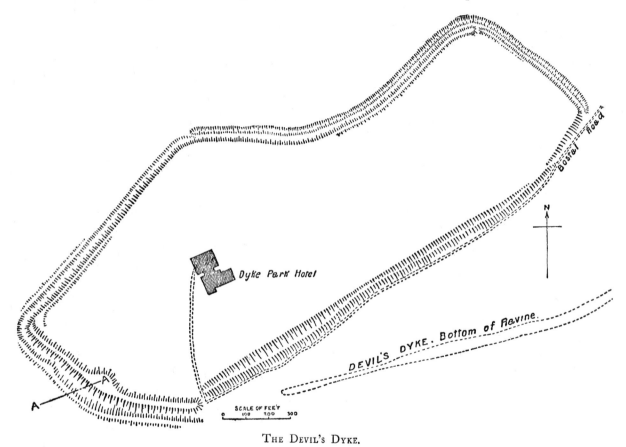

THE DEVIL'S DYKE.

made of a considerable size, and a deep ditch has been constructed on the outside.

This important part of the defences of the Devil's Dyke Camp is interesting as showing how very closely artificial work followed the natural features of the site, furnishing precisely those defensive features which the natural contour failed to give, and at the same time utilizing all those natural features which already existed. In this work the rampart and fosse are most developed about the middle of the south-west and south-south-west sides, where naturally there was a practically level surface extending from the main chain of the Downs to the spur which is now enclosed by the earthwork. A little to the north-west of this point the surface slopes towards the Weald, and the artificial work is of a much less formidable character in consequence. The highest point of the rampart, marked A on the plan, may have been an observation post.

The position of the enclosing earthworks on the slope of the hill all round is worthy of notice. These are judiciously placed, not along the top of the hill, but at a sufficient distance down the slope, to enable the defenders within the camp to command the approach to the work.

It will be seen, therefore, that this earthwork presents all the characteristics of a hill-top fortress in which the defences follow the natural line of the hill (Class B), and also features which would entitle us to place it among those works which are partly inaccessible by reason of precipices (Class A). It may be considered a good example of a hill-top promontory camp.

Neolithic implements, chips, cores, etc., are abundant. There seems to have been no source of water-supply in or near the camp, and, as far as one can now judge, no method of catching rainfall water. The absence of water, therefore, seems to be opposed to the idea that the camp was ever permanently occupied by a large number of people, whilst it would have been impossible for a small force to protect such a long line of defensive works against a determined enemy.

EDBURTON.—This little work is situated about two miles to the west of the Devil's Dyke. It is a curious example of a mount-and-bailey camp placed upon the top of the Downs, but as it presents no feature in any way related to hill-top camps it will be convenient to deal with it at a later stage in this article under Class E.

CHANCTONBURY RING.—This earthwork, which occupies a small part of a very prominent hill about $7\frac{1}{2}$ miles due west of the Devil's Dyke, is of oval form, conforming to the contour of the ground, which slopes gently from it on all sides except the north, where the slope is very steep. There is a rampart within a fosse, and traces of an entrance appear on the south-west and also on the east. The earthwork occupies an angle of the Downs, a narrow ridge which forms the crest of the Downs leading from the camp in a south-eastern direction, and another running in a western direction. Both of these ridges are defended by advanced works consisting of lines of rampart and outer fosse, and it is clear that these formed part of the defensive system of the camp, although the breastwork to the west does not seem to have been of much value from a military point of view. The breastwork to the south-east, however, is more complicated and formidable.

CHANCTONBURY RING.

General Pitt-Rivers points out that in addition to these outworks, which are similar to those of Wolstanbury, the entrance to the main intrench-ment is covered by three circles with slight depressions in the centres. A similar circle covers the opening in the outwork on the south-east. Between the mainwork and the south-eastern outwork there are two barrow-like mounds; whilst between the camp and the western work is another similar mound; still another is outside the western work. All these works, which are represented on the accompanying key-plan, are believed to be parts of the original arrangements for the defence of the camp and were intended also to cover communication with the water supply, which was a spring issuing forth at the foot of the hill about a quarter of a mile to the north-east of the camp. There is also a large hole to the south of the camp which may have been constructed as a reservoir for such rainwater as might be collected from the surface. Its position at the junction of two coombs suggests that this was its original purpose, but from certain remains found and after a deliberate examination of the site General Pitt-Rivers came to the conclusion that a regular well had been dug there, probably by the Romans. It is quite possible that there may have been a rainwater dish or tank here in neolithic times, to which period, it can hardly be doubted, this interesting camp and its outworks belong.

Chanctonbury Ring, to be properly understood, should be studied in connection with Mount Caburn and Wolstanbury Camp, with which it has several obvious points of similarity. As a post for observation and perhaps signalling it is as important as, if not more so than, Mount Caburn. It is, perhaps, the most conspicuous and prominent landmark of Sussex. There are few parts of the Wealden district of the county from which it is not visible. The characteristic group of dark foliaged trees, mainly beeches and firs, by which the height is crowned obscures, unfortunately, the chief part of the central oval earthwork, and it is to be feared that a considerable amount of disturbance and damage has been caused by the ramification of their roots in the soil. Unfortunately, too, the trees cut off much of what would otherwise be a very remarkable and extensive view from the ramparts of the camp.

Cissbury, High Down Camp, the Devil's Dyke and White Hawk Camp are all clearly visible from Chanctonbury Ring. There can be no question that in prehistoric times this was one of the most important look-out points in the south-east of England.

CISSBURY.—This earthwork occupies the top of an important hill practically midway between the sea-coast and the northern edge of the South Downs. Although the view from this eminence does not command a very extensive range of country, it is clearly visible from High Down Camp and Chanctonbury Ring, thus forming an important connecting link between the Weald and the sea-coast.

Beyond this, Cissbury is remarkable as affording evidences of ancient flint-mining, the manufacture of implements, and for its large size, the strength of its defensive works, and the indications of its having been continuously occupied for a long period of time. General Pitt-Rivers has described it as the principal stronghold of Sussex.

The formidable character of its ramparts is clearly visible from Worthing, but its size and strategic strength are only fully realized from an inspection on the spot. Its ramparts enclose an area of about sixty acres, and there are no less than four entrances to the camp. One entrance is on the eastern side where the narrow neck of land joins the camp. The ramparts here are specially strong to cover the entrance. Along the south-eastern side is another entrance, and almost at the southern extremity is a third. At both of these entrances the ramparts are developed in order to command the approach. A fourth entrance is near the most northern end of the camp.

Cissbury Camp shows considerable skill in the way the ramparts and fosses are planned. The ramparts are made not at the top of the

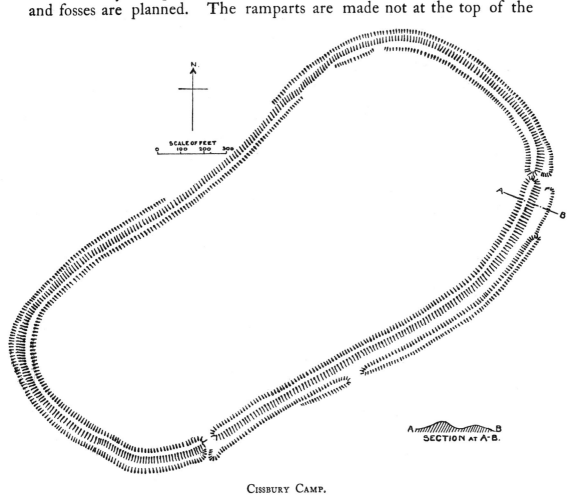

CISSBURY CAMP.

slope, where it would have been necessary to throw up a vast quantity of earth, but half-way down the slope, and the material removed from an internal ditch has been thrown outwards to form them, thus effecting a great economy of labour.

One curious feature which distinguishes Cissbury from many of the prehistoric camps of the South Downs is the large number of pits with which the slope on the western side of the area within the rampart is honeycombed. These pits, which vary from 20 to 70 feet in diameter, were carefully examined by General Pitt-Rivers[1] in 1867

[1] *Arch.* xlii. 53–76.

A HISTORY OF SUSSEX

and 1868. It was found that the depth of the pit was always proportioned to the diameter. Round the surface and also buried within the pits were large numbers of flakes and waste chips of flint as well as the rough blocks from which they had been struck. Full details of the discoveries are given in *Archæologia.*[1] The net results of the observations of General Pitt-Rivers tended to show that the holes had been dug for the purpose of procuring flint for implement making, and that they had been used as habitations at a subsequent period. Mr. E. H. Willett carried on further researches at Cissbury in 1873–5 which confirmed these theories. His paper was read before the Society of Antiquaries in 1875.[2]

THE TRUNDLE, ST. ROCHE'S HILL.—As far as situation and the extensive views obtainable from it are concerned, this earthwork may justly rank with Mount Caburn and Ditchling Beacon. Its form may be described as something between a circle and a six-sided enclosure.

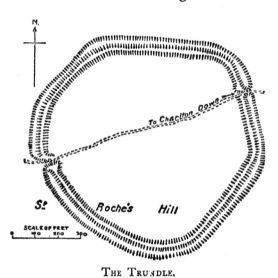

THE TRUNDLE.

It possesses a single rampart enclosed within a fosse, the former having been made by throwing the material from the ditch inwards. There are two entrances, namely, on the south-south-west and on the north-north-east. The view includes the most complete picture of the South Downs in West Sussex, which here are more wooded than those in the eastern and middle parts of the county. The view also includes a fine extent of sea-coast, the ramifications of Chichester Harbour, the Isle of Wight, etc.

The view, indeed, is extensive in every direction, and it is clear that at least one, if not the principal, purpose of the earthwork, was to afford an extensive look-out over the district. It is essentially a hill-top camp of early character, the defensive works following the contour of the hill in such a way as to get the greatest possible benefit from the natural slope. The rampart is boldly shown against the sky as one approaches the camp from the west.[3]

GOOSEHILL CAMP.—This is situated nearly two miles west of West Dean in Western Sussex. It is a more or less circular work, and stands at a height of about 500 feet above the sea. It forms one of the regular hill-top camps of the South Downs. Just to the south is Kingley Bottom, a place traditionally associated with 'Druidical' remains.

[1] *Arch.* xlii. [2] Ibid. xlv. pp. 337–48.
[3] There is a local tradition to the effect that the whole of the earthworks were thrown up by a great Roman army in twenty-four hours!

466

ANCIENT EARTHWORKS

HEYSHOTT.—About two miles south-south-east of Midhurst. There is a more or less circular work here.

HARROW HILL, also known as MOUNT HARRY, in the parish of Clapham. This is an oval work following the outline of a similarly shaped hill which rises suddenly from a level of some 250 ft. to 549 ft. above sea-level. It occupies a spur to the south of the South Downs. There are several small, shallow hollows near this camp, which were possibly the floors of dwellings. Although Harrow Hill earthwork is placed under Class B, it is quite possible that it may belong to Class G.

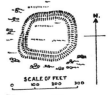

HARROW HILL, OR MOUNT HARRY.

HIGH DOWN CAMP.—This interesting little camp is situated on an isolated hill to the south of the South Downs and about four miles to the south-west of Cissbury. It is roughly of a quadrilateral form, occupying the top of the hill. On the south side, and in a lesser degree on the east and west sides, there is a double rampart, the ground being only slightly sloping on those sides. On the north side, however, where the ground slopes away more abruptly, the rampart is low and single. On the south-west side the earthen defensive works are not at present sufficient to have offered any serious obstacle to an attacking force, but probably the ramparts were stockaded originally, and it is also probable that the ramparts may have been lowered and levelled somewhat when the old windmill[1] stood here.

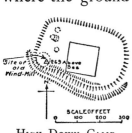

HIGH DOWN CAMP.

There are three or four shallow pits within the limits of the camp, some of which were excavated under the superintendence of General Pitt-Rivers and found to be of a sepulchral character.

There was a Saxon cemetery here, and during explorations of the site numerous interesting objects of glass, bronze, pottery, etc., have been found.[2]

The following are a few other Sussex camps which may be put under Class A.

ARUNDEL.—The general scheme of the earthworks of this well-known fortress belongs unquestionably to Class E, which comprises fortified mounts, either artificial or partly natural, with traces of an attached court or bailey, or of two or more such courts ; and the main part of the earthworks here will be dealt with under that section. But if the site of the castle and its precincts be carefully examined,[3] it will be found that although there is a moated mount with two large courts attached, there is to the north-west a deep fosse cutting off the whole of the castle site from the ridge of hill which extends to the north-

---

[1] The old miller, John Olliver, who died in 1793, at the age of eighty-four years, is buried under a square tomb in a field to the east of the site of his old windmill.

[2] See *Arch.* liv. 369–82 ; and lv. 203–14.

[3] The writer desires to express his obligations to the Duke of Norfolk, K.G., for kind permission to examine the castle and castle grounds, and to Mr. G. J. Heveningham, the Clerk of the Works at Arundel Castle, for kindly accompanying him and pointing out the position of the earthworks.

west. This is probably a work of a much earlier period than the erection of the mount and the building of the castle ; but whatever its date may be it clearly belongs to the type of defensive earthworks called Class A, and makes it a promontory fort comparable with the Devil's Dyke and the two others about to be described. The main earthworks of Arundel will be described under Class E.

BURPHAM.—This earthwork consists of a long narrow hill-top cut off to the north by a rampart and fosse which convert it into a promontory camp. A glance at the accompanying plan will enable one to judge of its form better than any description. This camp lies quite near one of the curved loops of the river Arun. The whole of the sides on the east, south, and west are naturally steep, but it is possible that their slopes may have been emphasized by artificial means.

The artificial rampart which completes the camp on the north side is broken about midway by an angle, at which was probably the entrance. This rampart is composed of chalky material, brought, perhaps, in baskets and thrown down in such a way that the contents of each basket might still be traced as a separate layer when the place was investigated some years ago.

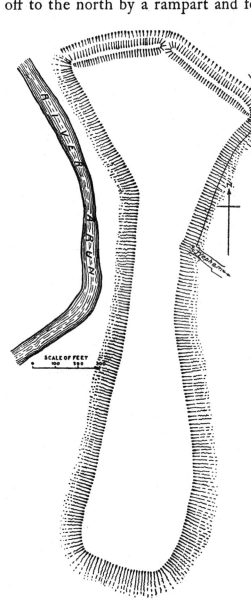

BURPHAM CAMP.

HASTINGS, EAST HILL.—The hill, which ends in a rather narrow point near the lift leading to East Hill, Hastings, marks the south-west extremity of an interesting specimen of a camp of Class A. Along the southern side the steep sandstone cliffs of the seashore form a sufficient natural defence. On the opposite side in an irregular line extending from the south-west to the north-east, the natural surface of the ground slopes abruptly to the north-west. So sharp is the slope that it seems probable that it has been artificially augmented by the cutting of a species of cliff which is now weathered and partly hidden by vegetation. The north-east side of the camp is formed by a rampart

468

and external fosse cut through the hard rock to a depth of from seven to eight feet. The removed material was thrown inwards so as to make the rampart almost perpendicular on its outer face. Inside, the slope leading up to the top of the rampart was gentle towards the southern end of the rampart, and within it are traces of earthworks, both parallel to the rampart and at right angles with it, which may have been parts of a supplementary defence of the south-eastern corner.

One feature of the hill-top camps of Sussex which stands out with peculiar clearness is the insufficiency of many of the actual earthen ramparts and fosses, as they now exist, for any serious purpose of defence. Indeed, it must be evident to any one who carefully considers the

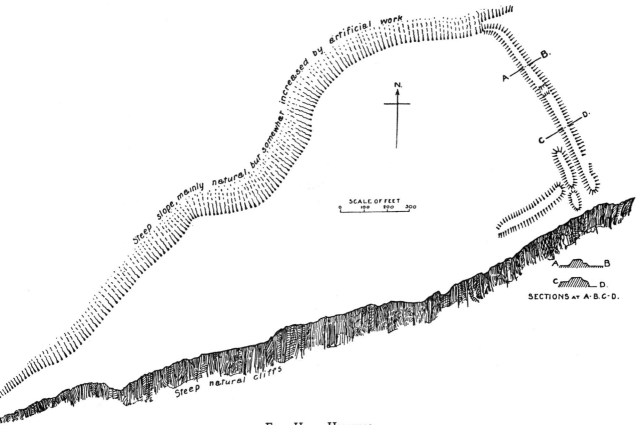

EAST HILL, HASTINGS.

question, that many of these camps or earthworks are not military works at all. They may have been extensive cattle-pens or enclosures, but their very extent, to say nothing of their inadequate bulwarks, is enough to show that they can never have been successfully defended against a powerful and resolute foe. The length of rampart could only have been held by such an army as would have been out of the question at the early age to which the earthworks obviously belong. The real purpose of such works as Ditchling Beacon, Wolstanbury, and Beltout, was apparently to provide a place of safety for cattle and men against wolves and possibly, human marauders. The thick, persistent hedge at the point on the slope of the Downs where pasture land meets the ancient Weald (now in most cases cultivated as arable land) is another indication of man's efforts to keep the Wealden wolves from the flocks on the grassy Downs, or perhaps to keep the flocks of the Downs from straying into the dense forests of the Weald.

The down-land formed the pasturage for the sheep and cattle of neolithic man ; the more sheltered valleys, near water, near food, and near fuel-supply, were evidently the home of such as were not actually engaged in tending the live stock on the Downs.

Under conditions such as these, the great value of observation-points commanding all possible approaches will be evident, and it is impossible to study the Sussex hill-top enclosures with any care without discovering how this idea of securing extensive views over all the surrounding country, or, where this was not possible, signalling posts from hill-top to hill-top, has entered into the policy of selecting sites and arranging defensive ramparts.

The defenced hilltops of Sussex furnish, in fact, a regular series of observation and signalling posts. Along the northern crest of the South Downs, overlooking many miles of Wealden scenery, are Ditchling Beacon, Wolstanbury, Devil's Dyke, Chanctonbury and the Trundle. An intermediate belt of camps, situated roughly about half-way between the crest of the Downs and the sea-coast, consists of Hollingbury and Cissbury, both communicating with the camps on the crest of the Downs, but not commanding a view over the Weald. Answering to these is a series of camps on and near the sea-coast, comprising Beltout, Seaford, Newhaven (destroyed), White Hawk, and High Down. There are three points which stand out on the crest of the South Downs with peculiar prominence, viz. Chanctonbury Ring, the Devil's Dyke Camp, and Ditchling Beacon, but the less prominent heights, such as White Hawk, Hollingbury, and Cissbury, will all be found to be equally visible from the different camps on or near the Downs. It is quite clear that there was in ancient times a regular system of signalling from the South Downs to the sea-coast.

SIMPLE ENCLOSED CAMPS
[Class C]

Of the rectangular Roman camps (Class C), Sussex appears to contain only one specimen, i.e. that of Hardham, although there are, of course, the walled towns of Chichester and Pevensey.

HARDHAM CAMP.—This interesting work has been much damaged by the making of the Mid-Sussex Railway through it and by other causes. When perfect it was nearly a true square, its sides respectively measuring 420 ft. and 435 ft. Its single line of rampart is only about four feet in height. The camp lies thirty-six feet above the level of the river Arun. A brief account of Hardham Camp, accompanied by fuller particulars of Romano-British interments in the neighbourhood, was read in 1863 by Dr. W. Boyd-Dawkins.[1]

[1] *Suss. Arch. Coll.* xvi. 52-64.

ANCIENT EARTHWORKS

Compared with hill-top camps the rectangular Roman camps present many striking differences. One of the chief of these is that whilst the earlier works occupy the whole of the available hilltop, the Roman works are limited in area and restricted in shape, being constructed, not with reference to site, but with reference to requirements. Again, the prehistoric works are situated, almost invariably, upon the highest summits of the hills, in positions frequently remote from water and sources of fuel, whereas the Romans seem always to have made a point of constructing their camps on level ground, and within easy reach of both fuel and water.

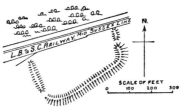

HARDHAM CAMP.

The number of the prehistoric camps, moreover, is much in excess of those which are known to have been occupied by the Romans.

Further, prehistoric camps occasionally contain traces of hut-circles, whilst the Roman camps do not contain them. The method of defending the entrance to the earlier camps, and the flint implements with which neolithic camps are generally associated, present striking contrasts to the Roman camps.

In the present condition of knowledge of early earthworks it is impossible to be certain as to the characteristics of Bronze Age camps and Prehistoric Iron Age camps, but as far as one can judge from the available evidence, Sussex does not contain any example which could be referred without doubt to either of these periods. Still, there is evidence that Hollingbury Camp was used during the Bronze Age and Mount Caburn during the age of prehistoric iron.

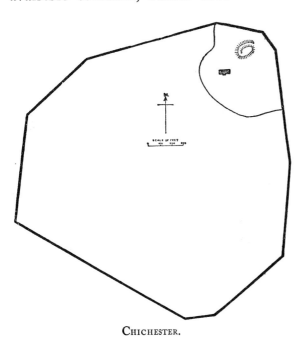

CHICHESTER.

Sussex possesses two walled fortresses or towns of undoubtedly Roman origin, namely Chichester and Pevensey, and there are earthworks of an interesting character in connection with both.

CHICHESTER.—The present town walls are largely of Roman construction, or on Roman foundations, and they are backed by a rampart, parts of which still remain. Some distance to the north of Chichester is an outwork of rampart known as 'The Broil,' consisting of two sides of a square said to be each a mile in length, but not now entirely visible.

471

PEVENSEY is remarkable for its magnificent specimens of Roman walls of coursed and faced masonry, and its south-western gateway. The actual earthworks of the place are mainly on the southern side, and

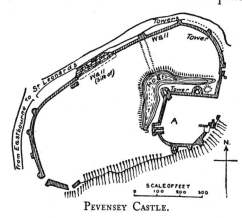

PEVENSEY CASTLE.

consist of a fairly well developed fosse extending from the west corner of the mediæval stronghold three-fourths of the way to the great Roman gateway.[1] Unfortunately this ditch has been considerably disturbed by a species of minor landslip carrying down with it large pieces of the Roman wall. Pevensey was probably occupied by William the Conqueror at an early period, like Hastings Castle. The massive walls built by the Romans were utilized to form the boundary of the castle bailey. The moat outside of this castle was probably constructed as an additional security, thus making it impossible to blow up the masonry by gunpowder or to damage it by means of the battering-ram.

CASTLE MOUNTS AND CASTLE MOUNTS WITH ATTACHED COURTS
[CLASSES D AND E]

For purposes of convenience these two classes will be considered together. Their characteristics are : (1) D, Forts consisting only of a mount with encircling ditch or fosse; and (2) E, Fortified mounts either artificial or partly natural, with traces of an attached court or bailey, or of two or more such courts.

Of Class D, Sussex possesses two examples, namely, Knepp Castle and Park Mount, Pulborough.

KNEPP CASTLE, in Shipley parish, occupies a low-lying site close to the river Adur. It consists, as will be seen from the plan, of little more than a mount, oval in plan, and surrounded by a fosse and rampart.

PARK MOUNT, PULBOROUGH.—This, like Knepp, is a simple mount encircled by a fosse, and strengthened by an enclosing rampart on the east, south and west sides.

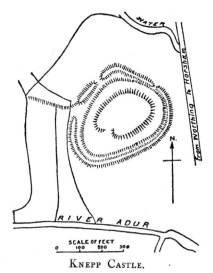

KNEPP CASTLE.

The mount itself has been considerably disturbed on the west side, where probably the material has been purposely removed. The whole place is

---

[1] There is a good account of the remains of Pevensey Castle in the sixth volume of the *Suss. Arch. Coll.* The paper, which was written by Mr. Mark Antony Lower, F.S.A., is accompanied by a ground-plan, and is entitled 'On Pevensey Castle, and the recent excavations there.'

now a copse, and a prolific growth of ferns, brambles, and other vegetation much obscures the earthworks. The point is peculiarly well suited for an observation-post, as it commands a view over a large area of the surrounding country.

It is noteworthy that both Knepp and Park Mount command two important Sussex rivers, the former being close to the Adur and the latter overlooking the Arun.

Sussex possesses several excellent examples of the moated mount and bailey type of fortress (Class E). Not only is the county rich in the number of these earthworks, but the variety of forms is almost equally remarkable.

Until about the year 1894, mounts of this class were generally regarded as Saxon works, identical in fact with the burhs mentioned in the Anglo-Saxon Chronicle ; but scrutiny of the records

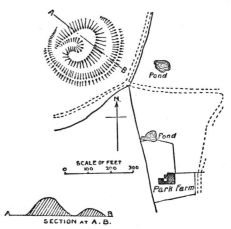

PARK MOUNT, PULBOROUGH.

and examination of the character and distribution of the earthworks tend to show that they were introduced by the Normans, or under Norman influence, in the time of Edward the Confessor.

ARUNDEL.—This magnificent castle presents a very excellent example of a fortress in which, although masonry has very largely superseded earthworks, it has not entirely obliterated them. The masonry of the castle, however, need not be taken into consideration in the present article, as only the earthen defences come within its scope.

The possibility of this having been a prehistoric camp of the promontory type has already been pointed out.

The moated mount is a fine example of this species of work. Its diameter at the base is 230 ft., whilst at the summit it is 90 ft. On the south side its height, measuring from the bottom of the ditch, is 70 ft., whilst on the north side, where the ground rises, it is about 50 ft. It is somewhat less in size than the

ARUNDEL CASTLE.

mound at Windsor Castle. Arundel possesses two baileys, occupying relatively the same positions in reference to the keep as those at Windsor to the Round Tower.

The steep slopes of the ground away from the castle, principally on its eastern, southern and south-western sides, are largely natural, but they have been emphasized by artificial work, and the castle is now entirely surrounded by steep slopes and fosses. The ditch, or moat of the great mount, forms the outer castle ditch on one part of the western

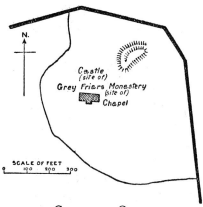

CHICHESTER CASTLE.

side. Inside the castle, unfortunately, a part of the moat has been filled up and converted into a lawn. There is no reason to suppose that this moat was ever filled with water; it seems always to have been dry.

CHICHESTER.—In addition to the defensive works surrounding the city, which are of Roman construction, a camp of the Class E type seems to have been built at the north-east corner within the walls. There are remains of a mount, but the building of the now destroyed Grey Friars Monastery, and other changes, have had the effect probably of obliterating the earthworks. The position of the castle just within the city wall is in accordance with the plan frequently adopted, and reminds one very forcibly of the arrangement at Canterbury.

BRAMBER, which stands in the valley of the Adur, is of a somewhat oval shape and surrounded by a fosse of great depth. Although there are wet ditches near the camp it does not seem probable that the great fosse round the castle was ever filled with water; indeed, the levels would not permit of it. The great ditch was probably always dry, and suggests a prehistoric origin. It is just possible that the Normans found an ancient earthwork already existing here, and converted it to their use, throwing up a large mound in the centre, as shown in the plan and section. The top of the mound forms an excellent look-out point commanding the river-valley, which is rather narrow at this point.

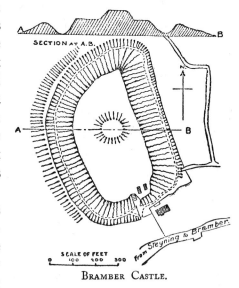

BRAMBER CASTLE.

Mr. G. T. Clark points out in his book on castles[1] that 'in the construction of the fortress (Bramber), advantage was taken of a knoll of the lower or grey chalk, roughly oval in figure, and about 120 ft. above the river. This was levelled on the top and scarped round the sides so as to form a more or less rounded area, 560 ft. north and south, by 280 ft. east and west. The scarp descended above 180 ft. at an angle of 45 ft. or a slope of one to one, into a ditch about 20 ft. wide at

[1] *Mediæval Military Architecture in England*, i. 268.

the bottom, and the opposite side of which, or counterscarp, rose about 40 ft. at a similar angle, so that the ditch at the counterscarp level was 100 ft. broad, and the crest of the scarp rose 30 ft. to 40 ft. above the ground opposite.' The conical mount is about 40 ft. high and 70 ft. in diameter at its summit.

LEWES.—This fortress, which stands in a favourable position for commanding the river Ouse and its valley, is remarkable as possessing two conical moated mounts, one at each end of the area enclosed by the castle walls. The mound to the south-west is now surmounted by the remains of the shell keep; that to the north-east, known as Brack Mount, has near the top a large fragment of flint walling, apparently overturned, but there are no traces of masonry on the top of the mound. Both still retain traces of the ditches or moats by which they were once surrounded.

The two mounds were probably suggested by the conformation of the ground. Mr. G. T. Clark[1] considers that each end of the knoll on which the castle stands was already a mound, and all the defenders, or rather makers, of the castle had to do was 'to pare and scarp its sides and slopes, to isolate it from the intervening platform by a ditch, and to pile up the earth so removed upon the central space. By this means two very respectable moated mounds were formed, each conical in figure, with a flat top, and with its circular and circumscribing ditch. Of the mounds so raised, partly natural and partly artificial, that to the south-west was about 130 feet above the northern plain, and that to the north-east about 110 feet. The next step was to defend the platform intervening between the two mounds. On the north front this was effected by scarping the already steep slope, which thus became almost inaccessible. The southern slope, less strong by nature, was protected by a strong bank of earth thrown up along its crest, below and outside of which was a formidable ditch, about 30 yards broad, and below and beyond it the ground occupied or to be occupied by the town.'

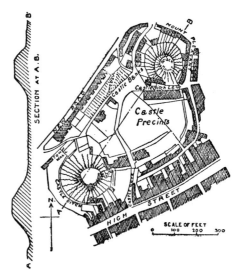

LEWES CASTLE.

The enclosed and defended area of the town may perhaps be considered to represent the outer bailey of the castle.

BURGHLOW CASTLE.—This is a mount and bailey castle situated quite near the river Cuckmere. The mount occupies the northern part of the castle area, the whole of which is surrounded by steep ground sloping away from the castle. In general arrangement Burghlow Castle is rather suggestive of Bramber, except that it is smaller and has no outer

[1] *Suss. Arch. Coll.* xxxiv. 58.

rampart. The object of Burghlow Castle was evidently to command the valley of the Cuckmere.[1]

EDBURTON.—This curious little work, situated on the top of the South Downs, about two miles to the west of the Devil's Dyke, has already been mentioned. It possesses a mount, and a well-defined bailey to the north of it. It is quite small, and stands alone on the Downs overlooking a large area of the Weald. There are no traces of masonry, and, as far as one can see, there is no supply of water near. Why it should be placed here is a mystery, unless, indeed, it was a signalling station visible perhaps from Pulborough and Knepp Castle.

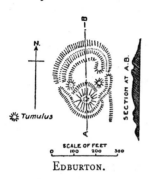

EDBURTON.

This camp lies practically on the level top of the Downs 600 feet above the sea. To the north is a steep descent of 100 feet in 70 yards. Beyond this point the land sinks even more rapidly to the level of 300 feet above the sea. On the verge of the fosse which separates the mount from the small bailey there are two hillocks, which may have been part of the scheme of defence, or perhaps they are merely the result of making a modern cart-road through the stronghold.

At a short distance to the east of Edburton camp there are indications of terraces, possibly once used for cultivation, on the hillside.

HASTINGS.—In addition to the promontory camp at Hastings already described, there are several interesting earthworks belonging to the castle on the west hill. These consist mainly of a mount and two, if not three, baileys attached. The mount is situated near the present entrance to the castle ruins, and although partly outside the walls, clearly belongs to the bailey in which the ruined walls of the castle stand. This mount is of very great interest from the fact that it is possibly the one depicted on the Bayeux Tapestry in the process of being thrown up. The part of the earthworks which may be considered the inmost bailey is separated from another bailey called Ladies' Parlour immediately to the north-east, and Mr. I. Chalkley Gould has called the writer's attention to traces of still another bailey extending further to the north and north-east.

HASTINGS CASTLE.

The bailey in which the castle ruins are situated has evidently suffered considerably from encroachments on the southern side. Whether those encroachments have been effected by the waves and influences of the weather seems doubtful. It seems more probable that a good deal of the cliff has been artificially cut away to make a convenient space

---

[1] The writer wishes to record his thanks to Mr. Duncan Montgomerie for notes as to Burghlow Castle.

for the buildings below. The plan of Hastings Castle published in Gross's *Antiquities*, about 1750, shows very irregular and jagged cliffs reaching to a roadway marked 'Road to Hastings,' which is close to the sea-beach. To the west of the castle there are indications of a ditch, marked on the plan, 'Ditch about an Hundred Feet Wide.'

The more important works of this class are the wet moats which surround the castles of Bodiam and Scotney. In connection with the former, Mr. Harold Sands, F.S.A.,[1] has discovered traces of a harbour between the river Rother and the castle. Hurstmonceux is surrounded by a dry moat.

HOMESTEAD MOATS

[CLASS F]

Homestead moats are found mainly in the Wealden parts of Sussex, but they are not numerous and do not present any points of special interest.

The following is a list of the Homestead moats of Sussex, arranged alphabetically under the names of the parishes in which they occur.

ARLINGTON.—Michelham Priory Moat (large) near the river Cuckmere.
    Claverham Moat.
    Moat near Sessingham Bridge.
    Moat at Willbees.
ASHINGTON.—Circular moat at Lower Buncton Farm.
BATTLE.—Moat at Netherfield Place.
BECKLEY.—Three sides of moat at Blossom Place.
BEXHILL.—Moat (?) near Cooding Farm.
BODIAM.—Circular moat just to the south of Kent Ditch.
BOSHAM.—Moat at Bosham.
    Remains of moat, etc., at Stonewall Farm.
BUXTED.—Moat to the north-east of Shepherd's Hill.
CHAILEY.—Remains, possibly those of a moat, at the Rectory, Chailey.
EASTBOURNE.—Moat in Eastbourne (old town).
EAST GRINSTEAD.—Rectangular moat at Brambletye House.
    Rectangular moat (?), containing water, on the south bank of Felbridge Water.
EDBURTON.—Moat (?) on site of Perching Manor-house.
ETCHINGHAM.—Moat formerly encircled the churchyard.
FRANT.—Moat at Moat Farm, Rumbold's Hill.
HELLINGLY.—Rectangular moat at Horselunges.
HENFIELD.—Moat at Streatham.
    Moat close to river Adur.
HORSHAM.—"The Castle" moat.
    "Moated House."
    Moat, near Grayland's Copse.
    Chelsworth Moat with remains of Chelsworth House.
    Remains of moat at Watling's Farm.
HUNSTON.—Moat at Hunston Manor House Farm.
IDEN.—Remains of moat at Moat Farm.
IFIELD.—Moat at Ifield Court.
    Moat at Ewhurst Place.
ISFIELD.—Circular moat to the south-west of the church.
LAUGHTON.—Moat at Laughton Place.

---

[1] *Sussex Arch. Coll.* vol. xlvi. pp. 114-133.

LITTLEHAMPTON.—Moat at Bailiffs Court (only two sides remaining).
  Moat to the north-west of Atherton.
NEWTIMBER.—Moat at Newtimber Place.
PAGHAM.—Remains of moat to the south-east of the church.
PLUMPTON.—Moat at Plumpton Place.
RUSPER.—Moat in Moat Copse.
RYE.—Site of Moat.
SALEHURST.—Moat (?) at Moat Farm.
SHERMANBURY.—Oval moat at Ewhurst Farm.
SLAUGHAM.—Moat at Slaugham Place.
TWINEHAM.—Moat at Moat Barn.
UPPER BEEDING.—Moat (two sides remaining) at Manor House.
WALDRON.—Regular circular moat in Middle Wood.
WARBLETON.—Moat close to the church.
WARTLING.—Moat enclosing supposed site of house, to the east of Kentland Fleet.
WEST GRINSTEAD.—Moat to the south-west of West Grinstead Park.
  Moat at Clothall's Farm.
  Moat at Moat Farm.
WEST HOATHLY.—Moat at Moat Farm.
WEST WITTERING.—Moat at Redlands Farm.
WISBOROUGH GREEN.—Moat at Drungewich Manor House.
WITHYHAM.—Moat at Blackham Court.
WIVELSFIELD.—Moat at Moat House.
WORTH.—Moat at Barn Wood.

UNCLASSIFIED EARTHWORKS

[CLASS X]

The following are brief particulars of other earthworks, which were probably of a defensive character originally :—

BUXTED.—At Shepherd's Hill is a work somewhat similar in character to that at Boreham Bridge, Wartling, but less symmetrical in form owing to its position on the slope of a hill. Mr. Charles Dawson, F.S.A., who has kindly furnished some particulars of it, states that the fosse on the higher side is about twenty feet deep, that on the lower ground being only six feet.

FALMER.—Mr. Herbert S. Toms has drawn the writer's attention to a curious work situated near Newmarket Plantation, Falmer. It is of singular construction, being a series of low banks with shallow fosse surrounding a Y-shaped valley, and enclosing a space about 500 feet long, and 460 feet broad. The question as to its ancient or modern date must await investigation.

HEATHFIELD.—This little camp, which lies quite away from the South Downs, is of oval form. Its greatest diameter, from north-east to south-west, is 140 ft., and its shortest diameter is 102 ft. Unfortunately very little of the earthwork now remains, the rampart having been purposely destroyed some years since by a former owner. It had a single rampart within a fosse.

The camp is not marked in the ordnance survey map (25 inches), but has been briefly described by Mr. John Lewis, F.S.A.[1]

---

[1] *Pro. Geologists' Assoc.* xvii. 174 (22 July 1901).

ANCIENT EARTHWORKS

MIDHURST.—St. Anne's Hill, close by the church at Midhurst, has some disturbed earthworks which probably represent a hill-top camp.

PAGHAM.—There are some irregular earthworks enclosed in a nearly quadrangular space by a wet ditch to the south-east of Pagham Church.

RACKHAM.—There is a long line of earthworks here, consisting of a rampart and remains of a fosse, possibly part of a boundary bank.

ROTHERFIELD, SAXONBURY HILL.—Here is an oval work, probably a camp.

SOMPTING.—About $1\frac{1}{2}$ miles north-north-east of Sompting church are two long lines of ramparts. The southern is an arc extending for upwards of a mile. There is a corresponding fosse on the convex or northern side. Opposed to this, about half a mile to the north, is another rampart and fosse, less well pronounced. Here the fosse is on the southern side, and the line is broken about the middle by an angle pointing to the south.

WARTLING.—The Ashbourn River, which falls into the sea near Pevensey, occupies a small portion of a fairly broad valley. In the middle of this valley and near the river, there is at Boreham Bridge, in the parish of Wartling, an interesting earthwork consisting of a circular convex platform raised somewhat above the level of the surrounding ground, and enclosed within a fairly deep but narrow trench or ditch. The whole of the surface within the enclosure is of slightly but unmistakably convex form, suggestive of a dry island for cattle and sheep in the wet weather, when much of the valley is flooded. Another, and, on the whole, perhaps more reasonable explanation is that it was intended to serve as a kind of crannog or marsh village. The work is locally known as 'Rat's Castle.'

WASHINGTON.—At Highden Clump there is a line of earthworks, possibly a boundary bank, which extends in a direction nearly north and south, and consists of a well-pronounced rampart with a fosse on the western side.

The earthworks somewhat to the south of Edburton, marked 'Roman Camp' on the ordnance survey map, are simply ancient field enclosures.

The tidal banks of the Arun and the Ouse, and the earthen banks on each side of the ancient road known as Stane Street, may be mentioned. The latter are very clearly seen at and near Bignor Hill.

TUMULI, BARROWS, ETC.

In conclusion, a word or two may be added in reference to sepulchral mounds, or barrows, in Sussex. These are found chiefly on the top of the South Downs, and there are several examples between Mount Harry near Lewes and the camp at Ditchling, and also between the Devil's Dyke and Edburton. There appear to be two pretty well-pronounced types, viz. (i.) low circular mounds, 30 feet or more in diameter and from 2 feet to 3 feet in height, and (ii.) circular mounds, about 20 feet in diameter and 2 feet 6 inches in height, with a kind of crater-shaped hollow near, but not actually on the centre. From the various remains found in them it appears that the former are probably of the Bronze Age, whilst the latter are Anglo-Saxon barrows.

The following is a list of the parishes in which barrows and tumuli have been noted. Most of them are probably sepulchral mounds, but excavations in the neighbourhood of Chanctonbury Ring and elsewhere have tended to show that some of the barrow-like mounds were connected with ancient defensive works.

Alciston (numerous)
Alfriston (numerous)
Arlington
Barlavington
Beddingham
Bepton
Bignor
Bishopstone
Burton
Bury
Chailey
Cocking
Easebourne
East Blatchington
Eastbourne, Beachy Head (numerous)
Eastdean (numerous)
East Lavington
Edburton
Falmer
Folkington
Friston
Glynde
Graffham
Hamsey (several)
Hangleton
Heyshott
Hove
Iford
Jevington
Kingston-by-Sea. Large mound known as Slonk Hill, and various others at Newmarket Hill, etc.

Lavant
Lewes
Litlington
Lullington
Newtimber
Old Shoreham
Ovingdean
Petworth
Piddinghoe
Piecombe
Plumpton
Portslade
Rodmell
Rottingdean
Seaford
South Malling
Stanmer
Storrington
Stoughton
Sutton
Treyford
Up Waltham
Walsingham
West Dean
West Firle (numerous)
West Stoke
Westmeston
Willingdon
Wilmington

The writer desires to express his obligations to numerous friends for their kind help and advice in the work of collecting materials for this paper, particularly to Mr. I. Chalkley Gould for kindly reading and revising what he has written ; and also to Mr. Charles Dawson, F.S.A., and Mr. John Lewis, F.S.A.

POLITICAL HISTORY

OF the reduction and colonization by the Romans of that portion of Britain which subsequently became Sussex no record has survived. General Pitt-Rivers considered that the results of his excavations on the Caburn[1] pointed to the British camp there having undergone a short siege by Roman troops, and suggested that it might have been one of the twenty 'oppida' captured by Vespasian during his expedition. But apart from such surmises, and from the conclusions that may be drawn from the prehistoric and other remains described elsewhere,[2] the history of what is now Sussex may be said to begin in the last quarter of the fifth century.

At this period the Romans had lately abandoned their colony of Britain, leaving behind them many long-enduring monuments alike of organization and of architecture. In the district with which we are here dealing the two most important relics of their rule were the city of Regnum, subsequently re-named Chichester, and the strong fortress town of Anderida, the westernmost defence of the 'Litus Saxonicum,' whose massive walls, after forming the outer defences of the medieval castle of Pevensey, still stand imposing even in decay. In 477 the Saxon Elle with his three sons Cymen, Wlencing and Cissa, and probably quite a small band of followers, landed in the extreme west of the present county at a place which was afterwards known as Cymen-esora[3] and established themselves there. The exact date at which they gained possession of Regnum, and gave it the name of Cissan-ceaster, is not known ; but they gradually extended their sway eastwards, driving the British into the dense forest of Andred, till in 485 the native chieftains, alarmed at the invaders' progress, assembled a strong force and met them in pitched battle on the banks of the Mercredesburn,[4] where a desperate struggle took place in which both sides suffered heavy losses and neither could claim the victory.[5] But Elle, obtaining fresh forces from his native land, continued his slow but irresistible advance till in 490 he laid siege to the stronghold of Anderida.[6]

Here he met with vigorous resistance ; the lofty walls and their desperate defenders repelled all attacks, while the neighbouring forest formed a perfect refuge for the Britons who swarmed out like bees to harass the Saxons whenever they attempted the assault of the fortress,

---

[1] *Arch.* xlvi. 476. [2] See sections on 'Early Man,' 'Earthworks,' and 'Roman Remains.'
[3] *Hen. of Huntingdon* (Rolls Ser.), 44. [4] Possibly the Ouse, see *Suss. Arch. Coll.* vii. 75.
[5] *Hen. of Huntingdon* (Rolls Ser.), 44. [6] Ibid. 45.

and being light of foot could escape to the woods when the enemy turned upon them. At last Elle divided his army into two portions, one to keep off these attacks, and the other to press the siege of the town. Famine did what force had failed to do, the place was taken, and the Saxons, enraged at their heavy losses, slew men, women and children, leaving not one alive, and destroyed the town.

From this year, 491, dates the establishment of the South Saxon kingdom, which at once reached the zenith of its power. Elle being the most influential of the contemporary Saxon chiefs in Britain was afterwards considered to have been the first Bretwalda,[1] though it is unlikely that he could have gained any such supremacy over the island as the later Bretwaldas held. On his death in 514, Cissa his son succeeded him and handed the kingdom on to his descendants, whose rule grew gradually feebler[2] until Sussex was absorbed into the rising kingdom of Wessex. This event possibly took place about 607,[3] when Ceolwulf, king of Wessex, fought a great battle with the men of Sussex, in which both sides lost heavily, but the advantage lay with Wessex.[4] A considerable degree of independence must have been preserved or regained by Sussex, as in 661 we have mention of Ethelwold, king of Sussex, who was persuaded in that year by Wulfhere of Mercia, who had over-run Wessex, to become a Christian, Wulfhere himself being his sponsor and rewarding him with the grant of the Isle of Wight and the province of the Meonwaras in Hampshire.[5] In 685, however, Cedwalla, king of Wessex, recovered the Isle of Wight and slew Ethelwold, but was driven out of the kingdom by the South Saxon generals (*duces*) Berthun and Audhun,[6] who continued to rule Sussex until the former was killed by Cedwalla.[7] At the same time the Sussex forces had lent their aid to Edric son of Egbert, and, after defeating and slaying King Lothere, had placed Edric on the throne of Kent.[8] Some forty years later this tendency to support other men's quarrels brought trouble upon the South Saxons. In 722 Ine, Cedwalla's son, having compelled Aldbricht his enemy to flee into Surrey and Sussex, where he apparently got together a sufficient following to become a source of danger to Ine, moved into Sussex and fought a successful action in which Aldbricht was killed.[9]

Although the South Saxons were apparently subject to, or at least within the sphere of influence of Wessex, they continued to have rulers of their own whose names are recorded only in contemporary charters, and who attest, for the most part indifferently, as ' Rex ' or ' Dux.' Thus Wattus occurs as king about 700, and Nunna, to whom coins are doubtfully ascribed,[10] about the same time ; Osmund and Ealdwulf, who appear as both ' Rex ' and ' Dux,' Ealweald and Ethelbert, who each attest as

[1] *Hen. of Huntingdon* (Rolls Ser.), 51.   [2] Ibid. 47.
[3] *Ric. de Cirencester* (Rolls Ser.), 43, says that Sussex fell to Ceaulin, king of Wessex, about 590.
[4] *Hen. of Huntingdon* (Rolls Ser.), 55.   [5] Ibid. 61.   [6] Ibid. 102.
[7] *Ric. de Cirencester* (Rolls Ser.), 203.
[8] *Hen. of Huntingdon* (Rolls Ser.), 105. William of Malmesbury names Edric as the successor of Ethelwold in Sussex. *Gesta Regum* (Rolls Ser.), 33.   [9] Ibid.
[10] Hawkins, *Silver Coins of England* (3rd ed.), 29.

'Rex,' occur in charters of doubtful authenticity from about 765 to 795.[1]

The kingdom of the South Saxons continued thus semi-independent until Egbert in 823 completed the consolidation of England by sending his son Ethelwulf to receive the submission of Kent, Surrey, Sussex and Essex.[2] These four kingdoms, or counties as they may now perhaps be considered, on Egbert's death in 836 formed the portion of his younger son Athelstan,[3] and in 855, on the death of Ethelwulf, they passed to his second son Ethelbert.[4] Ethelwulf himself was buried at Steyning,[5] though, as the chronicle states that his body was at Winchester,[6] it is probable that it was translated thither by his famous son Alfred, whose connection with Sussex is of considerable interest. It was at 'Dene' in this county that Asser, his friend and biographer, first made his royal master's acquaintance.[7] This is usually held to have been West Dean near Seaford, at which last named place tradition in the twelfth century asserted that Alfred once presided over a meeting of the Witan.[8] A large proportion of the lands bequeathed by his will[9] were in Sussex : thus to his nephew Ethelm he left the vills of Aldingbourne, Compton, Beeding, Beddingham (?) and Barnham ; to his other nephew, Ethelwold, that of Steyning ; and to Osferth his cousin the vills of Beckley, Rotherfield, Ditchling, Sutton, Lyminster, Angmering and Felpham.

Of the early plundering raids of the Danes no details relating to Sussex have been preserved, and the first occasion on which they appear is in 895 when a Danish force returning from the siege of Exeter attacked the men of Chichester and suffered a severe defeat at their hands, the townsmen, it is said, killing many hundreds of them and even capturing some of their ships.[10] Two years later two Danish ships, which had been damaged in a fierce encounter with Alfred's forces under the reeve Lucumon, were driven on to the Sussex shore, where their crews were captured and taken to Winchester and hanged.[11] In 897 Eadulf was appointed to protect Sussex from the Danes,[12] but he died the same year of the plague which was then raging.[13] After this for almost a hundred years there is a blank in the history of the county, till in 994 Olaf of Norway and Swegen of Denmark, failing in their attack on London, turned aside into Sussex and the neighbourhood and 'wrought the greatest evil that ever any army could do in burning and harrying and in man-slaying.'[14] Again, in 998, the Danes wintered in the Isle of Wight, and obtained their provisions by plundering Hampshire and Sussex,[15] the latter county being also ravaged in 1006 by a force which landed at Sandwich and was making its way to the favourite winter quarters in the Isle of Wight.[16]

[1] Searle, *Anglo-Saxon Kings and Nobles*, 269.
[2] *Ang. Sax. Chron.* (Rolls Ser.), ii. 53.   [3] Ibid. 55.   [4] Ibid. 54.
[5] Asser, *Life of King Alfred* (ed. Stevenson, 1904), p. 132.
[6] *Ang. Sax. Chron.* (Rolls Ser.), ii. 57.   [7] Asser, op. cit. cap. 79.   [8] Ibid. note.
[9] *Liber de Hyda* (Rolls Ser.), 531.   [10] *Ang. Sax. Chron.* (Rolls Ser.), ii. 72.
[11] Ibid. 74.   [12] *Ric. de Cirencester* (Rolls Ser.), ii. 48.
[13] *Ang. Sax. Chron.* (Rolls Ser.), ii. 73.   [14] Ibid. 106.   [15] Ibid. 108.
[16] *Walt. of Coventry* (Rolls Ser.), i. 29.

A HISTORY OF SUSSEX

At last, in 1009, Ethelred was so far roused from his customary inactivity as to assemble a powerful fleet at Sandwich, but with the perverse folly so characteristic of him he chose this particular moment to banish Wulfnoth 'child,' a South Saxon noble, probably the father of the great Earl Godwine,[1] on the false accusation of Brihtric, brother of the treacherous Edric. Wulfnoth collecting twenty ships, apparently part of the great fleet prepared against the Danes and possibly the South Saxon contingent, began to harry the coast; whereupon Brihtric, taking eighty of the assembled ships, set out to capture him, but a great storm arising, his vessels were driven on shore, where they were burnt by Wulfnoth.[2] As a result of this disaster the whole fleet dissolved, and nothing was done against the Danes, who in the autumn came against Canterbury, and would have taken it had they not been bought off. They then retired to the island and harried Hampshire and Sussex.[3] Two years later, in 1011, the district attacked by the Danes included Sussex and Hastings,[4] which is mentioned separately. The election of Cnut as King of England in 1017 at last gave Sussex rest.

In the fifty years following the accession of Cnut the history of Sussex is the history of the rise of two great rival powers—the native house of Godwine and the foreign influence of Normandy. How Godwine, who, as we have just seen, was probably a Sussex man by descent, rose to be the first man in the kingdom, holder of a wide earldom which included Sussex, and the father of sons whose earldoms covered the southern half of England, is well known. By the end of the Confessor's reign a third part of the county was in the hands of the house of Godwine, while Bosham was his chief residence. Two events of disastrous import are connected with Bosham. In 1049 Godwine and Harold had sailed in command of a small fleet in search of pirates, and cast anchor at Pevensey, where Harold apparently left the fleet and gave up his ship to his cousin Beorn; hither, then, came Swegen, Godwine's eldest son, hot with anger against Harold and Beorn who had opposed the restoration of his earldom; dissembling his treacherous intentions, he persuaded Beorn to ride with him to the King at Sandwich, and then changing his direction rode to Bosham, where he caused his cousin to be carried on board one of his vessels lying there, and murdered him. For this dastardly deed he was outlawed and declared 'Nithing' by the King and his whole army. The men of Hastings pursued him and caught two of his vessels,[5] but he himself escaped to Flanders, and was next year restored to his earldom. In 1051 he had again to fly from England, when banishment was pronounced against Godwine and all his house.[6] This banishment was of short duration, for in the summer of 1052 Godwine and Harold returned with a powerful fleet, receiving a hearty welcome from the men of Sussex, and especially those of Hastings,[7] and forced King Edward to restore their honours to them.

---

[1] See Freeman, *Norman Conquest*, vol. i. app. MM.
[2] *Ang. Sax. Chron.* (Rolls Ser.), ii. 114, 115. [3] Ibid. 115. [4] Ibid. 117.
[5] Freeman, *Norman Conquest*, ii. 102-5. [6] Ibid. 151. [7] Ibid. 322.

POLITICAL HISTORY

The second event connected with Bosham was more disastrous to the house of Godwine, for it was from that place that Harold set out, probably in 1064,[1] on the cruise which ended in his being wrecked on the coast of Ponthieu, and thus led to his taking the famous oath upon the relics renouncing his claim to the English crown in favour of William Duke of Normandy.

It has been stated above that one of the features of Sussex history during this period was the rise of Norman influence, the introduction of which by the Confessor laid the foundations of the Norman conquest of England ; and that this was so is clear, when we find that the great group of harbours at the east of the county—Hastings, Rye, and Winchelsea—and the mid-Sussex harbour of Steyning were all in the hands of the Norman Abbey of Fécamp, while at the west the King's favourite Norman chaplain Osbern, afterwards Bishop of Exeter, held the great estate of Bosham, which commanded the entrance to the harbour of Chichester.[2] It was not, however, to any of these ports that William steered his course when he set out to win the crown of England.

In January 1066 Edward the Confessor died, and Harold was immediately elected his successor. William at once formulated his claim to the throne, and entered into negotiations with neighbouring princes for the invasion of England. In May, Tostig, Harold's brother but William's ally, ravaged the coasts of the Isle of Wight, Sussex, and Kent ; Harold speedily called out the local forces—the 'fyrd'—to defend the coast, especially the ports of Hastings and Pevensey,[3] and kept them together for four months, but at the end of this period they could no longer be maintained in arms, and on September 8 the army was disbanded.[4] A fortnight later a force under Tostig and Harold Hardrada landed in the north of England and captured York, but Harold marching rapidly north utterly defeated the invaders at Stamford Bridge, killing their two leaders. Meanwhile William of Normandy was waiting anxiously at St. Valery, and praying for a favourable wind that he might cross to England ; and at last, after a month's delay, the south wind blew, and in the evening of Wednesday, October 27, his fleet set sail.[5] Early next morning the Duke's own ship, the *Mora*, cast anchor in Pevensey Bay and lay waiting for her consorts. Soon the whole fleet had assembled, and were drawn up on the beach ; William himself was the first to leap on shore, and in his haste stumbled and fell. Quick-witted as ever, he turned the ill-omened accident to good effect, exclaiming, 'By the splendour of God, I have taken seizin of my kingdom ; the earth of England is in my two hands.'

Following their general, the whole army rapidly disembarked. First the archers reconnoitred the ground while the knights mounted and formed up, but no resistance was met, so hastily throwing up an entrenchment within the Roman walls which had once surrounded

---

[1] Freeman, *Norman Conquest*, iii. 222. [2] Round, *Feudal England*, 319.
[3] Freeman, *Norman Conquest*, iii. 325. [4] Ibid. 338. [5] Ibid. 397.

A HISTORY OF SUSSEX

Anderida, the Duke mustered his troops and found that only two ships had gone astray—possibly the detachment cut up by the men of Romney. Leaving a small force to guard the ships the cavalry pressed on towards Hastings to secure forage and provisions for the army. As soon as the soldiers had occupied that town William caused them to construct a fortification with fosse and mound and wooden palisade, probably upon the commanding hill which is now crowned by the ruins of the later masonry castle.[1] Meanwhile the invading host plundered and ravaged the country round with fire and sword in the usual manner of troops in an enemy's territory,[2] driving the terror-struck inhabitants to seek refuge in the churches and cemeteries.

While the Norman army was landing at Pevensey a local thegn who had watched their movements took horse and rode to Harold's camp, and from Hastings another messenger sped north with the evil news.[3] The tidings reached Harold as he was feasting with his soldiers after the glorious victory of Stamford Bridge. He at once marched down to London, and remained there a week collecting reinforcements, drawing up plans for the coming campaign, and exchanging messages with the Norman Duke, to all of whose demands and wily suggestions of compromise he returned an indignant refusal.[4] Some of his counsellors advised the isolation of the invaders by ravaging the district round Hastings, and so cutting off supplies and compelling them to retire without fighting, but Harold determined to fight and to command the English troops in person.[5] Accordingly on the twelfth he left London and marched south towards Hastings through Kent and Sussex, and on the next day, Friday, occupied the position which he decided to defend— for it was his object to act on the defensive. The spot selected was well chosen ; some seven miles north-west of Hastings, the present road to London crosses, and is commanded by, a ridge of high land running east and west, of no great altitude but somewhat steep ; from the centre of this ridge on the London side a sort of isthmus runs back to the higher land, while on the side toward Hastings the ground is broken and undulating with marshy land in the hollows.[6]

On this ridge stands now the town and ruined abbey of Battle, and on it, then wild and desolate, marked only by an ancient apple-tree,[7] Harold drew up his men. His flanks were well protected by marsh and woodland, and he hastily strengthened his front by digging a fosse,[8] possibly covered with branches or in some way concealed, with three entries or passages for his skirmishers. Having done all that could be

---

[1] Freeman, *Norman Conquest*, iii. 407-11.

[2] There seems little proof of any exceptional harrying of the country as implied by Professor Freeman (ibid. 412).

[3] Ibid. 418.   [4] Ibid. 430-2.   [5] Ibid. 434-6.   [6] Ibid. 441-4.

[7] The site of the battle was that part of Battle afterwards known as Sandlake, or Sentlache, which Orderic adopted—Normanizing it as Senlac—for the name of the battle. Prof. Freeman pedantically rejected the name of Hastings, which had been applied to the battle for eight hundred years, in favour of Senlac—a name which, even if contemporary, was used by only one writer, and misspelled by him.

[8] According to Wace. For the destruction of Mr. Freeman's famous 'Palisade' by Mr. Round, see *Feudal England*, pp. 340-58.

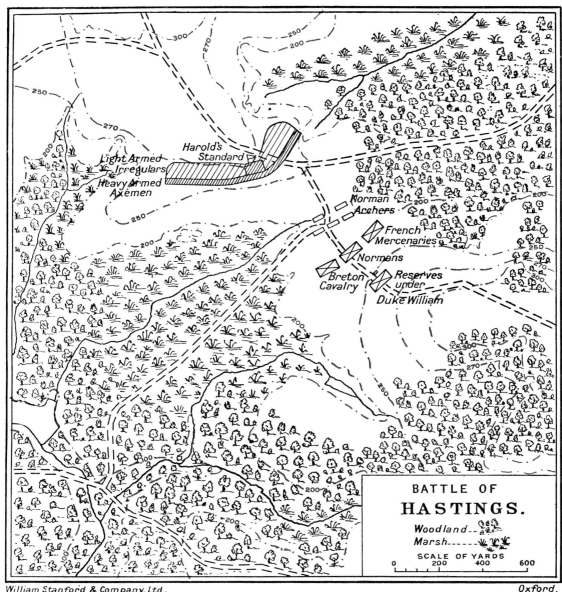

Light Armed
Irregulars
Heavy Armed
Axemen

Harold's
Standard

Norman
Archers

French
Mercenaries

Normans

Breton
Cavalry

Reserves
under
Duke William

BATTLE OF
HASTINGS.
Woodland
Marsh
SCALE OF YARDS
0   200   400   600

William Stanford & Company, Ltd.,   Oxford.

To face page 486.

done to make the position secure, the English soldiery gave themselves up to feasting, song, and minstrelsy, singing of their past victories, drinking to each other and shouting defiance of the enemy. In the rival camp the sterner temperament of the Normans, influenced by the semi-religious character given to their enterprise and the genuine piety of their leader, found expression in prayer : the princely bishops Odo of Bayeux and Geoffrey of Coutances, with other lesser priests and monks, went through the host administering the consolations of religion to all.[1]

When the morning of Saturday, October 14, dawned, William briefly addressed his troops, and then set them in motion. As they rode over the brow of Telham hill the English forces came into view on the ridge below. In the centre waved the national standard, the dragon of Wessex, and Harold's personal ensign of the fighting man : here were stationed Harold himself, his brothers Gurth and Leofwine, and probably Leofric, the aged Abbot of Peterborough, and Ælfwig, abbot of Winchester, with the house-carls—the picked troops of the army.[2] All along the brow of the ridge ran a line of heavy-armed infantry in close order, shoulder to shoulder and shield touching shield, forming a defensive wall, a living rampart[3] ; behind them were the light-armed troops and rustic levies, many with no better weapons than clubs and stones, and in the foreground were probably a number of skirmishers.

On Telham hill the Norman knights put on their armour, and once again the Duke showed his freedom from superstition, for in putting on his coat of mail the forepart was turned hindmost ; careless of the ill-omen he lightly said that it but signified that he who was now a Duke should be turned round into a King, and mounted forthwith upon his Spanish war-horse.[4] As he gazed upon his enemy's array he vowed that if God would grant him the victory he would build a great abbey where Harold's standard flew.[5] Then he and his host rode on ; on the left were the Breton cavalry under Alan of Brittany and Ralph of Wader of Norfolk, on the right were the French mercenaries with William Fitz-Osbern, Eustace of Boulogne, and probably Roger of Montgomery.[6] In the centre—where the consecrated banner was borne by Toustain of Bec—rode William himself and his brothers Odo, bishop of Bayeux, and Count Robert of Mortain, with many others whose names are famous in English history.[7]

As soon as the troops had reached the lower ground the gallant minstrel knight Taillefer[8] spurred forward, chanting the deeds of Charlemagne and the song of Roland and of Roncesvalles, tossing his sword in the air and catching it again as he rode on ; then dashing upon the English skirmishers he struck down two, but fell beneath the axe of a third. The overture was finished, and now the curtain rose on the

---

[1] Freeman, op. cit. 451.   [2] Ibid. 475–6.   [3] Round, op. cit. 346.
[4] Freeman, op. cit. 455–6.   [5] Ibid. 457.
[6] Although a story of his personal conflict with a gigantic Englishman is related by Wace (ibid. 494), some doubt exists whether he was actually present at the battle.
[7] Ibid. 458–66.   [8] Ibid. 478.

first act of the battle; rapidly the archers of Lisieux and Evreux swarmed forward, and with the aid of the cavalry drove the enemy's skirmishers back behind their shield-wall. Till that wall should be broken the cavalry could do nothing, so the archers continued to pour their shafts into the opposing mass, the English light-armed troops dashing out to drive their assailants back.[1] At last, maddened by the constant rain of arrows, to which with their smaller force of bowmen and slingers they could make little reply, the heavy-armed infantry on the English right[2] broke their line and joined in the charge upon their adversaries. For a moment success crowned their efforts; the archers and their cavalry supports fled, and even some of the Norman knights were seized with panic and turned their backs, crying that their Duke was slain and all lost. Count Eustace of Boulogne also turned craven and urged William to fly, but he, riding up from his position in the rear, where he had been watching the progress of the battle with his reserves, uncovered his head to show that he still lived, and soon checked the fugitives, while the war-like Bishop of Bayeux, wielding a great mace, helped to rally the disordered troops. Turning now upon their pursuers the cavalry rapidly drove them back,[3] following so hard upon them that English and French alike plunged into the fosse in front of Harold's line and filled it with their bodies.[4] Meanwhile William, taking advantage of the disorder in the shield wall, dashed forward with his picked knights against the English centre. As he reached it his horse fell, pierced by Gurth's javelin; but springing to his feet he struck Gurth to the ground, and seizing another charger from one of his knights, pressed on. Again his horse fell, and again he revenged its death upon its slayer; this time Count Eustace gave up his mount to his lord, and the attack was renewed. Leofwine, and many others, fell, but the English axes were not idle, and Harold above all was pre-eminent, striking horse and man to the ground with one blow.[5] The Norman attack was repulsed, and the disaster at the fosse, combined with the gallant defence of the centre, enabled the defenders to re-form their shield-wall.

Once more the attacking cavalry were faced by a barrier against which they could only surge uselessly. Again the archers poured in their shafts, but William had received a hint from the earlier accident and now laid a trap for the defenders. Again the English rushed upon the foe, and again the Norman host seemed to waver; all along the line the heavy infantry broke their ranks and charged down the hill. At first the Normans fled before them, but suddenly they wheeled round to the attack[6]; hastily the English tried to retreat to their position, but only

---

[1] Round, op. cit. 371–2.
[2] Freeman, op. cit. 482. Mr. Round says 'the whole host' (op. cit. 373).
[3] Ibid. 482–4.
[4] Round, op. cit. 374–80. The question of the position of this incident in the battle is a very difficult one; it seems to have been in connection with the Norman flight, but may have been either at the beginning or during the rally. The latter theory is perhaps the more probable.
[5] Freeman, op. cit. 484–8.　　[6] Ibid. 488–90.

BAYEUX TAPESTRY

(1) The arrival of the Normans at Pevensey. William's ship is distinguished by the square lantern on the top of its mast. The horses are disembarked, the ships drawn up on the beach, and the light cavalry hasten on to Hastings to forage.

(2) William holds a Council of War at Hastings with his brothers Odo and Robert, of whom the latter is apparently for instant action, while the former urges caution. William causes a mound, fortified with a wooden palisade, to be thrown up at Hastings. A messenger is shown announcing William's landing to Harold; also a typical instance of the Invaders' ravages round Hastings.

(3) The Normans leave Hastings. The spirited charger on the left is probably meant for the Arab steed presented to William by the King of Spain. The troops are armed with close-fitting coats of mail, conical helmets, kite-shaped shields and lances, some of which have pennons. On the right is shown William, armed with a war club; the figure behind him, also carrying a mace, is no doubt Odo of Bayeux.

To face p. 488.

BAYEUX TAPESTRY

(4) Vital the Scout announces the position of Harold's army. The Normans ride over the wooded hill of Telham; on the broken ground beyond Harold's scouts are watching, and bring news of William's approach to Harold himself, who is mounted and armed in the same manner as the Normans, but is distinguished by his moustaches.

(4) AND (5) William addresses his troops and sends them forward. In front are the archers, supported by light cavalry armed with javelins; the heavy cavalry, with their lances, follow.

(5) and (6) The battle begins, and an assault is made on the English shield-wall, from behind which the archers shoot, while on either side javelins are hurled. Where the opponents come to close quarters the English axes are vigorously plied, and the ground is covered with the dead and wounded. (6) and (7) The first Norman success; the English lines broken and Gyrth and Leofwine slain.

To face p. 488.

BAYEUX TAPESTRY

(7) Continuation of the struggle in which Gyrth and Leofwine fell. The figure striking down a horse is probably Harold. The disaster of the Malfosse, the ground apparently giving way under the Norman cavalry, who fall into the fosse with some of the English. (7) and (8) At the same time Bishop Odo, flourishing his mace, rallies the fugitives.

(8) William raises the front piece of his helmet to show his followers that he is still alive. The archers are shown in the lower border renewing their attack, and shooting up into the air. The Norman cavalry come to close quarters, and many of Harold's bodyguard are slain.

(9) The fight round the Dragon Standard. Harold staggers back, clutching the arrow which has pierced his eye. As he lies dead a knight strikes off his leg. The last handful of house-carls die fighting, and the Norman light cavalry, including mounted archers, drive before them the English levies, armed only with clubs, who fly on horseback or on foot into the woods. In the lower border are seen the spoilers of the slain.

To face p. 488.

to find that another force of cavalry had ridden round them and cut them off.[1]

Still the defenders of the ridge stood firm around their standard and repelled the attacking knights ; and still the remainder of the shield-wall—contracted, but not entirely broken up—received and checked the shafts of the bowmen, till as the dusk drew on there seemed a chance that Harold might, under cover of darkness, withdraw and raise another army. At last the Duke ordered his men to shoot up into the air so that their arrows should fall like rain upon the foe. The effect was terrible ; forced to expose either their bodies or their heads to the shafts, scores of English fell, and, worst disaster of all, Harold himself dropped to the ground in agony with an arrow piercing his eye.[2]

The Normans were not slow to profit by the disorder, and dashed in to render their victory complete. The English standard fell, and four knights cut their way to where the wounded Harold lay, and slew him. One knight added the indignity of striking off the dead king's leg, but William, angered at the unworthy deed, dismissed him from his army. Still the gallant band fought till all were either dead or disabled. The local levies fled in the gathering darkness, pursued by the victors, and the battlefield, and all England, remained in William's hands.[3]

Next morning search was made for Harold's body, but so mutilated was it and so thick lay the dead in that spot that none could recognize it till the fallen hero's mistress, Edith Swanneshals, came, who knew it by certain marks unknown to others. Sternly refusing all offers of ransom, the Conqueror ordered the body to be buried on the sea shore under a pile of stones[4] ; but afterwards—probably when the kingdom was assured to him and he could afford to be lenient—he relented and allowed it to be taken to the Minster of Holy Cross at Waltham, which Harold had founded.[5]

Of the partition of Sussex between the Conqueror's relations and other gallant followers, enough has already been said.[6] Nor does any other event of his reign call for mention here. When, however, William Rufus succeeded to the throne, to the exclusion of his elder brother Robert, Pevensey once more appears in history. Odo of Bayeux, Robert's principal supporter, escaped from Tunbridge Castle when Rufus besieged and took it, and fled to Pevensey, where his brother Count Robert of Mortain had erected a castle. The strong Roman walls, forming an outer defence to the palisaded Norman mound, defied all attacks, and it was not till food ran short and all hope of relief had

---

[1] Round, op. cit. 380–2.   [2] Freeman, op. cit. 497–8.

[3] Ibid. 499–502. Several writers relate that the Norman cavalry met with a reverse during the pursuit, being driven down a steep ravine ; but this seems to be only a misplaced version of the fosse disaster earlier in the day, especially as Count Eustace again appears as urging William to flee (ibid. 502–3. Round, op. cit. 378). A little bibliography of the long controversy on the battle was given by Mr. Round as an appendix to his paper on 'The Battle of Hastings' in *Suss. Arch. Coll.* xlii. 63. Since then have appeared his paper on 'Anglo-Norman Warfare' in *The Commune of London* (pp. 40–52), and Mr. F. Baring's note on 'The Battlefield of Hastings' in *Eng. Hist. Rev.* (1905) xx. 65–70.

[4] Freeman, op. cit. 512–4.   [5] Ibid. 518.

[6] See *Introduction to Domesday*, pp. 377–80

been destroyed by the defeat of the Norman fleet which had attempted to put to land and raise the siege, that Odo surrendered.[1]

Rebellion again broke out when Henry I. came to the throne, and the expectation that Robert of Normandy would attempt to land at Pevensey led to the King's assembling an army at that spot ; but the preparations were rendered vain by the Norman fleet directing its course to Portsmouth.[2] When Robert of Bellesme, son of Roger of Montgomery and lord of western Sussex, took up arms against his king in 1101, Arundel Castle was one of his three chief strongholds, and was the first attacked by Henry, who blockaded it and raised a fort to command it while he marched against Bridgenorth.[3] Robert being defeated and banished, his Sussex lands came into the hands of the King ; William Count of Mortain, son of Robert, being also concerned in this rebellion, forfeited his estate of Pevensey. Three of the six Sussex rapes thus fell into the King's hands, and he jealously kept for himself Arundel with its 'honour' throughout his reign, though at his death it passed to his Queen Adelais, on whom he had settled it in dower.[4] Part at least of the rape of Pevensey was granted to Richer de Laigle, who was in possession in 1130,[5] and from whose descendants it became known as 'the Honour of the Eagle.'

The two castles thus forfeited—Arundel and Pevensey—were the only two places in Sussex which played any notable part in the civil war of Stephen's reign. At Arundel the Empress Maud landed in the autumn of 1139, and there she was hospitably entertained by William d'Albini, who had married the Queen Dowager Adelais, while the Earl of Gloucester rode to Bristol to raise forces in her name. Stephen, out of courtesy to the Queen dowager, or as the result of treacherous advice, allowed Maud to pass unharmed to Bristol instead of besieging Arundel as he had first intended.[6]

Gilbert Earl of Pembroke acquired possession of the Castle and rape of Pevensey,[7] and in 1147 when Stephen marched against the fortress, he found it so strong with its formidable keep and powerful walls, washed on one side by the sea and difficult of access even by land, that he abandoned all idea of storming it, and left a force of ships and soldiers to blockade it.[8] After it had fallen into his hands he granted it first to his son Eustace, and on his death to his other son William, Count of Mortain and Earl of Warenne,[9] who had already acquired by his marriage the adjoining rape of Lewes, but who on the accession of Henry II. surrendered Pevensey with his other castles to the King.[10]

When John succeeded to the throne he was in Normandy, and the

---

[1] Freeman, *William Rufus*, i. 72–6.   [2] Ibid. ii. 404.
[3] Matt. Paris, *Chron. Majora* (Rolls Ser.), ii. 123.   [4] Ibid. 170.
[5] Pipe Roll, 31 Hen. I.
[6] *Chron. of Stephen, etc.* (Rolls Ser.), iii. 56.
[7] Round, *Studies on the Red Book of the Exchequer*, p. 7.
[8] *Chron. of Stephen, etc.* (Rolls Ser.), iii. 129.
[9] Round, *Ancient Charters* (Pipe Roll Soc.), 152 ; *Peerage Studies*, 169.
[10] Matt. Paris, *Chron. Majora* (Rolls Ser.), ii. 214.

coast of Sussex was the first spot of English ground on which he set foot as king, for in May 1199 he landed at Seaford.[1] By 16 June he was at Shoreham, whence a few days later he crossed to Normandy.[2] His restlessness and the rapidity of his movements, which were the subject of astonishment to his contemporaries, brought him not infrequently into the county ; thus in April 1206, on his way from Romney to Southampton, he was on successive days at Battle, Malling, Knepp, and Arundel : in 1208 he was at Aldingbourne, the Bishop of Chichester's manor, from 27 to 30 March, and was also there in the following January, and in May 1209, when he went on to Knepp for several days, also visiting Arundel, Bramber and Lewes. John again spent four days at Knepp in April 1211 ; and this was evidently his favourite residence in Sussex. It was a manor belonging to William de Braose, containing a small castle, probably used by the lords of Bramber as a hunting seat ; when John in 1208 began the quarrel with de Braose, which ended in the latter's flight to France and the death of his wife and son at Windsor, this manor, with others, was seized by the King and was not infrequently visited by him, the last occasion apparently being in January 1215.

The complete failure of John's continental campaigns, ending in the conquest of Normandy by Philip of France in 1205, led him to fear an invasion of England. Accordingly he summoned a council of the barons, who decided that an oath to keep the peace and defend the kingdom should be taken throughout the realm by all above the age of twelve ; at the same time it was ordained that head constables should be appointed for every county, and under them a constable for every hundred and borough, in addition to the usual constables of the castles, and that lists should be made of the armed men under each of the constables, who should be empowered to summon such levies when required for defence.[3] In addition to thus providing for infantry and irregulars, it was enacted that every nine knights throughout the country should equip and maintain a tenth knight on penalty of losing their fees.[4] While it is impossible to estimate even approximately the strength of the local levies in Sussex at this period, we can compute with some degree of accuracy the number of knights furnished by the county.[5] The greatest military tenant was the Earl of Arundel, who held the Honour of Arundel under a grant of Henry II, and owed the service of eighty-four and a half knights, of whom the honor of Petworth found twenty-two and a half, that of Halnaker twelve ; Earl Warenne provided sixty knights, the Count of Eu fifty-six, and Gilbert of Laigle thirty-five and a half of 'the honor of Mortain' (an honor distinguished by its 'small fees,' which were so far privileged that when any tax or aid was assessed upon knight's fees these 'small

[1] *Gerv. of Canterbury* (Rolls Ser.), ii. 92. Matthew Paris and other historians say Shoreham.
[2] *Itin.* printed in *Cal. Rot. Pat.* (Rec. Com.), i.
[3] *Gerv. of Canterbury* (Rolls Ser.), ii. 96, 97.   [4] Pat. 6 John, m. 2d.
[5] *Red Book of Exch.* (Rolls Ser.), passim ; *Testa de Nevill* (Rec. Com.), 222-4.

fees' paid only, approximately, two-thirds of the sum paid by the fees of other honors). William de Braose owed the service of ten knights only for his barony,[1] but over forty fees were held of him, and that number of knights would be available when the barony was in the King's hands. Finally there were the Bishop of Exeter, who was responsible for seven and a half knights for the chapelry of Bosham, the Bishop of Chichester, who held his barony by the service of four knights, and possibly another dozen knights not accounted for in the above-mentioned honors. Altogether, therefore, Sussex at the beginning of the thirteenth century had to furnish about two hundred and eighty, or, under the enactment of 1205, rather over three hundred fully equipped mounted men. An idea of the armament of the county forces may be obtained from an order sent in 1230 to Earl Warenne, Simon de Echingham, Amfrey de Feringes and the Sheriff of Sussex, to see that the 'array of arms' was kept within the county as ordained in King John's time,[2] namely, that every man having a knight's fee, or fifteen marks in property, should keep a corselet; for half a fee or ten marks of property, a hauberk; for forty shillings, an iron headpiece, a quilted jerkin (*perpunctum*) and a lance; for twenty shillings, a bow and arrows—unless he dwelt within the bounds of a forest, in which case (to preserve him from the temptation to poach) he should have a bill (*hachiam*) or a lance.

Besides the personal military service thus due from all, those who held certain property had to contribute towards the upkeep of the county defences; thus in 1205 the King ordered the citizens of Chichester and all who owed the service of enclosing part of the town to perform their duty by repairing the walls of the town.[3] In the same way many tenants of the honor of Bramber were bound to enclose a portion of the walls of Bramber castle,[4] and a similar custom existed, under the title 'heccage,' in connection with Pevensey castle.[5] To Pevensey castle also and to Hastings many manors contributed the service of 'castle ward.' There were also a few military serjeanties of no great importance, land near Eastbourne being held by the service of guarding the outer gate of Pevensey castle, and the tenant of an estate in Woolbeding being bound to attend the King as standard-bearer of the infantry in the county.[6] The naval forces of Sussex will be dealt with in another place,[7] so no more than note of their existence need be made here.

The warlike preparations of 1205 came to nothing, but about Easter 1213 there was again an alarm of invasion, and John hastened from Portsmouth by Arundel, Lewes and Battle to Dover, and thence back to Rye and Winchelsea,[8] where he stayed some three days and received the ambassadors of the French King, who appear to have landed at Seaford, as they were accompanied by the mayor and certain bur-

---

[1] *Testa de Nevill* (Rec. Com.), 126.   [2] Close, 14 Henry III. m. 5d.
[3] Pat. 6 John m. 5.   [4] Feet of Fines, Sussex, 50 Henry III.
[5] Salzmann, *Hist. of Hailsham*, 175.   [6] *Testa de Nevill* (Rec. Com.), 226.
[7] See section on 'Maritime Hist.'   [8] *Itinerary*.

gesses of that port.[1] While at Winchelsea John, who was posing at this time as the friend and protégé of the Pope, did not neglect the observances of religion and caused alms to be distributed and a hundred poor to be fed.[2] He then went on into Kent and collected an army which remained on the coast until news of King Philip's defeat in Flanders dispelled all fear of a French invasion. The next occasion on which John passed with his forces through the county his fortunes and his direction were alike changed. In May 1216 while he was in Kent he heard that Louis the Dauphin was landing in England ; resistance with the forces at his disposal was, for the time being, useless, so the King retired to Winchester, halting on the way at Seaford and Bramber and passing through Woolavington.[3] Sussex, as a whole, was a strong centre of loyalty ; the castle of Chichester was in the King's hands, and those of Arundel and Lewes were held by the Earl of Arundel and the Earl of Warenne, two of the greatest and most staunch of John's supporters. The lords of Pevensey and Hastings had each been in arms against the King, who had for a while put the latter castle into the hands of his faithful barons of the Cinque Ports,[4] but had subsequently given it back to the Count of Eu[5] ; Pevensey castle had also, apparently, been restored to Gilbert of Laigle.[6] John, however, took the precaution of dismantling the castle of Hastings, and probably also that of Pevensey.[7] The castles of Bramber and Knepp were, as we have already seen, also in the King's hands, and in May 1215, when the barons had secured possession of the city of London and John's fortunes were at their lowest, he wrote to Roland Bloet to take what forces he had at Knepp or could collect elsewhere and garrison the castle of Bramber with them, at the same time ordering the complete destruction of the dwellings (*domos*) of Knepp.[8] Either this last order was revoked or it did not apply to the castle, as four days later the King wrote to Bloet that if Earl Warenne or any of his men should come to him he should receive them into the castles of Knepp and Bramber.[9] In the following October these two castles were restored to Giles de Braose, bishop of Hereford,[10] who however died within a month, when the King restored Roland Bloet as constable of Knepp and appointed Wilkin Bloet to Bramber.[11] But when Louis began his victorious progress through the southern counties John sent orders for the castle of Knepp to be burnt without delay,[12] and it was apparently also his intention to destroy the castle at Chichester.[13] This latter, however, with all the other defences of Sussex, fell into the hands of his enemies, while, as a probable result, the Earl Warenne and the Earl of Arundel went over to the side of Louis. The men of the Cinque Ports

---

[1] Rot. Misae, 14 John (*Docts. Illustrative of Eng. Hist.*).   [2] Ibid.
[3] *Itinerary.*   [4] Pat. 15 John, m. 6.   [5] Pat. 16 John, m. 17.
[6] Pat. 18 John, m. 3. In October 1215 it was under care of the Earl of Arundel, and received a reinforcement from the King (Pat. 17 John, m. 14).
[7] *Ann. Mon.* (Rolls Ser.), iii. 46, 'destruxit castrum de " Eunesheye " et castrum de Hastinges.'
[8] Pat. 16 John, m. 1.   [9] Ibid.
[10] Pat. 17 John, m. 14.   [11] Pat. 17 John, m. 12.
[12] Pat. 18 John, m. 7.   [13] Pat. 1 Hen. III. m. 8.

remained loyally disposed but could not resist effectually, and John wrote to the barons of Winchelsea in June 1216 that if Louis should attack them they might ransom their town rather than that it should be burnt.[1] Subsequently, in September, he wrote to the barons of Hastings, Rye, Winchelsea, Pevensey and Shoreham, ordering them to return to their allegiance and offering to excuse the oath which they had taken to Louis under compulsion.[2] At the same time he sent a special letter of thanks to the men of Seaford for having remained faithful to him in spite of the pressure put upon them by Gilbert of Laigle, their lord. When John died in October, all Sussex was in the power of the French party, except for the gallant resistance made by one young soldier, William de Casingham, who, reviving the tactics employed by the British against Elle, took to the dense woods of the Weald and with a force of some thousand men constantly harried the invaders and slew many hundreds of them.

The death of John, and Louis' untactful promotion of his French followers at the expense of his English allies, caused the tide of popular feeling to turn strongly against the Dauphin and brought many of the rebellious barons back to their allegiance to the native royal house in the person of the young King Henry III. The King's party spared no efforts to recover the services of the more powerful lords by promises of free pardon and the like ; thus on 28 December 1216 a letter was sent to Gilbert of Laigle, urging him to return to his allegiance and promising that he should lose none of his estates, except that the King would for the time being take over the castle of Pevensey, because it would be so unpleasant for Gilbert if Louis should demand its surrender on the strength of the oath Gilbert had taken to him, but when the war should be over the King would see that justice was done him regarding the castle.[3]

About the end of February, 1217, the Earl Marshal, detaching Philip d'Aubigny to occupy Rye, marched on Winchelsea to hem in the Dauphin, who had taken refuge there and was hard pressed. But a French fleet enabled him to escape and to seize Rye.[4] Thence, however, he fled to France, leaving the Earl Marshal free to move westwards to Shoreham, whence he marched on Farnham, Knepp surrendering to him on the way.[5] From Farnham, which he captured, the King wrote to Reginald de Braose, desiring him to return to his allegiance.[6] The castles of Chichester and Winchester were next reduced,[7] the former being subsequently destroyed,[8] and at Chichester a truce was made by the legate and royal council, and the Earls of Arundel and Warenne rejoined the King, with William St. John, Peter Fitz-Herbert and

[1] Pat. 18 John, m. 7. [2] Ibid. m. 3. [3] Pat. 1 Hen. III. m. 14.
[4] On the last day of February the King wrote to the men of that town, saying that he had heard of the capture of their town by Louis, and bidding them to be of good cheer and not allow the enemy to take any hostage or pledge from them, as he would in a few days send an army under the Earl Marshal and other barons to drive out the French (Pat. 1 Hen. III. m. 13d.).
[5] L'histoire de Guillaume le Maréchal, iii. 220–3. [6] Ibid. m. 12d.
[7] Walter of Coventry (Rolls Ser.), ii. 236. [8] Pat. 1 Hen. III. 8.

494

others.[1] The last-named had a little while previously had a narrow escape from capture by the royalists, who surrounded a number of the rebels near Lewes and took prisoners two nephews of the Count of Nevers, William de Ponte Arche, Robert Savage and many others, 'but Peter Fitz-Herbert did then escape in a marvellous manner, for when the King's soldiers pursued him, his horse creeping up a steep and exceedingly lofty mountain, carried him over its summit, and so he escaped, " sed non in nomine Dei ! " '[3]

Amongst the barons captured at the battle of Lincoln, which, with the subsequent naval victory over Eustace the monk, decided the struggle in Henry's favour, were several who were more or less identified with Sussex, as William de Fiennes, Geoffrey and Walter St. Leger, Geoffrey de Say and Robert Marmion the younger.[4] Peace having been made with Louis and a general amnesty granted to the barons, orders were issued to Hubert de Burgh in his capacity of Warden of the Cinque Ports to cause those of Louis' followers who had been captured and imprisoned at Dover, Sandwich, Bulverhythe and Hastings to be liberated, either without ransom or at a price not exceeding one hundred marks, so that they might be exchanged for men of the Ports who had been taken prisoners.[5]

After Henry's firm establishment on the throne Sussex ceases for nearly fifty years from playing any notable part in the political history of the nation. Like the other counties it was concerned in the king's policy of favouritism and afforded opportunity for him to enrich his foreign courtiers. Thus the castle and manor of Pevensey were bestowed first on the Poitevin Peter de Rivallis,[6] and then, after being for a while in the hands of the Earl Marshal,[7] on the King's uncle Peter of Savoy[8]; Hastings was also granted to Peter of Savoy, and afterwards to Peter de Dreux, Duke of Brittany ; and John Mansel, the King's chief counsellor and one of the most unpopular of his party, held land in Wepham, and had licence to fortify his manor of Sedgewick in 1259.[9] When the feeling against the Poitevins had become so strong that Henry had to submit to their banishment in 1258, William de Valence, by means of bribes, induced Walter de Scotney, the steward of the Earl of Gloucester and a member of an old Sussex family, to administer poison to certain nobles assembled at a banquet in the Bishop of Winchester's palace. As a result of this treacherous action the Earl suffered a severe illness, and his brother William de Clare and some others died, for which Walter de Scotney was executed, and his Sussex estates forfeited.[10]

[1] Pat. 1 Hen. III. m. 10d.

[2] Louis had entrusted the counties of Sussex and Hants to the Count of Nevers, who by his tyranny made himself and his master hated (Ann. Mon. iii. 46).

[3] Gerv. of Canterbury (Rolls Ser.), ii. 112.   [4] Ibid. 111.
[5] Pat. 2 Hen. III. m. 3.   [6] Chart. R. 16 Hen. III. m. 5.
[7] Granted to him in 1234 (Chart. R. 19 Hen. III. m. 16) ; surrendered 1240 (Chart. R. 24 Hen. III. m. 2).   [8] Chart. R. 30 Hen. III. m. 6.
[9] Pat. 43 Hen. III. m. 15. In 1263 John Mansel fled to the Continent ' timens pelli suae ': Gerv. of Canterbury (Rolls Ser.), ii. 222. His Sussex property, bestowed on the younger Simon de Montfort, was subsequently recovered by John Savage.
[10] Blaauw, The Barons' War (ed. 1871), 72.

The enmity between the royalist and baronial parties continued to increase until in 1264, after the appeal to the King of France had resulted in the condemnation of the Oxford statutes, war broke out. The two leaders of the barons were Simon de Montfort Earl of Leicester and Gilbert de Clare Earl of Gloucester ; they each had some slight connexion with Sussex, the former holding the manor of Sheffield and the latter that of Rotherfield. At first the fortune of war favoured the royalists, who captured Northampton, Leicester and Nottingham, relieved the castle of Rochester which Earl Warenne had been gallantly defending against Montfort and seized the Earl of Gloucester's castle at Tonbridge.[1] London, on the other hand, being in the barons' hands and strongly favourable to their cause, Henry evidently considered it advisable to concentrate his forces where they would have the support of the local lords and their fortresses. For this purpose no county was more suitable than Sussex ; Lewes castle was in the hands of the King's devoted brother-in-law John de Warenne Earl of Surrey, and Pevensey and Hastings were held by his uncle Peter of Savoy ; and William de Braose of Bramber, and John Fitz-Alan of Arundel had both proved their loyalty by assisting in the defence of Rochester Castle. Accordingly at the beginning of May the royal army moved southwards from Tonbridge, passing through Robertsbridge,[2] where they plundered the abbey, obliging the monks to pay a heavy ransom for their lives, on to Battle, where, in spite of the loyal welcome given them by the abbey, they repeated their sacrilegious performances ; and so to Winchelsea,[3] where the King vainly endeavoured to secure the assistance of the Cinque Ports fleet, which was refused, though the hostages whom he took subsequently promised to obtain ships for his use, and were released on that understanding.[4] Meanwhile Montfort, with his army reinforced by a large contingent of Londoners, had left London on 6 May and was marching in the direction of Lewes, to which place the King now hastened, passing through Battle and Herstmonceux and reaching Lewes on 10 May.[5] The Earl of Warenne, with Prince Edward and others, were quartered in the castle, but the King preferred to take up his residence in the Cluniac priory. By 12 May the baronial forces had reached Fletching,[6] about nine miles north of Lewes, where they halted ; the choice of this locality was probably due to Earl Simon's possessing the manor of Sheffield in Fletching. Next day the bishops of London and Worcester were sent to the King to make a final effort for peace ; they were empowered to offer compensation for damages and to submit the question of what statutes should remain in force to a select committee of clergy. To this Henry replied by a letter of defiance, and another of similar import was sent by Richard King of the Romans and Prince Edward in the name of all the loyal barons.[7]

The bishops returned with this challenge to Montfort, who at once began to prepare his forces for the struggle. The Bishop of Worcester

[1] Blaauw, *The Barons' War* (ed. 1871), 125–33. [2] Ibid. 222. [3] Ibid. 133.
[4] Close, 48 Hen. III. m. 6d. [5] Blaauw, op. cit. 134. [6] Ibid. 139. [7] Ibid. 142, 159–62.

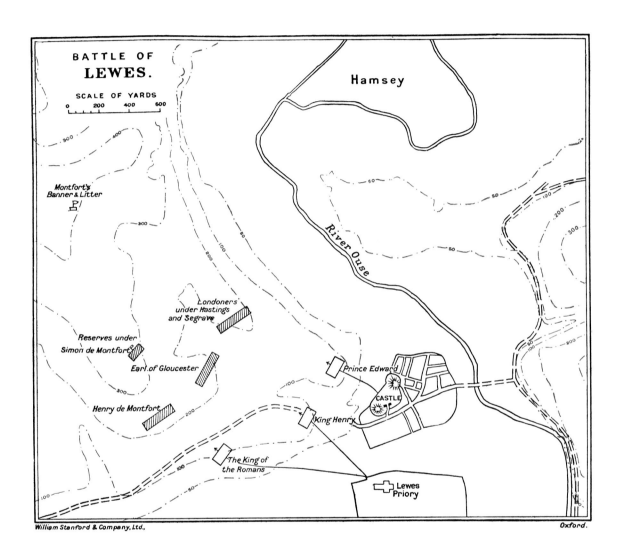

BATTLE OF
LEWES.

SCALE OF YARDS

0   200   400   600

Hamsey

River Ouse

Montfort's
Banner & Litter

Londoners
under Hastings
and Segrave

Reserves under
Simon de Montfort

Earl of Gloucester

Henry de Montfort

Prince Edward

CASTLE

King Henry

The King of
the Romans

Lewes
Priory

William Stanford & Company, Ltd.,   Oxford.

To face page 496.

went through the host giving absolution and encouraging all to fight for their just cause, while the Earl himself saw that all the commanders had full instruction for the morrow's march.[1] The frequency with which members of the same family were fighting in both armies rendered heraldic devices a source of confusion rather than an aid to identification, and it was therefore considered advisable for all the baronial troops to adopt a uniform badge, that chosen being the white cross, which had in other fields distinguished the English crusaders.[2]

Throughout Montfort's camp military alertness and discipline reigned, but a very different aspect was presented by the royalist forces lying at Lewes. Here drunkenness and dissolute licence were rife, and the priory courts and even the holy altars were desecrated by vicious profanity.[3]

Everything points to a total lack of discipline—military and moral— even the one picket posted on the hill, afterwards known as Mount Harry, commanding the barons' line of approach, was so ill-disciplined that the men composing it returned to Lewes, leaving only one of their number on duty.[4] Consequently when Montfort's forces, starting from Fletching before sunrise on Wednesday, 14 May, ascended the Downs about two miles north-west of Lewes the solitary outpost was captured asleep and made to give much useful information as to the royal army.[5] Pressing on in splendid order they bid fair to have surprised the royalists in their beds had it not been that scarcity of hay and corn had compelled certain foragers to start out early in the morning to obtain fresh supplies, who, returning hastily to the town, gave the alarm.[5] Before any of the King's troops could form up their enemies had come in sight of the priory tower. Here Earl Simon halted his army and after a brief address and prayer for victory set his lines in order and awaited the attack. He had the advantage of the ground, his flanks being defended by steep slopes, while along his front the enemy had to advance up a hill, not indeed steep but sufficient to handicap them in charging. On the left, upon the slope descending to the Wallands, were the Londoners under Nicholas de Segrave with Harvey de Boreham and Henry de Hastings, the latter of whom had been knighted with the Earl of Gloucester by Simon de Montfort on the way to the battle. The centre was under the Earl of Gloucester with John Fitz-John and William de Monchesney, and the right wing under Earl Simon's sons Henry and Guy, with whom were the younger Humphrey de Bohun and John de Burgh. The Earl of Leicester himself took command of the reserves, which were stationed on the higher ground commanding the whole field of battle.[6] With the barons were several Sussex men, as, for instance, Sir Henry Hussey of Harting and Jordan de Sackville, and we may be sure that there were present a large number of the local gentry, who can be shown by the evidence of records to have favoured the popular side, including such representative names as Ralph de Camoys, Richard de Amundeville,

[1] Blaauw, *The Barons' War* (ed. 1871), 163. [2] Ibid. 164. [3] Ibid. 166.
[4] Ibid. 171. [5] Ibid. [6] Ibid. 175–85.

John de Bohun of Midhurst, Matthew de Hastings, John de la Haye, John de la Lind, Waleran de Munceaux,[1] William Maufe, John Mucegros and William de Northye. The Sussex royalists, whose names have been recovered, and of whom most were probably present on this occasion, included, besides the lords of the castles already mentioned, William Aguillon of Perching castle, William Bardolf, Henry Percy of Petworth, Robert Pierpoint and Thomas de Audeham.[2]

While Montfort's troops were taking up the positions assigned them the royalists in Lewes were hastily arming and forming up. The first division to take the field was that forming the right wing under Prince Edward with the Earl of Warenne, William de Valence and the flower of the army; they had been quartered in the castle and had probably maintained better discipline than had been observed by the forces stationed at the priory. The left wing under the King of the Romans was now advancing towards the Ashcombe Hill, and in the centre where Henry himself was in command his standard of the golden dragon[3] had been unfurled, when the order to charge was given. Prince Edward, whose gallant spirit scarcely needed the spur of his personal animosity to the Londoners who were his present opponents, dashed impetuously up the slope and hurled his picked force of cavalry upon the half-disciplined and ill-armed levies of Hastings and Segrave who gave way before the furious attack, and broke and fled. Down the slopes of Offham Hill the victorious royalists pursued their flying foes and across the level ground towards Hamsey and Barcombe, where the waters of the Ouse added their complement to the tale of the slain.[4] At last, the rout of the Londoners being complete and the river probably checking the pursuit, the Prince recalled his men and turned back to rejoin the army, when his attention was caught by a small force of men close to the barons' camp on the summit of the Downs guarding Montfort's banner and his litter.[5]

The chance of killing or capturing the leader of the revolt, combined with the prospect of plundering the enemy's camp, induced the victorious force to direct their advance towards this spot and a desperate struggle ensued round the litter, in the course of which the standard-bearer, William le Blund, was slain. Within the car Simon de Montfort had placed certain prominent citizens of London who had opposed him, but in the excitement of the fight and their belief that they were dealing with Earl Simon himself, the royalists destroyed the car and its unfortunate occupants.[6] More time was spent in plundering the barons' camp, and it was late in the evening before Prince Edward's troops

[1] Custody of his lands and those of W. de Northye and of Geoffrey St. Leger had been granted to W. de Warenne on 30 April. (Pat. 48 Hen. III. m. 14.)

[2] Blaauw, op cit. passim; see also Pat. and Close R. etc.

[3] Said by Oxenedes and Rishanger to imply the resolution to give no quarter.

[4] Ibid. 194–5.

[5] This appears to have been a sort of large palanquin with the sides formed of grilles. It had been made for his use after he had injured his leg in the previous December, and so ill-informed were the royalists that they believed him to be still confined to it. Ibid. 173.

[6] Ibid. 196–7.

turned back, tired but exultant, to seek their friends, of whose success in the struggle proceeding out of their sight at the foot of the hills they appear to have had no doubt.

Meanwhile the fortunes of the rival parties had fared very differently on the other parts of the field. The left wing under the King of the Romans had pressed forward, but had been staggered by the shower of stones and arrows directed upon them from the high ground, and Montfort seeing his advantage hurled his reserves upon them. The fight was stern, but the advantage of the ground was with the barons, and also, probably, the advantage of better discipline; for if we may judge from the Dover Chronicle, the previous night's debauchery had unfitted many of the knights for fighting, as Henry Percy acknowledged that several knights on taking the field 'could scarcely see their opponents or hold their swords'; it is true the pious chronicler ascribes this to the influence of the spirits of St. Thomas of Canterbury and St. George,[1] rather than the wine of the Prior of Lewes. At last the royalists broke and fled; many leaders, including Fitz-Alan, Bardolf, Percy, Bohun,[2] and Robert Brus, John Comyn and John Balliol who were in command of the Scottish contingent, surrendered.[2] The King of the Romans, with his young son Edward, fled to a windmill, where he was captured by a young squire or knight, whom Robert of Gloucester calls Sir John de Befs.[3] This rather ignominious downfall of the avaricious and magnificent King was a subject of great delight to the people and political ballad-mongers of the time, whose mockery must have been very trying to the 'ever august' Richard.

The defeat of the left wing, and the absence of the right wing in its rash pursuit of the Londoners, left the centre, under King Henry, to bear the full weight of the attack by the concentrated forces of the barons. The fighting was desperate, Henry himself being in the thick of it and having two horses killed under him, besides being wounded severely; but here too at length the royal forces had to give way.[4] Their natural goal would have been the castle, but the barons seem to have worked round to the north and secured the Westgate, thus forcing them to seek refuge in the priory, whose great precinct wall constituted a formidable defence.

Thus, when Prince Edward and his comrades reached the town the castle, to which they first turned, and the priory, to which the Prince afterwards forced his way, were the only points not in the enemy's hands. Seeing the desperate state of affairs a large number of the royalist leaders, including the King's brothers, William de Valence and Guy de Lusignan, the Earl of Warenne and Hugh Bigot fled through the town and across the bridge over the Ouse, where many of the fugitives were drowned, to Pevensey castle and thence to France.[5] Their flight was dishonourable, but they could have done nothing to retrieve the day had they remained, and they were able to do much for

---

[1] *Gerv. of Canterbury* (Rolls Ser.), ii. 238.   [2] Blaauw, op. cit. 198.
[3] Ibid. 203.   [4] Ibid. 198.   [5] Ibid. 205.

their cause in France with the aid of the Queen, so that it may be considered as justified, or at least condoned, by the result.

For a while the contest continued, the castle repelling all attacks and its garrison setting fire to the town, to which the besiegers replied by firing the priory, whose church was with difficulty saved from destruction.[1] At last a truce was declared, at the suggestion of Earl Simon, and the decisive battle of Lewes was over. How many fell it is impossible to say with any certainty, but the lowest estimate would put the number at three thousand.[2] On the King's side two justiciaries, William de Wilton and Fulk Fitz-Warren, perished, and twenty-three barons were either taken or slain; while of the victors, besides William le Blund already mentioned, Ralph Heringot, a Sussex man, was the only baron who fell.[3]

Next day, Thursday, 15 May, the ecclesiastics appointed by either side to arrange the terms of peace met and drew up the famous treaty known as the Mise of Lewes.[4] Its terms are matters of national rather than local history, but we may note that the Bishop of Chichester, who had throughout given his support to the popular party, was chosen as the third of the three electors of the King's council, the other two being the Earls of Leicester and Gloucester. Prince Edward having been sent to Dover castle to be guarded by Henry de Montfort, the King was taken by Earl Simon on 17 May to Battle,[5] no longer with power to extort money from his entertainers as he had done on his last visit less than a fortnight before, and so to London. Following the transference of power there was naturally a transference of property, both regular as in the case of the royal grant of Peter of Savoy's lands to the Earl of Gloucester,[6] and irregular, as instanced by cases on the Assize and other Plea rolls, the principal 'robbers' in Sussex being Geoffrey St. Leger, Reynold de Tyreshers and John St. Alban,[7] and the principal sufferers Peter of Savoy, Thomas de Audham and Denise de Northeton.[8]

Immediately after the victory of Lewes, on 15 May, the garrison of Pevensey were commanded not to leave the castle without further orders,[9] and in July Hankin de Witsand, constable of Pevensey, John de la Rede and Hubert de Montreal were sent for to come to the King, in charge of William Maufe, to declare the truth about the injuries done by them in the district of Pevensey.[10] Later in the month John d'Abernon, who had superseded Roger de Loges as sheriff,[11] was ordered to take over the castle from the same three men and give them a safe-conduct to go either to the King or beyond seas.[12] They, however, refused to surrender it, and in September Henry Husee and others were ordered to guard the coast of Pevensey[13]—three hundred archers being

[1] Blaauw, op. cit. 208.　[2] Ibid. 211.　[3] Ibid. 210.　[4] Ibid. 215–7.
[5] Ibid. 222.　[6] Pat. 48 Hen. III. m. 8.　[7] Assize R. 1207.
[8] Apparently the same as the Denise of Pevensey, who at her own cost rebuilt the churches of Pevensey when they were injured during the siege of the castle (Mins. Accts. 1089–21).
[9] Pat. 48 Hen. III. m. 13.　[10] Ibid. m. 8.　[11] Ibid. m. 10.
[12] Ibid. m. 8d.　[13] Ibid. m. 4.

sent at the same time to garrison Winchelsea during the absence of its fleet at Sandwich.[1]   In the same month John Fitz-Alan, Robert St. John and others were ordered to come with horses and arms to assist the younger Simon de Montfort in besieging the castle.[2]   Simon was in command of this enterprise in November 1264,[3] when a payment of seven hundred marks was ordered to be made to him for the expenses of the siege.[4]   By the success of the royalists in bringing reinforcements of men and munitions by sea, the siege was prolonged,[5] and Simon was still occupied at Pevensey when orders were issued in the following March to summon Peter of Savoy at Pevensey, John de Warenne at Lewes, and Hugh Bigot at Bosham to attend the forthcoming parliament[6]—the historic parliament in which the cities and boroughs were to be represented for the first time ; and it was probably at Pevensey that in April 1265 he received his father's commands to cause John Fitz-Alan to surrender either his young son or his castle of Arundel as security for his good faith.[7]   The siege was fruitless, but one mark of it is still visible in the gap which exists in the southern wall which was thrown down at this time.[8]   When the royalist cause began to recover its strength Montfort decided that his countess, who had been in residence at Porchester castle, would be safer at Dover; accordingly in June 1265 she passed through Chichester to Bramber, and thence to Wilmington, where, at the priory, her son Simon appears to have met her and escorted her through Battle to Winchelsea and thence to Dover castle, which was under the command of her eldest son Henry, who, however, shortly afterwards left to join his father and fall with him at Evesham.[9]   Simon, also, in July was summoned to his father's aid, and raising the siege of Pevensey marched through Winchester to Kenilworth, where by his most unmilitary slackness he suffered a disastrous defeat which con- tributed largely to the 'débacle' at Evesham.   The Countess of Leicester, who continued to hold Dover, had with her several Sussex men ; there was a contingent of archers from Pevensey under John la Warre, who made himself so obnoxious to the royalists that the terms of composition for his estate were made particularly heavy ; a hundred sailors from Winchelsea, under Richard de Montfort; John de la Haye, who had been appointed constable of Rye and Winchelsea in August 1264; Waleran de Monceaux and Matthew de Hastings, the latter of whom seems to have had some share in the surrender of the castle to Prince Edward.[10]   After the fall of Dover, the Cinque Ports gave up the struggle, with the exception of Winchelsea, which was only taken by the Prince at the cost of much bloodshed.[11]   The pendulum had thus swung back again and the royalists, restored to power, seized and con- fiscated the estates of the fallen party; but by the Dict of Kenilworth the ' rebels ' were permitted to compound for their estates, and this

[1] Close, 48 Hen. III. m. 3.   [2] Pat. 48 Hen. III. m. 3d.
[3] Close, 49 Hen. III. m. 12d.   [4] Pat. 49 Hen. III. m. 29.
[5] Ibid. m. 28.   [6] Close, 29 Hen. III. m. 11.
[7] Pat. 49 Hen. III. m. 17.   [8] Exch. K.R. Accts. 479-15.
[9] Blaauw, op. cit. 323-4.   [10] Ibid. 325-6   [11] Ibid. 331.

appears to have been done in Sussex so fully that little change is notice-able in the position of the more prominent families. Amongst the royalists to whom the lands of the rebels were at first granted may be noted Imbert de Montreal, one of the gallant defenders of Pevensey, the recipient of the lands of William de Goldingham,[1] and of Gervase, William and Robert de Bestenoure,[2] who afterwards redeemed them by payment of £100.[3]

If the latter part of the reign of Henry III. was a period of anarchy and illegality, the converse is true of his successor's reign. The name of Edward I. is inseparably linked with the idea of law and order, and almost his first act on returning from the Holy Land to take up the reins of government in 1275 was to issue commissions and articles of inquiry for the great inquest whose returns are known as the Hundred Rolls.[4] The picture presented by these returns for the county of Sussex is a dark one of oppression and extortion ; from the sheriff to the catchpoll, from the earl to the bailiff of a petty manor, every officer seems to have used his position and power to wring money from those below him. But the remedy of such abuses was not the only, even if it was the principal, reason for this inquest, which was also intended to be an inquiry into the usurpation of royal rights and franchises by the nobles and manorial lords. The result of this investigation is seen more fully in the proceedings upon the writs 'de quo Warranto'[5] of 1278, which throw so much light on the local jurisdiction of Sussex and other counties. At the time that these writs were issued it is said to have been the King's intention to seize into his own hands all franchises and privileges exercised by prescription only and not by virtue of a royal charter, regranting such as he might see fit for payment. This ex-pedient for raising funds was, however, abandoned as a result of the opposition it aroused. The story of Earl Warenne drawing his rusty sword and vowing that as his ancestors had won their lands and privi-leges therewith so would he defend them, is well known ; it is true enough to the spirit of that and other noblemen, though its literal accuracy may well be doubted ; if made, the boast was an idle one for one whose name and lands had descended to him in the female line.

In taking a brief survey of local jurisdiction and privilege in Sussex at the end of the thirteenth century, we may first notice that of the fifty-three returns made at this time twenty, including many of the most comprehensive, relate to ecclesiastics, several of them being only connected with the county by the possession of small holdings. Thus the Abbot of Westminster at Parham, the Bishop of London at Lods-worth, the Templars at Compton, and the Hospitallers at Midhurst, recite all their well-known long lists of privileges. The Archbishop of Canterbury's extensive holding, though not mentioned, enjoyed the same

---

[1] He had acted as the younger Simon de Montfort's head bailiff of the district (Assize Roll, 1207).
[2] Supplementary Close R. 3.   [3] Close, 50 Hen. III. m. 10d.
[4] *Rotuli Hundredorum* (Rec. Com.), ii. 201–19.
[5] *Rotuli de Quo Warranto* (Rec. Com.), 749–63.

rights as the rest of his barony in Kent; and very wide powers were appurtenant to the abbey of Battle, the proceedings against whom are also wanting; the manors of each of these formed a peculiar jurisdiction possessing its own courts; prisoners taken on the archbishop's lands were sent to Maidstone gaol, though this removal to another county was subsequently considered to be contrary to the laws of the realm,[1] while the Abbot had his own gaol at Battle, and the justices in eyre had to come to Battle to try cases touching men of the Abbot's liberty.[2] There was also the peculiar jurisdiction of the Cinque Ports and their members, with the court of Shipweye. In the case of Pevensey, which was a member of Hastings, this led to much confusion, the barons claiming that the franchises of the Cinque Ports extended to all living within the Lowey—a district roughly including all the land within three miles of Pevensey castle—while the royal and county officers wished to limit them to the actual town and port. There was the further complication that Pevensey was the seat of the baronial court of the honor of Aquila, which was held at the castle gate for all tenants of the honor. The castle of Pevensey was the only place in the county where felons might be imprisoned for more than three days[3]; at Lewes the Earl had the right to keep them in the castle for three days, but must then send them to the castle of Guildford, which was the county gaol for Sussex and Surrey; and the same applied to Arundel castle, though in this latter case all felons arrested within the honor had to be brought to Arundel and delivered to the constable of the castle, who should then, after three days, send them on to Guildford. The Hundred Rolls mention that the constables of Petworth and Midhurst were fined for neglecting this custom and sending prisoners direct to Guildford. The absence of a gaol within the county was a cause of great inconvenience and expense and led not unfrequently to the escape of prisoners; an instance in which the sheriff was assaulted and a woman in his charge rescued—or abducted—is recorded. Similar cases appear to have been not unfrequent, the dense woods affording at once opportunity of escape and refuge for the fugitive, so that the borders of Sussex and Surrey were long infested with outlaws and robbers. It was not, however, until 1487 that the constant requests of the county were granted and a gaol established at Lewes.[4]

The jurisdiction exercised by the lords of the great honors was almost royal in its far-reaching extent. In several cases the rights of the lesser lords had been encroached upon by the greater; Peter of Savoy, when he held the honor of Aquila, established a monopoly of warren throughout a tract of country extending from Pevensey to the Ouse and from Glynde to the sea, and Earl Warenne had done the same for his whole barony, claiming warren in seventy vills and keeping armed retainers to prevent Robert Aguillon and other of his neighbours from hunting, and not even allowing his poor tenants to drive the wild

<hr>

[1] Assize R. 921, m. 8.   [2] Ibid. m. 1d.   [3] Ibid. m. 25.
[4] *Rot. Parl.* (Rec. Com.), vi. 388.

animals out of their crops. The earl gained his claim at the time of the Quo Warranto, pleading that when his ancestors lost their Norman lands of Warenne King John granted them universal warren for their English estates for the sake of the pun on their name, but the commons of Lewes petitioned against this decision, saying that the twelve jurors of every hundred in the rape had presented the Earl for encroaching, but he had been cleared on the finding of a single twelve who were his friends and were corrupted by him, and who had been challenged, unavailingly, as such by Robert Aguillon.[1] A similar monopoly of the right of wreck was successfully asserted by the lords of the rapes.

Beyond and behind the tangled system of privilege and feudal jurisdiction lay the hundred-courts, which in Sussex were entirely in private hands, being either appurtenant to the great baronies or granted to local lords, as in the case of Dumpford hundred held by Henry Hussey, Bexhill by the Bishop of Chichester, and the half hundred of Milton by John de la Haye ; and the county court, which had formerly been held at the central towns of Lewes and Shoreham, but, by the influence of the Earl of Cornwall, was at this time held at Chichester. The locus of the county court continued for some time unsettled, until in 1337, after a commission had been issued to make inquiries as to the most suitable spot, it was fixed at Chichester,[2] where it remained until 1504, when an act was passed for the county courts to be held alternately at Chichester and Lewes.

To the reign of Edward I. belongs also the commencement of the parliamentary history of Sussex, the first return [3] of the knights of the shire extant being for the parliament of 1290, when Henry Hussey and William de Echingham were elected, and the first return of the boroughs being in 1295, when members were returned from Chichester, Arundel, Lewes, Bramber, Shoreham and Horsham. The boroughs varied considerably in number and identity in later elections, Steyning being usually united to Bramber ; East Grinstead and Midhurst appear for the first time in January 1301, and all these eight boroughs sent representatives to the three parliaments between February 1358 and January 1361, but as a rule the number of boroughs taking part in any one election was not more than five or six. Seaford appears from 1298 to 1302, in 1325, and from 1366 to 1371, and again from 1396 to 1399, but then ceased to be a parliamentary borough till restored in 1640. Hastings, Rye and Winchelsea also sent members in right of their position as Cinque Ports. In 1299 the electors of Sussex refused to proceed in the absence of the archbishop and other magnates on the King's service beyond seas; and the county was again unrepresented in 1327, as the writs reached the sheriff too late to be published, as there was no county court before the date fixed for the assembly of parliament.

During the course of his reign Edward I. was not unfrequently

[1] Anct. Petition, 13780.   [2] Pat. 10 Edw. III. p. 1, m. 19d ; p. 2, m. 26.
[3] For these returns see *Suss. Arch. Coll.* xxx.

in Sussex,[1] the first occasion, apparently, being in 1276, when he spent the latter half of June at Chichester,[2] Aldingbourne and Lewes, afterwards going on to Battle and Winchelsea. In May 1278 he visited Stansted, Chichester, Petworth and Horsham; and in August 1281 was at Chichester and Binsted. Chichester appears to have been his favourite stopping place in Sussex, and he came there in July 1285 from Leeds castle, passing through Buckholt, Bramber and Arundel, and was again there in the following April, when he also visited Bosham and Midhurst, and in 1290 and 1294. In March 1292 he was at Ralph de Camoys' manor of Trotton, and in 1295 spent the first half of November at William de Echingham's manor of Udimore and at Winchelsea. In the spring of 1297 he passed through west Sussex, and in August of the same year stayed at Udimore while the fleet was preparing for the Flemish invasion, and here it was that the barons and prelates presented their petition against being summoned to do service in Flanders, and complaining of the excessive taxation, especially of the heavy tax on wool; Edward, however, refused to do anything for the time being, and eventually sailed from Winchelsea without his barons. It was during this visit that the king had an escape from death so remarkable as to almost justify the title of miracle applied to it by the chroniclers. The old town of Winchelsea having been destroyed by the great storm of 1287, it had been refounded by the King on a small hill rather more inland; the slope of the hill on the port side was very precipitous, and was only defended by an earth rampart of no great height; it happened that when the King was riding round this part of the town his horse took fright at a windmill and refused to go on; Edward urged it forward with whip and spurs, when it suddenly leaped over the rampart. Every one present was certain that the King must have been killed, but by wonderful good fortune the horse landed on its feet and slid uninjured along the miry surface of the lower road, so that its royal rider was able to return at once to his escort without even dismounting.[3]

In the summer of 1299 King Edward visited Uckfield, Lewes, Bramber, Arundel and Petworth, and was subsequently at Midhurst and East Grinstead; but his most important progress through Sussex was in September 1302, when he spent a fortnight in the county, going to Harting, East Dean, Chichester, Slindon, Arundel, Sele Priory, Bramber, Patcham, Lewes, Michelham Priory, Herstmonceux and Battle. His last recorded visit to the county in June 1305 was also of some duration and covered fresh ground, the halting places being Cocking, West Dean, Chichester, Arundel, Findon, Bramber, Clayton, Lewes, Horsted, Buxted and Mayfield.

The emptiness of the royal treasury in 1289 caused the King to decree the expulsion of all Jews from England; not only did their

[1] Gough, *Itinerary of King Edward the First.*
[2] He was present at the translation of St. Richard in the Cathedral.
[3] W. Rishanger, *Chron.* (Rolls Ser.), 173.

possessions thus fall to the Crown, but the popularity of the act enabled Edward to obtain a fresh subsidy from his already over-taxed Commons. As in the later instance of the 'popish recusants,' so with the Jews, their persecution was partly religious and partly political; alike as enemies of Christianity and as usurers and clippers of coin, they were regarded as undesirable subjects. They had never played so large a part in Sussex as in Norfolk and some other counties, but Deulebenie and Leo, Jews of Chichester, occur in 1190[1]; and Solomon, Benedict and Deulebenie, Jews of Chichester, occur with a number of other Jews probably belonging to the same place in 1199.[2] In 1272 the Jews of Chichester were taxed at 3 shillings, those of Arundel at the same, although they, like their brethren of Lewes who were assessed at 2 shillings, had 'nothing except some empty houses,' and those of Seaford at 2 shillings.[3] A tallage of a third of their goods was levied on the Jews in 1274, when the only two mentioned in Sussex were Moses son of Jose of Dogstrete (10 marks), and Jornin de Kanc' (20 marks)[4]; the former of these was amongst the Jews imprisoned in 1278 in the Tower for clipping coin,[5] and another Jew accused of the same offence was Sampson, a resident in Henhurst hundred.[6] Several Jews were also living at Hailsham[7] and carrying on the same nefarious trade in 1263 and in 1278; and if we may judge from the name of Aaron of Rye,[8] a prominent Jew of the period, Rye was also one of their resorts, though an order was issued in 1273 for their expulsion from Winchelsea on the ground that they were only allowed to live in places where they had been long established and that there had not previously been any Jews there.[9]

In the Welsh and Scottish wars of Edward I. the commons of Sussex played a naval rather than a military part; but they, of course, contributed with the rest of the kingdom towards the numerous subsidies of money and victuals for the army, and in 1295 William Dawtrey, William de Stoke and John de Mounceaus were commissioned to raise a force of four thousand archers and crossbowmen in Surrey and Sussex to assemble at Winchelsea in November[10]; this is the only notable levy of soldiers in the county recorded during this reign. At the same time that this force was raised a system of coastguards was established for the defence of the county against the French, who were now in alliance with Scotland; William Dawtrey was appointed warden of West Sussex and William de Stoke of East; under them was one mounted officer for each rape in command of from fourteen to twenty-four unmounted men, who were distributed amongst the various harbours along the coast.[11]

---

[1] Pipe R. 1 Ric. I.   [2] Ibid. 10 Ric. I.
[3] *Select Pleas of the Jewish Exchequer* (Selden Soc.), 69.   [4] Exch. Q. R. Accts. 249–18.
[5] Assize R. 921, m. 1.   [6] Ibid. m. 6.   [7] Salzmann, *Hist. of Hailsham*, 35.
[8] Selden Soc. op. cit. passim.   [9] Close 1 Edw. I. m. 7d.   [10] Pat. 23 Edw. I. m. 5.
[11] *Parl. Writs* (Rec. Com.), i. 274. The '*pedites*' assigned to the different '*rivagia*' were as follows: Chichester rape,—Horemouth (4), Selsey (4), Wittering and Coast of 'Cacan' (6); Arundel,—Felpham (4), Codelawe (10), Kingston-Tewkesbury (2); Bramber,—'Pende' (4), Shoreham (4), King-

POLITICAL HISTORY

It was, however, mainly on the gentry of Sussex that the burden of military service fell, and each of the numerous lists of summonses to join the royal armies contains names of the leading families of the county. Besides the nobility and baronage the representatives of the landed interest were called upon to take up arms, or else purchase exemption ; thus in 1278 all persons holding land to the value of twenty pounds were ordered to serve, and the return for Sussex shows that there were thirty members of this class,[1] many of whom are noted on the Assize Roll[2] of that year as holding knights' fees, but not being knights.

The castles of Hastings and Pevensey were in the King's hands, though the Count of Eu claimed the former in 1290 on the ground that it had been demised by his ancestress the Countess Alice to Henry III. only during the continuation of war with France ; it was, however, shown that the castle afterwards escheated to the Crown as 'lands of the Normans,' and the Count's claim was therefore rejected.[3] Besides local castles and forces, troops were sometimes called in from neighbouring districts to assist in the defence, and in 1299 the citizens of London, who had marched into Kent and Sussex to resist an invasion of the French, procured the King's letters patent that this service should not be drawn into a precedent.[4]

Under Edward II. the war with Scotland dragged on its slow disastrous course, and in August 1312 Nicholas Aucher was commissioned to raise in Kent and Sussex five hundred infantry,[5] a number increased in September to a thousand[6]; commissions to array the county forces for service against the Scots were also granted in September 1315 to William de Northoo and John de Hydeneye,[7] and in the following March to John de Ratingdene and Alan de Boxhull.[8] Again, in 1322, Henry Hussey and Nicholas Gentil were ordered to levy a force of five hundred men from Sussex and Surrey, excepting the city of Chichester, and take them to Newcastle.[9] In the same year, parliament having granted that every township in the kingdom should provide one man for the army, Peter fitz-Reynold and John de Ifeld were deputed to select suitable men in Sussex[10]; the armed footmen supplied by the boroughs on this occasion were—Arundel 2, Bramber and Steyning 2, Horsham 1, Lewes 4, and Midhurst 1.[11] Commission of array for 300 archers was shortly afterwards given to Robert de Echingham,[12] and next year Thomas Tregoz was ordered to array all able men in the county between the ages of sixteen and sixty.[13]

The conclusion of a truce for thirteen years with Robert Bruce in 1323 put an end to this drain upon the population and resources of the

ston (6) ; Lewes,—Aldrington (4), Brighton (4), Rottingdean (4), Newhaven (Mechingg) (6) ; Pevensey, —Seaford (4), Cuckmere (2), Eastbourne with Pevensey (12) ; Hastings,—Coding (6), Bexhill (4), Bulverhythe (4), Hastings (4), ' Clyveshend ' and Winchelsea (6).

[1] *Parl. Writs*, i. 216.   [2] Assize R. 921.   [3] *Rot. Parl.* (Rec. Com.), i. 23.
[4] Rymer, *Fœdera* (Rolls ed.), i. 903.   [5] Pat. 6 Edw. II. pl. m. 21.
[6] Ibid. m. 16.   [7] Pat. 9 Edw. II. p. 1, m. 22.   [8] Ibid. p. 2, m. 19.
[9] Pat. 15 Edw. II. p. 2, m. 20.   [10] Ibid. m. 11.   [11] Ibid. m. 9.
[12] Ibid. m. 8.   [13] Pat. 16 Edw. I. p. 1, m. 18.

country ; but besides external wars there was discontent and rebellion within the realm. As Prince of Wales Edward had developed a great affection for a dashing young Gascon squire, Piers Gaveston ; indeed during his banishment from his father's court in the summer of 1304, when he spent some time in Sussex, where he maintained a stud of horses at Ditchling, his chief regret was for the absence of his favourite.[1] On his accession he immediately began to shower his favours upon Piers, bestowing upon him amongst other things the city of Chichester,[2] until at last the English nobles united their forces to destroy the upstart. The Earl of Arundel was one of the leaders in this movement, but the Earl of Warenne was with difficulty persuaded to take part against the King.[3] The removal of one favourite only made room for others, and the place of Piers Gaveston was soon filled by the Despensers, to the younger of whom, son of the Earl of Winchester, the King granted the town of Shoreham[4] ; the earl himself, in 1324, obtained from Alina Mowbray a grant of the reversion of the castle and honor of Bramber on the death of her father William Braose, the tenant for life.[5] It was a dispute over the purchase of William Braose's Welsh estates that led to the rebellion of the Earls of Hereford and Lancaster. This rising ended in complete failure and involved several Sussex men in the ruin which overtook its leaders. Bartholomew de Badlesmere, who held a number of manors in this county, had fortified his castle of Leeds in Kent against the King, so that in October 1321 a royal summons was issued to the men of Essex, Hampshire, Surrey and Sussex to assemble for the capture of Leeds castle.[6] When it fell its constable Thomas Colepepper, a member of a family of note in Kent and Sussex and himself a landowner in the latter county, was sentenced and executed at Winchelsea[7] ; while, besides Bartholomew de Badlesmere, Francis de Audeham and Bartholomew Ashburnham, both belonging to Sussex, were condemned for treason.[8] Several other Sussex men lost their estates, and it seems that the whole county was somewhat disaffected, as in February 1322 the commonalty of knights and esquires of Sussex were fined £200 because some of them had failed to come to the place assigned them.[9] This probably refers to the summons already mentioned, unless it be connected with the assembling of the King's army at Cirencester in the previous December, to which Surrey and Sussex were ordered to send five hundred foot under John Dabernoun, Peter fitz-Reynold and John de Boudon.[10]

The accession of Edward III. put the kingdom for a while into the power of Queen Isabella and her favourite Roger Mortimer, till in 1330 the young King took the government into his own hands and seized and executed Mortimer, issuing at the same time commissions of array to resist the King's rebels to the mayor of Chichester and Bartho-

[1] *Suss. Arch. Coll.* ii.
[2] Chart. R. 1 Edw. II. no. 24.
[3] T. Walsingham, *Chron.* (Rolls Ser.), ii. 130, 131.
[4] Pat. 1 Edw. III. p. 2, m. 18.
[5] Pat. 17 Edw. II. p. 2, m. 9, 6.
[6] Rymer, *Fœdera* (Rolls ed.), ii. 457.
[7] Pat. 15 Ew. II. p. 2, m. 24d.
[8] Ibid. ; and Chanc. Misc. R. 17-4.
[9] Pat. 15 Edw. II. p. 2, m. 31.
[10] Ibid. p. 1, m. 7.

lomew de Burghersh.[1] Edward St. John, William de Northoo and Roger de Asshe were also appointed to arrest the King's rebels and those who harboured them in Sussex.[2]

The renewal of war with Scotland in 1335 caused a demand for sixty light horse to be supplied by the county, which were subsequently compounded for at 100 marks.[3] Nor was home defence neglected, for in 1336 the castles of Hastings, Pevensey, Lewes and Arundel were ordered to be put in a state of defence,[4] and in 1338 Henry and Roger Hussey, Thomas Braose and Thomas de Wemyll were commissioned to array the men of Sussex to defend the coast.[5] Next year the Earl of Arundel and two others were appointed to put the walls and defences of Chichester in order, the clergy undertaking to contribute part of the expense in view of the poverty of the citizens.[6] That these measures were not unnecessary is evident, for in 1339 Andrew Peverel, who was in command of the men-at-arms, light horse and archers of Pevensey rape, had to summon all his forces to repel an attempted landing by the crews of fifteen galleys and other vessels at Eastbourne.[7] These galleys were no doubt the same whose crews sacked the castle of Hastings, which ever since its bestowal upon the Duke of Brittany in 1264 had been allowed to fall into decay, the dukes taking the castle-ward rents but spending nothing on repairs.[8] Pevensey Castle had also suffered much from neglect, but occasional repairs were done, sufficient to keep it fencible, and a small garrison was thrown into it whenever invasion threatened, as for instance in 1370, when Sir John St. Clare on several occasions put in garrisons of about twenty or thirty men.[9] Ten years earlier, in 1360, orders were given to John de Saham to array all men-at-arms within the honor, then held by Queen Philippa, and in case of the castle being threatened to send them into it and, always leaving a sufficient force to hold it, to attack the invaders with the other troops.[10] In this same year the French did actually land in Sussex and captured Winchelsea, burning the town and treating the inhabitants with extreme brutality.

As King Edward had been in his nonage the unwilling subject of Mortimer's influence, so in his dotage he became the willing instrument of his third son, John of Gaunt. The predominant factor in English history during the close of this reign is the rise to almost absolute power of the enormously wealthy Duke of Lancaster; his estates spread into almost every county, and had been increased in 1372 by the grant of the honor of Aquila in Sussex, with the castle of Pevensey.[11] His rank and wealth combined made him the most influential man in the land, but his abuse of them made him the most hated. Consequently when in the spring of 1376 the emptiness of the exchequer compelled him

[1] Pat. 4 Edw. III. p. 1, m. 63.
[2] Ibid.
[3] Pat. 9 Edw. III. p. 1, m. 2.
[4] Rymer, *Feod.* ii. 940.
[5] Pat. 12 Edw. III. p. 2, m. 14d.
[6] Pat. 13 Edw. III. p. 1, m. 17.
[7] Assize R. 941, m. 8d.
[8] Inq. p.m. 13 Edw. III. 2nd Nos. 57.
[9] Mins. Accts. 1028-4.
[10] Pat. 34 Edw. III. p. 1, m. 22d.
[11] Dy. of Lanc. Royal Ch. 325.

to summon that parliament known as 'The Good Parliament' he was opposed both by the Commons and the nobles and suffered a complete temporary defeat. To this parliament Sussex[1] sent as knights of the shire William Fifhyde and Robert de Ore, both men of good family, but not otherwise noteworthy nor of previous parliamentary experience; the leader of the four lords chosen by the Commons to sit with them, Henry Percy, was also connected with Sussex, in which county he held the lordship of Petworth. When parliament had to be summoned again in January 1377 the Duke took care to ensure its subservience by causing the sheriffs to return, without election, members favourable to his interest; accordingly Sir John St. Clare and Robert Dalingrugge were sent up for Sussex, which they had represented on several previous occasions. The death of Edward deprived John of Gaunt of much of his power, and the opportunity of the assembling of Richard's first parliament in October 1377 was taken by many counties to return the members previously elected to the Good Parliament,[2] but this was not done by Sussex, which chose William Percy and Nicholas Wilcombe.

The reign of Richard II. opened disastrously for England and more especially for Sussex. The French had obtained command of the Channel and even captured the Isle of Wight, no doubt to the great alarm of the authorities at Chichester, who had just received orders to repair their walls, towers and gates and complete the new fosse.[3] The enemy, however, chose the eastern portion of the county for their attack, and, in spite of commissions to array archers and men-at-arms granted to the Earl of Arundel, the Abbot of Battle, John Montague, William Batsford, William Percy and Nicholas Wilcombe,[4] landed at Rye, which they took without much trouble; and after a stay of several days there, marched on Winchelsea and summoned the town to surrender. The gallant Abbot of Battle, however, who had taken command of the defence, refused the summons and offered so stout a resistance to the French that they gave up the assault and made their way to Hastings, which they found deserted and left in flames. Then not daring to advance inland they completed the sack of Rye and burnt it also to the ground. About the same time Rottingdean was the scene of another landing, but as the invaders were marching inland they were met by a small force under John of Cherlieu, prior of Lewes, Sir John Fallesley, Sir Thomas Cheyney and John Brocas; a desperate fight ensued, in which about a hundred of the defenders fell and all their leaders were captured, but the enemy had lost so heavily that although, according to Froissart,[5] their ships sailed up the estuary of the Ouse and actually anchored within sight of Lewes, they retired without attacking the town. The latter would have had to trust entirely to its walls and the gallantry of its burgesses, for the Earl of Arundel had fled, leaving the castle unprotected, and when the townsmen applied to him for aid

---

[1] *Suss. Arch. Coll.* xxxi. 97.   [2] Trevelyan, *England in the Age of Wycliffe,* 73.
[3] Pat. 1 Ric. II. p. 2, m. 20.   [4] Ibid. 1, m. 28d.
[5] Froissart, *Chron.* (ed. Johnes), ii. 182.

refused to send it unless they would pay the cost, in which case he promised four hundred lances. The Duke of Lancaster also, who was now playing the part of Achilles sulking in his tent, left the castle of Pevensey undefended, and when urged to send a force there said, 'Let them destroy it to the foundations, I have power to rebuild it again.'[1] This treacherous supineness of the local lords was again displayed in 1380, when the French made a successful attack on Winchelsea, driving back the Abbot of Battle, who had again come gallantly to its defence, capturing one of his monks and burning the town. On this occasion not only did the Earl of Arundel fail to render the assistance he could have given, but he prevented those, his inferiors in power but superiors in valour, who would have gone to the rescue.[2] Judging from his later success as admiral we may acquit the Earl of cowardice, but must conclude that he was guilty of acting from deliberate selfish policy in the interests of the Duke of Lancaster, who was at this time in treasonable correspondence with the enemy,[3] and whose designs may be conjectured from the statement of one of the French wounded left behind after the engagement at Rottingdean, that if John of Gaunt had been King of England there would have been no French raids.[4] Nor was the treachery of the nobles the only cause of weakness in the defence of the coast, for the numbers of the Commons had been terribly reduced by the devastations of the Black Death in 1349, and the two later outbreaks of plague in 1361 and 1366, so much so indeed that nine townships on the sea coast within the rape of Pevensey which had formerly been of great assistance in repelling invasions became desolate and uninhabited.[5]

The social condition of the peasantry at this time will be dealt with elsewhere,[6] but the corruption and incapability of the government and the burden of taxation and especially of the inquisitorial impost of the poll-tax are in themselves causes sufficient to explain the great rising of June 1381. This began in Kent and almost simultaneously in Essex, and rapidly spread to the neighbouring districts, Sussex and Bedford being mentioned by Froissart as the other counties which took a leading part in the movement; and this is confirmed by the appearance of Sussex as one of the five sources of the insurgents who destroyed the Savoy and murdered the Chancellor.[7] Few details of the rising in Sussex have been preserved, but they are sufficient to show that it possessed the usual features of being directed against the great spiritual and lay lords and especially against the Duke of Lancaster. Thus, the Abbot of St. Alban's farm buildings at Coombes were burnt down,[8] and the insurgents broke into the Earl of Arundel's castle of Lewes and destroyed the windows and gates and wrecked the buildings, burning rent-rolls and other muniments and appropriating ten casks of wine.[9]

---

[1] *Chron. Angliæ a Mon. Sancti Albani* (Rolls Ser.), 167-9.   [2] Ibid. 270.
[3] Ibid. 278.   [4] Ibid. 168.   [5] Mins. Accts. 7117.
[6] See section on 'Social and Economic History.'   [7] Pat. 4 Ric. II. p. 3, m. 4d.
[8] *Gesta Abbatum* (Rolls Ser.), iii. 363.   [9] Pat. 6 Ric. II. p. 2, m. 11d.

Arundel is twice mentioned by Froissart as a centre of revolt [1]; and in East Sussex the rising was assisted by the Duke of Lancaster's private enemies, Sir Edward Dalingrugge, Sir Thomas Sackville, and Sir Philip Medstede being concerned in burning a feodary and other muniments in the hands of the Duke's steward at Ringmer, and enforcing an oath that he would not hold any more courts.[2] Sir Edward pleaded that he only interfered to save the life of the steward, who would otherwise have been killed, but the jury found against him on this count and for hunting in the Duke's forest of Ashdown.[3]

As a result of the failure of the rising the county gaol at Guildford castle became dangerously full and the Earl of Arundel was ordered to keep a number of prisoners in his castles of Arundel and Lewes,[4] at the latter of which a felons' gaol was next year set up for two years.[5] Some of the insurgents from Kent having sought refuge in Sussex, a commission for their punishment was issued in October 1381 to the Earl of Arundel, Richard Poynings, Thomas Camoys, Edward St. John, Edward Dalingrugge and others.[6] Two Sussex men, John atte Hoth of Maresfield and John Mournour of Ferring were executed,[7] and when the act of general pardon was published eight others were excepted from its benefit, namely, Thomas Willot of Burwash, John Harry of Northicam, Stephen Holstock, Robert Hodge, John Jamyn of Warbleton, John Hunt, weaver, of Waldron, Thomas Cutbeard of Wadhurst, and Nicholas Basset of Hartfield.[8]

The danger of invasion continued to threaten Sussex throughout this reign; in 1385 Rye was ordered to be fortified and a tax was put on all fish landed on the neighbouring coasts to supply funds for this purpose.[9] Next year the county petitioned that the castle of Bramber should be garrisoned and further steps taken for the protection of the coast.[10] Possibly a result of this appeal was the licence granted in 1386 to Sir Edward Dalingrugge, who had made his fortune by serving in France under the celebrated Sir Robert Knolles, to crenellate his manor of Bodiam and make a castle for the defence of the adjacent country against the King's enemies.[11] Sir Edward is found serving on a commission of array with other local magnates in 1388,[12] and the commission for 1389 contains the name of Sir John Fallesley, who had been captured at Rottingdean in 1377.[13]

When Henry of Lancaster laid claim to the throne, Sussex did not come within the sphere of action of the contesting parties, but it is known that Lady Joan Pelham defended the castle of Pevensey on behalf of Henry against the local forces of Kent, Sussex, and Surrey, though the letter which she wrote on that occasion to her husband does not

[1] Froissart, *Chron.* (ed. Johnes), ii. 466, 475.
[2] Pat. 7 Ric. II. p. 2, m. 6d.
[3] Assize R. 947, No. 4.
[4] Pat. 5 Ric. II. p. 1, m. 32d.
[5] Ibid. p. 2, m. 12.
[6] Ibid. p. 1, m. 23d.
[7] Réville, *Le Soulèvement des Travailleurs*, pp. 233-4.
[8] *Rot. Parl.* (Rec. Com.), iii. 113.
[9] Pat. 8 Ric. II. p. 2, m. 539, 32d.
[10] *Rot. Parl.* (Rec. Com.), iii. 255.
[11] Pat. 9 Ric. II. p. 1, m. 23.
[12] Pat. 11 Ric. II. p. 1, m. 28d.
[13] Pat. 12 Ric. II. p. 1, m. 24d.

give us much information upon the matter.[1]   The reigns of the three
Henries contain little of importance for the political history of this
county, though it would be easy to compile a formidable list of Sussex
men who served their King in the French wars.   It is, however, enough
for our purpose to note that at the great victory of Agincourt the Earl
of Arundel numbered amongst his esquires members of such prominent
Sussex families as Lewkenore, Halsham, Waleys, Bartelot, Michelgrove,
Hussey, Covert, Culpepper, and William Wolf of Ashington, who took
prisoner the Sire de Bursegand, seneschal of France ; other Sussex men
served under Sir Thomas West, Sir Roger Fiennes and Lord Camoys ;
but Lord Poynings, Sir John Dalingrugge and Sir John Pelham, who
all served in other campaigns, were not present on this occasion.[2] Against
this picture of honourable, or even brilliant, service rendered by Sussex
soldiers must be set the terrible record of rapes, robberies and murders
done by the troops quartered in the county or passing through it on
their way to embark for France.[3]

The great event of the fifteenth century so far as Sussex is concerned
was the rebellion of Jack Cade in 1450.   The pitiable state of the
county, burdened with taxation, overrun with a brutal soldiery and
exposed to constant raids—the men of Tarring dared not even go to
neighbouring markets lest the French should take advantage of their
absence to burn the village,[4] as they had burnt Rye and Winchelsea in
1448,—combined with the socialistic, or communistic, teaching of
the Lollards, had produced a state of ferment within the county
which only required the presence of a leader to burst into active rebellion.   Such a leader was found in Jack Cade, who had been a servant
of Thomas Dacre of Heathfield, and who, assuming the name of
Mortimer, at the end of May began an abortive insurrection in Kent,
which he successfully revived in July.   That he had been for some
time organizing action is clear, for on 17 April one William Dalby of
Brookhampton and London came with others by his orders into the
forest of Worth and there harangued the populace in an extraordinary
rigmarole about the coming of ' a marvellous and terrible man of high
birth and of the ancient royal race, bearing on his arms [5] certain wild
beasts, namely, a red lion and a white lion ' with a force of two hundred
thousand armed men, and that this ' marvellous man ' would pursue the
' fox and leopard,' meaning King Henry, until he should obtain the
mastery and be crowned king.[6]   Unlike the Peasants' Rising of 1381,
this insurrection was aimed against the King, and while loyalty to
Richard had been the mark of the former, this was marked by enmity

---

[1] Horsfield, *Hist. of Suss.* i. 315.   [2] *Suss. Arch. Coll.* xv. 123–7.

[3] *Rot. Parl.* (Rec. Com.), iv. 251, 351.   [4] *Chart. R.* 22 Hen. VI.

[5] ' *Gerens in brachiis suis.*'   A fine example of dog-Latin.   This reference to Cade's arms is curious,
as he would naturally have assumed the arms as well as the name of Mortimer.

[6] Anct. Indictments, 122.   The account of this speech is much confused, the deponents having evidently been puzzled by the rather high-flown language.   Houndslow Heath is named, apparently as
the place where the battle between the ' marvellous man ' and the ' false and traitor king ' was to take
place.

towards Henry, for whom a contempt was felt which was probably well voiced by John and William Merfeld of Brightling, who ' in the open market the Sonday in the feste of Seynt Anne the xxviii yer of our saide sovereyn lorde falsly seide that the kynge was a naterell foole and wolde ofte tymes holde a staff in his handes with a bird on the ende playing therewith as a Foole.' [1] This enmity was clearly shown by the action of William Hovell of Sutton, gentleman, Richard Seynt of Pulborough, clerk, and a number of others who assembled at Chichester and issued proclamations summoning all the county on pain of death to join them in deposing the King and his lords.[2] The further aim of communism was also prominent. Thus John Clipsham, carpenter, and about a hundred others met in the woods near Hastings and elected captains and masters to depose the King, ' proposing as Lollards and heretics to hold all things in common '; and similar instances occurred at Horsham, Eastbourne and many other places. The election of ' captains ' was a noticeable feature of the rising; Cade himself was ' the captain of Kent,' and one John Cotyng, yeoman, ' calling himself captain of Burwash,' headed an attempt to break up the abbot's fair at Robertsbridge. The sheriff's tourn at Battle and the leet court at Sedlescombe were also broken up, and some of the gentry were attacked, one of the household of John Oxenbridge being killed, Sir John Pelham's chaplain being assaulted and laid up for six weeks, and William Frenyngham's house at Waldron being plundered of precious stones and other goods and himself held to ransom.[3]

A large contingent from Sussex evidently joined Cade's Kentish followers in their successful march on London, for after the rebels had been expelled from the city over four hundred Sussex men are named in the pardons issued on 7 July. That the rebels were no disorganized rabble is evident from these names, which include the Abbot of Battle and Prior of Lewes, with all their monks and servants, twenty-three gentlemen, of whom the most considerable were Bartholomew Bolney of West Firle, Colbrond of Wartling, Lunsford of Battle, Parker and Rakeley of Willingdon, Selwyn of Selmeston and Wolf of Ashington, the bailiffs and burgesses of Lewes, Seaford and Pevensey, the constables and inhabitants of eighteen hundreds and all the men of eight parishes.[4]

On the receipt of this general pardon Cade's followers broke up and returned to their homes, leaving him with only a handful of the more desperate at Rochester, whence he fled on 11 July, and being pursued by Alexander Iden, sheriff of Kent, was overtaken and slain in a garden at Heathfield. An attempt appears to have been made to revive the insurrection in Sussex by one Thomas Skynner, but no details of this second rising are preserved.[5]

For some little time there is little to record; in 1455 a commission, including the Earl of Arundel, Lord Delaware and Sir Richard Fenys,

---

[1] Anct. Indictments, 122.　　　[2] Ibid.　　　[3] Ibid.
[4] Suss. Arch. Coll. xviii.　　　　　　[5] The Antiquarian Magazine, iii. 168.

undertook the collection of money from the county for the defence of Calais,[1] and in 1461 the same three lords were ordered to bring all the armed forces of Sussex and Hampshire to aid against the ' mysruled and outrageous people in the northe parties of this reaume.'[2] The accession of Richard III. was marked by one act of resistance, and in November 1483 Sir Thomas Etchingham, Richard Leuknore of Brambletye, Thomas Oxenbridge and others were ordered to summon the men of Kent and Sussex to besiege the castle of Bodiam which the rebels were holding.[3] It was evidently taken, as in August 1484 Nicholas Rigby was granted the custody of the King's castle of Bodiam, late of Sir Thomas Leuknore, rebel[4]; but although the castle was then in Richard's hands its lord had received a general pardon in the previous May.[5] As Sir Thomas is there called ' of Trotton ' it was probably at his house that Edward IV had stayed in September 1479 on his way to Chichester.[6]

The reign of Henry VII is chiefly noticeable, so far as we are concerned, for the evil prominence of Edmund Dudley, a member of a Sussex family settled at Atherington at the mouth of the Arun. As the faithful instrument of the avaricious King's extortion he acquired an intense unpopularity for which he paid with his life in the first years of Henry VIII.

Two other Sussex men played prominent, and honourable, parts in Henry VIII.'s court, Sir John Gage of Firle being constable of the Tower, and Sir Anthony Browne Master of the Horse, each enjoying a large share of their royal master's favour and confidence, which they well merited. Sir Anthony, besides his princely house at Cowdray, became the possessor of the site of Battle Abbey at the dissolution of the monasteries. It may be noted in this connection that the dissolution in Sussex was not attended by any political disturbances but seems to have been generally acquiesced in, the leading gentry, though remaining faithful to the Roman Church, having no hesitation in participating in the plunder of the religious houses.

Henry on two occasions honoured certain Sussex lords with his presence. In August 1526 he paid a visit to the Earl of Northumberland at Petworth, where he made merry and showed himself very friendly to the local gentry.[7] Thence he removed to Arundel Castle, which he much liked, though it was then in great decay,[8] differing greatly from Petworth, which was one of the best appointed houses in the land, than which few were more neatly kept or had fairer and pleasanter walks. After Arundel the King went to Lord Delaware's house of Halnaker. His second visit to the county was in 1538, when he was again at Petworth and Arundel, and also at Cowdray.[9] Petworth, Cowdray and Halnaker were also visited in 1552 by Edward VI, who

---

[1] *Acts of P.C.* vi. 240.   [2] Ibid. 307.
[3] Pat. 1 Rich. III. p. 1, m. 3d.   [4] Pat. 2 Ric. III. p. 3, m. 9.
[5] Pat. 1 Ric. III. p. 4, m. 15.   [6] Pat. 17 Edw. IV. m. 20.
[7] *L. & P. Hen. VIII.* iv. 2368.   [8] Ibid. 2377.
[9] Ibid. xiii. (2), 1280.

describes the latter as 'a pretty house beside Chichester,' and refers to Cowdray as 'a goodly house of Sir Anthony Brown's where we were marvelously, yea rather excessively banketted.'[1] Some idea of the magnificence of Cowdray may be gathered from the details preserved of the entertainment offered Queen Elizabeth in 1593,[2] in which figure many of those quaintly elaborate 'conceits' so familiar in the pages of 'Kenilworth.'

But feasting and loyalty are only one side of the picture, and during the troubled year 1549, when rebellion was rife in Norfolk and Cornwall, Sussex was evidently disaffected, for Sir John Markham, writing early in August to the Earl of Rutland, refers to 'a general plague of rebelling,' and adds that 'Kent, Sussex, Essex, and all the parts near London have meekly confessed their folly and pray for the King's most gracious pardon.'[3] In the following May, however, the sheriffs of Kent and Sussex were warned of a conspiracy of the Commons of those counties to assemble at Heathfield on Whit Monday,[4] and in 1551 'one Flynt of Sussex' was in the Fleet as 'a seditious stirrer imprisoned for being a doer amongst the rebelles.'[5]

Outside troubles were also rife; the lord lieutenant of the county had been warned to see that the beacons were watched and the soldiers ready to assemble at an hour's notice,[6] and the authorities at Rye were busy fortifying their town, for which they asked leave to use the stone and mortar brought together for Camber Castle.[7] This latter was one of a series of block-houses erected along the south-east coast about 1540, and its ruins still testify to the low state of military architecture at this date.[8] It was apparently the only fort on the Sussex coast that was in use at this date; the castle at Pevensey had so fallen into decay that in June 1548 certain Scots lying at Dieppe considered it would fall an easy prey to any invader, while still strong enough to afford valuable assistance to a force occupying it.[9] This design, however, came to nothing, if indeed it had ever been seriously considered.

The history of Sussex during the reign of Elizabeth is almost entirely military, and resolves itself into a string of orders for the levying of troops, either for defence against invasion, or for warfare in Flanders and the Low Countries. The drain of men for the French wars was as great as in the time of the Edwards and Henries, but in this reign they were often required to assist the French king against the Spaniards. In 1562 the Earl of Arundel was ordered to raise 500 men in the county for foreign service,[10] and next year 2,000 men from Hants and Sussex were sent to Havre.[11] Another 300 were levied in 1577,[12] and

---

[1] *Suss. Arch. Coll.* x. 201.   [2] Ibid. v. 185-7.

[3] *Hist. MSS. Com Rep.* xii, pt. iv. p. 42.

[4] *Acts of P.C.* iii. 35.   [5] Ibid. 383.

[6] *Cal. S.P. Dom. Edw. VI.* Add. ii.   [7] Ibid. vii. 20.

[8] In 1540, 1,272 men were employed on the construction of this castle (*L. & P. Hen. VIII.* xv. 598). William Oxenbridge, as surveyor of the works, was paid £3,000 in 1542, and another £4,000 next year; but in less than a century the place was abandoned and in ruins.

[9] S.P. Dom. Edw. VI. iv. 13.

[10] *Cal. S.P. Dom. Eliz.* xxiv. 35.   [11] Ibid. xxix. 36.   [12] *Acts of P.C.* ix. 329.

150 recruits were raised for the Low Countries in 1587,[1] but now all attention was concentrated on the defence of the realm from the threatened Spanish invasion. In August, 1586, there had been rumours of a landing of the French in Sussex, and measures had been hastily taken to meet them.[2] Again, just a year later, Lord Buckhurst was ordered to put the county in a state of defence, a small supply of ordnance, six pieces only, being granted for the purpose.[3]

The total number of 'able men,' between the ages of sixteen and sixty, available for the defence of the county at this time was between six and seven thousand. In 1559 the muster roll showed 6,252 ;[4] in 1569 the total was 6,919, and included 1,876 archers, 4,533 pike and bill men, and 510 harquebussiers ;[5] in 1574 the total had gone down to 6,727, and the number of archers had fallen to 1,491, though by way of compensation the harquebussiers had doubled their numbers.[6] The archers continued to decrease, and in 1584 the council, hearing that archery was much decayed, ordered that special care should in future be taken of its maintenance.[7] They did not, however, underrate the value of firearms, and at the same time sent Captain John Vaughan to superintend the Sussex musters, and especially the shooting practice.[8] Orders were also given that, to avoid the great expense of maintaining the full force of militia, 2,000 of the most efficient men should be picked out and trained in shooting, but with as sparing a use as possible of the powder, to provide which a fund was to be raised in the county.[9] The method of training suggested was for a halberd to be set up in an open spot, and the men to pass in file, 'or as we term it in rancke as wild geese,' and as they pass to make as though they would fire. After a few trials it would be easy to see which of them had any notion of handling their weapons, and would repay further training. They were then to be taught skirmishing, how to carry their piece without endangering themselves or their neighbours, and how to put in the match. The next stage was actual firing, first with 'false fires,' that is to say with priming only, to accustom them to the flash, then with a half charge, and finally with the bullet. This scheme was nicely calculated to save powder, and also to encourage many who 'by reason of the churlishness of their peeces and not being made acquainted therewith by degrees are ever after so discouraged as eyther they wincke or pull their heads from the peece whereby they take no perfect levill but shoote at random.'[10] Corporals were to be appointed to every twenty men, and were to cause them to practise at butts erected in some convenient place, the targets being one yard and a half broad, and the range one hundred and fifty paces.[11] Whether any regular uniform existed at this time may be doubted, though the Hastings troops were ordered to be clad 'in cassockes of blewe clothe.'[12] In 1593, when 150 men were required

[1] *Acts of P.C.* xv. 118.
[2] Ibid. xiv. 212.
[3] *Cal. S.P. Dom. Eliz.* cciii. 14, 17, 18.
[4] Ibid. vi. 64.
[5] Ibid. li. 20.
[6] Ibid. xcviii. 12.
[7] Harl. MS. 703, f. 13.
[8] Ibid. f. 14.
[9] Ibid. and f. 15.
[10] Ibid. f. 16.
[11] Ibid. ff. 34–6.
[12] Ibid. f. 38.

for France, the county was to furnish 'coates of such cullours as you can best provide, and to be lyned least they might be occasyned to serve in the winter season.'[1]

When the coming of the Spanish Armada had become a certainty, Sussex was ordered to raise 4,000 foot and 260 horse, 2,500 of the foot being required for the main army, Sir Thomas Palmer having orders to conduct these to Croydon.[2] Of the officers Thomas Lewknour had served as a lieutenant both in Ireland and the Low Countries, and Captains John Vaughan, the muster-master, and William Henworthe were old soldiers.[3] Other men of military experience belonging to the county are noted by the Earl of Essex on the occasion of his expedition of 1596 : Sir Anthony Shirley had served in the Low Countries, where he was taken prisoner, and commanded all the English horse in Brittany,[4] where he fought divers times ; Sir Thomas Shirley the younger had a company of horse in the Low Country, and Sir Nicholas Pelham had been lieutenant in Sir William Pelham's company of horse, and afterwards captain, ' and hath done valiantly in all encounters.'[5] When this last named officer returned from Flanders in February 1597, Sir Francis Vere wrote to the Earl of Essex that ' he deserved exceeding well in the late service, and for a man of his worth none have received so small encouragement,'[6] and Count Maurice of Nassau also wrote in the same strain.[7] The officer however who, according to his own account, did most work in 1588 was Captain Humphrey Covert. He acted as muster-master to the forces in camp at Brighton, and was awarded for his good service a pension of a hundred pounds, which however in 1606 was eighteen years in arrear.[8]

Besides the troops assembled along the shore a number of small batteries afforded additional protection, as for instance the blockhouse at Brighton, which had been erected by the inhabitants early in this reign to prevent the recurrence of such incidents as the burning of the town in 1545 by the French, who at the same time ' sought to have sackt Seafoord,' but there the elder Sir Nicholas Pelham ' did repel 'em back aboord,' as his epitaph testifies. In the extreme east the blockhouse of Camber had a permanent garrison of some twelve soldiers, which could be increased on emergency by calling in the men of the two adjacent hundreds.[9] This fort was the object of the treacherous designs of the Jesuit, Father Darbysher, in France, who early in March 1588, suggested to Roger Walton, an English spy, that he, being well known in Sussex, ' should contrive that the blockhouse between Rye and Winchelsea should be given up to the Prince of Parma, which would be a great piece of service, and good for the small ships of France

---

[1] *Acts of P.C.* xxiv. 402.   [2] Harl. MS. 703, f. 54.
[3] *Foljambe MSS.* (Hist. MSS. Com.), Rep. xv (5), 40.
[4] Probably in 1592 when 1,000 men were sent from Sussex to join Sir John Norreys in Brittany (*Acts of P.C.* xxiii. 225) ; and 80 volunteers were enlisted for the same service (ibid. p. 273).
[5] *Cecil MSS.* (Hist. MSS. Com.), vi. 570.
[6] Ibid. vii. 84.   [7] Ibid. p. 85.
[8] Harl. MS. 703, f. 154.   [9] *Acts of P.C.* vi. 258.

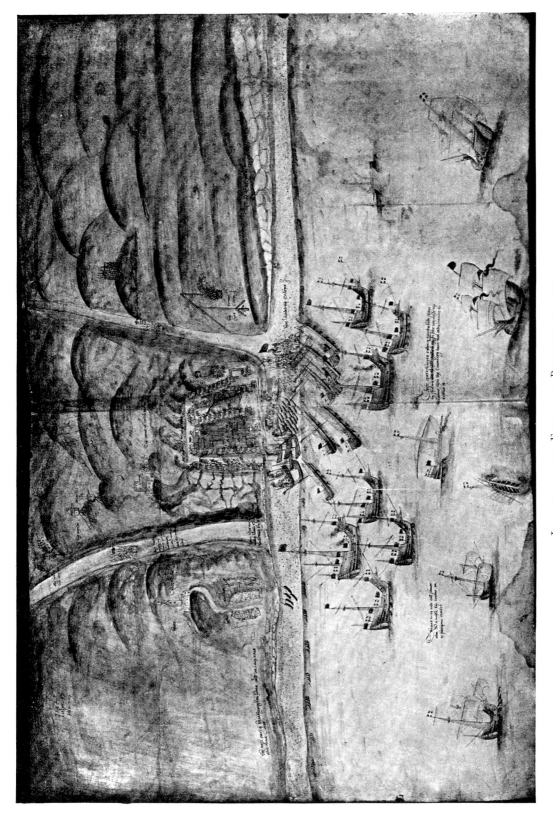

LANDING OF THE FRENCH AT BRIGHTON IN 1545

(From a Contemporary Painting in the British Museum—Corr. MS. Aug. I. i. 18.)

and Flanders to land men. One Wylforde is the governour, and by report a man that might be dealt with ; and if he would allow the fleet to land there he might have for himself and his soldiers any money in reason.'[1] The father added that 'there are many gentlemen in Sussex that are our friends,' and the spy notes in the margin the name of Thomas Leedes, a prominent recusant. Indeed, in spite of the general loyalty of the county, several Sussex men were involved in the various conspiracies of this reign. Thus in 1569 the Earl of Arundel, Lord Lumley, and Viscount Montague were all concerned in the Duke of Norfolk's plot, and it was even intended to carry off Mary, Queen of Scots, to Arundel Castle.[2] Nicholas Woolfe of Ashington was involved in Somerville's attempt of 1583, and when presented by the church-warden for not attending church called him 'a heretick,' and said that within a year he should 'singe a newe songe . . . or els he will frye with a fagot,' and that 'if all thinges had happened right as it was meante,' the queen would not be on the throne.[3] In the Throck-morton conspiracy of the next year the Earl of Northumberland's name was mentioned in connection with secret meetings with the Pagets at Petworth.[4]

On 28 July 1588, the Armada having passed the Sussex coast, orders were at once issued for the dismissal of the county forces,[5] and a week later the 2,000 men formerly sent to London returned,[6] the last sign of the military preparations being removed in October, when the beacons were discontinued.[7] Next year an English army was sent to assist Henri IV. of France, and Sussex was called on to supply 1,000 men, to serve under Sir John Burgh and Sir Nicholas Parker.[8] Arrangements were made for them to embark at Chichester, Arundel, New-haven and Rye, at which last port all the transports were to assemble ;[9] but when the troops arrived they were found to be so badly equipped that Lord Buckhurst had to re-arm most of them out of his own armoury, and a sharp letter was sent to the justices to explain how they came to make such a bad selection of men and arms.[10] This was not the only occasion on which such a complaint was made ; in 1585 the troops sent under Mr. Wilgoose to Gravesend were insufficient in number and had to be re-armed at the county's expense ;[11] and in 1591 Captains Christmas and Power complained of the soldiers sent from Sussex as 'lose and ragged fellows without apparrell, armour, weapon or money in theire purse,' and said that if Sir Nicholas Parker had not partly remedied their defects at his own expense they would have refused to take them. As it was they had expected trained men, but received 'a company of very rogues ragd without apparrell, without armour and in suche miserable case as they doubte the greate parte of them will starve for want and colde so sone as they are on the other syde.'[12] Several

[1] S.P. Dom. Eliz. ccix. 57.   [2] *Cecil MSS.* (Hist. MSS. Com.), i. 1456.
[3] S.P. Dom. Eliz. clxiii. 74.   [4] Ibid. clxxi. 79.
[5] *Acts of P.C.* xvi. 194.   [6] Ibid. p. 215.
[7] Ibid. p. 297.   [8] Ibid. xviii. 87.   [9] Ibid. p. 113.
[10] Ibid. p. 166.   [11] Harl. MSS. 703, f. 38.   [12] Ibid. f. 66.

of these ragged troops deserted while at Rye, and orders were issued for their arrest and punishment.[1]   Again in 1597 when Sir Nicholas Parker held a muster of three rapes, in the first muster only 160 trained men appeared out of 600 ; the other rapes however were better ; the arms were noted as poor, but the gentry were willing to supply deficiencies.[2] Finally, the Lord Admiral, writing to Cecil in 1599, complained very strongly of the lack of training and of numbers of the shire contingents, especially instancing Sussex with a nominal muster of 4,000 and an actual 2,000.[3]

The ' personnel ' of the troops could not be expected to reach a very high standard when the army was recruited by impressing all the ' sturdy rogues and vagabonds ' to serve.[4]   And even in the case of the more regular levies the standard was lowered by the readiness with which the commissioners allowed the person chosen to find unfit substitutes, or even, for a consideration, to escape altogether.[5]   To be steward to such an influential man as Lord Abergavenny was a sufficient excuse to avoid serving as an officer,[6] and in 1595 the captain of Chichester complained that ' the giving of liveries against the law ' interfered with the effectiveness of the musters.'[7]   Thus when a special force was brought together in February 1601, for the defence of the queen's person, on the occasion of the endeavour of the Earl of Essex to effect a ' coup d'état,' and 100 horse and 500 of the trained bands were sent for from Sussex, it was specially noted that as many as possible of the soldiers should be independent men, masters not servants.[8]

In spite of the crushing defeat of the Spanish Armada, danger of invasion, or at least of plundering raids, continued to exist during the last half of the reign of Elizabeth, and a descent of the Spaniards upon Cornwall in 1595 caused considerable alarm.   The officer in command at Chichester pointed out to the council the decayed state of the walls of that city, and urged their immediate repair.[9]   At this time arrangements were made for the mutual defence of the maritime counties, and Sussex was appointed to send 4,000 men into Kent or Hampshire if either were attacked ; the deputy lieutenants urged that they had only arms for 2,000, but were told that doubtless more could be raised from the inhabitants on emergency.[10]

The military history of the county during the reign of James I. and down to the beginning of the Civil War calls for little notice,[11] but reference may be made to an early example of a cadet corps, if the term may be used.   When Charles I. was at Chichester in the summer of 1627 he was pleased to observe the exercise of certain boys in the use of arms, and ' on his gracious reception of their

[1] *Acts of P.C.* xxii. 338.
[2] *Cecil MSS.* (Hist. MSS. Com.), vii. 206.
[3] Ibid. viii. 338.
[4] Harl. MSS. 703, f. 132.
[5] *Acts of P.C.* xxvii. 198.
[6] Ibid. vii. 129.
[7] *Cecil. MSS.* (Hist. MSS. Com.), v. 324.
[8] Harl. MSS. 703, f. 120.
[9] *Cecil MSS.* (Hist. MSS. Com.), v. 324.
[10] *Acts of P.C.* xxv. 71, 110.
[11] For orders and returns concerning musters and levies of soldiers from 1624 to 1631, see *Suss. Arch. Coll.* xl. 1–36.

active industry' request was made to him to bestow on them some small barrels of powder. This request the king was pleased to grant for their encouragement, and in the hope that the youth of other places might be stirred up to follow their example.[1]

An event of considerable importance was the decision taken in 1636 to appoint separate sheriffs for the counties of Sussex and Surrey.[2] The two counties had been under one sheriff from 1242 down to this date, with the exception of the period 1566 to 1571, when they had been temporarily divided, but from this time they remained separate. Another step in the direction of uniformity had been taken in 1584, when the holding of separate sessions in the several rapes was condemned, as a hindrance to business and as ' a thinge so singuler to y^rselves as but in yor shire onelie we doe not knowe of the like elswhere,' and orders were given for one general sessions to be held for the whole county.[3]

During this period we have several election petitions, showing that corruption and partiality which afterwards played so large a part in our parliamentary history were already rife. It would appear that in 1623 the mayor of Winchelsea procured the election of William Finch and the exclusion of Sir Alexander Temple by threatening and illegally disqualifying certain voters,[4] while the mayor of Arundel returned Sir George Chaworth in opposition to Richard Mills by reopening the poll after it had been taken, and continuing it until other voters for whom he had sent came in.[5] In 1640 Sir John Suckling was accused of getting himself returned for Bramber by threatening the better kind of electors and bribing the others,[6] and during the same election at Hastings there was open bribery—an offer, it is said, being made on behalf of Robert Reed that if elected he would give to the poor £20 down and £10 a year for life, and would also supply two barrels of powder for training the youths of the town.[7]

The question of ship-money does not play any large part in the political troubles of Sussex, as the county was a maritime one and had no fair ground for complaint against such a tax ; but the endeavour to raise money by irregular means was resented here as elsewhere, and the ' loan ' demanded in 1626 brought in only £120 from the whole county, the people pleading their poverty, but expressing willingness if required in regular parliamentary course to ' strain themselves beyond their abilities.'[8] Dissatisfaction with the king's counsellors, and especially with the Church, is also shown in the petition of the freeholders and inhabitants of Sussex to the House of Commons in 1641.[9]

When the Civil War, which had been long smouldering, actually blazed up in August 1642, the sympathies of east Sussex and of the mass of the poorer classes throughout the county were decidedly with the Parliament. In the west, however, the Royalist gentry were strong,

---

[1] *Cal. S.P. Dom. Chas. I.* lxxvii. 20.   [2] Ibid. cccxxvi. 63.
[3] Harl. MS. 703, f. 16.   [4] S.P. Dom. Add. xliii. 62.
[5] Ibid.   [6] *Hist. MSS. Com. Rep.* iv. 25.   [7] S.P. Dom. Chas. I. cccxlviii. 45.
[8] Ibid. xxxiii. 109.   [9] B.M. pressmark 669, f. 4.

and they further possessed the important stronghold of Arundel castle, although Chichester, like the Cinque Port towns and the borough of Lewes, was in the hands of the Puritan party, being under the leadership of William Cawley, a wealthy brewer. On 15 November 1642 William Cawley, Edward Higgons and Henry Chittey, who were in command of the trained bands, obtained ordnance from Portsmouth and fortified Chichester against the king's forces. The Royalist faction, however, were on the alert and at once seized the guns. That night Sir John Morley and other gentry offered to help to maintain order in the city, and on this pretence assembled in such strength as to compel the mayor to surrender the keys. The parliamentary leaders retired hastily to Portsmouth, and next day the sheriff, Sir Edward Ford, marched into Chichester with the trained bands and a hundred horse. Accompanied by Sir William Ford, Sir William Morley, Sir Edward Bishop, Thomas Leeds, member of parliament for Steyning, and now captain of horse for Arundel rape, Sir Thomas Bowyer, Bishop Henry King's brother and son, and many others, they seized the county magazine with ten barrels of powder from Portsmouth, and searched the houses of the adverse party for arms. The sheriff then, in order to put the local trained bands out of action, summoned them to Chichester on pretence of defending it from an attack by Prince Rupert, and when they came disarmed and detained them. As soon as news of this blow came to Portsmouth the governor sent Captains Swanley and Winford with a small force to retake the city, but the wind and tide failing they could not get beyond Thorney Island, and finding the garrison too strong, retired.[1]

Early in December Sir William Waller, having captured the Royalist castle of Farnham and the city of Winchester, prepared to attack Chichester. A party of cavalry under Lord Grandison endeavoured to assist the latter city, but being caught by Waller's troops near Winchester were obliged to surrender.[2] Another Royalist force under the Earl of Thanet suffered a complete defeat at Hayward's Heath while marching against Lewes,[3] which town Captain Ambrose Trayton had received orders to secure for the Parliament.[4] Making a sudden dash for Arundel Waller surprised the garrison under Sir Richard Leachford and Captain Goulding, blew in the gate of the castle, and captured it with all its stores for the loss of one man.[5] Waller then marched against Chichester and, repelling a sally of the garrison, planted his cannon on the high ground of the Broyle, afterwards bringing them close to the north gate, while a galling fire was kept up on the defenders from all sides, especially from the church of St. Pancras on the east. After eight days' siege the city surrendered on 29 December on the promise of 'quarter with honourable usage.'[6] The loss of Chichester was due partly to lack of ammunition, but more to the disaffection of

[1] Portland MSS. (Hist. MSS. Com.), i. 72.   [2] Cowper MSS. (Hist. MSS. Com.), ii. 327.
[3] Godwin, The Civil War in Hampshire (2nd ed.) p. 53.   [4] Ibid. p. 51.
[5] Suss. Arch. Coll. v. 41-2.   [6] Ibid. pp. 44-6.

the townspeople, who refused to serve in the ranks, so that the whole burden of the defence fell upon the fifty or sixty officers and gentry. Besides the leaders already mentioned there were taken the Bishop of Chichester, Thomas May, member for Midhurst, forty of Lord Crawford's troop of horse, and the recorder of Chichester, Christopher Lewknore. The interpretation of the terms of surrender caused some bitterness, as it was alleged that Waller had undertaken that the officers should go out of the town on horseback with their swords, and the common soldiers on foot, leaving their arms and colours undefaced; but he seized the officers as prisoners and robbed them,[1] stripping them of everything except the clothes upon their backs.[2] Great injury was done to Chichester by the destruction of the suburbs for the better defence of the city and in the attack,[3] and also by the victorious troops, who, under Sir Arthur Haselrig, wrought havoc in the cathedral, breaking the organs, defacing the monuments and plundering the treasury. In order to save the city from being plundered Waller demanded from the more wealthy inhabitants a quantity of plate, which with £900 worth of plate belonging to the Earl of Thanet, and as much more which the committee had sent to Portsmouth, was distributed amongst the soldiers as 'a month's donative.'[4]

During the early part of 1643 little happened in Sussex; in June orders were issued for the raising of a hundred horse in this county and Surrey for the use of the parliament, and recruiting evidently went on in the villages, as we hear of a riot at West Hoathly fair when Ancient Streater was beating for volunteers and was assaulted and the head of his drum knocked in.[5] Nor were the Royalists idle, for in August one Thomas Cotton, 'a dangerous papist,' was brought before Sir Thomas Pelham and other justices and found in possession of a warrant from Sir Edward Ford, the sheriff and now a captain of horse under Lord Hopton, authorizing him to seek contributions of horses, arms, plate or money for his majesty's service.[6] In September Colonel Herbert Morley, the most prominent Sussex parliamentarian, wrote to Lenthall of the danger that Southampton might fall, and that 'this may raise a storm in Sussex, which county is full of neuters and malignants, and I have ever observed neuters to turn malignants on such occasions.'

At the end of 1643 Lord Hopton was in command of a strong force of cavalry on the western borders of Sussex, and on 23 November a detachment of his horse belonging to Lord Crawford's regiment rode into South Harting and took up their quarters there. The same night 400 of Colonel Norton's parliamentarian dragoons also rode into the same village and made a fair bid to capture the whole force of their enemies; but the six Royalist officers, who were quartered in Sir John Caryll's house, Harting Place, slipping round to the rear of Norton's

---

[1] *Portland MSS.* (Hist. MSS. Com.), i. 84.
[2] *Ho. of Lords' MSS.* (Hist. MSS. Com.), Rep. vii. 444. [3] Ibid. p. 2.
[4] *Cal. S.P. Dom. Chas. I.* ccccxcvii. 99.
[5] *Portland MSS.* (Hist. MSS. Com.), i. 709. [6] Ibid. p. 126.

men, suddenly charged upon them shouting 'Follow, follow !' as if there were a troop behind them, and so startled the dragoons that they fled in disorder.[1] Harting Place seems to have been garrisoned at this time, and the king's soldiers pushed as far east as Petworth, but until 6 December nothing much was done.

On 6 December Sir Edward Ford and Sir Edward Bishop secured the town of Arundel and laid siege to the castle. The parliamentary officers made hasty efforts to raise troops at Horsham and elsewhere, while Captain Temple saw to the strengthening of the defences at Bramber and Shoreham. By 9 December some 500 or 600 horse and foot had been brought together under Colonel Morley and marched towards Houghton Bridge, but the night being dark and the where-abouts of the enemy uncertain the foot were sent into quarters at Parham, while the horse remained on the Downs, scouting.[2] Morley's force probably withdrew next day, as the castle had been surrendered by Captain Capcot on 9 December.[3] Lord Hopton also captured Cow-dray House, and endeavoured to push on to Lewes, but was beaten back by Colonel Morley. It was during this expedition that Captain James Temple ' defended the fort of Bramber against a bold and daring enemy, to the wonder of all the country.'[4] Another skirmish took place at Bramber about the same time, when the Royalists 'atempted Bramber bridge, but our brave Carleton and Evernden with his Dragoones, and our Coll. horse welcomed them with drakes and musketts, sending some 8 or 9 men to hell (I feare), and one trooper to Arundell Castle prisoner, and one of Captain Evernden's Dragoones to heaven ; all this while the enemy held the castle, and a party seised Wiston House, within a mile of Bramber Bridge.'[5] The Royalists appear also to have occupied Horsham, with the connivance of Thomas Middleton, the member for that borough and one of the Sussex Committee of Defence.[6]

Waller was not the man to sit idle all this while, and on 10 December started from Farnham, the next day driving the Royalists out of Cowdray House and occupying it himself.[7] The Cavaliers at Wiston also ' left the house and fled for theire lives, and in theire march at Findon left 3 carts loaden with plunder, the which (Morley's men) fetched home and refreshed (their) weary souldiers.'[8] On 13 December the siege of Arundel castle began ; the town was speedily captured and Waller's army, augmented by the regiments of Colonel Morley and Sir William Springett, now numbered 10,000 men, so that by the end of the month there was little doubt of the issue. The besieging troops made good use of the parish church of St. Nicholas, mounting artillery on its tower and firing thence into the castle, but the danger to the defenders lay principally in shortage of provisions and ammunition, which soon began to tell upon them. Lord Hopton made one desperate effort to raise the siege, advancing through North Marden to West Dean on 29 De-

[1] *Suss. Arch. Coll.* xxviii. 102–4. [2] Ibid. v. 57–8. [3] Ibid. xxviii. 100.
[4] Ibid. v. 154. [5] Ibid. ix. 52. [6] *Portland MSS.* (Hist. MSS. Com.), i. 183.
[7] *Suss. Arch. Coll.* xxviii. 106. [8] Ibid. ix. 52.

cember and next day appearing upon the Downs above Arundel, where he suffered a severe defeat.[1]   About a week earlier two or three hundred of Lord Crawford's men had been taken after a severe fight at South Harting.[2]   On 5 January 1644 the garrison were so reduced by hunger that Sir Edward Ford opened negotiations with Waller, who meanwhile courteously allowed some ladies who were in the castle to dine at his own table ; and on the morning of the next day Arundel castle was surrendered unconditionally.[3]   For his service Sir William Waller received the thanks of parliament and was promoted to be major-general.

In April 1644 Colonel Stapley was put in command at Chichester with orders to increase the garrison to 800 and to hasten the despatch of the county contingent to Waller.[4]   In June Colonel Apsley, by authority of Sir William Waller, took steps to raise a regiment in Sussex, but the gentry of the county objected on the ground that the burden of supporting the officers would annoy the county ; Sir William was therefore requested to cancel his commission to Apsley, which he did willingly ' the rather because I would not have anything to do with the gentlemen of Sussex, from whom I have received nothing but constant incivilities.'[5]   An urgent order had to be sent in September of this year to the committee of the associated counties of Surrey, Sussex, and Hampshire for the payment of their three troops of horse, who had been so long without pay that there was fear of their disbanding.[6]   The Sussex committee were also forbidden to proceed with the proposed demolition of Cowdray House, which would have a very bad effect on the county, but were directed to garrison the house.[7]   Mr. Cawley was accordingly put in command of 120 foot and ten horse at Cowdray.[8]   The committee again proposed in November to destroy a number of houses, but were told that it was inexpedient, and that since the decisive defeat of the king's troops at Newbury it was not necessary even to garrison the houses in question.[9]   Orders were also issued that the county forces should not be assembled till further notice,[10] and that Colonel Morley's regiment should be retained for the defence of the county.[11]

In January 1645 the Royalists were again in force on the western borders of Sussex, and the county troops were ordered to march against them ;[12] in May soldiers were sent from Chichester and Arundel to the siege of Basing House,[13] and next month the governor of Chichester, Colonel Algernon Sidney, had instructions to see to his fortifications.[14] A troop of horse was also raised at this time for the defence of west Sussex.[15]   The chief event of this year, however, was the rising of the clubmen.   A number of the countrymen who were not under arms on either side and had begun to experience the disastrous effects of civil war endeavoured to compel the contending parties to come to terms and

---

[1] *Suss. Arch. Coll.* xxviii. 108.   [2] Ibid. p. 109.
[3] Tierney, *Hist. of Arundel*, pp. 67–70.   [4] *Cal. S.P. Dom. Chas. I.* di. 65.
[5] Ibid. dii. 3, 7.   [6] Ibid. diii. 5.   [7] Ibid. 10   [8] Ibid.
[9] Ibid. 40.   [10] Ibid. 27.   [11] Ibid. 54.   [12] Ibid. dvi. 10.
[13] Ibid. dviii. 104.   [14] Ibid. 120.   [15] Ibid. dx. 2.

dismiss their respective armies. From their lack of pikes and firearms these irregular forces were called clubmen. In Hampshire this anti-war movement began about the end of August, and soon spread into Sussex, where one Aylen, a Mr. Peckham, and 'some of the Fords' were the ringleaders. The movement was warmly taken up in the villages of the south-west, especially round Eastergate and Walberton, and at Midhurst and Petworth. The clubmen to the number of about six hundred met on Runcton Down on Wednesday, 17 September, and arranged for a further muster on Bury Hill close to Arundel on the following Monday.[1] Instructions were sent to Colonel Norton to march into Sussex, where he was to be reinforced by 1,000 horse and also by the county trained bands, if their fidelity could be relied upon.[2] Meanwhile Captain Morley, then governor of Arundel, sent Major Young with a small force to fall upon the clubmen in their headquarters at Walberton, which they did before daybreak on Sunday, 21 September. This particular force was scattered, two 'malignant' ministers and a few others captured, and a man who tried to summon aid by ringing the church bell killed.[3] But the rising was not so easily quelled, and on 26 September Colonel Norton reported that he had put down the Hampshire clubmen successfully, and added: 'I hope this will be a warning to Sussex; if not we shall be ready to serve them the like trick.'[4] Yet on 13 October William Cawley complained that by reason of the clubmen's insurrection it was impossible to raise either men or money for Sir Thomas Fairfax's army, as they would not suffer any to be impressed, 'sending sometimes a constable or tithing-man with the blood running about his ears,' so that out of sixty-seven to be levied in the rape only twenty-seven had been secured and sent to General Cromwell at Winchester, while of £4,000 due less than £100 had been brought in.[5] He therefore requested that powers might be granted for the arrest of the ringleaders and the disarming of all; the conferring of which powers no doubt terminated the trouble.

The year 1648 saw a recrudescence of Royalist activity in Sussex. Early in June a petition of the knights, gentry, clergy and commons of Sussex was presented to the two Houses, desiring that the king might be treated with, the army paid off and disbanded, and no garrisons maintained.[6] The Royalists in the neighbourhood of Horsham supported this by threatening armed reprisals against all who had not joined in this petition, and emphasized their threats by putting a strong guard over the Horsham magazine and refusing to allow its removal to Arundel.[7] By 29 June the Cavaliers at Horsham had begun to arm and collect forces;[8] but Sir Michael Livesay's regiment of horse was ordered up from Kent and took the town with little trouble.[9] The insurgents,

[1] *A True Relation of the Rising of Clubmen in Sussex*, B.M. pressmark E302 (18).
[2] *Cal. S.P. Dom. Chas. I.* dx. 128, 139.   [3] The *True Relation*.
[4] *Hist. MSS. Com. Rep.* x. (6), 163.   [5] *Portland MSS.* (Hist. MSS. Com.), i. 289.
[6] *Ho. of Lords MSS.* (Hist. MSS. Com.), vii. 30.
[7] *Portland MSS.* (Hist. MSS. Com.), i. 465.   [8] Ibid. p. 719.
[9] *Cal. S.P. Dom. Chas. I.* xvi. 60, 61.

amongst whom William Marlett[1] and John Shelley of Sullington[2] are mentioned, were dispersed and fined, and the original suggestion of raising two troops of horse and a company of dragoons in the county to suppress the rising was negatived as unnecessary.[3] In August, however, a plot to seize Chichester was discovered, and the committee were warned to be vigilant ;[4] and about the same time Major Anthony Norton raised some sixty horse and foot and endeavoured to seize the magazine of Rye and to oppose the entrance of Major Gibbons by barricading Blackwell Wall.[5] Gibbons however secured the town and obtained an increase of his garrison.[6]

Livesay's regiment after the taking of Horsham caused great dissatisfaction by their 'disorders and plunderings without distinction of friend or enemy,'[7] and next year, being again quartered in the county though ordered for service in Ireland, proved a great burden 'both by their free quarter and their disorderly carriage.'[8] The grievance of free quarter was abolished by Cromwell, and in March 1652 we find £25 paid to Anne Denny, wife of George Goring, for three months' rent of Goring House for quartering soldiers,[9] but the disorders were an almost unavoidable accompaniment of the war, the principal sufferers being the loyal clergy.[10]

In September 1650 militia commissions for the county were issued for three captains of horse and eleven of foot, including one for Chichester,[11] and in August 1651, when Charles II. was marching southwards with the Scottish army, the Sussex militia were ordered to Oxford, two troops only being left in the county to preserve the peace.[12]

On 3 September 1651 was fought the decisive battle of Worcester, as a result of which Charles had to fly for his life. After a month spent in hiding and in slow journeys in disguise, the king, finding it impossible to obtain a boat at Bristol, determined to try the Sussex coast. Accordingly on 7 October Lord Wilmot came to Racton to arrange with Colonel Gounter for the king's escape. The colonel after considerable difficulty arranged with a Brighton skipper, Captain Tettersell, to carry the king, in the character of a man who had got into trouble over a duel, across to France. On Monday, 13 October, Colonel Gounter and his cousin and Lord Wilmot went coursing upon the Downs, and there met the king with Colonel Philips. The night was spent at Hambledon with Gounter's married sister, whose husband, Thomas Symonds, mistook Charles for a Roundhead, he having had his hair cropped for purposes of disguise. Next day they rode on, and as they were above Arundel met the governor, Captain Morley, while

[1] *Cal. of Com. for Advance of Money*, p. 1329.   [2] Ibid. p. 1238.
[3] *Ho. of Lords MSS.* (Hist. MSS. Com.), vii. 34.
[4] *Cal. S.P. Dom. Chas. I.* dxvi. 81.   [5] *Cal. of Com. for Adv. of Money*, p. 1351.
[6] *Cal. S.P. Dom. Chas. I.* dxv. 81.   [7] Ibid. p. 70.
[8] *Cal. S.P. Dom. Interregnum*, i. 32.   [9] Ibid. p. 592.
[10] See *Suss. Arch. Coll.* v. 73–9. Also the case of John Lewknor of West Dean, aged 19, who was robbed, stripped of his clothes and threatened with wounds by some parliamentary soldiers merely because some of his name were fighting on the king's side (*Cal. of Com. for Compounding*, p. 1215).
[11] *Cal. S.P. Dom. Interregnum*, i. 511.   [12] Ibid. xvi. 30, 33.

when they came down to Bramber they found the place full of soldiers. Riding boldly on they passed without arousing suspicion, and so came to Brighton, where they went to the George Inn. The host of the George caused fresh alarm to the party by recognizing the king and insisting upon kissing his hand. Further difficulties then arose, Captain Tettersell requiring most unreasonable terms, but at last all was settled, and by eight o'clock next morning the ship had set sail, and after a quick voyage Charles landed in safety at Fécamp.[1] Throughout the adventure Charles displayed much of that courage and coolness in danger which formed perhaps his most admirable quality.

The 'crowning mercy' of Worcester put an end to all fear of Royalist risings, and Captain Temple's Sussex troop of dragoons was disbanded,[2] and the garrison of Arundel castle reduced by half.[3] Next year the castle was disgarrisoned, its munitions sent to Portsmouth, and its defences blown up.[4] For six years peace reigned, and then the death of Oliver Cromwell restored the hopes of the king's party; schemes for insurrection broke out prematurely in different parts of the county, Chichester being one of the places whose capture was designed,[5] while Captain Culpepper tried to arrange for Charles to land at Brighton.[6] The Government, however, were still strong enough to cope with all these movements; companies were raised at Arundel, Chichester, Rye and Lewes, and Colonel Fagge was put in command of the Sussex forces,[7] while 2,000 men were sent down to Chichester and Arundel.[8] Early in August the Royalists were still in arms, though hitherto unsuccessful, and it was feared they might surprise Cowdray House, which was therefore garrisoned by a force of twenty men.[9] By the beginning of September all was quiet again and the troops were disbanded, though those at Rye under Captain Marshall and at Chichester under Major Clark were ordered to hold themselves in readiness to reassemble if required. The walls of Arundel and Chichester were at the same time ordered to be thoroughly demolished.[10]

In May 1659 Richard Cromwell found himself forced by a combination of circumstances which he could not withstand to resign the office of Protector, and Charles II. entered into peaceful possession of his kingdom in 1660. The Sussex gentry were not backward in offering him an address of congratulation.[11] The Puritan party, however, was still strong in the county, and even in 1663 the towns of Lewes and Chichester were particularly 'perverse'; so much so indeed that the trained bands had to be marched into Chichester to prevent an armed rising,[12] while a request was made for the justices to assist 'the honest party' at Lewes, as there was no militia in east Sussex.[13]

Measures were at once taken against the regicides; William Caw-

[1] *The Last Act in the Miraculous Story of His Majesty King Charles the Second's Escape*, by Col. Gounter of Racton.
[2] *Cal. S.P. Dom. Interreg.* xvi. 40.   [3] Ibid. xxiii. 13.   [4] Ibid. xli. 26, 153.
[5] Ibid. cciii. 92.   [6] Ibid. cciv.   [7] Ibid. cciii. 88.   [8] Ibid. 62.
[9] Ibid. cciv. 5.   [10] Ibid.   [11] *Cal. S.P. Dom. Chas. II.* i. 46.
[12] Ibid. lxxx. 99.   [13] Ibid. lxxx. 56.

ley, who had sat for Midhurst and Chichester, saved his life by flying to the Continent. John Downes, member for Arundel, and James Temple, member for Bramber, were sentenced to death, but respited and died in prison. Anthony Stapley had already died, in 1658, and William Goffe, the major-general in command of Sussex and one of Cromwell's House of Lords, escaped to America. Colonel Herbert Morley, although present at the trial of King Charles, did not affix his signature to the warrant. At the beginning of 1660 he was lieutenant of the Tower and was warned of coming events by the Royalist, John Evelyn, his old friend, but being over-cautious missed the opportunity of rendering the king good service, and had to buy his peace by paying £1,000.[1]

The prime necessity of appeasing the adverse party led alike to the pardon of the lesser offenders and the scanty rewarding of the loyal subjects who had suffered so much for the king's cause. Even the institution of the Order of the Royal Oak which had been contemplated by Charles was abandoned, although a list of its intended knights was compiled. This list includes the following Sussex men : Thomas Middleton, Walter Dobell, Edward and John Eversfield, two Lunsfords, members of the same family as Sir Thomas Lunsford, whose fame as a cannibal and eater of children is celebrated in *Hudibras*, Henry Goring, John May and Michelbourne of Stanmer.[2] Colonel Gounter, to whom the king largely owed his escape, received no reward, though some years later his widow was granted a life pension of £200 and his son a scholarship at New College, Oxford ; but Captain Nicholas Tettersell, whose part in the escape had been entirely a matter of self-interest, secured an annuity of £100 for himself and his children.[3]

It is not much to the credit of the county that it produced the infamous inventor of the Popish plot, Titus Oates. He was the son of the rector of All Saints', Hastings, and himself served as curate there until he had to fly the town, having been convicted of perjury and slander against the mayor. The feeling against the Papists aroused by Oates's pretended revelations was very bitter, and Mr. Bickley was put out of the commission of the peace for daring to throw doubt upon the story, and saying at a sessions dinner at Chichester that Oates had contradicted himself two and twenty times in his evidence.[4] Consequently when the Duke of Monmouth came to Chichester in February 1680 he was received as the Protestant champion with acclamation, bell-ringing, and bonfires, most of the cathedral clergy joining in the welcome, though the bishop, the mayor, and the greater part of the gentry discountenanced these proceedings.[5]

---

[1] *Suss. Arch. Coll.* v. 98–100.   [2] Ibid. p. 104.   [3] *Cal. S.P. Dom. Chas. II.* lxxxvi. 107.
[4] *Ho. of Lords MSS.* (Hist. MSS. Com.), Rep. xi. (2), 146.
[5] *Suss. Arch. Coll.* vii. 168–72. The duke's memory was long cherished amongst the populace, and when in 1698 a handsome young fellow, really the son of a Leicester inn-keeper, gave himself out to be the Duke of Monmouth, asserting that James II. had not really executed him, he was readily believed, receiving favours of all kinds from the Sussex yeomen and their wives, and even more than £500 in money (ibid. xxiv. 296–7).

A HISTORY OF SUSSEX

The trend of political and religious feeling in Sussex was again clearly shown in 1688, when James II., wishing to repeal the Test and Penal Statutes, and anxious to know whether he could obtain the support of Parliament for that purpose, caused three questions to be put to every justice of the peace. These questions were : (i.) If he should be chosen to serve in Parliament would he support the repeal of these statutes ? (ii.) Would he assist in the election of members pledged to their repeal ? (iii.) Will he live friendly with those of all persuasions ? For refusing to put these questions to the Sussex justices the Earl of Dorset was removed from the lieutenancy of the county and replaced by Viscount Montague. The replies must have been very unsatisfactory to the Crown, for although the third question was answered unanimously in the affirmative, only eight justices would assent to the first two, while almost every one in the eastern rapes definitely refused to agree thereto. Those in the western part of the county for the most part gave the politic answers that if elected they would vote as might seem best when the question came to be debated in the House, and that they would assist to elect such members as would best serve the interests of the country.[1]

When the news came to Chichester on 17 June 1689 that 'James 2nd, the papistical, was cut and runnd to across the sea,' the inhabitants were so delighted that they formed a club in imitation of the corporation, with a mayor, aldermen, town clerk, and so forth, to be called the 'Corporation of St. Pancras,' the one object of which was to meet and feast every 4 November, on the eve of the anniversary of the Gunpowder Plot.[2] A few of the county gentlemen remained faithful to James, the most notable being John Caryll of Harting, who accompanied his royal master into exile and was by him given the title of Baron Caryll of Dureford, but as a whole Sussex was strongly in favour of King William. For some little while there was fear of a French landing, and in July 1690 their ships came near enough in to throw a few shot into Hastings, and the militia were called out and several regiments of horse and foot sent into the county.[3] In the following January there was a report current that the Earl of Clarendon had drawn up a proclamation to be issued upon the landing of King James in Sussex,[4] but no such landing was attempted, and things soon settled down.

The eighteenth century was essentially the period of party government, and it is therefore during this time that we find most importance attached to the possession of a parliamentary seat, and in consequence a large amount of wire-pulling and manœuvring. The fullest and best account of any Sussex election is the description of that in 1734 compiled by Mr. Basil Williams from the Duke of Newcastle's papers in the British Museum.[5] The duke, by virtue of his wealth and the enormous extent of his lands, could practically control the return of about sixty or

[1] *Suss. Arch. Coll.* xxxi.
[2] Ibid. xxiv. 136–8. The corporation still existed at least as late as 1872.
[3] *Hist. MSS. Com. Rep.* xii. (7), 277.   [4] Ibid. p. 310.
[5] *Engl. Hist. Rev.* xii. 448–88.

530

seventy members, and was especially powerful in Sussex, which with its twenty-eight representatives was only surpassed numerically by three counties.[1] In no rôle did the duke shine more than in that of an electioneering agent, attending to every detail, consulted as to the best manner of bribing each individual elector, touring through the county in his six-horse coach, writing to bishops, noblemen, and commoners, pulling every conceivable wire and generally revelling in all the petty details of the business. His agents were also capable and energetic, especially Richard Burnett, who must have been invaluable, judging by the record of his cheerful activity. Henry Pelham, the duke's brother, who was standing for the county, was also an excellent and hard-working agent, but his fellow-candidate, James Butler, seems to have been a poor figurehead and more hindrance than help.[2] The two Tom Pelhams also, who were candidates for Lewes, were wretchedly incapable and could do nothing for themselves, Pelham of Lewes being apparently a valetudinarian,[3] while his namesake of Stanmer was known as 'Turk' Pelham, and drank himself to death in 1737.[4]

The methods of influencing voters in this election were very various, ranging from the grant of a living to the pardon of a popular smuggler; appointments to Government, and especially revenue, offices were numerous, while the drink bills incurred for constant treats were enormous. Threats of the loss of custom were used to wavering tradesmen, and in Lewes, where the voting was confined to householders rated on the poor books, unsatisfactory tenants were ejected and their places filled with those who would vote the right way, while care was taken that the parish officers who had control of the poor-books should be favourable.[5] Of violence there is scarcely a trace, and the conduct of the opposition candidates' supporters at Hailsham in burning Sir Robert Walpole in effigy is reprobated by both sides.[6] The result of the election was a triumph for the Duke of Newcastle and his business-like organization of corruption.

It would be easy to give a long list of cases of bribery from 1700, when Samuel Shepherd, member for Bramber, was unseated and committed to the Tower for that cause, down to the Chichester election of 1826, at which, although no definite giving of bribes can be alleged, the polling of less than 800 voters cost the three candidates nearly £9,000. The most remarkable case of corruption came to light at Shoreham in 1770. At the election of this year for the seat vacated by the death of Sir Samuel Cornish, three candidates came to the poll. Of these Thomas Rumbold obtained 87 votes and John Purling 37. The returning officer, Hugh Roberts, rejected 76 of Rumbold's votes and declared Purling elected. A committee being appointed to inquire into the officer's high-handed action, Roberts said that the votes rejected were those of the members of 'The Christian Society,' a society which under

[1] *Eng. Hist. Rev.* xii. 459.
[2] Ibid. p. 479.
[3] Ibid. p. 481.
[4] *Hist. MSS. Com. Rep.* xiv. (9), 9, 239.
[5] Williams, loc. cit. pp. 484-6.
[6] Ibid. p. 475.

the cloak of charity concerned itself solely with the corrupt manipulation of votes, and that the members on this occasion had undertaken to sell their support to the highest bidder, and had received £35 apiece from Mr. Rumbold's agent. Inquiry proved the truth of this statement ; Roberts escaped with a severe reprimand for his illegal action in disqualifying voters on his own motion, and all the members of the society were disfranchised, the franchise being for the future extended to all the 40s. freeholders in the rape of Bramber.[1]

Though corruption was possibly most highly organized at Shoreham it was almost equally rampant elsewhere. Thus in 1767 Arundel ' was sold for fifteen guineas pro vote to Mr. Crawford, who transferred her as was publickly said to a countryman of his . . . who was said to be negotiating the transfer of her to a third purchaser,'[2] and in 1780 Robinson wrote to Lord North, ' I will tell Sir Patrick Crawford that if he can secure the second seat at Arundel undoubtedly a friend is ready to give £3,000, but that I doubt that he will find that they must give Lord Surrey one member.'[3] As a result of a petition after this election of 1780 Sir Patrick was unseated and the existence was proved of a ' Malthouse Club,' of which the members had each received 30 guineas for his vote.

It is almost a surprise to find that there were any honest men connected with elections at that time, but the mayor of Arundel showed that he had the courage to do his duty in 1688. The Government had sent down a candidate to oppose the sitting members, and had also sent the notorious Lord Chancellor Jefferies to ensure his return. Upon Jefferies trying to interfere in the polling and cause a vote to be rejected, the mayor promptly gave him into the custody of the constable and caused him to be ejected. A somewhat similar case occurred in the county election of 1705, when the Dukes of Somerset and Richmond were turned out of the court by Sheriff Turner before he would take the poll.[4]

Sussex was one of the disturbed counties during the Reform agitation of 1830–1. By the Reform Bill of 1832 Bramber, East Grinstead, Seaford, Steyning and Winchelsea lost both their members, and Arundel, Horsham, Midhurst and Rye lost one member. Brighton received the right to return two, and the county was divided into East and West divisions, each returning two members. This arrangement held good until the Redistribution Bill of 1884, under which the county was arranged in six electoral divisions, Horsham, Chichester, East Grinstead, Lewes, Eastbourne and Rye, the borough of Hastings returning one member and Brighton two.

Out of the old trained bands, whose history in Sussex we have already traced down to the Restoration, rose the militia. The difference indeed was merely one of name until after the reorganization which followed the disgraceful failure of the northern militia in 1745. In

---

[1] *Suss. Arch. Coll.* xxvii. 90–5. [2] *Hist. MSS. Com. Rep.* x. (1) 409.
[3] Ibid. App. 6, 33. [4] *Harley Papers* (Hist. MSS. Com.), ii. 185.

that year, when the early successes of the Pretender's army alarmed the country, it being found impracticable to embody the Sussex militia at once, the gentry agreed to subscribe various sums, amounting to about £6,000, for the formation of a local force of volunteers, and a company was accordingly raised in Lewes rape under Colonel Thomas Sergison.[1] Thomas Hayley at the same time raised a company of foot known as the Chichester Blues.[2] From 1758 to 1762 many of the county forces were under arms, but the Sussex militia, who were at this time divided into East and West regiments and numbered 800 men,[3] were not embodied until 1778.[4]

Fear of a French invasion during 1778 and 1779 led to renewed military activity. Plans were formed for isolating any troops that might land, and depriving them of provisions by driving off all the cattle, sheep and corn to certain inland depôts, and thence still further inland if necessary, and destroying everything that could not be removed. Three regiments of dragoons were to be employed, with infantry, to harass the enemy while this was being done, and certain places were to be held as advance posts, such as Hollingbury and Cissbury Hills, Mount Caburn, the windmills at Beeding, Beddingham and Highdown, the castles of Arundel, Bramber and Pevensey, and Ore and Fairlight churches.[5] The gentry considered that the carrying out of these arrangements should be left to the lord lieutenant and his county officers, and protested strongly against its being put into the hands of General Peirson, the commander of the district in which Sussex lay.[6]

In 1779 the king sanctioned the raising of volunteers, and at a meeting of the leading county men held at the White Hart, Lewes, in November, it was agreed to raise 24 companies, each to contain at least 70 rank and file.[7] Only Sussex men were to be enrolled; the officers were to be gentry, and the sergeants active young farmers or their sons. Each company was to have three centres where the men were to meet every Sunday after church, to be taught the use and care of their firelocks. As no military punishments could be made use of, any one misbehaving was to be expelled, and any appearing drunk to be prosecuted for 'drunkenness on the Lord's day.' Prizes in kind to the value of half-a-crown were to be given to each detachment every week for shooting. Unfortunately no details of the troops then formed can be discovered.

The outbreak of the French Revolution was marked by a great influx of refugees into Sussex, about 1,100 landing in 1792, and when war broke out between England and France in 1793, and aliens were compelled, as a military precaution, to leave the coast, many of these settled at Lindfield and Cuckfield.[8] In August 1793 a great camp was formed at Brighton, and 7,000 men marched in from Ashdown Forest

---

[1] Add. MSS. 33058, f. 458.   [2] Dallaway, *Hist. of Western Sussex*, i. 181.
[3] Add. MSS. 33058, f. 602.   [4] Add. MSS. 33048, f. 307.
[5] Pelham MSS. in library of Suss. Arch. Soc.   [6] Ibid.   [7] Ibid.
[8] *Suss. Arch. Coll.* xxxv. 73.

and pitched their tents along the coast west of the town. For the sake of effect they were spread out in a long line, with the result that the North Devon and East Middlesex regiments had to encamp on a newly ploughed field, though there was excellent turf a little inland.[1]

The number of the Sussex militia was fixed by the 42nd Geo. III. cap. 90, at 803, each of the six rapes having its quota, and Brighton also. Its actual strength (counting, probably, the officers) was 840 strong, and the question of its transport was a serious one, as the tents were cumbersome and no limits were set to the impedimenta of the militia if they chose to pay for wagons; as in the case of some of our more recent wars, it was then said 'the Baggage waggon of a militia regiment resembles more the Removal of the Household Furniture of a Family than that of the Military Stores of an Army.'[2] Commissariat troubles also arose occasionally, and in April 1795 the Oxford militia stationed at Blatchington, resenting an insufficiency of food, mutinied, seized all the bread, flour and meat they could find at Seaford and in Bishopstone tide-mill, and then occupied Newhaven, where they were disarmed by the Lancashire Fencibles from Brighton and the Horse Artillery from Lewes. For this mutiny two men were shot at Goldstone Bottom near Brighton.[3]

Besides the great camp at Brighton, which in the autumn of 1794 contained about 15,000 men, there were troops stationed at Chichester, Arundel, Worthing, Seaford, Alfriston, Lewes, East Grinstead, Eastbourne, Hailsham, Pevensey, Bexhill (occupied for some time by Hanoverian soldiers), Battle, Hastings and elsewhere. While the danger of invasion was greatest, in 1803–4, and a descent was expected upon the flat coast of Pevensey Bay, a large camp was formed at Eastbourne under General Sir James Pulteney, entrenchments were thrown up along the coast for the emplacement of ninety-four 24-pounders, and the famous Martello towers, still to be seen, were erected on the coast from the Kentish border westward to Seaford. The Pevensey sluices were arranged so that the levels could be inundated, and the 'military canal' cut to cover the marshes east of Hastings. Extra temporary barracks were erected for 200 cavalry and 900 infantry at Hastings, and for the same number at Eastbourne. At last in October 1804 the Eastbourne camp broke up after a grand sham fight in which four regiments of foot, two squadrons of dragoons and the Sussex, Dorset, North Hants, Glamorgan and South Herts militia took part.[4]

The Sussex militia marched from Beachy Head to Colchester, and thence to South Shields, where in October 1806 the senior captain, John Garthwaite,[5] was court-martialled and dismissed for disrespectful behaviour to Colonel Newbury, who had succeeded Lord Chichester in the command.

Of the auxiliary forces raised during this period the first to be

[1] Parry, *Coast of Sussex*, p. 67. [2] Pelham MSS.
[3] Horsfield, *Hist. of Lewes*, i. 221. [4] Parry, *Coast of Sussex*, pp. 202–5.
[5] He published an account of the court-martial and a defence of his own character.

mentioned is the Sussex Fencible Cavalry, who were formed in April 1794. By the end of June there were 112 rank and file under Sir George Thomas, and in December 1795 they numbered 350. In January 1798 they were at Plymouth, and in the early summer of the same year they marched to Carlisle, and afterwards to Dumfries. Sir George Thomas was superseded in June 1799 by Major-General Garth, who was succeeded in August by Major-General Sir James Erskine, who was still in command when the troop was disbanded at Beverley, in April 1800.[1]

Infantry volunteer corps were formed in, or slightly before, 1798 at Arundel, Petworth, Seaford and Selsey, and others at Hastings, Rye and Winchelsea, which in 1803 amalgamated as the Cinque Ports Volunteers. In 1803 corps were also formed for Angmering, Bramber rape (North and South), Chichester, Hastings rape, Lewes rape (North and South), Littlehampton and Pevensey rape (North and South). Artillery corps also existed at Blatchington (1798 ; united with New-haven in 1803), Brighton (1803, ' The Prince of Wales's ' : the corps of ' Sea Fencibles ' are also mentioned as doing some fine practice shooting at Brighton battery in 1803[2]), Eastbourne (1803 ; ' a set of fine spirited fellows '[3]), and Rye (1804[4]). The county regiment of militia alone survived the great war ; and received the prefix of ' royal ' in 1830, when its strength was ten companies.

Of yeomanry, the Lewes corps was raised by Sir George Shiffner in 1795, and the Stanmer and Petworth troops about the same time. There were also troops at East Grinstead, Henfield, Midhurst and Parham, as well as at Ashburnham, where Lord St. Asaph had raised a troop in 1803. The corps with the greatest local reputation was that of the Sussex Guides ; and there was also a corps of horse artillery, commanded by the Duke of Richmond, whose services were confined to the district west of the Arun ; they served without pay and consisted of some sixty rank and file with two 3-pounder curricle guns and two $4\frac{1}{2}$-inch howitzers.[5] All these corps were disbanded after the great war ; but in the troublous winter of 1830–1 the Arundel and Bramber corps of three troops was raised by the Earl of Surrey, and the Petworth troop by Col. George Wyndham. Before the South African war the only yeomanry in Sussex formed part of the Duke of Cambridge's Own Middlesex regiment, but the county has now its own regiment of Imperial Yeomanry.

In 1805 Sussex for the first time gave its name to a regiment of the line. The 35th Foot was originally raised in Ireland in 1701, by an officer of William III, to which fact it owed its orange facings. In 1782, while serving in the West Indies, it received the title of the Dorsetshire regiment. It was recruited by a considerable contingent from the Sussex militia in 1799, when it served at Bergen and Alkmaer ; and was at Malta in 1800. In 1805 it became the Sussex regiment,

[1] W. O. Pay Lists.   [2] Parry, op. cit. p. 73.   [3] Ibid. p 202.
[4] W. O. Pay Lists.   [5] Ibid.

535

and two years later suffered severely in the Egyptian expedition.   The first battalion took part in the capture of the Ionian Islands in 1810 and remained in garrison at Corfu till 1818.   The second battalion was in the Walcheren expedition of 1809, served at Bergen-op-Zoom and Antwerp in 1813, and formed part of the reserves at Huy during the battle of Waterloo ; after taking part in the occupation of Paris it returned to England and was disbanded in October 1815.   In 1832 the Sussex regiment received the title of Royal, its facings being therefore changed to blue.   During the Indian Mutiny the Royal Sussex were badly cut up at Jagdespore in April 1858.

While the first battalion of the present Royal Sussex was thus constituted out of the 35th Foot, the second battalion was formed out of the East India Company's 3rd Bengal European Infantry, which was raised in 1854, served through the Mutiny and was incorporated, in 1861, in the British Army as the 107th Foot.   The third battalion was formed from the Royal Sussex Militia, and there are three volunteer battalions, namely, the late 1st Sussex Rifles with the Brighton College and Christ's Hospital cadet corps, the late 2nd Sussex Rifles with Hurstpierpoint, Lancing and Ardingly cadet corps, and the 1st Cinque Ports and Sussex with Eastbourne College cadets.   The regiment served at Abu Klea in 1884, with Sir Charles Wilson's expedition to Khartoum in 1885, and has since earned distinction on the Indian frontier and in South Africa.[1]

In 1900 the 3rd Brigade Cinque Ports Royal Garrison Artillery (Militia) were embodied as the Sussex R.G.A.   There are also two volunteer brigades of R.G.A., the first with headquarters at Brighton, and the second (heavy artillery) at Eastbourne, and the headquarters of the 2nd Cinque Ports R.G.A. are at St. Leonards.

APPENDIX

DIVISIONS OF THE COUNTY

Till the end of the eleventh century, and possibly later, it is probable that the county of Sussex possessed no exact northern boundary, the dense forest of Andredsweald rendering the accurate definition of the bounds between this county and the counties of Surrey, Hampshire and Kent a task of greater difficulty than advantage.   Evidence of this is shown in Domesday Book by the surveying of Worth and Lodsworth under Surrey, and also by the fact that the present parishes of North and South Ambersham, well within the limits of Sussex, were part of Hampshire as late as 1834.   On the east the estuary of the Rother, with its extensive marshes, formed a natural boundary, as the inlet of Chichester harbour did on the west. These bounds, once settled, appear to have remained unaltered until 1894, when the ecclesiastical parish of Broadwater Down was separated from Frant and included in the county of Kent.   The following year the Sussex portion of Lamberhurst was annexed to Kent, and the Kentish portion of Broomhill given to Sussex.

[1] Lawrence-Archer, *Regimental Records* ; and *Army List*.   A monument at Brighton and a memorial at Hastings have recently been erected in honour of the regiment's service in South Africa.

POLITICAL HISTORY

The division of the county into Rapes has already been dealt with,[1] and a note has also been made of the probable early existence of $42\frac{1}{2}$ hundreds, which had however been completely split up and re-arranged previous to 1086.[2] At the time of the Domesday Survey Sussex contained sixty hundreds, the greater part of which have continued down to the present time with little alteration. The following list shows the names of the Domesday hundreds, with their thirteenth century [3] and modern [4] equivalents :—

1086.	13th Century.	Modern.
Gestelinges.	Gestling.	Guestling.
Colespore.	Colespore, Golspurre.	Goldspur.
Babinrerode.[5]	Gosetrowe.	Gostrow.
Esseswelle.	Shoeswell.	Shoyswell.
Hauochesberie.	Hawkesbergh.[6]	Hawksborough.
Henhert.	Henehurst.	Henhurst, and Robertsbridge.
Staple.	Stapele.	Staple.
Hailesaltede.	{ Nederfeld ($\frac{1}{2}$), de Bello ($\frac{1}{2}$).	Netherfield, Battle.
Folsalre, Foxer	Foxelre, Foxelere.	Foxearle.
Baldeslei.	Baldeslowe.	Baldslow.
—— [7]	Nenefeud, Nymensfeud.	Ninfield.
Bexlei.	Bexle, Beause.	Bexhill.
Reredfelle.	Retherfeud.	Rotherfield.
Hertevel.	Hertfeud.	Hartfield.
Grenestede.	Grenestede, Estgrenestede.	East Grinstead.
Ristone.	{ Riston ($\frac{1}{2}$), La Denne ($\frac{1}{2}$).	Rushmonden,[8] Burleigh-Arches, and Danehill-Horsted (part).
Mellinges. } Framelle. }	Lokesfeld.	{ Loxfield Camden, Loxfield Dorset, Ringmer.
Edivestone.	Sepelake, Shepelake.	Shiplake.
Latille.	La Tille, Thille.	Dill.
Wandelmestrei.	{ Langebregge (in) Alciston.	Longbridge (part of), Alciston.
Auronhelle.[9]	Langebregge (in).	Longbridge (part of).
Wilendone.	Willindon, Wylendon.	Willingdon.
Pevensel.	Leucata de Pevenese.	Lowey of Pevensey.
Borne.	Burne, Estborne.	Eastbourne.
Flexberghe.	Faxeburgh, Faxberwe.	Flexborough, and Bishopstone.
Totenore.	Tottenore.	Totnore.
Estrat.	Strete.	Street.
Bercham.	Berecompe.	Barcombe.
Swaneberge.	{ Swanberg, Suthenore, Suthovere ($\frac{1}{2}$) [10]	Swanborough, Southover.
Homestreu.	Holmestre, Holmestrowe.	Holmstrow.
Welesmere. } Falemere. }	{ Whalesbon. Iwonesmere.[11]	Whalesbone. Youngsmere.
Prestetune.	Whalesbon (in).	Preston and Dean.
Burbece.	Burbeche, Burgebeche.	Burbeach.
Poninges.	Ponninges.	Poynings.
Eldritune.	Fisheresgate.	Fishergate.

[1] Introduction to Domesday, pp. 351-4   [2] Ibid. p. 360.
[3] The forms given are taken from 'Placita Coronæ,' the Hundred Rolls, etc.
[4] Taken from the index to Ordnance map.
[5] Occurs as Babirote on Pipe R. 31 Hen. I.
[6] Occurs as Hawkeswurth in 1262, Assize R. 912.
[7] No name is given to this Hundred in Domesday.
[8] Occurs in sixteenth century as Rushtonden.
[9] Occurs as Alrehelle in Pipe R. 31 Hen. I.
[10] Called Halimote of Southover in 1249 and 1262 ; Assize R. 909, 912.
[11] Occurs as Hywelesmere in 1249. Assize R. 909.

1086.	13th Century.	Modern.
Bottingelle.	Buntingehull, Bottynghill.	Buttinghill.
Windeham.	Wyndham.	Windham and Ewhurst.
Hamfelde.	Typenhok.	Tipnoak.
Tifeld.	Burbeche (in).	Singlecross, Burbeach and Horsham.
Grenestede.	Grenestede, Westgrenestede.	West Grinstead.
Staninges.	Staninges.	Steyning.
Bredford.	Bretford.	Brightford and Tarring.
Isewerit.	Esewrithe (½).	East Easwrith.
Isiwiridi.	Esewrithe (½).	West Easwrith.
Risberge.	Paling.	Poling and Patching.
Benestede.	Avesford.	Avisford.
Redrebruge.	Rotherbrigge	Rotherbridge.
Berie.	Bury.	Bury.
Eseburne.	Eseborne.	Easebourne.
Silletone.	Sengelton.[1]	Singleton with ⎱
Ghidentroi.	Burne, Westborne.	Westbourne. ⎰
Hamesford.	Demesford.	Dumpford.
Boseham.	Boseham.	Bosham.
Westringes. ⎱ Sumerlege. ⎰	Manewode.	Manhood.
Estocbridge.	Stockbridge with	Stockbridge with ⎱
Bocse. ⎱ Bosgrave. ⎰	Boxe.	Box. ⎰
Pageham.	Pageham.	Aldwick.

The two principal features noticeable in this list are the frequency with which the names of the hundreds alter between the time of Domesday and the thirteenth century, and the increase in their number by subdivision. The change of name was no doubt usually due to the selection of a fresh meeting-place for the hundred court more suited to changed conditions of population and other circumstances. A certain laxity of nomenclature is also noticeable even in Domesday in the case of the hundred afterwards known as Manhood— 'Westringes' manor being entered under 'Sumerlege' hundred and 'Sumerlege' manor under 'Westringes' hundred. The increase in the number of the hundreds was no doubt due in part to the growth of population rendering the larger districts inconvenient for administration, but still more to the creation of privileged districts in the hands of lords enjoying special franchises. Thus besides the abbot of Battle's hundreds of Alciston and Battle, the archbishop's hundreds of Loxfield, Ringmer, Aldwick and Patching, and the Bishop of Chichester's hundreds of Preston and Bishopstone, there were the Cinque Port liberties of Hastings (with a detached portion in Bexhill), Rye and Winchelsea, the Bishop of London's liberty of Lodsworth, and the Hospitallers' liberty of St. John in Midhurst and adjoining parishes.

The modern hundreds were for the most part reduced to their present form in, or before, the sixteenth century, but besides these here given others enjoyed a temporary existence ; thus in 1249 the hundred of Bykenaker is mentioned in the *Placita Coronæ*,[2] but no clue is given to its whereabouts or contents. The half-hundred of Milton (in Longbridge) occurs throughout the thirteenth century, and that of Hailsham occasionally in the later half of the sixteenth century, at which time a number of other so-called half-hundreds make desultory appearances.

The Sussex hundreds are for the most part compact and self-contained, but in a few instances, e.g. Rotherbridge and Bury, they possess small outlying members at some distance from the main body of the hundred, and that of Burbeach is divided into two portions, the northern being separated from the southern by the hundreds of Windham and Tipnoak. The modern hundred of Danehill-Horsted is, however, singularly discrete, its several portions lying in Horsted-Keynes, Selmeston, Tarring-Neville and Hellingly.

The detailed consideration of parochial boundaries and characteristics must be reserved for the topographical section, but attention may be called here to the general distribution of parishes throughout the county. In the case of Surrey Mr. Malden has pointed out [3] that the parishes near the Downs tend to run in strips which include a portion of down-land, a considerable extent of greensand and a portion of clay. This tendency is also to be observed

---

[1] Sometimes called a half-hundred. [2] Assize R. 909. [3] *V.C.H. Surrey*, ii. 6.

in Sussex in the case of the group of parishes bordering the Downs between the Arun and the Ouse, and stretching in an almost straight line from Amberley to Hamsey. But the main factor in the formation of the parishes in this county has been the woodland. The great extent of the forest of Andred, covering the whole of the north and much of the east of Sussex, has already been referred to,[1] and the gradual process of reclaiming and, as it were, colonizing this great forest tract is brought out in an interesting charter [2] of about 1100, by which Robert de Dene granted to the priory of Lewes certain lands, apparently near East Grinstead, which ' usque ad modernum tempus silve fuerunt.' As a natural result we find that the open country in the south and west contains a large number of small parishes, while in the heavily wooded northern district the parishes are few and large. Thus if a semicircle of eight miles radius be described, having Seaford as its centre and the sea coast as its base, nearly the whole of thirty-six parishes will be taken in, but a similar semicircle having the northern part of Rotherfield for its centre and the Surrey boundary as its base, will only take in nine parishes.

The parliamentary divisions have already been dealt with, and the following is a list of the unions : Battle, Brighton, Chailey, Chichester, Cuckfield, Eastbourne, East Grinstead, East Preston, Hailsham, Hastings, Horsham, Lewes, Midhurst, Newhaven, Petworth, Rye, Steyning, Thakeham, Ticehurst, Uckfield, Westbourne, West Firle, and West Hampnett.

---

[1] See pp. 365, 536.   [2] Printed by Mr. Round in *Suss. Arch. Coll.* xl. 68.

INDEX TO DOMESDAY OF SUSSEX

PERSONAL NAMES

PLACE NAMES

INDEX TO DOMESDAY